Solving Riddles and Untying Knots

Jonas C. Greenfield

חיים ליונה

Solving Riddles and Untying Knots

Biblical, Epigraphic, and Semitic Studies in Honor of Jonas C. Greenfield

Edited by

Ziony Zevit
Seymour Gitin
Michael Sokoloff

Winona Lake, Indiana
EISENBRAUNS
1995

Acknowledgments

This volume was made possible by a generous donation made in loving memory of Joanne Cotsen.

Additional support was given by the Dorot Foundation, with technical assistance provided by the University of Judaism and the W. F. Albright Institute of Archaeological Research.

Special thanks go to David Louvish of Jerusalem for his meticulous copy-editing of the volume and to Bella Greenfield for her encouragement and her assistance in compiling the biographical information.

Library of Congress Cataloging in Publication Data

Solving riddles and untying knots : biblical, epigraphic, and Semitic studies in honor of Jonas C. Greenfield / edited by Ziony Zevit, Seymour Gitin, Michael Sokoloff.

p. cm.

Includes bibliographical references and index.

ISBN 0-931464-93-5

1. Bible. O.T.—Criticism, interpretation, etc. 2. Dead Sea scrolls—Criticism, interpretation, etc. 3. Inscriptions, Semitic. 4. Semitic philology. I. Greenfield, Jonas C., 1926– . II. Zevit, Ziony. III. Gitin, Seymour. IV. Sokoloff, Michael. V. Title.

BS1192.S62 1995
221.6—dc20 95-16310
CIP

The paper used in this publication meets the minimum requirements of the American National Standard for Information Sciences—Permanence of Paper for Printed Library Materials, ANSI Z39.48-1984.♾™

Contents

Preface ix
Bibliography of the Published Writings of Jonas C. Greenfield ... xiii
Abbreviations xxix

BIBLE

Jes P. Asmussen • Copenhagen
Some Bird Names in the Judeo-Persian Translations of the Hebrew Bible 3
Joshua Blau • Israel Academy of Sciences and Humanities
The Monophthongization of Diphthongs as Reflected in the Use of Vowel Letters in the Pentateuch 7
Ariel A. Bloch • University of California at Berkeley
The Cedar and the Palm Tree: A Paired Male/Female Symbol in Hebrew and Aramaic 13
William M. Brinner • University of California at Berkeley
Some Problems in the Arabic Transmission of Biblical Names .. 19
Magen Broshi • Israel Museum and
Ada Yardeni • Hebrew University
On *netinim* and False Prophets 29
André Caquot • College de France, Paris
Grandeur et pureté du sacerdoce: Remarques sur le *Testament de Qahat* (4Q542) 39
Henri Cazelles • École Pratique des Hautes Études, Paris
Aḥiqar, *Ummân* and *Amun*, and Biblical Wisdom Texts 45
Riccardo Contini • University of Venice
Epistolary Evidence of Address Phenomena in Official and Biblical Aramaic 57
Moshe Greenberg • Hebrew University
The Etymology of נִדָּה '(Menstrual) Impurity' 69
William W. Hallo • Yale University
Slave Release in the Biblical World in Light of a New Text ... 79

Stephen A. Kaufman • Hebrew Union College, Cincinnati
Paragogic *nun* in Biblical Hebrew: Hypercorrection as a Clue to a Lost Scribal Practice 95
Michael L. Klein • Hebrew Union College, Jerusalem
A Fragment-Targum of *Onqelos* from the Cairo Genizah 101
Tryggve Kronholm • University of Uppsala
Abraham, the Physician: The Image of Abraham the Patriarch in the Genuine Hymns of Ephraem Syrus 107
Jacob Lassner • Northwestern University
Ritual Purity and Political Exile: Solomon, the Queen of Sheba, and the Events of 586 B.C.E. in a Yemenite Folktale .. 117
Baruch A. Levine • New York University
The Semantics of Loss: Two Exercises in Biblical Hebrew Lexicography 137
Peter Machinist • Harvard University
Fate, *miqreh*, and Reason: Some Reflections on Qohelet and Biblical Thought 159
Abraham Malamat • Hebrew University
A Recently Discovered Word for "Clan" in Mari and Its Hebrew Cognate 177
Émile Puech • Centre National de la Recherche Scientifique
Note de lexicographie hébraïque qumrânienne (*m-ṣw* / *yrwq*, *mḥšbym*, *śwṭ*) 181
Elisha Qimron • Ben-Gurion University of the Negev
A Work concerning Divine Providence: 4Q*413* 191
Nahum M. Sarna • Brandeis University
Variant Scriptural Readings in Liturgical Texts 203
Lawrence H. Schiffman • New York University
4QMysteries[a]: A Preliminary Edition and Translation 207
Stanislav Segert • University of California at Los Angeles
Poetic Structures in the Hebrew Sections of the Book of Daniel 261
Shaul Shaked • Hebrew University
Qumran: Some Iranian Connections 277
J. A. Soggin • Università di Roma—La Sapienza
Abraham and the Eastern Kings: On Genesis 14 283
Michael E. Stone • Hebrew University
A New Edition and Translation of the *Questions of Ezra* 293
Hayim Tadmor • Hebrew University
Was the Biblical *sārîs* a Eunuch? 317
Shemaryahu Talmon • Hebrew University
A Calendrical Document from Qumran Cave 4 (mišmarot D, 4Q*325*) 327

Jeffrey H. Tigay • University of Pennsylvania
לא נס לחה 'He Had Not Become Wrinkled' (Deuteronomy 34:7) 345
Emanuel Tov • Hebrew University
A Paraphrase of Exodus: 4Q*422* 351
J. P. Weinberg • Jerusalem
The Word *ndb* in the Bible: A Study in Historical Semantics and Biblical Thought 365

EPIGRAPHY

Shmuel Aḥituv • Ben-Gurion University of the Negev
Flour and Dough: Gleanings from the Arad Letters 379
Walter E. Aufrecht • The University of Lethbridge, Canada
A Phoenician Seal 385
Klaus Beyer • Heidelberg University
The Ammonite Tell Siran Bottle Inscription Reconsidered . . . 389
Frank Moore Cross • Harvard University
Paleography and the Date of the Tell Faḫariyeh Bilingual Inscription 393
Philippe Gignoux • École des Hautes Études, Paris
The Pahlavi Inscription on Mount Thomas Cross (South India) 411
André Lemaire • École Pratique des Hautes Études, Paris
The Xanthos Trilingual Revisited 423
E. Lipiński • Katholiek Universiteit Leuven
The Inscribed Marble Vessels from Kition 433
Philip Mayerson • New York University
Grain Prices in Late Antiquity and the Nature of the Evidence 443
Alan Millard • University of Liverpool
Latin in First-Century Palestine 451
Joseph Naveh • Hebrew University
Phoenician Ostraca from Tel Dor 459

SEMITICS

Tzvi Abusch • Brandeis University
The Socio-Religious Framework of the Babylonian Witchcraft Ceremony *Maqlû*: Some Observations on the Introductory Section of the Text, Part II 467

Maria Giulia Amadasi Guzzo • Università degli Studi di Roma
More on the Latin Personal Names Ending with
-*us* and -*ius* in Punic 495
Arnold J. Band • University of California at Los Angeles
Regelson, Pagis, and Wallach: Three Poems
on the Hebrew Language 505
M. A. Dandamayev • Institute for Oriental Studies, St. Petersburg
The Neo-Babylonian *tamkārū* 523
M. J. Geller • University College, London
An Eanna Tablet from Uruk in Cleveland 531
Victor Avigdor Hurowitz • Ben-Gurion University of the Negev
An Old Babylonian Bawdy Ballad 543
William L. Moran • Harvard University
Some Reflections on Amarna Politics 559
David I. Owen • Cornell University
Pasūri-Dagan and Ini-Teššup's Mother 573
Shalom M. Paul • Hebrew University
The "Plural of Ecstasy" in Mesopotamian and
Babylonian Love Poetry 585
Jack M. Sasson • University of North Carolina
Water beneath Straw: Adventures of a Prophetic Phrase
in the Mari Archives 599
Marcel Sigrist • École Biblique, Jerusalem
Some di-til-la Tablets in the British Museum 609
Aaron Skaist • Bar-Ilan University
Šīmu gamru: Its Function and History 619
Mark S. Smith • St. Joseph's University, Philadelphia
The God Athtar in the Ancient Near East and
His Place in KTU 1.6 I 627

Index of Authors 641
Index of Scripture 651
Index of Ancient Texts 659

Preface

Solving Riddles and Untying Knots: Biblical, Epigraphic, and Semitic Studies is dedicated to our teacher, colleague, and friend Jonas C. Greenfield on his 68th birthday as a token of our deep esteem and affection. All of us who have collaborated to make this volume possible, as well as so many others, have benefited greatly not only from Jonas's scholarly research but from his unstinted sharing of his knowledge, intellect, and experience. This volume, representing several fields of study, is intended to reflect the broad spectrum of Jonas's interests and pursuits.

Jonas Carl Greenfield, חיים יונה, was born on October 30, 1926, in New York City. He completed high school at *Mesivta Torah VaDaath* in Brooklyn and in 1949, received his B.A. in English literature from the City College of New York, winning the Ward Medal in English. In his graduate studies in English at Yale, he was greatly influenced by two professors of English, F. A. Pottle and Cleanth Brooks. In addition to the required course in Old English, Jonas was required to study a second early Indo-European language, and he chose Hittite. This brought him into contact with the distinguished Hittitologist and cuneiform scholar Albrecht Goetze, with whom he also studied Akkadian. In his classes, Jonas realized his true vocation and decided to transfer his attention from English to ancient Near Eastern studies.

Jonas's interest in Semitic languages had begun, however, at a much earlier age. He attributes his lifelong interest in Aramaic to his grandfather, who gave him a $50 *bar-mitzvah* gift for learning all of *Targum Onqelos.* Jonas, who is now the Caspar Levias Professor of Ancient Semitic Languages at the Hebrew University, bought Levias's grammar of Babylonian Aramaic at the age of 14. He began studying Arabic on his own soon thereafter. While a student at City College and the Yeshiva, he found time to attend classes in Arabic given by A. S. Yahuda and Moseh Perlmann at the New School for Social Research, where he also studied Comparative Semitics with Wolf Leslau. At Yale, his doctoral dissertation dealt with "The Lexical Status of Mishnaic Hebrew," and his thesis adviser was Julian Obermann. Harald Ingholt aroused his interest in archaeology and epigraphy. It was with Millar Burrows that he began his career in Dead Sea Scrolls research; Jonas was his assistant in correcting the second printing of the *Isaiah Scroll*. This marked the beginning of his career as a Scrolls scholar and editor; he has been commenting on and correcting other scholars' work on the Scrolls ever since. In addition to Goetze, Jonas was influenced by some of the most important orientalists of the mid-twentieth century: Sumerologist S. N. Kramer, Assyriologists E. A. Speiser, A. L. Oppenheim, and B. Landsberger; Iranist W. B. Henning; historian E. Bickerman; biblical scholar H. L. Ginsberg; and Arabist and Aramaicist F. Rosenthal.

Married in 1950, Jonas and his wife, Bella, have two daughters, Elisheva and Avigail, and six grandchildren. In 1954, while still a Ph.D. candidate, Jonas was awarded a Fulbright scholarship for the study of Old South Arabic with G. Ryckmans at Louvain, but instead he chose to teach at Brandeis University, where he introduced Ugaritic into the curriculum. He earned his Ph.D. from Yale in 1956 and accepted the invitation of his former teacher Wolf Leslau to go to UCLA as an Assistant Professor. There he introduced Ugaritic and Dead Sea Scrolls studies into the curriculum. During his nine years in Los Angeles, he was also associated with the University of Judaism. In 1963 and 1964 he was a Guggenheim Fellow and a Fulbright Travelling Scholar in Israel.

The Greenfields moved to Berkeley in 1965, where Jonas, by then a full professor, taught Near Eastern Studies, including Aramaic, Syriac, Ugaritic, and ancient Near Eastern history. In 1966, he began his 15-year association with the Jewish Publication Society as a member of the team of translators for the *Ketubim*. In 1968–69, he headed the University of California Program in Israel, while holding an American Council of Learned Societies/Social Science Research Council Fellowship for Semitic Studies.

The family made *aliya* in 1971, and since then Jonas has taught in the Department of Ancient Semitic Languages at the Hebrew University of Jerusalem. In 1976, he became the editor of the *Israel Exploration Journal*, the first nonarchaeologist to hold this post. He has been a long-term member of the editorial board of the *Bulletin of the American Schools of Oriental Research* and continues to maintain his relationship with the American Schools as a trustee of the W. F. Albright Institute of Archaeological Research in Jerusalem. He is a member of the Dead Sea Scrolls Supervisory Committee of the Israel Antiquities Authority and has also served on the editorial board of the American Oriental Society and the Society of Biblical Literature. He was vice-president in 1969 and president in 1970 of the Pacific Coast Section of the Society of Biblical Literature. He is a regular participant in the Rencontre Assyriologique and has traveled extensively to international Orientalist meetings and conferences, including those held in India, Iran, and Russia. For many years he has maintained personal contact with scholars in the former Eastern bloc nations. He is an honorary fellow of the Royal Danish Academy of Sciences and Letters and the Royal Asiatic Society. In 1994 Jonas was elected a member of the Israel Academy of Sciences and Humanities. Jonas's hobbies are walking in Jerusalem, talking, and collecting *Festschriften.*

Jonas's main contribution to biblical studies has been in the field of the semantics of Biblical Hebrew. In his first article, written in 1958 for the *Hebrew Union College Annual,* he noted that while medieval Jewish lexicographers had already applied a comparative methodology that used Mishnaic Hebrew, Aramaic, and Arabic to the understanding of the Bible, in the nineteenth and twentieth centuries the discovery of Akkadian, Ugaritic, and Phoenician texts produced new data for comparative linguistic study.

Jonas's work provides important models for the application of this new evidence. His articles demonstrate that the meaning of biblical words cannot be determined solely through an examination of the restricted biblical context but must be established by considering the larger context of Hebrew language studies within the framework of comparative Semitic lexicography. He contends that relying on the use of dictionaries of Semitic languages is insufficient for determining the meaning of Hebrew and other Semitic texts. A prime example of this was the widespread use during the 1950s and 1960s of Arabic dictionaries to interpret obscure Ugaritic words and subsequently retrojecting them onto Hebrew cognates, a practice that he opposed. He maintained that responsible scholarship requires the ability to understand the texts in their original language in order to apply the lexicographical data correctly.

After joining the Jewish Publication Society translation committee in 1966, working first on Psalms and later on Job, Jonas's concern with lexicographic issues became more sharply focused. It was also then that he began his wide-ranging Aramaic studies, including history and lexicography. These became the major theme of his subsequent publications and research interests. Jonas's Aramaic studies have not been limited to one particular dialect or period but encompass the entire breadth of Aramean culture from its earliest appearance in the Old Aramaic inscriptions through the great literary dialects of the first millennium C.E. Furthermore, he deals with this culture in its context, together with other contemporary contiguous ancient Near Eastern cultures. A dominant feature of these studies is the juxtaposition of diverse elements from the ancient Near East and their application to the issue at hand, be it legal, historical, religious, literary, etymological, or lexicographic. Jonas's articles are characterized by a wealth of relevant ancillary materials, as well as the latest literature on each subject from the most obscure of sources, making each article in itself a starting point for further study.

By the 1970s, the range of Jonas's research had expanded to include the documents discovered in the Dead Sea region of the Judean wilderness. This is best exemplified in his current work on the publications of the Babatha archive.

Jonas influenced his fields of study not only through his written articles and critical reviews, but also by his dynamic participation in the meetings of the American Oriental Society. In the 1960s and 1970s, scholars who presented papers at the annual meetings knew they must be well prepared because Greenfield would be in the audience. Jonas is a valued colleague to his contemporaries and is eagerly sought after as a mentor by junior scholars. He is able to provide them with relevant examples, bibliography, and ideas for further inquiry, all of which he culls effortlessly from his memory.

After making *aliya* in 1971, Jonas also became an important figure on the Israeli academic scene. His continuing influence on scholarship through personal contact and comment is reflected clearly in the many acknowledgments and expressions of thanks to him published in dissertations and books written in the USA, Israel, and Europe.

Ziony Zevit, University of Judaism
Seymour Gitin, W. F. Albright Institute
of Archaeological Research
Michael Sokoloff, Bar-Ilan University

This festschrift was to be presented to Jonas in Jerusalem in April 1995. But this was not to be. He died unexpectedly in his sleep at home on the 11th of Adar Sheni, March 13. He did, however, see the volume when he was given a bound copy of the proofs during a special presentation at the American Schools of Oriental Research reception in Chicago, November 1994. On April 12, Jonas was elected a member of the American Academy of Arts and Sciences. We shall miss Jonas and his wisdom and kindness.

תהא נשמתו צרורה בצרור החיים

Bibliography of Jonas C. Greenfield

Books

1. *The Psalms: A New Translation according to the Traditional Hebrew Text.* Philadelphia, 1973. [Member of translation committee for the Kethubim of the Jewish Publication Society; translation in conjunction with M. Greenberg, N. Sarna, et al.]
2. Prolegomenon to a reprint of H. Odeberg, *3 Enoch or The Hebrew Book of Enoch.* New York, 1973.
3. *Jews of Elephantine and Arameans of Syene* [fifth century B.C.E.; fifty Aramaic texts with Hebrew and English translation]. Jerusalem, 1974. [with B. Porten]
4. *The Book of Job: A New Translation according to the Traditional Text.* Philadelphia, 1980. With a chapter, "The Language of the Book." [Member of translation committee for the Kethubim of the Jewish Publication Society]
5. *Kethubim: The Writings.* Philadelphia, 1982. [Member of translation committee for the Kethubim of the Jewish Publication Society]
6. *The Bisitun Inscription of Darius the Great, Aramaic Version.* Corpus Inscriptionum Iranicarum 1/5/1. London, 1982–83. [with B. Porten]
7. Y. Yadin, N. Lewis, and J. C. Greenfield. *The Documents from the Bar Kokhba Period in the Cave of Letters, Volume 1: The Greek Papyri.* Jerusalem, 1989.
8. Y. Yadin, J. C. Greenfield, and A. Yardeni. *The Documents from the Bar Kokhba Period in the Cave of Letters, Volume 2: The Aramaic, Nabatean and Hebrew Texts.* [forthcoming]

Editorial Activities

Editor, *Israel Exploration Journal,* 1976–1995.

Associate editor, *Bulletin of the American Schools of Oriental Research,* 1969–71; contributing editor, 1991–1995.

Member of board of Society of Biblical Literature Monograph Series, 1969–75.

Coeditor

1. *New Directions in Biblical Archaeology.* New York, 1969; Anchor Books edition, 1971. [with D. N. Freedman]
2. *Studies in Hebrew and Semitic Languages* (E. Y. Kutscher Memorial Volume). Ramat Gan, 1980.

3. *Eretz-Israel* 14 (H. L. Ginsberg Volume; Jerusalem, 1978).
4. *Eretz-Israel* 16 (H. M. Orlinsky Volume; Jerusalem, 1982).
5. *Eretz-Israel* 18 (N. Avigad Volume; Jerusalem, 1985).
6. *Eretz-Israel* 20 (Y. Yadin Volume; Jerusalem, 1989).
7. *Eretz-Israel* 24 (A. Malamat Volume; Jerusalem, 1993).
8. *Studies in Judaica, Karaitica and Islamica Presented to Dr. Leon Nemoy* (Ramat Gan, 1982).
9. שיבת ציון, ימי שילטון פרס [The Restoration, the Persian Period]. *World History of the Jewish People* 1/6. Jerusalem, 1983.

Articles

1. "Lexicographical Notes I." *Hebrew Union College Annual* 29 (1958) 203–28.
2. "Lexicographical Notes II." *Hebrew Union College Annual* 30 (1959) 141–51.
3. "The Root 'GBL' in Mishnaic Hebrew and in the Hymnic Literature from Qumran." *Revue de Qumran* 2 (1960) 155–62.
4. "'Le Bain des brebis': Another Example and a Query." *Orientalia* 29 (1960) 98–102.
5. "The Preposition *B . . . Taḥat* . . . in Isaiah 57,5." *Zeitschrift für die Alttestamentliche Wissenschaft* 73 (1961) 226–28.
6. "Studies in Aramaic Lexicography I." *Journal of the American Oriental Society* 82 (1962) 290–99.
7. "בחינות לשוניות בכתובות ספירה" [Linguistic Criteria in the Sefîre Inscriptions]. *Lešonénu* 27–28 (1963–64) 303–13.
8. "Samaritan Hebrew and Aramaic in the Work of Professor Zeʾev Ben-Hayyim." *Biblica* 45 (1964) 261–68.
9. "Ugaritic *mdl* and Its Cognates." *Biblica* 45 (1964) 527–34.
10. "מסע נבוכדנאצר בספר יהודית" [Nebuchadnezzar's Campaign in the Book of Judith]. *Bulletin of the Israel Exploration Society* 28 (1964) 204–8.
11. "The Etymology of *Amtaḥat*." *Zeitschrift für die Alttestamentliche Wissenschaft* 77 (1965) 90–92.
12. "Stylistic Aspects of the Sefîre Treaty Inscriptions." *Acta Orientalia* 29 (1965) 1–18.
13. "Three Notes on the Sefîre Inscriptions." *Journal of Semitic Studies* 11 (1966) 98–105.
14. "Ugaritic Lexicographical Notes." *Journal of Cuneiform Studies* 21 (1967) 89–93.
15. "Some Aspects of Treaty Terminology in the Bible." Pp. 117–19 in *Proceedings of the Fourth World Congress of Jewish Studies*, Volume 1. Jerusalem, 1967.
16. "The *algummim/almuggim* Problem Re-examined." Pp. 83–89 in *Hebräische Wortforschung: Festschrift W. Baumgartner.* Vetus Testamentum Supplements 16. Leiden, 1967. [with Manfred Mayrhofer]
17. "The Aramaic Papyri from Hermopolis." *Zeitschrift für die Alttestamentliche Wissenschaft* 80 (1968) 216–31. [with B. Porten]
18. "קווים דיאלקטיים בארמית הקדומה" [Dialect Traits in Early Aramaic]. *Lešonénu* 32 (1968) 359–68.

19. "Some Glosses on the KRT Epic." *Eretz-Israel* 9 (W. F. Albright Volume; 1969) 60–65.
20. "Amurrite, Ugaritic, and Canaanite." Pp. 92–101 in *Proceedings of the International Conference on Semitic Studies, Jerusalem, 1965.* Jerusalem, 1969.
21. "The Small Caves of Qumran." *Journal of the American Oriental Society* 89 (1969) 128–41.
22. "The Guarantor at Elephantine-Syene." *Journal of the American Oriental Society* 89 (1969) 153–57. [with B. Porten]
23. "The 'Periphrastic Imperative' in Aramaic and Hebrew." *Israel Exploration Journal* 19 (1969) 199–210.
24. "**Hamarakara* > *ʾAmarkal*: The Use of an Iranian Loan Word in Hebrew and Aramaic." Pp. 180–86 in *W. B. Henning Memorial Volume.* London, 1970.
25. "Scripture and Inscription: The Literary and Rhetorical Element in Some Early Phoenician Inscriptions." Pp. 253–68 in *Near Eastern Studies in Honor of W. F. Albright.* Edited by H. Goedicke. Baltimore, 1971.
26. "Ugaritic Glosses." *Bulletin of the American Schools of Oriental Research* 200 (1970) 11–18. [with J. Blau]
27. "The Zakir Inscription and the Danklied." Pp. 174–91 in *Proceedings of the Fifth World Congress of Jewish Studies, Jerusalem, 1969,* Volume 1: *Ancient Near East, Bible, Archaeology, First Temple Period.* Jerusalem, 1971.
28. "The Background and Parallel to a Proverb of Aḥiqar." Pp. 49–59 in *Hommages à A. Dupont-Sommer.* Paris, 1972.
29. "Three Iranian Words in the Targum of Job from Qumran. *Zeitschrift der deutschen morgenländischen Gesellschaft* 122 (1972) 37–45. [with S. Shaked]
30. "Un rite religieux araméen et ses parallèles." *Revue biblique* 80 (1973) 46–52.
31. "מכתבי הרמופוליס" [The Hermopolis Letters]. *Qadmoniot* 7 (1974) 121–24. [with B. Porten]
32. "רטין מגושא" [The Mazdean Priest Murmurs]. Pp. 63–69 in *Joshua Finkel Festschrift.* New York, 1974.
33. "Standard Literary Aramaic." Pp. 281–89 in *Actes du premier congrès de linguistique sémitique et chamito-sémitique.* Paris, 1974.
34. "Hermopolis Letter 6." *Israel Oriental Studies* 4 (1974) 14–30. [with B. Porten]
35. "Notes on Some Aramaic and Mandaic Magic Bowls." *Journal of the Ancient Near Eastern Society of Columbia University* 5 (T. H. Gaster Festschrift; 1974) 149–56.
36. "מחקרים במונחי משפט בכתובות הקבר הנבטיות" [Studies in the Legal Terminology of the Nabatean Funerary Inscriptions]. Pp. 64–83 in *Ḥ. Yalon Memorial Volume.* Jerusalem, 1974.
37. "Iranian Vocabulary in Early Aramaic." Pp. 245–46 in *Commemoration Cyrus, Hommage Universel,* Volume 2. Leiden, 1974.
38. "The *Marzeaḥ* as a Social Institution." *Proceedings of the Internationale Tagung der Keilschriftforscher der sozialistischen Länder, Acta Antiqua* 22 (1974) 451–55.
39. "Iranian or Semitic?" Pp. 311–16 in *Monumentum H. S. Nyberg,* Volume 1. Leiden, 1975.

40. "The Aramaic God *Rammān/Rimmōn*." *Israel Exploration Journal* 26 (1976) 195–98.
41. "A New Corpus of Aramaic Texts from Egypt." *Journal of the American Oriental Society* 96 (1976) 131–35.
42. "*Nasû-nadānu* and Its Congeners." Pp. 87–91 in *Essays on the Ancient Near East: Studies in Memory of Jacob Joel Finkelstein.* Edited by M. de J. Ellis. Connecticut Academy of Arts and Sciences, Memoir 19; Hamden, 1977.
43. "The Enochic Pentateuch and the Date of the Similitudes." *Harvard Theological Review* 70 (1977) 51–65. [with M. E. Stone]
44. "On Some Iranian Terms in the Elephantine Papyri: Aspects of Continuity." *Acta Antiqua* 25 (= *Studies in Honor of J. Harmatta I*; 1977) 113–18.
45. "The Prepositions *ʿad-ʿal* in Aramaic and Hebrew." *Bulletin of the School of Oriental (and African) Studies* 40 (1977) 371–72.
46. "Some Reflections on the Vocabulary of Aramaic in Relationship to the Other Semitic Languages." Pp. 151–56 in *Atti del secondo congresso internazionale di linguistica camito-semitica, Firenze, 1974.* Florence, 1978.
47. "The Dialects of Early Aramaic." *Journal of Near Eastern Studies* 37 (1978) 93–99.
48. "The Meaning of פחז." Pp. 35–40 in *Studies in Bible and the Ancient Near East* (E. S. Loewenstamm Volume). Jerusalem, 1978.
49. "הערות לכתובת אזתוד (קאראטפה)" [Notes on the Asitawada (Karatepe) Inscription]. *Eretz-Israel* 14 (H. L. Ginsberg Volume; 1978) 74–77.
50. "Aramaic and Its Dialects." Pp. 29–43 in *Jewish Languages: Theme and Variations.* Edited by H. H. Paper. Cambridge, 1978.
51. "The Languages of Palestine, 200 B.C.E.–200 C.E." Pp. 143–54 in *Jewish Languages: Theme and Variations.* Edited by H. H. Paper. Cambridge, 1978.
52. "Remarks on the Aramaic Testament of Levi from the Geniza." *Revue biblique* 86 (1979) 214–30. [with M. E. Stone]
53. "The Root *šql* in Akkadian, Ugaritic and Aramaic." *Ugarit-Forschungen* 11 (1979) 325–27.
54. "Early Aramaic Poetry." *Journal of the Ancient Near Eastern Society of Columbia University* 11 (M. M. Bravmann Memorial Volume; 1979) 45–51.
55. "The Genesis Apocryphon: Observations on Some Words and Phrases." Pp. 22–29 in *Studies in Hebrew and Semitic Languages Dedicated to the Memory of Prof. E. Y. Kutscher.* Ramat Gan, 1980.
56. "A Mandaic 'Targum' to Psalm 114." Pp. 23–31 in *J. Heinemann Memorial Volume.* Jerusalem, 1980.
57. "Aramaic Studies and the Bible." Pp. 110–30 in *Congress Volume, Vienna, 1980.* Vetus Testamentum Supplements 32. Leiden, 1981.
58. "The Books of Enoch and the Traditions of Enoch." *Numen* 26 (1981) 89–103. [with M. E. Stone]
59. "Aḥiqar in the Book of Tobit." Pp. 329–36 in *De la Torah au Messie, Études . . . offertes à Henri Cazelles.* Paris, 1981.
60. "שתי מקראות לאור תקופתן—יחזקאל ט״ז 30 ומלאכי ג׳ 17" [Two Biblical Passages in the Light of Their Near Eastern Background: Ezekiel 16:30 and Malachi 3:17]. *Eretz-Israel* 16 (H. M. Orlinsky Volume; 1982) 56–61.

61. "A Hapax Legomenon: ממשק חרול." Pp. 79–82 in *Studies in Judaica, Karaitica and Islamica Presented to Dr. Leon Nemoy*. Ramat Gan, 1982.
62. "Some Notes on the Arsham Letters." Pp. 4–11 in *Irano-Judaica*. Jerusalem, 1982.
63. "Babylonian-Aramaic Relationship." Pp. 471–82 in *Mesopotamien und seine Nachbarn: Akten des XXVe Rencontre Assyriologique Internationale*, Volume 2. Edited by H.-J. Nissen and J. Renger. Berlin, 1982.
64. "הערות לכתובת הדו־לשונית מתל פח'ריה" [Some Observations on the Akkadian-Aramaic Bilingual from Tell Fekherye]. *Shnaton* 5–6 (1982) 119–29. [with A. Shaffer]
65. "A Bronze Phiale with a Phoenician Dedicatory Inscription." *Israel Exploration Journal* 32 (1982) 118–28. [with N. Avigad].
66. "*Adi balṭu*: Care for the Elderly and Its Rewards." Pp. 309–16 in Archiv für Orientforschung Beiheft 19. Graz, 1982.
67. "הנובלה ההיסטורית היהודית בתקופה הפרסית" [The Jewish Historical Novel in the Persian Period]. Pp. 203–9 in שיבת ציון, ימי שילטון פרס [The Restoration, the Persian Period]. *World History of the Jewish People* 1/6. Jerusalem, 1983.
68. "הלשון הארמית בתקופה הפרסית" [The Aramaic Language in the Persian Period]. Pp. 224–28 in שיבת ציון, ימי שילטון פרס [The Restoration, the Persian Period]. *World History of the Jewish People*. 1/6. Jerusalem, 1983.
69. "Aramaic *HNṢL* and Some Biblical Passages." Pp. 115–19 in *Meqor Ḥajjim: Festschrift G. Molin zu seinem 75. Geburtstag*. Edited by I. Seybold. Graz, 1983.
70. "Notes on the Akkadian-Aramaic Bilingual Statue from Tell Fekherye." *Iraq* 45 (R. Barnett Festschrift; 1983) 109–16. [with A. Shaffer]
71. "*QLQLTʾ*, *Tubkinnu*, Refuse Tips and Treasure Trove." *Anatolian Studies* 33 (1983) 123–29. [with A. Shaffer]
72. "Hebrew and Aramaic in the Persian Period." Pp. 115–29 in *The Cambridge History of Judaism*, Volume 1. Cambridge, 1984. [with J. Naveh]
73. "*Ana urditu kabāsu* = כבש לעבד." *Studia Orientalia* 55 (J. Arø Memorial Volume; 1984) 257–63.
74. "A Touch of Eden." Pp. 219–24 in *Orientalia J. Duchesne-Guillemin emerito oblata*. Leiden, 1984.
75. "Notes on the Phoenician Letter from Saqqara." *Orientalia* 53 (1984) 242–44.
76. "A Mandaic Miscellany." *Journal of the American Oriental Society* 104 (F. Rosenthal Volume; 1984) 81–85.
77. "Notes on the Early Aramaic Lexicon." *Orientalia Suecana* 33–35 (F. Rundgren Festschrift; 1984–86) 149–56.
78. "Aramaic in the Achaemenian Empire." Pp. 698–713 in *Cambridge History of Iran*, Volume 2: *The Median and Achaemenian Periods*. Cambridge, 1985.
79. "The Greek and Aramaic Fragments of a Levi Document." Pp. 457–69 in *The Testaments of the Twelve Patriarchs: A Commentary*. Edited by H. W. Hollander and M. de Jonge. Leiden, 1985.
80. "The Meaning of *TKWNH*." Pp. 81–85 in *Biblical and Related Studies Presented to Samuel Iwry*. Edited by Ann Kort and Scott Morschauser. Winona Lake, Indiana, 1985.

81. "Notes on the Curse Formulae of the Tell Fekherye Inscription." *Revue biblique* 92 (1985) 47–59. [with A. Shaffer]
82. "A Group of Phoenician City Seals." *Israel Exploration Journal* 35 (1985) 129–34.
83. "קמיע מנדעי בעל ארבע השבעות" [A Mandaic Lead Amulet with Four Incantations]. *Eretz-Israel* 18 (N. Avigad Volume; 1985) 97–107. [with J. Naveh]
84. "Baʿal's Throne and Isaiah 6:11." Pp. 193–98 in *Mélanges bibliques et orientaux en l'honneur de M. Mathias Delcor.* Alter Orient und Altes Testament 215. Neukirchen-Vluyn, 1985.
85. "The Seven Pillars of Wisdom (Proverbs 9:1): A Mistranslation." *Jewish Quarterly Review* 76 (M. Held Memorial Volume; 1985) 13–20.
86. "An Ancient Treaty Ritual and Its Targumic Echo." Pp. 391–97 in *Salvación en la Palabra: Homenaje al Prof. Alejandro Díez Macho.* Madrid, 1986.
87. "Aspects of Archives in the Achaemenid Period." Pp. 289–95 in *Cuneiform Archives and Libraries.* Edited by K. R. Veenhof. Leiden, 1986.
88. "Larnax tes Lapethou III Revisited." Pp. 391–40 in *Studia Phoenicia,* Volume 5. Edited by E. Lipiński. Louvain, 1987.
89. "The Epithets RBT//TRRT in the KRT Epic." Pp. 35–37 in *Perspectives on Language and Text: Essays and Poems in Honor of Francis I. Andersen's Sixtieth Birthday.* Edited by E. W. Conrad and E. G. Newing. Winona Lake, Indiana, 1987.
90. "Some Neo-Babylonian Women." Pp. 75–80 in *La Femme dans le Proche-Orient Antique.* Edited by J.-M. Durand. Paris, 1987.
91. "Aspects of Aramaic Religion." Pp. 67–78 in *Ancient Israelite Religion: Essays in Honor of Frank Moore Cross.* Edited by P. D. Miller et al. Philadelphia, 1987.
92. "The Verb *sallaṭa* in the Qurʾan in the Light of Aramaic Usage." *Jerusalem Studies in Arabic and Islam* 9 (Kister Jubilee Volume; 1987) 36–41.
93. "To Praise the Might of Hadad." Pp. 3–12 in *La Vie de la Parole, de l'Ancien au Nouveau Testament: Études . . . offertes à P. Grelot.* Paris, 1987.
94. "The Hebrew Bible and Canaanite Literature." Pp. 545–60 in *The Literary Guide to the Bible.* Edited by R. Alter and F. Kermode. Cambridge, 1987.
95. "Papyrus Yadin 18." *Israel Exploration Journal* 37 (1987) 229–50. [with N. Lewis and R. Katzoff]
96. "Smitten by Famine, Battered by Plague (Deuteronomy 32:24)." Pp. 151–52 in *Love and Death in the Ancient Near East: Essays in Honor of Marvin H. Pope.* Edited by J. H. Marks and R. M. Good. Guilford, Connecticut, 1987.
97. "North West Semitic Epigraphy and the Bible: Accomplishments." Pp. 1–7 in *Proceedings of the Ninth World Congress of Jewish Studies (1985), Panel Sessions: Hebrew and Aramaic Languages.* Edited by M. Bar-Asher. Jerusalem, 1988.
98. "Daily Life among the Jews in Egypt in the Fifth Century B.C.E." *Bulletin of the Israeli Academic Center in Cairo* 10 (1988) 14–16.
99. "Découvertes épigraphiques récentes au service de l'histoire, du retour de l'exil à Bar-Kokhba." Pp. 41–53 in *Archéologie, art et histoire de la Palestine.* Paris, 1988.

100. "The Words of Levi Son of Jacob in Damascus Document IV, Lines 15–19." *Revue de Qumran* 13 (1988) 319–22.
101. "Nergol *DḤŠPṬʾ*." Pp. 135–43 in *A Green Leaf* (J. P. Asmussen Volume). Leiden, 1989.
102. "On Mandaic Poetic Technique." Pp. 101–8 in *Studia Semitica necnon Iranica R. Macuch . . . dedicata.* Wiesbaden, 1989.
103. "Astrological Omen Texts in Jewish Palestinian Aramaic." *Journal of Near Eastern Studies* 48 (1989) 201–14. [with M. Sokoloff]
104. "Idiomatic Ancient Aramaic." Pp. 47–51 in *To Touch the Text: Biblical and Related Studies in Honor of Joseph A. Fitzmyer.* Edited by M. P. Horgan and P. J. Kobelski. New York, 1989.
105. "The 'Cluster' in Biblical Poetry." *Maarav* 5–6 (= *Sopher Mahir: Northwest Semitic Studies Presented to Stanislav Segert.* Edited by E. M. Cook. Winona Lake, Indiana, 1990) 159–68.
106. "The Aramaic Legal Texts of the Achaemenian Period." *Transeuphratène* 2 (1990) 35–92.
107. "Ben Sira 42.9–10 and Its Talmudic Paraphrase." Pp. 167–73 in *A Tribute to Geza Vermes.* Edited by P. R. Davies and R. T. White. Sheffield, 1990.
108. "Two Notes on the Aramaic Levi Document." Pp. 153–61 in *Of Scribes and Scrolls: Studies on the Hebrew Bible, Intertestamental Judaism, and Christian Origins Presented to John Strugnell.* Edited by H. W. Attridge, J. J. Collins, and T. H. Tobin. Lanham, Maryland, 1990. [with M. Stone]
109. "Two Proverbs of Aḥiqar." Pp. 195–201 in *Lingering over Words: Studies in Ancient Near Eastern Literature in Honor of William L. Moran.* Edited by I. T. Abusch, J. Huehnergard, and P. Steinkeller. Atlanta, 1990.
110. "לצורת המקור בשטרות הארמיים מואדי מורבעת ומנחל חבר" [The Infinitive in the Aramaic Documents from the Judean Desert]. Pp. 77–81 in *Studies on Hebrew and Other Semitic Languages in Honor of C. Rabin.* Edited by M. Goshen-Gottstein et al. Jerusalem, 1990.
111. "Asylum at Aleppo: A Note on Sfîre III, 4–7." Pp. 272–78 in *Ah, Assyria . . . : Studies in Assyrian History and Ancient Near Eastern Historiography Presented to Hayim Tadmor.* Edited by M. Cogan and I. Ephᶜal. Scripta Hierosolymitana 33. Jerusalem, 1990.
112. "Some Phoenician Words." *Semitica* 38 (= *Hommages à Maurice Sznycer,* Volume 1; 1990) 154–58.
113. "Philological Observations on the Deir ᶜAlla Inscriptions." Pp. 109–20 in *The Balaam Text from Deir ᶜAlla Re-evaluated: Proceedings of the International Symposium, Leiden, 1989.* Edited by J. Hoftijzer et al. Leiden, 1991.
114. "An Aramaic Inscription from Tyre from the Reign of Diocletian Preserved in the Palestinian Talmud." Pp. 499–502 in *Atti del II Congresso internazionale di studi fenici e punici, Roma, 1987.* Edited by E. Acquaro. Rome, 1991.
115. "Of Scribes, Scripts and Languages." Pp. 173–85 in *Phoinikeia Grammata: Lire et écrire en Méditeranée.* Edited by C. Baurain et al. Studia Phoenicia 9. Liège, 1991.

116. "Dove's Dung and the Price of Food: The Topoi of II Kings 6:24–7:2." Pp. 121–26 in *Storia e tradizioni di Israel: Scritti in onore di J. Alberto Soggin.* Brescia, 1991.
117. "*Kullu nafsin bima kasabat rahina*: The Use of *rhn* in Aramaic and Arabic." Pp. 221–79 in *Arabicus Felix: Luminosus Britannicus, Essays in Honour of A. F. L. Beeston on His Eightieth Birthday.* Edited by A. Jones. Exeter, 1991.
118. "Two Notes on the Apocryphal Psalms." Pp. 309–14 in *"Shaᶜarei Talmon": Studies in the Bible, Qumran, and the Ancient Near East Presented to Shemaryahu Talmon.* Edited by M. Fishbane, E. Tov, and W. W. Fields. Winona Lake, Indiana, 1992.
119. "The 'Defension Clause' in Some Documents from Naḥal Ḥever and Naḥal Ṣeᵓelim." *Revue de Qumran* 15 (Memorial Jean Starcky; 1992) 467–71.
120. "The Verbs for Washing in Aramaic." Pp. 588–94 in *Semitic Studies in Honor of Wolf Leslau.* Edited by A. Kaye. Wiesbaden, 1992.
121. "The Texts from Naḥal Ṣeᵓelim (Wadi Ṣeiyal)." Pp. 661–66 in *The Madrid Qumran Congress: Proceedings of the International Congress on the Dead Sea Scrolls, Madrid, 18–21 March, 1991.* Edited by J. Trebolle Barrera and L. Vegas Montaner. Studies on the Texts of the Desert of Judah 11. Leiden, 1992.
122. "The Genesis Apocryphon Column XII." Pp. 70–77 in *Studies in Qumran Aramaic.* Edited by T. Muraoka. Louvain, 1992. [with E. Qimron]
123. "The Contribution of Qumran Aramaic to the Aramaic Vocabulary." Pp. 78–98 in *Studies in Qumran Aramaic.* Edited by T. Muraoka. Louvain, 1992. [with M. Sokoloff]
124. "The Use of the Targum in a Mandaic Incantation Text." Pp. 79–82 in *"Open Thou Mine Eyes . . .": Essays on Aggadah and Judaica Presented to Rabbi William G. Braude on His Eightieth Birthday and Dedicated to His Memory.* Hoboken, 1992.
125. "Some Arabic Loanwords in the Aramaic and Nabatean Texts from Naḥal Ḥever." *Jerusalem Studies in Arabic and Islam* 15 (Joshua Blau Volume; 1992) 10–21.
126. "From the Workshop of the New Jewish Publication Society Ketuvim Translators." Pp. 147–63 in מנחה לנחום: *Biblical and Other Studies Presented to Naḥum Sarna.* Sheffield, 1993. [with M. Greenberg]
127. "Etymological Semantics." *Zeitschrift für Althebräistik* 6 (1993) 26–37. [ESF Workshop on the Semantics of Classical Hebrew]
128. "Some Glosses on the Sfîre Inscriptions." *Maarav* 7 (= *Let Your Colleagues Praise You: Studies in Memory of S. Gevirtz*; 1991) 141–47.
129. "The Aramean God Hadad." *Eretz-Israel* 24 (Abraham Malamat Volume; 1993) 54–61.
130. "The Prayer of Levi." *Journal of Biblical Literature* 112 (1993) 247–66. [with M. Stone].
131. "'Because He/She Did Not Know Letters': Remarks on a First Millennium C.E. Legal Expression." *Journal of the Ancient Near Eastern Society of Columbia University* 22 (= *Comparative Studies in Honor of Yohanan Muffs*; 1993) 39–44.
132. "The Qumran Scrolls Published and Unpublished." Pp. 378–82 in *Biblical Archaeology Today, 1990.* Jerusalem, 1993.

133. "The Babylonian Forerunner of a Mandaic Formula." Pp. 11–14 in *Kinattūtu ša darâti: R. Kutscher Memorial Volume.* Edited by A. Rainey. Tel Aviv, Journal of the Institute of Archaeology of Tel Aviv University, Occasional Publications 1. Tel Aviv, 1993.
134. "Deception Afoot" [review article of *The Dead Sea Scrolls Uncovered* by R. Eisenman and M. Wise (Shaftebury, 1993)]. *The Jerusalem Post,* February 17, 1993.
135. "Keret's Dream: *ḏhrt* and *hdrt.*" *Bulletin of the School of Oriental (and African) Studies* 57 (J. E. Wansbrough Volume; 1994) 87–92.
136. "*ʾatta porarta beʿozka yam* (Psalm 74:12a)." Pp. 113–19 in *Language, Theology and the Bible: Essays in Honour of James Barr.* Oxford, 1994.
137. "Apocryphes, pseudépigraphes et livres étranges de Qumrân." *Les Manuscrits de la Mer Morte: Les Dossiers d'archéologie* 189 (1994) 58–59.
138. "Babatha's *Ketubba.*" *Israel Exploration Journal* 44 (1994) 75–99. [with Y. Yadin and A. Yardeni]
139. "The First Manuscript of the Aramaic Levi Document from Qumran (4Q ArLevi^{a})." *Le Muséon* 107 (1994) 257–81. [with M. Stone]
140. "Babatha's Property and the Law of Succession in the Babatha Archive." *Zeitschrift für Papyrologie und Epigraphik* 104 (1994) 211–24. [with H. Cotton]
141. "The Wisdom of Aḥiqar." Pp. 43–52 in *Studies in Old Testament Wisdom and Related Literature: Essays in Honour of J. A. Emerton.* Edited by J. Day et al. Cambridge, 1995.
142. "The Names of the Zodiac in Aramaic and Hebrew." Pp. 95–101 in *Au carrefour des religions: Mélanges offerts à Phillipe Gignoux.* Res orientales 7. Edited by R. Gyselen. Paris, 1995.

In Press

143. "Aramaic and the Jews." In *Studia Aramaica: New Sources and New Approaches.* Journal of Semitic Studies Supplements 4. Manchester, 1995.
144. "Three Related Roots: *kms, kns,* and *knš.*" In *S. Morag Volume.* Jerusalem/ Madrid, 1995.
145. "The Receipt for a *Ketubba.*" In *M. Stern Memorial Volume.* Jerusalem, 1995. [with A. Yardeni]
146. "From *ʾlh rḥmn* to *ar-Raḥmān*: The Source of a Divine Epithet." In *Bridging the Worlds of Judaism and Islam: Papers in Honor of W. M. Brinner.* Berkeley, 1995.
147. "Apocrypha, Pseudepigrapha and Strange Texts at Qumran." In *J. Licht Memorial Volume.* Tel Aviv, 1995.
148. "P. Yadin 7: The Aramaic Gift Document from Naḥal Ḥever." *Eretz-Israel* 25 (J. Aviram Volume; 1995). [with Y. Yadin and A. Yardeni]
149. "An Astrological Text from Qumran (4Q318) and Reflections on Some Zodiacal Names." *Revue de Qumran* (1995). [with M. Sokoloff]
150. "The Second Manuscript of the Aramaic Levi Document from Qumran (4QArLevi^{b})," *Le Muséon* 108 (1995). [with M. Stone]

Articles in Encyclopedias

1. "Cheretites and Pelethites." P. 557 in *Interpreter's Dictionary of the Bible,* Volume 1. Nashville, 1962.
2. "Cyprus." Pp. 752–54 in *Interpreter's Dictionary of the Bible,* Volume 1. Nashville, 1962.
3. "Philistines." Pp. 791–95 in *Interpreter's Dictionary of the Bible,* Volume 3. Nashville, 1962.
4. "Philistines." P. 858 in *Encyclopedia Britannica,* Volume 17. Chicago, 1970.
5. "The History of Israel, Part II." Pp. 1026–31 in *Interpreter's One-Volume Commentary on the Bible.* Nashville, 1971.
6. "Aramaic." Pp. 39–44 in *Interpreter's Dictionary of the Bible, Supplementary Volume.* Nashville, 1976.
7. "רמון." Pp. 377–78 in *Encyclopaedia Biblica (Hebraica),* Volume 7. Jerusalem, 1976.
8. "שתר, שתר בזני." Pp. 270–72 in *Encyclopaedia Biblica (Hebraica),* Volume 8. Jerusalem, 1982.
9. "תמוז." Pp. 587–92 in *Encyclopaedia Biblica (Hebraica),* Volume 8. Jerusalem, 1982.
10. "תרשתא." P. 946 in *Encyclopaedia Biblica (Hebraica),* Volume 8. Jerusalem, 1982.
11. "Aramaic II: Aramaic Loanwords in Early Aramaic." Pp. 256–61 in *Encyclopaedia Iranica,* Volume 2. New York, 1987.
12. "ארמית." Pp. 196–200 in *Encyclopaedia Hebraica,* Supplementary Volume 2. Jerusalem, 1988.
13. *Encyclopaedia Judaica:* Various short articles.

Reviews

1. Cassuto, U., *The Goddess Anath* (Jerusalem, 1951 [Hebrew]). *American Journal of Archeology* 57 (1953) 223–24.
2. Gumpertz, Y. F., *Studies in Historical Phonetics of the Hebrew Language* (Jerusalem, 1953). *Journal of Biblical Literature* 75 (1956) 261.
3. Avi-Yonah, M. (ed.), *Sepher Yerushalayim* [The Book of Jerusalem], Volume 1: *The Natural Conditions and the History of the City from Its Origins to the Destruction of the Second Temple* (Jerusalem, 1956). *Journal of Biblical Literature* 76 (1957) 254–55.
4. Aharoni, Y., התנחלות שבטי ישראל בגליל העליון (Jerusalem, 1957). *Journal of Biblical Literature* 79 (1960) 71.
5. Schalit, A., *King Herod* (Jerusalem, 1960). *Journal of Biblical Literature* 80 (1961) 82–84.
6. Kaiser, O., *Die mythische Bedeutung des Meeres in Aegypten, Ugarit und Israel* (Berlin, 1959). *Journal of Biblical Literature* 80 (1961) 91–92.
7. Haran, M. (ed.), *Yehezkel Kaufmann Jubilee Volume* (Jerusalem, 1960). *Journal of Biblical Literature* 80 (1961) 296–97.
8. Brunner, G., *Der Nabuchodonosor der Buches Judith* (Berlin, 1959). *Journal of Biblical Literature* 80 (1961) 298.

9. Goshen-Gottstein, M. H., *The Qumran Scrolls and Their Linguistic Status* (Jerusalem, 1959). *Revue de Qumran* 3 (1961) 296–97.
10. Rabin, C., and Y. Yadin (eds.), *Essays on the Dead Sea Scrolls in Memory of E. L. Sukenik* (Jerusalem, 1961 [Hebrew]). *Revue de Qumran* 3 (1961) 457–62.
11. Ginsberg, H. L., קהלת (Tel Aviv, 1961). *Journal of Biblical Literature* 82 (1963) 351–53.
12. Biram, A., דברי ימי ישראל בזמן המקרא במסגרת תולדות המזרח הקדום (Haifa, 1962). *Journal of Biblical Literature* 82 (1963) 365.
13. Glanzman, G. S., and J. A. Fitzmyer, *An Introductory Bibliography for the Study of Scripture* (Westminster, 1961). *Journal of the American Oriental Society* 83 (1963) 244.
14. Stevenson, W. B., *Grammar of Palestinian Jewish Aramaic* (Oxford, 1962). *Journal of the American Oriental Society* 83 (1963) 244–45.
15. Clark, E., *The Selected Questions of Isho Bar Nun on the Pentateuch* (Leiden, 1962). *Journal of the American Oriental Society* 83 (1963) 245.
16. Drower, E. S., *The Canonical Prayerbook of the Mandaeans* (Leiden, 1959). *Journal of the American Oriental Society* 83 (1963) 246.
17. Drower, E. S., *The Coronation of the Great Sislam* (Leiden, 1963). *Journal of the American Oriental Society* 83 (1963) 246.
18. Drower, E. S., *The Secret Adam: A Study of Nasoraean Gnosis* (Oxford, 1960). *Journal of the American Oriental Society* 83 (1963) 246.
19. Segal, J. B., *The Hebrew Passover* (Oxford, 1963). *Journal of the American Oriental Society* 85 (1965) 255.
20. Albrektson, B., *Studies in the Text and Theology of the Book of Lamentations with a Critical Edition of the Peshitta Text* (Lund, 1963). *Journal of the American Oriental Society* 85 (1965) 255–56.
21. Thomas, W., and W. D. McHardy (eds.), *Hebrew and Semitic Studies Presented to Godfrey Rolles Driver in Celebration of His Seventieth Birthday* (Oxford, 1965). *Journal of the American Oriental Society* 85 (1965) 256–58.
22. Gordon, C. H., *Evidence for the Minoan Language* (Ventnor, 1966). *Journal of Biblical Literature* 86 (1967) 241–44.
23. Lieberman, S. et al., ספר חנוך ילון (*Henoch Yalon Jubilee Volume on the Occasion of His Seventy-Fifth Birthday*; Jerusalem, 1963). *Journal of the American Oriental Society* 87 (1967) 69–72.
24. Liverani, M., *Storia di Ugarit nell'eta degli archivi politici* (Rome, 1962). *Journal of the American Oriental Society* 87 (1967) 187–88.
25. McCullough, E. S. (ed.), *The Seed of Wisdom: Essays in Honour of T. J. Meek* (Toronto, 1964). *Journal of the American Oriental Society* 87 (1967) 188–89.
26. Kapelrud, A. S., *The Ras Shamra Discoveries and the Old Testament* (Norman, 1963). *Journal of the American Oriental Society* 87 (1967) 631–33.
27. Gordon, C. H., *Evidence for the Minoan Language* (Ventnor, 1966). *Journal of Biblical Literature* 86 (1967) 241–44.
28. Macuch, R., *Handbook of Classical and Modern Mandaic* (Berlin, 1965). *Oriens* 20 (1968) 391–94.
29. Weil, G. E., *Elie Levita: Humaniste et Massorète (1469–1549)* (Leiden, 1963). *Journal of the American Oriental Society* 88 (1968) 529–31.

30. Fitzmyer, J. A., *The Aramaic Inscriptions of Sefîre* (Rome, 1967). *Journal of Biblical Literature* 87 (1968) 240–41.
31. Wagner, M., *Die lexikalischen und grammatikalischen Aramäismen im alttestamentlichen Hebräisch* (Berlin, 1966). *Journal of Biblical Literature* 87 (1968) 232–34.
32. Dahood, M., *Ugaritic-Hebrew Philology* (Rome, 1965). *Journal of the American Oriental Society* 89 (1969) 174–78.
33. Yalon, H., *Studies in the Dead Sea Scrolls* (Jerusalem, 1967 [Hebrew]). *Revue de Qumran* 6 (1969) 571.
34. Katz, E., *Die Bedeutung des Hapax Legomenon de Qumraner Handschriften "HUAHA"* (Bratislava, 1966). *Revue de Qumran* 6 (1969) 572.
35. Weiss, R., המקרא בקומראן (Jerusalem, 1967). *Revue de Qumran* 6 (1969) 573.
36. Oxtoby, W. G., *Some Inscriptions of the Safaitic Bedouin* (New Haven, 1968). *Bulletin of the American Schools of Oriental Research* 198 (1970) 44.
37. Etheridge, J. W., *The Targums of Onkelos and Jonathan ben Uzziel on the Pentateuch, with the Fragments of the Jerusalem Targum from the Chaldee* (New York, 1968). *Journal of Biblical Literature* 89 (1970) 238–39.
38. Garbell, I., *The Jewish Neo-Aramaic Dialects of Persian Azerbaijan* (London, 1965). *Journal of the American Oriental Society* 90 (1970) 293–95.
39. Drower, E. S., *A Pair of Nasorean Commentaries* (Leiden, 1963). *Journal of the American Oriental Society* 90 (1970) 339–40.
40. Segal, J. B., *Edessa, "The Blessed City"* (Oxford, 1970). *Bulletin of the American Schools of Oriental Research* 203 (1971) 45.
41. *Archaeologica Iranica: Miscellanea in honorem R. Ghirshman* (Leiden, 1970). *Bulletin of the American Schools of Oriental Research* 203 (1971) 45.
42. *The Old Testament in Syriac according to the Peshitta Version, Sample Edition: Song of Songs-Tobit-4 Ezra* (Leiden, 1966). *Journal of the American Oriental Society* 91 (1971) 306–7.
43. Amir, D., *Ancient History of the Eastern Upper Galilee* (Kibbutz Dan, 1965). *Journal of Near Eastern Studies* 30 (1971) 158.
44. Allegro, J. M., and A. A. Anderson, *Qumrân Cave 4 I (4Q158–4Q186)* (DJD 5; Oxford, 1968). *Journal of Near Eastern Studies* 31 (1972) 56–58.
45. Black, M., *An Aramaic Approach to the Gospels* (Oxford, 1967). *Journal of Near Eastern Studies* 31 (1972) 58–61.
46. Galand, L. et al., *Inscriptions antiques du Maroc* (Paris, 1966). *Journal of Near Eastern Studies* 31 (1972) 119–20.
47. Schechter, S., *Documents of Jewish Sectaries, with a Prolegomenon by J. A. Fitzmyer* (New York, 1970). *Journal of Near Eastern Studies* 31 (1972) 344–46.
48. Arberry, A. J. (ed.), *Religion in the Middle East: Three Religions in Concord and Conflict* (Cambridge, 1969). *Journal of Near Eastern Studies* 32 (1973) 266–67.
49. Gibson, A. S., *Textbook of Syrian Semitic Inscriptions: Hebrew and Moabite Inscriptions* (Oxford, 1971). *Journal of the American Oriental Society* 94 (1974) 509–12.

50. H. Schneider et al., *The Old Testament in Syriac according to the Peshitta Version: Part IV, Fascicle 6* (Leiden, 1972). *Journal of the American Oriental Society* 94 (1974) 512–13.
51. Hrouda, B., *Handbuch der Archäologie, Vorderasien I: Mesopotamien, Babylonien, Iran und Anatolien* (Munich, 1971). *Israel Exploration Journal* 25 (1975) 56–59.
52. E. Neu and C. Rüster, *Tradition und Glaube, das frühe Christentum in seiner Umwelt: Festgabe für K. G. Kuhn* (Göttingen, 1971). *Bulletin of the American Schools of Oriental Research* 223 (1976) 74–75.
53. Neu, E., and C. Rüster (eds.), *Festschrift H. Otten* (Wiesbaden, 1973). *Bulletin of the American Schools of Oriental Research* 223 (1976) 76–77.
54. Bittel, K. et al. (eds.), *Anatolian Studies Presented to H. Güterbock on the Occasion of His Sixty-Fifth Birthday* (Istanbul, 1974). *Bulletin of the American Schools of Oriental Research* 223 (1976) 76–77.
55. Muffs, Y., *Studies in the Aramaic Legal Papyri from Elephantine* (New York, 1973). *Israel Exploration Journal* 26 (1976) 214–15.
56. Fitzmyer, J. A., *Essays on the Semitic Background of the New Testament* (London, 1971). *Journal of Near Eastern Studies* 35 (1976) 59–61.
57. Schwabe, M., and Lifshitz, B., *Beth She^carim, Volume 2: The Greek Inscriptions* (Jerusalem, 1967). *Journal of Near Eastern Studies* 35 (1976) 137–39.
58. Avigad, N., *Beth Sheᶜarim, Volume 3: The Archaeological Excavations during 1953–1958* (Jerusalem, 1967). *Journal of Near Eastern Studies* 35 (1976) 137–39.
59. De Vaux, R., *Archaeology and the Dead Sea Scrolls* (Oxford, 1973). *Journal of Near Eastern Studies* 35 (1976) 287–90.
60. Monsengwo, P. L., *La Notion de Nomos dans le Pentateuque grec* (Rome, 1973). *Journal of Biblical Literature* 95 (1976) 136–37.
61. Whitaker, R. E., *A Concordance of Ugaritic Literature* (Cambridge, 1971). *Journal of Cuneiform Studies* 29 (1977) 126.
62. Fisher, L. R., *The Claremont Ras Shamra Tablets* (Analecta Orientalia 48; Rome, 1972). *Journal of Cuneiform Studies* 29 (1977) 187–88.
63. Isbell, C. D., *Corpus of the Aramaic Incantation Bowls* (Missoula, Montana, 1975). *Journal of Biblical Literature* 96 (1977) 577–78.
64. Thompson, T. L., *The Historicity of the Patriarchal Narratives* (Beiheft zur Zeitschrift für die alttestamentliche Wissenschaft 133; Berlin, 1975). *Israel Exploration Journal* 27 (1977) 185–87.
65. Trevor, J. C., *Scrolls from Qumran Cave I: The Great Isaiah Scroll, The Order of the Community, The Pesher to Habakkuk, from Photographs by John C. Trevor* (Jerusalem, 1972). *Journal of Near Eastern Studies* 36 (1977) 215–16.
66. Frey, J. B., *Corpus of Jewish Inscriptions: Jewish Inscriptions from the Third Century* B.C. *to the Seventh Century* A.D. *Europe, Volume 1* (Rome, 1936). *Journal of the American Oriental Society* 98 (1978) 148–49.
67. Scholem, G., *Kabbalah* (New York, 1974). *Journal of the American Oriental Society* 98 (1978) 487–89.
68. Scholem, G., *Sabbatai Ṣevi: The Mystical Messiah 1626–1676* (Princeton, 1973). *Journal of the American Oriental Society* 98 (1978) 487–89.

69. Svedlund, G., *The Aramaic Portions of the Pesiqta de Rab Kahana with English Translation: Commentary and Introduction* (Uppsala, 1974). *Journal of the American Oriental Society* 98 (1978) 511–12.
70. Gibson, J. C. L., *Textbook of Syrian Semitic Inscriptions, Volume 2: Aramaic Inscriptions, Including Inscriptions in the Dialect of Zenjirli* (Oxford, 1975). *Israel Exploration Journal* 28 (1978) 287–89.
71. Lemaire, A., *Inscriptions hébraïques, Volume 1: Les Ostraca* (Littératures Anciennes de Proche-Orient 9; Paris, 1977). *Israel Exploration Journal* 29 (1979) 264.
72. Cross, F. M. et al. (eds.), *Magnalia Dei, the Mighty Acts of God: Essays on the Bible and Archaeology in Memory of G. E. Wright* (Garden City, 1976). *Bulletin of the American Schools of Oriental Research* 230 (1980) 83–84.
73. Beek, M. A. et al. (eds.), *Symbolae Biblicae et Mesopotamica: Francis Mario Theodoro de Liagre Böhl Dedicatae* (Leiden, 1973). *Bulletin of the American Schools of Oriental Research* 230 (1980) 84–85.
74. Powels, S., *Der Kalendar der Samaritaner anhand des Kitāb ḥisāb assinīn und anderer Handschriften* (Berlin, 1977). *Journal of Near Eastern Studies* 40 (1981) 148–51.
75. Gibson, J. C. L., *Canaanite Myths and Legends* (Edinburgh, 1978). *Israel Exploration Journal* 31 (1981) 254.
76. Bron, F., *Recherches sur les inscriptions phéniciennes de Karatepe* (Geneva, 1979). *Israel Exploration Journal* 32 (1982) 179–81.
77. Kronholm, T., *Motifs from Genesis 1–11 in the Genuine Hymns of Ephrem the Syrian* (Lund, 1978). *Journal of the American Oriental Society* 102 (1982) 190–91.
78. Tsereteli, K., *Grammatik der modernen assyrischen Sprache (Neuostaramäisch)* (Leipzig, 1978). *Journal of the American Oriental Society* 102 (1982) 209.
79. Ritter, W., *Turoyo, Die Volkssprache der syrischen Christen des Tur Abdin, B: Wörterbuch* (Beirut, 1979). *Journal of the American Oriental Society* 102 (1982) 406–7.
80. Bounni, A., and J. Teixidor, *Inventaire des inscriptions de Palmyre: Fascicle 12* (Damascus, 1977). *Journal of Near Eastern Studies* 41 (1982) 149.
81. Davies, R., *1QM, The War Scroll from Qumran: Its Structure and History* (Rome, 1977). *Journal of Near Eastern Studies* 41 (1982) 149.
82. Flusser, D., *The Josippon, Edited with Introduction, Commentary and Notes, Volume 2* (Jerusalem, 1980). *Immanuel* 15 (1982–83) 82–84.
83. Ulrich, E. C. Jr., *The Qumran Text of Samuel and Josephus* (Missoula, 1978). *Journal of Near Eastern Studies* 42 (1983) 67–68.
84. Charlesworth, J. H. (ed.), *The Old Testament Pseudepigrapha, Volume 1: Apocalyptic Literature and Testaments* (New York, 1983). *Israel Exploration Journal* 35 (1985) 209–10.
85. Charlesworth, J. H., *The Discovery of a Dead Sea Scroll (4Q Therapeia)* (Lubbock, Texas, 1985). *Israel Exploration Journal* 36 (1986) 118–19.
86. Krotkoff, G., *A Neo-Aramaic Dialect of Kurdistan: Texts, Grammar and Vocabulary* (New Haven, 1982). *Journal of the American Oriental Society* 106 (1986) 842–43.

87. Bergsträsser, G., *Introduction to the Semitic Languages: Text Specimens and Grammatical Sketches* (Winona Lake, Indiana, 1983). *Journal of the American Oriental Society* 106 (1986) 872.
88. Macuch, R., *Grammatik des Samaritanischen Aramäisch* (Berlin, 1982). *Journal of the American Oriental Society* 107 (1987) 332–33.
89. Clarke, E., J. C. Hurd, and F. Spitzer (eds.), *Targum Pseudo-Jonathan Pentateuch: Text and Concordance* (Hoboken, 1984). *Journal of the American Oriental Society* 107 (1987) 333–35.
90. Crown, A. D., *A Bibliography of the Samaritans* (Philadelphia, 1984). *Journal of the American Oriental Society* 107 (1987) 545–47.
91. Gubel, E., E. Lipiński, and B. Servais-Soyez (eds.), *Studia Phoenicia, Volumes 1–2* (Louvain, 1983). *Israel Exploration Journal* 38 (1988) 98–99.
92. Gubel, E., and E. Lipiński (eds.), *Studia Phoenicia, Volume 3* (Louvain, 1985). *Israel Exploration Journal* 38 (1988) 98–99.
93. Huffmon, H. B., F. A. Spina, and A. R. W. Green (eds.), *The Quest for the Kingdom of God: Studies in Honor of George E. Mendenhall* (Winona Lake, Indiana, 1983). *Bulletin of the American Schools of Oriental Research* 269 (1988) 92–94.
94. Meyers, C. E., and M. O'Connor, *The Word of the Lord Shall Go Forth: Essays in Honor of David Noel Freedman in Celebration of His Sixtieth Birthday* (Winona Lake, Indiana, 1983). *Bulletin of the American Schools of Oriental Research* 269 (1988) 92–94.
95. Seyrig, H., *Scripta Varia: Mélanges de archéologie et d'histoire* (Paris, 1983). *Israel Exploration Journal* 39 (1989) 121–22.
96. Seyrig, H., *Scripta Numismatica* (Paris, 1986). *Israel Exploration Journal* 39 (1989) 121–22.
97. Hajjar, Y., *La Triade d'Heliopolis-Baalbek* (Montreal, 1985). *Numen* 38 (1990) 280–83; reply to Y. Hajjar, *Numen* 39 (1991) 271–73.
98. Rothschild, J.-P., and G. D. Sixdenier (eds.), *Études samaritaines: Pentateuque et Targum, exégèse et philologie, chroniques* (Paris, 1988). *Israel Exploration Journal* 42 (1992) 125.
99. Crown, A. D., *The Samaritans* (Tübingen, 1989). *Israel Exploration Journal* 42 (1992) 125–26.
100. Appelbaum, S., *Judea in Hellenistic and Roman Times* (Leiden, 1989). *Israel Exploration Journal* 43 (1993) 76.
101. Broshi, M. (ed.), *The Damascus Document Reconsidered* (Jerusalem, 1992). *Israel Exploration Journal* 43 (1993) 76–77.
102. Charlesworth, J. H. (ed.), *Graphic Concordance to the Dead Sea Scrolls* (Louisville, 1991). *Israel Exploration Journal* 43 (1993) 76–77.
103. Hachlili, R. (ed.), *Ancient Synagogues in Israel: Third–Seventh Centuries* C.E. (Haifa and Oxford, 1989). *Israel Exploration Journal* 43 (1993) 77.

Archaeology: Various short reviews
Jewish Social Studies: Various short reviews
Middle Eastern Affairs: Various short reviews

Abbreviations

GENERAL

b.	Babylonian Talmud
BH	Biblical Hebrew
DSS	Dead Sea Scrolls
GE	Gilgamesh Epic
GNB	Good News Bible
JPSV	Jewish Publication Society Version
KJV	King James Version
LB	Late Babylonian
LXX	Septuagint
m.	Mishna
MA	Middle Assyrian
MB	Middle Babylonian
MH	Mishnaic Hebrew
MT	Masoretic Text
NAB	New American Bible
NB	Neo-Babylonian
NEB	New English Bible
NIV	New International Version
NJPSV	The New Jewish Publication Society Version
NRSV	New Revised Standard Version
OB	Old Babylonian
Pesh.	Peshiṭtaʾ
REB	Revised English Bible
RSV	Revised Standard Version
t.	Tosepta
Tg.	Targum
Vg.	Vulgate
y.	Jerusalem Talmud

MUSEUM SIGLA

A.	Preliminary Louvre Museum siglum for Mari tablets
BM	British Museum tablets
CBS	Tablets in the collections of the University Museum of the University of Pennsylvania, Philadelphia
HS	Tablets in the Hilprecht collection, Jena

K	Tablets in the Kouyunjik collection of the British Museum
MFA	Museum of Fine Arts, Boston
MLC	Tablets in the collections of the Morgan Library at Yale
Mus. Inv.	Museum Inventory number assigned to Qumran MSS in the Rockefeller Museum, Jerusalem
N	Tablets in the collections of the University Museum of the University of Pennsylvania, Philadelphia
NBC	Nies Babylonian Collection, Yale University
ND	Field numbers of tablets excavated at Nimrud (Kalḫu)
Ni	Tablets excavated at Nippur, in the collections of the Archaeological Museum of Istanbul
PAM	Palestinian Archaeological Museum photograph number
STT	Sultantepe Tablets

REFERENCE WORKS

AB	Anchor Bible
ABD	*Anchor Bible Dictionary*
ABL	R. F. Harper, *Assyrian and Babylonian Letters*
AcOr	*Acta Orientalia*
AfK	*Archiv für Keilschriftforschung*
AfO	*Archiv für Orientforschung*
AHw	W. von Soden, *Akkadisches Handwörterbuch* (Wiesbaden, 1965–1981)
AION	*Annali Istituto Universitario Orientale*
AJSL	*American Journal of Semitic Languages and Literature*
AJS Review	*Association for Jewish Studies Review*
ALUOS	*Annual of the Leeds University Oriental Society*
AnBib	Analecta Biblica
ANET	J. B. Pritchard (ed.), *Ancient Near Eastern Texts Relating to the Old Testament* (3d ed., Princeton, 1969)
ANETS	Ancient Near Eastern Texts and Studies
AnOr	Analecta orientalia
AnSt	*Anatolian Studies*
AOAT	Alter Orient und Altes Testament
AOS	American Oriental Series
AOS	Aula Orientalis Supplementa
ARM	Archives royales de Mari
ARMT	Archives royales de Mari Textes
ArOr	*Archiv orientální*
ARW	*Archiv für Religionswissenschaft*
AS	Assyriological Studies
ASJ	*Acta Sumerologica* (Japan)
ASTI	*Annual of the Swedish Theological Institute*
BA	*Biblical Archaeologist*
BAH	Bibliothèque archéologique et historique
BAM	F. Köcher, *Die babylonisch-assyrische Medizin*
BAR	*Biblical Archaeologist Reader*
BASOR	*Bulletin of the American Schools of Oriental Research*

BASP	*Bulletin of the American Society of Papyrologists*
BAW	B. Meissner, *Beiträge zum assyrischen Wörterbuch*
BDB	F. Brown, S. R. Driver, and C. A. Briggs, *Hebrew and English Lexicon of the Old Testament* (Oxford, 1907)
BE	Babylonian Expedition of the University of Pennsylvania, Series A: Cuneiform Texts
BETL	Bibliotheca ephemeridum theologicarum lovaniensium
BHK	R. Kittel (ed.), *Biblia Hebraica*
BHS	*Biblia Hebraica Stuttgartensia*
Bib	*Biblica*
BIE	*Bulletin de l'Institut d'Égypte*
BIN	*Babylonian Inscriptions in the Collection of J. B. Nies*
BiOr	*Bibliotheca orientalis*
BJS	Brown Judaic Studies
BK	*Bibel und Kirche*
BKAT	Biblischer Kommentar: Altes Testament
BN	*Biblische Notizen*
BSO(A)S	*Bulletin of the School of Oriental (and African) Studies*
BWL	W. G. Lambert, *Babylonian Wisdom Literature*
BZAW	Beihefte zur ZAW
CAD	*The Assyrian Dictionary of the Oriental Institute of the University of Chicago*
CBQ	*Catholic Biblical Quarterly*
CBQMS	Catholic Biblical Quarterly Monograph Series
CHJ	W. D. Davies and Louis Finkelstein (eds.), *Cambridge History of Judaism* (2 vols.; Cambridge: Cambridge University Press, 1984–90)
CIH	*Corpus inscriptionum himjariticarum*
CII	*Corpus inscriptionum iranicarum*
CIS	*Corpus inscriptionum semiticarum*
Cowley	Cowley, *Aramaic Papyri of the Fifth Century* B.C. (Oxford, 1923)
CRAI	*Comptes rendus de l'Académie des inscriptions et belles-lettres*
CRRAI	Compte rendu de la Rencontre assyriologique internationale
CSCO	Corpus scriptorum christianum orientalium
CT	Cuneiform Texts from the British Museum
CTA	A. Herdner, *Corpus des tablettes en cunéiformes alphabétiques*
CTN	Cuneiform Texts from Nimrud
DBSup	*Dictionnaire de la Bible, Supplément*
DISO	C.-F. Jean and J. Hoftijzer, *Dictionnaire des inscriptions sémitiques de l'ouest* (Leiden, 1965)
DJD	Discoveries in the Judaean Desert
EA	J. A. Knudtzon, *Die El-Amarna Tafeln* (2 vols.; ed. J. A. Knudtzon; Leipzig, 1915; reissue, Aalen, 1964)
EEA	S. Moscati, *Epigrafia ebraica antica 1935–1950* (Rome, 1951)
EI[1]	*Encyclopaedia of Islam* (Leiden, 1913–36)
EI[2]	*Encyclopaedia of Islam* (rev. ed.; Leiden, 1960–)
ErIsr	Eretz-Israel
ETh	*Études théologiques*
GAG	W. von Soden, *Grundriss der akkadischen Grammatik*

GCCI R. P. Dougherty, *Goucher College Cuneiform Inscriptions*
Gilgamesh OB P Pennsylvania tablet, OB version of Tablet II
GKC *Gesenius' Hebrew Grammar*, ed. E. Kautzsch, trans. A. E. Cowley
GLECS (Comptes rendus) Groupe linguistique d'études chamito-sémitiques
HALAT L. Koehler and W. Baumgartner et al., *Hebräisches und aramäisches Lexikon zum Alten Testament* (Leiden, 1967–1990)
HAR *Hebrew Annual Review*
HEO Hautes études orientales (Geneva and Paris)
HKAT Handkommentar zum Alten Testament
HR *History of Religions*
HSM Harvard Semitic Monographs
HSS Harvard Semitic Studies
HTR *Harvard Theological Review*
HUCA *Hebrew Union College Annual*
IAP D. Diringer, *Le iscrizioni antico-ebraiche Palestinesi* (Florence, 1934)
IB *Interpreter's Bible*
ICC International Critical Commentary
IDB G. A. Buttrick (ed.), *Interpreter's Dictionary of the Bible*
IDBSup Supplementary volume to *IDB*
IEJ *Israel Exploration Journal*
IF *Indogermanische Forschungen*
IOS *Israel Oriental Studies*
JA *Journal asiatique*
JANES(CU) *Journal of the Ancient Near Eastern Society (of Columbia University)*
JAOS *Journal of the American Oriental Society*
JBL *Journal of Biblical Literature*
JCS *Journal of Cuneiform Studies*
JEOL *Jaarbericht van het Vooraziatisch-Egyptisch Genootschap: Ex Oriente Lux*
JESHO *Journal of Economic and Social History of the Orient*
JHNES Johns Hopkins Near Eastern Studies
JJS *Journal of Jewish Studies*
JNES *Journal of Near Eastern Studies*
JPS Torah Commentary Jewish Publication Society Torah Commentary
JQR *Jewish Quarterly Review*
JRAS *Journal of of the Royal Asiatic Society*
JRT *Journal of Religious Thought*
JSJ *Journal for the Study of Judaism*
JSOT *Journal for the Study of the Old Testament*
JSOTSup Journal for the Study of the Old Testament Supplement Series
JSS *Journal of Semitic Studies*
JTS *Journal of Theological Studies*
KAI H. Donner and W. Röllig, *Kanaanäische und aramäische Inschriften*
KAR Keilinschriften aus Assur religiösen Inhalts
KB L. Koehler and W. Baumgartner, *Lexicon in Veteris Testamenti libros*
KBo Keilschrifttexte aus Boghazköi

KeH	Kurzgefasstes exegetisches Handbuch zum Alten Testament
KHC	Kürzer Hand-Commentar zum Alten Testament
KTU	M. Dietrich, O. Loretz, and J. Sanmartín, *Die keilalphabetischen Texte aus Ugarit* (AOAT 24; Neukirchen-Vluyn, 1976)
KUB	Keilschrifturkunden aus Boghazköi
LAPO	Littératures anciennes du Proche-Orient
Leš	*Lešonénu*
LKA	*Literarische Keilschrifttexte aus Assur*
MAD	Materials for the Assyrian Dictionary
MANL	*Memorie della Accademia Nazionale dei Lincei*
MARI	*Mari: Annales de recherches interdisciplinaires*
MDAIK	Mitteilungen des deutschen archäologischen Instituts, Abteilung Kairo
MDOG	Mitteilungen der deutschen Orient-Gesellschaft
MGWJ	*Monatsschrift für Geschichte und Wissenschaft des Judentums*
MIO	Mitteilungen des Instituts für Orientforschung
MMJ	*Metropolitan Museum Journal*
MS	Masoretic Studies
MSL	Materialien zum sumerischen Lexikon
NABU	*Nouvelles assyriologiques brèves et utilitaires*
NTS	*New Testament Studies*
OBO	Orbis biblicus et orientalis
OECT	Oxford Editions of Cuneiform Texts
OLA	Orientalia Lovaniensia Analecta
OLP	*Orientalia Loveniensia Periodica*
OLZ	*Orientalische Literaturzeitung*
Or	*Orientalia*
OrSuec	*Orientalia Suecana*
PAAJR	*Proceedings of the American Academy of Jewish Research*
PAPS	*Proceedings of the American Philosophical Society*
PBS	Publications of the Babylonian Section, University Museum, University of Pennsylvania
PEQ	*Palestine Exploration Quarterly*
PRU	Le Palais royal d'Ugarit
RA	*Revue d'assyriologie et d'archéologie orientale*
RAI	Rencontre assyriologique internationale
5 Rawl.	H. C. Rawlinson, *The Cuneiform Inscriptions of Western Asia*, vol. 5
RB	*Revue biblique*
RES	*Répertoire d'épigraphie sémitique* (Paris, 1905–68)
RelS	*Religious Studies*
RevQ	*Revue de Qumran*
RGG	*Die Religion in Geschichte und Gegenwart* (5 vols.; Tübingen, 1957–62)
RGTC	Répertoire géographique des textes cunéiformes
RHA	*Revue hittite et asianique*
RivB	*Rivista biblica*
RLA	*Reallexikon der Assyriologie*
RS	Ras Shamra texts
RSO	*Rivista degli studi orientali*

RSP	Ras Shamra Parallels
SAA	State Archives of Assyria
SBLDS	SBL Dissertation Series
SBLMS	Society of Biblical Literature Monograph Series
SBLRBS	Society of Biblical Literature Resources for Biblical Study
SBT	Studies in Biblical Theology
ScrHier	Scripta Hierosolymitana
SD	Studia et documenta ad iura orientis antiqui pertinentia
SEG	*Supplementum epigraphicum graecum*
SEL	Studi epigrafici et linguistici
Sem	*Semitica*
SGL	A. Falkenstein, *Sumerische Götterlieder*
SLB	*Studia ad tabulas cuneiformes collectas a F. M. Th. de Liagre Böhl pertinentia*
SRT	E. Chiera, *Sumerian Religious Texts*
SSN	Studia semitica neerlandica
StudOr	Studia Orientalia
TAPA	*Transactions of the American Philological Association*
TCL	Textes cunéiformes du Louvre
TCS	Texts from Cuneiform Sources
TDNT	G. Kittel and G. Friedrich (eds.), *Theological Dictionary of the New Testament*
THAT	E. Jenni and C. Westermann (eds.), *Theologische Handwörterbuch zum Alten Testament*
ThV	*Theologia Viatorum*
TIM	Texts in the Iraq Museum
TOB	*La Traduction oecuménique de la Bible*
TWAT	*Theologisches Wörterbuch zum Alten Testament*
UET	Ur Excavations, Texts
UF	*Ugarit-Forschungen*
UT	C. H. Gordon, *Ugaritic Textbook* (Rome, 1965)
VS	Vorderasiatische Schriftdenkmäler
VT	*Vetus Testamentum*
VTSup	Vetus Testamentum Supplements
WBC	Word Biblical Commentary
WO	*Die Welt des Orients*
WQW	S. Talmon, *The World of Qumran from Within* (Jerusalem and Leiden, 1989)
WTJ	*Westminster Theological Journal*
WVDOG	Wissenschaftliche Veröffentlichungen der deutschen Orient-gesellschaft
WZ	*Wissenschaftliche Zeitschrift der Martin-Luther-Universität*
WZKM	*Wiener Zeitschrift für die Kunde des Morgenlandes*
YNER	Yale Near Eastern Researches
YOR	Yale Oriental Series, Researches
YOS	Yale Oriental Series, Babylonian Texts
ZA	*Zeitschrift für Assyriologie*
ZAH	*Zeitschrift für Althebräistik*
ZÄS	*Zeitschrift für ägyptische Sprache und Altertumskunde*
ZAW	*Zeitschrift für die Alttestamentliche Wissenschaft*
ZDMG	*Zeitschrift der deutschen morgenländischen Gesellschaft*

Part I

Bible

Some Bird Names in the Judeo-Persian Translations of the Hebrew Bible

JES P. ASMUSSEN

In this article, I continue my studies of lexical points in Judeo-Persian. This contribution is concerned with names of birds.

Birds are often mentioned in the Hebrew Bible, both generally as 'birds' (*ᶜôp*, Judeo-Persian *murγ*; *ṣippôr* [*ṣippor*], Judeo-Persian *parande*) and specifically by their individual names (eagle, owl, and so on).

Highly interesting is the Judeo-Persian *sīmurγ* for *nešer* 'eagle', indicating that *sīmurγ* is not the mythological phoenix but the real eagle, *aquila*.[1] Also remarkable is the use of *ṭāwûs* (*ṭāβūs*) 'peacock', a loanword from Greek Ταῶς, for *ᶜayiṭ* 'bird of prey'.[2] The "real" peacock occurs only twice in the Bible, in 1 Kgs 10:22 and 2 Chr 9:21, in the plural: *tū(u)kiyyîm*. Thus the *Agrōn*, the fifteenth-century Hebrew–Judeo-Persian dictionary, has *tvkyym* = *ṭāwôs*.[3] The Judeo-Persian translation,[4] although it does not always reflect genuine tradition, has *ṭāōs hā* (1 Kgs 10:22).

The Judeo-Persian bird names listed below are taken from the Vatican Judeo-Persian Pentateuch (Vat.),[5] the British Museum Judeo-Persian Pentateuch (BM),[6] and the Judeo-Persian translation of Job.[7]

1. J. P. Asmussen, "Simurγ in Judeo-Persian Translations of the Hebrew Bible," *Acta Iranica* 30 (1990) 1–5.

2. J. P. Asmussen, "Ornithologisches aus den jüdisch-persischen Übersetzungen der hebräischen Bibel," in *Corolla Iranica* (Papers in honor of David Neil MacKenzie; ed. R. E. Emmerick and D. Weber; Frankfurt am Main, 1991) 1–2.

3. W. Bacher, "Ein hebräisch-persisches Wörterbuch aus dem 15. Jahrhundert," *ZAW* 16 (1896) 218.

4. Published by the British and Foreign Bible Society (London, 1905).

5. H. H. Paper, "The Vatican Judeo-Persian Pentateuch: Genesis," *AcOr* 28 (1964–65) 268–340; idem, "The Vatican Judeo-Persian Pentateuch: Exodus and Leviticus," *AcOr* 29/1–2 (1965) 75–181; idem, "The Vatican Judeo-Persian Pentateuch: Deuteronomy," *AcOr* 31 (1968) 55–113.

6. H. H. Paper, *A Judeo-Persian Pentateuch: The Text of the Oldest Judeo-Persian Pentateuch Translation British Museum Ms. Or. 5446* (Jerusalem, 1972). Quite a number of texts, up to Lev 11:20, are missing.

7. H. H. Paper, *A Judeo-Persian Book of Job* (The Israel Academy of Sciences and Humanities, Proceedings 5/12; Jerusalem, 1976).

1. *ᶜōrēb* 'raven'. Vat. Gen 8:7, Lev 11:15: *brᵓγ*.[8] Vat. Deut 14:14, however, has *byrᵓγ*, where BM has *klᵓg*. The Judeo-Persian Job 38:41 gives *brᵓγ* (Middle Persian *varāg*) but has *qylᵓγ* in the margin. This is New Persian *kalāγ, q(k)elāγ, kulāγ* 'raven' or 'crow', at any rate a bird of the *corvus* family.[9]

2. *peres* 'ossifrage'. Vat. Lev 11:13, Deut 14:12 *krks*; BM Deut 14:12 *krgs*: *karkas, kargas*; Middle Persian *karkās, kargās* 'vulture'.[10]

3. *ᶜozniyyâ* 'osprey'. Vat. Lev 11:13 and Deut 14:12 *ᶜvqᵓb*: *ᶜuqāb* 'eagle'.[11] The BM Deut 14:12 translates *mvšgyr*: *mūšgīr* 'a bird of prey of genus *Accipiter*'.[12]

4. *dāᵓâ* 'vulture'. Vat. Lev 11:14 *ᵓᵃlᵃh*: *ālah* 'eagle'.[13]

5. *ᵓayyâ* 'vulture, kite, hawk'. Vat. Lev 11:14 *ᵘzĕγᵃn*: *uzĕγan*, that is, *zaγan* 'vulture' or 'kite'.[14] The Judeo-Persian form seems to confirm Henning's suggestion: "A Persian word for 'vulture' of possibly Eastern Iranian origin is *zaγan* (for **zγan*): Saka *uysgana*, vulture[15] (Saka *-ys-* = *-z-*). The Vat. Deut 14:13 has *ᵓlh* for *ᵓayyâ* and is thus in agreement with Job 28:7: *aluh*.[16] The BM Deut 14:13 has *hvmᵓy, humāi*, "der sagenhafte Vogel Phönix; ein königlicher Adler—ein Pelikan."[17]

6. *rāᵓâ*, Deut 14:13 is apparently a mistake for *dāᵓâ*. The BM text leaves the word untranslated (*hrᵓh*), whereas the Vat. text has *xvdᵓvnd pr, xudāvand-i par* 'lord of the wing'!?

7. *bat hayyaᶜănâ* 'daughter of the desert', ostrich. In the Judeo-Persian translations *ᵓvštr, štvr mvrγ*: *uštur, šutur murγ*.[18]

8. *taḥmās*, Lev 11:16 and Deut 14:15, an unclean bird, difficult to identify (owl, swallow, cuckoo?). Vat. Lev 11:18 has *mškβrh*; Vat. Deut 14:15 *mvškβrh*: *mūšxᵛar* 'eagle, kite'??[19] BM Deut 14:15 gives *bᵓz, bāz* 'falcon, hawk'.[20]

8. P. Horn, "Zu den jüdisch-persischen Bibelübersetzungen," *Indo-germanische Forschungen* 2 (1893) 138.

9. U. Schapka, *Die persischen Vogelnamen* (Ph.D. diss., Würzburg, 1972) 218ff.

10. Ibid., 212.

11. Ibid., 170–71.

12. Ibid., 270.

13. Ibid., 8–9.

14. Ibid., 109.

15. W. B. Henning, "Sogdian Loan-Words in New Persian," *BSOAS* 10 (1940–42) 97 n. 2, with further references.

16. Schapka, *Die persischen Vogelnamen*, 8.

17. Ibid., 283–84.

18. Ibid., 154.

19. Ibid., 270.

20. Ibid., 13–14.

9. *tinšemet,* Lev 11:18, Deut 14:16, according to old tradition an owl species. Vat. Lev 11:18 and Deut 14:16 *prstvr*: *parrastū*(*k*) 'swallow'?[21] BM Deut 14:16 *hvd hvd, hudhud* 'hoopoe'.[22]

10. *šālāk,* Lev 11:17, Deut 14:17, probably 'pelican'. Vat. Lev 11:17 *lγlγ*: *laγlaγ* (*laklak, laglag, laqlaq*)[23] 'stork'; Vat. Deut 14:17 *kšᵓ mᵓhy*: *kašā māhī* 'fish catcher'; BM Deut 14:17 *lglg.*

21. Ibid., 36–37.
22. Ibid., 280–81.
23. Ibid., 242.

The Monophthongization of Diphthongs as Reflected in the Use of Vowel Letters in the Pentateuch

Joshua Blau

The medial diphthongs ay and aw were not simultaneously monophthongized. First aw shifted to ô, while under the same conditions ay was still preserved. This state of affairs is reflected in the spelling of the Pentateuch, the oldest layer of the Bible: medial ṣērê is spelled almost exclusively with yôd only when it developed from ay, and then it is almost invariably followed by yôd; whereas medial ḥôlam with wāw is used much less regularly, being spelled not infrequently without wāw even when it developed from ô, and marked by wāw, though less often, even when it reflects historical â.

There is hardly an element in biblical studies or Semitics in general in which Jonas Greenfield has not taken a personal interest. I therefore offer him this brief study, a side issue in diachronic biblical phonology.

It is my thesis that the medial diphthongs *ay* and *aw* were not simultaneously monophthongized. First *aw* shifted to *ô*, while, under the same conditions, *ay* was still preserved. Only later was *ay* monophthongized to *ê* under the very same conditions that had previously caused *aw* to shift to *ô*, thus creating the (historically incorrect) impression that the two diphthongs were simultaneously monophthongized.

The different rate of monophthongization need not surprise one. Instances of discrepancy in the behavior of diphthongs are well known. A case in point is Biblical Aramaic, in which also *aw* shifted to *ô* while *ay* was preserved in certain positions.[1]

Author's note: The system for transliteration of Biblical Hebrew used in this article is my own.

1. See, e.g., H. Bauer and P. Leander, *Grammatik des Biblisch-Aramäischen* (Halle, 1927) 37–38; S. Segert, *Altaramäische Grammatik* (Leipzig, 1975) 125ff.

The difference in the rate of monophthongization is reflected in the use of *matres lectionis* in the Pentateuch. The orthography of the Pentateuch was apparently fixed earlier than the spelling of the other books of the Bible;[2] it therefore reflects an earlier period of Hebrew. On the assumption that it still exhibits a stage of pronunciation in which medial *ay*, in contradistinction to medial *aw*, was preserved, we can recognize a regular pattern of what would otherwise seem to be arbitrary spelling habits.

The main difference between the behavior of the medial *ṣērê* and *ḥôlam* is twofold. Almost exclusively, medial *ṣērê* is spelled with *yôd* only in cases in which it developed from the diphthong *ay*, and then it is almost invariably spelled that way.[3] Medial *ḥôlam* with *wāw*, on the other hand, is used much less regularly; not only may it be spelled without *wāw* even if it developed from *aw*, but it may also, though less often, be marked by *wāw* when it reflects historical *â*. A convincing explanation of this different behavior of *ṣērê yôd* and *ḥôlam wāw* is that, when the orthography of the Pentateuch was fixed, medial *ay* had not yet become monophthongized, so that *yôd* had not yet become a vowel letter marking medial *ṣērê*; medial *aw*, however, had already shifted to *o*, so that *wāw* had already developed to indicate medial *ô*.

Admittedly, cases of long *ô* not arising from monophthongization are much more frequent than cases of long *ê* not stemming from *ay*. Yet even the somewhat restricted occurrence of long *ê* not due to monophthongization seems statistically significant, sufficiently so to establish that, at the time the orthography of the Pentateuch was fixed, medial *ay* was still a diphthong. The almost constant use of *yôd* marking medial *ṣērê* < *ay* points in the same direction. For details see below.

Some details should now be cited concerning the use of medial *ṣērê yôd* < *ay* in the Pentateuch. It clearly prevails in the plural/dual of nouns

2. See, e.g., F. I. Andersen and A. D. Forbes, *Spelling in the Hebrew Bible* (BibOr 41; Rome, 1986; hereafter AF) 313–14. Throughout this paper I have gratefully utilized the extensive statistics contained in that work. I believe that J. Barr's review (in *JSS* 33 [1988] 122–31) does not do justice to AF, which, of course, like every scholarly treatise, does have its weak points. Mainly, for my purposes, I missed the subdivision into groups of biblical books in many an orthographic type. *Obiter dictu*, on pp. 98–100, §3.4.3, AF mistook the Sephardic pronunciation used in the scholarly literature for the Tiberian as reflected in Masoretic vocalization. According to the latter, every *qāmeṣ*, pronounced according to the Sephardic pronunciation *a* or *o*, reflects a vowel like *å*, as against *ḥôlam o*. Therefore, according to the Tiberian tradition, *wāw* could not mark *qāmeṣ* [*qāṭān*]. Cf. also Y. Yahalom, *Leš* 52 (1988) 131 n. 54. At any rate, Barr's own book on biblical spelling (*The Variable Spellings of the Hebrew Bible* [Schweich Lectures of the British Academy, 1986; Oxford, 1989]) was of much less use for my purpose than AF.

3. Deviations either reflect special conditions or are statistically irrelevant; for some details see below.

preceding pronominal suffixes, as well as in prepositions with "plural" pronominal suffixes.[4]

Spellings like גּוֹיֵהֶם (four times in the Pentateuch; no cases with *plene* spelling are attested) reflect the well-known tendency to avoid double *yôd*. If this were a purely orthographic feature, one would assume that later, after the medial *ay* had shifted to *ê*, the original spelling *גּוֹיֵיהֶם was replaced by גּוֹיֵהֶם because of this tendency. It is also possible that **gōyayhem* was contracted comparatively early by dissimilation, and this is reflected in the orthography of the Pentateuch.[5]

Yet not only is medial *ê* < *ay* in nouns spelled so often with *yôd* that exceptions become statistically irrelevant,[6] but medial long *ê* which has not developed from *ay* is almost invariably written without *yôd*, thus attesting that *yôd* was not yet used to mark *ê* at the time the orthography of the Pentateuch was fixed. This is the case with nouns III-*yôd*, such as *miqnêhū* < **miqnayuhū* 'his cattle' and *śadêhū* < *śadayuhū* 'his field',[7] in which *ê* is not marked with *yôd* because the monophthongization of *ayu* occurred too early to affect even the spelling habits of the Pentateuch; this is also the case with nouns II-*wāw*/*yôd*, such as רֵק, עֵד, נֵר, מֵת, כֵּן, גֵּר.[8]

4. See AF, 170–73, types 13–14, and the analysis, 135ff., §5.5.4.

5. For the dissimilation of *yay*, cf., e.g., Bauer and Leander (*Grammatik*, 204, end), who treat the haplology of *ayayya*.

6. Nothing can be inferred from rare defective spellings of verbs III-*yôd* such as וְהִפְרֵתִי, 'and I shall make fruitful' because it may reflect original **wĕhip̄rītī* < **wĕhip̄rīytī*. As to pronominal suffixes following imperfect forms (as -*ē* [*hū*]), their etymon is more obscure. They may represent, e.g., short *i*; see, e.g., E. König, *Lehrgebäude der hebräischen Sprache* (Leipzig, 1885) 2.443 (cf. also G. Bergsträsser, *Hebräische Grammatik* [Leipzig, 1918–1929] 2.24, end; repr. Hildesheim, 1986, in one volume); at the time the spelling of the Pentateuch was fixed, *ṣērê* stemming from short *i* presumably represented a short vowel, the change being qualitative only. The same applies apparently to *ḥôlam* arising from short *u*. Accordingly, we will not deal with them in the framework of this paper. As to these pronominal suffixes following imperfect forms of verbs iii *yôd* (as in יִקְנֵהוּ), the origin of this form is not clear either: thus, the indicative might have influenced the short imperfect (**yiqnayuhū* might have affected **yiqnayhū*); the indicative itself was spelled defectively, because (see below) the monophthongization of *ayu* occurred too early to be reflected even in the orthography of the Pentateuch; moreover, ordinary verbs might have had an effect on III-*yôd*. Cf. also H. Bauer and P. Leander (*Historische Grammatik der hebräischen Sprache des Alten Testamentes* [Halle, 1922] 421), who derived it from short *i*.

7. Since the pronominal suffix -*ēhū* occurs with nouns III-*yôd* only, it was not influenced by other nouns. On the other hand, the spelling of, e.g. מַרְאֵיהֶן 'their appearance' has been adjusted to the spelling of plural nouns.

8. Although these nouns must be derived synchronically from roots II-*wāw*/*yôd*, their origin is not entirely clear. I would opt for deriving them partly from *awi*/*ayi*, partly from biliteral roots; cf. my "Origins of Open and Closed *e* in Proto-Syriac," *BSOAS* 32 (1969) 4. At any rate, they contain long *ṣērê*, since it is preserved even when remote from stress. Only outside the Pentateuch is *plene* spelling attested. On the other hand, while רֵק has to be derived from **rayiq* (if it is not originally biliteral), I am inclined to trace רֵיקָם (! invariably with *yôd*) back to **rayqam* because of its fixed *plene* spelling (a third pattern is reflected by רִיק < **riyq*).

In living languages one cannot always draw a sharp line between the preservation of diphthongs and monophthongization.[9] Even in dialects that preserve diphthongs they may be monophthongized in quick and unclear speech, and a dialectologist may come up against serious difficulties in the attempt to distinguish diphthongs from long vowels. Prepositions, by nature, are pronounced less distinctly than nouns, especially prepositions whose task is to indicate relations which, in languages with case systems, are represented by cases. This clearly applies to the preposition אֶל, which partly denotes what is referred to in Indo-Germanic tongues by the dative. Therefore, for example, **ʾilayhum* was apt to shift to אֲלֵיהֶם more quickly than the *ay* in nouns was monophthongized. This is probably why some two-thirds of the occurrences of *ʾel* with pronominal suffixes in the Pentateuch[10] are spelled without *yôd*, presumably because at the time the orthography of the Pentateuch was fixed, **ʾilay-* preceding pronominal suffixes had already shifted to *ʾilê*, whereas *ay* in general was still preserved.[11]

Since the preposition *ʿal* 'on' has a more independent meaning than *ʾel*, which, as stated, often indicates relation only (as do cases), its *ay* preceding pronominal suffixes was much less contracted; that is why only about 15 percent of its occurrences in the Pentateuch[12] are spelled defectively, much less than in the case of *ʾel*, yet much more than with ordinary nouns. In other words, first *ay* in *ʾel* was monophthongized, later in *ʿal*, and only later still was it affected in ordinary nouns.

It is well known that long *ḥôlam* emerged in Hebrew both by monophthongization of *aw* and by shift of stressed *â* to *ô*. Even in the Pentateuch, the feminine plural suffix *ôt* < *ât*, for example, is spelled in almost one-third of its occurrences with a *wāw*;[13] this minority of occurrences,[14] a substantial one, to be sure, proves that *aw* had already shifted to *ô*, and *wāw* developed to a *mater lectionis* marking medial *ô*.

9. See O. Jastrow's important observations in *Die mesopotamisch-arabischen* qəltu *Dialekte*, vol. 1: *Phonologie und Morphologie* (Wiesbaden, 1978) 77–78.

10. See AF, 171.

11. The third of the occurrences of *ʾelē* spelled plene probably reflects later adaptation to the spelling of nouns. In the other books of the Bible, *plene* spelling prevails, because in these books *ay* in general had been monophthongized and *yôd* had developed to be used as a vowel letter indicating medial *ṣērê*.

12. See AF, 172.

13. See AF, 11. Here are some other cases of *ô* < *â*: זְרוֹעַ is spelled with *wāw* four times in the Pentateuch; לָשׁוֹן only once; קוֹל (AF, 46–48) in the absolute singular is as a rule spelled plene, but with pronominal suffixes and in the plural it is spelled defectively (which indicates that its etymon is *qāl*, rather than *qawl*). In דּוֹר, too, *plene* spelling prevails.

14. The plene spelling of הֲלוֹא 'is not?' as against לֹא 'not' (AF, 186–87) is surprising. Perhaps it represents not (only) interrogative הֲ + לֹא, but (also) affinity with Biblical Aramaic

ô < *aw* is as a rule spelled with *wāw*. In some cases the *plene* spelling is so conspicuous that deviations from it need not be statistically significant. This is the case, for example, with יוֹם (only יָמִים in Num 9:22 is spelled defectively), שׁוֹר, תּוֹרָה, מוֹעֵד (spelled defectively in only seven of its very numerous occurrences), as well as in verbs I-*wāw* in *Hiphil*,[15] and *Niphal* past and participle. Sometimes, however, the minority of occurrences of defective spelling is conspicuous enough to indicate that *aw* had already shifted to *ô*. Thus תּוֹלְדוֹת occurs twenty-nine times in the Pentateuch, twenty-three of them with *plene* spelling and six defective (more than twenty percent!). This, together with the use of *wāw* in a substantial minority of occurrences to mark *ô* < *â*, leaves no doubt that, by the time the orthography of the Pentateuch was fixed, *aw* had already become monophthongized[16] and *wāw* had become a vowel letter to mark medial *ô*.[17]

אֱלוֹ 'lo' (see, e.g., Bauer and Leander, *Grammatik*, §71a; and the literature cited in W. Gesenius and F. Buhl, *Hebräisches und aramäisches Handwörterbuch über das Alte Testament* [16th ed.; Leipzig, 1915], Aramaic part, s.v. אֲלוֹ); in that case, the *ḥôlam* might reflect original *aw*.

The etymon of the verbal theme called *Polel* of II-*wāw/yôd* and geminate verbs (see AF, 196, type 45) is obscure (see my "Studies in Hebrew Verb Formation," *HUCA* 42 [1971] 147–51); in addition, one must take into consideration the possibility of vocalizing defectively spelled geminate verbs as *Piel* (see Bergstrasser, *Hebräische Grammatik* 2.140).

15. The defective spelling of אסף, etc. reflects a different history; see Bergsträsser, *Hebräische Grammatik* 2.79.

16. In contradistinction to *ay*.

17. Whereas *yôd* had not yet become a vowel letter indicating medial long *ṣērê*.

The Cedar and the Palm Tree: A Paired Male/Female Symbol in Hebrew and Aramaic

Ariel A. Bloch

There is limited evidence from two literary texts, one in Biblical Hebrew and the other in Aramaic, for the pairing of the cedar and the palm tree as male and female symbols, respectively. I discuss specific gender-related associations evoked by each tree, as well as—in the case of the palm—linguistic evidence for its "femaleness."

Trees and plants figure prominently in similes and metaphors about human beings in biblical poetry. The proverbial righteous person, for example, is said to thrive like a tree planted by streams of water (Ps 1:3, and cf. Jer 17:8). In a similar vein, a prosperous nation may be described as a vine whose branches reach beyond the sea (Isa 16:8, and cf. Ezek 31:3ff.) Associations of trees with human beings are probably so basic and natural to human imagination as to echo in one way or another in most of the world's cultures and literatures. On the other hand, the particular symbolism to be dealt with in this paper, involving the cedar and the palm tree, may well turn out be specific to Mediterranean cultures.

In the Song of Songs, the Shulamite concludes her detailed paean on her lover's physical attributes (5:10–15) with an enthusiastic exclamation, calling him *bāḥûr kā-ărāzîm* 'a man like a cedar'.[1] As in biblical

Author's note: I want to express special gratitude to my colleagues Daniel Foxvog, Wolfgang Heimpel, Anne Kilmer, and David Stronach for their helpful information about the various aspects connected with date palm symbolism and iconography in Mesopotamia and for bringing the relevant sources to my attention. My thanks also to my graduate students Ruth Kadish, Dan Reilly, and Lincoln Shlensky for many helpful suggestions and comments. Needless to say, responsibility for errors is mine alone.

1. Or alternatively 'distinguished as a cedar'. The plural *ʾărāzîm* is generic, denoting the species. Hence not 'as cedars', as in most translations. (The generic nature of *ʾărāzîm* in this expression is captured in the modern Hebrew equivalent *baḥur ka-ʾerez,* with *ʾerez* in the

imagery in general, the cedar in this expression evokes great strength and a majestic height, in harmony with other typical "male" characteristics attributed to the lover in that passage; compare "his thighs are marble pillars," and notice the various hard metals associated with parts of his body.[2] The cedar as a conventional male symbol continues to live on also in historically later expressions, as in the postbiblical *qāšeh kā-ʾerez* 'hard as a cedar', or the designation *ʾerez ha-lĕbānôn* 'cedar of Lebanon' for a man distinguished in Torah learning.[3]

The lover in turn views the Shulamite as a date palm: "I said in my heart, Let me climb into that palm tree and take hold of its branches. And oh, may your breasts be like clusters of grapes on a vine . . ." (7:9). In this verse the female aspect of the palm manifests itself not only in the association of the date clusters with breasts, but also in the erotic wish of the lover to climb that palm. In a more general sense, the association with a palm may also suggest a woman's tall, slender, proudly erect stature.

Another male/female pairing of the cedar and the palm occurs in the *Genesis Apocryphon*.[4] I am especially happy for the opportunity to discuss a passage of the *Genesis Apocryphon* in the Festschrift for Jonas Greenfield, since it was he who first drew my attention to the importance of these texts for linguistic and literary studies in Aramaic. Genesis 12 tells us that Abraham, fearing that the Egyptians might kill him in order to take the beautiful Sarai into Pharaoh's harem, demands of his wife to identify herself as his sister, so as to save his life (compare this story with the parallel story of Abimelech in Genesis 20). Now, col. XIX 14–21 of the *Genesis Apocryphon* offers a midrashic expansion of the biblical narrative, intended to provide an explanation of the reason Sarai had to lie to

---

sing.) For other plurals used in a generic sense in the Song, see 2:9, *ʿōper hā-ʾayyālîm*; lit. 'a young one of stags'; 4:15, *maʿyan gannîm*; 7:9, *tappûḥîm*; etc. Translations from the Song of Songs in this paper are based on Ariel and Chana Bloch, *The Song of Songs: A New Translation with an Introduction and Commentary, Afterword by Robert Alter*, to be published by Random House, 1995.

2. Of course, there is a lot of crossover between "male" and "female" traits in the Song of Songs, where both lovers are not infrequently described in terms more commonly associated with the opposite sex. See "Introduction," in Bloch and Bloch, *Song of Songs*. Also D. Fishelov, "The Song of Songs: Hard and Soft, Dynamic and Static," in *Studies in Poetic Simile* [Hebrew, manuscript].

3. A. Even-Shoshan, *Ha-Millon He-Ḥadaš* (Jerusalem, 1982). For the cedar as a male symbol consider also the midrashic tale about a custom of planting a cedar tree when a boy was born (H. N. Bialik and Y. H. Ravnitzky, *Sefer Ha-ʾAggadah* [Tel-Aviv, 1960] 156). (For a girl an acacia would be planted, *šiṭṭâ*, which differs from the female symbol dealt with in this paper.)

4. See J. A. Fitzmyer, *The Genesis Apocryphon of Qumran Cave I: A Commentary* (2d. ed.; Rome, 1971).

the Egyptians to save her husband's life. On the night before entering Egypt, we are told, Abraham had a dream about a cedar and a very beautiful date palm.[5] When some people came along intending to cut down the cedar but leave the date palm, the date palm remonstrated, and so the cedar was saved on account of the palm's intercession. (I leave out a number of details in this dream that are of no relevance to the specific topic under discussion.) The significance to the present subject is obvious: Abraham is the cedar, Sarai the date palm.

Fitzmyer suggests[6] that the two trees in this dream are drawn from Ps 92:13, "The righteous will blossom like a palm tree; he will grow high like a cedar in Lebanon," observing that rabbinical literature likewise tends to relate this particular verse to the story of Abraham and Sarai in Genesis 12. He also suggests the Song of Songs' male/female pairing of these two trees as an additional possible source of influence on the dream in the *Genesis Apocryphon.* Without denying in principle the possibility of intertextual influence, I would argue that Fitzmyer's approach leaves out an important aspect. An association of Ps 92:13 with Abraham and Sarai, as suggested by Fitzmyer, obviously *presupposes* a perception of a gender distinction between the two trees in the mind of those early exegetes who made this connection. For without such an association along gender lines, the attribution would have probably been the reverse, that is, *Abraham as the palm, *Sarai as the cedar, in conformity with the conventional order: Abraham and Sarai (= male and female, Gen 5:2, 7:16; Lev 3:1; and the many other ordered sequences, Moses and Aaron, etc.). Indeed, a gender distinction between these two trees may lie latent already in the Psalms verse itself. It is probably no coincidence that the palm is associated with budding and blossoming (*yipraḥ*), hence indirectly with the production of fruit, while the cedar is associated with height (*yiśgeh*).[7]

Apart from the general associations by which the palm could become a female symbol—the tree as the provider of a major source of nourishment; the date clusters as breasts; possible sexual and erotic connotations evoked by the palm, as in the Song; the palm tree's gracefully slender trunk—there is also linguistic support for the perception of the tree's inherent femaleness. While Hebrew *tamar* 'palm tree' is grammatically masculine, it is significant that the *name Tamar* is exclusively a woman's name (Gen 38:6; 2 Sam 13:1, 14:27, and passim). The creation of such a personal name from the word for the palm could have hardly

5. *ʾrz ḥd wtmrʾ ḥdʾ* [*yʾy*]ʾ [*śgyʾ*], in Fitzmyer's plausible restoration.
6. Fitzmyer, *Genesis Apocryphon,* 111
7. I owe this observation to Robert Alter.

come about without a perception of the tree's femaleness. Or, put differently, it is precisely when the tree is intimately associated with the human sphere—as in the process of naming—that its femaleness comes to the fore. Moreover, in the Aramaic of the *Genesis Apocryphon*, midrashic Hebrew, and Syriac, the word for 'palm' becomes overtly marked by the feminine ending, *tmrʾ/tmrtʾ, tĕmārâ, tĕmartāʾ* (Arabic *tamra* is a *nomen unitatis* and thus does not belong in the same category). Such historically secondary marking of originally unmarked nouns is a well-known linguistic development, often taking place when an object is perceived as female for some inherent iconic/symbolic factor. For example, the 'bow' is formally unmarked in Arabic *qaws* (reflecting Proto-Semitic **qawš*), but becomes secondarily marked by the feminine ending in most Semitic daughter languages, Hebrew *qešet*, Ethiopic *qast*, Syriac *qeštāʾ*, Assyrian *qaštu*.[8] (The association with femaleness is most probably connected with the bow's round shape, the fact that it "envelops" the arrow, etc.) Of course, such secondary overt gender marking may happen also with natural feminines, for example, French *soeur*, but Italian *sorella*.[9]

Finally, there is some support from Mesopotamia for the female symbolism of the palm tree. A vessel fragment from Lagash dating ca. 2400 B.C.E. shows a goddess holding a date cluster.[10] More specifically, Ishtar, the goddess of fertility and sexuality, is depicted on one cylinder seal as standing near a date palm and on another as holding the fruit-stalk of a date palm in her hand.[11] She is also described as "Ishtar, who envelops him (her lover) as the *sissinnu* the dates."[12] *Sissinnu* is the fruit-stalk (spadix, or reproductive organ) of the female palm tree. In order for the female tree to produce dates, pollen must be transferred to it from a male palm tree.[13] The association between the goddess and the date palm and, specifically, between her and the *sissinnu*, the palm's repro-

8. Brockelmann, *Grundriss*, 1.190.

9. For this phenomenon, see Y. Malkiel, "Diachronic Hypercharacterization in Romance," *Archivum Linguisticum* 9 (1957) 79–113; (1958) 1–36.

10. For a description, see M. Eiland, "Evidence for Pile Carpets in Cuneiform Sources. . . ," in *Oriental Carpet and Textile Studies* (Berkeley, 1993) 4.15.

11. R. M. Boehmer, *Die Entwicklung der Glyptik während der Akkad-Zeit* (Berlin, 1965) 307.

12. CAD S 325 s.v. *sissinnu*. The Heb. etymological cognate of the Akk. word is found in the Bible only in Song 7:9, *ʾōḥăzâ be-sansinnāyw*, lit., 'let me take hold of its [the date palm's] *sansinnîm*'. Athough the exact meaning of the *sansinnîm* is not clear (interpretations range from 'fruit-stalk' to 'topmost branches of the palm'), the very occurrence of the word in an unmistakably sexual context, with the date palm symbolizing the female, may well point to a "Mesopotamian connection" of this particular image.

13. For a depiction of the procedure of date palm pollination in ancient Mesopotamian iconography, see Eiland, "Evidence for Pile Carpets in Cuneiform Sources," 16–17.

ductive organ, is highly indicative of the the date palm as a symbol of female sexuality and reproductivity.

Let us return to the major point. Two texts, one in Biblical Hebrew and the other in Aramaic, provide evidence for the pairing of the cedar and the palm tree as male and female symbols, respectively. Certain gender-related associations evoked by these two trees determined their choice as contrasting gender symbols (including specific sexual connotations in the case of the date palm). There is also some linguistic, including onomastic, evidence for the inherent "femaleness" of the palm. We are dealing here with a basic phenomenon of human perception in which objects are considered masculine or feminine depending on a specific characteristic or on a particular human association evoked by the object. The underlying methodological argument is that, although this association may manifest itself in literary texts, as has been shown, the association itself is first of all a product of the human mind: a way chosen to perceive reality.

Some Problems in the Arabic Transmission of Biblical Names

William M. Brinner

A number of works already deal with the subject of the transmission of Biblical Hebrew names in the Qurʾān. Perhaps the most detailed of these is an article by Joseph Horovitz, written in 1925. The number of biblical names mentioned in the Qurʾān is, however, quite small when compared with the large onomasticon of the Hebrew Bible. In the present paper, therefore, I examine two Arabic works of a genre intentionally ignored by Horovitz, namely, the Qiṣaṣ al-anbiyāʾ, or 'tales of the prophets', in other words, those biblical figures who are called prophets in Islam. Three biblical name lists are presented: the grandsons of Noah, the sons of Jacob, and the sons of Ishmael. Whereas the Qurʾānic version of names are standardized, those of the qiṣaṣ-type are not. The influence of scribal error and oral transmission are examined.

Western readers of the Qurʾān who are acquainted with the Hebrew Bible notice that a considerable number of Qurʾānic narratives echo biblical themes, some more, some less closely. It is also easily noted that within these narratives we often find arabicized forms of biblical (i.e., Hebrew) names. In 1925 Joseph Horovitz published an article, "Jewish Proper Names and Derivatives in the Koran,"[1] summarizing and elaborating on the great amount of work, much of it in German, that had been done up to then on the subject, which may best be characterized as "the Jewish element in Islam, especially the Qurʾān."[2] In the seventy years that have elapsed since Horovitz wrote, scholarly attitudes have somewhat changed, and today one tends to look at elements that seem

1. J. Horovitz, "Jewish Proper Names and Derivatives in the Koran," *HUCA* 2 (1925) 145–227.

2. There is a rather large body of European scholarly literature from the mid-19th and early 20th centuries on this subject, beginning with the classic work by A. Geiger, *Was hat Mohammed aus dem Judenthume aufgenommen?* (2d ed.; Leipzig, 1902). See also D. Sidersky, *Les Origines des légendes musulmanes dans le Coran et dans les vies des prophètes* (Paris, 1933).

to be "Jewish" or "Christian" in some of early Islam as part of larger, shared cultural patterns common to a major part of the ancient and late antique Near East.[3]

In the aforementioned article, Horovitz intentionally limited himself to the Qurʾān and earlier Arabic literature, especially pre-Islamic poetry. By doing so, he deliberately omitted entries not only from the *Ḥadīth* (the traditional transmission of the words and deeds of the prophet Muhammad) and the *Sīra* (his biography), but also from the later literary genres of *tafsīr* (Qurʾān commentary) and *qiṣaṣ al-anbiyāʾ* (tales of the prophets, referred to henceforth as *qiṣaṣ*). He stated as his reason that "they reflect a later stage in the development of Islam than the Koran, and they therefore cannot be utilized as authentic material for the interpretation of the Koran."[4] Because this study does not concern itself with such interpretation, it is based precisely on that material.

All the aforementioned text genres, while generally following the Qurʾānic narratives quite closely, also incorporated large bodies of what was clearly borrowed material, often mentioned as coming from Jewish sources, hence called *Isrāʾīliyāt.*[5] These materials present an entirely different problem from the highly sensitive one of possible Jewish influence on or elements in the Qurʾān itself. Since the latter is believed by Muslims to be a divine revelation—the actual word of God—and not a product of human thought, composition, or intervention, the very idea of *any* human involvement in its composition is anathema. In Muslim belief, too, both the Torah and the Gospels were divinely revealed texts, of the same general origin as the uncreated and unaltered Qurʾān, but have suffered alteration and distortion at the hands of the rabbis and priests.[6] Almost as much as in the case of the Qurʾān itself, the *Ḥadīth* and *Sīra*, based largely on traditions going back to the Prophet himself, are therefore also considered by Muslims not to have been influenced by non-Muslim sources. This leaves the *qiṣaṣ* and *tafsīr* literature, which are clearly and admittedly the products of scholars who might have turned to Jews, Christians, and adherents of other faiths, as well as to recent converts to Islam, as sources for their exegesis of the Qurʾānic text and expansion of the narrative elements therein. The Qurʾānic narratives were all too often

3. The best concise presentation of a current view of this issue may be found in R. Firestone, *Journeys in Holy Lands: The Evolution of the Abraham-Ishmael Legends in Islamic Exegesis* (Albany, N.Y., 1990). See especially chaps. 1 and 2.

4. See Horovitz, "Jewish Proper Names," 145–46.

5. See Firestone, *Journeys in Holy Lands*, 13–15; G. Vajda, "Isrāʾīliyyāt," *EI*[2] 4.211–12; S. D. Goitein, "Isrāʾīliyyāt," *Tarbiz* 6 (1934–35) 89–101, 510–22.

6. On the question of Jewish and Christian altering (*taḥrīf*) of their original divine revelations, see Qurʾān 2:175, 179; 4:46; etc.; and F. Buhl, "*Taḥrīf*," *EI*[1] 7.618–19.

highly allusive and tantalizing in their brevity and their seeming reliance on the reader's previous acquaintance with the characters in the tales and knowledge of the main outline of the story. Hence the need to expand, elaborate, and explain.

In his lengthy article, Horovitz deals with a rather large number of personal and place-names, as well as some other terms, that occur in the Qurʾān. He mentions in passing that Jews and Christians had lived in the Arabian Peninsula for centuries before the coming of Muhammad, so that some names might have been well known among Arabic speakers. But since few of these names, if any, occur in the pre-Islamic poetry, he finds no real proof for this idea. However, he was able, in most cases, to trace the sources of those whose Arabic forms differ greatly from the Hebrew originals in the Bible to the Targum and Peshiṭta, less often to the Septuagint and to Ethiopic versions. He divided these names into several categories, beginning with those that were essentially the "same" as their Hebrew "originals," that is, usually showing the same consonantal structure: for example, Nūḥ, Lūṭ, Yaᶜqūb, Mājūj, Hāmān, Bābīl;[7] followed by those showing "small deviations," that is, in vocalization: for example, Yūsuf (also occurring as Yūsif), Madyan, Maryam, Baᶜl, Isrāʾīl, Ādam.[8] Listed under other names showing greater deviations, possibly under Syriac, Ethiopic, or Greek influence, are Isḥāq, Ismāᶜīl, Mūsā, Sabā (Sheba), Al-Yasaᶜ (Elisha), Ayyūb (Job), Jibrīl (Gabriel), Mīkāl (Michael), ᶜImrān (Amram), Hārūn (Aaron), Dāʾud/Dāwud (David), Yūnus (Jonah), Ilyās (Elijah), Yahūdhā, Finḥās, Samauʾal.[9] He also cites some forms that seem to have been created as pair-calques: ᶜĪsā (Jesus) / Mūsā (Moses); Ibrāhīm / Ismāᶜīl; Qārūn (Korah) / Hārūn (Aaron); Ṭālūt (Saul) / Jālūt (Goliath); Yājūj (Gog) / Mājūj (Magog); and Qābil (Cain, also rendered as Qayin in some Arabic texts) / Hābil (Abel).[10] Finally, there is a category that needs extensive reconstruction, including such names as Abraham's father, called ᶜĀzar, instead of Taraḥ (Terah), which also occurs, though less frequently. Scholarly opinion generally holds that this strange form arises from the name of Abraham's servant, Eliezer, due to a mistaken reading of the first element in the latter name, the Hebrew divine name *ʾel*, as the Arabic definite article *al-*, which was then omitted.[11]

While some of these names, such as Ibrāhīm, Ismāᶜīl, Hārūn, Mūsā, and Dāwud, have survived in regular Arabic/Islamic usage as personal

7. Horovitz, "Jewish Proper Names," 151.
8. Ibid., 152–53; regarding Yūsuf/Yūsif, see p. 153.
9. Ibid., 154–55.
10. See ibid., 160–65, for discussion of name pairs.
11. Ibid., 157.

names of Muslims down to the present, others are identified in the Arabic-speaking Islamic world as clearly Jewish or Christian personal names. ᶜĪsā, the form in which the name of Jesus appears in the Qurᵓān, has been used through the centuries as a Muslim personal name, because of the high standing accorded to the *Masīḥ*, that is, Christ, in the Qurᵓān.[12] Yet, Arabic-speaking Christians have generally avoided that form and have preferred to use Yasūᶜa (Yeshūᶜa) instead, and then only very rarely as a personal name.

Given the very large number of personal names that appear in the Hebrew Bible, one would expect them to occur much more frequently and in greater variety in Islamic religious texts. This is indeed the case if one looks at certain works that are mentioned above as outside the Qurᵓān itself, especially works such as the aforementioned *tafsīr*, or Qurᵓān commentaries, and *qiṣaṣ*, or "tales of the prophets," the latter stories often clearly influenced by or borrowed from the midrašic literature.

Without intending or attempting to achieve any degree of completeness, I have in this article several aims. First, I aim to present an idea of the richness of this material for the study of intercultural contact and influence, especially during the earliest Islamic centuries. It should also serve as a reminder of factors that are less apparent in the Qurᵓān, namely the strong, even determining influence on loanwords and names that make their way into Arabic, of the effort to arabize these names, that is, to fit them into Arabic nominal patterns, as well as the powerful effect of the phonetic differences between Hebrew and Arabic.

One other element that distinguishes biblical names found in the Qurᵓān from those in later texts is the important factor of possible scribal confusion and error, based on Arabic orthography and calligraphic styles and their influence on the way words eventually appear in later copies. The basic forms of many Arabic letters, each of which may stand for a very different phoneme, often lead to strange realizations of words transcribed from one language to the other. An example of this in two *qiṣaṣ* texts is the Arabic rendering of the place-name Hebron in several manuscripts of al-Ṭabarī's *Annales*[13] as *Jayrūn* جيرون and in other forms, as well

12. For possible sources of this form of the name, see G. C. Anawati, "ᶜĪsā," *EI*² 4.81–86.

13. Abū Jaᶜfar Muḥammad ibn Jarīr al-Ṭabarī (838–923), *Taᵓrīkh al-rusul wal-mulūk*, published as *Annales* (ed. M. J. De Goeje; 15 vols.; Leiden, 1879–1901). The first two volumes contain the *qiṣaṣ* material. An English translation of the entire work is being published, the first four volumes of which contain the *qiṣaṣ* material: *The History of Al-Ṭabarī* (Albany, N.Y., 1985-), vol. 1: *General Introduction* and *From the Creation to the Flood* (ed. F. Rosenthal, 1989); vol. 2: *Prophets and Patriarchs* (ed. W. M. Brinner, 1987); vol. 3: *The Children of Israel* (ed. W. M. Brinner, 1991); vol. 4: *The Ancient Kingdoms* (ed. M. Perlmann, 1987). Al-Ṭabarī intermingled these tales with Persian traditional history, both as prelude to and harbinger of the coming of Muḥammad and Islam.

as the expected *Ḥabrūn* حبرون;[14] it appears in the work known as *ʿArāʾis*, by al-Thaʿlabī, as *Jabrūn* جبرون.[15] The letters representing *j* ج and *ḥ* ح, as well as *y* ي and *b* ب, respectively, have the same form and are distinguished only by diacritic dots. As we see, one dot below the letter distinguishes *j* from *ḥ*, and two dots instead of one below the letter differentiate *y* from *b*.

Similarly, the Hebrew rendering *poṭifār* regularly becomes Arabic *qiṭfīr*, because *q* ق and *f* ف (*p* does not occur in the Arabic phonemic system), resembling each other in form, are distinguished only by their diacritic dots. But other phonemic variants appear as well: *qiṭfīr* قطفير becomes *iṭfīr* اطفير,[16] *qiṭṭīn* قطّين,[17] and *iṭfīn* اطفين[18] Explainable on the basis of common patterns in various Arabic dialects, these occurrences strongly suggest oral rather than purely written transmission.

The tales in the *qiṣaṣ* literature generally follow the chronological order of their biblical models. I say "generally" because at times the authors have their own ideas about the placement of certain figures, such as Job or Jonah, in the biblical chronology.[19] In other cases, especially in the ancient portions of al-Ṭabarī's monumental *History*, an effort is made to coordinate the chronology of biblical history with that of ancient Iran and to coordinate the dates of certain biblical figures with those of specific Iranian ones.[20] This is especially true of certain enigmatic individuals occurring in Qurʾānic narratives, such as Dhū l-Qarnayn ('the two-horned

14. In Ṭabarī, *Annales*, 1.343, 349, 371. Corrected in text from MSS that have *Jayrūn*, *Ḥayrūn*, and *Ḥayrān*; see 343 n. 1, 349 n. 1, and 371 n. c.

15. Aḥmad ibn Muḥammad al-Thaʿlabī (d. 1036), *Kitāb ʿArāʾis al-majālis fī qiṣaṣ al-anbiyāʾ* (Beirut, n.d.) 85–86.

16. The feature of the substitution of *q* by ʾ (glottal stop) is discussed by J. Cantineau, *Études de linguistique arabe* (Études arabes et islamiques: Études et documents 2; Paris, 1960) 69.

17. Here two separate phenomena are taking place: the assimilation of *t* and a following *f* and the substitution of *n* for *r*. Although the first is not discussed, many examples of the assimilation of *t* and various following consonants are given by Cantineau, *Études*, 42. For the substitution of *n* for *r*, see ibid., 50. See also H. Fleisch, *Traité de philologie arabe* (Beirut, 1961) 1.60.

18. The same as *iṭfīr* (n. 16) above, with an *n*/*r* substitution.

19. Thaʿlabī (*ʿArāʾis*, 135–44) places Job just before the birth of Moses and Jonah after the completion of the story of Jesus and the death of Mary, but before the People of the Cave (the Sleepers of Ephesus, ibid., 366–70). Ṭabarī (*Annales*, 1.361–65) places Job before the story of Joseph and Jonah after the People of the Cave, but before the story of the Apostles sent by Jesus to Antioch (ibid., 782–89).

20. Ṭabarī (*Annales*, 1.216) traces the genealogy of Yazdajird, the last Iranian ruler before the Islamic conquest, to Japheth, son of Noah. See also the story of Job, who is identified variously as a Byzantine and as an Israelite, the grandson of Isaac (in ibid., 1.361–64, 389). Jonah is placed in Arabia during the period of the "regional princes," as Perlmann translates *mulūk al-tawāʾif*. His story comes between that of the Seven Sleepers of Ephesus and the stories of Samson and St. George (see ibid., 1.782–88, 1201–2).

one'), who is made to fit into biblical and Iranian chronology and may be identified (though not always) with Alexander the Great;[21] or al-Khiḍr ('the green one'), who is somehow identified with a Qurʾānic tale about Moses, as well as being connected with the prophet Elijah.[22]

Only a few examples will be presented here, primarily to illustrate the richness of non-Qurʾānic sources for this study. We find in the *qiṣaṣ* collection by al-Thaʿlabī and the aforementioned ancient portions of the *History* by al-Ṭabarī lists of names of the descendants of Noah, the sons of Ishmael, and the sons of Jacob, almost all of them names that do not occur in the Qurʾān and have thus not survived in general Muslim usage. While the forms of many of these names fall into Horovitz's category of "the same" as the Hebrew, or of those showing "small deviations," others reflect some of the interesting features of Arabic phonemics, as well as problems rising from the influence of Arabic orthography and calligraphy, or from the influence of oral transmission on scribal practice, as mentioned above.

In the opening sections of al-Ṭabarī's work, in which he covers ancient history, we find the following passages about the sons of Noah (some variant readings from different manuscripts are given):

> There were born to . . . Yāfith يفيث [Japheth] seven men and a woman. Of the males born to him were Jūmar/Jawmar جومر . . . and Māriḥu (Māriju) مارح / مارج . . . and Wāʾil وائل . . . and Ḥawān حوان . . . and Tūbīl توبيل (Nūbīl نوبيل, Tūsil توسل) . . . and Hūshil/Hawshil هوشل (Hūshidh هوشذ) . . . and Tiras ترس . . . and Shabakah شبكة, [his] daughter . . .[23]
>
> . . . [Ham's wife] bore him three men: Kūsh كوش . . . Qūṭ قوط . . . and Kanʿān كنعان . . .[24]
>
> . . . [Shem's wife] bore him men: Arfakhshad ارفخشد . . . and Ashūdh اشوذ . . . and Lāwudh لاوذ . . . and ʿAwīlām (ʿUwaylām) عويلام. . . . Shem also had Aram ارم . . .[25]

21. See ibid., 1.201, 225ff. See, also, W. Montgomery Watt, "Al-Iskandar," *EI*² 4.127.

22. This is an interpretation of the narrative in Qurʾān 18:60–82. For its Jewish parallel, which involves R. Joshua ben Levi, see Nissim ben Jacob Ibn Shahin, *Hibbûr Yāfeh me-ha-Yešuʿah* (trans. H. Z. Hirschberg; Jerusalem, 1953). See also the English translation by W. M. Brinner, *An Elegant Composition concerning Relief after Adversity* (Yale Judaica Series 20; New Haven, 1977) 13–16. For its connection with the Alexander romance, see A. J. Wensinck, "Al-Khaḍir (Al-Khiḍr)," *EI*² 4.902–6, esp. 905.

23. Ṭabarī, *Annales*, 1.211.

24. Ibid., 1.212.

25. Ibid., 1.213.

Except for the following four instances, the differences in the names seem to stem from scribal error: (1) Jūmar/Jawmar (Hebrew: Gomer), both versions of which share the same consonantal form; (2) Tūbīl, which is clearly biblical Tubal;[26] (3) Ḥawān, which seems to be Yavan/Yawan; and (4) Tiras, which is the same as the Hebrew form. The names written as Māriḥu, Wāʾil, and Hūshil, however, pose difficulties. The biblical sons of Japheth not accounted for are Magog (in al-Ṭabarī's text both Mājūj and Yājūj are sons of Jūmar, hence grandsons of Yāfith, and are treated separately by him); Madai or Meshech, either of which may be Māriḥu; and Wāʾil may possibly be represented by Hūshil. The list, however, is full of problems.

Of the Hebrew names of the sons of Ham (Kush, Pūt, and Kĕnaʿan), as we have seen, only Put is a problem in Arabic, the *p-f/q* confusion mentioned above clearly being the cause.

As for the sons of Shem, Arpachshad and Aram show no problems. Hebrew Asshur as Asshūdh is clearly due to the very common problem of *r/dh* confusion by an Arabic scribe; Lud as Lāwudh, although similar, is a bit more complicated, as is ʿAwīlām/ʿUwaylām for Elam.[27]

A second list follows, the names of the sons of Jacob (certainly better known in Jewish and Christian tradition), as recorded by al-Ṭabarī and al-Thaʿlabī:

> The sons of Liyā ليا: Rūbīl روبيل,[28] Yahūdhā يهوذا, Shamʿūn سمعون / شمعون, Lāwī لاوي.
>
> The sons of Zilfa^{h} زلفة: Dān دان, Naftālī نفثالى / نفتالي, Zabālūn زبالون / زيبالون.[29]
>
> The sons of Bilha^{h} بلهة: Jād جاد, Yasḥar/Yashjar يشجر / يسحر,[30] Ashar اشر.

26. The "extreme ʾ*imāla*" (passage of *a* to *i*), as in Tūbal > Tūbīl, is discussed by Cantineau, *Études*, 91–99.

27. It is difficult to explain the insertion of long *ā* in *lāwudh*, or of the *wāw* in ʿ*Awīlām*. In Arabic ʿ*Uwaylām* would be the diminutive of ʿ*Awīlam*. The unpointed word may be read either way.

28. Ṭabarī, *Annales*, 1.355. This name also occurs as *Ribbīl*. On the *r/l* substitution, see Cantineau, *Études*, 50. As a general Semitic phenomenon, see D. O'Leary, *A Comparative Grammar of the Semitic Languages* (London, 1924) 64: Hebrew *ṣelem* = Arabic *ṣanam*. For further discussion, see n. 32 below.

29. Ṭabarī, *Annales*, 1.355. *Rubālūn* is found in Thaʿlabī, ʿ*Arāʾis*, 89.

30. Both forms are given by Ṭabarī: *Yasḥar* on p. 355, but note *c* has *Yashjar* in one MS, P(aris) n. 1468.

The sons of Rāḥīl راحيل: Yūsuf يوسف, Binyamin بنيامين (whose "real" name was Shaddād شداد).[31]

While the forms in which the names Dan, Naphtali, Gad, Asher, and Benjamin appear are "transparent," and those of Judah, Simeon, Levi, and Joseph can be seen to have "small deviations," the remaining three names are examples of problems referred to above.

The often-occurring Semitic substitution of *l* for *n* in Rūbīl/Ribbīl for Reuben is an attested feature in Arabic phonology and is not as rare as some Western grammarians have indicated in the relatively few studies that mention it.[32] In the examples I have collected, this substitution usually, but not always, occurs in loanwords or in colloquial/dialect usage.[33]

Rubālūn/Rayālūn for Zebulon represent problems of the Arabic writing system mentioned above: *z* ز and *r* ر are exactly the same in form with the sole addition of a dot to distinguish the sign for *z*. A similar problem occurs, as we have seen, with *y* and *b*.

The final problem in this group of names, Yashjar/Yashar for Yissachar, is again tied to the writing system: *s* س and *š* ش as well as *j* and *ḥ* (as already noted) being distinguished only by the addition of dots.

My final example is another list found in the *qiṣaṣ* literature, the sons of Ishmael in Gen 25:13–15, as given in two versions, those of al-Ṭabarī[34] and al-Thaᶜlabi.[35] Manuscript variants of the Arabic forms are given in parentheses (see chart, p. 27).

On the basis of all of these examples, most of the differences between the Hebrew and the Arabic versions are easily understood. What is important to point out is that when the scribes have differed greatly at times, as in Wuṭūr/Baṭūr, for example, or Ṭamā/Fīmā, the phenomenon is based on the peculiarities of the Arabic writing system. But where the consonantal skeleton of the Arabic word is drastically altered, as in the various changes wrought on *Qiṭfīr*, *Rūbīl*, and others, it may have been due to a scribe's not having copied a written text but having written from oral dictation and not having heard the correct consonant. Al-

31. Ṭabarī, *Annales*, 1.355. Thaᶜlabī (*ᶜArāᵓis*, 88) states that "Shaddād was his name in Arabic."

32. For a discussion of this *l/n* substitution, see Cantineau (*Études*, 53), who states that this often occurs in the vicinity of *r*, e.g., *ballūr* 'crystal' becomes *bennūr* in some dialects.

33. For examples of borrowed words: *burṭuᵓān* 'orange' for *burṭuqāl*, lit. 'Portugal'; *fingāl* for *finjān* 'cup'; *lifta* for Hebrew *neptoaḥ*; but *menīḥ* for literary Arabic *malīḥ* 'good, beautiful' and *embāriḥ* < *anbāriḥ* < *al-bāriḥa* 'yesterday'.

34. Ṭabarī, *Annales*, 1.351, variants from footnotes. On p. 352 he adds in the text itself the following variants: Qaydar, Adbāl, Mibshām, Dhūmā, Masā, Ḥadād, Taym, Yaṭūr (Qanṭar), Nāfis, and Qādaman.

35. Thaᶜlabī, *ᶜArāᵓis*, 88.

Genesis		*al-Ṭabarī*		*al-Thaʿlabī*	
Nebajoth	נביות	Nābit (Thābit)	نابت / ثابت	Nābitā	نابتا
Kedar	קדר	Qaydar	قيدر	Qaydhār	قيذار
Adbeel	אדבאל	Adbīl (Adīl)	ادبيل / اديل	Adbīl	ادبيل
Mibsam	מבשם	Mabshā (Mīshā)	مبشا / ميشا	Basām	بسام
Mishmā	משמע	Masmaʿ	مسمع	Masmaʿ	مسمع
Dumah	דומה	Dumā	دما	Dhūmā	ذوما
Massa	משא	Mās	ماس	Masā	مسا
Hadad	חדד	Adad	ادد	Ḥarā	حرا
Tema	תימא	Ṭamā (Ṭamān, Ṭamiyā)	طما / طمان / طميا	Fīmā	فيما
Jetur	יטור	Wuṭūr	وطور	Baṭūr	بطور
Nephish	נפיש	Nafīs (Qays)	نفيس / قيس	Nāfīs	نافس
Kedmah	קדמה	Qaydamān	قيدمان	Qaydmā	قيدما

though Horovitz is probably correct in tracing the Aramaic sources and other linguistic influences on the Qurʾānic deviations from the Biblical Hebrew names, when we look at the later Islamic literature, a small sample of which we have examined here, scribal errors and customary practices become equally important. Further study of these instances, which exist in abundance, will undoubtedly show many more cases both of miscopying due to the similarities of letter forms and of the influence of pronunciation due to writing from memory or from oral dictation, both factors not adequately studied hitherto.

On *netinim* and False Prophets

MAGEN BROSHI AND ADA YARDENI

Two Dead Sea Scroll fragments preserve remains of lists, one of netinim 'temple-servants' and the other of false prophets. At some time during the Second Commonwealth the status of the netinim declined drastically; it is suggested that the first fragment was part of a list of blemished people, unfit for marriage—a negative genealogical list. The false prophets listed in the second fragment range from Balaam to (most probably) Hananiah son of Azur, thus spanning the whole period from the Exodus to the fall of the First Temple.

Two tiny Dead Sea Scrolls fragments, though containing barely a dozen complete words, yield new information on the world of the Qumran sect. It is to be regretted that the fragments have been poorly preserved, but fortunately both retain their opening lines, which describe their content.

The first, a list of *netinim* 'temple-servants', is written in Hebrew and is most probably Qumranic, that is, Essene. The second, a list of false prophets, is in Aramaic. If Segert's rule is correct, that the Dead Sea sect used only Hebrew in their compositions,[1] the list is not sectarian, but its viewpoint was accepted at Qumran.

A List of netinim: 4Q340 (Negative 43407)

Description

This miniscule fragment (maximum measurements 4.5 × 2.9 cm.) was part of the upper right side of a leather scroll. The leather is wrinkled and

Author's note: This is a revised version of a Hebrew paper of the same title published in *Tarbiẓ* 62/1 (1993) 45–54. The second part of the present version has benefitted considerably from remarks made by Prof. E. Qimron ("On the Interpretation of the List of False Prophets," *Tarbiẓ* 63 [1994] 273–75).

1. S. Segret, "Die Sprachen-Fragen in der Qumrangemeinschaft," *Qumranprobleme: Vorträge des Leipziger Symopsions über Qumran-Probleme* (Berlin, 1963) 315–19; idem, "Sprächlische Bemerkungen zu einigen aramäische Texten von Qumran," *ArOr* 33 (1965) 190–206.

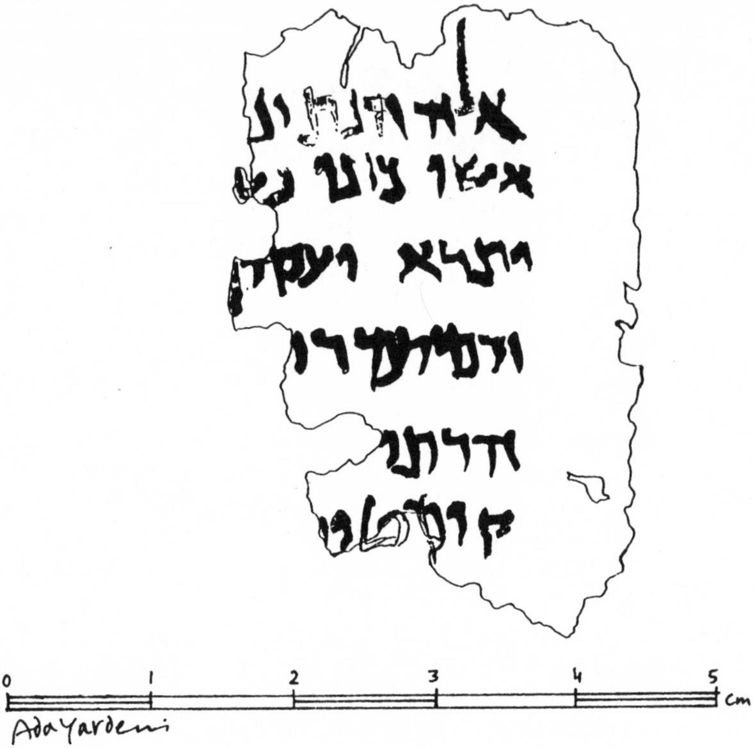

Figure 1. List of *netinim* (4Q*340*).

darkened, especially on the left. The upper margins (ca. 5 mm) and right end margins (ca. 7 mm) are preserved. In the middle, lengthwise, some 6 mm to the left of the right-hand margin, there is a trace of a fold. Of the Hebrew text, the beginnings of the first six lines have been preserved, written in Hasmonean formal script. There is no evidence of line tracing. The back is covered by paper, applied recently for conservation purposes. Thus there is no way of checking whether there was any writing on the reverse. On paleographic grounds, the document should be dated to about the first half of the first century B.C.E.

Decipherment

1. אלה הנתינ[ים]	1. אלה הנתינים
2. אשר כונו בש[מותיהם]	2. אשר כונו בשמותיהם
3. יתרא ו/יעקו/י.[ ]	3. יתרא

4. הסס̇ר ו/י[ ]
5. הרתו/י[ ]
6. קוו/י̇ך טו/י[ ] 6. . . .טו[ביה]

Translation

1. These are the *netin*[*im*]
2. Who were specified by [their na]mes
3. Ithra . . .
4. . . .
5. . . .
6. . . . To[biah]

Notes

Line 2. אשר כונו. This expression does not appear in the Bible, the Dead Sea Scrolls, or Rabbinic Hebrew.

שמותיהם. The Scrolls use both שמותיהם (CD II 13; IV 5) and שמותם (1QM IV 6, 7, and passim).

Line 3. יתרא. The name Ithra (NJPSV) is unknown fro the lists of *netinim* in Ezra–Nehemiah, but a person of this name is mentioned in the Bible as the husband of Abigail and father of Amasa (2 Sam 17:25; elsewhere—1 Kgs 2:5, 32; 1 Chr 2:17—the form is יתר). In Samuel he is described as an Israelite; in Chronicles as an Ishmaelite. The latter version seems superior, because there is no point in the appellation "Israelite" for a man who resides among Israelites. A foreign origin would accord with the prevalent conception regarding the ancestry of the *netinim.*[2]

ועקי/ו. At the end of the line there are traces of a long letter, which cannot be a *bet.* This precludes the very tempting reading עקוב, one of the *netinim* (Ezra 2:45), as well as the name of a family of gatekeepers (Ezra 2:42; Neh 7:45, 11:19; 1 Chr 9:17), who also belonged to the temple personnel during the Restoration.

We cannot propose plausible reconstructions of the other defective lines, except the last word in line 6, which may be read as טוביה. The children of Tobiah are mentioned among the returnees: ". . . who came up from Tel-melah . . . they were unable to tell whether their father's house and descent were Israelite" (Ezra 2:59–60, Neh 7:61–62). This name also suits a list of *netinim* who, as we shall try to show, were relegated to an inferior status because of their foreign origin.

2. The name was still used during the Second Commonwealth (by *natin*?). Cf. J. B. Frey, *CII* (Rome, 1952) 2.1301.

Significance of the List

Some time during the Second Commonwealth, the *netinim* suffered a drastic decline in status. During the Restoration there is not the slightest hint of discrimination against them: they migrated from Babylonia of their own free will, something they would not have done had they experienced discrimination. The *netinim* were also party to Nehemiah's Covenant and took upon themselves not to marry foreigners (this is the meaning of עמי הארצות, Neh 10:29), a clear proof that they enjoyed the same status as the rest of the people.[3]

The change in their status in later periods is reflected in the talmudic ruling prohibiting their marriage with unblemished Israelites; indeed, they were ranked together with *mamzerim* 'bastards' (*m. Qidd.* 4:1 et passim; and cf. parallels in the Talmuds). This is certainly not a late ruling; the fact that it is worded in Aramaic indicates a Second Commonwealth origin.[4] According to *m. Hor.* 3:8 (and *b. Hor.* 13a), a *mamzer* is superior to a *natin.*

That the *netinim* were a real entity even in later times may be deduced not only from literary sources (the Babylonian Talmud mentions a village called דורנוניתא whose inhabitants were descendants of *netinim*; *b. Qidd.* 70b) but also from an epigraphic find. A short inscription discovered at Tell el-Ful, on the northern outskirts of Jerusalem, reads חנניה בר חגב Hananiah Bar Hagab, most probably referring to a *natin.*[5] Not only does this name appear in Ezra and Nehemiah as the name of a *natin* (in conjunction with Hanan, Ezra 2:46; in Neh 7:48 the name is given as חגבא), but these are also names of *netinim* in Ugarit.[6] This inscription, dated to ca. 100 B.C.E., is roughly contemporaneous with our scroll.

We suggest that our scroll is a list of blemished people, unfit for marriage, a negative genealogical list. Rabbi Simeon b. Azzai, a sage active in the generation following the destruction of the Second Temple, states that he saw in Jerusalem a family register (literally, a genealogical scroll) in which was written: "so-and-so is a *mamzer* through [a sexual

3. B. A. Levine, "The Netinim," *JBL* 82 (1963) 207–12; idem, "Notes on the Hebrew Ostracon from Arad," *IEJ* (1969) 49–51; E. Puech, "The Tell el-Ful Jar Inscription and the Netinim," *BASOR* 261 (1986) 69–71.

4. J. N. Epstein, *Prolegomena ad litterase Tannaiticas* (Jerusalem and Tel Aviv, 1957) 54, 414–15 [Hebrew]. Cf. also: B. A. Levine, "Later Sources on the Nethinim," in *Orient and Occident: Essays Presented to C. H. Gordon on the Occasion of His Sixty-Fifth Birthday* (ed. H. Hoffner; Neukirchen-Vluyn, 1973) 101–7.

Levine (ibid., 103 n. 8) disagrees with Epstein and ascribes this *halakah* to the time of Ezra. It seems, however, that Epstein is correct. There is not a shred of evidence to suggest that the *netinim* were discriminated at the fifth century B.C.E. and certainly not to that extent.

5. See Puech, "The Tell el-Ful Jar Inscription."

6. See Levine, "Netinim," "Notes on the Hebrew Ostracon," and "Later Sources on the Nethinim."

union with] a married woman" (*m. Yebam.* 4:13).[7] At this time, normative Judaism was very strict in matters of genealogical purity, all the more so the Dead Sea Sect, who were notoriously extreme. Needless to say, some (plausibly most) of the sect's members led a more or less normal family life, as is attested in the *Damascus Document* (CD VII 6–9), as well as the *Rule of the Congregation* (1QSa I 4). As we are inclined to identify the sect with the Essenes, we may also cite Josephus' testimony concerning married Essenes (*JW* 2.161–69).[8]

We should mention here Baumgarten's ingenious suggestion that the term בני נכר (i.e., 'foreigners') in *Midraš 2 Samuel* 7 (= *Florilegium*; 4Q*174* I 4) refers to the *netinim*.[9] According to his interpretation, the *netinim* were to be excluded from the service of the eschatological temple. However, we do not believe that our list was composed in order to deal with the personnel of the eschatological temple. The problem of genealogical purity was certainly more urgent and relevant.

False Prophets: 4Q339 (Negative 43248)

The fragment (maximum measurements 8.3 × 5 cm.) comes from the upper left side of a document written on leather. The fragment was torn in two, almost in the middle. Parallel holes in the left sides of the upper and lower halves might have served to hold the two pieces together, indicating that it was folded along its width. A tear 3.3 cm. from the left side margin may indicate another fold. In this part, remains of the upper and lower margins have been preserved, as well as the left side margin. Remnants of a large rubbed-off black band may be seen along the margins. On the basis of these data we may suggest a reconstruction as a small square card, of original size ca. 8.5 × 7 cm., folded twice and perhaps even held together by a string passed through the holes. We have no parallels for such an arrangement and mention it just as a suggestion.

The document is very wrinkled and dark in color. Of the text, only the ends of nine lines, written in a formal Herodian hand, have been preserved. There are no remains of traced lines. The back is covered with paper applied recently for preservation purposes; hence we cannot say whether there was any writing on the reverse.

7. A. Büchler, "Purity and Family Impurity in Jerusalem Before 70 C.E.," *Studies in Jewish History* (London, 1956) 64–68 (= *Familie Reinheit und Familie Makel in Jerusalem vor Jahre 70* [A. Schwartz Festschrift; Berlin, 1917]) 133–62.

8. E. Schürer, *The History of the Jewish People in the Age of Jesus Christ* (rev. and ed. G. Vermes, F. Millar, and M. Black; Edinburgh, 1979) 2.570, 578.

9. See J. M. Baumgarten, "The Exclusion of the 'Netinim' and Proselytes in 4QFlorilegium," *Studies in the Qumran Law* (Leiden, 1977) 75–87. 4Q*Florilegium* was published in John M. Allegro, *Qumrân Cave 4: I (4Q158–4Q186)* (DJD 5; Oxford, 1986) 53–55.

Figure 2. List of false prophets (4Q*339*).

Decipherment and Suggested Reconstruction

1. נביאי [ש]קרא די קמו ב[ישראל]
2. בלעם [בן] בעור
3. [וה]זקן [די]בביתאל
4. [וצד]קיה בן כ[נ]ענה
5. [ואחא]ב בן ק[ול]יה
6. [וצד]קיה בן מ[ע]שיה
7. [ושמעיה הנ]חלמי
8. [וחנניה בן עז]ור
9. [ויוחנן בן שמ]עון

Translation

1. False prophets who arose in Israel
2. Balaam son of Beor
3. And the Old Man from Bethel
4. And Zedekiah son of Chenaanah
5. And Ahab son of Kolaiah
6. And Zedekiah son of Maaseiah
7. And Shemaiah the Nehelamite
8. And Hananiah son of Azur
9. And Johanan son of Simeon

Notes

Line 1. The expression נביאי שקר 'false prophets' does not occur in the Hebrew Bible, in Second Commonwealth Hebrew or in Aramaic epigraphy. It appears first in Mishnaic Hebrew (*m. Sanh.* 1:5 and passim). Thus, our document is the earliest Semitic source to use the expression. In Greek it occurs in the Septuagint version of the twelve minor prophets (Zech 13:2) and Jeremiah (several times)—a translation commonly held to have been made in the second century B.C.E.—in the form πσευδοπροφήτης.[10]

Line 2. בלעם בן בעור. Balaam son of Beor, the famous seer, is referred to frequently in the Bible (mostly in Numbers 22–24, as well as in

10. Y. A. Seligmann, "On the History and Nature of Prophesy in Israel," *ErIsr* 3 (1954) 125–32 [Hebrew].

Deuteronomy, Joshua, Micah, and Nehemiah). He is mentioned in the Deir ᶜAlla inscription[11] and is much discussed in the Talmud.[12]

For the talmudic sages, Balaam was a prophet, the last of seven who prophesied to the Gentiles, considered a counterpart to Moses (see *Numbers Rabba* 20) and even superior to him in certain respects (*Sipre*, end of *Deuteronomy*). The evil Balaam (*m. ᵓAbot* 5:19), who intended to curse Israel but was forced to bless them, is of course a negative figure, who deserves to open a list of false prophets, and not just because he is the first such prophet mentioned in the Bible.

Line 3. This, of course, has to do with the prophet of Bethel, described also as an old man (1 Kgs 13:11–31).[13]

Line 4. This is the Zedekiah son of Chenaanah, the prophet who promised Ahab victory against the Arameans at Ramoth-gilead (1 Kgs 22:1–28), 2 Chron 18:1–27).

Lines 5–6. These are the false prophets Ahab son of Kolaiah and Zedekiah son of Maaseiah, contemporaries and rivals of Jeremiah. Jeremiah accuses them, not only of prophesying a lie, but also of committing adultery with their neighbors' wives (Jer 29:21–24). Talmudic legends recount that these prophets tried to seduce Nebuchadnezzar's daughter (another version claims it was the queen; *b. Sanh.* 73.1).[14]

Line 7. Shemaiah the Nehelamite was a leader in Babylonia who announced that the return from the captivity was imminent (Jer 29:24–32). Jeremiah denounced him as a false prophet and foretold that he would "not have a man to dwell among [that] people" (v. 32).

Line 8. Though only two letters of this line have been preserved, the reconstruction seems fairly certain. Hananiah son of Azur, an adversary of Jeremiah, is an archetypical false prophet. His falsity was demonstrated not only by the fact that his prophesy was proven wrong six years after its utterance, but also by his death, as Jeremiah had predicted, in that very same year (Jer 28:17).[15]

Line 9. There is no biblical false prophet whose patronymic ends with עון. Therefore Qimron suggests that we ought to look for a later figure. If he is right in his ingenious idea that the letters עון represent

11. J. Hoftijzer and G. van der Kooij (eds.), *The Balaam Text from Deir ᶜAlla Re-evaluated* (Leiden, 1991). Up-to-date bibliography, 55–57.

12. On the image of Balaam in the talmudic literature, see L. Ginzberg, *Legends of the Jews* (Philadelphia, 1946–1947) vol. 7, in the index s.v. (pp. 55–56). See also E. E. Urbach, "Homilies of the Rabbis on the Prophets of the Nations and the Balaam Stories," *Tarbiẓ* 25 (1956) 272–89 [Hebrew; English summary, pp. iii–vii].

13. On the Bethel prophet, see Ginzberg, *Legends of the Jews*, 6.306–7.

14. Ibid., 4.278, 336–37.

15. Ibid., 4.297–98; 6.389 nn. 18–19.

שמעון, the only name with such an ending common in the Second Commonwealth, he may be also right in his guess that the full name is יוחנן בן שמעון. This is the Hebrew name of John Hyrcanus I, the ruler (ethnarch) of Judea and high priest (135–104 B.C.E.), son of Simeon the Hasmonean. Josephus tells us about his prophetic faculties: "He was the only man to unite in his person three of the highest privileges—the supreme command of the nation, the high priesthood, and the gift of prophecy. For so closely was he in touch with the Deity, that he was never ignorant of the future" (*J.W.* 1.2.8 §68–69; *Ant.* 13.10.7 §300, ed. H. St. J. Thackeray). The tradition about his supernatural powers was still preserved in a late rabbinic source, which claims that he heard a *bat kol,* a heavenly or divine voice that revealed God's will to man (*b. Soṭa* 33a). The author of our list may have regarded him as a false prophet. Though this is not a Qumranic composition, it agrees very well with their enmity to the leaders who were also high priests, and one of them, the "Wicked Priest," was their archenemy.[16]

16. On the various identifications of the "Wicked Priest" see P. R. Callaway, *The History of the Qumran Community* (Sheffield, 1988) 12–24.

Grandeur et pureté du sacerdoce: Remarques sur le *Testament de Qahat* (4Q542)

André Caquot

A new translation of the Aramaic Testament of Qahat was edited by É. Puech in RevQ 15 (1991). The 'great name' (I 1) is supposed to be the Tetragrammaton known and used by the priests. The word kilᵓayim (I 5) means 'hybrid', as a nickname for priests of doubtful extraction. Some minor points are also discussed (I 6–7, 7–8, 8–9; II 13).

M. Émile Puech a récemment donné l'*editio princeps* d'un important texte qoumrânien trop longtemps retenu par J. Starcky.[1] L'état de conservation du principal fragment et la qualité de son expression araméenne auraient cependant dû permettre une communication plus rapide digne de l'intérêt du document. Il contribue en effet à mettre en lumière certains aspects de l'idéologie cléricale essénienne. Légitimement soucieux de paléographie et des possibilités matérielles de restitution, E. Puech n'a pas développé le commentaire doctrinal que ce texte appelle. La présente note, qu'il m'est agréable d'offrir en hommage à Jonas C. Greenfield, vise à fournir quelques éléments pour ce commentaire.

Colonne I, ligne 1

On lit au début du texte une paraphrase du second verset de la bénédiction aaronide (Nombres 6:25) suivie d'une référence au "grand nom" de Dieu que Qahat doit communiquer. A la différence de Nombres 6:22–27, la bénédiction paraît réservée aux "fils" de Qahat (ligne 4),

1. Puech, "Le Testament de Qahat en araméen de la grotte 4 (4QTQahat)," *RevQ* 15 (*Mémorial Jean Starcky*; 1991) 23–54.

c'est-à-dire aux prêtres. C'est ce qui autorise à donner au "grand nom" une acception très précise qu'il n'a pas toujours à Qoumrân. En 1QM XI 2 et 4Q*504* 1–2 iv 9–10,[2] le "grand nom" n'est qu'une métonymie pour la personne même de Dieu (et aussi en 2 Baruch 5:1; 4 Esdras 4:25). Mais ici il s'agit du Tétragramme, que le grand prêtre doit articuler sur les victimes de Kippur (*Tosefta Yôm Hakkippûrîm* 2.2).[3] Quelques témoignages des pseudépigraphes[4] permettent d'entrevoir que les Esséniens partageaient la croyance dans les vertus théurgiques du "grand nom."[5]

Colonne I, ligne 2

La répétition au début de la ligne du verbe *wtndʿwnh* 'et vous le connaîtrez', peut être considérée comme accidentelle, c'est du moins l'opinion de l'éditeur. On peut toutefois se demander si l'auteur n'a pas voulu signifier deux choses: d'une part que les prêtres connaîtront le "grand nom" pour le prononcer correctement, et d'autre part qu'ils connaîtront Dieu lui-même. Dans la pensée essénienne, le prêtre est un "gnostique" (1QSb IV:27; *Testament de Lévi* 4:3, 18:3).

Colonne I, lignes 5–6

Qahat recommande à ses descendants de ne pas livrer leur héritage (*yrwtt-*) à des étrangers, ni leur "patrimoine" à des *kylʾyn*. L'héritage en question est sans doute celui dont parle Deutéronome 18:1, le revenu réservé aux prêtres. Le terme parallèle à 'héritage' *ʾḥsnwt-* doit être rendu par 'patrimoine' plutôt que par 'richesses', traduction retenue par É. Puech.[6] Mais le mot *kylʾyn* a fait le plus difficulté. L'éditeur n'a pas manqué de citer à ce propos le passage du *Testament* araméen *de Lévi*, d'après le fragment conservé à Cambridge (colonne *f*, ligne 10), où *kyl*[apparaît en parallèle à *nkry* 'étranger'. Le terme a été laissé sans traduc-

2. Voir M. Baillet, *Qumran Cave 4* (Oxford, 1982) 143.

3. Comparer les références au "grand nom" en *Jubilés* 23:21 et 36:7.

4. Ainsi *1 Hénoch* 55:2, 69:14–25; *Apocalypse d'Abraham* 10:4, 8.

5. Voir E. Urbach, *The Sages: Their Concepts and Beliefs* (Jerusalem, 1975) 124–34. Cette conception est bien illustrée dans les textes magiques (voir C. H. Gordon, *Or* 10 [1941] 273).

6. Dans le *Targoum Neofiti* de Deutéronome 18:1, *bʾḥsnwt* traduit l'hébreu *naḥălāh.* C'est donc une variante de *ʾḥsnh* de 18:1a, et un singulier plutôt qu'un pluriel. La traduction 'patrimoine' est justifiée parce que l'araméen d'Eléphantine *mhḥsn* recouvre la même réalité que le grec *klērouchos* 'détenteur d'un lot transmis par hérédité', selon H. Szubin et B. Porten, "Ancestral Estates in Aramaic Contracts: The Legal Significance of the Term *mhḥsn*," *JRAS* (1982) 3–9.

tion par J. C. Greenfield et M. Stone.[7] É. Puech l'interprète comme *kîlay* d'Isaïe 32:5 qu'il traduit par 'escroc' sur la foi d'une longue tradition.[8]

A mon sens, l'araméen *kylᵓyn* est identique à l'hébreu *kîlᵓayim* de Lévitique 19:19 désignant des espèces animales, des semences ou des textiles qu'on ne doit pas mêler, appliqué en Deutéronome 22:9 à l'ensemencement d'une vigne. Comme il s'agit d'un dérivé de la racine *klᵓ* dénotant la dualité, on pourrait penser que les *kylᵓyn* sont des individus "doubles" ayant comme il est dit plus loin dans notre texte (I 9) "un coeur et un coeur" (comparer Psaumes 12:3; 1QH IV 14; Siracide grec 1:28; *1 Hénoch* 91:1). Mais l'interprétation convenant le mieux au parallèle 'étrangers' est de voir ici un détournement satirique du sens pris par le terme technique *kîlᵓayim.* Lorsque le terme mishnique *kîlᵓayim* ressortit au règne animal il ne dénote pas seulement une espèce qu'il est interdit d'apparier à une autre,[9] mais aussi ce qui peut naître de ce genre d'unions contre nature. C'est en ce sens, en effet, que le terme peut être associé à la *ṭĕrēpâ* ou à la bête née par césarienne (*yôṣēᵓ dôpen*),[10] ou encore au *kôy,* un de ces hircocerfs qui hantaient l'imagination des anciens.[11] S'il est dit dans la *Tosefta* (*Berakot* 6.7) que les *kîlᵓayim* ne remontent pas aux six jours de la création, c'est qu'ils appartiennent à une création opérée par Adam qui selon la légende (*b. Pesaḥim* 54a) rapprocha deux espèces animales pour produire un mulet. Signalons qu'un texte à ce jour inédit (4Q*418*) présente les mots suivants, lisibles à la 7e ligne du fragment photographié au milieu et au bas de la planche 43.479: *wĕhāyâ kilᵓayim* [*ka*]*ppered* 'et ce fut un hybride comme le mulet'.

L'auteur du *Testament de Qahat* et celui du Testament araméen de Lévi ont repris le mot technique pour stigmatiser une descendance de Qahat qui aurait souillé, par des unions illicites, la pureté de son lignage. L'usage qui est fait ici de *kylᵓyn* rappelle celui de l'hébreu *mamzēr* en *1 Hénoch* 10:9 (selon le grec d'Akhmim et l'éthiopien) pour désigner les géants, 'bâtards' de créatures célestes et terrestres. Il semble que le texte inédit 4QMMT fasse suivre un rappel de la loi lévitique des *kilᵓayim* d'une allusion très précise à des unions matrimoniales condamnées qu'on reproche au clergé. L'association d'idées est celle qui justifie

7. Dans H. W. Hollander et M. de Jonge, *The Testaments of the Twelve Patriarchs: A Commentary* (Leyde, 1985) 468.

8. Symmaque *dolios,* Jérôme *fraudulens.* Rashi le rapproche de l'hébreu *nôkel* de Malachie 1:14.

9. S'agissant d'un individu, on trouve en ce sens l'expression *bar kilᵓayim* en *b. Berakot* 8*a.*

10. Nombreuses références: *Mishnah Zebaḥin* 8:1, 9:3, 14:2; *Bekorot* 9:4; *Temurah* 2:3, 6:1; *Tosefta Zebaḥin* 8.2, 9.5, 15.20.

11. *Mishnah Bekorot* 1:5; *Tosefta Ḥullin* 5.1; *Mekhilta sur Éxode* 13:13 (éd. Horovitz et Rabin, 71).

l'emploi d'une désignation de l'"hybride" dans ce passage du *Testament de Qahat.* La pureté de la caste sacerdotale a certainement obsédé plus d'un esprit de ce temps : on connaît le soupçon jeté sur Jean Hyrcan accusé d'être le fils d'une captive (Josèphe, *Ant.* 13.292)

Colonne I, lignes 6–7

É. Puech traduit 'et ils vous mépriseraient parce qu'ils seraient pour vous des résidents et qu'ils seraient sur vous des chefs'. Je propose de rattacher 'et ils vous mépriseraient' à la fin de la phrase précédente qui se terminerait ainsi et de comprendre la suite: 'Ceux qui sont pour vous des métèques deviendraient sur vous des chefs', le second *lhwn* de la ligne 7 étant précédé d'un *waw* d'apodose. Le nom *twtb* est défini par E. Puech comme un "calque de l'hébreu" *tôšāb*; il eût fallu rappeler qu'il apparaît dans l'araméen occidental ancien des "Proverbes d'Aḥiqar" (ligne 112 du papyrus d'Eléphantine) et aussi en syriaque, où il peut traduire l'hébreu *gēr* (ainsi dans la *Peshiṭta* d'Exode 2:22 et 12:48).[12]

Colonne I, lignes 7–8

La recommandation de s'attacher à la "parole de Jacob", aux "prescriptions d'Abraham" aussi bien qu'aux "ordonnances de Lévi" et à celles de Qahat rappelle qu'on a attribué aux deux patriarches nommés en premier lieu l'énoncé de règles que le clergé se doit de respecter. Le livre des *Jubilés* fait remonter à Abraham la réglementation des *sukkôt* (16:20–31) et une série d'instructions cultuelles (21:5–20), en particulier le règlement, non biblique, concernant le bois du sacrifice (21:12–14) auquel il est aussi fait référence en *Testament* (grec) *de Lévi* 9:12. Toujours selon les *Jubilés,* c'est Lévi qui institue la seconde dîme (32:9–15) et le Kippur (34:18–29). Le silence de cette phrase sur Isaac n'est pas fortuit: les *Jubilés* ne lui prêtent aucune initiative et d'après le *Testament* (grec) *de Lévi* (9:6–14), il ne fait que répéter des instructions d'Abraham.

Colonne I, lignes 8–9

La restitution de É. Puech: 'Soyez saints et purs de toute [impudicité] en masse' repose sur une traduction *dkyn mn* 'purs de' qui peut se recommander du targoum de Lévitique 16:30, *lĕdakkāʾāh yātkôn mikkôl ḥôbêkôn* 'pour vous purifier de tous vos péchés'. L'éditeur se reconnaît embarrassé par *brwb* qu'il traduit 'en masse'. Il s'agit sans doute d'un hé-

12. Voir R. Payne-Smith, *Thesaurus syriacus* (Oxford, 1879–1901) 1647.

braïsme, car on attendrait *brwbᵓ* comme dans l'adage *zîl bātar rûbāᵓ* 'suis la majorité' (*b. Ḥullin* 11a). Mais on peut se demander si *rwb* n'a pas le sens que lui donne la phrase déjà célèbre de 4QMMT, *pārašnû mērôb haᶜam* 'nous nous sommes séparés de la masse du peuple' et s'il ne faut pas donner à la préposition *mn*, devant la lacune, sa valeur de comparatif: 'soyez saints et purs plus que [quiconque] dans la masse'. On devrait alors restituer un indéfini comme *mn* au lieu de *znw* 'impudicité'.

Colonne II, ligne 13

La dernière phrase du grand fragment est obscurcie par la mutilation à gauche de la colonne. Jusqu'à la ligne 11, les restitutions proposées par É. Puech sont des plus vraisemblables: Qahat transmet à Amram et à ses fils les livres de Lévi afin qu'ils leur servent d'avertissement. A la fin de la ligne 12, la restitution 'afin que par eux vous fassiez attention [à toute impureté et à tout mal (?)]' doit être rejetée. Elle repose en effet sur une traduction erronée du début de la ligne 13: l'araméen *bᵓthylkwthwn ᶜmkwn* ne peut signifier 'en vous conduisant d'après eux', comme si l'on avait *bᵓthylkwtkwn ᶜmhwn*. Le suffixe *-hwn* se rapporte à des hommes qui se conduisent conformément à 'vous', c'est-à-dire à Qahat et à ses fils. Il est très imprudent de vouloir reconstituer des phrases entières d'un texte perdu sans parallèle, mais on sera certainement plus près de la vérité en supposant qu'à la fin de la ligne 12 Qahat recommandait aux siens non pas tant de se garder eux-mêmes que de veiller à ce que leur enseignement soit diffusé en Israël et ainsi 'grâce à eux [les livres] vous aurez un grand mérite parce qu'ils [Israël] se conduiront d'après vous [les prêtres]'. La phrase rappellerait la fonction pédagogique du clergé à laquelle les Esséniens paraissent avoir attaché de l'importance.[13]

Voici une traduction de ce fragment du *Testament de Qahat* reposant en grande partie sur celle de M. É. Puech, mais reprenant les observations présentées ci-dessus.

I 1. et Dieu des dieux pour tous les âges. Il fera briller Sa lumière sur vous, Il vous fera savoir Son grand nom

2. et vous le saurez. Et vous saurez de Lui qu'Il est le Dieu des âges, Seigneur de toutes les oeuvres et souverain

3. sur toutes choses en agissant sur elles selon Sa volonté. Il vous procurera la joie, et l'allégresse à vos fils dans les générations

13. Voir 1QSb IV 27, 1QH IV 27–29.

4. de justice, à toujours. Et maintenant, mes fils, veillez à l'héritage qui vous (a été) transmis
5. et que vous ont remis vos pères. Ne livrez pas votre héritage à des étrangers et votre patrimoine
6. à des hybrides: vous seriez abaissés et avilis à leurs yeux, et ils vous mépriseraient; ceux qui
7. sont pour vous des métèques deviendraient sur vous des chefs. Mais attachez-vous à la parole de Jacob
8. votre père et tenez ferme aux sentences d'Abraham, à la jurisprudence de Lévi et à la mienne. Soyez saints et purs,
9. plus que quic[onque] dans la masse, vous attachant à la vérité et marchant dans la droiture, non avec un coeur double,
10. mais avec un coeur pur et un esprit juste et bon. Vous me ferez parmi vous un bon renom, joie
11. pour Lévi, jubilation pour Jacob, allégresse pour Isaac, gloire pour Abraham, parce que vous aurez gardé
12. et fait progresser l'héritage que vous ont laissé vos pères, la vérité, la justice, la droiture,
13. la pure[té, la sa]inteté et la prêtrise, selon tout ce que je vous ai commandé, selon tout ce que

II 1. je vous ai enseigné, selon la vérité, dès maintenant et pour tous [les âges . . .]
2. toute parole de vérité viendra sur vo[us . . .]
3. la bénédiction éternelle demeurera sur vous et se[ra . . .]
4. subsistant pour toutes les générations des âges et vous ne [. . .] plus [. . .]
5. de votre châtiment, et vous subsisterez (*ou* vous vous lèverez) pour prononcer la sentence con[tre . . .]
6. et pour voir la faute de tous les coupables des âges [. . .]
7. et dans le feu et dans les abîmes et dans toutes les cavernes [. . .]
8. dans les [gén]érations de justice, et tous les enfants de l'iniqu[ité] passeront [. . .]
9. Et maintenant, Amram mon fils, je te recomman[de], moi [. . .]
10. et tes [f]ils à leurs fils, je recommande, moi [. . .]
11. et ils ont donné à Lévi mon père, et Lévi mon père m'[a donné . . .]
12. tous mes livres, en qualité de témoignage, et avec eux vous veillerez [. . .]
13. vous (aurez), grâce à eux, un grand mérite, parce qu'ils se conduiront à votre exemple.

Aḥiqar, *Ummân* and *Amun*, and Biblical Wisdom Texts

Henri Cazelles

What is the meaning of ʾāmôn in Prov 8:30? Is ḥokmâ an infant in arms or a master worker? According to van Dijk's discovery of Aḥiqar as an ummân in a Seleucid tablet, as well as studies by Greenfield and Parpola, it seems that the ḥokmâ in question, by whom kings rule and judges judge, is more a kind of steward than a baby.

Jonas Greenfield has surely earned a most prominent place among those specialists in West Semitic epigraphy and philology who have shown us how to determine the meaning of biblical terms by comparing them with documents from the ancient Orient and with the life they portray. In 1967, addressing the American Oriental Society, he analyzed the relationship between the Aramaic Wisdom of Aḥiqar and the book of Tobit, fragments of which had been found at Qumran, attesting to the long text.[1] Later he defined the background of Tobit and pointed out the parallel between Aḥiqar 156 and Prov 17:20b.[2] He returned to the subject still more recently,[3] examining two sentences from Aḥiqar (77 and v. 10 of the Syriac Aḥiqar).

After the translations by Grelot and Lindenberger, Kottsieper recently published the text and translation of lines 126–90, followed by 79–126 (in that order), with glossary and grammar.[4] Our main concern here

1. P. Skehan, *DBSup* 9 (1979) 818b; J. C. Greenfield, *Leš* 27/28 (1963–64) 303–13; idem, "Aḥiqar in the Book of Tobit," in *De la Torah au Messie: Mélanges H. Cazelles* (ed. J. Doré, P. Grelot, and M. Carrez; Paris, 1981) 329–36.

2. J. C. Greenfield, "The Background and Parallel to a Proverb of Aḥiqar," in *Hommages à A. Dupont-Sommer* (Paris, 1971) 49–59.

3. J. C. Greenfield, "Two Proverbs of Ahiqar," in *Lingering over Words: Studies in Ancient Near Eastern Literature in Honor of William L. Moran* (ed. T. Abusch, J. Huehnergard, and P. Steinkeller; HSS 37; Atlanta, 1990) 195–201.

4. P. Grelot, "Les Proverbes araméens d'Aḥiqar," *RB* 68 (1961) 178–94; J. M. Lindenberger, "The Aramaic Proverbs of Aḥiqar" (Ph.D. diss., Johns Hopkins University, 1974);

is with Greenfield's reference to a document from Sippar from the time of Esarhaddon, deciphered by J. van Dijk,[5] in which a certain Aba-Ninnu-dari, "called by the *Aḫlamê* Aḫuʾaqari," is mentioned as an *ummânu*. Though the name *Aba-Ninnu-dari* is unknown at the time of Esarhaddon, it is attested in the Middle Babylonian Period,[6] while the designation *aḫlamê* for the Arameans had become anachronistic by the Neo-Assyrian Period.[7] Thus, Lambert was probably right to consider the Babylonian "Counsels of Wisdom" as a prototype of our Aramaic Aḥiqar.[8]

I

But what is an *ummânu*? The term deserves attention, because it has been compared, not without reason, with the Hebrew word *ʾāmôn* in another wisdom text, Prov 8:30. We know of an *ummân*, also in the Middle Babylonian or Kassite Period, at the time of Nazimuruttaš;[9] but *ummânê* have been attested from the Old to the Neo-Babylonian Periods. The term was long thought to designate a master worker or craftsman, but its scope must be expanded: the contemporary of Nazimuruttaš was a scribe, who made extracts and selections.

Von Soden distinguishes two terms (AHw 1413, 1415): (1) *ummânu(m)*, also written *ummânnu*, which he relates to the West Semitic term *ʿam* 'people, body of men, army'; and (2) *ummiânum*, also written *ummênum, ummânum, ummannu*, meaning an artisan, ranging over a wide range of specializations (*Feldmesser, Handwerker, Fachmann, Künstler, Gelehrter, Geldgeber, Glaubiger*); the root is unknown.

In the Amorite of Mari, Bottéro and Finet[10] also distinguish between *ummânum* 'army' and *ummênu* 'craftsmen, skilled workers'. In some recently published texts, the plural *ummanâtum* designates armies,[11]

see also in J. H. Charlesworth (ed.), *The Old Testament Pseudepigrapha* (London, 1985) 2.479–507. I. Kottsieper, *Der Sprache der Aḥiqarsprüche* (Berlin, 1990).

5. J. van Dijk, in *Uruk: Vorläufiger Bericht* (ed. H. J. Lenzen; Berlin, 1962) 18.45, rev. 19–20.

6. 5 Rawl. 44, 111, 9′; cf. S. Parpola, *Letters from Assyrian Scholars* (Neukirchen, 1983) 2.450.

7. J. A. Brinkman, *A Political History of Post-Kassite Babylonia* (Rome, 1968) 278 n. 1799.

8. W. G. Lambert, *Babylonian Wisdom Literature* (Oxford, 1960) 90; cf. the address formula 'my son' and the parallel proverb.

9. W. G. Lambert, "Ancestors, Authors and Canonicity," *JCS* 11 (1957) 8.

10. J. Bottéro and A. Finet, *Répertoire analytique des tomes I à V* (ARMT 15; Paris, 1954) 191. The *Chicago Assyrian Dictionary* has not yet published the letter U.

11. J. M. Durand, in *MARI* V 164; ARM 1 85:17–19 (Dossin); cf. ARM 1 42: lines 42–43; P. Abrahami, *RAI* 38, 166, on the circulation of goods, people, and ideas in the Ancient Near East.

DUMU *ummiʾânim*, "those in charge of merchandise and valuables not only in transit but also when they are being sold or distributed." They are "frequently entrusted with sums of money belonging to several individuals. . . . It is often stated that the person in question is trustworthy."[12]

Under Esarhaddon, the *ummânê* were 'experts', craftsmen initiated into the secrets of the trade, known as *leʾuti.*[13] Parpola lists several 'scholars', high-ranking figures who belong to the "inner circle" revolving around the king; these *ummânê* are mentioned along with astrologers, exorcists, and doctors. One of them is called Esarhaddon's 'master'; another is the tutor of the heir to the throne, Assurbanipal.[14] On these grounds, Parpola suggests that an *ummânu* was "a trained expert of specific crafts."[15] This type of 'lettré'[16] corresponds in the lexical series to the Sumerian word written KI-SU-LU-SE-NIG, read UMME(A) where A is a suffix. The origin of the term is apparently Sumerian: the element *ânum* in the Akkadian ending was probably felt to enhance the bearer of the title.[17] The term may have passed from Akkadian into Aramaic, as did many others.[18] In West Semitic, however, the root was understood in the

12. C. Michel, "Transporteurs, responsables et propriétaires de convoi dans les tablettes paléo-assyriennes," *RAI* 38, 140. The equivalence *ummiʾânu* = *ummênu* is certain (AHw 1415b 3, 4).

13. CAD L, 161a; S. M. Moren translates 'able scholars' (*RA* 74 [1980] 190).

14. Parpola, *Letters from Assyrian Scholars*, xv–xvi. For the Old Assyrian Period, P. Garelli translates 'financier' (*Les Assyriens en Cappadoce* [Paris, 1963] 188, 244–45), and M. T. Larsen 'bankers' (*Old Assyrian Caravan Procedures* [Istanbul and Leiden, 1967] 96–97). For the Neo-Assyrian period, Parpola proposes 'master, teacher'. A DUMU (Akk. *mar* = 'son') *ummeʾanîm* is called *kēnum* (Larsen, *Old Assyrian Caravan*, 97: 'trustworthy'). Perhaps one should distinguish between *ummeʾânu* and DUMU *ummeʾânim*, the latter being executory agents (Garelli, *Les Assyriens*, 245 n. 4); but the expression may simply designate a member of the profession.

15. Parpola (*Letters from Assyrian Scholars*, 270), concerning the letter 279, 19.

16. See R. Labat, *Manuel d'épigraphie akkadienne* (5th ed.; Paris, 1976) 99.

17. The lexicographers distinguish the Akkadian *ummânu* meaning 'army' (KI-SU-LU-SE-NIG; cf. R. Borger, *Assyrisch-babylonische Zeichenliste* [AOAT 33; Neukirchen, 1978] no. 461) from another meaning '*Meister, Künstler*' (UM-MI/ME-A; ibid., no. 134). On the passage into Akkadian, see S. J. Lieberman, *The Sumerian Loanwords in Old Babylonian Akkadian* (Missoula, 1977) 514–15 no. 687; into Hebrew, see E. P. Lipiński, "Emprunts suméro-akkadiens en hébreu biblique," *ZAH* 1 (1988) 63: "The words *ʾâmôn* (Prov 8,30) and *ʾummân* (Cant 7,2) are perhaps merely dialectal forms or particular spellings borrowed from the Akkadian *ummânu*, 'master worker', a contracted form of *ummiânu*. This term derives in turn from the Sumerian UMMIA." Von Soden's statement (*GAG* §56r, p. 70) that the ending *-ânum* enhances the title-bearer's position is contested by I. Gelb, *BiOr* 13 (1955) 106. A. Finet ("Homme À SIKKUM et SIKKÂNUM d'apres ARM II,76 et I,113 (in De la Babylonie à l'Assyrie en passant par Mari)," in *Mélanges R. L. Kupper* [Liège, 1990] 148) explains it simply as signifying 'belonging'. I am indebted to M. J. Seux for his help on this matter.

18. I. Kottsieper, "Die literarische Aufnahme assyrischer Begenbenheiten in frühen aramäischen Texten," *RAI* 38, 283–89. He remarks that in the papyrus Amherst 64 (Aramaic/

sense of ʾ*mn* 'trust', which is attested only in Ugaritic, Hebrew, or South Semitic.[19]

In the West Semitic sphere of the second millennium B.C.E., the equivalents of the Akkadian *ummânu* are quite rare. They may be listed as follows:

1. Caquot[20] drew attention to an illegally excavated text in which a worker, probably a worker in metals, is called *lʾey bn ʾmyn*. In this expression we recognize the DUMU *ummiʾânim* of Mari, called an 'expert', the Akkadian *leʾutu* and the Ugaritic *leʾy*; this is all the more probable, because a syllabic text found in the "House of Tablets" in the south of the city (RS 22227) mentions *ummiʾâni*.[21]

2. Tablet 1 from Taᶜanak may contain the term *u-ma-nu* in line 20, according to Albright's reading and translation: 'If there (be) a wizard of Ashera, let him tell our fortunes and let me hear quickly, and the *omen* and the interpretation send to me'.[22] However, Hrozný's reading, *u-ba-nu*, seems certain, since the same sign is found in the same line. He interpreted it as an *omen*: "Wenn sich der Finger (= omen) der Ashirat zeigen wird, so moge man sich es einscharfen und befolgen."[23] Ebeling agrees more or less with Hrozný,[24] but Rainey, who knows the Taᶜanak texts well, not only reads *ubana* but sees no reference in the sentence to either Ashirat or an omen.[25]

II

Moving on to the first millennium with the Zindjirli texts (eighth century B.C.E.), we have two almost certain readings of ʾ*mn*,[26] but in a

Demotic) there are not only close parallels to Psalm 20, but also an echo of Assurbanipal's complaint against his brother's revolt.

19. J. Biella, *Dictionary of Old South Arabic: Sabaean Dialect* (Cambridge, Mass., 1982) 20; A. Beeston et al., *Sabaean Dictionary* (Louvain and Beirut, 1982) 6.

20. A. Caquot, *Annuaire Collège de France* 76 (1976) 462. The text itself was published in *Sem* 27 (1977) 7; incidentally, one should read there ᶜ*mn* (von Soden: *ummanu* 1), not ʾ*mn* (*ummê/anu* 2).

21. W. H. van Soldt, *Studies in the Akkadian of Ugarit* (Neukirchen-Vluyn, 1991) 392.

22. W. F. Albright, "A Prince of Taanach in the 5th Cent. B.C.," *BASOR* 94 (1944) 12–27; W. F. Albright (trans.), "Akkadian Letters," *ANET,* 490.

23. Hrozný, in E. Sellin, *Tell Taᶜannek* (Vienna, 1904) 113–14.

24. H. Gressmann and E. Ebeling, *Altorientalistiche Texte und Bilder zum Alten Testament* (Berlin, 1926) 1.371.

25. A. F. Rainey, "Verbal Usages in the Taanach Texts," *IOS* 7 (1977) 41.

26. Panammu I, 14; Panammu II, 21. But M. Lidzbarski (*Handbuch der nordsemitischen Epigraphik* [Weimar, 1898] 441) and Donner and Röllig (*KAI* no. 214,11) dot the *m* and *n* of Panammu I.

mutilated context. Both are preceded by *wāw*. Dion does not read them as two perfect tenses or even as two verbs with first *ʾalep*.[27] They might be considered as imperfect first-person singulars, like the *ʾḥz* of §19.2.[28] But Donner and Röllig do not translate it and consider the following clause, on line 12, as nominal. Lagrange translates *ʾmn* as 'sure alliance'.[29]

Also "very obscure," according to Lagrange, is another passage containing *ʾmn* (Panammu II; cf. *KAI* no. 215, 2). Neither Donner and Röllig nor Younger[30] translate it. The written form of the preceding context presents no difficulty: *wʾmr . bmšwt . wʾl . ybl . ʾmn*; not so the following context. Now *mšwt* is of uncertain meaning, and the verb *ybl* appears in three other passages of the inscription (lines 6, 14, 21).[31] In this case, however, *ybl* is preceded by *ʾl*, which in the Aramaic of Yaʾudi is always a preposition before a noun.[32] The passage must be speaking of some kind of 'bringing', in parallel with *mšwt*, which Lagrange associates with the root *nśʾ* 'to bring'. Here, as at Mari, the *ummānu* would be a person entrusted with transportation. Hence we might read: '(The king) said: Concerning the transportation and bringing (of funeral offerings for Panammu's tomb, according to the following lines), be an *ummān*'.

Would this clear up the difficult *ʾmyn* of the Saqqara Papyrus (end of seventh century B.C.E.)? The reading seems certain;[33] although the lower part of the first letter in Porten and Yardeni's collation seems to be damaged,[34] this is still the most likely version. The term is followed by a blank and thus ends the sentence.

The *y* is unusual. At this point in time, it might be the *mater lectionis* of *ummēn*,[35] particularly since the preceding word *šmyn* is not graphically

27. P.-E. Dion, *La Langue de Yaʾudi* (Waterloo, Ont., 1974) 210–56; G. Garbini, *L'aramaico antico* (Rome, 1956) 262.

28. Dion, *La Langue de Yaʾudi*, 120.

29. M. J. Lagrange, *Études sur les religions sémitiques* (2d ed.; Paris, 1905) 493.

30. K. L. Younger, "Panammuwa and Bar-Rakib: Two Structural Analyses," *JANES* 18 (1986) 96.

31. On *ybl* 'bring an offering' in Hebrew, see J. C. Greenfield, "Un Rite religieux araméen et ses parallèles," *RB* 80 (1973) 51.

32. Dion, *La Langue de Yaʾudi*, 163, §36.

33. A. Dupont-Sommer, "Un Papyrus araméen d'époque Saïte," *Sem* 1 (1948) 68, with photograph; B. Porten, *BA* 44 (1981) 36–42, line 3.

34. B. Porten and A. Yardeni, *Textbook of Aramaic Documents from Ancient Egypt*, vol. 1: *Letters* (Jerusalem, 1986) 6–7. However, according to the photographs in *Sem* 1, 68 and *BA* 44, 36, the vertical stroke of the letter reaches the upper horizontal at its midpoint and not at its end, indicating an *ʾalep* rather than a *wāw*. What is more, 'days of the heavens' is a fitting image of stability for Pharaoh, while wishing him long life like the 'days of the waters' (*wmyn*) is not very satisfactory. Donner and Röllig translate: 'Thron . . . des Pharao fest (machen) solange der Himmel steht!' (no. 266).

35. S. Segert, *Altaramäische Grammatik* (Leipzig, 1976) 2.4.3.1, p. 63.

similar to the word *šmyʾ* ('heavens') in the preceding line. Its shape is dictated by the reference in the same line to *bʿl šmym*, pronounced *Ba-al-sa-me-me* according to the treaty of Esarhaddon with Baal of Tyre (I,10).

The construction of the sentence poses a problem, because the latter halves of lines 2 and 3 are missing. The singular is inescapable here;[36] but is the vassal calling himself Pharaoh's trusted steward or could he be, rather, just wishing Pharaoh 'stability' (Dupont-Sommer) like 'the days of the heavens', in which case we might agree with Fitzmyer[37] that the unusual *ʾmyn* is an Aramaic adjectival form of the *ʾammin* pattern? The initial salutations in the letters of the princes of Canaan to Pharaoh (El-Amarna) often end with the vassal's protestation that he is the suzerain's servant. Hence the other alternative is not impossible; it might be understood as: 'I am a trustworthy steward of Pharaoh, who lives like the days of the heavens'.[38]

III

In the Aramaic dossier of Arshama, satrap of Egypt,[39] there are three certain cases of *ʾmn* as the equivalent of the Akkadian *ummênu* (*ummânu*). In 6:4 and 7:2, 6 the reference is not to an official but to a person of inferior rank, concerning whom the satrap is issuing instructions to his 'steward' (Grelot: 'intendant')[40] or 'officer' (Driver). The person in question is part of a *grd* (Driver: 'staff'; Grelot: 'Personnel'; Porten and Yardeni: 'domestic staff') that receives rations. In 6:2 *ʾmn* is in the singular; in 7:2, 6, in the plural. Driver thus translates 'craftsman', Grelot 'worker' (*ouvrier*); Grelot states that the workers in question are master artisans, even the architects of a building.[41] Porten and Yardeni translate 'artisan' (6:4) or 'craftsman' (7:2, 6, pl. *ʾmnn*); these craftsmen are said to be of 'all kinds' (races?).[42]

The Aḥiqar of the Elephantine Papyrus, also from the fifth century B.C.E., is not called an *ʾmn* but a 'scribe' (*spr*), 'wise man' (*ḥkym*), and

36. I was tempted to follow F. Vattioni, who interprets *ʾmyn* as a plural adjective, qualifying the heavens (*šmyn*) (*Il papiro di Saqqarah* [Studia papyrologica 5, July–Dec. 1966] 113). But the plural would call for two *n*'s, as in the Oxford papyrus (see n. 58).

37. J. A. Fitzmyer, "The Aramaean Letter of King Adon to the Egyptian Pharaoh," *Bib* 46 (1965) 50. The word *ḥššyr* in Dan 5:27 is similar in form.

38. Since Pharaoh was deified, vassal kings called themselves his *râbiṣu* (MAŠKIM) ('commissioners'); cf. J.-J. Seux, *Épithètes royales akkadiennes et sumériennes* (Paris, 1967) 233.

39. G. R. Driver, *Aramaic Documents of the 5th Century B.C.* (Oxford, 1954).

40. P. Grelot, *Documents araméens d'Égypte* (Paris, 1972) 67–68 and notes.

41. Ibid., 312 n. 1.

42. Porten and Yardeni, *Textbook* 1.114, 116.

mhyr. The latter term, well known from Ps 45:2, is a West Semitic term;[43] attested in the Kassite period (Ugarit, perhaps El-Amarna), it spread to Ramessid Egypt,[44] where the determinative is either a young man sucking his thumb, an armed man, a seated man, or even a boomerang. Often used in a military context, the term is also applied to an investigating judge, a groom, and several times to a scribe in the Satirical Letter (Papyrus Anastasi I); finally, it is also an epithet for Pharaoh. Thus its meanings are as varied as the *ummânu* of Aḥiqar in the second millennium B.C.E. Babylonian tablet. Like the *ummânu* of Esarhaddon, he carries a higher rank than simple craftsmen or workers, as is confirmed by onomastic research.[45]

IV

In Hebrew, the word *ʾommān* 'craftsman' is used in Cant 7:2. In Jer 52:15 we read that the remainder of the *ʾāmôn* were deported together with the remnant of the people, the "poorest in the land," and the defectors; the term thus denotes some well-defined element. As in Aramaic, the meaning of 'craftsmen' is suitable here, and Syriac inherited the term, translating *ḥāraš* in Exod 28:11 as *ʾômen.*[46] Elsewhere, the LXX translation of Prov 8:30 renders *ʾāmôn* as ἁρμόζουσα, a woman who regulates and organizes. Again in Alexandria, the Wisdom of Solomon (7:21) dubs Wisdom a τεχνίτις of all things, a companion of King Solomon, an unblemished mirror of divine activity. Since *ʾāmôn* is a masculine noun, Bonnard (but not Barucq)[47] associates the word with YHWH, not with the feminine *ḥokmâ.* But this does not correspond to the syntactic structure; moreover, the parallel *mĕśaḥeqet* is also feminine.

This is not the place to discuss the various emendations that have been proposed (by Savignac, Scott, De Boer, etc.), however interesting they may be, nor all the suggestions (by Gemser, von Rad, and others). One suggestion, however, more important than the rest, reads *ʾāmûn* for *ʾāmôn.* It is upheld by a rabbinic tradition that goes back to Aquila, who translates τιθενουμενη. This reading is philologically supported by the

43. J. Zorn, "LÚ PA.MA.ḪA.A in *EA* 162:74 and the Role of the *mhr* in Egypt and Ugarit," *JNES* 50 (1991) 129–38, esp. 133–34. Given the weakness of the Egyptian *r* at the time of the New Empire, *mahaa* would be *mhr,* corresponding to the Akkadian *râbiṣu.* W. L. Moran proposes 'commissaire' (*Les Lettres d'El Amarna* [Paris, 1987] 401); A. F. Rainey (*El Amarna Tablets 359–379* [Neukirchen-Vluyn, 1978] 2.85), following Albright, translates 'commissioner'.

44. Fourteen cases cited by Zorn, "LÚ PA.MA.ḪA.A," 133–34.

45. E.g., *ʿbdmhr* in the tablet of Ibn-Hani 77, 14, in *Syria* 56 (1979) 308.

46. Syriac scholars are unsure of the root of this term (oral communication, B. Aggoula). I believe it is a legacy of *ʾāmôn/ummânu.*

47. A. Barucq, *Le Livre des Proverbes* (Paris, 1964) 90, 235, quoting Bonnard.

masculine participle *ʾômēn* 'tutor' (2 Kgs 10:1, 5; Esth 2:7), 'protector' of a child or a weak person (Num 11:12; Isa 59:23), or the feminine participle meaning 'tutoress' (Ruth 4:16 in *TOB*) or 'wet nurse' (2 Sam 4:4). Aquila's reading assumes a passive participle of this root;[48] the sense of the root *ʾmn* 'to trust' would suffice to explain these forms.

H. P. Rüger has carefully traced the two traditions through rabbinic literature,[49] concluding: "The word *ʾāmôn* can be well translated as 'favorite' or 'foster-child.'" Plöger translates *Pflegling*, commenting: "dem Kontext entsprechend wird man eher an ein Kind als eine Helferin denken sollen."[50] A similar approach was taken by Toy, but not by Oesterley.

V

This interpretation also gains support from studies by Donner, Kayatz, and Keel;[51] they see in the *ḥokmâ* of Proverbs an echo of the Egyptian *Maât*, who would play and dance like a child before YHWH. But *Maât* is no infant or child in need of a wet-nurse or tutor. According to the reproductions in Keel's book, even when she plays and dances she is an accomplished young girl. Keel proves that there are sacred games and dances both in Egypt and in Israel. But, as Assmann has recently pointed out,[52] the concept of *Maât* appears in the Old Empire as an ideological expression of the fundamental political event that united all of Egypt from the Delta to the first cataract into a single power (*Herrschaft*). "*Maât* is identified with the will of the king,"[53] who implements social justice. "The foundation myth of the Egyptian state is the demiurgic god's installation of the king on earth with the instruction to implement *Maât*":[54] the king receives *Maât* and draws from it the strength to judge men and

48. The *ʾĕmûnîm* of Lam 4:5 should refer to the *yônēq* 'nursling' of the preceding verse, but the parallel colon with its reference to *maʿădannîm* is concerned with much older persons; cf. D. R. Hillers, *Lamentations* (AB 7A; New York, 1972) 75.

49. H. P. Rüger, "ʾAMÔN-Pflegekind: Zur Auslegungsgeschichte von Prov 8, 30a," in *Übersetzung und Deutung. Studien A. Reinhard Hulst* (Nijkerk, 1977) 154–61. Symmachus and Theodotion both render εστεριγμενη 'strengthen', corresponding to the Hebrew *sʿd* (Ps 104:15) and also *ʾmn* (Exod 17:12, etc.).

50. O. Plöger, *Sprüche Salomos* (BKAT 17; Neukirchen-Vluyn, 1984) 86–87, 94ff., 'Pflegen-Kind'; cf. A. Meinhold, *Die Sprüche 1: Sprüche Kapitel 1–15* (Zurich, 1991) 147.

51. H. Donner, "Die Religionsgeschichtlichen Ursprünge von Prov. Sal. 8, 22–31," *ZÄS* 82 (1957) 17ff.; C. Kayatz, *Studien zu Proverbien 1–9* (Neukirchen-Vluyn, 1966) 93–119; O. Keel, *Die Weisheit spielt vor Gott* (Fribourg [Switzerland], 1974) 21–30, reproductions 16, 17, 20.

52. J. Assmann, *Gerechtigkeit und Unsterblichkeit im Alten Ägypten* (Munich, 1990) 31.

53. J. Assmann, *Maât, l'Égypte pharaonique et l'idée de la justice sociale* (Paris, 1989) 66.

54. Ibid., 115–16.

offer sacrifices to the gods. Viziers, officials, and judges must also live by *Maât*, as the Oasis-dweller reminds the majordomo Rensi. Last, *Maât* is a daughter of Re^{c}, the demiurge who caused the beings and their forms to appear; it is *Maât* who guarantees the harmony of diverse forces, both in the physical universe and in society.[55]

Since, like the Egyptian *Maât*, the biblical *ḥokmâ* of Prov 8:22–31 is born, but of Yhwh (*ḥôlāltî*, vv. 24–25), as the very first of his works, and witnesses his cosmic activity, we cannot but agree with McKane and Gaster,[56] who interpret *ʾāmôn* as an *umānu*, that is, a vizier or steward, rather than a dancing child. Speaking of Aḥiqar, Greenfield has pointed out that the term designates not so much architects, but rather high-ranking scribes close to the postdiluvian kings and their successors. If this *ʾummān* (masc.) is said to be *mĕśaḥeqet* (fem.), that is because it is *ḥokmâ* personified, while the feminine *ummānātu* would simply denote an action.[57]

The root *śḥq* evokes a joyful laugh, possibly accompanied by a ritual dance; but only in particular instances are the performers children (Zech 8:5). When David dances before the Ark, he is not a child but a seasoned warrior. In the three etiological stories about Isaac's name, it is never the child himself who 'laughs' but either Sarah (Gen 18:12–15, J), Ishmael, his elder brother (Gen 21:9, E), or Abraham (Gen 17:17, P). In Ugarit it is the god El who laughs (KTU I,4 v. 25, etc.), and he is not the only god to laugh in cuneiform texts.[58]

Ḥokmâ, far from being a child, is described as the principle by which kings govern and subordinate authorities exercise their administrative functions. The oration of the personified Wisdom begins not at v. 22, but at v. 12, perhaps even before. Only in Prov 9:1, in a narrative style, does she become an architect and, like Solomon, invite people to her feast. She thus appears as an *ʾummān* / *ʾāmôn*, a high-ranking scribe, *ḥākkīm* and *māhîr*, like the Aramean Aḥiqar of Elephantine, but on a cosmic scale.

55. See the short article by S. Sauneron, in *Dictionnaire de la civilisation égyptienne* (ed. G. Posener; Paris, 1959) 156.

56. W. McKane, *Proverbs* (London, 1970) 357–58. McKane cites the parallel suggested by A. L. Oppenheim, according to which *mummu* ('Wisdom, Science') becomes *Mummu*, vizier of the god Apsu ("Enuma Eliš" I 31); see T. H. Gaster, in "Short Notes," *VT* 4 (1954) 77.

57. The words *śḥq* and *ṣḥq* are phonetic variants of the same term; cf. the name of Isaac, as related to Jacob/Israel (Gen 27:1, etc.), and in Amos 7:9 and 16 (cf. Jer 33:26); G. Castellino, "Il 'sorriso' di Dio nella Sacra Scrittura," in *Salvacíon en la Palabra . . . in memoriam A. Díez-Macho* (Madrid, 1986) 89.

58. H. Hirsch, "Über das Lachen der Götter," in *Zikir Shumim: Assyriological Studies Presented to F. R. Kraus* (Leiden, 1982) 110–20; M. Held, "A Faithful Lover in an Old Babylonian Dialogue," *JCS* 15 (1961) 20b (and the relationship between Akk. *ṣaḫum* and West Semitic *ṣḥq*); see also *ẓḥq* in Ugarit.

VI

It remains to be seen why the author of Proverbs 8 gives *ḥokmâ* the traits of the Egyptian *Maât*. McKane[59] disagrees with my earlier suggestion that it was a "liberation" of dynastic expectations. The formula was indeed not very apt, and I no longer hold that view. The question is: in the name of what doctrine did the successors of the *ḥăkāmîm* the 'wise men' receive their heritage, particularly the passages in praise of the king (Prov 16:10–15, 25:2–7), in the name of a personified *ḥokmâ* begotten by YHWH (Prov 8:24–25)?

These wise men worked during the exilic period, after the fall of the sacral monarchy.[60] Before that, *ḥokmā* was merely a quality—that of the god El in Ugarit, of the Phoenician, Aramaean, or Israelite kings like Solomon, or, last, of the king's counselors (Jer 18:18). With Ezekiel, the royal ideology was superseded by a distinction between sacred and profane, between prince and priest (Ezekiel 44–45). The Priestly Code embraced this doctrine when it designated two successors for Moses: Joshua for political affairs and Eleazar for the sacred function (Num 27:12–26).

Several important studies have recently been devoted to the conceptual, ideological, and theological framework of the Priestly Code.[61] One should not, however, ignore the political context that conditioned the Code. At that time Israel was faced with the problem of defending its identity, since political power was in foreign hands: Cyrus and Darius (Ezra 6) and Artaxerxes (Ezra 7:11–12; Daniel 7). Having distinguished between the two eternal covenants concluded by God the creator, with Noah for all mankind and with Abraham for his descendants, the Code distinguishes in Numbers 27 between political power and religious function. The Israelites' hope for the advent of a son of David was by no means opposed; but it was not an object of legislation.

Under the same circumstances, the Master of Wisdom of Proverbs 1–8 inherited ancient teachings in which Egypt had its share (Amenemopet) as much as Aḥiqar. Like a father or a prophet, he had to propose to the Israelite, exposed to the attraction of foreign wisdom, an education in the justice of the Prophets, to open the minds of simple people to discernment (1:2–6). He could not ignore the political problem. For him, there were no longer any 'wise' kings, ministers, or judges—*ḥăkāmîm*. But there was a *ḥokmâ* by which YHWH had "founded

59. McKane, *Proverbs*, 350.

60. H. Cazelles, *Le Messie de la Bible* (Paris, 1978) 109–23.

61. F. H. German, *The Theology of Ritual Space, Time and Status in the Priestly Theology* (Sheffield, 1990) 9.

the earth" and "established the heavens" (Prov 3:19–20). It was a "tree of life" that men could henceforth "grasp" (v. 18), a principle of government, a true *ummânu*, close to YHWH and begotten by Him. It was not beneath Him, like a child, but 'beside' him (*ʾṣlw*), like Potiphar's wife beside Joseph (Gen 39:15), the lean cows beside the fat (Gen 41:3), the Ark of YHWH beside the god Dagon (1 Sam 5:2). As the daughter of YHWH, she 'took delight' (*šʿšʿ*)[62] with men, like the "babe" in the country governed by the "shoot" of Jesse (Isa 11:9). She herself was no child, but, like an architect, built her house and invited the "simple" people to her feast to learn discernment (Prov 9:1–4).

62. The use of the term *šʿšʿym* in Prov 8:30–31 would have been a powerful argument for seeing *ḥokmâ* as a child (Isa 11:8, 66:12), if the psalmists had not also "taken delight" (94:19; 119:24, 77; etc.). The use of *ʾṣl* instead of *tḥt* seems to me to clinch the contrary argument.

Epistolary Evidence of Address Phenomena in Official and Biblical Aramaic

RICCARDO CONTINI

Terms and structures of address in ancient Semitic languages have not been investigated systematically until now, unlike, for instance, their Egyptian counterparts. In the light of recent progress in this field in general linguistics, two phenomena are here singled out and described in Official Aramaic epistolary usage and in Biblical Aramaic direct speech: (1) the fictive use of the kinship terms brother *and* sister *in address between equals or colleagues and even possibly between husband and wife (as a result of interference of Egyptian patterns of address); (2) the absence of person agreement in the sentence, owing to the use of honorific terms of address in third-person reference.*

Among Jonas Greenfield's many and insightful contributions to Northwest Semitic linguistics and stylistics, a good many are devoted to matters of epistolary phraseology.[1] It is from this area of his polymathic scholarship that the following pages derive their inspiration.

Author's note: The following abbreviations will be used in examples cited in the text (for other abbreviations see list at the beginning of this volume):

Adon = papyrus letter of King Adon to the Pharaoh, *editio princeps* by A. Dupont-Sommer, "Un papyrus araméen d'époque saîte découvert à Saqqarah," *Sem* 1 (1948) 43–68.

AP = papyri collected by A. Cowley, in *Aramaic Papyri of the Fifth Century* B.C. (Oxford, 1923).

Assur = Assur ostracon, *editio princeps* by M. Lidzbarski, "Ein aramäischer Brief aus der Zeit Ašurbanipals," *MDOG* 58 (1917) 50–52.

LH = Hermopolis papyri, *editio princeps* by E. Bresciani and M. Kamil, "Le Lettere aramaiche di Hermopoli," *MANL*, ser. 8, vol. 12/5 (1966) 361–428.

Pad = Padua papyri, *editio princeps* by E. Bresciani, "Papiri aramaici egiziani di epoca persiana presso il Museo Civico di Padova," *RSO* 35 (1960) 11–24.

1. See, e.g., his "'Periphrastic Imperative' in Aramaic and Hebrew," *IEJ* 19 (1969) 199–210; (with B. Porten) "The Aramaic Papyri from Hermopolis," *ZAW* 80 (1968) 216–31, and

Patterns of Address in First-Millennium B.C.E. *Aramaic Epistolary Literature*

The field of address, in the technical sense of "a speaker's linguistic reference to his/her collocutor(s),"[2] has received a great deal of scholarly attention in the last ten years. In particular, a team of linguists at the University of Kiel has been engaged in a research project on patterns and systems of address in all kinds of languages. They have designed a questionnaire, which was then used to interview informants on address behavior in their native languages, and compiled an annotated comprehensive bibliography of titles on the subject.[3]

Thanks to this extensive survey, it is easy to ascertain that much work has been done in the Semitic language family on modern Arabic dialects (particularly the Egyptian and Jordanian varieties) and rather less on Tigrinya and Amharic; nothing at all, apparently, on Modern Hebrew, Neo-Aramaic, and Modern South Arabian. The ancient Semitic languages seem to have been investigated very little from this particular angle,[4] whereas, for example, there is a monograph on the subject for Old Egyptian.[5] Actually, at least as far as ancient Semitic languages are concerned, some useful data that escaped the bibliographical net of the German sociolinguists' research group have been discussed in a variety of specialized nonlinguistic literature (e.g., biblical commentaries, assyriological or epigraphical publications, essays on medieval Hebrew and Arabic rhetoric). But it is certainly true that these data have never been systematically collected or considered in a general linguistic perspective. The gravest difficulty lies, of course, in gathering information on address in a dead, often poorly documented, language. In the case of first-

---

"Hermopolis Letter 6," *IOS* 4 (1974) 14–30; "Some Notes on the Arsham Letters," in *Irano-Judaica* (ed. S. Shaked; Jerusalem and Leiden, 1982) 4–11; "Notes on the Phoenician Letter from Saqqara," *Or* 53 (1984) 242–44.

2. F. Braun, *Terms of Address: Problems of Patterns and Usage in Various Languages and Cultures* (Berlin, 1988) 7. Its metalinguistic equivalents are French *allocution*, Italian *allocuzione*, German *Anrede*, and Spanish *tratamiento*: G. R. Cardona, *Dizionario di linguistica* (Rome, 1988) 31.

3. F. Braun, A. Kohz, and K. Schubert, *Anredeforschung: Kommentierte Bibliographie zur Soziolinguistik der Anrede* (Tübingen, 1986). The questionnaire is reprinted in Braun, *Terms of Address*, 195–252; among the most important publications of the Kiel group are also A. Kohz, *Linguistische Aspekte des Anredeverhaltens* (Tübingen, 1982); and W. Winter (ed.), *Anredeverhalten* (Tübingen, 1984).

4. The Kiel bibliography records only E. Littmann, "Anredeformen in erweiterter Bedeutung," in *Festgabe für Th. Nöldeke zum achtzigsten Geburtstage* (Göttingen, 1916) 95–111; and J. Østrup, *Orientalische Höflichkeit: Formen und Formeln im Islam* (Leipzig, 1929).

5. H. Grapow, *Wie die alten Ägypter sich anredeten, wie sie sich grüssten und wie sie miteinander sprachen* (Berlin, 1960).

millennium B.C.E. Aramaic, the typology of available written texts from which relevant data for direct linguistic interaction may be elicited seems to be severely restricted; considering the fact that drama, which might a priori be considered the most promising source, is a relatively recent acquisition in literatures in Semitic languages,[6] only epistolography and the few instances of direct speech allegedly quoted in narrative texts seem to be appropriate. To these may be added the fifth-century contracts from Elephantine, which, however, though styled as "I-you" direct speech, offer little or no information on address per se.[7]

In fact, epistolary literature represents a rich body of evidence of address phenomena in a dead (literary) language, even allowing for the standardization and stylization dictated by the genre: formal levels of speech also involve a similar standardization in address. Moreover, epistolography has always been accepted as a legitimate, indeed privileged, source of data on address in languages such as Greek and Latin,[8] so that I feel justified in using it to this end. Of course, I am well aware that this kind of evidence is far from permitting such a comprehensive inquiry as the analytical Kiel questionnaire; I shall confine my discussion here to two phenomena, until now only cursorily analyzed in this respect.

The Official Aramaic[9] epistolary corpus, although not as extensive by far as the Akkadian and Egyptian ones, nonetheless offers a fair amount of textual evidence, since it includes 56 letters on skin or papyrus and 41 on ostraca (which, however, yield little information on address because of their abbreviated style).[10] To these may be added, for

6. Upon first, cursory examination, the possible exception of dialogic poetry does not seem to repay investigation from this angle: on this long-lived literary genre see now the studies collected in G. J. Reinink and H. L. J. Vanstiphout (eds.), *Dispute Poems and Dialogues in the Ancient and Mediaeval Near East* (Louvain, 1991).

7. For a stylistic comparison between these documents and the Hebrew (epistolary) judicial plea from Meṣad Ḥašavyahu, see D. Pardee, *Handbook of Ancient Hebrew Letters* (Chico, Cal., 1982) 23.

8. See, e.g., H. Zilliacus, "Anredeformen" (*Jahrbuch für Antike und Christentum* 7 [1964] 167–82), as well as a number of titles quoted in Braun et al., *Anredeforschung*, 252–61.

9. I conventionally follow here the periodization of Aramaic proposed by J. A. Fitzmyer, "The Phases of the Aramaic Language," in *A Wandering Aramean: Collected Aramaic Essays* (Missoula, Mont., 1979) 57–84.

10. Cf. the catalog compiled by J. A. Fitzmyer, "Aramaic Epistolography," in *Studies in Ancient Letter Writing* (ed. J. L. White; Chico, Cal., 1982) = Semeia 22 (1981) 25–57. Aramaic letters have been much studied in the last 15 years: for further references see my survey, "I documenti aramaici dell'Egitto persiano e tolemaico," *RivB* 34 (1986) 73–109, esp. 78–79 n. 41; and P.-E. Dion, "Letters (Aramaic)," *ABD* (New York, 1992) 4.285–90; updated bibliography on individual texts in J. A. Fitzmyer and S. A. Kaufman, *An Aramaic Bibliography, Part I: Old, Official, and Biblical Aramaic* (Baltimore, 1992) 61–70 and passim. For this research I have used mainly the two Egyptian Aramaic *corpora* edited by B. Porten and J. C. Greenfield, *Jews*

the purpose of my inquiry, the 5 letters allegedly quoted in Ezra and the 2 in Daniel.[11]

Fictive Use of the Kinship Terms 'Brother' and 'Sister'

The different categories of Aramaic letters illustrate one of the most characteristic address phenomena, namely, the *fictive use of kinship terms* (KTs); that is, a KT is used to address someone who is not related to the speaker either by blood or by affinity, or even to address a relative with a term expressing a relationship different from the biological one.[12]

This use is well known in ancient Semitic address systems, and abundantly attested in the first millennium B.C.E. in Neo-Assyrian, Neo-Babylonian, Hebrew and Aramaic epistolography, particularly for the KT *ʾḥ* (/ *ʾḫ*) 'brother', conventionally employed as a term of address between correspondents of equal status or professional colleagues.[13] The same use is also known from other ancient Near Eastern address systems, particularly the Egyptian.[14]

Instances in the *praescriptio* or in the address of Official Aramaic letters are:

---

of Elephantine and Arameans of Syene (Jerusalem, 1980) [a rich selection of letters]; and by B. Porten and A. Yardeni, *Textbook of Aramaic Documents from Ancient Egypt*, vol. 1: *Letters* (Jerusalem, 1986) [complete except for ostraca].

11. While the latter are generally considered fictional, it has often been argued that the authenticity of the former is confirmed by the Elephantine findings. I believe the problem has been correctly restated by J. C. Greenfield, "Aramaic Studies and the Bible," in *Congress Volume, Vienna 1980* (VTSup 32; Leiden, 1981) 110–30 at 127: "It is not a question of authentification but rather of comparative typology."

12. Braun, *Terms of Address*, 9.

13. For Akkadian usage see, e.g., E. Salonen, *Die Gruss- und Höflichkeitsformeln in babylonisch-assyrischen Briefen* (StudOr, 38/1; Helsinki, 1967) 11; and F. B. Knutsson, "Cuneiform Letters and Social Conventions," in White, *Studies in Ancient Letter Writing*, 18. Neo-Assyrian instances may be gleaned in F. M. Fales and G. B. Lanfranchi, *Lettere dalla corte assira* (Venice, 1992) 25 (between the Assyrian king and other "great" kings), 108, 134, etc. (several formulaic and topical-literary parallels in letter writing between Elephantine and Neo-Assyrian Nineveh—none of them, however, specifically involving address phenomena—are illustrated in F. M. Fales, "Aramaic Letters and Neo-Assyrian Letters: Philological and Methodological Notes," *JAOS* 107 [1987] 451–69). Hebrew fictive use of *ʾḥ* may be documented in some of the Arad letters, which, however, Pardee (*Handbook of Ancient Hebrew Letters*, 49–50) prefers to interpret as literal designations of kinship. The same is attested for *ʾḫy* 'my brother' and *ʾḫty* 'my sister' in Ugaritic epistolary style; see, e.g., A. L. Kristensen, "Ugaritic Epistolary Formulas," *UF* 9 (1977) 143–58 at 147; and J. L. Cunchillos-Ilarri, *Estudios de epistolografía ugarítica* (Valencia, 1989) 101–2, 117, 164; but the field of address in Ugaritic has yet to be investigated in depth.

14. Grapow, *Ägypter*, 32ff.

Assur, 1: [*ʾl ʾlḥy prwr ʾḥwk bltr* 'to my "brother" Pirʾi-Amurri, your "brother" Bēl-ēṭir' (the two correspondents are high Assyrian officials, around 648)

AP 41, 5: *ʾl ʾḥy pl*[*ṭy br yʾlwš ʾḥwk hwšʿyh br ntn* 'to my "brother" Pil[ṭi son of Yaʾ]ush, your "brother" Hoshayah son of Nathan'

AP 21, 10: [*ʾl*] *ʾḥy ydnyh wknwth ḥylʾ yhwdyʾ ʾḥwkm ḥnny*[*h*] '[to] my "brothers" Yedanyah and his colleagues the Jewish garrison, your "brother" Ḥanany[ah]'

In family letters, however, it is often difficult or even impossible to decide whether a KT such as *ʾḥ* has its literal or displaced meaning. This uncertainty has given rise to many different reconstructions of the genealogical links between the people mentioned in the family correspondence from Hermopolis West. Subordinate to these reconstructions is the possibility that the KTs *ʾḥ* 'brother' and *ʾḥt* 'sister' may also have been used between husband and wife, for example:

LH 2, 1: *ʾl ʾḥty tšy mn ʾḥky mkbnt* 'to my "sister" Tashi from your "brother" Makkibanit'

LH 4, 1–2: *ʾl ʾḥty nnyḥm mn ʾḥky nbwšh* 'to my "sister" Nanayḥem for your "brother" Nabushe[zib]'

Although personally rather in favor of this interpretation,[15] I quite agree[16] that the case for it is not adequately proved, and probably never will be: the Hermopolis correspondence simply does not offer unequivocal evidence, nor can it be corroborated by external sources. However, it seems appropriate to point out that the use of sibling terms in address between husband and wife in Egyptian Aramaic is not too surprising a phenomenon if viewed in a general linguistic perspective, though it appears to be unusual in ancient Semitic address systems. Considering that the area of address is known from many, if not most, languages to be open to foreign influences, it would not be too daring to assume here the interference of a different address system, in which the fictive use of KTs extended to communication between husband and wife as well.

15. Advocated by, among others, P. Grelot, review of E. Bresciani and M. Kamil, "Le Lettere aramaiche di Hermopoli," in *RB* 74 (1967) 433 and *Documents araméens d'Égypte* (Paris, 1972) 146ff.; J. T. Milik, "Les Papyrus araméens d'Hermoupolis et les cultes syro-phéniciens en Égypte perse," *Bib* 48 (1967) 546–622, esp. 547ff.; J. C. L. Gibson, *Textbook of Syrian Semitic Inscriptions,* vol. 2: *Aramaic Inscriptions* (Oxford, 1975) 133; P.-E. Dion, "The Aramaic 'Family Letter' and Related Epistolary Forms in Other Oriental Languages and in Hellenistic Greek," in White, *Studies,* 59–76, esp. 60.

16. With Porten and Greenfield, "Hermopolis Letter 6," 30 (where, in any case, only the second occurrence is rejected).

Such a system is well known to have operated in ancient Egypt, where the old notion of "Geschwisterehe als rechtliche Einrichtung" licensed the use of sibling terms (*śn* 'brother', *śn.t* 'sister') as terms of address between lovers or married couples.[17] Obviously, the possible borrowing of this address phenomenon in epistolary style[18] would not imply that the milieu that produced the Hermopolis letters ever adopted the social practices that gave rise to it in ancient Egypt. As already observed, status and address structures easily reach across language boundaries, even between genealogically unrelated tongues: for instance, this very use of sibling terms between husband and wife, admittedly not very common in the world's languages, seems to be a typical areal feature of Southeast Asia, shared by members of different linguistic families.[19]

As a matter of fact, a quite certain occurrence of the fictive use of *ʾḥ* between wife and husband in Middle Aramaic has been pointed out by Greenfield[20] in the *Genesis Apocryphon*, 1QapGen II 9, where Bitenosh addresses her husband Lamech as *yʾ ʾḥy wyʾ mry* 'oh my brother and oh my lord'; in this document there would be no reason to assume Egyptian influence, but the mere reference to the fictive use of *ʾḥ* in Biblical Hebrew to denote "kinship, but not necessarily that of first degree"[21] does not seem to be an adequate explanation for its use between married people, unless supplemented by the consideration that, in the tradition of *Jubilees*, Bitenosh, as daughter of Methuselah's sister, is Lamech's first cousin.[22] The need to examine each case independently, stressed by Greenfield,[23] is again confirmed here.

17. Grapow, *Ägypter*, 19 and 28–30, with evidence from a variety of literary genres; relevant instances in epistolary usage may be found in *Letters from Ancient Egypt* (trans. E. F. Wente; ed. E. S. Meltzer; Atlanta, 1990) nos. 340, 353; cf., however, Dion, "Aramaic 'family letter,'" n. 27.

18. Already suggested by Grelot (*Documents araméens d'Égypte*, 146) and mentioned as a possibility by Porten and Greenfield ("Hermopolis Letter 6," 15).

19. See, e.g., M. B. Emeneau, review of C. P. Masica, *Defining a Linguistic Area: South Asia*, in *Language* 54 (1978) 201–10, esp. 206ff., with interesting remarks about the correlation of complex linguistic status patterns with elaborately hierarchical social structures and the notion of divine kingship: this appears to be a promising topic for an Egyptologist interested in ethnolinguistics.

20. Porten and Greenfield, "Hermopolis Letter 6," n. 2.

21. J. A. Fitzmyer, *The Genesis Apocryphon of Qumran Cave 1: A Commentary* (2d rev. ed.; Rome, 1971) 86.

22. As pertinently remarked by K. Beyer, *Die aramäischen Texte vom Toten Meer* (Göttingen, 1984) 167 n. 2. The fact that a woman addresses her husband as "my brother," in a text in which the episode of Abram and Sarai's deception of Pharaoh later plays such an important role, also seems to serve a purpose of literary irony.

23. Porten and Greenfield, "Hermopolis Letter 6," n. 3.

What may be considered reasonably certain is that the fictive use of *ʾḥ*/*ʾḥt* also extended to address between father and son, or between son and mother, as again evidenced in family letters:

Pad, 1, 1 (*praescriptio*): *ʾl bry šlmm* [*m*]*n ʾḥwk ʾwšʿ* 'to my son Shelomam [fr]om your "brother" Osea'; 14 (address): *ʾl ʾḥy šlmm br ʾ*[*w*]*šʿ ʾḥwk ʾwšʿ br pṭ*[. . .] 'to my "brother" Shelomam son of Osea, your "brother" Osea son of Peṭe[. . .]' (there is internal confirmation in the letter [lines 2, 9, 12] that Osea was in fact Shelomam's father).

LH 7 (emanating from a different family than the other letters), 1 (*praescriptio*): *ʾl ʾmy ʿtrdmry mn ʾḥwky ʾmy* 'to my mother ʿAtardimri from your "brother" Ami'; 5 (address): *ʾl ʾḥty ʿtrdy mn ʾḥw*[*ky ʾ*]*my* 'to my "sister" ʿAtardi from [your] "bro[ther" A]mi'.

As far as the epistolary evidence is concerned, on the other hand, there is no certain occurrence in Official Aramaic of a fictive use of the KTs 'father' and 'mother' as terms of address outside the bonds of blood or affinity.[24] The possibility that Nabushe[zib], who addresses Psami as 'my father' (*LH* 4, 14, quoted in the following section), was in fact his son-in-law does not contradict this statement.[25] Only a systematic survey of the use of 'brother' and 'father' as fictive terms of address in Biblical Hebrew, which lies outside the scope of this paper, would show whether it in fact reflects the variety of meanings—besides the merely biological one—that both lexemes show in their designative usage, as witnessed by the dictionaries.[26] Such a use is known in Akkadian and Ugaritic epistolary style,[27] as well as in modern Arabic dialects.[28] At any rate, this offers only comparative evidence for first-millennium B.C.E. Aramaic usage, since different speech communities may make different uses of identical or equivalent terms of address, as is easily verified by comparing, for

24. *Pace* J. P. Hayes and J. Hoftijzer, "Notae Hermopolitanae," *VT* 20 (1970) 98–106, at 104 and n. 2: cf. also Porten and Greenfield, "Hermopolis Letter 6," 14 and n. 1.

25. This filiation has been suggested by D. R. Hillers ("Redemption in Letters 6 and 2 from Hermopolis," *UF* 11 [1979] 379–82), while Porten and Greenfield ("Hermopolis Letter 6," 30) construe N. as P.'s stepson; in principle, both solutions are possible, as rightly stated by Grelot (*Documents araméens d'Égypte*, 147), who did not have to make a choice in his translation, since in French *beau-père* means both 'stepfather' and 'father-in-law'.

26. See, e.g., *HALAT* 1 s.vv. *ʾāb* and *ʾāḥ*. The monograph by Irene Lande, *Formelhafte Wendungen der Umgangssprache im AT* (Leiden, 1949), was unfortunately not available to me. The Pentateuch targums are concerned to make the fictive use of *ʾḥ* explicit, e.g., in *Tg. Ps-J.* Gen 31:46, "And Jacob said to *his sons whom he called* his brothers": cf. A. Samely, *The Interpretation of Speech in the Pentateuch Targums* (Tübingen, 1992) 9–10.

27. Salonen, *Höflichkeitsformeln*, 11; Cunchillos-Ilarri, *Epistolografía*, 305 (see index).

28. Braun, *Terms of Address*, 182ff. and 280ff.

example, the broad semantic spectrum of 'brother' and 'sister' as fictive terms of address in Egyptian and in other Arabic dialects.[29]

Honorific Terms of Address and Syntactic Irregularities

Like other ancient Semitic languages, Aramaic did not differentiate between simple or intimate pronouns of address and their polite or distant counterparts, as do many of the world's languages (e.g., French *tu* ~ *vous,* Italian *tu* ~ *Lei,* German *du* ~ *Sie,* etc.); these two types of pronoun are commonly designated by the symbols *T* and *V,* respectively, coined by Brown and Gilman.[30] To express deference in the communication of an inferior with a superior, however, first-millennium B.C.E. Aramaic had recourse to two correlated nouns of address, namely, *mry* 'my lord' for the addressee and *ᶜbdk* 'your servant' for the speaker (= the sender in epistolary style); the same two correlates occur, as is well known, in the address systems of other ancient Near Eastern languages, both Semitic, such as Akkadian, Ugaritic, and Hebrew; and non-Semitic, such as Egyptian.[31] This use is of course well represented in official letters, where it merely reflects a general characteristic of polite speech:[32]

> *AP* 30, 1: *ᵓl mrᵓn bgwhy pḥt yhwd ᶜbdyk ydnyh wknwth khnyᵓ zy byb byrtᵓ* 'to our lord Bagohi governor of Judah, your servants Yedanyah and his colleagues the priests who are in Elephantine the fortress'
>
> *AP* 17, 5: [*ᶜl*] *mrᵓn ᵓršm* [*z*]*y bmṣryn* [*ᶜb*]*dyk ᵓhmnš wknwth* '[to] our lord Arsames [w]ho is in Egypt, your [serv]ants Achaemenes and his colleagues'
>
> Ezra 4:11: *ᶜl ᵓrtḥššt mlkᵓ ᶜbdyk ᵓnš ᶜbr-nhrh* 'to king Artaxerxes, your servants men of Transpotamia'

29. See A. A. Dohaish and M. J. L. Young, "Modes of Address and Epistolary Forms in Saudi Arabia," *ALUOS* 7 (1969–73) [1975] 110–17; D. B. Parkinson, *Constructing the Social Context of Communication: Terms of Address in Egyptian Arabic* (Berlin, 1985) 85ff.; Braun, *Terms of Address,* 182ff.

30. R. W. Brown and A. Gilman, "The Pronouns of Power and Solidarity," in *Style in Language* (ed. T. A. Sebeok; New York, 1960) 253–76, 435–49.

31. Akkadian: Salonen, *Höflichkeitsformeln,* 10–11; Knutsson, "Cuneiform Letters," 19. Ugaritic: Cunchillos, idem, *Epistolografía,* 101–2, and passim. Hebrew: see H. Cazelles, "Formes de politesse en hébreu ancien," *GLECS* 7 (1954–57) 25–26; in epistolary style: Pardee, *Handbook of Ancient Hebrew Letters,* 157–58; a rather superficial sketch of the diachrony of linguistic politeness in Biblical Hebrew has been attempted by K. Ehlich, "On the Historicity of Politeness," in *Politeness in Language: Studies in History, Theory and Practice* (ed. R. J. Watts, S. Ide, and K. Ehlich; Berlin, 1992) 71–108, esp. 82–93. The literature on politeness in language—a field that coincides only in part with that of address—is very extensive; a good introduction may be found in P. Brown and S. C. Levinson, *Politeness: Some Universals in Language Usage* (2d ed.; Cambridge, 1987). Egyptian: S. Sauneron, "Formules de politesse en égyptien ancien," *GLECS* 7 (1954–57) 95–96; Grapow, *Ägypter,* 36–37, 182ff.

32. Cf. Pardee, *Handbook of Ancient Hebrew Letters,* 98; Knutsson, "Cuneiform Letters," 16.

Occasionally, these respectful terms of address may be employed (to stress a connotation of deference) in a familial context and so overlap with the more usual KTs or with the fictive use of 'brother' described in the preceding section:[33]

> *LH* 3, 1: *ʿl mrʾy psmy ʿbdk mkbnt* 'to my lord Psami, your servant Makkibanit'
>
> *LH* 4, 13: *šlm ʾby psmy mn ʿbdk nbwšh* 'greetings to my father Psami from your servant Nabushe[zib]' (see the preceding section for the two possible values of the KT 'father' in this case)

This honorific address between kinsmen is of course well attested in Biblical Hebrew. Perhaps its most famous occurrence, Jacob's addressing Esau as "my lord" and styling himself as "thy servant" (Gen 32:4–5), actually gave occasion to a beautiful anecdote, which shows rabbinic awareness of the social implications of address structures: R. Judah the Prince styles his letter to Emperor Antoninus in accordance with the respectful "your servant" / "our lord" address convention; when his scribe objects, "My master! Why do you belittle your dignity?" he quotes his "ancestor" Jacob's message to his brother (*Midraš Genesis Rabbạh* 75).[34]

The occurrence of nominal terms of address as bound forms (often called "indirect address")[35] in place of a T/V dichotomy, entailing honorific third-person reference for the addressee, may occasionally produce a lack of person concord in the sentence in Official Aramaic and Biblical Aramaic: like other sociolinguistically conditioned syntactic phenomena, this is generally overlooked in the grammars.[36] It usually appears as a switch from the respectful third person to the second, as evidenced both in epistolary style and in direct discourse in Daniel:

> *Adon*, 6: *ky mrʾ mlkn prʿh ydʿ ky ʿbdk* . . . 'for the lord of kings Pharaoh knows that *your* servant . . . '
>
> Ezra 4:14–15: *šlḥn whwdʿnʾ lmlkʾ* (15) *dy ybqr bspr dkrnyʾ dy ʾbhtk wthškḥ* . . . 'we have sent and informed *the king* (15) that *he* should search in the book of records of *your* fathers, and *you* will find . . . '
>
> Ezra 4:16: *mhwdʿyn ʾnḥnh lmlkʾ dy hn . . . ḥlqʾ bʿbr nhrʾ lʾ ʾyty lk* 'we inform *the king* that if . . . *you* will not have a portion in Transpotamia'

33. See also Porten and Greenfield ("Hermopolis Letter 6," n. 3), who mention Methuselah's addressing of Enoch, *yʾ ʾby wyʾ mry* 'oh my father and oh my lord', in 1QapGen II 24.

34. Text and discussion, with fuller references, in Pardee, *Handbook of Ancient Hebrew Letters*, 197ff.

35. Braun, *Terms of Address*, 12 and passim.

36. For syntactic irregularities due to polite address see, e.g., O. Jespersen, *The Philosophy of Grammar* (London, 1924) 193–94; B. Comrie, "Polite Plurals and Predicate Agreement," *Language* 51 (1975) 406–18.

Dan 2:30: *rzʾ dnh gly ly . . . ʿl dbrt dy pšrʾ lmlkʾ yhwdʿwn wrʿywny lbbk tndʿ* 'this secret has been revealed to me . . . in order that its meaning may be shown to *the king* and *you* may understand the thoughts of *your* heart' (in Daniel 2 and 3 the king is addressed about six times as often in the second person as in the third person: there are four instances of a lack of concord in coordinated sentences exhibiting the two types of address)

This phenomenon, or, in general, "modifications of language for the purpose of politeness," has sometimes been called *asteismos*,[37] a technical term of Greek rhetoric that, as far as I know, was introduced in biblical philology by the venerable Bede;[38] it was recently resurrected with the above-mentioned meaning by A. Díez Macho, who also referred to the equivalent value claimed for Arabic *ʾistithnāʾ* by the medieval Jewish philologist Abraham Ibn Ezra.[39] Since, however, the definition of ἀστεισμός (literally: 'urbanity') was by no means unambiguous even in classical tradition,[40] where it apparently expressed mainly (but not exclusively) 'self-irony',[41] I would suggest that the term be avoided in the context of either linguistic politeness in general, or the specific syntactic trait of lack of person agreement in respectful address structures. This last phenomenon occurs in Biblical Hebrew too (e.g., 1 Sam 25:31), but only a systematic survey would enable us to ascertain whether its use is actually as rare as has been suggested.[42] At least one occurrence may be gleaned from Ancient Hebrew epistolary style (*Lachish* 5, 6–7: *hšb ʿbdk hspr* (7) *m ʾl ʾdny* '*your* servant herewith returns the letters to *my* lord'[43]), probably arising from the contamination of second-person and deferential third-person address structures, since both were permitted with the characteristic self-abasement formula *my ʿbdk klb* 'who is your servant (but) a dog'.[44] It is quite clear that the Official Aramaic and Biblical Aramaic occurrences

37. See, e.g., S. A. Meier, *Speaking of Speaking: Marking Direct Discourse in the Hebrew Bible* (Leiden, 1992) 37.

38. Cf. E. R. Curtius, *Letteratura europea e Medio Evo latino* (Florence, 1992 [preferable to the German original, Bern, 1948, because of the excellent index]) 56–57, 332.

39. Díez Macho, "Paralelismo, enumeración, expolición, inciso, asteismo, hipérbole, incepción y transición," *Sefarad* 10 (1950) 150–52; idem, "L'Usage de la troisième personne au lieu de la première dans le Targum," in *Mélanges D. Barthélemy* (Göttingen, 1981) 84.

40. See H. G. Liddell and R. Scott, *A Greek-English Lexicon*, s.v.

41. See, e.g., H. Lausberg, *Handbuch der literarischen Rhetorik: Eine Grundlegung der Literaturwissenschaft* (Münich, 1960) §§583 / p. 303 and 1244 /s.v. *ironia*, pp. 729–30. A similar polysemy can be argued also for *ʾistithnāʾ*; see K. Gyekye, "The Term *istithnāʾ* in Arabic Logic," *JAOS* 92 (1972) 88–92.

42. Meier, *Speaking of Speaking*, 37.

43. Pardee, *Handbook of Ancient Hebrew Letters*, 96.

44. Ibid., 81 (with further references) and 98.

also result from the same kind of syntactical contamination between "plain" address in the second person and respectful in the third.

While first-millennium B.C.E. Aramaic does not exhibit the use of self-abasing appellatives for a speaker addressing a superior, as do, for example, Akkadian[45] and Hebrew, another characteristic phenomenon of polite address may possibly be traced in direct discourse in Biblical Aramaic, by interpreting Dan 2:36, *dnh ḥlmᵓ wpšrh nᵓmr*, as 'this is the dream and *I* shall say its meaning'. This sort of *pluralis humilitatis* (Rashi, who advocated this exegesis, called it *drk mwsr* 'polite form'),[46] fairly common in many languages,[47] is well known as a device of polite address in Classical and Egyptian Arabic.[48] The possible occurrence of this and other address structures in BH should be investigated anew in the light of recent progress of research on address in general linguistics.

45. Salonen, *Höflichkeitsformeln*, 62–63.

46. See J. A. Montgomery, *A Critical and Exegetical Commentary of the Book of Daniel* (Edinburgh, 1927) 171.

47. See, e.g., F. Slotty, "Der sog. Pluralis modestiae," *IF* 44 (1927) 155–90.

48. See M. Elchouémi, "Quelques moyens d'exprimer la politesse en arabe," *GLECS* 7 (1954–57) 34–37; and my own "Prefissi in *n-* di la persona singolare nelle lingue semitiche," in *Semitica: Serta philologica C. Tsereteli dicata* (Turin, 1993) 23–38, esp. 33–34.

The Etymology of נִדָּה '(Menstrual) Impurity'

Moshe Greenberg

Current uncertainty about the etymology of Biblical Hebrew נִדָּה *invites inquiry into the semitic field of ndd—morphologically its most natural etymon (cf.* בִּזָּה < בזז*)—in those languages closest to Hebrew in which documentation is ample and relatively clear. The following inquiry studies Targumic Aramaic and Peshiṭta Syriac renditions of Hebrew derivatives of ndd and the Hebrew and Aramaic equivalents of Syriac ndd in order to establish their semantic fields. The conclusion is that the base idea of ndd is 'distancing'—physical (e.g., flight from) and moral (e.g., abhorrence of)—and that this offers the least encumbered etymology for* נִדָּה. *The shift in the meaning of* נִדָּה *from Biblical Hebrew ([menstrual] impurity) to Mishnaic Hebrew (menstruous woman) is noted, with Ezekiel's usage a pivot.*

Recent studies of the etymology of נִדָּה '(menstrual) impurity' are inconclusive. Thus, Milgrom reviews the following possibilities (definitions and selection of citations are Milgrom's;[1] translations are from NJPSV or are mine):

> *ndd, Qal,* 'depart, flee, wander' (Isa 21:15: כי מפני חרבות נדדו 'for they have fled before swords' [NJPSV]); Hos 9:17: ימאסם אלהי כי לא שמעו לו ויהיו נדדים בגוים 'My God rejects them / Because they have not obeyed Him; / And they shall go wandering / Among the nations' [NJPSV].
>
> *Hiphil,* 'chase away' (Job 18:18: יהדפהו . . . ומתבל יְנִדֻּהוּ 'they thrust him . . . and drive him from the world'; cf. Ugaritic *ndd* 'to wander, go').[2]

Author's note: To a friend and co-worker, a Semitist of classic proportions, I dedicate these lines in affectionate admiration.

1. J. Milgrom, *Leviticus 1–16* (AB; New York, 1991) 744–45. See also J. Milgrom and D. P. Wright, "נִדָּה," *TWAT* 5.250–53.

2. A check of Ugaritic glossaries (*UT*; J. Aistleitner, *Wörterbuch der ugaritischen Sprache* [Berlin, 1965]; J. C. L. Gibson, *Canaanite Myths and Legends* [Edinburgh; 1978]), texts, and

Alternatively, Milgrom cites Koehler and Baumgartner[3] for a derivation from:

> *ndh, Piel,* 'chase away, put aside' (Isa 66[so read]:5: אחיכם שׂנאיכם מנַדֵּיכם 'Your kinsmen who hate you / Who spurn you' [NJPSV]); Amos 6:3: המנַדִּים ליום רע 'you ward off [thought of] a day of woe' [NJPSV]); cf. Ugaritic *ndy*[?] 'drive out', Akkadian *nadû* 'throw, cast down').

Milgrom associates the nominal form with derivatives of double *ᶜayin* roots such as גִּזָּה, זִמָּה (from גזז, זמם). But he notes the affinity of such roots with *lamed he* roots (e.g., שגה/שגג) in order to keep open the alternative derivation (from נדה). He defines נִדָּה as 'expulsion, elimination', i.e., discharge of menstrual blood, which came to mean on the one hand menstrual impurity (and impurity in general), and on the other the menstruant herself, excluded from society.

Equally recent is Levine's derivation of נִדָּה from נדה, cognate with Akkadian *nadû* 'throw' and a variant of Hebrew נזה 'spatter'; he defines it as the flow of blood that leaves the menstruant's body, rather than referring it to the menstruant herself who is 'cast off'.[4] As to morphology, he calls it a *Niphal*-based construction (presumably passive), but then goes on to say that, as applied to a menstruant, it means "one who is spilling blood" (active).[5]

The *Hebräisches und Aramäisches Lexicon zum Alten Testament*[6] adds to the confusion by postulating two roots.

---

translations (add to the foregoing H. L. Ginsberg, in J. B. Pritchard, *ANET*; A. Caquot et al., *Textes Ougaritiques: I, Mythes et Légendes* [Paris, 1974]) reveals disagreement over what words belong to *ndd,* as well as ways to define them. Gibson's glossary divides the data among three entries: *nd*(*y*) 'escape', *nd* < *nwd* 'fled', and *ndd* 'hastened away'. The semantic range of the definitions is so narrow that one wonders whether the small number of verb-forms may not be derived from a common root that denoted motion of some kind ('proceed, stand up, go'). As with Hebrew *niddâ,* increase of linguistic data multiplies possibilities of etymology and the number of homonymous roots. Such proliferation is not assuring. See the judicious treatment of homonymy in J. Barr, *Comparative Philology and the Text of the Old Testament* (Oxford, 1968) 125–55. Yet another root *ydy* 'drive away' is posited for Ugaritic; see below, note 22.

3. Koehler and Baumgartner, *Lexicon in Veteris Testamenti libros* (2d ed.; Leiden, 1958) 596.

4. B. A. Levine, *Leviticus* (JPS Torah Commentary; Philadelphia, 1989) 97; idem, *Numbers 1–20* (AB 4; New York, 1993) 463–64.

5. Levine, *Numbers 1–20,* 464. Whether the second element of the combination מֵי נִדָּה 'water of lustration' (NJPSV) is the same word as the object of this inquiry (as both Milgrom and Levine maintain) is disputed; I shall not enter the dispute. Z. Ben-Ḥayyim argues against identifying the two words, in "ᶜErke Milim," *Tarbiẓ* 50 (1981) 199–200 (my thanks to the editorial reader who called my attention to this item).

6. W. Baumgartner et al., *HALAT* (Leiden, 1983) 635–36.

ndd: (I) 'flee, wander about, move', to which it connects the Ugaritic *ndd*[7] and in addition Arabic *nadda* 'run away' and Syriac *Afʿel* of *ndd* 'drive away'; (II) undefined but associated with Syriac (unspecified) and ? (= perhaps) with Arabic *nad^{h}d^{h}a* 'urinate'. From *ndh* II is derived נִדָּה, with which Syriac *nedd^{e}ta* 'filth' and *n^{e}diduta* 'abomination' are cognate.

With this confused picture one may compare an earlier generation's derivation of נִדָּה from *ndd* (I) 'retreat, flee, wander', listing as cognates only Aramaic *ndd* 'hate, abominate, shrink from' and Arabic *nadda* 'run away'. Accordingly, נִדָּה is defined in BDB as 'impurity (as abhorrent, shunned)'; so too in Gesenius-Buhl, *Handwörterbuch über das Alte Testament.*[8] These earlier lexicons could not have utilized as yet undiscovered Ugaritic; they invoked Akkadian *nadû* 'throw' for an etymology of the *Piel* verb *niddâ* in Amos 6:3 and Isa 66:5.[9]

Since the most straightforward morphological analysis of *niddâ* 'impurity' is as a noun derived from the geminate root *ndd*, it deserves first hearing among the claimants to the title of etymon. What follows is such a hearing, displaying the range of senses of derivatives of *ndd* in Hebrew and its closest relative, Aramaic (for the problematic Ugaritic evidence see n. 2, above). Examination of Hebrew words translated in the Peshiṭta by derivatives of Syriac *ndd* and Peshiṭta and Targumic Aramaic equivalents of Hebrew *ndd* will yield contours of a semantic field, interlocking with one or two other terms, the whole picture pointing in the direction of the earlier etymology and suggesting an alternative basic meaning of the root (see chart, pp. 72–73).[10]

Set 1–5 equates Heb. *ndd* and Syr. *ndd*; the dictionary definition of the Syriac 'loathe', works in 3–5, but it is hard to fit that meaning onto 1–2, where parallelism and the Targum suggest 'removed (themselves), went away'. In this light 1–5 could as well mean 'distance/remove oneself', as the Targum expressly renders it in 3–4, or even (in an augmented sense) 'flee', as the Targum expressly renders it in 5 (= NJPSV in 2). The *Aphel* *ʾnd* with 'sleep' as object (no. 6), that is, 'drive sleep away', can only be causative of 'go away, flee'. This is assured by the variant [continued on p. 74]

7. See Milgrom, *Levitucs 1–16*, 744–45.

8. *W. Gesenius' hebräisches und aramäisches Handwörterbuch über das Alte Testament*, revised by F. Buhl (17th ed.; Berlin, 1915 and later reprints).

9. See Milgrom and Levine, summarized above, pp. 69–70.

10. In gathering the following data, beside Even-Shoshan's concordance to Hebrew Scriptures and Payne-Smith's *Thesaurus Syriacus*, I used: Ch. Y. Kasovski, קונקורדנציה לתרגום אנקלוס [*Concordance to Targum Onqelos*] (Jerusalem, 1986); W. Strothmann, *Konkordanz zur Syrischen Bibel: Die Propheten* (Wiesbaden, 1984); M. M. Winter, *A Concordance to the Peshitta Version of Ben Sira* (Leiden, 1976). I make no claim to completeness.

Syriac/Hebrew	NJPSV	Targums[11]
Syr. *ndd* = Heb. *ndd*		
Peal		
1. Isa 22:3: נדדו . . . ברחו	'departed'	
Pesh. נדו . . . ערקו		איטלטלו . . . ערקו
2. Isa 33:3: נדדו . . . נָפְצו	'have fled'	
Pesh. נדו . . . אתבדרו		איתברו . . . אתבדרא
3. Hos 7:13: אוי להם כי נדדו ממני	'straying'	
Pesh. דנדו מני		אתרחקו מדחלתי[12]
4. Nah 3:7: כל רֹאַיִךְ יִדּוֹד ממך	'recoil'	
Pesh. ננד מנכי		יתרחק מנך
5. Ps 31:12: רֹאַי בחוץ נדדו ממני	'avoid'	
Pesh. נדין הוו מני		ערקין מן קדמי
Aphel		
6. Isa 38:15: אֱדַּדֶּה כל שנותי	'All my sleep had fled' (Note: uncertain)	
Pesh. ואנד כלה שנתי	['I drive away all my sleep'][13]	
7. Cf. Sir 40:8b ועתרא מנד שנתהון	['wealth drives away their sleep']	
Sir 42:9b ובצפתה מנדא/מפרדא שנתה	['by worry over her his sleep is driven away']	
Syr. *ndd* = Heb. *n/yq*^{c}		
8. Jer 6:8: תֵּקַע נפשי ממך	'come to loathe'	
Pesh. תנד נפשי מנכי		ירחק מימרי יתיך
9. Ezek 23:17: וַתֵּקַע נפשה מהם	'turned from them in disgust'	
Pesh. ונדת נפשה מנהון		קצת נפשה בהון
10. Ezek 23:18: ותקע נפשי . . . כאשר נקעה נפשי	'turned in disgust . . . disgusted'	
Pesh. ונדת . . . איך דנדת		ורחיק מימרי . . . כמא דרחיק
11. Ezek 23:28: שנאת . . . נקעה נפשך	'hate . . . turned in disgust'	
Pesh. דסנית . . . דנדת		דסנית . . . דקצת נפשך בהון

11. A. Sperber's edition, *The Bible in Aramaic* vols. 1–4A (Leiden, 1959–1968) is cited (only *Onqelos* is cited for the Pentateuch), supplemented by P. de Lagarde, *Hagiographa Chaldaice* (Osnabrück, 1967 [reprint of 1873 ed.]).

12. Cf. Jer 2:5 רחקו מעלי = Pesh. דאתרחקו מני = Tg. אתרחקו מדחלתי.

13. Understanding the MT as did Joseph Kara, who, comparing Gen 31:40 (no. 16 in the table), paraphrases: מנודד אנכי מכל שנותי 'I am distanced from all my sleeps'. Targum departs from the text.

Syriac/Hebrew	NJPSV	Targums
Syr. *nedd^{e}ta*ʾ '[object of] abhorrence' = Heb. *niddâ*		
12. Lam 1:17: היתה . . . לנדה	'a thing unclean'	
Pesh. הות נדתה		הות . . . דמיא לאתתא מרחקא
Heb. *ndd* = Syr. *(ʾt)rḥq* 'move/be far'		
13. Isa 10:31: נדדה מדמנה	'ran away'	
Pesh. אתרחקת		אתברו
Hiphil		
14. Job 18:18: יהדפהו . . . ינדהו	'thrust . . . driven'	
Pesh. יסחפונה . . . ירחקונה		יהדפוניה . . . יגלוניה
Heb. *ndd* = Syr. *ʿrq* 'flee'		
15. Job 15:23: נֹדד הוא ללחם	'wanders about'	
Pesh. ערק		מנדד
Heb. *ndd* = Syr. *prd* 'flee'		
16. Gen 31:40 וַתִּדַּד שנתי מעיני	'fled'	
Pesh. פרדת שנתי מן עיני		ונדת
17. Jer 4:25: וכל עוף השמים נדדו	'have fled'	
Pesh. וכלה פרחתא דשמיא פרדת		איטלטלו
18. Job 20:8: וְיֻדַּד כחזיון לילה	'banished'	
Pesh. ונפרד איך חזוא דליליא		ויגלי
19. Esth 6:1: נדדה שנת המלך	'deserted'	
Pesh. פרדת שנתה דמלכא		נדת
Aphel		
20. Cf. Sir 42:9b var. מפרדא cited above in no. 7		
Heb. *ndd* = Syr. *(ʾt)bdr* 'be scattered'		
21. Isa 21:15: מפני חרבות נדדו	'have fled'	
Pesh. אתבדרו		ערקו
22. Jer 9:9: נדדו הלכו	'have fled'	
Pesh. אתבדרו ואזלו		אטלטלו גלו
Heb. *tʿb* = Syr. *rḥq*		
23. Deut 23:8: לא תתעב	'abhor'	
Pesh. תרחקיוהי		תרחק
Heb. *gʿl* = Syr. *rḥq*		
24. Lev 26:44: לא געלתים	'spurn'	
Pesh. רחקת אנון		ארחיקינון

*mprd*ʾ 'driven away' (7, 20; cf. the *Peal* of *prd* in the related idiom—with sleep as subject—in 16, 19 = Targum *ndd*). I conclude that Peshiṭta Syriac recognized a common meaning for Heb. and Syr. *ndd*, namely, 'distance oneself, flee, recoil from'.

Set 8–11 shows the common dictionary definition of Syr. *ndd* 'abhor, loathe', rendering a Hebrew idiom meaning 'turn away from in disgust' synonymous with Heb. **שנא** 'hate' (see 11). With God as subject and speaker in 8 and 10, the Targum renders 'my word **רחיק** rejected/abhorred (lit. 'put far away') you'; compare this with 23–24, where the Peshiṭta and Targum both render by **רחק** (*Pael, Aphel*) the Heb. **תעב** 'abominate' and **געל** 'spurn'. I conclude that, in Peshiṭta Syriac, *ndd* 'abhor' is a maximized semantic extension of the base idea 'distance oneself from'.

Syriac and Hebrew meet once more in 12, where Heb *niddâ* in the general sense of an abominated/polluted thing is rendered by its Syriac cognate *nedd*ᵉ*ta*ʾ.

Sets 13–19 show the Peshiṭta and Targum understanding Heb. *ndd* as connoting movement to a distance—flight (**פרד, ערק, רחק**), restless wandering, exile (**גלא, טלטל**). An ultimate extension of the idea is 21–22, in which the flight and distancing ends in scattering (cf. the gradation of verbs parallel to *ndd* in 1 [**ברח**] and 2 [**נפץ**]).[14]

How does all this bear on **נִדָּה**?

Targumic Aramaic renders **נדה** 'menstrual impurity' by **ריחרק**, literally, 'distancing, separation' (e.g., Lev 15:19ff.). In Lev 20:21, where **נדה** means an impure act (NJPSV: 'an indecency'), it is rendered by the passive *Pael* participle **מרחק(א)**, literally, 'that which is put far off'. But **מרחק(א)** is a targumic translation of **תועבה** 'abomination' (e.g., Deut 7:26, 24:4; Isa 1:13; Prov 21:27)[15] and of **פגול** 'an offensive/unclean thing' (Lev 7:18, 19:7). The semantic range of targumic **רחק** accords with that of Heb. and Syr. root *ndd*, all pointing to a base concept of distancing, both physical (moving away from) and moral (recoiling from, abhorring).[16]

The simple noun formation *niddâ* is on the geminate root pattern seen in *bizzâ* 'spoliation, spoil', *zimmâ* 'depravity, a (usually sexually) depraved act', *sibbâ* 'turn of events'. Its basic sense will be (like its targumic

14. Note the relation between Syr. **פרד** 'flee' and Heb. **נפרד** 'separate oneself'; see H. Yalon, "**פרד שמשמעותו רץ**" ["*prd* Meaning 'run'"], *Bulletin of Hebrew Language Studies* 1/1 (Jerusalem, 1937) 6–7.

15. In 2 Kgs 23:13 **תועבת** = Targ. **ריחוק**. Within Hebrew the two roots are synonymous in Job 30:10: **תעבוני רחקו ממני**.

16. So Ibn Janaḥ, on the basis of Hebrew alone; see Abū al-Walīd Marwān Ibn Janāḥ, **ספר השרשים** (ed. W. Bacher; Berlin, 1896) 286.

equivalent) 'distancing, apartness', specifically, the separation of women from certain social contacts during their menstrual 'impurity'. It is an abstract term referring to the ritually impure state of the menstruant, thus: "she shall remain בנדתה in her menstrual impurity seven days" (Lev 15:19; so vv. 20, 33); "And if a man lies with her, her menstrual impurity נדתה is communicated to him" (v. 24, so v. 25, על נדתה = על עת נדתה 'beyond the period of her menstrual impurity').

Since נִדָּה is a kind of טֻמְאָה '(ritual) uncleanness', there is a point to the apparently tautologous construct phrase (כ)טֻמאת נדתה '(like) the uncleanness of her menstrual impurity' (Lev 15:26); in (ב)נדת טמאתה (18:19) the members are inverted, as happens with synonymous construct pairs.[17]

The term for menstruant in Biblical Hebrew is the euphemism (אִשָּׁה) דָּוָה 'an infirm woman' (Lev 15:33, 20:18; cf. 12:2: "she shall be unclean as at the time of נִדַּת דְּו‍ֹתָהּ the menstrual impurity of her infirmity"; Isa 30:22).

The data summarized in the preceding three paragraphs are derived primarily from the priestly stratum of the Pentateuch and, excepting Lev 20:21 ('an indecency'), bear the specific sense of menstrual impurity. Elsewhere the usage is ramified. The specific sense recurs in Ezek 22:10: "one (fem.) unclean through menstrual impurity טְמֵאַת הַנִּדָּה." The generalized sense 'uncleanness/impurity' is found in Ezra 9:11 ("a land of impurity ארץ נדה because of the impurity of בְּנִדַּת the peoples of the land"). A concretization of this sense, 'an unclean/abhorrent thing' (as in Leviticus) is found in late literature: Ezek 7:19–20, Lam 1:17 (no. 12 above), and 2 Chr 29:5. But in Ezekiel the start of a new concretization can be seen: in אשה נדה of Ezek 18:6, the word נדה, in apposition to the word אשה, denotes an embodiment of menstrual impurity—"a woman, a menstruant = a menstruous woman'—on the pattern of אשה זונה 'a harlot (woman)'.[18] In Ezek 36:17 it is an open question whether כְּטֻמאת הנדה means 'like the uncleanness of menstrual impurity' (as in Lev 15:26) or, as most translators take it, 'like the uncleanness of a menstruant'. What is clear is that Ezekiel's אשה נדה foreshadows postbiblical Hebrew usage:

17. On such inversion see H. Yalon, פרקי לשון [*Studies in the Hebrew Language*] (Jerusalem, 1971) 158, 330.

18. *Tg. Ezek.* 18:6, אתא טְמאה imitates the Hebrew, in that the second, appositional member, basically an abstract term ('impurity'), here denotes an embodiment of the abstraction. The Aramaic phrase is literally 'a woman, an impure thing' = 'an impure woman'. The same Aramaic noun pair renders Hebrew דוה in Lev 20:18, while טומאתא alone renders דוה in Isa 30:22. The targumists in these passages seem to show awareness of the originally abstract sense of נִדָּה, while at the same time being aware that in their time נדה served for Biblical Hebrew's דוה (on this shift, see ahead).

while in the Qumran writings the generalized senses predominate,[19] in Mishnaic Hebrew the concrete sense 'menstruant' prevails, even appearing in the plural in the neo-form נִדּוֹת 'menstruants'.[20] *Tg. Lam.* 1:17 (no. 12, above) renders לנדה היתה by 'was like a menstruous woman', in accord with mishnaic usage.

Summing up the argument to this point: The morphology of *niddâ* immediately suggests an etymology from *ndd.* The semantic fields of Heb. and Syr. *ndd* indicate a basic meaning 'distance oneself' with negative connotation, as in flight or from disgust or abhorrence. Heb. *niddâ* appears to contain both ideas: distancing and separation due to abhorrence. The term has a specific abstract reference to menstrual impurity (as abhorrent [to males] and entailing separation of the sexes). It has a generic abstract reference to the state of "impurity," and a generic concrete reference to an "impure thing/act" (what is to be kept apart, abhorred). The generic senses occur almost exclusively in biblical and Qumran nonlegal contexts; the specific abstract sense 'menstrual impurity' prevails in priestly legal texts. For the specific, concrete 'menstruant', Biblical Hebrew employs the euphemistic *dawâ.* In Mishnaic Hebrew, *dawâ* is replaced by *niddâ,* which no longer denotes a state but the menstruant herself (or, rarely, her blood). The first sign of this shift in usage occurs in Ezek 18:6—in accord with other evidence of the pivotal character of Ezekiel's language.[21]

Milgrom and Levine, quoted at the start of this study, favor *ndh* as the etymon of *niddâ,* cognates being Ugaritic *ndy* 'remove, drive away', Akkadian *nadû* 'cast down, reject, expel'. Both scholars take the discharged blood to be the primary reference of *niddâ* (its "expulsion" or outflow) but differ in their morphological analysis. Milgrom admits that the noun pattern belongs to geminate roots; Levine speaks of a *Niphal* (presumably passive) formation, by which he evidently means **nindâ* in the sense of 'outcast/spilled (blood)'. But since Levine expressly avoids taking the woman as the outcast, there is no explanation for the feminine form of the word (for *dam* 'blood' is masculine). Nor is it advisable to overrule Levine and take the outcast woman as the reference, for as we have seen, Biblical Hebrew uses *dawâ* for the menstruous woman, and

19. See J. Licht, מגילת הסרכים [*The Rule Scroll*] (Jerusalem, 1965) 96; Y. Yadin, *The Temple Scroll* (Jerusalem, 1983) 2.192–93; B. Nitzan, מגילת פשר חבקוק [*Pesher Habakkuk*] (Jerusalem, 1986) 90–91.

20. See Ch. Y. Kasovsky, אוצר לשון המשנה [*Thesaurus Mishnae*] (Jerusalem, 1958) 3.1179–80. Much less frequent is the sense "menstrual flow" (e.g., *m. Ber.* 3:6).

21. A. Hurvitz, *A Linguistic Study of the Relationship between the Priestly Source and the Book of Ezekiel* (Paris, 1982), esp. 150–51. By the age of the Tannaim, *dawâ* had fallen into such disuse that it had to be glossed in the schools: *Sipra Qedošim* 11.1 (Lev 20:18): אין דוה אלא נדה '*dawâ* means *niddâ*'.

only Mishnaic Hebrew converted *niddâ* to that meaning. The hypothesis that the etymon is *ndd* 'distancing, separation' has the least morphological and semantic obstacles in its way.

The existence of a primary Hebrew root *ndh* is postulated on the basis of two *Piel* participial forms:

Syriac/Hebrew	NJPSV	Targums
Isa 66:5: שֹׂנְאֵיכֶם מְנַדֵּיכֶם	'who hate you,	סנאיכון
Pesh. סנאיכון מסליניכון	who spurn you'	מרחקיכון
Amos 6:3: הַמְנַדִּים לְיוֹם רָע	'you ward off [the thought of] a day of woe' (with note, "meaning of Hebrew uncertain")	מרחקין
Pesh. מסכין	'hoping/waiting for'	

Certainly, the natural parsing of these participles derives them from *ndh*; but there are noteworthy affinities between the Hebrew-Aramaic-Syriac configurations of these two words and the Hebrew-Aramaic-Syriac configurations of *ndd* set out at the beginning of this inquiry:

- in the Isaiah passage, the Hebrew sequence שנא—נדה recalls the Peshiṭta sequence of סנא—נדד in no. 11;
- in the Peshiṭta of that passage, מסלינין 'who spurn' for Hebrew מנדים associates with its rendering of generic נדה in Ezek 7:19, 20 by מסליא 'a rejected thing';
- the Targum renders both participles by רחק, its common equivalent of *ndd* derivatives.

Would it be going too far to suggest that, at least for these Semitic translators, these two *Piel* participles appeared to be denominatives of נִדָּה: 'treat as (menstrual) impurity, recoil from in disgust, thrust far away'?[22]

22. Reviews of past discussion of המנדים in Amos appear in S. M. Paul, *Amos* (Hermeneia; Minneapolis, 1991) 204 n. 31; M. Weiss, ספר עמוס [*The Book of Amos*] (Jerusalem, 1992) 2.357 n. 70. The word *ydy* in the Ras Ibn Hani text, derived from *ndy* according to P. Bordreuil and A. Caquot ("Les Textes en cunéiformes alphabétiques decouverts en 1978 à Ibn Hani," *Syria* 57 [1980] 346–47, to which Paul refers in his note), is derived from a root *ydy* 'drive away' according to J. C. de Moor ("An Incantation against Evil Spirits (Ras Ibn Hani 78/20)," *UF* 12 [1980] 430) and Y. Avishur ("The Ghost-Expelling Incantation from Ugarit (Ras Ibn Hani 78/20)," *UF* 13 [1981] 16 n. 11, referring to H. L. Ginsberg's study of the root in "Ugaritico-Phoenicia," *JANESCU* 5 [1973] 132–34).

Slave Release in the Biblical World in Light of a New Text

William W. Hallo

The provisions for the release of debt-slaves (and the treatment of other slaves) are reviewed in the light of the evidence of the Laws of Hammurapi and the "edicts" of his successors, as well as biblical and postbiblical legislation. A fragmentary cuneiform text is identified as part of the concluding paragraph of the Edict of Samsu-iluna, which bears on this subject and is edited in this connection.

In the course of cataloging the Nies Babylonian Collection at Yale, I was struck by the cuneiform fragment presented herewith, in spite of its small size (fig. 1),[1] for its penultimate line could readily be restored as *an-du-r*[*a-ru*] or *an-du-r*[*a-ar-šu*], inviting comparison with the Edict of Ammi-ṣaduqa and other royal dispositions of Old Babylonian times, as F. R. Kraus designated them in the second of his magisterial studies of the genre.[2] And indeed, the sliver of text proved to parallel portions of all three known examples of the genre: §3′ of the Edict of Samsu-iluna;[3]

Author's note: This paper is dedicated to Jonas C. Greenfield in recognition of many decades of friendship and collegiality. Its substance was presented to the 40th Rencontre Assyriologique Internationale (Leiden, July 8, 1993) and benefited from the comments of colleagues there. I am deeply grateful to Barry L. Eichler for reading an earlier draft of my manuscript and offering several constructive suggestions, identified as his in what follows.

1. Cataloging of the entire Yale Babylonian Collection is proceeding under successive grants from the National Endowment for the Humanities. The Nies Babylonian Collection (NBC) was tackled first.

2. F. R. Kraus, *Königliche Verfügungen in altbabylonischer Zeit* (Studia et Documenta 11; Leiden, 1984); previously, idem, *Ein Edikt des Königs Ammi-ṣaduqa von Babylon* (Studia et Documenta 5; Leiden, 1958). Hereinafter cited as SD 11 and SD 5, respectively. For an important review article of SD 11, see S. J. Lieberman, "Royal 'Reforms' of the Amurrite Dynasty," *BiOr* 46 (1989) 241–59 (ref. courtesy Hayim Tadmor), hereinafter cited as *BiOr* 46.

3. SD 11, 154–57.

Figure 1. NBC 8618.

§H of "Edict X,"[4] which Kraus tentatively assigned to Ammi-ditana;[5] and §21 of the Edict of Ammi-ṣaduqa.[6]

Kraus restored §21 on the basis partly of the earlier edicts and partly of §20 of the Edict of Ammi-ṣaduqa. None of its thirteen lines is fully preserved and, despite the duplicates and parallels, two of its lines remained incomplete in his restoration. The new text remedies this situation only in part. It measures a mere 70 × 23 × 6 mm. (= $2\frac{7}{8} \times \frac{7}{8} \times \frac{1}{4}$ inches). It preserves the beginnings of eleven lines, corresponding to the last ten and one-half lines of §21. These are followed by a double dividing line, a blank space, another dividing line, and finally what appears to be another blank space (see copy). Then the fragment breaks off.

Since the other side of the fragment is entirely lost, it is no help in determining whether the preserved side is the obverse or reverse of a tablet. But the disposition of the lines on the preserved side strongly suggests that nothing, or at most a colophon, followed the last dividing line. If so, the preserved lines represent the conclusion of a text. This in turn would tend to make the fragment a duplicate of the Edict of Samsu-iluna, where the corresponding paragraph (§3′) also marks the conclusion of the text. In both of the later edicts, the corresponding paragraph (§H in Edict X and §21 in the Edict of Ammi-ṣaduqa) is followed by at least one more paragraph.

The assignment to Samsu-iluna also makes sense in terms of the assumed provenience of the fragment. Its accession number, NBC 8618, places it in the context of the archives from Lagaba, a group of some 210 texts in the Nies Babylonian Collection at Yale acquired in 1933–34 and assigned numbers between NBC 6252 and NBC 8913.[7] On the basis of a combination of internal and external indices, these texts can be assigned to two discrete and unequal groups, the smaller one originating in Lagaba[8] and the other, much larger one, sent there from Babylon.[9] Some of the texts are letters, and thus undated, but all the dated texts at

4. Ibid., 161.

5. Ibid., 293. Lieberman (*BiOr* 46, 251) considers Abi-eshuh an equally plausible candidate. R. F. G. Sweet ("Some Observations on the Edict of Ammiṣaduqa Prompted by Text C," in *The Archaeology of Jordan and Other Studies Presented to Siegfried H. Horn* [ed. L. T. Geraty and L. G. Herr; Berrien Springs, 1986] 579–600, esp. 589–60 n. 26) finds a possible "reason to regard BM 78259 as part of the edict of Ammiṣaduqa."

6. Ibid., 180–82.

7. MLC 1955 and NBC 11507, among texts at Yale, are also thought to come from Lagaba.

8. Notably the records of a certain Ili-u-Shamash, and "A draft for an Old Babylonian seal inscription" published by Gary Beckman, *NABU* 1988: 50 no. 72.

9. Notably the letters and sealed letter-orders of Saggil-mansum (to Marduk-muballiṭ and others).

Yale that are thought to come from Lagaba, 131 in all, date to the reign of Samsu-iluna, beginning with his fourth year[10] and ending with his eighth.[11] I owe these data to Oded Tammuz, who is preparing the entire archive for publication.

If the new fragment is indeed from Lagaba, then it is significant that the other Yale texts from Lagaba represent one or more archives that ended precisely in the eighth year of Samsu-iluna, the very year whose date formula appears on the Sippar exemplar of the Edict of Samsu-iluna, the only one hitherto known. In this connection, Kraus remarked: "It remains unclear how the date x .III. Samsu-iluna 8 in col. I lines 1′–10′ is to be evaluated for the dating of the edict."[12] It now becomes at least conceivable that the vague "release" commemorated in the name of the king's second year was not translated into the specific legislation of the Edict until his eighth year, at which time it was circulated widely in the entire kingdom, including Sippar and Lagaba. That the Edict of the eighth year was entirely discrete from the edict commemorated in the name of the second is a conceivable alternative,[13] but a less likely one, given allusions to an edict in two letters from the Lagaba archive.

These letters, which Tammuz has identified as belonging to the archive, include one, NBC 8702, with a broken date, which simply provides that a loan of one sheqel of silver for four plowing oxen (*i-ni-a-tim*) be repaid at harvest time on penalty of applying the royal edict (*ú-ul i-na-a-di-in ṣi-im-da-at sar-*[*ri-im*]).[14] But the other, NBC 6311, is more revealing. It is a letter of 27 lines, reporting a lawsuit that involved renting a field for cultivation in return for a specified portion of the yield. It actually quotes the Edict, saying (lines 15–18): "As you know, according to the edict of my lord (or perhaps we should translate, 'at the time covered by the edict of my lord'), he who collects and receives (repayment of a loan) must return (it)" (*ki-ma ti-du-ú / i-na ṣi-im-da-at be-lí-ia / ša ú-ša-ad-di-nu-ú-ma il-qu-ú / ú-ta-ar*). As also seen by Dominique Charpin,[15] this is probably an allusion to the Edict of Ammi-ṣaduqa §4 or its presumable antecedent in the Edict of Samsu-iluna. It raises interesting new questions regarding

10. NBC 8738. One text. NBC 8819, is dated MU AMAR.KIN Ú.RE.EŠ(?), which, by comparison with CT 48, 35, may be a variant for Samsu-iluna 2; cf. J. J. Finkelstein, CT 48 ad loc.

11. Eleven Lagaba texts were copied by A. Goetze and will be published in YOS 15 (forthcoming). One of them (YOS 15 90) is dated Samsu-iluna 22 but is from the collection of the late E. A. Speiser and not part of the Yale Babylonian Collection.

12. "Wie das Datum x .III. Samsu-iluna 8, I 1′–10′, für die Datierung des Edikts zu verwerten ist, bleibt unklar" (Kraus, SD 11, 69 [3]).

13. As implied especially by Lieberman, *BiOr* 46, 251–58.

14. Oded Tammuz, *The Archives from Lagaba* (Ph.D. diss., Yale University, 1993) 435–36.

15. Communication of 7 April 1993. He also cites TCL 17 76, last discussed by Kraus, SD 11, 66–67.

the much-debated sense of *ṣimdatum/ṣimdat šarrim*, which cannot be gone into here.[16] More importantly, it would represent the first verbatim citation of any Old Babylonian legal corpus in a contemporary archival context; even the Laws of Hammurapi are at most alluded to obliquely and then only in a single letter.[17]

Paragraph 4 of the Edict of Ammi-ṣaduqa provides that someone who, beginning in the last month of the last year of his predecessor, has 'demanded and collected repayment of a loan outside of the season for collection must, because he had demanded and collected repayment outside of the season for collection, return that which he has received (*ša ú-ša-ad-di-nu-ma il-qú-ú ú-ta-ar*). He who does not return (it) according to the royal edict (*a-na ṣi-im-da-at šar*-RUM) will die'.[18] That a corresponding provision was originally part of the Edict of Samsu-iluna cannot, as yet, be proved, but it seems highly probable, given the tendency of the later edicts (as emphasized by Charpin)[19] to imitate the earlier ones in general, and given the near identity of the opening paragraph of both edicts in particular, both alike limiting the powers of the 'collection agent' (*mušaddinu*). As Stephen Lieberman noted, only the motivating clause is different in the two edicts.[20] In the earlier one it is 'because the king has established justice' (*aššum šarrum mīšaram* (*ina mātim*?) *iškunu*), a phrase that recurs like a Leitmotif in all the edicts;[21] in the later one it is 'in order to strengthen them (the indicated classes of citizens) and to deal justly with them' (*ana danānišunu u išariš apālišunu*), a phrase already largely familiar from a virtually identical context in a well-known letter of Samsu-iluna.[22] All in all, we may safely conclude that the new fragment represents the last paragraph of the Edict of Samsu-iluna.

The last seven lines of the new text correspond almost sign for sign with the last paragraph (3′) of the Edict of Samsu-iluna, as far as the latter is preserved, even in line division. The only divergence is *ú-lu-ma* in

16. See for now the latest discussions by M. de J. Ellis, "*ṣimdatu* in Old Babylonian Sources," *JCS* 24 (1972) 74–82; Kraus, "Akkadische Wörter und Ausdrücke, XII. *ṣimdatum/ṣimdat šarrim*," *RA* 73 (1979) 51–62; idem, SD 11, 8–14.

17. Or. Inst. A 3529 (unpubl.); cited CAD N 364f.

18. Cf. SD 11, 170–71.

19. *AfO* 34 (1987) 41–44.

20. *BiOr* 46, 253. On such clauses see in general W. W. Hallo in *Lingering over Words: Studies in Ancient Near Eastern Literature in Honor of William L. Moran* (ed. T. Abusch et al.; HSS 37; Atlanta, 1990) 205–6; previously S. M. Paul, *Studies in the Book of the Covenant*... (VTSup 18; Leiden, 1970) 16–19.

21. Paragraph 1 in Samsu-iluna, §§E and F in "Edict X," and §§2, 3, 12, 14, 15, 16, 19, and 20 in Ammi-ṣaduqa.

22. TCL 17 76; translated by W. L. Moran, "Akkadian Letters," *ANET*, 627; and last treated by Kraus, SD 11, 66–67; Lieberman, *BiOr* 46, 253–55.

line 4′ of the Edict for *ú-lu* in the new text.[23] The same seven lines also exactly correspond to §21 of the Edict of Ammi-ṣaduqa as restored by Kraus and thus help to confirm his restorations; even the tiny divergence just noted for the earlier edict does not apply here. But the first four lines of the new exemplar diverge more significantly from §21 as restored by Kraus. Both texts are juxtaposed here, together with the corresponding lines from §20.

NBC 8618 (1′–4′)	Ammi-ṣaduqa §21 (B v 38–vi 2)	Ammi-ṣaduqa §20 (B v 26–28)
	[DUMU *I-d*] *a-ma-ra-az*^{KI}	[DUMU *I-da*] *-ma-ra-az*^{KI}
DUMU UNUG.K[I	DUMU UNUG.KI	DUMU UNUG.KI
	[DUMU Ì].SI.IN.NA.KI	[DUMU Ì.SI.I]N.NA.KI
DUMU KI.SUR.RA	DUMU KI.SUR.RA.KI	DUMU KI.SUR.RA.KI
	DUMU MURGU.K[I	[DUMU MURGU.K]I
ù DUMU *ma-tim*		*i-il-tum i-il-šu-ma*
a-na ši-im-	*š* [*a*] *ši-*[*im-*	

Accordingly, the new exemplar should be restored to read as follows:

[*šum-ma* GEME.ARAD *wi-li-id* É]
[DUMU *Nu-um-hi-a* DUMU E-mu-ut-ba-lum^{KI}]
[DUMU *I-da-ma-ra-az*^{KI}]
DUMU UNUG.KI [DUMU Ì.SI.IN.NA.KI]
DUMU KI.SUR.RA.[KI DUMU MURGU.KI]
ù DUMU *ma-ti*[*m*]
a-na ši-im [*ga-mi-ir*]
a-na KÙ.BABBAR *i*[*n-na-di-in*]
ú-lu a-na ki-[*iš-ša-tim*]
ik-ka-š[*i-iš*]
ú-lu a-na m[*a-an-za-za-ni*]
in-ne-[*zi-ib*]
an-du-r [*a-ar-šu*]
ú-ul iš-[*ša-ak-ka-an*]

If a slave-woman (or) slave—"born in the house"
(of ?!/ or ?!) a citizen of Numhia, a citizen of Emutbal,

23. The same divergence was noted between the edicts of Samsu-iluna and Ammi-ṣaduqa by Lieberman, *BiOr* 46, 252.

a citizen of Idamaraz
a citizen of Uruk, a citizen of Isin,
a citizen of Kisurra, a citizen of Malgium,
or a "citizen of the land"—
for a full price
is sold for money,
or else is made to work off a debt,[24]
or else is deposited as security:[25]
his release
will not be granted.

The general drift of this provision was elucidated by Kraus. According to the preceding paragraph (Ammi-ṣaduqa §20), the free men ('citizens') of the said cities were subject to royal release from debt-slavery, usually proclaimed in the first full year of a king's reign and commemorated in the name of the second year.[26] Slaves born in the houses of such citizens, however, did not enjoy this privilege, or, to state it another way, their owners were relieved of the burden of freeing them.[27]

Two new details emerge from the fragment, small as it is. One is the specification that the sale, which along with distraint and pawning is a contingency subject to the said exemption, must be 'for a full price' (*ana šim* [*gamir*]). This understanding of the text, suggested by B. L. Eichler, rests on a conjectural restoration; so far, it is otherwise attested (in this absolute form) only in peripheral Akkadian (Susa, Mari, Alalakh) for the Old Babylonian period.[28] But it reflects the standard Sumerian formula ŠAM.TI.LA.NI/BI.ŠÈ and is certainly preferable to the likeliest alternative restoration, *a-na ši-im-*[*ti-šu il-li-ik*] '(if) he goes to his fate (i.e., dies)', since that would imply a fourth contingency and one *not*, like the others, separated from the next one by *ú-lu* 'or'.

The other new detail is the addition of the 'citizen of the land' (*mār mātim*) to the roster of citizens of specific cities and countries listed in §20. Here, too, the reading is not above all suspicion, but there are no

24. On *kiššātu* and its Sumerian equivalents (zašda, ašda, ziz-da, za-az-da) see in detail SD 11, 266–77; previously R. Westbrook and C. Wilcke, *AfO* 25 (1972–77) 111–21; Wilcke, *RA* 73 (1979) 95–96; P. Steinkeller, *RA* 74 (1980) 178–79.

25. On *mazzazānu*, see in detail B. L. Eichler, *Indenture at Nuzi* (YNER 5; New Haven, 1973) 49–88.

26. Cf. below, n. 58.

27. On the general subject of debt and its consequences in Mesopotamia, see the instructive inaugural address by M. Stol, *Een Babylonier maakt schulden* (Amsterdam: Vrije Universiteit, 1983).

28. CAD G 37ab, s.v. *gamru*; AHw, s.v. *gamru*(*m*) 1a. Klaas R. Veenhof tells me it occurs at least twice in Old Assyrian.

likely alternatives. The possibility of a syllabic spelling for Malgium (MURGU.KI)[29] is excluded by the traces of the preserved signs. A further argument against it is the absence of 'and' (*ù*) before the city name in the preserved portion of §21; such a connective would be expected before the last member of a lengthy series, and the space in §21 (though not in §20) allows for another member after Malgium there.

As for the sense of *mār mātim*, once more we owe its elucidation to Kraus. In another work,[30] he studied all conceivable combinations of 'son' with other nouns in the genitive—excepting only 'son of NN'.[31] *Mār mātim* is mentioned, if only in passing,[32] but a quick check of the dictionaries reveals that it occurs with some frequency in Old Babylonian, at least in the plural: 'citizens of the land' are found in letters from Mari, Shemshara, later Ugarit,[33] and twice in the Laws of Hammurapi, virtually in the last two paragraphs (§§280–81).

The last point is interesting in itself, given the comparable position of the paragraph containing the expression in one or more of the edicts. But beyond that, §280 provides that, in the case of a slave bought abroad, 'if the slave and slave-woman are citizens of the land (*mārū mātim*), without (payment of) any money their release will be granted (*andurāršunu iššakkan*)', using the identical idiom as the Edict. Paragraph 281 provides that, 'if they are citizens of another country (*mārū mātim šanītim*), their foreign owner may redeem them from the Babylonian who bought them abroad'. Paragraph 282, the last of the Laws, provides that 'if a slave has said to his master, "You are not my master," he (i.e., his master) shall prove him as his slave and his master shall cut off his ear'.

The burden of these paragraphs has long been the subject of learned legal comment, and it is not my purpose to add my layman's glosses. Suffice it to call attention to two studies, one old, the other fresh off the press. In 1951, F. M. T. de Liagre Böhl published a letter from his own collection, now part of the collection of the Netherlands Institute for the

29. Usually written with *ma-al-* but occasionally with *mà-al-*; see B. Groneberg, RGTC 3 (1980) 156–57; and most recently, D. I. Owen and R. Westbrook, *ZA* 82 (1992) 204 and 206, line 3. The alleged spelling with *mal-* is disputed by Charpin, *AfO* 34 (1987) 42 n. 46.

30. *Vom Mesopotamischen Menschen der altbabylonischen Zeit und seiner Welt* (Mededelingen der Koninklijke Nederlands Akademie van Wetenschappen, Afd. Letterkunde, n.s. 36/3; Amsterdam and London, 1973).

31. For this exception see W. W. Hallo apud B. Buchanan, *Early Near Eastern Seals in the Yale Babylonian Collection* (New Haven and London, 1981) 441 and n. 6; idem, *The Book of the People* (BJS 225; Atlanta, 1991) 140 and n. 102.

32. Kraus, *Vom Mesopotamischen Menschen*, 76.

33. Mari: ARM 1 43; Shemshara: J. Laessoe, *The Shemshara Tablets: A Preliminary Report* (The Royal Danish Academy of Sciences and Letters, Arkaeologisk-kunsthistoriske Meddelelser 4/3; Copenhagen, 1959) No. 15:9; and Ugarit: PRU 3 11:4.

Near East at Leiden, written by King Samsu-iluna to a certain Ibbi-Shahan, which effectively prohibited the purchase of men or women who were citizens of Idamaraz or Arraphum.[34] Two years later he provided a revised edition of the letter.[35] R. Frankena reedited the text in 1968[36] and commented on it ten years later, noting the possibility that the letter, like other documents in the Leiden Collection that mention Ibbi-Shahan, may belong to the archives of Lagaba.[37] Kraus discussed the letter in 1984, though unsure of its relevance to either the Laws of Hammurapi or the Edicts.[38] But it may at least be of interest that it names "citizens of Idamaraz," that it dates to Samsu-iluna, and that it may have been found in Lagaba. All three considerations establish a possible contact with the Yale fragment of the Edict of Samsu-iluna, thus providing another bridge between it and §§280–81 of the Laws of Hammurapi.

Paragraph 282 of the Laws of Hammurapi is discussed in the context of a new study on "marking slaves in the Bible in the light of Akkadian sources" by Victor (Avigdor) Hurowitz.[39] This wide-ranging study draws on rituals and incantations as well as legal texts to compare and contrast the cutting off of the ear in the case of the rebellious Babylonian slave with the piercing of the ear of the Hebrew slave who rejects release from slavery. Such a Hebrew slave becomes a "slave for life" (Exod 21:6).[40] In passing it may be noted that the biblical law is essentially the first law in the Book of the Covenant (cf. Exod 24:7), illustrating the fact long ago pointed out by R. H. Pfeiffer that the casuistic legislation of the Pentateuch tends to reverse the order of the Laws of Hammurapi.[41]

Such a "slave for life" may or may not be synonymous with the *yĕlîd bāyit,* the 'house-born slave' who is contrasted with the slave purchased for money in the Bible.[42] But he is very likely the functional equivalent of the Akkadian (*w*)*ilid bītim, ilitti bītim,* the 'house-born slave' with whom

34. F. M. T. de Liagre Böhl, "Ein Brief des Königs Samsu-iluna von Babylon (± 1685–1648 v. Chr.)," *BiOr* 8 (1951) 50–56.

35. Idem, *Opera minora* (Groningen and Djakarta, 1953) 364–74, 515–16.

36. R. Frankena, *Briefe aus der Leidener Sammlung* (Altbabylonische Briefe 3; Leiden, 1968) no. 1.

37. Idem, *Kommentar zu den altbabylonischen Briefen aus Lagaba und anderen Orten* (SLB 4; Leiden, 1978) 1–3.

38. SD 11, 72–74. Cf. also M. Heltzer, Über . . . Einfuhr fremdländischer Sklaven . . . ," *UF* 8 (1976) 443–45.

39. V. Hurowitz, " 'His Master Shall Pierce His Ear with an Awl' (Exodus 21.6): Marking Slaves in the Bible in the Light of Akkadian Sources," *PAAJR* 58 (1992) 47–77.

40. *wĕ ᶜăbādô lĕ ᶜôlām*; cf. the *ᶜebed ᶜôlām* of Deut 15:17.

41. R. H. Pfeiffer, *Introduction to the Old Testament* (New York, 1941, 1948) 213–15; previously idem, *AJSL* 36 (1920) 310–15.

42. Gen 17:12–13, 23, 27; cf. Lev 22:11. I am grateful to Barry Eichler for reminding me of the concept.

§21 of the Edict of Ammi-ṣaduqa begins. According to Kraus, the distinctive character of the "house-born slave" (so-called) was that he essentially and permanently remained a slave unless his master chose formally to release him, whereas a free citizen who had become a slave through indebtedness, or otherwise, could gain his release without his owner's action, either by purchasing his freedom, by judicial review of his status, or by royal edict.[43]

It would be hard to improve on Kraus's description, but I venture to add the lexical evidence. Akkadian *ilitti bītim* translates Sumerian EMEDU (AMA.TU, AMA.A.TU; cf. AMA.TU.A),[44] which in turn is equated also with Akkadian (*w*)*ardum*, the general word for 'slave', and with *dušmû*, interpreted as 'a slave born in the house'.

What all this suggests is that all three classes of slaves enjoyed some kind of protected status: (1) the "house-born slave," by analogy with the "slave for life" of biblical law whose ear was pierced before the door or doorpost of the master's house, "admitting him to the full religious privileges of the family";[45] (2) the citizen of a specific city or country such as Idamaraz, by analogy with Samsu-iluna's letter to Ibbi-Shahan; and (3) the "citizen of the land," by analogy with §§280–81 of the Laws of Hammurapi.

Paragraph 117 of the Laws of Hammurapi, in addition, provided for the routine freeing of debt-slaves after three years of service to their creditor, at least if they belonged to the class of free men, that is, if they were the wife, son, or daughter of an *awīlum*.[46] The Edict of Ammi-ṣaduqa (§20) extended the privilege to the citizens of designated cities, tribes, and countries without specifying prior service of a given duration. Instead, the next paragraph limited the privilege in some other way.

Kraus thought it was by withholding it from the house-born slaves belonging to the same classes of citizens mentioned in §20. But he acknowledged the grammatical or at least stylistic difficulties of this interpretation, which requires an implicit genitive (*ša*) to be understood before a long series of recta.[47] Another interpretation was offered by Eichler, who implicitly differed from Kraus on just this point, to judge by his translation,

43. SD 11, 280–84.

44. See for now A. L. Oppenheim, *Catalogue of the Cuneiform Texts of the Wilberforce Eames Collection* (AOS 32; New Haven, 1948) 87–88; Bendt Alster, *The Instructions of Suruppak* (Mesopotamia 2; Copenhagen, 1974) 103.

45. S. R. Driver, *The Book of Exodus* (Cambridge, 1911), cited by Hurowitz, "His Master," 53.

46. See most recently J. Fleischman, "The Authority of the Paterfamilias according to CH 117," in *Bar-Ilan Studies in Assyriology Dedicated to Pinḥas Artzi* (ed. J. Klein and A. Skaist; Bar-Ilan Studies in Near Eastern Language and Culture; Ramat Gan, 1990) 249–53, with earlier literature; but note the reservations of S. J. Lieberman, *JAOS* 112 (1992) 689.

47. SD 11, 278–79; previously SD 5, 41. Followed in this respect by Lieberman, *BiOr* 46, 250.

although he did not explicitly point out the difference. According to Eichler, the series beginning with DUMU *nu-um-hi-a* consists entirely of appositions to *wilid bītim*, thus implying that the slaves, not their masters, were citizens or natives of the designated places.[48] Eichler's rendering was ignored, in its turn, by Kraus in his otherwise exhaustive review of the literature on these paragraphs that had appeared between his first and second editions of the Edict.

A third explanation was offered by Yonah Bar-Maoz and by Charpin in his review article of Kraus's book.[49] Following Driver and Miles,[50] they take *andurāru* (and its Sumerian equivalent AMA.AR.GI_4) to refer, *not* to liberation or release from (debt-)slavery as such, but to restoration to a previous status. In the case of a free-born citizen, such restoration indeed implied liberation, and in fact §20 expressly says so (*uššur*),[51] albeit *before* mentioning the restoration. But in the case of one born into slavery (*wilid bītim*), it meant restoration to his previous owner. Paragraph 21 of the Edict of Ammi-ṣaduqa specifically ruled out this kind of restoration: once sold or distrained or pawned to a new owner, such a slave would not revert to a previous owner. This solution is certainly enlightening, but it does not solve the syntactic and stylistic problem raised by Kraus's reading, nor does it qualify as an example of royal solicitude for the weak and the oppressed.

Thus it may be legitimate to pose alternative solutions to all three proposals. Perhaps the "house-born slave" is the first member of a series of appositional phrases specifying the kinds of slaves (GEME ARAD)[52] subject to the provisions of §21, and the "citizen of the land" is its last member—all alike subject to "exemption" from release. If so, the difference between §§20 and 21 is to be sought elsewhere than either Kraus's or Eichler's interpretation, or even Charpin's. Conceivably it is the presence in §20—and the absence in §21—of the motivating clause 'because the

48. Eichler, *Indenture at Nuzi*, 80–83. Eichler translates DUMU *nu-um-hi-a* as 'a citizen of Numhia' in §20, *wi-li-id* É DUMU *nu-um-hi-a* as 'a houseborn slave from Numhia' in §21; cf. CAD I 71c: 'a house-born slave, a native of Numhia'. Orally, Eichler points out that his rendering leaves open whether all or only the last class of slaves is referred to by the geographic specifications; what counts is that DUMU is used, like LÚ elsewhere, to indicate provenience.

49. D. Charpin, "Les Décrets royaux à l'époque Paléo-Babylonienne, à propos d'un ouvrage récent," *AfO* 34 (1987) 36–41.

50. G. R. Driver and John C. Miles, *The Babylonian Laws* (2 vols.; Oxford, 1952–55) 1.225, 229, 485–86. Cf. Yonah Bar-Maoz, "The Edict of Ammiṣadūqa," in *Studies in Hebrew and Semitic Languages Dedicated to Prof. Eduard Yechezkel Kutscher* (ed. Gad B. Sarfatti et al.; Ramat-Gan: Bar-Ilan University Press, 1980) 40–74 [in Hebrew; English summary pp. lviii–ix], esp. pp. 64–65 and n. 76; Charpin, *AfO* 34, 37 n. 4.

51. Charpin, *AfO* 34, 37 n. 5, accepting the restoration of the line by Kraus.

52. Lieberman treats these two terms as a single logogram with the Akkadian reading *aštapirum* and the meaning 'slave' (*BiOr* 46, 249–50).

king established justice for the land' (*aššum šarrum mīšaram ana mātim iškunu*). Absent this one-time celebration of the new king's accession, or a specific royal edict on a subsequent occasion, there is no longer any automatic release from debt-slavery. To paraphrase D. O. Edzard, the edicts applied to debts of only one given year each and left untouched any debts incurred thereafter.[53]

Or again, perhaps the crucial difference between the two paragraphs is the presumable presence in the second and absence in the first of the specification *ana šīm gamir* 'for a full price'. As shown most recently by Raymond Westbrook,[54] one technical meaning of this phrase, or consequence of its inclusion in a contract, is to put a sale of real estate beyond possibility of redemption. Conceivably, it would similarly put a slave sale beyond the reach even of a royal proclamation of *andurārum.*

Regardless of which of these explanations ultimately accounts best for the contrast between §§20 and 21,[55] one thing seems clear: by these paragraphs, Samsu-iluna effectively abrogated the benign provisions of §117 of the Laws of Hammurapi. I am not insisting that they were actually and necessarily enforced, or even intended for enforcement, as argued most recently and most forcefully by W. F. Leemans,[56] only that, however well intentioned, they may have proved unworkable in practice. By limiting debt-slavery to three years, they could well have discouraged the extension of credit in the first place. Apparently the automatic release from debt-slavery was replaced, within months of Hammurapi's death[57] and certainly no later than the first full year of the reign of Samsu-iluna, his son and successor, by the special release which gave its name to his second year. The Sumerian of the date formula in question (AMA.AR.GI KI.EN.GI KI.URI IN.NI.GAR) corresponds to the *andurāram ana mātim šakānum* of the edicts.

As Landsberger showed, subsequent kings of the dynasty implied the same in the date formulas of *their* second year, albeit less explicitly, by

53. D. O. Edzard, "'Soziale Reformen' im Zweistromland bis ca. 1600 v. Chr.: Realität oder literarischer Topos?" in *Wirtschaft und Gesellschaft im Alten Vorderasien* (ed. J. Harmatta and G. Komoróczy; Budapest, 1976), repr. from *Acta Academiae Scientiarum Hungaricae* 22 (1974) 145–56, esp. p. 153. Cf. already Kraus, SD 5, 240, 246.

54. R. Westbrook, "The Price Factor in the Redemption of Land," *Revue internationale des droits de l'antiquité* 32 (1985) 97–127; repr. in idem, *Property and the Family in Biblical Law* (JSOTSup 113; Sheffield, 1991) chap. 5. The functional equivalent in Hebrew is *kesep mālēʾ* (Gen 23:9; 1 Chr 21:22, 24); see ibid., 24–30, 106–7.

55. Note a somewhat comparable contrast, similarly motivated, between §§10 and 11 of the Edict of Ammi-ṣaduqa, as elucidated by Kraus, SD 11, 230–32.

56. W. F. Leemans, "Quelques considerations à propos d'une étude récente du droit du Proche-Orient ancien," *BiOr* 48 (1991) 409–37, esp. cc. 414–20.

57. Charpin, "La *Mîšarum* à l'avènement de Samsu-iluna," *NABU* 4 (1988) 52–53, no. 76.

assuming the epithet "shepherd."[58] If they reigned long enough, they might repeat the release at intervals thereafter. The much-debated "periodicity" of such royal actions was thus dependent on royal longevity as well as royal whim;[59] indeed their effectiveness may have depended on the very unpredictability of their timing.[60] I would argue that while Samsu-iluna and his successors extended release from debt-slavery with one hand, so to speak (i.e., in their first year and at more or less lengthy intervals thereafter), they withdrew it with the other (i.e., in all the other years of their reigns). This appears to be the burden of the new text and its longer-known parallels.

Now it is also clear why the coverage of the new text and its parallels is broader: whereas the edicts extended *release* only to citizens of specified cities, tribes, and lands, *exemption* from release extended not only to these same citizens but also, and more generally, to *all* slaves, male and female, house-born or free-born, citizens of the specified geographical units and of the country as a whole. If this interpretation is correct, it raises the possibility that the edicts of Samsu-iluna and his successors were intended to replace or modify as much as to supplement or reinforce the Laws of Hammurapi, though doing so subtly, given the high prestige of the older legislation. By the same token, it diminishes correspondingly the likelihood that an edict of Hammurapi himself may yet be discovered.[61]

The general thrust of the Old Babylonian release legislation has long been recognized as being closely paralleled by later Egyptian and especially Israelite legislation, beginning with the biblical institution of *šĕmiṭṭâ*, or remission of debts, every seventh year (Deut 15:1–3) and release from debt-slavery in the seventh year of service (Deut 15:12–15; cf. Exod 21:2–4). In both the Covenant Code and Deuteronomy, the latter provision immediately precedes the provision for a "slave for life" (Exod 21:5–6, Deut 15:16–18) noted earlier. The parallels have been assembled many times, most recently and systematically by Moshe Weinfeld at the

58. B. Landsberger, "The Date List of the Babylonian King Samsu-ditana by Samuel I. Feigin (1893–1950)," *JNES* 14 (1955) 137–60, esp. 146–47.

59. Lieberman, *BiOr* 46, 251–58. Previously Hannes Olivier, "The Periodicity of the *mēšarum* Again," in *Text and Context: Old Testament and Semitic Studies for F. C. Fensham* (ed. W. Claassen; JSOTSup 48; Sheffield, 1988) 227–35; G. Komoróczy, "Zur Frage der Periodizität der altbabylonischen *mīšarum*-Erlässe," in *Societies and Languages of the Ancient Near East: Studies in Honor of I. M. Diakonoff* (ed. M. A. Dandamayev et al.; Warminster, 1982) 196–295; J. J. Finkelstein, "The Periodicity of the *misharum*-Act," *Studies in Honor of Benno Landsberger on His Seventy-Fifth Birthday* (AS 16; Chicago, 1965) 243–46.

60. Charpin, "L'Application des edits de *mîšarum*: Traces documentaires," *NABU* 3 (1992) 57–58, no. 76.

61. Charpin, *AfO* 34, 44 end. Cf. below, p. 93.

25th Rencontre Assyriologique[62] and need not be reviewed here. Rather, I wish to point to a parallel in the later evolution of the Babylonian and biblical institutions, respectively.

That the mandatory release of debt-slaves encountered difficulties is already clear from biblical passages urging its observance (e.g., Deut 15:18) or denouncing its nonobservance (Jer 34:14). The same was true of the institutionalized remission of debts in the sabbatical year (cf. Deut 15:7–11). Hence the postbiblical reform instituted by Hillel and enshrined in the Mishna, which was known as *prosbul* or *pruzbul*, probably from the Greek πρὸς βουλῇ (βουλευτῶν) 'before the assembly (of counselors)'.[63] It assured the availability of credit in the face of an imminent sabbatical year by circumventing the biblical provisions for it.[64]

Just so, it is here suggested, Samsu-iluna and later Old Babylonian kings circumvented §117 of the Laws of Hammurapi by confining the release from debt-slavery to the first year of reign and to such special occasions as were subsequently proclaimed by royal edict.

The questions raised here relating to slave release cannot, of course, be finally resolved in isolation, but only in the context of the general relationship between the Laws of Hammurapi and the edicts of his successors. This relationship has barely been addressed since J. J. Finkelstein's review article of SD 5.[65] Finkelstein emphasized that the edicts were frequently alluded to in the contemporaneous letters and contracts, the "law codes" never, that the edicts were typically in apodictic form, the codes in casuistic or conditional form, that the edicts were typically proclaimed at the beginning of a new reign, the laws at the end, that the edicts involved practical measures of limited duration but strict enforcement, the laws ideal provisions of eternal applicability but without judicial impact, that the edicts were circulated in clay tablet copies like other administrative measures, and the laws (we could add) in monumental guise. From these and other indications, he concluded that the edicts were authentic legislative acts, while the laws were pious "apologies" or last testaments rendered to the gods and to future generations by the aged king. The edicts of the royal accession (and of subsequent occasions

62. M. Weinfeld, " 'Justice and Righteousness' in Ancient Israel against the Background of 'Social Reforms' in the Ancient Near East," in *Mesopotamien und seine Nachbarn* (ed. H.-J. Nissen and J. Renger; RAI 25; Berlin, 1982) 491–519.

63. However, Sweet ("Some Observations on the Edict of Ammiṣaduqa," 580) derives it from Greek προσβολή.

64. A. Rothkoff, "Prosbul," *Encyclopaedia Judaica* 13.1182–83. Cf. the symposium on *prozbul* with P. Schiffman, D. Kraemer, and D. M. Gordis in *S'vara: A Journal of Philosophy, Law, and Judaism* 2/2 (1991) 61–73 (reference courtesy James E. Ponet).

65. J. J. Finkelstein, "Ammiṣaduqa's Edict and the Babylonian 'Law Codes,' " *JCS* 15 (1961) 91–104.

of the royal lifetime) were part of the royal claim to the epithet "shepherd" or "king of justice" of which the Laws were the final summing up.

In light of these considerations, it is tempting to attribute an edict even to Hammurapi himself. A letter from Lu-Ninurta to Shamash-hazir dating from his reign declares: "The edict(!) of the king, as you know, (provides that as to) a field, purchases are restored (to the seller)' (*ṣi-im-da-at šar-ri-im / ki-ma ti-du-ú-ma /* A.ŠÀ-*lum ši-ma-tum tu-ur-ra*),[66] in language uncannily anticipating NBC 6311.[67] Given Shamash-hazir's involvement with the conquered province of Larsa, it is even possible that this reference alludes to the debt-release (and slave-release?) proclaimed for Larsa by Hammurapi in the middle of his thirty-second year, immediately after his conquest of Larsa and his assumption of rule in the province at the same time.[68]

But on present evidence, this remains no more than a hypothesis. Whether Hammurapi issued an edict or not, and whether it applied beyond Larsa or not, we cannot know, since we have as of now no edict in his name. By the same token, we have as of now no "law codes" attributable to his successors. Hence their edicts should be considered not so much early credits toward royal claims of judicial solicitude to be made later in the context of "law codes" in general but rather reactions to the earlier Laws of Hammurapi in particular.[69]

66. Kraus, *Altbabylonische Briefe* 4 (1968) no. 56; cf. idem, SD 11, 60.

67. See the text on p. 82.

68. Marc van de Mieroop, "The Reign of Rim-Sin," *JCS* 87 (1993) 47–69, esp. p. 61 and n. 69, citing Charpin, *NABU* (1991) no. 102 and (1992) no. 76.

69. Gregory C. Chirichigno, *Debt-Slavery in Israel and the Ancient Near East* (JSOTSup 141; Sheffield, 1993) appeared too late to be incorporated here.

negative imperative construction after אַל. In many poetic contexts it is also found outside of pause, where it is probably more often than not simply to be explained as the poetic use of a stylistic variant, be it for metrical or other reasons. Here we will concentrate rather on the prose material, for which reliance upon simple stylistic variation will not suffice.

Our solution assumes that we are dealing here with a living scribal tradition, not necessarily with a living linguistic phenomenon. The intent of this scribal tradition was surely to reflect earlier, authentic linguistic traditions, or perhaps even alternative dialects of Hebrew. In any case, at the stage of Hebrew reflected in the scribal tradition, the imperfect indicative forms with final long vowel did end in final *nun*, but the *nun* was not always pronounced! Anyone familiar with the colloquial Semitic languages knows that words within a clause are not isolated units. Related words are joined to one another in long phrases, with connecting vowels added if necessary. Verbs are regularly joined with following prepositions into single units, and within these units phonological changes occur with little if any regard to word boundary. That such *sandhi* phenomena obtained in Late Biblical Hebrew as well is demonstrated by numerous aspects of the Tiberian Masoretic tradition, such as the vocalization and stress changes in the construct state, euphonic *dageš*, and thematic *pataḥ* for expected *ṣere* in *Piel* and *Hithpael* forms closely bound to the following word. In the case of the paragogic *nun*, we are dealing with a much earlier stage of the language, to be sure, but the principle is the same. *Nun* assimilates to a following consonant in Hebrew; thus, in spoken Hebrew, an imperfect with long vowel would have been followed by a doubled initial consonant (the ancient consonantal Hebrew orthography would not indicate that doubling, of course); but in pause the now-final *nun* remains, in both pronunciation and orthography.

The scribal curriculum of Ancient Israel must have included a lesson detailing when and when not to add a paragogic *nun*, in conformity with ancient practice. That one was to use it in pause is clear; but when otherwise? The attested usages with actual imperfect indicatives cannot help us, nor can the analysis of those cases wherein the *nun* is absent when otherwise expected. Clearly, the ancient form was in the process of disappearing from the Hebrew language in biblical times, and later scribes surely "modernized" many texts by "correcting" these forms (along with other well-known changes, such as the insertion of *matres lectionis* and vocabulary substitution), as is demonstrated by examples of passages in Chronicles where the *nun* found in the parallel texts in Kings is missing.[3] The correct key is to be found rather by looking at the clearly erroneous

3. Cf. Gesenius and Kautsch, *Hebräische Grammatik* (22d edition; Leipzig, 1878) 106 n. 1.

examples; for, fortunately for us, some of the scribes whose work has come down to us seem to have missed (or at least misunderstood) some of the details of the lesson on paragogic *nun*. From their errors, it turns out, we are able to deduce the rule. Indeed, it is only by assuming the existence of such a scribal rule that we may account for some of the totally unexpected biblical forms with paragogic *nun*.

The errors (hypercorrections) in question are those instances in which the paragogic *nun* is found on a verbal form other than an indicative imperfect. Not surprisingly, perhaps, all of these "errors" are found in only two books, Deuteronomy and Judges, suggestive of a shared scribal history.[4] The following are the examples with *waw* consecutive:

Deut 1:22 וַתִּקְרְבוּן אֵלַי כֻּלְּכֶם
Deut 4:11 וַתִּקְרְבוּן וַתַּעַמְדוּן תַּחַת הָהָר
Deut 5:23 וַיְהִי כְּשָׁמְעֲכֶם . . . וַתִּקְרְבוּן אֵלַי
Judg 8:1 וַיְרִיבוּן אִתּוֹ בְּחָזְקָה׃
Judg 11:18 וַיַּחֲנוּן בְּעֵבֶר אַרְנוֹן וְלֹא־בָאוּ בִּגְבוּל מוֹאָב

In two cases the *nun* occurs on a perfect, albeit a perfect whose consonantal shape is identical with the corresponding imperfect:

Deut 8:3 וַיְעַנְּךָ וַיַּרְעִבֶךָ וַיַּאֲכִלְךָ אֶת־הַמָּן אֲשֶׁר לֹא־יָדַעְתָּ וְלֹא יָדְעוּן אֲבֹתֶיךָ
Deut 8:16 הַמַּאֲכִלְךָ מָן בַּמִּדְבָּר אֲשֶׁר לֹא־יָדְעוּן אֲבֹתֶיךָ לְמַעַן עַנֹּתְךָ

Surely, the fact that in five of the seven examples the final *nun* is followed by *ʾalep* can be no coincidence.[5] The *ʾalep* must be the definitive factor. The scribal rule was something like: the final *nun* of the imper-

4. There appear to be three additional imperfect consecutive forms in the MT, but all are patent errors and must be excluded from our discussion. At Ezek 44:8,

וְלֹא שְׁמַרְתֶּם מִשְׁמֶרֶת קָדָשָׁי וַתְּשִׂימוּן לְשֹׁמְרֵי מִשְׁמַרְתִּי בְּמִקְדָּשִׁי לָכֶם

the *nun* of וַתְּשִׂימוּן is surely intended to be the 3d fem. pl. pronominal suffix, with משמרת treated as a plural. In Amos 6:3,

הַמְנַדִּים לְיוֹם רָע וַתַּגִּישׁוּן שֶׁבֶת חָמָס

the verb ותגישון is surely to be emended to the participle ומגישין, parallel to המנדים. Finally, at Isa 41:5,

רָאוּ אִיִּים וְיִירָאוּ קְצוֹת הָאָרֶץ יֶחֱרָדוּ קָרְבוּ וַיֶּאֱתָיוּן

the Masoretes have pointed the preformative form ויאתיון as a consecutive, since it appears (from the conjoined perfect) to be in a past context. (This is a ubiquitous and quite erroneous Masoretic practice.) In fact, the form is no more past than either of the other two imperfects in the line, and the *waw* should be pointed with *šĕwa*, simply another example of the paragogic form in pause.

5. Of the remaining two examples, the first (Deut 4:11) is easily explained away inasmuch as the form ותקרבון is identical to the form in the preceding and following examples. Surely it is simple scribal accommodation to those forms, while the *nun* of ותעמדון is scribal accommodation to ותקרבון. Judg 11:18, on the other hand, is not easily explained.

fect indicative normally assimilates to the initial consonant of the next word, but it is written in pause and when the next word begins with a consonant that does not allow assimilation, specifically *ʾalep* (and probably *ʿayin*).[6] Earlier authors and scribes still distinguished long and short imperfect forms in their language and would not fail to recognize forms that could have the *nun*—silent or not. Later authors and scribes, such as those responsible for the Priestly material of the Torah, did not use the *nun*-bearing forms at all. In the intermediate period, when the formal distinction between the imperfect and the jussive/preterite was no longer a part of the language, errors in the application of the scribal rule were likely to be made. So they were.

6. In itself, this is not a novel idea, to be sure. As noted by Hoftijzer (*Function and Use of the Imperfect Forms*, 27 n. 98), many years ago F. Böttcher recognized the frequency with which the *nun* precedes certain other letters. (According to Böttcher, the *nun* is used "für lautlich bequemen Anschluss vor א, ע, ה, נ, מ." Hoftijzer's claim that M. Lambert disproved Böttcher is false. Lambert merely argued that the use before *ʾalep* and *ʿayin* was due to the large number of prepositions that begin with those letters. Whether this is true or not is simply irrelevant.) My purpose is not so much to demonstrate that this old idea is, in fact, correct, but rather to stress the importance of *sandhi* and scribal practice in the tradition of Biblical Hebrew. The method itself should be applicable to the solution of other similar problems as well.

A Fragment-Targum of *Onqelos* from the Cairo Genizah

Michael L. Klein

The phenomenon of "fragment-targum" has been known for hundreds of years, among Ashkenazic and Sephardic manuscripts, as well as among the fragments of oriental manuscripts from the Cairo Genizah. However, the previously known fragment-targums were all extracts of the Palestinian Targum to the Pentateuch. This article presents the first extant example of fragment-targum of Onqelos. A comparison with the Palestinian fragment-targums to Numbers 16–18 indicates that this is a unique text and that there is no textual or redactional relationship between it and its Palestinian counterparts, except for the fact that they may both be categorized as fragment-targums.

Targumic studies have enjoyed a rejuvenation in recent decades. Early fragments of targum to Leviticus and Job were discovered among the Dead Sea Scrolls. A complete exemplar of a Palestinian targum was identified among the Hebrew manuscripts of the Vatican Library. Numerous fragments of Palestinian targum and fragment-targum, expansive targumic toseftas, and liturgical targumic poems have turned up in the various collections of Cairo Genizah manuscripts throughout the world. All of these have contributed to the philological study of Jewish Aramaic, rabbinic exegesis of the Bible, medieval Jewish liturgy, and the synagogal and academic settings of targumic literature—subjects on which Jonas Greenfield has himself made significant contributions.

The phenomenon of "fragment-targum" has been known for hundreds of years[1] but is not fully understood to this very day. Scholars have yet to discover the rationale behind these sporadic collections of single words, phrases, verses, and even brief passages of targum. What is known is that such selective anthologizing was quite common, since at least three

1. The first printed edition of a fragment-targum appeared in the Bomberg Rabbinic Bible (Venice, 1517–18). The first modern edition was published by M. Ginsburger, as *Das Fragmententhargum* (Berlin, 1899).

or four major textual families of fragment-targum have survived.[2] Moreover, the medieval copying of these collections, and by inference their use for study or in the synagogue, was indeed widespread. Ashkenazic and Sephardic manuscripts, as well as fragments of Oriental manuscripts from the Cairo Genizah, have come down to us.[3]

The fragment-targums known until most recently were all extracts of the *Palestinian* Targum to the Pentateuch. Therefore, it came as a pleasant surprise when, in the process of preparing a descriptive catalog of targum manuscripts in the Cambridge Genizah collections,[4] I stumbled on a leaf of the first known exemplar of fragment-targum of *Onqelos*. The brief catalog description of the new manuscript reads as follows:

> C.U.L. T-S B 12.20
> Numbers 16:1–18:27
> Paper; 1 leaf; 18.2 × 13.0 cm; 1 column; 19 lines; Oriental semi-cursive script, with occasional square letters (especially *ʾaleph*); 12–13 Century; very sporadic Tiberian vocalization; divine name יי׳; contains a single Hebrew *lemma* (17:24) and sporadic insertions of Saʿadya's Judeo-Arabic translation; bottom line contains only one word, verso blank.

The leaf begins with the opening verse of a *parašâ* and ends abruptly with only a single word on the last line; the verso of the leaf is entirely blank. These facts raise the question of whether the fragment was part of a more extensive work or merely a single (experimental?) page.

The appended comparative chart indicates that, from among a total of 90 biblical verses between Num 16:1 and 18:27, passages from only 14 verses of *Onqelos* were included in this fragment-targum. Only seven of these are the same verses for which either of the extant Palestinian fragment-targums preserves passages. In two instances (16:13 and 17:3), the phrases preserved for verses common to the present manuscript and the other fragment-targums are mutually exclusive. It is therefore clear that

2. See M. L. Klein, *The Fragment-Targums of the Pentateuch*, vol. 1: *Introductory Essays* (AnBib 76; Rome, 1980) 14–42; and idem, *Genizah Manuscripts of Palestinian Targum to the Pentateuch* (Cincinnati: 1986) 1.xxvi. See also the basic study: idem, "The Extant Sources of the Fragmentary Targum to the Pentateuch," *HUCA* 46 (1975) 115–37. An attempt to solve the mystery of their rationale that came to my attention after this article was submitted is Ronald M. Campbell, *A Fragment-Targum without a Purpose? The Raison-d'être of MS. Vatican Ebr. 440* (Ph.D. dissertation, Northwestern University, Evanston, Ill., 1994 [advisor: P. V. M. Flesher]).

3. *Ashkenazic*: MSS Vatican Ebr. 440, Nürnberg-Stadtbibliothek Solger 2,2° and Leipzig-Universität B.H. fol. 1.

Sephardic: MS Paris Bibliothèque nationale Hébr. 110.

Oriental: MSS British Library Or. 10794 and Cambridge University Library (C.U.L.) T-S AS 72.75–77.

4. M. L. Klein, *Targumic Manuscripts in the Cambridge Genizah Collections* (Cambridge, 1992).

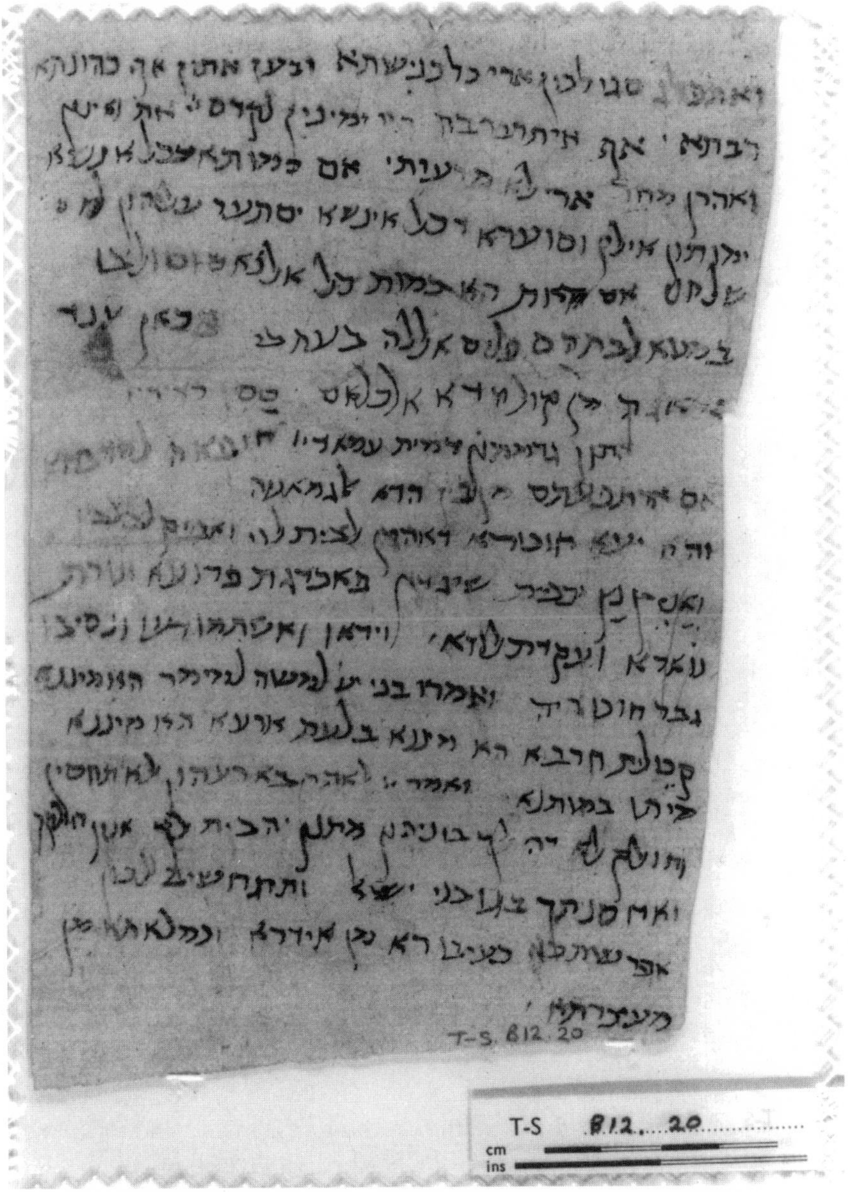

Figure 1. C.U.L. MS T-S B 12.20.
Courtesy of the Syndics of Cambridge University Library.

no textual or redactional relationship exists between the present manuscript and its Palestinian counterparts, except for the fact that they may both be categorized as fragment-targums.[5]

C.U.L. MS T-S B 12.20

Numbers

1. (16:1) ואתפלג (3) סגי לכון איי כל כנישתא (10) ובען אתון אף כהונתא
2. רבתא׳ (13) אף אתרברבה (16) הוו זמינין לקדם י״י את ואינון
3. ואהרן מחר (28) ארי לא מרעותי (29) אם כמותא דכל אנשא
4. ימותון אילין וסוערא דכל אינשא יסתער עליהון לא י[״י]
5. שלחני אם מאת הא כמות כל אלנאס וטולבו
6. במטאלבתהם פליס אללה בעת בי (31) פכאן ענד
7. פראגה מן קול הדא אלכלאם (17:3) טַסִין רדידין חופאה למדבחא
8. (6) אתון גרמתון דמית עמא דיו
9. (10) אם ארתפעתם מן בין הדא אלגמאעה
10. (23) והא יעא חוטרא דאהרן לבית לוי ואפיק לבלבין
11. וְאַנֵיץ נַץ וכפית שיגדין פאכרגת פרועא ונורת
12. נוארא ועקדת לוזא׳ (24) ויראו ואשתמודעו ונסיבו
13. גבר חוטריה (27) ואמרו בני יש׳ למשה למימר הא מיננא
14. קטֵלית חרבא הא מיננא בלעת ארעא הא מיננא
15. מיתו במותנא (18:20) ואמר יי׳ לאהרן בארעהון לא תחסין
16. וחולק לא יהי לך ביניהון מתנן יהבית לך אנון חולקך
17. ואחסנתך בגו בני ישראל (27) ותתחשיב לכון
18. אפרשתכון כעיבורא מן אידרא וכמלאתא מן
19. מעצרתא׳

Translation

1. (Num 16:1) And he separated (3) Enough for you! for all the community (10) and you also seek the high priesthood
2. (13) also rule [over us] (16) stand ready before the Lord—you, they
3. and Aaron tomorrow (28) but not of my devising. (29) If these [persons] die
4. the death of all mankind, and the fate of all mankind befalls them, then God has not
5. sent me. [Arabic: If these die the death of all mankind and they
6. share a common fate(?), then Allah has not spoken(?) to me. When he had
7. finished all of this speech] (17:3) flat-hammered sheets as plating for the altar
8. (6) you have caused the death of the Lord's people

5. The numbers in parentheses in the Aramaic text and in the English translation are the biblical citations of chapter and verse. The numbers in the margins are the line numbers in the manuscript.

9. (10) [Arabic: remove(?) yourselves from among this people]
10. (23) And the staff of Aaron of the house of Levi had sprouted and brought forth buds,
11. produced blossoms, and borne almonds [Arabic: brought forth buds,
12. produced blossoms and borne almonds]. (24) And they saw: And they made acknowledgment, and each one
13. took his staff. (27) And the Israelites said to Moses as follows: Some of us
14. were killed by the sword, some of us were swallowed up by the earth and some of us
15. died in the plague. (18:20) And the Lord said to Aaron: You shall not have an inheritance in their land
16. nor shall you have a portion among them; I have given you [priestly] gifts—they shall be your inherited
17. portion among the Israelites (27) and that which you set apart
18. will be considered for you as grain from the threshing floor and as the rich juice
19. from the wine press.

Comparative Chart of Verses Preserved

	T-S B 12.20		Palestinian Fragment-Targums	
	Onqelos	Sa^{c}adya	Paris 110	Vatican 440
Numbers				
16: 1	•	-	•	•
3	•	-	-	-
10	•	-	-	-
13	•	-	•	-
15	-	-	•	•
16	•	-	-	-
22	-	-	-	•
28	•	-	•	•
29	•	•	-	•
31	-	•	-	-
17: 3	•	-	•	•
6	•	-	-	-
10	-	•	-	•
23	•	•	•	•
24	•	-	-	-
27	•	-	-	•
18:12	-	-	-	•
20	•	-	-	-
27	•	-	-	-

Abraham, the Physician: The Image of Abraham the Patriarch in the Genuine Hymns of Ephraem Syrus

Tryggve Kronholm

Ephraem Syrus (ca. 306–73 c.e.), the foremost poet of the ancient Syrian Church, was decidedly anti-Jewish in his approach to the Scriptures and the divine election of the people of Israel. In a number of previous studies I have tried to demonstrate that Ephraem's exposition of stories and details from the biblical Urgeschichte (Genesis 1–11) was, ironically, profoundly indebted to traditional Jewish hermeneutics. In the present article I continue these studies by presenting a first survey of the relevant source material concerning Ephraem's hymnic portrayal of Abraham the Patriarch. A scrutiny of these texts and fragments displays that Ephraem basically conceives Abram/Abraham in terms of a renowned physician (ʾsyʾ mšbḥnʾ), treating various patients and sickly areas by means of the word of truth (mltʾ dqwštʾ). The different aspects of this medical activity, as depicted by Ephraem, are revealed in constant comparison with parallel texts and concepts in rabbinical sources. The investigation shows that the anti-Jewish Church Father, even in these respects, was a disciple of the synagogue, not necessarily in a direct manner, but more probably within the framework of general indebtedness of classical Syrian Christendom to contemporary Jewish tradition and hermeneutics.

In a series of previous studies I have tried to elucidate the ironical fact that Ephraem Syrus (ca. 306–73 c.e.), decidedly an anti-Jewish Church

Author's note: For standard abbreviations, see the list at the beginning of this volume. The following abbreviations are used for the works of Ephraem Syrus; all works cited were edited by E. Beck, with the exception of the commentary to Genesis (CSCO 152–53; ed. R.-M. Tonneau; Louvain, 1955]): *Azym, Crucif & Resurr = Paschahymnen (de Azymis, de Crucifixione, de Resurrectione)* (CSCO 248–49; Louvain, 1964); *CH = Hymnen contra Haereses* (CSCO 169–70; Louvain, 1957); *CNis* I–II = *Carmina Nisibena* (CSCO 218–29, 240–41; Louvain, 1961–63); *Eccl = Hymnen de Ecclesia* (CSCO 198–99; Louvain, 1960); *HdF = Hymnen de Fide* (CSCO 154–55; Louvain, 1955); *Nat & Soq = Hymnen de Nativitate* (CSCO 186–87; Louvain, 1959); *Parad & Jul = Hymnen de Paradiso und contra Julianum* (CSCO 174–75; Louvain, 1957); *Virg = Hymnen de Virginitate* (CSCO 223–24; Louvain, 1962).

Father, was greatly indebted to Jewish traditional hermeneutics in his exposition of stories and details from the biblical *Urgeschichte* (Genesis 1–11), not merely in his exegetical works and his sermons but, above all, in his poems.[1]

In this paper, designed as a tribute to my esteemed friend, the *Doctor linguarum semiticarum,* Professor Jonas C. Greenfield of Jerusalem, I intend to continue these studies by presenting the first survey of the relevant source material concerning Ephraem's hymnic portrayal of Abraham the Patriarch, particularly in its traditio-historical relation to rabbinic exegesis.

Within the traditions of the Hebrew Bible, the Abraham-Isaac cycle essentially encompasses the material of Genesis 12–25(26) (or, more precisely, Gen 11:10–26:35). As is well known, the historicity of these patriarchal narratives has been greatly disputed in modern critical scholarship.[2] Moreover, analysis of their literary structure has gradually displayed that the composition of Genesis 12–25(26) is extremely entangled, and, accordingly, scholarly conclusions differ on fundamental issues.[3]

It is also universally agreed that the Abraham-Isaac cycle played a most significant and varied role in subsequent religious history, not merely in the later books of the Hebrew Bible, in the apocrypha and pseudepigrapha, but also (admittedly in expanded and reinterpreted forms) in the legends of ancient and medieval Judaism,[4] the New Testament,[5] the pa-

1. See especially T. Kronholm, "The Trees of Paradise in the Hymns of Ephraem Syrus," *ASTI* 11 (1977–78) 48–56; idem, *Motifs from Genesis 1–11 in the Genuine Hymns of Ephrem the Syrian: With Particular Reference to the Influence of Jewish Exegetical Tradition* (D.D. Diss., Lund, 1978); "Paradiset hos Ephraem Syrus," *Religion och Bibel* 37 (1978) 44–54; "Inslag av judisk tradition hos en anti-judisk kyrkofader (Ephraem Syrus)," *Nordisk Judaistik / Scandinavian Jewish Studies* 2 (1979) 15–25; "Judisk tradition hos kyrkofäderna och kristen tradition hos rabbinerna . . . ," in *Patristica Nordica 1 . . . (Lund 25–28 augusti 1981)* (Lund, 1982) 34–65.

2. See, e.g., T. L. Thompson, *The Historicity of the Patriarchal Narratives: The Quest for the Historical Abraham* (BZAW 133; Berlin, 1974); N. P. Lemche, *Early Israel: Anthropological and Historical Studies on the Israelite Society before the Monarchy* (VTSup 37; Leiden, 1988); idem, *Ancient Israel: A New History of Israelite Society* (Biblical Seminar 5; Sheffield, 1988).

3. See, e.g., H. Gunkel, *Genesis* (3d ed.; HKAT 1; Göttingen: 1922); idem, "Abraham," *RGG* 2/1 (1927) 65–68; M. Noth, *Überlieferungsgeschichte des Pentateuch* (3d ed.; Stuttgart, 1949; 1966); A. Jepsen, "Zur Überlieferungsgeschichte der Vätergeschichte," *WZ* (Leipzig) 2/3 (1953–54) 267–81; A. Weiser, "Abraham," *RGG*[3] 1+1 (1957) 68–71; R. Kilian, *Die vorpriesterlichen Abrahamsüberlieferungen* (Bonn, 1966), esp. 279–83; R. de Vaux, *Histoire ancienne d'Israël* 1 (Paris, 1971); C. Westermann, *Genesis 12–36* (BKAT 1/2; Neukirchen-Vluyn: 1977–81); T. L. Thompson, *The Origin Tradition of Ancient Israel: I, The Literary Formation of Genesis and Exodus 1–23* (JSOTSup. 55; Sheffield, 1987).

4. Cf. especially L. Ginzberg, *The Legends of the Jews* (trans. H. Szold; Philadelphia, 1968 [repr.]), index (vol. 7), s.v.

5. J. Jeremias, "'Αβρααμ," *TWNT* 1.7–9.

tristic literature, in the Qurʾān,[6] no less, and Islamic legend, as well as in the pertinent iconography and religious art.[7]

The Church Father Ephraem Syrus holds a prominent position in the transmission of this Jewish-Christian Abraham tradition. In fact, the exposition of the patriarchal narratives in Ephraem's genuine poems go into numerous details, some of which are of minor significance from a traditio-historical perspective. In many instances, however, Ephraem's indebtedness to Jewish exegetical tradition is obvious.[8] Ephraem's interests in this respect do not focus solely on the traditions found in the Hebrew Bible. For natural reasons, he also considers the patriarchs from the perspective of the New Testament. Even then, he reveals his profound indebtedness to rabbinic hermeneutical tradition.

It is, of course, impossible to base Ephraem's hymnic expositions concerning Abraham on one formula. But a clearly dominating feature is that of Abraham as a physician.[9] For an excellent point of departure we turn to Ephraem's treatment of Gen 11:31 in one of his *Carmina Nisibena*:

> Abram, the famous physician [*ʾsyʾ*], arrived at Haran, which had fallen ill [*dkryhʾ hwt*].
> He investigated it [*gšh*] and then immediately continued, turning to the land of Canaan.
> He came to Egypt, and investigated [*sʿrh*] the entire body. He stopped; he bandaged [it, *ʾṣb*] and cured [it, *ʾsy*] with the word of truth [*bmltʾ dqwštʾ*].
> Now, since [the treatment of] Abram was not enough for you,
> [oh Haran], who will be sufficient to [cure] you,
> (oh Haran), who enjoys [your] (her) sickness [*kwrhnh*].[10]

In this hymn, then, Abram is described as a renowned physician (*ʾsyʾ mšbḥʾ*) who turns to a couple of sickly bodies, namely, Haran and Egypt. As an experienced doctor, he investigates both his patients carefully. In

6. S. Goitein, *Ha-Islam šel Muhammad* (Jerusalem, 1956); Y. Moubarac, *Abraham dans le Coran* (Paris, 1958).

7. For general references, see H. Rosenau, "Abraham, in the Arts," *EncJud* 2.122–24; R. Paret, "Ibrāhim," *EI*² 3.980a–81b.

8. See, e.g., D. Gerson, "Die Commentarien des Ephraem Syrus im Verhältnis zur jüdischen Exegese: Ein Beitrag zur Geschichte der Exegese," *MGWJ* 17 (1868) 15–33, 64–72, 98–109, 141–49; S. Hidal, *Interpretatio Syriaca: Die Kommentare des heiligen Ephräm des Syrers zu Genesis und Exodus . . .* (Lund, 1974); R. Murray, *Symbols of Church and Kingdom: A Study of Early Syriac Tradition* (Cambridge 1975); Kronholm, *Motifs from Genesis 1–11*; and cf. also A. Levene (ed.), *The Early Syrian Fathers on Genesis from a Syriac MS. on the Pentateuch in the Mingana Collection . . .* (London, 1951).

9. See Gerson, "Die Commentarien," 30ff.

10. *CNis* XXXIV 1.

the case of Egypt, he is reported to have cured the entire country; but in the case of Haran, his treatment failed.

To Ephraem, the doctor of these sickly areas stems personally from the vicinity of Qardu (Gen 8:4, according to the Peshiṭta), just like Noah and even Adam, the first man.[11] And very much like the rabbis, Ephraem describes Abraham as the "friend" of God,[12] a man of a unique "faith," a child of "light," and a member of the genuine tradition of divine salvation.[13] It is immediately obvious that the words referring to the physician's visit to Egypt are concerned primarily with the encounter between Abram/Sarah and the Egyptian Pharaoh, that is, the brief narrative of the *Gefährdung der Ahnfrau* (12:10–20; with partial parallels in 20:1–8 and 26:1–11).

Ephraem treats this story in several hymnic contexts. In one, he finds Abram and Sarah at the court of the Pharaoh. The couple, otherwise known for honesty, try to conceal the truth concerning their relationship in a threatening situation, but they remain, in Ephraem's view, absolutely honorable.[14] In another poem where Ephraem places Abram in the same situation, he describes the patriarch as a homeless "vagabond" (*glwyᵓ*),[15] whom Sarah nevertheless prefers to Pharaoh, toward whom she has even begun to feel a certain amount of hatred (*snt*).[16] In a third context Ephraem goes so far as to claim that the very will of Abram's wife remained pure in Pharaoh's bosom.[17]

But the point of most significance is that Doctor Abra[ha]m, on his visit to Egypt, really did find the country sickly, investigated it thoroughly, and cured it with 'the word of truth' (*mltᵓ dqwštᵓ*),[18] a phrase later echoed in the Qurᵓānic expression 'speaker of truth' (*ṣiddīq*), within the framework of texts from the second and third Meccan periods.[19]

The biblical background for this idea is undisputably the verse *waynaggaᶜ* Yʜᴡʜ *ᵓet-Parᶜoh nĕgaᶜim gĕdolim wĕᵓet-beyto ᶜal-dĕbar Saray ᵓešet ᵓAbram* (Gen 12:17). In the traditional *midraš* (*Gen. Rab.* 41:2), this verse is taken to imply that the Egyptians were stricken by a most disturbing skin

11. *Crucif* VII 7; on Qardu in rabbinic sources see, e.g., *Targums Neophyti I, Onqelos,* and *Pseudo-Jonathan* ad Gen 8:4; Ginzberg, *Legends of the Jews*, 5 186; Kronholm, *Motifs from Genesis 1–11*, 200–203 for further sources.

12. *HdF* V 17.

13. E.g., *CH* XXIV 22; XXV 6; *HdF* V 17; XXI 6; LXXXVII 3.

14. *Virg* XXII 16–17; ad Gen 12:13; cf. 20:5.

15. Cf. *Jul* IV 8; *CNis* XLIII 3.

16. *Nat* XX, 4, ad Gen 12:15.

17. *Virg* I 9, ad Gen 12:15.

18. *CNis* XXXIV 1.

19. Compare Qurᵓan 37:83–98, 26:69–89, 19:41–50, 43:26–28, 21:51–73, 29:16–27, 6:74–84. And see Paret, "Ibrāhim," 980a.

disease, as defined by the Palestinian Amora Reš Lakiš,[20] in the name of the Tanna Bar Qappara:[21] "Pharaoh was smitten by *raathan*," a disease that, in particular, severely hinders cohabitation with a woman (*Lev. Rab.* 16:1). In addition, the Amora Rab Aḥa from Lydda[22] notes that the scriptural words *ʾet-beyto* suggest that the very walls of the Pharaoh's house were smitten with plague, together with the ruler's household. And R. Levi, the well-known Palestinian Amora of the third generation,[23] expounds that the angel of the Lord was standing all that night with a whip in his hand, saying to Sarah: 'When you say, Strike!, I will strike, and when you say, Desist!, I will desist' (*ʾyn ʾnrt mḥy ʾyn ʾnrt nyšbq šbyqnʾ*). Further rabbinic sources intimate that the Pharaoh was smitten with a kind of leprosy.[24] All these rabbinic texts are unanimous in defining Egypt as a patient smitten by disease. Although the biblical text intimates that Pharaoh thought he was legally entitled to take Sarah, the *midraš* claims that the reason for the plagues was that Sarah *had* in fact disclosed to him that she was a married woman; in spite of this, the *midraš* asserts, Pharaoh did not wish to relinquish her (*Gen. Rab.* 41:2). This point is hardly discernible in the Genesis text itself.

Ephraem concludes that all the Egyptian diseases were healed by Abram, in his adherence to truth (Gen 12:17–20). It is noteworthy that while Jewish commentators of the Middle Ages, such as Naḥmanides, criticize Abram for bringing his pious wife close to sin on account of his fear, neither Ephraem nor the ancient rabbinic authorities express any criticism whatsoever of Abram. He simply stands out as the truthful and good physician.

In the Melchizedek episode (Gen 14:17–24) Abram's role is fairly passive. Ephraem views the pericope from a typological perspective (especially Gen 14:18). Following traditional Jewish exegesis, he regards Melchizedek as a figure of perfection (cf. *melek šalem*, Gen 14:18). Very much like Abram, Melchizedek is seen as a *typos*: he looks forward to the Perfect One, as did Abram.[25] Melchizedek was a priestly *typos*, who did not sacrifice any flesh or drink offerings: his perfection was displayed in his offerings of bread and wine, pointing to the perfect priesthood.[26]

20. H. L. Strack and G. Stemberger, *Einleitung in Talmud und Midrasch* (7th ed.; Munich, 1982) 91.

21. Ibid., 88.

22. Ibid., 98.

23. Ibid., 94.

24. *Midraš Tanḥuma* (ed. Buber), p. 66; *Yal. Gen.* §68.

25. *Nat* I 25; *Eccl* XI 3; cf. also *Nat* IX 3; Gerson, "Die Commentarien," 28–29.

26. *Azym* II 7–8; in rabbinic tradition, see, e.g., *Gen. Rab.* 43:6.

Ephraem treats both Abram and Melchizedek as *typoi,* representatives of ultimate healing, mediators who turn something imperfect into perfection, wholeness, soundness. The most far-reaching and profound healing effected by Abram was, according to Ephraem, his gradual and ultimately full reception of the divine promise: the seed of the true people of Israel in this world. As Melchizedek, out of divine love, was granted a perfect 'priesthood' (*kwmrwtʾ*), Abram was given a 'promise' of universal dimensions (*mwlknʾ*).[27] Although he initially questioned this promise,[28] Abram subsequently received confirmation thereof through divine revelation, connected with another offering scene.[29] Henceforth, Abram and his seed were inseparable, his seed being the medicine of life to all humanity.[30]

The Egyptian background returns curiously in Ephraem's exposition of the story of Hagar and Ishmael (Genesis 16, 21:9–21), where the divine "promise" continues to be in focus. Ephraem views Hagar, "the Egyptian woman" (Gen 21:9), as the daughter of Pharaoh, a view occasionally met with in Jewish tradition.[31] Ephraem emphasizes that Saray/Sarah, against her nature, was jealous, though not of her husband's concubine but of Ishmael, in view of the promised seed.[32] And, following the Peshiṭta *ad* Gen 16:12, Ephraem depicts Ishmael as a 'wild ass' in the desert (*ʿrdʾ*);[33] a 'rebel' (*mrwdʾ*) watered from a desert spring.[34] This view of Ishmael comes close to that expressed by Reš Lakiš: "[Ishmael was] a real wild ass of a man. All [human beings] rob [their fellowmen] of money, but he robs souls" (*Gen. Rab.* 45:9; cf. *Yal. Gen.*, §79). Throughout, the point remains that Abram's son Ishmael was the son of the Egyptian woman, not the son of the divine "promise," and therefore not the "seed" of salvation and healing.

To Ephraem, all this is merely a background to the story of the wondrous, first fulfillment of the "promise," Abraham being by that time 100 years of age and Sarah 90.[35] The messengers of the fulfillment were three 'spiritual guardians' (*ʿyrʾ rwḥnʾ*),[36] who approached Abraham at the holy tree of Mamre.[37] Ephraem does not go into details about the relation

27. *Eccl* XI 3, and cf. ed. note 4, ad Gen 15:4. And cf. Gerson, "Die Commentarien," 107.
28. Cf. *Parad.* XII 5.
29. *Soq* III 8; cf. *Gen. Rab.* 44:9, 14–16; *b. Meg.* 31b.
30. Cf. *Gen. Rab.* 40:6; *Midraš Tanḥuma* (ed. Buber), p. 70.
31. Cf. Gerson, "Die Commentarien," 65, 98ff.
32. *Nat* XX 1.
33. *Epiph* VIII 14; *Nat* XIII 17; *Eccl* XLIII 2.
34. *Epiph* VIII 14; cf. *CH* XLI 8.
35. Cf. *Nat* XX 5; *Eccl* XXIV 2–5[6]; cf. *CNis* XIX 1.
36. *HdF* X 11.
37. Cf. *Soq* III 10.

between the messengers and their heavenly Lord. He only notes that Abraham, amazingly, offered 'a calf to the angels' (*ʿglʾ lʿyrʾ*), that is, he offered flesh to creatures of spirit and fire.[38] Accordingly, Abraham himself stands out as a generous and health-restoring host,[39] as well as a lover of the poor,[40] all motifs frequently expounded by the ancient rabbis.[41] In this context Abraham is the medium of heavenly compassion, generosity, and life; he is the divinely guided physician.

Ephraem also depicts Abraham's mercy, displayed in his prayer for Sodom.[42] To the rabbis Abraham's compassion in that context was indeed inspired by divine compassion, particularly in connection with Abraham's sickness and weakness due to his having just been circumcised. Thus, for example, in *b. Soṭa* 14a this idea is expressed by the Palestinian Amora R. Ḥama ben R. Ḥanina:[43] "The Holy One, blessed be He, and his servants visited the sick, since it is said: And the Lord appeared unto him, etc. [Gen 18:1]. Thou shalt also visit the sick." [44] Thus, Abraham's mercy was inspired by God himself.

On the margin of Ephraem's interest in Abraham the physician, even Lot, the son of Abram's brother Haran, plays a role. Ephraem pays a certain amount of attention to the threat offered by the population of Sodom to the heavenly messengers, when Lot ultimately found himself forced to offer his two daughters for his visitors' welfare; likewise, he treats the subsequent fate of Sodom, including Lot's incest.[45] The focus is placed on the difference between the seed of the incestuous liaison *and* the seed of the promise.[46] Most curiously, Ephraem, normally a grim moralist, who uses even the story of Lot and his daughters as an opportunity to warn against the desire for wine, since it was certainly because of the wine that "the women stole the fruit of the womb,"[47] nevertheless tries hard to justify Lot's incest with his two daughters.[48] This is a basic point in the total conception of the Abraham tradition, and, partially, it

38. *HdF* X 11; cf. *Crucif* III 7. And cf. W. Cramer, *Die Engelvorstellungen bei Ephräm des Syrer* (Orientalia Christiana Analecta 173; Rome, 1965).

39. Cf. *Abr* (= CSCO 322) IV [10-]11.

40. *Nat* I 84.

41. E.g., *m. Šabb.* 18:1; *b. Šabb.* 127a; *b. B. Meṣ.* 87a; *Gen. Rab.* 48:10; *Yal. Gen.* §8.

42. *Parad* I 12; *Virg* XLIV 1; *HdF* LVI 5–6, ad Gen 18:15–33; cf. *Nat* II 18.

43. Strack-Stemberger, *Einleitung*, 92.

44. For related dicta by R. Ḥama's contemporary R. Simlai, see *Midraš Tanḥuma* (ed. Buber), p. 83.

45. Ad Gen 19:1–29; *CNis* LXXII 5; XLI 16; [*Abr* (= CSCO 322) XV 14]; *HdF* LXXXI 13; *CNis* XXXV 7; and cf. even *Virg* XXXVIII 13; *CNis* LVII 7–9; *Virg* XXXVIII 9.

46. *Virg* XXXVIII; *Crucif* V 9.

47. *Virg* I 11.

48. Ad Gen 19:30–38; *Virg* XXXVIII; cf. also *CNis* LVII 7–9.

has its pendant in Ephraem's likewise remarkable defense of the adultery of Tamar.[49] Neither Tamar nor Lot's daughters were, according to Ephraem, acting out of pure selfishness or illicit desire, but primarily out of righteousness. In the case of Lot's daughters, this righteousness caused the creation of two peoples, necessary component parts of the salvation history, whereas the conduct of Tamar is explained solely in view of the genuine seed of Israel, once promised to Abraham.

The Aqedah episode (Genesis 22) is often used in Ephraem's hymns, especially for its typological aspects.[50] Although Isaac for three days had pained his father with words of supplication,[51] the divine plan must be executed, the promised seed must survive: Abraham was bound to stand the test, and his seed was bound to become the drug of life in history.

The people of Haran are the focus of Ephraem's exposition of Genesis 24. Ephraem claims that Abraham, whom he styles "the honorable one" (*hdyr ᵓpᵓ*),[52] in his wisdom and subtlety bought the avaricious people of Haran by means of generous gifts.[53] Ephraem further notes that Isaac prayed on account of his wife Rebekah, in order that she should conceive.[54] In the center of his thoughts we find, again, the idea of the promised seed, through which Abraham was ultimately going to heal the world with blessing, in accordance with the divine promise:

> Merely one is his seed, the one that blesses everything.[55]

Haran was the point of departure for Abraham's health-restoring mission, that is, for the promised "leaven" of Abraham to penetrate the Near East.[56] Haran was also an important site in the subsequent fulfillment of the divine promise of healing, although the city itself remained an enemy of genuine remedy.[57] But in the history of salvation, the history of Israel, Abraham the physician was to have a parallel in Moses the physician. Admittedly, the two doctors of Israel worked from different perspectives, but with the same goal:

49. See T. Kronholm, "Holy Adultery: The Interpretation of the Story of Judah and Tamar (Gen 38) in the Genuine Hymns of Ephraem Syrus (ca. 306–373)," *OrSuec* 40 (1991) 149–63.

50. *CNis* LXIII 1–4; LXX 4–6; LXXII 3; *Virg* XLIX 11; *Nat* XVIII 30; VIII 13; *HdF* LVI 3–6; *Soq* III 8, 10; *Crucif* II 7; cf. Gerson, "Die Comentarien," 99.

51. *Virg* XLIX 11.

52. *CNis* XXXI 10–12.

53. *CNis* XXXI 1, 10–12, 15–16; XXXII 2; *Epiph* VII 4.

54. *Nat* XX 2.

55. *Nat* XX 2; cf. Gal 3:16.

56. *CNis* XXXIII 12–13; *Virg* XLIX 7–8; cf. Matt 13:33.

57. *CNis* XXXIV 7.

> As Abraham, the physician, who came and healed [all the body],
> from the head [downwards],
> thus Moses cured the body from the feet [upwards].[58]

Adhering to traditional rabbinic terminology, Ephraem notes, finally, that the people of Israel are "the daughter of Abraham,"[59] a daughter who has received all divine medicine and blessing for the world—first, admittedly, in *typoi* and parables, but then, gradually, the power of full and perfect healing. And the first medium of this national and universal healing is Abraham the physician.

58. *CNis* XXXIV 7; cf. *CH* XI 11–13.
59. *CNis* XIII 11; *Nat* XIV 19; *Resurr* III [1-]2; cf., however, *Epiph* V 3.

Ritual Purity and Political Exile: Solomon, the Queen of Sheba, and the Events of 586 B.C.E. in a Yemenite Folktale

JACOB LASSNER

In this article I deal with the cause of the Babylonian conquest and captivity as seen from the perspective of an eighteenth-century Yemenite folkloric text. In a bizarre series of linkages, the author, a certain Saadiah ben Joseph, understands sexual politics and behavior, the Babylonian conquest and the loss of Jewish sovereignty, the exile of the Jews, and procreation and divine order, as all part of a single moral construct that gave meaning to the past and, by implication, the present and the future.

Arguably the most talked-of tragic moment in Jewish experience has been the conquest of Jerusalem by Nebuchadnezzar in 586 B.C.E. This event, which led to the destruction of the temple and the expulsion of the Israelites from the sacred soil of their ancestors, has become the quintessential topos for many subsequent calamities afflicting God's chosen people. In this article I deal with a highly imaginative explanation for the circumstances of that year, as seen from the perspective of an eighteenth-century C.E. Yemenite text, an enchanting folkloric tale attributed to a certain Saadiah ben Joseph.

In a bizarre series of linkages, Saadiah understood sexual politics and behavior, the Babylonian conquest and loss of Jewish sovereignty, the exile of the Jews by Nebuchadnezzar, and procreation and divine order as together being part of a single moral construct. This explanation, cobbled together from seemingly disparate themes, makes for an overdetermined interpretation of events. Needless to say, Saadiah's version of events will not displace the established wisdom of modern biblical

Author's note: This article is an expansion of remarks found in a chapter of my book, *Demonizing the Queen of Sheba* (Chicago, 1993).

scholarship. There is, nevertheless, much in this story to exercise a historian's imagination, because it illustrates the manner in which folkloric material may reflect, ever so poignantly, a historical consciousness that fuses residual memories of dramatic political events with deep symbolic meanings. In this case, these meanings are associated with religious, social, and sexual behavior. The references are to exile and ritual purity; the pollution of sacred space in the land of Israel with menstruation; the politics of gender and family with natural order; defending political boundaries with procreation; and, were that not enough, establishing cultural barriers to protect Jews and Judaism against assimilative tendencies in times of perceived weakness. All this may be teased from a single tale, told in but a few pages and in a style and language that is accessible to a wide range of readers.

The Yemenite Tale

The Yemenite tale in question was discovered by Y. Avida in the library of the Jewish Theological Seminary of America. Among the various items examined by Avida during a trip to New York almost forty years ago was Enelow 874, a unique Hebrew manuscript dated to the beginning of the eighteenth century C.E. and attributed to a certain Saadiah ben Joseph. Within the larger text, Avida uncovered what he thought to be a discrete Yemenite version of one of the more dramatic incidents in the ongoing war between men and women, namely, the celebrated visit of the Queen of Sheba to King Solomon's court—a tale told in numerous versions, especially in Ethiopic, Jewish, and Arabic literature. The Yemenite version of the Solomonic story was subsequently published by Avida in the Festschrift for Simha Assaf under the title "*Maʿăśeh malkat Šĕbāʾ*."[1] As have many items written specifically for Festschriften, Avida's piece seems to have faded from sight. It is mentioned briefly in a popular book that treats the Queen of Sheba in Jewish, Muslim, Ethiopic, and Western Christian traditions, all within 160 pages, including footnotes, bibliography, and index.[2] But, other than Avida's short and schematic study, no detailed analysis of the Yemenite text has appeared.

Avida divided the tale into three distinct episodes for which he provided the following rubrics: "The Story of the Queen of Sheba and How She Acquired the Realm," "Solomon's War with One of the Island Kings," and in reference to her celebrated visit, "King Solomon and the Queen

1. Y. Avida, "*Maʿăśeh malkat Šĕbāʾ*," *Sefer Assaf* (ed. U. Cassuto et al.; Jerusalem, 1953) 1–17.

2. J. B. Pritchard (ed.), *Solomon and Sheba* (London, 1974) esp. 65–145.

of Sheba." The latter two episodes, that is, the war and visit, appear sequentially in the manuscript; the story of the queen's origins, considered by Avida to be an integral part of the larger tale, is recorded separately many pages removed from the segments pertaining to Solomon.[3]

One might best describe the text as presented by Avida as lightly annotated. His footnotes and commentary are generally limited to identifying the numerous allusions to biblical passages and phrases, particularly in the segment describing the queen's visit to Solomon's court, where scripture is ingeniously spliced into folkloric narrative to produce subtle meanings. The story of the queen's origins he regards as being derived from an Islamic tale, but his brief references to the *Thousand and One Nights* and to Turkish folklore are false leads.[4] Put less charitably and as succinctly as possible, there is little reason to suppose any linkage between the Muslim sources referred to by Avida and the Jewish text that he edited. A more detailed study of Islamic sources was promised, but I am not aware that any such study was ever published by Avida or, for that matter, by anyone else. Be that as it may, I found Arabic parallels to the Hebrew account of the queen's origins in Diyārbakrī's *K. al-Khamīs,* a sixteenth-century Muslim work on biblical events and persons; in Ibn al-Athīr's universal history of the twelfth century, the *Kāmil fī-Taʾrīkh*; and, moving backwards in time, in the *Murūj al-dhahab,* Masʿūdī's tenth-century compilation of wide-ranging historical and belletristic traditions.[5] There are also probable linkages between the Yemenite account of Solomon's island campaign and medieval Arabic sources, but all this is a subject for another occasion.[6]

My concern here is with the final segment: the story of the queen's visit in Saadiah's text, a tale of competing intellects, carnal knowledge, and if I am not mistaken, a case of ritual impurity and risky sex that affected the fate of the entire Israelite nation.[7] I refer here to Solomon's legendary appetite for women and how, in the circumstances of the queen's visit, the need to gratify his sexual desires ultimately led to Nebuchadnezzar's conquest, the destruction of the temple, and the Babylonian captivity. Strange as it may seem to us, this Yemenite author,

3. Avida, "*Maʿăśeh,*" 1.

4. Ibid., 2.

5. *Khamīs* (Cairo, 1884) 1.276–77; *Kāmil* (Beirut, 1965–67) 1.231; *Murūj* (Paris, 1861–77) 3.152.

6. Thaʿlabī, *ʿArāʾis,* 322ff.; Kisāʾī, *Qiṣaṣ,* 293–95; Tabarī, *Annales* 1/2.586–94; Yaʿqūbī, *Historiae* 1.63–64; Diyārbakrī, *Khamīs* 1.283–84; Zamakhsharī, *Kashshāf* (Calcutta, 1856) 1236; Balʿamī, *Taʾrīkh* (Zotenberg) 4.24–26; G. Salzberger, *Die Salomo-Sage in der semitischen Literatur* (Berlin and Heidelberg, 1907).

7. Avida, "*Maʿăśeh,*" 5–7, 11–15.

reflecting the values of his society, understood the hierarchical politics of gender, dangerous sexual activity, and the fate of the Jewish people and their state, as being part of a single historiographical construct. There are no identifiable eighteenth-century markers in this formulation, nor is it entirely certain in what ways Saadiah's account is a distinctive Yemenite tale. What may be said is that the relevant sections of Enelow 874 comprise a text juxtaposing various traditional attitudes of Near Eastern Jewry; it is also part of a wider story with Jewish, Islamic, and even universal linkages. Above all, this is a story of a woman challenging a man in defiance of social convention and natural order, and the consequences of that challenge to the well-being of Israel and its polity. In this sense, the text reflects the inner logic of cultural codes governing attitudes towards sexual and other political hierarchies—attitudes that give rise, in turn, to a bizarre and titillating explanation for the calamity of 586 B.C.E.

Ritual Impurity: Female Blood as a Pollutant

Briefly stated, the tale of the queen's visit follows a familiar script, albeit with certain significant variations. As in the biblical account, 1 Kgs 10:1–13, the prototype for all subsequent Jewish versions, she took with her 120 talents of pure gold, great quantities of spices, precious stones, and sandalwood. Having arrived at the Israelite court, she probed Solomon's famed intelligence with a number of riddles, all of which are reported in earlier Jewish sources: the *Midraš Proverbs*, the *Midraš ha-Ḥêfeṣ*, and the Aramaic *Targūm Šênî* to the book of Esther.[8] The game of wits begins.

> "What are they?" she asks. "Seven depart and nine enter; two give succor but only one partakes."

The riddle, familiar to readers of midrashic literature, elicits a contemptuous response from the "wisest of all men." As our author, Saadiah, indicates, the king, whose remarkable wisdom surpasses that of Ethan the Ezrahite and of Heman, Chalkol, and Darda, the sons of Mahol, and indeed of all the legendary wise men of the East, was not to be troubled by

8. *Midraš Proverbs* (ed. Buber) 40–41, (ed. Visotzky) 4–7; for *Midraš ha-Ḥêfeṣ*, see S. Schechter, "The Riddles of Solomon in Rabbinic Literature," *Folklore* 1 (1890) 349–58, including edition, translation, and commentary; the *Targūm Šênî* has been edited a number of times. A new edition based on all known manuscripts has been published by B. Grossfeld (New York, 1994). The text found in the supplement to the volume on the Five Scrolls in *Miqrāʾôt Gĕdōlôt* is cited here because it is the most accessible to readers. See MG (repr. Rabbinowitz; New York) 6.2a–b. The most recent translation and commentary is the one by B. Grossfeld, *The Two Targums of Esther* (Collegeville, Minn., 1991).

so trivial a question. Unlike the other more familiar accounts, which present Solomon as willing if not eager to take up the queen's challenge, Saadiah reports that the king's first inclination was to ignore the question altogether. At first glance, readers might think the test not worthy of Solomon's intelligence—an insulting challenge requiring no response. Did she really expect to stump the great king with the prattle of females? For, as the author reminds us through Solomon, such riddles are the fare of women chatting (idly) in the moonlight.[9]

We are not informed by either Saadiah or his interlocutor, the king of Israel, why this particular riddle should suggest a moonlight chat between women. Indeed, none of the other versions of the queen's visit draws attention to any such chat. Perhaps the added comment attributed to Solomon is innocuous, but Jewish folkloric accounts tend to be carefully constructed and highly allusive. The economy of language and thought does not suggest an innocuous interpolation. Saadiah's reference to women conversing begs for an explanation, however speculative.[10] Regarding the nocturnal female prattlers, the reference to the moon (*lĕbānâ*) may be a play on words that suggests the period of the month when women uncertain of their ritual purity are denied their husband's companionship in accordance with Jewish law. Scripture refers to seven days of menstruation, to which the rabbis added additional days when women "wore white" while continuing to examine themselves for lingering signs of blood, that is the period of *libbun* (based on Hebrew *laban* 'white'). The wearing of white, ironically the color of purity, was a visual marker for males that they were to keep their distance from a woman suspected of menstrual discharge.[11] Might Solomon's quip about the idle prattle of females in the moonlight (*ballĕbānâ*) be understood as a woman chatting with a friend wearing white (read *bĕlibbūnâ*)? Orthographically, *lĕbānâ* and *libbūnâ*, both derived from the same Hebrew root, are easily confused, especially if the short vowels are omitted, as was the custom in Hebrew script and as is the case in Saadiah's tale. If we were to assume, therefore, that the passage in question reflects a suggestive play on words or perhaps a scribal error, might we be allowed to entertain an

9. Avida, "*Maᶜăśeh,*" 5.

10. Avida suggests a connection to *b. Ber.* 3a, though no connection is evident by comparing the texts. Note also the expression *mōzĕrōt ballĕbānâ* in *b. Soṭa* 6b.

11. Based on Lev 15:19–33, 18:19; Ezek 18:6, 22:10. See *EncJud* 12.1141ff. s.v. *niddah* for a summary of these complex issues; also H. Eilberg-Schwartz (*The Savage in Judaism* [Bloomington, 1990], esp. 177–95), who combines the insights of anthropology with a reading of traditional Jewish sources on ritual pollution; and the anthropologist M. Douglas (*Purity and Danger* [London, 1966]), who broadly links laws of purity to the condition of the body politic. Despite the informed discussion of anthropologists, the laws of purity remain problematic to scholars.

additional thought, however playful and imaginative. Is Saadiah suggesting that the Queen of Sheba herself might have come to Jerusalem when her purity was in doubt—that is to say, when she was "wearing white"? Or perhaps Saadiah wished to convey that the queen deliberately chose white garb to mislead Solomon into thinking that she was still observing her menses. The theme of disguised appearances, particularly in regard to dressing, is prominent in all the stories of the queen's visit. Were it indeed the author's intention to indicate that the queen wore white, for whatever reason, how does a reading of *libbūnâ* for *lĕ bānâ* affect the message of the larger tale and the manner in which it unfolds? More specifically, how does the alternative reading link Solomon's strange silence when the queen tries to test him with Nebuchadnezzar's conquest of Jerusalem and the exile of the Israelites to Babylonia in 586 B.C.E.?

The king was reluctant to respond to the queen's riddle. Now, the Yemenite author was surely aware that Jews are supposed to avoid contact and even idle conversation with women during their monthly cycle. The Jews of Islamic lands were particularly strict regarding the segregating of women during their monthly cycle, and according to anecdotal evidence, traditional Yemenites were and continue to be the strictest of all. Would Saadiah not have assumed, therefore, that the all-wise Solomon also would have known of God's intention and would have embraced the sentiments of the rabbis who prescribed that women isolate themselves from men when impure? Commenting on the biblical verse, "Do not approach a women when she is impure in order to reveal her nakedness [that is, to have intercourse]" (Lev 18:19), the authorities ask, "May her husband perhaps embrace her or kiss her or engage her in idle chatter?" The question, a rhetorical device to explicate a principle of rabbinic jurisprudence, namely the construction of a hedge around the law in order to preserve its basic intent (*sĕyag la-tōrâ*), evokes a swift and final response from the rabbis: "Scripture says, 'Do not approach [her].'"[12] Apropos of this seemingly harsh interpretation (the biblical text speaks only of contact to engage in penetrative sex) there is the well-known rabbinic dictum that enjoins men to 'eschew conversation with women' (*ʾal tarbeh śîḥâ ʿim hā-iššâ*). Some talmudic variants explain this oft-cited but inherently puzzling statement with a gloss: *bĕniddātāh* 'when she is ritually impure'.[13] That is to say, even innocent conversation may be an inducement to sexual activity and so talking to women when they are (or might be) ritually impure was not condoned. If the queen

12. *ʾAbot R. Nat.* 8ff. (ed. Schechter), which also notes that it is not even possible for an unclean woman to sleep on a couch next to her husband fully clothed or to dress or apply makeup in a way that will make her alluring to men.

13. Ibid.

were indeed wearing white, as I have chosen to suppose, one would then understand why in Saadiah's account Solomon's first inclination was to decline comment altogether, even though he was asked a direct question. The king was simply following the dictates of Jewish law, in this case a rabbinic interpretation that serves as a gloss to a well-known biblical statute.

This, however, was no ordinary situation; there was danger in following the dictates of Jewish practice. Speaking through Solomon, the author suggests that the queen was likely to conclude that failure to respond to her riddle reflected an inability to do so. That is, a mute response would be for the queen a clear sign that she had triumphed in their game of wits. And so Solomon must answer her question. It is implied that had he refused to respond she would have shamed him and all other men, in defiance of natural order as well as his kingdom and, worse yet, his God. Were Solomon to have remained silent, she would have declared herself the victor with all that such a victory implied. One may sympathize with Solomon, given the difficult situation in which he was placed. He had no recourse but to answer her, but on what authority? How could he avoid being accused of transgressing Jewish law, albeit for the sake of defending sexual hierarchy, his people, and his God?

One need not conclude that, in answering the queen's riddles, Solomon was taking excessive license with the law as Saadiah and the rabbis understood it. Were a precedent needed for talking to a woman suspected of ritual impurity (that is while she was wearing white), the wise king could easily fall back on the authority of Hebrew Scripture. In answering the queen's riddle, Saadiah ben Joseph has Solomon quote from his very own composition, the book of Proverbs: "Answer a dullard in accord with his folly lest he consider himself wise" (Prov 26:5). A prooftext from scripture is all that Solomon would have needed to defend his response to the queen, the rabbinic stricture eschewing conversation with women notwithstanding. In legal terms, he would have been justified because direct biblical authority, that is a "commandment *middĕ*ˀ*ôraytā* " is privileged over a rabbinic dictum, a "commandment *middĕrabbānān*." Although strictly speaking the verse from Proverbs is a didactic comment and not a positive commandment, Saadiah exercises literary license to suggest that it may be understood as a legal precept (that is, if I am not making an irresponsible claim on our source). The Yemenite author, speaking through the quoting of scripture by the king, will not allow the queen any excuse to be haughty, let alone give her reason to doubt the Israelite or his God. As in the biblical account, which serves as the skeletal structure of the Yemenite and all other versions, the king replies in order to win the queen's respect and then obeisance.

Saadiah's narrative suggests that the Queen of Sheba might have been familiar with Jewish ritual practice. And why not? Like Solomon, she was possessed of great intelligence and knowledge. Seen in this light, the pagan queen wore white deliberately and then tested Solomon while cleverly and audaciously invoking his obligation to remain silent and sexually distant. Had he followed the precepts of Jewish law and ignored her, she would have triumphed despite his vaunted intelligence and sexual prowess. If this were indeed the queen's ploy, as presented by Saadiah, he may be seen as drawing on the famous story of Beruriah, the learned and testy wife of Rabbi Meir, who invoked the rabbinic dictum *ʾal tarbeh śîḥâ ʿim hā-iššâ* when dealing with Rabbi Jose the Galilean. Rabbi Jose, a mere scholar, passed his test with a mute response, thereby protecting his scholarly reputation. Solomon, the world's wisest man, was playing a game for much higher stakes and thus found it necessary to answer her directly.[14]

Turning to the business at hand, Solomon responds to her query as he does in the earlier midrashic sources but with one significant difference: "Seven depart refers to the days of wearing white" (note the specific mention here of *libbūn*; the other versions speak more generally of *niddâ*, the comprehensive legal rubric that governs menstruation and purity).[15] The rest of the riddle means: "Nine enter refers to the months of pregnancy. After the woman gives birth, the two breasts will give succor to the child."

The answer, correctly given, indicates to an alert reader how appropriate the riddle is to women amusing a lonely friend or relative who is observing herself for residual discharges of blood, their company made necessary because her husband must keep his distance. He cannot partake of meals with her or even sleep next to her while she is fully clothed on a couch.[16] Indeed, some sources called for her total isolation at a "house of uncleanliness."[17] Commenting on the verse: "Concerning she who is afflicted with menstruation . . ." the rabbis say, "all the days of her impurity let her remain isolated (from men)."[18] The Babylonian authorities were somewhat more lenient than their Palestinian colleagues in the matter of segregating women. They allowed the afflicted female to continue with her household chores, but they denied her the privilege of washing her husband's body (let alone enjoying it), making his bed (let alone occupying it), or filling his wine cup (let alone sharing it in his

14. *B. ʿErub.* 53b.
15. That is, in *Midraš Proverbs* and *Midraš ha-Ḥêfeṣ*. See n. 8 above.
16. *ʾAbot R. Nat.* 8.
17. *Y. Nid.* 7.4.
18. *ʾAbot R. Nat.* 8.

company). Be that as it may, the Palestinian view, which called for more stringent segregation, was the view widely accepted by the Jews of Islamic lands, Yemen included.

Solomon thought the queen's riddle the mere prattle of females, but the telling of such riddles and other amusements may have been an important part of women's culture during their period of segregation. For the impure woman and those empathetic to her condition, this particular amusement speaks of a time of reunion. Soon she will have no need of lady friends with whom to chat in the absence of men, however meaningful the company of women may have been. The period of waiting will be over. Free of any signs of blood, she will abandon her white garments, purify herself in the ritual bath, and then return to her husband's bed. Finally, if all goes well, she will become pregnant and give birth and, having done that, she will nurture her child; all this is implied in the riddle. In such fashion, she will fulfill what God ordained in his blessing to Adam and Eve: "be fruitful and multiply" and "fill the earth and take dominion over it" (Gen 1:28). The riddle, which is suggestive of Jewish tradition and society, makes it abundantly clear that sexual relations should lead to procreation and that for women the essence of marriage is to bear and nurture children.[19]

Despite much discussion, the deeper symbolic meaning of menstruation in Jewish law remains and will no doubt always remain problematic. I am inclined to follow the modern scholars who argue that the flow of menstrual fluid in a woman represents a missed opportunity for reproduction, there being no perceived chance of conception during the menstrual cycle. This being the case, sexual relations with women during the period of *niddâ* would seem to represent a waste of semen. One ought to note in this respect the fate of the biblical Onan who "spilled his seed" rather than consummate relations with his wife Tamar in a levirate marriage following the death of his brother Er, her first husband. Rather than perpetuate his brother's line according to biblical custom and law, Onan preferred to practice coitus interruptus, an act that occasioned God's vengeance against him, while earning for Tamar the reputation of a killer-wife. The story, part of the larger tale of Judah and Tamar, which will be cited shortly, is emblematic of the Hebrew Bible's heavy emphasis on procreation and its links to human biology (Gen 38:6–30).[20]

19. The most detailed explication of this verse in Jewish tradition is the explanation of J. Cohen, "*Be Fertile and Increase, Fill the Earth and Master It*": *The Ancient and Medieval Career of a Biblical Text* (Ithaca, 1989).

20. For an extensive study of this tale, see M. Friedman, "Tamar, A Symbol of Life: The 'Killer Wife' Superstition in the Bible and Jewish Tradition," *AJS Review* 15 (1990) 23–62.

A recent anthropological study of Near Eastern Jewish women, in this case traditional Moroccans living in Israel, tends to reinforce a symbolic linkage between the laws of ritual purity and the imperative to procreate.[21] "Menstrual blood . . . signifies [for these Moroccan women] the potential of conception, the construction of the Jewish household and the continuity of the Jewish people . . . . It becomes a symbol of Jewish identity as it marks them from their Muslim neighbors who practice less stringent regulations [as well as] the expression and symbol of the feminine essence. . . ."[22] For all those familiar with Jewish tradition, the views of the Moroccan women would appear to be based on precedents from scripture and rabbinic tradition.

Biological Imperatives

Bearing children was not a matter to be taken lightly. Following the Flood and the near extinction of humankind and all living creatures, God repeated his blessing to the survivors. The very same blessing of fertility reverberates in the later covenant between Abraham and God, an act that directly links the Almighty with those who were to become his chosen people and their rulers, the Israelites and their kings. God's blessing was similarly granted to Isaac; to Jacob, the eponymous ancestor of the Israelite tribes; and by extension to the larger polity, the people of Israel. The survival of the species, a matter of universal concern, thus became a special concern of Israel's society and its cultural guardians.[23]

By invoking procreation the queen's riddle will lead us, however indirectly, to the related themes of Jewish sovereignty and exile and as we shall see, ultimately to the events of 586 B.C.E. When Jeremiah anticipates the return of the people of Samaria taken captive in 722 B.C.E., he says in God's name: "And I myself will gather the remnants of my flock from all the lands to which I have exiled them, and I shall bring them back to

21. R. Wasserfall, "Menstruation and Identity: The Meaning of Niddah for Moroccan Women Immigrants to Israel," in *People of the Body* (ed. H. Eilberg-Schwartz; New York, 1992) 309–28.

22. Ibid., 312ff.

23. Gen 17:19–21, 28:3–4, 35:11–12, 47:27, 48:3–4; Lev 26:9; Jer 3:16, 23:3; Ezek 36:9–11. For a discussion of these passages, see Cohen, *Be Fertile and Increase*, 25–35. On the linkage between the Lord's blessing and the need for human resources in the Israelite period, see C. Meyers, *Discovering Eve* (Oxford, 1988). She contends that the hill country of premonarchic Israel was underpopulated and gave rise to a complex interweaving of societal resources and needs that encouraged large families. For Meyers, the end result was the value system embodied in the Genesis narratives, which valorize procreation. For the perceived need to maintain a critical mass in the postbiblical period, see Cohen, *Be Fertile and Increase*, 124–26.

their pasture where they shall be *fruitful and multiply*" (Jer 23:3; see also 3:16). Jeremiah then goes on to prophesy the coming emergence of a "true branch of David's line," a king who will prosper in a land made secure (Jer 23:5). As if resonating to these words, the prophet Ezekiel speaks of still another exiled community, the people in Babylonian captivity, and envisages a time when God will restore the land of Israel to its former state: "I [that is, God] will settle [on the land] a large population . . . the entire house of Israel; the towns shall be resettled and the ruined sites rebuilt. I will multiply men and beasts upon [it], and they shall *multiply and be fruitful* . . . and you shall know that I am the Lord" (Ezek 36:9–11).

The central text upon which both these prophecies rest is Leviticus 26, which speaks of a covenantal relationship between the people of Israel and their God. The Israelites are obliged to carry out Yahweh's commandments; in return, God will control nature to their advantage and secure their polity by increasing their numbers and delivering them from their enemies. He summarizes this by saying, "I [God] shall look with favor upon you and make you fruitful and multiply you . . . . [According to our covenant] I will be your God and you shall be my people" (Lev 26:9). For Israel procreation is a ubiquitous metaphor for divine commitment to their well-being and sovereignty. Indeed, a theologian not afraid of taking excessive liberties with scripture might give the biblical text a modern gloss and explicate "fill[ing] the earth and [taking] dominion over it" as referring to the Israelite settlement of ancient Palestine and, linked to that, the establishment of Jewish sovereignty within its geographical boundaries.

There were pragmatic concerns, to be sure, that occasioned biblical and postbiblical attitudes towards procreation. At all times the ancient Israelites and their successors were numerically and geographically a small political entity. For the most part the people of Israel were incapable of enacting an independent foreign policy and were subject as well to the encroachment of assimilative tendencies. The Roman destruction of Jewish sovereignty in 70 C.E. and the beginnings of a two thousand–year diaspora served to exacerbate already pronounced feelings of insecurity. Numbers represented a hedge against a loss of political control and then later against religious leakage. By rabbinic times, procreation was considered by learned scholars to be part of Mosaic legislation. Hence, producing offspring was not only pleasurable and/or desirable, it had become encumbant on Jewish men and, by implication, Jewish women, because men alone cannot reproduce the species. Legend had it that the refusal of a single Jew to conform to this legislation might occasion the Divine Presence to abandon the people called Israel. The queen's riddle suggests, ever so poignantly, that childbearing and nurture are the proper roles for women. There is a lesson in this for a woman who denies sexual hierarchy and prefers to rule men instead.[24]

The Queen of Sheba is no ordinary woman, however. She has not achieved or exercised power by shrinking from the prospect of extended combat with men. In the segment that relates the queen's origins, she is portrayed as outwitting men easily and as becoming a world conqueror upon the death of her husband. She is, therefore, a proper analog and future rival of the great Solomon, who in Jewish scripture and lore extended the influence and borders of the Israelite state to an extent never seen before or thereafter. Indeed, without this symmetry of powerful and intellectually gifted rivals, the story would lose much of its appeal to reading or listening audiences.

And so she questions the Israelite once again, this time with a riddle concerning procreation that brings us still closer to Nebuchadnezzar and the events of 586 B.C.E.:

> [To what does this refer?] A child asked his mother, "Who is my father?" The mother answers, "Your father is my father and your grandfather is my husband. You are my son and I am your sister."

As in earlier Jewish sources where the riddle is cited, the king answers succinctly and with confidence:

> No doubt the reference is to Ammon and Moab who were descended from Lot.

They were, as readers no doubt recalled, the offspring of Lot's daughters, those incestuous females who slept with their father to become pregnant (Gen 19:31–35). The unnatural act was performed when the women feared for the continuity of their family, because they saw no men with whom to propagate the species following the destruction of Sodom and Gomorrah. Saadiah's readers, or those who might have listened to oral versions of his tale, were no doubt aware of the linkage between the figures of the riddle and Solomon himself. Moab was the ancestor of Naomi, mother-in-law of Ruth; and Ruth married Boaz the descendant of Amminadab, whose son was leader of the tribe of Judah during the sojourn in the wilderness. Out of the union of Ruth and Boaz came the Davidic line of ancient Israel (Ruth 4:19–20, 1 Chr 2:10). That is to say, David was the great-grandson of Ruth, and Solomon the great great-grandson. Thus, had it not been for the willingness of Lot's daugh-

24. *B. Yebam.* 64a.

ter to engage in licentious, indeed unnatural behavior in order to follow the imperative of procreation and preserve her father's line, there would have been no David and no Solomon, no Israelite Jerusalem, no temple, and no Jewish sovereignty.

Parenthetically, Amminadab, the more remote ancestor of the Davidic line, was the descendant of Perez, who was also the issue of an illicit relationship. The reference is to Judah and his daughter-in-law Tamar.[25] This sexual encounter was occasioned by Tamar's desire to perpetuate Judah's line after the premature death of his sons, Er and Onan, her previous husbands. Had it not been for Tamar's ingenious scheme to disguise herself in order to bed down with her father-in-law, there would have been no Boaz to marry Ruth. And so, both the maternal and the paternal sides of the Israelite royal family reflect the extent to which the cultural imperative to reproduce transcended even illicit relations. It is perhaps no coincidence that the story of Judah and Tamar is central to one of the queen's riddles in the *Midraš ha-Ḥêfeṣ*, an earlier text of Yemenite provenance that describes the historic encounter between the two sovereigns. In any case, the theme of all three riddles links procreation with Jewish destiny—in the latter two riddles with the ruling family itself, hence with Jewish sovereignty—and suggests that the primary function of women is reproduction and nurture.[26]

Bested a second time, the queen is still not satisfied. Following a pattern in other Jewish (and also Islamic)[27] sources, she presents Solomon with a visual problem. She dresses and bejewels male and female children in an identical fashion and then asks the king to distinguish between the sexes. This he does by distributing roasted grains and nuts among them. The boys grab them and, running off, go their merry way. The narrative suggests that boys will always be boys. On the other hand, the girls place them on their laps and sit well behaved. Needless to say, girls will always be girls—that is, in the view of Saadiah. There is no missing the point of the queen's riddle or of Solomon's brilliant response. Were Solomon unable to distinguish male from female, he would have failed the test that, by its very nature, is designed to show women are equal to men. Indeed, in other sources the children are dressed in Israelite purple, the royal colors, a not very subtle sign that women may even be allowed to rule. But all this is foolishness on the queen's part. Disguised appearances cannot hide what nature has decreed even in

25. See n. 20 above.

26. *Midr. ha-Ḥêfeṣ*, 349.

27. For example Thaᶜlabī, *ᶜArāʾis* 316; Kisāʾī, *Qiṣaṣ* 287; Zamakhsharī, *Kashshāf* 1026; Balᶜamī, *Taʾrīkh* 4.16; Diyārbakrī, *Khamīs* 1.278–79. For a fuller list of parallel Arabic sources as well as a detailed explication of the texts, see Lassner, *Demonizing the Queen of Sheba*, 79–80.

childhood, before the sexes are more prominently differentiated by hairiness, voice, physical stature, and the like. Once again, Solomon reads cultural (or as Saadiah understood them, natural) codes with consummate accuracy. In God's design, aggressiveness and power are reserved for the male species. No doubt, the Queen of Sheba is a most impressive woman, but she is not able to master the most impressive of men. At least, such is the conventional wisdom of this tradition and all the other traditions of the queen's encounter with Solomon. Her remaining riddle, in this text a direct translation from the Aramaic *Targūm Šênî* also dealing with disguised appearances, is dismissed as easily as the others. Having lost the game of wits, she must concede the match, and as in the biblical account, she then sings the Israelite's praise and that of his God.

Risky Sex

The Queen of Sheba is still a woman who rules over men. Indeed, her reputation as a conqueror of peoples and domains exceeds that of her husband, the late ruler of Sheba. There is something unnatural in a woman acting as though she were a man. Thus, she will have to submit to Solomon in a fashion that establishes his primacy over her and with that, the primacy of Israelites over others. This conquest will take place in the royal bedchamber. When it comes to sexual prowess, Solomon is a *surhomme du monde*, a notion suggested by the biblical story of his thousand wives and concubines and the numerous legends of his potency to which the story gave rise (1 Kgs 11:3).[28] The very thought that a man could satisfy a thousand women as did King Solomon boggles the imagination.

The presumptive signs for this conquest are seemingly positive. Our Yemenite source, unlike all the other variant accounts, stresses that the queen is currently unmarried and therefore available (there is a possible reference here to Solomon's father, David, who had an affair with Solomon's future mother when she was still married to Uriah the Hittite, a well-known story that brought humiliation upon King David and suffering to his people [2 Samuel 11–12 and Psalm 51]. In other words, the laws that govern sex apply even to the kings of Israel). As luck would have it, the queen is not only unmarried, she is also exceedingly beautiful (an opportunity to combine duty with pleasure). But there is a rumor that occasions Solomon's concern. As in other accounts, he has heard that she, the suspected daughter of a jinni, has hairy legs (a symbol of

28. On Solomon's lovemaking, see *Midr. Song of Songs Rab.* 9 (ed. S. Dunsky). For Islamic legends of his potency, see Lassner, *Demonizing the Queen of Sheba*, 85–86.

her mixed breeding and of her arrogating male prerogative to rule).[29] Were Saadiah familiar with the version of this episode recorded in the *Stories of Ben Sira*, a pseudonymous and exceedingly popular medieval Hebrew work of wisdom and fables, his Solomon would have had additional cause for concern.[30] The author of the *Stories* asks us to remember that this historic encounter took place at a time when Israelite women removed all the hair ordinarily covered by their garments. With this comment, he seems to echo a rabbinic view that the daughters of Israel shaved their private parts because such hair was considered exceedingly dangerous to men.[31] Sex with an unshaven woman was risky sex. One had only to recall the story of Solomon's half-brother Amnon who, in raping his half-sister Tamar (not to be confused with Judah's daughter-in-law), became entangled in her pubic hair and wound up with mutilated genitalia, an unconventional way to suffer castration that exercised the imagination of the rabbis.[32] In any case, the reader is led to believe that hirsute women are considered threatening to men and an anomaly in God's given universe.

In Saadiah's rendering of events, Solomon is forced to investigate the rumor by means of an elaborate scheme, also familiar from other accounts, particularly the Islamic sources. He constructs a marble clearing upon which water is splashed, giving the impression that the entire floor is a pond. The queen, convinced that she is facing a real body of water, lifts her garments to cross over and reveals her hairy legs.[33] At this, Solomon supplies her with cosmetics (with which to make herself alluring) and also with a depilatory to remove the (dangerous) hair. And so, thanks to the depilatory, a lime paste made of an arsenic base and labeled 'miracle in lime' (*nēs bĕsîd*),[34] she comes to him and he sleeps with her. The presumption is that she is now suitably feminine and pure, that is, disarmed and desirable. One may note in this connection the language of Pseudo–Ben Sira: "Her skin was made pure."[35] The use of the Hebrew verb *thr* reinforces the notion that the hairiness of women was

29. See *Targūm Šênî* in *Miqrāʾôt Gĕdōlôt* 6:2b; Pseudo–Ben Sira (*Sippūrê Ben Sira* [Jerusalem, 1984] 217–18). For Islamic versions, see Lassner, *Demonizing the Queen of Sheba*, 82–86.

30. I rely on the recent edition of E. Yassif. For other versions under different names, see *EncJud* 4.548–50. This work is not to be confused with that of the ancient Ben Sira. It is henceforth referred to as Ps. Ben Sira, as distinct from the latter.

31. Ps. Ben Sira, 218.

32. 2 Samuel 13; *b. Sanh.* 21a.

33. See *Targūm Šênî* in *Miqrāʾôt Gĕdōlôt* 6:2b. Islamic parallels are found in Lassner, *Demonizing the Queen of Sheba*, 60–61, 82ff.

34. The meaning of *nēs bĕsîd* is problematic, but it is clear that the author is speaking of a depilatory.

35. Ps. Ben Sira, 218.

not simply a matter of esthetics but one of ritual purity, the initial theme that elicited our concern.

The Events of 586 B.C.E.

At this point one wants to ask, what does all that has been discussed above and, more generally, what does the theme of ritual purity have to do with interpreting the events of 586 B.C.E.? In the end, Solomon's moment of pleasure will come to haunt the Israelites. As in the *Stories of Ben Sira,* Saadiah's queen becomes pregnant and gives birth to, of all people, Nebuchadnezzar. The implications of Solomon's unbridled passion were perfectly clear to all Jews familiar with this bizarre tradition of Nebuchadnezzar's origins. Setting aside the 400 years that separate the age of Solomon from this alleged son, who, needless to say, is not attested as the Israelite's offspring in the biblical text, the historical fact remains: in the end, the Babylonian ruler destroys the temple and the house of Solomon, his father, avenging thereby the indignity that has been brought on his illustrious mother. Solomon is repayed in full for disempowering the Queen of Sheba.[36]

Saadiah ends the love tryst with a clever and most appropriate postscript based on Isa 49:17: "Those who ravage you and leave you waste will depart from you." Any learned Jew would have recognized the biblical passage and its context. Quoted in full, the verse reads: "Swiftly your children are coming. Those who ravage you and leave you waste will depart from you." The verse itself is part of an extended text in which the prophet foretells the redemption of Zion, previously laid waste by the Babylonian monarch. "The children swiftly coming" is thus a reference to the return of the Babylonian exiles to Mother Zion; the "departure of those who ravaged her and laid her waste" refers to the defeat and withdrawal of Jerusalem's Babylonian conqerors.

Saadiah is not interested, however, in happy stories of redemption. His is the tale of the world's wisest monarch, who is nevertheless not smart enough to keep his distance when dealing with a clever and enticingly beautiful female. Solomon should have been content with besting her in a game of wits. The contest in the royal bedchamber shifts the match to a playing field on which women are all too dangerous. In this instance Solomon wins the game and beds the queen on his terms, that is without hair and in full makeup, but she wins the match when Nebuchadnezzar lays his father's kingdom waste. And so the words of Isaiah concerning Mother Zion are cited by Saadiah ben Joseph as though they

36. See E. Ullendorff, *The Bawdy Bible* (Oxford, 1979) 428.

are being stood on their head. "Those who ravage you and leave you waste" still refers to the Babylonians, or in this case Nebuchadnezzar himself. But the phrase 'shall depart from you' (*mimmēk yēṣēʾû*) is understood by Saadiah to mean 'shall issue forth from you'. Hence, the reference is not to the flight of the Babylonians as the exile is about to end but to the birth of their monarch, the tyrant, who, in a perverse twist of fate, is sired by Israel's illustrious king.

The feminization of Zion and by extension the entire land of Israel, a theme widespread in the prophetic writings, makes that twist of fate seem even more perverse at second glance. By ravaging the land thus anthropomorphized, Nebuchadnezzar may be seen as reenacting the role of his father, Solomon, whose ultimate conquest of the Sheban queen takes place in the royal bedchamber. The inescapable symmetry is made all the more ironic if one considers the possibility that the Queen of Sheba may have come to Solomon when she was "wearing white" as did women observing themselves for residual discharges of blood. Reflecting on the Babylonian conquest, the author of Lamentations describes Jerusalem as 'ritually unclean' (*hāyĕtâ . . . lĕniddâ*), 'her skirts defiled with [the stain] of her impurity' (*ṭumʾātāh bĕšûle(y)hā*) (Lam 1:8–9, 17). Utilizing vivid images of ritual impurity, Ezekiel describes the land as having been defiled by those whose actions were in God's sight 'like the uncleanliness of a menstruating woman' (*kĕṭumʾat hanniddâ*) (Ezek 36:17). Somewhat later, as the exiles prepare to return from Babylonia, Ezra informs them that they will take possession of a 'land made impure by the impurity of [their ancestors' captors]' (*ʾereṣ niddâ hîʾ bĕniddat ʿammê haʾărāṣôt*) (Ezra 9:11). These prophetic passages were known to all literate Jews, and certainly to the Yemenites, who have always been famous for their capacity to cite scripture from memory. The symbolism evoked by the trenchant references to *niddâ*, that is, 'ritual impurity', was easily accessible to Saadiah's readers. Consequently, Nebuchadnezzar would have been seen as possessing a female Zion who is clearly afflicted with menstruation, her condition made obvious by her stained garments. Be this as it may, her evident distress would seem to have no bearing on his lustful and rapacious behavior; one cannot imagine Nebuchadnezzar being constrained by Jewish laws of ritual purity. Symbolically he does indeed repay Solomon in kind.

Solomon, on the other hand, cannot be so cavalier with the constraints of Jewish law and practice. Were the Queen of Sheba wearing white, that is, were she, like Zion, similarly marked by her garment, we may underscore Solomon's most inappropriate, indeed most sinful conduct. But then again Solomon is the quintessential lover and when it comes to lovemaking the great king of the Israelites is known to take excessive risks. Commenting on the biblical verse, "Among the many nations there was not a king like him . . . yet foreign wives caused even him to sin," Rabbi Eliezer, son of Jose the Galilean, explains: "The verse informs us that Solomon had intercourse with them [that is foreign women] when they were ritually impure . . . ."[37] It is one thing to forego disdain and engage the queen in conversation during her monthly cycle because it is necessary to put her in her place for the sake of men, Israel, and God. Answering her riddles is therefore understandable, if not imperative, despite the stringent rabbinic interpretation of the laws of purity. It is another matter to bed her, especially if there is even the slightest possibility that she is ritually impure. Clearly, the king's passion has ruled his senses—that is, if, in this case, Saadiah's account does indeed suggest that the queen might have been wearing white. By having intercourse with a woman suspected of menstruating, he is putting his own ritual purity at risk, the blood of a woman being a pollutant to men who come into direct contact with it. To risk this knowingly is a grave offence according to Jewish law. Even if one gives Solomon the benefit of the doubt, that is, assumes that he is going against the law to establish male dominance and restore God's divine scheme for the sexes, his is a most reckless act. Were the queen wearing white, he should keep his distance.

This conjecture that the queen was observing herself for residual discharges of blood, which is admittedly a speculative reading of Saadiah's account, calls for further conjecture and analysis by modern readers. The punishment for wanton disregard of the laws of purity is *kārēt*, from the Hebrew root *krt*, meaning 'to cut, cut off or down' (Lev 18:29). An enigmatic biblical concept, understood by the rabbis as 'premature demise [brought about by divine intervention]', *kārēt* may also reflect an ancient practice of 'banishment', that is, being cut off from one's homeland and polity. All this being the case, the person resulting from the carnal act, Nebuchadnezzar, carries out the judgment of *kārēt* himself.

37. *Midr. Song of Songs* 9. In the larger discussion of Solomon's behavior, there is the suggestion that in his activities with women he was not sensitive to Jewish practice. Note the commentary on 1 Kgs 11:1–2: "King Solomon loved many foreign women . . . of the nations concerning which the Lord said, 'You shall not mingle with them nor shall they mingle with you; for surely they will turn away your hearts after their god'; Solomon clung to them [the foreign women] out of love." Rabbi Joshua ben Levi understood this to mean that Solomon allied himself with these foreign women, though forbidden by Deut 7:3–4: "You shall not marry among them nor give your daughter to their son or take for your son their daughter. [For they will turn your son from me and he shall worship foreign Gods; whereupon the wrath of God will be upon you and he will quickly destroy you.]" Rabbi Simeon ben Jochai understood love to mean fornication, that is, Solomon was driven by unbridled passion. On the other hand, Rabbi Jose ben Halafta suggests that Solomon loved them in order to "draw them close, convert them and bring them under the wings of the Divine Presence."

After laying the land waste and destroying the temple, the Babylonian monarch exiles the Israelites, thus denying his father's other progeny the privilege of ruling their people and living in their own land. Following the Babylonian conquest, the Davidic monarchy comes to a sudden end. Here is a still greater and perhaps ultimate irony. In putting the queen in her place, Solomon carries out God's charge to uphold the world as it is and as it should be. Men are meant to rule over women. This fact, because it is the natural order of things, is a biological as well as political imperative (in any event, this is how the author sees the world). But by creating a complex biology for women, God has established a natural phenomenon that grants them power that it denies men. This is to say, the biological cycle of women allows for both child-bearing and ritual pollution. As the quintessential naturalist—a reputation already established in the Hebrew Bible—Solomon is aware of all these issues when he gives in to carnal pleasure. By his moral failing, he is personally responsible for the catastrophe of 586 B.C.E.

Additional Musings

Solomon's career, as illustrated in the books of Kings and Chronicles, is essentially a play of three acts: the obtaining of the throne and the consolidation of power; the formation of an aggressive foreign policy designed to expand Israelite influence; and finally the tragic events of Solomon's later rule when, owing to his laxity, Israel's stringent monotheism is compromised by the inroads of assimilation. In each part of this drama there are foreign women who serve as markers for the time. At the outset of his career, there is his marriage to the Egyptian Pharoah's daughter (1 Kgs 11:1–8). Once he is well established in power, there is the visit of the Queen of Sheba. And, in the final act he falls victim during his old age to his passion for foreign women. That is, he allows his beloved foreign wives and concubines to "turn his heart after other Gods" (1 Kgs 11:1–8).

In each instance there is, according to Jewish tradition, a price to pay for involvement with foreign women. Because he allows polytheism to enter his kingdom, the unified and powerful realm that is largely his achievement is undone. Following his death, the Israelite polity is divided, and half of the former realm is lost to the Davidic family. His offspring dwell in Judea with their capital in Jerusalem; one of his servants starts a rival dynasty in the northern parts of the land (1 Kings 12–14). As we have seen, the interlude with the Queen of Sheba brings the bitter fruit of Nebuchadnezzar, that is, the destruction of the temple, the loss of Jewish sovereignty, and exile. Finally, moving backwards in time, there is his marriage to the Pharaoh's daughter, an event that is to occasion the final and most disastrous consequence of Solomon's involvement with foreign women.

The rabbis report[38] that at the moment of the union, the angel Gabriel descended from the heavens and placed a reed in the sea. The reed then gathered a great sandbank around it, upon which was built the city of Rome. Hence, the marriage to the foreign queen, the descendant of the great enemy of Solomon's ancestors, gave rise to the future and most destructive of all Israel's enemies, the empire that would destroy the Second Temple, end Jewish sovereignty on the sacred soil of Palestine called *ereṣ yiśrā᾿ēl*, and initiate a diaspora that would continue for two millennia. The long-range implications of dealing with foreign women, menstruating or otherwise, are obviously calamitous in the eyes of the authors. Having pursued dangerous liaisons with the opposite sex, often in total disregard of the laws of purity, Solomon occasions no less than three national disasters, the Babylonian captivity among them.

Unfortunately for Solomon, those responsible for chronicling and otherwise commenting about his life and times wrote from the perspective of later ages and values, when the paradigms explaining Jewish experience were firmly fixed. The Israelites of early monarchic times were not concerned with marriages to foreign women and were, it would appear, given to a religious syncretism that was unacceptable to later writers of the Hebrew Bible and their postbiblical successors. Seen from the perspective of postexilic Judaism, that is, the periods following both the Assyrian and Babylonian captivities, the integrity of shattered Israelite polities required identifiable markers enabling the faithful to distinguish between the people chosen by God and their ways, and the polytheist "others" and their ways. These markers, which included strict regulations concerning marriage, dietary laws, and a host of ritual practices, were then legitimized by an appeal to a sacred history, an appeal that combined residual memories of an authentic past with fictive elements of a tendentious contemporary historiography. The rabbis, in turn, continued this process, drawing a hedge around the earlier legislation to preserve what was perceived as its basic intent, while substituting imaginative legends and folkloric tales for the vivid and highly schematic narratives of the biblical chroniclers. In both biblical and postbiblical writings, the retelling of the past produced a history that was at the same time remembered, embellished, and all too often, invented. How else would a religious culture with a revealed tradition in need of continuous and changing interpretation reflect about a history that modern Western scholars see as the sum of discrete occurrences, each with its own context?

38. *B. Sanh.* 21b.

The Semantics of Loss: Two Exercises in Biblical Hebrew Lexicography

Baruch A. Levine

This study examines two Biblical Hebrew lexemes whose meaning has not been fully realized. It is shown that Biblical Hebrew ḥālaq 'to be lost, disappear, perish' is a homonym of ḥālaq 'to split, divide, apportion'. Proper recognition of its nature alters our understanding of a number of biblical passages. It is further shown that the semantic range of Biblical Hebrew ʾābad encompasses the meanings of two probable Akkadian cognates, abātu A 'to destroy, ruin' and abātu B, a stative verb connoting absence and flight. Failure to recognize these two sets of meanings for the verb ʾābad has likewise prevented a proper understanding of certain biblical passages.

My first introduction to the scholarship of Jonas Greenfield was in the form of his two early articles, both entitled "Lexicographical Notes."[1] These studies, which have been followed by many similarly enlightening inquiries into the meanings of words, are models of method and analysis and have set a lasting standard of excellence and insight. It is therefore appropriate in a study honoring Jonas Greenfield to engage in further lexicographical inquiry.

Among the problems that complicate the lexicographical analysis of Biblical Hebrew (henceforth BH) is that of homonyms. The first of our two exercises focuses on a proposed homonym, BH *ḥālaq* 'to be lost, to disappear, to perish', and it is therefore important to discuss the arguments for and against the acknowledgment of homonyms in a given language. Some lexicographers of the Semitic languages have held that

Author's note: I wish to thank my colleague Anson Rainey for discussing the problems treated in this article with me. At one point I even discussed the verb *ḥālaq* with Jonas Greenfield himself; as always, his comments were most enlightening.

1. J. C. Greenfield, "Lexicographical Notes I," *HUCA* 29 (1958) 159–203; idem, "Lexicographical Notes II," *HUCA* 30 (1959) 141–51.

originally homonymous roots tend to coalesce in time, a process sometimes referred to as "contamination," and as a result they lose their distinctive meanings. In this view, biblical writers may no longer have been aware of distinctive roots and meanings, even when they were clearly identifiable. This approach to etymology and semantics hardly encourages the search for or acknowledgment of homonyms in BH; in fact, the very existence of homonyms as a phenomenon of language is often downplayed by Semitists in favor of polysemic connotations, all deriving from a single root.

The present investigation proceeds from the assumption that the phonemic inventory produced by speakers of a given language and recorded by its writers in literate societies is actually fairly limited. This situation gives rise to homophones and homographs, words that sound alike and/or are written alike but have no etymological connection to each other.

It would be logical to postulate such a process for BH, which is known to us solely from written documents and whose alphabet represents a shortened version of what was a longer West Semitic orthography. It was inevitable that certain originally distinct phonemes would combine. But, even when no such orthographic or phonic reduction in the writing system is to be assumed, we may have genuinely homonymous roots merely because the phonemic inventory of BH was limited. Furthermore, the dialectology of BH shows a high degree of interpenetration with other Semitic languages, so that lexicographical input from diverse sources may have added to the number of homonyms.

In the case of BH there is yet another factor that tends to impede the identification of homonymous lexemes, namely, the Masoretic vocalization system—the reading of the biblical text as it has been received. Long ago H. L. Ginsberg illustrated by clear examples how this system masks morphological realizations of known roots in BH (such as the internal *Qal* passive, for example) and at times even reads functional lexemes out of existence.[2] It is all well and good to try to understand the basis for the Masoretic pointings, but the lexicographer should not be restrained from considering alternative readings of the same orthographic text that would reveal new meanings.

The second of our examples provides a subtle contrast to the phenomenon of homonyms, representing an instance of what has been called "dialectal interpenetration." We have learned that BH *ʾābad* enjoys a broader semantic range than had been thought, for as it turns out it connotes not only substantial loss, but absence and distance as aspects of

2. H. L. Ginsberg, "Behind the Masoret," *Tarbiz* 5 (1933–3) 208–23 [Hebrew].

loss. As such, BH *ʾābad* comprehends the semantic range of two Akkadian roots, *abātu* A, primarily an active-transitive verb consistently connoting substantial loss, ruin, destruction, death; and *abātu* B, which connotes only absence, flight, vanishing, and the like. In other words, BH *ʾābad* may in some instances mean what Akkadian *abātu* B means. In fact, BH *ʾābad* may be cognate with both of these homonymous Akkadian roots, which are occasionally confused even in Akkadian itself. An awareness of the lexicographical situation in Akkadian suggested that we were missing something in our understanding of the semantic range of BH *ʾābad*. An investigation of Ugaritic *abd* shows that the situation in BH had been anticipated, because Ugaritic *abd* also expresses both meanings: substantial loss as death, and loss as removal and distancing.

It is my overall experience that, more often than not, biblical writers exhibited considerable subtlety in their choice of words and that, consequently, the modern reader of the Hebrew Bible ought not to be content with surface meanings and leveled translations. Both of the present exercises will, it is hoped, endorse this perception.

Biblical Hebrew ḥlq

Loss as Absence and as Extinction: Biblical Hebrew *ḥālaq* 'to disappear, be lost, to perish'; *ḥillēq* 'to disperse, drive away, to destroy, to cause the loss of land'.

A perusal of the lexica, from Gesenius[3] to *HALAT*,[4] shows that the etymology of the BH root *ḥ-l-q* is complex. Two definitions have dominated the discussion of BH *ḥ-l-q* until relatively recently, as we learn from the presentation of these phemonena in *HALAT*: (1) *ḥ-l-q* I, a stative verb 'to be smooth', and in the *Hiphil*, with active-transitive force: 'to smoothen', in various ways, ranging from hammering metal (Isa 41:7), to speaking with a smooth tongue. (2) *ḥ-l-q* II, an active-transitive verb 'to split, divide, apportion', connotations clearly attested in BH both in the simple stem and in the *Piel*, with intensive force.

HALAT adds *ḥ-l-q* III 'to be lost, die, perish', citing cognates in Ugaritic, Akkadian, Ethiopic, and Tigre. However, only Lam 4:16, together with Ps 17:14, itself not a valid example, are singled out as possibly attesting this root in BH, even though more is now known about the workings of this verb.

3. H. F. W. Gesenius, *Thesaurus Philologicus* (Leipzig, 1835) 483–85.
4. L. Koehler and W. Baumgartner, *HALAT* (4 vols.; Leiden, 1967–90) 1.309–10.

It is not my purpose here to attempt a full resolution of the etymological problems attendant upon BH *ḥ-l-q* in its various realizations. On the face of it, the meanings listed for both *ḥ-l-q* I and II in *HALAT*'s classification are attested for Arabic *ḫalaqa*, which means both 'to smoothen' and 'to divide, measure, form'.[5] It is customary, however, for Arabic lexicographers to list homographic roots under the same entry, and it is likely that Arabic *ḫalaqa* itself may express more than one original root.

In any event, my concern here is with Ugaritic *ḫlq* and Akkadian *ḫalāqu* and what they have to teach us about BH usage. Whatever we decide about other sets of meanings, this set is clear and unambiguous in Ugaritic and Akkadian. I will now examine the usage of the root that *HALAT* lists as *ḥ-l-q* III and to trace its path in BH. In my view, there is no valid basis for associating BH *ḥ-l-q* III, the cognate of Akkadian *ḫalāqu* and Ugaritic *ḫlq*, with notions of division, apportionment, or smoothness; it is simply a separate root, notwithstanding its phonetic identity with Arabic *ḫalaqa*.

Comparative Evidence

I begin with the ancient Near Eastern comparative evidence as background. Ugaritic poetry attests *ḫlq* as a parallel word to *mt* 'he died, he is dead'. This comparative observation on the meaning of BH *ḥ-l-q* was first offered by Dahood,[6] who cited a passage in the myth of Baal and Mot,[7] where we read of the death of Baal:

mǵny.lbᶜl.
npl.la/rṣ.
mt.aliyn.bᶜl
ḫlq.zbl.bᶜl.arṣ

We two arrived at Baal,
He had fallen to the ground.
"Dead is Mighty Baal;
Perished is the prince, lord of earth!"[8]

5. *Lane's Arabic-English Lexicon* (London, 1855) 1.799–803, s.v. *ḫalaqa*. Lane lists the first meaning of Arabic *ḫalaqa* as 'to measure' and then proceeds to notions of creation, bringing things into existence according to a model. Meaning 12 is 'it was, or became smooth', in the sense of being without fractures or being worn smooth. There are nouns such as *ḫalqun* 'a share or portion' and adjectives like *aḫlaqun* 'smooth'.

6. M. Dahood, "Hebrew-Ugaritic Lexicography II," *Bib* 45 (1964) 408; idem, "Hebrew-Ugaritic Lexicography IV," *Bib* 47 (1966) 406.

7. J. C. L. Gibson, *Canaanite Myths and Legends* (2d ed.; Edinburgh, 1978) 73 (5 vi 8–10).

8. Text: ibid.; my translation.

As noted by Dahood, Ugaritic *ḫlq* is cognate with Akkadian *ḫalāqu* 'to disappear, vanish, to become missing or lost, to perish; to escape, flee'. The Mesopotamian lexical series list as synonyms of *ḫālaqu* Akkadian *nabūtu* 'fled, gone' (from *abātu* B) and *narqū* 'distant, away'. Sumerian ba.úš ba.an.záḫ is translated *im-tu-ut iḫ-li-iq* 'he died, he perished', which immediately recalls the Ugaritic parallelism *mt*//*ḫlq* (CAD H 36–40). In the D-stem, Akkadian *ḫulluqu* has a wide range of meanings, including 'to cause a loss, allow to escape, remove, destroy, ruin'.[9]

It is telling that the Semitic root realized as Akkadian *ḫalāqu* and as Ugaritic *ḫlq* also occurs in the El Amarna correspondence. Furthermore, in the El Amarna dialect it develops distinctive connotations and is cast both in the usual Akkadian morphology and in West Semitic verbal patterns. These facts of distribution and morphology demonstrate the rootedness of this verb in West Semitic, quite apart from its occurrence in Ugaritic and BH.

Albright[10] recognized a West Semitic *yiqṭal* form of *ḫalāqu* in EA 274:14, the third-person feminine singular *tiḫlaq*, in a passage later cited by M. Greenberg[11] because of its relevance to the Hapiru question:

> *yi-ki-im* LUGAL *be-li* KUR-*šu iš-tu qa-te* LÚ.MEŠ SA.GAZ.MEŠ *la-a te-eḫ-la-*[*a*]*q* URU.KI URU *Ṣa-pu-na*
>
> Let the king, my lord, rescue his land from the hands of the SA.GAZ (= Ḫapiru). Let not your city, Ṣapuna, be lost.

A. F. Rainey explains that the standard Akkadian G-stem of the present future would be *iḫalliq* in the relevant clause, since the thematic vowel of this verb is *-i-* and since in Akkadian *ālu* 'city', the antecedent of the verb, is masculine.[12] But in West Semitic languages, words for 'city' are feminine, and since the Barth-Ginsberg law applies, the thematic vowel of the G-stem becomes *-a-*. The form *tiḫlaq*, with 'city' as antecedent, must therefore represent the third feminine singular.

9. F. C. Fensham ("Malediction and Benediction in Ancient Near Eastern Vassal-Treaties and the Old Testament," *ZAW* 74 [1962] 5) calls attention to the use of Akkadian *ḫalāqu* in the curse sections of vassal treaties found at Ugarit, where D-stem *ḫulluqu* may characterize in a general way the specified destruction to be brought upon all who violate the treaty.

10. W. F. Albright, "Two Little Understood Amarna Letters from the Middle Jordan Valley," *BASOR* 89 (1943) 17 n. 60.

11. M. Greenberg, *The Ḫab/piru* (AOS 39; New Haven, 1955) 46.

12. A. F. Rainey, "The Barth-Ginsberg Law in the Amarna Tablets," *ErIsr* 14 (Ginsberg Volume; 1978) 11.

There are additional attestations of the verb *ḫalāqu* in the West Semitic morphological pattern, including D-stem forms. An example occurs in EA 197:33–34:

> *u an-nu-ú PN qa-du PN yu-ḫa-li-qu* KUR *A-bi*
>
> And now, whereas PN together with PN caused the loss of the land of Apu . . .

So much for the verb *ḫalāqu* in West Semitic morphology. Moran, in his discussion of EA 197, offers a further insight concerning usage of the verb *ḫalāqu* in the El Amarna correspondence. It seems that D-Stem *ḫulluqu*, however it may be cast morphologically, always has as its direct object a location, a land, or a city. This leads Moran to state: "The 'destruction' is not necessarily material, but most often the loss by the Egyptians of political control."[13] When G-stem *ḫalāqu* has as its subject a place, as is the case in EA 274:14 cited above, this is also the functional sense of the verb.

In summary, we are able to trace the extended history and the wide distribution of cognates of BH *ḥ-l-q* in West Semitic, in Ugaritic, and in the El Amarna dialect. We are not dealing with merely another Akkadian cognate, although even such a situation ought not to deter us from the enterprise of comparative lexicography.

Biblical Evidence

The following suggested attestations of BH *ḥ-l-q* (III) are presented for consideration.

ḥālaq libbām (Hos 10:2)

It is this occurrence of a verb *ḥālaq* that first suggested to me the presence in BH of a cognate of Akkadian *ḫalāqu* 'to disappear, to vanish, to become missing or lost, to perish', although I was later to learn that others had found the realization of this root elsewhere in the Hebrew Bible. In the course of assessing Ginsberg's theory of Hosean influences on Deuteronomy,[14] I found myself attempting to make sense out of Hos 10:1–8, a powerful critique of northern Israelite religiosity in the third quarter of the eighth century B.C.E.[15]

13. W. L. Moran, *Les Lettres d'El Amarna* (Littératures anciennes du Proche-Orient 13; Paris, 1987) 289 n. 1.

14. H. L. Ginsberg, *The Israelian Heritage of Judaism* (New York, 1982) 19–24.

15. B. A. Levine, Review of *The Israelian Heritage of Judaism*, by H. L. Ginsberg, in *AJS Review* 12 (1987) 143–57.

Hos 10:1–2, which opens the oracle, presents a mixed metaphor in which Northern Israel is compared to a vine that had been fruitful but was now ravaged and broken. The more prosperous this society became, the more altars and cultic stelae were erected. But the lavish endowment of the cult came to an abrupt halt when the fortunes of the society changed dramatically for the worse. The people promptly turned against the royally sponsored cult and tore down their altars. I translate as follows:

> Israel is a ravaged vine;
> His fruit is like him (*piryô yišweh lô*).
> As his fruit increased,
> So did he proliferate altars.
> But their devotion is lost (*ḥālaq libbām*),
> Now that they have experienced misfortune.
> He pulls down their altars,
> Ruins their cultic stelae (Hos 10:1–2).[16]

The Hebrew *ḥālaq libbām* in v. 2 has usually been taken in one of two ways: to some it meant 'their heart is deceitful', a notion derived from *HALAT*'s *ḥ-l-q* I 'to be smooth, slick'. Just as smooth lips, tongues, and mouths speak deceitfully (Ps 55:22; Prov 2:16, 5:10, 7:5, 26:28), so would a 'smooth' heart be untrue. Thus, Ps 12:3: *śĕpat ḥălāqôt bĕlēb wālēb yĕdabbērû* 'with smoothened lips, they speak with two minds (literally: with one heart and another)'. Alternatively, *ḥālaq libbām* has been taken to mean 'their heart is divided', in the sense of being uncommitted, disloyal, from *ḥ-l-q* II 'to be split, divided'. This would, however, constitute a virtually unique case of the stative sense for *ḥ-l-q* 'to divide, apportion', which elsewhere has active-transitive force in the simple stem.

Perusing the concordances and the lexica, one will usually find *ḥālaq libbām* of Hos 10:2 listed under two entries, with a question mark in both! Some have even suggested vocalizing consonantal *ḥlq* as a *Pual* form, *ḥullaq*, to produce the sense of being divided.

Undoubtedly sensitive to the weakness of existing renditions, the translators of the NJPSV took this verse differently. The metaphor of the vine was carried over into v. 2, so that it is "the heart" of the vine that is split, not the hearts of the people. A note refers the reader to 2 Sam 18:14,

16. In this translation the Hebrew words *ʿattâ yeʾĕšāmû* in Hos 10:2, which follow *ḥālaq libbām*, are understood as stating the cause for Northern Israel's loss of devotion. Misfortune undermined faith. (In the NJPSV, misfortune is conveyed by the words *ḥālaq libbām* 'their boughs are split'.) The stative verb *ʾāšēm* may connote the punishment of guilt incurred, not just the guilt itself or feelings of guilt. As a matter of fact, the connotation of punishment seems to be part of Hosea's diction (cf. Hos 4:15, 14:1).

where we read that Absalom was caught by his hair in the branches of an oak tree and remained alive 'in the thickness of the oak' (*bĕlēb hāʾēlâ*).

Still others have suggested emending *ḥālaq* to *ḥālap* 'to pass away', conveying the sense that the heart of the people, namely, their devotion or affection, had left them. This interpretation is certainly closer to what we would expect in context and, curiously, it is one of the precise connotations conveyed by Akkadian *ḫalāqu*, making it unnecessary and undoubtedly incorrect to emend the Masoretic Text.

There are two principal sets of emotions, attitudes, and resulting relationships expressed by Hebrew *lēb* 'heart, mind' that may shed light on the meaning of enigmatic *ḥālaq libbām* in Hos 10:2, once the Akkadian-Semitic meanings of *ḫalāqu* 'to pass away, flee, disappear' are brought to bear on the interpretation of this verse. The two are courage and devotion. With respect to both, notions of closeness and distance and of fullness and loss alternate in biblical usage. Hebrew *lēb* as 'courage' is not difficult to document. Thus Jer 4:9: 'It shall happen on that day, speech of YHWH, that the courage of the king shall be lost and the courage of the princes (*yōʾbad lēb hammelek wĕlēb haśśārîm*); that the priests shall be desolate, and the prophets shall be stunned'. This is, of course, the image of "losing heart," and the fact that the stative verb *ʾābad* is used to express this emotional state is significant. After all, Akkadian *abātu* B 'to be lost, perish' is a synonym of *ḫalāqu* in the Sumero-Akkadian lexical series, as noted above. The loss of courage is also conveyed by the idiom *nāpal lēb* 'the heart fell' (1 Sam 17:32); and 'to discourage' others, to nullify their courage, is conveyed by the idiom *hēnîʾ lēb* (Num 32:7, 9; cf. similar images in Josh 14:8; Isa 35:3–4, 46:8; Jer 48:41, 49:22). It is possible, therefore, that *ḥālaq libbām* in Hos 10:2 means 'they lost their courage'.[17]

But it is probably the loss of devotion that best suits the immediate context of Hos 10:2 after all. In Isa 29:13–14 this state of mind is conveyed by the image of the distant heart:

> The LORD said:
>
> Whereas this people draws near in [the words of] of his mouth, and with his lips honors me, he has distanced his heart from me (*wĕlibbô riḥaq mimmennî*), so that their worship of me is merely the practiced duty of men—for that reason do I persist in dazing this people, dazing them over and again, so that the

17. CAD H 37, in the lexical section, cites OB LU part 4:21: lú.šà.šu.gul.ag = *ša li-ib-*⸢*ba-šu*⸣ *ḫu-ul-*⸢*lu-qu*⸣ 'one whose heart has vanished', perhaps a coward or a weakling. This is close to being an exact parallel to BH *ḥālaq libbām*, but because there is no context to inform us clearly what 'vanished heart' means, we are back where we started.

wisdom of his sages is lost, and the discernment of his analysts is obscured.

Actually, one could just as well read *wĕlibbô rāḥaq mimmennî* 'though his heart has become distant from me', introducing the stative sense of the simple stem, instead of the *Piel riḥaq*. In any event, usage of the verb *rāḥaq* 'to be distant' recalls the fact, noted above, that one of the synonyms of Akkadian *ḫalāqu* in the Sumero-Akkadian lexical series is *narqū* 'distant'. One is reminded of Jer 12:2b: 'You are near in their mouth, but distant (*wĕrāḥôq*) from their kidneys'.

That the image of the distant heart is a way of expressing loss of devotion is reflected in such idioms as 'to steal away the heart' (*gānab lēb)* in 2 Sam 15:16 and 'to remove the heart' (*hēsîr lēb*) in Job 12:24, as well as 'to turn the heart away' (*hēšîb lēb*) in Ezra 6:22. Conversely, restoration of loyalty is expressed as 'the heart shall return' (*wĕšāb lēb*), in 1 Kgs 12:27. This idea is expressed most dramatically in Mal 3:24: "He shall 'restore the heart' (*wĕhēšîb lēb*) of fathers to sons, and the heart of sons to their fathers," and so forth.

Come to think of it, Hos 10:1–2 appears to resonate the thought earlier conveyed in Hos 7:11:

> Ephraim behaved like a stray pigeon,
> Showing no fidelity (*ʾên lēb);*
> They called out to Egypt,
> They went to Assyria.

Masoretic *wayyēḥālēq ʿălêhem laylâ* (Gen 14:15)

As the consonants are pointed, this *Niphal* form, derived by the Masoretes from *ḥ-l-q* 'to divide', is usually taken to convey the sense of detachment, of deployment in units. I would translate: 'He detached himself against them at night, he and his officers, and slew them'. Abram had mustered his forces (if that is what *wayyāreq* in the preceding verse means), attacked the invading kings, and routed them, pursuing them to a point all the way north of Damascus.

And yet this rendering is somewhat forced and glosses over a syntactic and a morphological irregularity. We would expect the *Niphal* of *ḥ-l-q* 'to divide, apportion' to refer to something that happened to Abram and his forces; that they were themselves split up or divided into units. In similar circumstances, we read that Jacob split up his children (the Hebrew is *wayyaḥaṣ* 'he divided in half') when he saw Esau and his forces approaching (Gen 33:1). And yet, the occurrence of the *Niphal* in an indirect object clause, *wayyēḥāleq ᶜălêhem,* inevitably carries the action to the others, to 'them', and the *Niphal* thus loses its reflexive force. The verb now impacts its object, and this is strange for the *Niphal* stem.

If we are free to vocalize the verb as a *Qal* form and accordingly read *wayyeḥelaq ᶜălêhem laylâ,* deriving the resultant form from *ḥ-l-q* III in the sense 'to flee', the following translation becomes possible: 'He fled past them at night, he and his officers, and slew them'. Reference to nighttime is, after all, suggestive of stealth, and we would have a typical maneuver whereby one force moves behind the other and then attacks.

Masoretic *ᵓêzeh hadderek yēḥāleq ᵓôr* (Job 38:24)

The problems in this descriptive statement are similar to those we encountered in Gen 14:15, where a *Niphal* pointing also occurs. Here it seems almost compelling to vocalize the verb as a *Qal* form and to read *yeḥĕlaq ᶜôr,* deriving the verbal form from *ḥ-l-q* III 'to flee, vanish, be lost', which yields the translation: 'Where is the path by which light vanishes?' This is the second instance where the Masoretes used a *Niphal* pointing in their effort to elicit meaning, most probably because they did not know of BH *ḥ-l-q* III, the cognate of Akkadian *ḫalāqu* and Ugaritic *ḫlq.*

In anticipation of what will be discussed presently, the complete verse should be translated, because, among other things, it shows the similarity in meaning of *ḥ-l-q* III in the *Piel* stem (*ḥillēq*) and Hebrew *hēpîṣ* 'to disperse'. I would therefore render Job 38:24 as follows: 'Where is the path by which light vanishes, [by which] the East wind is driven (*yāpēṣ*) over the earth?'

I have taken *Hiphil yāpēṣ* as an elliptical stative. Of course, one could also take consonantal *yḥlq* as a *Piel* form and translate: 'Where is the path by which "he" disperses (*yĕḥallēq*) light; [by which] "he" drives the East wind over the earth?'

Masoretic *laḥăliq miššām bĕtôk hāᶜām* (Jer 37:12)

As pointed by the Masoretes, the Hebrew *laḥăliq* would represent a syncopated form of *lĕhaḥăliq,* the *Hiphil* stem. It is inconclusively derived either from *ḥ-l-q* I 'to be smooth', hence causative *Hiphil* 'to smoothen', or as a *Hiphil* stative, 'to slip'; or from the root *ḥ-l-q* 'to divide', hence 'to break away', or the like. I would accordingly translate '. . . to slip away from there / to break away from there in the midst of the people'. Concordances and lexicons often list the unique form *laḥăliq* under more than one entry, with question marks.

Why not vocalize consonantal *lḥlq* as the *Qal* infinitive *laḥălôq* and derive this form from *ḥ-l-q* III 'to flee, be lost'? This would yield a clear sense: 'Jeremiah departed from Jerusalem to travel to the land of Benjamin, so as to flee (*laḥălôq*) from there in the midst of the people'.[18]

Perhaps the most enlightening results of postulating the verbal root *ḥ-l-q* III become evident in the Masoretic *Piel* realizations, which yield connotations very similar to those known for the D-stem *ḫulluqu* 'to make disappear, cause a loss, ruin, destroy' in Akkadian and West Semitic. In any number of instances, what has usually been understood as an intensive connotation of *ḥālaq* 'to divide, cut' should probably be understood as having a causative sense, transmitted by the *Piel* stem, of *ḥ-l-q* III. We have already raised this possibility in the discussion of Jer 37:12. Following are clear examples.

ʾăḥallĕqēm bĕyaʿăqōb waʾăpîṣēm bĕyiśrāʾēl (Gen 49:7)

Assuming the root *ḥ-l-q* I 'to divide', this passage has usually been translated along the following lines: 'I shall apportion them / divide them up in Jacob, I shall disperse them in Israel'. Reference is, of course, to the brothers Simeon and Levi, cursed by their father for their violence (Gen 34:25–31). They were to lose their own territories, only to become pariahs among the tribes of Israel.

Would not Jacob's dire words have more force and the parallelism be closer if we were to derive the *Piel ʾăḥallĕqēm* from *ḥ-l-q* III? We could then translate: 'I shall disperse them in Jacob, I shall scatter them in Israel'. This was one of the verses cited by Dahood and others as indicating the presence in BH of a cognate of Akkadian *ḫalāqu*, as is Lam 4:16, which follows.

pĕnê Yhwh *ḥillĕqām, lōʾ yôsîp lĕhabbîṭām* (Lam 4:16)

Once again, deriving the *Piel ḥillĕqām* from *ḥ-l-q* III would yield a superior translation: 'Yhwh's countenance has made them disappear / banished them from sight; He will look upon them no more'.

Masoretic *ḥăbālîm yĕḥallēq bĕʾappô* (Job 21:17)

Dahood cites this enigmatic clause as an example of *ḥ-l-q* III in BH, and he correctly favors a sense other than 'pain, pangs' for Hebrew *ḥăbālîm*. However, the Masoretes probably understood consonantal *ḥblym*

18. Actually, Gesenius (*Thesaurus Philologicus*, 483 [under *Hiphil*, 2]) had the meaning of *laḥălîq* in Jer 37:12 right. He quotes Qimḥi, among others, suggesting the Latin translation *evadendi*. He compares *Hiphil heḥĕlîq* to the Hebrew verbs *mālaṭ* and *pālaṭ*, which connote flight and escape. Of course, he was not aware of Akkadian *ḫalāqu*.

to mean just that, 'pain (the abstract plural), pangs' (Jer 13:8, 22:23, 49:24; Job 39:3), yielding the translation: 'He deals out pain (*ḥăbālîm yĕḥallēq*) in his wrath'.

Now, the Masoretes surely knew of a verbal root *ḥ-b-l* 'to damage, injure, oppress', which is frequently realized in the *Piel* stem, with intensive force (Isa 13:5, 54:16; Mic 2:10; Ps 140:6[?]; Qoh 5:5). For all we know, the sense of 'pain' is itself derived from this very root, as may be the derivation of the name given to Zechariah's second rod, *ḥōbĕlîm* (Zech 11:7, 24). In any event, the Masoretes did not associate *ḥăbālîm* in Job 21:17b with this known root, probably because they did not know of the root we are calling *ḥ-l-q* III. It is quite simple to vocalize consonantal *ḥblym* as *ḥabbālîm*, the *Piel* participle, 'oppressors, robbers' (or possibly as the *Qal* participle *ḥōbĕlîm*). This translation would produce a much better reading of Job 21:17–18:

> How often is the lamp of the wicked extinguished,
> Does their downfall overtake them.
> He drives away oppressors (*wĕḥabbālîm yĕḥallēq*) in his wrath;
> They shall be as straw before the wind,
> Like chaff spirited away by a storm.

wĕʾet ʾarṣî ḥillēqû (Joel 4:2 [3:2])

It is quite possible that the distinctive connotation of *ḫalāqu* in the El Amarna dialect, that of ruin conceived as deprival of political control over a city or land, is expressed in the oracle of Joel 4:1–9 [3:1–9]. The context is mixed, with notions of dividing spoils interacting with realities of exile, so that it is difficult to determine the precise sense of *ḥillēqû* in v. 2. To appreciate this ambiguity it is best to translate vv. 1–3 as I understand them:

> For, behold, in those days and in that time,
> When I shall restore the captivity of Judah and Jerusalem—
> I shall assemble all of the nations,
> And bring them down to the valley of Jehoshapat.
> I shall bring them to trial on the matter of Israel,
>   the people who are my possession,
> Whom they dispersed (*pizzĕrû*) among the nations;
> And [concerning] my land [which] they *expropriated* (*ḥillēqû*).
> They cast lots over my people;
> They traded the young boy for a harlot,
> And the young girl for wine to drink.

The oracle goes on in vv. 4–9 to speak of God's future punishment of the Tyreans and Sidonians, who had occupied Philistia and sold Judeans into slavery to the Ionian Greeks. God will restore his exiled people and, in retribution, the Judeans will then sell young Tyreans and Sidonians to far-off Arabia.

Now, it is certainly proper in context to translate *wĕʾet ʾarṣî ḥillēqû* in Joel 4:2b [3:2b]: 'They divided up my land'. The reference to casting lots over the people in v. 3 might suggest this rendering: the conquerors divided the land among themselves just as they traded the people as slaves.

And yet it would also yield a harmonious translation if we were to understand *Piel ḥillēqû*, as we have, to convey the sense of Akkadian *ḫulluqu* in the El Amarna correspondence, where a land or a city is the direct object. The Tyreans and Sidonians took control of the land; they "ruined" it by depriving the Judeans of control over it.

Biblical Hebrew ʾbd

Loss, Reversible and Irreversible: *ʾābad* 'to flee / to perish'; *ʾibbēd* 'to disperse / to ruin'; and *heʾĕbîd* 'to banish / to destroy'.

The semantic field of BH *ʾābad*, in the simple stem as well as in the *Piel ʾibbēd* and in the *Hiphil heʾĕbîd*, ranges all the way from notions of distance, absence, and separation, 'to flee, be lost, exiled', to notions of extinction, 'to perish, be lost, die, cease to exist'. These sets of meanings are decidedly compatible with each other; they represent a semantic progression or syndrome, and there is therefore no reason to posit two roots in Hebrew. Actually, Akkadian *ḫalāqu*, investigated above, shares a similar semantic range, connoting both loss as disappearing and being missing, and loss as perishing and ceasing to exist. Even in English usage the notion of loss may convey both of these realities.

And yet, Akkadian employs two separate cognates of BH *ʾābad* to comprehend the same semantic range: (1) *abātu* A, basically an active transitive verb meaning 'to destroy, ruin', and in less frequent stative realizations, 'to collapse, fall down'. This verb seems always to connote substantial loss or ruin; (2) *abātu* B, a stative verb attested only in the G-stem and N-stem, which means 'to run away, flee', namely, to be 'lost' from sight or distant. Its principal synonyms in the Mesopotamian lexical series are adjectival *narqū* 'remote', *naparku* 'to abscond, escape', and most significantly, *ḫalāqu* 'to disappear, vanish'. In other words, Akkadian *abātu* A and B, taken together, achieve a semantic range similar in scope to BH *ʾābad*, nothwithstanding aspectual differences between BH *ʾābad* and Akkadian *abātu* A (CAD A/1 41–47).

What is being posited for BH *ʾābad* is actually attested, in a less complete way, for Ugaritic *abd*. In the G-stem and its derivatives, Ugaritic *abd* means 'to perish, die'. Thus, we read in the "Keret Epic" about successive deaths in the hero's family:

wbtmhn.šp̮ḥ.yitbd
wb.pḫyrh.yrṯ

So, in its entirety a family perished,
And from the whole of it—an heir.[19]

What is remarkable in Ugaritic usage is that the D-stem of the verb *abd* has the meaning 'to remove, cast off', in the same way that BH generates the *Piel* connotation 'to disperse'. In a composite Ugaritic magical text, KTU 1.100 + 1.107, recently investigated by Levine and de Tarragon,[20] the infinitive absolute of the D-stem of *abd* recurs in a magical formula for healing venomous snake bites. The gods repeatedly urge the snake charmer on with the following words:

lnh. mlḫš. abd
lnh. ydy. ḥmt

From it (= the snake) let the charmer remove;
From it—let him cast off venom.

The parallelism of *abd*//*ydy* (from *n-d-y* 'to cast off') establishes the sense of D-stem *abd*. The venom was not to be destroyed as such, but rather gathered up in the projected magical procedures of which the magical text speaks.[21]

An awareness of the existence of two roots in Akkadian and of the Ugaritic evidence allows us to resolve most of the ambiguities of BH usage of *ʾābad*, in all of its realized stems. Such perceptions open the door to a clearer understanding of biblical statements on war and conquest, on divine punishment of Israel and of the nations, and on biblical views of history and destiny. This is so whether one concludes that cognates of both of the Akkadian homonyms have coalesced in BH, or whether one decides that, like Akkadian *ḫalāqu*, BH *ʾābad* had an intrinsically broad semantic range that embraces the connotations expressed by both of the Akkadian homonyms. Armed with comparative information, we can sort out two discrete sets of meanings.

19. Gibson, *Canaanite Myths*, 82 (4 i 24–25); my translation.

20. B. A. Levine and J.-M. de Tarragon, "Shapshu Cries Out in Heaven: Dealing with Snake Bites at Ugarit (KTU 1.100 + 1.107)," *RB* 95 (1988) 481–518.

21. Ibid., 496 nn. to line 8.

The notion of loss as ruin and extinction is expressed unambiguously in such biblical passages as Joel 1:11, which describes devastated fields and a ruined harvest: *kî ʾābad qĕṣîr śādeh* 'for the harvest of fields has perished / is ruined'. Similarly, 2 Kgs 9:8 refers to the punitive murder of the wicked house of Ahab: "And the entire house of Ahab shall perish (*wĕʾābad*)!" That is to say, they shall die.

It is the notion of substantial, irreversible loss that generates the causative-factitive reflex 'to destroy, ruin, terminate' in the *Piel* and *Hiphil* stems *ʾibbēd* and *heʾĕbîd*, respectively. This unambiguous sense is expressed in many biblical passages that speak of laying waste to physical structures and of killing human beings (including *Piel*: Num 33:52; Deut 12:2; 2 Kgs 19:18//Isa 37:19; 2 Kgs 21:3; Ezek 6:3, and 22:27; and *Hiphil*: 2 Kgs 10:19; Jer 1:10, 18:7, and 31:28).

Contrast the sense of the simple stem in Joel 1:11 and 2 Kgs 9:8 with the sense of participial *ʾôbēd* in Deut 26:5, correctly translated by Albright[22] as follows: *ʾărammî ʾōbēd ʾābî* 'my ancestor was a fugitive Aramean' (or, 'my ancestor was an Aramean fugitive'). Unfortunately, Albright offered no lexicographical background to explain his rendering. In any event, Jacob's clan did not cease to exist. As Deut 26:5 proceeds to inform us, "and he voyaged southward to Egypt," where he became a large clan.

What recommends seeing a cognate relationship between participial *ʾōbēd* in Deut 26:5 and Akkadian *abātu* B is the occurrence of Akkadian terms meaning 'fugitive(s), deportee(s)' that are formed precisely on the N-stem of *abātu* B 'to flee', namely, *munnabtu, nunnabtūtu,* and related *naʾbūtu.* The phenomenon of the *munnabtūtu* was recently discussed by G. Buccellati, who notes the abundance of references to such uprooted fugitives in Syro-Mesopotamian documents of the Late Bronze Age. Such ancient *deracinés* were a factor in what Buccellati refers to as a cosmopolitan age, before the formation of world empires.[23]

Similar sociopolitical patterns are evident in the Neo-Assyrian Period, a fact that may be more relevant after all to the interpretation of the Deuteronomic creed. In citing the unusual identification, *ʾărammî ʾōbēd* of Deut 26:5, Mazar calls passing attention to a reference in the annals of Sennacherib to "Aramean fugitives."[24] An investigation of this passage has proved to be most enlightening.

Reviewing his eighth campaign in Babylonia, Sennacherib speaks of a certain Shuzubu, a Chaldean, who had rebelled. In a tone reminiscent

22. W. F. Albright, *From the Stone Age to Christianity* (Baltimore, 1940) 181.

23. G. Buccellati, "*ʿApīrū* and Munnabtūtu: The Stateless of the First Cosmopolitan Age," *JNES* 36 (1977) 146–47.

24. B. Mazar, "The Aramean Empire and Its Relations with Israel," *BA* 25 (1962) 98–120.

of what Judg 9:4 has to say about Abimelech's band and what 1 Sam 22:2 has to say about David's men, Sennacherib characterizes Shuzubu's motley entourage:

> lú *A-ra-me ḫal-qu mun-nab-tú a-mir da-me ḫab-bi-lu ṣi-ru-uš-šu ip-ḫu-ru-ma*
>
> Aramean fugitives, the deportee, the murderer, the robber, around him they gathered.[25]

We have, therefore, a parallel in Akkadian of BH *ʾărammî ʾōbēd,* in the plural lú *aramē ḫalqū,* an equivalence that once again points to the interaction of Akkadian *ḫalāqu* and *abātu* B in describing forced migration. Furthermore, the passage in Sennacherib's annals groups together the *munnabtu* 'the deportee' and the Arameans characterized as *ḫalqū* 'fugitives'. It is this sociopolitical context that more accurately characterizes Jacob and his clan, rather than the nomadic way of life, an interpretation early attached to Deut 26:5.[26] This context also informs the relatively late oracle preserved in Isa 27:13:

> It shall happen on that day that a great ram's horn shall be blown, and the fugitives in the land of Assyria (*hāʾōbĕdîm bĕʾereṣ ʾaššûr*) and the deportees in the land of Egypt (*wĕhanniddāḥîm bĕʾereṣ miṣrāyim*) shall come and bow down to YHWH at the holy mountain, in Jerusalem.

The parallelism of *ʾōbĕdîm//niddāḥîm* clarifies the functional sense of the verb *ʾābad.* By whatever words they were described, exile and deportation represented a well-tested policy employed by and against Arameans, Philistines, and Phoenicians during the first half of the first millennium B.C.E., if Amos chap. 1 is any indication. Thus, the God of Israel will bring about the exile of Aram (Amos 1:5) and do the same to the Philistines of Gaza, Ashdod, and Ekron, who for their part had sent large local populations into exile to Edom (Amos 1:6–8). In the same way, the Tyreans were to be punished for deporting a large population from the Levantine coast to Edom (Amos 1:9–10).

An expressive biblical metaphor that reflects these ancient realities of exile and deportation is that of stray animals, "lost" from the flock, those whom a good shepherd would never abandon and would seek to round up. The image of 'stray flocks' (*ṣōʾn ʾōbĕdôt*) became a metaphor for way-

25. D. Luckenbill, *The Annals of Sennacherib* (Chicago, 1924) 42 (col. V, lines 22–23).

26. M. A. Beek, *Das Problem des aramäischen Stammvaters (Deut. xxvi, 5)* (OTS 8; Leiden, 1950) 193–212.

ward Israel, led astray by their shepherds (Jer 50:6–7). In Ezekiel 34 we find the metaphor of improperly tended flocks, who are allowed to wander off without being rounded up, ultimately to be lost for good:

> Oh son of man, prophesy concerning the shepherds of Israel, and say to them, to the shepherds: Thus says the LORD, YHWH: Oh, shepherds of Israel, who have been tending them: Are not the shepherds supposed to tend the flocks? . . . Yet, you failed to strengthen the weak sheep, and the ill one you did not heal, and the one with broken limb you did not bandage, and the outcast (*hanniddaḥat*) you did not bring back, and the stray (*hāʾōbedet*) you did not retrieve (*lōʾ biqqaštem*). So they dispersed (*wattĕpûṣênâ*) without a shepherd (Ezek 34:2–5a, with deletions).

But the God of Israel will rectify the situation and do what a devoted shepherd should:

> I shall tend my flock, and I shall enable them to lie down, says the LORD, YHWH. I shall retrieve the stray (*ʾet hāʾōbedet ʾăbaqqēš*), and the outcast (*hanniddaḥat*) I shall bring back . . ." (Ezek 34:15–16; and cf. 1 Sam 9:3, 20; Ps 119:76).

Now, Akkadian attests only the G-stem and the N-stem of *abātu* B, as has been noted. For the meanings 'to destroy, lay waste, ruin' Akkadian relies exclusively on *abātu* A, in both the G-stem and the D-stem. But along with meanings we would associate with Akkadian *abātu* A, BH generated another set of *Piel* and *Hiphil* meanings that we would associate semantically with Akkadian *abātu* B. Instead of connoting destruction and ruin, these derived forms convey the sense of expulsion and exile. This semantic development was anticipated in Ugaritic, as we have already observed.

The starting point for a discussion of this set of meanings in BH is Jer 23:1–4, which may be seen as an active, causative reflex of Ezek 34:2–5, 15–16, presented above. There, the simple stem predominates; here, the derived stem. In literary-historical perspective, Jer 23:1–4 undoubtedly antedated Ezekiel 34, but for purposes of analyzing the *Piel* forms in BH, it was logical to discuss the simple stems of Ezek 34:2–5 first. But now, observe how Jer 23:1–4 emerges as a counterpoint to Ezekiel 34, so that *Piel ʾibbēd* conveys the active sense of scattering and dispersing flocks:

> Oh shepherds who disperse and scatter (*mĕʾabbĕdîm ûmĕpiṣîm*) the flock of my pasturing, says YHWH. Therefore, thus says YHWH,

> God of Israel, concerning the shepherds who tend my people: You have scattered (*hăpiṣōtem*) my flock, and you have driven them out and have not taken account of them. I hereby hold you to account for the evil of your deeds, says YHWH. I shall gather in the remnant of my flock from all of the lands to which I have banished them and I shall restore them to their sheepfolds, and they shall be fruitful amd increase. I shall place over them shepherds who will tend them, so that they will no longer be afraid or terrified, nor shall they be unaccounted for.

Now, *abātu* B is a synonym of *ḫalāqu* 'to be lost, disappear' in the Mesopotamian lexical series, and, indeed, the parallelism of *ʾibbēd//hēpîṣ* in Ezekiel 34 recalls the synonymous parallelism of *ḥillēq//hēpîṣ* in Gen 49:7, where the objects of the verbs were tribes of people, not flocks.

In view of the repeated use of the verb *biqqēš* 'to seek out, retrieve' as a contrast to *ʾibbēd* 'to disperse, drive out' in the metaphor of the shepherd and his flock, it occurs to me that we have been missing something in our understanding of Qoh 3:5–6, which, inter alia, resonates this very metaphor:

> A time to cast away stones,
> and a time to gather stones.
> A time to embrace,
> and a time to hold back from embracing.
> A time to seek out (*ʿēt lĕbaqqēš*),
> and a time to drive away (*ʿēt lĕʾabbēd*).
> A time to retain,
> and a time to throw away.

So much for the *Piel*, *ʾibbēd* 'to drive away, exile, deport, disperse'. Let us now examine attestations of the *Hiphil*, *heʾĕbîd* in the sense of 'deport, banish, expel', reflecting the same sociopolitical realities that informed the *Piel*.

In writing a commentary on Leviticus, I encountered a problem in Lev 26:41, part of the protracted admonition that serves as an epilogue to the Holiness Code. This modified execration text heaps disaster upon disaster in projecting the consequences of Israel's repeated failure to submit to the divine will. Finally, God decrees exile for his people. As received in the Masoretic Text, Lev 26:41 reads:

> I, moreover, will act with hostility toward them, and I will bring them (*wĕhēbēʾtî ʾōtām*) into the land of their enemies. Perhaps then at last will their thickened heart submit, and they will expiate their transgression.

Since late antiquity it has been recognized that the threatened punishment of exile would not likely be expressed as bringing a people into the land of their enemies, since the verb *hēbîʾ* in BH so often connotes restoration and the attainment of a sought-after destination. Furthermore, the usual syntax is *hēbîʾ ʾel* or *hēbîʾ l-* 'to bring to', *hēbîʾ* + a locative accusative, or even *hēbîʾ min* 'to bring back from', but not *hēbîʾ b-*. The Septuagint translates: καὶ ἀπολῶ αὐτοὺς 'and I will destroy them', undoubtedly reflecting a Hebrew text that read *wĕhaʾăbadtî ʾōtām* instead of *wĕhēbēʾtî ʾōtām*. On this basis, the original text would have threatened that God will bring about the destruction of his own exiled people. Some have postulated that the Hebrew text was consciously emended in antiquity so as to avoid this very idea, thereby producing the text that reads *wĕhēbēʾtî*.

A question remains, however: How is it that the Hebrew text, read and translated by the Septuagint authors and emended by late redactors, would have contained such thoughts in the first place? The truth is that it did not! Most likely, the Septuagint translators misunderstood the meaning of *wĕhaʾăbadtî* in their Hebrew text and failed to perceive the nexus of vv. 38 and 41 precisely because they did not know of an alternate set of meanings borne by the *Qal ʾābad*, namely, 'to flee, wander away', or of the *Hiphil hĕʾebîd* 'to banish, scatter, cause to flee'. They knew only the meaning 'to destroy, ruin' for the *Hiphil* of BH *ʾābad* and, indeed, translated the *Qal* form *waʾabadtem baggōyim* in Lev 26:38 as καὶ ἀπολεῖσθε ἐν τοῖς ἔθνεσιν 'and you will perish among the nations'.

The same limitation of knowledge was what stimulated the redactors to emend the text from *wĕhaʾăbadtî* to *wĕhēbēʾtî*, if, indeed, this is what occurred. Had they correctly understood what the biblical author intended to say, they would not have been troubled by the *Hiphil* of BH *ʾābad*.

More accurately, the text used by the Septuagint translators meant the following:

> You will vanish (*waʾăbadtem*) among the nations, and the land of your enemies will consume you (v. 38).
>
> And I will disperse them (*wĕhaʾăbadtî ʾōtām*) in the land of their enemies (v. 41).

In effect, Lev 26:41 is an alternate way of expressing the thoughts conveyed in Lev 26:33 within an earlier section of the admonition: "And you—I shall scatter (*ʾĕzāreh*) among the nations," and so forth. The present interpretation has the advantage of removing the apparent contradiction between v. 38 and the verses that follow. If *waʾăbadtem* in v. 38

connotes actual extinction, how is it that vv. 39–41 speak of survivors who are contrite and confess their transgressions? One is more or less compelled to assume a process of redaction whereby the severity of an earlier statement was subsequently mitigated. However, if properly understood, the simple stem *ʾābad* in v. 38 and original *Hiphil wĕhaʾăbadtî* in v. 41 both connote exile or deportation, not extinction, and so it is relevant to speak subsequently of exiled remnants and their ultimate fate.[27]

Soon after my work on the final chapters of Leviticus, I found myself studying the poetic sections of Numbers. Bearing in mind what I had learned, namely, that Akkadian *abātu* B connoted flight and remoteness, I expected that in contexts of conquest and war the BH *Hiphil heʾĕbîd,* might convey something like the *Piel ʾibbēd,* namely, 'to banish, deport, disperse'.

In Balaam's fourth oration (Num 24:15–19) we are told that in the future a mighty Israelite warrior-king will conquer Moab and Edom-Seir. The following will be the consequences for Edom-Seir:

> Edom shall be a dispossessed land (*yĕrēšâ*),
> Seir—a land dispossessed by its enemies (*yĕrēšâ ʾōyĕbāyw*);
> While Israel is triumphant.
> Jacob will subjugate them (*wi*[*y*]*rōdēm yaʿăqōb*),
> And deport survivors (*wĕheʾĕbîd śārîd)* from ʿAr.

The overall context indicates the pattern of conquest and dispossession—of subjugation, not of annihilation per se. In a similar vein, Zeph 2:5 is probably predicting that the God of Israel will exile the Philistines from the coastal region:

> Oh, inhabitants of the coastal strip,
> the nation of Cretans;
> The oracle of YHWH [is spoken] against you,
> Canaan, land of the Philistines:
> "I shall depopulate you (*wĕhaʾăbadtîk*),
> Leaving no inhabitants!"

The concluding statement quotes the actual oracle. The prophet goes on to describe how the coastal strip will be reduced to grazing land and

27. In my commentary (*Leviticus* [JPS Torah Commentary; Philadelphia, 1989] 190–92, 275–81), I was still groping with the semantics of BH *ʾābad* and could only suggest, logically, that this verb might not connote total destruction but only a stage in the process. In the light of what has been learned since, the literary interpretation of the Epilogue to the Holiness Code (Lev 26:3–26) will have to be revised.

to predict how the God of Israel will in due time resettle the remnant of Judah in the former territory of the Philistines.

The question of whether, in any given statement, *Hiphil heʾĕbîd* connotes destruction or whether it connotes exile is consequential for our understanding of biblical notions of conquest and of biblical policies for the treatment of native populations. Included as relevant is the Deuteronomist's program for the conquest of Canaan, where such language is employed (Deut 8:20, 9:3). The same ambiguity surrounding *Hiphil heʾĕbîd* affects our understanding of the verb *hikrît* 'to cut off', used by Deuteronomy in speaking of what the God of Israel will do to the Canaanite peoples (Deut 12:29, 19:1). Were the Canaanites to be killed off systematically, or were they to be systematically deported, exiled from the land? It also remains to explore, with the same question in mind, the oracles of Ezekiel 25 against the interior peoples—Ammon, Moab and Edom—where *heʾĕbîd* and *hikrît* occur both separately and in parallelism (Ezek 25:7; and cf. Jer 49:38). Based on my understanding of the semantic range of BH *ʾābad*, it is my view that *Hiphil* forms functioned as part of the political vocabulary and, like such verbs as *Hiphil hôrîš* 'to dispossess' (Deut 9:1, 18:12) and *riḥēq* (Isa 6:12), *hirḥîq* (Ezek 11:16) 'to expel afar', realistically connote deportation rather than annihilation. The same would be true of God's admonition to Israel: exile, not extinction is the threatened punishment.

The interaction of *hikrît* and *heʾĕbîd* also comes into play in the formulation of the penalty of banishment in priestly law. In almost all cases, the law will state: (a) "that person shall be cut off (*wĕnikrĕtâ hannepeš hahîʾ*) from among 'her' kinfolk" (Gen 17:14; Exod 12:15, 19; Lev 7:20); or (b) "I will cause to be cut off (*wĕhikrattî*)" that person (Lev 17:10, 20:3–6). There is little doubt that banishment or ostracism, rather than death, was originally intended as the punishment for the relevant religious offenses. And so, when we encounter a unique instance in Lev 23:30, where instead of *wĕhikrattî*, we read *wĕhaʾăbadtî ʾet hannepeš hahîʾ miqqereb ʿammāh,* we are prompted to translate: 'I will banish that person from among "her" kinfolk'. Banishment is the exile of the individual and his family.

Conclusion

The two exercises here presented illustrate, in a small way, the abundant possibilities afforded by comparative lexicography for adding to our understanding of the Hebrew Bible. Beyond lexicography and philology, the investigation of unrecognized meanings helps to clarify major themes in biblical literature and to bring into focus biblical perceptions of human experience.

The connotations attendant upon the BH roots *ḥ-l-q* and ᵓ*-b-d* relate predominantly to the dire, catastrophic aspect of history and to the down side of human experience. These two roots connote loss, but their precise interpretation reveals that such loss is not always perceived as absolute. These roots also embrace more hopeful connotations: a people exiled may be restored, and those who are distant may return.

Fate, *miqreh*, and Reason: Some Reflections on Qohelet and Biblical Thought

PETER MACHINIST

This paper begins with a discussion of the understanding of fate in religious traditions generally and then in the Hebrew Bible particularly, calling attention to two issues: the relationship between fate and morally guided action on the one hand and the control of fate on the other, whether by a god or gods or by an impersonal, metadivine force. The paper then focuses more closely on the book of Qohelet, which represents perhaps the most explicit and elaborate biblical treatment of fate. An examination of the principal term involved, miqreh, along with several related terms, suggests that for Qohelet death is the overwhelming issue, which serves as the defining boundary for a concept of fate, even as it allows little or no room for the possibility of morally guided action. Even more significant, in reaching these conclusions, Qohelet puts great emphasis on the use of rationality. The paper then discusses how this rationality is expressed in Qohelet and the implications of its presence there—a presence that is not really paralleled elsewhere in the Hebrew Bible—for a possible connection with Greek culture.

Introduction

Fate is a concept that has invited uneasiness when brought into the study of ancient Israelite thought. More than once scholars have argued that it was not merely absent from ancient Israel as reflected in our only real source on the matter, the Hebrew Bible, but fundamentally contradictory to the Israelite world view.[1] If there is an exception, it is usually

Author's note: I should like to thank my student, Hindy Najman, for her critical reading of the manuscript and her most helpful discussion of it with me.

1. See, e.g., A. E. Suffrin, "Fate (Jewish)," in *Encyclopaedia of Religion and Ethics* (New York, 1912) 5.793: "Based on the OT, which on the whole acknowledges freedom of choice, Judaism does not, and consistently cannot, hold the pagan doctrine of Fate."

considered to be in the book of Qohelet. I venture here to reconsider this issue, first by surveying what we might say about fate in the Bible as a whole and then by focusing on the case of Qohelet. In particular, our attention will be directed to a key term in Qohelet, *miqreh*, and through it we shall try to determine what relevance fate may have to the book's perspective and meaning and, in this regard, whether the book is congruent with the rest of biblical literature.

We cannot begin, however, without at least a brief look at definition, all the more because fate has been one of the more slippery terms in cultural parlance. In such instances, one usually goes to the handbooks, and so let me quote a recent characterization by Kees Bolle, in the *Encyclopaedia of Religion*:

> [T]he term fate denotes the idea that everything in human lives, in society, and in the world itself takes place according to a set, immutable pattern . . . . in whatever variation, language, or shade of meaning it occurs, [fate] always retains a basic element of mystery. Fate may be in the hands of some powerful, superhuman being; it may be superior to the gods; it may be accessible to some select individuals. But, quite differently from the case of philosophical determinism, vis-à-vis fate, not only is a certain knowledge possible but also a certain "negotiation" with or even an aversion of fate's decrees.[2]

There are several notions at work in this definition. (1) The lives, at least of humans, move according to preset patterns. (2) The patterns are set and controlled by a superhuman force or forces. (3) The knowledge of these patterns and of the relationships among patterns is only partially accessible to humans at best. And (4), while there is an inevitability to the patterns, events, and behaviors within them occurring as predetermined, there may be points where the patterns can be changed, whether by the superhuman force or by humans with its help. One might add a fifth point: regularly a distinction is made between fate and luck or chance, the latter understood as events with no determination, the former with maximum determination. Yet the interesting thing is that the two concepts often appear within the same framework, as opposed to a concept of morals, in which action is understood to be self-generated and events move along on the basis of reward or punishment by higher forces. The coexistence of fate and luck is not an accident(!). For what looks like luck is often conceived of as an action within a preset pattern whose meaning remains unknown to the humans experiencing it. Although fate and luck, therefore, are not identical, they should be kept together as facets of the same perspective.

2. K. W. Bolle, "Fate," *Encyclopedia of Religion* (New York, 1987) 5.290.

Two areas of ambiguity regularly accompany the definition just given. First, what is the identity of the superhuman force controlling fate? Is it a deity or a group of deities, or is fate an emanation of a "higher" force, to which even the gods are subject? Second, how does the determination of behavior essential to the notion of fate square with the moralistic view that events in the world occur as humans are rewarded or punished by divine forces for their obedience or disobedience to divine will? These two ambiguities are related, for the underlying question is the control of the patterns of action and who or what is responsible: are the gods subject to a higher order; are humans? What, in short, is determined and what is the determiner?

Fate in Ancient Israel—An Overview

The important point in this discussion, as various critics have seen, is the coexistence of perspectives. Religious traditions, it would appear, are not governed totally either by fate or by morally guided action; the situation is normally if not always mixed, and it is the differing balances of fate and morality—the ways the two are present and play off against one another—that serve as the distinguishing mark of each tradition. How, then, does ancient Israel, as reflected in the Hebrew Bible, fit here?

The answer must begin with the salient feature of the biblical religious picture, the sovereignty of the Israelite God. To be sure, the affirmation of this sovereignty in the Hebrew Bible is made against a background of occasional challenges to and qualifications of it, but Yehezkel Kaufmann at least exaggerates in the correct direction when he says, "The Bible knows only one supreme law: the will of God."[3] The question, then, is how the Bible conceives of the manifestation of this divine sovereignty to humans. Here the two perspectives we have been discussing may serve as guides.

Thus, sovereignty may be imagined in moralistic terms: God's demand for human behavior that comports with the rules he has established and revealed and his response when such behavior does or does not appear. That this moralism pervades the biblical text needs hardly any demonstration; one might only recall how it is conceptualized in the covenant with Israel, wherein human actions are given a certain autonomy that can influence, even as they are judged by, God.[4]

3. Y. Kaufmann, *The Religion of Israel* (trans. and abridg. Moshe Greenberg; Chicago, 1960) 73.

4. See, e.g., Jer 26:19, where it is recalled that because Hezekiah and Judah listened to the prophet Micah and turned to God, God in turn 'repented', i.e., 'changed his mind' (*wayyinnāḥem*) about the "evil" he had planned for Judah. This response, however, is not limited

But what of the predetermination and control of events—fate, as we have come to know it? By the Second Temple Period, it is clear that there were Jewish groups that affirmed this as part of God's sovereignty. Perhaps the best-known example is the section on the "Two Spirits" from the so-called *Manual of Discipline* from Qumran:

> From the God of Knowledge comes all that is and shall be. Before ever they [= humanity] existed He established their whole design [*kol maḥšabtam*], and when, as ordained for them, they came into being, it is in accord with His glorious design [*kĕmaḥšebet kĕbôdô*] that they accomplish their task without change [*wĕʾên lĕhiššānôt*] (1QS III 15–16).[5]

Nothing in the Hebrew Bible is quite as explicit and as dramatic as this, but we do have some hints:

(1) There are a number of references, scattered throughout the biblical text, to God's 'plan' (*ʿēṣâ, maḥăšābâ*), which he 'intends' (*yāʿaṣ*) or 'plans' (*ḥāšab*) for human history or, more precisely, for various phases of it. These references, studied by Bertil Albrektson and Wolfgang Werner among others,[6] are reflected as well in certain narratives, like that of Joseph, which subtly or directly describe God as controlling events to his predetermined end. As Joseph says upon finally revealing himself to his brothers:

> And now do not be distressed, or angry with yourselves, because you sold me here; for God sent me before you to preserve life (Gen 45:5, RSV).

(2) Other, scattered references, last collected by Shalom Paul, refer to a heavenly book or roster in which God writes the deeds and ends, for good or for evil, of humans.[7] As Paul and others have made clear, there is ample precedent for such heavenly ledgers elsewhere in the pre-Hellenistic Near East, notably Mesopotamia, and they are elaborated upon in postbiblical Jewish and Christian texts. Significantly, the biblical and later references reveal a certain oscillation about these books concerning whether they record predetermined ends, or rewards and pun-

---

to Israel/Judah in the Bible. As noted, e.g., in Jonah 3:10, God also 'repents' (*wayyinnāḥem*) when the people of Nineveh 'return' (*šābû*) from their "evil" way.

5. See *Scrolls from Qumran Cave I* (Jerusalem, 1972) pls. 130–31; best edition by J. Licht, *Megillat Hassĕrakîm* (Jerusalem, 1965) 90–91. The translation is taken from G. Vermes, *The Dead Sea Scrolls in English* (3d ed.; New York and London, 1987) 64.

6. B. Albrektson, *History and the Gods* (Coniectanea Biblica Old Testament Series 1; Lund, 1967) chap. 5; W. Werner, *Studien zur alttestamentlichen Vorstellung vom Plan Jahwes* (BZAW 173; Berlin, 1988).

7. S. M. Paul, "Heavenly Tablets and the Book of Life," *JANESCU* 5 (1973) 345–53, with a listing of previous scholarship.

ishments that may be changed by the deity in accordance with an individual's behavior.

(3) There are occasional allusions to luck, an event that, as we have seen, may befall a person unsuspectingly, that is, without his understanding why, even if he acknowledges that in some way God is behind it. Here we should include the terms *gād* and *ʾāšēr*, whose use as the names of tribal eponyms leads to punning on the "good luck" involved (Gen 30:11, 13; compare also the mention of *gād* and *mĕnî* in Isa 65:11, which many have identified as deities of fate);[8] and perhaps the word 'life' (*ḥayyîm*), which, as Baudissin argued long ago, may carry the connotation of 'good luck, well-being' (Mal 2:5f.?).[9]

(4) Finally, one should note the occurrences of *gôrāl*, describing the 'lot' that a human could cast to reveal an event or phenomenon already decreed by divine will (e.g., Josh 18:6, 8, 10). The word *gôral* can then come to mean the 'lot' of a person's life, that is, the 'fate' or character of his life that God has given him; and as such, it may be a synonym of *ḥēleq* and *mānâ*, as in Ps 16:5, where all three appear. In the book of Esther yet another synonym of *gôrāl* is introduced, the loanword *pûr*, which appears to designate the favorable moment, presumably arranged by the deity, for humans to enact their plans (Esth 3:7, 9:24).[10]

All these hints—of plans, heavenly books, luck, and lots—are, it should be emphasized, regularly associated by the biblical writers with the sovereign agency of the Israelite God. The matter is concisely expressed in Prov 16:33: "The lot (*gôrāl*) is cast into the lap (*ḥêq*), but the whole disposing thereof is of the Lord (*ûmēYHWH kol-mišpāṭô*)."[11] As Kaufmann has seen with particular force,[12] the Bible is unusual in that it does not seem to reckon with an impersonal, metadivine realm, from which fate might emanate,[13] as found in various other religious traditions, including

8. For the most recent review of the evidence, see W. A. Maier, "Gad," *ABD* 2.863–64; idem, "Meni," *ABD* 4.695.

9. W. W. Baudissin, "Alttestamentliches *ḥajjīm* 'Leben' in der Bedeutung von 'Glück,' " in *Festschrift Eduard Sachau* (ed. G. Weil; Berlin, 1915) 143–61.

10. For recent studies of *gôrāl* and *pûr*, see W. Dommershausen, "Goral," *TWAT* 1.991–98; and W. W. Hallo, "The First Purim," *BA* 46 (1983) 19–29. I thank Ziony Zevit for his suggestion about the meaning of *pûr* in Esther.

11. Brought to my attention by Y. M. Grintz, *EncJud* 13.1280, whose felicitous translation I use.

12. Kaufmann, *Religion of Israel*, 72–73. Compare the fuller treatment in his original Hebrew work, *Tôlĕdôt Hāʾĕmûnâ Hayyiśrĕʾēlît* (Jerusalem and Tel Aviv, 1937) 1/2.448–49.

13. One possible exception might be 1 Sam 6:9, but on this see below, p. 169. For a second possible exception one might go to the passages about *pûr* = *gôrāl* in Esther (3:7, 9:24) noted earlier, which do not explicitly associate it and its activity with a deity. Indeed, as is well known, there is no mention of the Israelite god or other deities at all in the book. Yet this lack of explicitness must be set against Esth 4:14, which, with many commentators (e.g.,

the nonbiblical ancient Near East. Indeed, it is precisely this biblical aversion to an impersonal realm beyond the gods that has been seized upon by some scholars to make little of, if not to dismiss altogether, the role of fate in the biblical world view and so to ignore the very real option in religious traditions, as we have seen, that fate may also be associated with particular deities.[14] In fact, it is not uncommon to have both kinds of fate, or better, both perspectives on fate, coexist in a given tradition: the impersonal, metadivine force and the force controlled by deities. An example, within the nonbiblical Near East, may be found in Mesopotamia.[15]

If the biblical God, then, is responsible for fate, how can we correlate this with the other side of the biblical picture we have examined, God's concern for morally accountable action? The Bible offers no easy and consistent answer, and the difficulty and tension involved in providing one are exemplified in the ambiguity noted above about whether the human "fates" recorded in the heavenly books can be changed. One may also note the narrative of the Exodus plagues, with its oscillating explanation for Pharaoh's refusal to let the Israelites leave their Egyptian abode: God had (pre)determined to harden Pharaoh's heart, or Pharaoh himself hardened his own heart.[16] The point is that such tensions are common to all religious traditions in which fate and moralism co-

---

C. A. Moore, *Esther* [AB 7B; Garden City, N.Y., 1971] 50), I take to indicate that the author of Esther does understand the Israelite god to be operating, in fact controlling the whole, behind the scenes as it were, not unrelated to the pattern in other biblical narratives like that of Joseph. On this basis, it makes sense to suppose that the deity would be understood behind the *pûr* in particular, all the more because in 9:24–26 Haman's expectations for the *pûr* turn out exactly the reverse, to his undoing and the benefit of the Jews, and thus in illustration of the "relief and deliverance from another place" that was signaled in 4:14.

14. So, for example, Suffrin, cited in n. 1 above.

15. Thus, gods like Ea/Enki or Marduk, or the great gods as a group, may be said to 'determine' (*šâmu*) or 'pronounce' (*nabû*) the 'fate' (*šīmtu*) of human individuals or communities (see *šâmu* or *šiāmum, šīmtu* in AHw 1225, 1239; CAD Š/1 359b–363a). On the other hand, in such myths as Enuma eliš and Anzu, there is a 'tablet of fates' (*ṭup šīmāti*) that exists independent of the gods, whose possession by a god gives him power to control, virtually, the workings of the cosmos. For a discussion of "fate" in Mesopotamia and the terms used to describe it, see, e.g., A. L. Oppenheim, *Ancient Mesopotamia: Portrait of a Dead Civilization* (revised ed. completed by E. Reiner; Chicago, 1977) 201–6; and F. Rochberg-Halton, "Fate and Divination in Mesopotamia," in *Vorträge . . . 28. Rencontre Assyriologique Internationale in Wien 6.–10. Juli 1981* (AfO Beiheft 19; 1982) 363–71. Yehezkel Kaufmann, it may be noted, was unwilling to concede much room to individual gods in Mesopotamia and other "pagan" religions controlling fate; for him, these were cultures pervaded by the notion of an impersonal, metadivine realm of fate, just as, by contrast, Israel was pervaded by the notion of a single, all-powerful god without such a realm, who thus controlled fate. See Kaufmann, *Religion of Israel* 21–22, 32–33, 38, 73.

16. For an interesting attempt to make sense of this treatment of Pharaoh in the context of other biblical, Mesopotamian, and later Jewish texts, see T. Frymer-Kensky, "Hattêʾôlôgyâ šel Hāʾāsôn: Šĕʾêlat Haṣṣedeq Hahîstôrî," *Beer-Sheva* 3 (1988) 121–24.

exist, reflecting, one may suppose, the persistent clash between the human will to system and the often harsh reality of disorder.[17]

Nonetheless, as in other traditions, so the Bible is not without efforts to provide some correlation between these two perspectives. Let us turn, therefore, to one text, which forms perhaps the most explicit and elaborate biblical attack on the problem.

Qohelet and Fate

The text is Qohelet (Ecclesiastes in the Greek biblical tradition), and within it the following group of words invite attention: *miqreh* ('happening'); *qārâ* ('to happen'); *pegaʿ* ('meeting'); *ʿēt* ('appointed time'); *zĕman* ('time'); *ʿôlām* ('eternity'); *ḥēleq* ('portion, share'); *maʿăśeh* ('doing'); *ḥešbôn* ('reckoning'); *kĕbār* ('already'); *ʾaḥărît* and *sôp* ('end'); and *rōʾš* and *rēʾšît* ('beginning'). These words form for Qohelet a kind of semantic field, treating what I would call "patterned time." Most of them recur throughout the book, often in clusters as word pairs or in parallel clauses; and this recurrence, which also characterizes a number of other terms in other semantic groupings, is what brings the individual sections of Qohelet together into a larger coherence. The coherence, in other words, does not seem to result from any overall, systematic structure to the book, apart from the *inclusio* established by verses 1:2 and 12:8 and the possibility, worked out by Addison G. Wright, of *gematria*-like groupings by numbers of verses.[18]

A full study of this semantic field is beyond the scope of the present paper. Our discussion, rather, will center on two of the terms involved, with occasional reference to the others: *miqreh* and its verbal root, *qārâ*. The former occurs seven times in Qohelet (2:14, 15; 3:19–20; 9:2, 3), the latter, three times, two of them with *miqreh* (2:14, 15) and once without but with two other "patterned time" terms, *ʿēt* and *pegaʿ* (9:11).[19] Let us begin with a collection of the relevant passages:

17. On this tension as expressed in biblical and later Jewish tradition, with a brief, but insightful discussion of the ways various postbiblical thinkers tried to resolve it, see D. Winston, "Free Will," in *Contemporary Jewish Thought* (ed. A. A. Cohen and P. Mendes-Flohr; New York, 1987) 269–73.

18. This does not mean, of course, that there are no smaller units in Qohelet, for they obviously do exist, e.g., 3:1–8. As for Addison G. Wright's proposal, see "The Riddle of the Sphinx: The Structure of the Book of Qoheleth," *CBQ* 30 (1968) 313–34; "The Riddle of the Sphinx Revisited: Numerical Patterns in the Book of Qoheleth," *CBQ* 42 (1980) 38–51; and "Additional Numerical Patterns in Qoheleth," *CBQ* 45 (1983) 32–43. One recent, and negative, reaction to Wright's proposal is found in M. V. Fox, *Qohelet and His Contradictions* (JSOTSup 71 / Bible and Literature Series 18; Sheffield, 1989) 155–57, 162.

19. Compare the studies of *miqreh* and *qārâ* by H. Ringgren, *TWAT* 7.172–75; and S. Amsler, in *THAT* 2.681–84. There is also the more wide-ranging study of J. Barr, *Biblical Words for Time* (SBT 33; London, 1962), which, however, does not include our two words.

2:14. The wise man has eyes in his head, but the fool walks in darkness. But I have to acknowledge that one *miqreh* happens to (*yiqreh*) them all.

2:15. And I realized that like the *miqreh* of the fool, so too will it happen even to me (*yiqrēnî*). So why then have I been so exceedingly wise? And I realized (thus) that this too is vanity.

3:19–20. For the *miqreh* of humankind and the *miqreh* of beasts are indeed one *miqreh.* As the one dies, so the other, and there is one breath to all. And there is no advantage of humans over beasts, for all is vanity. All go to one place; all was from dust, and all returns to dust.

9:2. One *miqreh* is for all: for the righteous and the wicked, for the good and the evil, for the clean and the unclean, for the one who sacrifices and the one who does not. As is the good, so is the sinner, the one who swears an oath as the one who shuns an oath.

9:3. This is an evil in all that is done under the sun, for one *miqreh* is for all . . . .

9:11. I observed again under the sun that the race does not (belong) to the fleet, nor battle to the warriors, nor again bread to the wise, nor again wealth to the discerning, nor again favor to the knowing, but time (*ᶜēt*) and meeting (*pegaᶜ*) happen to (*yiqreh*) all of them.

Two initial observations on these passages may be made:

(1) The word *miqreh* is here, as its root would suggest, an 'occurrence'—not just any occurrence, but one that is predetermined and defines the life events of humans and animals. It becomes, thus, an abstract concept, and we are not wrong in translating it 'fate'.

(2) The 'occurrence' in question is death, whose salient characteristic, the book proposes, is that it cuts across all moral categories of humans. The argument here is made a fortiori by the observation that death cuts across the human-animal division as well. It is the one clearly immutable event in all life.

If we now take these observations and put them in relation to the other time words and against the book of Qohelet as a whole, several further conclusions follow:

(1) Death as included in *miqreh* is simply the final point (compare the use also of *ᶜēt* for this point in Qoh 7:17) in a planned pattern of activity for each human (and animal), otherwise to be labeled his *maᶜăśeh* (3:11; 8:14, 17; 9:10).[20]

20. Note particularly the statement in Qoh 9:10 that there is no *maᶜăśeh* in Sheol, i.e., after death. See further n. 28 below.

(2) Each one's pattern is under the control of God, who has determined, or better, predetermined it (3:11; cf. 9:1) and knows how it relates to the patterns of others.

(3) These are, in turn, part of the larger pattern of God's activity, his *maᶜăśeh* (3:11, 8:17, 11:5).[21]

(4) The contours of this larger, divine pattern cannot be discerned or affected by humans (3:11, 7:13, 8:17, 11:5), neither can humans grasp their own individual patterns, because God will not allow it, except in regard to the final point, death (3:11, 6:12, 7:14, etc.). In short, humans are unable to figure it all out (compare, for instance, the use of *ḥokmâ* in 7:23). This includes what may survive beyond death, either physically or in terms of memory and influence: humans cannot know whether there is such survival or if there is, of what it consists, and so cannot rely on it (3:21–22; 7:14; 9:4, 10; 11:8).

(5) Humans are left, therefore, to enjoy as they can their *ḥēleq*, that is, what is granted to them by God as part of their activity while alive (2:10, 21; 3:22; 5:17, 18; 9:6, 9). This *ḥēleq* constitutes the limited arena of a person's freedom to act, but rewards and punishments play no significant, no enduring role in the scheme, because their effects are canceled out by the deaths of the persons concerned (e.g., 9:5–6 and 2:21, in which an individual who has not toiled for it is left to enjoy the *ḥēleq* of one who has but has died).

The observations we have been discussing, it should be emphasized, are not found in the book of Qohelet in the form of a systematically arranged treatise on time patterns and human and divine order. But when we consider them together, it is plain that they are the product of systematic, conscious, abstract reasoning on this issue. Qohelet starts with the one clear, final point in the pattern, death, and works backward as far as he can to its beginning, in life. He does not start with birth and work forward, because that would leave him in an open-ended situation of intellectual chaos.[22] The use of this reasoning is deliberately signaled

21. It is true that none of the occurrences of *miqreh* and *qārâ* in Qohelet is explicitly connected with God, but this does not mean that the author has left open the question of God's control of *miqreh*, as Ringgren supposes (*TWAT* 7.175). For, if *miqreh* is the end point of all patterns of activity (the *maᶜăśeh*), God, affirms Qohelet, is the one in control of those patterns, See, for example, 3:11: "He (= God) has made everything (*hakkōl*) appropriate (*yāpeh*: literally, 'beautiful') in its time (*bĕᶜittô*), whereby the word *hakkōl* 'everything' should be connected with 'the *maᶜăśeh*' at the end of the verse, "which God has made from beginning to end."

22. One might compare the celebrated remark of the Greek political leader, Solon, as given in Herodotus: 'Until (a man) die, refrain from calling him happy; (call him) only lucky' (*prin d'an teleutesę, epischein mēde kaleein kō olbion, all'eutychea*) (C. Hude, *Herodoti Historiae: Libri I–IV* [Oxford, 1912] 1.32.7–8).

by our author at several places in the text, for example: 'I set my mind to inquire and to explore in wisdom (*wĕnātattî ʾet-libbî lidrôš wĕlātûr baḥokmâ*) all that is done under the sun' (1:13); or: 'I pondered in my mind (literally: I said in my heart [*ʾāmartî ʾănî bĕlibbî*]), "Let me now test you (*ʾănassĕkâ*) on (the matter of) pleasure, and investigate (literally: and see [*ûrĕʾēh*]) good"' (2:1); or: 'All this I tested by means of wisdom (*nissîtî baḥokmâ*)' (7:23). And the point of it all is finally to show the limitations of the process: reason—or to use the most common label for it in Qohelet, *ḥokmâ* (e.g., 1:13; 2:3; 7:23, 25; for other terms, see below)—used to explore the boundaries of reason (see especially 1:12–2:26 and 7:23–28).

What to make of the intellectual process we have described? The object on which Qohelet focuses it, death, is of course a common topos in biblical and other Near Eastern literatures of virtually all periods, where it likewise may be associated with divine control and used to define the boundaries of life. Compare, for example, Ps 39:5:

> Yahweh, let me know my end (*qiṣṣî*)
> And the measure of my days—what it is.[23]

But within this broad background, the distinctiveness of the approach or formulation of Qohelet, at least for biblical/Israelite tradition, becomes clear if we compare the occurrences of *miqreh* in the Bible outside of Qohelet. There are three of them, along with one for the related noun, *qāreh*:[24]

Ruth 2:3. And she (= Ruth) went off and came to glean in the field behind the harvesters. She happened upon the portion of the field belonging to Boaz, of the family of Elimelech (literally: And her *miqreh* happened upon the portion of the field belonging to Boaz, of the family of Elimelech [*wayyiqer miqrehā ḥelqat haśśādeh lĕbōʿaz ʾăšer mimmišpaḥat ʾĕlîmelek*]).

23. Brought to my attention by O. Kaiser and E. Lohse, *Death and Life* (Biblical Encounters Series; Nashville, 1981) 20.

24. One might also note here the word *qerî*, which occurs seven times in the Hebrew Bible, all in Leviticus 26 (vv. 21, 23, 24, 27, 28, 40, 41; I thank Hindy Najman for suggesting that I look at *qerî* in the present context). In these verses *qerî* means 'hostility', in the idiom 'to act (literally, 'walk') hostilely toward another'. Many have suggested (e.g., Amsler, *THAT* 2.682) that its root is the same *qrh* as for our *miqreh/qāreh*. Were that so, *qerî* might be understood to connect semantically with *qrh* as 'hostile occurrence, confrontation', but such a meaning helps us little with the meaning of *miqreh/qāreh*, discussed below. The separation from *miqreh/qāreh* would be even more pronounced if the root of *qerî* is, in fact, not *qrh*, but *qrr* 'to be cold' (thus, 'coldness' > 'hostility'), as argued most recently by B. A. Levine, *Leviticus* (JPS Torah Commentary; Philadelphia, 1989) 186.

1 Sam 6:9. And take notice: if the border traversed by it (= the Ark in the wagon) takes it up to Beth Shemesh, then he (= God) is the one who caused this great disaster for us. But if it does not, then we shall know that it was not his hand which reached out against us; it was (rather) a *miqreh* for us.

1 Sam 20:26. (When David did not appear as expected at Saul's court on the Festival of the New Moon) Saul did not say anything on that day, for he thought (*ʾāmar*), "(There has been) a *miqreh,* (and) he has become unclean."[25]

Deut 23:11. For if there is a man among you who is not clean because of a *qāreh* of the night and he goes out of the camp, then he shall not come (back) into the camp.

In these four passages, it is clear, *miqreh/qāreh* describes an occurrence that to humans is unexpected because they cannot foresee or control it and cannot understand, at least at the time of occurrence, the reason for it.[26] If one is inclined, therefore, to translate the terms as 'chance' or luck', this need not automatically exclude divine determination or predetermination, as our earlier discussion, based on other biblical and more general considerations, has shown.[27] To be sure, how God fits into our passages is not made explicit. But at least in Ruth 2:3, one may assume that he is the "behind-the-scene" cause of Ruth's *miqreh,* for the thrust of the Ruth narrative as a whole is God's guidance of Ruth to a new life with Boaz. In 1 Sam 6:9, on the other hand, God and *miqreh* appear to be envisaged as two possible and contrasting causes for a particular action, but even here we may ask whether this is a contrast accepted by the biblical author, given that it is put forward in a statement made by "pagan" Philistines, not Israelites.[28]

Whatever one decides about God in these passages, their agreement that a *miqreh* or *qāreh* is something people cannot foresee or grasp is presented, one should note, not only in the concrete, but in the more

25. On the excision of the final clause, *hûʾ kî-lōʾ āhôr,* as a doublet arising from conflation, see P. Kyle McCarter, Jr., *I Samuel* (AB 8; Garden City, N.Y., 1980) 338 ad loc., following S. Talmon, "Double Readings in the Massoretic Text," *Textus* 1 (1960) 173–74.

26. Note that in Ruth 2:3 this meaning is expressed by the combination of *miqreh* with the cognate verb *qārâ.*

27. Note also the use of the cognate verb *qārâ* in Gen 24:12 and 27:20. In these verses *qārâ* occurs in the Hiphil, with God as the subject, and describes God's ability to cause 'good luck/success' (literally, 'to make things happen') for Abraham's servant and for Jacob.

28. That the biblical author did not accept the contrast as legitimate is suggested by his demonstration in the subsequent narration that the action in question was caused by God, not by a *miqreh* (compare 1 Sam 6:12 with 6:9).

abstract. That is to say, our passages not only speak of single "occurrences" of *miqreh/qāreh*, but also understand these terms as indicative of a certain *type* of occurrence (1 Sam 6:9, 20:26; Deut 23:11), or, in the case of Ruth 2:3, as a *type* of phenomenon that appears to characterize individuals and govern the "occurrences" that "befall" them. In these respects, our passages certainly provide the semantic tradition on which Qohelet could draw for his use of *miqreh*, namely, as a type of occurrence befalling humans that is beyond their control and understanding, or as a characteristic of humans and animals that marks their activities (note the same conjunction of the noun *miqreh* and the verb *qārah* in Qoh 2:14, 15 as in Ruth 2:3). Yet it is equally clear how Qohelet is different from these other passages. For it identifies *miqreh* not just with any unforeseen and uncontrolled 'occurrence', but exclusively with death,[29] and death becomes, then, the predetermined defining point of an abstract notion: *miqreh* as the pattern of time that each individual lives out. Put another way, if there is abstraction in the ways *miqreh* is used in 1 Sam 6:9, 20:26; Ruth 2:3; and Deut 23:11, the abstraction is only hinted at and not worked out. In Qohelet, however, it is made explicit and elaborated: the larger system of time in which *miqreh* is embedded now brought forward as the direct object of reflection.

This move toward a more explicit conceptualization and abstraction is confirmed by at least three others of the words for patterned time in Qohelet. The first is *ḥešbôn* (7:25, 27; 9:10), which carries in our book the sense of 'considered assessment of life, that is, what is arrived at by a deliberate process of reckoning' (7:27–28; maybe 7:25; and 9:10) or, apparently, 'the reckoning process itself' (9:10; possibly 7:25).[30] The word *ḥešbôn* is unique to Qohelet in the biblical corpus, and this uniqueness becomes clearer when one compares other forms of the underlying root *ḥšb*, both verbal and nominal, elsewhere in the Bible. For although the other forms certainly provide the ground for Qohelet's usage (e.g., 'to devise, consider the meaning of' [Ps 77:6]; 'thought, plan'), none of

29. Cf. M. Hengel, *Judentum und Hellenismus* (2d ed.; Wissenschaftliche Untersuchungen zum Neuen Testament 10; Tübingen, 1969) 220.

30. Qoh 9:10 says that in the realm of death, Sheol, to which humans go, there are no *maᶜăśeh, ḥešbôn, daᶜat,* and *ḥokmâ.* This makes the best sense if we understand that what is absent in death are not only the products of reckoning, knowledge, and wisdom, but also the capacity to exercise these faculties. (For other possible occurrences of this dual use of *ḥokmâ* and *ḥešbôn*, see 7:25). As for *maᶜăśeh* in 9:10, one could by analogy understand it in the same dual way, as both the planned pattern of activity and the capacity to operate in such a pattern, which together cease with death. It should be added that Fox also recognizes the dual use of *ḥešbôn* in Qohelet, remarking in *Qohelet*, 241, that the word "refers to both the process of reckoning and the solution reached."

them seems to approach the level of abstraction, of self-reflexivity, that Qoh 9:10 gives to *ḥešbôn.*[31]

As for the word *maᶜăśeh,* it, unlike *ḥešbôn,* does occur in other books of the Bible but once more is not used there as it is in Qohelet. Its normal meaning outside of Qohelet—and this is found in Qohelet as well (e.g., 1:14; 2:4, 11)—is 'a deed' or work', which certainly underlies, yet is far from the specialized extension Qohelet uses: 'a planned life pattern of activity characteristic of each individual and God' (e.g., 3:11; 7:13; 8:14, 17). Closer to this latter sense is the meaning 'occupation, characteristic lifestyle' that is found in a few biblical texts (Gen 46:33, 47:3; Judg 13:12). Even in these passages, however, one misses the linkage to a generalized system of time on which Qohelet focuses.[32]

Finally, there is the word *ᶜôlām,* which can occur in Qohelet in the meanings it has elsewhere in the Hebrew Bible, 'eternity (usually in the prepositional phrase *lĕᶜôlām* 'forever'), ancient times' (1:4, 10; 3:14; 9:6; 12:5).[33] But in an admittedly difficult passage, 3:11, Qohelet seems once more to have taken the meaning to a new level of abstraction and self-consciousness. Here *ᶜôlām* is not simply 'eternity', but the 'ability to

31. Thus, *maḥăšābâ* (pl. *maḥăšābôt*), as noted above, may be used to describe God's 'plan' or 'plans' in history (e.g., Isa 55:8–9; Jer 18:11). While this certainly carries with it some abstraction, it is still a usage tied to particular plans and does not involve a consideration of the *process* of planning, which *ḥešbôn* appears to have in Qoh 9:10 and perhaps 7:25. Likewise, the verb *ḥšb* in the sense 'to consider the meaning of', as in Ps 77:6, refers to reflecting on the meaning of events, but not, again, to the process of reflection itself.

One other form of *ḥšb* needs to be recognized here. It is *ḥiššĕbōnôt* (plural of an unattested singular, *ḥiššābôn*), whose two biblical occurrences include 2 Chr 26:15 and Qohelet itself, in 7:29. In the Chronicles text *ḥiššĕbōnôt* describes 'devices' for conducting siege warfare. In other words, it refers to particular, concrete objects. In the Qohelet verse it is part of an observation in which the author opines, "Only mark this: I have found that God has made humans upright/straightforward (*yāšār*), and/but they have (constantly) sought many *ḥiššĕbōnôt.*" Admittedly the meaning of this is difficult, but since the verse comes just after others that mention *ḥešbôn* (7:25, 27), it is probably to be understood with them. On that basis, I suggest that like *ḥešbôn* (see above, n. 30) *ḥiššĕbōnôt* refers here to the reckoning, both the process and the product achieved, that humans undertake to make sense of life. The plural would then indicate individual and repeated efforts at such reckoning, all finally futile, which are to be connected or contrasted in some way with the condition of "uprightness" or "straightforwardness" that God has allotted to humans (see the discussions, e.g., in G. Ogden, *Qoheleth* [Readings, a New Biblical Commentary; Sheffield, 1987] 124; and Fox, *Qohelet,* 243). Should this understanding be correct, *ḥiššĕbōnôt* in Qoh 7:29 would be distinguished from 2 Chr 26:15 precisely as another example of abstraction in the use of the root *ḥšb.*

32. The distance, in terms of level of abstraction, between Qohelet's use of *maᶜăśeh* and other biblical occurrences becomes even greater if we understand *maᶜăśeh* in Qoh 9:10 as the capacity to exercise *maᶜăśeh* as well as the *maᶜăśeh* that results: see above, n. 30.

33. The emphasis in Qohelet seems to be on something that is fixed and unchanging, as opposed to that which is constantly in flux or in cycle and that cannot, therefore, be relied on by humans: see, e.g., 1:4.

consider and reflect on the concept of eternity',[34] which God has put into the minds (*lēb*) of human beings 'so that' (*mibbĕlî ʾăšer*), paradoxically, they are able to see that they cannot discover the nature of God's own pattern of activity, his *maʿăśeh*. In other words, *ʿôlām* in 3:11, like 'wisdom' (*ḥokmâ*) elsewhere in the book (e.g., 1:13; 2:21 within the context of 1:12–2:23; 7:23; 9:10; cf. also *ḥešbôn* above), seems to be the capacity God gives humans to be able to discover the limits of their understanding. The word *ʿôlām*, it would appear, allows the discovery of limits precisely because it gives human beings an awareness of the 'eternal' that lies beyond.[35]

In Qohelet, thus, we witness the beginnings of a technical vocabulary created or adapted to deal with the problem of time in human existence. Not everything is new: certain words like *ʿēt* ('appointed time') seem to be taken over more or less directly from existing usage (compare, e.g., Ps 102:13). But the use of *miqreh*, *ḥešbôn*, *maʿăśeh*, and *ʿôlām* suggests the new intellectual groping in Qohelet—the systematic, reflective character of the book's attack on the time problem, its disciplined meditation on the implications of death for the nature of the divine order and humanity's place in that order. So overwhelming in Qohelet's meditation is the presence of death as the divinely predetermined point in all existence, the only clear and certain point that humans can know by the application of their reason, that while it does not eliminate no-

34. See Ogden, *Qoheleth*, 55, who translates *ʿôlām* in 3:11 as 'a consciousness of the eternal', though with a somewhat different view of the matter from what is proposed here.

35. The interpretation of 3:11 just offered is tentative, as is any of this verse. For other possibilities, see the commentaries, e.g., G. A. Barton, *The Book of Ecclesiastes* (ICC; Edinburgh and New York, 1908) 105; and R. Gordis, *Koheleth: The Man and His World* (3d ed.; New York, 1968) 231–32; and for the occurrences of *ʿôlām* as a whole in Qohelet and elsewhere in the Bible and the ancient Semitic languages, see E. Jenni, "Das Wort *ʿōlām* im Alten Testament," *ZAW* 64 (1952) 197–248; *ZAW* 65 (1953) 1–34, especially 22–29 (Qohelet).

One might be tempted to translate the crucial part of Qoh 3:11 as 'He (= God) has put *hāʿôlām* into their minds, without which man cannot find out the *maʿăśeh* that God has done from beginning to end'. This rendering of *mibbĕlî ʾăšer . . . lōʾ* does not require the interpretation of *lōʾ* as a pleonasm, which would be the case for the alternative translation, 'so that man cannot find out . . . .' Which of the two translations is preferable? The first, 'without which man . . .', yields the meaning that God has made it possible for humans to understand the *maʿăśeh*, a meaning that is not found elsewhere in Qohelet. Indeed, such a meaning would contradict the tenor of a number of other passages in the book, such as 11:5, and especially 8:17, which refers to exactly the same issue and says, "I saw all the *maʿăśeh* of God, that man is not able to find out the *maʿăśeh* which was done / occurred (*naʿăśeh*) under the sun." For 8:17, in other words, what humans are able to perceive of God's activity is precisely that it and every other activity is unknowable. This would also be the meaning of 3:11, if one were to adopt the second translation of it above, 'so that man cannot find out . . .'. I choose, therefore, to adopt this translation and thus to bring 3:11 into conformity with the rest of Qohelet.

tions of good and evil human behavior, it loosens their attachment to any scheme of reward and punishment and so moves to relativize their value to one another. In other words, in Qohelet human reason seems to be the first standard of judgment, and applying reason to the perennial tension between fate and morally accountable action appears to tip the balance toward fate. If one is to bring morally accountable action back into the picture as an active notion guiding human behavior and its relationship to the divine, then, Qohelet seems to be saying, it will have to be done on other grounds than what reason recommends.[36]

This emphasis on reason and the construction of a rational argument about the subject of fate stands out as highly unusual, if not unique in the biblical Hebrew corpus. Put another way, what is significant in Qohelet is not simply the concern with the subject matter on which human reason focuses and the conclusions it yields, but an awareness of, a reflection on the reasoning process itself. This is indicated, as we have seen, in Qohelet's explicit remarks about his investigative approach in such passages as 1:13, 2:1, and 7:23, with the recurrent reference to terms like *lēb/lēbāb* ('heart' > 'mind'), *nsh* ('to test'), and *twr* ('to explore').[37] But even more, the emphasis is revealed in the three nouns we have examined: *ḥokmâ, ḥešbôn* and *ᶜôlām,* all of which appear to describe both the product and the process of reason.[38]

36. See, thus, the end of the book, long puzzling to readers, wherein the advice is given: "A final word (after) everything has been heard—fear God and keep His commandments, for this is (what) man is all about. For God will bring every deed (*maᶜăśeh*) into judgment, including (*ᶜal,* on which cf. 11:9, as Fox [*Qohelet,* 329] has seen) every secret one, whether good or bad" (12:13–14). The point here, whether made by a later editor of the book or by its original author, seems to be that in the final analysis, after reason can go no further (note the end of the previous verse [v. 12], "much reflection is a weariness of the flesh"), all a (Israelite) person has is faith, faith in God and his willingness to abide by his commandments, as known from tradition, that he will judge the good and the bad and reward them appropriately.

37. *Lēb/Lēbāb* in Qohelet sometimes means literally 'the heart' (e.g., 7:3, 4; 9:7), but more often, it appears, refers to 'the mind, mental faculties' (e.g., 1:13, 17; 2:1, 3, 15; 7:25; 9:1; 10:2). For *nsh,* see 2:1 and 7:23. On *twr,* 1:13; 2:3; 7:25; and possibly 9:1, if one emends, with BDB 1064b, MT *bûr* to *tûr.* The word *twr,* it should be added, is significant in that its biblical attestations outside of Qohelet all seem to denote 'exploring' or 'seeking out' something physical, like land (e.g., Num 13:2, 16:7; Judg 1:23) or 'roaming' through a physical space (e.g., Job 39:8). Only in Qohelet is *twr* used to describe the process of rational inquiry. This shift in usage thus parallels the shifts represented by *ḥešbôn* and *ᶜôlām,* as argued above.

38. For *ḥokmâ*: e.g., 1:16–17, 2:12–13, 9:10 (product); 2:21, 7:23, 10:10 (process). For *ḥešbôn*: 7:27–28 (product). For *ᶜôlām*: 1:4, 10; 3:14; 9:6; 12:5 (product); 3:11 (process). See also n. 30 above on 9:10 and 7:25 and n. 31 on 7:29, in which *ḥokmâ* and *ḥešbôn,* as well as *daᶜat, maᶜăśeh,* and *ḥiššěbōnôt,* all appear to designate both product and process.

How, finally, are we to explain the origin and context of Qohelet's preoccupation with fate and its workings? The answer is not easily found or agreed upon, and a full discussion really requires a separate study. But perhaps a word or two might be ventured by way of conclusion. As is well known, Qohelet's attention to fate has reminded more than one commentator of the traditions of the Hellenistic period; similarly for other features, such as the use of the term *hebel*.[39] But it should be plain by now that in assessing influences on Qohelet, one cannot avoid taking account of the native Israelite tradition of *miqreh* and, more broadly, of fate, which clearly shows that these, in some way, were talked about well before Hellenistic contact and that Qohelet was an heir to that discussion. To be sure, we cannot disregard the significance of Qohelet's elaboration on and more explicit thinking about the issue of fate, yet it is equally clear that his discussion is only at the beginning stages of a rational inquiry, far from a full-blown systematic analysis, at least in the way it is expressed. Further, while *miqreh* in Qohelet echoes some of the meanings of the terms used for fate in Hellenistic culture—the all-embracing determinism of *heimarmenē*, the equally embracing control of *tychē*, the connection with death of *moira*—it is equivalent to none of these terms. For example, *miqreh* is never hypostatized in Qohelet: it thus is not *tychē* or like *tychē*, which could be personified as a goddess and was widely revered as such in the Hellenistic period.[40]

All of this suggests that if we are to consider Greek, specifically, Hellenistic, influence on Qohelet's use of *miqreh*, and I think we may, we must be circumspect, for the influence may reside not so much in the use of *miqreh* for fate per se, as in the ability to write about *miqreh* in a way that indicates both a rational process at work and, even more, a reflection on what that rationality consists of. We have here, in short, a concern for "second-order" thinking such as marked Greek thought from the pre-Socratics onward and that otherwise is hardly to be noticed in the written remains of the pre-Hellenistic Near East.[41] Yet, as a last

39. The most recent comprehensive discussions of Qohelet and Hellenistic thought are by Hengel (*Judentum und Hellenismus*, 210–40, with 220–21 on *miqreh*), and R. Braun (*Kohelet und die frühhellenistische Populärphilosophie* [BZAW 130; Berlin, 1973]), who discusses *hebel*, specifically, on pp. 45–46. The possible connections with the Greek world and the nature of the connections we should look for have provoked a long-standing debate, still unresolved, which is concisely chronicled in D. Michel, *Qohelet* (Erträge der Forschung 258; Darmstadt, 1988) 58–65.

40. For a brief view of the Greek terms, with references to fuller studies, see K. Ziegler and W. Sontheimer (eds.), *Der Kleine Pauly* (Munich, 1979) 2.972–73; 3.1391–96; 5.1016; N. G. L. Hammond and H. H. Scullard (eds.), *The Oxford Classical Dictionary* (2d ed.; Oxford, 1970) 430–32, 1100–1101; and Hengel, *Judentum und Hellenismus*, 230.

41. Cf. Hengel (*Judentum und Hellenismus*, 232), who proposes that "Seine (viz., Qohel et's) unvoreingenommene, distanzierte Beobachtung und sein streng rationales, logisches

point, the incipient character of the expression of this thinking in Qohelet may indicate a still early, incomplete exposure to Greek tradition, of the sort that we might imagine in the third century B.C.E., the Ptolemaic period of Palestinian history, to which in fact many would on other grounds date Qohelet.[42]

Denken" as applied to the "radikalen Kritik der Vergeltungslehre der traditionellen Weisheit" constitute one of the points of contact of Qohelet with the "Geist des frühen Hellenismus." On Greek second-order thinking, see S. N. Eisenstadt (ed.), *The Origins and Diversity of Axial Age Civilizations* (SUNY Series in Near Eastern Studies; Albany, 1986) chap. 1 (Y. Elkana, "The Emergence of Second-Order Thinking in Classical Greece"), chap. 2 (C. Meier, "The Emergence of an Autonomous Intelligence among the Greeks"), and chap. 3 (S. C. Humphreys, "Dynamics of the Greek Breakthrough: The Dialogue between Philosophy and Religion"). In addition, G. E. R. Lloyd, *Magic, Reason and Experience: Studies in the Origins and Development of Greek Science* (Cambridge, 1979); and idem, *Demystifying Mentalities* (Cambridge, 1990), especially chap. 3. Lloyd has occasional comments as well on the ancient Near East. For more extended treatment of the Near East and how its written sources might be interpreted, see, with specific reference to Mesopotamia, P. Machinist, in Eisenstadt, *Origins and Diversity,* chap. 7 ("On Self-Consciousness in Mesopotamia"); and M. T. Larsen, "The Babylonian Lukewarm Mind: Reflections on Science, Divination and Literacy," in *Language, Literature, and History: Philological and Historical Studies Presented to Erica Reiner* (ed. F. Rochberg-Halton; AOS 67; New Haven, 1987) 203–25.

42. E.g., Elias Bickerman, *Four Strange Books of the Bible* (New York, 1967) 141–67, especially 141.

A Recently Discovered Word for "Clan" in Mari and Its Hebrew Cognate

Abraham Malamat

As expected, the word lîmum at Mari, 'clan, tribal unit', has finally appeared. The Lim names were exclusively divinized family names and did not refer to real deities. In several new Mari texts, the West Semitic word lîmum is attested. It is a cognate of Ugaritic lʾim and of Hebrew lĕʾōm 'clan, tribe, people'. In Akkadian lîmum also means 'the figure 1000, a multitude'. The Biblical Hebrew word ʾelep '1000' is also a synonym for 'clan' and is thus a semantic parallel to Akkadian, including the Akkadian of Mari.

Since the very beginnings of the Mari discoveries in the 1930s, various personal names have appeared that incorporate the theophoric element Lim, such as Yahdun-Lim and Zimri-Lim, the kings of Mari, and Yarim-Lim, the ruler of Aleppo, and many more.[1] Outside Mari as well, Lim names are plentiful, mostly in the Old Babylonian Period. Recently, some earlier Lim names have also appeared at Ebla, spelled there *li-im*.[2] Yet the deity Lim proper, that is, outside personal names, has so far not been attested. Thus we may have in "Lim" only a divinized name, rather than a real deity. The case is similar to that of the name Hammurapi or Ammurapi, where Hammu (*ʿammu*) is again exclusively a divinized family or clan, but not an actual deity.

Accordingly, the Lim names, like the Ammu names, never carry the DINGIR determinative, perhaps a sign of their weakened theophoric character, denoting a deity of lower rank. Lim is never written in Mari with a Sumerogram and always with a syllabic spelling, such as *li-um*, *li-im* (see n. 4).

1. On Lim in short, see M. Krebernik, "Lim," *RLA* 7.25ff. For the above Lim names and many others, see M. Birot, *ARM* 16/1 (1979), Noms de personnes. See also I. J. Gelb et al., *Computer-Aided Analysis of Amorite* (AS 21; Chicago, 1980) 145–46.

2. E.g., A. Archi, "Die ersten zehn Könige von Ebla," *ZA* 76 (1986) 213–17.

Surprisingly, Durand and Marello have now published new Mari letters attesting to a West Semitic word *lîmum*, spelled syllabically *li-im*, meaning a 'clan or a tribal unit'. In one instance in the Marello letter (A. 1146, line 21),[3] silver was passed on to a clan. In a second instance (line 24) the clan is said to have been assembled in its entirety in the city of Hen, which was situated in a seminomadic environment of the Upper Habur. Certain other aspects of this document are also of interest, but they lie outside the scope of this note. The Durand letter mentions the annihilation of a certain clan or tribe (M. 6060).[4] A further recent occurrence of *lîmum* is still unpublished (A. 2090), but both Durand and Marello refer to it.[5] The clan in question was situated in the country of Zalmaqum and migrated from there to the lowland.

Lîmum has occurred previously in lexical texts, where it is parallel to the noun *nîrum*, also meaning 'a clan'.[6] The synonym now appears in a Mari text, published by Lafont.[7] The text contains a list of people, including the idiom *nîrum*, referring twice to a large number of women. Text 12 records 70 mí *ni-ru-um*, and text 19 mentions a *ni-ru-um* of 74 women. These were perhaps not simply groups, but rather formal assembles or even clans.

It is of interest that in Ugarit, or rather, Ugaritic, we encounter the vocable *lʾim* (*ʾalep* with *ḥîreq*), also referring to a people or clan,[8] a form identical with the Mari word. On the other hand, the archaic and poetic expression *lĕʾōm* (pl. *lĕʾummîm*) for a tribal unit or even an entire people[9] is frequently attested in Biblical Hebrew. Like the Hebrew kinship groups *gôy*, *ʾummâ*, *ḥeber*, and *ʿamm*, thus *lĕʾōm* in time came to expand its scope to encompass entire peoples or nations, contrary to its original narrow gentilic sense as still attested at Mari. While at Ugarit the Mari vowel of *lîmum* is retained, in the Bible it changes to *o/u*, like *mʾid* 'much' in Ugaritic and *mĕʾōd* in Hebrew. *Lîmum* has hardly any connection with the biblical archaic form *lmw* (Deut 32:3, etc.)[10] or with the

3. P. Marello, "Vie nomade," *Mémoires NABU* 1 (1992) 115–25.

4. J.-M. Durand, "Precurseurs syriens . . . ," *Marchand, diplomates et empereurs (Mélanges P. Garelli)* (Paris, 1991) 50–53.

5. Durand, ibid., 53; Marello, "Vie nomade," 119,e.

6. CAD N/2, 263 s.v. *nîru* E; CAD L, 198 s.v. *lîmu* C.

7. B. Lafont, "Le *ṣâbum* du roi de Mari," *Miscellania babyloniaca (Mélanges M. Birot)* (Paris, 1985) 174 (no. 12), 176 (no. 19).

8. C. H. Gordon, *UT* 426b.

9. *HALAT* 2.488; *TWAT* 4.411ff. The word *lĕʾummîm* appears once in the Bible as the name of a specific tribe (Gen 25:3).

10. *HALAT* 2.505. But see E. Lipiński ("Le Dieu Lim," in *15ᵉ Rencontre assyriologique internationale* [Liège, 1967] 150–60), who equates *lmw* with Lim and takes it as an epithet of the God of Israel. Cf. similarly G. Dossin, "À propos du dieu Lim," *Syria* 55 (1978) 327–32.

personal name Lemuel, Lemoel (*lmwʾl*) (Prov 31:1, 4), as sometimes assumed[11] (unless we propose a metathesis). In the Bible we apparently have not only an etymological parallel with Mari but also a semantic one. *Lîmum* in Akkadian, including Mari Akkadian, also stands for the number 1000,[12] which may designate a multitude.[13]

Now, one of the common synonyms in the Bible for a clan or a tribe is *ʾelep*.[14] The most common explanation of *ʾelep* is 1000. Thus *lîmum* may be equivalent not only to *lĕʾōm* but also to *ʾelep*. The concept of 1000, a typological number for multitude, may represent a tribe or clan, or perhaps, more precisely, the military potential of these entities.

11. Cf. most recently S. C. Layton (*Archaic Features of Canaanite Personal Names in the Hebrew Bible* [Atlanta, 1990] 190–91), who translates 'Lim is God' instead of 'God is for him' or the like, as suggested to me by A. Shaffer.

12. AHw 553b; CAD L 197.

13. Cf., e.g., *Recueil É. Dhorme: Études bibliques et orientales* (Paris, 1951) 70.

14. *HALAT* 1.58 s.v. אלף III; D. R. Meyer and H. Donner (eds.), *Wilhelm Gesenius: Hebräisches und Aramäisches Handwörterbuch über das Alte Testament* (18th ed.; Berlin, 1987) 68 s.v. אלף III; J. Pedersen, *Israel: Its Life and Culture* (London, 1926 [repr. 1946 as 4 vols. in 2]) 1.50. For the typical biblical passages with *ʾelep*, see above and in S. Bendor, *The Bet-Ab in Israel*. . . (Oranim and Haifa, 1986) 38–39, 55 [Hebrew].

Note de lexicographie hébraïque qumrânienne (*m-ṣw/yrwq, mḥšbym, śwṭ*)

Émile Puech*

Cette note propose d'expliquer trois mots rares attestés en hébreu dans des textes hymniques qumrâniens, de la Règle de la Communauté (1QS), des Hymnes (1QS), des Paroles des Luminaires (4Q504), et des Cantiques du Sage (4Q511). Le mot mṣw/yrwq, forme qiṭṭul probable de ṣrq, désigne une 'pincée de pâte' (de pain, d'argile . . .) et se rendrait assez bien en français par 'pâton', sens qui s'impose dans un contexte de potier. De la racine ḥšb 'tisser', le substantif mḥšbym en relation avec les abîmes signifie très vraisemblablement les 'fissures, sillons, replis, dédales' des fonds abyssins. Enfin, la racine sémitique šw/yṭ a, dans plusieurs exemples en hébreu biblique et qumrânien, comme ailleurs en araméen, syriaque, ge^{c}ez et arabe, le sens de 'brûler, consumer, cuire', ici dans des exemples en rapport avec l'image d'une coulée incandescente.

Dans ce volume en l'honneur du Professeur Greenfield, linguiste éminent, nous nous proposons bien modestement d'étudier de plus près la signification de quelques mots hébreux d'après leurs attestations qumrâniennes.

mṣw/yrwq

La lecture et le sens du substantif *mṣwrwq* ont posé problème dans les attestations actuellement repérées. En 1QS XI 21, l'éditeur Burrows a lu *mṣwr rq* (ce qui a entraîné la même lecture en 4QS^{j} 1, 8 d'après le fichier du Musée Rockefeller mais avec un *circellus* sur le second *reš*). Cependant en 1QS une lecture *mṣwrwq* ne saurait souffrir de discussion, malgré Kuhn[1] qui lit sûrement (?) d'après la photographie *mṣyrwq*, lecture habituellement retenue par bien des commentateurs par la suite, et

* Centre National de la Recherche Scientifique.

1. K. G. Kuhn, *Konkordanz zu den Qumrantexten* (Göttingen, 1960) 131 n. 4.

en partie du moins d'après 1QH XX 35 (= XII 32) que l'éditeur Sukenik a lu *mṣydwq*, de même col. XXIII 36 (= fg. 2, 16).[2] Dans ce cas au moins, le *reš* qui est d'un ductus différent de celui du *dalet* dans cette écriture, est certain,[3] tout comme en 1QH XXIII 28 et 36 (= fg. 2, 8 et 16), et on pourrait hésiter tout au plus entre *mṣy/wrwq*, puisque dans cette main ces deux lettres sont souvent non distinctes. Cependant, là encore, certains ont discuté la lecture de Sukenik pour retenir soit *mṣwrwq*, soit *mṣyryq*.[4] La dernière attestation en 4Q*511* 28–29, 3 a été lue par l'éditeur Baillet *mṣyrwq* avec un point sur le *yod*.[5]

Quoi qu'il en soit de ce point somme toute mineur, la difficulté principale vient de ce que la racine semble inconnue, mais des commentateurs ont noté l'ordre inversé des consonnes radicales dans le mot qui suit en 1QS XI 21, *whwʾh mṣwrwq ḥmr qwrṣ* et en 4Q*511* 28–29, 3, *wʾny mṣyrwq yṣr*[4] [*ḥmr*] *qwrṣty*.[6] La dernière remarque de Baillet est sans aucun doute judicieuse: "Mais peut-être vaut-il mieux comprendre le mem initial comme préposition. Cf. *mḥmr qrṣty* en Job 33:6 et ici même le parallélisme avec *wmḥwšk mgbly*."[7]

2. E. L. Sukenik, *The Dead Sea Scrolls of the Hebrew University* (Jerusalem, 1955). Nous citons les colonnes et lignes de 1QH non d'après l'édition qui n'a pas retrouvé la mise en ordre originale des colonnes et des fragments, mais d'après notre reconstruction du rouleau exposée dans "Quelques aspects de la restauration du Rouleau des Hymnes (1QH)" (*JJS* 39 [1988] 38–55), ou dans "Un Hymne essénien en partie retrouvé et les béatitudes, 1QH V 12–VI 18 (= col. XIII–XIV 7) et 4QBéat." (*RevQ* 13 [1988] 59–88), et nous mettons l'ancienne numérotation entre parenthèses.

3. La traduction d'A. Dupont-Sommer ("Le Livre des Hymnes découvert près de la mer Morte [1QH]," *Sem* 7 [1957] 84) laisse entendre que cet auteur lisait sans difficulté *mṣydyq* 'hors de la justice' supposant probablement deux *yod* comme *matres lectionis* pour le son ê, de même au fg. 2, 16, mais au fg. 2, 8, il lit: *wmṣw*[*wt ʾmt* (p. 105).

4. Voir par exemple J. Carmignac dans *Les Textes de Qumrân traduits et annotés, I: La Règle de la Communauté, la Règle de la Guerre, les Hymnes* (par J. Carmignac et P. Guilbert; Paris, 1961) 267 n. 58.

5. M. Baillet, *Qumrân Grotte 4: III (4Q482–4Q520)* (DJD 7; Oxford, 1982) 235. L'éditeur précise "*yod* plutôt que *waw*, d'après la largeur de la lettre, en partie détruite." A vrai dire, la pl. LXI ne nous permet pas de trancher en toute certitude car la tête de la lettre qui ne paraît pas toucher le *reš* ne semble pas triangulaire ou pointue mais arrondie, pouvant faire hésiter entre *waw* et *yod*. Mais jusqu'à preuve de consultation de l'original, nous faisons confiance à la perspicacité de l'éditeur qui a vu les traces d'encre et non les seules taches de la reproduction, toujours sujettes à discussion.

6. Baillet (ibid.) écrit: "Le sens est obscur. La racine *ṣrq* ne semble attestée dans aucune langue sémitique. Mais les radicales sont, dans l'ordre inverse, celles de *qrṣ* qui figure ensuite ici et en 1QS XI 21. Donc peut-être une forme de caractère cabalistique et faisant jeu de mots avec *qrṣ*. On pourrait encore penser à un mot composé (= *mṣ yrwq*) ou à une origine étrangère (grec μάσσω 'pétrir' ?)."

7. Nous lisons ensuite *wmḥwšk mgb*[*ly nd*]*h* ⟨ *w*]*ʿwh* ⟩ *wʿwlh btkmy bśry* 'et de ténèbres est [ma] pétrissu[re, soui]llure ⟨[et] ruine⟩ et iniquité sont dans mes membres de chair', voir notre recension en *RB* 95 (1988) 410.

Jusqu'à présent, les exemples repérés se coulent toujours dans l'image de l'argile et d'une fabrication—modelage façonné en cette matière. Il semble que le mot puisse s'expliquer à partir des emplois du ge^cez et de l'arabe *ṣaraqa* signifiant 'faire l'aumône, pétrir un gâteau, couper une tranche de gâteau, rendre fin', voir en Tigrane et en Amharique, *ṣariq* 'petite pièce de monnaie', et en arabe *ṣaraq* 'fin, mince'.[8] On a même rapproché *ṣarīqa* de l'araméen *serīqīn* 'gâteau fin'.[9] N'est-il pas surprenant en effet que l'hébreu *qrṣ* qui suit le mot en question et dont les radicales sont dans l'ordre inverse, signifie 'pincer (de l'argile), séparer', d'où 'modeler' en Job 33:6, *qērēṣ* 'miche (de pain)' et *qrṣ* 'diviser (la pâte)', de même l'akkadien *karāṣu* et *qarāšu*.[10] Les deux mots composés des mêmes consonnes dans l'ordre inverse paraissent être visiblement en étroite relation. Il en résulte que le sens fondamental de la racine *ṣrq* semble être celui de 'rendre fin, rendre mince, émincir', et de 'pétrir (un gâteau, une pâte)'.

Dans l'ordre inversé des radicales, le substantif devrait alors désigner soit la pâte (à modeler, à façonner, à émincir, à séparer en tranches) ou mieux une pincée (de pâte) de laquelle est tiré ou façonné un élément, une pièce (de poterie, un gâteau, une miche) et dans ce cas le *mem* serait à lire comme préposition, *m-ṣw/yrwq* parallèle à *m-ḥmr* (Job) et à *m-ḥwšk* en 4Q*511* 28–29 (très probablement aussi en 1QH XX et XXIII), soit à la rigueur le résultat de la pincée, la pièce elle-même, une tranche, miche, poterie (petite ou/et fine?), extraite et façonnée, telle une tranche de pâte. La première solution nous semble bien préférable. On obtient alors la forme *quṭṭul* préférable à celle d'un substantif à préformante *m-*, peut-être même la forme *qiṭṭul* si la graphie de 4Q*511* permettait de trancher, mais *y* < *w* pourrait s'expliquer par dissimilation, comparer 1QIsa[a] 43:17, *^cwzwz* pour le TM *^czwz* (*^cizûz*)[11] où la graphie est indiscutable. Cette forme *^cwzwz* devrait expliquer aussi la graphie d'au moins bon nombre des exemples qumrâniens à lire apparemment *mṣwrwq*.

Cette 'pincée' de pâte ou quantité prélevée par la (les) main(s) qui traduit le sens fondamental de la racine *qrṣ* en relation avec une 'pâte (pain, argile, . . .)' devrait se rendre en français par le substantif 'pâton'

8. W. Leslau, *Comparative Dictionary of Ge^cez (Classical Ethiopic) Ge^cez-English / English-Ge^cez with an Index of Semitic Roots* (Wiesbaden, 1987) 564; F. Steingass, *The Student's Arabic English Dictionary* (London, 1884) 580.

9. S. Fraenkel, *Die aramäischen Fremdwörter im Arabischen* (Leiden, 1886) 186 n. 2.

10. CAD K 209 s, *karāṣu*: 'to pinch off (clay), to break off' et citant l'exemple, "I pinched off from the potter's clay the clay (to make a figurine of) her" *Maqlû* III 17, p. 210; CAD Q 128, *qarāšu*: 'to trim, carve (meat), to make dough into loaves (?)'.

11. Voir E. Y. Kutscher, *The Language and Linguistic Background of the Isaiah Scroll (1QIsa[a])* (Leiden, 1974) 52–53; et P. Joüon, *Grammaire de l'hébreu biblique* (Rome, 1923) §88.

qui désigne un morceau de pâte prélevé pour former un pain ou une pièce de céramique.[12]

Cette explication permettrait de comprendre ainsi:

Litt. Et lui, de la poussière est sa pétrissure[13]
et nourriture de vermine son (dernier) séjour.
Et lui, du pâton [22]d'argile il est modelé
et vers la poussière est son inclination (1QS XI 21–22).

Selon ma connaissance ⟨j'ai parlé⟩,
(moi qui suis) du pâton de modelage d'argile,
[36]et que dirai-je. . . . (1QH XX 35s [= XII 32s]).

Mais Toi, [28][mon Dieu, tu as établi le mode]lage de l'argile
et du pâton [tu (m'?) as façonné] pour ton bon plaisir
(1QH XXIII 27–28 [= fg. 2, 7–8]).[14]

Tu as fait merveilleusement cela pour ta gloire
et du pâton [37][tu as modelé/façonné. . . .
(1QH XXIII 36s [= fg. 2, 16s]).[15]

Et moi, du pâton du modelage d' [4][argile] j'ai été façonné,
et de ténèbres est [ma] pétrissu[re,
soui]llure [⟨et] ruine⟩ et iniquité sont dans mes membres de chair
(4Q*511* 28–29, 3–4).

mḥšbym

L'hymne 1QH XI 20–37 (= III 19–36) contient plusieurs mots difficiles et plus ou moins bien compris. Ce sont d'une part les *mḥšby*

12. Voir par ex. E. Littré (*Dictionnaire de la langue française* [Paris, 1881] 3.1007), qui distingue *paton*: 2° "terme de potier. Motte de terre qui sert à faire une oreille, un manche, une anse à une pièce de poterie" (dérivé de patte, mais non destinée à fabriquer un objet en lui-même), de *pâton*: 2° "morceau de pâte que le boulanger agite avec force en pétrissant"; le *Grand dictionnaire encyclopédique Larousse* 8 (Paris, 1984) 7888b, *pâton*: "morceau de pâte . . ."; et le *Dictionnaire illustré multilingue de la céramique du Proche Orient Ancien* (sous la direction de M. Yon), coll. *Maison de l'Orient Méditerranéen* n° 10 (Série Archéologique 7; Lyon, 1981) 181, "*paton*: masse d'argile préparée que va travailler le potier." Le mot *pâton* (à dériver de pâte comme en Occitan) devrait désigner la petite portion (tranche de pâte) prélevée de la masse par le boulanger ou le potier et destinée à la fabrication d'une unité: un pain, un objet en argile, céramique, poterie, figurine, etc. Ce mot rendrait alors parfaitement compte du sens fondamental de la racine *ṣrq* (fin, mince, tranche) en rapport direct avec le sens de sa racine aux consonnes inversées, *qrṣ* (pincer, diviser [de la pâte] . . .).

13. Voir J. C. Greenfield ("The Root 'GBL' in Mishnaic Hebrew and in the Hymnic Literature from Qumran," *RevQ* 2 [1960] 155–62, 162 n. 33), l'auteur comprend *mṣwr* ('to fashion') et *rq* lu *rēq* ('empty'), à la suite de la lecture de l'éditeur.

14. Etant donné la séquence normale, restaurer [*qrṣth* ou *qrṣtny*].

15. Restaurer de même [*qrṣth*. . . .

thwm ou *ʾrṣ* (lignes 33–34 (= 32–33) et, d'autre part les deux emplois de *tšwṭ*, lignes 31, 37 (= 30, 36).

> 33*wybqʿw lʾbdwn nḥly blyʿl*
> *wyhmw mḥšby thwm bhmwn gwršy rpš*
> *wʾrṣ* 34*tṣrḥ ʿl hhwwh hnhyh btbl*
> *wkwl mḥšbyh yrwʿw.*

La lecture *mḥšby*(*-h*) est certaine mais la traduction retenue ne fait guère de sens.[16] Aussi corrige-t-on souvent en *mḥškym* d'après Ps 74:20 (*mḥšky ʾrṣ*), 88:7 (*bmḥškym bmṣlwt*), et 143:3 (*hwšybny bmḥškym kmty ʿwlm*), qui désignent des "lieux obscurs, des recoins (des profondeurs) de la terre.[17] Mais la lecture *mḥšbym* qui s'impose en 1QH se retrouve en 4Q*511* 37, 4 où elle est, là encore, certaine: 3. . . *wtḥwl hʾrṣ*[4. . . *y*]*rwʿw kwl mḥšbyh wkw*[*l* (*ʾšr ʿlyh?*),[18] et en 4Q*504* 1–2 vii 7, *lšmym hʾrṣ wkwl mḥšbyh*[.[19]

S'il est déconseillé de corriger la lecture dans tous ces cas actuellement publiés, il est recommandé de donner un sens acceptable à ce

16. Voir par ex. Carmignac, *Les Textes de Qumrân*, 202 s, "et les ingénieuses (créatures) de l'abîme" renvoyant à 1QH V 26 (= XIII 12) où cet auteur a placé avec raison le fg. 20 mais où il est supposé lire (ligne 4) *mḥšbym*, corrigeant(?) à tort la bonne lecture faite dans "Compléments au texte des Hymnes de Qumrân" (*RevQ* 2 [1960] 267–76, 268), mais la note 1 est reprise dans le commentaire de 1961 à tel point qu'il ne semble pas distinguer les deux formes. En fait, la lecture *mḥšbwtm* est certaine et il n'y a pas lieu de retenir cet emploi (pour les lectures, voir notre étude, "Un hymne essénien en partie retrouvé et les béatitudes, 1QH V 12–VI 18 [= cols. XIII–XIV 7] et 4QBéat.," *RevQ* 13 [1988] 59–88). Voir encore par exemple M. Delcor, *Les Hymnes de Qumrân (Hodayot): Texte hébreu, Introduction, Traduction, Commentaire* (Paris, 1962) 113: 'les êtres pensants de l'abîme'; B. P. Kittel, *The Hymns of Qumran: Translation and Commentary* (SBLDS 50; Chico, Cal., 1981) 59, 'the schemers of the abyss. . . .' J. Licht (*The Thanksgiving Scroll, A Scroll from the Wilderness of Judaea: Text, Introduction, Commentary and Glossary* [en *ʿIvrît*] [Jerusalem, 1957] in loco) comprend 'les profondeurs cachées' à l'image des pensées secrètes du coeur de l'homme.

17. Ainsi A. Dupont-Sommer, "Le Livre des Hymnes," 40, 'et ⟨les recoins⟩ de l'Abîme', suivi par E. Lohse, *Die Texte aus Qumran: Hebräisch und Deutsch* (Darmstadt, 1971) 123, 'und die Tiefen der Urflut'; H. W. Kuhn, *Enderwartung und gegenwärtiges Heil: Untersuchungen zu dem Gemeinden von Qumran, mit einem Anhang über Eschatologie und Gegenwart in der Verkündigung Jesu* (Studien zum Umwelt des N.T. 4; Göttingen, 1966) 41, etc.

18. Lecture de Baillet (*Qumrân Grotte 4*, 239), mais rendue par ']tous ses êtres pensants [so]nt malmenés, et tou[t ce qui est sur elle. . .]'.

19. Baillet (ibid., 150) propose avec raison *mḥšbyh* plutôt que *mḥškyh* qui était sa lecture dans l'étude "Un Recueil liturgique de Qumrân, Grotte 4: 'Les Paroles des Luminaires' " (*RB* 68 [1961] 195–250, sp. 234). En effet, il est manifeste que dans ce manuscrit le *bet* a plusieurs formes tandis que le *kaf* médial est, lui, de module constant. Mais l'auteur traduit encore 'et tous ses *êtres pensants*[', et signale dans le commentaire "on est tenté de lire *mḥškyh* 'ses antres', cf. Ps. 74:20, mais *mḥšbyh* 'ses êtres pensants' semble meilleur: cf. 1QH iii 32–3." Cependant le passage et la ligne qui semble devoir se compléter ainsi [*hymym wthwm*] 8*rbh wʾbdwn whmym* . . . ne paraissent pas favorables à cette traduction.

mot, autre que 'êtres pensants'. De fait, comme le note justement un lexique récent,[20] le sens fondamental ou premier de la racine *ḥšb* n'est pas 'considérer, estimer, imaginer', mais 'tisser', d'où le sens de "sangle, bande (tissée)" pour *ḥšb.* Dans ce cas, les *mḥšby thwm* de 1QH XI 33 (= III 32) ou *mḥšby* (*h*)*ʾrṣ* de 1QH XI 34 (= III 33), de 4Q*511* 37, 4 et de 4Q*504* 1–2 vii 7 doivent désigner de préférence les 'réseaux abyssaux' comparables à un tissage ou à des écheveaux entremêlés. Ce sont vraisemblablement des *dédales de sillons* et *de fissures* dans les recoins ou profondeurs de la terre, des replis cachés qui les font assimiler au *thwm rbh* 'Grand Abîme'.[21] D'où la proposition de traduction:

> Et les torrents de Bélial s'engouffreront dans l'Abaddôn,
> les fissures de l'Abîme mugiront d'un grondement d'éruptions
> de boue.
> La terre [34]hurlera au sujet de la calamité survenant au monde,
> toutes ses fissures crieront (1QH XI 33–34 [= III 32–33]).

>][7]aux cieux, la terre et toutes ses fissures,[les mers,]Grand
> [8][Abîme] et Abaddôn et les eaux et tout ce qu'elles[contiennent
> (4Q*504* 1–2 VII 7).

> [3]. . . et seront ébranlées] leurs [fon]dations
> et frémira la terre[. . .
> [4]et]crieront toutes ses fissures et tou[t . . . (4Q*511* 37, 3–4).

šwṭ

Le même hymne contient deux emplois d'une racine *šwṭ,* 1QH XI 31, 37 (= III 30, 36). Dans une autre étude,[22] nous avons proposé de comprendre ces deux emplois à l'inaccompli féminin avec *ʾš* pour sujet à la ligne 31 (= 30) et avec *mlḥmh* à la ligne 37 (= 36), comme 'consumer, embraser, brûler',[23] en les rattachant à la racine *śwṭ* que nous avions déjà identifiée dans les traités araméens de Sfiré 1 A 24.[24] Même si

20. *HALAT* 1.345 s.

21. Ces *mḥšbym* 'fissures, sillons, canaux, replis (de l'Abîme)' semblent bien être connus et rendus par le Pseudo-Philon, *tunc expergefactus est abyssus de* venis suis *et omnes fluctus maris* . . . (Liber Antiquitatum Biblicarum 32, 8), qui nous conseillerait, à sa manière, de ne pas corriger la lecture matérielle du mot en *mḥškym.*

22. E. Puech, "La Racine *śyṭ-šʾṭ* en araméen et en hébreu: A propos de Sfiré 1 A 24, 1QH^a iii 30 et 36 (= xi 31 et 37) et Ezéchiel," *RevQ* 11 (1983) 367–78.

23. E. J. Pryke ("Eschatology in the Dead Sea Scrolls," *The Scrolls and Christianity: Historical and Theological Significance* [SPCK Theological Collections 11; London, 1969] 45–57, sp. 54) traduit par 'burnt' mais sans explication.

24. E. Puech, "Les Inscriptions araméennes I et III de Sfiré: Nouvelles lectures," *RB* 89 (1982) 576–87. Cette signification qui s'impose dans ce passage est passée inaperçue dans *HALAT* 4.1336–37. Le sens de 'manquer' proposé par C. Jean and J. Hoftijzer (*Dictionnaire*

on ne retenait pas le sens de 'brûler' pour les emplois de *šᵓṭ* en Ezéchiel, au profit du sens plus habituel de 'mépriser' que confirme l'emploi araméen du Testament araméen de Lévi (Cambridge e 21, *wdy šᵓyṭ ḥwkmth*), cette signification s'impose dans ces deux passages des Hymnes, à l'exclusion du sens habituellement retenu de 'fouetter'[25] ou même de 'envelopper'.[26] L'image du feu destructeur où *tšwṭ* est employé en parallèle à *bᵓš ᵓwklt,* ligne 30 (= 29) et à *tᵓwkl,* lignes 31–32 (= 30–31) que précise la destruction complète *ᶜd klh,* ligne 37 (= 36), est alors celle du déluge de feu des temps eschatologiques qui constitue le pendant du déluge d'eau aux origines.

En faveur de cette signification, on pourrait faire appel à Isa 28:15 et 18, *šwṭ šwṭp ky yᶜb(w)r*[27] *l(w)ᵓ ybwᵓnw,* repris en 1QH XIV 38 (= VI 35), *wbᶜbwr šwṭ šwṭp bl ybwᵓ bmbṣr,*[28] que nous avions laissé de côté dans notre étude précédente. Les traductions 'flot destructeur/dévastateur' (Bible du Centenaire), 'fléau menaçant/dévastant, flot dévastateur' (Bible de Jérusalem), 'flot inondant' (Dhorme), 'fléau déchaîné'[29] (TOB), 'fouet dévastateur' (Dupont-Sommer), 'fléau torrentiel' (Carmignac), 'sausende Geissel' (Lohse), et 'plötzliche Wasserflut' (*HALAT*). . . , ne sont pas des plus recommandables et ne font pas justice aux passages en question. On ne voit pas comment un 'fouet, fléau' (*šwṭ*) peut produire l'effet de *rms* 'fouler, écraser par terre' en Isa 28:18, *whyytm lw lmrms.* En revanche, une traduction littérale 'et vous deviendrez pour lui une foulée/chaussée', donc 'et vous lui servirez de chaussée', c'est-à-dire de lieu de passage, ne préjuge pas de l'image, flot, fleuve de feu, coulée incandescente (de lave), etc. Les LXX ont rendu par καταιγις 'tempête, ouragan' (voir 28:2–3), Théodotion par κατακλυσμος 'cataclysme', la syrohexaplaire par *ᶜlᶜlᵓ* 'ouragan', mais Aquila par μαστιξ 'fouet', le latin par *flagellum,* la Peshiṭta par *šwṭᵓ* et le targum *knḥl mgbr* 'comme un torrent débordant'. Cependant, l'emploi de 1QH XIV 38 (= VI 35) est plus précis puisque, dans la ligne suivante, il est question de 'comme la pierre] pour le crépi et comme la poutre pour le feu'. Cette même dévastation ou

---

des Inscriptions sémitiques de l'Ouest [Leiden, 1965] 293) ne va pas sans difficulté et n'a aucune étymologie ou racine apparentée dans d'autres langues sémitiques.

25. Dupont-Sommer, "Le Livre des Hymnes," 40–41.

26. Carmignac, *Les Textes de Qumrân,* 202.

27. Le Texte Massorétique lit au v. 15, *šyṭ šwṭp ky ᶜbr* (avec deux fautes de scribe) mais au v. 18 *šwṭ šwṭp ky yᶜbr,* et 1QIsa[a], *šyṭ šwṭp ky ybwr* (avec deux fautes de scribe) au v. 15 et la leçon *šwṭ šwṭp ky yᶜbwr* au v. 18. Les deux fautes de scribe dans les deux textes s'expliquent par la confusion des *waw-yod* dans une copie antérieure d'une part, et d'autre part par une écriture phonétique, soit oubli de *yod* (haplographie) en TM, soit élision du *ᶜaïn* entre deux sons -a- en 1QIsa[a].

28. Nous lisons sûrement *wbᶜbwr,* non *wmᶜbyr* de l'éditeur Sukenik.

29. Mais est-on autorisé à donner à la racine hébraïque le sens abstrait que le mot possède en français?

consumation de la pierre et de la poutre par le feu peut se retrouver en Isa 29:6 où les images de l'ouragan et de la tempête sont accompagnées de celles d'une flamme de feu dévorant. L'image d'un incendie, d'une flamme de feu, d'une coulée de laves incandescentes dévorant et débordant pour exécuter le jugement de Dieu est des plus courantes dans la Bible, Isa 66:15s, Deut 32:22. . . . Le sens de "coulée (incandescente, consumante)"[30] suit manifestement mieux le contexte que 'fléau/fouet' en Isaïe 28 et 1QH XIV (= VI) et renforcerait, si besoin était, le sens de 'brûler, consumer' proposé pour *śy* / *wṭ* en 1QH XI 31, 37 (= III 30, 36) d'après le sens de *soṭ-syṭ* en syriaque et en ge^{c}ez et de *šawwaṭa* en arabe. Noter qu'en 1QH XIV 33 (= VI 32) *yrmwsw* correspond à *lmrms* d'Isa 28:18 et qu'il s'adapte bien au passage d'une coulée de matériau lourd incandescent traçant une chaussée, écrasant et aplanissant tout, et débordant de ses rives. En Isaïe 28–29, les images d'une coulée d'eau et de feu seraient associées: orage-torrents-lave (28:2, 15, 17–18; 29:6; voir Isa 34:9 à propos de la fin d'Edom).

Comme confirmation de ce sens de la racine *śwṭ* pourrait-on ajouter la traduction en ge^{c}ez de Sira 8:13 où $^{\supset}$*itešuṭ* rend le grec εκκαιε et l'hébreu *tṣlḥ*,[31] voir le latin *incendas*? Faut-il comprendre $^{\supset}$*itešuṭ* $^{\supset}$*esatomu laḫate*$^{\supset}$*an* 'ne répands pas le feu des pécheurs', en donnant à la racine le sens plus fréquent de 'répandre', ou mieux 'n'allume pas le feu des pécheurs afin que tu ne te brûles pas à leur flamme' (*kama* $^{\supset}$*ita*^{c}*ay banadomu::*) en donnant encore une fois à cette racine le sens de 'brûler'?[32] On sait que le syriaque *syṭ-soṭ* traduit l'hébreu *ḥrh* en Job 30:30, et que l'arabe *šwṭ* (*šawwaṭa*) ou mieux *šyṭ* signifient 'brûler, cuire, rôtir',[33] sens de la racine qui convient parfaitement en Sfiré 1 A 24.[34]

En définitive, ne faudrait-il pas isoler une racine sémitique *šy*/ *wṭ* avec la valeur de 'brûler, enflammer, consumer, cuire' qui semble rendre parfaitement compte de ces quelques emplois repérés?

> Et quand passera la coulée débordante,
> elle n'entrera pas dans la forteresse . . . (1QH XIV 38 [= VI 35]).
>
> La coulée débordante, quand elle passera, vous lui serez
> une chaussée (Isa 28:18; voir v. 15).

30. A comprendre de coulée incandescente (de laves, de minerai . . .).

31. Voir notre étude "Sur la racine ṢLḤ en hébreu et en araméen," *Sem* 21 (1971) 5–19, sp. 10s, n. 6.

32. Dans cette étude nous n'avions pas osé proposer ce sens aussi pour le ge^{c}ez.

33. Voir E. W. Lane, *Arabic-English Lexicon* (London and Edinburgh, 1867) 4.1618–19, *šwṭ-šawwaṭa*; 1630–31, *šyṭ*.

34. Voir Puech, "La Racine *śyṭ-š*$^{\supset}$*ṭ*" et "Les Inscriptions araméennes": "et que ses sept ⟨panetières⟩ s'en aillent tandis que brûle le pain, et qu'il ne soit pas emmagasiné!"

[30]Alors les torrents de Bélial déborderont sur toutes les rives élevées
par un feu dévorant toutes leurs irrigations
pour détruire tout arbre vert [31]ou sec de leurs canaux,
et il consumera par des tourbillons de flamme
jusqu'à la disparition de tout ce qui s'y abreuve. . . .

La guerre des héros [37]célestes consumera le monde
et elle ne cessera pas jusqu'à l'extermination fatale, définitive et sans pareille (1QH XI 30–31, 37 [= III 29–30, 36]).

Que le Professeur J. C. Greenfield trouve ici l'expression de notre reconnaissance pour l'émulation sans cesse renouvelée dans l'étude de racines sémitiques à la connaissance desquelles il a, pour sa part, tant contribué!

A Work concerning Divine Providence: 4Q*413*

ELISHA QIMRON

4Q413 is a scroll from Qumran, only four lines of which have been preserved. This article consists of a transcription and restoration of the text, accompanied by a short commentary. Two features are discussed at length:

(1) The expression הלך אחר משמע אוזניו ומראה עיניו. *This expression, alluding to Isa 11:3, designates a person who is acting according to his own (in contrast to God's) will. The meaning given here to this biblical expression helps us to reconstruct and understand a fragmentary pesher on this verse of Isaiah (4Q161 frgs. 8–10, lines 21–23) and other texts from Qumran that are dependent on Isaiah 11. The passage in Isaiah was apparently interpreted in the Dead Sea Scrolls as dealing with the war of the messianic king at the end of days, and the sentence in Isa 11:3,* ולא למראה עיניו ישפוט ולא למשמע אזניו יוכיח, *was taken to mean that the king could not start a war without the permission of the priests.*

(2) The spelling פועלות *instead of* פעולות *'acts' conforms to the pronunciation in the Tiberian tradition. In this tradition a šĕwāʾ before a guttural was pronounced like the vowel of the guttural. Accordingly, words like* פְּעֻלָּה *were pronounced puʿullâ. Presumably this was also the case in the Hebrew of the Dead Sea Scrolls. In this type of Hebrew, the wāw in words like* פעולה *is placed after the guttural or before it, and one rarely finds plene phonetic spelling, as in* כוהונות *'priesthood', pronounced kuhunnot (4Q400 1 ii 19).*

Description of the Manuscript

Only two fragments of this manuscript, each containing four lines, have survived. Both fragments have upper margins. The larger one also has a left margin and the smaller one a right margin. Even though the two fragments do not join, they evidently belong to the top of the same column (see photograph [p. 193] and transcription). The script is Herodian.

Contents and Literary Genre

It is difficult fully to determine the nature of this work on the basis of such a short text. The four preserved lines contain an appeal (in the first person) exhorting the reader to consider carefully the historical events of the past, which demonstrate that whoever followed God has been rewarded, while whoever did not has failed to survive. This concept of divine providence is commonly found in other Dead Sea literary works, such as the *Damascus Document* (in the "Admonition"). Cf. also 1QS III 13–25, the epilogue of MMT and 1Q*27*.

The Text

1. מׄזׄמׄתׄ ד[עת מצאו] וחוכמה אלמדכמה והתבוננו בדרכי אנוש ובפועלות
2. בני אדׄ[ם כי באהבת]אׄלׄ את איש הרבה לו נחלה בׄדעת אמתו וכפי גועלו
3. כל רעׄ[ההולך אחר מ]שׄמע אוזניו ומראה עינו בלׄ יחיה *vacat* ועתה
4. חסד[ ]רׄיׄאשונים ובינו בׄשׄני ד[ור ו]דׄור כאשר גלה אל

vacat[ ]ל[ ] [ ]ל[ ] [

TRANSLATION

1. . . . a plan of [knowledge find] and wisdom let me teach you, and (thus) contemplate the conduct of man and the actions of
2. people. [For whenever] God [favored] a person He increased his share in the knowledge of His truth; and as He despised
3. every wicked individual [who would follow] what his ears hear and what his eyes see (that wicked individual) would not survive *(vacat)*. And now
4. . . . of the former years and contemplate (the events of) past generations as God has revealed.

COMMENTS

Line 1

מזמת. Both the word מזמה and the following related term חוכמה are used in the sectarian Dead Sea Scrolls in reference to divine providence. For the restoration, see Prov 8:12.

וחוכמה. The plene orthography of this word occurs thirteen times in the nonbiblical Dead Sea Scrolls (both published and unpublished).

It represents an early *quṭla* pattern, as does its Tiberian and Babylonian vocalization. The alternative spelling of this word (חכמה) is, however, more frequent in the Dead Sea Scrolls (twenty-eight times), and perhaps attests to another early pattern, for example *ḥikma* as in Syriac, Arabic, Samaritan Aramaic,[1] and perhaps Qumran Aramaic.[2] Several cases of *ḥakma* are found in Hebrew.[3] It is less likely that all the cases of חכמה (without *waw*) are defective spellings, since some of them occur in manuscripts that consistently mark any *u*/*o* vowel with a *waw*.

אלמדכמה. Cf. Ps 34:12: יראת ה׳ אלמדכם. The long pronominal suffix is typical of Dead Sea Scrolls Hebrew.[4]

והתבוננו. *Hitpolel* forms of the root בין occur in Biblical Hebrew, in Dead Sea Scrolls Hebrew (and Aramaic), in the book of Ben-Sira, and (rarely) in Mishnaic Hebrew.[5]

בדרכי אנוש ובפועלות בני אד[ם]. The word דרך here means 'conduct'. It occurs here parallel to פְּעֻלָּה. I have not found such parallelism anywhere else, but I did find ארחות//פְּעֻלּוֹת in Ps 17:4 (cf. also 1QS IV 15, 1QpHab VIII 13). The word אנוש occurs in Biblical Hebrew exclusively in poetry. In the Dead Sea Scrolls it is found in prose as well. For the spelling פועלות for פעולות, see appendix 2 below.

1. E. Y. Kutscher, *Hebrew and Aramaic Studies* (Jerusalem, 1977) 276 [Hebrew part].

2. I have found the form חכמה fourteen times, and חוכמה only once.

3. E. Qimron, *A Grammar of the Hebrew Language of the Dead Sea Scrolls* (Ph.D. diss., Hebrew University, 1976) 43 n. 27 [Heb.].

4. See E. Qimron, *The Hebrew of the Dead Sea Scrolls* (HSS 29; Atlanta, 1986) §322.17 [henceforth HDSS].

5. See M. Moreshet, "Polel/Hitpolel in Mishnaic Hebrew and in Aramaic," *Bar-Ilan* 18–19 (1981) 248–69 [Heb.].

Line 2

אל [באהבת]. I have restored באהבת according to CD VIII 16: באהבת אל את הראשנים . . . ובשונאו את בוני החיץ. The word אל here and in line 4 is written in paleo-Hebrew script, as is the case in other scrolls.

את איש 'a person'. The use of את before the indefinite object is peculiar. Cf. the somewhat similar construction (with *lamed* rather than את) ואהבת חסד לאיש (1QS V 25; 4QS[d] reads ואהבת חסד without the object).[6]

הרבה לו נחלה. Similar expressions occur in the Bible and in the Dead Sea Scrolls: לרב תרבה נחלתו (Num 26:54; cf. 33:54); . . . באי[ש לפי נחלת איש בין רוב למועט) הרביתה נחלתו בדעת אמתכה (1QH X 28–29): (1QS IV 16); וכפי נחלת איש באמת יצדק (1QS IV 24). Note that the suffix in נחלתו in the biblical sources and in 1QH is equivalent to לו in our text. Compare עינים להם ולא יראו (Ps 115:5) to ידיהם ולא ימישון (115:7).

בדעת אמתו. The combination דעת + אמת occurs in 1QH X 28–29 cited above and in 1QS IX 17. Similar combinations occur elsewhere. The juxtaposition of נחלה + אמת also occurs in 1QS IV 24.

וכפי גועלו. The word כפי is equivalent to לפי or to the prepositions כ and ב. It is relatively more frequent in the Dead Sea Scrolls than in the Bible, especially before an infinitive. The word גועלו should be parsed as an inflected infinitive, rather than a *quṭl* noun (בגֹעַל נפשך Ezek 16:5). The verb געל is an antonym of אהב.

Line 3

ההולך אחר מ]שמע אוזניו ומראה עינו]. This expression is taken from Isa 11:3: ולא למראה עיניו ישפוט ולא למשמע אזניו יוכיח. The form מִשְׁמָע is unique in the Bible, while מַרְאֶה is common, occurring frequently in the combinations מראה עיניך, מראה עיניה, and the like. The passage in Isaiah 11 deals with the Messianic King, stating that he will judge through God's inspiration. The expression under discussion is generally taken as a metaphor for human frailty. At first glance the usage of this expression in our text seems different from its usage in Isaiah. Yet this is not necessarily the case. Fortunately, we have a *pesher* on this biblical text that informs us about the ways in which the expressions under discussion were interpreted by the Qumran sectarians. In the appendix, I will attempt to demonstrate that the *pesher* interpreted this expression as a metaphor for a person acting according to his own will (in contrast to God's will). This is apparently the meaning of the expression here. It is an attribute for an evil person, who acts independently rather than following God's com-

6. Cf. M. Kister, "Biblical Phrases and Hidden Biblical Interpretations and Pesharim," in *The Dead Sea Scrolls: Forty Years of Research* (ed. D. Dimant and U. Rappaport; Jerusalem and Leiden, 1992) 30.

mands. Compare Isa 33:15, אטם אזנו משמע דמים ועצם עיניו מראות ברע (referring to a righteous person), and 1QH VII 2–4, שעו עיני מראות רע אוזני משמוע דמים השם לבבי ממחשבת רוע.

בל יחיה. The negative בל occurs twenty-seven times in the Dead Sea Scrolls (both published and unpublished), always before an imperfect tense. In the Bible, it occurs sixty times, before various verbal forms. In Mishnaic Hebrew, it is not used freely but rather always in the combination בל תעשה (or יעשה) in the sense of a prohibitive law.

Line 4

. . . ובינו. In restoring the beginning of this line, I assume that the conjunctive *waw* in ובינו suggests that another imperative form with a similar meaning (such as זכורו) stood here (cf. Deut 32:7 זכר ימות עולם בינו שנות דור ודור. This would also be consistent with the occurrence of ועתה (after the *vacat* in line 3); ועתה indicates that the action expressed by the verb that follows is actual. This verb is frequently in the imperative (or, the jussive), as in CD I 1, ועתה שמעו כל יודעי צדק ובינו במעשי אל. It thus appears that the beginning of the line contained a sentence parallel to ובינו בשני דור ודור. (Parallelism is typical of this text.) The word חסד, which is materially quite certain, seems, however, to be inconsistent with this suggestion. The only solution that occurs to me is to take חסד as an abbreviation of בני חסד (one of the epithets of the Dead Sea sect; 1QH VII 20) and to restore ועתה חסד [זכורו ימים] ר^א^ישונים 'And now, members of the covenant, contemplate (the events of) the days gone by. . . .' Compare with Sir 41:11, הבל אדם בגויתו אך שם חסד לא יכרת.

For the imperative *Qal* בינו, see CD I 1. The introduction of the object of בין by ב in the *Hiphil* and *Qal* is typical of the Dead Sea Scrolls and of late Biblical Hebrew.[7] The masculine plural of שנה is used here instead of the archaic feminine plural form, used especially in biblical poetry as in, for example, the biblical parallel source, Deut 32:7.

כאשר גלה אל. The word אל is written in paleo-Hebrew script. The blank space left at the beginning of line 5 shows that אל is the last word of the sentence. The verb thus has no object. Compare 1QS VIII 16: כאשר גלו הנביאים ברוח קודשו.

Appendix 1

The use of the expression (הלך אחר) משמע אוזניו ומראה עיניו in the present text helps us to reconstruct and understand the *pesher* on Isa 11:3

7. See A. Hurvitz, *The Transition Period in Biblical Hebrew* (Jerusalem, 1972) 136–37 [Hebrew]; HDSS, 88.

Table 1

The Temple Scroll	*The Pesher*
1. על פיהו יצא ועל פיהו יבוא . . .	ועל פיהם [יצא להלחם עם אויביו]
2. ולוא יצא עד יבוא לפני הכוהן הגדול	[ו]עמו יצא אחד מכוהני השם
3. לוא יצא מעצת לבו עד אשר ישאל במשפט האורים והתומים	ואשר אמר לוא [למראה עיניו ישפוט] ולא למשמע אוזניו יוכיח פשרו אשר [ישאל לדברי הכוהנים] וכאשר יורוהו כן ישפוט

(= 4Q*161* frgs. 8–10, lines 21–23).[8] The latter text includes a special interpretation of that verse, which strikingly agrees with the sectarian law concerning the king found in the *Temple Scroll* (LVIII 15–21). Here is a reconstruction of the *pesher* as supported by the *Temple Scroll's* parallel:

ואשר אמר לוא
[למראה עיניו ישפוט] ולוא למשמע אוזניו יוכיח פשרו אשר
[ישמע לדברי הכוהנים] וכאשר יורוהו כן ישפוט ועל פיהם
[יצא להלחם עם אויביו ו]עמו יצא אחד מכוהני השם ובידו בגדי

The similarity of the *pesher* and the *Temple Scroll*, which helps to reconstruct the former, is demonstrated in table 1 (above).

If the third passage in the *pesher* is truly parallel to that of the *Temple Scroll*, then the expression under discussion must be equivalent to מעצת לבו of the *Temple Scroll*.[9] If my reconstruction of the *pesher* is correct, it should be assumed that the words ישפוט and יוכיח in the biblical source were interpreted as designating 'quarrel, fight, punish', rather than intellectual judging.[10]

8. J. M. Allegro, *Qumrân Cave 4: I* (*4Q158–4Q186*) (DJD 5; Leiden, 1968) 14.

9. Another equivalent is שרירות לב; see E. Qimron, "Biblical Philology and the Dead Sea Scrolls," *Tarbiẓ* 53 (1989) 313 [Hebrew]; for an etymology of שרירות which fits this interpretation, see L. Kopf, *Studies in Arabic and Hebrew Lexicography* (Jerusalem, 1976) 224. Note also 1QS IX 2 וזולת רצון אל לו (= לא) יחפץ. The preceding sentence, והריחו ביראת ה', may also be interpreted to this effect.

10. Cf. Ps 149:7: לעשות נקמה בגוים תוכחות בלאמים. This sectarian interpretation is peculiar and differs markedly from other interpretations, for example, from the rabbinic interpretation in the *b. Sanh.* 93a. The passage in Isaiah is also used in the blessing of the Messianic King in 1QSb V 20–29 (DJD 1.127–28). This text likewise refers to the execution of justice and the subduing of the nations as a goal of the Messianic King. This is also the

One may wonder whether the comparison between these two sources is adequate. The *Temple Scroll* deals with any king, while the *pesher* deals with the Messianic King. There are indications, however, that the sectarians treated both alike. On the one hand they concluded from Isa 11:3[11] that no king might start a war without the permission of the priests, and on the other, they concluded from the law of the king in Deut 17:18–20 that the Messianic King should study the Torah. This is the source for the *pesher* on רוח דעת (Isa 11:2) ואל יסומכנו ב[דעת] תורה (4Q*161* frgs. 8–10, line 18). Cf. also the ascription of מדע תורה to the "leader of Israel" in MMT (C 28).

My reconstruction is further supported by a *pesher* on Hab 1:12–13: ה׳ למשפט שמתו וצור להוכיח יסדתו טהור עינים מראות רע. This passage contains expressions similar to those of Isa 11:3 (underlined). Here is the entire passage from 1QpHab V 1–8:

> [אלהי קדושי לוא נמות ה׳] למשפט שמתו וצור למוכיחו יסדתו טהור ע׳נים
> מראות ברע והבט אל עמל לוא תוכל פשר הדבר אשר לוא יכלה אל את עמו
> ביד הגוים וביד בחירו יתן אל את משפט כול הגוים ובתוכחתם יאשמו
> כל רשעי עמו אשר שמרו את מצוותו בצר למו כיא הוא אשר אמר טהור
> עינים מראות ברע פשרו אשר לוא זנו אחר עיניהם בקץ הרשעה

---

case in 4Q*285* frg. 7, lines 2–4: ויצא חוטר מגזע ישי [. . .] צמח דויד ונשפטו את [. . .] והמיתו נשיא העדה צמ[ח דויד . . . ח]לל[י] כתיי[ם] (see G. Vermes, *JJS* 43 [1992] 86–90). The word המיתו corresponds to ימית רשע in Isaiah. From the words חללי כתיי[ם] we may infer that the Messianic King is the leader of Israel in the eschatological war against the Kittim. The leader of the Kittim is Gog. This may be inferred from the fragmentary *pesher* on Isaiah cited above. In this *pesher* the word מגוג occurs in connection with the war of the Messianic King (4Q*161* frgs. 8–10, line 20: ובכל הג[ואי]ם ימשול ומגוג [. . .] העמים תשפוט חרבו; it is immaterial whether one reads מָגוֹג or מְגוֹג, since Gog is the king of Magog. Gog is also mentioned in 1QM XI 16 in connection with the eschatological war: [בע]שותכה שפטים בגוג ובכול קהלו. In the 4Q*285* fragments there are expressions known from the description of the war of Gog in Ezekiel 38–39: e.g., על הרי ישראל and להם קברי[ם]. These expressions will be dealt with by B. Nitzan in a forthcoming article. A. Tal has directed my attention to the Samaritan version in Num 24:7: וירם מגוג מלכו in a verse referring to the Messianic King. The Samaritan pronunciation tradition is *magog*; their interpretations fluctuate; see Z. Ben-Hayyim, *The Literary and Oral Tradition of Hebrew and Aramaic amongst the Samaritans* (Jerusalem, 1961) vol. 3/part I, 86. The evidence of Qumran implies that Gog was taken as the adversary of the Messianic King and that he was the king of the Kittim (both are sons of Japhet; cf. Gen 10:1 and 1QM XVIII 2: ונפלו בני יפת לאין קום וכתיים יכתו לאין [. . .]). The identification of Gog as the adversary of the Messianic King is found in rabbinic sources (*b. Sanh.* 94a.).

11. And from other biblical sources as well, such as Num 27:21 and 1 Sam 30:7–8; cf. also 4Q*376* 1 ii–iii (J. Strugnell, "Moses-Pseudoepigrapha at Qumran: 4Q375, 4Q376 and Similar Works," in *Archaeology and History in the Dead Sea Scrolls: The New York University Conference in Memory of Yigael Yadin* [ed. L. H. Schiffman; Sheffield, 1990] 237).

This passage has been considered crux interpretorum.[12] In the light of our text, however, it becomes clear, as we shall now see.

In this text the biblical word ברע (MT רע) was interpreted as an adverb (= בקץ הרשעה; cf. בצר למו above; and cf. also Isa 33:15), while the expression טהור עינים מראות was perhaps taken as טהור מראות עינים and thus interpreted אשר לא זנו אחר עיניהם. This passage clearly refers to the eschatological war, like the passage from the *pesher* on Isaiah.[13]

It should finally be noted that the interpretation given in the *pesher* on Isaiah is not as farfetched as it first seems. There is a similar expression with approximately the same meaning in Qoh 11:9: והלך בדרכי לבך ובמראי עיניך. Thus, Ibn Ezra writes ,"and the interpretation of this verse is like ולא תתורו אחרי לבבכם ואחרי עיניכם."[14]

Thus, the peculiar use of the expression הלך אחר משמע אזניו ומראה עיניו has helped us to explore the peculiar interpretation given in the Dead Sea Scrolls to the Messianic passage in Isaiah 11.

Appendix 2

The form ובפועלות looks like a variant of ובפעולות. The noun פְּעֻלָּה belongs to the pattern קְטֻלָּה (← *quṭulla** ← *quṭula** ← *quṭulat**).[15] The form in our text is not an error, since it occurs two (or even three) times in 1QIsa[a] (see table below). The word is regularly spelled in the Dead Sea Scrolls, however, with a *waw* after the *ᶜayin* rather than before it (see table 2, p. 199).

At first glance, ובפועלות does not seem to conform either to פְּעֻלָּה of the Tiberian (or Babylonian) tradition or the assumed earlier form of this word, *puᶜula.* A thorough study of the evidence, however, suggests that it does indeed correspond to both these forms. What was the form of the Proto-Semitic *quṭulat* pattern in Dead Sea Scrolls tradition? Nouns of this pattern appear in the Dead Sea Scrolls in four different spellings, as shown in table 2.

The form קטלה (occurring mostly in biblical scrolls) is a defective spelling and should be disregarded here. The other three spellings might a priori be regarded as reflecting three separate forms. Alterna-

12. W. H. Brownlee, *The Midrash Pesher of Habakkuk* (Ann Arbor, 1979) 84–90. H. W. Basser, "Pesher Hadavar: The Truth of the Matter," *RevQ* 13 (1988) 398–400.

13. See. B. Nitzan, מגילת פשר חבקוק ממגילות מדבר יהודה (Jerusalem, 1986) 64–65.

14. Cf. R. Gordis, *Koheleth: The Man and His World* (New York, 1955). Onkelos renders ולא תתורו אחרי לבבכם ואחרי עיניכם (Num 15:39): ולא תטעון בתר הרהור לבכון ובתר חזו עיניכון; cf. Rashi to this verse. Note also the expression כראות עיניו in Modern Hebrew. On the combination of דרך + לב and the significance of the pronominal suffix attached to the word לב see Kister, "Biblical Phrases and Hidden Biblical Interpretations and Pesharim," 32–33.

15. H. Bauer and P. Leander, *Historische Grammatik der hebräischen Sprache des Alten Testamentes* (Halle, 1922) 469.

Table 2

קטולה	קטלה	קוטלה	קוטולה
פעולה (more than 20 times)	פעלה (7 times)	פועלה (1QIsa[a] 49:4, 65:7, and perhaps 61:8)[16]	
פקודה (more than 20 times)	פקדה (3 times)		
חנופה (twice)	חנפה (once)		
	אחזה (7 times)[18]	אוחזה[17]	
כהונה (9 times)		כוהנה (4Q*400* frg. 2, line 5)	כוהונה (4Q*400* 1 ii 19)
עמורה (4Q*172* frg. 4, line 3)		עומרם (5 times)	
קדושה (?) (1QS III 7)[19]			
כבודה (1QpH X 11)[20]			
	גאלה (4 times)		

tively, קוטלה and קטולה could be taken as defective spellings of קוטולה,[21] which corresponds to the assumed early form of this pattern.[22] The first solution is unlikely. The second seems more promising, but it cannot serve as a general explanation, since the spelling קוטלה always occurs

16. The *ᶜayin* seems to be written over a *waw.*
17. לאוחזת עולם (1QS XI 7).
18. Once אזתם (11QpaleoLev 25:32).
19. As in Mishnaic Hebrew; 4QS[a] reads וברוח קודשו.
20. Commentators suggest בעבור כְּבוֹדֹה and are divided on the question of the antecedent of the suffix. For the interpretation of this word as כְּבֵדָה, cf. בעבור הון (1QpHab VIII 10–11).
21. See below.
22. See Bauer and Leander, *Historische Grammitik,* 469.

when the second or first consonant is a guttural, while other nouns of this pattern have no *waw* after their first root consonant.

Even though the form קוטולה corresponds to the assumed early form of the pattern under discussion, it does not represent a form earlier than the Tiberian. (Such an explanation would not account for the fact that all examples of קוט(ו)לה involve gutturals.) Rather, קוטולה corresponds basically to the Tiberian pattern. In Tiberian tradition, words like פְּעֻלָּה were pronounced with two consecutive *u* vowels, since the *šĕwāʾ* before the guttural was realized as the following vowel.[23]

The forms פועלה and פעולה are then both defective spellings of פועולה. As Kutscher pointed out, the Dead Sea Scrolls scribes sometimes marked with *waw* only one of two consecutive vowels *u/o* in a single word.[24] In the pattern under discussion we fortunately have one case of plene spelling (כוהונה), which establishes the existence in it of two consecutive *u* vowels.

In Greek and Latin transliterations of Hebrew, words of this pattern have the form *qoṭolla*.[25] The evidence in the Dead Sea Scrolls, however, does not correspond to that of these transliterations, since all the instances of **quṭulla* involve gutturals. That the *u* vowel after the first consonant does not represent the original vowel but is rather a realization of a *šĕwāʾ* is confirmed by evidence from words of other patterns in which the "Tiberian" *šĕwāʾ* before a guttural is pronounced like the vowel of the guttural. In some of these patterns the vowel before the guttural does not correspond to the original one.

The phenomenon occurs in more than ten words. Here are three examples:[26]

(1) The *yod* in the word בחירי 'chosen ones' is sometimes misplaced before the *ḥet*: ביחרי (1QS IX 17); this reading is materially preferable to the possible alternative בוחרי, in the editions; 4QS[d] reads בחירי; ב(י)ח̇ר̇י (4QS[d] VIII 6); and apparently also כול ביחרי רצונֿך (1QH XIV 21, according to E. Puech, "Un hymne essénién en partie retrouvé et les béati-

23. See S. Morag, *The Hebrew Language Tradition of the Yemenite Jews* (Jerusalem, 1963) 148–74 [Heb.]; Y. Yahalom, *Leš* 34 (1970) 55–56.

24. E. Y. Kutscher, *The Language and Linguistic Background of the Isaiah Scroll (1QIsa[a])* (Leiden, 1974) 503–4; idem, in *Leš* 22 (1958) 105. In the latter discussion, Kutscher claims that this phenomenon is typical of short words. I would rather say that it is virtually a general rule but confined to the basic form of the word (namely, the form without suffixes). Words with suffixes may have two (or even three) consecutive *o/u* vowels (one of the basic form and one of the suffix (e.g., כתובו, יכתובו, יבואו, יכתובוהו).

25. See my dissertation, *A Grammar of the Hebrew Language of the Dead Sea Scrolls*, 108 n. 91; add to the references cited there: Kutscher, *Language and Linguistic Background*, 113–14.

26. See Ibid., 500–501.

tudes," *RevQ* 13 [1988] 64; Puech reads בוחרי). These spellings are best explained as reflecting the pronunciation *biḥire.*

(2) The personal name מַעַזְיָהוּ, 1 Chr 24:18 (= מַעַזְיָה, Neh 10:9), occurs in 4Q*321* II 3 in the form מעוזיה (a form known also from the Elephantine papyri, e.g., Cowley 23:2).[27] This name occurs in another spelling מועזיה (4Q*321* IV 8, V 2). This variant suggests that the actual pronunciation at Qumran was *Moᶜozia* (cf. Moozias in the Septuagint of 1 Chr 24:18).

(3) In a manuscript of the *Hôdāyôt Scroll* from Cave 4, one finds the form יועדני (4Q*427* 7 i 9). The context is broken and does not enable us to establish the meaning of the word. Fortunately, we have a similar text reading ומי יועדני וידמה במשפטי (4Q*491* 11 i 17).[28] The word יועדני seems to have a meaning similar to that of the word וידמה which follows in 4Q*491.* It is best derived from the root עוד with the meaning 'connect'.[29] The form יועדני is therefore a by-spelling of יעודני, both pronounced *yuᶜudeni.*

In the place-name עמורה (עומרם), which belongs to the קְטֻלָּה pattern,[30] it is the first consonant that is a guttural. In this case the vowel following the guttural became identical to the vowel of the following syllable. This phenomenon is attested in other words in the Dead Sea Scrolls. Good examples are: עוברי (pronounced *ᶜobori,* 1QIsa[a] 23:6),[31] יע˺בורנו (1QIsa[a] 35:8), [למי]העוד 4Q*364,* but עדולם 4Q*522* i 11; cf. Οδολλαμίτην in the Septuagint [Gen 38:1]).

The pronunciation *quṭulla* in the Dead Sea Scrolls evolved from assimilation and involves vowel harmony. Vowel harmony near gutturals is a well-established phenomenon in Hebrew (cf. also Ugaritic), for example, in forms such as יַעֲבֹד, וַחֲמִשָּׁה, מָעֳמָד, and in the pronunciation of the *šĕwāʾ* before a guttural (mentioned above). The same phenomenon occurs in forms like בַּבַּיִת (← *bahabbayit* ← *bĕhabbayit*) and מַהְלְכִים (← *mahalĕkim* ← *mĕhalĕkim* ← *mĕhallĕkim*).[32]

27. Cf. *Encyclopedia Biblica* 5.191 [Hebrew].

28. On the relationship between these two texts, see E. Schuller, "A Hymn from a Cave Four Hodayot Manuscript: 4Q427 7 i + ii," *JBL* 112 (1993) 605–28.

29. Cf. M. Zeidel, חקרי לשון (Jerusalem, 1986) 22–23. Zeidel cites Lam 2:13 and Jer 49:19, 50:54, where עוד occurs in similar contexts. In the light of the forms in the Dead Sea Scrolls, the forms in these passages as they appear in the consonantal text may be interpreted as *Qal* of עוד in the patterns יקול and יקיל. The vocalization of the forms, however, is problematical. See also H. Yalon, *The Dead Sea Scrolls: Philological Essays* (Jerusalem, 1967) 86 [Hebrew].

30. Γομορρα in the Septuagint; *emirra* in the Samaritan tradition.

31. Cf. Kutscher, *Language and Linguistic Background,* 194.

32. M. Lambert, *Traité de grammaire hebraïque* (Paris, 1938) 293, 295, 321; R. Kutscher, "מַהְלְכִים ואחיותיה," *Leš* 26 (1962) 93–96.

My analysis of the evidence differs somewhat from that of Kutscher.[33] Kutscher believed that the pronunciation of this pattern in 1QIsa[a] was similar to that of the Greek and Latin transliterations. He admitted, however, that all the examples in this scroll involve gutturals. In my opinion, the analysis of all the evidence for this pattern suggests that the pronunciation was similar to that of the Tiberian. The form כוהונ[ת] suggests that the actual pronunciation of such words (with guttural second root consonants) was *ku-un-na*, or something similar, rather than *kun-na*.

33. See n. 24 above.

Variant Scriptural Readings in Liturgical Texts

NAHUM M. SARNA

In this study I examine some instances of textual variants found in scriptural citations used in liturgical compositions. These correspond to one or more early independent witnesses to the Biblical Hebrew text—the Qumran materials, the Greek and Latin translations, and the Syro-Palestinian Targum and rabbinic sources.

In his studies on the Passover Haggadah, Daniel Goldschmidt observes that biblical citations in the liturgy often vary from our traditional received Hebrew text.[1] He notes that in many instances changes were intentionally made on contextual grounds or in order to accommodate the congregational setting of the prayer in which the scriptural verse is cited.[2] An obvious and well-known variant introduced into the liturgy for theological reasons is the citation of Isa 45:7. The text there reads:

> I form light and create darkness;
> I make peace and create evil (Hebrew *rā*ᶜ).

In the daily Jewish liturgy the final word of the verse was replaced by 'all things' (Hebrew *hakkōl*), a change that is mentioned in the Talmud, *b. Ber.* 11b.[3] However, there are several instances of liturgical variant readings for which none of the above-mentioned reasons can be valid. Some occur in the Passover Haggadah.

1. D. Goldschmidt, *The Passover Haggadah: Its Sources and History* (Jerusalem, 1960) 15–16 [Heb.].

2. Ibid., 16 n. 9.

3. Jer 10:16 has the phrase *yôṣēr hakkōl*, not *bôrēᵓ hakkōl*. Ben Sira (51:24) cites the Jeremiah form; see M. H. Segal, *Sefer Ben Sira Ha-Šalem* (Jerusalem, 1960) 355 and the note ad loc. on p. 356.

A famous issue that has long troubled the commentators on the Haggadah is the apparent lack of difference between the question asked of the father by the "wise son" and the one posed by the "wicked son." The former cites Deut 6:20, "What mean the decrees, laws, and rules that the Lord our God has enjoined upon you (Hebrew *ʾetkem*)?" The latter cites Exod 12:26, "What does this rite mean to you (Hebrew *lākem*)?" Each employs a mode of speech that seems to exclude the speaker himself, yet only the "wicked son" is rebuked. Much ink has been spilled and plenty of mental gymnastics performed in attempts to resolve the dilemma. However, as has often been noted, a variant form of the text of Deut 6:20 appears in the ancient versions and rabbinic sources. Both the Septuagint[4] and the Vulgate[5] render 'enjoined upon us', not 'upon you'. The Hebrew text underlying both versions must have read *ʾōtānû*. What is particularly interesting is that the Palestinian Talmud,[6] the Mekilta de-Rabbi Ishmael,[7] and Maimonides' version of the Passover Haggadah, both in the early printed editions and in the Yemenite manuscripts,[8] all feature the same reading as is presupposed by the Septuagint and the Vulgate, contrary to our so-called Masoretic Text of the Torah. Such a plethora of independent witnesses are a certain indication that these sources represent the original Hebrew version of the Deuteronomy passage quoted by the "wise son" in the Haggadah. Later scribes harmonized the text with the MT, thereby creating the dilemma, to the delight of pilpulists.[9]

Another biblical citation in the Haggadah that does not conform in every detail to our standard Hebrew Bibles is Deut 6:21. It appears in the

4. LXX: ὅσα ἐνετείλατω κύριος ὁ θεὸς ἡμῶν ἡμῖν.

5. Vulgate: quae praecepit Dominus Deus noster nobis.

6. *Y. Pesaḥ.* 10:4 (37d).

7. Ed. H. S. Horovitz and I. A. Rabin (2d ed.; Jerusalem, 1960), *Boʾ* XVIII, p. 73 and n. 13 (ed. M. Friedmann, Ish Shalom; Vienna, 1870; repr. 1968) 22b and n. 22. See also ed. J. Z. Lauterbach (Philadelphia, 1933) 1.166 and note.

8. *Sefer Ha-Zĕmannim, Hilkot Ḥameṣ U-Maṣâh,* chap. 8, "*Nosaḥ Ha-Haggadah*"; cf. ed. S. Frankel (Jerusalem, 1978) 2.349 (variae) and 766 ad loc.; see also *Rambam La-ʿAm,* vol. 2: *Sefer Zĕmannim* (Jerusalem, 1957), and 445 n. 4: also Goldschmidt, *Haggadah,* 29 n. 22.

9. M. Kasher, *Haggadah Šelemah* (3d ed.; Jerusalem, 1967) introduction, chap. 22, 120–23; Goldschmidt, *Haggadah.* All attempts to explain the widespread reading *ʾōtānû* as a later "correction," made in order to clarify the difference between the questions of the two sons, are nullified by the Septuagint and Vulgate versions, neither of which could have had any connection with the Haggadah.

⟦*Added in proof.* Since submitting this contribution to the editors, I have received the memorial volume for Moshe Goshen-Gottstein, *Studies in Bible and Exegesis* (Ramat Gan, 1993), vol. 3 [Heb.]. I note that Prof. Y. Maori, in "Rabbinic Midrash as a Witness of Textual Variants of the Hebrew Bible . . ." (pp. 267–86), also deals with the problem of the text of Deut 6:20. Unfortunately, the book arrived too late for me to refer to it in this study.⟧

ᶜăbādîm hāyînû passage. The received text reads, "We were slaves to Pharaoh in Egypt, and the Lord brought us out from Egypt with a mighty hand." The Haggadah version reads, "We were slaves to Pharaoh in Egypt and the Lord our God brought us out from there with a mighty hand and with an outstretched arm." The variants are immediately apparent: "our God" has been added; in place of "from Egypt," we read "from there"; and a further addition is "and with an outstretched arm." This form of the citation appears in all versions of the Haggadah. With the exception of the phrase "our God," this text is identical with that of the Septuagint. It was clearly also the version from which the Syro-Palestinian Targum was made.[10] Once again, the variant Hebrew text, and not the received MT, has served as the source for the Haggadah version.

Another example of the same phenomenon may well occur in the seventeenth benediction of the statutory, regular Amidah, or *Šĕmôneh ᶜEśrēh* prayer, often simply termed in rabbinic sources *tefillah*,[11] the prayer par excellence. This paragraph consists of a petition for the reinstatement of the ancient temple service. It concludes as follows, "May our eyes behold Your return to Zion in mercy. . . ." No biblical verse corresponds exactly to the wording of this prayer; it is a composite. Isa 33:17 and Ps 17:2 are the only biblical passages in which the phrase 'the eyes behold'[12] occurs using the same Hebrew verb as in the above-cited benediction, and either may have served as the source. The phrase 'return to Zion' appears in Isa 52:8, which reads, "For every eye shall behold when the Lord returns to Zion."

Since this latter phrase is unique in the Bible, it appears most likely that the formulation of the particular Amidah benediction under discussion was influenced, conceptually and textually, by this verse. In that case, it may be asked whether the additional phrase 'in mercy' (Hebrew *bĕraḥămîm*) is original to the benediction or is a later scribal amplification of the biblical clause. The weight of evidence favors the first possibility. The Greek version renders the phrase in question, "When the Lord shall have mercy upon Zion."[13] This presupposes an underlying

10. See M. H. Goshen-Gottstein (ed.), *The Bible in the SyroPalestinian Version* (Jerusalem, 1973) 39. A similar text appears in the MT of Deut 5:15, but this relates to the Sabbath, not to the Passover; cf. also Deut 26:8, which refers to the ceremony of the bringing of the first-fruits. There the text simply reads, "the Lord brought us out of Egypt." According to Goldschmidt, (*Haggadah*, 16 n. 11), Saadiah cites the verse with the addition of "our God."

11. *M. Ber.* 2:4, 3:1; *m. Šabb.* 1:2; et al.

12. I. Abrahams (*A Companion to the Authorized Daily Prayer Book* [rev. ed.; London, 1932] lxvi), observes that the first clause of the above-cited concluding entreaty "is paralleled by Micah 4:1." This remark ignores the negative context of this verse, which refers to the national enemies who maliciously desire to feast their eyes on the destruction of Israel.

13. ἡνίκα ἂν ἐλεήσῃ κυριὸς τὴν Σιών.

Hebrew text close to that of the seventeenth benediction of the Amidah. It can hardly be coincidental that the great *Isaiah Scroll* from Qumran (1QIsa[a]), like the prayer book, adds the word *bĕraḥămîm,*[14] reading in Isa 52:8, "When the Lord returns to Zion in mercy." Once again, the liturgy preserves a pre-Masoretic Hebrew text.

14. Cf. Zech 1:16. It is noteworthy that the *Job* targum from Qumran ([ed. M. Sokoloff; Ramat Gan, 1974] 102, line 3) also adds *bĕraḥămîm* to Job 42:10.

4QMysteries^{a}: A Preliminary Edition and Translation

Lawrence H. Schiffman

4Q299 (Mysteries^{a}), 4Q300 (Mysteries^{b}), and 1Q27 (Livre des mystères) are manuscripts of the same text, a meditation on various aspects of the mysteries of the natural order and the divine role in the history and future of the universe. This text is closely related in both terminology and content to the Sapiential Texts, especially to 4Q416–419. Both groups of texts share a similar emphasis on wisdom, which includes the natural phenomena and the events of history. This paper represents the preliminary publication of the text, translation and commentary on 4Q299 (Mysteries^{a}) that the author is editing for the series Discoveries in the Judaean Desert.

The texts entitled "Mysteries" consist of four manuscripts. Three of these, 1Q*27*, 4Q*299* (Myst^{a}), and 4Q*300* (Myst^{b}), can definitely be shown to be one and the same text. The fourth, 4Q*301* (Myst^{c}), was classified as part of this same composition by J. T. Milik, although no definite overlap in text exists. The close parallels between this last text and *hekhalot* literature, parallels not found in the other three manuscripts, have led me to take a more cautious view of this matter; accordingly, I prefer to reserve judgment on the relevance of 4Q*301* at this time.

It is certain that this work is of similar genre and content to the so-called Sapiential Texts, especially 4Q*416–419*, designated Sapiential Work I^{c}.[1] Terms such as רז נהיה, הבט, התבונן, and numerous others tie these

Author's note: I wish to thank Erik Larson of New York University for supplying the technical information on which the physical description of the manuscript below is based. Professor Elisha Qimron of Ben Gurion University was kind enough to review the transcription and made valuable suggestions and corrections. His help is greatly appreciated. Most of this study was completed during my tenure as a Fellow of the Annenberg Research Institute in 1992–93.

1. On this genre, see T. Elgvin, "Admonition Texts from Qumran Cave 4," in *Methods of Investigation of the Dead Sea Scrolls and the Khirbet Qumran Site: Present Realities and Future Prospects* (ed. M. Wise et al.; Annals of the New York Academy of Sciences 722; New York, 1994).

texts together. At the same time, the lack of any textual overlap, considering the extent of the preserved material in both texts, makes it extremely unlikely that these constitute parts of the same text.

The title, *Mysteries*, is derived from the occurrence in these texts of the term רזים. Numerous studies of the use of this term in Qumran literature have been undertaken.[2] Without entering into the wider issues raised by its use, I should like to emphasize that in this text it refers to the mysteries of creation, that is, the natural order of things that depends on God's wisdom, and to the mysteries of the divine role in the processes of history. Indeed, wisdom is another motif that occurs in these documents, and its importance lies in being the source from which the divine mysteries emerge. All the natural phenomena and events of history are seen here as part of the divine wisdom.

The first exemplar of this material to be discussed was published by R. de Vaux in a very preliminary manner with little analysis.[3] Even before the formal publication by J. T. Milik in 1955,[4] an important study by I. Rabinowitz had set forth the basic interpretation of the document and its poetic structure.[5] The document that is represented in 1Q*27*, 4Q*299* and *300*, with which we are dealing here, is definitely poetic and is part of a type of reflective (i.e., nonliturgical) poetry to which many Qumran compositions belong. Parts of 1Q*27* were republished by J. Licht in his edition and commentary on the *Hôdāyôt Scroll*,[6] and much of 4Q*299–301* appears in the preliminary edition of B. Z. Wacholder and M. G. Abegg,[7] which presents an improved version of the transcriptions that Milik prepared for the Preliminary Concordance. The present edition for now maintains the fragment numbers used by Milik in the concordance and followed by Wacholder and Abegg, although in the final edition they may be changed. Further, I have assigned numbers to the fragments not in the concordance in accord with their placement on the most recent photo-

2. See, e.g., R. E. Brown, *The Semitic Background of the Term "Mystery" in the New Testament* (Philadelphia, 1968), esp. 22–30; B. Rigaux, "Révélation des mystères et perfection à Qumrân et dans le Nouveau Testament," *NTS* 4 (1957–58) 237–62.

3. "La Grotte des manuscrits Hébreux," *RB* 56 (1949) 605–9, pl. XVII; cf. J. T. Milik, "Elenchus textuum ex Caverna Maris Mortui," *Verbum Domini* 39 (1952) 42–43.

4. D. Barthélemy, J. T. Milik, et al., *Qumran Cave 1* (DJD 1; Oxford, 1955) 102–7, pls. XXI–XXII. English translation of col. I is available in G. Vermes, *The Dead Sea Scrolls in English* (London, 1987) 239. Spanish translation in F. García Martínez, *Textos de Qumrán* (Madrid, 1992) 411–13; English translation in idem, *The Dead Sea Scrolls Translated* (Leiden, 1994) 399–401.

5. I. Rabinowitz, "The Authorship, Audience and Date of the de Vaux Fragment of an Unknown Work," *JBL* 71 (1952) 19–32.

6. J. Licht, מגילת ההודיות (Jerusalem, 1957) 242.

7. B. Z. Wacholder and M. G. Abegg, *A Preliminary Edition of the Unpublished Dead Sea Scrolls: The Hebrew and Aramaic Texts from Cave Four, Fascicle Two* (Washington, D.C., 1992) 1–37.

graphs. I have placed an asterisk after the number of each "unconcorded" fragment to indicate that these numbers were assigned by me.

In this paper I am endeavoring to provide an edition of 4Q*299* (Myst[a]), aided in its reconstruction by parallels in 1Q*27* and 4Q*300*. In the case of one extensive passage, I am providing a poetic reconstruction. Where appropriate, fragments are provided with introductory remarks, textual notes and commentary, although for many of the fragments only the text and translation are given.[8] Some improvements in the readings and restorations have been possible, although these have not been of great significance. It is impossible to determine, as far as I can see, the order in which the material stood in the original composition.

The manuscript is somewhat irregular in line heights (the measurement of the top of one line to the one below), averaging 0.6–0.7 cm, with extremes varying between 0.4 cm and 1.0 cm. Average letter height is 0.2 cm, but letters of 0.3 cm are not uncommon. Dry lines, both horizontal and vertical, are clearly visible on several of the fragments preserved on PAM 43.389 (Inv. no. 605), and the writing is suspended from them. Dry lines are extremely difficult to make out on the material preserved on other plates. Intercolumnar margins are 0.8 cm, and the bottom margin is 1.7 cm. The color of the leather is tannish-brown, becoming dark brown where stained (as on the two top pieces of PAM 43.389, the original fragments of which are now almost illegible to the naked eye). The leather is of medium thickness, and the writing is on the hair side, as is usual in Qumran manuscripts. On some of the fragments parts of the surface have flaked off, resulting in the loss of letters or parts of letters. F. M. Cross has identified the script as developed Herodian semiformal.[9] The orthography is mixed, including Qumran-type forms and forms usual in Masoretic Hebrew. Accordingly, 4QMysteries[a] should be seen as a part of the sectarian corpus.

Fragment 1 + 1Q27, Column I

Because the text directly above our fragment is available in 1Q*27*, and since the first three lines or so overlap, we are justified in restoring the text above based on 1Q*27*. While I have not provided here a restored

8. I felt free to include only those components appropriate for the particular fragments, so that some may have textual notes and no commentary, others the reverse. It is expected that the notes and commentary will expand greatly as discussion of these texts ensues. A revised edition will appear in DJD.

9. For a complete list of available photographs, see S. Reed with M. Lundberg and M. B. Phelps, *The Dead Sea Scrolls Catalogue: Documents, Photographs, and Museum Inventory Numbers* (SBLRBS 32; Atlanta, 1994) 94. My edition was based primarily on PAM 43.389–93, which are far more legible than the actual manuscripts, which I examined as well.

version of the Hebrew text, I do include the full restoration in my translation. I have followed an approximate line length in this restoration and have numbered the restored material with zeros preceding the numbers, following the method used by Yadin in the *Temple Scroll.* On the other hand, we can in no way be certain that this restored text appeared on the same column above our text from 4Q*299*. Some or all of it may have appeared on the preceding column. In determining the line lengths of the restored lines, I followed the line lengths of lines 1–3, which may be restored to 55–58 letter spaces. A few additional words, the position of which cannot be definitely established, are available in another parallel fragment, 4Q*300* frg. 3. These have also been added at the beginning of the text in italics. Underlined text represents parallels in the second manuscript. Braces have been used to designate restorations within bracketed material. Note that here we have overlaps between all three exemplars of this text.

Fragment 1

1. [ומזה יודע לכמה כי לוא ישוב אחור הלוא כול העמי]ם̇ שנאו עול/
2. [וביד כולמה יתהלך הלוא מפי כול לאומים שמע]ה̇אמת היש שפה ולשן/
3. [מחזקת בה מי גוי חפץ אשר יעושקנו חזק ממנו]מ̇י̊ גוי אשר לוא גז̇ל̊/
4. [הון]ב̊ית מולדים נש̇ט̊ר̊ה̇○/
5. [ ]אנשי מחשבת לכול/
6. [ ]○○ ם̇ נ̇בחנה דברים/
7. [ ]ל̊[תו]צ̊אותם/
8. [ ]ולכ̇[ול]
9. [ ]○[

Translation

01. [everything]

02. [*in order that they would know (the difference) between good and evil,*[10] *{falsehood and}* truth,]

03. [. . . mysteries of transgression, *all their wisdom.* But they did not know the mystery of that which was coming into being,[11] and the former things]

10. The motif of distinguishing between good and evil is common in this literature. Cf. 4Q*416* 1 15 (Wacholder and Abegg 2.54); 4Q*417* 2 i 8 (p. 66); 4Q*418* 2 7 (p. 78), 43 5–6 (p. 90).

11. The term רז נהיה, found throughout the wisdom texts and mysteries from Qumran and in the sectarian corpus as well, is discussed by Elgvin. I cannot accept his translation

04. [they did not consider. And they did not know what is to come upon them. And they did not save]

05. [their lives from the mystery that was coming into being. And this shall be the sign to you that it is taking place: when the begotten of unrighteousness are delivered up, and wickedness is removed]

06. [from before righteousness, as {da}rkness is removed from before light.
(Then,) just as smoke wholly ceases and is {no more}, so shall wickedness cease]

07. [forever, and righteousness shall be revealed as the sun (throughout) the full measure of the world. And all the adherents of the mysteries of {Belial}[12] are to be no]

08. [more. But knowledge shall fill the world, nor shall folly ever{more} be there. The thing is certain to come, and true is the oracle.]

1. [And from this you will know that it will not be reversed: Do not all the people]s hate iniquity?
2. [But it goes on at the hands of all of them. Does not the] truthful [report (issue) from the mouth of all the nations?] Is there a language or a tongue [which
3. upholds it? What nation (is there which) desires that (one which is) stronger than it should oppress it?] What nation (is there) which has not stolen
4. [property . . .] time of birth . . .
5. . . . men of (evil) devices for all
6. . . . it has been tested, the words
7. . . . according to [that which re]sults from them
8. . . . and for all . . .

Textual Notes

Lines 1–4. Restored based on 1Q*27* 1 i 8–12.

Line 2. כולמה. 1Q*27*: כולמ[ה].

Line 2. ולשן. 1Q*27*: ולשון.

'Mystery of Being', however. This term, as can be seen from 4Q*418* 123 3 (Wacholder and Abegg 2.115) and such sectarian texts as 1QS III 15 and XI 3–4, takes in the entire past, present and future. Therefore, we take נהְיָה as a participle and translate accordingly.

12. Although the text has פלא, it is obvious from the context that it must be emended to בליעל or some synonym. My final edition will analyze the 1Q*27* material in greater detail.

Lines 3–4. [הון] מי גוי אשר לוא גזל. 1Q*27* has a longer text: מי יחפץ כי יגזל ברשע הונו מי גוי אשר לוא עשק רעה[ו] איפה עם אשר לוא גזל הון 'Who would desire to be wickedly robbed of his property? Who is the nation which has not extorted from [its] neighbor an ephah, the people which has not stolen [property]?'

Line 4. [הון]. In 1Q*27* there follows ל]אחר, as restored by Milik.

Line 4. ונשטרה. The reading is extremely doubtful, because no interpretation can be suggested.

Line 7.]ל[. Reading with Wacholder and Abegg.

Line 7. תו]צאותם. Cf. 1Q*27* line 12 as read by Milik: [. . . הו ותוצאות יית.

COMMENTARY

Lines 1–4. The text seeks to point out the hypocrisy of human beings, who claim to seek to do good but instead do evil.[13]

Line 1. יודע לכמה. *Niphal* verb. The expression יודע לכם occurs only in Ezek 36:32.

Line 1. ישוב אחור. For the *Qal* of שוב + this adverb, see Ps 9:4, 56:10, Lam 1:8. This same expression occurs in the Sapiential Texts. See 4Q*520* 1 ii 4 (Wacholder and Abegg 2.159), 4Q*421* 1 ii 15 (p. 162) and 1QH XIII 19. Cf. also the benedictions after the reading of the Haftarah (*Sop.* 13:10 [ed. Higger, 246–47]), אחור לא ישוב ריקם '(your word) will not return unfulfilled' (cf. Isa 55:11, where אחור does not occur).

Line 1. שנאו עול. Cf. Isa 61:8, שנא גזל בעולה, speaking of God.[14] If instead of *ʿolah* the text is vocalized *ʿawlah*, it may be translated, 'hates iniquitous theft'.

Line 2. שפה ולשן. Rabinowitz[15] notes that the author has blended both the literal and figurative meaning of the words, which can designate 'peoples'. Cf. Isa 28:11; Ezek 3:5, 6.

Line 3. יעושקנו. See Qimron §311.13g.[16]

Line 3. חזק ממנו. Cf. 2 Kgs 3:26, Jer 31:11, Ps 35:10.

Line 4. בית מולדים. This enigmatic phrase must be taken as referring to the time of birth, which is seen to affect the future and nature of the

13. Cf. Milik, DJD 1.105.
14. Rabinowitz, "Authorship, Audience, and Date," 29.
15. Ibid.
16. E. Qimron, *The Hebrew of the Dead Sea Scrolls* (HSS 29; Atlanta, 1986).

individual. Compare *Tg. Onq.* to Gen 40:20 בית ולדא, paralleled by *Tg. Ps.-J.* יום גנוסא, translating יום הלדת. Note also מולדי עת in 1QH XII 8. The sense of מולד as the 'time of birth' is behind the regular use of this word for the onset ('birth') of the new moon in rabbinic parlance. While we cannot prove that this is the correct interpretation, other possibilities do not seem preferable. In Sapiential Work I[a] and I[b], two manuscripts of the same text, an identical passage states, דרוש מולדיו[17] ואז תדע נחלתו 'investigate his time of birth and then you will know his lot', or, his nature.[18] This seems to be the same usage. The phrase בית מולדים occurs several times in the Sapiential and Mysteries Texts. Compare 4Q*415* 2 ii 9 (Wacholder and Abegg 2.45).

Line 7. תוצאות. Milik suggests 'expenses',[19] but such an interpretation is refuted by the usage of this word in the Sapiential Texts.

POETIC RENDERING

[*in order that they would know (the difference)*
between good and evil,
{*falsehood and*} truth,]

[(That they would understand the) mysteries of transgression,
(with) *all their wisdom.*

But they did not know the mystery of that which was coming
into being,
and the former things] [they did not consider.

Nor did they know what is to come upon them.
And they did not save] [their lives from the mystery that was
coming into being.

And this shall be the sign to you that it is taking place:

When the begotten of unrighteousness are delivered up,
and wickedness is removed] [from before righteousness,
as {da}rkness is removed from before light.

(Then,) just as smoke wholly ceases and is {no more},
so shall wickedness cease] [forever,

and righteousness shall be revealed as the sun
(throughout) the full measure of the world.
And all the adherents of the mysteries of {Belial} will be no] [more.

17. So I[b]. I[a] has מולדו.
18. I[b]: 4Q*416* 2 iii 9–10 (Wacholder and Abegg 2.57); I[a]: 4Q*418* 9 8–9 (p. 81).
19. Milik, DJD 1.105.

But knowledge shall fill the world,
nor shall folly ever{more} be there.

The thing is certain to come,
and true is the oracle.]

[And from this you will know that it will not be reversed:

Do not all the people]s hate iniquity?
[But it goes on at the hands of all of them.

But does not the] truthful [report (issue) from the mouth of all the nations?]
Is there a language or a tongue [which upholds it?

What nation desires that a stronger one should oppress it?]
(Yet) what nation (is there) which has not stolen [property (from another)]

. . . time of birth

. . . men of (evil) devices for all

. . . it has been tested, the words

. . . according to [that which re]sults from them

. . . and for . . .

SUMMARY

Human beings were given wisdom in order that they should discern the difference between good and evil, and truth and falsehood. Despite this wisdom, which should have been sufficient, people failed to realize what would happen in the future, since they did not properly grasp the significance of the events of the past. Yet there is a sign from God that the end of days is about to dawn. For at that time all the wicked and evil itself will be eliminated and will cease forever. Then knowledge of God will fill the earth. How can one be certain that the end of days is really at hand? It is because of the hypocrisy of all the nations. All nations claim to revile evil but commit it themselves against their neighbors. We should note that this passage is reminiscent of tannaitic teachings that on the eve of the messianic era, חצפא יסגי 'impudence will be abundant'.

Fragment 3 + 1Q27, Column II

It appears that the order originally proposed for the fragments of 4Q*299* is incorrect. Column II of 1Q*27* preserves a text that continues after 4Q*299* frg. 1, lines 4–8 (which are not paralleled in 1Q*27* col. I, but follow it). No proposed line length would allow the placement of the substantial 4Q*299* frg. 2 between the end of frg. 1 and col. II of 1Q*27*. We therefore reproduce frg. 3 here, restoring text above it and below it (in the English translation) with 1Q*27* col. II. Since the right margin of 1Q*27* col. II is preserved, we are able to calculate the relative position of the words as they would have appeared in 4Q*299*, and this will be provided in the final publication. For now, we reproduce this fragmentary text according to its line divisions in 1Q*27* col. II. Accordingly, the line numbers of that column appear here in parentheses. When 1Q*27* parallels 4Q*299*, the 1Q text is underlined here.

Fragment 3

1.]לׄא יצׄלׄחׄ[לכול כן כול טוב ממונׄו ברו?
2. ?ו]יגל בלוא ה[ון ונמכר בלוא מחיר כי
3. ?יש]וׄה בה מהׄ[מ?   מׄחים כי אם כול
4.]◦◦◦◦[

01 (1). [ ]

02 (2). And [ ] they set up (?) the calculation[s[20]

03 (3). . . . what advantage is there to [

04 (4). except one who does good and one who does evil, if [

1.]he will not succeed [in anything, thus, all good is his property (?).[
2. and he will be] exiled without pro[perty (i.e. payment) and sold without a price, for
3. . . . will be wo]rth it. How [. . . except every
4.]. . . .[

(8). amount (?) and it will not be worth any price [

(9). *vacat*

(10). for all the nations [

(11). The Lord knew every [

(12). . . . [

20. Milik: 'les comptes sont satisfaisants' (DJD 1.105).

TEXTUAL NOTES

Lines 1–3. This fragment overlaps with 1Q*27* 1 ii 5–7, and restorations have been made accordingly.

COMMENTARY

Line 1. לא יצלח [לכול. Jer 13:7. Perhaps translate 'it will not be good [for anything . . . .'

Line 2. בלוא מחיר. Cf. Isa 55:1, Jer 15:13. Deut 28:68 may lie behind this line from a conceptual point of view, as it describes the exile of Israel to Egypt, where they will be sold into slavery to their enemies, but no one will purchase them.

SUMMARY

The passage appears to concentrate on the fate of the evildoer who will be sold into slavery and exiled, in fulfillment of the Torah's prophecy.

Fragment 2

The material presently identified as frg. 2 is a composite of three pieces. I have labeled these as frgs. 2a, 2b, and 2c. Fragment 2a preserves a few remnants of col. I, which I will treat first. Fragment 2a col. II is parallel to and may be restored with 4Q*300* frg. 5. Accordingly, it is possible to prove that frg. 2c is to be joined to 2a at the upper left-hand corner. Further, we may then restore additional material in the translation above frg. 2a+c from 4Q*300* frg. 5.[21] For now, my restoration of the text immediately preceding 4Q*299* frg. 2a col. II maintains the line distribution of 4Q*300* frg. 5.

Fragment 2b preserves some text which Milik, in the concordance, followed by Wacholder and Abegg, took as part of frg. 2a, col. I, lines 13–18. It does indeed preserve the leftmost part of a column and the left margin. Yet it preserves only two letters of its second column. Since these two letters cannot be successfully placed in frg. 2a col. II, we have no choice but to disconnect this fragment and treat it separately. Fragment 2a has a small overlap with 4Q*300* frg. 1 that allows us to restore portions of the text above and to gain additional words below, difficult as they are to place at this point in our research. Overlaps with 4Q*300* are underlined. Only exacting calculations will make their definitive location possible.

21. The continuation of that fragment, in turn, may be reconstructed from 4Q*299* frg. 2a+c, with which we are presently dealing.

Fragment 2a, Column I

1.]

2.]

3.] ○

4.]הוא/

5.]מׄה

6–12.

Translation

1–3. [. . .]

4. . . .]he

5. . . .]what (?)

Textual Notes

Lines 3–5. The leftmost portion of this column is preserved on frg. 2a, as is the narrow margin separating the columns.

Line 1. The surviving letter was read as a *he* with a circle over it by Milik (Wacholder and Abegg).

Fragments 2a + 2c, Column II + 4Q*300* Fragment 5

1. [ ]○ הא ○[[אביון]

2. /מה נקרא ה֯] [הו ומעש]]

3. /וכול מעשה צ֯ד֯י֯ק֯ הטמׄ]אה ומה [נׄקרא לאדׄ]ם]

4. /חכם וצדיק כי לוא לאיש֯] [ה֯ ולׄו֯]א ?ה חכמה נכחדת כי]

5. /אם חוכמת עורמת רוע ומ֯]חשבת בליעל

6. /מעשה אשר לוא יעשה עׄו֯דׄ כׄיׄא אׄם]

7. /דׄ֯בר עושו ומה {ו}הוא אשר יעשה ג]בר

8. /הׄמרה את דבר עושו ימחה שמו מפי כולׄ]

9. /[erasure] שמעו תומכי ○]

10. /עולם ומזמות כול מעשה ומׄחׄ]שבות

11. /כול רז ומ֯כׄ֯ין כול מחשבת עושה כולׄ] הנהיות

12. /הו֯]אה מק[דׄם עולם הואה שמו ולׄע֯]ולם

13. ותׄש] [לׄ [מ]חשבת בית מולדים פתח לפ֯]ניהם

14. [ ]○שׄ֯בו כי לבנו בחן וינחילנו]

15. [ ]כ֯ו֯ל רז וחבלי כול מעשה ומה]

16. [ומה]ע֯מים כ֯[י] ב֯ראם ומעש֯]יהמה

TRANSLATION

01 (1).] a thought of discernment

02 (2).] judgment, because of property

1.] . . . [poor.]
2. What shall we call the[person?] his [ ] and [his?] deeds [ ]
3. and every action of the righteous is im[pure]. [And how] shall we call a per[son . . .]
4. wise and righteous, for not to a person[ ] and no[t hidden wisdom, ex-]
5. cept the wisdom of evil cunning and the de[vices of Belial.
6. a deed which should not be done again, except[
7. the command of his Creator. But what is it which a m[an] shall do [
8. violated the command of his Creator, his name shall be erased from the mouths of every [
9. *erasure* Listen O those who hold fast [
10. eternity, and the schemes of every creature. And the de[vices
11. every mystery and every plan. He causes everything [which comes into being.
12. H[e is from be]fore eternity; the Lord is his name, and for e[ternity
13. [ ] [p]lan of the time of birth he opened be[fore them
14.] . . . for he tested our heart, and he caused us to inherit [
15.] every mystery and the tribulations of every creature. And how [
16. and what are] the peoples [that] he created them, and [their] deed[s

TEXTUAL NOTES

Line 4. Restore after לאיש] either חוכמ[ה, תושי[ה, or תבונ[ה.

Line 4. ומ]זמת. An alternative restoration is ומ[חשבת. Cf. 1QH II 16–17.

Line 7. והוא. Deleting the first *waw,* which is clearly a scribal error.

Line 7. The end of line 7 must have contained Hebrew text meaning either 'since he' or 'whoever'.

Line 8. Perhaps restore at the end [בשר or a similar word.

Line 10. The line must have ended with a verb of the sense of 'He sets out'.

Line 11. הנהיות. An alternative restoration is הבריאות.

Line 12. The restoration in Wacholder and Abegg, taken from Milik's reading, is too short to fill the lacuna.

COMMENTARY

Line 3. מעשה צדיק. Cf. Qoh 8:14.

Line 4. חכם וצדיק. Cf. Qoh 9:1.

Line 6. מעשה אשר לוא יעשה. Cf. Gen 20:9, Isa 19:15.

Line 8. ימחה שמו. Deut 25:6; cf. 29:19.

Line 9. שמעו. A regular form of address in hortatory and wisdom texts known from the Qumran sect. This formula is used in CD I 1; II 2, 14; 1QH I 35, often with (ו)עתה, which also figures prominently in our text.

Line 12. Cf. Exod 15:3. הואה here serves as a substitute for the Tetragrammaton.[22]

Line 14. לבנו בחן. Cf. Jer 12:3; Ps 7:10, 17:3; Prov 17:3.

Line 15. כול רז. Cf. Dan 4:6.

SUMMARY

This passage begins with a set of rhetorical questions. Such questions, beginning with מה 'what' or 'how' are typical of the rhetoric of the Qumran sapiential literature. 4Q*301* also has a series of such questions. In our passage, they are intended to bemoan the person whose wisdom serves only his wickedness. From line 8 on we have a hortatory speech, addressed to the righteous who hold fast to eternity. It emphasizes the all-knowing quality of God, who sets forth the fate of all humanity. Here we encounter the familar concept of predestination, found in the Qumran sectarian corpus.

Fragment 2b

]יה∘∘∘∘∘ם .1

]תסתם מ֯כ֯ם/ .2

22. Cf. L. H. Schiffman, *Sectarian Law in the Dead Sea Scrolls: Courts, Testimony, and the Penal Code* (BJS 33; Chico, Cal., 1983) 100–101 n. 16.

[○ שמעו כי מה/ .3
[○ ○א שמה/ .4
[שׯוׄ ○ ○רׯזי עד/ .5
[○ מׯעשוׄ יה○] .6

Translation

01 (1). [ ] magicians, who teach transgression, say the parable and relate the riddle before it is spoken. And then you will know, if you have looked

02 (2). and the signs (?) of hea[ven . . .] your foolishness, for it is sealed from you. [Se]aled is the vision. And you did not look at the eternal secrets, and you did not contemplate with understanding.

03 (3). Th[en] you shall say [. . .] for you did not look at the root of wisdom. And if you should open the vision,

1.] it will be kept secret from you
2. all your wisdom, for yours is the para{ble}] . . . listen for what
3. is hidden wisdom(?) . . .] . . . there
4. still you will not be] . . . eternal secrets
5. vision] . . . his deeds . . . [

Commentary

Line 2. תסתם. Cf. Dan 8:26; 12:4, 9; Ps 51:8.

Summary

Fragment 2b relates further evidence of the signs of the impending end. It may therefore eventually have to be placed with the restored frg. 1. It asserts that the signs are in the heavens but that they are not comprehended. They are unavailable even if one tries to understand the "vision," for it is hidden wisdom.

Fragment 4

לב]לתי המוׯ[.1
[○מו בתׄ] .2
]אׯרׯץׄ וכמהׄוׯ ל[.3
י]דׯע ונספרוׯ רישׯ[ונות .4
]אינה לשׄלםׯ[.5

TRANSLATION

1. so as] not to [
2. [. . .]
3.] land, and like it . . . [
4. k]new, and the first [things] were related (?) [
5.] is not to pay(?)[

COMMENTARY

Line 4. ריש]ונות. Cf. Isa 41:22; 43:9, 18; 46:9; and 48:3, where this term refers to the events of the past. BDB 911a interprets it in Isa 42:9 as referring to 'earlier predictions'.

Fragment 5

1. מאור]וׄת כוכבים לז[כר]ו֯ן שמ֯[ו
2. גב]ו֯רות רזי אור ודרכי חוש֯[ך
3.]ב֯דׄין מועדי חׄום עׄם קצ֯[י
4. מבוא יום]ומוצא לילהׄ[ ]ל[
5.]ובית מולדיׄם[

TRANSLATION

1. the light]s of the stars for the reme[mb]rance of [his] name[
2. the migh]ty mysteries of light and the ways of darkne[ss
3.] . . . the seasons of warmth as well as the period[s of
4. the coming in of day] and the going out of night[
5.]and the times of birth of the creatures[

bottom margin

TEXTUAL NOTES

Line 1. The restoration עבו]דת כוכבים '(star worship)' in Wacholder and Abegg, originally suggested by Milik, does not fit the context, as the text is dealing here with the wonders of creation.

Line 4. The restoration is conjectural, but this must be the sense of the text.

Commentary

Line 1. לז[כר]ון שמ[ו. Cf. Mal 3:16.

Line 2. ודרכי חוש[ך. Cf. Prov 2:13. This same phrase is found in 1QS III 21 and IV 11.

Line 3. Cf. Gen 8:22.

Line 4. Cf. Ps 19:7; 4Q*418* 123 ii 2 (Wacholder and Abegg 2.115); 1QS X 10; 1QH XII 4, 7.

Summary

It is asserted here that God's wonders are beyond the ken of humanity. The heavenly bodies and the seasons are called forth as evidence of God's hidden wisdom.

Fragment 6

This fragment preserves the left side of the right column, so that the intercolumnar space is also entirely preserved. The text preserved of col. I consists, therefore, of the ends of the lines.

Fragment 6, Column I

[מים/	.1
[מרותם/	.2
[○○ם לעבודתם יחזקו/	.3
ברק[ים עשה לנצח גשמים/	.4
מי[○ם ובמשורה ישקו/	.5
[י̊אמר̊ להם ויתנו/	.6
[בגברתו ברא/	.7
[א̊] [○ל [ה]ר̊יה וכול/	.8
[○ ○ כֹל צאצאיהָ/	.9
[מ̊טברו פרש/	.10
[○○○דם עת בעת/	.11
[ר̊ להרות לכול/	.12
[כֹי מעפר מבניתם/	.13
[○כול מקו̊יהם וחדר/	.14
[נת̊ן ממשל לחזק/	.15
[○ת כול גבורה/	.16
[ומ̊חזק כול/	.17

]◦ עבודת גבר/ .18

עב]ודתו/ .19

TRANSLATION

1.]water (?)
2.]their (?)
3.] . . . their task. They will strengthen
4. cloud]s he made for eternal rain
5. wate]r, and according to measure they shall drink.
6.]He will say to them, and they will give
7.] in his might he created
8.]its mountains and
9.] . . . all its descendents
10.]it spread out from its omphalos (?)
11.] . . . for each and every time
12.] to water all
13.] for they are constructed of dust
14.] all their hopes (?) and the chamber (?)
15.] he permitted to rule to strengthen
16.]s of all might
17.] he held fast to all
18.] the work of a man
19.] his [wo]rk

TEXTUAL NOTES

Line 9. The *he* at the end of the line was written above the *yod* for lack of space at the end of the line.

COMMENTARY

Line 4. ברק]ים עשה. Cf. Jer 10:13, 51:16; Ps 135:7.

Line 5. מי]ם ובמשורה. Cf. Ezek 4:11, 16 (where שתה appears instead of שקה, as in our text). Cf. also the *Baraita*ᵓ *Qinyan Torah,* preserved as ᵓ*Abot* 6:4, ומים במשורה תשתה 'you will drink water by measure', describing the hard life of a sage of the Torah.

Line 11. Similar phrasing occurs in CD XII 19–21(עת ועת), referring to the progression or evolution of the law with the times. Compare also 1QS IX 13–14.[23]

Line 13. מבניתם. The noun מבנית is found in 1QH VII 4, 9 and 1QS XI 9, and three times in the *Angelic Liturgy*, 4Q*403* 1 i 41, 4Q*405* 14–15 i 6, 11QShirShabb 2-1-9 9.

Line 14. מקויהם. Or 'their cisterns'.

Fragment 6, Column II

This fragment preserves the right side of the left column. The text preserved of col. II consists, therefore, of the beginnings of the lines.

1. ל]וׄא ○○○ [
2. /ועליכם החי ○ [
3. /אוילי כסה ○ [
4. /נסתרה מכול תומכ֯[י
5. /מה אב לבנים מאי֯ש֯[
6. /כיא אם ארץ להדר ○ [
7. /ממנו כי אם רוח ○ע֯[
8. /עמים מ֯היׄא אשר֯[
9. /אשר אין ל○○ [
10. /חוש[ך] ו֯א[ור
11. /כן יהיה כ֯[
12. /לב רעׄו וׄאׄוׄלׄבׄ מ○ [
13. /מאיש נואׄל הון ○ [
14. /לפי תׄבאוׄת ומה בׄ○ [
15. /מׄוׄדה או תכלית י֯[
16. /תׄכון אחד ולוא ישׄ[
17. /מׄשפט כן ירד המ[
18. /ואם דשׄ יוסיף ל[
19. /הוא י○ [ ]ל[ ]מׄ[
20. /○○ל[

TRANSLATION

1. n]ot . . . [
2. and upon you, the live (?)[

23. L. H. Schiffman, *The Halakhah at Qumran* (Leiden, 1975) 25, 43–44.

3. the fools of . . . [
4. hidden from all those who hold fast [to
5. Why is a father (better) for children than (another) man[
6. except the land to beautify (?) [
7. from it, except the spirit of [
8. peoples. What is it that [
9. which has not [
10. darkne[ss] and li[ght
11. thus may it be like [
12. the heart of his neighbor, and he ambushes . . . [
13. from a foolish man property, property [
14. according to the crops. And how . . . [
15. property, or the end of [
16. one measure and it will not [
17. judgment, thus may the . . . go down [
18. and if he threshed, he shall add to [
19. property, and . . . [
20. [. . .]

TEXTUAL NOTES

Line 7. Perhaps restore at the end רוח [ה]ע[ול.

Line 8. מה היא = מהיא.

COMMENTARY

Line 3. אוילי כסה. Cf. Prov 12:16.

Line 5. אב לבנים. Isa 38:19.

Line 13. נואָל. This word for a 'fool' appears in some readings in the genizah manuscripts of Sir 37:19. Only the verbal usage of this root, יאל, occurs in the Bible.

Line 14. לפי תבאות. Cf. Lev 25:15–16.

Line 16. Or 'he will not'.

Line 16. תכון in the sectarian texts has the complex meaning of that which God has apportioned, 'measure' or 'lot'. Here it no doubt refers to the allotted fates of God's people, according to the lots he has placed them in.

Line 17. For משפט in the sectarian scrolls, see Schiffman, *Halakhah at Qumran*, 42–47.

Line 19. מודה. The Qumran form for biblical מאד.

Summary

Column I evokes as evidence of God's mysteries his creation of the irrigation of the earth, based on rain and flowing streams. The end of the column seems to discuss God's endowing man with the arts of civilization.

Column II is illusive. It is a series of questions that rhetorically emphasize aspects of God's creation, such as parent-child relationships, which cannot be thoroughly fathomed by human beings. The second part (lines 12–19) seems to discuss the ability of man to grow crops, but the context is insufficient for further explication.

Fragment 7

This fragment may be further reconstructed in light of 4Q*300* 6–7, which has definite overlaps with it (some of these are underlined below). The exact relationship is extremely difficult to determine.

.1 [ ]ה֯וא א֯[

.2 [ ]קרוב [

.3 /]מה הוא רחו[ק֯ לאיש ממעש֯]ה

.4 /מ֯ו֯ל֯ א֯י֯ש֯ והוא ר֯ח֯וק מ◦ [ואין לענה]

.5 /לנגדו מנו֯טר֯]לנ[ק֯]ו[ם בלוא מ֯ש֯]פט

.6 /אש֯]ר מ[ע֯ל ועשה֯ [

Translation

1.]he [
2.] close [
3. [What is furth]er from a person than an act [of
4. to a(nother) person and he is far from [. . . and there is no (greater) poison]
5. before him than bearing a grudge [to a]ve[n]ge unjustly[
6. wh[o tr]espassed and did [

Commentary

Line 5. Such grudges are prohibited by the law of reproof of CD IX 2–8, as well as by CD VII 2–3 and XIV 22.[24]

24. See Schiffman, *Sectarian Law*, 90–98.

Line 5. מנוטר [לנ]ק[ו]ם. Cf. Lev 19:18 and Nah 1:2.

Line 5. בלוא מש]פט. Jer 22:13; Ezek 22:29; Prov 13:23, 16:8.

Line 6. מ]על ועשה. Cf. Ezek 18:24.

SUMMARY

This fragment also contains rhetorical questions. It clearly castigates one who bears a grudge. It is in accord with the biblical tradition, while emphasizing a principle stressed in the *Zadokite Fragments* as well.

Fragment 8

]ה֯וא הכין ע[.1
]◦ פלג שכל֯ם[.2
]ן֯ הוא ◦[.3
]בה מ[.4
]◦◦ ומה֯ יתבונן גׄב֯[ר] בלוא יׄדׄע֯ ולוא שמע [.5
ה]ב֯ינה יצר לבנ[ו] ברוב שכל גלה אוזננו ונש֯[מעה .6
]י֯צ֯ר בינה ל֯כ֯ו֯ל רודפי דעת ו֯הׄ◦[.7
]כ֯ו֯ל שכל מעולם הוא לוא יׄשנה֯[.8
ה]סׄגיר בעד עׄד מים ל֯בל[תי .9
]ש֯מים ממעל לשמים ◦[.10
]ל[.11

TRANSLATION

1.] he prepared [
2.] a portion of their knowledge [
3.] he [
4.] . . . [
5.] And how can a ma[n] understand who did not know and did not hear [
6. the] discernment, the inclination of our heart. With great intelligence he opened our ears, so that we [would hear
7. the inclination of understanding for all who pursue knowledge, and the [
8.] all intelligence is from eternity; it will not be changed[
9.] he shut them up before (the) waters, so as [not to
10.] heaven above heaven [
11.]. . .[

Textual Notes

Line 6. ונש]מעה. An alternative restoration is ונש]כילה.

Line 9. After בעד the scribe wrote עד again in error.

Commentary

Line 6. יצר לבנ[ו]. Cf. Gen 6:5, 8:21.

Summary

This excerpt emphasizes the notion that all knowledge and discernment comes from God. All is at the same time predestined. At the end the fragment appears to turn to the wonders of creation.

Fragment 9

1.]םׄ הא◦[
2.]◦ שרים לי זרח א֯[ר]ץ֯ ל֯מׄ[
3. מ]לך נכבׄד֯ והדר מלכותו מ֯לא֯[
4.]א עם כול צב֯[א
5.]אׄרך א[פים

Translation

1.]. . .[
2.] princes to Me, to shine (?), the la[n]d to [
3. (the) K]ing who is honored, and the majesty of his kingdom fills[
4.]with all the ho[st
5.]long su[ffering

Textual Notes

Line 1. ם[. Also possible is כי.

Line 4. צב]א. The reading and restoration are conjectural.

Commentary

Line 3. מ]לך נכבד. Cf. 2 Sam 6:20.

Line 3. והדר מלכותו. Ps 145:2.

Fragment 10

]מלך [.1
] וגב[ו]רי חיל יחזקו מ[עמד .2
ר]ם על כול גואים ישרא[ל .3
] ◦ וליצור ולחשוב[.4
]ושופטים לכול לא[ומים .5
] ◦ על כול מספרם ◦ [.6
]ל[ ] ◦ ושופטים בין אביו[ן .7
]אתם לתכן כול עבודת[.8
]כול ממ[ש]לותם [.9
] יומם[.10
]מו ומחש[בותם .11

TRANSLATION

1.]king [
2.]and mi[gh]ty warriors shall take (their) [stand
3. ex]alted over all the nations. Israel [
4.] and to fashion and to think [
5.] and judges for all the na[tions
6.] according to all their numbers [
7.]. . . judges between a poor ma[n
8.]. . . for the measure of all work of [
9.] all of their dom[i]nion [
10.] by day[
11.] and their th[oughts

COMMENTARY

Line 2. יחזקו מ[עמד. Cf. 1QSa II 4–5; 1QM XIV 6; 1QH IV 36, V 29–30; cf. 1QS I 17.[25]

Line 4. Cf. Jer 18:11.

SUMMARY

Both frgs. 9 and 10 refer to the king, presumably God. God is described in 10 as having set up the rulers for all the nations. Israel is apparently to be contrasted in some way.

25. On מעמד, see L. H. Schiffman, *The Eschatological Community of the Dead Sea Scrolls: A Study of the Rule of the Congregation* (SBLMS 38; Atlanta, 1989) 28–29.

Fragment 11[26]

This fragment, as listed in Wacholder and Abegg, following Milik's entries in the concordance, is made up of two pieces, which I have numbered 11a and 11b. I am providing separate transcriptions for each, followed by a reconstruction according to Milik's view.

Fragment 11a

]ח֯ול בין הׄש֯◦[.1
י]שׂראל ואתכם[.2
ה/מ]לכו בה֯[.3

1.] . . . between . . . [
2. [I]srael, and you [
3.] walked in it (or ruled over it)

Fragment 11b

]המשיל אתכם[.1
]ם ◦[.2

1.]. . .[
2.]he made you rule (or he likened you)
3.]. . .[

Fragment 11a + b

1.]. . . between . . .[
2.]he made you rule (or he likened you) [I]srael, and you [
3.]. . . walked in it (or ruled over it)

COMMENTARY

Line 1. Perhaps read]◦הׄט֯ and restore: בין קודש ל]חול בין הטמ[א לטהור 'between the holy and the] profane, between the impu[re and the pure'.

Line 2. אתכם. A verb for this direct object pronoun must follow in the lacuna.

26. Immediately to the left of frg. 10 on PAM 43.390 there are two virtually illegible fragments, which I hope to include in the final edition.

Fragment 12

2]מלׄקוש ל֯ ○[
3]○לי֯ה ובסוד֯ ○[
bottom margin

1.]. . .[
2.] latter rain for [
3.]. . . and in the counsel of [

bottom margin

TEXTUAL NOTES

Line 3. The last letter may be a *pe.* If so, perhaps read ובסוד[י פ]לא.

Fragment 13

2]לו֯א֯ יׄגע[ח]ז֯ק֯[ות]ל֯כ֯ו֯[ל
3][ ]יׄחזק ○○לׄ○[ ]יתׄ֯ם לשמׄע ○○ם[
bottom margin

1.] he shall not touch[. . . st]rong for al[l
2.]*vacat* He will strengthen . . . to hear . . . [

bottom margin

Fragment 14

1]עשה ○[
2]רוחכׄם[
3]○○○[

1.] he did (or made)[
2.]your spirit[
3.] . . . [

Fragment 15

Although readable text is preserved only on col. I of this fragment, it appears that to the left of the margin there was writing on a second column. This margin, assuming that it was one, is considerably wider than the one in frgs. 2a, 2b, and 6, raising the question of whether this indeed was a second column (rather than the end of a sheet) or if, perhaps, this fragment does not belong to 4QMyst[a].

Fragment 15, Column I

]עשה[.1
/מחוכמה[.2
bottom margin

1.]he did [
2.]from (or because of) wisdom

bottom margin

Fragment 15, Column II

]○[.1
vacat .2

Fragment 16

]ישלים פשע[.1
]בו וביום[.2
]מהטות[ ]אהב[.3

1.] he shall complete (or requite?) (the) transgression [
2.] in it, and on the day [
3.] I shall tur[n] from inclining [

Fragment 17

] המשל[.1
]○○ [.2

1.] the parable (or ruling) [
2.]. .[

Textual Notes

Line 1. Perhaps read ומשל.

Fragment 18

]חוק תכונם כיא אם[.1
]משקל לתכון ○○○[.2
]יחד רובם אם[.3

1.]the allotment of their measure, except[
2.]the weight, according to the measure of[
3.]together, most of them if[

Textual Notes

Line 3. רובם Perhaps read ריבם ‘their dispute’.

Fragment 19

]○○ם[ ]נן ב[.1
] גליהם ביד ○[.2
]○ לוא כול כוח וכ[.3
]ואוצר כול[.4

1.]. . .[
2.] their heaps in the hand of [
3.] not every power and [
4.] and the one who stores up everything [

Commentary

Line 4. Cf. Hos 13:15.

Fragment 20

]מפי[.1
] למחי○[.2
]○י מ○[.3

1.] from the mouth of [
2.]. . .[
3.]. . .[

Fragment 21

.1]○○[
.2] הוא א֯[
.3]מ֯ו֯ד֯ה מנ֯[
.4]○ נפש [
.5]○ה ארׄכ֯ה֯[

1.]. . .[
2.] he [
3.]property [
4.] person [
5.] its length [

Fragment 22

.1]○○○[
.2]היאה מ֯[
.3 א]שר ה[
.4]○[

1.]. . .[
2.]it is [
3. wh]ich (?) the[
4.]. . .[

Fragment 23

.1]○○[
.2]םׄ תפ֯[
.3]א לוא[
.4]○יׄ רש[

1.]. . .[
2.]. . .[
3.] not[
4.]. . .[

Fragment 24

מ/מו]של ○[.1
]ו̇נספרה֯[.2
]○○ת לוא֯[.3
]○ מ̇צ̇[.4

1. ru]les [
2.]and let us recount[
3.]. . . not[
4.]. . .[

Fragment 25

]ו̇א ○[.1
]ה על מ○[.2
]○ מה מ[.3
]אבן מ○[.4
]○ ○[.5

1.] . . . [
2.] on [
3.] what [
4.]stone [
5.]. . .[

Fragment 26

]   [.1
]א֯ הילודים[.2
]ת̇מהו כן ילו̇ד֯[.3

2.] those who are born[
3.]they were astonished, thus one who is born[

TEXTUAL NOTES

Line 3. Ps 48:6. Perhaps restore י]תמהו or ו]תמהו 'they will be astonished' or 'and they were astonished'. At the end of the line, perhaps restore ילוד[ים 'those who are born'.

COMMENTARY

Line 2. The vocalization הַיִּלּוֹדִים occurs in Jer 16:3, and הַיְלוּדִים occurs in 1 Chr 14:4.

Fragment 27*

1.]○○מ○[
2.]○○○ ○ל ים֯[
3.]ובמדה ח֯י֯ כ֯ל[
4.]○○ י֯ש֯ב֯י֯ע[

1.]. . .[
2.]. . .[
3.]every living thing, and in a measure[
4.]he will swear [

COMMENTARY

Line 4. This line may also be translated, 'he will satisfy'. Cf the use of the *Hiphil* of שבע in Ps 145:16, where כל חי appears, as it does in line 3 of our text.

Fragment 28

We were not able to locate a photograph of this fragment, so we reproduce it based on the transcription of Milik compiled by Wacholder and Abegg.

1.]   [
2.]בׄש֯למו֯ א֯[
3.]○מ בח֯ו֯שך וׄשך[ח
4.]○ לוא ה֯מוסר֯[
5.]הׄוסיׄף ○○[

1.]. . .[
2.] when he completes[
3. da]rkness in darkness [
4.]the teaching (he) did not [
5.] he added[

TEXTUAL NOTES

Line 4. Perhaps restore ל]קח or ל]קחו 'he did not ac[cept' or 'they did not ac[cept'. The verb לקח followed by the object מוסר is regular in biblical usage.

COMMENTARY

Line 3. Cf. Qoh 6:4.

Fragment 28a*

.1 [◦ן י̊◦]
.2 [בּ̊כול ◦ ◦]
.3 [◦ עוד ◦ ◦ ◦]
.4 [בידך]

1.]. . .[
2.]in all [
3.] still [
4.]in your hand[

COMMENTARY

Line 4. Perhaps referring to God's control over the affairs of man and the world.

Fragment 29

.1 [◦◦◦]
.2 [◦שלו מה הוא המצו̊[ה
.3 מ]חזיק ותולד̊ות המ[
.4 [א̇◦] [מ̊שקל̇]

1.]. . .[
2.] . . . what is the command[ment (?)
3. he h]olds fast, and the generations of the [
4.] weight[

Fragment 30

1.]○○ ○[
2. י]צ֯רו ובמח○[
3.]○○שׄוי ואם ינשא[
4.]מה גבורה בלוא[

1.]. . .[
2.]his inclination and . . . [
3.] . . . and if he will bear[
4.]what is might without[

Fragment 31

1.]○○מה יכון נ○[
2.]תו֯ ואם יהפכ֯[ו
3.]○ מׄב֯י֯ןׄ ○[

1.] . . . he will establish [
2.] his [. . .], and if [they] will turn[
3.] understands [

Fragment 32

1. א]ל הדעות[
2.]בׄיד מלאכ[י

1. G]od of knowledge[
2.]in the hand of the messenger[s

Textual Notes

Line 2. Perhaps restore]ביד מלאכ[י קודש.

Commentary

Line 1. For this designation of God, see 1 Sam 2:3 and 1QS III 15; 1QH I 26, XII 10, and frg. 4 15. It occurs as well in the sapiential material from Qumran, such as 4Q*417* 2 i 8 (Wacholder and Abegg 2.66); 4Q*418* 43 6 (p. 90); 55 5 (p. 94).

Line 2. Or, 'through the agency of the prophets'. This is probably the correct meaning, as the fragment refers to God's making known his teachings through the biblical prophets. Cf. 2 Chr 36:15, where מלאך, literally 'messenger', also designates a prophet. Cf. also 1QS III 21, IV 12.

Fragment 33

]לכל כ̇○[.1
ה]ו̇א יהיה[.2
]○○ ○[.3

1.]to all [
2. h]e will be[
3.]. . .[

Fragment 34

]○[.1
]כ̊ול מע̇שה̇ ה[.2
]פת̇ח בפ○ ○[.3

1.]. . .[
2.]every deed of the[
3.]He opened [

TEXTUAL NOTES

Line 3. The attractive reading בפני]יהם 'before them' is unlikely in light of the traces.

COMMENTARY

Line 2. Hebrew מעשה may also refer to 'creature'.

Line 3. We understand this line to refer to God's having revealed his wisdom to man.

Fragment 35

]○ לפני ○○[.1
]בה אוש○[.2
]○○ם ○[.3

1.] before [
2.]. . .[
3.]. . .[

Fragment 36

.1]בׄנׄי יש֯[ראל
.2]לתכונם ◦[
.3]◦ד ◦◦[

1.]the children of Is[rael
2.]according to their measure [
3.] . . . [

Fragment 39[27]

.1]ב֯ה מׄ[
.2]◦ד כי אם֯[
.3]ליׄהא לוא[
.4]◦ החכמה[

1.]. . .[
2.] except[
3.] . . . not[
4.] the wisdom[

Fragment 40

.1 ◦ש֯ו֯ם֯
.2]תׄומכי ר[זי
.3]התב֯[וננו
.4]ם֯ תו[

1.]. . .[
2.]those who hold fast to the sec[rets
3.] investigate [
4]. . .[

Commentary

Line 3. Or, ‘they investigated’. The *Polal* of בון appears throughout the sapiential corpus from Qumran, meaning ‘to examine closely in order to discern the truth’; cf. 4Q*413* 1 1 (Wacholder and Abegg 2.43).

27. Fragments 37 and 38* preserve no translatable words.

Fragment 41

]לי ומ◦[.1
]◦ מעש[י/ה .2
]ועתה[.3

1.]. . .[
2.] creature(s)[of
3.]And now[

COMMENTARY

Line 3. ועתה. This must have been the beginning of a section of a wisdom speech. This word serves to introduce such speeches, often beginning after a *vacat* indicating a new paragraph, throughout this literature. Cf. 4Q*413* 1 3 (Wacholder and Abegg 2.43); 4Q*418* 69 ii 5 (p. 97).

Fragment 42

]ה לבם[.1
]אמרו ◦[.2
ג]בורה [.3

1.] their heart [
2.]they said [
3. m]ight [

Fragment 43

]◦ ◦[.1
]א בוננ◦[.2
]הוא ◦[.3
]◦[.4

1.]. . .[
2.]investigate [
3.]he [
4.]. . .[

TEXTUAL NOTES

Line 2. Probably read בוננו. Also possible are בוננת or בוננתם. See commentary to frg. 40, line 3.

Fragment 44[28]

1.]ש֯פ֯[
2.]ולברכ֯[
3.]ול֯ב֯[

Fragment 45

1. כו]ל֯ עוׄב֯[רי
2.]ו֯בכ֯ול מ◦ [
3.]יׄם֯[

1. al]l who pas[s
2.]and in every [
3.]. . .[

Textual Notes

Line 1. Perhaps restore עוב]רי דרך 'travellers'.

Line 3. The preserved portion of this line, apparently the masculine plural ending, would require that it be preceded with a noun.

Fragment 48[29]

1.]מלאכׄ[י

1.]messenger[s of

Commentary

Line 1. See commentary to frg. 32, line 2.

Fragment 49

1. ◦◦ [
2. ◦◦◦◦ [
3. /איש נו֯◦ [
4. /בכוׄר[

1. . . . [
2. . . . [

28. Fragment 44 has no translatable word. Perhaps read in 44, line 2: ולברכ]ה.
29. Fragments 46* and 47* have no complete words.

3. man [
4. in the furnace[

COMMENTARY

Line 4. The notion that man is refined through suffering is often expressed in terms of his having gone through a furnace. Cf. CD VIII 26 and 1QH V 16.

Fragment 50

[ת֯וׄע֯בׄו֯ת] .1
[בׄקודשו֯ ○○] .2
[ה בכם ○○○] .3
[○דׄ ואין שם למו֯ע]ד .4
[מׄשפט כיא צדי֯ק] .5
ג]בׄו֯ר֯תו וחזק[.6
[לאל לנקום נׄקׄם] .7
[וריב על חזק ע] .8
א]ל ובשמים מדור[ו .9
[○םׄ *vacat*] .10
[יכם אשמיע֯] .11
[בׄו֯ עם מלך] .12

bottom margin

1.]abominations[
2.]in his holiness [
3.] among you [
4.] and there is no name for the peri[od
5.]judgment for he is righteous[
6.]his [m]ight and the power[
7.] to God to exact vengence[
8.] and a dispute against the strong [
9. G]od, and in the heavens is [his] dwelling[
10.] . . . *vacat*[
11.]your [. . .] I will announce[
12.]him (?) with the king[

bottom margin

TEXTUAL NOTES

Line 12.]בו[. Perhaps read]כי[.

COMMENTARY

Line 7. Cf. Num 31:2; Ezek 24:8, 25:12.

SUMMARY

This fragment deals with the coming judgment, in which God will avenge the violation of his law. From the heavens he will exact punishment, in an age so terrible that it does not even have a name. After that, redemption will be announced.

Fragment 51

1.]○○תׄ מ[
2.]ם֯ עשוק וגזול ב○○○[
3.]○ה֯ו כיא אהבת ח֯ס֯ד[
4.]○ בכוׄל ○○○ ל○○[
5.]○ ○○ ○○

1.]. . .[
2.] persecuted and robbed by [
3.] for lovingkindness[
4.] in all . . . to[
5.]. . .[

COMMENTARY

Line 2. עשוק וגזול. Deut 28:29; cf. Jer 22:3.

Line 3. אהבת חסד. Mic 6:8. The phrase is common in sectarian texts. Cf. 1QS II 24, V 4, V 25, VIII 2, X 27; CD XIII 18; 4Q*418* 169 3, and 170 3 (Wacholder and Abegg 2.128).

Fragment 52

1.]קודשוׄ ○○○○[
2. המשפ]טים הצדיק֯יׄם֯[
3.]○הנו כיא המ[
4.]א֯שר ב֯ח֯ר֯ו֯ ב֯ה○ א֯[

עבו]ד̇ת קודשו ו̇לכפ̊ר ע̊ל ○ ○ [.5

]עליהם ל[.6

bottom margin

1.] his holiness . . . [
2.]the righteous [judg]ments[
3.] . . . for . . . [
4.]which they chose [
5.]his holy [serv]ice, and to atone for [
6.]upon them to[

bottom margin

TEXTUAL NOTES

Line 4. בחר. Perhaps read ראו.

COMMENTARY

Line 2. Deut 4:8. Cf. 4Q*412* 3 1 (Wacholder and Abegg 2.42); 4Q*418* 121 1 (p. 113), 214 2 (p. 140).

Fragment 53

]○[.1

] שׁ̊ו̇פטם במשפט̊י[.2

י]חזיקו ביד ○○○○[.3

]○ל○○[ ]○[.4

1.]. . .[
2.]their judgment according to the regulations[
3. t]hey shall hold fast to the . . . [
4.]. . .[

COMMENTARY

Line 3. Cf. Judg 7:20.

Fragment 54

]○[.1

]נו בה[.2

]אשר יעשה[.3

4.]יׄע את אש[ר
5.]○○ ○○○[

1.]. . .[
2.] in it[
3.]which he will do[
4.] that whi[ch
5.]. . .[

Fragment 55

1.]○עׯ ○○[
2.]○ השיב ל○[

bottom margin

1.]. . .[
2.] he answered to [

bottom margin

Fragment 56

1. /יׄקׄדׯש ○[ ] ○[
2. /בׄמשפט יריב א[ת
3. /בכול עוברי פיׄהׯ[ו
4. /עוזרי רשעה[
5. /○○○ עׄׯושי[
6. *vacat* [
7. /○○○ ונריבה ריב○[

1. he will sanctify [
2. with justice he will contend wi[th
3. against all those who violate [his] command[
4. those who aid (in doing) evil[
5. . . . those who do[
6. *vacat*
7. . . . and let us contend in dispute

TEXTUAL NOTES

Line 3. Literally, 'who violate [his] mouth'.

Line 4. Perhaps read ריבו 'his (God's) dispute'.

COMMENTARY

Line 2. Cf. Mic 7:9.

SUMMARY

Again we encounter the motif of God's doing justice against those who violate his commandments.

Fragment 57

]○○○○ ○○[.1
]רצה ופקוׄדׄ[.2
[סגולה מכול [העמים .3
[וכול מלכי עׄמׄיׄ]ם .4
]○ ○[.5

1.]. . .[
2.]favor (?) and remember[
3.]treasure from among all [the nations
4.]and all the kings of the nation[s
5.]. . .[

TEXTUAL NOTES

Line 3. Restored with Exod 19:5; Deut 7:6, 14:2.

COMMENTARY

Line 4. מלכי עמי]ם. Gen 17:16.

Fragment 58

]○שׄ○○○הׄ ○○○הׄ[.1
]○ בחׄוקים[.2

1.]. . .[
2.]in the laws [

Fragment 59

]○ ○○[.1
]וא וריב ר[.2
] ועתה מ○ *vacat* [.3
]שנאיכה לוא יוכל[ו .4
]לחצרו[תי]המה למ○[.5
]○[.6

1.]. . .[
2.] and dispute [
3.]*vacat* And now, [
4.]your [e]nemies will not be abl[e
5.]to their courtyard[s
6.]. . .[

COMMENTARY

Line 3. Note ועתה, the customary beginning to the wisdom speech.

Fragment 60

Fragment 60 appears in the concordance under that number. It is not found on the latest photographic plate but is on PAM 41.321. Instead, PAM 43.392 includes another fragment, which I have numbered 60*.

]שמעו ו○○[.1
]○○ובל ○ל ד○[.2
]וישמילנו [.3
]כבודו [.4
]א[.5

1.]Listen and [
2.]. . .[
3. and he will cause us to turn aside to the left (?) [
4.]his glory [
5.]. . .[

COMMENTARY

Line 1. The common introduction to a hortatory speech, as noted above.

Line 3. The *Hiphil* of שמאל means 'to turn from the true way' (BDB 970a).

Line 4. Taking the reference here as referring to the divine presence, designated by כבוד in Qumran sectarian texts.

Fragment 60*

]השמים ל[.1

]גים קדו[ש .2

]○○ ○הבל ○[.3

]○○[.4

]א[.5

1.]the heavens to[
2.] . . . hol[y
3.] . . . vanity [
4.]. . .[
5.]. . .[

Fragment 61

]○○○○[ ]○[.1

]○ינו שיד הואה[.2

מ[חסור ולמחיר[.3

]○○○ מעלים עי[ן .4

]○לת לגויתו וא○[.5

]ת ו○[.6

1.]. . .[
2.]. . . he[
3. l]ack, and for the price of[
4.] . . . they avert the ey[e
5.] . . . to his body [
6.]. . .[

Textual Notes

Line 3. מ]חסור. This word is very common in the sapiential texts, for example, 4Q*416* 1 4 and 6 (Wacholder and Abegg 2.54) and is the most likely restoration here.

Commentary

Line 4. Cf. Lev 20:4, Ezek 22:26, Prov 28:27 (preceded by מחסור; cf. line 3).

Fragment 62

[∘∘ם ולׄשׁוׄנׄוׄ]ת .1

[לׄ משפחות] .2

[∘ל ישרא]ל .3

[∘ יתנו] .4

[לׄ .5

1.] . . . tongues [
2.] families[
3.] Israe[l
4.] they will give[
5.]. . .[

Textual Notes

Line 1. Perhaps read עמי]ם ולשונו[ת.

Line 2. Restore האׄדמה], הארץ] or הארצות].

Line 3. Read either על or כול.

Commentary

Lines 1–2. Both these terms most likely designate the peoples of the earth. In some way the text contrasts them with Israel (line 3).

Fragment 63

.1

[∘ כול משפחותׄ] .2

[∘ע עמׄו מכוהן ∘] .3

[ליׄםׄ כל ר] .4

[∘∘∘] .5

1.]. . .[
2.] all the families of[
3.] with him, from a priest [
4.] . . . all [
5.]. . .[

Textual Notes

Line 3. The supralinear correction cannot be interpreted since it is only partly preserved. The word עמו, here translated 'with him', can also be 'his people'.

Fragment 64

.1 יש]ראׄל ועםׄ[
.2]° לׄבני ישרׄ[אל
.3 ע]בודתו ל[
.4]ם ידע[

1. Is]rael and the nation[
2.] to the children of Isra[el
3.]his [s]ervice to[
4.] he (or they) knew[

Fragment 65

It is possible that this fragment has been misplaced, as it deals with the Day of Atonement or some similar ritual. The same is the case with frg. 75. On the other hand, 1Q*27* frgs. 3 and 6 deal with priestly and sacrificial matters, as do 4Q*419* 1 1–8 (Wacholder and Abegg 2.155) and 4Q*421* 13 1–6 (p. 165).

.1 א]חת בשנהׄ[
.2 אור]יׄם ותומים[
.3]° כול האדם[

bottom margin

1. O]nce in the year[
2. Ur]im and Thummim[
3.] every person[

bottom margin

Commentary

Line 1. Cf. Lev 16:34 regarding the annual character of the Day of Atonement rituals.

Fragment 66

1. [◦תם חוק̊]
2. [לו̊א ידעתם ◦]
3. [לחול ו̇את]ם
4. [ל עם אשמה̊]

1.] . . . the law[
2.]you did not know [
3.]to that which is nonsacral, but yo[u
4.] with guilt[

Commentary

Line 2. Cf. Deut 11:28, 13:3, 14; Jer 33:3; Ezek 32:9.

Line 3. לחול[. Or 'to the sand'.

Fragment 67

1. /שבי פש̇]ע
2. /צ̊ר̇ב לכם ומ̊[
3. /נאצתה ו̊[
4. /ו̊י̊שפ̊ר ל̇[

1. those who have repented from transgress[ion
2. it burnt you and [
3. you reviled and[
4. and it was pleasing for[

Commentary

Line 1. Isa 59:20.

Fragment 68

1. הו]א̇ קדוש הו̊א̊[
2. ג]ב̊ורי צדק [

3. י]דעו כיאׄ[
4.]◦ על פ[

1. H]e is holy, he[
2. h]eroes of righteousness[
3.]they knew that[
4.] upon [

Textual Notes

Line 3. Or ‘will know’.

Commentary

Line 1. קדוש הוא. 2 Kgs 4:9, referring to a man; Ps 99:3, 5, referring to God.

Fragment 69

1.]◦ ◦[
2.]◦יׄ ואין[
3.]אׄל הדׄעׄ[ות
4.]◦ ל[

1.]. . .[
2.] and there is no[
3.]God of know[ledge
4.]. . .[

Fragment 70

1.]◦נׄוׄ[
2.]מׄשה פנים אבני[
3.]לזׄכׄר קדושׄיםׄ על [
4.]ל◦ וגב[
5.]◦◦דׄ◦[

1.]. . .[
2.]Moses, a face, stones of[
3. a remembrance of the holy ones, upon [
4.]. . .[
5.]. . .[

COMMENTARY

Line 3. זכר קדושים. Cf. Ps 30:5, 97:12. The word קדושים most likely refers to angels.

Fragment 71

1.]○○ל תכלת[
2.]כבוד לפתוח̇[

1.] . . . blue[
2.] honor, to open[

Fragment 72

1.]○ ו̇מ○[
2.]מ̇פיהו לפת[וח
3. /כול אבות העדה[
4. /וב○○○ בין איש[
5.]ה[

1.]. . .[
2.]from his mouth, to op[en
3. all the fathers of the congregation[
4. and in . . . between each (or a man) [
5.]. . .[

TEXTUAL NOTES

Line 4. Perhaps restore ובריב בין איש] לרעהו.

COMMENTARY

Line 2. Cf. Prov 24:7.

Line 3. אבות העדה. Num 31:26. Cf. 1QSa I 16, 24; II 16; 1QM II 1, 7; III 4; and Schiffman, *Eschatological Community*, 21, 53, where אבות are taken as 'clans, households'.

Fragment 73

1.]○○ איש̊[
2.]כ̇ול בידכם[
3.]○ ו̊ה̊ו̊א[

1.] a man[
2.]all in your hands[
3.] and he[

COMMENTARY

Line 2. Cf. Gen 9:2; Josh 9:11.

Fragment 74

]ח֯וקתיה[.1
]גׄבולותיה[.2
]○○○○○י֯ם֯[.3

1.]its laws[
2.]its boundaries[
3.]. . .[

Fragment 75

It is questionable whether this fragment is part of this composition, since it appears to be describing Aaron and the offering of sacrifices. See the introductory remark to frg. 65.

]○ם[.1
]י֯שרים [.2
]ד֯רך חיים [.3
]○וׄ רצונו הל[.4
]ארץ צביו והׄוא ○[.5
]באהליהם ואהרון מ[.6
ריח נ]י֯חוח לזכרון נב○[.7
] כול העמים ○○[.8
]ליׄו להיׄ[ות]ל[.9

bottom margin

1.]. . .[
2.]the upright [
3.]way of life [
4.]his will [
5.]his chosen land, and he [

6.]in their tents, and Aaron [
7. a fragrant of]fering as a remembrance of . . . [
8.] all the nations
9.] to b[e] for[

bottom margin

Commentary

Line 3. Cf. Jer 21:8, Prov 6:23.

Line 5. ארץ צביו. Cf. Jer 3:19; Ezek 20:6, 15; 25:9; Dan 11:16, 41.

Fragment 76

]◦◦ קרא א̊[.1
]ועתה פ̇[.2
מ]שׁ̇פ̇ט̊י̊ צדק[.3
]◦◦[.4

1.] he called [
2.] And now, [
3. l]aws of righteousness[
4.]. . .[

Commentary

Line 2. The familiar wisdom introduction.

Line 3. Isa 58:2; Ps 119:7, 106, 164.

Fragment 77

]ה̊ארץ למ◦[.1
]◦ ישפוט̊ ש̊[.2

1.]the land to [
2.] he will judge [

Fragment 78*

]◦ז̊ו̊ת [.1
] ישים[.2

3.]◦י֯ת֯י֯ ישראל[
4.]◦יו֯ם ֯יי֯מס[
5.]◦לים וק◦[

1.]. . .[
2.] he will put[
3.]. . . Israel[
4.]day (?) . . .[
5.]. . .[

Fragment 79

1.]◦ ◦[
2.]בקדם ◦[
3.]◦ית ב◦[
4.]ברית ה◦[
5. ?עבו]ד֯ת קוד[ש

1.]. . .[
2.]before [
3.]. . .[
4.]the covenant of the [
5.]the [ser]vice (?) of holine[ss

Textual Notes

Line 5. Perhaps restore קודשו 'his holiness' or קודשך 'your holiness'.

Fragment 81*[30]

1.] [
2.] [
3.]יצ [
4.]ם לך [

1.]. . .[
2.]. . .[
3.]. . .[
4.] to you [

30. Fragment 80* has no translatable text.

Fragment 82

1.]○○○○[
2.]שיתׄ מ○[
3.]הוא ○[

1.]. . .[
2.]. . .[
3.]he [

Fragment 83

1.]○○[
2.]דׄת בלחמם֯[
3.]○וׄ ○○○[

1.]. . .[
2.] in their bread [
3.]. . .[

Fragment 84

1. ע]בודׄת֯ [
2.]קדשו ○[
3.]○ מ֯[

1. se]rvice of the [
2.]his holiness [
3.]. . .[

Fragment 85*

1.]ם [
2.]ימים י[
3.] א[

1.]. . .[
2.]days (?) [
3.]. . .[

Fragment 93[31]

1.] יושבי֯[
2.]○○○[

1.] those who dwell in[
2.]. . .[

Fragment 95[32]

1.] לכול ל○○[
2.] עש֯ה[
3.]○[

1.]to all to [
2.]he did
3.]. . .[

Fragment 97*[33]

1.] יב [
2.]לוא בא[
3.] נ [

1.]. . .[
2.]not in [
3.]. . .[

Fragment 98*

1. ל]וא [
2.] קר ○[

1. n]ot [
2.]. . .[

31. Fragments 86*–92* have no complete words.
32. Fragment 94* has no complete words.
33. Fragment 96* has no complete words.

Fragment 102*[34]

.1 [ ]
.2 [אבר]הם
.3 [ ]

1.] . . . [
2.]Abra[ham (?)
3.]. . .[

34. Frgs. 99*–101* have no complete words.

Poetic Structures in the Hebrew Sections of the Book of Daniel

Stanislav Segert

In the Stuttgart editions of the Hebrew Bible, as well as some translations and commentaries, passages in Daniel 8–12 that are considered poetry are printed as lines of poetic verse. These sections are examined here according to various criteria: parallelism, which is weakened in postexilic poetry; word pairs; and prosodic regularity according to an alternation or accentuation system. Such features are attested in Daniel 8:23–26, 9:24–27, and 12:1–3. These sections, which conclude reports of visions, enhance the message of those visions by the poetic structuring. A quantitative comparison of the frequency of poetic features in the three poetic sections and in Dan 11:2–45 demonstrates the prosaic character of the latter. However, the division of prose texts into short segments, corresponding to poetic cola, furthers understanding of the text. This may be seen in Vulgate editions, in Buber's German translations, and in some translations by his followers. Poetic structuring has always aided the memorizing of religious texts. Further study of Hebrew biblical poetry from the postexilic period may benefit both from application of various methods and from a comparison with Hebrew and Aramaic texts from that period which are now becoming accessible, such as the Qumran scrolls and the Egyptian Papyrus Amherst 63.

Graphic Arrangement of Poetry

Because the study of poetry in the Hebrew Bible concentrates on the earlier stages, later developments receive inadequate attention. Consequently, the characteristics of poetry from the later biblical period have not been clearly observed and defined, nor have the dividing lines been traced between this poetry and prose.

It is generally accepted that the Hebrew chaps. 8–12 in the book of Daniel are the latest part of the canon of the Hebrew Bible. Since Porphyry, they have been dated to the early Maccabean period, ca. 165 B.C.E.[1]

1. O. Eissfeldt, *The Old Testament: An Introduction* (New York, 1976) 520–22; J. A. Soggin, *Introduction to the Old Testament* (London, 1976) 409–10.

The introductory Hebrew section, 1:1–2:4a, contains no poetic passages, and its genre and date need not be discussed here.

In the Stuttgart editions of the Hebrew Bible, three passages in the Hebrew part of Daniel are marked as poetry by graphic arrangement: verses are set in lines, and cola are separated by spaces. The 1937 and 1976 editions, prepared by Walter Baumgartner, exhibit the same arrangement. The passages printed as poetry are: 8:23–26, 9:24–27/2, and 12:1–3.[2] Recent translations differ considerably in the graphic arrangement of these sections. Some set all three passages as prose, others print all or most as poetry, and a few indicate additional verses as poetic passages. Even translations that indicate poetry in the book of Daniel by graphic means do so less frequently for the Hebrew than for the Aramaic sections.

No poetic passages are marked in Daniel 8–12 in the following translations: Jewish Publication Society 1917 (JPS) and 1982 (NJPSV), Good News Bible (GNB, 1979), New International Version (NIV, 1978), and the French translation by F. Michaéli (Pléiade, 1959); the same is true of the commentaries by Vellas (1966), Delcor (1971), Porteous (1965), and Hartman and Di Lella (1978). In translations that acknowledge the poetic character of some passages, there is much disagreement about what is poetry. The New Revised Standard Version (NRSV, 1989) presents only verses in chap. 8 as poetry; the earlier Revised Standard Version (RSV) of 1952 has no verse arrangements. The Chicago translation (1939) presents only verses from chap. 9, Plöger's commentary only those from chap. 12.[3] Two poetic passages from chaps. 8–9 are printed as poetry in the Jerusalem Bible, French and English, as are 10:5bc–6. Two poetic passages in chaps. 8 and 12 appear in the New English Bible (NEB, 1970) and the Revised English Bible (REB, 1989). Only two verses, 9:24 and 12:3, are considered poetry in Montgomery's commentary (1927). The three passages in BHS are rendered as poetry in the New American Bible (NAB, 1990), the Czech Bible (1990), and the Slovak *Biblia* (1979) translations, as well as in the commentaries by Goldingay (excluding 8:26) and Lacoque (1979; excluding 9:24 but adding 12:4). Bentzen, in his 1937 commentary, added 11:2–45 (with some hesitation) and 12:4 to the three

2. In this paper, a BHS verse number may be followed by a slash and a number that indicates poetic line number(s). For example, 27/2 means v. 27, line 2. Cola are indicated by the letters *a*, *b*, and *c*.

3. The commentaries cited below are as follows: A. Bentzen, *Daniel* (Tübingen, 1937; 2d ed., 1952); M. Delcor, *Le Livre de Daniel* (Paris, 1971); J. E. Goldingay, *Daniel* (WBC 30; Dallas, 1989); L. F. Hartman and A. A. Di Lella, *The Book of Daniel* (AB 23; Garden City, N.Y., 1978); A. Lacoque, *The Book of Daniel* (Atlanta [1976] 1979); J. A. Montgomery, *The Book of Daniel* (ICC; Edinburgh, 1927); O. Plöger, *Das Buch Daniel* (Gütersloh, 1965); N. W. Porteous, *Daniel: A Commentary* (OTL; Philadelphia [1962] 1965); V. M. Vellas, *Daniēl* (Hermēneia Palaias Diathēkēs 7; Athens, 1966).

passages; but in the 1952 edition he did not lay out either 9:25–26 or the passage from chap. 11 as poetry.

This rather complicated survey identifies the following as poetic passages: those marked as such by Baumgartner in the Stuttgart Bibles, 8:23–26, 9:24–27/1–2, 12:1–3; and in addition those considered to be poetic by only some translators, 9:27/3, 10:5b–6, and 12:4, as well as 11:2–45.

Poetic Structures and Features

All sections set as poetry should be examined according to the various criteria that may be used to determine the poetic character of a text. The most objective of these is syntactic analysis, which delimits poetic units (cola and verses) that coincide with syntactic units. In parallel constructions, syntactic relations are enhanced by semantic connections. Some features appear more frequently in poetry than in prose: semantic connections expressed through word pairs and the phonetic enhancement of cohesion by alliteration, assonance, and rhyme. The second criterion raises some difficulties: it is not always clear what kind of prosody was applied to a poetic composition, since we are not sufficiently familiar with the pronunciation and accentuation of Hebrew during the different periods.

Although these criteria are valid for identifying Hebrew poetry from the period of the monarchy or earlier, their application to postexilic poetry is often difficult and leads to uncertain results. Similar uncertainty hinders attempts to assign allegedly poetic passages to literary genres that exhibit formal poetic characteristics.

Syntactic and semantic cohesion, expressed most obviously by parallelism, is considerably weakened in postexilic poetry. In Lamentations 5 verses with parallelism prevail: only 3 of the 22 symmetric verses do not use parallelism. But in chap. 4 of the same book, only half of 44 asymmetric bicola are structured by patterns of parallelism. This lower frequency is due to the asymmetric *qînâ* verses. Psalm 137, which is certainly postexilic, contains no verses structured in parallelism in Hans Bardtke's 1969 edition.[4] In the Wisdom of Ben Sira, a Hebrew poetic book from the beginning of the second century B.C.E., roughly contemporary with the Hebrew part of Daniel, verses with parallelism prevail, continuing the tradition of canonical wisdom poetry.

The accentuation of preexilic posody was based on natural word stress. Accented syllables in a colon (usually three, often two or four)

4. Bardtke was the editor of the book of Psalms (1969) now included in the complete BHS (1967–77) edition.

were separated by one to three nonstressed syllables. This system is assumed by a majority of scholars for postexilic poetry as well. (Bentzen in both editions of his commentary on Daniel conveniently presents the number of accents in the cola and verses.)

For the language and structuring of postexilic Hebrew poetry, however, one must reckon with the heavy impact of Aramaic. This is especially to be expected in the book of Daniel, half of which is in Aramaic. Aramaic influence on Hebrew may be observed, on the one hand, in the tendency to reduce or eliminate short vowels, and on the other hand in the preservation of some vowels by lengthening. The result was a language in which short vowels occurred only in closed syllables (*CVC*), while long vowels occurred in open syllables ($C\bar{V}$) and in closed syllables ($C\bar{V}C$) at the end of words. Because reduced vowels apparently did not count in prosody, the language of late postexilic Hebrew poetry consisted of syllables of the same prosodic value.

This functional equivalence, as well as the weakening of word stress, also ascribable to Aramaic influence, made it possible to introduce alternation prosody:[5] stressed and unstressed syllables alternated regularly without regard for natural word stress; only the last prosodic accent of a colon had to coincide with the word stress. The number of accents in symmetric verses is mostly 4 + 4, and in asymmetric verses 4 + 3. Such verses are well attested in the book of Nehemiah: symmetric 3 + 3 in the complaint of the Judeans working on the wall of Jerusalem (4:4),[6] asymmetric (4 + 3, 4 + 3, 3) in the warning of Nehemiah (6:10). Symmetric verses with 4 + 4 accents may also be observed in the Aramaic sections of Daniel, especially in 3:33 and 4:31–32. In Ben Sira alternating symmetric verses are well attested in the Praise of the Fathers (chaps. 44–49), especially in the rhymed introductory section 44:1–9.[7]

Word pairs are not unique to poetry, but they are more frequent in structured poetry than in rhetorical prose. Word pairs (synonymous, complementary, or antithetic) appear as elements of parallelistic structures in adjacent cola or verses or as coordinated clause components or constituents. Word repetition is rare in older biblical poetry, being limited to words specified by expressions of similar semantic characteristics. In postexilic poetry repetition of identical words and roots is more frequent, and

5. Cf. S. Segert, "Vorarbeiten zur hebräischen Metrik, I-II," *ArOr* 21 (1953) 481–542, esp. 511, 527, and 541–42.

6. J. Blenkinsopp (*Ezra-Nehemiah: A Commentary* [OTL; Philadelphia, 1988] 248–49) considers this passage to be composed in *qînâ* or lament form (3 + 2). But the immediate vicinity of the stresses of the first two words, unseparated by an unstressed syllable, violates the rules of accentuation prosody.

7. Segert, "Vorarbeiten," 538–39.

it gains frequency as the use of parallelistic patterns decreases. Repetition contributes to the cohesion of poetic structures.

Specific words and morphemes with certain syntactic functions, such as the relative *ʾšr*, the *nota accusativi ʾt* that introduces determined objects, and the article *h-/ha(C)-/*, have attracted attention.[8] They appear only rarely in "classical" Biblical Hebrew poetry but are significantly represented in postexilic poetry and thus cannot serve as criteria to distinguish it from prose.

Phonetic embellishments such as cohesion, alliteration, assonance, and rhyme, are represented in all stages of Hebrew poetry.[9] Repetition may also be considered a phonetic effect, even though it may not have been intended as such.

Since opinions about the poetic character of various passages in the Hebrew parts of the book of Daniel are far from unanimous, each of the passages we have specified may be examined according to the above criteria. Only as the poetic passages are tentatively delimited by formal criteria may the role of poetic features be evaluated properly. The use of poetic devices in some prose sections should also be observed.

All three allegedly poetic passages in the second part of the book of Daniel (8:23–26, 9:24–27, and 12:1–3) have the same function: they serve as the climax of visions. In this position they attract attention by their effective, compact structuring. In the following discussion, I will use the arrangement of cola and verses in Baumgartner's edition and the accent counts in Bentzen's commentary of 1952.[10]

Daniel 8:23–26

23. When their kingdoms are at an end,
when the transgressors' [measure] has been filled,
Then a king will arise, impudent
and understanding intrigues.

8. Cf. D. N. Freedman, "Pottery, Poetry, and Prophecy: An Essay on Biblical Poetry," in *Pottery, Poetry, and Prophecy: Studies in Early Hebrew Poetry* (ed. D. N. Freedman; Winona Lake, Ind., 1980) 1–22, esp. 2. In n. 4 Freedman mentions that Albright routinely eliminated these particles in his reconstructions of Hebrew poetry. See F. I. Andersen and A. D. Forbes, "'Prose Particle' Counts of the Hebrew Bible," in *The Word of the Lord Shall Go Forth: Essays in Honor of David Noel Freedman in Celebration of His Sixtieth Birthday* (ed. C. L. Myers and M. O'Connor; Winona Lake, Ind., 1983) 165–83; counts of these particles in each chapter of the Hebrew Bible are given on pp. 172–83.

9. Cf. S. Segert, "Assonance and Rhyme in Hebrew Poetry," *MAARAV* 8 (*Let Your Colleagues Praise You: Studies in Memory of Stanley Gevirtz*; part 2; ed. R. J. Ratner et al.; 1992) 171–81.

10. My English translations mostly follow the NJPSV; or, for more literal renderings, also the JPSV. Some Hebrew poetic features are presented in new, more literal translations.

24. And his power will be strong, not by his power,
and he shall destroy wonderfully;
and he shall prosper and do;
And he shall destroy mighty ones
and the people of holy ones.
25. By his cunning,
he will use deceit successfully,
And he will make great plans,
will destroy many, taking them unawares,
And he will rise up against the chief of chiefs,
and he will be broken without hand.
26. And the vision of evening and morning which has been told
is true, But you, shut up the vision,
for it pertains to far-off days.

This poetic passage is presented by Baumgartner in nine poetic verses, mostly bicola, except 24/1, which is marked by spaces as a tricolon. Bentzen gives the following number of word accents: 23: 2 + 2, 3 + 2; 24: 2 + 2, 2 + 2; 25: 3 + 3, 2 + 3, 3 + 3; 26: 3 + 3, 3 + 3. For vv. 24–25 Bentzen introduces changes based on the Greek Septuagint version.[11] Application of alternation prosody indicates a majority of 3 + 3 accents: in 23/1–2, 25/2–3, 26/1–2. The Masoretic Text of the other verses may be scanned as follows: 24/1: 2 + 2, 3 + 3; 24/2: 2 + 2; 25/1: 2 + 3. If these verses, as emended, are excluded from the conclusion, the alternation system gives more regular results than prosody based on the normal accents of words.

Some bicola in parallelism are bound by words that are parallel both in their semantic relationship and in their syntactic function, while other parallel structures are rather relaxed. The adverbial modifiers in 23/1 are closely connected,

(a) *bʾḥryt* 'at an end' || (b) *khtm* 'at being filled',

as are their substantival attributes, the first specifying a general term, the second evaluating it,

(a) *mlkwtm* 'their kingdoms' || (b) *hpšʿym* 'the transgressors'.

The king in 23/2 is characterized by complementary adjectival attributes,

(a) *ʿz-pnym* 'strong of face'/'impudent' || (b) *mbyn ḥydwt* 'understanding intrigues'.

11. Compare his commentaries on Daniel of 1937 (p. 38) and of 1952 (p. 60).

In the Masoretic Text, the parallel structuring may be observed in four cola:

24/1a	*wᶜṣm kḥw*	'and his power will be strong'	A colon
24/1b	*nplᵓwt yšḥyt*	'and he shall destroy wonderfully'	B colon
24/1c	*whṣlyḥ wᶜśh*	'and he shall prosper and do'	A colon
24/2a	*whšḥyt ᶜṣwmym*	'and he shall destroy mighty ones'	B colon

Both parallelistic bicola are mutually parallel.

The last bicolon, 25/3, is in antithetic parallelism:

(a)	*wᶜl-śr-śrym yᶜmd*	'and he will rise up against the chief of chiefs'
(b)	*wbᵓps yd yšbr*	'and he will be broken without hand'

Cola 25/1b, 25/2a, and 25/2b seem parallel in meaning, but their relationship is difficult to establish, because of the uncertainty of 25/1a.[12]

There are no parallelisms in 8:26. In both bicola the (b) cola are subordinate clauses.

An additional word pair appears in 26/1a, functioning as a substantival attribute: *hᶜrb whbqr* '(of) evening and morning'.

The repetition in 24/1a serves to express antithesis: *kḥw wlᵓ bkḥw* 'power, not by his power'. Repeated and related words meaning '(and) he will destroy' are somewhat distant: in 24/1b and 25/2b *yšḥyt*, in 24/2a *whšḥyt*.

There are only two instances of the "nonpoetic" article, in 26/1a.

The features of parallelism in nearly all these verses corroborate the poetic character of the climax of the vision in 8:23–26. The most frequent prosodic features are bicola with three accented syllables, alternating with unstressed syllables in each colon; this regularity supports the poetic structuring.

Daniel 9:24–27

24. Seventy weeks have been decreed
upon your people, and upon your holy city,
To finish the transgression,
and to make an end of sin,
and to purify iniquity,
And to usher in eternal righteousness,
and to seal vision and prophet,
and to anoint holy of holies.
25. And you must know and you must understand:
From the issuance of the word,

12. Colon 8:25/1a is linked with 24/2b in BHS and by Bentzen, *Daniel* (1952), 60.

to restore and rebuild Jerusalem,
until the anointed leader, is seven weeks;
And for sixty-two weeks,
it will be built again,
square and moat,
but in a time of distress.
26. And after the sixty-two weeks,
the anointed one will be cut off and will be no more,
And the city and the sanctuary
will be destroyed by the army of a leader that will come;
But its end will come through a flood,
and till the end of the war
an appalling thing is decreed.
27. And he will make a firm covenant with many
for one week,
And for half a week
he will suspend the sacrifice and the meal offering;
And at the corner [of the altar] (?) will be an appalling abomination,
until the decreed destruction will be poured down
upon the appalling thing.

While opinions regarding the extent of the poetic passages in Daniel 8 are nearly unanimous, there are slight disagreements regarding the poetry at the end of chap. 9. Most translations and commentaries that consider this passage to be poetry set vv. 24–27 in verse lines, but some parts are set as prose: 27/3 in Baumgartner's Hebrew edition, as well as in the Czech Bible; vv. 25–27 by Montgomery and the Slovak translation; vv. 25–26 by Bentzen; v. 24 by Lacoque.

Scansion according to alternation prosody yields less regular results for 9:24–27 than for the end of chap. 8. Thus we have 9:24: 4 + 4, 2 + 3 + 3, 4 + 3 + 3; 9:25: 2, 3 + 2 + 4 (according to spaces in BHS 3 + 4 + 2), 4 + 4 + 3 (according to BHS spaces 3 + 3 + 2 + 3); 9:26: 5 + 4, 2 + 4, 2 + 3 + 3; 9:27: 3 + 2, 2 + 3, 4 + 3 + 3 (in BHS, a prose line). Bentzen's accentuation prosody indicates various regular verses: 9:24: 3 + 3, 2 + 2 + 2, 3 + 3 + 3; 9:27: 3 + 2, 3 + 2, 3 + 2.

Verses in parallelism:

9:24/2a	*lklʾ hpšʿ*	'to finish the transgression'	A colon
b	*wlḥtm ḥṭʾwt*	'and to make an end of sin / liquidate the sin'	B colon
c	*wlkpr ʿwn*	'and to purify/avert iniquity'	C colon

The next tricolon, 24/3, uses positive terms opposite to 24/2:

(a)	*wlhbyʾ ṣdq ʿlmym*	'and to usher in righteousness of eternity'	A colon
(b)	*wlḥtm ḥzwn wnbyʾ*	'and to seal vision and prophet'	B colon
(c)	*wlmšḥ qdš qdšym*	'and to anoint holy of holies'	C colon

The specification of time intervals by consecutive numbers of time units hinders the use of parallel structures. One example occurs in 9:25/2: (a) "from the issuance of the word," (c) "until the anointed leader." Coordinated phrases and word pairs, however, help to overcome this difficulty: 9:24/1b, "for your people and for your city of holiness"; 25/1, "and you must know and you must understand"; 25/3c, "square and moat"; 26/1b, "the anointed will be cut off and will be no more"; 26/2a, "the city and the sanctuary"; 27/2b, "the sacrifice and the meal offering."

Forms of *bny* 'to build' in 25/2b and 25/3b are paired with immediately preceding words derived from *šwb* 'to return'. Though the first of the latter, in *Hiphil*, is understood as 'to restore' and the second as a kind of auxiliary verb rendered in translations by the adverb 'again', these closely connected verbal forms may be considered word pairs, at least in their poetic function.

Repetitions contribute to cohesion. The word 'week' is represented three times in the plural, *sbʿym*: 24/1a, 25/2d, 26/1a; and twice in the singular, *šbwʿ*: 27/1b, 27/2a. The effect is reinforced by semantically and phonetically related words for numbers, 'seventy' *šbʿym*, 24/1a; and 'seven' *šbʿh*, 25/2d. The word for 'leader', *ngyd*, appears in 26/2b and 25/2c, in the latter colon paired with *mšyḥ* 'anointed', also attested in 26/1b; the verb *mšḥ* 'to anoint' is used in 24/3c. The root *šmm*, meaning 'appall', occurs in 27/3a, 27/3c, and 26/3c, in the last two occurrences linked with *Niphal* formations of *ḥrṣ* 'decreed'.

All these features demonstrate the markedly poetic character of 9:24–27. Though the numbering does not favor the use of features of parallelism, the sequence of numbers contributes to cohesion: "seventy," 24/1a; "seven," 25/2d; "sixty-two," 25/3a and 26/1a; "one," 27/1b; "half," 27/2a.

Only six instances of the article may be listed as "nonpoetic" features.

Daniel 12:1–3

1. And at that time shall appear
the great prince Michael,
who stands by the the sons of your people.
And it will be a time of trouble,
such as has never been since the nation came into being,

till that time.
And at that time your people will be rescued,
all who are found inscribed in the book.
2. And many of those who sleep
in the dust of the earth will awake,
some to eternal life,
and some to reproaches and to eternal abhorrence.
3. And the knowledgeable will shine like the brightness of the firmament,
And those leading the many to righteousness
will be like the stars for ever and ever.

Scholars are not in agreement about the number of verses to be considered poetry at the beginning of chap. 12. Bentzen adds v. 4 to the first three verses, as does Lacoque (but he deletes the first part of v. 1). Montgomery considers only v. 4 to be poetry.

In BHS v. 1 is printed in four lines, each representing one bicolon, but the content indicates that there are two opening tricola, one about Michael, the other about "the time of trouble." This structuring is scanned by Bentzen: 3 + 3 + 3, 3 + 3 + 3. The alternation approach yields less regular results: 4 + 4 + 4, 3 + 4 + 3. The number of stresses at the end of v. 1 are 4 + 3 and 5 + 4, respectively. Neither of the two prosody systems yields regularity in vv. 2 and 3. The accentuation system yields for v. 2: 4 + 3 + 4; for v. 3: 2 + 2, 2 + 3. The alternation system yields for v. 2: 3 + 3, 3 + 3 + 2; for v. 3: 3 + 3, 4 + 4. Bentzen gives the following accent count in v. 4: 4 + 4, 2 + 2. The corresponding figures according to alternation prosody would be: 3, 2 + 2 + 2, 2 + 2.

A contrastive parallelism occurs in 12:2/2, which uses two the same words in both cola, *ʾlh* 'these/some' and *ʿlm* 'eternity': (a) 'some to eternal life' || (b) 'some to reproaches and eternal abhorrence'. The bicola in v. 3 are mutually parallel: both 'knowledgeable ones' and 'those leading to righteousness' 'will shine' like 'the brightness of the firmament' or 'stars'. There is an obvious parallelism in v. 4: 'shut up the words' || 'seal the book'. A rather relaxed parallelism occurs at the end of of the same verse, if the verb in *Polel, šwṭ* 'to range far and wide', is interpreted as 'to attempt to investigate', which would be parallel to 'knowledge will increase'. Such a parallelism is reflected in the Greek version of Theodotion, 'many will be instructed and the knowledge will be augmented'. The rendering in the Vulgate is not in parallelism: '*pertransibunt plurimi et augebitur scientia* 'many will pass by . . .'. An antithetical parallelism appears in the quotation *multi pertransibunt, sed augebitur scientia,*[13] in which the verb is interpreted as 'they will pass away'.

13. This quotation is based on an oral tradition heard by the author in a discussion of the history of science.

A repetition appears in 12:1/4a, *wbʿt hhyʾ* 'and at that time', after 12:1/3b, *ʿd hʿt hhyʾ* 'to that time'. Perfect forms of the verb *hyy* 'to be' appear in 12:1: *Qal* in 2b, *Niphal* in 3a; both cola actually belong to the same tricolon. In 12:3/1 the verb *zhr* 'to shine' is followed by a noun derived from the same root.

The frequency of the article is relatively high: it occurs eight times in vv. 1–3 and twice in v. 4. The relative *ʾšr* occurs in 12:1/3a.

Though there are relatively few poetic features in 12:1–3 compared to the sections in chaps. 8 and 9 considered previously, the function of this passage as the conclusion of the vision in chaps. 10–11 supports its characterization as poetry. This does not fully apply to 12:4, but the appeal in 8:26 may be cited as an analogous poetic form.

The Jerusalem Bible, in both the French and English versions, sets the description of "the man dressed in linen," 10:5bc–6, in poetic lines. Verse 5 ends with two cola describing his clothing: "dressed in linen" || "his loins gird in gold of Uphaz." Verse 6 contains five comparisons characterizing his appearance: "body," "face," "eyes," "arms and legs," and "sound of his voice." Most of these cola have three stressed syllables, if scanned according to alternation prosody. The comparison of arms and legs has two such cola.

Both prosodic regularity and the use of the typical poetic device of comparison characterize this description as poetry. It may possibly be a quote from an older poem.

Poetry or Prose?

Only in the first (1937) edition of Bentzen's commentary is the prophecy—actually *vaticinium ex eventu*—in Dan 11:2–45 set as poetry, with the accents indicated. However, Bentzen himself considered the "metric articulation" very uncertain for chaps. 11 and 12, arranging his translation according to sense units to facilitate an understanding of the content.[14] While retaining this division in the second (1952) edition of his commentary, he abandoned his admittedly uncertain metrical articulation.[15]

A simple comparison of the frequency of poetic and nonpoetic features helps not only to determine the structure of Dan 11:2–45, but also to distinguish poetic passages from prose.

For this quantitative approach, I will use the prose lines in BHS. The rather rhetorical prose of 11:2–45 is printed on 63 lines. The poetic passages we have already discussed comprise some 20 lines: (approximately)

14. Bentzen, *Daniel* (1937), 45 and n. 1.
15. Bentzen (1952) 77.

5 lines for 8:23–26, 9 for 9:24–27, and 6 for 12:1–4; these three poetic passages contain 4 + 4 + 3, for a total of 11, parallel bicola or tricola. In chap. 11, three times as long, only 7 such structures may be found, some of them quite relaxed. In the three poetic passages there are 13 word pairs apart from those in structures of parallelism: 4 in chap. 8, 8 in chap. 9, and one in chap. 12. The number of word pairs in chap. 11 is 20. This disproportionate number of typical poetic features clearly demonstrates the difference between poetry and prose in the Hebrew sections of the book of Daniel.

Repetition of identical words and the connection of words derived from the same root contribute to cohesion in both poetry and rhetorical prose. There are 13 such instances (2 + 8 + 3) in the poetic passages in Daniel 8, 9, and 12; this number corresponds to the frequency of these features in the prose of chap. 11, where there are 26 of them.

The grammatical elements rightly considered nonpoetic in older poetry—the article, *nota accusativi,* and the relative *ᵓšr*—are attested in postexilic poetry. They occur in the poetic passages in Daniel: 2 in chap. 8, 6 in chap. 9, and 11 in chap. 12. Fourty-four occur in 11:2–45: the *nota accusativi* occurs once, *ᵓšr* 4 times, and the article 39 times. But nearly half of the articles are attached to nouns indicating 'south' (*h*)*ngb* (9 occurrences) and 'north' (*h*)*ṣpwn* (7 occurrences). This criterion of "nonpoetic" words is irrelevant for characterizing Hebrew poetry of the postexilic period.

The literary genre of chap. 11, revelation by an angel, did not require the use of poetic structuring. Similar revelations and visions in 8:1–22, 9:20–23, and 10:1–11:2a are presented in prose, with only their climactic conclusions in the poetic vein.

Bentzen's attempt to express poetic structuring by the number of accents produces rather irregular results.[16] Only a few verses seem regular: 11:10, 3 + 3, 3 + 3; 11:24, four times 4 + 3; 11:35, 2 + 2 + 2 + 2; 11:40, twice 4 + 4. Alternation prosody also yields irregular results. These analyses support the majority opinion: Dan 11:2–45 is prose.

Criteria for distinguishing poetry from prose may also be used to test the final section of the book of Daniel, the last revelation, 12:5–13. More than half of this passage consists of 4 sections of direct speech. Such an apportionment of smaller units is not convenient for structures in parallelism; the longest speech, vv. 9–13, contains only 2 instances of parallelism, both in v. 10. There is one example of synonymous parallelism in the middle of v. 7. A long repetition is used at the end of v. 5. Other contributions to cohesion are word pairs: complementary words in vv. 7 and

16. Bentzen (1937) 45.

9 and 3 synonymous words in the parallelism of v. 10. In the entire section, which is printed on 12 lines, there are 15 articles, one *nota accusativi*, and 2 relative pronouns. Though syntactic units with 4 alternation accents prevail in vv. 5–7, their loose connections do not allow one to establish poetic verse structures.

The genres presented as poetry in the Hebrew sections of Daniel are also distinguished as poetry in the Aramaic sections of the book too.[17] The most relevant passages in the visions are 4:7–9, 11–14; 7:9–10, 13–14, and 23–27. Just as the visions of the Hebrew chapters end with poetic verses, the narratives in the Aramaic sections close with liturgical praises: 3:33; 4:31–32; 6:27–28. The benediction in 2:20–23 is also structured as poetry.

The criteria applied to the poetry in the Hebrew sections of Daniel may also be used to determine the poetic character of passages in other clearly postexilic books, such as Neh 9:5–37. Although the cola and verses are not uniform in number of accents, syntactic articulation and the use of poetic features explain why this prayer, which reflects historical traditions, is considered poetry.[18]

The criteria we have used to distinguish postexilic Hebrew poetry from prose may be summarized as follows. The coincidence of prose units—cola and combinations of cola (= poetic verses)—with syntactic units is the most objective criterion of poetry and is the first test to be applied to a passage. A second criterion, prosodic regularity, may be observed, though it is not always as uniform as in older poetry. Poetic cohesion is supported by the use of parallelism and repetition of words and roots and enhanced by repetition or similarity of sounds.

Attempts to distinguish poetry from prose in the Hebrew Bible may be affected by bias brought from the researcher's acquaintance with poetry in his native language or, on the other hand, from a study of poetry that is strictly distinguished from prose by its form, as in ancient Greek and Latin. Foreign and anachronistic standards should be carefully avoided. It would also be interesting to establish a continuum, proceeding from less structured to firmly structured literary units.

Functions of Poetry

Two questions arise here: What is gained by trying to distinguish and define poetry in the Hebrew Bible? Do such efforts help to improve our

17. According to the graphic arrangement in BHS.

18. S. Segert, "History and Poetry: Poetic Patterns in Nehemiah 9:5–37," in *Storia e tradizioni di Israele: Scritti in onore di J. Alberto Soggin* (ed. D. Garrone and F. Israel; Brescia, 1991) 255–65.

understanding and interpretation of the text? Both questions may be answered in the affirmative. The contribution of such analyses to interpretation is demonstrable not only in the recognition of poetic devices and their functions, but also in passages of uncertain poetic character. A good example is Dan 11:2–45. As stated, Bentzen treated this chapter in his 1937 commentary as poetry, while in his second (1952) edition, he abandoned rhythmic articulation, but he retained the division into short segments (corresponding to poetic cola) in his German translation, in order to facilitate understanding.[19]

In the Stuttgart edition of the Vulgate,[20] the lines are arranged in syntactic units in both prose and poetic sections, a layout that furthers the understanding of the Latin translation. The similar graphic arrangement of Martin Buber's German translation[21] also contributes to a better understanding of the text and of Buber's efforts to render the Hebrew original faithfully.

A translator who recognizes the organic syntactic units rather than focusing on the individual words and translating them literally, is better equipped to understand the content and to render it adequately in the target language. Relationships between segments also become more evident. The translator is thus able to penetrate more deeply into the structure of the text and consequently enabled better to interpret its message.[22]

While the function of poetry in books of the Hebrew Bible that are totally poetry may be defined more clearly, it is not always clear what function or functions may be attributed to poetic passages in prose contexts. The use of poetry in the book of Daniel provides one answer: poetic structuring was used to emphasize the most relevant messages in a vision. Another function of poetry was to accentuate religious feelings in prayers and confessions. Furthermore, specific literary genres, expressing specific religious messages, required the use of poetic forms (cf. the use of asymmetric verses in Lamentations).

In periods when religious messages depended mainly on oral transmission, poetic structuring aided memory of the text. Those who composed poetic structures stored in their memories inventories of word

19. Bentzen, *Daniel* (1937), 45 and (1952), 77.

20. R. Weber (ed.), *Biblia Sacra iuxta Vulgatam versionem* (Stuttgart, 1969).

21. M. Buber (trans.), *Die Schrift* (1925–37; repr. Heidelberg, 1954–62).

22. This was my approach in my Czech translation of the Five Megilloth, *Pět svátečních svitků* (Praha, 1958), not only with regard to the poetic books of Song of Songs (with J. Seifert), Lamentations (with V. Závada), and Ecclesiastes (with V. Kubíčková), but also for the prose books of Ruth and Esther. Thanks to David Flusser, I had the opportunity of discussing this kind of presentation with Martin Buber in the spring of 1964.

pairs and techniques suitable for poetic structuring. The results were presented orally, only later being recorded in writing.

Memorization, often based on reading aloud, has always been and is still being used for study in various religions all over the world.[23] It is facilitated by poetic structuring. This function of poetry can be tested on modern hearers. Such tests, especially with native speakers of Hebrew, may well help to elucidate certain communicative functions of poetic devices, such as parallelism, as they were perceived by the original hearers.[24] This application of psycholinguistics may provide additional insights into the traditional literary analysis of poetry, as well as correctives to modern methods.

Further study of Biblical Hebrew poetry from the postexilic period may benefit both from application of different methodological approaches and from comparison with nonbiblical Hebrew and Aramaic poetic texts that have recently become accessible, from the Qumran scrolls and the Egyptian Papyrus Amherst 63.[25]

Appendix: Survey of Poetic Features in Daniel 8–12

Passage	Poetic Units		Parallelisms	Additional Word Pairs	Repetitions
	Bicola	Tricola			
8:23–26	8	1	3 + 2?	4	2
9:24–27/2	6	4	2 + 1?	7 + 2?	6
9:27/3?		1	1	1	2
(10:5bc–6)	3?	1?	3	1	
12:1–3	5	2	3 + 1?	1	3
12:4 ?	1?	1?			

23. In the spring of 1964, Jonas Greenfield, then on sabbatical leave from the University of California, Los Angeles, introduced me to students reading the Talmud in an ultra-orthodox neighborhood of Jerusalem.

24. Z. Zevit ("Roman Jakobson, Psycholinguistics, and Biblical Poetry," *JBL* 109 [1990] 385–401) provides a basis for this kind of research.

25. See R. C. Steiner, "The Aramaic Text in Demotic Script: The Liturgy of a New Year's Festival Imported from Bethel to Syene by Exiles from Rash," *JAOS* 112 (1992) 362–63, with bibliography in n. 1; S. Segert, "Preliminary Notes on the Structure of the Aramaic Poems in the Papyrus Amherst 63," *UF* 18 (1986) 271–99.

Qumran: Some Iranian Connections

Shaul Shaked

In this article I discuss a number of proper names and nouns that occur in writings discovered at Qumran, for which an Iranian origin may plausibly be suggested. The words discussed are ʾwšy, (ʾ)bdny, and pnbd. The names are bgsrw, bgwšy, and ptryzʾ.

J. T. Milik recently published a number of new fragments from Qumran that he describes as "proto-Esther."[1] These fragments from the fourth cave at Qumran form part of a curious narrative of the goings-on in the Persian royal court, and in this they bear a strong resemblance to Esther, but there the resemblance seems to end. The narrative itself is quite different, the characters are not the same as those that we have in the book of Esther, and there is no reason to suppose that this narrative preceded that of the book of Esther or that there was a dependence in the opposite direction, namely that the book of Esther influenced the new narrative. What we can deduce quite certainly from the existence of this new book is that the book of Esther was not unique in Jewish literature in reporting real or imaginary intrigues at the royal court of Persia. To some extent this type of literature must have been familiar already because of the books of Daniel and Ezra. But these two books have a completely different and very serious thrust. The book of Esther and the new book, by contrast, belong to a more lighthearted type of composition. Although

Author's note: I make a distinction between transcriptions, which I indicate by italic type, and transliterations (i.e., letter-by-letter romanizations of the original alphabet), which I indicate by bold type.

1. J. T. Milik, "Les modèles araméens du livre d'Esther dans la grotte 4 de Qumran," *RevQ* 59 (1992) 321–99. Another, less reliable edition is found in R. H. Eisenman and M. Wise, *The Dead Sea Scrolls Uncovered: The First Complete Translation and Interpretation of 50 Key Documents Withheld for over 35 Years* (New York, 1992) 101ff. I should like to thank Jonas Greenfield, in whose honor this volume is being published, for being among the first to draw my attention to Milik's publication.

it may have a clear moral at its end, the narrative in these books serves its own end, being told at least partly for sheer entertainment.

The new book from Qumran must have belonged to a genre, or at least sub-genre, in which events having some bearing on the fate of the Jews or individual Jews were reported. One other work which may be said to belong to the larger genre of which Esther and the new book form part is the book of Tobit, which tells of events in roughly the same historical period.

Apart from the considerable interest that the book holds by itself, the new work thus has the great merit of saving the book of Esther from its isolation as a composition comparable to no other work in Jewish literature.

From an Iranian point of view, it is obvious that one should first concentrate on the proper names. These are, for the most part, evidently of Iranian origin. The names ***bgsrw***, ***bgwšy***, and ***ptryzʾ*** have a strong Iranian color and may be explained as Iranian names, even though none of them has yet been attested in the onomastics of the Iranian sources.

bgsrw: This is evidently Iranian Baga-srū or Baga-srava-, which would roughly mean 'listening to the god' (or, more specifically, 'listening to Baga'). This has already been recognized by Milik,[2] who compares the name to the Slavonic Bogoslav and Greek Theoklēs.

bgwšy: The name may be interpreted as Baga-uši- 'having the ear (or understanding) of the god (or of Baga, as a specific name of a god)'. Milik[3] refers to Josephus, who mentions a Samaritan enemy of the Jews, Bagōses. This could well be the same name.

ptryzʾ: This name should most likely be interpreted as **pitar-raij-* 'pleasing to (his) father'. For the second element, compare Sogd. *ryž-*, NP *rīža,* from Old Iranian **raig-*. If the fourth letter is a *waw,* the name may be interpreted as **pitar-rvaz-* 'joy to (his) father'. In the edition of Eisenman and Wise,[4] this word is transcribed ***ptrwnʾ***, and inexplicably romanized as Fratervana.

The second category of probable Iranian words is common nouns. It seems likely that the word ***ʾwšy***, apparently a singular noun, is in this category. It appears in the genitive construction ***ʾwšy mlkʾ***. Given its context, Milik translates it 'messenger of the king'. He attempts to explain it[5] from the verb *ěwaš,* attested in the Babylonian Talmud, and accordingly determines its primary sense as being '(public) crier, announcer'. The talmudic verb is, however, a denominative from another Iranian

2. Milik, "Les modèles araméens," 351.
3. Ibid., 350–51.
4. Eisenman and Wise, *The Dead Sea Scrolls Uncovered,* 101.
5. Milik, "Les Modèles araméens," 331–32, 370–72.

word (of Parthian origin)[6] and seems hardly suitable for the context. The word *ʾwšy* could well be a borrowing from the Old Iranian word for 'ear, intelligence, understanding'. That word is *uš-* (n.) but is almost exclusively used in the dual. The form *uši* could well be a dual form, used as a singular in Aramaic. If this is true, we would have here a variant of the well-known term for the 'ears of the king', already attested in Aramaic as *gwšk.*[7] One may, however, assume that there was a difference in the application of these two Iranian titles. Since the Iranian term *uš* has a more intellectual connotation, it is quite likely that it was applied to a highly placed official of the king.

Two other Qumran words that have caused difficulty may be interpreted on the assumption that they are borrowings from the Iranian. One is the somewhat mysterious word ***bdny*** (pl.), which is quite widely used in a number of Qumran writings, notably in the *Songs of the Sabbath Sacrifice* and in the *War Scroll.*[8] The Qumran word has been translated, from its presumed meaning in the context, as 'forms, figures, appearance'. It seems possible to explain it from Old Iranian **abidaēnā-*, which has a meaning quite close to the sense required for the Hebrew word. The descendants of the putative Old Iranian word are chiefly Manichaean Parthian ***ʾbdyn***, Manichaean Middle Persian ***ʾywyn***, with the reconstructed reading for Pahlavi and Manichaean Middle Persian *ēwēn.* The word in Middle Iranian means 'style, mode, form, ritual'. It is not entirely surprising that the word should have lost its initial vowel in the Hebrew context. The initial vowel is nevertheless attested in one occurrence of the word, written ***ʾbdny.***

It may be interesting to explore whether another word, attested in Hebrew and Aramaic, is not related. The Targum often translates various Biblical Hebrew words that denote magic, such as the Hebrew *baddîm, ôb,* and so on, by ***bdyn***, vocalized *biddîn.* This form may possibly be considered as another reflection of the Iranian word for 'style, form'. One magic text, published in a new volume of Aramaic spells, carries the seemingly related form in Aramaic, ***bydynʾ*** (which can also be read ***bwdynʾ***).[9]

6. Cf. S. Shaked, "Iranian Elements in Middle Aramaic: Some Particles and Verbs," in *Medioiranica: Proceedings of the International Colloquium Organized by the Katholieke Universiteit Leuven from the 21st to the 23rd of May 1900* (ed. W. Skalmowski and A. van Tongerloo; Leuven, 1993) 147–56.

7. For a discussion of this term, see S. Shaked, "Two Judaeo-Iranian Contributions" (in *Irano-Judaica* [ed. S. Shaked; Jerusalem, 1992] 292–322, esp. 301–2), where a reference to Schaeder's classical study of the title is made.

8. Cf. C. Newsom, *Songs of the Sabbath Sacrifice: A Critical Edition* (HSS 27; Atlanta, 1985) 235, 283–85.

9. Cf. J. Naveh and S. Shaked, *Magic Spells and Formulae: Aramaic Incantations of Late Antiquity* (Jerusalem, 1993) 79–80, no. A 23.

The last word to be discussed in this group is ***pnbd***, as I believe the reading should be. It occurs in 2Q*26*, where the text is as follows:

1. חדא מן תרתי לחמא יהיבת [ל]כ[הן ראשא]
2. עמה ואחריתא [...י]היבת לתנינא די קאם פנבד [...]

The translation provided by the original editor is:

> (je regardais) jusqu'à ce que l'un des deux pains fût donné [au grand prêtre]. . . . avec lui, et l'autre fût donné à son second qui se tenait debout (à part?).[10]

The commentary by the editor runs as follows: "le *pé* étant certain, le mot ne peut être qu'un emprunt iranien ou une faute de copiste pour מן בד." In his preliminary edition of the fragment, Baillet already experimented with an Iranian derivation, which he himself rightly rejected.[11]

The same text occurs also in 11QNJ.[12] We lack an additional context that might clarify the role of the second priest who stands ***pnbd***. The alternative translation, 'à part', is based on the possibility of a scribal corruption from *min bad*. This is excluded, however, by the occurrence of the same spelling in another manuscript. The translation 'debout' is mere guesswork, based apparently on the (failed) etymology with which Baillet experimented in his preliminary edition. The suggestion that the word is a borrowing from Iranian is, however, worthy of serious consideration.

At the outset, it is impossible to find an Iranian word that has the same form as the Aramaic *pnbd*. It is possible, however, to suggest a fairly plausible Iranian connection, which would make the word related to a common Persian word with a strong ritual connection. The Persian word in question is *paywand*, which denotes, among other things, 'connection, relationship, association', used specifically to indicate a ritual connection between two priests while they perform a ritual that needs to be performed by more than one priest. The word *paywand*, etymologically derived from **pati-band-*, shows the typical phonetic development that gives as a result the Middle and New Persian form *paywand*. If we assume a vari-

10. M. Baillet, J. T. Milik, and R. de Vaux, *Les 'Petites grottes' de Qumran* (DJD 3; Oxford, 1962) 86–87.

11. M. Baillet, "Fragments araméens de Qumrân 2: Description de la Jérusalem Nouvelle," *RB* 62 (1955) 222–45, esp. 235–36.

12. Cf. F. García Martínez, "The Last Surviving Columns of 11QNJ," in *The Scriptures and the Scrolls: Studies in Honour of A. S. van der Woude . . .* (ed. F. Carcía Martínez et al., VTSup 49; Leiden, 1992) 185. The same fragment was published previously by B. Jongeling, "Publication provisoire d'un fragment provenant de la grotte 11 de Qumrân (11QJér Nouv ar)," *JSJ* 1 (1970) 58–64; "Note additionnelle," ibid., 185–86.

ant form of **pati-band-*, with a second preverb *ni,* we may reconstruct **pati-ni-band-*, a form not otherwise attested, but certainly within the range of linguistic possibility. This might have roughly the same sense as *paywand,* that is, 'association, connection'. The preverb *pati* shows a development to *pa* before *-n-* in the word *panāh* 'protection', if the accepted etymology of the word is still valid.[13]

The fact that the Aramaic word does not have an *-n-* before the final letter does not constitute a serious obstacle to this etymology. The Persian form may have been transmitted in its zero grade (though this is unlikely in this form), or the *-n-* may have been assimilated to the final *d* in Aramaic, a common phonetic occurrence in Semitic.

If this suggestion is accepted, the meaning of the Aramaic word *pnbd* may be not 'separate(ly)', but its opposite, 'in close proximity, in association (with the first priest)'. The text is too fragmentary to tell whether this is a ritual requirement or, what seems more likely, just a descriptive adjective.

The presence of Persian words in the manuscripts found at Qumran should no longer cause surprise. That the words are unattested elsewhere in Hebrew or Aramaic does not mean that the language used in Qumran was under stronger Persian influence than other types of Hebrew or Aramaic. It only shows how deficient our knowledge of the language of the period still is. In the case of the new narrative it is possible that the text was originally written not in Palestine but somewhere in the East, closer to the royal Iranian court.

13. The word is derived from **pati-nāθa-*; cf. P. Gignoux, *Iranisches Personennamenbuch*, vol. 2: *Mitteliranische Personennamen*; Fasc. 2: *Noms propres sassanides en moyen-perse épigraphique* (ed. M. Mayrhofer and R. Schmitt; Österreichische Akademie der Wissenschaften, Phil.-hist. Klasse; Vienna, 1986) 144, no. 744. P. O. Skjærvø, "L'Inscription d'Abnūn et l'imparfait en moyen-perse," *Studia Iranica* 21 (1992) 153–60, esp. 155, notes the possibility that the word could be derived from **upanāya-*, in view of the orthography ***pnʾy***.

Abraham and the Eastern Kings: On Genesis 14

J. A. Soggin

In this paper I try to avoid approaches that have been called "false cues" in the past. The story is certainly late and no connection with early or late documents may be found. The center of the story is the Malkî-ṣedeq episode; it should be interpreted either as Hasmonean kings attempting to acquire legitimacy or as the Jerusalem priesthood claiming tithes and submission from the Hasmoneans. It will be the task of future scholarship to ascertain which is the right alternative.

Introduction

Genesis 14 is one of the texts that cannot be assigned with even minimal certainty to any of the traditional Pentateuchal sources by those who maintain the Documentary Hypothesis. At the beginning of our century the trend was to associate the chapter with P, but some have recently dated it even later than P, while other authors have found Dtr elements in the text.[1] In all these cases the composition of the chapter is assigned a relatively late date.

Gunkel drew attention to the fact that the whole story seems to reflect the style of Jewish popular legends during the Persian and Hellenistic periods.[2] But a new trend became manifest in the 1960s, in Speiser's important commentary, followed later by Sarna and several

1. Those who associate the chapter with P: H. Gunkel, *Genesis* (Göttingen, 1901; 3d ed., 1910); O. Procksch, *Die Genesis* (Leipzig and Erlangen, 1913; 2d–3d eds., 1924). Those who date it later than P: R. de Vaux, *Histoire ancienne d'Israel* (2 vols.; Paris, 1970) 1.208–12; J. Ha, *Genesis 15* (Berlin, 1989) 202–6. Those who have found Dtr elements in the text: e.g., M. Astour, "Political and Cosmic Symbolism in Genesis 14 and its Babylonian Sources," in *Biblical Motifs, Origins and Transformations* (ed. A. Altman; Cambridge, Mass., 1966) 65–112; J. Van Seters, *Abraham in History and Tradition* (New Haven and London, 1975).

2. Gunkel, *Genesis,* 189–90.

other authors:[3] vv. 1–11, they maintain, were a kind of translation, not without misunderstandings and later editorial additions, of an ancient cuneiform text the original of which has, however, not been found and is probably no longer extant. A similar thesis was proposed as early as 1843 by Heinrich Georg August Ewald (1803–75), followed by several authors, some of them orientalists.[4]

But, as is well known, the text does not stop at v. 11. Verses 12–13 connect it, although "loosely" (Speiser), with Abraham's family captured at Sodom and in vv. 14ff., with the Patriarch's expedition against the kings, in which he rescued his relatives and part of the loot. On his return journey to Mamrē (vv. 18–20), he was met first by the king of Sodom and then by the king of Salem. To the latter he paid a tithe of his own possessions, probably not of the booty, which he returned to its legitimate owners. The story concludes by stressing the patriarch's modesty and unselfishness: like a great and noble king, he did not need to enrich himself and could, therefore, return everything to the original owners, keeping for himself and his allies only as much as was necessary to defray the expenses.[5] Thus, whatever the supposed antiquity of vv. 1–11, the function of these verses is now to introduce the main subjects:[6] Abraham's victory, his encounter with the king of Salem and his unselfishness.

There are several elements worth noticing in the text: the names are considerably different in the Greek of the LXX (as also happens elsewhere); according to Josephus (*Ant.* 1.171ff.), the war is supposed to have been fought only between the Assyrians and the Sodomites. There are also some variant readings in the LXX and in 1QapGen that contrast favorably with the rather clumsy Hebrew style of the Masoretic Text. Whether the expression *bîmê* 'in the time(s) of . . .', followed by a royal name, may be a translation of the Akkadian *enūma* . . . 'when . . .', as argued by Speiser, should be taken into consideration, although there are other more likely explanations, such as translating it 'Once upon a time. . . .'

Only two names of the eastern countries involved are clearly understood: *šinᶜār* was the current term in Hebrew for Mesopotamia (see, inter

3. E. A. Speiser, *Genesis* (Garden City, N.Y., 1964). Cf. already W. F. Albright, "Abraham the Hebrew," *BASOR* 163 (1961) 46–57; N. M. Sarna, *Understanding Genesis* (New York, 1966).

4. For details see W. Schatz, *Genesis 14: Eine Untersuchung* (Bern and Frankfurt a/M, 1972); C. Westermann, *Genesis 12–36* (BKAT 1/2; Neukirchen-Vluyn, 1981; Eng. trans.: Minneapolis, 1985).

5. J. Muffs, "Abraham, the Noble Warrior," *JJS* 33 (1982) 81–107.

6. Thus, rightly, J. Skinner, *A Critical and Exegetical Commentary on the Book of Genesis* (ICC; 2d ed.; Edinburgh, 1930).

alia, Gen 11:1ff.), a reading that is endorsed by 1QapGen, which has the almost synonymous *bābel* (LXX has only a transliteration of the Hebrew, Σενναάρ, as in Gen 11:1ff.); *ᶜêlām* is the ancient name for Persia, the region east of Mesopotamia. But the other eastern names have until now defied identification. For Hebrew *ᵓellāsār*, the Vulgate has *rex Ponti*, that is, some kingdom on the Black Sea, while *gôyîm* may mean anything (see p. 289 below). The same applies to the names of the four kings: no reasonable, even tentative, identification has been offered to this date, although many suggestions have been made.[7]

Topography and Ethnography

The itinerary, where it may be reconstructed, is also disconcerting, as Skinner has rightly noted in his commentary, followed by von Rad.[8] From the east toward the Dead Sea region they moved first through the Transjordanian Highlands, following what was called (until modern times) the 'King's Highway' (*tarīq as-sulṭāni*), along which Numbers locates the final itinerary of the Exodus, but during the Exodus obviously in the opposite direction. At the Gulf of Aqaba, the expedition turned toward the northwest until *qādēš* (*ᶜain el-qudeirat*, on the border between Canaan and Egypt, coord. 096-006), moving after that to the northeast, this time directly toward its destination. The extravagance of this itinerary has been compared to the extravagant itinerary in the deuterocanonical book of Judith. In Judith there are also many unknown places, while the few identifiable ones make no sense. In Genesis 14 there is, however, a notable difference: the first part of the itinerary, in Transjordan, would be quite sensible if the expeditionary army descended from there directly toward the Dead Sea, say through one of the main wadis. At the end of the Early Bronze Age (ca. the 23d century B.C.E.) and at the end of the Late Bronze Age (ca. the 13th century B.C.E.), the region had many villages along the road, as clearly shown by Nelson Glueck in the 1930s and the 1940s.[9] But should Abraham be dated as early or as late as that? Furthermore, the itinerary from Aqaba to the Dead Sea remains unexplainable.

Among the identifiable localities, I mention the following. On the King's Highway: *ᶜaštĕrôt qarnayim*, now *tell ᶜaštāra* on the Haurān, coord. 243-244; *hām*, today's *hām*, coord. 226-213, near Irbid; *qiryātayim*, today, either *qaryatîn* south of *el-kerāk* or *qaryat el-mehāyet*, coord. 220-128. Other

7. See, e.g., R. T. O'Callaghan, *Aram Naharaim* (Rome, 1948) 31f.
8. Skinner, *A Critical and Exegetical Commentary*; G. von Rad, *Das erste Buch Moses: Genesis* (9th ed.; Göttingen, 1972; English translation: Philadelphia and London, 1972).
9. N. Glueck, *AASOR* 18–19 (1939) 264ff.

places are: *ʾēl-pāʾrān*, probably on the site of today's Aqaba or Eilat; *qādēš* has been dealt with above; *tāmār* is usually identified with *ʿain huṣb*, coord. 173-024.

The conquered peoples are the ones mentioned in Deut 2:10–12 and traditionally associated with Transjordan before the settlement of the Ammonites, Edomites, and Moabites; it is impossible to identify them with any known ethnic or political group. This led Noth and von Rad to the conclusion that Genesis 14 is a more or less learned construction rather than a traditional recollection of events;[10] R. de Vaux similarly concludes that Genesis 14 cannot be used to reconstruct historical events.[11] The only contemporary scholar besides Speiser and Sarna (and the authors they quote) who maintains that at least the first part of the itinerary is historical is Y. Aharoni.[12]

Canaanite City-States

As far as the Canaanite city-states and their sovereigns are concerned, the situation is not substantially different: not one of the localities mentioned has been even tentatively identified, although there are some *tulul* in the region, nor is there any evidence of a densely populated area. The only exception is *belaʿ/ṣōʿar*, provided that the identification of the two localities as implied by the text itself is tenable: *tell eṣ-ṣāfî*, coord. 194-049. The only reference to them is in the deuterocanonical Wis 10:6 as 'Five Cities' (πεντάπολις).

The name of Sodom has been preserved in the Arab name *ğebel usdūm*, coord. 187-053; but, like the Arab name of the lake, *baḥr lūṭ*, it derives from the biblical narrative.

The names of the first two Canaanite kings were associated by later Jewish exegetes with the roots *rāʿaʿ* and *rāšaʿ*, respectively 'the wicked' and 'the impious', and were therefore considered names created ad hoc for pedagogical reasons. However, the etymology is a different one and has been associated with Arabic *baraʿa*, the shouting of the victorious, and *biršaʿam* 'gallant'; all are good West Semitic names attested in the second millennium B.C.E.

Textual Problems

Further textual elements may be noted. In v. 3, notice the use of *ḥābar*, which in conjunction with the preposition *ʾel* normally indicates a

10. M. Noth, *Überlieferungsgeschichte des Pentateuch* (Stuttgart, 1948) 170; von Rad, *Das erste Buch Moses*.

11. De Vaux, *Histoire*, 1.211.

12. Aharoni, *The Land of the Bible* (Philadelphia, 1966) 127ff.

person one is joining; we have, therefore, an unusual construction.[13] In v. 5 the reading *zamzummîm*, as in Deut 2:20, has been suggested, following 1QapGen and Σ, instead of *hazzûzîm*, but the question arises whether it is worth correcting a text that is in any case dubious. In v. 6, notice that *śēᶜîr* stands as a gloss to *bĕharĕrām*. The proposal by the Samaritan Pentateuch and the ancient versions to read *bĕharĕrê* instead appears to be a lectio facilior. The repetition of *beʾĕrôt* in v. 10 indicates an unusually great quantity.[14] In Hellenistic and Roman times the region was known for its virtual monopoly on the production of bitumen. For the incomprehensible *herâ*, the reading *haharâ* 'toward the hill country' has been suggested. In v. 13 Abraham is called *hāᶜibrî*,[15] which seems to mean here nothing more than 'descended from *ᶜēber*' (Gen 10:24 and 11:16).[16] This qualification is unique in the patriarchal traditions and should not be linked, therefore, with ethnic movements or social upheavals in the second millennium. It is interesting to note that Mamre appears here as the name of a person, while elsewhere it is always the name of a locality. In v. 14 Lot is the *ʾāḥ* of Abraham, but this word should not be rendered 'brother'. It is used here (and elsewhere) generically to indicate a 'relative'. The word **ḥānîk* appears only here in this form and is probably an Egyptian loanword.[17] It has been identified by Albright[18] in a West Semitic text, tablet 6 from Tell Taᶜanāk (second half of the fifteenth century B.C.E.), where the expression *ḥa-na-ku-u-ka* 'your retainers' is found. The root *ḥānak* developed into the meanings 'to consecrate, to dedicate' and also 'to instigate'. In v. 19 the root *qānâ* may mean 'to acquire' (therefore, in the participle *qal*, 'lord of') and 'to create', 'to produce' (therefore 'Creator'). In the Phoenician inscription from Karatepe (ca. 720 B.C.E., *KAI* no. 26), III 18, the expression *ʾl qn ʾrṣ* appears. In our text 'lord' and 'creator' would yield equally good translations, although some prefer 'creator'.[19] In the Hebrew Bible the expression is usually connected with Jerusalem.

13. As already examined by GKC §119ee/p. 384.

14. Cf. GKC §123e/p. 396.

15. But cf. the LXX ὁ περάτης; similarly Aquila, 'the Euphratian'.

16. As suggested by J. de Fraine, *Genesis* (Roermond and Maastricht, 1963).

17. T. O. Lambdin, "Egyptian Loan Words in the Old Testament," *JAOS* 73 (1953) 145–55.

18. W. F. Albright, "A Prince of Taanach in the Fifteenth Century B.C.," *BASOR* 94 (1944) 24.

19. M. Metzger, "Eigentumsdeklaration und Schöpfungsaussage," in *"Wenn nicht jetzt, wann dann?" Aufsätze für H.-J. Kraus zum 65. Geburtstag* (ed. H.-G. Geyer et al.; Neukirchen-Vluyn, 1983) 37–51.

Old or Recent?

It is obvious, and therefore generally admitted, that Genesis 14 comprises at least three components: (a) the expedition of the Kings from the East, (b) the involvement of Abraham, and (c) his encounter with the Kings of Sodom and Salem. And while the association between the expedition and Abraham is probably secondary, the matter of the encounter with the King of Salem is more complex. For all the artistic value of the story, the reader cannot escape a feeling of artificiality: in reality, things do not work so easily and trimly! How and why these elements have been put together I should like now to try to discover.

A first disconcerting element is that, while there is a certain agreement among most biblical scholars about the fictitious and late character of the narrative, this conclusion, as we have seen, is not universally shared among orientalists. A certain number of orientalists tend to consider the narrative to be the product of an ancient tradition, even if later it was readapted to permit its use for the glorification of Abraham. There is, however, a certain unanimity in the admission that the text does not fit into the present context and that it contains many mysterious elements, in references to persons, but also to sites and places of departure, transit, and arrival. Another element is that no clues are given regarding the reasons for the present context of the story or for its transmission. The fact that most biblical scholars consider the text in a much more critical way than many orientalists remains baffling nevertheless. One wonders whether biblical scholars should be accused of being hypercritical, showing excessive caution and skepticism, perhaps fearing to become apologetical or, worse, to be considered "fundamentalists," or whether orientalists should be accused of levity or lack of responsibility in a field beyond their direct competence?

On the other hand, proponents of the substantial antiquity of Genesis 14 cannot avoid suggesting at least probable identifications for the persons mentioned with others known from the history of the ancient Near East and offering reasonable explanations for the events and localities. In other words, it is their duty to produce a list of the events and persons referred to, that is, to indicate which expedition of eastern kings lies behind the events referred to in the biblical text and when an expedition was mounted against other kings in the Dead Sea area. An explanation must be found, furthermore, for the description of their itinerary, and how, having started along the King's Highway in Transjordan, they traveled to the Dead Sea region via Kadesh, instead of going the shortest and easiest way. It is necessary, finally, to state the oriental sources from which the tradition was taken or adapted. All this seems to me an impossible mission: the antiquity, at least, of the tradition cannot be verified, and, as we shall see, there are strong grounds for its rejection.

As far as the alleged ancient sources of the text are concerned, two "false cues" were discerned by Emerton.[20] First is the claim that the text is a reworking of an ancient epic document, as maintained by Albright and others before him; the second is that it is the product of translation, possibly involving mistakes, of an original cuneiform document (see above, p. 283).

As already mentioned, none of the individuals listed can be identified, even tentatively, as the commentaries have clearly shown. Particularly strange is the expression "King of the *gôyîm*." The ingenious explanations proposed—equating it with the *ummān manda*[21] or comparing it with the word Hyksos[22] and supposing that the aim of the expedition was a war against Egypt—testify more to the authors' imagination than to their scientific acumen. It seems, rather, that the reference to the four Kings is intended to establish the universal character of the expedition, as the number four represents the four parts of the heavens.

In other words, nothing is known of a joint campaign of a Mesopotamian and an Elamite king, accompanied by two other, unknown sovereigns, and this applies to the third, the second, and the first millennia B.C.E. But there is a period in which an expedition like this would at least have been possible: the Persian period, when Mesopotamia, Elam (= Persia), and the surrounding countries were united under a common crown, that is, the Median and Persian Empire.[23] Of course, the fact that something is possible certainly does not mean that it really happened!

Even less is known of the Canaanite kings from the Dead Sea region. The presumption, of course, is that the shores of the lake were densely populated before the catastrophe described in Genesis 19 destroyed everything (cf. Gen 13:10f.); but there is no evidence whatsoever for this, and everything we know militates against it.

Enter Abraham

Because of the capture of Lot by the eastern armies, Abraham finds himself involved in the conflict, which otherwise would hardly have interested him. He pursues them and, after a brief skirmish, probably with their rearguard, succeeds in recapturing Lot and the greater part of the

20. J. A. Emerton, "Some False Cues in the Study of Genesis XIV," *VT* 21 (1971) 24–27.
21. AHw 1413; this suggestion is due to Speiser.
22. F. Cornelius, "Genesis XIV," *ZAW* 72 (1960) 1–7.
23. This has been rightly stressed by J. Van Seters, *Abraham in History and Tradition*, 296.

loot. Strangely enough, the pursuit follows what is known to be the traditional northern border of the Davidic-Solomonic empire, so that the campaign reminds one of David's wars in Syria; and the reference to Dan in v. 14 (cf. Judg 18:29) is an interesting anachronism. The indirect connection with David and his campaigns is stressed by the reference to Jerusalem and its king, who bears a name related to *ṣādôq*. It should be stressed that this is probably a reference to Jerusalem, as is also true in 1QapGen,[24] as opposed to an interesting attempt to identify Salem with a generic "City of Justice" that is introduced to contrast with Sodom, the "City of Evil."[25] Salem is also a name attested for other places (cf. Gen 33:18, where, however, other translations are possible).

Perhaps this episode of Abraham's battle offers the clue for solving the problem of this chapter. In his commentary, Procksch already pointed out that this section, far from being simply an independent insert interrupting the context (as it might appear *prima facie*),[26] is in reality the key element for the whole chapter. From a formal point of view, Melchizedek (*malkî-ṣedeq*) interrupts the encounter between Abraham and the King of Sodom, but from the point of view of substance it is worthwhile working on the hypothesis that this section, far from being a simple insert at the wrong place, is in reality the central element of the story around which the other episodes have been assembled or even created. That this was done in a rather clumsy way from the formal point of view may be regrettable, but that is another question. What, then, was the aim of the redaction?

An explanation that takes this episode fully into account was proposed by Nyberg in 1938:[27] he supposes that in this chapter Abraham prefigures King David, while Melchizedek represents Zadok (*ṣādôq*), the priest who appears only after the conquest of Jerusalem and is later appointed by Solomon to replace Abiathar, the other priest (1 Kgs 2:24ff.). Thus a new dynasty of priests was founded, for which the author of 1 Chr 6:27–41 created a genealogy going back to Aaron. Nyberg even

24. As suggested by J. A. Emerton, "The Site of Salem, the City of Melchizedek (Genesis XIV 18)," *Studies in the Pentateuch* (VTSup 41; Leiden, 1990) 45–71; idem, "Some Problems in Genesis XIV," ibid., 73–102; K. Baltzer, "Jerusalem in den Erzväter-Geschichten der Genesis? . . . ," in *Die hebräische Bibel und ihre zweifache Nachgeschichte: Festschrift für R. Rendtorff zum 65. Geburtstag* (ed. E. Blum et al.; Neukirchen-Vluyn, 1990) 3–12.

25. See G. J. Wenham, *Genesis 1–15* (WBC; Waco, Tex., 1987); and independently H. Jagersma, "Salem, la ville de Melchisédech," *Ad Veritatem* 24 (1990) 5–11.

26. As still maintained by von Rad, *Das erste Buch Moses*, and W. Zimmerli, *1 Mose 12–25* (Zurich, 1976).

27. H. S. Nyberg, "Studien zum Religionskampf im Alten Testament," *ARW* 35 (1938) 329–87.

suggests that David may have taken the concept of sacral kingship from the priestly King of Jerusalem (Melchizedek).

There is considerable evidence that Nyberg was on the right track. The real problem with his proposal, however, is the early dating of the whole episode. The story is also hinted at in Psalm 110, with its explicit reference to Melchizedek. But can this psalm be considered ancient, or is it simply archaizing? There are many important arguments against its antiquity, summarized recently by Donner.[28] Two more can be added. (1) It is in Hellenistic and Roman times (in the Apocalyptic writings, at Qumrān, and in the New Testament, for example in the so-called Epistle to the Hebrews 5:2ff., 7:8ff.) that speculations about Malkî-ṣedeq become frequent. Earlier, the character is never referred to. (2) It is during post-biblical times that the asphalt of the region is mentioned repeatedly.

Would it be foolish to see in the Abraham-Melchizedek episode an attempt by the Hasmonean Kings to acquire the legitimacy that had always been denied to them and an attempt to link their reign to an "ancient" tradition, going back as far as the Patriarchs and the legendary King of Jerusalem? Another possibility is the opposite of this: perhaps the Jerusalem priesthood was claiming tithes and submission from the Hasmonean Kings. Research will be necessary to find out which, if either, of these two theses is the most likely. One must admit that the hypothesis of this paper makes all tesserae of the complex mosaic fall into place. At least a sensible working hypothesis such as this would aid research more than traditional interpretations, which have hitherto led scholars nowhere.

28. H. Donner, "Der verlässliche Prophet: Betrachtungen zu I Makk 14,41 und zu Ps 110," in *Prophetie und geschichtliche Wirklichkeit im alten Israel: Festschrift für Siegfried Herrmann zum 65. Geburtstag* (ed. R. Liwak and S. Wagner; Stuttgart, 1991) 89–98.

A New Edition and Translation of the *Questions of Ezra*

Michael E. Stone

This neglected apocryphon is of considerable interest. It belongs to the literature that developed around the figure of Ezra after the completion of 4 Ezra. It presents a dialogue between the seer and an angel, touching on the post-mortem fate of souls. An ascent of the righteous soul through the seven heavens to the presence of God is described, as well as ceremonies which can free souls from subjection to Satan.

The text survives in two recensions. The longer Recension A is incomplete and the shorter Recension B supplements it at crucial points. Both recensions are presented in a synoptic edition, with apparatus criticus. A carefully revised English translation and a new commentary are added in the hope that they will form a solid basis for further study of this intriguing document.

The *Questions of Ezra*, one of the lesser known of the apocryphal writings, is of enough inherent interest and raises enough intriguing questions to be worthy of a new edition and translation. I dedicate them with great affection to Jonas Greenfield, a redoubtable scholar and a close friend, in the hope that he, and others too, may find some points of interest in them. The work is to be viewed in a number of contexts which make it of interest to scholars in a number of areas.

The *Questions of Ezra* is one of a group of four "later" apocrypha attributed to the prophet Ezra. The other documents of this group are *The Greek Apocalypse of Ezra, The Vision of Ezra,* and *The Apocalypse of Sedrach.* These apocalypses, some of which have made their way into modern collections of Pseudepigrapha, are all derived in one measure or another from *Fourth Ezra,* a Jewish work written in the last decade of the first century C.E. They form a part of the even more extensive literature that came to be associated with the name of Ezra in the first millennium C.E., including documents of astrological and calendary, as well as apocalyptic character.[1] The importance of the Ezra materials in early medieval Christianity contrasts with the rather lesser development of these traditions in earlier Jewish writing.

By the examination of the later apocalypses associated with Ezra, which draw upon the earlier Jewish work, *Fourth Ezra,* it is possible to see which aspects of that work were of interest in the later contexts of transmission and which were ignored. The figure of Ezra undergoes a metamorphosis from Scribe of the Torah to apocalyptic visionary, to revealer of astrological and calendrical secrets, and eventually into the Erra Pater, from whose writing the *Farmer's Almanac* drew much of its ultimate inspiration. From an analysis of this selectivity of borrowing and of the character of the transformation of the Ezra figure, much is to be learned about what was of importance and what was not in the Middle Ages.[2]

Thus, one aspect of the importance of the work is that it is representative of the rather extensive medieval Ezra apocrypha. Another dimension should be mentioned, the fact that this work contains a description of an ascent to the heavens. The ascent to the heavens is, of course, a *topos* in Jewish apocalyptic literature from the third century B.C.E. on and was the inheritance of Christian apocalyptic literature on the one hand and of the Merkabah mystical writings on the other. Thus, no little interest inheres in literature describing ascents to heaven. The description of the ascent in *Questions of Ezra* has been little studied. It draws its general inspiration from the ascent in 4 Ezra 7:80–99 but differs from it in both general atmosphere and in details of the description. The character of the ascent in *Questions of Ezra* and its affinities and lack of affinities are discussed in detail in the commentary below. It should be remarked that in many features this description has no parallels either in the Jewish apocalyptic literature or in other Christian or more specifically Armenian works.

Thus, quite apart from illustrating how one biblical figure was understood and transmuted in later thinking—itself a matter of interest to scholars of the Bible—the *Questions of Ezra* is of considerable interest to students of the apocalyptic and mystical traditions in Judaism and Christianity.

1. See, in general and with further bibliography, M. E. Stone, *Fourth Ezra: A Commentary on the Fourth Book of Ezra* (Hermeneia; Minneapolis, 1990) 43–47 (hereafter Stone, *Fourth Ezra*).

2. On the changes in the understanding of Ezra, as well as on the more general use of the later apocalypses as a "diagnostic tool" for early medieval concerns, see M. E. Stone, "The Metamorphosis of Ezra: Jewish Apocalypse and Mediaeval Vision," *JTS* 33 (1982) 1–18. Concerning the tradition of Erra Pater and the *Farmer's Almanac,* see the intriguing article of E. A. Matter, "The 'Revelatio Esdrae' in Latin and English Traditions," *Revue Bénédictine* 92 (1982) 379–87.

Previous Editions and the Present Edition

The work first became known through the printing of one recension of it by S. Yovsēp'ianc' in his collection of Armenian apocrypha, published at the end of the last century. He printed the document from a single copy in the Library of the Mechitarist Fathers in Venice. This was MS no. 570, a *Ritual* (*Maštoc'*) copied in 1208 C.E., and the text occurs on folios 203r-206v.[3] A page is missing from the manuscript at the division between §10 and §11 of the text, and the text is incomplete at the end.[4] Yovsēp'ianc' 's text was translated into English by J. Issaverdens in 1900.[5] No other manuscript of the long recension, dubbed Recension A, has been discovered.

A vulgar text of Recension B was first printed in the fourth recension of the Armenian *Menologium* in Constantinople in 1730.[6] A second printing of Recension B in an Armenian journal added to it the witness of another manuscript of the seventeenth century.[7] English translations of the two recensions were published in *Old Testament Pseudepigrapha*.[8] A third witness to the text of the short recension has been consulted here, and a critical apparatus showing the readings of these three witnesses to Recension B has been prepared.[9]

The following sigla are used for the witnesses to the short recension:

Y *Yaysmawurk'* (ed. 1730)
O Oxford, Bodleian, MS Marsh 438, vol. 3, fol. 402r
V Vienna Mechitarist MS 10, 16th century (Dashian, *Catalog*, 79–80)

3. S. Yovsēp'ianc', *Uncanonical Books of the Old Testament* (Venice, 1896) 300–303 [in Armenian]. B. Sarghissian and S. Sargsian give a description of the manuscript in *Grand Catalogue of the Armenian Manuscripts of the Mechitarist Library in Venice* (Venice, 1966) 2.55–66 [in Armenian].

4. See B. Sarghissian, *Studies on the Uncanonical Books of the Old Testament* (Venice, 1898) 453 [in Armenian].

5. J. Issaverdens, *The Uncanonical Writings of the Old Testament Found in the Armenian MSS. of the Library of St. Lazarus* (2d ed.; Venice, 1932) 505–9.

6. Grigor Xlat'ec'i (1403), *Yaysmawurk'* (Menologium) (Constantinople, 1730) 424–25. On the history of the Armenian Menologium, see J. Mércérian, "Introduction à l'étude des Synaxaires arméniens," *Bulletin arménologique* (Mélanges de l'Université de S. Joseph 40; Beirut, 1953).

7. Bodleian Library, Oxford (MS Marsh 438, vol. 3, fol. 402). The Menologium text was reprinted by M. E. Stone with the variants of the Oxford manuscript in "Two New Discoveries Concerning the Uncanonical Ezra Books," *Sion* 52 (1978) 54–60 [in Armenian].

8. M. E. Stone, "Questions of Ezra," in J. H. Charlesworth, *Old Testament Pseudepigrapha* (New York, 1983) 1.591–98.

9. Vienna, Mechitarist Library, no. 10 of the year 1208 C.E.; printed by J. Dashian in *Catalog der armenischen Handschriften in der Mechitaristen-Bibliothek zu Wien* (Haupt-Catalog der armenischen Handschriften 1/2, Vienna, 1895) 1.79–80 [in Armenian]. This manuscript is older than the fourth recension of the Menologium, showing that Grigor Xlat'ec'i drew on an existing source.

In the present edition, the two recensions and carefully revised translations of them are printed in a synoptic form. A new commentary on both recensions has been prepared, and some remarks of a more general character set the work into the context of the apocryphal Ezra literature. This presentation of the material will, it is hoped, form a sound working basis for further studies of this apocryphon.

Recension B is considerably shorter than Recension A and contains no material corresponding to A 11–30. However, even in sections of the document where the two recensions run parallel, it does contain a good deal of material that is not present in the longer recension. Moreover, it preserves text at the two points where the manuscript of Recension A has physical lacunae, that is, following A 10 and at the end.

In addition to the texts enumerated above, the existence of two further Armenian Ezra writings should be mentioned. One is the so-called Book of Esdras. This is, in fact, a translation into Armenian of the Latin translation of 6 Ezra (4 Ezra chap. 16).[10] More significant are the extensive passages found in the Armenian version of 4 Ezra that do not occur in any other version. The majority of these originated in Greek and were translated into Armenian as part of the recension of 4 Ezra that stands behind the Armenian version of that work.[11]

Character of the Work, Its Original Language and Date

Questions of Ezra is dependent, first and foremost, on 4 Ezra, from which it draws its character as series of questions posed by the seer and angelic responses. Moreover, its central interest in the fate of human souls after death derives directly from 4 Ezra.[12] Naturally, it is also influenced by language, terminology, and expressions deriving from the Scriptures, as was virtually all the Armenian apocryphal literature; the most striking instances are noted in the commentary. A third source of influence upon *Questions of Ezra* may have been the Byzantine apocalypses that were also dependent on 4 Ezra, in particular the trio of works entitled *Greek Ezra Apocalypse*, *Apocalypse of Sedrach*, and *Vision of Ezra*.[13] Parallels have been pointed out between *Questions of Ezra* and other elenchic works preserved

10. M. E. Stone, "The Book of Esdras," *Journal of the Society for Armenian Studies* 4 (1988–89) 209–12.

11. M. E. Stone, *The Armenian Version of 4 Ezra* (University of Pennsylvania Armenian Texts and Studies 1; Missoula, 1979); idem, *Textual Commentary on the Armenian Version of 4 Ezra* (Septuagint and Cognate Studies 34; Atlanta, 1990). One passage was studied in detail in idem, "Some Features of the Armenian Version of IV Ezra," *Le Muséon* 79 (1966) 387–400.

12. Detailed points of similarity are documented in the commentary below.

13. A description of these works, with further bibliographical indications, may be found in Stone, *Fourth Ezra* 43–46.

in Armenian, but it is far from certain that these works in fact were a source of *Questions of Ezra*.[14]

It is impossible to determine whether the work was composed in Armenian or is translated from Greek. In either case, it is clearly Christian as it stands before us. Moreover, its date is unknown; but it doubtless derives from the Byzantine Period, as its affinity with the other Byzantine Ezra apocalypses indicates. It contains remarkable descriptions of the ascent of the soul through seven heavens and of the environs of the Godhead. These set it squarely in the ascent tradition that, originating in the Second Temple Period, continued in later Jewish and Christian sources.

Two types of material have been discerned in this work. One is the ascent narrative (A 16–30) and the other a dialogue between Ezra and the angel (A 1–10, B 4 or its original, A 11–15, B 6 or its original, A 31–40 and B 10–14 or its original). These may reflect different source documents or traditions, but it is noteworthy that parallels to 4 Ezra are found throughout.

Text of Recension A	**Text of Recension B**
ՀԱՐՑԱՔՆՆՈՒԹԻՒՆ ԵԶՐԻ ՄԱՐԳԱՐԷԻՆ ԸՆԴ ՀՐԵՇՏԱԿԻ ՏԵԱՌՆ ՎԱՍՆ ՀՈԳՈՑ ՄԱՐԴԿԱՆ	ՅԱՅՍՄ ԱՒՈՒՐ ՅԻՇԱՏԱԿ ՏԵՍԼԵԱՆ ԵԶՐԻ ՄԱՐԳԱՐԷԻՆ ԶՈՐ ԵՏԵՍ ՎԱՍՆ ՀՈԳՈՑ
1. *Տեսանէր Եզր մարգարէն զհրեշտակ Աստուծոյ, եւ հարցանէր զնա բան առ բան. եւ հրեշտակն մատուցանէր նմա եւ ասէր զոր ինչ լինելոց է ի կատարածին:*	1. *Սա ետես զհրեշտակն Աստուծոյ*
2. *Եհարց մարգարէն ցհրեշտակն եւ ասէ՝ թէ Զի՞նչ պատրաստեալ է Աստուած արդարոց եւ մեղաւորաց. եւ ի ժամանակին՝ յորում հասանէ օր վախճանին, ի՞նչ լինիցին կամ ու՞ր երթան, ի պատի՞ւ եթէ ի տանջանս:*	*եւ եհարց վասն արդարոց եւ մեղաւորաց երբ ելանեն յաշխարհէս:*

14. These parallels were pointed out by B. Sarghissian (*Studies on the Uncanonical Books*, 465–69, 475–78) and further discussed by Stone ("Questions of Ezra," 592).

3. Պատասխանի ետ Հրեշտակն եւ ասէ ցմարգարէն. Պատրաստեալ է արդարոցն ուրախութիւն մեծ եւ լոյս յաւիտենից, եւ մեղաւորացն պատրաստեալ է գխաւարն արտաքին եւ գՀուրն յաւիտենից:	2. Ասէ Հրեշտակն. Արդարոցն լոյս է եւ Հանգիստ, կեանք յաւիտենական, իսկ մեղաւորացն տանջանք անվախճան:
4. Ասէ մարգարէն ցՀրեշտակն. Տէր, ո՞վ է որ ոչ իցէ մեղուցեալ Աստուծոյ ի կենդանեաց.	
5. եւ թէ այդ այդպէս իցէ, ապա երանի է անասնոց եւ թռչնոց՝ որ ոչ մնան յարութեան, եւ ոչ ակն ունին վախճանին:	3. Ասէ Եզր. Եթէ այդ այդպէս իցէ, ապա երանի անասնոց եւ գազանաց երկրի՝ եւ սողնոց եւ թռչնոց երկնից, որ ոչ մնան յարութեան եւ դատաստանի:
6. Եթէ զարդարսն՝ որ ամենայն տանջանացն Համբերեցին, եւ զմարգարէսն եւ զառաքեալսն եւ զմարտիրոսն պսակեսցես՝ յորժամ զգայլաՀազն առնոյին, եւ ծեծէին ռամք զերեսս նոցա՝ մինչեւ երեւէին երիկամունք նոցա. նոքա վասն քո չարչարեցան.	
7. մեզ մեղաւորացս ողորմեա, որ գրաւեալ եմք եւ ըմբռնեալ ի ձեռն սատանայի:	
8. Պատասխանի ետ Հրեշտակն եւ ասէ. Եթէ ոք քան զքեզ ի վեր է, մի յաւելուս խօսել ընդ նմա, եթէ ոչ՝ մեծ չար լինիցի քեզ:	4. Ասէ Հրեշտակն. Մեղանչես զայդ ասելով,
	զի ամենայն ինչ վասն մարդոյն է արարեալ Աստուած, եւ զմարդն վասն Աստուծոյ

	եւ յորս ուր գտանէ Աստուած զմարդն, այնու դատի:
9. Ասէ մարգարէն ցհրեշտակն. Տէր, սակաւիկ մի յաւելում խօսել ընդ քեզ, արա ինձ պատասխանի:	5. Ասէ Եզր.
10. Յորժամ հասանի օր վախճանին եւ առնու զհոգին, ի տեղի տանջանա՞ց կարգէ զնա, եթէ ի տեղի պատուոյ՝ մինչեւ ի գալուստն[	Յորժամ առնուս զհոգիս մարդկան, ու՞ր տանիս:
]	6. Ասէ հրեշտակն. Զարդարոց հոգիսն տանիմ յերկրպագութիւն Աստուծոյ եւ կայացնեմ ի յօդդ վերին, եւ հոգիք մեղաւորացն ըմբռնին ի դիւաց եւ յօդս են արգելած:
11. Պատասխանի ետ հրեշտակն եւ ասէ. Մի մնայք մինչեւ ի յօր վախճանին. այլ որպէս արծիւ թռուցեալ փութացարուք գործել զբարիս եւ զողորմութիւնս:	
12. Զի աճեղ է օրն այն ստիպող եւ պահանջող. ոչ զորդիս տայ հոգալ եւ ոչ զինչս:	
13. Գայ հասանէ յանկարծակի, որպէս գերիվար է անողորմ եւ անաչառ, յանկարծահաս անկասկած: Եթէ լայ եւ եթէ ողբայ, ոչ ինչ լինիցի նմա ողորմութիւն:	
14. Այլ յորժամ հասանի օր վախճանին, բարի հոգոյն բարի հրեշտակ գայ եւ չարին չար. որպէս առաքեալ ոմն ի թագաւորացն առ չարագործսն եւ առ բարեգործսն,	

բարոյն բարի հատուցանէ եւ չարին չար·

15. *Նոյնպէս եւ բարի հոգոյն բարի հրեշտակ գայ, եւ չարին չար։ Ոչ եթէ հրշտակն է չար, այլ իւրաքանչիւր գործքն։*

16. *Առնու զհոգին՝ տանի ընդ արեւելս, ընդ եղեամն, ընդ ձիւն, ընդ խաւար, ընդ կարկուտ, ընդ սառն, ընդ մրրիկ, ընդ գունդս սատանայի, ընդ փտակս եւ ընդ հողմն սաստիկ անձրեւացն, ընդ ահեղ եւ ընդ զարմանալի ճանապարհսն, ընդ անձուկ կապանս եւ ընդ բարձրահամ լեռունս անցուցանեն։*

17. *Ով զարմանալի ճանապարհն. զի ոտն հետ ոտին է, եւ առաջի նորա հրեղէն գետք են։*

18. *Զարմանայր մարգարէն եւ ասէր. Ով զարմանալի եւ սոսկալի ճանապարհն այն։*

19. *Ասէ հրշտակն. Յայն ճանապարհն եւթն բանակք դիւաց կան, եւ եւթն աշտիճանք աստուածութեանն, եթէ ընդ այն կարեմ անցուցանել։*

20. *Քանզի առաջին օթեւանքն չար են եւ զարմանալի. երկուքն ահեղ եւ անպատումն. երեքն դժոխք են եւ սառամանիք. չորքն կռիւք են եւ պատերազմունք. ի հինգն ապա քննումն. եթէ արդար է՝ լուսաւորի, եւ եթէ մեղաւոր է՝ մթանայ. ի վեցն*

ապա պայծառանայ հոգի
արդարոյն իբրեւ զարեգակն.

21. յետ֊ն ապա տարեալ
հասուցանեմ զնա յերկրպա-
գութիւն մեծի աթոռոյ աս-
տուածութեանն, ընդդէմ
դրախտին՝ յանդիման փառացն
Աստուծոյ, ուր գերազանցիկ
լոյսն է։

22. Ասէ մարգարէն ցհրեշ-
տակն. Տէր իմ, երբ ընդ
այնպիսի արհաւիրքն, ընդ
կռիւքն, ընդ պատերազմունքն,
ընդ տապախառինքն անցու-
ցանես զնա, ընդէ՞ր ոչ հան-
դիպեցուցանես զնա աստուա-
ծութեանն՝ քան աթոռոյն
միայն հասուցանես։

23. Ասէ հրեշտակն ցմարգարէն.
Դու ի սնոտի մարդկանէ ես
եւ զմարդկան բնութիւն
խորհիս։

24. Ես հրեշտակ եմ եւ հանա-
պազ Աստուծոյ եմ ծառայել,
եւ ոչ եմ տեսեալ զերեսս
Աստուծոյ. դու զիա՞րդ ասես
հանդիպեցուցանել զմարդ
մեղաւոր առաջի աստուա-
ծութեանն։

25. Զի ահեղ եւ զարմանալի
է աստուածութիւնն, եւ ո՞վ
իշխեսցէ հայել ընդդէմ
անեղին աստուածութեանն։

26. Եթէ հայեսցի ոք, իբրեւ
զմոմ հալեսցի յերեսացն
Աստուծոյ. զի հրեղէն է աս-
տուածութիւնն եւ զարմանալի.
քանզի այսպիսի պահապանք
կան շուրջ զաթոռոյ աստուա-
ծութեանն։

27. *Կայանք են, մանասրուանք են, խոռոչք են, հրեղէնք են, կամարազգեստք են, լապտերք են:*	
28. *Անդ որոտմունք են, անդ շարժմունք են, անդ կռիւք են, անդ պատերազմունք են, անդ տապախառինք են, շրջախոռոչք են, զեռունք են, հրեղենազգեստք են, բոցեռացք են, հրեղենագունդք են:*	
29. *Շուրջ զնովաւ սերոբէքն անմարմին, քերոբէքն վեցթեւեան. երկու թեւօքն զդէմսն ծածկեն եւ երկու թեւօքն զոտսն եւ երկու թեւօքն թռուցեալ աղաղակեն՝ սուրբ սուրբ (սուրբ) տէր զօրութեանց, լի են երկինք եւ երկիր փառօք քո:*	
30. *Այսպիսի պահապանք կան շուրջ զաթոռոյ աստուածութեանն:*	
31. *Եհարց մարգարէն ցհրշտակն եւ ասէ. Տէր, զի՞նչ լինիցիմք. զի մեղաւորք եմք ամենեքեան եւ ըմբռնեալ ի ձեռս սատանայի: Արդ ի՞ւ զերծանիմք, կամ ո՛վ հանէ զմեզ ի ձեռաց նորա:*	7. *Ասէ Եզր. Եւ հոգին որ կալցի ի սատանայէ, ե՞րբ ազատի:*
32. *Պատասխանի ետ հրշտակն եւ ասէ. Եթէ ոք մնայ յետ մեռանելոյն, հայր, կամ մայր, կամ եղբայր, կամ քոյր, կամ որդի, կամ դուստր, եւ կամ այլ ոք ի քրիստոնէից, եւ աղօթս մատուցանէ՝ պահօք տվօք քառասնօք, մեծ հանկիստ եւ ողորմութիւն լինի ի ձեռն զենմանն Քրիստոսի.*	8. *Ասէ հրեշտակն. Եթէ իցէ ոք հոգւոյն ի յաշխարհիս բարի յիշատակ որ աղօթիւք եւ ողորմութեամբ թափէ զնա ի սատանայէ:*

33. զի Քրիստոս վասն մեր պատարագեցաւ ի վերայ խաչին, եւ զվեց դարուն զհոգիքն ի ձեռաց սատանայի կորզեաց:

34. Որչափ ի ձեռն սրբամատոյց քահանային հոգին ազատի, եթէ քահանայն այսպէս կատարէ զքառասունսն՝ որպէս հաճոյ լինի Աստուծոյ.

35. զքառասուն օր յեկեղեցին կացցէ եւ ոչ ի հրապարակս երթալով. այլ ի ժամէ ի ժամ զերգս մարգարէին Դաւթի կատարեսցէ հանդերձ օրհնութեամբ:

36. Սա է՝ որ հանէ զմեզ ի ձեռաց սատանայի: Ապա եթէ ոչ՝ տալ ի յաղքատս:

37. Զի աղօթքն ձեր այսպէս է. որպէս ելանէ մշակն՝ երթայ սերմանել, եւ ելանէ բոյս զուարթ եւ վայելուչ, եւ կամի առնել արդիւնս բազումս, եւ ելանէ փուշ եւ որոմն եւ հեղձուցանեն, եւ ոչ տայ ժողովեալ արդիւնս բազումս.

38. Նոյնպէս եւ դուք յորժամ երթայք ի դուռն եկեղեցոյն եւ կամիք աղօթս մատուցանել առաջի աստուածութեանն, ելանեն հոգք աշխարհիս եւ պատրանք մեծութեան, եւ հեղձուցանեն զձեզ. եւ ոչ տայ սերմանել արդիւնս բազում:

39. Զի եթէ աղօթքն ձեր այսպէս էր՝ որպէս Մովսէս ելաց աւուրս քառասուն, եւ

9. Ասէ Եզր. Որո՞վ իրօք: Ասէ հրեշտակն. Աղօթիւք, ողորմութեամբ եւ պատարագօք:

բերան ընդ բերան խօսեցաւ ընդ Աստուծոյ,

40. *նոյնպէս եւ Եղիա Հրեղէն կառօք յերկինքն վերացաւ, նոյնպէս եւ Դանիէլ եկաց ի գուբ առ[իւծոց*

10. *Ասէ մարգարէն. Եւս թէ չկենայ Հոգւոյ մեղաւորին՝ բարի յիշատակ որ օժանդակ է նմա, զի՞նչ լինիցի այն Հոգին:*

11. *Ասէ Հրեշտակն. Մնայ այնպիսին՝ ի ձեռն սատանայի մինչ ի գալուստ Քրիստոսի, յորժամ Հնչէ փողն Գաբրիէլի.*

12. *յայնժամ ազատին Հոգիքն ի ձեռացն սատանայի, եւ սլանան յօդիցդ ի վայր*

13. *եւ գան միանան յիւրաքանչիւր մարմին Հողացեալ զոր ձայն փողոյն շինէ եւ զարթուցանէ եւ նորագէ:*

14. *Եւ ընդ առաջ վերացուցանէ Քրիստոսի Աստուծոյ մերոյ որ գայ ի դատել զերկիր, այս է զարդարս եւ զմեղաւորս եւ Հատուցանէ ըստ իւրաքանչիւր գործոց:*

Colophon *Աղերսանօք Հոգեպատում մարգարէիցն քոց անճառելիդ Աստուած, ողորմեա ստացողի գրոյս:*

Apparatus of Recension B

1. *սա ետես*] *ետես եզր դպիր* O | *զՀրեշտակ տեառն* O V | *երբ ելանեն*] *յորժամ փոխին* O + *ի* V

2. *սաց*] *ասէ* O V | *եւ կեանք* O *ի կեանքն* V | *յաւիտենականք* O | *իսկ*] *եւ* O | *տանջանք անվախճան*] *հուր եւ խաւար եւ դժոխքն յաւիտենական* O V : cf A 3
3. *երանի*] + *է* O : cf A 5 | *եւ սողնոց*] › O *սողնոց* V | *թռչնոց երկնից*] *երկնից թռչնոց* O | *յարութեան եւ*] › V : contrast A 5
4. *զամենայն* O V | *արարեալ է* O : secondary | *ուր*] › O | *աստուածն*] *աստուած* O V | *զմարդն*] precedes *յորս* O
5. *յորժամ առնուս զհոգիս մարդկան*] *զհոգիս մարդկան յորժամ առնուս* O | *զհոգիս մարդկան*] *զհոգին* V
6. *կայացնեմ ի*] *ընակեցուցանեմ* O *կայան է մի* V | *յօդտ* O | *դիւացն* O | *եւ յօդս*] *եւ յաւդտ* O *եւ յաւդս* V : *աւ* for *օ* hence throughout in O V
7. *եզր*] *մարգարէն* O | *եւ – սատանայէ*] › V | *կալցի*] *ըմպ-նի* O | *ազատի*] *զերծանի* O
8. *ի յաշխարհս բարի յիշատակ*] *բարի յիշատակ ի յաշխարհս* V | *ի*] › O | *բարի – ողորմութեամբ*] › O | *նա թափէ* O
9. totum › V | *եզր*] *մարգարէն* O | *աղօթիւք*] › O
10. *եւս թէ*] *եւ թէ* O *եթէ* V | *չկենայ*] V *կենայ* Y *չունի* O | *հոգւոյ*] *հոգի* O | *բարի*] *զոք* O | *որ*] *իւր* O | *այն հոգին*] *նմա* O
11. *գալուստն* O V
12. *յաւդիցտ* O
13. *հողացեալ մարմին* O V | *ձայն փողոյն*] *փողն* O | *չինէ*] *հնչէ* V | *եւ նորագէ*] › O *նորոգէ* V
14. *մերոյ*] › O | *զերկիր այս է*] › O | *զմեղաւորսն*] › V | *հա տուցեալ* V | *ըստ*] › O

Colophon › O V

Translation of Recension A	**Translation of Recension B**
THE QUESTIONS OF THE PROPHET EZRA OF THE ANGEL OF THE LORD CONCERNING HUMAN SOULS	ON THAT DAY, THE MEMORIAL OF THE VISION OF EZRA THE PROPHET WHICH HE SAW CONCERNING SOULS
1. Ezra the prophet saw the angel of God and asked him one question after another. And the angel approached him and said what is going to take place at the consummation.	1. He saw the angel of God

2. The prophet asked the angel and said, "What has God prepared for the righteous and the sinners? And at the time when the day of death arrives, what will become of them? Where do they go, to honor or to tortures?"	and asked concerning the righteous and sinners when they go forth from this world.
3. The angel replied and said to the prophet, "He has prepared great joy and eternal light for the righteous and for the sinners he has prepared the outer darkness and the eternal fire."	2. The angel said, "For the righteous there is light and rest, eternal life, but for the sinners, unending tortures."
4. The prophet said to the angel, "Lord, who of the living has not sinned against God?	
5. And if that is so, then blessed are the beasts and the birds who do not await resurrection nor do they hope for death (or: the end).	3. Ezra said, "If that is so, then blessed are the animals and the beasts of the field and the creeping things and the birds of heaven who do not await resurrection and judgment."
6. If you will crown the righteous and the prophets and the apostles and the martyrs, who endured every torture when (people) were taking flint and hammers were pounding their bodies until their innards were visible—they were tortured for your sake—(then)	
7. have mercy upon us sinners who have been seized and captured by Satan."	
8. The angel replied and said, "If there is someone above you, do not talk with him any more, otherwise great evil will befall you."	4. The angel said, "You sin in saying this,
	for God has made everything for the sake of humans and humans

	for the sake of God. And in those things in which God finds a human, by that is he judged."
9. The prophet said to the angel, "Lord, I would speak a little more with you, reply to me!	5. Ezra said,
10. When the day of death arrives and he takes the soul, will he assign it to the place of punishment or to the place of honor until the coming[	"When you take the souls of men, where will you bring (them)?"
]	6. The angel said, "I bring the souls of the righteous to worship God and establish them in that upper atmosphere, and the souls of the sinners are seized by the demons and are imprisoned in the atmosphere."
11. The angel replied and said, "Do not wait until the day of death, but like a flying eagle hasten to do good deeds and mercy.	
12. For that day is fearsome, urgent, and exacting. It does not permit care of children or of possessions.	
13. It arrives suddenly; it is like a merciless and impartial captor, unexpected, without doubt. Even if one weeps or mourns, there will be no mercy for him.	
14. But when the day of death arrives, a good angel comes to the good soul and an evil one to the evil. Just as someone sent by the kings to doers of evil deeds and good deeds recompenses good to the good and evil to the evil,	

15. even in the same way a good angel comes to the good soul and an evil one to the evil: not that the angel is evil, but each (person's) deeds (are evil).

16. He takes the soul, brings it through the east; they pass through frost, through snow, through darkness, through hail, through ice, through storm, through hosts of Satan, through streams, and through the wind of terrible rains, through the fearsome and wondrous paths, through narrow defiles, and through high mountains.

17. O, wondrous way, for one foot is behind the other and before it are fiery rivers!"

18. The prophet was amazed and said, "O, that wondrous and terrible way!"

19. The angel said, "To that way there are seven camps of demons and seven steps to the Divinity, if I can make (someone) pass along it.

20. Because the first lodgings are evil and wondrous; the second fearsome and indescribable; the third are hell and icy cold; the fourth are quarrels and wars; in the fifth, then, investigation — if he is righteous he shines and if he is a sinner, he is darkened; in the sixth, then, the soul of the righteous one sparkles like the sun;

21. in the seventh, then, having brought (it) I make it approach the worship of the great throne of the Divinity, opposite the Garden, facing the glory of God where the sublime light is."

22. The prophet said to the angel, "My lord, when you cause it to pass through such terrors—through the quarrels, through the wars, through the burning heat—why do you not cause it to meet the Divinity, rather than causing it only to approach the throne?"

23. The angel said to the prophet, "You are one of the worthless humans and you think according to human nature.

24. I am an angel and I perpetually serve God, and I have not seen the face of God. How do you say that a sinful human should be caused to meet the Divinity?

25. For the Divinity is fearsome and wondrous and who dares to look towards the uncreated Divinity?

26. If anyone looks he will melt like wax before the face of God: for the Divinity is fiery and wondrous. Because such guardians stand around the throne of the Divinity:

27. there are stations, there are . . ., there are hollows, there are fiery ones, there are girdle-wearers, there are lanterns.

28 There there are thunders, there there are earthquakes, there there are quarrels, there there are wars, there there are burning heats. There are turning hollows, there are creeping things, there are fire-wearers, there are flame-swarming ones, there are fiery hosts.

29. Around it are incorporeal seraphs, six-winged cherubs: with two wings they cover (their) face

and with two wings (their) feet and flying with two they cry, 'Holy, Holy, (Holy) Lord of Hosts, the heaven and earth are full of your glory.'	
30. Such guardians stand around the throne of the Divinity."	
31. The prophet asked the angel and said, "Lord, what will become of us, for we are all sinners and seized in the power of Satan. Now, by what means are we delivered or who brings us forth from his power?"	7. Ezra said, "And when is the soul which will be seized by Satan freed?"
32. The angel answered and said, "If someone remains after death, father or mother or brother or sister or son or daughter or any other Christian, who offers prayers with forty days' fast, there is great rest and mercy through the sacrifice of Christ.	8. The angel said, "If there is someone in this world as a good memorial for the soul, who releases it from Satan through prayer and (acts of) mercy."
33. For Christ was sacrificed for our sake upon the Cross and for six ages he delivered souls from the power of Satan.	
34. How the soul is freed through a priest making a reverent offering, if the priest completes the forty days in such a way as is pleasing to God!	9. Ezra said, "By what means?" The angel said, "By prayer, by (acts of) mercy, and by masses."
35. For forty days let him remain in the church, not going in the public places, but from time to time let him recite the songs of the prophet David together with the odes.	
36. It is this which extracts us from the power of Satan. If not, giving to the poor.	
37. For your prayers are thus: just as a farmer sets forth, goes to sow and	

the shoot comes forth joyous and graceful and desires to produce numerous fruit, and thorns and weeds also come forth and choke (it) and do not let numerous fruit be gathered in.

38. Similarly also you, when you go inside the church and desire to offer prayers before the Divinity, the cares of this world and the deceit of wealth come forth and choke you and do not let numerous fruit be sown.

39. For if your prayer were such as Moses wept for forty days and spoke with God mouth to mouth,

40. likewise also Elijah was taken up to heaven in a fiery chariot, likewise Daniel also pray[ed] in the li[ons'] den [

10. The prophet said, "If no good memorial remains for the sinner's soul to help him, what will become of that soul?"

11. The angel said, "Such a one remains in the power of Satan until the coming of Christ, when the trumpet of Gabriel sounds.

12. Then the souls are freed from the power of Satan and soar down from that atmosphere.

13. And they come and are united each with its body which had been returned to dust and which the sound of the trumpet builds and arouses and renews.

14. And it raises (it) up before Christ our God who comes to judge the earth, that is the righteous and

the wicked, and requites each for their deeds."

Colophon: Through the petition of your inspired prophets, ineffable God, have pity upon the commissioner of this writing!

Commentary

A 1. բան առ բան 'one question after another'. Literally 'matter by matter.'

մատուցանէր. The factitive is anomalous and the context requires an intransitive meaning; see commentary on A 16.

A 2. վախճանին 'of death'. The word could also be translated 'of the end.' However, 'death' seems the more likely interpretation; cf. B 1 and the use of this word in A 6, 10, 11, etc. Moreover, A 14–17, B 6–8 and 11–14 seem to refer to an intermediate state of the souls. The question closely resembles that in 4 Ezra 7:75.

պատիւ 'honor'. Honor or glory form part of the reward of the souls (see Stone, *Fourth Ezra*, 244–45) though the term պատիւ 'honor' in this connection is unusual; cf., however, A 10, below. The word տանջանս 'tortures' is a common technical term for eschatological punishment (see Stone, *Fourth Ezra*, 72, 240–41).

A 3. Compare this verse with 4 Ezra 7:38.

պատրաստեալ է2° 'he has prepared2°'. This verb is obviously transitive, as the two following accusatives indicate. In the earlier part of the verse the identical form could be either passive or active, and we have translated it as active. Similar uses of the periphrastic perfect are rather common in both recensions. The term 'prepared' is often applied to eschatological things (see Stone, *Fourth Ezra*, 199; and idem, *Textual Commentary*, xx–xxi, on the use of the term in Armenian).

զխաւարն արտաքին 'outer darkness'. See Matt 8:12, 22:13, 25:30, and particularly *Greek Ezra Apocalypse* 1:24, 4:38.

A 4. Literally: 'who is there of the living who . . .'. This question resembles 4 Ezra 3:35, *Greek Ezra Apocalypse* 5:26.

A 5. Compare the idea and the wording with 4 Ezra 7:66: զի ոչ յարութեան ակն ունին եւ ոչ դատաստանաց մնան 'for they do not hope for resurrection, nor do they await judgments'. Compare also

Greek Ezra Apocalypse 1:21–23. Perhaps *Questions of Ezra* is dependent here on a text like Armenian and Arabic² of 4 Ezra: see Stone, *Textual Commentary*, 170.

A 6. եթէ . . . պսակեսցես 'If you will crown'. The Armenian is difficult here. եթէ is best taken as introducing a conditional sentence. The language and terms describing the martyrs' deaths are very like descriptions of the murder of Abel in *History of Abel and Cain* §27 and *History of the Forefathers* §§24–27.[15] Moreover, according to §26 of the latter text and *Abel* §3 the murder weapon is a flint (գայլահազ), as it is here. For the crown, cf. *Greek Ezra Apocalypse* 6:21.

գերեսս 'bodies'. This meaning is listed in the dictionaries and is demanded by the context.

երիկամունք 'innards'. The word literally means 'kidneys'.

A 7. The general idea should be compared with 4 Ezra 8:26–28.

B 4. The idea that creation was for the sake of humankind is widespread; see Stone, *Fourth Ezra*, 188–189. The expression 'And those things in which God finds man, by that is he judged' seems to be adapted from a sentence attributed to the lost apocryphon of Ezekiel (and to other sources) which reads in one form: ἐν οἷς γὰρ εὕρω ὑμᾶς . . . ἐπὶ τούτοις καὶ κρινῶ.[16] There is some grammatical roughness in this sentence; յորս 'in those things' is plural and այնու 'by that' is singular. This may be the result of the adaptation of the quotation to its context in *Questions of Ezra.*

A 9. Compare 4 Ezra 8:42.

A 10. գալուստն 'coming'. This word could also be translated 'Parousia,' but since the text breaks off here and a page is missing from the manuscript, its exact meaning remains uncertain. Perhaps B 6 preserves something of the missing text. This verse repeats the question of A 2, which resembles 4 Ezra 7:75.

B 6. This view about the fate of the souls and the demons who inhabit the atmosphere and imprison the souls there is quite unique. See the comments of Stone, 'Questions of Ezra,' 394. The form կայացնեմ 'I establish' is medieval.

15. These works are to be found in M.E. Stone, *Armenian Apocrypha: Relating to Adam and Eve* (Jerusalem, forthcoming).

16. This is from Clement Alex. *quis div. salv.* 40:1f. This saying exists in many forms and with many attributions: see D. Satran, M. E. Stone, and B. G. Wright, *Apocryphal Ezekiel* (Early Judaism and its Literature; Atlanta, forthcoming) 28–29, where the evidence is set forth in detail.

A 11. 'wait'. Both verbs in this section are plural, while the person addressed in A 8–9 is singular. Since a page has been lost following v. 10, clearly material intervened which would account for this change.

A 13. տայ 'permit'. On this use, see commentary on A 37.

գայ հասանէ 'it arrives'. Armenian actually has a hendiadys, literally 'it comes it arrives'. This is not an uncommon construction. Issaverdens translates: 'It cometh suddenly and without pity and without respect it carries away its captive suddenly and unexpectedly.' We propose a correction of Yovsēp'ianc' 's word division, from գերի վարէ 'it takes captive' to գերիվար է 'it is a captor', which removes the chief difficulties.

A 14. This verse presents the idea of two angels, cf. *Apoc. Paul* 11–16; *2 Apoc. Bar.* 51:1–6; *T. Abraham* A 17:7, B 13:13.

A 15. The first part of this verse repeats part of A14.

իւրաքանչիւր գործքն 'each (person's) deeds (are evil)'. The Armenian expression is very elliptical, but this seems to be its meaning. The structure of the sentence resembles Armenian 4 Ezra 8:62L.

A 16. անցուցանեն 'they pass'. Literally: 'they make it pass.' This use of the factitive for the indicative may also be observed in A 1 and see also 4 Ezra Armenian 6:1C, 1I; and 12:6. A preliminary journey of the soul is intended, preceding the ascent to the Godhead, which is described in vv. 19–21.

A 17. The idea of a narrow path leading to the heavenly city, with fire at its side, is found in 4 Ezra 7:8, which probably inspired the present verse.

A 19. աշտիճանք աստուածութեանն 'steps to the Divinity'. Literally 'steps of the Divinity'. Apparently the 'seven camps of demons' and 'the seven steps to the Divinity' refer to the seven good and bad stages of the ascent of the souls and are based on 4 Ezra 7:81–99.[17] Most of the heavens or lodgings that are described have aspects of reward or punishment. Do the 'lodgings' (օթեւանք), an odd term here, correspond to the lodgings, *mansiones,* in which itineraries were reckoned in antiquity?[18]

A 20. լուսաւորի . . . մթանայ 'he shines' . . . 'he is darkened'. Issaverdens interprets this of the heavens, but the parallel with 4 Ezra 7:79 and 7:125 is inescapable.

իբրեւ զարեգակն 'like the sun'. Cf. 4 Ezra 7:97.

A 21. This vision in the seventh heaven resembles 4 Ezra 7:87, 98. The soul is opposite Eden, in which God's throne resides, cf. *2 Enoch*

17. Cf. Stone, 'Questions of Ezra,' 597. On the term 'steps', see Stone, *Fourth Ezra*, 243.
18. See E. D. Hunt, *Holy Land Pilgrimage in the Later Roman Empire* (Oxford, 1982).

8:1–8; *Death of Adam* 17; *Life of Adam and Eve* [44](22):4. Light is, of course, typical of the environs of the divinity.

A 23. Հրշտակն 'angel'. This spelling, sometimes encountered in this manuscript, is not unusual in medieval manuscripts.[19] This verse is drawn from 4 Ezra 4:10–11 (cf. Stone, *Fourth Ezra*, 85–86).

A 24. զերեսս Աստուծոյ 'the face of God'. Compare this view with Exod 33:20. Observe, however, the revelation of the face of God in *2 Enoch* 22:1–2, *Apocalypse of Sedrach* 2:4, and 4 Ezra 7:98 (Stone, *Fourth Ezra*, 245–46).

A 25. իշխեսցէ 'dares' or 'is able.'

A 26. հալեսցի 'he will melt'. A typical feature of God's presence; cf. 4 Ezra 13:4 (of the Messiah); Mic 1:4; Ps 68:3, 97:5.

A 27. These names of angelic classes are unparalleled. Issaverdens translates the latter part of the verse less literally: 'and around His throne there are such fiery guardians, as chambers of fire . . ., there are igneous hollows, vaulted ways full of lamps'. The word մանասրուանք has no satisfactory etymology and does not appear in the dictionaries.

A 28. Perhaps the words from 'thunders' to 'heats' are misplaced (cf. vv. 18, 20). They are formulated differently from those that precede and follow them.

A 29. This is a citation of Isa 6:2–3 and is, of course, commonplace as angelic praise.

A 30. The verse repeats the end of A 26.

A 31. Compare A 7.

A 32. Հայր 'father'. The passage is clearly constructed on 4 Ezra 7:102–105; see also a similar issue in 1 Cor 15:9.

Հանկիստ 'rest'. This spelling is frequent in manuscripts. The 'great rest and mercy' are those of the deceased.

A 33. զվեց դարուն 'for six ages'. This refers to the idea that the world will last 6,000 years and Christ will come in the middle of the sixth millennium: see *Life of Adam and Eve* 44 and the discussion in the 'Introduction' to *History of Adam and His Grandsons.*[20] The text is confused and perhaps should read something like 'in the sixth age'.

զհոգիքն '(our) souls'. The form is medieval Armenian.

19. See, e.g., the *Miscellany* of Mexit'ar Ayrivanec'i, Matenadaran no. 1500 (1272–88 C.E.).

20. To be published in Stone, *Adam and Eve,* forthcoming.

A 35. *կատարեսցէ* 'recite'. Literally 'complete' or 'carry out.'

A 36. *ապա եթէ ոչ* 'if not'. That is, if the above procedure does not take place.

A 37. *տայ* 'let'. Normally this verb would mean 'cause' in such constructions. The use in A 2 and A 38 resembles the use here.

A 38. This verse depends on Matt 13:22. Agricultural parables are common in ancient Jewish and Christian literature.

A 39. The reference to Moses combines Exod 24:18, 33:1; and Num 12:8. For Elijah see 2 Kings 2:1–2 and for Daniel, Daniel 6. Note the overall resemblance of this passage to 4 Ezra 7:106–10.

B 11. *փողն գաբրիէլի* 'the trumpet of Gabriel'. A feature of the coming of the eschaton in Jewish and Christian sources.

B 12. Compare A 6.

B 13. This verse resembles 4 Ezra 7:31–32. The form *նորագէ* 'renews' is corrupt for *նորոգէ*.

B 14. Compare 4 Ezra 7:34–38.

Colophon. It is impossible to know whether this short colophon was the work of the compiler or of the copyist.

Was the Biblical *sārîs* a Eunuch?

HAYIM TADMOR

In this paper I examine the evidence for the specific character of the sārîs/sārîsîm in the Hebrew Bible. It is suggested that, like the terms ša rēši / šūt rēši, which referred to officials at the court of the Assyrian kings, the term sārîs, borrowed from Akkadian, denoted a eunuch in both preexilic and postexilic periods. It is further suggested that the term and the institution were borrowed from Akkadian or, more specifically, Western Akkadian through the mediation of Phoenician. The borrowing presumably took place before the eighth century B.C.E.*, when the Assyrians imposed their rule over Israel and Judah.*

The specific nature and role of officials designated as *ša rēši* / *šūt rēši* at the courts of the Assyrian kings in the time of the Empire has been the concern of several studies in the last decades.[1] The core of the problem is whether all these officials, only a certain segment of them, or perhaps even none of them[2] were eunuchs. Another aspect of the problem relates to pictorial representations, mainly on Assyrian monuments and cylinder seals: were the beardless courtiers depicted there merely young

1. E.g., J. V. Kinnier-Wilson, *The Nimrud Wine Lists* (CTN 1; London, 1972) 46–48; A. L. Oppenheim, "A Note on *ša rēši*," *JANESCU* 5 (1973) 267–79 (with a correction in *RA* 68 [1974] 95); P. Garelli, "Remarques sur l'administration de l'Empire assyrien," *RA* 68 (1974) 128–40; M. Heltzer, "On the Akkadian term *rēšu* in Ugarit," *IOS* 4 (1974) 4–11; S. Parpola, *Letters from Assyrian Scholars to the Kings Esarhaddon and Assurbanipal* (Neukirchen-Vluyn, 1983) 2.20–21; H. Tadmor, "Rab-saris and Rab-shakeh in 2 Kings 18," in *The Word of the Lord Shall Go Forth: Essays in Honor of David Noel Freedman in Celebration of His Sixtieth Birthday* (ed. C. L. Meyers and M. O'Connor; Winona Lake, Ind., 1983) 279–85; J. A. Brinkman and Stephanie Dalley, "A Royal Kudurru from the Reign of *Aššur-nādin-šumi*," *ZA* 78 (1988) 85–86, with some further bibliographical references (cf. also T. Abusch, *Harper's Bible Dictionary* [San Francisco, 1985] 849).

2. So, rather emphatically, W. von Soden, AHw 974a (9) *ša šūt rēši* 'etwa (Hoch-)Kommissare; keine Eunuchen!' However, the crucial passage *kīma šūt rēši la ālidi nīlka lībal* 'Like the eunuch who does not beget, may your semen dry up' (CT 23,10:14) [CAD N/2 234a] is not quoted in that entry.

pages[3] and clean-shaven adults, or were they emasculated males, in contradistinction to the bearded ones?[4] Both designations, *ša rēši* and *ša ziqni*, were often used as a merism to denote the entire body of courtiers of the Assyrian monarchs under the empire.[5] I believe that the cumulative evidence gleaned from the Assyro-Babylonian records justifies the view that in the Neo-Assyrian empire the *ša rēši* officials (or *šūt rēši*, their Neo-Assyrian semantic equivalent) were usually eunuchs and that the term should be rendered as such in translation, rather than 'head officers', 'officials', or the like.[6]

Strangely enough, the evidence concerning the term *sārîs* in the Hebrew Bible has thus far not played any significant role in Assyriological discussions, though both protagonists and opponents of the pan-eunuch view agree that the Hebrew term is a loan from the Akkadian *ša rēši*.[7] As such, it has been thought to bear no independent value for the pertinent Assyriological discussion.

I propose, therefore, a reappraisal of the biblical evidence. If it could be shown that, on most occasions, *sārîs/sārîsîm* in the Hebrew Bible stands for 'eunuch(s)', such evidence would have a direct bearing on the meaning of the original Akkadian term. This brief investigation is dedicated to my friend and colleague, Jonas Greenfield, who in the course of his long scholarly career has masterfully elucidated numerous complex issues of borrowings (as well as other linguistic phenomena) in ancient Semitic languages.

3. See Oppenheim, "A Note on *ša rēši*," 333.

4. J. Reade, "The Neo-Assyrian Court and Army: Evidence from Sculptures," *Iraq* 34 (1972) 91–92, 95, 100.

5. CAD Z 127; Oppenheim, "A Note on *ša rēši*," 333.

6. Of special significance in this connection is the reference to the "successors" of the *ša rēši* courtiers mentioned in a Neo-Assyrian prophecy, K.883:4–5, newly edited by A. Ivančik in *NABU* (1993) no. 2, 40–42 (following an unpublished edition of K. Deller). The goddess Mulissu promises Ashurbanipal, still a crown prince, that he will exercise royal authority 'over the sons of the bearded (*ša ziqni*) and over the *ḫalpēte* of the eunuchs (*ša rēši*)'. Ivančik quotes Deller's proposal to take *ḫalpēte* from the common West Semitic *ḥlf* 'replace, change, substitute', and translates 'successeurs'; so also Parpola, *Letters*, 2.117, note on 129:8. [The singular LÚ *ḫalpu*, an Aramaic loanword in Neo-Babylonian, is actually attested: von Soden, AHw 313a s.v. *ḫalpu* III, 'Ersatzman'; cf. also *ḥalîfā* = 'replacement, substitute' in Mishnaic Hebrew.] The implication of this passage is clear: while the (present) bearded courtiers are to be succeeded by their sons, the eunuchs will have only 'replacements'. The evidence concerning the *ša rēši* and *ša rēš šarri* in Babylonia, especially in the late second millennium, is much more complex; see Brinkman and Dalley, "A Royal Kudurru." In a forthcoming study Dr. Dalley discusses the place of the *ša rēši* in the Middle Assyrian and Neo-Assyrian texts. I am grateful to her for allowing me the opportunity to read her manuscript prior to its publication. As it happens, her views are at variance with those submitted in the present paper.

7. Already stated by F. Delitzsch, *Assyrische Handwörterbuch* (Leipzig, 1896) 694; H. Zimmern, "Über Bäcker und Mundschenk im Altsemitisch," *ZDMG* 53 (1899) 116 and BDB, 710.

The biblical material pertaining to *sārîsîm* may be grouped into several categories. To the first group I assign references to *sārîsîm* who were connected with the queen's quarters and were in the service of the queen. Analogy to the practice at the courts of Assyrian and Persian kings (as well as to the practices at the later Roman, Byzantine, and Ottoman courts) would suggest that such officials were eunuchs. The foremost example in this category appears in 2 Kings 9, in the story of the encounter between Queen Jezebel and Jehu, the rebel king.[8] When Jehu approached the royal palace in Jezreel, having killed the monarch (Jezebel's son and his kinsman [cousin or nephew], the king of Judah), Jezebel addressed him derisively: "Is all well, Zimri, murderer of your master?" Enraged, Jehu shouted, "Who is on my side, who?" Then, "Two or three *sārîsîm* leaned out of the window toward him. 'Throw her down,' he ordered. They threw her down, and her blood spattered on the wall and on the horses" (2 Kgs 9:31–33). Who were these *sārîsîm* of the queen? It is very unlikely that any other males but eunuchs would be permitted to move freely in Jezebel's private quarters.[9] Though we are unfamiliar with the regulations at the court of Tyre, Jezebel's home, it is known that in contemporary Assyria the only males permitted to enter the royal harem were eunuchs, and the efficacy of their castration was periodically checked and verified.[10]

The next case of *sārîsîm* in the service of the queen comes from texts relating to the last days of Judah. The *sārîsîm* are listed in conjunction with the *gĕbîrâ*, the king's mother, deported by Nebuchadnezzar after Jehoiachin's submission: "King Jeconiah, the Queen Mother, the *sārîsîm*, the officials of Judah and Jerusalem . . . " (Jer 29:2); and in the parallel passage: "Jehoiachin . . . the king's mother, the royal wives, the *sārîsîm* and 'the notables of the land' " (2 Kgs 24:15). The rendering 'eunuchs', as in the Septuagint and the Vulgate, is, I believe, the most plausible in this context.[11] The same seems to be true of Jer 41:16, where the people taken to Egypt by Ishmael son of Nethaniah are listed in the following manner: "men, soldiers, women, children and *sārîsîm*."[12] The distinction

8. The story is a part of the Elisha pericope, from the time of the Jehu dynasty: A. Rofé, *The Prophetical Stories* (Jerusalem, 1988) 79–86.

9. The LXX, Vg., and most of the modern versions, beginning with the KJV, translate here 'eunuchs'.

10. E. Weidner, "Hof- und Harems-Erlasse assyrischer Könige aus dem 2. Jahrtausend v. Chr." *AfO* 17 (1956) 276: 50; 286: 98, 100; Oppenheim, "A Note on *ša rēši*," 330; von Soden, AHw 609a, 613a s.v. *marruru*; CAD M/1 440–41 s.v. *mazziz pani*; M/2 223 s.v. *murruru*.

11. Here, however, except for the NEB and a few other critical translations, the English versions, starting with the KJV, translate 'officers' or 'officials'.

12. Note that in a parallel passage, in Jer 43:8, the text reads: "men, women, children and *king's daughters*."

here is according to gender and age. The *sārîsîm* are clearly a separate category alongside males, females, and minors and are rendered 'eunuchs' in the ancient and modern translations.

The second group of texts would include the other preexilic or exilic references to *sārîsîm* as royal officials, none of whom are specifically connected with the queen. In these cases there is no way to judge from the context alone whether they were eunuchs. In 1 Sam 8:14–15, Samuel warns that the future king will confiscate fields, vineyards, and olive groves, giving them to his servants (*ʿăbādāyw*); furthermore, he will take a tithe of the grain and vine and will give it to his *sārîsîm* and his servants (as above, *ʿăbādāyw*). A distinction is thus kept here between the *sārîsîm* and the royal servants (*ʿabdê hammelek*). We do not know why the ancient author chose this specific terminology.[13] The latter term referred in the biblical period to royal/state officials, including those of high standing. If these were exclusively in the service of the king, could it that *sārîsîm* refers here to those who attended the queen?

A similar problem exists in the case of Jer 34:19, where *sārîsîm* are listed as a separate category among the nobles (*śārîm*) of Judah and of Jerusalem, the priests and all 'the people of the land' (*ʿam haʾareṣ*), who participated in the solemn ceremony of oath taking when Zedekiah proclaimed a release of the slaves. Modern biblical translations render *sārîsîm* as 'royal courtiers' in general, but it could equally well be argued that it means 'eunuchs'.

In several other places in 1 and 2 Kings and Jeremiah, an individual *sārîs* is referred to as a royal officer: a king of Israel sends a *sārîs* (literally, 'one *sārîs*') to summon Micaiah son of Imlah (1 Kgs 22:9); another king assigns a *sārîs* to accompany the woman whose son Elisha had revived (2 Kgs 8:6); and later, in Judah, a *sārîs* is in command of the soldiers in Jerusalem on the eve of, or just after, its fall (2 Kgs 25:19).[14] Again, one cannot tell from the context whether these were eunuchs, though the titles of Nathan-melech the *sārîs* (2 Kgs 23:1) and of Ebed-melech the Nubian, *ʾîš-sārîs* (Jer 38:7), are rendered 'eunuch' in both ancient and modern translations.[15]

13. It is very questionable whether 1 Samuel 8 is of an early date and reflects the royal practice in the Canaanite city-states (cf. I. Mendelsohn, "Samuel's Denunciation of Kingship in the Light of the Akkadian Documents of Ugarit," *BASOR* 143 [1956] 17–22) or of a much later date. F. Crüsemann (*Der Widerstand gegen das Königtum* [Neukirchen-Vluyn, 1978] 66–68) considers v. 15 to be secondary/editorial expansion. P. K. McCarter (*I Samuel* [AB 8; Garden City, N.Y., 1980] 158–59) takes *sārîsîm* as 'officers', since he follows the view that this was also the original meaning of *ša rēši* in Akkadian.

14. Note that in the Neo-Assyrian Empire the Chief Eunuch, *rab ša rēši,* served as the commander-in-chief; see Tadmor, "Rab-saris," 282 n. 17.

15. Was a Nubian eunuch an exception or were eunuchs usually recruited from among non-Israelites? In any event, emasculated persons were not admitted to the "congregation of the Lord," Deut 23:1.

The last, and unquestionably the most difficult case in texts of the second group, is that of Potiphar the *sārîs* and high court official of the Pharaoh of Egypt in Gen 37:36 and 39:1. Here *sārîs* is usually rendered 'courtier' rather than 'eunuch', the main reason being the fact that Potiphar had a wife. Egyptologists who have treated this story have noted that there is hardly any evidence of native castrates at the court in Pharaonic Egypt.[16] This may well be so, but Joseph's story was composed, after all, by a Hebrew speaker and was addressed to an Israelite audience. The drama in the story of Joseph and Potiphar's wife, whether it originates from a late Egyptian milieu or not, is embedded in the fact that the wife of a royal eunuch was strongly tempted by the handsome young slave in her husband's service. Indeed, one wonders whether the masterful portrayal of Potiphar as a eunuch (in all but name) in Thomas Mann's *Joseph in Egypt* is not much closer to the spirit of the story than a modern scholar would like to admit. But was it at all possible for a eunuch to marry? We have no direct evidence of marriage among eunuchs in Assyria, but there are examples of that practice in later empires where, in certain cases, the eunuchs married and adopted children.[17] In any event, the fact that Potiphar was married cannot serve as central evidence for the claim that *sārîs* in preexilic Biblical Hebrew does not mean 'eunuch'.

The identity of *sārîsîm* in the postexilic contexts, our third group of texts, presents less of a problem. There is an explicit reference to a *sārîs* as a castrate in Second (or Third) Isaiah (56:3–4): "And let not the eunuch say, 'I am a withered tree.' " He is consoled by the prophet that, by keeping the Lord's covenant, he will earn a 'memorial monument' (*yād*) and an everlasting name (*šēm*) for himself, "better than sons or daughters, that shall not perish." The pun here is on the word 'name' (*šēm*) which in Akkadian meant a 'male successor', in conjunction with the

16. G. E. Kadish, "Eunuchs in Ancient Egypt," in *Studies in Honor of John A. Wilson* (Chicago, 1969) 55–62; D. B. Redford, *A Study of the Biblical Story of Joseph* (VTSup 20; Leiden, 1970) 51, 200–201; idem, *Egypt, Canaan and Israel in Ancient Times* (Princeton, 1992) 425 (cf. also M. Görg, "Die Amtstitel des Potiphar," *BN* 53 [1990] 14–20).

17. From Achaemenid Persia, at least one high-ranking court eunuch, Artoxares the Paphlagonian, who served under Artaxerxes I and Darius II, is said to have been married (F. W. König, *Die Persika des Ktesias von Knidos* [AfO Beiheft 18; Gratz, 1972] 21 §53 and p. 88; P. Guyot, *Eunuchen als Sklaven und Freigelassene in der griechisch-römischen Antike* [Stuttgart, 1980] 185–86). In the Byzantine Empire certain categories of court eunuchs of high standing were permitted to marry, adopt children, and bequeath them their wealth (R. Guillard, "Les Eunuchs dans l'Empire Byzantin," *Études Byzantines* 1 [1943] 201). In China, where eunuchs exercised political, often unlimited, authority, especially under the Later Han Dynasty, many eunuchs married, acquired concubines, and bequeathed their adopted sons enormous wealth (T. Ch'u, *Han Social Structure* [Seattle and London, 1972] 100, 236, 436 n. 117, 470 n. 334, 478; cf. also T. Mitamura, *Chinese Eunuchs: The Structure and Intimate Politics* [Rutland, Vermont, and Tokyo, 1972] 113–26).

word used for 'perish' (*yikkārēt*),[18] the very verb that defines castration in Deut 23:1. It is true that a Neo-Babylonian or early Achaemenid Persian milieu is described here, but the meaning of the Hebrew *sārîs*, defining a class of royal servants, could not have changed drastically in the course of the century that separated the editors of Kings and Jeremiah from the author of Isaiah 56. The Babylonian milieu is also addressed by the compiler of 2 Kgs 20:18: Hezekiah's offspring will serve as "*sārîsîm* at the palace of the King of Babylon," probably meaning here 'eunuchs'.[19] The chief of the eunuchs, *śar hassārîsîm*, is the person who changes the names of Daniel and his compatriots at the court of the Nebuchadnezzar in the early layer of the Daniel story (Dan 1:3, 7, 10, 18), composed most likely towards the close of the Persian Period.[20] From about the same period we find numerous references to *sārîsîm* in the book of Esther, which is set in the milieu of the Persian court. There the royal *sārîs*, "guardian of the women" (Esth 2:3), was undoubtedly a eunuch. The same title, as applied to other servants dispatched by King Ahasuerus or standing in attendance before him (1:12, 15; 2:21; 4:5; 6:14; 7:9), is usually rendered 'eunuchs' in recent biblical translations, very much in line with the description of the Persian royal court given by the classical authors.[21]

To sum up the evidence discussed so far, I believe it very likely that the term *sārîs* stands for 'eunuch', not only in texts from the Neo-Babylonian and Achaemenid milieus, but also in texts describing the Israelite and Judean royal courts. There is no conclusive evidence that might militate against this view, and a point of semantics may be added to support it. It is very hard to imagine how *sārîs* could have borne two simultaneous meanings in Biblical Hebrew: that of royal courtier (not castrated) and that of a (court) eunuch. No development from general to specific may be discerned in the biblical evidence. Moreover, Biblical Hebrew already possessed indigenous terminology for royal courtiers/

18. See also the comment of J. Blenkinsopp, "Second Isaiah: Prophet of Universalism," *JSOT* 41 (1988) 95 and 102 n. 35.

19. For the date of this text see R. E. Clements, *Isaiah and the Deliverance of Jerusalem* (JSOTSup 13; Sheffield, 1980) 66–68; M. Cogan and H. Tadmor, *II Kings* (AB 11; New York, 1988) 262–63. Contrast: B. Oded, "The Babylonian Embassy Narrative (Isaiah 32 = II Kings 20:12–18): Historical Event but Fictitious Prophecy?" *Shnaton* 9 (1987) 115–26 [Hebrew].

20. See E. Bickerman, *Four Strange Books of the Bible* (New York, 1967) 91–92.

21. E.g., Herodotus 3.77; 6.32; 8.104–5; Xenophon *Cyr.* 7.5, 60–65. The advantages of employing eunuchs are highly praised by Cyrus, Xenophon's literary hero (ibid.). More examples may be adduced from Ktesias, *Persica.* For evidence from Xenophon and Ktesias, see D. L. Gera, *Xenophon's Cyropaedia: Style, Genre, Literary Technique* (Oxford, 1993) 203–5, 218, 254–59, 287–89. Some eunuchs in the emperor's service wielded power and rose to the rank of satraps, occasionally becoming unchallenged autocrats: see, e.g., D. M. Lewis, *Sparta and Persia* (Leiden, 1977) 21–22, 81; Guyot, "Eunuchen," 80–91.

officers (*ᶜabdê hammelek, śārîm,* etc.). There would have been no reason to borrow it had a Hebrew equivalent to 'eunuchs' existed in the language and in practice.

I opened this discussion with the commonly accepted assertion that *sārîs* is a loanword from the Akkadian *ša rēši.*[22] This point, however, should be considered in the wider context of the question of the borrowing of Assyrian or Babylonian titles in Biblical Hebrew.

In the Persian period, some Akkadian terminology for state functionaries found its way into late Hebrew through the mediation of Aramaic. This is especially true of *sĕgān* (pl. *sĕgānîm*), from *šaknu* 'commissioner', and of *peḥâ* (pl. *pāḥôt*), from *pāḫātu, bēl piḫāti,* 'governor'.[23] Both terms refer to Persian officials, irrespective of whether they were Jews or Iranians. However, an examination of titles of high officials in the courts of the kings of Judah and Israel shows that there is not one case of a similar borrowing of an Akkadian term, adjusting it only to the phonetic and grammatical rules of the Hebrew. The title *ᵓăšer ᶜal habbāyit,* majordomo, the royal steward, at the courts of the kings of Israel and Judah might have been coined after Egyptian or Mesopotamian models, but in the title the Hebrew calque was used.[24] The untranslated though slightly Hebraized Assyrian titles *rab-šāqeh, rab-sārîs,* and *tartān* in the story of Sennacherib's invasion of Judah (2 Kgs 18:17)[25] are employed exclusively for Assyrian, not Judean officials, and so are the titles of *paḥôt* for governors and *qĕrōbîm,* for Assyrian *ša qurūbuti,* royal adjutants, bodyguard (Ezek 23:5, 12).[26] What is described in the latter text is the reality of Assyrian officialdom ruling a client kingdom.

The only Akkadian term for a state functionary in the Neo-Assyrian period that was actually borrowed in Biblical Hebrew is *ṣîrîm,* from Neo-Assyrian *ṣirâni* 'ambassadors'. This was a regular borrowing in a period when kings of Israel were constantly sending ambassadors to Assyria, beginning, as it appears, in the early eighth century. These ambassadors were part of the numerous foreign envoys at the Assyrian court, attested already from the days of Ashurnasirpal II. Isa 18:2, the earliest occurrence

22. See S. A. Kaufman, *The Akkadian Influence on Aramaic* (AS 19; Chicago, 1974) 100.

23. Ibid., 82, 97–98; J. N. Postgate, "The Place of the *šaknu* in Assyrian Government," *AnSt* 30 (1980) 67–76.

24. R. de Vaux, *Ancient Israel: Its Life and Institutions* (London, 1961) 129–30; T. D. N. Mettinger, *Solomonic State Officials* (Lund, 1971) 70–79. Cf. *ša muḫḫi bīti* (CAD B 296) and *ša muḫḫi ekalli* (CAD E 62), attested from the Middle Assyrian Period onward.

25. Cogan and Tadmor, *II Kings,* 229–30.

26. G. R. Driver, "Problems in Aramaic and Hebrew Texts," *Miscellenea Orientalia Dedicata Antonio Deimel* (AnOr 12; Rome, 1935) 60–61.

of this loan term, purposely interchanges *ṣîrîm*, the new term, and *malʾăkîm*, the Hebrew term.[27]

It would thus seem highly unlikely that the term *ša rēši* for an Israelite or Judean courtier was borrowed from Assyrian practice during the short period when Israelites and Judeans were clients of the emperors of Assyria. The borrowing must antedate the rise of the Assyrian Empire and would belong to the early layer of borrowings from Akkadian, probably Western Akkadian.[28]

It is difficult to identify an early historical contact between Western Akkadian and Biblical Hebrew. One possibility is that it entered Hebrew, perhaps northern Hebrew, from the early Northwest Semitic usage, through contacts with the Canaanite city-states, together with certain other pre-Israelite social terms (e.g., *mas* 'corvée').[29] Another possibility is that it was borrowed later, through Phoenician mediation.[30] If this hypothesis is accepted, one may suggest that the term *sārîsîm*, together with its bearers, the class of castrated courtiers, were introduced into Israel by the Phoenician princess Jezebel during the reign of Ahab. It is at this time that we witness the growing role of the queen and queen mother in the kingdom of Israel, similar to developments in Assyria in the days of Sammu-ramat (Semiramis), wife of Shamsi-adad IV and mother of Adad-nerari III, the powerful queen mother. It was also at about this time that very influential eunuchs (the most famous of them being Nergal [or Palil]-eresh, the "strong-man" under Adad-nerari III and his immediate successors) rose to power,[31] something unprecedented, as far as we know, in Assyria. But the vicissitudes of the high Assyrian *ša rēši* officials are obviously beyond the topic of the present discussion. My attempt here is to

27. H. Tadmor, in *Bible and Jewish History: Studies . . . Dedicated to the Memory of Jacob Liver* (ed. B. Uffenheimer; Tel Aviv, 1971) 225 n. 13; and independently P. Machinist, "The Image of Assyria in First Isaiah," *JAOS* 103 (1983) 730 n. 65.

28. The uncontracted long vowel in the propenultima of the pl. *sārîsîm* is very irregular and calls for explanation. One might speculate whether it retained the length of *ša*, often written *ša-a* (*rēši*) in Western Akkadian (for the evidence from Ugarit, see J. Huehnergard, *The Akkadian of Ugarit* [Atlanta, 1989] 60 n. 121). Huehnergard, who is skeptical about this possibility, regards the plene of *ša* as a graphic rather than phonetic phenomenon (personal communication).

29. A. F. Rainey, "Compulsory Labour Gangs in Ancient Israel," *IEJ* 20 (1970) 191–202.

30. I leave open the question of the *š* > *s* shift in early Northwest Semitic, especially in Phoenician.

31. See provisionally H. Tadmor, "The Historical Inscriptions of Adad-nirari III," *Iraq* 35 (1973) 147–48; J. Reade, in *Assyrian Royal Inscriptions: New Horizons* (ed. F. M. Fales; Orientis Antiqui Collection 17; Rome, 1981) 158–59; H. D. Galter, "Ein Inschrift des Gouverneurs Nergal-ereš in Yale," *Iraq* 52 (1990) 47–48.

show that the biblical evidence is, in all of its aspects, relevant to the wider issue of the meaning of the Akkadian term.[32]

Added in proof. After this paper had gone to press, two further points came to my attention:

(a) As to Potiphar's being a eunuch, see J. L. Kugel, *In Potiphar's House* (San Francisco, 1990) 75–76.

(b) Regarding the translation of Isa 56:5, S. Talmon takes יד ושם as a hendiadys, meaning 'a memorial stele' ("יד ושם: *gilgulei maṭbeᶜa lashon*," in *Studies in Bible Dedicated to the Memory of U. Cassuto on the 100th Anniversary of His Birth* [ed. H. Beinart and S. E. Loewenstamm; Jerusalem, 1987] 137–41 [Hebrew]). More recently, Sara Japhet has made another suggestion, namely, to render *yād* as 'share' ("יד ושם [Isa 56:5]: A Different Proposal," *MAARAV* 8 [1992] 65–80). The passage would then mean: the eunuchs will have 'a share and a name' in the Temple and its precincts.

32. Thanks are due to Mordechai Cogan, Miriam Tadmor, and Jeffrey Tigay, who read this paper and offered valuable criticism.

A Calendrical Document from Qumran Cave 4 (mišmarot D, 4Q*325*)

Shemaryahu Talmon

Some twenty fragmentary calendrical documents help to fill out the mosaic-like picture of the Covenanters' solar ephemeris that results from the collation of calendar-related references in major Qumran writings. Concomitantly, these documents attest to the Covenanters' high rating of "proper chronology," which governs the execution of ritual acts. Their adherence to a solar calendar, which differed from mainstream Judaism's lunar calendar, prevented their participation in the sacrificial temple service and triggered the institutionalization of "prayer" as an alternative form of worship.

The reconstructed calendrical fragment published here illustrates the Covenanters' method of synchronizing festivals and holy seasons, in this instance "sabbaths" and the "beginnings of the months," with the one-week turns of service of the 'priestly courses' (mišmarot) in a six-year cycle. The rotating system facilitated the adjustment of the biblical roster of 24 priestly courses (1 Chr 24:7–19) to the solar year of 364 days, which is constituted of 52 weeks.

Whereas 1 Enoch and Jubilees refer to basic principles that underlie the 364-day solar calendar, the detailed calendrical registers from the Qumran caves address diverse aspects of private and public life. The difference suggests that this calendar determined, de facto, the life pattern of the individual Covenanter and of the community.

Introduction

Fragments of numerous documents pertaining to calendrical matters have turned up among the Qumran writings, especially among the fragments that emanated from Cave 4.[1] These remains of ancient timetables help in filling out the mosaic-like picture that emerges from the

1. J. T. Milik identified these fragments and referred to some of them in his publications. See, inter alia, J. T. Milik, "Le Travail d'édition des manuscrits de Désert de Juda," *Volume du Congrès Strasbourg 1956* (VTSup 4; Leiden, 1957) 25; idem, *Ten Years of Discovery in the Wilderness of Judaea* (trans. J. Strugnell; London, 1959) 107–13.

collation of calendar-related references in major Qumran writings, such as 1QS, CD, 1QpHab, 1QH, and the more-detailed exposition in the *Temple Scroll* (11QTemple). The considerable number of calendrical records and statements attests to the great importance of "proper chronology" in the world view of the Covenanters' community. Their messianic-millenarian expectations[2] derive from and depend on an accurately defined succession of stages in history,[3] קצי עולמים (1QS IV 16; 1QM I 8–9), קיצי אל (1QpHab VII 12–13), or קצי נצח (1QH I 24–25) and similar expressions, culminating in the 'new age' קץ נחרצה ועשות חדשה (1QS IV 25).[4] The correct execution of halakhic rulings is subject to precise timing, and so is the efficacy of ritual acts, foremost the offering of sacrifices. Since the schedule of sacrifices in the Jerusalem Temple was adjusted to the lunar year of 354 days, the observance of a solar calendar of 364 days (see below, pp. 343–32) prevented the Covenanters from participating in the sacrificial services.

An additional difficulty was caused by the fact that in the temple 24 priestly courses took turns in carrying out the sacrificial rituals in accordance with the enumeration of the names of 24 priestly families in the postexilic roster preserved in 1 Chr 24:7–19. Rabbinic sources ascribe the division of the priesthood into 24 courses to "the prophets" (*b. ʿArak.* 12b), who are accredited with having developed an earlier arrangement, presumably introduced by Moses, who is reported to have established 8 (*m. Taʿan.* 1:2) or 16 courses (*b. Taʿan.* 27a). Each *mišmar* served alone for one week every half-year and thus covered all in all 336 days per annum. The remaining 18 days were taken care of by having several courses share in the service on festivals (*m. Sukk.* 5:6–8; *b. Sukk.* 55b–56b; *b. Moʿed Qaṭ.* 17b; etc.).

In contrast to this, the Covenanters' solar year of 364 days necessitated the appointment of 52 priestly courses per annum to serve during

2. See S. Talmon, "Waiting for the Messiah: The Conceptual Universe of the Qumran Covenanters," in *Judaisms and Their Messiahs* (ed. J. Neusner, W. S. Green, and E. Frerichs; New York and Cambridge, 1988) 11–137; idem, "The Calendar of the Covenanters of the Judean Desert," in *Aspects of the Dead Sea Scrolls* (ed. C. Rabin and Y. Yadin; ScrHier 4; Jerusalem, 1958) 162ff.; repr. in S. Talmon, *The World of Qumran from Within* (hereafter *WQW*) (Jerusalem and Leiden, 1989) 147–50, 273–300; idem, "The New Covenanters of Qumran," *Scientific American* 225/5 (1971) 73–81.

3. A schema of the subdivision of historical time into ten jubilees appears to underlie a composition in which Melchizedek, the royal priest of old (Gen 14:18–20; cf. Ps 110:1–7), is accorded the role of supreme judge in the age to come (11QMelch). See M. de Jonge and A. S. van der Woude, "11QMelchizedek and the New Testament," *NTS* 12 (1965–66) 301–26; J. T. Milik, "*Milkî-ṣedeq* et *Milkî-rešaʿ* dans les anciens écrits juifs et chrétiens," *JJS* 23 (1972) 95–144; P. J. Kobelski, *Melchizedek and Melchirešaʿ* (CBQMS 10; Washington, D.C., 1981). Further: S. Talmon, "Between the Bible and the Mishna," *WQW,* 36–51, with additional bibliography.

4. S. Talmon, "קֵץ *qeṣ*," *TWAT* 7 (1990) 84–92; idem, *WQW,* 45–48.

the 52 weeks, each course officiating for one week every half-year. Since the Covenanters were committed to never deviating from a biblical tradition, a system had to be devised that would allow for the application of the prototype of 24 priestly courses to the solar year of 52 weeks. They solved the problem by establishing a six-year cycle with a staggered rotation of the *mišmarot.* In this system the 4 weeks by which the solar calendar exceeds the lunar year of 48 weeks are covered by 4 courses that serve each for one additional week, in other words, officiate 3 times in a given year. This arrangement evidently underlies the comment in the *War Scroll* (1QM II 1): "The fathers of the community are fifty-two. The major priests shall be appointed after the High Priest and his deputy in twelve courses to serve constantly before God. And the twenty-six heads of courses shall serve in their appointed term" (1QM II 1–2). The seemingly baffling statement does not refer to the 24 priestly families enumerated in 1 Chronicles 24 but rather to the 26 courses that actually served, each for one week every half-year, and in conjunction make up the "fifty-two fathers of the community."[5] Concurrently, the Covenanters filled the void in their religious life that resulted from the abstention from participation in the temple ritual by introducing "institutionalized prayer" as a substitute for the "temporarily" suspended sacrificial acts.[6]

For these reasons, calendar-related notations are accorded a place of prominence at the conclusion of a Qumran work, as in 1QS X and 11QPs[a] XVI, or at its very beginning, as in 11QTemple and 4QMMT. This proliferation of calendrical documents in the Covenanters' collection of writings throws additional and welcome light on the "calendar controversy," which was a major cause of internal rift and dissent among Second Temple Jewry.[7]

Description of 4Q325

Four fragments have been identified as belonging to 4Q*325*. Two larger ones, (a) and (b), are of a light-brown color, while two smaller ones, (c) and (d), are of a dark-brown, almost black color. On the

5. I withdraw a suggestion offered at a time when only rudimentary information on the rosters of priestly courses was available, namely, that the Covenanters added two משמרות to the biblical roster. See my "Calendar of the Covenanters," *WQW,* 157–62.

6. S. Talmon, "The Emergence of Institutionalized Prayer in Israel in Light of Qumran Literature," in *Qumrân, sa piété, sa théologie, et son milieu* (ed. M. Delcor; BETL 46; Louvain, 1978) 265–84 = *WQW,* 200–243.

7. I raised this issue in the early stages of Qumran research. See S. Talmon, "Yom Hakippurim in the Habakkuk Scroll," *Bib* 32 (1951) 549–63 = *WQW,* 186–99; idem, "Calendar of the Covenanters."

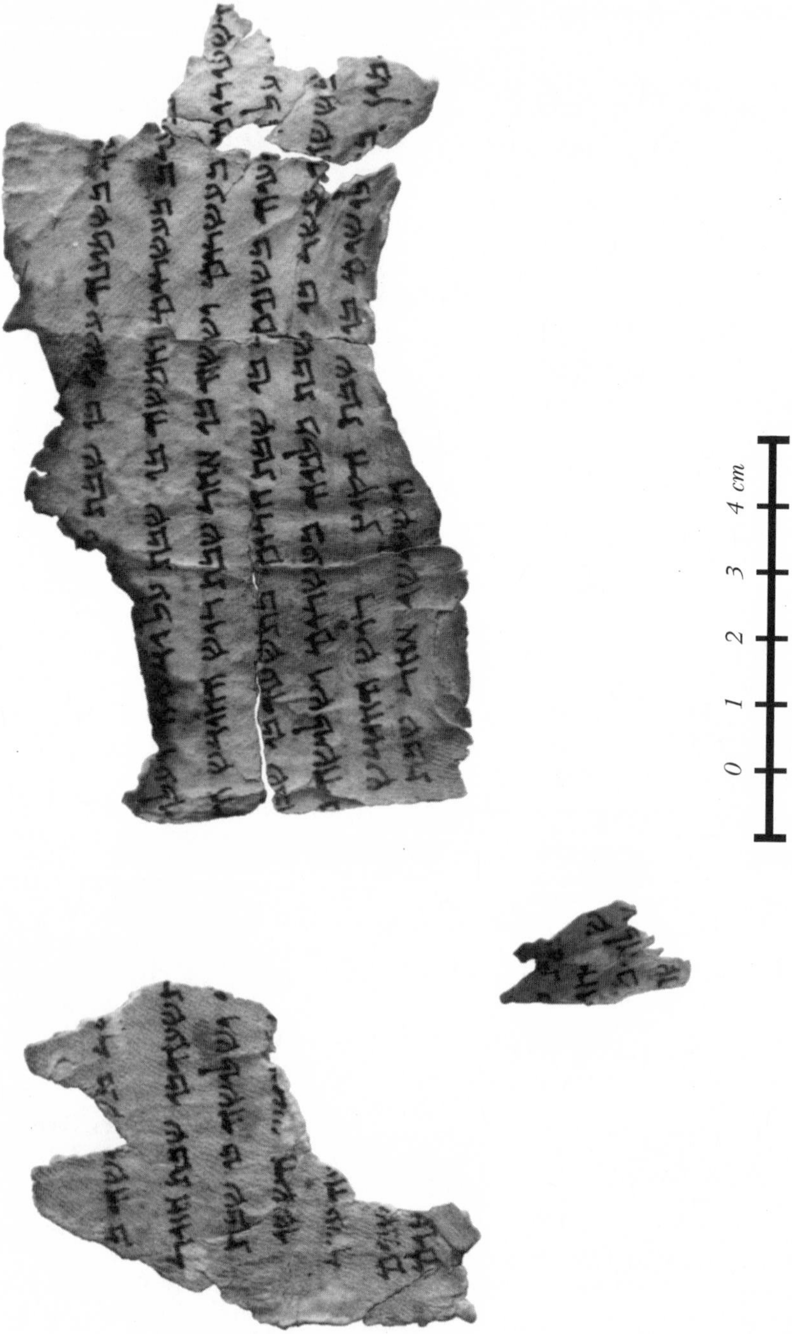

Figure 1. Mišmarot D, 4Q*325*.

strength of its contours and the partial words it contains, frg. (c), which measures 1.9 × 3.4 cm., could be joined to the lower right-hand part of (a), with only a small gap remaining between them.[8] Therefore, in the ensuing discussion (c) will be considered a part of (a).

Photograph

The larger fragments (a + c) and (b) may comfortably be placed in their respective original positions in the scroll. But the few legible letters on the small fragment, (d), which measures 1.3 × 2.6 cm., do not suffice to establish its original place in the document.

The composite fragment (a + c) is 10.6 cm. wide and 6.0 high.[9] The similarly uneven edges at the top and the bottom and the equally uneven right-hand edge seem to have resulted from deterioration. The straight edge on the left-hand side appears to attest to breakage of the material. A line caused by a partial split of the leather surface runs horizontally for some 4.0 cm. from the middle of the left-hand edge. A similar line crosses the fragment vertically at its middle, from top to bottom.

The right part of the top margin is extant to a length of 5.3 cm. and a height of 1.1 cm., the left part of the bottom margin to the extent of 4.2 × 0.6 cm. No traces of the side margins are extant. On the right-hand side, the beginnings of the written lines are lost, while on the left-hand side the writing comes up to the very edge of the fragment. The right half of the lower edge is missing altogether, apparently due to a fault in the material. As a result, the writing on the bottom line extends only over about one-third of its left part.

Fragment (b) measures 4.5 × 6.2 cm. Its contours are rather uneven, except for the straight lower half of the left-hand edge, which may have resulted from breakage along a series of needle holes where the thread had disintegrated. The thin line of an incipient split runs from top to bottom in the left-hand part of the fragment. Another such line runs through the right-hand part from top to bottom, then turns upwards toward the left-hand edge and ends at a quarter of its height. The broken top margin is extant to a height of 0.9 cm., and the left side margin to a width of 0.6–1.0 cm. Therefore, as said, in this fragment all line-endings are preserved.

Fragment (d) measures 0.9 × 2.5 cm. The few remaining letters of four lines permit the restoration of several words, which fit well into the vocabulary of 4Q*325*:

8. The join shown in photograph 43.333 constitutes a definite improvement on a previous attempt to combine the pieces, as shown in a photograph of an earlier series (42.332).

9. All measurements given pertain to the maximal widths and heights of the fragments.

1. ש]בת בׄ[לגה
2. [רו]ש [הׄ]חו]דׄש
3. אׄלה מ[ו֯
4.]שׄר֯

Line 1. ש]בת. In 4Q*325* this term is followed exclusively by one of three vocables: על, (חודש) רוש, or the name of a priestly course. The trace of the first letter in the word after ש]בת appears to be the remnant of a *bet.* If this is indeed the case, we can restore only the name of a משמר, because the restitution of על or רוש would be excluded. Therefore, the most plausible reconstruction is בׄ[לגה, the only name of a priestly course that begins with a *bet.*

Line 2. The proximity of the phrases ש]בת בׄ[לגה and [רו]ש [הׄ]חו]דש suggests that the fragment relates to the first turn of duty of Bilgah in the first year of the cycle, when this *mišmar* served from the 26th of the fourth month to the 2d of the fifth month, with רוש החודש falling on the 3d day of its service. Accordingly, the partly preserved, partly restored text of frg. (d) could be accommodated in the bottom lines of the reconstructed second column (see below, pp. 328–29). However, the letters preserved in lines 3–4 preclude a positioning of the fragment at that juncture.

Line 3. The trace of a letter at the right-hand side of the fragment seems to be the top of an *ʾalep,* rather than of a *šin.* It is clearly followed by לה מ.

Line 4. The first letter is evidently *šin,* followed by what appears to be the right-hand vertical stroke of *reš.*

The Writing

Each of frgs. (a) and (b) contains part of seven written lines. The line-endings on the left are mostly intact, especially on frg. (a). In contrast, the line-beginnings on the right side of the columns are missing, in frg. (b) to a very large extent. A space of 0.3–0.4 cm. divides one line from the other. Between line 1 and line 2 this space is slightly wider, 0.5 cm. on frg. (a) and 0.6 on frg. (b). The remains of four lines on frg. (d) are equally spaced.

Words are separated from one another by a fairly regular space of the width of one letter, amounting to 0.2, and in some instances to 0.3 cm., as, for example, in (a), lines 2, 6, and 7; and (b), line 2. A caesura in (a), line 6, measuring 0.8 cm., is evidently intended to separate the term רוש החודש, which opens a new section, from the phrase שבת הקוץ, with which the preceding one ends. In contrast, the large gap that extends over two-thirds of the bottom line of frg. (a) and thus cuts off the ordinal number השלישי (beginning of line 7) from רויש החודש (end of line 6) presumably resulted from a flaw in the oddly shaped vellum.

On the whole, the individual letters are regularly executed. With the exception of the very thin letters, ו, ז, י, ן, and the especially long ones, ל, ן, ץ, ק, which protrude above or below the lines respectively, most letters exhibit the apparently traditional measurement of 2 × 2 mm., which puts the "squareness" of the Hebrew alphabet into relief.

Measurements

On the basis of above data, we may assess the original dimensions of the two columns of the document partly preserved in frgs. (a + c) and (b).

Fragment (a): The almost completely extant third line holds 34 letters and 8 separators between words, or in other words, 42 spaces. By accurately positioning the words in line 3 in relation to lines 2 and 4, we are led to conclude that three additional spaces must be assumed in this line, which thus held altogether 45 spaces. A similar result is achieved by gauging the length of lines 2, 4, and 5.

The preserved lettering in line 3 extends over 10.6 cm. The reconstructed text, which holds 13 letters and 2 word-separators, covers approximately 2.8 cm. It follows that line 3 originally held 47 letters and 10 word-separators, and that it was ca. 13.4 cm. long. Judging by the left margin of frg. (b), in part preserved to a width of 1.0 cm., we may assume that the side margin of (a) originally measured ca. 1.2 cm. It follows that, when intact, col. I would have attained a width of ca. 14.5 cm.[10]

Fragment (b): The proposed reconstruction of the text implies that the lines of this fragment were perceptibly shorter than those of frg. (a). On the basis of the preserved line-endings and the restored text, we conclude that each of lines 4–5 contained 37 letters and 9 intervals between words, or, 46 spaces and was ca. 9.2 cm. long. Together with the margin, the column was approximately 10.0–10.5 cm. wide. A similar width may be calculated for line 6, which holds 39 + 9 = 48 spaces, taking up 9.6 + 1.2 cm., or ca. 10.8 cm. in all.

Since in both fragments all seven lines are partially extant, as well as sizable parts of the top and bottom margins, it may be established that the scroll stood approximately 7.0 cm. high.

The length of the part of the scroll that presumably contained the six-year service cycle of the priestly courses,[11] may be assessed on the basis of

10. In calculating the width of a column, only one side margin is taken into account, since every margin is shared by two adjacent columns.

11. We have no way of establishing whether this part was preceded or succeeded by some other calendrical composition, as is the case with 4Q*321*. See S. Talmon and I. Knohl,

the following considerations. As shown in the proposed reconstruction, the roster of courses and festivals of one year may be accommodated in somewhat less than 6 columns. Accordingly, approximately 35 columns would be required to record the entire six-year cycle. We have established the width of the partly extant cols. I and III at ca. 14.5 and 11.0 cm., respectively. With this fluctuation taken into account, the length of (this part of) the scroll would have come to ca. 75–80 cm.[12]

Paleography and Date

The regularly executed lettering evinces the hand of a trained scribe. Several prominent characteristics suggest that the scroll was penned in an "early formal Herodian script": The vertical lines at the bottom of the letter *šin* meet in a protruding spike, as, for example, in the *šin* of שבת and the first *šin* of השלישי in frg. (a), lines 1, 7; and several letters *šin* in frg. (b), lines 1–4. The thickened head of the upward stroke of *lamed* bends slightly to the left, as in על and ועלו in frg. (a) line 1. Other characteristics are the slight incline of the right-hand stroke of *mem* (passim) and the rectangular bend of the left down-stroke of *taw* (passim). Accordingly, 4Q*325* may be dated to the last third of the last century B.C.E.[13]

Orthography

The document does not exhibit the notable plene spelling that typifies Qumran scribal practice. However, in two instances (line 6), it offers a plene instead of the MT defective spelling: חרים in frg. (a), line 4, instead of חָרִם (1 Chr 24:8);[14] and מ[י]מין instead of מִיָּמִן (1 Chr 24:9; Ezra 10:25; Neh 10:8, but Neh 12:5: מימין).[15] On the other hand, frg. (a) has the spelling (החודש) רוש twice,[16] comparable to the spelling רֹשי השנים (miš F[a] 4Q*328* I 1) and רשונה with the elision of *ʾalep* (e.g., 1QS II 19–20; VI 5, 8; VII 19).

"Fragments of a Calendrical Scroll from Qumran: Miš B (4Q321[a])," *Tarbiz* 60 (1992) 505–21 [Hebrew]. An English version is published as "A Calendrical Scroll from a Qumran Cave: *Mišmarot* B[a], 4Q*321*," in *Pomegranates and Golden Bells: Studies in Biblical, Jewish, and Near Eastern Ritual, Law, and Literature in Honor of Jacob Milgrom* (ed. D. P. Wright, D. N. Freedman, and A. Hurvitz; Winona Lake, Ind., 1995) 267–302.

12. (3 × 14.5 = 43.5 cm.) + (3 × 11.0 = 33 cm.) = 76.5 cm.

13. See F. M. Cross, "The Development of the Jewish Scripts," in *The Bible and the Ancient Near East: Essays in Honor of William Foxwell Albright* (ed. G. E. Wright; Garden City, N.Y., 1961; repr. Winona Lake, Ind., 1979) 133–202, chart on pp. 137–39, line 4.

14. Thus in all other biblical occurrences of the name.

15. Pace BHS.

16. The defective spelling רוש (כוהני/ נשיאי) prevails in the *Songs of the Sabbath Sacrifice* (4Q*405*).

The Text

The scroll presumably contained a six-year roster of the sabbaths, the "beginnings of the month(s)," and the special Qumran harvest festivals, coupled with the names of priestly courses that served on each of these days. As far as may be ascertained, the major biblical festivals were not itemized in 4Q*325*.

In frg. (a) the pertinent dates and priestly courses for the first two months of the first year[17] in the cycle are enumerated. The list ends with the mention of the "beginning (or: the first) of the third month." The reconstructed frg. (b) records the appropriate data for the fifth and sixth months. Therefore, we may assume that frg. (a) constituted col. I of the scroll or of this specific component,[18] and frg. (b) col. III. Accordingly, in the no-longer-extant col. II, the sabbaths, harvest festivals, and priestly courses that fall in the third and fourth months must have been specified. The overall account follows a recurrent pattern, so that we are able to reconstruct, to within a high degree of certainty, the text of that intervening column, in fact of the entire missing latter part of the scroll, in which the appropriate data for the second half-year were given.[19] Since Qumran sources do not record any harvest festival for this period, and since in our document the biblical festivals (such as fall in the seventh month) are not recorded, the roster of sabbaths and priestly courses was presumably punctuated only by references to the "first of the month(s)."

The small frg. (d) probably stems from one of the reconstructed columns (see above, pp. 331–32). However, as stated, no definite placement may be suggested on the basis of the few legible letters that are preserved.

Column I

1. השנה הראשו]נ֯ה בשמונה עשר בו שבת עׄ[ל יויריב
2.]בׄערב בעשרים וחמשה בו שבת על ידעיה ועלו[
3. מועד] הׄשעורים בעשרים וששה בו אחר שבת רוש החודש השׄ[ני
4. בששה ב֯ו֯] על [יׄ]דׄעיה בשנים בו שבת חרים בתשעה בו שבתׄ
5. שעורים] בששה עשר בו שבת מלכיה בעשרים ושלושה בׄ[ו
6. שבת מי]מין בשׄלושים בו שבת הקוץ רוש החודש
7. השלישי אחר שבת

17. If the restoration of השנה הראשו]נה], proposed below, is correct.

18. As stated, we cannot rule out the possibility that this roster was preceded by some other list or lists, just as in 4Q*321* two different accounts are combined. See Talmon and Knohl, "Fragments of a Calendrical Scroll."

19. In order to differentiate the partly extant columns from the altogether reconstructed ones, a zero 0 is prefixed to the numbers of the latter. See below, p. 340.

TRANSLATION[20]

1. The first ye]ar. On the eighteenth in it {= the first month, falls the} sabbath {on which} ent[ers Joiarib
2.]in the evening. On the twenty-fifth in it {falls the} sabbath {on which} enters Jedaiah and enter[
3. The festival of] the {first} grain {falls} on the twenty-sixth in it after {the} sabbath. The first of the second mon[th
4. {falls} on the sixth {day} in it {= the week of service in which} entered Jedaiah. On the second in it {= the second month, falls} Sabbath Harim.[21] On the ninth in it {falls} Sabbath
5. [Seorim. On the sixteenth in it {falls} Sabbath Malchijah. On the twenty-third of [it
6. {falls} Sabbath Mi]jamin. On the thir[ti]eth in it {falls} Sabbath Hakkoz. The first of the third
7. month {falls} after {the} sabbath

Line 1. I propose to restore השנה הראשו]נ̊ה̇ or השנה הרשו]נ̊ה̇ at the beginning of the line, as in 4Q*321* IV 8. The first legible letter is without doubt *he,* preceded by a partially preserved *nun.* The remaining letter traces cannot be read שי, as proposed by Wacholder and Abegg, who extracted this reading from the hand concordance and ensuingly restored the erroneous reading [ביום שלו]שי. Subsequently, they also entered another unwarranted ביום שלישי in line 2.[22] Here, as in other instances, Eisenman and Wise seem simply to have copied Wacholder and Abegg's restorations,[23] although they emphatically assert that they "have depended on no one else's work."[24] The untenable reading [ביום שלי]שי then led them to surmise that "fragment 1 concerns the period from Passover (1/14) until the first sabbath of the third month."[25] However, as stated, the biblical festivals are not recorded at all in this document. Eisenman and Wise did not attempt to interpret their reading [ביום שלישי] בערב in line 2 and justifiably so, because it cannot be explained. The phrase could refer only to the last day of Passover, which falls on the 21st of the first month, namely, between Sabbath Joiarib on the 18th and Sabbath Jedaiah on the 25th. However, the last day of Passover and also the last day of

20. Legend: Square brackets [ ] indicate lacunae in the text, curly brackets { } explanatory translation additions.

21. I capitalize *Sabbath* when the day is identified by the ensuing name of a *mišmar.*

22. B. Z. Wacholder and M. G. Abegg, *A Preliminary Edition of the Unpublished Dead Sea Scrolls* (Washington, 1991) 86.

23. R. Eisenman and M. Wise, *The Dead Sea Scrolls Uncovered* (Shaftesbury, 1992) 127.

24. Ibid., 9.

25. Ibid., 127.

the Sukkot Festival, which earn special mention in biblical ritual legislation (Exod 12:16, Lev 23:8, Num 28:18, Deut 16:8, Lev 23:39, Neh 8:18), are never itemized in Qumran calendrical documents.[26]

השנה הראשו]נׄהׄ. Before this opening phrase or superscription, a gap of 10–12 spaces must be presumed, unless it was preceded by the reference to החודש הר(א)שון 'the first month', with an inversion of the usual order, השנה הר(א)שונה החודש הראשון.[27]

בשמונה עשר. In this document the explication of the day always precedes the pronoun בו, which refers to the month, in this instance the first month, and the reference to the שבת that falls on that date, followed by the name of the priestly course.

עׄ]ל. A technical term that defines the entrance of a priestly course into the temple to begin its service. In other documents (e.g., miš C^{a-d}, 4Q*322–324*[a]) the term ביאת is employed, for which compare 2 Kgs 11:4–9. In rabbinic literature נכנס prevails in this context (*b. Ber.* 12a; *Sukk.* 52b, 56b; *Taᶜan.* 17a), but also עלה is used: הגיע זמן משמר לעלות כהנים ולוים עולים לירושלים (*b. Taᶜan.* 27a); שאפי׳ יהויריב ראש משמרת עולה לא ידחה ידעיה ממקומו (*b. Taᶜan.* 27a; cf. *Yebam.* 101a; *ᶜArak.* 13a).

יויריב]. I restored the short form, which prevails in other Qumran calendrical documents, as opposed to the longer form יהויריב in 1 Chr 24:7 and rabbinic literature. The proposed restoration of the text is virtually certain since the enumeration of the sabbaths of the priestly courses forms the framework of this document.

The account does not begin with the first day of the year, nor are the names of the 3 courses recorded that served during the first 18 days of the first month, namely, גמול (4 days), דליה, and מע(ו)זיה.[28] Rather, by opening with the mention of Joiarib, the list follows closely the roster of priestly courses in 1 Chr 24:7–18. In contrast, in the roster of priestly families who returned from the exile, Joiarib is placed 17th (Neh 12:6). The promotion of Joiarib to the head of the list was construed as corroborating the assumption that the 1 Chronicles version derives from the Maccabean Period and evidences a preference for this priestly house, which was presumably related to the Hasmoneans (1 Macc 2:1, 14:29;

26. This conspicuous absence needs to be considered separately.

27. As restored in 4Q*321* at the beginning of col. I, on the strength of the reading השנה ה[שנ]ית [הראשון (col. I 6), that is: The second year. The first {month}. See Talmon and Knohl, "Fragments of a Calendrical Scroll."

28. The forms מעוזיה and מעזיה (Neh 10:9; cf. 1 Chr 24:18—מעזיהו) are used in Qumran documents indiscriminately, one next to the other. See Talmon and Knohl, "Fragments of a Calendrical Scroll."

Josephus, *Life* 1.2).[29] But the argument is tenuous. The order of service of the priestly courses was subject to rotation (in the Qumran tradition in a six-year cycle). There is also no reason to doubt the veracity of the talmudic report that "the course of Joiarib was officiating when the Temple was destroyed" (*b. Taᶜan.* 29b; *ᶜArak.* 11b).

We must posit a gap of some 10–11 spaces at the end of line 1, and another of approximately 20 spaces at the beginning of line 2, unless these lines contained a portion of text that can no longer be retrieved.

Line 2. בׄערב. As in rabbinic tradition (*t. Sukk.* 4.24–25 [Zuck. 200, 10–13]; *y. Yoma* 2.39b; *b. Yoma* 26a; *b. Sukk.* 56b; cf. *ᶜArak.* 11b, *Taᶜan.* 29b; et al.), the turn of duty of a priestly course began and ended on the afternoon of a sabbath, and this שבת was named after it. However, the counting of a course's days of service began on the ensuing Sunday morning. Since this was the rule, the fact is mentioned only once, at the beginning of the document.[30]

ועלו. Thus also Eisenman and Wise. Wacholder and Abegg reproduce the concordance reading ועלי]ן, which is presumably erroneous. The third-person plural of the verb is not easily explained, since its subject is missing. It was possibly followed by the names of further משמרות, if in a week in which a festival fell more than one priestly course served, as attested in rabbinic tradition (*b. Sukk.* 56b, *Moᶜed Qat.* 17b).

Line 3. In the week of service of Jedaiah, on the 26th day of the first month, falls the 'Waving of the Omer' הנף העומר (4Q*321* V 4, 9; VI 7; 4Q*513* 3–4 [DJD 7.289]; 11QTemple XI 10, XVIII 9–12; XLIII 6; et al.),[31] here designated מועד] הׄשעורים, as in miš Eª I 4 (4Q*326*): ב26 בו מועד שׄ[עורים]. In 4Q*365ª* I 1 it appears to be named מועד הבכור]ים לדגן.[32]

In addition to the seriatim recording of the sabbaths and the "beginnings of the months," the document also lists the special Qumran festivals of the gathering of grapes and olives respectively, together with the "festival of the wood offering"[33] next to the festival of the barley harvest and presumedly the festival of the wheat harvest,[34] the only biblical feast mentioned. It should be noted that the three particular Qumran holy

29. See E. Schürer, *A History of the Jewish People in the Age of Jesus Christ* (175 B.C.–A.D. 135) (rev. and ed. by G. Vermes, F. Millar, and M. Black; Edinburgh, 1979) 2.245–50.

30. Therefore, בערב does not disprove my thesis that the Covenanters reckoned the day from the morning. See S. Talmon, "The Reckoning of the Day in Judaism of Biblical and Early Post-biblical Times: From the Morning or from the Evening?" in *Essays in Memory of Sarah Kamin* (ed. S. Japhet; Jerusalem, 1993) 109–29 [Heb.].

31. See Talmon, "Calendar of the Covenanters."

32. This unpublished document is quoted here, courtesy of Sidnie A. White.

33. See below frg. (b), col. III, line 7.

34. See below, col. 0II, line 2.

seasons are not recorded in *mišmarot* rosters, such as 4Q*320* and 4Q*321*, which register solely the biblical holy seasons, including הנף העומר and לחם בכורים or לחם תנופה, namely, חג השבועות (Lev 23:9–21), and the course in whose turn of service each falls.[35]

אחר שבת. Weekdays are referred to by cardinal numbers (see above), with the exception of the first day of the week, which is always called אחר שבת 'after the sabbath'. In Qumran literature this term is synonymous with the biblical designation ממחרת השבת (Lev 23:11, 15, 16). The term אחר שבת highlights a prominent feature of the Covenanters' calendar. Their starting point for counting 49 days from עמר התנופה the 'Waving of the Omer', ממחרת השבת, until the 'Festival of the First Wheat', לחם הבכורים (Lev 23:9–21), was always the first day of the week, actually the first Sunday after Passover, which falls on the 26th day of the first month. In other traditions, the count began on the Sunday within the week of Passover. Rabbinic law, on the other hand, took ממחרת השבת to refer to the morning after the first day of the Maṣṣot Festival, which may fall on any day of the week except Sunday, Wednesday,[36] or Friday.

רוש החודש. The 'first (or: the beginning) of the month', not 'new moon', since a solar calendar is involved.[37]

הש]ני. In contrast to the days of the month or the days in the week of service of a priestly course, the months are always designated by ordinal numbers.

Line 4. בששה בו]. The reference to the 'beginning of the month' precedes the reference to the day on which it falls in the week of service of the משמר, whereas as stated, the reference to a שבת is preceded by the date on which it falls.

Following the concordance, Wacholder and Abegg restored ביום] שׁי[ש, a patently wrong reading. The two dots before על are not the remains of the heads of the letters שי, but rather of בו. Eisenman and Wise again copied this restoration, even printing [הש]שי as if the letters שי were in fact extant. Wacholder and Abegg carefully indicated by superimposed

35. See Talmon and Knohl, "Fragments of a Calendrical Scroll." The most complete roster of "holy seasons" may be found in 4Q*326*, reconstructed on the basis of the extant fragments of the scroll. However, like 4Q*327*, that document does not mention names of priestly courses at all.

36. It should be noted that in the Covenanters' calendar, the Maṣṣot Festival always falls on a Wednesday. See Talmon, "Calendar of the Covenanters," *WQW*, 153–63.

37. The term 'new moon', which prevails in translations of *Jubilees* and *1 Enoch*, should accordingly be emended to 'beginning of the month', as in J. C. VanderKam's edition of *The Book of Jubilees* (Corpus Scriptorum Christianorum Orientalium 511, Scriptores Aethiopici 88; Louvain, 1989).

dots that they, or the concordance entry, propose to *restore* שׁ̇̇י. The glaring fallaciousness of reading ביום ש[שי] is proven by the fact that in our document, the noun יום 'day' is never employed. Days of the month and of the week of service of a priestly course are always designated by a number, in all instances by a cardinal and never by an ordinal number (see above, note on הש[ני]). The proposed restoration בששה] בוֹ tallies with this practice. In other *mišmarot* lists, as in some calendrical fragments, יום is employed as a component of the designation of a festival, such as [ב]יום השבׄת, יום הבכורים, יום הזכרון, יום הכיפורים (4Q*321* V 2, 6; VI 9), חג המצות יום רבי[עי], [י]ום הׄ[שבועות].[38]

על [י]ד̇עיה. When the a reference to the sabbath of a course is interrupted by a reference to a festival or to the 'beginning of the (next) month', the account resumes with the repetition of the name of the course listed before the insertion.

[י]ד̇עיה. Rabbinic traditions reflect a rivalry between this course and the course of יויריב. See *b. B. Qam.* 110a; *b. Ta^can.* 27b; *b. ^cArak.* 13a.

חרים. MT 1 Chr 24:8 has the defective spelling חרִם, but LXX(B) Χαρηβ possibly reflects the plene spelling חרים. Compare line 6, מי[מין], and MT 1 Chr 24:9, מִימִן.

Line 7. The long gap at the beginning of line 7 was presumably caused by a fault in the leather (see above, pp. 332–33).

Column 0II

1. [על הקוץ בשבעה בו שבת אביה בארבעה עשר בו שבת]
2. [על ישוע מועד החטים בחמשה עשר בו אחר שבת על]
3. [ישוע בעשרים ואחד בו שבת שכניה בעשרים ושמונה]
4. [בו שבת על אלישיב רוש החודש הרביעי בארבעה בו]
5. [על אלישיב בארבעה בו שבת יקים באחד עשר בו]
6. [שבת חופה בשמונה עשר בו שבת ישבאב בעשרים]
7. [וחמשה בו שבת בלגה רוש החודש החמשי אחר שבת]

TRANSLATION

1. [{in the week of service in which} entered Hakkoz. On the seventh in it {= the third month, falls} Sabbath Abijah. On the fourteenth in it {falls the} sabbath]

38. Practically every instance in which Eisenman and Wacholder restored יום in a *mišmarot* fragment is a blunder (e.g., 4Q*323^a* frg. 2 2; 3 3 [p. 123]; 4Q*323^c* frg. 1, line 4 [p. 124]). I shall discuss this technical terminology in detail in a separate publication.

2. [{on which} enters Jeshuah. The feast of the {first} wheat falls on the fifteenth in it after the sabbath {on which} entered]
3. [Jeshuah. On the twenty-first in it {falls} Sabbath Shecaniah. On the twenty-eighth]
4. [in it {falls the} Sabbath {on which} enters Eliashib. The first of the fourth month {falls} on the fourth {day} in it]
5. [{= the week of service in which} entered Eliashib. On the fourth in it {= the fourth month, falls} Sabbath Jakim. On the eleventh in it]
6. [{falls} Sabbath Huppah. On the eighteenth in it {falls} Sabbath Jeshebeab. On the twenty-]
7. [fifth in it {falls} Sabbath Bilgah. After {the} Sabbath {falls} the first of the fifth month]

Line 1. The reconstruction of this column follows the pattern of col. I. Line-divisions are conjectural.

Line 2. מועד החטים, the second annual harvest festival, with which ends the counting of 50 days from הנף העמר. This festival is variously designated in the *Temple Scroll*: לחם חטים . . . ביכורים (XVIII 13–14); חג הביכורים לדגן החטים (XLIII 6–7); חג ש[בועות הוא חג בכורים] (XIX 9). It is conjoined with the festivals of "the first wine" and "the first oil" in the triad ימי הביכורים לדגן לתי[רוש וליצהר (XLIII 3; cf. 4Q*261* [DJD 3.300]; 4Q*508* 13 [DJD 7.181]). In other Qumran writings, it is also referred to by the designations יום הביכורים (4Q*509* 131 ii 5), תפלה ליום ה[בכורים] (DJD 7.201 and several unpublished documents), or חג השבועים (miš A, 4Q*320*; miš B[a], 4Q*321*; 11QTemple XI 11, XXXVIII 4, LX 6, et al.).

Column III

1. [בששה בו על בלגה בשנים בו שבת על א]מׄר בשׄ[ל]וׄשה ב[ו
2. [מועד התירוש אחר שבת על אמר ב]תשעה בו שבת חזיר
3. [בששה עשר בו שבת הפצץ בעשרי]םׄ ושלושה בו שבת
4. [פתחיה בשלושים בו שבת על יחזקאל רו]שׄ [ה]חׄוׄדׄשׄ הששי
5. [אחר שבת על יחזקאל בשבעה בו שבת יכין בארב]עׄה עשׄר
6. [בו שבת גמול בעשרים ואחד בו שבת דליה בעשרים ו]שנים
7. [בו מועד היצהר אחר מועד היצהר מועד קרבן הע]צים

TRANSLATION

1. [on the sixth {day} in it {the week of service in which} entered Bilgah. On the second in it {= the fifth month, falls the} sabbath {on which} enters Imm]er. On the thi[r]d of [it
2. [{falls} the festival of the {first} wine after {the} sabbath (in the week in which} entered Immer. On] the ninth in it {falls} Sabbath Hezir.

3. On the sixteenth in it {falls} Sabbath Aphses. On the twenty]-third in it {falls} Sabbath
4. [Pethahiah. On the thirtieth in it {falls the} sabbath {on which} enters Jehezkel. The first of the] sixth month
5. [{falls} after {the} sabbath {on which} entered Jehezkel. On the seventh in it {= the sixth month, falls} Sabbath Jachin. On the fo]urteenth
6. [in it {falls} Sabbath Gamul. On the twenty-first in it {falls} Sabbath Delaiah. On the twenty]-second
7. [in it {falls} the festival of the {first} oil. After the festival of the {first} oil {falls} the festival of the offering of the w]ood.

Line 1. This column too is reconstructed in accordance with col. I. The length of the lines can be established on the basis of their extant endings.

The left upper part of a *mem* that precedes a *reš* makes the restoration אמר certain.

Line 2. מועד התירוש] 'the festival of the new wine', יין חדש (11QTemple XXI 7–10), the first of the Covenanters' special harvest festivals (see 11QTemple XXI 8, XLIII 1–4; 4Q*261* [DJD 3.300]; 4Q*508* 13 [DJD 7.181]).

Line 7. מועד היצהר] (4Q*261* [DJD 3.300]; 4Q*364*; 4Q*508* 13 [DJD 7.181]; 11QTemple XLIII 1, 9; et al.) or מועד השמן (4Q*327*), the *yaḥad*'s second special festival, at which the 'new oil' שמן חדש was offered (11QTemple XXI 14, XXII 4, XLIII 10; 4Q*365*^{a} I 1; et al.).[39]

מועד קרבן הע[צים], the third of the Covenanters' particular festivals (11QTemple XLIII 1–4; 4Q*327* II 9; 4Q*365*^{a} 23, line 9, cf. line 5). Wood was a sine qua non of the sacrificial service. Neh 10:35 relates that members of the postexilic community volunteered the supply of wood for the temple. In biblical times, 'wood cutters' חטבי עצים, like 'water carriers' שאבי מים, fulfilled important, albeit subsidiary, cultic functions at the 'altar of Yhwh' מזבח ה' (Josh 9:27b), on behalf of the entire community (9:27a, cf. 9:21; Deut 29:10), as a secondary echelon of the Levites (Ezra 2:43–54 = Neh 7:46–56).[40] In the *Testament of Levi* Abraham is accredited with having identified twelve aromatic species of wood, suited for the

39. The festivals of 'the new wine' and of 'the new oil' are presumably rooted in an earlier tradition. It is more than unlikely that the Covenanters innovated such festivals at Qumran under desert conditions that are certainly not propitious for the cultivation of vineyards and olive groves.

40. The potential linkage of the postexilic נתינים (Ezra 2:43–54 = Neh 7:46–56) with the Gibeonites of whom Joshua 9 speaks, can be mentioned here only en passant.

purpose, as long as they were "free of worms" (*T. Levi* 35:9–21, 36:19–21).[41] In rabbinic literature, the offering of wood is recurrently mentioned (*m. Šeqal.* 6:4; *b. Hor.* 20b; *b. Ta*ᶜ*an.* 28b; et al.). It was evidently much appreciated. On a day on which the wood offering was brought, the convocation of the laical מעמד was suspended (*m. Ta*ᶜ*an.* 4:4, 6). The מעמד was customarily "paired" with the concurrent priestly course that served in the temple. But no specific festival is mentioned in these contexts. However, it cannot be doubted that the Covenanters did not "innovate" this festival or the holy seasons of the first wine and the first oil, which must obviously have had a Sitz im Leben in a predominantly agricultural society. Rather, they gave a lease on life to customs that rabbinic tradition did not preserve, for reasons that can no longer be ascertained.[42]

Postscript

The foregoing presentation of 4Q*325* (miš D) reveals a telling difference between the Qumran calendrical documents and passages in *1 Enoch* and *Jubilees,* which are related to the very same solar calendar of 364 days.[43] The comments in the apocryphal books pertain, on the whole, to the basic principles of the solar calendar and its overall structure. They aim at presenting it as the exclusively legitimate Jewish chronometric system. The authors never tire of holding up this ephemeris as being infinitely superior to the lunar calendar to which the mainstream community adhered. But they do not delve into details, nor do they dwell on facets of the actual socioreligious rift in contemporary Judaism, triggered by the solar versus lunar calendar controversy. At no point do the apocryphal books reflect the realities of calendar controversy in a true-to-life setting. *1 Enoch* and *Jubilees* do not convey the picture of a structured community that promulgated the 364-day solar calendar and was engaged in a tangible dispute with another *Strömung,* or other *Strömungen,* in a contemporary Judaism that rejected this time system in favor of the 354-day lunar calendar.

41. See K. Beyer, *Die aramäischen Texte vom Toten Meer, samt den Inschriften aus Palästina, dem Testament Levis aus der Kairoer Genisa, der Fastenrolle und den alten talmudischen Zitaten* (Göttingen, 1984) 199–200.

42. It is of interest to note that in the detailed description of Noah's celebration of the feast day at the beginning of a new year, the author of *Jubilees* (7:1–6) adds oil and wine to the sacrifice, which, in regard to the animals offered on the occasion, reflects Abraham's covenant sacrifice (Gen 15:9–10).

43. My comments are aimed only at the calendar proper, to the exclusion of astronomical details in which the "Book of the Heavenly Luminaries" (*1 Enoch* 72–82) abounds.

The very opposite holds true for the literature of the Covenanters. As stated, not one calendrical Qumran document conveys a full-fledged picture of the solar calendar, commenting on and summarizing its structure.[44] Every one of the diverse sources dwells solely on selected features of the phenomenon. But all have a bearing on specific facets of the Covenanters' communal organization and cultic life.

In sum, behind *Jubilees* and *1 Enoch* stand undeterminable groups in ancient Judaism of the "Enoch circles" type. In contrast, the Qumran documents emanate from a structured socioreligious entity. The authors of *1 Enoch* and *Jubilees* concern themselves predominantly with "calendar-orthodoxy"; Qumran authors with "calendar-praxis." The apocryphal works echo theory; the Qumran writings breathe actuality.

44. I would suggest that the itemized roster of "David's Compositions" (J. A. Sanders, *The Psalms Scroll of Qumran Cave 11* [DJD 4; Leiden, 1965] 48, 91–93 [11QPs[a] XVI]) in an indirect way comes closest to a comprehensive presentation of the 364-day calendar

לא נס לחה 'He Had Not Become Wrinkled' (Deuteronomy 34:7)

Jeffrey H. Tigay

The statement in Deut 34:7 that, when Moses died at the age of 120, לא נס לחה *has been given a variety of interpretations, most commonly that Moses' 'moisture' in the sense of 'natural force' or 'vigor' had not left him. However, there is no evidence that* לח *means 'vigor', and in any case, according to Deut 31:2, Moses had lost his vigor.*

In this article I argue that in Deut 34:7 לח *'moisture' refers to lubricity in the sense of freshness and smoothness of the skin; despite his extreme old age, Moses' skin had not become wrinkled. This interpretation, first proposed by Ibn Ezra, is supported by the semantic parallel of Northwest Semitic* עדן, *which, as Jonas Greenfield showed, connotes luxuriance, particularly liquid luxuriance, and is used in the Talmud to refer to "the lubricious quality of the skin due to its being moist and freshened," that is, unwrinkled. On the basis of this interpretation, it is likely that the verb* נס *does not mean 'departed' but, as suggested by Ibn Janaḥ and R. Joseph Qimḥi, 'dried up', cognate to Arabic nassa (n-s-s) 'to dry up', used of bread.*

According to Deut 34:7, when Moses died at the age of 120 "his eyes were undimmed" and, the text adds, לא נס לחה. The latter phrase has been given a variety of interpretations. Several ancient translations—perhaps influenced by the parallel term *eyes*, referring to a facial feature—assumed that לחה was derived from לחי 'cheek, jaw' and took the phrase to mean that Moses' cheeks did not become sunken or that he did not lose the teeth of

Author's note: Jonas Greenfield's article "A Touch of Eden," which inspired the present article, provides an apt metaphor for Jonas Greenfield himself as a scholar and as a colleague. For students of every branch of Semitic studies, Jonas Greenfield's publications have been extraordinarily suggestive, filled as they are with כל עץ נחמד למראה and, especially, נחמד להשכיל. As a colleague, his implicit motto has been מכל עץ הגן אכול תאכל. No scholar surpasses him in the unstinting generosity of his assistance and advice. It is a pleasure to take part in this tribute to a seminal scholar and a dear friend.

his jaws.[1] However, as R. Joseph Qimḥi observed, this is morphologically excluded, since לחֹה lacks the final *yod*, which is preserved in the suffixed forms of לחי, as in לחיו in Job 40:26 (cf. לחיה in Lam 1:2).[2]

By far the best known interpretation, proferred by the medieval grammarians[3] and found in most English translations[4] is that Moses' 'natural force' or 'vigor' did not leave him. This interpretation is based on the derivation of לחֹה from לח 'fresh, moist',[5] and נס from נוס 'flee', hence 'depart'. This derivation of לחֹה is unproblematic, but there are two difficulties with taking 'moisture' to mean 'vigor':

(a) There is no evidence for the use of לח to mean 'vigor'. That it had such a meaning might be argued on the basis of the cognate לחלוחית 'moistness' in Rabbinic Hebrew.[6] A number of passages in rabbinic literature use לחלוחית to describe people who have not lost their youthful vigor. For example, R. Eleazar explains that Joab did not follow Absalom because עדיין ליחלוחית של דוד קיימת 'David was still in possession of his vigor' (*b. Sanh.* 49a). However, the spelling לחלוחית is not certain. In the other three passages where this usage is found, all in *Midraš Genesis Rabbah*, the London manuscript that served as the basis for the Theodor-Albeck edition reads לכל(ו)כית instead of לחלוחית. For example, in *Gen. Rab.* 48:16, R. Ammi explains the difference between two verses saying that Abraham was old: כאן זקנה שיש בה לכלכית, להלן זקנה שאין בה לכלכית 'Here [in Gen 18:11] it refers to old age where there is still vigor;

1. LXX, Χελυνια 'jaw, lip' (H. G. Liddell and R. Scott, eds., *A Greek-English Lexicon* [rev. H. S. Jones; Oxford, 1985] 1987, col. ii, s.v. Χελυνη); *Targum Jonathan*, ניבי ליסתיה 'the teeth of his jaws'; Vulgate, *dentes* 'teeth'; Peshiṭta, לא אתקמטו פכוהי 'his cheeks had not become sunken, or shriveled'. Cf. *Midraš Tannaim*, p. 227 top (הא בלחייו שלמתים נפסק; *Midraš Hagadol* has a variant נפרק); Rabbenu Meyuḥas, המתים להשמט לחייהם. Some of the targums interpret in a more general way that it was simply Moses' facial appearance that had not changed. Thus the *Fragment Targum* renders לא אישתנו זיויהון דאפוי; *Targum Neofiti*, לא אשתניו זיווהון דאפוי; and *Onqelos*, לא שנא זיו יקרא דאפוהי (interestingly, the *Fragment Targum* and *Onqelos* use exactly the same terms for the skin of Moses's face in Exod 34:29–35, and Neofiti uses זיו איקרהון, as does *Onqelos* here). This view is found in *Midraš Lekaḥ Ṭov* (כי קרן עור פניו, שלא נשתנה אדמות פניו מדמות שהיה מהר סיני) and Rashi (ולא נהפך תאר פניו).

2. ספר הגלוי, H. J. Mathews (ed.), *Sepher Ha-galuj* (Berlin, 1887) 8 (ref. courtesy of Uri Melammed). See also Isa 50:6; Hos 11:4; Job 16:10; Cant 1:10, 5:13; and Ezek 29:4.

3. See the dictionaries of Ibn Janaḥ and Qimḥi (s.v. לוח and נוס), the translation of Saadia (רטובתה), and the *Samaritan Targum* (רטובה).

4. The KJV, Leeser, and the RSV have 'natural force'; Moffatt, NEB, NAB, and the *Jerusalem Bible* have 'vigor'; the NIV has 'strength'.

5. Cf. renditions of this phrase as 'freshness' (Luzzatto: 'freschezza'; Field, *Hexapla*: *viror* ['greenness']; Yehoash: פרישקייט; Keil-Delitzsch).

6. See A. van Selms, "A Forgotten God: Laḥ," in *Studia Biblica et Semitica: Theodoro Christiano Vriezen . . . Dedicata* (Wageningen, 1966) 318–26 (ref. courtesy of Uri Melammed). Rashi implicitly compares לחֹה with לחלוחית in its literal sense of 'moistness'; see below, n. 10.

later [in 24:1] it refers to old age where there is no vigor'.[7] לחלוחית and לכלוכית may be two separate words, not necessarily related to each other, despite the fact that they share the meaning 'moistness'. Hence, if the original form of the one used for 'vigor' was indeed spelled with *kap*, it may not be related to biblical לח. This would explain why none of the targums or commentaries of the talmudic period rendered, or glossed, לחה with the rabbinic word; had it been spelled לחלוחית at the time, it would have been natural for them to do so.

(b) If the rabbinic term is unrelated to biblical לח, it is nevertheless semantically parallel to the alleged meaning of לח in Deut 34:7. However, an equally serious objection to לחה meaning 'vigor' is that, according to Deut 31:2, Moses had in fact lost his vigor. Some scholars have inferred from the putative inconsistency that 34:7b is not Deuteronomic,[8] thus circumventing the problem. However, there are no other grounds for separating v. 7b from its context and assigning it to a different source. As G. A. Smith observed, "the phrase cannot be assigned to one source more than another."[9] Even if the phrase were demonstrably non-Deuteronomic, it would not necessarily follow that its source disagreed with Deuteronomy's very plausible assertion that Moses had been weakened by extreme old age. Hence it would be best to find a suitable connotation of 'moistness' that does not entail an inconsistency with Deut 31:2.

In fact, 'natural force' or 'vigor' is not the only possible connotation of moistness. R. Eliezer b. Yaakov in the *Sipre* took the phrase to mean that Moses' body did not dry up, but this is based on his view that the passage refers to the preservation of Moses's body after death.[10] Albright took 'moistness' as referring to sexual power, which Moses allegedly had not lost at the age of 120.[11] However, this hardly suits the context (we

7. Ed. Theodor-Albeck, 493. See also *Gen. Rab.* 61:2 and 79:1 (ed. Theodor-Albeck, 658 and 938). MS Vat. 30 reads לכל(ו)כית in the first two passages; in the third it reads לחלוחית (presumably either the scribe or the author of the midraš chose a spelling that matched כלח in Job 5:26, which the midraš is interpreting). For the verb לכלך see M. Sokoloff, *A Dictionary of Palestinian Jewish Aramaic* (Ramat-Gan, 1990) 283; H. Yalon, פרקי לשון (Jerusalem, 1971) 412–13. Similar variant readings are found in the Ibn Tibbon translation of Maimonides' *Guide*, III:46: the main text reads ומלכלכים, and a variant reads ומלחלחים (New York, 1946) 58a.

8. See, for example, the commentaries of Dillmann (KeH, 2d ed., 1886), Bertholet (KHC, 1899) and Steuernagel (HKAT, 2d ed., 1923).

9. Cambridge Bible (1918).

10. *Sifre Deuteronomy* (ed. L. Finkelstein) 429. He is followed by Rashi, who paraphrases לחלוחית שבו, שלא שלט בו רקבון (decomposition).

11. W. F. Albright ("The 'Natural Force' of Moses in the Light of Ugaritic," *BASOR* 94 [1944] 32–35), perhaps inspired by 'virility' in *The Bible: An American Translation* (repr. Chicago, 1975).

never hear that Moses fathered children after leaving Midian, let alone in old age), and Albright later abandoned the suggestion.[12]

No better ideas are suggested by the closest parallels to Deut 34:7, namely, the descriptions of Adad-guppi, mother of Nabonidus, who lived to the age of 104, and Si'-gabbar, priest of Nerab. Adad-guppi's inscription states that to the end of her life, "my eyesight was good, my hearing excellent, my hands and feet were sound, my words well chosen, food and drink agreed with me, and my mind happy." Si'-gabbar's inscription states that until the day of his death, "[his] mouth was not seized, preventing speech" and that he was able to see his descendants with his own eyes. Both of these descriptions refer to the retention of eyesight, as does Deut 34:7 but none of the other faculties described could be described as a retention of 'moistness'.[13]

In his study of the Northwest Semitic root עדן on the basis of the bilingual Akkadian-Aramaic inscription from Tell Fakherye in Syria, Jonas Greenfield provides an important clue to the meaning of 'moistness' in Deut 34:7. He shows that עדן connotes luxuriance, particularly liquid luxuriance, and that it was used to refer to freshness and smoothness of the skin.[14] This is indeed an appropriate connotation of moistness in the context of aging. According to *The Wellness Encyclopedia* of the University of California, Berkeley:

> With age, the skin gradually loses its elasticity and becomes thinner and drier. Because of the effect of gravity, skin may begin to sag . . . these developments affect facial skin, causing wrinkles and bags under the eyes . . . a moisturizer can help make the skin feel smooth, temporarily prevent moisture loss from the cells, and decrease the fine lines caused by dryness . . . .[15]

12. According to Marvin H. Pope in RSP III, 369.

13. See the translations in *ANET* (A. L. Oppenheim [trans.], "Babylonian and Assyrian Historical Texts," 561c; and F. Rosenthal [trans.], "Canaanite and Aramaic Inscriptions," 661d); and the study by H. Tawil, "Some Literary Elements in the Opening Sections of the Hadad, Zakir, and Nerab II Inscriptions in the Light of East and West Semitic Royal Inscriptions," *Or* 43 (1974) 60–63. Other descriptions of old age cited by Tawil are no more suggestive, nor is 2 Sam 19:36. Another characteristic of Moses paralleled in royal inscriptions is his ענוה (Num 12:3) 'piety'; see the comment of J. Milgrom, *Numbers* (*JPS Torah Commentary* [Philadelphia, 1990] ad loc.), and then the remarks of Tawil, "Some Literary Elements," 51–55.

14. J. C. Greenfield, "A Touch of Eden," in *Orientalia J. Duchesne-Guillemin Emerito Oblata* (Leiden, 1984) 223–24.

15. *The Wellness Encyclopedia*, from the Editors of the University of California, Berkeley, *Wellness Newsletter* (Boston, 1991) 287.

Greenfield notes that (1) in Ugaritic, the verb ᶜ*dn* is used for providing luxuriant rainfall; (2) in Rabbinic Hebrew it is used for freshening the skin and body by lubricating them with oil and for rain freshening soil and grass; (3) in Sarah's comment in Gen 18:12, אחרי בלותי היתה לי עדנה, the noun עדנה is used in contrast to בלותי 'I am withered' and refers to "the lubricious quality of the skin due to its being moist and freshened"; and (4) this was understood in the Talmud, which describes the fulfillment of Sarah's words thus: "After the skin had withered (נתבלה) and wrinkles multiplied, the skin was freshened (נתעדן) and the wrinkles became smooth, and beauty returned" (*b. B. Meṣ.* 87a; נתעדן is used the same way in the identical description of Jochebed's rejuvenation in *b. B. Bat.* 120a). In sum, the restoration of moistness to Sarah's skin led to the disappearance of her wrinkles. This suggests that Moses' moistness, לחה, may also refer to unwrinkled skin.

In fact, this is how Ibn Ezra interprets לא נס לחה. He comments that לחה is derived from לח 'moistness' and explains, 'for dryness overcomes the aged; and נס means the opposite of stretch (tight)' (כי היבשות תתגבר על הזקן, וטעם "נס" הפך מתח). Although his comment is characteristically terse, it is convincingly explained in the supercommentaries. According to Solomon Zalman Netter, Ibn Ezra understands נס here not as 'flight' but as shriveling and dryness, the opposite of tightness and smoothness, meaning that Moses' moistness did not shrivel and dry up but remained as it was, for when the face is full of moistness the skin is stretched out, but the reverse is true when the moistness of the face departs: it shrivels.[16] Another supercommentator, Judah Leib Krinski, held that Ibn Ezra did understand נס as 'departed', but otherwise he agreed with Netter: a young person's skin is full of moistness and is therefore stretched over his flesh, but in old age the moistness departs and his skin becomes wrinkled. Krinski even cited Rashbam's comment on Sarah's statement in Gen 18:12, a comment that is simply a verbatim quotation from *b. B. Meṣ.* 87a, cited above. In sum, Krinski concluded, Ibn Ezra means that Moses never showed visible signs of old age, since his moistness never departed and his skin remained as smooth as in his youth.[17]

Ibn Ezra's explanation, I believe, is the correct one. It is consistent with Deut 31:2 and now has the support of an apt semantic parallel in the use of עדן.

16. Netter's supercommentary was first published in 1859. I am citing it from the Ḥoreb edition of *Miqraᵓot Gedolot* (London and New York, 1948).

17. חומש מחוקקי יהודה (1907–28).

Netter's and Krinski's disagreement over the meaning of נס leads us back to one further contribution of the medieval grammarians to the understanding of לא נס לחֹה. A verb meaning 'flee' is far from being a natural predicate for 'moistness'. According to Ibn Janaḥ and R. Joseph Qimḥi, נס in Deut 34:7 is not from נוס 'flee' but from a different verb, cognate to Arabic *nassa* (*n-s-s*) 'dry up', used of bread.[18] The same explanation is proposed by Ehrlich, who notes that it requires vocalizing the *nun* with a *pataḥ* instead of a *qameṣ*.[19]

All of the above considerations indicate that לא נס לחֹה means that the moistness of Moses's skin had not dried up, that he had not become wrinkled in his old age but retained the smoothness of his skin to the end of his life.

18. *Sepher Ha-galuj*, 8, cited by R. David Qimḥi, ספר השרשים, 423 s.v. נוס. For the Arabic verb, see Freytag 4:270. Ibn Janaḥ says the same, though he concedes that derivation from נוס (meaning העברה) is tolerable.

19. A. B. Ehrlich, *Randglossen zur hebräischen Bibel* (repr. Hildesheim, 1968) 392. See GKC §67a, b, and bb.

A Paraphrase of Exodus: 4Q*422*

Emanuel Tov

4Q 422 contains a paraphrase of the beginning chapters of Genesis (frgs. 1–9) and Exodus (frg. 10a–e). In this article I will deal with the Exodus section, which contains a paraphrase of a section of the book of Exodus (the plagues and some of the events leading up to them). The wording of the Bible is often recognizable in single words and phrases, and at the same time one notices elements reflecting exegesis of the biblical text. It is not clear whether the text once covered larger sections of Exodus. The sequence of the plagues is close to that of Exodus and Psalm 105. At the same time, in the description of the plagues, the wording of 4Q 422 depends in the first place on the historical Psalm 78, second on Psalm 105, and third on the account in Exodus. The text displays no signs of the special exegesis or ideas of the Qumran community. The article contains an introduction to 4Q 422, as well as a transcription, translation, and commentary.

4Q*422* contains a paraphrase of the beginning chapters of Genesis (frgs. 1–9) and Exodus (frgs. 10a–e), followed by at least one sheet. Both sections derived from one composition, written by the same hand and deriving from the same scroll (cf. the similar shape of the fragments).[1] The final publication of this composition will be produced jointly by T. Elgvin and me. Elgvin will be responsible for the section on Genesis, and I will be responsible for the section on Exodus. The present article, dedicated to J. C. Greenfield, deals only with Exodus. At an earlier stage these fragments were named "Traditions on Genesis," even though the fragments transcribed below pertain to the book of Exodus.

Author's note: I am grateful to E. Qimron, who greatly improved our understanding of this document by placing four of the fragments in the correct sequence and by improving several readings. I further benefited a great deal from remarks by E. Larson.

1. This issue is treated in detail in a forthcoming DJD edition (volume 13). The Genesis and Exodus fragments have one additional significant phenomenon in common: the two layers of writing on some fragments (on which see below).

The Exodus section contains a paraphrase of a section of the book of Exodus (the plagues and some of the events leading up to them). The wording of the Bible is often recognizable in single words and phrases, and at the same time one notices elements reflecting exegesis of the biblical text (for both, see the comments). Other elements in the text, not understandable because of its fragmentary condition, are probably exegetical as well. It is not clear whether the fragments once covered larger sections of Exodus. The sequence of the plagues is close to that of Exodus and also to Psalm 105, on which see the comments. At the same time, in the description of the plagues, the wording of 4Q*422* depends in the first place on the historical Psalm 78, second on Psalm 105, and third on the account in Exodus. The text displays no signs of the special exegesis or ideas of the Qumran community.

Physical Description (Exodus Fragments)

The color of the leather is faded brown. The left margin measures 1.4 cm, followed by stitches at the end of the sheet. The right margin is partially preserved. The distance between the lines is 0.7–0.9 cm from the base of one line to the base of the next. The fragments are extremely translucent. An additional layer of writing, discernible at the ends of the lines of the columns on frg. 10e and quite visible on photograph PAM 42.820, is now very faint on the fragment itself. This writing starts at a certain point on the fragment, some two cm before the end of the writing block, parallel to most lines of the fragment. The stitching and guide dots are more visible on photograph PAM 42.820 than on the later photograph PAM 43.540. The length of the writing block may be calculated as an average of 85 spaces on the basis of frg. 10, lines 8–10. In absolute terms, the length of the line is 16 cm. Among the Qumran fragments a column block of this size is considered above average. The fragments of 4Q*422* are arranged in three columns, of which the Exodus fragments constitute col. III.

In calculating the length of the lines the following assumptions are taken into consideration:[2]

2. Fragments 10b and d constitute part of the reconstruction, which juxtaposes the six fragments into a column structure. Among other things, frg. 10b contains a phrase in line 6 referring to the third plague in the Exodus account, and frg. 10d reflects a phrase in line 10 describing the plague of the locusts. In our view, these fragments fit perfectly into the reconstruction. At the same time, according to information provided by J. Strugnell, when the fragments were found, frg. 10d was on top of frg. 10b, and indeed the two fragments have similar elements. This position may indicate that these two fragments belonged to different layers and hence different columns. If this information is correct, the fragments would have to be arranged differently, but this seems less likely from the point of view of content.

a b c d e

Figure 1. 4Q422. PAM 43.540. Courtesy of the Israel Antiquities Authority.

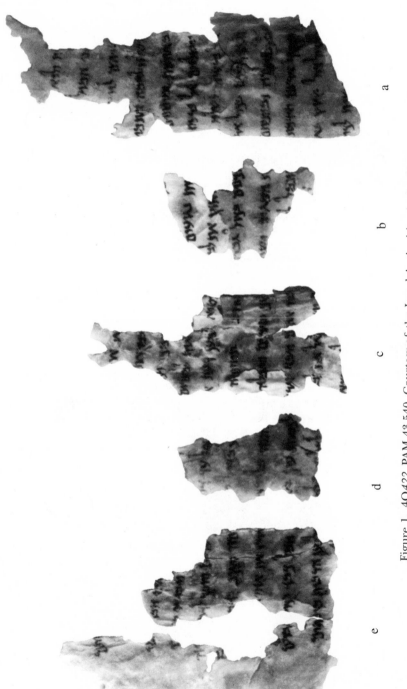

1. Fragment 10b was situated very close to frg. 10a because of the context created by the beginning of line 8.
2. According to frg. 10, lines 7–10, three or four letters are missing between frgs. 10b and 10c.
3. The distance between frgs. 10c and 10d varies in accordance with the shape of the fragments from 4 or 5 letters to 1 letter. The remainder of a letter to the right of לכסות on line 10 probably is the *he* of the preceding word ארב֯ה֯, so that in this line the fragments are close to each other.
4. In frg. 10, lines 9 and 11, three spaces were lacking between frgs. 10d and 10e.

Orthography and Morphology

The fragments reflect the so-called Qumran practice of orthography and morphology. For the pronominal suffix of the third-person plural, see להמה in frg. 10, line 4; מ֯ימׄ]יהמה in frg. 10, line 7; [בב]תיהמה and פ[ ]המה in frg. 10, line 8;[3] and מקׄניהמה and ב֯[בתי]המה in frg. 10, line 9. Note further the spellings מו]שה in frg. 10, line 4; פרעוה in frg. 10, lines 6–7; לוא in frg. 10, line 1; and כול in frg. 10, lines 8, 10, 11, 12. The word ליוא]ר in frg. 10, line 3 should probably be viewed as an unusual spelling of ליאר 'to the Nile', analogous to such spellings as מואדה. The word ר֯שית[, *si vera lectio,* in frg. 10, line 12, is a typical Qumran spelling for ראשית. The evidence for the Qumran practice is admittedly limited, but there are no spellings or forms contradicting the assumption that 4Q*422* is written in the Qumran practice, with the exception of ב]נׄיהם in frg. 10, line 3. Note further the defective spelling of חסל in line 10, possibly reflecting *ḥasal* rather than *ḥasil.*

Fragment 10a–e

(Mus. Inv. 166 [earlier numbers SL 59, 62], PAM 40.966, 41.478, 41.856, 42.820*, 43.540)

top margin

1.	[ ]ת ולוא [		[
2.	[ש]תׄי המיל]דות	[? *vac*]	*vac* [
3.	[ב]נׄיהם ליוא[ר] ◦ [	]אר או[	א]ותם
4.	[ו]ישלח להמה את מוׄ]שה	ויראה]במראת[הסנה הבוער ?	◦ [

3. For similar cases of a *he* added to the final *mem*, see J. P. Siegel, *The Scribes of Qumran: Studies in the Early History of Jewish Scribal Customs, with Special Reference to the Qumran Biblical Scrolls and to the Tannaitic Traditions of Massekheth Soferim* (Ph.D. diss., Brandeis University, 1972) 134ff.

.5 באותות ומופתים[ ]ת֯מכו ועׄ[
] ∘∘∘ חבר֯[ ]מרׄ

.6 וישלחם אל פרעוה֯[ ]∘ות נגועים [ ] נ֯פ֯[ל]אות למצרים[ ]ד֯[
] ויביאו ד֯ב֯ר֯ו

.7 אל פרעוה לשלח א֯[ת עמם ו]יחזק את לב[ו ל]חׄטוא למען דעת
א[נשי ישר]אל עד דו[רות]עול֯ם ויופך לדם[מימ]יהמ֯ה

.8 הצפרדעים בכול ארצ֯[ם ?] וכנים בכול גבול֯[ם]עׄרוב [בב]תיהסה
ו֯[יפג]ע בכול פ[ ]הסה ויגוף בדב[ר את/כול]

.9 מקׄניׄהסה ובהמתם ל֯[מו]תׄ הסגירׄ ישי[ת חו]שכ בארצׄם ואפלה
ב֯[בתי]הסה בלירא[ה] איש את אחיוׄ[ויך]

.10 בברד ארצם ואדמת[ם ב]חנמל לה֯[אביד כו]ל֯ פרי אוכׄ[ל]ם ויבא ארב֯ה֯
לכסות עין ה֯אׄ[רצ] חסל כבד בכול֯ גׄבולם

.11 לאכול כול ירוק בא[רצם]לׄ[ ]ם֯ ויח֯[זק]אל את לב [פרעו]ה֯
לבׄל֯ת֯י֯[ש]לח[ם]ו֯למׄען הרבות מופתים

.12 [ויך בכורם]ר֯שית לכו[ל אונם]ל∘[ ]∘הא[ ]ל֯[ ] ∘ ל[
]∘[[

Notes on Readings

At the end of line 5, in the margin, slightly below the last letter, as well as above the last word in line 10, there may be remnants of several letters, eaten out in the leather.

Furthermore, in frg. 10e several lines of additional letters are visible, very close to the bottom of the preceding lines (especially on photograph PAM 42.820) between most lines of the text. The additional writing starts at exactly the same point in the line, about 1 cm from the left edge of the fragment. The following letters may be read, all being imprints of words on frg. 10c:

1. מכו (between lines 5–6) from תמכו 10c, line 5
2. אות (between lines 6–7) from נפלאות 10c, line 6
3. למען (between lines 7–8) from 10c, line 7
4. בבתי (between lines 8–9) from בבתיהסה 10c, line 8
5. רצם וא (between lines 9–10) from בארצם ואפלה 10c, line 9
6. לם בא (between lines 10–11) from אוכלם ויבא 10c, line 10

An additional layer of writing is similarly visible on other fragments of 4Q*422*, as analyzed by T. Elgvin in the forthcoming DJD publication.

Lines 7–8. Note the *he* written vertically in the margin between these two lines. The letter is preceded by what looks like a horizontal line together with a hole in the leather with a minute speck of ink. The line is visible on photograph PAM 42.820, but not on the later photograph, PAM 43.540, or on the fragment itself. Following a suggestion by E. Qimron, I read מימ]יהמ̊ה, assuming that the last two letters were written vertically. Vertical writing of letters in the margin is not unprecedented (cf. cols. XXVIII, XXX, and XXXII in 1QIsa[a]), but it is surprising here, since there would have been space for two letters after the last *he* on the line.

Line 7. לב]ו. The speck of ink above the *bet* on photograph PAM 42.820 is probably too high to represent a *waw.*

Line 9. הסגיר̇. There seems to be a crossbar at the bottom of the last letter, but it nevertheless does not have the shape of a *bet.*

Translation

1.]and not [
2. the t[wo] mid[wives
3. their so[ns] to the Nile [. . .]them
4. [and] He sent them Mo[ses . . . and He appeared] in the vision of[the burning bush ?]
5. with signs and wonders[. . .] ? [
6. [and] He sent them to Pharaoh[. . .] . . . plagues . . . [won]ders for the Egyptians[. . .]and they reported His word
7. to Pharaoh to let [their people go. And] he hardened [his] heart [so that he would] sin in order that the pe[ople of Isra]el would know ⟨it⟩ until eternal gene[rations]. He turned their [water] to blood.
8. The frogs [were] in all [their] land and lice throughout [their] territory, gnats (?) [in] their [hou]ses and [they afflic]ted all their . . . and He smote with pestilen[ce all]
9. their livestock and their animals He delivered to d[eat]h. He plac[ed dark]ness in their land and gloom in their [houses] in order that no one would be able to see the others.[And He smote]
10. their land with frost and [their] land [with] hail to des[troy al]l the fruit which they eat. And He brought the locust to cover the face of the ear[th], heavy locust in all of their territory,
11. to eat every plant in the la[nd . . . ,] and God har[dened] the heart of [Phara]oh as to not let [them] go and in order to multiply wonders.
12. [And He afflicted their firstborn,]the prime of al[l their strength

Comments

Fragment 10 first briefly mentions several events leading up to the description of the plagues: the two midwives, the throwing of the sons of the Israelites into the Nile, the appearance of God (in the burning bush?), the sending of Moses and Aaron to Pharaoh, and the hardening of Pharaoh's heart. Then 4Q*422* describes the plagues in detail, beginning with the plague of the blood.

The basic sequence of the plagues is that of Exodus, as distinct from Psalms 78 and 105. Missing from the list is the plague of the boils.[4] Note that this plague is the only one that is not mentioned in Psalm 105 and one of the four plagues not mentioned in Psalm 78. In the sequence of the last four plagues one notes the following divergence from the account in Exodus:

Plague	*Exodus*	*4Q422*
blood	1	1
frogs	2	2
lice	3	3
gnats (?)	4	4
pestilence	5	5
boils	6	- ?
hail	7	7
locusts	8	8
darkness	9	6
firstborn	10	9

In the description of the last four plagues, the plague of darkness is mentioned before the plagues of hail, locusts, and the firstborn. In this respect the sequence of 4Q*422* is identical with that of Psalm 105, where the last plagues appear in the following sequence: hail (vv. 32–33), locusts (34–35), and death of the firstborn (36).[5]

Line 2. ש[ת̇י המיל]דות. For the two midwives, cf. Exod 1:15–22. The exact phrase does not occur in the Bible.

Line 3. ב[נ̇יהם ליוא]ר. Cf. Exod 1:22.

Line 4. ו[ישלח להמה את מו̇]שה. Cf. Ps 105:26: שלח משה עבדו אהרן אשר בחר בו. See further Exod 3:15.

Line 4. ויראה [במראת] הסנה הבוער?. The single preserved word probably referred to one of the appearances of God to Moses. According to the sequence of events recorded in 4Q*422*, the text probably refers to

4. See, however, the comments on line 7.

5. For a recent analysis of the description of the plagues in Exodus and elsewhere in the Bible, see Z. Zevit, "The Priestly Redaction and Interpretation of the Plague Narrative in Exodus," *JQR* 66 (1976) 193–211 (with bibliography).

Exod 3:3, where מראה refers to God's appearance in the burning bush. On the other hand, according to the sequence of events in Exodus, God first appears to Moses, and only afterwards is Moses sent to his people. Here the sequence is reversed. Possibly 4Q*422* first refers to the sending of Moses referred to in chap. 3 and afterwards to the appearance of God in chap. 6.

Line 5. באותות ומופתים[. The phrase occurs in Exod 7:3; Deut 4:34, 6:22, 7:19, 29:2, 34:11; Jer 32:20; Ps 78:43, 105:27, 135:9; and Neh 9:10, always with reference to the miracles performed in Egypt. The phrase is also used in 4Q*392* 2 2 ("liturgical work"). According to the sequence of the events in this text, this phrase in 4Q*422* probably refers to the wonders of Moses (compare האתת in Exod 4:30) performed for the people or before Pharaoh (compare מופת in 7:9). In any event, this line is probably not referring to the ten plagues, which are mentioned below, from line 6 onward.

Line 6. וישלחם אל פרעוׄה[. 'And He sent them [that is, Moses and Aaron] to Pharaoh'. The names of Moses and Aaron were probably mentioned in the lacuna at the end of line 5.

Line 6.]◦ות נגועים. A possible reconstruction is להר]א֯ות נגועים 'to show plagues (. . . to the Egyptians)'.

Line 6. נגועים. This word serves as the plural of נֶגַע 'stroke, plague'.[6] This noun occurs in the biblical account of the plagues only with reference to the death of the firstborn.

Line 6.]נ֯פ֯[ל]אות למצרים[. Cf. Ps 135:9: שלח אתות ומפתים בתוככי מצרים. Possibly unidentified frg. O,]םׄ מופ]תים, should to be placed in the lacuna after this phrase.

Line 7. לשלח א֯]ת עמם. Cf. Exod 4:23; 5:1; 7:16, 26; 8:16; 9:1, 13; 10:3.

Line 7. ו]יחזק את לב[ו. Cf. Exod 7:13: ויחזק לב פרעה. In the present context Pharaoh hardens his own heart, as in Exod 7:13, before the plagues take place, while in the course of the description of the plagues God hardens his heart (thus line 11 here; see below). Cf. Exod 9:12: ויחזק יהוה את לב פרעה. See further Exod 10:20, 27; 11:10; 14:8.

Line 7. למען דעת א[נשי ישר]אל עד דו[רות]עו֯לם. Less likely: א[יש ישר]אל. Unlikely: א[ל ישר]אל or א[לוהי ישר]אל. E. Qimron suggests א[ת יד]אל. The reconstruction of the last word in the line, מימ]יהמ֯ה, requires an antecedent referring to the land of Egypt, but that word cannot easily be

6. See E. Qimron, *The Hebrew of the Dead Sea Scrolls* (HSS 29; Atlanta, 1986) 111.

fit into the present context. For the wording of the preserved and reconstructed text, see Judg 3:2, למען דעת דרות בני ישראל and Gen 9:12, לדרת עולם. In the biblical text the idea of sinning is mentioned only as part of the description of the plague of hail (Exod 9:27) and of the description immediately after that plague (Exod 9:34). In 4Q*422*, the sinning is mentioned before the detailed description of the plagues. According to the reconstructed text, the purpose of the plagues was to be an everlasting reminder to the Israelites. See further frg. 5 10–11 in the Genesis section of this composition:]אות לדור[ות] עולם.

Line 7. ויופך לדם [מים]יהמה. See notes on readings. Cf. Ps 105:29, הפך את מימיהם לדם; Ps 78:44, ויהפך לדם יאריהם; and secondarily also Exod 7:20, ויהפכו כל המים אשר ביאר לדם. Alternatively, one may reconstruct [יאור]יהמה on the basis of Ps 78:44, ויהפך לדם יאריהם. Note that the suffix of this word has no immediate antecedent in the present reconstruction, but it probably referred to the Egyptians mentioned in line 6. Ideally 'Egypt' is reconstructed in the lacuna earlier in this line, but no reading suggests itself readily (the text would have to read 'Egypt' or 'the God of Egypt' in the lacuna of למען דעת א[   ]אל עד דו[רות]עולם). The form ויופך as a future of הפך is known from Rabbinic Hebrew, derived from a secondary root, אפך, as in Aramaic. For a similar form, see 4Q*501* 4 ויופכו.[7]

Line 8. הצפרדעים בכול ארצ[ם ?]. Cf. Exod 8:1, הצפרדעים על ארץ מצרים (see also 8:3); as well as Ps 105:30, שרץ ארצם צפרדעים.

Line 8. וכנים בכול גבול[ם]. Cf. Ps 105:31, אמר ויבא ערב כנים בכל גבולם, and secondarily also Exod 8:13.

Line 8. ערוב [בב]תיהמה. Cf. Exod 8:17, ומלאו בתי מצרים את הערב (see also 8:20).

Line 8. ו[יפג]ע בכול פ[ ]המה. Possibly read: ○ [ויפג]ע. An attractive alternative reconstruction (by E. Qimron) of the first word would be ו[היה נג]ע, implying the plague of the boils, otherwise not mentioned in this document. Elsewhere that plague is not called נגע.

Line 8. פ[ ]המה. Possible reconstructions are פ[רותי]המה '(they afflicted all) their fruits' or פ[ני]המה '(they afflicted all) their faces'.

Line 8. ויגוף בדב[ר. Cf. Exod 9:3 and Ps 78:50, though not for the exact wording. For the use of ויגוף with regard to the plague of pestilence, see מגפה (Exod 9:14), used in the Bible only with reference to that plague.

7. See Qimron, *Hebrew of the Dead Sea Scrolls*, 98.

Line 9. מקׄנׄיהםה ובהמתם. Cf. Exod 9:19, 20, referring to the plague of hail (see also 9:22, 25; Ps 78:48, בעירם ומקניהם).

Line 9. ובהמתם ל֯[מו]תׄ הסגירׄ. This stich, like the next one, refers to the plague of the pestilence. For the use of הסגיר with reference to the plague of pestilence, see Ps 78:50, and see further v. 48 there, where the same verb is used with reference to hail. For the parallelism of דבר and מות in 4Q*422*, see the same verse: לא חשך ממות נפשם וחיתם לדבר הסגיר.

Line 9. ישי[ת חו]שך בארצׄם ואפלה ב֯[בתי]הםה. Or: ישי[ם. For the phrase, see Exod 10:22, ויהי חשך אפלה בכל ארץ מצרים שלשת ימים, as well as Ps 105:28, שלח חשך.

Line 9. בליראֹ[ה] איש את אחיוׄן[. Also possible: אחיהׄ[ו. For the phrase, see Exod 10:23, לא ראו איש את אחיו. Note the absence of a space between בל and ירא[ה]. The word בל occurs in the account of the plagues in Ps 78:44 in the description of the first plague: ונזליהם בל ישתיון.

Lines 9–10. [ויך] בברד ארצם. See Ps 78:47 for a similar phrase.

Line 10. ואדמת[ם ב]חנמל. There is room for a verb in the lacuna, such as הכה.

Line 10. ב]חנמל. See Ps 78:47, where the same word occurs, likewise in parallelism with ברד.

Line 10. לה֯[אביד כו]ל֯ פרי אוכׄ[ל]ם. Either לה֯[שחית or לה֯[שמיד would be possible, but the reconstruction is based on a text recorded in the *Preliminary Concordance* as חנמל ל[ו]אׄ אבד֯[. The last two words have now been lost and cannot be verified. See further Ps 105:35: ויאכל פרי אדמתם.

Line 10. ויבא ארב֯ה֯ לכסות עין ה֯א֯[רצ. Cf. Exod 10:4b–5a: הנני מביא מחר ארבה בגבלך וכסה את עין הארץ.

Line 10. ויבא. In accordance with the sequence of the verbs in this section (see the last paragraph in this article), the causative 'and He brought' is expected here rather than 'and ⟨the locust⟩ came'. Furthermore, in the plene writing of this document the latter form would have been written as ויבוא.

Line 10. חסל כבד בכול֯ גׄבולם. For the parallelism, cf. Ps 78:46, ויתן לחסיל יבולם ויגיעם לארבה. Note that also in Exod 10:14 the locust is called 'heavy'.

Line 10. חסל. This word probably reflects *ḥasal,* rather than *ḥasil,* as in the MT. For the parallelism of חסל and ארבה, cf. Ps 78:46.

Line 11. לאכול כול ירוק באֹ[רצם]לׄ[ ]ם֯. Cf. Exod 10:15, ויאכל את כל עשב הארץ and Ps 105:35, ויאכל כל עשב בארצם ויאכל פרי אדמתם,

especially for a possible reconstruction: לאכול כול ירוק בא[רצם]ל[אכול פרי אדמת]ם.

Line 11. ירוק. Cf. Exod 10:15 where יֶרֶק is mentioned in connection with the plague of the locusts (also 10:5 according to the Sam. Pent., 12). 4Q*422* uses ירוק instead, literally 'green', with the same meaning as 'vegetable', as in Palestinian Aramaic.[8] For the same interchange, see Isa 15:6, where for יֶרֶק in the MT, 1QIsa[a] reads ירוק.

Line 11. ויח]זק [אל את לב [פרעו]ה. Cf. Exod 9:12: ויחזק יהוה את לב פרעה. God's hardening of Pharaoh's heart is mentioned here after the plague of locusts (line 8), as in Exod 10:20. In the Exodus account this phrase also recurs after the plagues of blood (Exod 7:22), pestilence (9:12), and darkness (10:27), as well as in 11:10, after the last plague. Line 11 of 4Q*422* paraphrases the adjacent verses, Exod 11:9–10. For the different conceptions of the hardening of the heart in 4Q*422*, see the remark on line 7 above.

Line 11. לבלתי[ש]לח[ם]. Cf. Exod 9:12, 10:20, referring to Pharaoh's refusal to let the Israelites go as a result of the hardening of his heart, as in the present context.

Line 11.]ולמען הרבות מופתים . Cf. Exod 11:9: למען רבות מופתי בארץ מצרים. The implications of the paraphrase in this line are similar to the context in Exodus. God hardened Pharaoh's heart for a certain purpose, both in order to let him sin (line 7) and in order to inflict a multitude of plagues on the Egyptians. Only that multitude of plagues could convince Pharaoh that he should let the Hebrews go, but God knew in advance that Pharaoh would not listen. Note the variation of רבות in Exodus and הרבות in 4Q*422*, without difference in meaning. For the latter, see 7:3, והרביתי את אתתי ואת מופתי.

Line 12. ויך בכורם]רשית לכו[ל אונם]. Cf. Ps 105:36 and 78:51. The hardening of Pharaoh's heart in line 11 leads here into the plague of the firstborn, as in Exod 10:27, preceding the description of the death of the firstborn in chap. 11.

Literary Patterns

The account moves quickly from one event to the next, indicating each episode with a few words, pausing only at the description of the plagues and describing each plague separately. It is not impossible that

8. See E. Y. Kutscher, *The Language and Linguistic Background of the Isaiah Scroll* (*1QIs*[a]) (Leiden, 1974) 202.

the episode of the plagues formed the main topic of the Exodus section of 4Q*422*.

The description of the plagues is structured in a poetical parallelistic form, similar to that of Psalms 78 and 105. Within this description, 4Q*422* elaborates on the biblical text with synonymously parallel phrases. After the plague of blood, three distichs follow, in which two, one, and one plagues, respectively, are mentioned. These three distichs are followed by three tristichs, each describing one plague: darkness, hail, and locusts. Within these tristichs the first two stichs describe the plague in synonymous words, and the third describes an additional feature. 4Q*422* thus reflects distinctive poetic features.

ויופך לדם[מימ]יהמ֯ה
הצפרדעים בכול ארצ֯[ם ?]
]עׄרוב [בב]תיהסה
ויגוף בדב[ר את/כול] מקׄניׄהסה
ישי[ת חו]שכ בארצׄם
ויך] בברד ארצם
ויבא ארב֯ה֯ לכסות עין ה֯אׄ[רצ]

וכנים בכול גבול֯[ם
ו֯[יפג]ע בכול פ[ ]הסה
ובהמתם ל֯[מו]תׄ הסגירׄ
ואפלה ב֯[בתי]הסה
ואדמת[ם ב]חנמל
חסל כבד בכול֯ גׄבולם

בליׄרא[ה] איש את אחיוׄ[
לה֯[אביד כו]ל֯ פרי אוכׄ[ל]ם
לאכול כול ירוק בא[רצם

Dependence on the Biblical Wording in the Account of the Plagues

The notes on the text provide biblical parallels for the wording used in 4Q*422*. In this section the text depends in the first place on the historical Psalm 78, second on Psalm 105, and third on the account in Exodus.

Line 7. ויופך לדם[מימ]יהמ֯ה. Cf. Ps 105:29, הפך את מימיהם לדם, and Ps 78:44, ויהפך לדם יאריהם, and secondarily also Exod 7:20, ויהפכו כל המים אשר ביאר לדם.

Line 8. הצפרדעים בכול ארצ֯[ם]. Cf. Ps 105:30, שרץ ארצם צפרדעים, and Exod 8:1, הצפרדעים בארץ מצרים (see also 8:2-3).

Line 8. וכנים בכול גבול֯[ם. Cf. Ps 105:31, אמר ויבא ערב כנים בכל גבולם.

Line 8. עׄרוב [בב]תיהסה. Cf. Exod 8:17, ומלאו בתי מצרים את הערב and Ps 78:45, ישלח בהם ערב.

Lines 8–9. ויגוף בדב[ר את/כול] מקׄניׄהסה ובהמתם ל֯[מו]תׄ הסגירׄ. For the use of ויגוף with regard to the plague of pestilence, cf. מגפה (Exod 9:14), used only with regard to that plague. See further Ps 78:48, where הסגיר is used and where a similar pair of synonyms is used, though with reference to another plague, hail: ויסגר לברד בעירם ומקניהם לרשפים. See also Ps 78:50, where this verb is used in connection with pestilence: וחיתם לדבר הסגיר. For the parallelism of דבר and מות in 4Q*422*, cf. the same verse: לא חשך ממות נפשם וחיתם לדבר הסגיר.

Line 9. ישי[ת חו]שכ בארצ̇ם ואפלה ב̊[בתי]הםה. Cf. Exod 10:22: ויהי חשך אפלה בכל ארץ מצרים שלשת ימים. The pair of juxtaposed and synonymous nouns is broken down in 4Q*422* in accordance with the "break-up pattern."[9]

Line 9. בלירא[ה] איש את אחיו̇]. Cf. Exod 10:23, לוא ראו איש את אחיו.

Lines 9–10. ויך] בברד ארצם ואדמת[ם ב]חנמל. Cf. Ps 78:47 for a similar pattern of parallelism and for similar phrases: יהרג בברד גפנם ושקמותם בחנמל. Note that חנמל does not occur either in the Exodus account or in Psalm 105.

Line 10. ויבא ארב̊ה̊ לכסות עין ה̊א̇[רצ] חסל כבד בכול̊ ג̇בולם. Cf. Exod 10:5: וכסה את עין הארץ. See Ps 78:46 for a similar pattern of parallelism: ויתן לחסיל יבולם ויגיעם לארבה.

Line 11. לאכול כול ירוק בא[רצם. Cf. Exod 10:15, ויאכל את כל עשב הארץ, and Ps 105:35, ויאכל כל עשב בארצם ויאכל פרי אדמתם.

Style

In the description of the plagues, as elsewhere in this composition, God's actions are described in short sentences with God as the subject of the verb, just as in the historical psalms, but unlike the Exodus account. Third-person verbal forms are rarely found in this part of the Exodus narrative (see, however, ויהפך יהוה רוח ים חזק מאד in Exod 10:19). In the Exodus account, situations rather than actions are depicted. On the other hand, in 4Q*422* one finds: line 7, ויופך; line 8, ויגוף; line 9, הסגיר̇; line 9, ישי]ת; line 10, ויבא (= וַיָּבֵא); as well as a few reconstructed verbs.

9. Cf. E. Z. Melamed, "Break-up of Stereotype Phrases as an Artistic Device in Biblical Poetry," in *Studies in the Bible* (ScrHier 8; ed. C. Rabin; Jerusalem, 1961) 115–53.

The Word *ndb* in the Bible: A Study in Historical Semantics and Biblical Thought

J. P. Weinberg

A survey of the usages of the root ndb as a component in ancient Jewish personal names and an analysis of the usages of all its derivatives in the Bible lead to the conclusion that it was a significant key word in biblical vocabulary, especially in exilic and preexilic times. Diachronically considered, ndb and its derivatives display an obvious trend toward monosemy, denoting mainly freewill and voluntary actions in different realms. The development was a linguistic manifestation of the growing role and importance of freewill and voluntary action in all realms and on all levels of Jewish life after 586 B.C.E.

What could be worth reviewing and discussing about the usage and meaning of *ndb*? This root and its derivatives are usually interpreted and translated with some unanimity by modern biblical scholars: 'sich freiwillig entschliessen, sich stellen, spenden'; 'decide, enlist, present oneself, give a freewill offering, offer voluntarily, volunteer'; and so on.[1] But a consensus does not always presuppose the solution, and indeed the goal of this article is to elucidate the practical, social, political, religious, and ideological applications and functions of *ndb* and its manifold derivatives, especially in the postexilic citizen/temple/community of Judea.[2]

Author's note: It is always tempting, but also risky, to try to characterize a person and his actions in one comprehensive word or expression. This can nonetheless be done for Jonas Greenfield: the root *ndb* denotes one of his prevailing personality traits. Hence the following review of the usage and meaning of this root conforms to the scientific interest of a dear colleague and friend.

1. All our interpretations and translations of *ndb* and its derivatives are taken (unless otherwise specified) from: W. Baumgartner et al., *Hebräisches und aramäisches Lexikon zum Alten Testament* (4 vols.; Leiden, 1967–90); and L. Holladay, *A Concise Hebrew and Aramaic Lexicon of the Old Testament* (Leiden, 1971).

2. J. Weinberg, *The Citizen-Temple-Community* (JSOTSup 151; Sheffield, 1992).

I shall begin this review with an analysis of the usage of *ndb* in the ancient Jewish onomasticon, because it is easier to determine the chronological framework and historical and socioideological background of a personal name. The data thus obtained may be used to investigate other occurrences of *ndb* and its derivatives.

The Root ndb Is a Component of Some Seven Personal Names in the Bible and in Ancient Hebrew Epigraphy

(1) The personal name *ʾăbînādāb* (*ʾāb* + *ndb* 'Vater hat sich freiwillig gezeigt'[3]) occurs thirteen times, denoting four different persons: (a) a Judahite, son of Jesse and brother of David (1 Sam 16:8, 17:13; 1 Chr 2:13); (b) a Benjaminite, son of Saul (1 Sam 31:2; 1 Chr 8:33, 9:39, 10:2); (c) an inhabitant of the Benjaminite town of Gibea, father of Elazar, who served the Shrine during the reign of Saul and at the beginning of David's kingdom (1 Sam 7:1; 2 Sam 6:3, 4; 1 Chr 13:7); and (d) the son of Abinadab appears in the authentic list of Solomon's district governors (*nîṣābîm*),[4] as governor of the fourth district of Dor and the king's son-in-law (1 Kgs 4:11). There are no real grounds to doubt the authenticity of this information about the persons named *ʾăbînādāb* and their historicity. They should be dated to the 11th–10th centuries B.C.E.; at least three of them belonged to the tribes of Judah and Benjamin, the clans of David and Saul, and were closely connected with the royal government.

(2) *ʾăḥînādāb* (*ʾāḥ* + *ndb* 'mein Bruder ist edel, hat sich freigebig gezeigt') is mentioned in the Bible only once, denoting one Ahinadab, son of Iddo (1 Kgs 4:14), governor of the seventh district of Mahanaim,[5] evidently a historical person, connected with Solomon's royal administration and consequently dated to the second half of the tenth century B.C.E.

(3) *yĕhônādāb-yônādāb* (*yhwh* + *ndb* 'Jahwe zeigt sich freigebig'[6]) occurs in the Bible fifteen times, denoting two people: (a) Jonadab, son of Shima, "the brother of David," described as a 'very wise man (*ḥākām*)', who played a significant but ambiguous role in the conflict between David's

3. M. Noth, *Die israelitischen Personennamen im Rahmen der gemeinsemitischen Namengebung* (Stuttgart, 1928) 193; J. D. Fowler, *Theophoric Personal Names in Ancient Hebrew: A Comparative Study* (Sheffield, 1988) 44–48, 82, 351.

4. Y. Aharoni, "Mĕḥôzôt yiśrāʾēl wîhûdâ," in *Bîmê bayit riʾšôn: Malkûyôt yiśrāʾēl wîhûdâ* (Jerusalem, 1961) 110–15; F. Pintore, "I dodici intendenti di Salomone," *RSO* 45 (1970) 177–207; Z. Kallai, *Historical Geography of the Bible: The Tribal Territories of Israel* (Jerusalem and Leiden, 1968) 40–72.

5. Noth, *Die israelitischen Personennamen*, 193; Fowler, *Theophoric Personal Names*, 46–48, 82, 173, 351.

6. Noth, *Die israelitischen Personennamen*, 193; Fowler, *Theophoric Personal Names*, 32–38, 82, 161, 351.

sons Amnon and Absholom (2 Sam 13:3, 5, 32, 35); and (b) Jehonadab, son of Rechab, leader and teacher of the famous Rechabites (1 Chr 2:55),[7] who lived in the mid-ninth century B.C.E. (2 Kgs 10:15; Jer 35:6, 8ff.). There is no doubt about the historicity of both people, who lived in the first half of the tenth and middle of the ninth centuries B.C.E., were both Judahites engaged in political activities, one distinguished mainly for his secular wisdom, the other for his piety.

(4) *nĕdabyâ-nĕdabyāhû-nādāb* (*ndb* + *yhwh* 'Jahwe ist freigebig'[8]) occurs in the Bible twenty-one times, denoting five different persons: (a) Nadab, son of Aaron, who for some ritual infringement was condemned to die childless (Exod 6:23; 24:1, 9; 28:1; Lev 10:1; Num 3:2, 4; 26:60, 61; 1 Chr 5:29; 24:1, 2); he and his brother Abihu may have been eponyms of once influential priestly collectives, which later disappeared or were deprived of their priesthood;[9] (b) Nadab, a member-chain of the preexilic genealogy of the Benjaminites, who lived in Gibeon (1 Chr 8:30, 9:36); (c) Nadab, a member-chain of the preexilic Judahites-Jerahmeelites (1 Chr 2:28, 30); (d) Nadab, son of Jeroboam I, king of Israel at the end of the tenth century B.C.E. (1 Kgs 14:20; 15:25, 27, 31); and (e) Nedabiah, son of Shealtiel, of the postexilic Davidides (1 Chr 3:18). Except for Aaron's son Nadab the historicity of all the other bearers of this name, including those referred to in the Judahite and Benjaminite genealogies,[10] is beyond doubt. They all belonged to the elite of the tribes of Judah and Benjamin and may be dated between the tenth and sixth centuries B.C.E. The name *ndbyhw* also appears in an inscription on a half-shekel weight found in the postexilic solar shrine at Lachish (*/l/ndb/yhw*)[11] and on an ostracon from late preexilic Arad (*mšlm/bn ndbyhw*).[12] The epigraphic data indicate the prevalence of the name

7. S. Abramsky, "Bêt harêkābîm: gênêʾalogiyâ wĕṣibyôn ḥebrātî," *ErIsr* 8 (Sukenik Volume; Jerusalem, 1967) 255–64; F. S. Frick, "The Rechabites Reconsidered," *JBL* 90 (1971) 279–87.

8. Noth, *Die israelitischen Personennamen,* 193; Fowler, *Theophoric Personal Names,* 82, 161, 351.

9. A. H. J. Gunneweg, *Leviten und Priester: Hauptlinien der Traditionsbildung und Geschichte des israelitisch-jüdischen Kultpersonals* (Göttingen, 1965) 86ff.; M. Haran, *Temples and Temple-Service in Ancient Israel: An Inquiry into Biblical Cult Phenomena and the Historical Setting of the Priestly School* (repr.; Winona Lake, Ind., 1985) 69ff.

10. On the considerable degree of authenticity of the genealogies in Chronicles see A. Demsky, "The Genealogy of Gibeon (1 Chronicles 9:35–44): Biblical and Epigraphic Considerations," *BASOR* 202 (1971) 16–23; J. P. Weinberg, "Das Wesen und die funktionelle Bestimmung der Listen in 1 Chr. 1–9," *ZAW* 93 (1981) 103–4, 111; H. G. M. Williamson, "Sources and Redaction in the Chronicler's Genealogy of Judah," *JBL* 98 (1979) 351–59.

11. Y. Aharoni, "Trial Excavation in the 'Solar Shrine' at Lachish: Preliminary Report," *IEJ* 18 (1968) 164–65.

12. A. Lemaire, *Inscriptions hébraïques, tome 1: Les Ostraca* (LAPO 9; Paris, 1977) 206, no. 39, 3.

nĕdabyâ-nĕdabyāhû-nādāb in the late preexilic–early postexilic periods, mainly in the elite Judahite milieu.

(5) *ᶜammînādāb* (*ᶜam* + *ndb* 'Mein Vatersbruder zeigt sich freigebig'[13]) occurs in the Bible fifteen times, denoting three different people: (a) the father of Elisheba, wife of Aaron (Exod 6:23), and of Nahshon, the *naśîᵓ* of the Judahites (Num 1:7; 2:3; 7:12, 17; 10:14) and an ancestor of David (1 Chr 2:10; Ruth 4:19, 20); (b) a member-chain of the genealogy of the Levites-Kehatites (1 Chr 6:7); and (c) a bearer of the name is mentioned as a chief (*śār*) of the Levites-Uzielites who participated in David's transfer of the Ark to Jerusalem (1 Chr 15:10, 11). Although one may justifiably question the historicity of some of the bearers of the name Amminadab, the name itself seems to have been popular in the milieu of the premonarchic–early monarchic Judahite elite and Levites-Kehatites. In epigraphy, *ᶜmndb mlk bn ᶜmn* ('Amminadab, king of the Ammonites') is mentioned in a late seventh-century B.C.E. inscription[14] and in another approximately contemporary inscription (*lᵓdnplṭ / ᶜbd ᶜmndb*).[15]

(6) The name *ᵓlndb*, obviously the Elohistic version of *yĕhônādāb-yônādāb*,[16] appears only in a non-Hebrew, perhaps Phoenician inscription from the eighth century B.C.E. (*/ l / ᵓlndb bn ᵓlydn.*).[17]

(7) The name *ndbᵓl*, obviously the Elohistic version of *nĕdabyâ-nĕdabyāhû*, appears only in epigraphy: on a seal from Ammon, from the eighth or seventh century B.C.E. (*/ l / ndbᵓ l / bn ᵓdmdm*),[18] on another Ammonite seal, from the seventh century B.C.E. (*ndbᵓl / bn ᶜmsᵓl*),[19] and on a seal from the vicinity of Hebron, from the sixth century B.C.E. (*lbqš b / n ndbᵓl*).[20]

This review demonstrates that names with the component *ndb* were particularly popular in monarchic and early postexilic times, but almost exclusively among the Judahites, Benjaminites and Aaronides-Levites, mainly among the social and political elite of these groups—the Davidides, the Saulides, and others. It was also common among the elite of the

13. Noth, *Die israelitischen Personennamen*, 193; Fowler, *Theophoric Personal Names*, 48–50, 82, 351.

14. H. O. Thompson and F. Zayadine, "The Tell Siran Inscription," *BASOR* 212 (1973) 5–11; C. Krahmalkov, "An Ammonite Lyric Poem," *BASOR* 223 (1976) 55–57; W. H. Shea, "The Siran Inscription: Amminadab's Drinking Song," *PEQ* 110 (1978) 107–12.

15. D. Diringer, *Le iscrizioni antico-ebraiche Palestinesi* (Florence, 1934) 253–55, no. 98.

16. Fowler, *Theophoric Personal Names*, 38–44.

17. N. Avigad, "Qĕbûṣat ḥôtāmôt ᶜivrîyim," *ErIsr* 9 (Albright Volume; Jerusalem, 1969) 8, no. 20.

18. Diringer, *Le iscrizioni*, 188–89, no. 29.

19. N. Avigad, "Leqeṭ ḥôtāmôt ᶜatîqîm," *Yediᶜot* 25 (1961) 241; J. Naveh, "Kĕtôvôt kĕnaᶜăniyôt wĕᶜivriyôt (1960–1964)," *Leš* 30 (1965) 79.

20. S. Moscati, *Epigrafia ebraica antica 1935–1950* (Rome, 1951) 64, no. 41.

neighboring Ammonites. In view of the activities and characteristics of some of the bearers of these names—the wisdom of Jonadab, son of Shima (our no. 3a), the piety and virtue of Jonadab, son of Rehab (no. 3b), the generosity of Amminadab (no. 5a; cf. Num 7:12ff.), as well as the social and political status of most of them—we may conclude that the names represent an essential feature of the persons so named: their nobility as a quality granted by God, provenience, and deeds.

Derivatives of the Root <u>*ndb*</u> *and Their Biblical Usages*

(1) The noun *nĕdîbâ* ('Edles, Würde'; 'something noble, honor') occurs only three times in the Bible. It appears twice in the eschatological prophecy of Isaiah (32:8) about the future righteous and just kingdom and is associated there with *ṣedeq* (32:1), *mišpāṭ* (32:1, 7) and other words of this semantic-ideological field;[21] it is opposed to *nābāl* (32:5), which denotes: "homo nihili; Unmensch, Nichtmensch; nabal ist wer in irgendeinem Lebensbereich negativ dasteht, nicht gibt, nicht hilft, nicht ehrt, nicht ist."[22] Although a preexilic, 1-Isaian attribution of Isa 32:1–8 cannot be excluded, a later, exilic, 2-Isaian provenience is not impossible.[23] The third occurrence of *nĕdîbâ* in Job 30:15, where it denotes the hero's past, now lost well-being, is surely postexilic.[24] Thus, the word *nĕdîbâ* is used only in late preexilic, exilic, and postexilic prophetic and wisdom literature, designating the totality of important positive human qualities.

(2) The word *nādîb* ('willig, jeder in seiner Kunstfertigkeit Bereitwillige, der aus freiem Entschluss Spendende, der Edle'; 'willing, one who is generous, noble') appears in the Bible as a noun twenty-one times, but as an adjective only five times. As a noun, *nādîb* is used in poetical-liturgical (Num 21:18; 1 Sam 2:8; Ps 47:10, 83:12; etc.), prophetical (Isa 13:2; 32:5, 8) and poetical-lyrical (Cant 7:2, etc.) contexts and in wisdom literature (Prov 8:16; 17:7, 26; Job 12:21; 21:28; etc.) but never in the historical and legal parts of the Bible. We may therefore assume that *nādîb* is not a term with a well-defined social, political, or legal sense, but rather a poetic expression, without a specific or fixed meaning. The word is used, as a rule, in a relationship of comparison or opposition, paired

21. J. Crüseman, "Jahwes Gerechtigkeit (*ṣĕdāqā / ṣädäq*) im Alten Testament," *ETh* 36 (1976) 427–50; D. Kendall, "The Usage of *Mišpaṭ* in Isaiah 59," *ZAW* 96 (1984) 391–405; M. Weinfeld, *Mišpaṭ uṣĕdāqâ bĕyiśrāʾēl ûbâ ʿammîm* (Jerusalem, 1985) 2ff.

22. G. Gerleman, "Der Nicht-Mensch: Erwägungen zur hebräischen Wurzel *nbl*," *VT* 24 (1974) 150–53.

23. O. Eissfeldt, *Einleitung in das Alte Testament* (Tübingen, 1964) 426ff.

24. G. Fohrer, *Das Buch Hiob* (Berlin, 1988) 419–20.

with such semantically polyvalent words as *ṣādîq* ('not guilty, guiltless, innocent, just, righteous'; Prov 17:26), *ʾěbyôn* ('needy, poor, oppressed', in a religious, moral sense; Ps 107:40–41, 113:7–8, etc.), *rāšāʿ* ('guilty, transgressor, impious, evildoer before God'; Job 21:28, 34:18), *nābāl* (see above; Prov 17:7, Isa 32:5), and so on. We can agree with Gerleman[25] that *nādîb* is not only 'der freigebige' but also 'der an keine bestimmte amtliche Funktion gebundene, gunsterweisende Herr, der Gönner'. It should also be stressed that most occurrences of the noun *nādîb* occur in the postexilic parts of the Bible.

The adjective *nādîb*, unlike the noun, is used mainly (four out of five times) in two compact religious-legal (Exod 35:5, 22)[26] and historical (1 Chr 28:21, 2 Chr 29:31) texts,[27] each clearly of exilic-postexilic provenience. In contrast to the diverse usages of the noun, the adjective occurs four times in connection with human sacral-ritual activities. It is used twice (Exod 35:5, 22) in connection with observance of the fully institutionalized, regular, obligatory, and normative duty of *těrûmâ*, so that the voluntary element is naturally restricted. In Chronicles, however, *nādîb* is associated with such noninstitutionalized and one-time sacral-ritual actions as David's preparations for building the temple and the contributions of the priests and Levites (1 Chr 28:21) or Hezekiah's cleansing and rededication of the temple (2 Chr 29:31),[28] where there is much more scope for a display of free, voluntary decision by the participants. This semantic nuance of voluntariness in the adjective *nādîb* is explicitly reinforced by its usage three times in *status constructus* with the word *lēb* (Exod 35:5, 22; 2 Chr 29:31), which the Bible considers not only an organ of the human body, but also the seat of man's emotional and intellectual functions and activities, including decision, volition, and so on.[29]

We may therefore conclude that the noun/adjective *nādîb* was used primarily in exilic and postexilic times and that it was associated not only with institutionalized, regular, obligatory and normative sacral-liturgical activities, which offer only limited scope for the expression of free will and voluntary action, but also with noninstitutionalized, singly

25. Gerleman, "Der Nicht-Mensch," 156–58.

26. K. Koch, *Die Priesterschrift: Von Exodus 25 bis Leviticus 16* (Göttingen, 1959) 96ff.; Eissfeldt, *Einleitung in das Alte Testament*, 310–18; H. Utzschneider, *Das Heiligtum und das Gesetz: Studien zur Bedeutung der Sinaitischen Heiligtumstexte (Ex 25–40; Lev 8–9)* (Göttingen, 1988) 243–46, 296–97.

27. J. P. Weinberg, "Das Eigengut in den Chronikbüchern," *OLP* 10 (1979) 179–81.

28. R. de Vaux, *Ancient Israel* (New York, 1965) 2.435; H. H. Rowley, *Worship in Ancient Israel* (London, 1967) 126.

29. J. P. Weinberg, "Der Mensch im Weltbild des Chronisten: Sein Körper," *OLP* 13 (1982) 85–86; H. W. Wolff, *Anthropologie des Alten Testaments* (Munich, 1984) 68–90.

performed sacral and liturgical acts, where much depends on a person's free, voluntary decision.

(3) A further derivative of *ndb* is the noun *nĕdābâ* ('freier Antrieb, willige, spontan gegebene Gabe'; 'free inclination, voluntary gift, free-will offering, given spontaneously'). It occurs twenty-six times in the Bible: thirteen times in the Pentateuch (Exod 35:29; 36:3; Lev 7:16; 22:18, 21, 23; Num 15:3; 29:39; Deut 12:6; etc.); four times in prophetic sayings (Ezek 46:12, Hos 14:5, Amos 4:5); four times in Psalms (54:8, 68:10, 110:3, 119:108); three times in Ezra (1:4, 3:5, 8:28); and twice in the Chronicler's *Eigengut* (2 Chr 31:14, 35:8). Although some of these texts (approximately seven: Amos 4:5, Hos 14:5, Deut 12:6; etc.) may be attributed to the preexilic period, most of them (ca. 17/19: Exod 35:29; Lev 22:18; Ezek 46:12; Ezra 1:4, 3:5; etc.) are clearly of exilic or post-exilic provenience. While most of the occurrences (23 times) of *nĕdābâ* are associated with different sacral-ritual acts, one cannot ignore that the noun also denotes God's love for his people (Hos 14:5) and his benevolent gift of rain (Ps 68:10), and on a third occasion (Ps 119:108) *nĕdābâ* is a saying addressed to God. Twelve times *nĕdābâ* is associated with the most significant kinds of sacral-ritual act, sacrifices and gifts practiced in pre- and postexilic Jahwism: *tĕrûmâ* (Exod 36:3, Deut 12:6, etc.), *ᶜôlâ* (Lev 22:18, Num 15:3, etc.), *šĕlāmîm* (Num 29:39, Ezek 46:12, etc.), and others, all institutionalized, obligatory, regular and normative.[30] Eleven times, however (Lev 7:16, 22:18; Num 15:3; Deut 12:6; etc.), *nĕdābâ* is linked with *nēder* ('Gelübde'; 'vow'), which is 'a promise to give or to consecrate to God a person or a thing',[31] in any case a freewill, noninstitutionalized and irregular sacral-liturgical act. Hence *nĕdābâ* was increasingly used, it seems, to denote partly or wholly free-will, voluntary sacral and liturgical acts.

(4) The verb √*ndb* occurs seventeen times in the Bible, three in *Qal* and fourteen in *Hithpael*. All the instances of √*ndb* in *Qal* ('antreiben'; 'urge on, prompt') occur in the exilic-postexilic Holiness Code (Exod 25:2; 35:21, 29),[32] where the verb denotes an essentially institutionalized, obligatory, regular and normative sacral-liturgical act—the contribution of the *tĕrûmâ* to the tabernacle and the service there.[33] Nevertheless, its frequent coupling with the nouns *lēb*[34] and *rûaḥ* ('Hauch, Atem, Luft, Wind, Weltseite, Lebensträger, Sinn, Gesinnung, geistige Verfassung'; 'breath, wind, direction, mind, disposition, temper'), which in a human

30. De Vaux, *Ancient Israel*, 415ff.; Haran, *Temples and Temple-Service*, 205ff.
31. De Vaux, *Ancient Israel*, 465–66.
32. See n. 26 above.
33. See n. 28 above.
34. See n. 29 above.

context also denote "Träger energischer Aktionen des Willens."[35] underlines its association with freewill and voluntary human action, as explicitly expressed by the same root in *Hithpael.*

In this mode √*ndb* occurs only in historical texts (Judg 5:2, 9; Ezra 1:6; 2:68; 3:5; Neh 11:2; 1 Chr 29:5, 6, 9, 14, 17; 2 Chr 17:16). With the exception of the early, preexilic Song of Deborah (Judg 5:2, 9),[36] these instances all date to the middle or second half of the fifth century B.C.E. In *Hithpael,* √*ndb* denotes only noninstitutionalized, irregular or single activities and acts, such as David's preparation for the building of the first temple (1 Chr 29:6ff.) or the erection of the second temple and the organization of its services (Ezra 1:6, 2:68, etc.). The root *ndb* in *Hithpael* also appears in contexts that are not explicitly sacral-liturgical, such as participation in the synoikism of Jerusalem (Neh 11:2). In many of the texts listed (Ezra 1:6; 3:5; 1 Chr 29:9, 14, 17, etc.), the semantic nuance of free will and voluntary action is explicit. Hence it seems justifiable to conclude that √*ndb* in *Hithpael* is peculiar to the postexilic vocabulary, where it denotes free, voluntary acts, mainly in the sacral area but also in the profane.

Summarizing this analysis of the root *ndb* and its derivatives, we may conclude that it was a significant key word in biblical vocabulary, especially in the exilic and postexilic periods. It was not as monosemous as is sometimes supposed but possessed rather a limited polysemy or diffuse monosemy, with an obvious trend toward expressed monosemy, denoting freewill, voluntary human deeds and actions in different realms. This semantic evolution is, I believe, a linguistic manifestation and token of a significant phenomenon in Jewish history, life, and mentality after 586 B.C.E., namely, the increasing role and importance of freewill, voluntary action in all areas and on all levels of the people's existence.

Freewill and Voluntary Action in Exilic and Postexilic Times

Because I will discuss this problem in detail in a forthcoming book,[37] I restrict myself here to a few examples demonstrating the significant and even decisive role of the principle of freewill and voluntary action in the life of the Jewish people in exilic and postexilic times.

(1) An important aftermath of the catastrophe of 586 B.C.E. was the dispersion and disappearance of two fundamental institutions of preexilic Jewish society, the *bêt ʾāb*[38] and the *mišpāḥâ.* Any individual's affilia-

35. Wolff, *Anthropologie des Alten Testaments,* 65.

36. Eissfeldt, *Einleitung in das Alte Testament,* 134.

37. J. P. Weinberg, *Der Chronist in seiner Mitwelt* (forthcoming).

38. S. Bendor, *Bêt hāʾāv bĕyiśrāʾēl lĕmin hahitnaḥălût wĕʿad sôf yĕmê hammĕlûkâ* (Haifa, 1986) 17ff.

tion with both institutions was predetermined by birth and provenience. It was a sine qua non for the nation's survival and the preservation of its national identity, for both the deportees in Babylonia and the remnant in Babylonian Judea, that the previous, Gentile-based institutions be replaced by some others. These were the *bêt ʾăbôt*[39] among the deportees in Babylonia and what I have called the "community named by toponyms" among the remnant in Babylonian Judea.[40] The new institutions were essentially different, the first being an agnatic formation and the second a local, territorial one; but they had a basic feature in common: affiliation with them depended mainly on the free choice of individuals and/or families. Of course, the voluntary element should not be exaggerated, as individuals' choices and decisions were influenced by objective conditions and factors. Nevertheless, free will and voluntariness played a substantial role in the formation and functioning of these basic institutions of the postexilic Jewish society, especially of the *bêt ʾăbôt*.

(2) A substantial component of national mentality and ideology after 586 B.C.E. was the hope ideology and/or theology,[41] though it was by no means—and could not be—homogeneous and uniform. The time of fulfillment of the *tiqwâ* ('Erwartung, Hoffnung, glückliche Aussicht'; 'expectation, hope') and its content were bones of contention: while the so-called "false prophets" Hananiah and his colleagues promised salvation in the nearest future, Jeremiah warned that seventy years would pass till its advent (Jeremiah 28–29). The two answers represented not only different attitudes toward the nation's present, but also different notions about its future. Among the Jews in Babylonian Judea, the hope of renewing the *status quo ante* prevailed, rebuilding the temple, restoring the Davidic kingdom, and so on; there was a distinct orientation toward continuity. On the other hand, the "restoration plan" of Ezekiel 40–48, which evidently expressed the hopes, expectations, and intentions of the exiles and perhaps also of the first returnees,[42] was permeated by an obvious orientation toward discontinuity. It aimed at noticeable innovations such as strict separation of the secular and sacral and radical changes in the status and functions of the head of the future state, to mention only two. In both the main centers of Jewish existence,

39. J. P. Weinberg, "Das *bēit ʾābōt* im 6.-4. Jh. v. u. Z.," *VT* 23 (1973) 412–14.

40. J. P. Weinberg, "Kollektivy, nazvannye po mestnostyam v akheminidskoi Yudeye," *ArOr* 42 (1974) 241–53.

41. C. Westermann, "Das Hoffen im Alten Testament," *ThV* 6 (1952–53) 19–70; W. Zimmerli, *Der Mensch und seine Hoffnung im Alten Testament* (Göttingen and Zürich, 1968) 7–18; D. L. Smith, *The Religion of the Landless* (Bloomington, 1989) 129ff.

42. H. Gese, *Der Verfassungsentwurf des Ezechiel (Kap. 40–48): Traditionsgeschichtlich untersucht* (Tübingen, 1957) 6ff.; W. Zimmerli, "Planungen für den Wiederaufbau nach der Katastrophe von 587," *VT* 18 (1968) 229–55; G. Ch. Macholz, "Noch einmal: Planungen für den Wiederaufbau nach der Katastrophe von 587," *VT* 19 (1969) 322–52.

Babylonia and Judea, the Exile was a time of strained, even overstrained, hopes and expectations, that faced both individuals and groups with the need to choose between the different types of *tiqwâ*. Subjective factors such as free choice and voluntary decision play a substantial role in the genesis of every state, but they become especially crucial in the situation of the *Nullpunkt*,[43] when the goal is the restoration of a lost state. Such was the situation on the eve and after 538 B.C.E. We are therefore probably justified in assuming that free choice and voluntary decision played a very substantial role in the genesis and formation of the postexilic Judean citizen/temple/community.

(3) Cyrus's edict (Ezra 1:1–4, 6:3–5) gave the exiles permission to return to Judea and rebuild the temple, promising financial support from the Persian state. Neither version of the edict contains any hint of general, compulsory repatriation, organized by the state and embracing all exiles. Quite the contrary: the keywords of the edict, 'Anyone of you of all his people—may his God be with him, and let him go up to Jerusalem . . .' (*mî bākem mikol ᶜammô yĕhî ᵓĕlōhāyw ᶜimmô wĕyaᶜal lîrûšālayim* . . . , Ezra 1:3), prove that the repatriation was proposed and realized as a wholly voluntary action, dependent only on the free choice and volition of individuals or families. This thesis is confirmed by the fact that the repatriation was not an isolated event but a protracted process, and that by no means did all of the exiles return to Judea. The fundamental principle of free choice and voluntary decision also played a significant role in the subsequent development of the postexilic citizen/temple/community: there is convincing evidence that most members of the "communities named by toponyms" joined the postexilic community as an act of free will; moreover, the participation of individuals and *battê ᵓăbôt* in the reconstruction of the Jerusalem city wall, in the synoikism of Jerusalem, and so forth, was characterized by the same voluntary spirit.

(4) I have suggested elsewhere[44] that the mentality of the Jewish people underwent a radical change during the exilic and postexilic periods: instead of the acknowledgement of and quest for strict monism, obligatory uniformity and homogeneity of doing and thinking as a sine qua non, there emerged a recognition that pluralism, diversity, and heterogeneity of doing and thinking was permissible and possible, within certain limits. Of course, such pluralism necessarily presupposes the possibility and necessity of free choice and voluntary decision between different modes of doing and thinking.

43. Zimmerli, "Planungen für den Wiederaufbau," 229.

44. J. P. Weinberg, "Die Mentalität der Jerusalemischen Bürger-Temple-Gemeinde des 6.-4. Jh. v. u. z.," *Transeuphratène* 5 (1992) 133–41.

Though these examples are by no means exhaustive, they provide sufficient grounds for the hypothesis that freewill and voluntary action, the notion and principle represented by *ndb* and its derivatives, played a substantial role in all realms and on all levels of Jewish life in exilic and postexilic times. The principle has remained no less significant in later periods of Jewish history, especially during the twentieth century, when the need to exercise free will and make voluntary decisions has become one of the fundamental features of our national existence.

Part II

Epigraphy

Flour and Dough: Gleanings from the Arad Letters

Shmuel Aḥituv

*The paper deals with some terms in the Arad Letters. In Arad Letter 1, ͑ôd means 'surplus'. It is a noun also attested in Mishnaic Hebrew in the plural. The Hiphil of rkb is used for loading movables onto a beast of burden, a meaning unattested in Biblical Hebrew and attested only once in the Jerusalem Talmud (for the scape-goat). ͗Aggān here and in Isa 22:24–25 is not a krater but some sort of storage jar. In Arad Letter 3 bāṣēq is not dough but grains of wheat. It is compared to Ugaritic bṣql 'ear of grain', parallel to šblt and to biblical *bṣqln in 2 Kgs 4:42.*

Arad 1:5–9

ומעוד הקמח הראשון תרכב ‎ıı‏ קמח לעשת להם לחם

The general meaning of the order given to Elyashib is quite clear.[1] He was told to give the *Kittiyîm*—most probably Greek mercenaries in Judean service—a certain quantity of flour (1 *ḥōmer, kōr*?) for bread. However, various terms and details of the text require explanation.

The term עוד occurs four times in the Arad correspondence: here and in 2:7, 5:3, and 21:8. In ostraca 2 and 21, the term will bear the translation 'yet' or 'still', thus ואם עוד 'and if there is yet/still. . . .' However, neither our text nor 5:1–4 (אל אלישב ועת שלח מאתך מעוד הקמח ה[ר]א[שן]), can bear such a translation. In these two instances עוד means 'surplus'. Elyashib was ordered to provide the *Kittiyîm* with flour from the remaining first-grade surplus under his charge in the Arad granaries.[2]

1. For the Arad Letters, see Y. Aharoni, *Arad Inscriptions* (Jerusalem, 1981) (henceforth: *AI*).

2. See my *Handbook of Ancient Hebrew Inscriptions* ([Jerusalem, 1992] 56 [Heb.]) and lately also G. B. Sarfatti, "The Inscriptions of the Biblical Period and Mishnaic Hebrew," in *Israel Yeivin Festschrift* (= *Language Studies* 5–6; Jerusalem, 1992; ed. M. Bar-Asher) 60–61 ([Heb.] English summary, XV).

This meaning of עוד is not attested in the Bible, but it does occur in the Mishna. Tractate *m. Ter.* 4:7 records a debate regarding the neutralization of heave-offering (*tĕrûmāh*) that has become mixed with nonsanctified produce:

רבי אליעזר אומר תרומה עולה באחד ומאה. רבי יהושע אומר במאה וָעוד.
ועוד זה אין לו שִׁעור. רבי יוסי בן משולם אומר: ועוד—קב למאה סאה.

R. Eliezer says: Heave-offering becomes neutralized in a hundred and one parts. R. Joshua says: In somewhat more than a hundred; and this "somewhat more" has no prescribed measure. R. Jose b. Meshullam says: This "somewhat more" must be [at least] one *kab* to a hundred *seahs*. . . .[3]

The Mishna even attests to a plural form of the noun עוד. Thus, in *m. Menaḥ.* 7:2:

הנזירות היתה באה שתי ידות במצה שבתודה: חלות ורקיקים ואין בה רבוכה;
נמצאו עשרה קבים ירושלמיות שהן ששה עשרונות ועֲדָנַיִן.

For the Nazirite's offering they brought twice as much of what was unleavened as for the Thank-offering—cakes and wafers, but not soaked cakes; thus there were ten *kabs*, Jerusalem measure, which are six Tenths and something over.[4]

Another unfamiliar linguistic usage is presented by the word תרכב. B. Otzen's proposal to translate it as 'auf einem Wagen laden'[5] has already been refuted by Aharoni, who maintains that it cannot mean to load onto a chariot or cart and suggests that it means loading onto donkeys.[6] Compare this with Arad 3:2–6: וצוך חנניה על באר שבע עם משא צמד חמרים 'and Ḥananyahu ordered you: "Go to Beer Sheba with a burden of a pair of donkeys"'. The word תרכב (*tarkib*) is *Hiphil*, jussive of רכ״ב. The *Hiphil* of רכ״ב for loading something onto a cart is attested only in the story of bringing the Ark to Jerusalem (2 Sam 6:3, 1 Chr 13:7), but never for loading something onto a beast of burden. The form is commonly used for putting a person into a chariot (Gen 41:43, 2 Kgs 10:16, et al.) or onto a beast of burden, such as a mule (1 Kgs 1:33) or a horse (Esth 6:9). However, while there is no biblical evidence for the use of the *Hiphil* of רכ״ב for loading goods onto a beast of burden, such use is attested in postbiblical Hebrew. In the Jerusalem Talmud, *y. Yoma* 6.3

3. H. Danby, trans., *The Mishnah* (Oxford, 1933) 57.

4. Ibid., 500.

5. B. Otzen, "Noch einmal das Wort TRKB auf einem Arad Ostracon," *VT* 20 (1970) 239–40.

6. *AI*, 13.

(43c), we read concerning the scapegoat: חלה המשתלח מרכיבו על החמור 'If the scapegoat became ill, he should load it onto a donkey'. Similarly, in the Tosepta, *t. Yoma* 4(3):14 (Zuck. 188[7]) we read: שאלו את ר' אליע' הרי שחלה שעיר המשתלח מהו להרכיבו 'They asked R. Eliezer: If the scapegoat becomes ill, is it permitted to load it onto. . . ?'.[8]

It is possible that the lack of biblical attestation to the use of the *Hiphil* of רכ"ב for loading inanimate objects onto a beast of burden is purely coincidental, as is the fact that it is only attested once in post-biblical Hebrew.

For whom was Elyashib ordered to provide flour? Aharoni and Lemaire speculate about the identity of the recipients referred to by להם;[9] they also ask whether the reference is to a special method of baking bread, unlike that used by the Judeans.[10] If Aharoni's restoration of letter 5:5–7 [קמ]ח [לעשת] לחם ל[כ]ת[ים] 'flou[r to make] bread for the [*Ki*]*tti*[*yîm*]' is correct, then להם is 'for them', that is, the same *Kittiyîm* mentioned above. See also 2:7–8, ונתת להם 'and you shall give them', the *Kittiyîm* mentioned in lines 1–2. However, there is no way of knowing why the writer mentioned both here and in 5:5–7 that the flour was for baking bread. Most probably he had no special intention in mentioning the purpose of the flour. Such draft letters should not be read as though they were elaborate, thought-out literary pieces. The *Kittiyîm* did not eat special bread; they ate the ordinary bread issued to them by Elyashib (cf. letters 2 and 10).

Arad 1:9–10

This letter ends with a *nota bene*: מיין האגנת תתן 'From the wine of the *ʾaggānōt* you will give'. The word *ʾaggānōt* is the plural of אגן, which is commonly taken to mean 'a large banquet bowl or crater'.[11] It is identified as the Greek *kratēr*, in which wine and water were mixed before being served. It might refer to a large, deep, two-handled bowl.

7. *Tosephta, Based on the Erfurt and Vienna Codices* (ed. M. S. Zuckermandel; 2d. ed.; Jerusalem, 1937).

8. It is possible, however, that the question put to R. Eliezer was not about loading the scapegoat onto another animal, but about carrying it on one's shoulders. This is the interpretation given in the Babylonian Talmud, *b. Yoma* 66b: שאלו את רבי אליעזר חלה מהו שירכיבו על כתפו . . . וחכמים אומרים חלה מרכיבו על כתפו 'They asked R. Eliezer: If it (i.e., the scapegoat) became ill, is it permitted to carry it on one's shoulder. . . . And the Sages say: If it became ill, he should carry it on his shoulder'.

9. *AI*, 14.

10. A. Lemaire, *Inscriptions hébraïques*, vol. 1: *Les Ostraca* (Paris, 1977) 158–59.

11. Cf. A. M. Honeyman, "The Pottery Vessels of the Old Testament," *PEQ* (1939) 78–79; J. L. Kelso, *The Ceramic Vocabulary of the Old Testament* (New Haven, 1948) 15–16.

Cant 7:3 certainly refers to a mixing bowl, and the vessel mentioned in Exod 24:6 fits this description well. An actual *ʾgn*-vessel was found in Palmyra with the word *ʾgn* inscribed on it. The vessel was a crater, approximately 60 cm tall, with an inner diameter of approximately 56 cm, quite a large vessel. It is inscribed with the name of King Odenath (*ʾdnyt mlkʾ*), who lived at the beginning of the first century C.E.[12] Another small fragment of an *ʾgn*-vessel was discovered in Kition (Cyprus), inscribed with *hʾgn hz ʾ*[*š* 'This *ʾagan* wh[ich . . . dedicated'.[13]

Aharoni has proposed that יין האגנת was "a certain type of wine preserved or diluted in these vessels."[14] However, in ancient times wine was always diluted with water, and sometimes spiced, before it was served, so it is unlikely that the term refers to a specific type of wine. Nor can the term refer to wine stored in crater-like vessels, since wine was stored only in narrow-necked jars which could be sealed with stoppers. It can only be concluded that the *ʾaggān* of Arad was not the *ʾaggān* of Exod 24:6 or Cant 7:3, nor was it the *ʾgnʾ* of the Palmyrenes and the *ʾgn* from Kition.[15] We might be faced with a usage specific to Arad, or with what is described in Isa 22:24–25, where *ʾaggānot*-vessels are hanging on a peg. Crater-like vessels were never hung on pegs, but rather stacked on shelves. In view of all this, it seems that here too the *ʾaggān* is some sort of storage jar.

Arad 3:3–6

וצוך חנניהו על באר שבע עם משא צמד חמרם וצרר אתם בצק

> And Ḥananyahu has ordered you: "Go to Beer Sheba with a burden of a pair of donkeys and load them with dough."

Aharoni has interpreted this letter as dealing with an emergency, so that dough, rather than flour, was sent from Arad to Beer Sheba.[16] However, this interpretation is improbable. The distance from Arad to Beer Sheba is approximately 30 km, i.e., a long day's march. During such a

12. H. Ingolt-J. Starcky, "Recuil des inscriptions sémitiques de cette region," in *La Palmyrène du nord-ouest* (ed. D. Schlumberger; Paris, 1951) 60 (description: no. 36), 151 (inscription: no. 21), pl. XXV:3–6.

13. M. G. Amadasi Guzzo and V. Karageorghis, *Fouilles des Kition,* vol. 3: *Inscriptions phéniciennes* (Nicosia, 1977) 168–69, pl. XXII, 6.

14. *AI,* 14.

15. Comparison with mishnaic and talmudic material does not help in this case. The talmudic *ʾaggan* is a huge vessel, a basin in which one can even bathe. Cf. Y. Brand, *Klei ha-Ḥeres be-Sifrut ha-Talmud* (Ceramics in Talmudic Literature) (Jerusalem, 1953) VI–VIII [Heb.].

16. *AI,* 18.

journey dough would not ferment, but rather dry up. Furthermore, even in an emergency there is no need to send dough, as it takes only a few minutes to knead the flour and water and bake the dough into unleavened bread.

I propose that בצק be equated with the Ugaritic *bṣql* and with **bṣqln* of 2 Kgs 4:42 (וכרמל בצקלנו). In the Ugaritic cycle of Aqhat there is a description of the hero Dan'il in the dry field, embracing and kissing an ear of grain. The description appears twice. In the first occurrence the ear of grain is called *bṣql* and in the second, *šblt* (1 Aqht 61–74). The parallel description led Cassuto to equate *bṣql* and *šblt* 'ear of grain' and reconstruct **bṣqln* in 2 Kgs 4:42.[17]

I suggest that *bāṣĕq* here is not dough but 'grains of wheat', that is, the contents of the ripe ears. The ripe ears were called *bṣql* because they were swollen, from בצ"ק 'to be swollen'. The word *bṣql* is composed of *bṣq* with the suffix-*l*. Formation of nouns with suffixed-*l* is attested also in כרמל 'vineyard-(land?)' from כרם 'vineyard'; ערפל 'dark (rain?) cloud' from ערף* 'cloud' (cf. Akkadian *urpatu, urpu,* 'cloud'[18]).

If my suggestion is correct, then בצק is the same as חטם 'wheat', mentioned already in line 7.

17. U. Cassuto, "Daniel and the Ears of Corn: An Episode from Tablet I D of Ras Shamra," *Biblical and Oriental Studies,* vol. 2: *Bible and Oriental Texts* (Jerusalem, 1975) 195–97, esp. 197.

18. W. von Soden, *Akkadisches Handwörterbuch* (Wiesbaden, 1981) 3.1432.

A Phoenician Seal

Walter E. Aufrecht

This essay presents the initial publication of a Phoenician seal of unknown provenance inscribed with two roosters and the name ḥrṣ 'Gold'. The seal is dated to the eighth century B.C.E. *on the basis of its paleography and onomastics.*

It is a pleasure to dedicate these brief remarks to Jonas Greenfield, a colleague and friend who has contributed greatly to the study of Semitic languages. I am indebted to Eli Borowski of Jerusalem for permission to publish this seal from the collection of the Bible Lands Museum, Jerusalem.

This scaraboid stamp seal, of unknown provenance, is made of transparent rock crystal. It measures 2 × 1.8 × 1.2 cm and is perforated along its length. The edges are slightly damaged on all sides. The curved side of the seal is carved in the form of a scarab. The flat side depicts two roosters facing each other, standing on a single line that represents the ground. The letters of the name *ḥrṣ* are grouped around the roosters. The motif of roosters is not common in glyptic art. They are depicted on two Hebrew seals, with engraving inferior to what is displayed here,[1] and two cylinder seals from the Neo-Babylonian Period.[2]

Paleographically, the *reš* is undistinguished. The *ṣade* is the classical form, found in Phoenician inscriptions of the ninth and eighth centuries B.C.E.[3] The Phoenician *ṣade* quickly evolved into the form with a

Author's note: Research for this paper was supported by funds from the Social Sciences and Humanities Research Council of Canada.

1. See R. Hestrin and M. Dayagi-Mendels, *Inscribed Seals* (Jerusalem, 1979) nos. 5 and 6.
2. W. S. McCullough, "Fowl," *IDB* 2.323.
3. See, for example, a cylinder seal found at Karatepe, originally classified as Aramaic by H. T. Bossert, *Karatepe* (Istanbul, 1946) pl. 4:37; but reclassified as Phoenician by A. Dupont-Sommer, *Jahrbuch für kleinasiatische Forschung* 1 (1950) 43–45.

Above: Face of seal of *ḥrṣ*.
Below: Impression of seal of *ḥrṣ*.

more jagged, *Z*-shaped head.[4] The classical form is found on a seventh century B.C.E. Ammonite seal,[5] but not on Aramaic seals, which exhibit a variety of forms,[6] or on Hebrew seals, which shorten the left down-stroke and add a downward tick to the cross-stroke.[7] The three-bar *ḥet,* not attested in the transjordanian script traditions, is found on Hebrew and Phoenician seals from the eighth to the sixth centuries B.C.E. and on Aramaic seals up to the beginning of the seventh century B.C.E., when it is replaced by the two- and one-bar forms. In the Aramaic series, it is common for both vertical shafts to extend above the top cross-line as on our seal,[8] but this feature is also found on seals and impressions classified as Phoenician and Hebrew.[9]

The word *ḥrṣ*, meaning 'gold', is found in Ugaritic, Phoenician, and Punic.[10] The seal appears to be the first attestation of this word as a proper name. It is possible that the word identifies the profession of the owner, that is, 'goldsmith', but the absence of the definite article makes this less likely.

On the basis of these paleographic and onomastic criteria, the seal may be classified as Phoenician, from the eighth century B.C.E.

4. See, for example, the early seventh-century B.C.E. seal published by N. Avigad, "Notes on Some Inscribed Syro-Phoenician Seals," *BASOR* 189 (1968)45 (fig.), 47–49. Unfortunately, the *ṣade* on that seal is written backwards, thereby diminishing its diagnostic usefulness.

5. W. E. Aufrecht, *A Corpus of Ammonite Inscriptions* (Lewiston, N.Y., 1989) no. 18.

6. For examples, see L. G. Herr, *The Scripts of Ancient Northwest Semitic Seals* (Missoula, Mont., 1978) fig. 31.

7. A possible exception is the *ṣade* on a Hebrew seal published by M. deVogué, *Mélanges d'archéologie oriental* (Paris, 1868) 140 no. 42. Unfortunately, this letter is also written backwards.

8. For examples, see Herr, *Scripts of Ancient Northwest Semitic Seals,* fig. 27.

9. Phoenician: Hestrin and Dayagi-Mendels, *Inscribed Seals,* nos. 118 and 119; P. Bordreuil, *Catalogue des sceaux ouest-sémitiques inscrits* (Paris, 1986) nos. 2 and 27. Hebrew: Hestrin and Dayagi-Mendels, *Inscribed Seals,* nos. 14, 17, 19, 21, 25; Bordreuil, *Catalogue,* no. 46; Herr, *Scripts of Ancient Northwest Semitic Seals,* 133 no. 119, 139 no. 135, 147 no. 158.

10. Ugaritic: see *UT* 405 no. 1014; I am indebted to Professor Frank M. Cross for calling these examples to my attention. Phoenician: *KAI* nos. 10:5; 11:1; 24:12; 60:3 and 5. Punic: *CIS* I 327:4–5.

The Ammonite Tell Siran Bottle Inscription Reconsidered

KLAUS BEYER

The author offers several new suggestions for the translation of the Ammonite bottle inscription.

In 1972, a bronze bottle, 10 cm. in length, was found on the outskirts of Amman. It contained a sample of roasted wheat and cereal grains. On the bottle's side was an inscription which is in fact the only reasonably long and completely preserved Ammonite inscription known. According to J. Naveh, its Aramaic-Ammonite script dates to the period around 667 B.C.E.[1] (less likely is F. M. Cross's date of around 600 B.C.E.). The most recent edition is found in W. E. Aufrecht's *Corpus of Ammonite Inscriptions*,[2] which also contains a bibliography of no less than ninety-nine items on this inscription alone. In spite of this, it seems to me that not everything necessary has yet been said. With the present contribution I now launch the second hundred contributions and wish for the jubilarian, Jonas Greenfield, that his scientific productivity may continue to grow as steadily and retain the same vitality as has the discussion over this inscription.

TRANSCRIPTION

1. מעבד עמנדב מלך בן עמן
2. בן הצלאל ' מלך בן עמן
3. בן עמנדב מלך בן עמן
4. הכרם ' וה'גנת ' והאתחר

Editors' note: The German manuscript of this article was translated by A. Livingstone.

1. J. Naveh, *Early History of the Alphabet* (2d ed.; Leiden and Jerusalem, 1987) 110–11.
2. W. E. Aufrecht, *A Corpus of Ammonite Inscriptions* (Lewiston, N.Y., 1989) 203–11.

5. ואשחת
6. יגל וישמח
7. ביומת רבם ובשנת
8. רחקת

TRANSLITERATION

(1) *mōᶜabád ᶜAmmīnadáb mèlk bànē ᶜAmmṓn*
(2) *bèn Heṣṣīlᵓél mèlk bànē ᶜAmmṓn*
(3) *bèn ᶜAmmīnadáb mèlk bànē ᶜAmmṓn*
(4) *hak-karm wahag-gánnat wahaᵓᵓTḤR* (5) *waᵓŠḤṓt*
(6) *yagī́lū wayaśamméḫū*
(7) *beyawamṓt rabbī́m wabešanṓt* (8) *raḥoqṓt*

TRANSLATION

(1) That which Amminadab, the king of the Ammonites,
(2) the son of Hessilel, the king of the Ammonites,
(3) the son of Amminadab, the king of the Ammonites, has laid out
(4) are the vineyard, the garden, the orchard (5) and cisterns.
(6) May they cause joy and pleasure
(7) for many days and in (8) far off years.

COMMENTARY

Lines 1–8. While the inscription was divided into six lines in the "Vorlage" according to its meaning, the artisan lacked sufficient space for lines 4 and 7.

Line 1. In the neighboring Hebrew the only words attested from the root *ᶜbd* are the verb *ᶜabad* 'work, serve', the masc. noun *ᶜabd* (pattern: *qaṭl*), 'slave', and the feminine noun *ᶜebōdā* (pattern: *qiṭāl*), 'labor'. The rare and late (Ezra, Nehemiah, Job, Qoheleth) derivatives *ᶜobād* (preceded by assimilated *mèn* 'part of') and *maᶜbād* 'deed, product' (to which *ᶜabdūt* 'servitude', belongs) are Aramaic and should therefore not be presumed in Ammonite. So the remaining possibility is proclitic *mō*, 'what?' in the meaning 'that which'; cf. C. Brockelmann, *Hebräische Syntax* (Neukirchen, 1956) §154. For writings with *mīm* alone in Canaanite and Aramaic, cf. C.-F. Jean and J. Hoftijzer, *Dictionnaire des inscriptions sémitiques de lᵓouest* (Leiden, 1965) 114 (+ Deir ᶜAlla II 13 around 800 B.C.E.; Hermopolis Papyrus 5:7 around 500 B.C.E.).

Lines 4–5. The only comparable list of agricultural installations from Palestine (of course, several centuries later) is Qoh 2:4–6 (H. O. Thompson and F. Zayadine, "The Tell Siran Inscription," *BASOR* 212 [1973] 10). On the basis of this one would expect an orchard in the third position. Many etymologies of *ʾTḪR* are possible. The cisterns mentioned at the end of the sequence of installations would of course have been present in each of them; for this reason the word stands in the plural and is indeterminate. All four (nonmilitary) installations of the king should be in the same line, but there was insufficient space, although line 4 continues to the base of the bottle. So the last word stands alone in line 5; the same has happened in line 8.

Line 6. The verbal forms are in the C- and D-stems (cf. Aufrecht, *Corpus of Ammonite Inscriptions,* 210). Unaccented long vowels in final position are not indicated (here: *-ē, -ū*); cf. K. Beyer, *Die aramäischen Texte vom Toten Meer* (Göttingen, 1984, + Supplement 1994) 409.

Paleography and the Date of the Tell Faḫariyeh Bilingual Inscription

Frank Moore Cross

Among the striking and remarkable features of the Tell Faḫariyeh Inscription is the script chosen by the scribe in which to engrave the Aramaic version. It is an exemplar of Linear Phoenician at an early stage of its development. Were there no contrary evidence, the paleographer would date the script in the Phoenician series in the late eleventh century B.C.E. *It has no significant features that characterize the extant Aramaic scripts of the early, middle, and late ninth century* B.C.E. *The Aramaic scripts of the ninth century are well known, and the sequence of the Aramaic scripts is fixed in date by external as well as typological data. In this series is the Gozan Pedestal Inscription from the late tenth century or the beginning of the ninth century* B.C.E. *(from the Kapara period at Gozan), an inscription recently rescued for paleographical analysis thanks to newly-found photographs. Its existence is a mortal blow to notions that the Faḫariyeh script belongs to a peripheral pocket of archaism. At the same time, very strong arguments exist for dating the Tell Faḫariyeh text to the third quarter of the ninth century (ca. 840–825* B.C.E.*). In view of these conflicting data, how is the issue of the date of the inscription to be resolved?*

Among the striking and remarkable features of the Tell Faḫariyeh Inscription is the script chosen by the scribe in which to engrave the

Author's note: This is a revised version of a paper read at a panel discussion held on July 21, 1982, at the Hebrew University of Jerusalem, in which Jonas Greenfield, Joseph Naveh, Aaron Shaffer, Hayim Tadmor, and I participated. I am pleased to be able to present it in homage to Jonas Greenfield. His contributions to the study of the Tell Faḫariyeh text have been many and include the following papers: J. C. Greenfield and A. Shaffer, "Notes on the Bilingual Inscription from Tell Fekherye," *Shnaton* 5–6 (1982) 119–29; J. C. Greenfield and A. Shaffer, "QLQLTᵓ, TUBKINNU, Refuse Tips and Treasure Trove," *Anatolian Studies* 33 (1983) 123–29; J. C. Greenfield and A. Shaffer,"Notes on the Akkadian-Aramaic Bilingual Statue from Tell Fekheryeh, *Iraq* 45 (1983) 109–16; J. C. Greenfield, "A Touch of Eden," *Orientalia J. Duchesne-Guillemin emerito oblata* (Leiden, 1984) 219–24; J. C. Greenfield and A. Shaffer, "Notes on the Curse Formulae of the Tell Fekherye Inscription," *RB* 92 (1985) 47–59.

Aramaic version.[1] It is an exemplar of Linear Phoenician at an early stage of its development. It has no significant features that characterize the extant Aramaic scripts of the early, middle, and late ninth century B.C.E. The Aramaic scripts of the ninth century are well known, and the sequence of the Aramaic scripts is fixed in date by external as well as typological data. In this series are the Gozan Pedestal Inscription from the late tenth century or the beginning of the ninth century B.C.E. (from the Kapara period at Gozan),[2] the ᶜÊn Gev Inscription (second quarter of the ninth century),[3] the contemporary Jar Inscription from Dan,[4] the Bir Hadad Inscription (ca. 850 B.C.E.),[5] the Aramaic Stele from Dan (shortly before 842 B.C.E. as proved by new fragments),[6] the Amman Cita-

1. The *editio princeps* is A. Abou-Assaf, P. Bordreuil, and A. R. Millard, *La Statue de Tell Fekherye et son inscription bilingue assyro-araméenne* (Études Assyriologiques, Cahier 7; Paris, 1982). For bibliography, see John Huehnergard's review of the above-mentioned volume in *BASOR* 261 (1986) 91–95; W. E. Aufrecht and G. J. Hamilton, "The Tell Fakhariyah Bilingual Inscription: A Bibliography," *Newsletter for Targumic and Cognate Studies Supplement* 4 (1988) 1–7; and S. Layton, "Old Aramaic Inscriptions" (edited by D. Pardee), *BA* 51 (1988) 172–89.

2. For bibliography and a discussion of the date, see below.

3. See B. Mazar, A. Biran, M. Dothan, and I. Dunayevsky, "ᶜEin Gev: Excavations in 1961," *IEJ* (1964) 27–29, and pl. 13B. The inscription is on a jar from Stratum III dated by the excavators to 886–841 (or 838) B.C.E.; and J. C. L. Gibson, *Textbook of Syrian Semitic Inscriptions*, vol. 2: *Aramaic Inscriptions* [hereafter Gibson II] (Oxford, 1975) no. 3.

4. N. Avigad, "An Inscribed Bowl from Dan," *PEQ* 100 (1968) 42–44 and pl. 18; and Gibson II, no. 4.

5. See F. M. Cross, "The Stele Dedicated to Melcarth by Ben Hadad," *BASOR* 205 (1972) 36–42; E. Lipiński, *Studies in Aramaic Inscriptions and Onomastics I* (OLA 1; Louvain, 1974) 15–19; Gibson II, no. 1; P. Bordreuil and J. Teixidor, "Nouvel examen de l'inscription de Bar-Hadad," *Aula Orientalis* 1 (1983) 271–76; A. Lemaire, "La Stèle araméenne de Barhadad," *Or* 53 (1984) 337–49; Layton, "Old Aramaic Inscriptions," 172–89; G. G. G. Reinhold, "The Bir-Hadad Stele and the Biblical Kings of Aram," *Andrews University Seminary Studies* 24 (1986) 115–26; and W. T. Pitard, "The Identity of the Bir Hadad of the Melqart Stele," *BASOR* 272 (1988) 3–21 (with bibliography).

I cannot accept Pitard's new reading of the patronymic of the Ben Hadad of the inscription. I do not like the stance of the *taw* he reconstructs; I see a *zayin*. Further, I think the sequence [ ] *mš*[is clear, and I find the element *hmk* implausible in a personal name. I still should argue that we can read in line 2: *br ᶜzr*[ ]*mš*[. In 1972 I proposed alternate readings. One of these I still prefer: *br ᶜzr* [.] ⌜*d*⌝ *mš*[*qyᵓ br*], reading the whole, 'The stele which Bir Hadad, son of ᶜEzer (ᶜIðr), the Damascene, son of the king of Aram, set up to his lord Milqart to whom he made a vow and who heard his voice'. We take the Bir-Hadad of the inscription to be the son and crown prince or co-regent of (Hadad-)Idri (ᶜIðr), who flourished ca. 870–842 B.C.E.

6. See provisionally J. Naveh and A. Biran, "An Aramaic Stela Fragment from Tel Dan," *IEJ* 43 (1993) 82–98; and E. Puech, "La stele araméenne de Dan: Bar Hadad II et la coalition des Omrides e de la maison de David," *RB* 101 (1994) 215–41. In a lecture at Harvard University in November 1994, Prof. Biran showed photographs of new fragments of the stele that appear to demonstrate that the stele comes from the reigns of Joram of Israel and Ahaziah of Judah. These data should silence those who wish to date the Stele of Bir Hadad and

del Inscription (mid-ninth century B.C.E.),[7] the Kilamuwa Inscription (ca. 925 B.C.E.),[8] the four Ḥazaʾel inscriptions (ca. 825 B.C.E.),[9] the Luristan Bronze Jug Inscription (ca. 800 B.C.E.),[10] and the Zakkur Inscription (ca. 800–775 B.C.E.).[11] The Old Canaanite and Early Linear Phoenician series of scripts is also richly illustrated and closely fixed in date by a network of interlocking historical, archaeological, and typological evidence. The fortuitous circumstance that the military elite of Canaan chose to inscribe bronze arrowheads with their names in the eleventh century has provided a corpus of some twenty published inscriptions that span the eleventh century, and more exist in museums and private hands.[12] Other tenth- and ninth-century texts in Linear Phoenician are in good supply. As I have said, while the language of the Faḫariyeh text is Aramaic, it is not written in an Aramaic script—unless that term is misused to apply to the script, properly called Linear Phoenician, which was used by Phoenicians, Israelites, and Aramaeans in the late eleventh and early tenth centuries B.C.E. Rather it is written in Phoenician. This phenomenon, inscriptions composed in one language but written down in the script of another, is not unique. The Kilamuwa Inscription is written in the Aramaic script though its language is Phoenician, and the Amman Citadel Inscription uses an Aramaic script to record a text in Canaanite (Ammonite); some would argue that the

---

the Dan Stele in the last quarter of the ninth century or even at the beginning of the eighth century.

7. For bibliography, see W. E. Aufrecht, *A Corpus of Ammonite Inscriptions* (ANETS 4; Lewiston, N.Y., 1989) 154–63, no. 59. See also my paleographical analysis of the inscription in my paper, "Epigraphic Notes on the Ammān Citadel Inscription," *BASOR* 193 (1969) 13–19.

8. *KAI* no. 24. Note that the inscription is engraved in Aramaic script, not Phoenician, although the language is Phoenician.

9. See E. Puech, "L'ivoire inscrit d'Arslan Tash et les rois de Damas," *RB* 88 (1981) 544–62 and pls. 12 and 13; H. Kyrieleis and W. Röllig, "Ein altorientalischer Pferdeschmuck aus dem Heraion von Samos," *Mitteilungen des Deutschen Archäologischen Instituts, Athenische Abteilung* 103 (1988) 37–75 and pls. 9–15; F. Bron and A. Lemaire, "Les inscriptions araméennes de Hazäel," *RA* 83 (1989) 35–44; and I. Ephʿal and J. Naveh, "Hazael's Booty Inscriptions," *IEJ* 39 (1989) 192–200 and pls. 24–25.

10. See A. Dupont-Sommer, "Trois inscriptions araméennes inédites sur des bronzes du Luristan," *Iranica antiqua IV* (ed. P. Ghirshman and L. Vande Berghe; Leiden, 1964) 106–88, esp. 106–11 and pls. 33–34; Gibson II, no. 11 (with bibliography).

11. *KAI* no. 202; Gibson II, no. 5 , with bibliography, to which should be added J. C. Greenfield, "The Zakir Inscription and the Danklied," *Proceedings of the Fifth World Congress of Jewish Studies* (Jerusalem, 1969) 1.174–79; J. F. Ross, "Prophecy in Hamath, Israel, and Mari," *HTR* 63 (1970) 1–28; and Lipiński, *Studies in Aramaic Inscriptions and Onomastics I.*

12. See the list and bibliography in F. M. Cross, "An Inscribed Arrowhead of the Eleventh Century BCE in the Bible Lands Museum in Jerusalem," *ErIsr* 23 (1992) 21*–26*.

Gezer Calendar, written in a Hebrew dialect, is composed in the Phoenician script. Although it exhibits one or two peculiar features, the Tell Faḫariyeh script fits perfectly into the Phoenician series, and were there no contrary evidence, paleographers would assign it to the end of the eleventh century B.C.E. While there are a few letter forms, notably the *kap* and *pe*, that are typologically earlier, the letters of the script are stabilized in right-to-left, horizontal stances, a standardization that emerged in Phoenician in the late eleventh century B.C.E. when multidirectional styles of writing finally died out.

To be sure, we are in the general period when the Aramaeans borrowed the Linear Phoenician script. The cluster of typological features that came to characterize the national Aramaic script no doubt emerged slowly and became fully recognizable only at the beginning of the ninth century B.C.E. One must observe, however, that Phoenician continued to influence the Aramaic script for a century or a century and a half after its borrowing, so that the ninth-century Aramaic script exhibits some features that evolved in tenth-century Phoenician. One may argue that in the far northeastern periphery of the Aramaic realm, archaic features remained long after the Aramaeans initially borrowed the script from the Phoenicians. The difficulty with such an argument is that Aramaic inscriptions of the ninth century are widely distributed, including epigraphs from central Transjordan in the south to Zinčirlı in the north; and distributed, even if not engraved locally, from Samos in the Aegean to Luristan in the far east. A number of our Old Aramaic inscriptions have been found on the trade route that runs from Aleppo to Carchemish, from Carchemish to Arslan Tash, from Arslan Tash to Haran and Gozan. All our ninth-century Aramaic texts, however, prove to belong to the standard, homogeneous Aramaic series, with little hint of the kind of archaism found in the new text from Faḫariyeh.

An even greater hindrance to the notion of a peripheral pocket of archaism is the existence of the Gozan Pedestal Inscription. The object itself was destroyed in the Second World War. A poor drawing of it was published by Johannes Friedrich in 1940 and an equally bad drawing by R. A. Bowman in 1941.[13] Neither was really usable for either decipherment or paleographical analysis. Fortunately, two photographs were found in 1986, together with a plaster impression of a squeeze of the inscription. These have now been published by G. Dankwarth and Christa Müller.[14] They transcribe:

13. J. Friedrich et al., "Die Inschriften vom Tell Halaf," *AfO* 6 (Berlin, 1940) 69–70, pl. 29; and R. A. Bowman, "The Old Aramaic Alphabet at Tell Halaf: The Date of the 'Altar' Inscription," *AJSL* 48 (1941) 359–67.

14. G. Dankwarth and Christa Müller, "Zur altaramäischen 'Altar'-Inschrift von Tell Ḥalaf," *AfO* 35 (1988) 74–78 (with bibliography).

FMC

Figure 1. A Drawing of the Gozan Pedestal Inscription from ca. 900 B.C.E.

zdmt | *b*^{c}*m* [*x* | |] | *zy* | *k*(*z*) | | *ḥy* [*xxx*] | | (empty)

They read the beginning of the inscription *za damūt(a)* ‘dies ist das (Stand)-Bild’ and favor an interpretation, “Dieses (ist das) Bild des (st. c.) PN/GN?, welches (+ Verbalform) PN.” So far I believe they are correct. However, the inscription yields at least another letter, which they have misread. After *kap* on the third side of the pedestal there is a clear if lightly engraved *nun* and traces of another letter at the corner. I should read:

(1) *zdmt* | *b*^{c}*m*[*r*]
(2) | *zy* | *kn*⌜*n*⌝ [|]
(3) *ḥy* [ ]
(4) [empty]

This is the image of B^{c}m[r?] which Ḥayyā [. . .]set up.

The root *kwn*, excessively rare in Aramaic, appears here evidently in the R-stem, precisely as in the Tell Faḫariyeh inscription, of setting up an image. The name Ḥayyā is spelled as it is on the Kilamuwa Gold Sheath. We should expect Ḥayyā$^{\supset}$ (as in the large Kilamuwa Inscription). Similarly we should have expected *z*$^{\supset}$, rather than *z* for *zā*$^{\supset}$, the feminine form of the demonstrative pronoun. We may speculate that the personal name in line 1 should be reconstructed as *B*^{c}*mr* and analyzed as composed of a preposition plus a noun (the theophoric element omitted): *Bi-*^{c}*im*[*r*]. Compare the local personal name found in the Tell Halaf texts in Akkadian transcription, *bi-im-me-r-a-a* and *bi-im-ra-a*, and the Hebrew personal name ^{c}Omri.[15]

The inscription was found in the Kapara levels at Gozan, which predate Assyrian domination and are now generally dated to the late tenth

15. Friedrich et al., “Inschriften vom Tell Halaf,” 105, Vs. 2; 105, Rs. 4.

century or, at the latest, the beginning of the ninth century.[16] The script of the Gozan Inscription shows archaic features. The *mem* in particular is archaic, but like the letters *zayin*, *dalet*, and *yod*, may easily fit into tenth-century Linear Phoenician. In the ninth-century Aramaic script, the *dalet* has grown a short tail, and the tail of *yod* no longer droops. The form of *zayin* changes little until the third quarter of the ninth century, when the *Z*-form develops, first seen in the Ḥazaᵓel inscriptions (once on the Horse ornaments) and in the Zakkur text of the turn of the ninth century B.C.E. Most notable is the *K*-form *kap* in the Gozan text. This form develops from the trident form, which appears first at the beginning of the eleventh century (ᶜIzbet Ṣarṭah), and is found in tenth-century Hebrew, in early Greek and, with a lengthening leg, in ninth-century Aramaic. In Phoenician it is absent from most eleventh- and all tenth-century inscriptions, being replaced with a three-fingered form (i.e., a trident without handle). The vertical downstroke of *taw* in the Gozan text has lengthened beyond the earlier *X*-form. This is an Aramaic trait (in this period). Both Hebrew and Phoenician *taw* retain an *X*-form, in Hebrew for centuries, in Phoenician through the ninth century. The *nun* is difficult to use since it is faint in the photograph of the cast. If my drawing is correct, its tail has begun to lengthen. This is a trait found in tenth-century Hebrew (the Timnah Graffito) and in ninth-century Aramaic. The *ḥet* is crudely made but probably was drawn with three horizontal bars, though the top one is obscured, with clear "break-throughs" downward below the lowest horizontal bar. It is a form that replaces the box-form *ḥet*s in the Phoenician of the eleventh century.

The Gozan Inscription reflects the evolution of the Aramaic script in the tenth century, under the partial influence of the Phoenician character. It also exhibits distinct innovations of the Aramaic script which, in the course of the first half of the ninth century, will create a wholly individual national Aramaic script. The script of the text from Gozan, the capital city of Hadad-yiθᶜī, whose image is on the Tell Faḫariyeh statue, underlines the anomaly of the script on the statue inscription—if one argues for a date in the second half of the ninth century for the Tell Faḫariyeh statue, more than a half century after the Gozan text. And it decimates the notion that the Faḫariyeh script is a peripheral Aramaic script. The Gozan script is precisely what is anticipated for the Aramaic

16. See W. F. Albright, "The Date of the Kapara Period at Gozan (Tell Halaf)," *Anatolian Studies* 6 (The Garstang Volume; 1956) 75–85; and recently, I. Winter "North Syrian Ivories and Tell Halaf Reliefs: The Impact of Luxury Goods upon 'Major' Arts," *Essays in Ancient Civilization Presented to Helene J. Kantor* (ed. A. Leonard Jr. and B. B. Williams; Studies in Ancient Oriental Civilization 47; Chicago, 1989) 321–32 and pls. 62–66.

character (anywhere in the Aramaean realm) as it begins its separation from Linear Phoenician at the end of the tenth century B.C.E.

There are certain other traits of the Tell Faḫariyeh Aramaic text that are uniquely archaic. The inscription uses word dividers or syntactical dividers, the vertical stroke (found no later than the Meshaᶜ Inscription of ca. 940 B.C.E.) and two or three vertically arranged dots, to divide words. Such dots, as Joseph Naveh has observed, characterized Proto-Canaanite and Old Greek, and effectively disappeared in the tenth century B.C.E. in West Semitic epigraphs. The use of *samek* for the notation of the phoneme [*θ*] contrasts with the use of *šin* in all other extant Old Aramaic texts. While the phenomenon has given rise to various explanations,[17] the easiest and most parsimonious one is to suppose that it reflects historical phonetic development. We know from Egyptian and Akkadian transcriptions that *samek* shifted from a median affricative, [*ts*] or [*tš*], to a simple sibilant, [*s*], in this general period (in the interval of the XIX–XX Dynasties of Egypt). West Semitic *samek* [*s̊*] is transcribed in Egyptian by the hieroglyphic *ṯ* [*č*]; the equation also operates in the reverse direction. Later, the equation changes, and Egyptian *ś* is rendered by *s̊*, *samek*, having shifted from the affricate to the sibilant. The same shift is reflected in the Amarna transcription of *samek* [*s̊*] by *z* (i.e., *zu*, *zi*, etc.); in later Assyrian by the transcription *š*, pronounced [*s*] (= Hebrew *samek*). An example is the name of the town, Phoenician/Hebrew *ʾōs̊ō* (< **ʾās̊ā*), Palaeo-Tyre, is transcribed in Hieroglyphic by *ỉwčw*, *uzu* in Amarna, and *ušu* in Assyrian transcriptions. The sound change seems to have swept through West Semitic. Before the shift, *samek* may have seemed to the Aramaeans a more suitable notation for *θ*, *šin* a more suitable sign after the shift of *samek* from its affricative value to a simple sibilant. There are also some archaic grammatical elements to be noted, including the use of the *Gt*, so-called, and the prefixed precative *lamed* with the imperfect verb; we shall leave these matters of grammar to another occasion. They are, however, of considerable interest. On the other hand the full development of the article in the Tell Faḫariyeh Inscription is an advanced trait in Aramaic and remarkable.

Despite the archaic features of the script of the Tell Faḫariyeh Inscription, there are strong arguments for a date in the third quarter of the ninth century (ca. 840–825), in the time of the Amman Citadel Inscription (mid-ninth century), the Kilamuwa Inscription (ca. 825 B.C.E.) and the Ḥazaʾel inscriptions (842–806). The Tell Faḫariyeh Inscription

17. See, for example, G. A. Rendsburg, "The Ammonite Phoneme /Ṯ/," *BASOR* 269 (1988) 73–79.

would be later than the Ben (Bir) Hadad and the ᶜÊn Gev inscriptions from the first half of the ninth century and considerably later than the neighboring inscription from Gozan from the end of the tenth century. None of these arguments for a late date stem from paleographical arguments; in fact they are in conflict with them. The Tell Faḫariyeh script does not fit into the Aramaic series from the Gozan text to the Ḥazaᵓel inscriptions and, a fortiori, into the sequence of Aramaic scripts of the second half of the ninth century.

The arguments for dating the Tell Faḫariyeh Inscription in the third quarter of the ninth century are as follows.

(a) The closest parallels to features of artistic style found in the sculpture point to the ninth century B.C.E. Assyrianizing elements appear stronger in the Faḫariyeh image than in the Kapara sculptures of the tenth century. There are also peculiar features in the art of the Faḫariyeh image. It is not fully Assyrianizing in style. In any case, caution is required in relying on the typology of artistic features, in view of the paucity of comparative materials of the eleventh and early tenth centuries, after Assyrian hegemony under Tiglath-pileser I (1115–1077).

(b) Certain features of Assyrian orthography and linguistic usage are characteristic of the inscriptions of Assur-naṣir-pal or of roughly contemporary Assyrian royal inscriptions. Yet once again we are faced with little in the way of comparable Assyrian royal inscriptions of a similar genre from the late eleventh and tenth centuries when Assyria was in decline. It has been observed by Stephen Kaufman that the cuneiform script of the Tell Faḫariyeh Inscription is more evolved than that of the Kapara cuneiform texts.[18] I am wary of arguments based on Akkadian paleography. The typological sequence of styles of cuneiform scripts in this period is little studied, or, in any case, studies are not published. On the other hand the archaism of the vertical writing of the cuneiform is surprising, an instance of radical archaizing.

(c) Šamaš-nūrī (Sās-nūrī) appears in the eponym lists in the seventeenth year of Assur-naṣir-pal II, 866 B.C.E., at the place expected for the governor of Gozan, following the name of the governor of Tušḫan. It is tempting simply to identify Šamaš-nūrī of the eponym list with Šamaš-nūrī , the father of Hadad-yiθᶜī, and to date the statue and its inscription ca. 840 B.C.E. or a decade or two later, in the reign of Shalmaneser III (858–824 B.C.E.). To be sure, the repetition of dynastic names in Assyria and in the Aramaic city-states in this period is notorious. Identical throne names succeed one another (the sequence of Ben Hadads), and papponymy is practiced. So certitude eludes us.

18. Stephen Kaufman, "Reflections on the Assyrian-Aramaic Bilingual from Tell Fakhariyeh," *Maarav* 3 (1982) 140.

(d) The system of *ʾimmôt haq-qĕrîʾāh,* matres lectionis, used in the Tell Faḫariyeh Inscription is the fully developed Aramaic orthographic system, not the purely consonantal orthography of either earlier or later Phoenician. However, the orthography is much more plene than anticipated, and indeed more plene than the orthography of ninth- through seventh-century texts in Aramaic.[19] In the final position, *waw* is used for *-ū*; *yod* for *-ī*; and *hē* for *-ā*, *ē*, and **ō*. *ʾAlep* is not used as a mater lectionis. *Waw* and *yod* are also used sporadically as internal *matres lectiones*, especially in foreign words or names (as elsewhere in Old Aramaic) and in nouns or verbs derived from so-called 2d and 3d *waw/yod* roots, a phenomenon attested in Old Aramaic and early Hebrew, but with relative infrequency. Indeed twice in the Faḫariyeh text, *yod* is used to mark the masculine plural ending *-īn* , a usage wholly unexpected in Old Aramaic or, for that matter, in epigraphic Imperial Aramaic.

In the monograph *Early Hebrew Orthography,*[20] now forty years old and antiquated at many points, we argued that the Aramaeans, some time after their borrowing of the Phoenician alphabet in the eleventh century, invented a system of matres lectionis, notably the use of *waw, yod,* and *he* to mark final vowels, and that this Aramaic orthographic system was borrowed by Israel, probably in the early ninth century. Earlier Israel had used both the Phoenician Linear script and consonantal orthography of the Phoenician chancelleries. All evidence subsequently accumulated from both Israel and Aram, including now the Gozan and Tell Faḫariyeh texts, has supported this conclusion.

We contended also that the development of this orthography took place early and rapidly, as did the development of Greek orthographic innovation. However, it is unlikely that the system was adopted overnight even in the major Aramaic city-states. One might argue on this basis that the orthographic features of the Tell Faḫariyeh text point to a ninth-century date. I must confess, however, that I find the argument weak, to be used only to support other stronger arguments. I still prefer an eleventh-century date for the time of origin of the Aramaic orthographic system. The late tenth-century Gozan text reflects the new system, at least in part (*zy* for *ðî*). As a matter of fact, it is not difficult to argue that the Faḫariyeh orthography, with its extraordinarily full use of internal matres lectionis (much fuller than the more or less standardized Aramaic orthography of later centuries) reflects a time of experimentation at the beginning of the use of vowel letters.

19. See F. I. Andersen and D. N. Freedman, "The Orthography of the Aramaic Portion of the Tell Fekherye Bilingual," in *Text and Context: Old Testament and Semitic Studies for J. C. Fensham* (ed. W. Claasen; JSOTSup 48; Sheffield, 1988) 9–49.

20. F. M. Cross and D. N. Freedman, *Early Hebrew Orthography: The Epigraphic Evidence* (New Haven, 1952).

While the evidence drawn from the cuneiform text for a ninth-century date has been discussed extensively in early publications, only a few papers have engaged in serious paleographical analysis.[21] One notes that in the ninth century the Phoenician and Aramaic (as well as Hebrew) scripts have diverged to form distinct typological series. These independent "national scripts" are not to be mixed or used indiscriminately in paleographical analysis. This can lead, and has led, only to confusion.

The *ʾalep* of the Faḫariyeh Inscription, a *V* rotated 90 degrees that cuts through a vertical stroke, has an interesting history. It is the standard twelfth-century form, surviving into the early eleventh century in extant texts. It is replaced in Phoenicia and Palestine with a short-lived variant—the rotated *V* touching the vertical at its point, not cutting through—which dominates in the eleventh century, and in Phoenicia proper is the exclusive form in the tenth century. The older form, which presumably never died out of usage, reappears in early Greek, in the tenth century in Hebrew, and in ninth-century Phoenician.

Bet shows only slight change from the late eleventh century into the ninth century. The right downward stroke of the "head" is slowly lengthening below the "head," and the lower diagonal stroke begins well below the "head," branching off to the left from the right vertical. The normal form in the eleventh century has the lower diagonal drawn directly from the right lower corner of the head. The Faḫariyeh *bet* is identical with the *bet* of the tenth-century Byblus inscriptions that continues in Hebrew and Aramaic in the tenth and ninth centuries.

Gimel is not in rapid change in this period, and exhibits no distinctive characters that distinguish Phoenician and Aramaic.

21. See, in particular, the studies of J. Naveh, "The Date of the Tell Fakhariyeh Inscription: A Palaeographical Analysis of the Aramaic Text," *Shnaton* 5–6 (1982–83) 131–40; "Proto-Canaanite, Archaic Greek and the Script of the Aramaic Text on the Tell Fakhariyah Statue," in *Ancient Israelite Religion: Essays in Honor of Frank Moore Cross* (ed. P. D. Miller, P. D. Hanson, and S. D. McBride; Philadelphia, 1987) 101–13; and "Semitic Epigraphy and the Antiquity of the Greek Alphabet," *Kadmos* 30 (1991) 143–52. Cf. S. A. Kaufman, "The Pitfalls of Typology: On the Early History of the Alphabet," *HUCA* 57 (1986) 1–14; and E. Lipiński, "Epigraphy in Crisis," *BAR* 17 (1990) 42–43, 49, and 57. The drawings of the Nora Fragment in this article are wretched, whether the work of Lipiński or some other, I know not. Compare the drawing made from photographs and directly from the stone in F. M. Cross, "The Oldest Phoenician Inscription from Sardinia: The Fragmentary Stele from Nora," in *"Working with No Data": Semitic and Egyptian Studies Presented to Thomas O. Lambdin* (ed. David M. Golomb; Winona Lake, Ind., 1987) 65–74. The crisis in epigraphy is in fact the crumbling of the paradigm—clung to by classical epigraphists since its enunciation in most impressive form by Rhys Carpenter in 1933—which holds that the Greek alphabet was borrowed from the Phoenicians in the course of the eighth century B.C.E. This paradigm, with its origins in an older generation of classicists' anti-Phoenician bias, cannot comprehend the new data. Yet remarkably even some Orientalists continue to wave the banner, *ex Oriente nox*.

The letter *dalet,* more or less an equilateral triangle in the Tell Faḫariyeh hand, a form that developed by the mid-eleventh century, is found in early Greek, in Phoenician and Hebrew inscriptions of the tenth century, and in the Gozan Inscription. It is not found in ninth-century Aramaic. The *dalet* with a tail is fully developed in the Ben Hadad, Amman Citadel, and Kilamuwa inscriptions. Hebrew (including the Mešaᶜ script) retains the archaic form into the eighth century B.C.E.

The letter *he* has some advanced traits. In many exemplars we find a rotation of the letter counterclockwise from the vertical, the horizontals inclining downward to the left. This counterclockwise shift of stance is observed first of all in ninth-century Phoenician, Hebrew, and Aramaic, in such letters as *ᵓalep, he, ḥet, samek, qop,* and *reš.* It is probably an earlier shift of stance, a new fashion, by chance not extant in the lapidary texts we possess, to judge from its distribution through the descendants of Linear Phoenician. One should not overlook the fact that the crude *ḥet* of the Gozan text shows this shift of stance, though I should not wish to make too much of it.

The *waw* in the Faḫariyeh text is paralleled precisely only by the *waw* of an unpublished inscribed arrowhead from the Hecht Collection.[22] Its next closest parallels are to Greek forms.

Zayin in our text is indistinguishable from Phoenician forms of the eleventh and early tenth centuries B.C.E. Its vertical stroke is long, the two crossbars short. Later, the vertical shortens in the course of the ninth century in Aramaic, and in the third quarter of the ninth century the *Z*-form makes its appearance (the Ḥazaᵓel Inscription from Samos and the Zakkur Inscription). The only *zayin* in Aramaic comparable to the *zayin* of Tell Faḫariyeh is that of the Gozan Pedestal Inscription.

The *ḥet* of the Faḫariyeh script is remarkable for its vertical stance, which distinguishes it from the late tenth- and ninth-century Aramaic scripts. One notes, however, that it belongs with the tenth-century Phoenician forms of *ḥet,* not with the eleventh-century "box" forms of the letter.

Ṭet in our text uses a form that shows no perceptible change from ca. 1100, when it first appears in our inscriptions, until the early ninth century, when in Aramaic the *X* in the circle loses a crossbar (Ben Hadad and Amman Citadel inscriptions). In Phoenician and Hebrew the archaic form persists throughout the ninth century; it also appears in the Tel Dan Bowl inscription (a very formal script), and returns sporadically in eighth-century Aramaic texts.

Yod shows little change in the time frame of our interest.

22. I plan to publish the piece shortly in a forthcoming volume of *Eretz-Israel.*

EARLY PHOENICIAN SCRIPTS

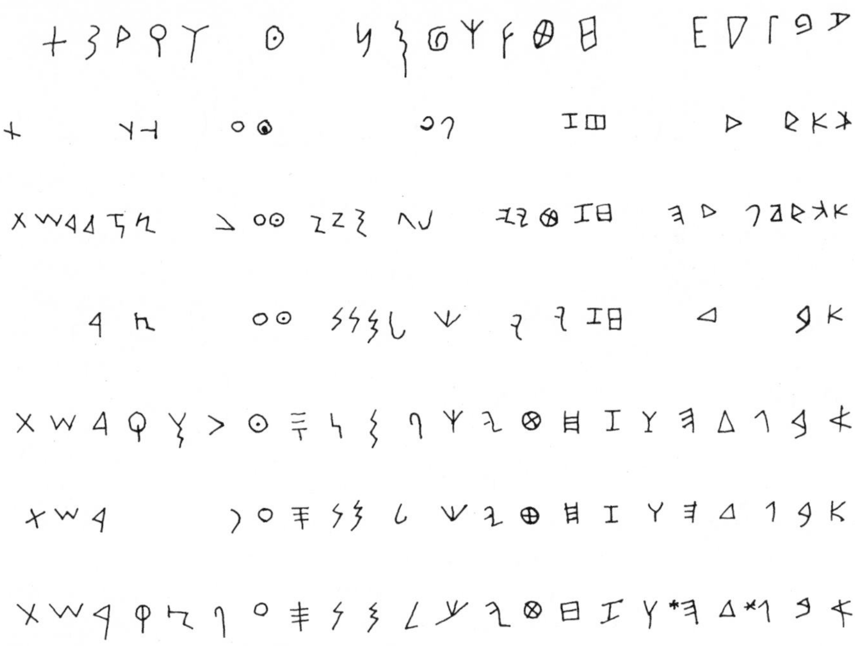

Figure 2. The Early Phoenician Scripts.
Line 1. From the ᶜIzbet Ṣarṭah Ostracon of ca. 1100 B.C.E.
Line 2. From the ᵓEl-Ḫaḍr Arrowheads of the Early 11th Century B.C.E.
Line 3. From Inscribed Arrowheads of the Mid-11th Century B.C.E.
Line 4. From Inscribed Arrowheads of the Late 11th Century B.C.E.
Line 5. From the Tell Faḫariyeh Inscription
Line 6. From the ᵓAḥiram Inscription of ca. 100–975 B.C.E.
Line 7. From the Gezer Calendar of the 10th Century B.C.E.

The trident-shaped *kap* of the Tell Faḫariyeh script is known only from the ᶜIzbet Ṣarṭah Abecedary from the beginning of the eleventh century B.C.E.[23] The earliest Aramaic inscription has the *K*-form *kap* (Gozan), and this form develops, the vertical leg lengthening and rotating clockwise in the course of the ninth century in Aramaic and Hebrew.

23. See F. M. Cross, "Newly-Found Inscriptions in Old Canaanite and Early Phoencian Scripts," *BASOR* 238 (1980) 1–20 and bibliography.

EARLY ARAMAIC SCRIPTS

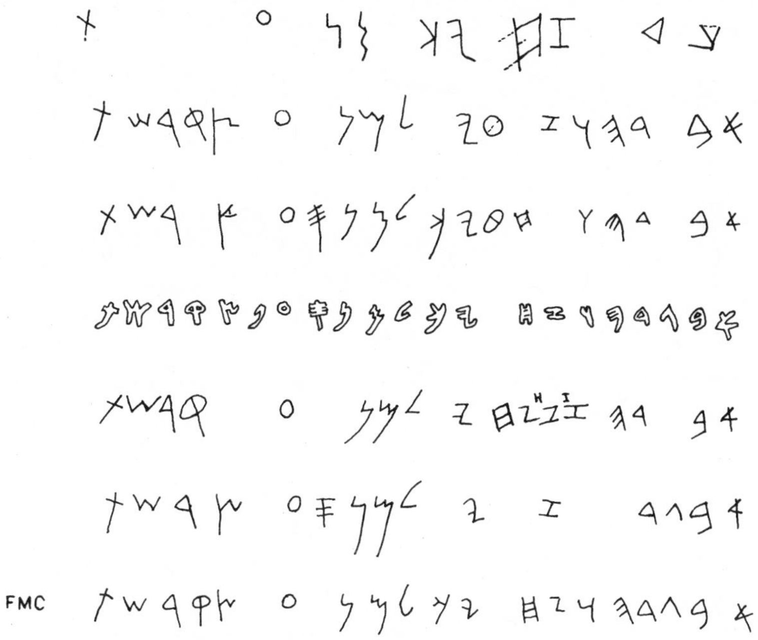

Figure 3. The Early Aramaic Scripts.
Line 1. From the Gozan Pedestal Inscription of ca. 900 B.C.E.
Line 2. From the Ben Hadad Inscription of ca. 950 B.C.E.
Line 3. From the Amman Citadel Inscription of the Mid-9th Century B.C.E.
Line 4. From the Kilamuwa Inscription of ca. 925 B.C.E.
Line 5. From the Ḥazaʾel Inscriptions (H = Horse Ornament, I = Ivory) of ca. 925 B.C.E.
Line 6. From the Luristan Bronze Jug of ca. 800 B.C.E.
Line 7. From the Zakkur Inscription of ca. 800–775 B.C.E.

The Tell Faḫariyeh *kap* thus shows no affinities with ninth-century Aramaic and none with the late tenth-century text from Gozan next door. It cannot be fitted into the Aramaic sequence.

The looped, "upside-down" *lamed* has analogs in the Phoenician script of the El-Ḫaḍr arrowheads of the beginning of the eleventh century,[24] in a text in Early Linear Phoenician of the eleventh century to be

24. For the ʾEl Ḫaḍr arrowheads, see my paper, ibid., and its bibliography.

published by Kyle McCarter (two exemplars), in a Phoenician arrowhead of the mid-eleventh century, and in old Greek. It reflects the period of multidirectional writing, when stances rotated. There is no parallel in later Phoenician or in later Aramaic.

The *mem* of Tell Faḫariyeh has precise parallels in late eleventh-century texts (Crete, Byblus B), and there are comparable forms in the Byblus texts of the late eleventh and tenth centuries B.C.E. The Gozan Inscription also provides two close parallels. The form differs *toto caelo* from the Aramaic *mems* of the early-, mid,- and late-ninth century B.C.E.

The *nun*, with the lower vertical of roughly equal length to that of the upper vertical, and a highly vertical stance, is a very early type. It belongs with eleventh-century *nuns*; later, in the Aramaic sequence, from Gozan to Zakkur, the lower leg of *nun* lengthens. In fact this lengthening is found in tenth-century Phoenician and Hebrew.

The *samek* is similar to the *samek* of the Cretan Cup (dated by the writer and Lipiński to ca. 1000 B.C.E.),[25] although it must be noted that the form revives in the ninth and eighth centuries. Evidently the *samek* with the vertical cutting the three horizontals and the *samek* with the vertical drawn below the horizontals are biforms, the latter adapted to lapidary scripts or to scripts written in relief.

The *ᶜayin* with the "pupil," the point in the center, is rare after the end of the eleventh century. It is found in Greek. In scripts of the ninth century it has been identified in the Ben Hadad Inscription, but the reading is not certain. The Gozan text has the typologically later, simple circle for *ᶜayin*.

Pe is precisely paralleled by the Phoenician *pe* of the *Banayaᵓ rab ᵓalp* Arrowhead of the mid-eleventh century B.C.E. and by no other extant form.[26] Nothing remotely comparable is found in the sequence of ninth-century Aramaic texts.

The strange *ṣade* of the Tell Faḫariyeh inscription is not found elsewhere in extant Phoenician or Aramaic inscriptions. A variety of *ṣade*s appear in the twelfth–eleventh century. Their form is rather fluid. And of course in the older pictographs there must have been at least two signs for the two or more phonemes that merged in Phoenician *ṣade*. A sign from the Carian alphabet (derived from the Greek), given the value *ṣ* by Friedrich, has been compared to the Tell Faḫariyeh *ṣade*.

25. E. Lipiński, "Notes d'épigraphie phénicienne et punique," *OLP* 14 (1983) 129–65. Cf. my comments in "Phoenicians in the West: The Early Epigraphic Evidence," *Studies in Sardinian Archaeology, Volume II: Sardinia in the Mediterranean* (ed. Miriam S. Balmuth; Ann Arbor, 1986) 124 (postscript).

26. See F. M. Cross, "Newly Discovered Arrowheads of the Eleventh Century BCE," *The Israel Museum Journal* 10 (1992) 57–61 and figs. 2–3.

The form of *qop* is archaic, the leg not breaking fully through the circular head. The form is found elsewhere only in the ᶜIzbet Ṣarṭah Abecedary at the beginning of the eleventh century. In ninth-century Aramaic and Phoenician, the leg bisects the circle, and the vertical rotates counterclockwise.

Reš with its large head and short leg has its closest typological parallels to eleventh-century Phoenician forms, and to early Greek.

The *X*-shaped *taw* is found in early Phoenician. However, in earliest Aramaic (Gozan), the leg lengthens, and this long-legged form is the only form found in ninth-century Aramaic.

Let me emphasize that all these comparisons have placed the Faḫariyeh alphabet in the sequence of early Phoenician scripts. Some letters have their best or exact parallels with eleventh-century Phoenician forms: *kap, lamed, pe, qop,* and *reš.* Another group of letters exhibits the characters of Phoenician signs that bridge the eleventh and tenth centuries: *ᵓalep, dalet, waw, zayin, ḥet, mem, nun, samek, ᶜayin* (?), and *taw.* Two letters have forms that survive both in Aramaic and Phoenician into the tenth century: *zayin* and *mem,* differentiating only in the ninth century. A few signs have forms that evolve little if at all in the tenth–ninth centuries and have no typological features that distinguish them in Phoenician and Aramaic: *bet, gimel, he* (?), and *yod.* None of the Faḫariyeh signs possesses a form that belongs exclusively to the Aramaic typological series or exhibits a letter that is found only in the sequence of Aramaic characters of the ninth century.

Also typologically important are two general traits often overlooked even by epigraphists. In the Faḫariyeh script, the letters exhibit a strong verticality of stance, a style that is tenth-century and earlier in Linear Phoenician, and that gives way to the rotation counterclockwise of a number of letters at the end of the tenth century and characterizes ninth-century Phoenician and especially ninth-century Aramaic: *ᵓalep, bet, he, ḥet, yod (samek, ṣade), qop,* and *reš.* Similarly, a number of letters contemporaneously rotate clockwise: *kap, lamed, mem, nun, pe* (and *taw*). This major cluster of stylistic features that marks the transition from tenth-century to ninth-century forms is undetectable in the Tell Faḫariyeh script. The second general trait of the Faḫariyeh script may be expressed negatively: the scribe in making his letters shows no tendency to lengthen final downstrokes. This is the case, too, in tenth-century and earlier Phoenician. But the lengthening of the final downstroke of a letter, notably in the letters *ᵓalep, dalet, he, kap, mem, nun, reš,* and *taw,* characterizes the evolution in the Aramaic script of the ninth century B.C.E.

I should draw the following conclusions from the data we have reviewed:

(a) Arguments for a date in the third quarter of the ninth century, ca. 840–825, for the Tell Faḫariyeh Bilingual Inscription are several and strong; at the same time, we are faced with a paucity of comparable materials of late eleventh- and tenth-century date with which to compare the statue and its two inscriptions.

(b) The paleographic analysis of the script places it unambiguously in a known typological sequence. The Aramaic text is written in a characteristic, early Linear Phoenician script, and falls in the typological sequence among inscriptions of the end of the eleventh or the beginning of the tenth century B.C.E. There are a few remarkable archaisms in the script, letter forms of *kap* and *pe*, for example, that do not appear after the early eleventh century.

(c) We are faced with alternatives.

(1) A ninth-century scribe copied earlier script models from Aramaic monuments of the late eleventh century, before the recently borrowed Linear Phoenician script had begun to evolve into the Aramaic character and become a separate national style. He ignored the Aramaic script used by contemporary scribes, notably the script found in the monuments of Ben Hadad, the Amman Citadel Inscription, the Kilamuwa Inscription, the Ḥazaʾel texts, the Luristan Jug, and the Zakkur Inscription. He ignored even the earlier script tradition of his fellow scribe in Gozan, which, while exhibiting traits closer to its Phoenician forebear, is still far more advanced than that of the Faḫariyeh hand. The script of the Faḫariyeh inscription is not a peripheral survival of the old Phoenician script. If indeed it were composed in the second half of the ninth century, it is a remarkable piece of archaizing. The scribe has copied the earlier script with remarkable fidelity, with few if any slips into the style of his own day. He has also used an archaic tradition in the representation of the phoneme we represent as [θ] by *samek* rather than *šin*, and resurrected long-forgotten word dividers.

(2) The alternative is to conclude that the inscription should be dated by the style of its Phoenician script: that the inscription in fact derives from the late eleventh or early tenth century B.C.E. In that case, it would represent the style of script used by the Aramaeans in the century after it was borrowed from Phoenician chancelleries—before the development of the ninth-century Aramaic character.

If the latter alternative is taken, we should have to place Hadad-yiθʿī, son of Šamaš-nūrī, ancestor of the Šamaš-nūrī who was governor of Gozan under Assur-naṣir-pal II in 866, in the interval after the Assyrians had lost sway over Gozan following the death of Tiglath-pileser I in 1077 B.C.E. and before the rise of the dynasty of Ḫadyānu and Kapara in the late tenth century. It would have been a period when Assyrian cultural influence was still strong but fading, before the emergence of the peculiar Kapara culture. It has been remarked that Hadad-yiθᶜi does not sound like a vassal, certainly not like a pious vassal. The Assyrian title *šākin māti* in the Akkadian text (rather than king), is the only hint of such, and in fact the title was used and known in the West in the thirteenth–tenth centuries (ʾAḥiram, ca. 1000–975 B.C.E.) and need not carry overtones of vassalage.

I am not sure, after all, that the data is sufficient to decide firmly between the alternatives we have laid down. One thing is certain. The script is typologically pure Phoenician, the Phoenician character of the end of the eleventh century B.C.E. It has no traits of the Aramaic script of the late tenth, or early, middle, and late ninth century B.C.E. At the same time I am inclined to the view that the text is indeed a triumph of archaism. I am not sure my reasons are rational. I am not impressed by arguments that depend on likenesses in style and language between the statue and cuneiform text of the Tell Faḫariyeh Inscription and ninth-century Assyrian statues and texts. One requires in any typological series, whether it be linguistic usage or formulas, art motifs, or script, that we know the typological characters that go before as well as those that follow. The paucity of monuments in the interval between Tiglath-pileser I and the Kapara period is therefore a grave hindrance to reaching a firm conclusion.

It is, finally, the coincidence of the appearance of the name Šamaš-nūrī in the Tell Faḫariyeh text and in the eponym list that tips the balance. To be sure, Aramaean (and Assyrian) dynasties repeat dynastic names ad nauseam. But one hesitates to argue that fate is so cruel as to produce an inscription in which we are misled by the repetition of dynastic names.

The Pahlavi Inscription on Mount Thomas Cross (South India)

Philippe Gignoux

Though the St. Thomas Mount Church Pahlavi inscription has frequently been interpreted, some words have yet to be understood correctly, particularly proper nouns. In this article I am suggesting new readings and interpretations. I am also publishing a two-word inscription from Kanheri.

Before Father Jean de Menasce passed away, he entrusted to me, as one of his last students, his project of publishing the Pahlavi inscriptions from South India in a fascicle of the *Corpus Inscriptionum Iranicarum* (*CII*), for which he had collected many photographs and related scholarly literature.[1]

Some years later, D. N. MacKenzie put at my disposal a large number of photographs collected in South India by Mrs. M. Leese for the benefit of *CII*.[2] Years have passed, and though I have been busy with other research, due to an earlier commitment to Father de Menasce, the project was not forgotten. Only at my seminar at l'École Pratique des Hautes Études (1991–92) was I able to study the Pahlavi inscriptions again.[3]

Author's note: This modest contribution is dedicated to that esteemed scholar, Professor Jonas Greenfield, with whom I have had many deeply appreciated meetings in Jerusalem and elsewhere.

1. In a letter dated June 16, 1972, he wrote to me: "Bivar m'a écrit pour me dire que le comité directeur du C.I.I. est d'accord pour accueillir nos Inscriptions Pehlevies de l'Inde, proposant aussi d'y ajouter telles autres inscriptions qui n'auraient pas trouvé place ailleurs." He was referring specifically to certain late funerary Pahlavi inscriptions, but because of his death in November 1973, our common project was abandoned.

2. I am grateful to N. Sims-Williams, Secretary of the board of the *CII*, for having sent me a copy of Mrs. Leese's report, dated March 18, 1974, and to D. N. MacKenzie for permission to publish here some photos that are the property of the *CII*.

3. See *Annuaire de l'École Pratique des Hautes Études, Section des sciences religieuses* 100 (1991–92) 177–78.

The material includes six inscribed crosses, visitors' inscriptions in the Kanheri caves, and a trilingual text on a copper plate (known as the "Quilon plate"). I will confine my attention to the most important of the crosses, the one in St. Thomas Mount Church, in the region of Mylapore (nearly seven miles from the town). The other five are thought to be reproductions of the original Thomas Cross,[4] and their inscriptions are in such difficult script as to be almost undecipherable. Many scholars, from the sixteenth century onwards, have published the Mount Thomas Cross.

In an article on the typology of crosses in the Chaldean Church, Jean Dauvillier[5] distinguished four types: Maltese crosses, which may be found all over Asia (Russian Turkestan, Tibet, Ladakh, etc.); crosses surmounting a lotus, represented by the famous Si-ngan-fou Stele[6] and by the Zaitoun Chinese harbor crosses;[7] "fleury crosses," of which type are the Indian crosses; and finally, crosses with lobed branches. Because of their decoration, these crosses are known as "victorious"; they are peculiar to the Nestorian churches, in contrast to other churches (Eastern and Latin), which commonly represent the crucified Jesus on their crosses.

As mentioned, I would like to limit myself to the St. Thomas Cross. While this Pahlavi inscription (fig. 1) has been deciphered quite frequently, to my mind, it has not received until now a definitive interpretation. I shall first list the different publications of the text and then compare the most accurate. We may dismiss the fantastic reading of Fr. Gaspar Coelho (1561)[8] and jump to the end of the nineteenth century. A. C. Burnell was the first European scholar to attempt a translation in 1873, having first identified the inscription as Pahlavi; he was followed by M. Haug, who dated the cross to ca. 650 C.E.,[9] and in the same year,

4. See T. K. Joseph, *Malabar Christians and Their Ancient Documents* (Trivandrum, 1929) passim.

5. Jean Dauvillier, "Les Croix triomphales dans l'ancienne Eglise chaldéenne," *Eleona* (1956) 11–17; reproduced in *Histoire et institutions des Eglises orientales au Moyen Age* (London: Variorum Reprints, 1983) 10.11–17.

6. See now the *editio princeps*: Paul Pelliot, *Recherches sur les Chrétiens d'Asie Centrale et d'Extrême-Orient, II, 1: La Stèle de Si-Ngan-Fou* (Oeuvres posthumes de Paul Pelliot; Paris: Éditions de la Fondation Singer-Polignac, 1984).

7. See J. Foster, "Crosses from the Walls of Zaitun," *JRAS* (1954) 1–25, 17 pls., with Syriac and Arabic inscriptions, dated 13th–14th century.

8. See L. M. Shouriah, *Blood on the Mount* (Madras, 1950) 23, who cites a very strange translation by a Brahman scholar. He then quotes a few interpretations by European scholars, noting that "they are never found to tally with one another" (p. 24).

9. According to Joseph (*Malabar Christians,* 29) the cross is "assigned by experts to the 7th–8th century on palaeographic grounds." M. Haug, *Die Allgemeine Zeitung* (Munich: January 29, 1874); repr. in *Indian Antiquary* 111 (1874) 308–16. I take these references from B. T.

E. W. West.[10] Baron de Harlez then offered a new translation.[11]

In 1896, West again deciphered the inscription, after acquiring ink impressions of the different crosses. In 1914, Dastur D. Peshotan Sanjana, the first Parsi scholar to take an interest in this Christian document, gave his interpretation.[12] J. J. Modi wrote a note on the inscription in 1924 and later another paper on the same subject.[13] In the same year a Jesuit Father, H. Hosten, reviewed the work that had been done up to that time.

The next studies[14] were published by C. P. T. Winckworth and E. Herzfeld;[15] T. K. Joseph, who added some observations to the Winckworth article,[16] and later, in 1950, published an interpretation given to him by Henning;[17] H. S. Nyberg, in a review of Joseph, *Malabar Christians*;[18] L. Shouriah, who did not decide between the different interpretations he quoted;[19] B. T. Anklesaria, who presumably adopted the Winckworth or Nyberg reading but added some inaccurate interpretations;[20] W. B. Henning;[21] and R. Sharp of Shiraz gave his version in a Persian work.[22] Finally in 1970, G. Gropp published an interesting article on the St. Thomas inscription.[23]

Before I compare the best and more recent interpretations of the inscription, I must give the transliteration and meaning of the Syriac line

---

Anklesaria, "The Pahlavi Inscription on the Crosses in Southern India," *Journal of the K. R. Cama Oriental Institute* 39 (1958) 64–107.

10. West published a review of Burnell (see Anklesaria, "The Pahlavi Inscription," 66).

11. In *Proceedings of the Eighth International Congress of Orientalists* (Paris, 1892).

12. In the *Sir J. J. Madressa Jubilee Volume* (ed. J. J. Modi).

13. J. J. Modi, in the *Annual Report of the Archaeological Department* (Travancore State, 1923–24) 4–7; *Journal of the Bombay Royal Asiatic Society*, 1926.

14. Not mentioned in Anklesaria's 1958 article, as though the later work had no value.

15. Winckworth ad Herzfeld, "A New Interpretation of the Pahlavi Cross-Inscription of Southern India," *JTS* 30 (April 1929) 238–39 (originally a paper read at the 17th International Congress of Orientalists, 1928); see Joseph, *Malabar Christians*, 27–28.

16. In the *Kerala Society Papers*, series 3, 1929.

17. T. K. Joseph, "Christian and Non-Christian Crosses in Ancient India," *Journal of Indian History*, 38/2 (1950) 111–22 (see p. 111 n. 1).

18. Nyberg, in *Le Monde Oriental* 26/27 (1932) 349–50.

19. Ibid., 24–25.

20. Ibid., 67–70.

21. Henning, *Handbuch der Orientalistik*, vol. 4: *Linguistik* (1958) 51.

22. A. ᶜEbād and A. Hekmat, *Naqš-e Pārsī bar ahjār-e Hend* (Persian Inscriptions on Indian Stones) (Tehran, 1959).

23. G. Gropp, "Die Pahlavi-Inschrift auf dem Thomas-Kreuz in Madras," *Archäologische Mitteilungen aus Iran* n.s. 3 (1970) 267–71. Mrs. Leese, in her report to MacKenzie (see n. 2 above), lists translations from a guest book in the Kottayam Church, ending with the Winckworth and Herzfeld version.

inscribed on the lower part of the niche in which the decorated cross is standing:

> *ly dyn lʾ nhwʾ ly d-ʾštbhr ʾlʾ ʾn b-⟨z⟩qyph*[24] *d-mrnyšwʿ mšyḥʾ*

> For me, let me never boast, if not of the Cross of our Lord Jesus Christ (Gal 6:14).[25]

This quotation is certainly apt for the stele but not for the Pahlavi text.

I want first to recall the most recent translations of the Pahlavi inscription before rejecting what I consider from a paleographical or semantical point of view to be irrelevant.

> My Lord Christ, have mercy upon Afras son of Chaharbukht, the Syrian who cut this.—Winckworth and Herzfeld (1929)

> Mr. Winckworth's interpretation is simple, natural, and credible and has every chance of holding the field hereafter. "Who cut this" may perhaps have to be changed into "Who got this cut," or "who caused this to be set up," or "who presented this."—Joseph (1929) and Nyberg (1932)

> My Lord Christ, have mercy upon Afras, son of Chaharbukht, son of Geewargis, who arranged this (or set this up).[26]— Henning (1958)

> Unser Herr Messias erbarme sich über Gabriel, den Sohn des Chaharbokht, den Enkel des Durzad, der dies (Kreuz) anfertigte.—Gropp (1970)

The main differences occur in the reading of the proper names and at the end of the text, in the last verbal form.

The name of the man who commissioned or made the monument has been understood as *Āfrāh*, which means 'teaching, doctrine'. Henning noted the unlikelihood of the term as a personal name,[27] suggesting other readings, such as *spdʾs, spyʾs,* or *dypdʾs* = *Devadāsa.* He concluded that the son was an Indian, the father a Persian, and the grandfather a Syrian. I believe this is quite impossible on ethnic and historical grounds: the cross would have been made by a Christian Indian, whose father was Mazdean (?) or a convert to Christianity, but his grandfather would have had a Syriac (Syro-Palestinian) name!

24. Nobody up to now has noticed the lack of this /z/, which is essential for an understanding of the sentence.

25. Joseph (*Malabar Christians,* 28 n. 33) translates this Syriac Peshiṭta verse.

26. Anklesaria's translation is totally erroneous (*Malabar Christians,* 70): "Lord Anointed Saviour too and supreme revelation too—of four apostles. Syrians whom saved this."

27. Henning, *Handbuch,* 51 n. 4.

In fact, the first letter of the name can only be read as *s*, linked to a following *p* or *c*, but neither *spdʾs* nor *spyʾs* can be plausibly interpreted. Thus Gropp's reading must also be rejected for paleographical reasons, though *Gabriel* would be a good candidate for the name.

Now it seems clear to me that the first letters of the word in question should be read as *spl-*. Perhaps, then, the name may be spelled, not SPLʾ (the ideogram for *dibīr*, which is first a title), but *splyš*⟨*w*⟩, which may represent the Syriac proper name *Sabr-Išōʿ*, meaning 'Hope in Jesus' or 'Jesus (is my) hope', a very common name in the Nestorian or Syrian milieu: it was the name of five patriarchs, from the sixth to the thirteenth centuries. It is also attested in the Si-Ngan-Fou stele.[28]

All scholars agree on the interpretation of the patronymic: it is a compound name, whose meaning is quite obvious, namely, *Cahār-bōxt* 'Saved by the Four', but what is meant by *four* is dubious, probably a series of gods. Parallels in Sassanian onomastics are well known: *Sēbōxt* 'Saved by the Three', referring to the Holy Trinity in a Christian context or to a Mazdean triad of gods (?).[29] *Panj-bōxt* may refer to a Manichaean pentad.[30]

The word following the patronymic Cahār-bōxt is the most difficult to read. It is most unlikely to be a grandfather's name, to my mind, because such an ascending line is extremely rare in Iranian epigraphy. Hence the word is presumably an epithet or adjective and not a proper name. The scholars cited above have proposed the following readings: (1) *swryʾy* (Winckworth) agrees only with the two first letters; (2) *gywlgys* (Henning) is impossible from the start; (3) *dwrzʾd* (Gropp) must be rejected for the same reason; moreover it should be spelled *dwrzʾt*. In addition, the name *dwrzʾd* is not known elsewhere, though it might mean 'afar born'. Gropp is right, however, in his identification of a *z* in the middle of the word;[31] therefore, as he wrote, Anklesaria's reading *swlyʾy* is impossible.

I propose to read this enigmatic word as *swlzʾd*, which I suggest is a nickname, in Persian *Sūr-zay* 'who has mighty weapons'.[32] This Persian epithet would be appropriate in conjunction with a Mazdean name.

28. Pelliot, *La Stèle de Si-Ngan-Fou,* 59, no. 26. See also two charters given in the ninth century by the king of Quilon to the Christian church in Quilon, which was built by a Persian Christian merchant named *Maruvan Sabrišōʿ*; see T. K. Joseph, *Malabar Christian Copper Plates* (Trivandrum, 1925) 13, 16; idem, *Malabar Christians*, 30.

29. See P. Gignoux, *Noms propres sassanides en moyen-perse épigraphique* (Iranisches Personennamenbuch, 2, fasc. 2; Vienna, 1986) no. 833, p. 157.

30. See ibid., no. 751, p. 145.

31. See Gropp, "Die Pahlavi Inschrift," 268.

32. See D. N. MacKenzie, *A Concise Pahlavi Dictionary* (London, 1971; reprint: 1986) 98: *zay* < *av. zaya-* 'instrument, weapon'.

Last, the verbal form at the end of the sentence has been variously read and translated. Henning proposed *wnˀrt*, which fits the meaning but not the reading, because the first letter is undubitably *b*, as proved by the Koṭṭayam inscription (fig. 2). Gropp has the ideogram *BᶜYDt'* for *kard* 'made', but this form is only conjectural; one would have expected *ᶜBYDWN*. Because the word begins with *b*, Nyberg's reading seems correct, that is, *bwlyt* = *burīd* 'has cut'. However, in consideration of the graphy, we must apparently read *bwylm*, which may represent Pahlavi *burēm*, first-person singular (or plural). The verb may perhaps be an error for **bwlym/t*. Be that as it may, my interpretation is as follows:

> *MRᶜHmn mšyḥˀ ˀpḥšˀd QDM splyš ⟨wᶜ⟩ Y cḥˀlbwḥt Y swlzˀd MNW *bwlym ZNH*

> My Lord Christ, have mercy upon Sabrišōᶜ, son of Cahār-bōxt the mighty (lit. 'who has mighty weapons'), (I) who carved (lit. 'cut') this.

Thus, the inscription clearly has nothing to do with the legend of St. Thomas in India. It refers only to the making of a decorated cross by a pious Christian, probably about the seventh-eighth century; this dating is based on epigraphic grounds.

To conclude I would like to decipher a small inscription, inscribed twice on a pillar in the veranda of the Kanheri Cave. The two lines of the text may be read as follows:

1. *ˀpˀngwsnsp'*
2. *Y plḥwˀn*

that is,

Ābān-Gušnasp,
son of Farrox[33]

This is the name of a visitor who, like many others, came to the place in the eleventh century and left his father's and his name carved on the rock.[34]

33. The first name has not yet been added to my *Noms propres*, but the meaning is obvious. For the patronymic, see *Noms propres*, no. 352, p. 82.

34. The lists of visitors have been generally well deciphered by E. W. West, "The Pahlavi Inscriptions at Kanheri," *Indian Antiquary* (1880) 265–68. Republication is desirable, but we need good photos. However, I hope to collect them in a supplement to my *Noms propres*, together with other names from recent epigraphical sources.

Figure 1. St. Thomas Mount Church: Stone tablet with cross and Pahlavi inscription (photo permission of the *Corpus Inscriptionum Iranicarum*).

Figure 2. St. Thomas Mount Church: Lower right of stone tablet with the end of the inscription.

Figure 3. St. Thomas Mount Church: Upper right of stone tablet with the beginning of the inscription.

Figure 4. St. Thomas Mount Church: Upper left of stone tablet.

Figure 5. St. Thomas Mount Church: Lower left of stone tablet.

Figure 6. Koṭṭayam Valiyapalli Church: Syriac inscription.

Figure 7. Kanheri: Pahlavi inscription on veranda pillar.

Figure 8. Kanheri: Pahlavi inscription on veranda pillar.

The Xanthos Trilingual Revisited

André Lemaire

Paleographical and philological remarks try to clarify several problems of the Aramaic text. Pixodaro(s)' edict/dātāh (lines 6–18) is introduced by ʾmr (end of line 5). A clarification of the meaning of mhḥsn (line 19) and ylmhnṣl (lines 20, 23, 26), as well as a proposed double emendation in line 22, aid in understanding lines 19–27: the priest Simias initiated the engraving of this inscription (line 19a), the purpose of which was to protect his property.

Twenty years after its discovery in the summer of 1973, not all the difficulties of the famous Xanthos trilingual have been solved. This Greek, Lycian, and Aramaic trilingual certainly has contributed to a better understanding of the Lycian language, especially thanks to the pioneering work of E. Laroche, in collaboration with H. Metzger and A. Dupont-Sommer for the Greek and Aramaic texts. Although there are still problems with the Lycian text, I shall rather try to deal here with difficulties in the Aramaic text as a tribute to J. C. Greenfield, who chose Aramaic as his favorite field of research. Taking as a basis the *editio princeps* of A. Dupont-Sommer,[1] I shall present several paleographical and philological remarks, before offering a new translation.[2]

Aramaic Text

1. BYRḤ SYWN ŠNT ḤD
2. ʾRTḤŠSŠ MLKʾ
3. BʾWRN BYRTʾ PGSWD[R]

1. A. Dupont-Sommer, "IIIe partie: L'Inscription araméenne," in *Fouilles de Xanthos VI: La Stèle trilingue du Létôon* [hereafter abbrev. as *Xanthos VI*] (ed. H. Metzger, E. Laroche, A. Dupont-Sommer, and M. Mayrhofer; Paris, 1979) 129–78, pls. XVI–XXIII.

2. At some future opportunity, I shall discuss the long-debated problem of the date of the inscription.

4. BR KTMNW ḤŠTRPNʾ
5. ZY BKRK WTRMYL *ʾMR*
6. ʾTʿŠTW BʿLY ʾWRN
7. *K/DR/NPʾ* LMʿBD LKNDWṢ
8. ʾLHʾ KBYDŠY WKNWTH
9. WʿBDW KMRʾ LSYMYN
10. BR KDWRS WʾYTY B*Y/G*[*T?*]
11. ZY BʿLY ʾ!WRN YHBW
12. LKNDWṢ ʾLHʾ WŠNH BŠ
13. NH MN MTʾ YHYBN KSP
14. [M]NH ḤD WPLG KMRʾ! ZNH
15. ZBḤ LRʾ!Š YRḤʾ NQWH
16. LKNDWṢ ʾLHʾ W*DBḤ*
17. ŠNH BŠNH TWR / WDMʾ
18.]ZNH ŠBYQ ZY LH
19. DTH DK KTB ZY MHḤ!SN ʾP
20. HN ʾYŠ MTWM YHNṢL
21. MN KNDWṢ ʾLHʾ ʾW MN
22. KMRʾ [*Z*]NH WY*H!*⟨*WY*⟩ MN KNDWS
23. ʾLHʾ WKNWTH MHNṢL
24. WMN ʾLH⟨*Y*⟩ʾ LʾTW ʾRTMWŠ
25. ḤŠTRPTY WʾḤWRN ⟨*ʾ*⟩YŠ
26. MHNṢL Wʾ!LH ʾLHYʾ
27. YBʿWN MNH

Paleographical and Philological Remarks

At the middle of line 3, *byrtʾ* corresponds to Greek *polis* (line 12): it is a 'city' or 'fortified town', rather than a simple 'citadel' or 'stronghold'.[3]

At the end of the same line, Dupont-Sommer was in doubt as to the length of the lacuna, but there is clearly room for only one letter: *reš*. The alternative reading proposed by Dupont-Sommer, *pgswd*[*rw*],[4] must be rejected on paleographical as well as phonological[5] grounds.

At the end of line 5, Dupont-Sommer's reading *ʾmr* 'said' has been disputed by J. Teixidor,[6] who reads only the *ʾalep*. However, there is clearly

3. Cf. A. Lemaire and H. Lozachmeur, "*Bīrāh/birtāʾ* en araméen," *Syria* 64 (1987) 261–66.

4. *Xanthos VI*, 140.

5. Cf. Greek *Pixōdaros* (and not *Pixōdarōs*) and Lycian *Pigesere/Pichesere*.

6. J. Teixidor, "Bulletin d'épigraphie sémitique," *Syria* 52 (1975) 261–95, esp. 287–88 = *Bulletin d'épigraphie sémitique (1964–1980)* (BAH 127; Paris, 1986) 339–40; cf. also "The Aramaic Text of the Trilingual Stele from Xanthos," *JNES* 37 (1978) 181–85, esp. 181.

space and the remains of two letters after the *ʾalep*, and the photographs corroborate Dupont-Sommer's personal examination of the inscription to read *ʾmr.* Furthermore, this verb makes good sense in the context: it introduces the official (written) declaration of the satrap.

In line 6, Dupont-Sommer's translation of *ʾtʿštw* 'they have thought, contemplated' is closer to the ambiguous Greek word *edoxe* and seems better than 'they have instituted'.[7] Even in *Cowley* 30,23, *ʾtʿšt* does not refer to a 'decision' but only to 'take thought for (that temple)': Bigvai, governor of Judea, had no power to decide whether to (re)build a temple in Yeb/Elephantine. The meaning of *ʾtʿštw* is important for an understanding of the political relations between the people of Xanthos and Pixodaros: the project of the people of Xanthos had to be confirmed by Pixodaros for it to be enacted.

At the end of line 6, *bʿly ʾwrn* (cf. also line 11) is a West-Semitic designation for the the citizens/authorities of a town or country. It is already attested in eighth-century Aramaic;[8] the *bʿly* of a town or of a country may constitute a political assembly.[9]

At the beginning of line 7, only *pe* and *ʾalep* are sure. The first two letters could be *dalet, kap, reš,* or *nun.*[10] The reading *krpʾ* is uncertain, especially since the Iranian word **karpa* is not attested elsewhere; therefore, the interpretation 'rite, cult' is still very uncertain.[11] Indeed, the Greek ('altar') and Lycian ('sanctuary') seem to refer to something more concrete. One should note also that while *ʿbd* may mean 'worship (a god)' in Hebrew and Judeo-Aramaic, this meaning is apparently not attested in Imperial Aramaic, and the general meaning 'to make' would fit better here if *--pʾ* designates something concrete.

At the end of line 7, *kndwṣ* (lines 7, 12, 16, 21; cf. *kndws,* line 22) clearly corresponds to Lycian (or rather Caunian/Carian) *chētawati* (cf. Luwian *hantawati*)[12] 'king'. However, it is considered in the Aramaic text as the personal name of a deity. It should not, therefore, be translated 'king', even if the Greek text has *basilei* (line 7). In Aramaic, 'king'

7. Pace Teixidor, ibid., 182, but with P. Frei, Review of *Xanthos VI,* in *BiOr* 38 (1981) cols. 366–67.

8. Cf. *bʿly ktk, bʿly ʾrpd*: Sfiré I A 4; I B 4–5; cf. III, 23.26; see A. Lemaire and J.-M. Durand, "Les Inscriptions araméennes de Sfiré et l'Assyrie de Shamshi-ilu" (HEO 20; Geneva and Paris, 1984) 113–31.

9. Cf. M. Sznycer, "L'Assemblée du peuple dans les cités puniques d'après les témoignages épigraphiques," *Sem* 25 (1975) 47–68, esp. 65.

10. *Xanthos VI,* 145 does not mention *nun*; but see the shape of *nun* in *kndwṣ* (same line).

11. The reading *dnpʾ* would not be impossible (cf. perhaps Iranian *dāna-*).

12. *Xanthos VI,* 105–6, 145. One wonders whether the transcription with final *-ṣ* could correspond to a (Luwian nominative?) ending *-tis* > *t(i)s* > *ṣ*.

would have been written *mlk*(ᵓ), but this word has already been used for Artaxerxes (line 2), and the redactor may have avoided it consciously, since it might create confusion. Furthermore, he specified the category of the name: *ᵓlhᵓ* 'the god', which does not appear in the Greek text.

In line 8, one would expect *kbydšyᵓ* if it had been related to *ᵓlhᵓ*; so *kbydšy* may have been directly connected with *kndwṣ*. Furthermore, it is difficult to accept an Aramaic ethnicon *-šy*;[13] *kbydšy* could be rather an ethnicon of *kbydš*, perhaps a transcription of Lydian *chbide* with a (Luwian nominative?) ending *-is*. So one may propose to translate *kndwṣ ᵓlhᵓ kbydšy* as 'the god Kandawats Caunian', rather than 'the King, the God of Caunos'.[14]

At the end of line 8, Dupont-Sommer reads *knwth*, while Teixidor and Neumann[15] have only *wr*[. .]. The reading *knwth* is clear enough if one takes into account that a *taw* was added above the line of writing. This reading is confirmed by the same word in line 23. Aramaic *knwth* 'his colleagues' corresponds to Greek *Arkesimai* and to Lycian *ArKKazuma*[16] *chētawati*. *Arkesimas*/*ArKKazuma* looks like a theonym, but Aramaic *knwth* is a common name, with a personal suffix relating to 'Kandawats'. One wonders whether *knwth* is not a translation[17] of Lycian *ArKKazuma chētawati*. In that case, *ArKKazuma*/*ArWWazuma*, probably of Carian origin,[18] would mean 'colleague(s)'.

At the end of line 10, it is paleographically possible to hesitate between three possible readings: *by*[*t*], *by*,[19] and *bg*.[20] Either *by* or *byt* may designate a 'house' or a piece of 'property, a plot of land,' while *bāga* would be an Iranian loanword meaning 'estate', which is about the same thing. The context makes a choice between these three possible readings difficult.

The verb *yhb* 'to give' appears twice in the following lines, once in the active form, *bᶜly ᵓwrn yhbw* (line 11), and once in the passive form, *mn mtᵓ yhybn* (line 13). Dupont-Sommer translated *mtᵓ* as 'town' because

13. Against *Xanthos VI*, 145.

14. *Xanthos VI*, 145.

15. *Teixidor*, "Aramaic Text of Trilingual Stele," 181; G. Neumann, *Neufunde Likischer Inschriften seit 1901* (Vienna, 1979) 46.

16. Ibid., 44 prefers the transcription *ArWWazuma* (see already O. Carruba, "Commentario alla trilingue licio-greco-aramaica di Xanthos," *Studi Miceni ed Egeo-Anatolici* 18 [1977] 273–318, esp. 294). On this problem of transcription, see also L. Sanz Mingote, "La escritura licia: Una propuesta de transcripción," *Aula Orientalis* 7 (1989) 95–103, esp. 97, 103.

17. Cf. the translation in the Greek text of *chētawati* by *basilei*, while it is simply rendered by *kndwṣ* 'Kandawats' in Aramaic.

18. Cf. Laroche, *Xanthos VI*, 57, 114.

19. *Xanthos VI*, 147.

20. Teixidor, "Aramaic Text of Trilingual Stele," 181 n. 1.

of the corresponding Greek word *polis,* but *mtᵓ*, an Akkadian loanword in Aramaic, means 'country' and not 'town' in Imperial Aramaic.[21] A comparison of the two formulae with *yhb* makes it likely that the assembly of the *bᶜly ᵓwrn* represented not only the city of Orna but also the surrounding country.[22]

The last word of line 16 is very difficult to read and interpret. The first letter may be *dalet/reš/kap* or *nun*; the second is a clear enough *bet,* but the third one is strange. Dupont-Sommer proposed, tentatively, to read it as a *ṣade* and to interpret the word as *rbṣ*, a verb parallel to *zbḥ* 'to sacrifice' (line 15):[23] "Nous proposons donc, sous toute réserve, le verbe RBṢ (racine II) 'asperger, saupoudrer', d'où peut-être 'immoler'. . . .[24] Teixidor reads only "*r*[. .]."[25] However, as Dupont-Sommer made it clear, his reference to *rbṣ* II 'sprinkle', hence 'sacrifice'(?), seems very dubious, and it seems convenient to seek another solution. The last letter may also be interpreted as a *ḥet* (cf. *zbḥ,* line 15), with a short vertical stroke (cf. *mhḥsn,* line 19)[26] and the last word read as *dbḥ* 'sacrifice', which is an alternative writing of *zbḥ* (line 15). This simple alternative reading would explain why the Greek and Persian texts used only one verb meaning 'to sacrifice'. It is moreover possible, since the variant writings *d/z* for **ḏ* are well attested during the Persian Period, sometimes in the same inscription.[27] Indeed, note for example, *znh* (lines 14, 18), *dk* (line 19), and *zy* (lines 18, 19) in this inscription.

The sentence of line 19, *dth dk ktb zy mhḥsn,* has been interpreted in various ways:

(a) Dupont-Sommer translates: 'Cette loi-ci, il (Pixôdaro) (l')a inscrite, (lui) qui est maître (de la décision)'.[28] However, this would mean that the subject had not been mentioned since line 3, and this is really difficult to accept. Furthermore, the interpretation of *zy mhḥsn* 'master (of the decision)' is more a reference to the Greek text *Pixôtaros de kurios estô* than a translation of the Aramaic where, with this meaning, one would expect *mrᵓ* or *bᶜl ṭᶜm.*

21. Cf. S. A. Kaufman, *The Akkadian Influence on Aramaic* (AS 19; Chicago, 1974) 71; I. Kottsieper, *Die Sprache der Ahiqarspruche* (BZAW 194; Berlin, 1990) 243–44. However, *mtᵓ* 'town' is well attested in both Jewish Babylonian Aramaic and Mandaic.

22. Cf. the *perioikoi* in the Greek text. On this last word in Lycia, cf. I. Hahn, "Periöken und Periökenbesitz in Lykien," *Klio* 63 (1981) 51–61.

23. The Greek and Lycian texts have only one verb for *zbḥ* and *rbṣ*(?): *thuein* and *kumezidi.*

24. *Xanthos VI,* 150.

25. *Teixidor,* "Aramaic Text of Trilingual Stele," 180.

26. Cf. also *Xanthos VI,* 163: "Les deux signes *ṣadé* et *ḥêt* peuvent arriver à se confondre si la haste de droite du *ḥêt* est indûment raccourcie."

27. Cf. S. Segert, *Altaramäische Grammatik* (Leipzig, 1975) 92, §3.2.7.5.3.

28. *Xanthos VI,* 137.

(b) Teixidor translates: 'This edict (hereby) inscribed is the one that conveys the title to the property'.[29] In this case, *ktb* would be a passive participle with a defective writing. Although the full writing *yhybn* appears in line 13, such a defective writing might not be impossible. However, *dth* is feminine,[30] and the passive participle should also be feminine. Furthermore, the *Haphel* participle *mhḥsn* is generally related to a person and not to a writ.

Now recent studies of the *Haphel* participle of *ḥsn* in Imperial Aramaic[31] have clearly shown that Aramaic *yaḥsēn* is parallel to Hebrew *yinḥal* and that a *mhḥsn* is a 'hereditary property-holder'. But who owns the property here? The first part of the inscription indicates the god Kandawats and (or rather, i.e.) his priest Simias;[32] this last one is the true owner, as indicated by the last sentence of Pixodaros: *wdmʾ znh šbyq zy lh* (line 18) 'and this domain which is freed is *his*'. This interpretation is confirmed by the Greek text, which shows that Simias and his heirs were to be the true owners of the domain. In such a case, one may very well understand that Simias was interested in engraving the edict of Pixodaros, which gave him a domain free of taxes.

The next sentence is probably to be understood in this context. As already shown by Greenfield,[33] in Aramaic documents of the Persian Period, *hnṣl* means 'to remove, to take (back)', or 'to reclaim' what has been given; it is specified several times that what has been given cannot be reclaimed. This meaning fits perfectly here:

1. *hnṣl* is preceded by the verb 'to give', attested twice (*yhbw*, line 11, and *yhybn*, line 13);
2. *hnṣl* is followed by *mn* + PN.

In the middle of line 22, Dupont-Sommer reads *nhwyʾ*, which he interprets as an emphatic *Niphal* participle and translates 'le prêtre (alors) existant'.[34] However, as he pointed out, the *Niphal* of the verb *hwh* is not attested in Aramaic; in fact, the existence of *Niphal* in Imperial Aramaic

29. Teixidor, "Aramaic Text of Trilingual Stele," 184.

30. Cf. Dan 2:13, 15.

31. See H. Z. Szubin and B. Porten, "'Ancestral Estates' in Aramaic Contracts: The Legal Significance of the Term *mhḥsn*," *JRAS* (1982) 3–9; see also B. Porten and H. Z. Szubin, "Hereditary Leases in Aramaic Letters," *BiOr* 42 (1985) cols. 283–88; see P. Grelot, "Essai de restauration du papyrus A.P. 26," *Sem* 20 (1970) 23–31, esp. 30–31.

32. Teixidor ("Aramaic Text of Trilingual Stele," 184) explains "(i.e. the god's)," but the god does not act by himself: the priest Simias is acting in his name and both are clearly associated (cf. line 21: *mn kndwṣ ʾlhʾ ʾw mn kmrʾ*).

33. J Greenfield, "Aramaic HNṢL and Some Biblical Passages," in *Meqor hajjim: Festschrift G. Molin* (Graz, 1983) 116–19; cf. also H. Z. Szubin and B. Porten, "A Life Estate of Usufruct: A New Interpretation of Kraeling 6," *BASOR* 269 (1988) 29–45, esp. 41.

34. *Xanthos VI*, 154.

is doubtful.[35] Furthermore, the translation 'the existing priest' seems strange and has no parallel. Teixidor proposed, rather, to interpret *nhwy*ᵓ as an imperfect with the prefix *n-* (well known in Syriac); it would be connected to the two participles *mhnṣl*.[36] However, the prefix *n-* is attested only in Syriac, while in Biblical Aramaic, and perhaps in Arebsun, we have the prefix *l-*.[37] Furthermore, one would expect *nhwh*/ᵓ/*y*, but not *nhwy*ᵓ; and, in that case, the final ᵓ*alep* would be very difficult to explain.

Faced with such difficulties in interpreting the reading *nhwy*ᵓ, one wonders whether it should not be corrected, even if such a solution seems rather desperate. In fact, one could think of two mistakes made by the engraver: (1) There is some space between *kmr*ᵓ and *nh*. . . . , and, because at the beginning of line 14 the engraver may have forgotten to engrave a (small) letter: the place could well fit a *zayin*, which is only a vertical stroke. This correction would give the demonstrative ⟨*z*⟩*nh*, not out of place after the emphatical *kmr*ᵓ (cf. *kmr*ᵓ *znh*, line 14). (2) The reading of the letter after *wy* is uncertain. The shape looks like that of a *gimel*,[38] and the reading ᵓ*alep* is Dupont-Sommer's correction. However, another correction is possible: the missing stroke could be a vertical stroke inside the angle, which would produce a *he*.[39] The word *wyh* does not seem to make sense here. If *waw* is an apodosis *waw* (after a conditional sentence beginning with ᵓ*p hn*), one would expect the jussive *yh*⟨*wy*⟩ 'let him be . . .': one might propose correcting a mistake due to haplography, reading *wyh*⟨*wy*⟩ . . . *mhnṣl* (*Hophal* participle). In that passive apodosis, the subject is probably the man (ᵓ*yš*: line 20) who took (anything) away (*yhnṣl*).[40] Needless to say, this second emendation is conjectural.

The gods of the sanctuary are mentioned in the last conditional sentence, beginning with *waw*.[41] Teixidor proposed emending ᵓ*lh*ᵓ (line 24) in the plural ᵓ*lh*⟨*y*⟩ᵓ;[42] this small emendation seems reasonable, since ᵓ*alep* and *yod* are confused several times in this inscription. A similar conjectural emendation could be made at the end of line 25, correcting the reading to ⟨ᵓ⟩*yš* or ᵓ⟨*y*⟩*š* (cf. ᵓ*yš*, line 20).

35. Cf. P. Leander, *Laut- und Formenlehre der Ägyptisch-aramäischen* (Hildesheim, 1966 = Göteborg, 1928) §21b; Segert, *Grammatik*, 257, §5.6.7.3.7.

36. Teixidor, "Aramaic Text of Trilingual Stele," 184; Review of *Xanthos VI*, in *Syria* 56 (1979) 394, no. 162.

37. Cf. Segert, *Altaramäische Grammatik*, 297: §5.7.8.1.6.

38. See *Xanthos VI*, 154.

39. Cf. the *he* of ⟨*z*⟩*nh* just before *wy*.

40. Cf. R. Contini, Review of *Xanthos VI*, in *OrAnt* 20 (1981) 233; Frei, Review of *Xanthos VI*, col. 368.

41. Cf. Segert, *Altaramäische Grammatik*, §7.5.4.2.

42. Teixidor, "Aramaic Text of Trilingual Stele," 184 n. 21.

At the end of line 26, Dupont-Sommer understood *ʾlh ʾlhyʾ* as referring to Kandawats and his colleagues. However, *ʾlh ʾlhyʾ* means 'these gods'[43] and refers, rather, to 'the god(s) Leto, Artemis, Ḥšatrapati . . .' (lines 24–25).

At the end of the inscription, *ʾlh ʾlhyʾ ybʿwn mnh* is parallel to the Cilician inscriptions of Keseçek Köyü (*wybʿh lh šhr wšmš*) and Gözneh (*wybʿwn lh bʿl šmyn rbʾ šhr wšmš*). However, there is a difference in the formula: here the verb *bʿh* is followed by *mn* (and not by *l*). In fact, here *bʿh* is probably a *Qal* and not a *Paʿel*,[44] and the suffix *-h* is not the object of the verb *bʿh*. The object of lines 24–27 seems to be implied, that is, the stele with the inscription (*dātāh*), which is put under the protection of the gods of the main sanctuary.

Translation

1–5. In the month of Siwan, year one of King Artaxerxes, in the fortified city of Orna, Pixodaro(s) son of Katamno(s), the satrap in Caria and Lycia, said/promulgated:

6–18. "The 'citizens' of Orna have contemplated *instituting a cult/making a chapel* (?) to the god Kandawats Caunian and his colleagues. And they made Simias son of Koddorosi priest. And there is a *property* which the 'citizens' of Orna gave to the god Kandawats. Year after year a ⟨mi⟩na and a half of silver will be given by the country. This priest will sacrifice to the god Kandawats a sheep for the new moon, and he will *sacrifice* every year an ox. And this domain, which is his own, is freed."

19a. The property-holder has written this law.

19b–23. Furthermore, if ever someone takes (anything) away from the god Kandawats or from ⟨*t*⟩*his* priest, *let him be* taken away by the god Kandawats and his colleagues.

24–27. And whoever takes (anything/the stele?) away from the god⟨*s*⟩ Leto, Artemis, Ḥšatrapati and others, these gods will seek (for it) from him.

Even without a detailed analysis of the differences between the Aramaic and Greek texts, it seems fairly clear that the Greek text represents the position of the local authorities, with two archontes of Lycia and a governor of Xanthos established or confirmed by Pixodaros at their head; their proposition has still to be promulgated by the satrap: *Pixôtaros de kurios estô* (line 35). However, lines 6–18 of the Aramaic inscription

43. Ibid., 184.
44. Cf. Dan 2:16, 18, 49; 7:16.

represent the official position/response/rescript of Pixodaros promulgating this religious law (*dātāh*). The Aramaic inscription also mentions (line 19a) that the law was engraved on the order of "the property-holder," the priest Simias, who probably thought it the best way of avoiding any reclamation. The same priest probably added the two maledictions in lines 19b–23 and 24–27, putting his property under the protection of his gods and of the great gods of the main sanctuary of Orna, where the stele was erected.

However, even if the Aramaic text is clearly the official text, being placed in the center between the Greek and Lycian texts,[45] one should note that though it is the longest monumental inscription in Imperial Aramaic, it is not very well engraved. Without going into the details of a paleographic analysis,[46] I would state that one may clearly discern many mistakes in this beautiful, official stele.

1. One letter (*taw*) was forgotten and later added above the line (end of line 8).

2. At least one (*mem* at the beginning of line 14) if not two (*zayin*, line 22) letters were not engraved, though the engraver left space for them. These letters were probably written in ink by the scribe who wrote the model, but the engraver later forgot to engrave them.

3. Several letters are probably missing by haplography: two letters in line 22, *wyh*⟨*wy*⟩; one letter in line 23, *ᵓlh*⟨*y*⟩*ᵓ*; and one letter at the end of line 25, *ᵓ*⟨*y*⟩*š* or ⟨*ᵓ*⟩*yš*; the last two mistakes being a consequence of the easy confusion between the shapes of *ᵓalep* and *yod* (infra).

4. The small upper right stroke of *ᵓalep* is sometimes missing (lines 11, 14, 15, 26); thus they are easily confused with *yod* or *gimel*.

5. Similarly, the middle stroke of the *he*[47] is probably missing in the middle of line 22, so that this letter is easily confused with *gimel*, *yod*, or *ᵓalep*.

6. Several letters present anomalous shapes: *lamed* in line 9, *ṣade*/*ḥet* at the end of lines 16 and 19, *bet* at the beginning of line 27; moreover, the shape of the *samek* is peculiar, to say the least.

7. Especially from line 19 downward, the lines of writing tend to slope down on the left.

8. In the last line, the spaces between *waw* and *nun*, and *nun* and *he* are unusual.

This large number of mistakes is all the more surprising, because the inscription is engraved on a beautiful stele, and the Greek inscription is

45. *Xanthos VI*, 133.

46. Cf. the remarks above (pp. 424–29) and Dupont-Sommer's comments.

47. The shape of the *he* in this inscription seems to be influenced by the Lycian *e*.

a generally well-engraved *stoichēdon.*[48] The engraver probably did not know Aramaic and was not used to engraving Aramaic inscriptions. This is not surprising since, at Xanthos, "moins de 5% des textes inscrits d'époque archaïque et classique sont en araméen. Cette langue apparaît essentiellement comme l'instrument de l'empire."[49]

48. *Xanthos VI,* 32.

49. C. Le Roy, "Araméen, lycien et grec: Pluralité des langues et pluralité des cultures," *Hethetica* 8 (1987) 263–66, esp. 264.

The Inscribed Marble Vessels from Kition

E. Lipiński

A number of Phoenician inscriptions on fragments of white marble, found on the site of Eshmun-Melqart's sanctuary at Kition, reproduce a dedicatory formula that is reconstructed here on the basis of recent reeditions of the fragments in question. The possible aim of these offerings of marble bowls and the nature of the deity so honored are further examined.

The Cesnola collection in the Metropolitan Museum of Art, New York, comprises a number of Phoenician inscriptions on fragments of white marble bowls, which occasionally show a spout or a handle. The inscriptions are engraved in a single line around the rim; one is written in two lines on the belly of the bowl. All the pieces were found between 1869 and 1871 and seem to derive from a single site, a small sanctuary of the Phoenician deity Eshmun-Melqart, which occupied the low hill called Batsalos among the salt lagoons southeast of ancient Kition.[1]

Although the dedications are very fragmentary, they are sufficient to restore a whole formula, which Ernest Renan proposed reading as follows: "On the X day of the month Y in the year Z of Pumayyaton, king of Kition and Idalion, son of king Milkyaton, king of Kition and Idalion, N son of NN vowed this gift to his Lord, to Eshmun-Melqart, for he heard his voice; may he bless."[2] Not all the bowls bore the full formula, while others had additional data, such as the donor's official title. The new publication of these inscriptions by M. G. Amadasi Guzzo,[3] on the one hand, and by J. Teixidor,[4] on the other, has provided an opportunity to

1. For information on the site where these bowls were found, see G. Colonna Ceccaldi, "Découvertes de Chypre," *Revue archéologique* n.s. 11/21 (1870) 24–27.

2. *CIS* I, vol. 1, p. 48.

3. M. G. Amadasi Guzzo and V. Karageorghis, *Fouilles de Kition*, vol. 3: *Inscriptions phéniciennes* (Nicosia, 1977) A 5–25 and E 3.

4. J. Teixidor, "The Phoenician Inscriptions of the Cesnola Collection," *MMJ* 11 (1976) 55–70.

restore the formula anew in the light of all the available fragments, but neither editor has made the attempt. The purpose of this paper is to attempt a fresh restoration of the formula and to propose an interpretation. This was greatly facilitated by the photographs kindly supplied by the Metropolitan Museum of Art (figs. 1, 2, p. 437), which also provided the writer with a photograph of fragment 74.51.2275; this most likely belongs to the same group, but the inscription is unfortunately illegible.

Since Teixidor's publication in *The Metropolitan Museum Journal* is useful mainly because of the excellent quality of the photographs, a synoptic view of the numbering of the inscriptions in Amadasi Guzzo's *Corpus* and in Teixidor's article (*MMJ*) may be useful:

Corpus	*MMJ*	*Corpus*	*MMJ*
A 5	14	A 16	5
A 6	1	A 17	4
A 7	2	A 18	7
A 8	3	A 19	18
A 9	9	A 20	17
A 10	11	A 21	6
A 11	(lost)	A 22	8
A 12	15	A 23	10
A 13	(lost)	A 24	(lost)
A 14	16	A 25	13
A 15	12	E 3	(Louvre)

The name of the marble vessels offered to Eshmun-Melqart has never been established, although fragments of at least eighteen different bowls have been recovered, as noted in 1872 by Schröder.[5] Two fragments, A 11 and A 24, were already lost at that time, and it is therefore impossible either to determine whether they belonged to one of the eighteen bowls or to collate the readings. In any case, some fragments seem to have preserved, at least partially, the key word of the inscription. The best example is A 19, the photograph of which in *MMJ* 18 allows us to read *bn bʿlr]m*[6] *qʾḥt[* without any hesitation and accordingly to

5. P. Schröder, "Über einige Fragmente phönikischer Inschriften aus Cypern," *Monatsberichte der Königlichen Preussischen Akademie der Wissenschaften zu Berlin: Phil.-hist. Klasse* (1872) 330–41 and pls. I–III.

6. King Milkyaton's father was called *bʿlrm* and bore no royal title, as seen in *CIS* I 88 = Amadasi Guzzo and Karageorghis, *Fouilles de Kition*, vol. 3, F 1, line 2; *CIS* I 90 line 1, and

restore *q̇*(ʾ)*ḥt* in A 20, as proposed by Hall.[7] We can further restore [*qʾḥ*]*t z* ʾ[*š ytn*] in A 17, in the light of ʾ*š ytn* [ʿ*bdrš*]*p bn* ʾ[in A 18. This implies that *qʾḥt* designates the marble vessels on which the inscriptions were engraved.

Now, a common Egyptian word for 'vessel' is *ḳrḥ.t*, also spelled *ḳꜣḥ.t*,[8] since the weak consonant *r* tends to be replaced in writing by *ꜣ* and was most likely pronounced as a glottal stop. This word, already attested in the time of the Old Empire, appears in Biblical Hebrew as *qallaḥat*[9] and in Coptic as *čalaht* or, perhaps better, *ǧalaht*.[10] Although the latter is believed to be a loanword from Semitic,[11] it, in turn, should be considered an old loanword from Egyptian, as suggested by the coexistence of the forms *qlḥt* and *qʾḥt* in "Canaanite," best explained as independently originating from the same Egyptian word *ḳrḥ.t* 'vessel'. If this explanation of *qʾḥt* is correct, the key word of the Phoenician dedicatory inscriptions from Kition simply means 'vessel'.

The size of the bowls varied considerably, allowing for additional elements in the basic formula. The diameter of some bowls could be established approximately, thus: ca. 23 cm for A 23, 80 cm for A 18, 85 cm for A 6, 90 cm for A 20, 120 cm for A 9, and 140 cm for A 5, giving circumferences of ca. 72 cm, 2.5 m, 2.7 m, 2.8 m, 3.8 m, and 4.4 m, respectively. The bowl to which fragment A 23 belonged was smaller, and its belly consequently bore two lines of text. Fragment A 16 apparently preserves an extension of the basic formula: [*qʾḥt w*] *ml*ʾ *z* [ʿ*š ytn* . . .] 'this is [the vessel and] the contents [that gave N son of NN]'. This additional element indicates that the bowls dedicated to Eshmun-Melqart were not empty, but it does not reveal the nature of the contents. Other additional elements are provided by A 9 and A 21, which specify the donor's

---

from the new Kition inscription published by M. Yon and M. Sznycer, "Une inscription phénicienne royale de Kition (Chypre)," *CRAI* (1991) 791–823.

7. I. H. Hall, "More Phoenician Inscriptions in New York," *Hebraica* 2 (1885–86) 240–43 (see p. 243, no. XVIII).

8. A. Erman and H. Grapow, *Wörterbuch der ägyptischen Sprache* (Berlin, 1931; reprint, 1971) 5.62–63.

9. 1 Sam 2:14, Mic 3:3.

10. W. Westendorf, *Koptisches Handwörterbuch* (Heidelberg, 1965–77) 454; J. Černý, *Coptic Etymological Dictionary* (Cambridge, 1976) 329; W. Vycichl, *Dictionnaire étymologique de la langue copte* (Louvain, 1983) 339–40.

11. This opinion, defended already by P. A. de Lagarde (*Übersicht über die im Aramäischen, Arabischen und Hebräischen übliche Bildung der Nomina* [Abhandlungen der Königlichen Gesellschaft der Wissenschaften zu Göttingen 35; Göttingen, 1889] 1.88), is followed by J. Černý and W. Vycichl (see n. 10).

official title: *ml*[*ṣ*] *krsym* (A 9) 'the interpreter of the Cretans',[12] and *rb ṣlm* (A 21), perhaps 'the chief of the roasters'.[13]

A synoptic view of the material at our disposal may be useful before we attempt to restore the formula.

Dating formula

A 6	[*bymm*] *2̇9 lyrḥ*[. . . *bšnt*]	*4 lmlk mlk*[*ytn*	*mlk kty*]	*wʾdyl b*[*n bʿlrm* . .][14]
A 5A	[*bymm* . . *lyrḥ* . . .	*bšnt* . . .*lml*] *k̇ mlkytn*	[. . .]	
A 7	[*bymm* . . *lyrḥ* . . .	*bšnt* . . .*lm*] *lk mlkytn*	*m*[*lk kty*	*wʾdyl* . . .]
A 8	[*bymm* . . *lyrḥ* . . .	*bšnt* . . .*lmlk mlkytn*]	*mlk kty*	*wʾd*[*yl* . . .]
A 19	[*bymm* . . *lyrḥ* . . .	*bšnt* . . .*lmlk mlkytn*	*mlk kty*	*wʾdyl bn bʿlr*] *m*

Dedication

A 19	[. . . *bn bʿlr*] *m qʾḥt*	[*z*	*ʾš ytn* . . .]
A 20	[. . . . .] *q̇*(*ʾ*) *ḥt*[15]		
A 17	[. . . *bn bʿlrm qʾḥ*] *ṫ*	*z*	*ʾ*[*š ytn* . . .]
A 16	[. . . *bn bʿlrm qʾḥt w*] *mlʾ*	*z*[	*ʾš ytn* . . .]
A 18			*ʾš ytn* [*ʿbdrš*] *p bn ʾ*[. . .]
A 23,1			*ʾ*[*š ytn* . . .]

12. Cf. E. Lipiński, "Notes d'épigraphie phénicienne et punique," *OLP* 14 (1983) 129–65 and pls. II-VI (see pp. 146–52). In a private communication, M. Heltzer rightly pointed to the Ὀνάσανδρος Κρής in Cyprus in the fourth century B.C.E. (*SEG* XXVIII 1302). Y. Garfinkel ("*MLṢ HKRSM* in Phoenician Inscriptions from Cyprus, the *QRSY* in Arad, *HKRSYM* in Egypt, and *BNY QYRS* in the Bible," *JNES* 47 [1988] 27–34) pays little attention to the different spellings and the different historical contexts.

13. The root *ṣly* means 'to roast'. The function of a *rb ṣlm* would originally have been quite similar to that of a *rab ṭabbāḥīm*, etymologically 'chief of the butchers' or 'of the cooks'. The plural of the active participle *Qal* of *ṣly* is in fact *ṣlm*, just as the *bnm* of the Kition inscription C 1, A 4 are 'builders' or 'architects'. The title of *rb ṣlm* was not yet recognized by M. Sznycer, "Les noms de métier et de fonction chez les Phéniciens de Kition d'après les témoignages épigraphiques," in *Chypre: La vie quotidienne de l'Antiquité à nos jours* (Paris, 1985) 79–86.

14. The inclination of the stroke seems to justify Teixidor's reading "20 + 9" ("Phoenician Inscriptions of the Cesnola Collection," 56); cf. A 29 (pl. VIII, 1), line 1, where "20" and "10" are written next to each other. The usual reading "10 + 9" was proposed by Hall ("More Phoenician Inscriptions," 241, V), followed by L. Palma di Cesnola (*A Descriptive Atlas of the Cesnola Collection of Cypriote Antiquities in the Metropolitan Museum of Art* [New York, 1903], vol. 3, pl. 122:5), and by *RES* no. 1531, and by Amadasi Guzzo and Karageorghis, *Fouilles de Kition*, vol. 3, A 6. At the end of the fragment one should read *b* instead of *m*, as shown clearly by the photograph in *MMJ* 1.

15. The word *q̇*(*ʾ*)*ḥt* in A 20 is followed by an anepigraphic space that suggests that nothing is missing after this word. If this assumption is correct, one should think of a formula similar to that of *CIS* I 95, from Lapethos. This would give a text like [*lʾšmn mlqrt* N *bn* NN *ytn ʾt*] *q̇*(*ʾ*)*ḥt*.

Figure 1. Fragment A 5B.

Figure 2. Fragment A 25.

Donor's and god's names

A 5B	[. *b*]*ṅ ʿbdmrny*	*lʾdny lʾšmn mlq*[*rt* . . .]
A 9	[*bn ršp*]*ytn ml*[*ṣ*] *krsym*	*l*[*ʾdny lʾšmn mlqrt* . . .]
A 18C	[*ʾšmnʾd*]*ṅy bn ʾ*[. . .]	
A 21	[. . . . . *bn* . . . .]*k rb ṣlm*	*l̇*[*ʾdny* . . .][16]
A 22	[. . . . .] *bn* [. . .]	
E 3	[. . .]*ytn bn ʿbd*[. . .]	
A 25	[. . . . . *bn* . . *m*]*lqrt*	*lʾdny lʾšmn* [*mlqrt* . . .]
A 10	[. . . .]	*lʾdny lʾšmn ml*[*qrt* . . .][17]
A 11	[. . . .	*lʾdny l*]*ʾšmn ml*[*qrt* . . .]
A 15	[. . . .	*lʾdny lʾš*]*mn ml*[*qrt* . . .]
A 23,2	[. . . .]	*lʾ*[*dny* . . .]
A 12	[. . . .	*lʾdny lʾšmn ml*]*qrt ybrk*
A 13	[. . . .	*lʾdny lʾšmn*] *mlqrt y*[*brk*]
A 14	[. . . .	*lʾdny lʾšmn ml*]*q̇rt yḃ*[*rk*]
A 24	[. . . .	*kšmʿ*] *qlm* [*ybrk*]

In light of this synoptic view of the fragmentary inscriptions, we propose the following reconstruction of the basic formula:

> *bymm* X *lyrḥ* Y *bšnt* Z *lmlk mlkytn mlk kty wʾdyl bn bʿlrm qʾḥt* (*wmlʾ*) *z ʾš ytn* N *bn* NN (title) *lʾdny lʾšmn mlqrt* (*kšmʿ qlm*) *ybrk*
>
> On the X day of the month Y in the year Z of King Milkyaton, king of Kition and Idalion, son of Baalrom, this is the vessel (and the contents) that N son of NN (title) gave to his Lord, to Eshmun-Melqart(, for he heard their voice); may he bless!

The anepigraphic space preceding *ʾš ytn* in A 18 and A 23 suggests a shorter formula, omitting the date and the name of the object.

In 1894, besides the fragments of the marble bowls unearthed by Palma di Cesnola, the site of the Eshmun-Melqart shrine yielded a fragment of a terracotta bowl inscribed with a formula comparable with the inscriptions of the marble vessels. The fragment, now in the Cyprus Museum in Nicosia (inv. Inscr. Ph. 13), has been reedited, together with other

16. Teixidor's reading *ndr.lm* ("Phoenician Inscriptions of the Cesnola Collection," 58), based on a confusion of the letters *b, d, r,* is certainly erroneous.

17. Teixidor's reading *lʾšmn wl*[*mlqrt*] is not correct, despite the difference between the very cursive *mem* of *ʾšmn* and the *mem* of *ml*[*qrt*], whose head and shaft form an acute angle; the center line, easily recognizable in the photograph of *MMJ* 11, precludes the interpretation of the letter as *waw*.

Kition inscriptions, by Amadasi Guzzo (D 10).[18] The beginnings of the two lines of the text are lost and their length is unknown. In addition, it is not clear whether *mlqrt* in line 1 is the theophorous element of a proper name or the end of the formula [*lʾdny lʾšmn*] *mlqrt*. The second line, written in larger letters, preserves the concluding words of common dedicatory inscriptions: [*k šmʿ q*]*l ybrk* 'for he heard (his) voice; may he bless!'

One wonders, of course, what were the purpose and the content (*mlʾ*) of the bowls offered to Eshmun-Melqart. The inscriptions give no clue in this respect; we might just surmise, for example, that the vessels were used for the planting of the ephemeral "Gardens of Adonis," the epithet that constantly precedes the name of Eshmun-Melqart. This ritual tradition remained alive in popular circles in Cyprus until the present century,[19] and traces of the practice have even been detected in the celebrations of St. Lazarus on the eve of Palm Sunday, as well as of Whitsunday and of the Feast of the Virgin Mary's Assumption. There were probably considerable local variations in the date of the Cypro-Phoenician festival; the name of the month is always missing in the inscriptions from Kition, even in A 6, which preserves the beginning of the date formula. Therefore, association with an Adonis festival remains purely conjectural. In addition, the occasional traces of a spout or handle on the fragments[20] suggest rather that the bowls were supposed to be filled with wine for libations,[21] with water for ablutions,[22] or with some other liquid. The libation was the most frequent form of sacrifice in the ancient world; in this rite, two kinds of vessel were used, a wine jug and a libation bowl. However, the shape, the size, and weight of the marble vessels from Kition do not favor their use as libation *phialai*. It is also unlikely that plain water was offered to the deity in these white marble bowls. Considering that the offerings were made to Eshmun-Melqart, that Eshmun's name is related to the word *šmn* 'oil',[23] and that oil offerings (*zbḥ šmn*) are attested in the Phoenician-Punic milieu, namely, at Carthage,[24] we might

18. Amadasi Guzzo and Karageorghis, *Fouilles de Kition*, 3.137–39 (where the previous literature is listed).

19. W. Baumgartner, *Zum Alten Testament und seiner Umwelt* (Leiden, 1959) 263.

20. See, e.g., Amadasi Guzzo and Karageorghis, *Fouilles de Kition*, vol. 3, pls. V:2; VII:1 and 2.

21. A libation bowl with a Phoenician inscription was published by N. Avigad and J. C. Greenfield, "A Bronze *phialē* with a Phoenician Dedicatory Inscription," *IEJ* 32 (1982) 118–28 and pl. 12 A.

22. A servitor carrying a vase of a similar size, with water for ablutions, is represented on a Neo-Assyrian bas-relief. Cf. *Encyclopédie photographique de l'art* (Paris, 1935) 1.315.

23. E. Lipiński, "Eshmun, 'Healer'," *AION* 33 (1973) 161–83.

24. *CIS* I 165 = *KAI* no. 69:12; *CIS* I 167 = *KAI* no. 74:9.

surmise that it was oil, perhaps for anointing,[25] that was presented to the god in these marble vessels. We may wonder if there may be a connection of sorts between the use of marble, the cultic function of the vessels, and ritual impurity, as in Second Temple Period Jerusalem. Stone vessels were not liable to impurity and hence could be reused safely.

The composite name Eshmun-Melqart suggests the worship of an originally Cypriot deity whose features were not matched by a single Phoenician god. One should probably consider him as a god of healing, identified with Eshmun and perhaps connected with the salt lagoons, but also appealed to as warder-off of evils and victor over them, somewhat after the fashion of a Heracles ἀλεξίκακος and καλλίνικος. These characteristics would support the association with Heracles-Melqart, who is represented on the coins of Kition advancing with bow and club, a lion's skin hanging behind him.[26]

Reference should also be made to the limestone statues of a smiting god wearing lion-skin and brandishing a club. Attested from the sixth century on in many Cypriot sanctuaries, as well as on the Levantine coast, he is characterized by a small lion that he is holding by the tail, while the animal is holding up its head as if to bite the god.[27] This detail, typical of the Egyptian god Shed "the Savior," merged with Horus-the-Savior in the Late Period[28] and later 'Shed the Healer' *Šdrpʾ* on the Syro-Phoenician Amrit stela,[29] and seems to imply that the god's Heraclean

25. The deprivation of oil for anointing is mentioned in connection with Melqart and Eshmun in the curses of Esarhaddon's treaty with Baal, king of Tyre. Cf. S. Parpola and K. Watanabe, *Neo-Assyrian Treaties and Loyalty Oaths* (SAA 2; Helsinki, 1988) no. 5, IV, 14′–17′: "May Melqart and Eshmun . . . take away the oil for your anointing."

26. See, e.g., B. V. Head and G. F. Hill, *A Guide to the Principal Coins of the Greeks* (London, 1932) pls. 9:48 and 49. For a good enlarged reproduction of Pumayyaton's gold coin, with the "Heraclean" deity wearing a lion's skin and holding a club and a bow, see V. Karageorghis, *Kition: Mycenaean and Phoenician Discoveries in Cyprus* (London, 1976) fig. 94.

27. Cf. M. Yon, "À propos de l'Héraklès de Chypre," in *Iconographie classique et identités régionales* (ed. L. Kahil, C. Augé, and P. Linant de Bellefonds; Bulletin de correspondance hellénique, Supplements 14; Paris, 1986) 287–97. Material relating to this iconography has been collected by C. Jourdain-Annequin, *Héraclès-Melqart à Amrith—Recherches iconographiques: Contribution à l'étude d'un syncrétisme* (BAH 142; Paris, 1992). Of course, the name given to the deity is unwarranted.

28. G. Loukianoff, "Le Dieu Ched," *BIE* 13 (1930–31) 67–84; B. Bruyère, *Rapport sur les fouilles de Deir el Médineh (1935–1940)* (Fouilles de l'Institut français d'archéologie orientale 20/3; Cairo, 1952) 138–70; A. Caquot, "Chadrapha: À propos de quelques articles récents," *Syria* 29 (1952) 74–88, in particular 74–77 and 85–88; H. Brunner, "Eine Dankstele an Upuaut," *MDAIK* 16 (1958) 5–19, in particular 16–19; D. Meeks, in *Génies, anges et démons* (Sources orientales 8; Paris, 1971) 56–57; H. Brunner, "Sched," *Lexikon der Ägyptologie*, vol. 5 (Wiesbaden, 1984) 547–49.

29. A reproduction of the stela can be found in J. Teixidor, "Stèle votive" (in *Au Pays de Baal et d'Astarté: 10.000 ans d'art en Syrie* [Paris, 1983] 222–23, no. 255) and a decipherment

equipment is only a Greek disguise for a Cypriot or Cypro-Egyptian deity, inspired by iconographic similarities and by Heracles' supposed ability to avert evils of all kinds.

In conclusion, Eshmun-Melqart might be the local Phoenician name of the divine "Savior" and "Healer" represented in contemporaneous Cypriot art as a "Heraclean" smiting god and integrated by the Phoenicians of Kition into their own pantheon.

---

of the inscription in E. Puech, "Les inscriptions phéniciennes d'Amrit et les dieux guérisseurs du sanctuaire" (*Syria* 63 [1986] 327–42 [see 336–37]).

Grain Prices in Late Antiquity and the Nature of the Evidence

Philip Mayerson

In attempting to gain some insight into the state of health of the ancient world, sociologists, economists, and climatologists seek out, among other data, the price of basic foodstuffs. For late antiquity (the period between the fourth and the eighth centuries C.E.*) the statistical evidence for the price of wheat and barley is sparse, but fortunately it is based, unlike an earlier period, on a fairly stable monetary system. However, a cautionary note is needed. The price of grain is essentially a minor factor in revealing how well, or poorly, a community, a province, or even an empire, bears up under the vagaries of weather, parasitic insects, fungi, political unrest, speculators, creditors, epidemics, shortage of labor, or an inadequate infrastructure.*

Within the several disciplines that attempt to seek a broader view of the ancient economic, social, or climatological conditions during a specific period of time and place, an eagerly sought datum is the price of basic foodstuffs such as wheat and barley. To that end literary sources (both sacred and secular) and epigraphic and papyrological documents are scoured for the desired statistical evidence. For the Near East in late antiquity (Egypt and North Africa included) the results are quite sparse and uneven. Inscriptional evidence is lacking, with one exception. The papyrological documents from Egypt yield an abundance of material, generally in the form of receipts that represent record-keeping rather than informative comments on price movements. From two writers of the fourth century, a Roman emperor and a historian, we know of benefactions in the form of grain distributions at set prices to two cities suffering from severe food shortages. As for sacred or quasi-sacred literature, there is very limited evidence from the sages of the Talmud or the saints of the early monastic movement. However, in spite of the paucity of the statistical evidence, there is one advantage in dealing with evidence from late antiquity, and that is a monetary system based on the gold *solidus* that provided reasonably stable prices for almost 400 years, from the mid-fourth century C.E. to the time of the Umayyad caliphs. Prior to that time, rising inflation over a period of a century and more distorted meaningful values for the price system.

The following is a list of known prices for wheat and barley as given in the sources from the fourth century to the time of the Umayyads. A brief description is also given of the recorded events that caused serious fluctuations in prices.

(1) The Emperor Julian recounts that when the Syrian city of Antioch suffered from a shortage of grain due to a number of droughts, he brought in large quantities of wheat from neighboring cities and from Egypt on which he set a price not of 10 *modii* per *solidus* but of 15 *modii.*[1]

(2) The historian Ammianus Marcellinus reports that during the reign of Valentinian I (ca. 371) there was a famine in the city of Carthage. The proconsul Hymetius sold wheat from the public granaries at the rate of 10 *modii* to the *solidus.* Shortly thereafter, when crops had improved, he replaced what he had taken (in the open market) at the rate of 30 *modii* to the *solidus.*[2]

(3) In 445, Valentinian III issued an edict setting a commuted rate for wheat at 40 *modii* per *solidus.*[3]

(4) In the Egyptian papyri from the fifth to the seventh centuries, prices for wheat, depending on market conditions, ranged from as little as 8 *artabae* (ca. 26 *modii*) to as much as 15 *artabae* (ca. 50 *modii*) to the *solidus*; most sales were in the range of 10–12 *artabae* (ca. 33–40 *modii*). Barley, cheaper than wheat, sold in one instance for 30 *modii* to the *solidus,* but under what might be called normal conditions, 16–18 *artabae* (ca. 50–60 *modii*) to the *solidus.*[4]

(5) An account of a shortage of wheat in Egypt comes from the biographer of Pachomius, the celebrated founder of organized monasti-

1. *Misopogon* 369 (*The Works of Emperor Julian* [ed. W. C. Wright; LCL] II, pp. 502–5). The emperor, attempting to show his magnanimity by offering 15 *modii,* fell afoul of speculators who purchased the grain and sold it for exorbitant sums. Julian further states that even in good times wheat rarely sold for that amount. When he attempted to fix prices he incurred the ill will of the rich, who were prevented from selling their stored grain at inflated prices. (The *modius* is a Roman measure, approximately the equivalent of a peck.)

2. Marcellinus (*Amianus Marcellinus* [ed. J. C. Rolfe; LCL] III) XXXVIII.1.17–18, p. 99.

3. *Novella* XIII, par. 4 (*Codex Theodosianus* [ed. P. M. Meyer; Hildesheim, 1990] 2.95).

4. A. C. Johnson and L. C. West, *Byzantine Egypt: Economic Studies* (Princeton, 1949) 173–76. The Egyptian *artaba* is highly variable in terms of *modii.* For the period in question, I convert one *artaba* into $3\frac{1}{3}$ *modii,* which is at the lower end of the range. For a discussion of the problem of converting the *artaba* into *modii,* see R. P. Duncan-Jones, "The Choenix, the Artaba, and the Modius," *ZPE* 21 (1976) 43–51.

cism. He tells of a time when no wheat could be found in all of Egypt. Pachomius sent out a fellow monk with 100 *solidii* to go to the cities and villages to purchase supplies of wheat for the monastery. In one city he came upon a (supposedly) devout official in charge of the public granary, who offered the monk, who had only 100 *solidi*, 200 *solidi* worth of wheat at the rate of 13 *artabae* (ca. 43 *modii*) to the *solidus*. The monk was told that the public wheat was not needed at that time and that it could be replaced at the next harvest. Pachomius berated the monk for his speculative undertaking and for threatening the monastery with debt and slavery in the event that the money or the wheat could not be replaced. The transaction was repudiated, and with the money given to him by Pachomius, the monk purchased wheat at the rate of $5\frac{1}{2}$ *artabae* (ca. 18 *modii*) to the *solidus*. This episode is said to have taken place in the second quarter of the fourth century.[5]

(6) A chronicle attributed to St. Joshua the Stylite provides first-hand data on prices of wheat and barley for several critical years of the late fifth and early sixth centuries in the city of Edessa (modern Urfa), the capital of the province of Oshroene in Mesopotamia. Surrounded by a fertile plain, the city prospered from its agricultural economy, though subject to periodic droughts, invasions by locusts, desiccating winds, and earthquakes. St. Joshua believed that these calamities were visited on the community as retribution for its profligate and sinful ways. Be that as it may, the information he provides is detailed in terms of conditions of supply and demand as they affected the price structure of both wheat and barley.

For the year 494–95, as though to set a benchmark for prices, Joshua states that wheat sold at the rate of 30 *modii* and barley 50 *modii* to the *solidus*. In May of 499, locusts invaded the region and laid their eggs in the ground; these hatched in March of 500, and the locusts devastated the region of its vegetation. As a result, the price of grain rose about eightfold: 4 *modii* to the *solidus*; barley, 6 *modii* to the *solidus*. As conditions worsened, prices soared: wheat sold for 13 *kabs* (= *sextarii*) per *solidus* and barley 18 *kabs* per *solidus*. In other words, wheat sold for less than 1 *modius* to the *solidus* and barley little more than 1 *modius* to the *solidus*. After the harvest for the year 501, wheat sold for only 5 *modii* per *solidus*. No mention is made of the price for barley.

The year 501–2 looked highly promising for the people of Edessa, since abundant rains had produced strong growth of the planted seed, but in May of 502, before reaping time, a desiccating wind reduced the

5. F. Halkin, *Sancti Pachomii Vitae Graecae* (*Subsidia hagiographica* 19; Brussels, 1932) 147–49, §§ 21–22.

yield so that wheat sold at 12 *modii* to the *solidus* and barley 22 *modii* to the *solidus,* less than half the rate they sold for in 494–95.

St. Joshua has only one more datum on grain prices. He states that up to the year 504–5, wheat had sold at the rate of 4 *modii* per *solidus* and barley 6 *modii,* but after the harvest of 505, wheat was sold at the rate of 6 *modii* to the *solidus* and barley at the rate of 10 *modii.* For the years between 501 and 504, Joshua gives no indication of the conditions that held production down to this level.[6]

(7) Turning to Palestine where, unlike Egypt and Edessa, water resources were highly variable, we possess two notices regarding the price of wheat from two regions separated by several hundred kilometers and by as many years. One item is from the Jerusalem Talmud, dated to the mid-fourth century; the other (hitherto uncommented upon) consists of two papyrological documents from the Negev, clearly dated to the Umayyad period of the late seventh century.

In the Jerusalem Talmud (*y. B. Qam.* 9:5), R. Jonah reports the case of a man who was given 8 *dinars* (= *solidi*) to buy wheat at Tiberias but chose instead to buy it at Sepphoris. We are told that the man would have received 25 *modii* (to the *solidus*), but since he bought it in Sepphoris, he only received 20 *modii.* It is apparent in this instance that the price in these two locations was determined by a number of variables, such as availability, business practices, transportation, and so forth, but not by a severe shortage.[7]

(8) The papyrological documents uncovered at Nessana, a site deep in the Negev close to the Sinai border, record a number of requisitions of wheat and oil to be turned over to Arab officials. Out of a total of seven extant documents of this kind, one, *P. Ness.* 65, dated to 675–76, gives a price of $13\frac{2}{3}$ *solidi* as the total value (as the *adaeratio* rate) of 207 *modii* of wheat and 207 *sextarii* of oil.[8]

The other document, *P. Ness.* 69, dated to 680–81(?), is an account of a food allowance for Arab troops. A portion of the total amount, 407 *modii* of wheat and 407 *sextarii* of oil, is commuted (?) to $27\frac{1}{8}$ *solidi.*[9]

If we were to extrapolate the price of oil from these two documents, we would be left with a fairly good approximation of the price of wheat for this early postconquest period. I have taken the price of 40 *sextarii*

6. W. Wright (ed.), *The Chronicon of Joshua the Stylite* (Amsterdam, 1968; reprint of 1882 Cambridge edition) 17, 28–29, 34–35, 69. See also H. Leclair, "Crises économique à Edessa (494–506) d'après la chronique du pseudo-Josué le Stylite," *Pallas* 27 (1980) 89–100.

7. See D. Sperber, *Roman Palestine 200–400: Money and Prices* (Ramat-Gan, 1974) 31.

8. C. J. Kraemer, Jr. (ed.), *Excavations at Nessana: Non-literary Papyri* (Princeton, 1958) 191–93.

9. Ibid., 199–201.

per *solidus* from the Egyptian documents as representing the price of oil in Nessana, fully aware that olives did not flourish in Egypt, but neither did they in the semi-arid Negev. By using this figure for *P. Ness.* 65, 205 *sextarii* of oil would be valued at 5.1 *solidi,* leaving the net cost of wheat to be 8.5 *solidi* for 205 *modii,* or an average price of ca. 24 *modii* per *solidus.* By using the same calculation for *P. Ness.* 69, 407 *sextarii* of oil would be valued at 10.2 *solidi,* leaving the net cost of 407 *modii* of wheat at 17 *solidi,* or ca. 23–24 *modii* per *solidus.*

The following table summarizes in terms of *modii* per *solidus* the narrative evidence for prices of wheat and barley (when available).

Modii per Solidus

	Wheat	*Barley*	*Conditions and Dates*
Egypt	30–40	50–60	"Normal"
	18		Shortage (4th century C.E.)
Syria	15		Shortage (363)
Africa	10		Famine
	30		ca. 371
	40		Edict of 445
Edessa	30	50	"Normal"?
	4	6	Locusts (500)
	5		501
	12	22	Dry winds (502)
	4	6	Up to 504–5
	6	10	505
Palestine	25–20		ca. 351
	23–24		675–76; 680–81?

The above figures represent a broad picture of grain prices in geographical settings that vary considerably in methods of obtaining the basic prerequisite for grain production, water. Egypt relied on the annual flood of the Nile; all the other regions depended on rainfall. Egypt and North Africa generally had sufficient moisture for their crops, as evidenced by the number of years they served as grain suppliers for the cities of Rome and Byzantium. Edessa lay in the agriculturally productive region of Oshroene; its fields were well watered and produced abundant crops of cereals, vegetables, and fruit.[10] Under so-called normal conditions, a *solidus* could purchase 30–40 *modii* of wheat in Egypt, North Africa, or Edessa. The situation in Palestine, however, offers a paradox. The price of wheat in Tiberias and Sepphoris, 20–25 *modii* per *solidus*, is matched by the commuted rate at Nessana of 23–24 *modii* per *solidus*. Sepphoris in the Galilee and Tiberias by the Kinneret had adequate amounts of rainfall to produce good crops of grain. Nessana, on the other hand, situated in an arid zone, with an annual rainfall of only 85–100 mm. (less than 4 inches), matched the two cities in the north of Palestine in the prices for wheat. The answer to the paradox is found in the laborious technique used by the ancient inhabitants of the Negev highlands to harvest wadi floodwater and distribute it over their terraced fields.[11] Other documents from the Nessana archive, especially *P. Ness.* 82, show the success achieved by these desert inhabitants in raising crops of wheat and barley under the most difficult conditions.[12]

What substantive generalization may we derive from this scattering of statistics, covering approximately 300 years, regarding climate change or other causes of shortages in the food supply system? The evidence does not lend itself to one. P. Garnsey, examining famine and food supply in the Greco-Roman world at large, comes to the conclusion, admittedly on deficient evidence, that "famines were rare but that subsistence crises falling short of famine were common."[13] This statement applies not only to the world of antiquity but to the modern world as well. Farmer and nonfarmer alike are hostage to the vagaries of weather, parasitic insects and fungi, earth movements, political unrest, speculators, creditors, epidemics, and the availability of labor. Where there is an infrastructure of stored surplus, of adequate transport, and of governmental regulation and assistance, food-supply crises can be alleviated. The ability of the Emperòr Julian to summon supplies from neighboring cities and from Egypt and have them shipped to Antioch demonstrates this principle on a small scale. At Edessa, during the famine of 500, the bishop interceded with the emperor to remit a portion of the taxes; the governor of the city authorized the release of grain from the public granaries and provided a small amount of bread for the poor; and the emperor provided a substantial sum of money for the needy.[14] Food, grants of money, remission of taxes, and other corporate acts of concern

10. J. B. Segal, *Edessa, "The Blessed City"* (Oxford, 1970) 141; see also 120–21.

11. P. Mayerson, "The Agricultural Regime," *Excavations at Nessana* (London, 1962) 1.219–24; 239–49.

12. Ibid., 227–31.

13. P. Garnsey, *Famine and Food Supply in the Greco-Roman World* (Cambridge, 1988) 6.

14. Wright, *Chronicon of Joshua the Stylite*, 29–31.

reduce the distress of a suffering population to some extent. However, without an ability to petition a caring central government, or when living under conditions of anarchy, a population, ancient or modern, experiencing a food crisis, has no alternative but to rely on whatever resources are at hand and/or on prayer.

Latin in First-Century Palestine

Alan Millard

A curious feature of the Gospels is the occurrence of Latin words in the Greek text of each one, giving, in some cases, the earliest examples of those words current in Greek. Recent publications show there was a little knowledge of Latin in first-century Palestine, although Latinisms are absent from literary works. There was resistance to Latin words among Greek writers in Egypt, but several appear in documents of the Second Revolt found in the Judean Desert. Accordingly, it is argued, the Latin words in the Gospels may reflect colloquial use of the first century in Palestine, even during the lifetime of Jesus.

Aramaic, Hebrew, and Greek are now recognized as languages current in first-century Palestine. The discoveries of the past half-century have expanded our appreciation of the situation in various ways and put to rest contrary views some had espoused earlier. While Hebrew continued in use for religious debate and writing and for daily conversation in some circles, Aramaic was the common language at almost every level, with Greek rivaling it in the larger centers; anyone wanting to reach a wider public in the Roman world would need Greek.[1] The presence of a fourth language, Latin, the official language of the ruling power, has received less attention, for there has been little evidence for its currency in comparison with the other three. If the ordinary citizens of Judea, Samaria, and Galilee knew of Latin, few are likely to have learned to speak or read it actively. Educated Roman-born government officials and military commanders commonly spoke and wrote Greek; Latin had little role in their work. Thus a standard textbook states, "In Palestine . . . Latin made no major inroads until the later period of the empire," then shows that it might have appeared occasionally in notices set up by imperial

1. See Jonas Greenfield's overview, "Languages of Palestine, 200 B.C.E.–200 C.E.," in *Jewish Languages: Theme and Variations* (ed. H. H. Paper; New York, 1978) 143–54; and James Barr's survey, "Hebrew, Aramaic and Greek in the Hellenistic Age," *CHJ* 2.79–114.

authorities.[2] Three cases are reported in Josephus' *Antiquities*, edicts of Caesar and of Mark Antony, all with parallel Greek versions. To them is to be added the famous notice at the temple enclosure in Jerusalem, that warned Gentiles against entering the sacred area. None of these monuments has survived. There is, however, the well-known inscription of Pilate found at Caesarea in 1961, which originally bore a dedication in honor of Tiberius by PONTIUS PILATUS PRAEFECTUS IUDAEAE. "But the spread of Latin in Palestine in the early period of Roman rule did not extend far beyond official uses of this kind."[3] All these display Latin as the language of the ruling power, and that, presumably, was the governor's intention in writing the title for Jesus' cross in Latin (John 19:19, 20). In daily life the most familiar occurrence of Latin was the legends on imperial coins, mainly the silver *denarius* and, for the wealthy, the gold *aureus*. The "tribute penny" shown to Jesus at his request was such a denarius, with the emperor's titles in Latin around his bust (Matt 22:19ff.).

Roman soldiers, it might be thought, would speak Latin. This was true for many, but before the Jewish Revolt of 67–73 C.E., the garrisons in Palestine were drawn mainly from local non-Jewish residents, with some from nearby territories. They would have spoken Greek or Aramaic. Only after the fall of Jerusalem was the Tenth Legion Fretensis stationed in the land, stamping its name on tiles made for its forts and using Latin more generally. Before that time the number of Romans in the land was small. While the governors, who came from the educated equestrian class, certainly knew and used Latin, they probably spoke Greek and read Greek as freely and easily. If we could uncover the private bookshelves of Pilate or one of his colleagues, they might hold a few scrolls of Homer, Plato, or Euripides, as well as Latin works. Among the latter might be a copy of the recently published patriotic work that Virgil had finished in approximately 19 B.C.E. to honor the Emperor Augustus, the *Aeneid*. All this is speculation; the only place where books belonging to high officials might be found today is Egypt, but even there the great stores of papyrus manuscripts do not come from the main center of government, Alexandria; their provenances are outlying provincial centers and villages, so they only reveal the books lesser officials were reading. The Latin works among them are very few.

2. See E. Schürer, *The History of the Jewish People in the Age of Jesus Christ* (3 vols; rev. and ed. G. Vermes, F. Millar, and M. Black; Edinburgh, 1979) 2.80. For a summary account of Latin in first-century Palestine, see J. A. Fitzmyer, "The Languages of Palestine in the First Century A.D.," in *A Wandering Aramean: Collected Aramaic Essays* (Missoula, 1979) 29–56; repr. from *CBQ* 32 (1970) 501–31.

3. Ibid.

Yet there were some humbler people who had knowledge of Latin in first-century Palestine. They were servants in the household of Herod. Evidence for this surprising fact comes from the excavations at Massada. A large number of inscribed potsherds came to light, the majority with Aramaic, Hebrew, or Greek on them.[4] Some were pieces of large wine jars. These amphorae were specially labeled: C. SENTIO SATURNINO CONSULE PHILONIANUM DE L. LAENI FUNDO REGI HERODI IUDAICO 'In the consulate of C. Sentius Saturninus, Philonian wine from the estate of L. Laenius, for Herod the Jewish king'.[5] The wine merchants or shippers in Italy naturally wrote in their own language. When the wine reached King Herod's cellars, his butler, at least, would need to know enough Latin to select the vintage his master demanded or liked. Jars labeled with consular dates for four different years have been found: Saturninus's of 19 B.C.E., others from 27, 26, and 14 B.C.E. The same need faced others in Herod's kitchens, for one jar was found marked GARUM 'fish sauce', another ME, probably for *mella* 'honey', and a third MAL, for *mala* 'apples'.[6] It is not hard to imagine a servant's terror if he were to serve the tyrant a sweet or fruit when he expected a savory! Massada was only one of Herod's many castles, so similar supplies almost certainly went into the stores and cellars in Caesarea, Jerusalem, Herodium, and the others, requiring similar recognition of their labels.

Latin, then, could be seen written in early first-century Palestine in very formal, Roman contexts, in the more well-to-do areas of the markets, or where expensive luxuries were imported from Italy—for Herod's life-style was not restricted to him alone. After 70 C.E., Roman soldiers conducted business in Latin and possibly read books in Latin. At Massada, papyrus fragments indicating both activities lay in the ruined buildings that belonged to the Roman garrison. They included a legionary's note of pay received and expenses paid; parts of four letters; a piece listing sick men, bandages, and medicaments; and fragments bearing only a few words or characters.

Massada's manuscripts can be studied today because of the accidents of their preservation in an arid climate and their discovery; even so, they are surely only a small part of the documents that once existed there. When only a single find is made like this, it is impossible to draw general conclusions. The garrison at Massada may have been unique in its day, perhaps the only one in which a soldier had a line or two of Virgil on a

4. Y. Yadin, J. Naveh, and Y. Meshorer, *Masada I: The Aramaic and Hebrew Ostraca and Jar Inscriptions; The Coins of Masada* (The Masada Reports; Jerusalem, 1989); H. M. Cotton and J. Geiger, *Masada II: The Latin and Greek Documents* (The Masada Reports; Jerusalem, 1989).

5. Ibid., 140–58, nos. 804–16.

6. Ibid., 166–67, no. 826; 139, no. 800; 163–64, no. 822.

strip of papyrus.[7] On the other hand, Latin writing like this may have been commonplace among all first-century Roman garrisons, as indeed probability suggests it was. Discoveries in other parts of the empire from the succeeding centuries assure us that this was indeed the case.

After the fall of Jerusalem, as Roman rule was more firmly imposed, the presence of Latin grew. The papyri from the "Cave of Letters," written during the first quarter of the second century, make this clear. The degree of Latin influence apparent in them surprised the scholars who edited them, for it is more marked there than in any other of the Eastern provinces. The Latinisms are both syntactical and lexical, the latter including βασιλικά (*basilica*, no. 16: lines 2, 4), ἀπο ἀκτῶν (*ab/ex actis*, no. 12: lines 1, 4), πραισίδιον (*praesidium*, no. 11: lines 6, 19), τριβουνάλιον (*tribunal*, no. 14: lines 12–13, 31). There are also Latin terms for money (the most common being, δηνάριον, *denarius*) and dates.[8]

It is appropriate to set the presence of Latinisms in the four Gospels in the context of these firsthand testimonies to Latin in early Roman Palestine, concentrating on the lexical material. There is a long history of comment on this phenomenon.[9] The material is conveniently displayed in the Blass-Debrunner grammar.[10] Several of the words are terms for measures or money, others refer to military matters, while some are not easily explained. Their presence distinguishes the Gospels from the Hebrew and Aramaic books among the Dead Sea Scrolls, mostly written in the first century B.C.E. and up to 65 C.E., which have no Greek or Latin loanwords,[11] and from the first-century Jewish writers Philo and Josephus, whose extant writings in Greek rarely exhibit the same loanwords as the Gospels.[12] Of the eighteen Latin words in the Gospels, ten occur in Mark, which has more Latinisms "than any other original Greek literary text," lending support to the long-standing suggestion that Mark's Gospel was written in Rome.[13] Either the number of Latinisms in the

7. Ibid., 31–35, no. 721.

8. N. Lewis and J. C. Greenfield (eds.), *The Documents from the Bar Kokhba Period in the Cave of Letters: Greek Papyri* (Judean Desert Studies; Jerusalem, 1989) 16–19.

9. For example, J. H. Thayer, "Language of the New Testament," in J. Hastings (ed.), *Dictionary of the Bible* (Edinburgh, 1898–1904) 3.40; F. F. Bruce, "Languages (Latin)," in *ABD* 4.221; A. T. Robertson, *A Grammar of the Greek New Testament in the Light of Historical Research* (3d ed.; London: 1919) 108–11.

10. F. Blass, A. Debrunner, and F. Rohrkopf, *Grammatik des neutestamentlichen Griechisch* (14th ed.; Göttingen, 1975) 6–9.

11. E. Qimron, *The Hebrew of the Dead Sea Scrolls* (HSS 29; Atlanta, 1986) 117.

12. See A. Schlatter, *Der Evangelist Matthäus* (Stuttgart, 1929) 816; *Der Evangelist Johannes* (Stuttgart, 1930) 393; *Das Evangelium des Lukas* (Stuttgart, 1931) 710.

13. M. Hengel, *Studies in the Gospel of Mark* (London, 1985) 28, 29, with references to earlier studies.

Gospels indicates that they were all composed in an area of strong Latin influence, such as Rome, or the Latin elements reflect the linguistic situation of early first-century Palestine. If the former is true, then the difference between the Gospels and the rest of the New Testament in this feature is striking, for there are only nine additional Latin words in the remaining books.

The distribution of the Latin words in the Gospels is interesting. Hengel has drawn attention to Mark's explanations in Latin at two points: κοδράντης, *quadrans* to elucidate the widow's "two mites" in 12:42; and πραιτώριον, *praetorium* for the governor's hall in 15:16.[14] Yet Matthew has both terms without any qualifying phrases (5:26 and 27:27), the former in a passage without parallel in Mark, "until you have paid the last *quadrans*." While Mark's Latinisms are the most striking, Latin words in Matthew are as many, and not all occur in parallel passages. In addition to *quadrans* in 5:26, he has κουστωδία, *custodia* for the guard on Jesus' tomb (27:65, 66; 28:11) and μίλιον, *milia* 'mile' in 5:41. His Gospel shares no Latin words with Luke or John, except the frequent *denarius*, which is common to all (fourteen times). Luke has the fewest Latin words, often giving a Greek equivalent where parallel passages have a Latin word. Thus Luke 8:16 has σκεῦος where Mark 4:21 and Matt 5:15 have μόδιος, *modius* for a measuring vessel; he has φόρος (20:22) where they have κῆνσος, *census* (Mark 12:14; Matt 17:25, 22:17); he has παιδεύειν (23:16, 22) where they have φραγελλοῦν, *flagellare* (Mark 15:15, Matt 27:26). For Matthew's κοδράντης (5:26) Luke has λεπτόν (12:59). On one occasion Luke writes a Greek word where John has a Latin: the accusation placed on the cross is ἐπιγραφή in Luke 23:38, while John terms it τίτλος, *tit(u)lus* (19:19, 20). Luke shares with John the scarf, σουδάριον, *sudarium* (Luke 19:20; John 11:44, 20:7), which reappears in Acts 19:19. Luke's preference for Greek words may accord with his style, generally considered to be the most polished of the New Testament narratives. In this respect he may stand with Philo and Josephus, all concerned with writing Greek well, in order to gain favor with their educated patrons or audiences. The Gospel of John has four Latin words absent from the Synoptic Gospels: λέντιον, *linteum* 'towel' (13:4, 5); λίτρα, *libra* 'pound weight' (12:3, 19:39); τίτλος, *tit(u)lus*, 'title' (19:19, 20); φραγέλλιον, *flagellium* 'whip' (2:15).

An investigation of these words in the standard Greek-English lexicon[15] and the *Thesaurus Linguae Graecae*[16] reveals the remarkable fact that

14. Ibid.

15. H. G. Liddell and R. Scott, *Greek-English Lexicon* (rev. H. S. Jones, with supplement; Oxford, 1968).

16. The check with the Ibycus computer program was made for me by Tim Freeman at Tyndale House, Cambridge.

several do not occur in any Greek texts earlier than the first century C.E., and some of them occur only in the Gospels. They are:

census, κῆνσος: only in Mark and Matthew
quadrans, κοδράντης: in Heron (first century B.C.E.), Mark, and Matthew
custodia, κουστωδία: in Oxyrhynchus Papyrus 294.20 (22 C.E.) and Matthew
sextarius, ξέστης (as a cup): only in Mark
praetorium, πραιτώριον: only in Mark and Matthew
sudarium, σουδάριον: in the Life of Aesop (first century C.E.), Luke, and John
speculator, σπεκουλάτωρ: only in Mark
tit(u)lus, τίτλος: only in John
flagellium, φραγέλλιον: only in John
flagellare, φραγελλοῦν: only in Mark and Matthew

As noted, several of these words relate to military and administrative activities (*census, custodia, flagellium, flagellare, praetorium, speculator, tit(u)lus*) and so could have become familiar wherever Rome ruled, as would coins and measures (*as, denarius, libra, milia, modius*). The occurrence of all these words, and others, in unofficial writings concerning events in a marginal region of Rome's empire is unexpected; it is all the more surprising to find that the words are distributed across the four Gospels and to find that two Gospels use the same word in different passages. Seventeen words in forty-two occurrences provide insufficient basis for any firm conclusion (leaving aside the fourteen cases of *denarius*). They do indicate a milieu for the Gospel writers in which Latin words were taken into Greek without great hesitation. This might have been anywhere in the Eastern Mediterranean, but the only country to give a large collection of comparable material, Egypt, showed a strong resistance to accepting either Latin or native words into Greek. In reviewing a study of the subject, the papyrologist J. G. Keenan observed, "the penetration of Latin terms into everyday Egyptian Greek was limited, artificial and superficial" except for clothing, weights and measures, and coins; "clothing was, as so often, an object of concern in a military context."[17] The two Latin words for clothing in the Gospel, *linteum* and *sudarium*, do not have a strong military association, but might have been imported by military personnel. Texts from Palmyra display a similar

17. J. G. Keenan, review of *Il lessico latino nel greco d'Egitto* (2d ed.; Barcelona: 1991), by S. Davis, in *BASP* 29 (1992) 219–20.

range of military and administrative words taken from Latin, including *centurion* (*qntryn*ʾ) and *legio* (*lgywn*ʾ). An inscription from 51 C.E. thanks a Palmyrene for gifts worth 150 and 120 *denarii* revealing that the Roman coin was already circulating there. The famous Tariff of Palmyra, issued in 137, refers to an edict from the time of Germanicus, about 18 C.E., mentioning the *denarius* and the *as* (*dnr* and ʾ*sr* = ἀσσάριον).[18] In Palestine the Bar Kochba Period documents reveal no resistance to loanwords there, and the epigraphic evidence at Massada displays some Latin presence a hundred years earlier, as noted above. With its particularly mixed population and its small area, Palestine was perhaps more open to foreign influences in its languages. This applies to Hebrew as well as to Greek. Latinisms are absent from literary works such as the Dead Sea Scrolls and relatively rare in rabbinic works put into writing from about the end of the second century C.E. onwards.[19] On the other hand, some found their way through Greek into ordinary life. Not surprisingly, the word *denarius* is found in several of the "Cave of Letters" documents, with a Hebrew plural ending, *dînarîn*, and that form is found in the Mishna and other rabbinic texts of the third century beside *quadrans*, *as*, and various measures (*qodrantis* and ʾ*issar* in *t. B. Bat.* 5:12, the latter already in *m. Qidd.* 1:1; *môdyā*ʾ in the Mishna, *lîṭrā*ʾ in the Tosepta). More noteworthy are the appearances of *porgal, flagellium* in the Tosepta and Mekilta of the third century and of *sphiklator, speculator* in *Sipre* 91 and the *midrašim* of the same and later centuries, with the sense of 'executioner'. Apart from Mark 6:27, the second word is not found in Greek writings;[20] the former is found after the Gospels in a second-century papyrus and in the works of Origen. In addition, Mishnaic Hebrew *sûdarîn* is surely *sudarium*, despite Jastrow's objection.[21]

Latin words apparently entered the Greek and local languages of Palestine in a larger quantity than can be seen in other areas. Although their numbers are small and the sources unevenly scattered in time, they

18. See J. Teixidor, *Un port romain du désert: Palmyre et son commerce d'Auguste à Caracalla* (= *Semitica* 34) (Paris, 1984) 49–50, for the dedication to Bel; 80–81, for the tariff referring to the earlier edict.

19. S. Lieberman (*Hellenism in Jewish Palestine* [New York, 1962] 17) observed, "The Palestinian Rabbis certainly did not know Latin. Except for military and judiciary terms (as well as names of objects imported from Latin speaking countries) which are usually also extant in Syriac and later Greek, Latin words are less than scarce in rabbinic literature."

20. The word does occur on a Greek tombstone of perhaps the third century C.E. See J. and L. Robert, "Bulletin Epigraphique,"*Revue des Études grecques* 72 (1959) 214 no. 260.

21. M. Jastrow, *A Dictionary of the Targumim . . .* (New York, 1926) 962a. For the 140 or so Greek and Latin loanwords in Rabbinic Hebrew, see now *The Historical Dictionary of the Hebrew Language: Materials for the Dictionary, Series I 200 B.C.E.–300 C.E.* (Jerusalem, 1988) microfiche 91.

seem to allow us to suggest that the presence of Latin words in the Gospels reflects the linguistic picture of Palestine in the first century C.E. The Latinate explanations Mark supplies, κοδράντης and πραιτώριον, may indicate an origin in Rome, as Hengel has argued (see above, p. 454), yet the use of the same words by Matthew may imply they were more widely known and that Mark was simply helping the general reader outside Palestine by adding greater precision. Since it is generally agreed that the Gospels were written shortly after 70 C.E. (Mark possibly before that date),[22] it would be hard to argue for the authors making a special feature of introducing Latin terms that might alienate Jewish readers, Christian or not, terms used by the conquerors of Jerusalem. We may deduce, therefore, that such Latin words as the ones used in the Gospels were current in the Greek spoken in Palestine early in the first century C.E., even during the lifetime of Jesus of Nazareth.

22. See the opinions gathered in standard works such as W. G. Kümmel, *Introduction to the New Testament* (London, 1966).

Phoenician Ostraca from Tel Dor

JOSEPH NAVEH

The paper deals with four Phoenician ostraca from Tel Dor. Because they are in a very poor state of preservation, the readings are suggested with a great amount of reservation.

Four ink-written Phoenician ostraca were found At Tel Dor in 1985 (A and B), 1987 (C), and 1992 (D).[1] Although the script is in a very poor state, what has been preserved indicates that they were written in the cursive style in the fifth or fourth century B.C.E. The decipherment of any Phoenician text is hindered by the Phoenician scribal practice of *scriptio continua* and defective spelling. The reading of Phoenician cursive, in which different letters tend to assimilate to each other, is even more difficult. If, in addition, parts of the script have been effaced, as in our case, then the reading is problematic indeed. Therefore, although the excavators provided me with excellent photographs, the following tentative readings are suggested here with considerable reservation.

Ostracon A 33608/1

The fragment measures approximately 11.5 × 9 cm. Six lines of writing, of which only the end of the text can be transliterated (figs. 1–2):

4. . . . כנאמרעב.כ
5. האיעצכמאשטבת
6. כמי . . ת

These characters can perhaps be divided and the text reconstructed and translated as follows:

1. My thanks are due to Ephraim Stern for entrusting me with the publication of these sherds.

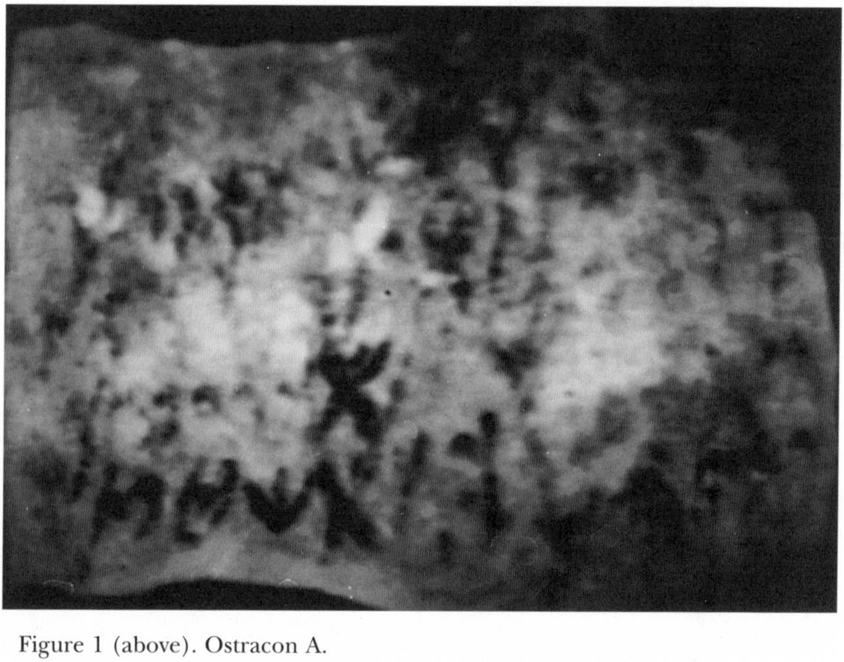

Figure 1 (above). Ostracon A.
Figure 2 (below). Ostracon A (Photo by the Israel Police Laboratory).

Figure 3. Ostracon B.

4. . . . כן אמר עב[ד]ך
5. הא יעצך מאש טבת־
6. ך מי[. .]ת

4. [. . .] so said your ser[vant]:
5. he advised you what your bene-
6. fit de[serve]s (?)

Should this reading be correct, at least in part, the text seems to have been part of a letter.

Ostracon B 33646

This ostracon measures approximately 8 × 7 cm. It is a badly preserved list in four lines, which may be read as follows (fig. 3):

1. לאהל. . .
2. בד צ . . ם ||[ ]
3. בד צ.ם [ ]
4. צ . . [ ]

Line 1. אהל, meaning 'tent' or 'family', seems to be a personal name, as in 1 Chr 3:20 and on a bulla from the City of David that reads: לאליקם בן אוהל.[2] אהל may also be part of a name; see the Phoenician proper name אהלבעל[3] and biblical אהליאב, אהליבמה, as well as fem. אהלה, אהליבה. A seal found in a burial cave on the slopes of Mount Zion in Jerusalem is inscribed: לחמיאהל בת מנחם.[4]

Line 2. The reading בד is not certain, but any other possibility that comes to mind is less probable. בד, meaning 'in the hand of', may be part of a personal name; thus one may read בדצ[ד].[5] However, since at the end of the line there are a *mem* and numerals, it seems likely that the word ending with *mem* (the sign of plural) begins with a *ṣadê*, and the letters preceding it form the word בד. Tentatively one may read here: [+]2 בד צרפם 'in the hand of (the) goldsmiths 2[+]'.

Line 3. The text in this line seems similar, if not identical, to that of line 2.

Line 4. The fact that lines 2–4 all contain words (or the same word repeated) beginning with *ṣadê* is intriguing. Unfortunately, I do not know how to read it/them.

Ostracon C 64963

The sherd measures approximately 8 × 6 cm. Writing is visible in three lines, which may perhaps be read (fig. 4):

[ ]|| ʒʒ כדם .1	42[+] jars
[ ]||| ¬ ʒ כדם .2	33[+] jars
[ ]כד .3	[ ] jars[s]

This text, listing numbers of jars, seems to be an account. In line 3 there are faint traces that may perhaps be reconstructed [ ]\|\| ʒ כדם '22[+] jars'.

Ostracon D 108150

This piece is approximately 10 × 8.5 cm. There are traces of five lines of writing. In the first two lines one may perhaps read (fig. 5):

2. Y. Shiloh, "A Group of Hebrew Bullae from the City of David," *IEJ* 36 (1986) 29, no. 29. The spelling אוהל is one of the very rare preexilic examples of medial *o* marked by *waw.*

3. F. L. Benz, *Personal Names in the Phoenician and Punic Inscriptions* (Rome, 1972) 60, 262.

4. D. Davies and A. Kloner, "A Burial Cave of the Late Israelite Period on the Slopes of Mt. Zion," *Qadmoniot* 41 (1978) 18–19 [Hebrew].

5. Benz, *Personal Names,* 88, 283–86, 398.

Figure 4. Ostracon C.

Figure 5. Ostracon D.

[מ]לקרת . . כד עבדאס וא [ ].1
||| → ם[עבדב]על ע כד[ ].2

This fragmentary text may belong to a list of amounts of certain goods, given by various individuals in jars. The only clear name is עבדאס, meaning 'the servant of Isis'.[6]

6. See ibid., 149, 271–72.

Part III

Semitics

The Socio-Religious Framework of the Babylonian Witchcraft Ceremony *Maqlû*: Some Observations on the Introductory Section of the Text, Part II

Tzvi Abusch

This essay continues the author's interpretation of the introductory section of the Maqlû text and is part of his reconstruction of the social and ideological framework of this Mesopotamian antiwitchcraft ceremony. The introductory incantations (I 1-72) seek the indictment and imprisonment of witches in preparation for their judgment and execution. Underlying this demand is the existence of a social compact (māmītu) and its breach by the witches. The present essay focuses especially on the mythic/religious dimension of I 37-60. After a brief statement of the purpose and legal setting of the ceremony, an interpretation of the speaker's mission is presented. The metaphors invoked and ritual actions undertaken by the speaker to achieve his goals are discussed, and the speaker's transformation, ascent to heaven, and mission to the netherworld, as well as the topographical/cosmic framework in which he operates are examined. In addition, the paper points to the existence in the introductory incantations of several themes that are central to biblical prophecy.

This paper will focus upon several of the introductory incantations in the Babylonian magical series *Maqlû* (I 37–72) and discuss the mythic framework and religious experience underlying this section of the text.

Author's note: My analysis of *Maqlû* I 37–72 was the subject of several invited lectures presented in 1990. A condensed version of part II was read at the Eleventh World Congress of Jewish Studies, Jerusalem, 1993, under the title "Babylonian Magical Literature and Biblical Prophetic Literature: A Shared Cosmic-Legal Framework." Part I will appear elsewhere; a condensed version of that part was read at the 201st meeting of the American Oriental Society, Berkeley, 1991, under the title "Observations on the Cosmology, Imagery, and Social Setting of *Maqlû*." My work on these studies was supported by an NEH Fellowship. I wish to express particular gratitude to Kathryn Kravitz for valuable assistance and suggestions during the preparation of this essay. I also thank Diane Feinman Baum for a number of improvements in the final draft.

Starting from the calendrical setting and purpose of the text that I have established elsewhere, I will examine first the legal setting, then the personal experience of the participant (his transformation, ascent to heaven, and mission to the netherworld), and finally the cosmic framework in which he acts.

Professor Jonas C. Greenfield is one of the leading students of Near Eastern literature in this generation. While attaining an admired mastery of a number of the individual fields that make up Near Eastern, Semitic, and biblical studies, he has emphasized the value of seeing the fields of ancient Near Eastern studies in relationship to each other and of using one to elucidate the other. It is a pleasure to dedicate this study to Jonas Greenfield; I thus express my affection for a dear colleague and friend. But the present study is also intended as one more demonstration of the organic unity of the ancient Near East, a unity that forms the basis of Jonas's comparative studies and informs so much of his work.

Thus, my purpose here is not only to discuss an Akkadian text, but also to point to the existence therein of ideas and themes that are sometimes found in biblical prophetic literature and appear here in a single organic form. Scholars have previously noted ancient Near Eastern parallels to biblical prophetic forms and themes and argued that the basic forms of biblical prophetic literature existed already in Near Eastern literature.[1] Here I hope to explicate a Mesopotamian religious text that contains a dense cluster of themes reminiscent of prophetic literature and shapes them into a coherent construction. Since I allude to the biblical materials rather than discuss them in detail—I shall note parallels to the *rîv* pattern, the charge of the prophetic messenger, and cosmic theophany—I should mention at the outset that the Mesopotamian and biblical texts cited contain similar patterns and seem to be contemporaneous and to belong to the cultural world of the Assyrian Empire; thus, beyond typological and phenomenological similarities, I believe that they reflect a common historical matrix and social ideology.

Introduction

Tablets I–VIII of the *Maqlû* series record the text of almost one hundred incantations. These incantations constitute the legomenon of a single coherent ritual or ceremony.[2] The introduction to *Maqlû* (I 1–72)

1. See, e.g., the important survey article by M. Weinfeld, "Ancient Near Eastern Patterns in Prophetic Literature," *VT* 27 (1977) 178–95, where Weinfeld has drawn together many ancient Near Eastern parallels.

2. See T. Abusch, "Mesopotamian Anti-Witchcraft Literature: Texts and Studies. Part I, The Nature of *Maqlû*: Its Character, Divisions and Calendrical Setting," *JNES* 33 (1974) 251–62.

is perhaps the main passage that establishes the character and defines the context of the standard version of the *Maqlû* ceremony. In my estimation, it was created in the first millennium, was added to one of the latest versions of the text, and encapsulates its conceptual world.[3] The introduction comprises five incantations, which form three units: I 1–36, 37–60, and 61–72. The opening incantation, I 1–36, is an address to the gods of the night sky; the next group of three incantations (I 37–41, 42–49, 50–60) takes the netherworld as its focus but actually addresses and draws together the heavens and the netherworld; and, finally, the fifth incantation is a call to the powers of nature.

The whole introductory section, but especially I 37–72, is fraught with difficulties.[4] Still, let us undertake the task of reconstructing a few aspects of the context and thought of this sequence of incantations, though we must always bear in mind the degree of speculation involved in the enterprise and the uncertain nature of some of the results. We concern ourselves first with the legal setting, as revealed especially in the second and fifth incantations (I 37–41, 61–72), and then with the transformation of the speaker and the cosmic setting, especially as revealed in the third and fourth incantations (I 42–49, 50–60).

The text of the second through the fifth incantations, I 37–72, reads:[5]

Incantation 2 (I 37–41)

> Netherworld, netherworld, yea netherworld,
> Gilgamesh is the enforcer of your oath.
> Whatever you have done,[6] I know,

3. For the history of *Maqlû*, see especially Abusch, "The Demonic Image of the Witch in Standard Babylonian Literature: The Reworking of Popular Conceptions by Learned Exorcists," in *Religion, Science, and Magic in Concert and in Conflict* (ed. J. Neusner et al.; New York and Oxford, 1989) 27–58; "An Early Form of the Witchcraft Ritual *Maqlû* and the Origin of a Babylonian Magical Ceremony," in *Lingering Over Words: Studies in Ancient Near Eastern Literature in Honor of William L. Moran* (ed. T. Abusch et al.; HSS 37; Atlanta, 1990) 1–57; and "The Ritual Tablet and Rubrics of *Maqlû*: Towards the History of the Series," in *Ah Assyria . . . : Studies in Assyrian History and Ancient Near Eastern Historiography Presented to Hayim Tadmor* (ed. M. Cogan and I. Eph^{c}al; ScrHier 33; Jerusalem, 1991) 233–53.

4. Elsewhere I will set out in detail the many difficulties that this passage presents.

5. For the Akkadian text, see Excursus I, below, pp. 490–75. Here I limit myself to a few comments on the translation.

6. The manuscripts consistently write the verb *epēšu* here as if it were a preterite. I would have preferred to treat the verb as a durative, as it appears in lines 40–41, and to translate 'whatever you do', in part because of the stylistic feature in incantations 2–4 of parallel, even repetitive, lines and words. There seems to be some confusion here; simply note the occurrence in lines 39–41 of "preterite" forms for this verb in the two northern manuscripts A 43 (Assur: lines 39–40) and *STT*, vol. 1, no. 78 (Sultantepe: lines 39–41), and confusion in the Sultantepe text even over the grammatical person of the verb in lines 40 (3d person) and 41 (1st person).

Whatever I do, you do not know,
Whatever my witches do, there will be no
one to[7] overlook, undo, release.

Incantation 3 (42–49)

My city is Zabban, my city is Zabban,
Of my city Zabban, two are its gates:
One for the rising of the sun, the second for the setting of the sun,
One for the rising of the sun, the second for the setting of the sun.
Raising up a broken palm frond and *maštakal* plant,
I offer water to the gods of the sky (and say):
"As I purify you yourselves,
May you purify me myself."

Incantation 4 (50–60)

I have enclosed the ford, I have enclosed the quay,
I have enclosed (therein) the witchcraft of all the lands.
Anu and Antu have sent me, (saying):
"Whom shall we (lit., I) send to Bēlet-ṣēri?"
Place locks on the mouth of my warlock and witch,
Place the sealing[8] of the sage of the gods, Marduk,
When they call to you, do not answer them,
When they speak to you, do not listen to them,
When I call to you, answer me,
When I speak to you, listen to me.
By the command of Anu, Antu, and Bēlet-ṣēri.

Incantation 5 (61–72)

I am sent and I will go, I am commissioned and I will speak,
Asalluḫi, lord of exorcism, has sent me against my warlock
and witch.
You of the heavens, pay heed! You of the netherworld, listen!
You of the river, pay heed! You of the dry land, listen to my speech!
....
When I present the testimony against my warlock and witch,
May the ox set at ease (the judge); may the sheep set at ease
(the judge).
May their testimony be dismissed but mine stand up (under
scrutiny).

7. Lit., 'they (var. it) will have no one to. . . .'

8. For the translation 'sealing' instead of 'incantation', see W. Farber, "*Mannam lušpur ana Enkidu*: Some New Thoughts about an Old Motif," *JNES* 49 (1990) 321 n. 76.

When I present (my) testimony, may their testimony not prevent mine from being effective.
By the command of Asalluḫi, lord of exorcism.

Elsewhere I have established the setting and purpose of the *Maqlû* ceremony.[9] We need to recall these before turning to the details of the passage. The *Maqlû* ceremony was performed, principally at night, during a festival of the dead at the end of the month of *Abu*, a time of year when ghosts return from the netherworld. At that time, spirits move back and forth between the netherworld and this world, the living and the dead interact, and there can be judgments in this world by both heavenly and netherworld deities who have power over the dead. The purpose of the *Maqlû* ceremony is to judge, punish, and expel all witches. Dead witches are unearthed and held captive; live witches are killed. All are then utterly destroyed. Hence, the destruction of the witch's corpse by burning or feeding to animals or, alternatively, the removal of her bones from the grave. The witches are thus expelled and permanently deprived of the possibility of burial. They are thus prevented from finding a place in the netherworld and are permanently eliminated from the cosmos. *Maqlû*'s approach to the witch fits well with the calendrical setting of the text, for with the appearance of ghosts, both live witches and dead witches may be judged and punished. And, in keeping with its setting and purpose, the very beginning of the work is directed to the nighttime sky and its gods and to the netherworld and its gods. The work thus takes on an astral and chthonic character and orientation and assumes a cosmic setting.

Legal Setting

Still, the ritual activities are clothed in a legal guise and constitute some form of judgment and execution. Central to the introductory section is the indictment of the witches and their imprisonment, prior to and in anticipation of their subsequent judgment and execution in the following sections of the work. In the opening five incantations, the accuser attempts to gain the assistance of the heavens in support of his accusation and to persuade the netherworld that the shades of witches should not be allowed into that realm. In their present setting, these incantations serve to recall, invoke, and impose a divinely sanctioned oath and curse and to secure the imprisonment of the witches.

9. See my "Mesopotamian Anti-Witchcraft Literature" and "The Socio-Religious Framework, Part I."

But what is the justification for the indictment, destruction, and permanent exclusion of the witch? Elsewhere, I deal with this legal and ideological question at some length,[10] and I shall here present my understanding in a less detailed form.

Already the use of the term *māmītu* 'oath' in our second incantation, as well as the variety and totality of punishments later in the series, suggest the operation here of a social/ideological framework different from and more comprehensive than that of the normal witchcraft ceremony. There is a special juridical context in operation here, as is clear from the appearance already in these early incantations of contractual terminology and of natural forces as witnesses.

The second incantation invokes the *māmītu* and builds on and proceeds from this adjuration:

> Netherworld, netherworld, yea netherworld,
> Gilgamesh is the enforcer of your oath.
> . . . .
> Whatever my witches do, there will be no one to overlook, undo, release.

In this incantation, the speaker invokes the netherworld and then declares that the witches are under an oath administered and enforced by Gilgamesh; hence, it is an oath sanctioned by the netherworld. In the preceding incantation (I 1–36), the speaker implicitly invoked an oath sanctioned by the gods of the heavens when he invoked the gods of the night sky and accused the witches of performing evil witchcraft.[11] The oath by the netherworld is thus perhaps part of the standard pattern of adjurations by the pair heaven and netherworld: e.g., zi.an.na hé.pàd zi.ki.a hé.pàd: *niš šamê lū tamâta niš erṣeti lū tamâta* 'Be you adjured by heaven, be you adjured by earth'. In any case, in the second and fourth incantations, the *māmītu* is placed explicitly under the sanction and execution of netherworld authorities, Gilgamesh and Bēlet-ṣēri.

Broadly speaking, *māmītu* refers not only to oaths and curses but also to rules. In my estimation, the *māmītu* here designates stipulations, a code of behavior, to which members of society, including the witches, have been bound by oath under the threat of punishment. This *māmītu* is authorized and guaranteed by the powers of the heavens and the netherworld. I would suggest that we are dealing here with a social compact or contract directed against hostile behavior. The compact prohibits behav-

10. See "Socio-Religious Framework, Part I."

11. For a detailed analysis of this incantation, see T. Abusch, *Babylonian Witchcraft Literature: Case Studies* (BJS 132; Atlanta, 1987) x–xii and 85–147.

ior of an antisocial, seditious nature, behavior which either refers to or is construed as the performance of witchcraft.[12] All members of society have entered the compact and are bound to abide by the rules of social order. Hence, the frequent statement in prayers and incantations that witches have committed evil or various forms of witchcraft against their victim (*aššu īpuša lemnēti išteʾa lā banâti* 'Because evil did she perform against me and harm has she sought against me . . .'),[13] an accusation that has on occasion been expanded to include the charge that the witch has performed witchcraft (= evil) against the victim although he had not performed witchcraft against her (*ᵈŠamaš aššu lā ēpušaššimma šī īpušanni* / *ᵈŠamaš aššu lā asḫuraššimma šī isḫuranni*[14]). Because they have disregarded the terms of the compact by their antisocial behavior, the witches have broken a *māmītu* of the heavens and the netherworld, are accused of breaking the social compact, and are to be punished and excluded from the organized community of humanity, which encompasses the living and the dead.

That a compact and its breach underlie our text agrees with the invocation of the heavens and the netherworld in the speaker's indictment of the witches. It also explains and is confirmed by the call upon the forces of nature in the fifth incantation (I 61–72). The heavens and the netherworld are invoked because they sanction the compact; the forces of nature are then called upon because they witnessed the compact. Here, in a form not very different from the biblical *rîv* pattern, the speaker calls upon the forces of nature to function as witnesses and support him in his legal confrontation.

I am sent and I will go, I am commissioned and I will speak,
Asalluḫi, lord of exorcism, has sent me against my warlock and witch.
You of the heavens, pay heed! You of the netherworld, listen!
You of the river, pay heed! You of the dry land, listen to my speech!
. . . .
When I present the testimony against my warlock and witch,
. . . .

12. It probably also requires obedience and loyalty to the divine, governmental, and social authorities and structures.

13. *Maqlû* I 18. There are many additional examples; see, simply, the examples cited in W. Mayer, *Untersuchungen zur Formensprache der babylonischen "Gebetsbeschwörungen"* (Studia Pohl: Series Maior 5; Rome, 1976) 91–92 (d).

14. J. Laessøe, *Studies on the Assyrian Ritual and Series bît rimki* (Copenhagen, 1955) 36–44 (and further duplicates): 49–50. See also *Maqlû* II 199–200 and *LKA* 155, rev. 25 // K3394+, rev. 10.

May their testimony be dismissed but mine stand up (under scrutiny).
When I present (my) testimony, may their testimony not prevent mine from being effective.

The forces of nature are thus asked to help the plaintiff during the presentation of his case against the witches. Perhaps they present testimony and, by their testimony, support the plaintiff's case and confirm his claim that the witches have broken the agreement to which they were bound. But, in any case, they serve as an audience and prevent the witches from interfering with the plaintiff's presentation.

What we are dealing with here in *Maqlû* is not unlike the treaty forms, ideology, and procedures of the Neo-Assyrian Empire.[15] There, too, the individual who has broken the political or social agreement must be punished regardless of whether he is living or dead. Hence, the execution and corporeal destruction of treaty transgressors and the disinterment and destruction of those who had seemingly escaped by dying. Similarly, in *Maqlû*, witches, whether living or dead, are criminals, and are therefore punished and permanently excluded from the universal community. The similarities suggest that the *Maqlû* passage and the treaties are the result of common literary activity and share a world of social thought.[16]

Having been accused of breaking the social compact, the witches, for their part, wish to cancel the *māmītu*: its oath, obligations, and curses. It is to this that the speaker refers when, in line 41, he informs the witches that there will be no one to overlook, release, absolve. This line does not mean that the speaker will be unable to find someone to release the witchcraft. Such a reading would be nonsense in an antiwitchcraft incantation, for there the victim of witchcraft normally seeks the release of what the witch has done and expresses the belief that, indeed, her acts can be released. Rather, its context is that of the earlier invocation of the oath; line 41 thus provides excellent support of my construction of the materials. Knowing what the witches are doing (cf. lines 39–40) and that they will try to render the oath inoperative, the speaker now assures the witches that they will find no one who will disregard or revoke the *māmītu* and absolve and free them from its oath, obligations, and curse. A similar

15. See "Socio-Religious Framework, Part I"; cf., e.g., S. Parpola and K. Watanabe, *Neo-Assyrian Treaties and Loyalty Oaths* (SAA 2; Helsinki, 1988), passim, especially pp. xxii–xxiii; and E. Cassin, "Le mort: Valeur et représentation en mésopotamie ancienne," in *La mort, les morts dans les sociétés anciennes* (ed. G. Gnoli and J.-P. Vernant; Cambridge, 1982) 355–72, especially 358–59.

16. Moreover, the compact to which groups and individuals were bound is not unlike the covenant of Israel, and the speaker who goes forth against the witches is not unlike the prophet who chastises Israel and calls it to judgment.

idea recurs in Esarhaddon's vassal treaty, where the partners to a treaty are told in words reminiscent of our line that they may not seek release from the oath, obligations, and imprecations.[17] Note, moreover, that Middle Assyrian Law A §47 suggests that a similar social obligation applied also to individual citizens and that it, too, could not be released.[18]

Mission of the Speaker

The speaker's mission here in *Maqlû* is to invoke and enforce the compact. The first incantation was directed to the heavens against live witches. In the second, the *māmītu* of the netherworld is invoked against dead witches; having invoked it, the speaker must ensure its preservation and enforcement. Having told the dead witches that, regardless of what they do, they will not be able to undo the *māmītu,* he must now frustrate any attempt that they might make: he must prevent any divine being from aiding the witches and revoking the *māmītu;* and he must ensure that the dead witches who had ascended during the festival of the dead be confined for trial at a point between heaven and the netherworld and not be permitted to return to the netherworld.[19] To this end, he undertakes the activities described in the third and fourth incantations. In the third, he calls upon the gods of the sky for their assistance; then, in the fourth, he calls upon the netherworld goddess Bēlet-ṣēri for her assistance. He imagines himself able to address and interact with the gods of both cosmic regions and to journey to both.

Most notably, he must approach the netherworld goddess Bēlet-ṣēri,[20] perhaps at the "ford" and "quay" where, according to the opening

17. See simply Parpola and Watanabe, *Neo-Assyrian Treaties,* 43–44: 373–84 and 44: 397–99 (Esarhaddon's Succession Treaty), as well as p. 22: 11′ (Esarhaddon's Accession Treaty).

18. Note, moreover, the witchcraft connection of that law.

19. Ghosts and demons travel back and forth between the netherworld and the upper world. In this regard, they resemble the sun, the moon, and the stars; the latter travel a circuit between the heavens and the netherworld, spending part of their time below the horizon, together with the denizens of the netherworld, and the rest of their time above the horizon, together with the inhabitants of this world. Also, the dead witch returns to this world: she is a human being and, as such, her ghost may ascend, especially during the festival at the end of *Abu;* moreover, in one of her manifestations, the witch of *Maqlû* also possesses supernatural, demonic form and power (cf. Abusch, "Demonic Image," 38–50).

20. For Bēlet-ṣēri, see the dated but still valuable discussion in K. Tallqvist, *Sumerisch-akkadische Namen der Totenwelt* (StudOr 5/4; Helsinki, 1934) 17–22, especially 18–20. I assume that Bēlet-ṣēri appears here in the role of scribe of the netherworld. (So, too, e.g., B. Landsberger, in *Textbuch zur Religionsgeschichte* [ed. E. Lehmann and H. Haas; 1912] 126 n. 4.) As the scribe of the netherworld, she is identified with (Geštin)/Geštin.anna/Nin. Geštin/Nin.Geštin.anna. (For the Sumerian goddess, see D. O. Edzard, "Geštinanna," *RLA* 3.299–301; and more recently M. J. Geller, *Forerunners to UDUG-HUL: Sumerian Exorcistic*

lines of the fourth incantation, the speaker has confined the witches who have tried to enter the habitation of the living from outside:

> I have enclosed the ford, I have enclosed the quay,
> I have enclosed (therein) the witchcraft of all the lands.

As we know from other texts, the *nēberu* 'ford' or 'pass' is stationed as a passageway or transit point on the eastern horizon, at the entrance to the heavens.[21] Here, in our text, the pass or ford serves as an entry-point

---

Incantations [Freiburger Altorientalische Studien 12; Stuttgart, 1985] p. 89 ad line 48 and p. 100 ad line 284.) Bēlet-ṣēri occurs in this role in both bilingual and unilingual Akkadian texts. Note that she is also equated with gašan.gú.edin.na, and these form the epithets of Gubarra/Ašratu, the wife of Martu/Amurru. (For references to this goddess, see recently D. O. Edzard, "Martu (Mardu).A.Gott," *RLA* 7.435–36: §§3–4.) More specifically, I assume that Bēlet-ṣēri here has the authority to abrogate the *māmītu* (see below, n. 39).

(On a literal level, Bēlet-ṣēri 'Mistress of the Steppe' may simply be the lady in charge of the steppe, a habitat of bandits, nomads, and demons, and thus a chaotic realm separate from and opposed to the ordered world of humans; this region, moreover, is sometimes seen as leading to, or as the equivalent of, the netherworld [chaos-death/order-life]. Given Geštinanna's role as a dream interpreter, her identification with wine, and the association of dreams with the steppe [the steppe or the netherworld as a place whence dreams come and wither they go], I wonder whether one of the numinous forces behind Geštinanna: Bēlet-ṣēri may not have been the dream experience itself and whether, perhaps, the goddess herself once functioned as a bringer of dreams. This would agree, perhaps, with the necromantic characteristics of the speaker's address to Bēlet-ṣēri [see below, n. 37].)

Note the appearance of Bēlet-ṣēri in Neo-Assyrian penalty clauses. Especially in view of the first-millennium date that I have posited for these introductory incantations, a better understanding of her nature and function in the Neo-Assyrian texts may eventually require a modification of our present understanding of her function here in *Maqlû*. (For references, see K. Deller, "Review of R. de Vaux, *Les Sacrifices de l'Ancien Testament*," *Or* n.s. 34 [1965] 382-86, especially 383-84: text types 2, 3, and 4; and B. Menzel, *Assyrische Tempel* [Studia Pohl: Series Maior 10; Rome, 1981] vol. 2, T. 194ff. [see nos. 146, 147, 180, and 257 listed on T. 195]; cf. M. Weinfeld, "The Worship of Molech and of the Queen of Heaven and Its Background," *UF* 4 [1972] 144-49; M. Cogan, *Imperialism and Religion: Assyria, Judah and Israel in the Eighth and Seventh Centuries* B.C.E. [SBLMS 19; Missoula, 1974] 81-83; and J. Day, *Molech: A God of Human Sacrifice in the Old Testament* [Cambridge, 1989] 41-46.) Moreover, if Deller's reading of the god's name in the penalty clause as ^{d}*Adad-milki* rather than ^{d}Sin is correct (but note that the reading ^{d}Sin has been preferred by, e.g., S. A. Kaufman, "The Enigmatic Adad-milki," *JNES* 37 [1978] 101-9; W. G. Lambert in Day, *Molech*, 43; and T. Kwasman and S. Parpola, *Legal Transactions of the Royal Court of Nineveh, Part I* [SAA 6; Helsinki, 1991] 92) and Bēlet-ṣēri stands alongside Adad-(Milki) in these penalty clauses, then, especially in view of the association of Bēlet-ṣēri and Martu (see above) and the connection between Martu and Adad (see especially Deller, "Review," 384), attention should be drawn in this context to the central place of the cult of Adad in the city Zabban (see below, Excursus II, n. 75).

21. See "Enūma Eliš" V 1–10 and MUL.APIN I i 37; cf., provisionally, H. Hunger and D. Pingree, MUL.APIN: *An Astronomical Compendium in Cuneiform* (AfO Beiheft 24; Horn, 1989) 139. Elsewhere, together with Wayne Horowitz, I hope to examine the astronomical/astral aspects of *Maqlû*.

from the netherworld into the heavens or from the heavens into the netherworld for those spirits who, like planets, move in retrograde motion. The quay is, therefore, a place to imprison[22] and hold back those who would follow a cosmic circuit but now cannot go either forward into the inhabited world (and then on into the netherworld) or backward into the netherworld.[23] Here, where the two worlds meet, the subsequent trial or judgment of the confined witches will perhaps also take place.[24]

The speaker must come to Bēlet-ṣēri as a messenger of the gods, at whose behest he asks for her support. But he is a member of the laity and not a priest. Thus, he is not automatically a messenger of the gods. To understand how he may become their messenger, we must turn back to his interaction with the gods of the sky. Here, then, we take up the experience and acts of the speaker, leaving for later his location, Zabban.

In the opening incantation, the speaker, standing on a rooftop, had invoked the gods of the night sky and perhaps received an oracular response from them. Still standing on a roof, the speaker in the third incantation again faces the gods of the night sky, the stars. In lines 46–47, he says:

> Raising up a broken palm frond and mashtakal plant,
> I offer water to the gods of the sky.

22. In my opinion, the *kāru* 'quay' in our text also serves as a jail in which prisoners—here, the witches—are held prior to trial. In this context, note the jail in the "Hymn to Nungal" and its female jailor. For that text, see Å. Sjöberg, "Nungal in the Ekur," *AfO* 24 (1974) 19–46 and "Miscellaneous Sumerian Texts, II," *JCS* 29 (1977) 3–6 as well as B. Alster and C. B. F. Walker, "Some Sumerian Literary Texts in the British Museum," in *DUMU-E_2-DUB-BA-A: Studies in Honor of Åke W. Sjöberg* (ed. H. Behrens et al.; Occasional Publications of the Samuel Noah Kramer Fund 11; Philadelphia, 1989) 7-10, and references there, p. 7, to further duplicates. For studies that treat the prison, jailor, and juridical aspects, see T. S. Frymer-Kensky, "The Nungal-Hymn and the Ekur-Prison," *JESHO* 20 (1977) 78-89, and "*Inclusio* in Sumerian," *RA* 79 (1985) 93-94; and M. Civil, "On Mesopotamian Jails and Their Lady Warden," in *The Tablet and the Scroll: Near Eastern Studies in Honor of William W. Hallo* (ed. M. E. Cohen et al.; Bethesda, Md., 1993) 72-78. Bēlet-ṣēri and Nungal seem to share some characteristics and functions. (Here, I may note one correspondence between the "Hymn to Nungal" and this *Maqlû* incantation: compare line 48, in Civil's translation, 'No powerful ones knows (how to say) "open up this door!," incantations for it are ineffective' [p. 73], with *Maqlû* I 54-55 // VII 10-11. With Bēlet-ṣēri's role as scribe, cf. the "Hymn to Nungal," line 77.) We should, of course, not forget other allusions to the *kāru* as a place of confinement and of judicial activities. See, for example, the citation from the great Enlil hymn (A. Falkenstein, *SGL* I, no. 1) in Frymer-Kensky, "Nungal Hymn," 86.

23. Should we also compare the prison house for the stars at the end of the heaven and earth in *1 Enoch* 18:12–16?

24. It seems likely that the ford and quay in our text are connected to the waters, or river, that lead to and from the netherworld. For these waters, cf., e.g., T. S. Frymer-Kensky, "The Judicial Ordeal in the Ancient Near East" (Ph.D. dissertation, Yale University, 1977) vol. 2:583–613, especially 592–604.

The offer perhaps takes the form of sprinkling water towards the heavens. In the following two lines, he then says to the gods:

> As I purify you yourselves,
> May you purify me myself.

It is to the previously mentioned act of giving water that he alludes when he tells the gods that he has purified them; now he asks them to purify him in turn.

The purpose of this purification may be construed in several ways,[25] but here, I think, purification is requested by the speaker primarily so that he may be incorporated into the court of the gods of the night sky.[26]

25. For example: (1) As preparation for an eventual dream incubation. Cf., e.g., *STT,* vol. 1, 73: 83, where the sprinkling of water to specific stars is contextually linked to the request for a dream incubation (see E. Reiner, "Fortune-Telling in Mesopotamia," *JNES* 19 [1960] 27). (Is it possible that in the first incantation, I 1–36—as in some other addresses to stars—the participant hoped for a response in the form of a dream; for addresses to stars that are intended to elicit such an outcome, see, e.g., *STT,* vol. 1, 73: 44–51 [Reiner, "Fortune-Telling," 32–33].) (2) As protection against demonic forces, generally, and witchcraft, specifically. (3) As reaffirmation of the judgment of innocence given previously in the first incantation (21–26) and there symbolized by a purification in the presence of the gods of the night sky. (4) As preparation for entering the world of the gods; see immediately below.

26. Given that the purpose of the purification is to incorporate the speaker into the divine company, one might speculate that perhaps with his comment about sprinkling water and purification ('As I purify you yourselves, May you purify me myself'), the speaker is alluding to a "mouth-washing" ceremony, which he had performed in order to prepare an image to receive the divine presence, and now asks the gods that they, in turn, transform him into a divinity. However, there is no explicit warrant for this construction (but cf. *STT,* vol. 1, 83, obv. 10′). For a recent discussion of mouth-washing, especially in relation to priests and prophets, see V. Hurowitz, "Isaiah's Impure Lips and Their Purification in Light of Akkadian Sources," *HUCA* 60 (1989) 39–89.

I would note, as an aside, that the underlying concept or experience here of ascent to the world of the gods is also found in early Jewish Apocalyptic and Hekhalot literatures, where the participant ascends to heaven to join the divine world (cf., e.g., I. Gruenwald, *Apocalyptic and Merkavah Mysticism* [Leiden, 1980], especially 32–51, 98–109, and 119–21), and in early Pythagoreanism and in Hellenistic literature, where the soul at death returns to the heavens and is to be found among or as one of the stars (cf., e.g., W. Burkert, *Lore and Science in Ancient Pythagoreanism* [Cambridge, 1972] 350–64). These traditions, it should be noted, are linked, in one way or another, to ancient Mesopotamia and are rooted in an ecstatic, trance, or dream experience.

Earlier I noted that the purification may also have served to prepare the speaker for a dream or, preferably, a vision. This is also suggested by Geštinanna/Bēlet-ṣēri's association with dreams, the necromantic character of his address to Bēlet-ṣēri (see below), and the appearance of the dead in dreams or in the form of dream images (cf., e.g., A. L. Oppenheim, *The Interpretation of Dreams in the Ancient Near East* [Transactions of the American Philosophical Society 46/3; Philadelphia, 1956] 236; and I. L. Finkel, "Necromancy in Ancient Mesopotamia," *AfO* 29 [1983] 13: 4′ and 8′ and discussion there).

The speaker is located in Zabban, a cosmic area that connects heaven and the netherworld and guards the passes and/or gates of the heavens through which the sun and stars rise and set. He is thus stationed in a place from which he can ascend into heaven and then descend to the netherworld. But to enter the netherworld he must assume the identity of an astral body that routinely travels through the heavens and the netherworld. On a mythological level, that is, he must become a member of the company of the stars, the heavenly host or retinue of Anu and Antu, for only then can he serve as their emissary and present himself as he does in lines 52–53: "Anu and Antu have sent me saying, 'Whom shall I send to Bēlet-ṣēri?' " Hence he asks the gods to purify him, thus preparing him for incorporation into their company. At his request, the gods of the sky prepare him, induct him, and introduce him into the presence of Anu and Antu. The latter, in turn, commission him as their messenger, thus providing him with the authorization and support that he requires in order to travel to Bēlet-ṣēri.

The situation is not unlike the induction of Isaiah;[27] the prophet is purified so that he may participate in the divine court and serve as the Lord's emissary:

> Then one of the seraphim flew to me carrying in his hand a glowing coal. . . . He touched my mouth with it and said, "See, this has touched your lips; your iniquity is removed, and your sin is wiped away." Then I heard the Lord saying, "Whom shall I send? Who will go for me?" And I answered, "Here am I; send me." He said, "Go and tell this people. . . ."[28]

Having joined the gods of the night sky, taken on the identity of a heavenly body, and ascended into the sky, Isaiah's Babylonian counterpart now descends to address Bēlet-ṣēri in the netherworld.

In the fourth incantation (50–60), he comes to Bēlet-ṣēri. The exigencies of the moment required that the participant reach Bēlet-ṣēri and be heard by her. But, as noted earlier, the speaker was not a regular priestly or divine messenger, and ordinary folk may not move back and forth between this world and the netherworld and present themselves to netherworld officials. The speaker can achieve his purpose only if he comes as an authorized agent of the gods of the sky. In fact, the very

27. Already K. Tallqvist (*Die assyrische Beschwörungsserie Maqlû* [Acta Societatis Scientiarum Fennicae 20/6; Leipzig, 1895] 1.121) cited this Isaiah passage in connection with I 50–60: "Sein verhältniss zu den obergöttern giebt er kund mit den worten (*mannu lušpur ana* ^{il}*Bêlit ṣêri*), welche lebhaft an diejenigen worte erinnern, durch welche der prophet Jesaias sich als der gesandte Jahves Israel präsentirt Jes. 6, 8. . . ." See pp. 120–21 for Tallqvist's attempt to make sense of our incantations.

28. Isa 6:6–9 (translation: NEB).

formula of introduction that he uses when he reaches Bēlet-ṣēri —^{d}*anu u antu išpurūʾinni* / *mannu lušpur ana* ^{d}*Bēlet-ṣēri* 'Anu and Antu have sent me, (saying) "Whom shall I send to Bēlet-ṣēri?"' (52–53)—makes clear that he has now become a member of the heavenly court and a messenger of the gods.

To grasp fully the significance of this formula of introduction (52–53), we must notice that this formula is unusual and seems, moreover, to disrupt the surrounding lines (50–51, 54–55). An examination of these formulaic and structural anomalies will help us attain a better understanding of the narrative/mythic situation. The formula in our text is not the normal form of introduction used by a regular messenger. Indeed, it seems to be a neologism, perhaps created especially for our text and formed by the conflation of two discrete formulae: (1) ^{d}*anu u antu išpurūʾinni* 'Anu and Antu have sent me' (line 52), which normally introduces speeches of regular messengers in narratives (e.g., myths) as well as of regular priests in Sumerian prayers and incantations; and (2) *mannu lušpur* 'whom shall I send?' (line 53), which otherwise occurs alone in Akkadian incantations, where it appears not as a quote in the mouth of a messenger, but as the opening words of ritual instructions.[29]

The use of the new formula supports my reconstruction of the narrative context of the third and fourth incantations, for it proves that the speaker is not a regular divine or priestly messenger, but rather an ordinary human being or layman whose ad hoc commission has been required by his present circumstances. The formulation is meant to explain to the addressee why he/she does not recognize the messenger and, therefore, represents the induction scene of an ad hoc messenger ("*mannu lušpur* . . ."); thus, it demonstrates to the addressee that although the speaker is irregular, he is nonetheless a legitimate and authorized messenger.

A comparable conflation occurs in the myth "Nergal and Ereshkigal." In myths, the messenger does not normally repeat the introductory *luš-purka* 'I will send you' when quoting his master's original speech, instructions, and message, for he is a regular messenger and need not provide proof of his commission. But when Nergal seeks to escape from the netherworld and leave Ereshkigal without her permission, the doorkeeper is understandably suspicious and hesitates to allow one who was not a regular emissary to leave the netherworld. Nergal must, therefore, present himself as a legitimate messenger, who is unknown because he has only recently been commissioned; he therefore uses a formula similar to ours: [^{d}*ereškigal bē*]*letka* [*išpuranni*] *umm*[*a ana šamê*] *ša* ^{d}*an*[*im abini lušpurka*]

29. For the *mannam lušpur* formula, see most recently Farber, "*Mannam lušpur,*" 299–321; for our text, see 304–5.

'[Ereshkigal] your [mis]tress [has sent me saying], "[I would send you to the heaven] of Anu [our father]"...' (*STT*, vol. 1, 28, IV 23′–24′).[30] It has the desired effect and seems to allay the doorkeeper's suspicions. This usage supports our interpretation of the formula in *Maqlû* I 52–53.

Furthermore, alongside the formulaic anomalies of lines 52–53, our incantation contains structural anomalies that suggest that the formula of introduction was inserted secondarily between lines 50–51 and 54–55; thus the incantation itself provides additional support for our understanding of lines 52–53 as a neologism, created in order to convey the legitimation of a new messenger. This suggestion is confirmed by *Maqlû* VII 8–11, lines that are part of an incantation added to *Maqlû* at the same time as our own incantation and belong to the same recensional stage as our passage.[31] They read:

ṣalil nēbiru ṣalil kāru
mārī malāḫi kališunu ṣallū
eli dalti u sikkūri nadû ḫargullū
nadât šipassun ša ^{d}*siris u* ^{d}*ningišzida*

The ford is asleep, the quay is asleep,
The sailors, all of them, are asleep.
Upon the door and bolt, locks are placed,
Applied is the sealing of Siris and Ningishzida.

This passage parallels and is probably the prototype of our lines; thus VII 8-9 // I 50-51:

ṣalil nēbiru ṣalil kāru // akla nēbiru aktali kāru[32]
mārī malāḫi kališunu ṣallū // akli ipšīšina ša kališina mātāti

and VII 10–11 // I 54–55:

eli dalti u sikkūri nadû ḫargullū // ana pī kaššāpiya u kaššāptiya idî ḫargullī
nadât šipassun ša ^{d}*siris u* ^{d}*ningišzida // idî šipassu ša apkal ilī* ^{d}*marduk*

30. For the restoration, see O. R. Gurney, "The Sultantepe Tablets VII: The Myth of Nergal and Ereshkigal," *AnSt* 10 (1960) 118. The restoration is retained in recent translations: see M. Hutter, *Altorientalische Vorstellungen von der Unterwelt: Literar- und religionsgeschichtliche Überlegungen zu "Nergal und Ereškigal"* (OBO 63; Freiburg and Göttingen, 1985) 26, and B. R. Foster, *Before the Muses: An Anthology of Akkadian Literature* (Bethesda, Md., 1993) 1.423, whose translation I have quoted.

31. See Abusch, "Ritual Tablet and Rubrics," 251–52.

32. The parallelism of VII 8–9 and I 50–51 further proves that *kalû* in I 50–51 should be translated 'to enclose' and not 'to keep out', or the like, because VII 8–9 clearly places the sailors (= outsiders = witches) inside the pass and quay.

The integrity of VII 8–11 indicates the primacy of I 50–51 + 54–55 and the secondary nature of I 52–53, thus demonstrating that the present text of I 50–55 is a secondary construction and that I 52–53 is an intentional intrusion, now separating lines that elsewhere appear together.[33]

In lines 52–53, then, the speaker presents himself to Bēlet-ṣēri as a fully-accredited messenger of the sky gods and presents his credentials. The legitimation of his mission is thus conveyed by the (secondary) insertion of his credentials, the aforementioned neologism, between lines 50–51 (his statement that he has imprisoned the witches in the pass and quay prior to their trial) and lines 54ff. (his actual request of Bēlet-ṣēri).[34]

Having restrained the witches in the pass and quay between the heavens and the netherworld, the messenger turns to Bēlet-ṣēri because her approval is necessary for entrance into the infernal realm. She guards, at least figuratively, the entrance to the netherworld and perhaps also governs the prison-house.[35] In effect, the speaker is an imperial messenger, sent by the king to a provincial official responsible for controlling the population on the border. His purpose is to keep the witches confined prior to trial here in the pass and quay, at the entrance to the netherworld, and to prevent the witches from persuading netherworld officers to abrogate the oath.

His request to Bēlet-ṣēri reads:

Place locks on the mouth of my warlock and witch,
Place the sealing of the sage of the gods, Marduk,
When they call to you, do not answer them,

33. Farber ("*Mannam lušpur*," 304–5) and I, independently, reached the conclusion that our formula here in *Maqlû* is a special construction created by the composer of *Maqlû* for our incantation. Given that our starting points, arguments, and evidence are different, our analyses, I believe, are mutually supportive and confirm the essential correctness of the conclusion.

34. The occurrence of an "enclosure" metaphor in both lines 50–51 and lines 54–55 constitutes a further indication of the close connection between the statement that he has enclosed the witches (50–51) and the request to Bēlet-ṣēri that she silence them (54–55), especially since the metaphor is unnatural in and has been extended to 54–55. Having affirmed in lines 50–51 that the witches are enclosed, the composer extends the locking metaphor and finds a new application for it in lines 54–55. There, the speaker asks Bēlet-ṣēri to make fast the lock, but the object is now not the original door of the primary image and motif but rather the witch's mouth. He has thus transferred the placement of *hargullu* and *šipassu* from the door to the speech organs: the mouth is now closed, locked, and sealed. (Perhaps this reflects a change of attitude regarding the manner in which the witch might harm others: evil produced elsewhere by means of action is now produced by means of speech—the evil mouth both curses and vilifies and also argues convincingly in a court[room] context.)

35. The goddess is thus the guardian of those who are in limbo and await the determination of whether they are to enter/reenter the netherworld.

When they speak to you, do not listen to them,
When I call to you, answer me.
When I speak to you, listen to me.
By the command of Anu, Antu, and Bēlet-ṣēri.

Here he asks Bēlet-ṣēri to silence the witches (54–55), not to heed their requests (56–57), but to heed his (58–59).[36] Like the necromancer[37] who calls to the dead for information, so too both the messenger and the witches will call to Bēlet-ṣēri in the netherworld for a response. Thus, I would construe his petition[38] as follows: The dead witches will request of Bēlet-ṣēri that she assist them in the subsequent legal contest by confirming their innocence of the charge, that she abrogate the *māmītu* if necessary, and that she allow them into the netherworld. He asks that Bēlet-ṣēri not heed the witches' call for assistance but instead respond to his call. He calls upon Bēlet-ṣēri to keep them imprisoned, to sustain the ban invoked against them, and not to heed their request to abrogate it.[39] In this manner, the witches are to be kept confined for the trial and prevented either from entering heaven and attacking the earth and/or from returning to the netherworld and finding a haven there.[40]

36. Just as earlier the plaintiff first accused the witch of gagging him so that he would not be able to speak out against her and then, in turn, magically destroyed her speech organs (I 31–33), so here in lines 54–55 he renders her speech organs ineffective and then asks Bēlet-ṣēri to find her speech not effective, but to find his speech effective.

37. That our incantation draws upon necromancy ceremonies, I infer from similarities between this incantation and several of those edited by Finkel, "Necromancy," 1–17. Compare the sequence *šasû-apālu* 'to call, to answer' in lines 56 and 58 with Finkel, "Necromancy," 8: 13′ ([(xx)] *tašassima ippalka*) and p. 9, II 4′–5′ and 10′.

38. The meaning of this petition is not immediately clear, for we are not told the content of the witches' request or of his request—what Bēlet-ṣēri is to ignore and what she is to heed.

39. K. van der Toorn, *Sin and Sanction in Israel and Mesopotamia* (SSN 22; Assen/Maastricht, 1985) 138–39 has noted the association of Bēlet-ṣēri with the *Šurpu* ritual. That Bēlet-ṣēri has the authority to abrogate the *māmītu* is thus further suggested by this association because the central purpose of the *Šurpu* ritual is the undoing of the *māmītu*. (Many years ago, I already noticed that 79-7-8, 71, the text edited and discussed by van der Toorn in *Sin and Sanction* and known to me then from Geers' copy [D 74], supported my interpretation of Bēlet-ṣēri's role here in *Maqlû* as one who had the authority to release the *māmītu* and had to be dissuaded from exercising that authority in respect to the witches. While I am not certain now why I construed 79-7-8, 71 in this manner, I suspect that it was because I read or misread 6′ as] x la at-me *ana pašāri asḫurki*.)

40. Confined in prison until trial, the witches would have also been prevented from inflicting harm; thus, a further reason for imprisoning the witches may have been to protect the patient or victim—here, the witches' adversary. In one regard perhaps, Bēlet-ṣēri functions here not so very differently from Ningishzida, who as *guzalû erṣeti rapašti* is both policeman and jailor and as such protects the innocent, takes evil forces captive, and keeps them under guard in jail; it is perhaps not a coincidence that Ningishzida appears in VII 1–22 (see VII 11 and 15).

The man identifies with the stars in order to become a messenger of the heavenly court. There are other reasons, as well, for his identification with the gods of the night sky, the stars. But whereas his role as a messenger takes place on a sociocosmic level, these other factors operate on psychological and phenomenological levels. We seem to have here a mixture of the experience of ecstatic trance with the function of a messenger: one wonders whether the speaker's soul has left his body and traveled to the supernatural world. But we must leave these aspects for another occasion and turn instead to a discussion of the cosmological setting of our text.

Cosmic Framework

The setting and description of Zabban are central to our text. Historical sources contain references to a city Zabban; it is, therefore, possible that our lines refer to the terrestrial city Zabban. In a detailed study of numerous references to Zabban, E. Weidner concluded that the city was to be located not on the lower Zab, but rather near the place where the Shatt el-Adheim breaks through the Jebel Ḥamrīn.[41] Regarding the *Maqlû* passage I 42–45, Weidner observed that, "Es ist zwar unklar, wie der Zusammenhang zu fassen ist, doch dürfte soviel deutlich sein, dass die Stadt auch in der Beschwörungskunst eine bestimmte Rolle gespielt hat."[42] I, too, have experienced difficulty and frustration in my attempts to understand the context. Still, one must persist in the attempt, even if it remains an exercise in imagination.

It may be possible to reconstruct a setting for the function of Zabban here if we assume that our text has the perspective and bias of an historical work such as the "Synchronistic History" and recall that, at certain periods, Zabban was located on the border between Assyria and Babylonia.[43] The aforementioned "History" is a pro-Assyrian work that treats conflicts between Assyria and Babylonia as arising from violations of

41. E. Weidner, "Simurrum und Zaban," *AfO* 15 (1945–50) 75–80; for the location, see p. 79. For text references to Zabban, discussions of the location, and previous bibliography, see also S. Parpola, *Neo-Assyrian Toponyms* (AOAT 6; Kevelaer/Neukirchen-Vluyn, 1970) 379; and the various volumes of *Répertoire Géographique des Textes Cunéiformes* (Wiesbaden), e.g., B. Groneberg et al., *Répertoire* 3.256 (OB; 1980); R. Zadok, *Répertoire* 8.332 (NB and LB; 1985); and especially Kh. Nashef, *Répertoire* 5.279–80 (MB and MA; 1982).

42. Weidner, "Simurrum und Zaban," 76–77.

43. Zabban was sometimes on the Babylonian side of the border (e.g., during the reign of Adad-nirari II and Aššurnaṣirpal II [cf. J. A. Brinkman, *A Political History of Post-Kassite Babylonia* [AnOr 43; Rome, 1968] 180–81, 188–89, and 188 n. 1151]), sometimes on the Assyrian side (e.g., during the reign of Šamši-Adad V [cf. Brinkman, *Political History*, 208 n. 1292]).

Assyro-Babylonian border agreements or treaties that were drawn up under oath.[44] Especially in view of the occurrence in this Chronicle of the term *māmītu* (Grayson, *Chronicles,* 158, I 4′) and the city Zabban (162, II 11),[45] we may wonder whether the conjuction here in *Maqlû* of Zabban (I 42–45) and *māmītu* (I 38) might not indicate that also our *Maqlû* text reflects a concern with a violation of an agreement between Assyria and Babylonia. Perhaps we should construct the following scenario. Assuming that, at the time of writing, Zabban was situated on the Assyrian side of the border and served to define it, we may imagine our speaker standing at this border post and defending it against the encroaching Babylonians. He sees them as a demonic, alien force that threatens the imperial structure by virtue of their violation of sworn border agreements, and tries to hold them at the border. The text thus treats the infraction of an oath sworn to maintain the structure of the Assyrian Empire and serves to uphold that structure.

While our reconstruction provides an interesting scenario, we would be remiss if we did not consider additional possibilities as well, especially since a number of characteristics of our text suggest that the geographical setting of the city might well be cosmic. Among these characteristics are the following: our ceremony is set in a festival centered on the movement of spirits between the netherworld and this world; it focuses on the expulsion of witches from the organized cosmos; this enterprise encompasses the heavens and the netherworld; and, finally, it presents the speaker as a member of the divine court, who travels between the several cosmic realms. Since the city Zabban is a major point upon which the regions are focused and around which they revolve, it is more than likely that the city possesses an imagined cosmic significance rather than, or in addition to, an actual terrestrial one.

Let us examine the text more closely from this point of view. The text states that the city contains two gates, one for the rising of the sun and the other for its setting (I 43–45):

ša āliya Zabban šitta abullātīšu
ištīt ana ṣīt šamši šanītu ana erēb šamši
ištīt ana ṣīt šamši šanītu ana erēb šamši

44. For this characterization of the Synchronistic History, see A. K. Grayson, *Assyrian and Babylonian Chronicles* (TCS 5; Locust Valley, N.Y., 1975) 51–53; note particularly 158–59, I 1′–7′ and references on p. 53 n. 17. Cf. J. A. Brinkman, "Political Covenants, Treaties, and Loyalty Oaths in Babylonia and between Assyria and Babylonia," in *I Trattati nel Mondo Antico Forma Ideologia Funzione* (ed. L. Canfora, M. Liverani, and C. Zaccagnini; Rome, 1990) 81–112, especially 86–89.

45. The occurrence p. 164, II 15′ requires emendation; see simply 164, note to II 15′.

This statement is intended to emphasize less the direction of the earthly city's gates, and more the fact that the city faces, perhaps even contains, the very gates through which the sun rises and sets.[46] These gates are on the horizon, and through them pass the sun and other heavenly bodies when they enter and leave the sky. Through these gates the heavenly bodies enter the heavens from the netherworld when they rise and return to the netherworld when they set. Thus, the gates of Zabban lead into the heavens and the netherworld, and the city, together with its "inhabitant," guards the entrances into and out of those regions.

In lines 50–51 of the following incantation, mention is made of *kāru* ('quay') and *nēberu* ('pass'); in this quay and pass, the messenger claims to have imprisoned the witches that have come from all over the world. These structures are associated with Zabban;[47] presumably, then, also the city is located on a body of water. Confirmation of this location may possibly be provided by an ancient commentary on these *Maqlû* incantations, which seems to state that Zabban is situated on the 'shores': *mā Zabban aššum kibrāti nadi.*[48] The commentary then associates Zabban explicitly with a *kāru: mā ša imitti Zabbanma ša šumēli kāru karku* (?) 'On the right is Zabban, on the left the quay is. . . .'[49] As noted earlier, also the quay and pass have cosmic significance; if this is correct, the shores and city would also possess such significance, and it is perhaps to such a quality that the commentary alludes.

Zabban thus possesses forms, features, and functions often associated with cosmic structures. Note, moreover, that, especially in regard to the rising and the setting of the sun, Zabban in our text is described like and has a significance similar to the mythic Mount Māshu of the "Epic of Gilgamesh":

> The name of the mountain is Mashu.
> When [he arrived] at the mountain range of Mashu,
> Which daily keeps watch over sun[rise and sunset]—
> Whose peaks [reach to] the vault of heaven
> (And) whose breasts reach to the nether world below—
> Scorpion-men guard its gate,

46. Cf. the *Maqlû* commentary KAR 94:22, as read by G. Meier, "Studien zur Beschwörungssammlung Maqlû," *AfO* 21 (1966) 71: "*šá ina lìb-bi* UD *napâḫi ana šikin siḫpi-šu iq-bu-u*"; instead of a form of *napāḫu* for ZI, perhaps read ZI: *tebû.*

47. They remain associated with the city even in the unlikely event that they are not actually part of the city.

48. I read the third and fourth words in KAR 94:20 not as *ana mu-x-ra-a-ti* with Meier ("Studien," 71) but as *aššum ki*[*b*]*!-ra-a-ti,* where *aššum* = 1 MU or DIŠ (= *ana*).MU= *šum*. Even so, the line requires collation.

49. KAR 94:23, as read by Meier, ibid.

Whose terror is awesome and whose glance was death.
Their shimmering halo sweeps the mountains
That at sunrise and sunset keep watch over the sun.[50]

In keeping with its description and function, Zabban is to be understood as having a cosmic character and location. We may describe the picture as follows. Zabban is a cosmic locale, situated on the cosmic shore beyond which are stationed the forces of chaos. The city is linked to the heavens and the netherworld. Whether simply leading from the earth into the heavens or actually encompassing the earth and the heavens, the city connects the world above the horizon with the netherworld by means of the gates for the rising and the setting of the sun. Also, the quay and pass are cosmic. Located on the horizon, they serve as entry points through which cosmic travelers and ghosts normally pass, without hindrance, from the netherworld into the heavens, but where they may also be temporarily imprisoned.

This picture, of course, is only general and approximate; still, at this point in the analysis, I can see two possible avenues of speculation that might lead to some further understanding of Zabban. The first is to associate it with the *zabbu,* a cultic functionary who is known to enter ecstatic trances.[51] Perhaps the city of Zabban is simply the city of the *zabbu.*

The second is to associate it with Northwest Semitic *Ṣapān,* biblical *Ṣāphôn,* and to read the name not as *zab-ban,* but as *Ṣap-pan.*[52] I note only that the location of "Zabban" on the shore, at the entrances to the heavens and the netherworld or depths, is quite evocative; it recalls the divine abodes of Canaanite literature, the homes of El and Baal.[53] Of course, if

50. GE, Tablet IX ii 1–9. Translation: E. A. Speiser, "Akkadian Myths and Epics," *ANET,* 88.

51. For this functionary, see Finkel, "Necromancy," 12–13 (Excursus I).

52. No manuscript of the *Maqlû* text writes the name with the ⟨ba⟩ sign (e.g., *ZAB/ZA-AB-*ba-an*). Thus, there is no orthographic evidence in any of the manuscripts that contradicts the assumption of /p/ rather than /b/ and the transcription ⟨pp⟩ rather than ⟨bb⟩. For a double writing of the second consonant of *Ṣapān* in an Akkadian context, see E. Lipiński, "El's Abode: Mythological Traditions Related to Mount Hermon and to the Mountains of Armenia," *OLP* 2 (1971) 61 and n. 243; cf. C. Grave, "The Etymology of Northwest Semitic *ṣapānu*," *UF* 12 (1980) 227.

53. For the cosmic mountain in Canaan and Israel, see R. J. Clifford, *The Cosmic Mountain in Canaan and the Old Testament* (HSM 4; Cambridge, 1972). Note, for example, the following picture of El's abode: "Then they set face / Toward El at the sources of the Two Rivers, / In the midst of the pools of the Double-Deep" (Clifford, *Cosmic Mountain,* 48), and cf., e.g., F. M. Cross, *Canaanite Myth and Hebrew Epic* (Cambridge, 1973) 37–38, where Cross describes El's abode as follows: "The picture of ʾĒl's abode . . . places it at the cosmic mount of assembly in the north at whose base the cosmic waters well up; there the council of ʾĒl meets in his Tabernacle of assembly (biblical *ʾōhel môʿēd*) on the shore of sea. . . . The

the incantation was composed in the first millennium, a form with *ā*, rather than the Canaanite ō, would suppose an Aramaic context compatible with the mode of contact of Assyria with the West. While influenced by Canaanite models, our composer would have viewed the cosmos through Mesopotamian eyes and transformed a cosmic mountain into a cosmic city. Hence, Mount *Ṣāphôn* has become the city *Ṣappān*.[54]

But whether "Zabban" is a normal terrestrial city, the city of the zabbu, the city *Ṣappān*, or a combination of these three, here in *Maqlû* it is a cosmic locale, an *Axis Mundi* that connects the earth, heavens, and netherworld and draws together the human, divine, and infernal communities. Here the speaker is not only at the point of contact between the earth and the night sky but also at the point where heaven, earth, and the netherworld meet. For this reason, perhaps, the composer chose such a city as the jumping-off point for the incantation.

The speaker is on earth but he is also in the heavens. In some sense, his vision is like Isaiah's vision of God, a vision which is both terrestrial and heavenly: "I beheld my Lord seated on a high and lofty throne; and the skirts of His robe filled the Temple" (Isa 6:1).[55] Moreover, in the guise of a star that rises in the east and sets in the west (*Maqlû* I 42–45), he imagines himself able to address and interact with the gods of the sky and the netherworld and to journey to both (46–60). His circuit recalls

---

mythic pattern which couples the cosmic river(s) with the Mount of God, the place where the gates of heaven and the watery passage into hell are found, may be applied to any great mountain with springs at its foot or side where a sanctuary of ᵓĒl (or Yahweh) exists." For a detailed discussion of El's abode, see M. H. Pope, *El in the Ugaritic Texts* (Leiden, 1955) 61–81; see also Lipiński, "El's Abode," 13–69. El's two sons, šaḥar and šalim (Dawn and Dusk) may well be connected with our *ṣīt šamši* and *erēb šamši*.

For further discussion of the cosmic mountain in ancient Israel, see J. D. Levenson's chapter, "Zion as the Cosmic Mountain," in *Sinai and Zion* (Minneapolis, 1985) 111–37, especially 122–26, where, particularly with references to *Ṣāphôn*, Levenson discusses Zion as the junction between heaven, earth, and the netherworld. By treating Zabban as cosmic, I do not mean to imply that the city is the cosmos, but rather that the city has cosmic characteristics. An admonition about cosmic mountains applies equally well here: "In the case of the cosmic mountain, it should be noted at the outset that the term 'cosmic' can be misleading. Clifford's point is not that the cosmos is envisioned in ancient Canaan as a mountain, but rather that a mountain is given characteristics and potencies of cosmic, that is, of an infinite and universal scope" (Levenson, *Sinai and Zion*, 111).

For a recent discussion of the etymology of *Ṣapān*, see Grave, "Etymology," 221–29; cf. also E. Lipiński, "*Ṣāpôn*," *TWAT* 6.1093–1102. I am, of course, not unaware of late writings of Baᶜal-Ṣapān as *Baᶜal-ṣa-pu-na* (see Lipiński, "El's Abode," 63 and n. 252; and Grave, "Etymology," 222; cf. Zadok, *Répertoire*, 8.278), but this is a consequence of the Canaanite shift of ā > ō.

54. See Excursus II for a continuation of my line of speculation that links Zabban with *Ṣāphôn*.

55. Translation: NJPSV.

Isa 14:12ff., where the king of Babylon, the bright morning star, scales the heavens where the stars are located, rises up to the mountain of the divine council in the distant *Ṣāphôn*, and then is brought down to Sheol, the netherworld.

Like Isaiah 14, the *Maqlû* text is also anti-Babylonian. By contrast, however, the cosmic traveler in *Maqlû* is presented in a positive light and is seen functioning in the service of the Assyrian Empire. For, more specifically, the city "Zabban" also represents the Assyrian Empire, an imperial structure that must control chaos and hold back evil. The text underscores the importance of holding back and punishing those who threaten the structure and fabric of Assyrian society.[56]

The crossing and quay are the entrances to the city, to the civilized empire (Assyria or one of its outposts), to the cosmos (comprising the organized terrestrial world and heavens). The theme of controlling the quay and crossing may derive from the activity of levying taxes or duties on travel and transport at the transit points of quay and crossing.[57] But here this usage has been even further expanded: the *nēbiru* and *kāru* now function first as entry points, on the terrestrial level, to the city and empire, and then as transit points from the netherworld into this world. The speaker is able to control the pass and, by extension, the quay leading from the netherworld into the heavens. As mentioned earlier, he is in effect an imperial messenger or officer sent by the central authorities of the human empire or the cosmos to the border in order to deal with the illegal entry of alien or dangerous populations or enemies. These enemies try to enter through the quay and take over the city, the empire, and/or the cosmos but are caught and imprisoned in the quay. In this holding place, the man of "Zabban" encloses the witches coming from the netherworld and prevents them from entering the visible organized world, be it the heavens, the empire, or the city.

But whether a political reading is correct or not, it remains true that here in *Maqlû* "Zabban" is both a terrestrial and a cosmic intersection. Like all places on earth, it is a point of connection between this world and the netherworld, a place where the living and the dead meet, where in the festival of the dead the two human communities come together.

56. I should mentioned that it remains unclear, to me at least, whether the power of the city derives from its function as a linchpin at the center or from its location on the border between either Assyria and Babylonia or the Empire and the outside world.

57. Compare, for example, the granting of exemption from this levy in Neo-Assyrian grants in J. N. Postgate, *Neo-Assyrian Royal Grants and Decrees* (Studia Pohl: Series Maior 1; Rome, 1969) 10 and text references there, and 15–16. Note, for purposes of dating, the comment there, p. 12: "The sequence *ina miksi kāri nēbiri* . . . . occurs in the Sargon text here for the first time. . . ."

But, in addition, it draws together earth, heaven, and the netherworld.[58] The cosmic "Zabban" allows the human to ascend into the heavens, to become an astral divinity, and to descend to the netherworld in order to enlist its help.

Here I would end this section of my exposition. I am not unaware of its speculative nature, but all the same I hope that I have given a coherent reading to several incantations and conveyed some of the biblical images that they evoke in me.

Excursus I

Incantations 2–5 (I 37–72)[59]

erṣetu erṣetu erṣetumma
ᵈgilgameš bēl māmītikunu
mimmû attunu tēpušā[60] *anāku īde*
mimmû anāku eppušu attunu ul tīdâ
mimmû kaššāpātīya ippušā ēgâ pāṭira pāšira lā išâ[61]

ālī zabban ālī zabban
ša āliya zabban šitta abullātīšu
ištīt ana ṣīt ᵈšamši šanītu ana erēb ᵈšamši
ištīt ana ṣīt ᵈšamši šanītu ana erēb ᵈšamši
anāku era ḫaṣba maštakal našâku
ana ilī ša šamê mê anamdin
kīma anāku ana kâšunu ullalukunūši
attunu yâši ullilāʾinni

akla nēberu aktali kāru
akli ipšīšina ša kališina mātāti
ᵈanu u antu išpurūʾinni
mannu lušpur ana ᵈbēlet ṣēri

58. Note further that the connection of the earth with the heavens and the netherworld can be understood to exist on either a horizontal or a vertical plane; thus, e.g., one may travel from the earth to the netherworld on an east-west plane (horizontal), but, alternatively, the grave itself or a mountain may connect the earth, heaven, and netherworld (vertical).

59. See provisionally, G. Meier, *Die assyrische Beschwörungssammlung Maqlû* (AfO Beiheft 2; Berlin, 1937), and idem, "Studien." The text given here is a transcription of what I deem to be the standard text. Occasionally, I note a variant or a reading to explain my choice.

60. Perhaps read *teppušā*; see above, n. 6.

61. Var., *ul iraššī*.

ana pī kaššāpiya u kaššāptiya idî hargullī
idî šipassu ša apkal ilī ^{d}*marduk*
lilsâkima[62] *lā tappilīšināti*
liqbânikkimma lā tašemmêšināti
lulsikima apulinni
luqbâkkimma šimînni yâši [63]
ina qibīt iqbû ^{d}*anu antu u* ^{d}*bēlet ṣēri*

šaprāku allak uʾʾurāku adabbub
ana līt kaššāpiya u kaššāptiya ^{d}*Asalluḫi bēl āšipūti išpuranni*
ša šamê qūlā ša erṣeti šimâ
ša nāri qūlāni ša nābali šimâ pī⸢*ya*⸣ (?)[64]
. . . .

adi amāt kaššāpiya u kaššāptiya aqabbû
alpu ipaššar immeru ipaššar
amāssunu lippaširma amātī lā ippaššar
adi amāt aqabbû amāssunu ana pān amātiya lā ipparrik
ina qibīt ^{d}*Asalluḫi bēl āšipūti*

Excursus II

Continuing the line of speculation linking "Zabban" and *Ṣāphôn*, I should here note that a number of features in the text seem to indicate that the earthly seaport city of Tyre may have been in the composer's

62. With one exception, manuscripts read: *lilsâkima;* only *STT* 78 reads *lilsânikkimma.* Although *šasû* can take dative suffixes, here the full dative form seems to have been written under the influence of *liqbânikkimma* of the following line. Ironically, *STT* 78 accidentally omits ⟨*kim*⟩ in that word and instead reads *liq-ba-nik-*⟨*kim*⟩*-ma.*

63. No manuscript reads *ia-a-ti* found in Meier's edition (this is another example of an unshaded sign [= restoration] in Tallqvist's copy being read as if it were an extant sign). The only clear reading preserved is in *STT* 78: *a-a-ši* and K43+, where the word should be read as *ia-a-*⸢*ši*⸣.

64. As far as I can see, a clear INIM-*su* is not to be found in any manuscript. Tallqvist based himself on IV *R*^{2}, pl. 49 = K43+, where, however, -*su* is partially restored. Note that on grounds of sense, a third-person suffix is unexpected and if extant, would have to be emended, since it would refer to the victim in the third person (as would a priest) but in fact the victim is the speaker and should be referred to in the first person. (If extant, a third-person pronoun referring to the victim might indicate that the present recension of the incantation derives from an earlier form recited by a priest prior to its adaptation here in *Maqlû* for recital by a victim.) My reading of a photograph of K43+ indicates that the signs should perhaps be read instead as: KA-⸢*ia*⸣ = *pīya*, cf., *KAR* 71, rev. 2. In *STT* 78 this last word in the line seems to be missing, but an examination of a photograph of the tablet indicates that it might have been lost in the break at the end of the line.

mind or, at least, provided him with images when he composed the incantations and developed their imagery. That this idea is not farfetched, as such, is suggested by the actual conjunction of *Maqlû* and the earthly city Tyre in the reign of Esarhaddon: *Maqlû* was performed for King Esarhaddon,[65] the same Assyrian king who concluded a vassal treaty with Baᶜal of Tyre in 676[66] but remained concerned with that city and was even forced to conquer it five years later.[67] Both the geographical location of Tyre ("in the midst/heart of the seas") as well as its thematic associations are suggestive. In the present context, moreover, it is striking that in the eighth and seventh centuries Tyre is mentioned in connection with control of the quays of other coastal cities. Thus, in the reign of Tiglath-Pileser III, an official in the West writes to the Assyrian king regarding the Tyrians' rights to enter and leave any quays and quay-houses they wish and to bring down wood from Mount Lebanon, as well as regarding his own control of the taxing of "the quays of all Mount Lebanon" and of those who bring down wood.[68] And in the reign of Esarhaddon, we find that one of the foci of his treaty with Tyre is the issue of Tyrians' rights to enter quays of various cities; it also mentions overnight stays of Tyrian sailors in their own ships in these quays as well as the ultimate Assyrian control over the Tyrians.[69]

The occurrence of the quay in a similar context in *Maqlû* and in these other texts (*nēberu* 'pass' also occurs together with *kāru* 'quay' in taxation contexts in Neo-Assyrian texts[70]) takes on even greater significance in view of the further observation that Esarhaddon's treaty with Tyre contains, in IV 10–13,[71] lines that are similar to *Maqlû* III 133–37: *ša makurrišina libbatiq ašalša / markassa lippaṭirma tarkullaša linnasiḫ /* (. . .) */ edû* (. . .) *ana tâmati lišēṣišināti / šamrūtu agû elišina lītellilû.*[72]

These shared lines point to a connection between the two texts and suggest that the composer of *Maqlû* had some association with the Phoe-

65. See Abusch, "Mesopotamian Anti-Witchcraft Literature," 259; and S. Parpola, *Letters from Assyrian Scholars to the Kings Esarhaddon and Assurbanipal, Part 2: Commentary and Appendices* (AOAT 5/2; Kevelaer/Neukirchen-Vluyn, 1983) 203-4.

66. For this treaty, see Parpola and Watanabe, *Neo-Assyrian Treaties*, 24–27.

67. Ibid., pp. xxix and l n. 12. Again, in 662, Assurbanipal was required to mount a campaign against Tyre.

68. See ND 2715: 3–14, reedited J. N. Postgate, *Taxation and Conscription in the Assyrian Empire* (Studia Pohl: Series Maior 3; Rome, 1974) 390–93. (Note also the use of *naṣāru* and *maṣṣartu* in lines 13 and 14.)

69. Parpola and Watanabe, *Neo-Assyrian Treaties*, 25–27, III 18′–26′.

70. See Postgate, *Neo-Assyrian Royal Grants*, 10 c and 12.

71. For these lines, see Parpola and Watanabe, *Neo-Assyrian Treaties*, 27.

72. For the text of these lines, see provisionally Meier, "Studien," 74–75; as well as *Spätbabylonische Texte aus Uruk*, vol. 3, no. 74 A; and *OECT*, vol. 11, no. 44.

nician shore and drew some of his imagery from western sailing and seagoing practices. In the incantation III 128–39, the text looks upon and treats the witches as if they were sailors. This certainly agrees with the appearance of sailors, instead of witches, in *Maqlû* VII 8–9: *ṣalil nēbiru ṣalil kāru / mārī malāḫi kališunu ṣallū.* As noted earlier, these are the very lines that served as a prototype of I 50–51, where the speaker claims to have imprisoned the witches who have come from all over the world:

VII 8: *ṣalil nēbiru ṣalil kāru*	// I 50: *akla nēbiru aktali kāru*
VII 9: *mārī malāḫi kališunu ṣallū*	// I 51: *akli ipšīšina ša kališina mātāti*

VII 8–9 are the more original lines, and the sailors, the more original topos. Here in *Maqlû*, the sailors are presented sleeping in the quay, thus the circle of connection with Tyre is completed, for, as noted above, Esarhaddon's treaty with Ba^{c}al of Tyre talks of the Tyrian sailors' staying overnight in their own ships in foreign quays (III 22′ff.).

Especially in view of the links with Isaiah 14 previously noted, I would be remiss here if I omitted reference to the related Ezek 28:1–10, a prophecy against the king of Tyre, and to the cosmic imagery that underlay this and other oracles against Tyre. Basing himself on Ugaritic materials about El and Ba^{c}al, M. H. Pope has reconstructed a myth that runs as follows: Originally, El was the head of the pantheon and lived on the mount of assembly, Mount *Ṣāphôn,* but was deposed by Ba^{c}al and banished to an infernal abode "at the springs of the (two) rivers, in the midst of the channels of the (two) deeps." From this netherworld abode, El then tried to regain his former position by using the sea, Yamm, but he failed in this attempt.[73] In Ezek 28:1–10, following Pope's analysis, the Tyrian king (and people) makes a claim to the divinity of El and to his former elevation but will not succeed and will instead be cast (back) into the watery depths where El now resides.

If, then, the Canaanite cosmic mountain *Ṣāphôn* has become the Mesopotamian cosmic city *Ṣappān* and Tyrian aggressiveness vis-à-vis coastal ports and mountains is associated with El's attempt to recapture Mount *Ṣāphôn,* a composer (here, the composer of *Maqlû*) drawing upon this material could view the Tyrians as constituting the enemy from the depths or the netherworld who wish to gain control of the land. The sailors become the enemy witches who bring witchcraft from foreign lands, witches who are not only foreign but are also imbued with a demonic

73. Pope, *El,* 82–104, especially 92–99 and 102–3; cf. also R. R. Wilson, "The Death of the King of Tyre: The Editorial History of Ezekiel 28," in *Love and Death in the Ancient Near East: Essays in Honor of Marvin H. Pope* (ed. J. H. Marks and R. M. Good; Guilford, Conn., 1987) 211–14.

and cosmic character comparable to that found in VI 136–38 // 145–47.[74] As noted earlier, these enemies try to enter through the quay and take over this world, be it the city, the empire, or the cosmos, but they are caught and imprisoned in the quay. Perhaps it is the man of "Zabban" who is particularly able to control the pass and quay leading from the netherworld into the heavens. He encloses the witches coming from the netherworld in this holding place and prevents them from entering this world, generally, and the heavens, specifically.

In view, then, of the location of "Zabban" on the shore, of its association with harbors to which travelers (< sailors) from all "lands" tried to gain access and wherein they were then confined, and of the various connections between Tyre and *Ṣāphôn* and between Tyre and *Maqlû*, we may wonder if the composer did not also draw upon terrestrial and cosmic images that relate both to Tyre and to *Ṣāphôn* and bring them together. But whatever the case, the city "Zabban,"[75] whether on the border between Assyria and Babylonia or on land facing the western Mediterranean shore, represents the imperial structure of the Assyrian Empire—more broadly, the terrestrial earth and heaven—that must control chaos and hold back evil.

74. "Ha! my witch, my informer, / Who blows back and forth over all lands, / Crosses to and fro over all mountains."

75. In view of the identification of the sea (and the sailors = the witches) with El and of *Ṣāphôn*/"Zabban" (and the speaker) with Ba^{c}al = Haddu, is it of significance that the main god of the earthly city Zabban is Adad? For the temple names of Adad of Zabban, see Weidner, "Simurrum und Zaban," 76, especially nn. 18–20; and recently A. R. George, *Babylonian Topographical Texts* (OLA 40; Louvain, 1992) 180–83, lines 183–84a, with the observation (p. 465) that "the temple names represent the god's frightening aspect as thunderstorm."

More on the Latin Personal Names Ending with *-us* and *-ius* in Punic

Maria Giulia Amadasi Guzzo

The present work attempts to recognize the system used in Punic to render the endings -us and -ius of Latin personal names. The regularity in the correspondence of Latin -us / Punic -ʾ (seldom -h) and Latin -ius / Punic -y(ʾ) has long been noticed; for instance: Donatus = dn(ʿ)tʾ, Tiberius = tbry. However, the problem of the Latin forms underlying the Punic spellings is still open: the Latin vocative ending and a spoken pronunciation have been proposed. Examination of dated evidence shows that, after a period of exact transcriptions in Punic of Latin names in the nominative case (for instance rwps and rʾps = Rufus), foreign endings were adapted to Punic othographic rules, that is, to the system of marking with -ʾ suffixes consisting of a vowel, and spelling with -y(ʾ) suffixes in -y + a vowel. The conclusion drawn is that, at the very beginning of the first century c.e.*, Latin personal names (in the same way as Latin common nouns such as podium = pʾdy, denarius/i = dnʿryʾ) were really "punicized" and not transcribed from a given case or a spoken form.*

Latin personal names may be found in several Late Punic inscriptions, particularly those written in Neo-Punic.[1] Their orthography is quite regular, though there are also some exceptions. Analytical studies of the Latin personal names in Punic writing have been undertaken during the past decades.[2] One particular problem discussed in these studies is

Author's note: This study is the development of a suggestion formulated in a paper on Latin personal names in Punic inscriptions, read in 1990, in Sassari, at the *Sesta giornata di studi camito-semitici e indoeuropei.* I am grateful to C. de Simone, who read the Italian version of this paper.

1. Only a few of them are in F. L. Benz, *Personal Names in the Phoenician and Punic Inscriptions* (Studia Pohl: Series Minor 8; Rome, 1983); on the other hand they are studied and listed in K. Jongeling, *Names in Neo-Punic Inscriptions* (Ph.D. dissertation, Univ. of Groningen, 1984), quoted hereafter as *NNPI.*

2. See, in particular, J. Friedrich, "Griechisches und römisches in phönizischem und punischem Gewande," in *Festschrift O. Eissfeldt* (ed. J. Fuck; Halle-Saale, 1947) 109–24, esp.

the rendering in Punic of the Latin endings *-us* and *-ius*. The correspondence of *-ʾ* for Latin *-us* and of *-y* for Latin *-ius* is consistent: for example, *dnṭʾ* and *dnʿṭʾ* for *Donatus IPT* 17 (12),[3] 86 (51); *mʿrsʾ* for *Marsus IPT* 52 (44 t), 71; *sʿbynʾ* for *Sabinus IPT* 28 (33), 23 (29); *bqy* for *Boccius IPT* 38 (44 f); *gʿy* for *Caius IPT* 26 (31); *srwy* for *Servius*; *slpqy* for *Sulpicius IPT* 74; and so on. But while the orthographic conventions used to render Latin names are quite well known, the Latin original forms are still being discussed. The reexamination of the problem offered here aims at proving that a clue to understanding the Punic spellings is the identification of the orthographic system to which Latin names conform in the Neo-Punic inscriptions. As a secondary conclusion, one might observe that the exact pronunciation of the Latin names as they appear in Punic is a problem that is independent from the othographic one.

G. Levi Della Vida was the first scholar to notice the regular orthography employed in Punic to render Latin personal names ending in *-us*. Already in 1934–35, when he published the Late Punic inscription of Bitia (Sardinia),[4] which contains a dating formula based on Antoninus Pius's reign (161–80 C.E.),[5] he pointed out that the ending *-us* of Latin names was systematically written with final *-h*; he also observed that *h* in this inscription corresponds to the vowel *e*, as is proved by the transcription of *Aurelius* as *ʿwrhly* and of *Peducaeus* as *phdwqʿyh*. The Latin names attested in the Bitia inscription are: *qʿysr mʿrqh ʿwrhly ʿnṭnynh* [*ʿ*]*wgsṭh* (line 1) = *Caesar Marcus Aurelius Antoninus Augustus*; *mʿrqh phdwqʿyh plʿwṭy*

115–22; idem, "Vulgärpunisch und Vulgärlatein in den neupunischen Inschriften," *Cahiers de Byrsa* 3 (1953) 99–111, esp. 104–11 (French translation by J. Ferron, in the same volume, pp. 229–39); J. G. Février, "La prononciation punique des noms propres latins en *-us* et en *-ius*," *JA* (1953) 465–71; J. Friedrich, "Punische Studien, 3: Griechische und römische Personennamen in den punischen Inschriften," *ZDMG* 107 (1957) 292–94; cf. also J. Friedrich and W. Röllig, *Phönizisch-punische Grammatik* (2d ed.; AnOr 46; Rome, 1970) §210 (hereafter *PPG*²); W. Röllig, "Das punische im Römischen Reich," in G. Neumann and J. Untermann (eds.), *Die Sprachen im Römischen Reich der Kaiserzeit* (Beihefte der Bonner Jahrbücher 40; Köln/Bonn, 1980) 283–99, esp. 291–95; Jongeling, *NNPI*, in particular 93–109.

3. The abbreviation designates G. Levi Della Vida and M. G. Amadasi Guzzo, *Iscrizioni puniche della Tripolitania (1927–1967)* (Rome, 1987; hereafter *IPT*); the number in parentheses corresponds to the previous numbering by Levi Della Vida.

4. Cf. G. Levi della Vida, "L'iscrizione punica di Bitia in Sardegna," *Atti della Reale Accademia delle Scienze di Torino* 70 (1934–35) 185–98.

5. The possibility that the emperor mentioned was Caracalla (211–17), who has the same names (*Marcus Aurelius Antoninus*), seems to be excluded. One *suffes*, in fact, apparently bears the *cognomen* "the Roman" (line 3, *bbʿl hrʾmy*), which might mean that the right of citizenship had not yet been granted to everyone (I owe this observation to A. Mastino, whom I wish to thank).

(line 4) = *Marcus Peducaeus Plautius*; *pʾmpʿy phls* (line 6) = *Pompeius Felix*;[6] *sʿṭwrnynh* (line 7) = *Saturninus*.[7] The same ending *e* of a Latin name in *-us* was identified in a Latino-Punic inscription (that is, in Punic written in Latin letters)[8] republished in *KAI* no. 178, which has *Rogate* for *Rogatus*. The explanation given for this *e* was that Latin names had entered Punic in the *-e* form of the vocative case, "which certainly stems from the fact that the vocative is precisely the form in which personal names are more frequently heard."[9] The same opinion was maintained shortly later, in an edition of two Neo-Punic inscriptions from Leptis Magna, *IPT* 21 (27) and 22 (28),[10] where imperial personal names and Latin names adopted by private citizens appear. The first ones show the *-us* ending rendered by *samek*, while the others, with the exception of *Rufus*, written *rwps* (see below, pp. 500–501), have the correspondence *-us* = *ʾ*.[11] According to Levi Della Vida, the difference in spelling (*samek* instead of *ʾalep*) might correspond to the adoption through a literary medium of the first names (those of the emperor and of the members of his family), through the spoken language of the second ones (the names of natives who had adopted a Latin *cognomen*).

The problem of the Punic rendering of Latin names in *-us* and in *-ius* was later dealt with several times by J. Friedrich. In his first study, in 1947 (see n. 2), he proposed that the spelling with *-y*, corresponding to a pronunciation *-i*, might have been a transposition of a "vulgar Latin" ("vulgärlateinisch") form; on the other hand, for the spelling with *-ʾ*, corresponding to a pronunciation *-e*, he excluded a transcription on the basis of the vocative and suggested, instead, a derivation from previous Etruscan onomastic forms ending with *-e*. He advanced the same explanation in his Phoenician and Punic grammar (see n. 2). Going back to the same question in 1953, Friedrich slightly changed his position, admitting that names in *-us* transcribed with *-ʾ* might be derived from the

6. Note in *Pompeius* the us of *ʿy* for the diphthong *ei*; cf. Jongeling, *NNPI*, 102; *phls* should be the vulgar Latin *Felis*; J. G. Février suggests, on the contrary, *Pullius*; idem, "La prononciation punique," 466; cf. also K. Jongeling, "Survival of Punic," in E. Devijver and E. Lipiński (eds.), *Studia Phoenicia X* (Louvain, 1989) 367.

7. We must also recall *ʿwyṭyʿn* (line 5), which might be an "irregular" spelling of *Avitianus*.

8. Cf. G. Levi Della Vida, "Sulle iscrizioni 'latino-libiche' della Tripolitania," *OrAnt* 2 (1963) 65–94.

9. Levi Della Vida, "L'iscrizione punica," 192; see in particular n. 2.

10. G. Levi Della Vida, "Due iscrizioni imperiali neopuniche di Leptis Magna," *Africa Italiana* 6 (1935) 7 n. 1, quoting E. Littmann, "Anredeformen in erweiterter Bedeutung," *Nachrichten von der Königlichen Gesellschaft der Wissenschaften zu Göttingen, phil.-hist. Klasse* (1916) 93–111.

11. Levi Della Vida points out, however, that in Africa this consonant often indicates the vowel *o* ("Due iscrizioni imperiali," 7 n. 1).

vocative Latin case, passed from the spoken to the written language; as to names in *-y*, he maintained his hypothesis of transcription from "vulgar Latin" forms.[12] In 1957, finally, Friedrich seemed also to relate names originally in *-ius*, transcribed by means of a *-y*, to the vocative of the spoken language.[13] The same interpretation, although expressed with caution, is adopted in W. Röllig's study, as well as in Jongeling's onomastic repertory.[14]

A different opinion was expressed by J. G. Février. In his 1953 article (see n. 2), he proposed that Latin names were transcribed on the basis of Punic spoken forms: transcriptions with *-s* of names in *-us* and *-ius* and with *-yʾ* of names in *-ius* allowed him to trace a development of Punic spelling from the correct pronunciation of the names in the nominative to a pronunciation *-iu*, transcribed *-yʾ*, then *-i*, transcribed *-y*, of names in *-ius*; for the names in *-us* he reconstructed a pronunciation *-u* > *-ö*, transcribed *-ʾ* in North Africa, *-h* at Bitia, *-e* in the Latino-Punic inscriptions. Therefore, Punic must have adopted nominative forms, whose pronunciation and transcription were gradually modified. This reconstruction was not accepted by Friedrich.[15]

The explanation that Latin names passed into Punic in the vocative form is difficult to accept because, as Friedrich pointed out in his first article, there are no examples of the written use of that case in Latin or in the derived languages, even though one might observe that derivatives of Latin forms in the Romance languages and adoptions of foreign onomastic forms in Semitic languages need not necessarily be considered as equivalent.[16] On the other hand, we still have the problem of the frequent use in Africa of *ʾ* = *o* and of the apparent nonvocative form of the transcriptions of names in *-ius*. It was probably these observations, together with spellings *-yʾ* for names in *-ius* and *-s* for names in *-us*,[17] that led Février to reconstruct a pronunciation different from that of the vocative case for names in *-us* as well. Besides, Levi Della Vida himself does not deal specifically with the spelling of the names in *-ius*, and proposes, for those in *-us*, an eventual passage from an *-o*(*m*) (accusative) ending to an *-e* ending.[18]

12. Friedrich, "Vulgärpunisch und Vulgärlatein," 110.

13. Friedrich, "Punische Studien, 3," 293.

14. Röllig, "Das punische im Römischen Reich," 291–93; Jongeling, *NNPI*, 97.

15. Friedrich, "Vulgärpunisch und Vulgärlatein," 293; without a detailed discussion.

16. Littmann, ("Anrederformen in erweiterter Bedeutung") mentions in particular the passage into the written language of vocative forms such as "domine" or "monsieur"; a series of names, especially Greek, in -ος and -ιος, spelled in Syriac with final *-ʾ* and *-y*, do not necessarily go back to vocative originals .

17. Février's examples of the transcription of names in *-ius* by *-s* are very doubtful. See "La prononciation punique."

18. Levi Della Vida, "Due iscrizioni imperiali," 7 n. 1.

In order to clarify the situation, we must observe, first, that the explanations given until now take it for granted that Latin names were transcribed in Punic according to given Latin forms or Punic pronunciations; it is never suggested that they have been "punicized," that is, adapted to the local orthographic system.[19] To demonstrate this hypothesis, it is useful to reexamine briefly the conventions used to transcribe foreign names in Phoenician and Punic before the Roman Period and, finally, to consider the attestations of Latin names in dated inscriptions, comparing their spelling with the orthographic rules of Punic.

Transcriptions of foreign names in Phoenician are known since the ninth century B.C.E. (Kilamuwa, *KAI* no. 24); they are frequent in the Hellenistic Period, particularly as concerns Greek personal names, whose passage into Phoenician was studied specifically.[20] Here one finds occasional, but not casual, use of *matres lectionis* and frequent transcription of the nominative ending as a sibilant. Since 1964 we have had the evidence of the Etruscan and Punic inscriptions from Pyrgi, dating from ca. 500 B.C.E. regarding Etruscan-Italic names that were adopted in Punic, to which Friedrich attributed the -ʾ spelling of the Roman Period. The Punic version (*KAI* no. 277) contains names whose original forms are found in the Etruscan inscriptions. The donor is the ruler of Caere, called in Etruscan *Θefarie(i) Velia/unas*, and in Punic *tbryʾ wlynš*. The Punic text offers an accurate transcription, in which one may observe exact reproductions of the endings: Etruscan *-ie* is indicated by *-yʾ* and *-as* is indicated by *-š*. Punic *b* reproduces a realization as a voiced bilabial spirant of a voiceless spirant in the Etruscan consonant system.[21] This adaptation shows that the name of the "king" of Caere was transcribed from a spoken form, probably on the specific occasion of the redaction of the Punic text. Similarly, the name of the town of Caere, in Punic *kyšryʾ*, seems to go back to an Etruscan original that has not survived and whose ending, transcribed *-yʾ*, must again be reconstructed as *-ie*.[22]

19. Recall that in Greek inscriptions Phoenician names generally receive the endings of the Greek cases; cf. next note.

20. C. Bonnet in M. G. Amadasi Guzzo and C. Bonnet, "Anthroponymes phéniciens et anthroponymes grecs: Remarques sur leur correspondances," *SEL* 8 (1991) 1–21 (with previous bibliography).

21. Etruscan does not have phonemic opposition between voiceless and voiced consonants; see in particular C. de Simone, "Il nome del Tevere: Contributo per la storia delle più antiche relazioni tra le genti latino-italiche ed etrusche," *Studi Etruschi* 43 (1975) 119–57, in particular 139.

22. The form of the original place-name, perhaps **Khaisr(a)ie* (= **Kaisuraie*), has been discussed several times; cf. C. de Simone, "Ancora sul nome di *Caere*," *Studi Etruschi* 44 (1976) 163–84 (in particular 170); cf. now the adjective form *Caisriva*, at Caere itself (ca. 340 B.C.E.?), singled out by G. Proietti, "L'ipogeo monumentale dei Tamsnie: Considerazioni sul nome etrusco di Caere e sulla magistratura cerite del IV secolo," *Studi Etruschi* 51 (1983)

The Pyrgi text presents a transcription of Etruscan-Italic personal names different from the adaptation of Latin names in Punic as generally attested in the Roman Period. Apart from *-ie* rendered as *-yʾ* (while in Roman names in *-ius* one usually has simply *-y*, but see below, pp. 501–2), the final sibilant is preserved when present in the original language, being rendered in Punic not by *samek*, as usually happens in the Roman Period, but by *šin*, as attested in the Hellenistic Phoenician inscriptions containing Greek names.[23] Finally, in Roman times, the Punic transcription of voiceless dentals and velars does not exactly correspond to what is attested at Pyrgi.[24] One must conclude, therefore, that there developed, in this later period, a different and partially new orthographic tradition.

As a matter of fact, the evidence of dated Punic inscriptions shows that the spelling of Latin endings changed during the first century B.C.E., soon becoming quite steady (although some oscillations remained). This is proved by inscriptions from Tripolitania, which may be dated on the basis of the year of the ruling emperor or proconsul. The earliest ones, from 8 B.C.E. (*IPT* 21 [27]) and from 1–2 C.E. (*IPT* 24 [30]), both have a corresponding Latin text.[25] The first, already quoted, contains the name of Caesar Augustus, transcribed as *qʿysr ʿwgsṭs*. At the end of the text the two yearly *suffetes* are mentioned; the second is named *ḥnbʿl bn ḥmlkt ṭbḥpy rwps*, which in Latin is *Annobal Himilcho* (corrected over a previous *Imilchonis*) *f*(*ilius*) *Tapapius Rufus.*[26] In Punic, as previously in Phoenician and at Pyrgi, one has a true transcription of *Rufus* as *rwps*, where (as in *ʿwgsṭs* = *Augustus*) the Latin ending *-us* corresponds to *-s*.

The second inscription, *IPT* 24 (30), mentions the same person, whose name is written this time *ḥnbʿl bn ḥmlkt ṭbḥpy rʾps* and, in Latin, which has two versions *IRT* 321 and *IRT* 322: once *Annobal Rufus* . . . (titles) . . . *Himilchonis Tapapi f*(*ilius*); and once *Annobal* . . . (titles) . . . *Hi-*

557–71 (de Simone presents as a formal parallel the name *Manθureie*, in "Rivista di Epigrafia etrusca," *Studi Etruschi* 56 [1989–90] 360–61. I thank him for the information).

23. A typical example is *ptlmyš* for Πτολεμαιος; cf. *KAI* nos. 42 and 43 (contrast with *ptlmys* in *KAI* no. 19 and *KAI* no. 40; cf. C. Bonnet, "Anthroponymes phéniciens et anthroponymes grecs," 12–13).

24. *t* = *ṭ*; *k* = *q*, cf. *PPG*^{2}, §37. Pyrgi has Etruscan θ = *t*; *k* = *q*.

25. J. M. Reynolds and J. B. Ward Perkins, *The Inscriptions of Roman Tripolitania* (Rome/London, 1952) 319, 321–22 (cf. 323) (hereafter *IRT*).

26. The correction of *Himilcho* from original gen. *Imilchonis* (written instead of *Himilchonis*) shows that the Latin translator was more interested in transcribing the initial Punic consonant than in adapting the name to Latin morphology; the same care is not verified in the case of *ḥnbʿl* = *Annobal.*

milchonis Tapapi f(ilius) Rufus.[27] The suffix *-us* is again rendered as *-s*, but less usually, ʾ is equivalent to *u.*[28]

Slightly later, between 14 and 19 C.E.,[29] the inscription *IPT* 22 (28) presents the following personal names: *ʿwgsṭs* = *Augustus*; *ṭbry ʿwgsṭs* = *Tiberius Augustus*; *grmʿnyqs* = *Germanicus*; *drʾss* = *Drusus*; *sʿṭrnynʾ* = *Saturninus*, the name of the first *suffes*; [ ]*ryqlʾ* = an incomplete name, but certainly in *-us*, of the second *suffes.*[30] We therefore have here transcription with *-s* of the ending of the names of the imperial family and of the title *Augustus.* The ruling emperor's name, *Tiberius*, however, does not have the Latin nominative ending and is rendered according to the abovementioned correspondence *-ius* = *-y*. The ending *-us* in the Latin names of the *suffetes* is also rendered *-ʾ*, according to the "rule."

The inscription *IPT* 76 (6), found at Ras el-Haddağa, may be dated to 15–19 C.E. thanks to the name of the proconsul of the African province, Lucius Aelius Lamia, which appears in Punic as *lwqy ʿyly lʿmyʿ*. As in the case of Tiberius (previous inscription), the names in *-ius* are "regularly" rendered with *-y*.

The next dated document, from Leptis Magna, dates from 92 C.E., according to the formula of the Latin version. It is an honorary inscription, *IPT* 27 (32), corresponding to *IRT* 318 and 347. The name of the person in whose honor the text was carved is in Latin (*IRT* 347): *Ti(berius) Claudius Quir(ina tribu) Sestius Ti(beri) Claudi Sesti f(ilius)*; in Punic only the patronymic has been partially preserved:]*bn ṭybry q*[*lʿwdy ssty*]. Tiberius Claudius holds, inter alia, the office of *flamen divi Vespasiani*, in Punic *z*[*bḥ lʾlm*] *wʾspʿsyʿnʾ*. Clearly therefore, in this period the name in *-us* of the emperor is also rendered in Punic with a final *-ʾ*; moreover, the orthography of the first syllable makes it quite likely that the final *-ʾ* might represent *e*.

Thus, over a period of a few decades, Latin names, in their passage into Punic, underwent the following evolution: during the first, short period they were transcribed, with names in *-us* keeping the Latin nominative ending (we do not have transcriptions of names in *-ius* before

27. It is therefore sure here that the son (that is, the *suffes*) bears the name *ḥnbʿl rwlʾps*, while his father bears the name *ḥmlkt ṭbḥpy* (but in *IRT* 319, corresponding to *IPT* 21 [27] *Annobal* himself is *Tapapius Rufus*).

28. On the use of *ʾalep* as a vowel, cf. *PPG*^{2}, §§107, 108.1; Jongeling, "Survival of Punic," 365–70; M. G. Amadasi Guzzo, "Aleph *mater lectionis* en punique," *Actes du 3ᵉ Congrès international d'études phéniciennes et puniques, Tunis 1991* (in press).

29. For the dating: the emperor is Tiberius Claudius Nero (14–37 C.E.); Germanicus, who died in 19 C.E., is named as the appointed successor to the throne; Livia (Claudia Livia Iulia, called Livilla), Nero's daughter, is also mentioned (her memory was damned in 32 C.E.).

30. The dating formula is: *špṭm bʿlytn bn ḥnʾ g. sʿṭrnynʾ wbdmlqrt bn bdmlqrt ṭbḥpy* [ ]*ryqlʾ*.

Tiberius's times).[31] Already under Tiberius, the name of the emperor, as well as those in *-ius* of the proconsul in Africa, besides the Latin names of the local *suffetes,* in *-us,* were spelled with final *-y* and *-ʾ*; on the other hand, the names in *-us* of the members of the imperial family kept the nominative ending, rendered with *samek* (the title *Augustus* also kept the final sibilant). Therefore, adaptation to Punic seems to have occurred for some Latin names: locally employed names and the familiar names of the ruling emperor and the proconsul. By the end of the first century C.E., Emperor Vespasian's name also has the ending rendered *-ʾ*; later, at Bitia, all names in *-us* end with *-h,* and those in *-ius* end with *-y.*

It follows that Latin names in *-us* and *-ius,* once their use became common, were no longer transcribed in their original form, but rather adapted to Punic orthography, according to a system to which they were undoubtedly assimilated. This system may be identified with the regular Punic way of denoting a purely vocalic ending (whatever its quality) by means of *-ʾ* and the ending *y* + final vowel by *-y.* The last orthography is already of Phoenician proper and is found in the suffix personal pronoun (possessive and direct object) of the 3d-person masculine and feminine singular, as well as in the endings of hypocoristic personal names and of adjectives (frequently in nisbe formations).[32] The use of *-ʾ* with the function of final vowel is, on the other hand, rare in Phoenicia; however, it is a characteristic ending in hypocoristic personal names.[33] But the regular use of final *-ʾ* as a vowel is an innovation peculiar to Punic; it is, in particular, the regular way to mark the pronominal suffix of the 3d-person masculine and feminine singular, when it is only a vocalic one. At this stage we have the following system: the vocalic suffix (*-ō* and *-ā*) is marked by *-ʾ*; the suffix in *y* + vowel (*-yū* > *-yō̆* and *-yā*) is marked by *-y.*[34] The Punic usage might be a systematization of spelling peculiar to the above-mentioned hypocoristic names (where the ending *-ʾ* was originally a consonant), occurring occasionally in the transcription of foreign personal names.

31. Names in *-is* are apparently transcribed with *s* or *š*; cf., e.g., *nbls* = *Nobilis, wrylš* = *Virilis* (cf. Jongeling. *NNPI,* 96); those in *-ens* with *s/š,* e.g., *wʾls/š* = *Valens* (cf. *NNPI,* 93, 164–65).

32. Cf. *PPG*^{2}, §§112.1.I.c.β, 2; 190.4, 5; 204–5; for the suffix pronouns, see also W. R. Garr, *Dialect Geography of Syria-Palestine 1000–586 B.C.E.* (Philadelphia, 1986) 55, 101–2, 110–11.

33. See, e.g., Benz, *Personal Names,* 232–42.

34. See in particular C. R. Krahmalkov, "Observations on the Affixing of Possessive Pronouns in Punic," *RSO* 44 (1969) 181–86; idem, "The Object Pronouns of the Third Person in Phoenician and Punic," *Rivista di Studi Fenici* 2 (1974) 39–43; J. Huehnergard, "The Development of the Third Person Suffixes in Phoenician," *MAARAV* 7 (1991) 183–94; C. R. Krahmalkov, "Language, Phoenician," *ABD* 4.223.

It is likely that the Punic spelling of originally foreign common nouns, of which we have only a few examples, conformed to the same system. Witness, again in inscriptions from Tripolitania, the following already well-known cases: *pʾdy* = *podium* (*IPT* 27 [32], 92 C.E.) and *dnʿryʾ* = *denarius* or pl. *denarii* (*IPT* 17 [12], undetermined date,[35] and perhaps *IPT* 25), considered by Friedrich to be derived from vulgar Latin forms (**podī* and *denario*, attested in *IRT* 906, 3).[36] The pronunciation of the ending as -*i* + vowel is made clear in the spelling *dnʿryʾ*, which perhaps aims at differentiating the singular from the plural, whatever the underlying Latin form. The same spelling, -*yʾ*, may, in fact, indicate in Late Punic the pronominal suffix of the 3d-person singular, specifying, by means of the *mater lectionis* *ʾalep*, the pronunciation as a consonant *y* + vowel. For example:

1. In the case of the possessive suffix *lʾḥyʾ* 'for his brother', *IPT* 10 (2); and *lʾbyʾ* 'for his father', *IPT* 79 (38);
2. In the case of the direct object suffix *yqṣyʾ* 'he will eradicate it', *CIS* I 3784; *ybrkyʾ* 'may they bless him', *CIS* I 3604, 3709, 4503, 4963; *rpyʾ* 'he healed him' (**rapāyū̆/ō̆*), *KAI* no. 66 (= *CIS* I 143).[37]

Thus, while it is possible to maintain that the -ʾ and -*y* spellings of the Latin names in -*us* and in -*ius* point to their orthographic "punicization," it is more difficult to establish their real pronunciation, given the ambiguity of the Punic system with regard to the annotation of vowels: in particular, *ʾalep* is used, especially at the beginning of the late Punic evidence, for any vowel (see n. 28). Levi Della Vida and Friedrich favor the pronunciation -*e*. Besides *Rogate* of the Latino-Punic *KAI* no. 178, which appears in the same form in an inscription from Bir ed-Dréder,[38] we may recall *Amice* of *IRT* 827 and *Macrine* of *KAI* no. 179 (*IRT* 889). For names in -*ius*, the -*y* spelling might point to a pronunciation *i* + vowel;

35. It is perhaps contemporary with *IRT* 599—two benches with Latin inscriptions from the same *termae* of Hadrian; however, the date of these inscriptions is not known: like those with Punic inscriptions, the benches are reused (they are dated in *IRT* during the first century C.E.).

36. Cf. Friedrich, "Vulgärpunisch und Vulgärlatein," 111; idem, "Kleinigkeiten zum Phönizischen, Punischen, und Numidischen," *ZDMG* 114 (1964) 227–28; also *PPG*^{2}, §208; and H. Jean and J. Hoftijzer, *Dictionnaire des inscriptions sémitiques de l'Ouest* (Leiden, 1960–65) 59.

37. Examples in Amadasi Guzzo, "Aleph *mater lectionis* en punique"; add *pʿmʾt* 'times', *IPT* 21 (27), where ʾ = *ō*.

38. R. Goodchild, "La necropoli romano-libica di Bir ed-Dréder," *Quaderni di Archeologia della Libia* 3 (1954) 98–107 n. 5. List of personal names in Latino-Punic inscriptions in Levi Della Vida, "Sulle iscrizioni 'latino-libiche' della Tripolitania," 93–94.

however, in Latino-Punic inscriptions, these names (if they do not keep the original ending, e.g., *Flabius* and *Iulius*),[39] present forms with an *-i* ending (*Cecili, Flabi, Licini, Marci*).[40] But the presence, at least in a period preceding the Latino-Punic inscriptions, of a vowel after *-i* seems to be demonstrated by Punic examples ending in *-yʾ* (therefore concordant with *dnʿryʾ*), some of which were already cited by Février (see n. 2) in order to propose an evolution in pronunciation *-iu* > *-i*. These examples,[41] whose number is limited, cannot be placed in a chronological sequence from *-yʾ* to *-y*. It seems, rather, that *-yʾ* simply shows greater accuracy in the graphic rendering of the final vowel (in parallel with what is observed in the *-yʾ* spellings of the suffix pronoun *-yū̆/-yā* of Punic).

Once again, as for the ending of names in *-us*, the inscription from Bitia hints at a pronunciation *-ie,* in view of the transcription of *Peducaeus* as *phdwqʿyh* (on the other hand, *Pompeius* is *pʾmpʿy*): here the constant employment of *h* with the function of Latin *e* makes a phonetic realization **Peducaie* quite likely. An evolution of pronunciation, with the final vowel dropped, is possible in the course of time: this stage might be reflected in the Latino-Punic inscriptions.

In conclusion, I propose that the Punic spellings *-ʾ* and *-y*(*ʾ*) of the endings of the Latin names in *-us* and *-ius* are not transcriptions of a definite Latin form, but adaptations of Latin suffixes (of personal names, as well as common, masculine, and neuter nouns) to Punic orthography, which reproduced them according to its own system. Their pronunciation appears to be at least similar[42] to *-e* in the case of the ending *-us* and to *-ie* for the endings *-ius* / *-ium*; the latter probably passed to *-i* in a recent period (Latino-Punic inscriptions). It is likely that these pronunciations correspond to "punicized" rather than Latin forms.

39. Forms attested at Bir ed-Dréder, cf. Goodchild, "*La necropoli romano-libica di Bir ed-Dréder,*" 91–107 nn. 3, 13, 14, 17; 5, 6.

40. *IRT* 877, 886 a, 889 (if not *Flabida*); R. Bartoccini, "Rinvenimenti vari di interesse archeologico in Tripolitania (1920–25)," *Africa Italiana* 1 (1927) 233; *IRT* 877.

41. The correspondences are not always sure, cf. Jongeling, *NNPI*, 93–96; moreover, the general list at the end, pp. 147–212 (*wyqṭryʾ* = *Victrius*, *lʾryʾ*= *Lurius*, *lʿbyʾ* = *Labbaeus*, *phlyʾ* = *Pullius*, add *wʿlryʾ* = *Valerius*, mentioned on p. 96).

42. An evolution in the pronunciation of the kind outlined by Février or Levi Della Vida (see above, pp. 496 and 498 and nn. 2 and 18) seems plausible.

Regelson, Pagis, Wallach: Three Poems on the Hebrew Language

Arnold J. Band

While poems about the writing of poetry are fairly common and are well attested in Modern Hebrew literature, poems that actually employ the linguistic peculiarities of the Hebrew language as their theme are relatively rare. Three examples of this type of poem are discussed in this paper: "Hakukot otiyotayikh," by Abraham Regelson; "Targilim beʿivrit shimushit," by Dan Pagis; and "Ivrit," by Yonah Wallach. A comparison of these three poems reveals not only the specific poetics of each poet, but the development of the poetic capacity of the Hebrew language during the past fifty years.

Self-consciousness and self-reflexivity are two of the hallmarks of European poetry, at least since the beginning of the Romantic Period, and the critical literature on the poetics of self-reflexivity is enormous. Among the various genres exhibiting self-reflexivity few are as obvious or pervasive as poems about the writing of poetry. In Hebrew literature we find such poems since the early modern classics: for example, Bialik, Tchernichowski, and Steinberg.[1] Far less frequent, though still illuminating, are Hebrew poems that take as their theme the linguistic peculiarities of Hebrew and their potential meanings. That grammar is meaningful in poetry and functions as a type of trope we have learned over the years from the many articles of Roman Jakobson;[2] I am interested here not in grammar considered generically, but in the poets'

Editors' note: In this article the Library of Congress system is used for transliteration of Hebrew.

1. Ruth Kartun-Blum has collected and discussed many of these poems about poetry in two volumes: הַשִּׁירָה בִּרְאִי עַצְמָהּ (*Poetry in Its Own Mirror* [Tel Aviv, 1982]) and (*Self-Reflexive Poetry: Forty Years* [Tel Aviv, 1989]).

2. Jakobson's main theoretical article on this issue is "Poetry of Grammar and Grammar of Poetry," *Lingua* 21 (1968) 597–609. It has been collected in volume 2 of his *Selected Writings* (The Hague, 1968).

exploration of grammatic and lexical features that are peculiar to Hebrew. The self-reflexivity is particularized in the poet's conscious exploitation of the grammatical properties of the Hebrew language; the grammatical pecularities are thus thematized and become metaphors for crucial aspects of human existence. Similar examples may exist in other languages, but I (and my colleagues) have not found any to date.

To demonstrate this subgenre of modern poetry, I will discuss three examples, poems written in the past fifty years, precisely the period that has seen such a phenomenal expansion in the expressive capacities of the Hebrew language and the efflorescence of Hebrew literary creativity that has both profited from and contributed to it. The poems, strategically selected to raise a variety of issues, are: חֲקוּקוֹת אוֹתִיּוֹתַיִךְ ("Inscribed Are Your Letters") by Abraham Regelson, 1946; תַּרְגִּילִים בְּעִבְרִית שִׁמּוּשִׁית ("Exercises in Daily Hebrew") by Dan Pagis, 1982; and עִבְרִית ("Hebrew") by Yonah Wallach, 1985.[3]

"Inscribed Are Your Letters"

Abraham Regelson was one of the prominent figures during the richest period of Hebrew literary creativity in America, 1914–48. His biography is characteristic of most of the Hebrew writers in America: born in Minsk in 1896, he immigrated with his family to New York in 1905 and was educated in American schools; he spent most of his life until 1948 in New York and finally settled in Israel in 1949, where he died in 1981. Regelson's poetics should be understood as the extreme poetic expression of the *Tarbut Ivrit* (Hebrew Culture) movement, which attempted to propagate a specific Hebrew national ideology in America during this period.[4] Always elitist and restricted to small cadres of dedicated, obsessed Hebraists, the *Tarbut Ivrit* and later the *Histadrut Ivrit* (The Hebrew Organization) insisted that Hebrew was the national language of the Jewish people and that without it, there could be no meaningful national existence for Jews anywhere. To achieve the profound Hebraization of the Jewish people, these Hebraists cultivated Hebrew language and literature and invested heroic efforts in education. Though the Tarbut Ivrit ideologues could claim some remarkable achievements before

3. (a) Abraham Regelson, חֲקוּקוֹת אוֹתִיּוֹתַיִךְ in *Hakukot otiyotayikh* (Tel Aviv, 1964) 7–26 (first published in *HaTekufah* [New York, 1946] vols. 30–31); (b) Dan Pagis, תַּרְגִּילִים בְּעִבְרִית שִׁמּוּשִׁית in *Shirim* (Jerusalem, 1991) 211–13 (first published in *Milim nirdafot* [Tel Aviv, 1982]); (c) Yonah Wallach, עִבְרִית in *Tat hakarah niftahat kemo menifah* (Tel Aviv, 1992) 180–82 (first published in *Tsurot* [Tel Aviv, 1985]).

4. For recent articles by Alan Mintz and Ezra Spicehandler on the *Tarbut Ivrit*, see *Hebrew in America* (ed. Alan Mintz; Detroit, 1993). Also see Benjamin Harshav's *Language in Time of Revolution* (Berkeley, 1993).

חֲקוּקוֹת אוֹתִיּוֹתַיִךְ

א.

חֲקוּקוֹת אוֹתִיּוֹתַיִךְ בְּתַבְנִית עוֹלָמִי, רְחִימָה בַּלְּשׁוֹנוֹת!
חַרְצָן בְּזַג, עִנְבָּל בְּזוֹג, רָזֵךְ רַחֲשְׁתִּי, הוֹ עִבְרִית,
מִכָּל תָּאֳרֵי תֵבֵל־שַׁדַּי וְאָפְנֵיהֶם:
אַתְּ בְּצֶדֶק וְכוֹכָב! אַתְּ בְּשַׁבְּתַי וּמַאֲדִים!
אַתְּ בְּאוֹר הַגַּלְגַּל, עוֹלֶה עַד אַרְיֵה, בְּטֶרֶם יָרֵחַ יָעֹז!
אַתְּ בְּיָרֵחַ קְצוּץ־לֶחִי, נוֹסֵעַ עַל פְּנֵי שׁוֹר, תְּאוֹמִים, עַקְרָב!
אַתְּ בַּנּוֹפְלִים סִרְטוּטֵי־אֵשׁ, יוֹצְאֵי נֵבֶל וְיוֹצְאֵי בְתוּלָה!
אַתְּ בְּכוֹכֶבֶת, יִפְעָה בוֹדֶדֶת,
מְבַשֶּׂרֶת תִּזְמוֹרֶת צִפֳּרִים וְחָזוּת זְרִיחָה;
אַתְּ בַּחַמָּה הַמְּלֵאָה, וּבַדְּשָׁאִים הָרְטֻבִּים,
מְשַׂגְשְׂגֵי בְּעִרְבּוּבְיָה וְאִישׁ־אִישׁ מֵהֶם אֶל חֻקַּת מִינֵהוּ חָרֵד:
פּוּאָה, אַבְרָשׁ וְיוֹעֶזֶר, כַּרְשִׁינָה וְאֶפְעוֹן,
וְשׁוֹכְנֵיהֶם מִן הַכְּנִמִּיּוֹת, הַנַּקָּרִים, הַחִפּוּשִׁיּוֹת,
מַטּוֹת הַחַרְגּוֹל וְעֶדְרֵי הַפַּרְפָּר,
וּבוֹלְשֵׁיהֶם הַשְּׂעִירִים, זַמְזָמֵי־צָהֳרַיִם,
זוֹ דְּבוֹרָה, עָבָה וְרָוָה, וְזוֹ צִרְעָה, צִמְרִיַּת פַּסִּים לְגֵו צָנוּם;
אַתְּ בְּשִׂיחִים וְאִילָנוֹת, אִם בְּדוּדֵי־כֵפִים וְאִם חֲבוּרֵי־יְעָרוֹת,
דַּפְנָה הֲרָרִית, צַפְצָפָה, מֵילָה אֲחוֹת־זַיִת,
תּוּת, אַמְזוֹג וּתְאַשּׁוּר, אַלּוֹן־שָׁנִי וְדֶבְדְּבָן שָׁחוֹר,
וִירָקֵי הַמַּחַט, אֹרֶן, תָּרְנִית וְאַשּׁוּחַ, צֶאֱצָאֵי אִצְטְרוֹבָל — —
בַּכֹּל אֲגַשְׁשֵׁךְ אוֹר מִתְגַּשֵּׁם,
בַּכֹּל אַשִּׂיגֵךְ שֵׂכֶל מִתְנוֹצֵץ.

ב.

כִּי מִיַּלְדוּתִי הִרְחַפְתִּנִי עַל פְּנֵי תֹהוּ־תְהוֹם,
אִתָּךְ לָצֶקֶת, לְהַקְפִּיא, לְהַדְשִׁיא, לְהַחֲיוֹת וּלְדוֹבֵב,
אִתָּךְ לִפְסוֹק "כִּי טוֹב" וְלִשְׁבּוֹת שַׁבַּת־יוֹצְרִים;
עַל יָדֵךְ נֶאֱרַשְׂתִּי בְּאַהֲבַת אָבוֹת,
עִם גַּפְנֵךְ יָרַדְתִּי מִצְרַיְמָה, וּמִמִּצְרַיִם הֵסַעְתִּי;
אִתָּךְ פָּסַלְתִּי בָּהָר לוּחוֹת אֱלֹהִים לִבְנֵי־אֱנוֹשׁ,
אִתָּךְ פַּעֲמַיִם נִטַּעְתִּי לְהוֹד, נִשְׂרַפְתִּי לְעִי, וְגֹרַשְׁתִּי לְקָלוֹן,
שָׁמֹר בִּנְזוּפַי לוּז־תּוֹרָה וְטַל־חָזוֹן לְחַיּוֹת מֵתֵי לַפְּקִידָה,
אִתָּךְ הֵהַנְתִּי גֶּשֶׁת וְתַקֵּן פְּגַם־אֱלֹהַּ,
הֶעֱדֵר שְׁלוֹם־מַלְכוּתוֹ מִבָּאֵי־אָרֶץ, —
וַתִּהְיִי לִי לְשׁוֹן בְּרִיאָה, לְשׁוֹן הִתְגַּלּוּת וּלְשׁוֹן קֵץ־הַיָּמִים.

ג.

כְּאוֹהֵב, מוֹנֶה שִׁבְחֵי גְבוּרָתוֹ, וּבִטּוּיוֹ קָצֵר מֵרִגְשׁוֹ,
כֵּן דַּחַף־לִי לֶאֱרוֹשׁ מַעֲלוֹתַיִךְ, וְאִם אֲמַסְכְּנֵךְ בִּתְהִלָּתִי.
הֵן הַבּוֹלְטוֹת וְהַשְׁלְדִיּוֹת בְּגֵוֵךְ אֲרַמֵּז,
וְאֶדֹּם מִן הַקִּמְטִיּוֹת וְהַבֵּין־פִּרְקִיּוֹת,
הַדָּם וְהַלֵּחַ וְהַמֵּחַ עַל תְּעָלוֹת־זְרִימוֹתֵיהֶם —
הַגַּע אֶצְבָּעַי אֶל פְּאוֹת דִּקְדּוּקַיִךְ,
וְאַתְּ הֲלֹא בִּפְסוּקַיִךְ פֵּשֶׁר־יָפְיֵךְ וּבְסִגְנוֹנוֹתַיִךְ שַׂעֲרוֹת־עֻזֵּךְ.
מַה־מָּה מִיִּקְרוֹת מִלּוֹתַיִךְ אֶלְקֹט, —
וּמִי יְשַׁחֵר סִתְרֵי תְמוּנַת אוֹתִיּוֹתַיִךְ, חִטּוּב־צַלְעוֹתֵיהֶן וְאָהֳלִיאָבוּת־חֲלוּלֵיהֶן,
וּמִי יָסֹּק אֶל גֹּבַהּ תְּנוּעוֹתַיִךְ, מַזָּלוֹת מַנְהִיגִים לָאוֹתִיּוֹת,
וְכַמַּזָּלוֹת בָּרָקִיעַ זָעֲרוּ לָעַיִן, גַּם כִּי עָצְמוּ בִּמְאֹד־מְאֹד?
וּמִי יִרְגֹּל עַד חֶבְיוֹן טְעָ508מַיִךְ,
וְהֵם נְשָׁמוֹת לַתְּנוּעוֹת, מַנְגִּינוֹת לַכּוֹכָבִים?

ד.

רָצִיתִי בִּנְיָנַיִךְ,
קַלֵּךְ הָעוֹשֶׂה בְּפַשְׁטוּת, לוֹקֶה בְחֶטְאוֹ וְקָם בְּצִדְקוֹ,
וְהוּא בָּן וְכוֹתֵב מַה פָּעַל אֵל;
נִפְעָלֵךְ הַנִּכְנָע לַסֵּבֶל, וְנִשְׁבָּר, וְנִשְׁאָר בֶּאֱמוּנָתוֹ, וְסוֹפוֹ — נוֹשַׁע;
פִּעֲלֵךְ הַמְחַזֵּק יָדַיִם, הַמְעַשֶּׂה לְמִצְווֹת וַחֲסָדִים,
יְסַקְּלֵךְ מִנְּגָפִים וִימַלְאֵךְ טוֹבִים;
פֻּעֲלֵךְ הַמְלֻמָּד, מְקֻטָּר וּמְעֻטָּר בְּיוֹם יְדֻבַּר בּוֹ, וּבִכְרָמָיו יְרֻנַּן וִירֹעָע;
הִפְעִילֵךְ הַמַּשְׂכִּיל וְהַמֵּיטִיב,
אֵין כָּמוֹהוּ מַנְעִיל יָחֵף וּמַלְבִּישׁ עֵרוֹם וּמַאֲכִיל רָעֵב,
וְהוּא מַרְנִין בְּגַנָּיו:
עָלָיו מוֹרִיקִים, נִצָּנָיו מַלְבִּינִים וּמַוְרִידִים, וּפֵרוֹתָיו מַאֲדִימִים;
הָפְעֲלֵךְ, מָשְׁזָר בַּמּוּחָשׁ וּבַמּוּכָח, וּבוֹ הַמֻּחְלָט יֻבַּע;
הִתְפַּעֲלֵךְ — מַה־מְּאֹד אֶשְׁתּוֹמֵם עָלָיו, כִּי רֶכֶב וְשֶׁכֶב בּוֹ הִתְאַחָדוּ,
בְּצוּרוֹ יִדַּבֵּק וְעוֹלָמִית לֹא יִטַּמֵּא, בֵּין תְּמִימִים יִתַּמָּם,
בּוֹ יִכּוֹנֵן מִקְדָּשׁ, וּבְמִקְרָאָיו, נְשָׁמָה,
הִזְדַּכְּכִי, הִסְתַּכְּלִי לְאַחֲרִיתֵךְ, הִצְטָעֲרִי עַל זְדוֹנוֹתַיִךְ וְהִשְׁתַּלְּמִי בִּזְכֻיּוֹת,
הֵן רַק פָּעֳלֵךְ תִּשְׂתַּכָּרִי.

the dissipation of the "movement" after the establishment of the State of Israel, it was, in retrospect, a valiant but misguided attempt to endow language and literature with all the emotional and intellectual passions of a total cultural life which, under normal circumstances, would include all aspects of human existence. The Hebraists in America could all speak Hebrew but had no viable Hebrew-speaking society in which they might live (except in Israel, where many settled between 1948 and 1951) and thus invested all the passions of their minds in the Hebrew language and its literature, which became for them a surrogate religion. The cultivation of Hebrew was a mitsvah, while mistakes in Hebrew were heinous sins. Their Hebrew was not shaped by a speech community but rather by prodigious reading in the immense literary resources of Hebrew literature of all periods. Their Hebrew style was inordinately rich and, at times, precious.

Regelson's חֲקוּקוֹת אוֹתִיּוֹתַיִךְ ("Inscribed Are Your Letters") is a formidable paean to the Hebrew language (he calls it a הִמְנוֹן, a hymn or paean) covering twenty pages, subdivided into twenty chapters. The verses are lengthy (about eighteen syllables) and unrhymed, Whitmanesque in their sweep. If a poem of such dimensions seems anachronistic to us today, it should be remembered that when Regelson wrote this הִמְנוֹן, the lengthy poem called the "poemah" was still normative in Hebrew poetry. As a paean to the Hebrew language, the poem is much more subtle than a simple recitation of the language's aesthetics or antiquity, qualities one would expect to find in such a paean. Regelson depicts a language that is identical with both the physical world and his own personality. The poet's very being is mediated through this language, which is also the linguistic medium through which he perceives reality.

The opening line summarizes what we will find in the entire poem: חֲקוּקוֹת אוֹתִיּוֹתַיִךְ בְּתַבְנִית עוֹלָמִי, רְחִימָה בַּלְּשׁוֹנוֹת! ('Inscribed are your letters in the pattern of my world, beloved among languages!'). The inscription of the Hebrew letters in the pattern of the poet's world is then the clarion opening to an elaborate personal mythology that embraces personality, world, and language. This mythology is intertextually related to that of the thirteenth-century Kabbalist, Abraham Abulafia, in whose contemplative mysticism the letters of the Hebrew alphabet play a crucial role.[5] Regelson, not a religious mystic but a secular Hebraist, clearly

5. The most comprehensive study of Abraham Abulafia's mystical philosophy is Moshe Idel's *Mystical Experience in Abraham Abulafia* (Albany, 1988). The mystical doctrine of the Hebrew letters is treated in detail, as is the doctrine of the Urim and Thummim. One of Regelson's contemporaries in New York, the Hebrew poet Moshe Feinstein, wrote a complete epic poem on Abulafia. Though fully published in 1956 as a separate volume, chapters appeared earlier. Gershom Scholem's pioneering lectures on the major trends in Jewish mysticism were delivered in New York in 1938 and published there in English in 1941. The publication contains a substantial chapter on Abulafia.

found elements of Abulafia's speculations useful for his poetry about the Hebrew language. By declaring that Hebrew is inscribed in a lengthy, rich catalog of natural phenomena—celestial bodies, plants, insects—all called by their specific names in an orgy of linguistic desire, the poet creates and governs the world of his own being through the very enunciation of the specific Hebrew names of objects. Were names in any other language inscribed in the pattern of the world, they would be meaningless to him. He elaborates on this mystical power of Hebrew words in his life in the second chapter, which ends with the sweeping assertion: וַתִּהְיִי לִי לְשׁוֹן בְּרִיאָה לְשׁוֹן הִתְגַּלּוּת וּלְשׁוֹן קֵץ־הַיָּמִים ('You are for me the language of creation, the language of revelation, the language of final redemption').

In the third chapter he extends his mythology even further by attempting to describe his beloved Hebrew as if she were a beloved woman. The description of the female body is an act of linguistic possession and certain limbs are compared to grammatical terms. The configuration of the Hebrew language, the poet's beloved, as a female body clearly echoes the Kabbalistic image of the world of Sefirot constructed as a human body (again the echoes of Abulafia are evident) and allows the poet to dedicate chapters four through fifteen to the mystical beauty of specific features of Hebrew grammar. Chapter four tells of his love for her varied moods, her *binyanim* (verbal meaning classes); in chapter five we learn of the subtlety of her tenses; in chapter six, of the wonders of the *gezarot* (verbal sound classes); in seven, of the *mishkalim* (noun classes); in eleven, the peculiarities of gendering objects; in fifteen, the absorption of Aramaic words or Greek phrases in common Hebrew usage. In each case, Regelson lavishes a prodigious wealth of Hebrew poetic description on aspects of language that one usually regards merely as items to be mastered in a language course. Turning these into objects of adoration and poetic ecstasy is not only a poetic tour de force; it is evidence of a veneration of Hebrew that transcends the ordinary.

Continuing the quasi-mystical adoration of Hebrew, Regelson opens chapter sixteen with a striking apostrophe to Hebrew: אוּרִים וְתֻמִּים אֲשֶׁר לָאֻמָּה! ('Urim and Thummim of the nation!'). The evocation of the mystical jewels on the breastplate of the high priest in the temple in association with the Hebrew language is doubtless taken from Abulafia, who regarded the letters as manifestations of the Urim and Thummim. The difference, though, is significant: for Abulafia, the letters, like the Urim and Thummim, are devices for mystical contemplation, while for Regelson the letters are manifestations of the genius of the Jewish people, since the great texts of the Jews were written in Hebrew. This insight inspires him to survey the function of Hebrew from antiquity through the Zionist revitalization of the language.

The historical sweep provides the bridge to the next chapter, which deals with exile, a dark period that allowed, nevertheless, an enrichment of culture and a revitalization of language. The evocation of exile prompts a digressive lament for the children who have been burned and will never be privileged to learn Hebrew. The language itself has thus lost the great potential writers of the future who would have continued to add to her literary treaures. One assumes that this chapter, probably written in 1943–45 like the rest of the poem, refers to the slaughter of European Jewry. The composition of this paean to the language is therefore an affirmation of historical continuity and creativity despite the terrible losses of the period.

As he approaches the end of this vast paean, Regelson raises two questions couched in biblical language: first, who should be privileged to ascend the glorious mountains of the Hebrew language (an echo of Psalms)? Second, what are the cardinal sins against the language (from the opening chapter of Amos)? The faithful Hebraist should have three virtues (chapter eighteen): first, he should be morally sensitive to all people; second, he should be faithful to the Jewish people and their aspirations; third, he should continually study and thus master the classical Hebrew texts of all periods. The three cardinal sins (chapter nineteen) are not the opposite of the lofty ideals of the three virtues but seem to refer to specific contemporary persons: (1) those who write false memorials for the sake of money; (2) those who reject linguistic innovation; (3) those who would restrict the Hebrew language to refined, elegant subjects only. In the last two Regelson seems to be answering his critics, since he was fond of creating new words.

A rancorous, even bitter tone permeates the last chapter, which is a veiled confession. The poet declares again his devotion to the Hebrew language but complains that his own people have chained him like a galley slave, and he has not the strength to recount "the deeds of the Lord" in Hebrew. He confesses the sin of his double exile: of the Jew from his land and the narrator from his story. He prays for a return to the land where Hebrew is spoken and he can return to his creativity, to work alongside a long list of laborers who labor—naturally—in Hebrew. In the act of Hebrew labor אֱלֹהַּ מִתְגַּלֵּם־מִתְגַּלֶּה וְעוֹלָם מִתְעַלֶּה־מִתְאַלֵּהַּ ('God incarnates-disappears and the world transcends and becomes divine').

The complicated play of words in this poetic closure is no less important than the quasi-messianic wish expressed; for the prodigious play with the Hebrew language is the concrete proof of the poet's creative power and the capacity of this specific language to inscribe itself compellingly in the universe. The argument that lends structure and coherence to this sprawling hymn is by no means as impressive as the dazzling richness of the language with its enormous lexical range, its grammatical flexibility, its subtle echoes of texts of all periods and genres. If the language of poetry may be defined as language that calls attention to itself, that is, it is not merely a mode of communicating ideas or sentiments, Regelson's Hebrew in חֲקוּקוֹת אוֹתִיּוֹתַיִךְ calls attention to itself, not only as poetic language, but as Hebrew poetic language. The Hebraic aspects of the language are constantly paraded before the reader both in the ideas conveyed in the individual chapters and in the linguistic signals the reader receives. As such, this poem is the quintessential product of the ideology of Tarbut Ivrit; it embodies its heroic attempts to create a new world by an act of both will and intellect but succeeds in restricting entrance to that world to very few readers.

"Exercises in Daily Hebrew"

If Regelson's חֲקוּקוֹת אוֹתִיּוֹתַיִךְ is a comprehensive hymn to the Hebrew language presented in detail as the linguistic embodiment of the poet's personality, Dan Pagis's תַּרְגִּילִים בְּעִבְרִית שִׁמּוּשִׁית ("Exercises in Daily [lit. practical] Hebrew") is a sardonic critique of the debasement of the Hebrew language, and by extension of all language, by politics and politicians. The poem, minimalistic in style, parodies a set of lessons in the Hebrew language, and since the teaching of the Hebrew language has been a major project of acculturation conducted by the Israeli government since 1948, the poem is also a critique of certain aspects of Israeli life. The voice we hear is that of the teacher speaking to the students in his language class and indirectly to us, the readers. Both the opening and closure of the poem are marked by the phrase שָׁלוֹם שָׁלוֹם, a truncated echo of the phrase in Jer 6:14 and 8:11: שָׁלוֹם שָׁלוֹם וְאֵין שָׁלוֹם ('Peace, peace, when there is no peace!'). This phrase binds together all the themes of the poem: the seemingly innocent greeting of the teacher to the class of Hebrew language students is ironized as we progress in the poem and begin to realize that we are reading a bitter lament on the murderous wars that beset Israel and the attendant contamination of the Hebrew language. Since the poem was composed in 1982, it was most likely occasioned by the Lebanese War, which had been given the grotesquely ironic (to Pagis) code name שְׁלוֹם הַגָּלִיל ('The Galilee Peace').

The motto of the poem encapsulates the theme, tone, and method of the poem. We read: הֲשָׁלוֹם לָךְ? הֲרָצַחְתָּ וְגַם יָרָשְׁתָּ? ('How are you [Are you at peace]? Have you killed and also later possessed?') While the main phrase referring to murder and expropriation is obviously taken literally from the encounter of Elijah and Ahab in 1 Kgs 21:19, the salutation ?הֲשָׁלוֹם לָךְ echoes many biblical and postbiblical passages. The juxtaposition of the two phrases is surely ironic, since the salutation does not comport with the accusatory tone of the main statement. The explanation for the bizarre juxtaposition is found in the parentheses that follow, where we are informed that the interrogative statements in the motto are an "example of interrogative sentences in a grammar book." The motto thus comprises a poignant commentary on the contradiction between the acquisition of language, hence of culture, and murder and expropriation of property. That all these acts may be combined indiscriminately by the same formal marker, the interrogative enclitic הֲ, suggests the formal moral neutrality of linguistic statements, a notion that clearly disturbs the poet. Each of the eleven enumerated stanzas of the poem develops this basic notion by teaching, as it were, a point of Hebrew grammar; conversely, in each stanza, each statement, however neutral on first reading, assumes added connotations because of its contextualization in this poem. This phenomenon, familiar to any sensitive reader of poetry, is also one of the linguistic lessons of the poem.

This semantic dynamic of poetic language is featured in the very first stanza of the poem, where we encounter one of the standard statements found in all Hebrew grammar books: "In Hebrew there is a past and future tense, but no present, only a present participle (medial)."[6] Here, the absence of the present tense suggests the dependence of the present upon past experiences and future aspirations. The poem, rendered in a minimalistic style, does not elaborate on this point, which becomes increasingly crucial as we progress into the poem. In this stanza, we are rushed on to confront a new linguistic item: the מִשְׁפָּט, which means of course 'the sentence', but can also imply 'justice or judgment'. This second meaning is corroborated by the examples of sentences presented in the second stanza: אֶרֶץ אוֹכֶלֶת יוֹשְׁבֶיהָ ('a land [which] devours its inhabitants'); אוֹהֲבֶיהָ אוֹכְלִים אֶת אוֹהֲבֶיהָ ('those who love her devour those who love her').[7] The two examples of basic sentences/judgments, the building blocks to rational, civilized discourse, are statements of violence, both natural and human. The violence exists not only in the

6. שָׁלוֹם, שָׁלוֹם. בְּעִבְרִית יֵשׁ עָבָר וְעָתִיד,
אֲבָל אֵין הוֹוֶה, רַק בֵּינוֹנִי.
עַכְשָׁו נַעֲבֹר לַמִּשְׁפָּט.

7. אֶרֶץ אוֹכֶלֶת יוֹשְׁבֶיהָ.
אוֹהֲבֶיהָ אוֹכְלִים אֶת אוֹהֲבֶיהָ.
הֲפֹךְ אֶת הַכֹּל לְעָתִיד.

present participle, but also in the future even though disguised as a grammatical exercise by the putative teacher of the grammar lesson we are taking: הֲפֹךְ אֶת הַכֹּל לְעָתִיד ('Convert all to the future tense').

The stark critique of the first two stanzas is modulated in the next three: three, four, and five. In stanza three an explanation of modes, declarative, imperative, and interrogative, utilizes morally neutral clichés as examples.[8] The demonstration of independent versus dependent clauses in the fourth stanza uses a classic example of a dilemma that implies the moral quandary of the poet: אוֹי לִי אִם אֹמַר, אוֹי לִי אִם לֹא אֹמַר ('Woe is me if I speak, woe is me if I don't speak').[9] The list of greetings and polite statements in stanza five ends subtly with a dissonant, brief dialogue conveying the impersonality and rudeness of bureacratic life: the narrator who asks, "Is this the place?" is told, "Come back tomorrow." While the obvious violence of the first two stanzas is softened in this cluster of three stanzas, the nexus between language acquisition and culture—or lack thereof—is still pervasive.

The potential decline of civilization is presented in stanzas six, seven, and eight: six is ostensibly a "short composition"; seven is a "conversation drill"; eight is "an exercise in precise diction." The locale of the action in all three is a cemetery, perhaps a military cemetery in Israel where the student of language (and life) went for a walk with his class. Here, too, the minimalist poetics are used to great effect; again ostensibly neutral statements explode with meaning. The student, for instance, asks someone, apparently in the cemetery, "Where did we err (in our walk)?" The question's broader meaning is: Where did we err on our life's path so that it has ended in a cemetery where the child (of the next stanza) needs help in finding his father's grave? The poet's analysis of the loss of life in the cemetery is captured in the exercises (stanza eight) in which the student is instructed to be precise in his diction. He should not use לְחִנָּם ('for nothing') where the context calls for לַשָּׁוְא ('in vain'); the first derives from the world of exchange, meaning that you have received something for nothing, while the dead have already paid with their lives and have actually died לַשָּׁוְא.

This demand for subtley and propriety in the distinction between the meanings of words is the poet's moral stance, the moral responsibility, in effect, of all poetry. This moral obligation is demonstrated in

8. אֲרָצוֹת זָבוֹת חָלָב וּדְבָשׁ. זֶה חִוּוּי.
אִם תִּרְאֶה אוֹתָם, מְסֹר לָהֶם דַּ"שׁ, זֶה צִוּוּי.
וְעַכְשָׁו מִשְׁפַּט שְׁאֵלָה: מָה חָדָשׁ?

9. אוֹי לִי אִם אֹמַר, אוֹי לִי אִם לֹא אֹמַר.
אֱמֹר מַה כָּאן מִשְׁפָּט עִקָּרִי וּמַה טָפֵל שֶׁל תְּנַאי.

the parade of twenty-four Hebrew synonyms expressing moral outrage and disgust in stanza nine. We should not forget that the Hebrew term for 'synonyms' שֵׁמוֹת נִרְדָּפִים is also the name given to the entire volume in which this specific poem is found. Here too the possibility of a second meaning is offered, since the term שֵׁמוֹת נִרְדָּפִים, taken literally, could mean 'words that are persecuted', a remote possibility, to be sure, but one suggested by the semantic range of the list of synonyms selected as examples. Clearly the problem of synonyms, and more broadly of semantics, is a central obsession of Pagis in this period and for that matter throughout his career.

Following the format of grammar books, Pagis has planted several instructions for language exercises in this poem. We have seen one in stanza two, "Convert all verbs to the future tense," and another one in stanza eight, "Be precise in your language." In stanza ten the student is instructed, עַטֵּר לְשׁוֹנְךָ בְּנִיבִים ('Adorn your language with aphorisms'), a somewhat amusing instruction coming from Pagis, who investigated the use of aphorisms and formal epithets in Medieval Hebrew poetry. All the aphorisms suggested, however, imply a degree of aggressiveness and hostility, beginning with אַל תְּהִי מָתוֹק פֶּן יִבְלָעוּךָ ('Don't be sweet lest they swallow you up') and ending with the motto of the poem, already discussed above, הֲשָׁלוֹם לְךָ? הֲרָצַחְתָּ וְגַם יָרָשְׁתָּ?. The final stanza gives the student a final "little exercise as a conclusion": הַבְחֵן יָפֶה בַּהֶבְדֵּל בֵּין שְׁתֵּי הַמִּלִּים: שָׁלוֹם שָׁלוֹם ('Distinguish clearly between two words: Shalom, shalom'). The two words the student and the reader are asked to distinguish clearly are, ironically, identical. Ordinarily, the student is told that the word *shalom* means 'peace' and by extension 'peace be with you' or 'Hello/Goodbye'. Given the overall meaning of the poem and the identity of the poem, it should be obvious that we are asked to distinguish not between the primary and secondary or extended meaning, but between the true meaning of the word 'peace' and a false meaning of the word. The "Exercise in Daily Hebrew" is then a declaration of what is truly useful in language in the eyes of the poet: the preservation of clear distinctions about the true meanings of words and their relation to reality.

"Hebrew"

Yonah Wallach's poem עִבְרִית ("Hebrew") was written only a few years after Pagis's תַּרְגִּילִים בְּעִבְרִית שִׁמּוּשִׁית, yet in theme and tone it manifests a different world of poetics. This difference may be due to the specific generations, origins, and genders of the poets. Pagis, born in Bukovina in 1930, learned Hebrew after World War II in transit camps and in a kibbutz; Wallach, born in 1946, was reared in Israel with a fairly typical Israeli education. Pagis was a professor of Medieval Hebrew Literature at the Hebrew University, while Wallach was closely associated with the pop culture of the period. Finally, Pagis was obviously a man and Wallach was a woman. (Both poets died of cancer: Wallach in 1985 and Pagis in 1986.) The gender difference is crucial for our understanding of this poem, which exploits the inherent gendered nature of the Hebrew language to explore a variety of sentiments generated by gender differences. Wallach also makes greater use of daily speech idioms and rhythms than does Pagis; she is far less concerned with maintaining consecutive discourse than is Pagis and thus often pushes the borders of coherence beyond the limits of ready comprehension. One does not expect a Wallach poem to proceed by traditional logical steps, one idea or image linked coherently to the next. The poem is more likely to be comprised of a rush of pithy statements, driven by associations not always clear to the reader. Metaphors and allusions are often willfully hermetic and playful. The poem עִבְרִית, for instance, is a digressive monologue that runs on for 79 verses without any formal breaks or structures. The ensemble of verses, at times internally self-contradictory, yields nonetheless a poetic statement moving in its emotional intensity and complexity—even when it is not entirely comprehensible.

The complexity of this poem stems not only from Wallach's poetic style, but even more from her adventurous, often rapturous, exploration of three parallel and frequently confused notions of gender and/or sexuality: there is the basic biological gender distinction, male and female, ordained by nature; there is the constructed gender system embedded in language, more richly so in Hebrew than in English; and there are the constructed gender relations one finds in society, the product of historical experience. Wallach shifts freely and playfully from one level to the next and thus spins a loose web of meanings and sentiments engendered by the aspects of gender felt in the Hebrew language experience. I am aware that in my attempt to give coherence to the poem, to perform the critic's task, I must expect only partial success and in a sense must do violence to the poetics of this poem.

Not specifically mentioned in the poem, but integral to it, is the fact that Hebrew, though more "gendered" than English (as referred to in the opening of the poem), does not distinguish as English does between the grammatical terms masculine / feminine and the biological terms male / female. In Hebrew זָכָר means both 'masculine' and 'male' while נְקֵבָה means both 'feminine' and 'female'. The word מִין means both 'gender' and 'sex' or, for that matter, 'kind'. Furthermore, the word עִבְרִית, the Hebrew language, is obviously feminine and allows easy

עברית

בִּשְׁמוֹת מִין יֵשׁ לְאַנְגְּלִית כָּל הָאֶפְשָׁרֻיּוֹת
כָּל אֲנִי — בְּפֹעַל
הוּא כָּל אֶפְשָׁרוּת בְּמִין
וְכָל אַתְּ הִיא אַתָּה
וְכָל אֲנִי הוּא בְּלִי מִין
וְאֵין הֶבְדֵּל בֵּין אַתְּ וְאַתָּה
וְכָל הַדְּבָרִים הֵם זֶה — לֹא אִישׁ לֹא אִשָּׁה
לֹא צָרִיךְ לַחְשֹׁב לִפְנֵי שֶׁמִּתְיַחֲסִים לְמִין
עִבְרִית הִיא סֶקְסְמַנְיַאקִית
עִבְרִית מַפְלָה לְרָעָה אוֹ לְטוֹבָה
מְפַרְגֶּנֶת נוֹתֶנֶת פְּרִיבִילֶגְיוֹת
עִם חֶשְׁבּוֹן אָרֹךְ מֵהַגָּלוּת
בְּרַבִּים יֵשׁ זְכוּת קְדִימָה לָהֶם
עִם הַרְבֵּה דַּקּוּת וְסוֹד כָּמוּס
בְּיָחִיד הַסִּכּוּיִים שָׁוִים
מִי אוֹמֵר שֶׁכָּלוּ כָּל הַקִּצִּים
עִבְרִית הִיא סֶקְסְמַנְיַאקִית
רוֹצָה לָדַעַת מִי מְדַבֵּר
כִּמְעַט מַרְאֶה כִּמְעַט תְּמוּנָה
מַה שֶּׁאָסוּר בְּכָל הַתּוֹרָה
לְפָחוֹת לִרְאוֹת אֶת הַמִּין
הָעִבְרִית מְצִיצָה מִבַּעַד לְחוֹר הַמַּנְעוּל
כָּמוֹנִי לְאִמָּא שֶׁלָּךְ וְלָךְ
כְּשֶׁהֱיִיתֶן מִתְרַחֲצוֹת אָז בַּצְּרִיף
לְאִמֵּךְ הָיָה תַּחַת גָּדוֹל
אֲבָל אַף פַּעַם לֹא הִפְסַקְתִּי לַחְשֹׁב
הַיָּמִים עָבְרוּ כַּחֲלֹף הַטּוּשִׁים
נִשְׁאַרְתְּ יַלְדָּה רָזָה וּמְסֻבֶּנֶת
אַחַר כָּךְ סְתַמְתֶּן אֶת כָּל הַחוֹרִים
סְתַמְתֶּן אֶת כָּל הַפִּרְצוֹת
הָעִבְרִית מְצִיצָה לָךְ מֵחוֹר הַמַּנְעוּל
הַשָּׂפָה רוֹאָה אוֹתָךְ עֵירֻמָּה
אָבִי לֹא הִרְשָׁה לִי לִרְאוֹת
הוּא סוֹבֵב אֶת גַּבּוֹ כְּשֶׁהִשְׁתִּין
אַף פַּעַם לֹא רָאִיתִי אוֹתוֹ טוּשׁ מַמָּשׁ
תָּמִיד הוּא הֶחְבִּיא אֶת הַמִּין

כְּמוֹ שֶׁרַבִּים מַחְבִּיא אִשָּׁה
כְּמוֹ שֶׁקָּהָל הוּא זָכָר בְּגוּפִים
כְּמוֹ שֶׁמִּלָּה הִיא זָכָר וּנְקֵבָה
אֵין כְּמוֹ אֵלּוּ דְּבָרִים מְתוּקִים
הָעִבְרִית הִיא אִשָּׁה מִתְרַחֶצֶת
הָעִבְרִית הִיא בַּת־שֶׁבַע נְקִיָּה
הָעִבְרִית הִיא פֶּסֶל שֶׁלֹּא פּוֹסֵל
יֵשׁ לָהּ נְקֻדּוֹת חֵן קְטַנּוֹת וְסִימָנֵי לֵדָה
כְּכֹל שֶׁהִיא מִתְבַּגֶּרֶת הִיא יוֹתֵר יָפָה
הַשִּׁפּוּט שֶׁלָּהּ הוּא פְּרֶהִיסְטוֹרִי לִפְעָמִים
נוֹיְרוֹזָה כָּזֹאת הִיא לְטוֹבָה
תַּגִּיד לִי בְּזָכָר תַּגִּיד לִי בִּנְקֵבָה
כָּל אֲנִי יַלְדוּתִי בֵּיצִית בְּטֶרֶם הַפְרָיָה
עַל מִין אֶפְשָׁר לִפְסֹחַ
עַל מִין אֶפְשָׁר לְוַתֵּר
מִי יַגִּיד מִינוֹ שֶׁל אֶפְרוֹחַ?
הָאִישׁ שֶׁהַטֶּבַע יוֹצֵר
לִפְנֵי שֶׁהָטְבַּע בּוֹ פֹּעַל מֻטֶּה.
זִכָּרוֹן הוּא זָכָר
יוֹצֵר מִינִים
תּוֹלָדָה הָעִקָּר
כִּי הִיא הַחַיִּים
עִבְרִית הִיא סֶקְסְמַנְיַאקִית
וּמַה שֶּׁתַּגֵּדְנָה בִּטְרוּנְיָה פֶמִינִיסְטִיּוֹת
הַמְחַפְּשׂוֹת גֵּרוּיִים מִחוּץ לַשָּׂפָה
בְּאִינְטוֹנַצְיָה הַנּוֹתֶנֶת פֵּרוּשׁ לַדְּבָרִים
סִימָנִים רַק שֶׁל זָכָר וּנְקֵבָה בְּמִשְׁפָּט
יִתְּנוּ יְחָסִים מִינִיִּים מְשֻׁנִּים
עַל כָּל נְקֵבָה סִימָן, עַל זָכָר סִימָן אַחֵר
כְּשֶׁגַּם כָּל פֹּעַל וּבִנְיָן מְסֻמָּנִים
מָה עוֹשֶׂה הָאִישׁ לָאִשָּׁה
מַה הוּא מְקַבֵּל בִּתְמוּרָה
אֵיזֶה כֹּחַ הִיא מַפְעִילָה עָלָיו
וְאֵיזֶה סִימָן נִתַּן לָעֶצֶם
וּלְשֵׁם עֶצֶם מֻפְשָׁט וְלַמִּלִּיּוֹת
נְקַבֵּל מִין מִשְׂחַק טֶבַע
הִתְרַחֲשׁוּת נַפְשִׁית כְּיַעַר צָעִיר
מִשְׂחָק שֶׁל כֹּחוֹת טֶבַע כְּלָלִיִּים

שֶׁמֵּהֶם נִגְזָרִים כָּל הַפְּרָטִים
סִימָנִים כְּלָלִיִּים לִכְלַל הָאֵרוּעִים
שֶׁאֶפְשָׁרִי שֶׁיִּקְרוּ בִּזְמַן מִן הַזְּמַנִּים
תִּרְאֶה אֵיזֶה גּוּף יֵשׁ לַשָּׂפָה וּמִדּוֹת
אֹהַב אוֹתָהּ עַכְשָׁו בְּלִי כְּסוּת לָשׁוֹן

identification of the poetess, Yonah Wallach, with the language that is the medium of her expression. The tension created by this merging of meanings and the persistent gendering of nouns, verbs, and modifiers energizes much of the associative flow and wordplay in the poem. We notice, for example, that this long poem is loosely organized around three occurrences of one striking, comic verse, actually the motto of the poem: עִבְרִית הִיא סֶקְסְמַנְיַאקִית ('Hebrew is a [fem.] sex-maniac').

This verse appears for the first time after the initial 8 lines of the poem, in which we learn that English (unlike Hebrew) pays scant attention to gender: in English, nouns for instance are usually neuter; the pronouns *I* and *you* have no specific gender; things normally have no sex. Consequently, in English, one does not have to think about gender/sex, but "Hebrew is a sex-maniac" since it is obsessed with gender/sex and draws distinctions that are often judgmental (that is, masculine/male is privileged over feminine/female particularly in the plural) and are based on long linguistic traditions. Like Pagis, Wallach expands grammar rules to comprise general statements about society. In line 13, for instance, she declares that "in the plural, the masculine takes precedence" (i.e., a group of individual nouns in both masculine and feminine will take a masculine verb or modifier in the plural), while in the singular "the prospects are equal," since the gender of the noun in the singular is always reflected in the accompanying verb or modifier. These grammatical observations are the first intimations in the poem of a feminist position, which becomes the focal point of the last 20 lines (60–79).

The motto line serves as a loose link between the passages of the poem. The first occurrence (line 9) links the first passage (lines 1–8), on the genderless qualities of English, and the second passage, on the gendered aspects of Hebrew (lines 10–16). The second occurrence (line 17) introduces a lengthy passage that shifts subtly from theme to theme for some 40 lines. We begin with a statement that Hebrew רוֹצָה לָדַעַת מִי מְדַבֵּר ('wants to know who is speaking'), because of its constant obsession with gender, and thus, by association Hebrew is impiously concrete, sexually frank, and even a voyeur looking through a keyhole. This is an idea that elicits an 8-line digression in which the poetess refers to her own peeking at the feminine reader and the reader's mother through a keyhole when the two of them used to bathe. And while one may plug a real keyhole so that no one can see through it, we learn in lines 31–32:

הָעִבְרִית מְצִיצָה לָךְ מֵחוֹר הַמַּנְעוּל
הַשָּׂפָה רוֹאָה אוֹתָךְ עֵירֻמָּה

Hebrew peeps at you from the keyhole
the language sees you [fem.] naked.

Childhood memories are evoked again as the poetess describes her father turning away from her so that she could not see his sex when he urinated, כְּמוֹ שֶׁרַבִּים מַחְבִּיא אִשָּׁה ('just as the plural [in Hebrew] hides the female'). Hebrew is then considered: a woman bathing; Bath-Sheba clean; a statue that doesn't sculpt (or forbid). Developing the female personification, Wallach declares that she (Hebrew) becomes more beautiful as she matures and that her judgment is "prehistoric," as manifested in the sharp distinctions she draws between masculine and feminine, though the first person was a man before he was grammatically modified—another hermetic, playful insight. This historical excursus concludes with a striking quatrain (55–58), the most rhythmically coherent passage of the entire poem:

זִכָּרוֹן הוּא זָכָר
יוֹצֵר מִינִים
תּוֹלָדָה הָעִקָּר
כִּי הִיא הַחַיִּים

Memory is masculine
creating genders (sexes)
generation (history) is the cardinal principle
for she is life.

At this point we encounter for the third time the linking motto verse, עִבְרִית הִיא סֶקְסְמַנְיַאקִית, which can again refer either backwards or forwards in the development of the poem. Reading forward from this last appearance of the motto, one encounters the most challenging section of the poem, twenty often brilliant verses, each more or less coherent, but some maintaining the most tenuous links to the surrounding verses. The femininity of Hebrew, its powerful sexuality, conjures up a "feminist" argument that is not fully articulated and seems to be rejected by the poetess. Hence the difficulty of the final portion of the poem. "The feminists," with whom Wallach obviously disagrees, argue against the invidious gender distinction in society (the third level of gender distinctions we have mentioned above) and attribute it to the gender differences embedded in the Hebrew language. Wallach seems to counter that gender differences in language are only internal linguistic signs and if the signs for masculine and feminine in language were taken literally, they would produce in life "strange sexual relations." She would rather regard this linguistic gender differentiation as the potential play of the forces of nature as represented in language. From this play of natural forces, all details and signs are determined and will shape the totality of all possible events in the future. This revelation inspires the poet to declare that she would love the Hebrew language now because of its body and features, visible without the cover of linguistic differentiation.

* * * * * * * *

While these three poems are not fully representative of the range of twentieth-century Hebrew poetry (there are, for instance, no poems of Alterman or Amichai here), one may investigate a variety of interesting poetic aspects by comparing them with one another. At present I shall restrict my considerations to the nature of poetic language employed.

The level of poetic language varies radically from poem to poem and is eloquent evidence of what Regelson hails: the expressive capacities of Hebrew over the past fifty years. Regelson's own poetic style is blatantly literary, lexically rich, even precious, rife with rare words and his own neologisms. In its literariness, it evokes Hebrew texts of all periods and addresses the literate Hebraist; the lexical difficulties of this poetic language are daunting and comprise a serious challenge for the average Hebrew reader today. By privileging the historical literary text, it slights language generated by any coherent speech community, specifically the one crystallizing in Israel during his career.

Wallach's poetic diction stands at the other end of the spectrum: though the Hebrew is always correct, the syntax and lexical range clearly derives from conversation (she even composed lyrics for a rock band), albeit conversation at such a sophisticated level that many lines become poignantly aphoristic. Her phrases are often clusters of words—three, four, or five—held together by a kernel idea or emotion, which seems to well up suddenly from the unconscious. In עִבְרִית, for instance, each cluster is a verse, but the sequence between verses is not always evident.

The lexical range is by no means as wide as that of Regelson, but the combination of pithy, even fragmentary phrases dealing with the most intimate topics creates an emotional and even intellectual effect that is immediate and profound.

Pagis's poetic language is a remarkable fusion of the literary and the conversational, particularly in his poem תַּרְגִּילִים בְּעִבְרִית שִׁמּוּשִׁית, a parody of a Hebrew language lesson. The poem is a deftly wrought mélange of very simple statements or commands and instances of high literary sophistication, such as veiled references to known literary texts or seemingly simple statements with powerful, secondary meanings. Pagis's diction is ordinarily more complex and extensive than in this poem, but even in this one the reader is always aware that he or she is listening to a poetic voice in full command of both literary Hebrew and the nuances of speech diction. The self-consciousness of the use of Hebrew in a Pagis poem is often so acute that the workings of the self-consciousness become a prominent feature in the poem.

Pagis's poem, then, is emblematic of much of Hebrew poetry of the past 100 years: immensely literate, but increasingly exploiting speech rhythms, fully conscious of the rapid development of the language and the consequent demands to balance the literate with the conversational, history with the potential audiences of future generations. Though his immediate subject in תַּרְגִּילִים בְּעִבְרִית שִׁמּוּשִׁית is the debasement of language by politicians in a time of war, the more enduring theme is the dignity and probity of the Hebrew language, based on its past achievements and future aspirations. In this sense too, "in Hebrew there is a past and a future, but no present tense, only a medial participle."

The Neo-Babylonian *tamkārū*

M. A. DANDAMAYEV

This paper is an analysis of Neo-Babylonian documents published over the last twenty years that concern the tamkārū 'merchants'. While during the third and second millennia B.C.E. *the Mesopotamian tamkārū were professional merchants who acted as agents of the palace or temple, a considerable change occurred in their role during the first millennium* B.C.E. *Although some were still employed by the palace and temple, they were now generally independent merchants engaged in domestic and international commerce, operating with their own resources and at their own risk. However, alongside the tamkārū, numerous business firms, such as the famous Egibi and Murašû houses, flourished during the period under consideration. This strong competition substantially decreased the role of the professional merchants.*

More than twenty years ago I discussed some thirty Neo-Babylonian documents containing information about professional merchants (*tamkāru*, pl. *tamkārū*).[1] The aim of this paper is to consider the operations of *tamkārū* as reflected in first-millennium B.C.E. Babylonian texts published since that paper appeared in 1971.

Author's note: Abbreviations used in this article are as follows:

Camb. J. N. Strassmaier, *Inschriften von Cambyses, König von Babylon* (Leipzig, 1890)
Dar. J. N. Strassmaier, *Inschriften von Darius, König von Babylon* (Leipzig, 1897)
Lab. B. T. A. Evetts, *Inscriptions of the Reigns of Evil-Merodach (B.C. 562–559), Neriglissar (B.C. 559–555) and Laborosoarchod (B.C. 555)* (Leipzig, 1892)
Nbk. J. N. Strassmaier, *Inschriften von Nabuchodonosor, König von Babylon* (Leipzig, 1889)
Nbn. J. N. Strassmaier, *Inschriften von Nabonidus, König von Babylon* (Leipzig, 1889)
TMH *Texte und Materialien der Frau Professor Hilprecht Collection of Babylonian Antiquities im Eigentum der Universität Jena* (Leipzig)
VS *Vorderasiatische Schriftdenkmäler der Königlichen Museen zu Berlin* (Leipzig)

1. See M. A. Dandamayev, "Die Rolle des *tamkārum* in Babylonien im 2. und 1. Jahrtausend v.u.Z.," in *Beiträge zur sozialen Structur des alten Vorderasien* (ed. H. Klengel; Schriften zur Geschichte und Kultur des Alten Orients 1; Berlin, 1971) 69–78.

Royal Merchants

A certain Sin-aḫa-iddin, son of Iniṭaja, is referred to as a merchant in several documents, drafted in Sippar under Nebuchadnezzar II and Nabonidus. These texts are as follows (for transliterations see Appendix).

Four talents 20 minas of wool are sold for 1 mina of silver (to) Sin-aḫa-iddin and Nabû-zera-ukin, the merchant(s?). Silver is paid to the *qīpu*-official. Ten minas of wool are issued to Marduk-eresh the carpenter. The 16th day of the month Arahsamna, the 36th year of Nebuchadnezzar, king of Babylon (CT 55, 763).

Kalbaia, son of Shamash-eresh, owes [. . . *kur*] 1 *pān* 1 *sūtu* of barley to Shamash-iqisha, son of Shamash-aḫa-iddin. He will deliver the barley in its principal sum in the month Ajaru. The barley is for a business enterprise of Sin-aḫa-iddin, son of Iniṭaja, the royal merchant.[2] Witnesses (names of two persons) and scribe (name). The 4th day of the [month . . .], the 5th year of [Nabo]nidus, king of Babylon (CT 55, 173).

Bel-eriba, son of Inṣarahesh [. . .] and (a woman named) Ummajan [. . .] owe 5 *kur* of barley to Shamash-iqisha, son of Shamash-aḫa-iddin [and] Sin-aḫa-iddin, son of Iniṭaja, the royal merchant. They must pay the barley in full in the month Ajaru at the gate of the storehouse [. . .]. They will stand as guarantors for each other. Witnesses (names of two persons) and scribe (name). [Sippar?]. The 10th day of the month Arahsamna, the 12th year of Nabonidus. Each [has received] one [copy of the document] (CT 55, 96).

These documents, drafted in the 36th regnal year of Nebuchadnezzar II (569 B.C.E.) and the 5th and 12th years of Nabonidus (551 and 544 B.C.E.), all refer to Sin-aḫa-iddin, son of Iniṭaja. In the earliest of the three (CT 55, 763), he and Nabû-zera-ukin are designated as *tamkārū*. Because the title stands in the singular, however, it may refer to Nabû-zera-ukin only. In any case, Sin-aḫa-iddin was apparently not yet in royal service.

All three documents come from the archives of the Ebabbar Temple in Sippar. According to CT 55, 763, in 569 the temple sold 130 kilograms of wool to Sin-aḫa-iddin and his partner for 500 grams of silver. In CT 55, 173, Sin-aḫa-iddin is referred to as a 'royal merchant'. As seen from the text, Kalbaia took a loan in barley in order to participate in a business enterprise of Sin-aḫa-iddin. Finally, in CT 55, 96, the royal merchant Sin-aḫa-iddin and his business partner Shamash-iqisha issued a loan of 900 liters of barley to two private persons.

2. Line 9: LÚ DAM-GÀR LUGAL.

Now a certain Shamash-eriba and Sin-aḫa-iddin (without patronymic) are mentioned in VS VI, 287, as having paid 145 *kur* of dates, equivalent to 2 minas 25 (?) shekels of silver, to their contracting party for 75 sheep. The document is not dated, and nothing is known of its provenance. But Sin-aḫa-iddin's activity in this text is typical of a *tamkāru*, and he was probably identical with Sin-aḫa-iddin son of Iniṭaja. As seen from this document, 1 *kur* (180 liters) of barley cost approximately 1 shekel of silver, and 1 sheep cost about 2 shekels of silver; these were normal prices under Nabonidus. In all probability, therefore, this text dates to the same period as the other documents discussed above and was drafted in Sippar.

Nabû-zera-ukin, Sin-aḫa-iddin's business partner, is also referred to in Nbn. 877, as a creditor who issued a loan of 63 *kur* of dates in the 14th year of Nabonidus; he also appears in CT 57, 508 (the date is broken off), and in CT 55, 420 (the 11th year of Nabonidus), as a seller of sheep. Both texts come from the Ebabbar Temple archives in Sippar.

Shamash-iqisha, son of Shamash-aḫa-iddin, Sin-aḫa-iddin's other business partner, is mentioned in many documents drafted in Sippar. For example, in the first year of Nabonidus, he sold several oxen to the Ebabbar Temple as regular offerings (CT 55, 699). In the same year, he sold 2 more oxen to the temple (CT 55, 692). According to another document, the Ebabbar administration paid him 1 mina of silver for oxen (CT 55, 68; the reign of Nabonidus, the year is broken off); and later, in the fifth year of Darius I (517 B.C.E.), he was again issued 35 shekels of silver "as price for the oxen" (Dar. 186). In the first year of Nebuchadnezzar IV (521 B.C.E.), he was paid by the same temple administration 1 mina 30 shekels of silver for sheep. To judge from the sum he received, he sold some 40 sheep (CT 57, 118; see also Nbn. 249). According to Nbn. 205, drafted in the fifth year of Nabonidus in Āl Shamash, near Sippar, he issued a loan in barley to a certain Zerija and his mother.

Finally, in the twelfth year of Nabonidus, he granted a monetary loan to a certain Shamash-eresh at the rate of twenty percent a year. In addition, a slave and his wife, belonging to the debtor, were used as security (CT 55, 99; see also Lab. 5).

The Ebabbar Temple and Merchants

The next four texts are also from the Ebabbar archives in Sippar.

> Two full-grown sheep (and) 3 male lambs are bought for $\frac{1}{3}$ mina $\frac{1}{2}$ shekel of white silver from Nabû-bel-[uballiṭ?] the merchant; he is paid. The 28th day of the month Addaru, the 25th year of Darius, king of Babylon, king of lands (CT 55, 608).

Thus, in 487 B.C.E., the Ebabbar Temple bought 5 sheep and lambs from a *tamkāru* for $20\frac{1}{2}$ shekels of silver (see also CT 55, 483).

> The chief *tamkāru*[3] gave one piece of linen fabric for (the god) Shamash to the clothes mender Bunene-shimanni. The 21st day of the month Abu, the 13th year of Nabonidus, king of Babylon (CT 55, 823).

CT 56, 551 records various sums of silver issued to several persons to buy a garment (TÚG-KUR-RA), which was to be given to 'archers at the disposal of a *tamkāru*'.[4] These archers apparently accompanied a merchant (or merchants) on some commercial trip authorized by the Ebabbar Temple. The enterprise was probably considered dangerous. The date of the document is unknown.

CT 57, 23 is an itemized account of temple expenditures, including 12 shekels of silver issued to a *tamkāru* (line 6). The text is not dated.

The Eanna Temple and Merchants

The next two documents come from the archives of the Eanna Temple in Uruk. The first, however, was drafted in Babylon in the second regnal year of Amel-Marduk (560 B.C.E.).[5] It records that the temple was to deliver 80 talents (2.4 tons) of wool to 'Libluṭ and Ippaija, the royal merchant'.[6] The title apparently refers to Ippaija only. The temple officials (*qīpu*, estate manager and accountant) stood as guarantors for each other that the wool would be delivered to Libluṭ and Ippaija in Uruk at a specified time. They were obviously paid in Babylon for the wool.

A document drafted in the second year of Nergal-shar-uṣur (558 B.C.E.) records various temple expenditures.[7] Inter alia, it notes that 12 shekels of silver were issued to a *tamkāru* named Nabû-bel-uṣur for 12 *kur* of barley that he had sold to the Eanna Temple.

Some Conclusions

To conclude, I shall dwell briefly on a few documents drafted in Babylon, Ur, Uruk, Kish, and other places, some of which I discussed in detail in my previous paper.

3. Line 2: LÚ GAL DAM-GÀR[MEŠ].
4. Line 3: LÚ ÉRIN.MEŠ *šá* GIŠ.BAN *la*-IGI DAM-GÀR.
5. R. H. Sack, "Some Remarks on Sin-iddina and Zērija, *qīpu* and *šatammu* of Eanna in Erech," *ZA* 66 (1977) 286.
6. Line 2: LÚ DAM-GÀR *šá* LUGAL.
7. F. Joannès, *Textes économiques de la Babylonie récente* (Paris, 1982) 246ff., no. 60.

The Eanna Temple bought some gold from a *tamkāru* (GCCI II, 26). *Tamkārū* sold fish (YOS 7, 151) and slaves (TCL 12 32). Certain persons called 'great *tamkārū*'[8] owned a field. In the fragmentary TMH 2/3 266, a *tamkāru* bought a field. Sometimes *tamkārū* are mentioned as creditors of loans in barley, dates, or vegetable oil (see, e.g., UET IV, 104). One *tamkāru* sold 22 baskets of alum, which was usually brought from Egypt (TMH 2/3 251). There were *tamkārū* who specialized in date and sheep trade.[9] And *tamkārū* are listed among the witnesses in several legal and business documents.[10]

An important post under the Neo-Babylonian kings was that of the 'royal merchant' (*tamkār šarri*), who was responsible for the sale of commodities belonging to the palace, as well as for the acquisition of goods needed by the royal household.[11] One royal merchant is listed among freeborn persons (*mār-banê*) who made a decision regarding a debtor's obligations (VS VI, 63). A certain Ina-eshe-eṭir, son of Nadin, was ordered to buy some gold for Nebuchadnezzar II (Nbk. 127). Seventeen years later he is mentioned as a witness in Babylon, but without his title 'royal merchant' (Nbk. 334). In all probability, he had by then been retired from service. Another royal merchant stood as guarantor for a debtor (Nbn. 17). Several documents show royal merchants also acting as independent contracting parties, making profits for themselves (granting loans, selling commodities, etc.).[12] A royal merchant rented out his land for 48 *kur* of dates (VS III, 18). Sometimes royal merchants were issued provision for their service (Nbn. 464).

An important official was 'chief of merchants' (LÚ *rab tamkārū*). Under Nebuchadnezzar II, this post was occupied by a certain Hanunu (i.e., Hanno), a person of Phoenician origin.[13] An Iranian named Artarush bore the same title under Cambyses.[14]

The title 'royal merchant' does not appear in texts of the Achaemenid period. In the second half of the fifth century B.C.E., however, some merchants in the Nippur area came together to form a special corporation (*ḫaṭru*), dependent on the state administration. They received allotments of state land and paid taxes. According to one document, "fields

8. GCCI II, 407:2: LÚ DAM-GÀR GAL-*ti*.

9. Nbn. 887:2–3: LÚ DAM-GÀR ZÚ-LUM-MA; Dar. 141:10: LÚ DAM-GÀR UDU-NÍTA.

10. See, e.g., *OECT* 10, 120:10–11, etc.

11. Cf. L. Shiff, *The Nur-Sin Archive: Private Entrepreneurship in Babylon, 603–507 B.C.* (Ph.D. diss., University of Pennsylvania, 1987) 53–54.

12. CT 55, nos. 96, 173, etc.

13. E. Unger, *Babylon: Die heilige Stadt nach der Beschreibung der Babylonier* (2d ed.; Berlin, 1970) 285, line 19; cf. A. L. Oppenheim, *Ancient Mesopotamia* (Chicago, 1964) 94.

14. Camb. 384. This document, although written in Babylonian, was drafted in Humadeshu, in the Persepolis area in Iran.

belonging to the corporation of the *tamkārū*" were rented out.[15] The exact nature of their obligations is not indicated in the documents. They were apparently engaged in trade as state-employed agents. The corporation was headed by persons bearing the title LÚ *šaknu ša* LÚ *tamkārū*[16] ('superintendent of the merchants'), designated by the royal administration. One document also mentions a 'merchant of the governor'.[17]

As we have seen, in the Neo-Babylonian and Achaemenid periods merchants are referred to as either *tamkārū* and royal (or governor's) *tamkārū*, or *tamkārū* of dates or sheep, attesting to some degree of specialization. They bought and sold slaves, fish, gold, and so on. The temples, too, used the services of the *tamkārū*, selling them their agricultural production surpluses and buying various items from them.

Some *tamkārū* were apparently also engaged in international commerce (at least, selling Egyptian alum in Babylonia). It is possible that during the sixth century B.C.E. international commerce and large-scale trading operations remained largely in the hands of the professional merchants.[18] However, their role decreased substantially during the periods under consideration. They probably needed to compete with many business firms, including the famous Egibi and Murašû firms. These firms not only carried out various operations (granting loans, buying and selling houses and fields on behalf of other people, paying off debts of third parties) but were also involved in domestic and international trade. Interestingly, the members of these firms were not referred to as *tamkārū*, although they were engaged, inter alia, in domestic and international commerce. It would seem that the strong competition from such business houses caused the decline in the role of the *tamkārū*.

Appendix: Selected Texts in Transliteration

CT 55, 96

1. 5 KÙR ŠE.BAR *šá* ^{md}UTU-BA-*šá*
2. A-*šú šá* ^{md}UTU ŠEŠ-MU [. . .]
3. [*u* ^{md}]XXX-ŠEŠ-MU A-*šú šá* ^{m}*In-nu-ṭa-i-na-a*ᵓ
4. LÚ DAM.GÀR LUGAL AŠ UGU ^{md}EN-SU
5. A-*šú šá* ^{m}*In-ṣa-ra-ḫe-eš* [. . .]

15. *BE* X, 54:4. Cf. M. W. Stolper, *Entrepreneurs and Empire: The Murašû Archive, the Murašû Firm, and Persian Rule in Babylonia* (Leiden, 1985) 78.

16. See *PBS* 2/I, 195:6, 10 and upper edge.

17. VS VI, 252:15: LÚ DAM-GÀR *šá* LÚ *ša-kìn*.

18. Cf. A. L. Oppenheim, "Essay on Overland Trade in the First Millennium B.C.," *JCS* 21 (1967) 239–40; Shiff, *The Nur-Sin Archive*, 53–54.

6. *u* ^{f}*Um-ma-a-an* [. . .]
7. AŠ ITI GU_4 ŠE-BAR TIL [. . .]MEŠ
8. AŠ KA *ka-lak-ku* [. . .]
9. SUM-*nu* ? 1 *pu-ut* 2-*i na-šu-ú*
10. LÚ *mu-kin*$_7$ ^{m}*Aš-la-a* A-[*šú*]
11. *šá* ^{md}AG-BA-*šá* A LÚ SANGA ^{d}UTU
12. ^{md}AG-ZÁLAG-*ir* A-*šú šá* ^{m}*Ri-ḫe-e-tum*
13. LÚ UMBISAG ^{md}UTU-*na-ṣir* A-*šú šá*
14. [. . .]-*da-ti* A LÚ [. . .]
15. [. . .]KI ITI APIN U_4 10 [KAM]
16. [MU 1]2 KAM ^{d}AG-I
17. *I-en pu-ut ta-*[. . .]

CT 55, 173

1. [. . . KÙR] 1 (PI) BAN ŠE-BAR *šá*
2. ^{md}UTU-BA-*šá* A-*šú šá*
3. ^{md}UTU-ŠEŠ-MU AŠ *muḫ-ḫi*
4. ^{m}*Kal-ba-a* A-*šú šá*
5. ^{md}UTU-KAM AŠ ITI GU_4
6. ŠE-BAR AŠ SAG-DU-*šú*
7. *i-nam-din*
8. ŠE-BAR *šá* KASKAL^{II} *šá* ^{md}XXX-PAP-MU A-*šú šá* ^{m}*I-ni-ṭa-a-a-a*ʾ
9. LÚ DAM-GÀR LUGAL
10. LÚ *mu-kin*$_7$ ^{md}U-GUR-TIN(*iṭ*)
11. A-*šú šá* ^{md}AG-NUMUN-MU
12. ^{m}[. . .]-ZÁLAG(*ir*) A-*šú šá* ^{m}*Ri-ḫe-e-tú*
13. [LÚ] UMBISAG ^{m}ḪI.GA-*ia* A-*šú šá*
14. [. . .]-^{d}UTU
15. [ITI . . .] U_4 4 KAM MU 5 KAM
16. [^{md}AG]-I LUGAL E.KI

CT 55, 608

1. 2 UDU-NÍTA GAL-*ú*.MEŠ
2. 3 UDU-NÍTA *ka-lu-mu*.MEŠ
3. *a-na* $\frac{1}{3}$ MA.NA $\frac{1}{2}$ GÍN
4. KÙ-BABBAR BABBAR-*ú* AŠ ŠU^{II} ^{md}AG-EN-[TIN?]
5. LÚ DAM-GÀR SUM-*na* SUR
6. ITI ŠE U_4 28 KAM
7. MU 25 KAM
8. ^{m}*Da-ri-ja-muš*
9. LUGAL TIN.TIR.KI LUGAL KUR.KUR

CT 55, 763

1. 4 GUN 20 MA.NA
2. SÍK.ḪI.A *a-na* 1 MA.NA KÙ-BABBAR
3. [md]XXX-ŠEŠ-MU
4. *u* [md]AG-NUMUN-GIN LÚ DAM-GÀR
5. SUM-*na* KÙ-BABBAR *a-na*
6. LÚ *qí-i-pi* SUM-*na*
7. 10 MA.NA SÍK.ḪI.A [d]ŠÚ-KAM-EŠ
8. LÚ NAGAR SUM-*na*
9. ITI APIN U_4 16 KAM
10. MU 36 KAM
11. [md]AG-NÍG-DU-URÌ LUGAL TIN.TIR.KI

CT 55, 823

1. 1 GADA *šal-ḫi* [. . .]
2. *šá* LÚ GAL DAM-GÀR [MEŠ]
3. *a-na* [d]UTU *id-din-nu*
4. AŠ *pa-ni* [md]ḪAR-*ši-man-ni*
5. LÚ *mu-ka-bu-ú*
6. ITI NE U_4 21 KAM
7. MU 13 KAM [d]AG-I
8. LUGAL E.KI

An Eanna Tablet from Uruk in Cleveland

M. J. Geller

The only Neo-Babylonian tablet from among the small cuneiform collection of the Cleveland Public Library is surprisingly important for the information it provides about a prominent official in Achaemenid Uruk, namely Šum-ukīn, who is well known from other tablets mostly in the Yale Babylonian Collection. Although this document is a legal suit against Šum-ukīn's second wife, his first wife, also mentioned in this document, is known from other documents and letters, and the tablet partially elucidates Šum-ukīn's domestic affairs. Moreover, the court case provides significant details regarding the income derived from temple rituals, which is the subject of the present litigation.

The tablet edited below has resided in the Cleveland Public Library as part of the large collection of Orientalia and chess pieces collected by John Griswold White, the benefactor of the White Collection, who died in 1925. The tablet was in pieces and required restoration, the process of which has obscured many possible readings on the tablet. Nevertheless, the tablet, a court case from the Eanna Temple of Uruk, originally belonged to the archives found mainly in the Yale Babylonian Collection and represents an important new addition to the published corpus.

This court case from Uruk's Eanna Temple was important enough to be tried before the chief temple administrators, the *šatammu* and *bēl piqitti*, as well as both the general assembly (*puḫru*) and court (*kiništu*) of priests. The case was brought against the second wife and widow of Šum-ukīn, a prominent and wealthy *fermier général* of the Eanna Temple. The widow's claim to Šum-ukīn's temple income from the *ḫarû*-ritual is the main focus of this litigation.

Author's note: I wish to thank Alice Loranth for permission to publish this tablet and for the generous assistance of her staff in the White Collection of the Cleveland Public Library. I am also indebted to Karlheinz Kessler and G. van Driel for detailed suggestions and corrections and to Irving Finkel, Paul-Alain Beaulieu, and C. Wunsch for additional corrections and advice. Thanks are also due to Sam Hoenig for the excellent photographs.

Cleveland Public Library, White Collection 036422

1. [^{f}*Li-i*ʾ]*-du-*ʾ*u* DUMU.⸢SAL⸣ *šá* ^{md}*Šamaš*-DÙ.ŠEŠ ⸢DUMU-*šú*⸣ *šá* ^{md}*Nabû-na-din-*[MU ....]-AN *a-na*

2. [UKKIN-*šú*]*-nu lí-qa-a-ta* ^{md}*Nabû*-GIN.⸢DUMU.NITA LÚ.ŠÀ.TAM⸣ [É.AN.NA DUMU] ^{m}*Na-di-nu*

3. [A ^{m}*D*]*a-bi-bi ù* ^{md}*Nabû*-ŠEŠ.MU LÚ.SAG.LUGAL LÚ. EN [*pi-qit-tu*$_4$ É.A]N.NA *ár-ka-at*

4. [^{f}*L*]*i-i*ʾ*-du-*ʾ*u iš-ta-a*ʾ*-lu-ma* LÚ.KU$_4$.É ^{d}INNIN U[NUG^{ki} LÚ.DUMU.DÙ.MEŠ] *ù* LÚ *ki-niš-ti*

5. [É.AN].NA *šá ṭe-e-me* [*š*]*á* ^{f}*Li-i*ʾ*-*[*d*]*u-*[ʾ*u*] *ḫa-ar-*[*ṣu*(*-ú*) LÚ.KU$_4$.É.MEŠ] *u* UKKIN-*šú-nu a-na*

6. [^{m}*Nabû*-G]IN.DUMU.NITA LÚ.ŠÀ.TAM É.AN.NA ⸢*ù*⸣ [^{md}*Nabû*-ŠEŠ.MU LÚ.E]N *p*[*i-qi*]*t* É.AN.NA

7. [*i*]*q-*[*b*]*u-ú um-ma i-na* MU.5.KAM ^{m}*Nabû*-IM.TUK *ḫa-ru*[*-ú šá* DINGIR.MEŠ *u* ^{d}INNIN].MEŠ *šá i-*⸢*na*⸣ TIN.TIR^{ki}

8. [*ù Bá*]*r-*⸢*sipa*^{ki} *ḫa-ar*⸣*-ṣi ina lìb-bi il-q*[*a- x x x x x* ^{m}M]U.GI.N[A] DUMU-*šú šá* ^{m}EN-NUMUN

9. [DA]M *maḫrû*(IGI-*ú*) ⸢*šá* ^{f}*Bu-*ʾ*i-i-tu*$_4$ *a*⸣*-di* M[U.X.KAM ^{f}*Li-i*ʾ*-du-*ʾ*u i-ḫu-uz-ma* (?) DUMU ù] DUMU.SAL *la tu-lid-su ár-ki* MU.10.KÁM *šá* ^{m}MU⟨GI.NA⟩

10. [*a-n*]*a šim-tu*$_4$ *il-li-*⸢*ku a-di 3 x*⸣ [...... DAM-*šú* ^{f}*Li-i*ʾ*-du-*ʾ*u* DUMU.SAL *šá* ^{m}]^{d}*Šamaš*-DÙ.ŠEŠ

11. [*a*]*-na* DAM-*ú-tu la tu-ši-ib-ma* [.................. *a-na*] *na-da-nu*

12. [*šá*] *ḫa-re-e šá ina* TIN.TIR^{ki} *ù Bár-sipa*^{ki} [x x ^{f}*Li-i*ʾ*-du*]*-ú* DUMU.SAL.A.NI

13. [*šá*] ^{md}*Šamaš*-DÙ.ŠEŠ *šá ina ḫa-re-e par-ṣi la z*[*i-za-at*$^{?}$ x x x] ⸢^{túg}*di*⸣*-du taḫ-ḫa-líp-ma*

14. [*ta*]*l-ti-*⸢*el*⸣*-a*(?) *par-ṣi a-na bit-a-nu* [*šá* É.AN.NA (?) *i*]*t*$^{?}$*-ḫi-ni-ma a-na* É *ḫi-il-ṣi*

15. *š*[*á*] ⸢É⸣.AN.NA *te-ru-ub* [^{md}*Na*]*bû*-GIN.DUMU.NITA ⸢LÚ.ŠÀ.TAM⸣ É.⸢AN.NA⸣ *ù* [^{md}*Nab*]*û*-ŠEŠ.MU LÚ EN *p*[*i-q*]*it* É.AN.NA *it-ti*

16. LÚ.KU$_4$.É.MEŠ *ù* LÚ *ki-niš-tu*$_4$ É.AN.NA *im-tal-ku-ma* [x x (x) *ù* LÚ].KU$_4$.⟨É⟩ É.AN.NA *iq-*[*bu-ú*] ^{f}*Li-i*ʾ*-du-ú*

17. *ina* ^{túg}*di-du a-*[*na naḫ-lu-pi*] *tel-te-el-*⸢*lu*⸣*-*ʾ*u a-na* É *ḫi-il-ṣi*

18. *šá* ⸢É⸣.AN.[NA *te-er-ru-ub* . . . . . .].

reverse

1. (erased)

2. (erased) ^{lú}*mu-kin-nu* ^{md}*Marduk*.MU.MU DUMU-*šú šá*
^{md}*Nabû*-ŠEŠ.⸢MEŠ.TIN⸣-*iṭ*

3. DUMU ^{m}TIN ^{m}ÌR-^{d}*Marduk* DUMU-*šú šá* ^{m}*Zi-*[*ri-i*]*a* DUMU ^{m}*E-gi-bi*
^{md}*Sîn*-URU$_4$-*eš* DUMU-*šú šá* ^{md}*Nabû*-MU.SI.SÁ

4. DUMU ^{m}DÙ.DINGIR ^{m}ÌR-^{d}*Bēl* DUMU-*šú šá* ^{m}[*Ṣil-la*]-⸢*a*⸣ DUMU
^{m}MU.^{d}PAP.SUKKAL ^{md}*Nabû*-MU.GAR-*un* DUMU-*šú šá*

5. ^{md}*Nabû*-DÙ.ŠEŠ DUMU ^{m}ŠEŠ.DÙ-*i* *š*[*á*] [^{md}*Šam*]*aš*-DU.[D]UMU.NITA
DUMU-*šú šá* ^{md}DI.KUD.ŠEŠ.MEŠ.MU DUMU ^{m}*Ši-gu-ú-a*

6. ^{m}*Na-di-nu* DUMU-*šú šá* ^{md}*Bēl*-ŠEŠ.MEŠ.B[A-*š*]*á* DUMU ⸢^{m}*E*⸣-*gi-bi*
^{m}*La-ba-a-ši*-^{d}*Marduk* DUMU-*šú šá* ^{m}ÌR-^{d}*Bēl* DUMU ^{m}*E-gi-*⸢*bi*⸣

7. ^{m}GI-^{d}*Marduk* DUMU-*šú šá* ^{m}ÌR-^{d}*Nabû* DUMU *šangû*(LÚ.É.BAR) ^{d}*Nabû*
[^{m}]^{d}*Nabû*-DÙ.ŠEŠ DUMU-*šú šá* ^{m}*Kab-ti-ia* DUMU ^{m}TIN

8. ^{m}DA-^{d}*Marduk* DUMU-*šú šá* ^{md}*Nabû*-MU.GIN DUMU-*š*[*ú*] ^{m}⸢*E*$^{!}$-*ṭi-ru*
^{md}*Šamaš*-ŠID⸣.ÙRU DUMU-*šú šá* ^{md}*Marduk*-DUB.NUMUN DUMU
^{md}*Sîn*-TI.A.ŠI

9. ^{md}*Nabû*-NUMUN.SI.SÁ DUMU-*šú šá* ^{md}*Nabû*-GIN.DUMU.NITA DUMU
[^{m}]^{d}*Sîn*-TI.A.ŠI ^{m}ÌR-*ia* DUMU-*šú* ⸢*šá*⸣ ^{m}GAR.MU DUMU ^{m}ŠU-^{d}*Na-na-a*

10. ^{md}INNIN.ŠEŠ.MU DUMU-*šú šá* ^{md}*Nabû-mu-še-tíq*-UD.DA [DUMU
^{m}]ŠU-^{d}*Na-na-a* ^{md}[*I*]*n-nin*-MU.ŠEŠ DUMU-*šú šá* ^{m}*Gi-mil-lu*

11. DUMU ^{m}ŠU-^{d}*Na-na-a* ^{md}*In-nin*-DUMU.NITA.⸢ÙRU DUMU⸣-*šú šá*
^{m}*Nabû*-TIN-*su*-E DUMU ^{m}*É-kur-za-kir*

12. ^{md}*A-nu*-MU.DÙ DUMU-*šú* ^{md}*Nabû*-KAR-*ir* DUMU
^{md}*Nabû-ša*[*r-ḫ*]*i*-DINGIR.MEŠ ^{md}*A-*[*nu*]-ŠEŠ.MU DUMU-*šú šá* ^{m}ŠU
DUMU ^{m}*Kur-i*

13. $^{m⸢d⸣}$*In-nin*-MU.ÙRU DUMU-*šú šá* ^{m}ŠU DUMU ^{m}*Kur-*⸢*i*⸣

14. ⸢^{m}ÌR⸣-^{d}*Marduk* DUB.SAR DUMU-*šú šá* ^{md}*Marduk*-MU.MU DUMU
^{md}*Bēl*-DUMU.NITA.Ù[R]U UNUG^{ki} ^{iti}AB UD.14.KAM MU.⸢5⸣.KAM
^{m}*Ku-ra-áš* LUG[AL] TIN.TIR^{ki} LUGAL KUR.KUR

TRANSLATION

Li[⊃]idu, daughter of Šamaš-tabni-aḫi, son of Nabû-nādin-[. . . , descendant of . .]-ili was taken to the [assembly]. Nabû-mukīn-apli, administrator of the [Eanna, son] of Nadinu, descendant of Dabibi, and Nabû-aḫ-iddin, royal chief officer, chief [overseer of the] Eanna, made an official inquiry about Li⊃idu. The opinion of the priests of Ishtar of Uruk, [citizens,] and the court (*kiništu*) of Eanna being clarified regarding (the case) of Li⊃idu, [the priests] and their assembly spoke thus to Nabû-mukīn-apli, administrator of the Eanna, and [Nabû-aḫ-iddin, chief] overseer of Eanna:

"In the fifth year of Nabonidus, regarding the *ḫarû*-ritual [of the gods and goddesses], which has been clarified in Babylon and Borsippa: one derived (an income) from it. Šum-ukīn son of Bēl-zēri, the former husband of Bu⊃iti, until year [x had married Li⊃idu, but she] did not bear him [son or] daughter. Ten years after Šum-ukīn went to his fate, and until three ..[.., his (second) wife(?) Li⊃idu, daughter of] Šamaš-tabni-aḫi, did not remarry (lit. dwell in matrimony)." [In order to] give [. . . . . of] the *ḫarû*-ritual which [. . .] in Babylon and Borsippa, Li⊃idu daughter of Šamaš-tabni-aḫi, who had no *share* in the *ḫarû*-ritual rite [. . .], had dressed in a *dīdū*,-garment and had *adorned herself,* she . . . the rite into the *bītānu* [of the Eanna (?)], and she entered the *bīt ḫilṣi* of the Eanna. Nabû-mukīn-apli, administrator of the Eanna and Nabû-aḫ-iddin, chief overseer of the Eanna, together with the priests and court of the Eanna considered the matter and [. . . and] priests spoke: "Li⊃idu will [/will not] *adorn herself* [by dressing] in a *dīdū*-garment, and [she will/will not enter] the *bīt ḫilṣi* of Eanna [. . . .]."

rev. (witnesses)

Arad-Marduk, the scribe, son of Marduk-aḫ-iddin, son of Bel-apla-uṣur of Uruk, 14th of Abu, fifth year of Cyrus, king of Babylon and king of the lands.

COMMENTARY

Line 1. Šamaš-tabni-aḫi appears in an Uruk temple account (Pohl, AnOr 9 no. 8:7) from Nabn. year 3.

Line 2. The official Nabû-mukīn-apli is attested as *šatammu Eanna* from Cyrus year 4 until Cambyses year 6; cf. H. Kümmel, *Familie, Beruf, und Amt im spätbabylonischen Uruk* (Berlin, 1979) 143.

One might alternatively restore *a-na* [IGI-*šú*]-*nu,* although both restorations share the disadvantage of employing a pronoun -*šunu* without an antecedent. The term *lí-qa-a-ta* is unusual in such contexts, indicating that this case was brought against Liʾidu, who was being summoned to court.

Line 3. For the expression *arku . . . šaʾālu,* see CAD A/2 277b s.v. *arku.*

Nabû-aḫ-iddin was *ša rēši šarri bēl piqitti Eanna* from Nabn. year 17 until the 4th year of Cambyses (see Kümmel, *Familie,* 144). He was appointed to the administration of the Eanna together with Nabû-mukīn-zēri, the brother of Nabû-mukīn-apli (the *šatammu Eanna* of our text), in a reorganization of the Eanna at the troubled end of Nabonidus's reign; see P.-A. Beaulieu, *The Reign of Nabonidus, King of Babylon 556–539* BC (YNER 10; New Haven, Conn., 1989) 221.

Line 4. The restoration of *mār bāni* is based on a similar court case from Uruk before the priests of Ishtar, the *kiništu* of the Eanna, and the *mār bāni.* Cf. I. Spar, "Three Neo-Babylonian Trial Depositions from Uruk," in *Studies in Honor of Tom B. Jones* (ed. M. Powell and R. H. Sack; AOAT 203; Neukirchen-Vluyn, 1979) 165:20–21 (reference courtesy K. Kessler).

Line 5. For similar wording, cf. R. P. Dougherty, YOS 6 224:17–18; cf. idem., *The Širkûtu of Babylonian Deities* (YOR 5/2; New Haven, Conn., 1923) 36: FPN_1 *ṭe-e-mu šá* PN_2 *ummi-ia ù* PN_3 *ummi ummi-ia ḫar-ṣa-at* '(a woman) PN was certain "regarding the case of PN my mother and PN my grandmother"'.

Lines 7–8. There are several grammatical and contextual difficulties in these lines, for which a tentative translation is being offered here. Two clauses appear to be joined syntactically, namely *ḫarû ša . . . ḫarṣi* 'the ḫ.-ritual has been clarified', followed by *ina libbi ilqa*['he took from it'. The first clause lacks the expected subjunctive ending on the verb, while the second clause lacks a subject. Despite these difficulties, the clauses appear to be an attempt to state the position of the *ḫarû*-ritual in the fifth year of Nabonidus, and the implication of the context is that Šum-ukīn himself was the beneficiary of the ritual.

The suggestion that Šum-ukīn derived an income from the *ḫarû* ritual is confirmed by a letter (Contenau, TCL 12 115:11 = E. Ebeling, *Neubabylonische Briefe* [Munich, 1949] 340) that refers to the *ḫa-ru-ú šá* ^{m}*Šum-ukīn.* The letter is addressed to Nabû-aḫ-iddina, the same *bēl piqitti* of Eanna mentioned in our text. The fact that the *ḫarû*-ritual referred to in this text belongs to Babylon and Borsippa may reflect Šum-ukīn's financial interests outside Uruk; see the general comments below.

Line 9. For the restoration of this line, cf. T. G. Pinches, "The Law of Inheritance in Ancient Babylonia," *Hebraica* 3 (1886–87) 15:4, a court case in which a man claims that *áš-šá-ti a-ḫu-uz-ma* DUMU *u* DUMU.SAL *la tul-du* 'I married but she bore me neither son nor daughter'. In this latter case, however, the husband seeks to adopt his wife's son by a previous marriage: PN DUMU DAM-*ia šá la-pa-ni* PN_2 *mu-ti-šú mah-ru-ú tu-li-du* 'PN the son of my wife whom she bore to PN_2, her former husband'.

Line 13. CAD D 135 is uncertain in its definition of a *dīdū*, describing it generally as 'a piece of female apparel covering the hips', without evidence of its being cultic clothing.

Line 14. The verb *tal-te-el-a* is tentatively taken here as a 3d fem. sing. Gt preterite form of *šâlu* 'to coat, smear' (CAD Š/1 282b), and the same verb appears in the present-future as *tel-te-el-lu-ʾu* (line 17). Alternatively, one could restore the first sign as [*i*]*l*-, thus giving better vowel harmony but not explaining the use of a masculine verbal form. For the *bītānu*, see F. Joannes, "Les temples de Sippar et leurs trésors à l'époque néo-babylonienne," *RA* 86 (1992) 168–69, although our text suggests that Liʾidu gained access to the inner sanctum of the temple, following CAD B 274, rendering *bītānu* as 'inner quarter' of the temple.

The statement that Liʾidu 'entered the *bīt hilṣi* of the Eanna' suggests that she participated in the ritual in order to derive an income from it, which is the reason why this case is brought against her, to determine her eligibility or legitimacy.

Lines 17–18. It is possible that the gaps negate these clauses.

Rev. 2–13. The witnesses to this court case were distinguished members of the Uruk Temple bureaucracy, judging by the names appearing in Kümmel, *Familie* (150ff. et passim), although documentation of their respective offices is beyond the scope of the present study.

Rev. 14. The scribe is known from YOS 6 230:13, where he appears as a witness rather than as a scribe, in a text dated to the Nabn. year 12. In other texts from the reign of both Cyrus and Cambyses he functions, as here, as 'scribe of the Eanna' (see Kümmel, *Familie,* 111 and 144). The latest reference to this scribe occurs in Darius's accession year (see D. Weisberg, *Guild Structure and Political Allegiance in Early Achaemenid Mesopotamia* [New Haven, 1967] 64: 18–19 [reference courtesy K. Kessler]).

The date is damaged and could represent either the 5th or 6th year of Cyrus.

General Comments

Šum-ukīn, son of Bēl-zēri, descendant of Basiya, left an extensive archive, mostly from Uruk, which has been discussed by D. Cocquerillat.[1] Records in which Šum-ukīn appears include the purchase of a slave,[2] a

1. D. Cocquerillat, *Palmeraies et cultures de l'Eanna d'Uruk* (Berlin, 1968) 56–57, 74–75, 91ff., et passim.

2. YOS 6 5.

house rental,[3] and many tax claims involving the property of the Eanna Temple of Uruk; Šum-ukīn collected temple imposts of barley and dates from temple lands for at least the first four years of Nabonidus's reign.[4] He himself was no stranger to litigation, since he was sued by tenant farmers regarding agreements he had made with them, although he himself did not bother to appear in court.[5] Šum-ukīn's prominence as ^{lú}*ša muḫḫi sūti ša* ^{d}*Bēlti ša Uruk* is further indicated by the fact that he had his own *bēl piqitti*,[6] and his wealth is indicated by the reference to his own estate (Tabini-ša-Šum-ukīn), from which he collects taxes on behalf of the Eanna Temple.[7] In a document recently published by C. Wunsch,[8] dating from Nabn. year 4, Šum-ukīn is involved in the local onion trade in Šahrīnu, a site between Babylon and Borsippa, while a letter to Šum-ukīn reveals his financial interests in Babylon.[9]

Šum-ukīn's first wife Buʾiti is known from an interesting document,[10] in which one Hannaʾ, a *zakītu* of the Eanna, belongs to Buʾiti, daughter of Šapî-Bēl and wife of Šum-ukīn. The *zakītu* Hannaʾ brands two of her daughters to be given (presumably as servants) to Buʾiti and to another woman, Liʾudu-Nanâ, who is likely to be the same Liʾidu featuring as the litigant of our court case; the document is dated to the 8th year of Nabonidus. Although the relationship between Buʾiti and Liʾidu is not specified, it is likely that they were both wives of Šum-ukīn, since polygamy was allowed in cases in which the first wife was childless; our court case suggests that the second wife, Liʾidu, also never bore children to Šum-ukīn (line 9), which is plausible in a case of male sterility or sexual impotence. It is conceivable, therefore, that in Nabn. year 8, both wives were living in Šum-ukīn's household, but by Cyrus year 5, Liʾidu was the only survivor, since she was the younger woman and had not remarried after Šum-ukīn's death (lines 10–11). Liʾidu was claiming an income from the *ḫarû* ritual, on the grounds that she remained a widow.

According to our text, dated to the 5th (or possibly 6th) year of Cyrus, Šum-ukīn himself died ten years earlier, in approximately Nabn. year 12. This information can be confirmed by following the career of Šum-ukīn's "partner," Kalbā son of Iqīša. In Nabonidus's first year, Šum-ukīn and Kalbā were granted royal permission in duplicate contracts

3. Ibid., 6 85.

4. Cf., inter alia, ibid., 6 12, 35–36, 43–45, 47, 49, 78, 84, 242, and BIN 1 97.

5. YOS 6 78.

6. Ibid. 6 6:4.

7. Ibid. 6 45:3, 15.

8. C. Wunsch, *Die Urkunden des babylonischen Geschäftsmannes Iddin-Marduk* (Groningen, 1993) vol. 2, no. 134.

9. YOS 3 46.

10. YOS 6 129 (= Dougherty, *Širkûtu*, 43).

from Uruk and Larsa to cultivate Eanna Temple land.[11] The last record of Šum-ukīn's dealings was in Nabn. year 11, in a tablet compiling Šum-ukīn's accounts and agreements for collection of dates in years 8, 9, and 10 of Nabonidus, in partnership with Kalbā, *ina sūti ša* ᵐ*Šum-ukīn u* ᵐ*Kalbā*.[12]

Furthermore, Kalbā wrote a letter to Buʾiti, addressing her as "mother," and refers in the same letter to Šum-ukīn;[13] Kümmel suggests that Šum-ukīn may have been Kalbā's uncle.[14] On the assumption that Kalba's reference to Buʾiti as "mother" was merely politeness, it seems likely that Šum-ukīn's younger partner and kinsman Kalbā eventually took over his position in the Eanna Temple of collecting rents, and by the last year of Nabonidus's reign (year 17), Kalbā had succeeded Šum-ukīn in the office of ˡᵘ́*ša muḫḫi sūti ša* ᵈ*Bēlti ša Uruk*.[15] Beaulieu, however, has drawn attention to the fact that by this time Kalbā had accrued large debts to the Eanna,[16] but despite these reverses, Kalbā was still acting in the same official capacity in Cyrus's 2d year.[17]

Appendix

According to collations of YOS 6 129, the following corrections of the edition in Dougherty, *Širkûtu*, 43, should be noted:

YOS 6 129:2: Read *še-en-de-e-ti* (against Dougherty's reading *ṣab-ti* 'prisoner' of Buʾiti).

Ibid.: 3: Read the name as Šum-ukīn (MU.GIN), as in our text, and not Zēr-ukīn. Cf. Kümmel, *Familie*, 106 n. 77.

Ibid.: 4: Read the name as ᶠ*Ina-*ᵈ*Na-na-a-ul-ta-ra-aḫ*, with no break until the end of the line.

Ibid.: 6: Read *tal-ṭu-ru* LÚ.T[UR].MEŠ *šá* [*šá-ṭa*]-*ri*.

Ibid.: 7: Read *še-en-de-*[*e-ti*].

11. Cf. W. Schwenzner, "Beiträge zur Kultur- und Wirtschaftsgeschichte des Alten Orients," *AfK* 2, 107ff.; Beaulieu, *Reign of Nabonidus*, 118, 124, and 126; G. Frame, "Nabonidus, Nabû-šarru-uṣur, and the Eanna Temple," *ZA* 81 (1991) 59–61; Cocquerillat, *Palmeraies et cultures de l'Eanna d'Uruk*, 38–39; and F. Joannes, *Textes économiques de la babylonie récente* (Paris, 1982) 130–53 (for a detailed discussion of this text and Šum-ukīn's career).

12. YOS 6 242:5.

13. YOS 3 22; cf. Ebeling, *Neubabylonische Briefe*, no. 22.

14. Kümmel, *Familie*, 106.

15. YOS 6 207; cf. Kümmel, *Familie*, 105 n. 58.

16. Beaulieu, *Reign of Nabonidus*, 118, citing YOS 3, no. 2.

17. YOS 7 23:1; and Dougherty, GCCI II, 98.

Obverse

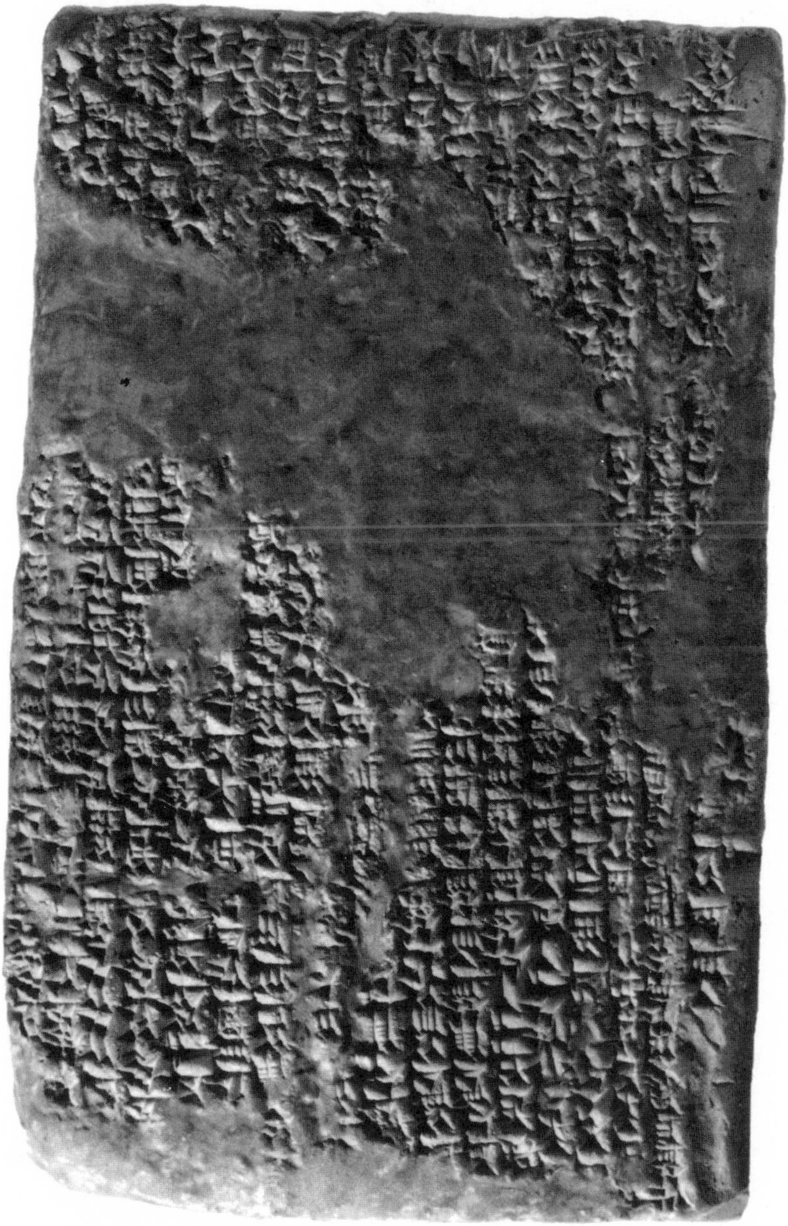

Reverse

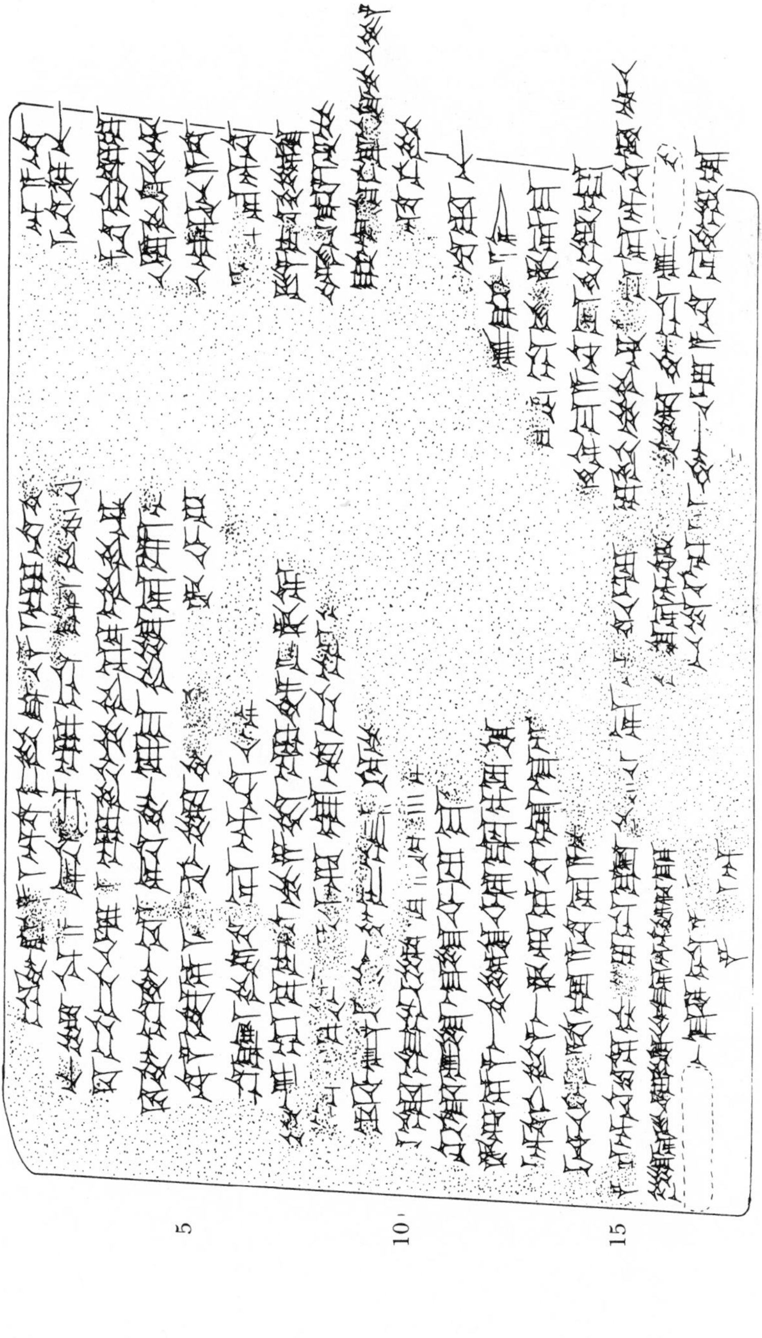

CPL 036422 obv.

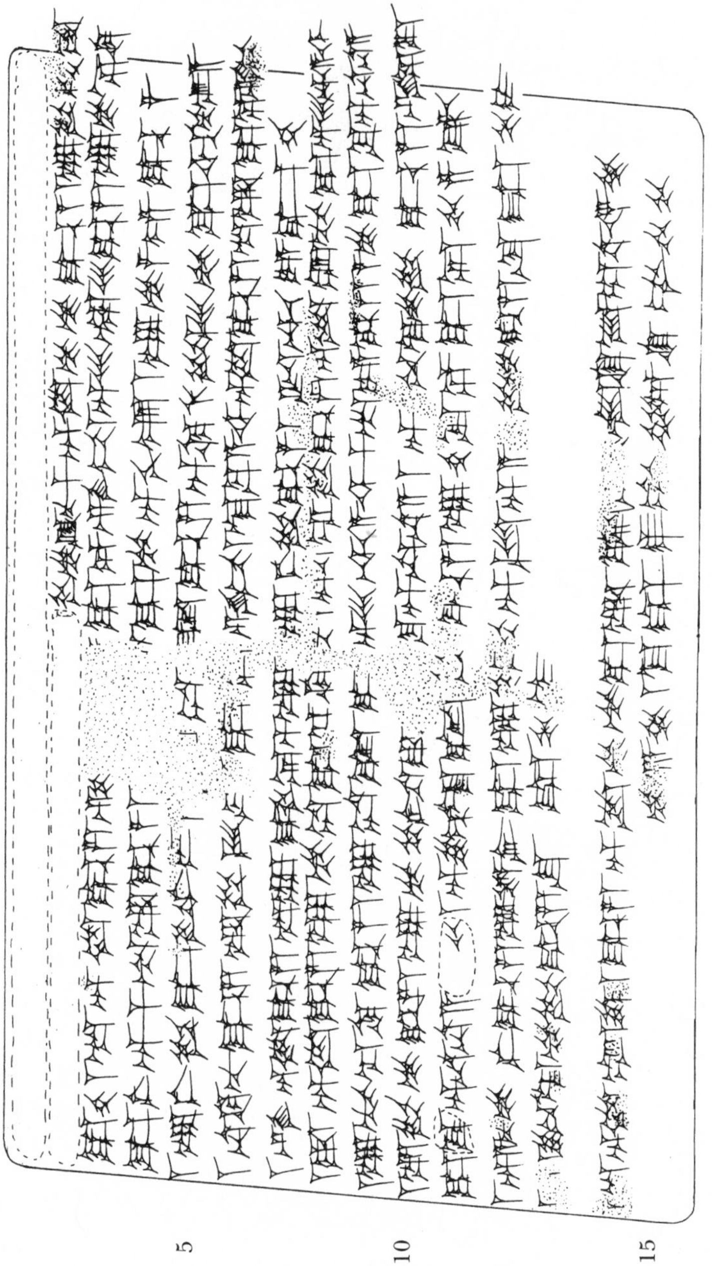

CPL 036422 rev.

An Old Babylonian Bawdy Ballad

Victor Avigdor Hurowitz

HS 1879, published recently by W. von Soden, is a twenty-line tablet from the first year of Hammurapi, designated by its colophon as a pārum ša Ištar. The meaning of this term and the function of the text are unknown, but the work itself is a short and very lewd ballad. It describes graphically a massive sexual tryst between a female named Ištar and 120 young men. This article is an explication of the text that discusses its tone, language, content, plot, and meaning, illuminating them with the help of other Mesopotamian and ancient Near Eastern literature of sexual content.

Introduction

W. von Soden recently published a "*pārum*-Preislied für Ištar" from the Hilprecht collection in Jena (HS 1879).[1] In the introduction and textual notes he illuminates the orthography, grammar, and date of composition, the syllable count of the verses, the meter of the refrain, and other such essential aspects of the text. The brief "discussion" of the composition that follows the philological notes revolves solely around the question of its genre. The size and shape of the tablet are said to mark it as an excerpt tablet, while the refrain and the reference to the goddess Ištar would be characteristic of a long cult song. The word

Author's note: The text to be discussed here came to my attention in 1992 while I was on sabbatical leave at the Annenberg Research Institute for Jewish Studies in Philadelphia. I am grateful to the institute for their generous support of my research and the wonderful surroundings provided. I joyfully dedicate this study to my teacher Jonas Greenfield, who was also a fellow at ARI that year.

1. W. von Soden, "Ein spät-altbabylonisches *pārum*-Preislied für Ištar," *Or* n.s. 60 (1991) 339–43, pl. CVI. Although not published until now, this text is cited at the relevant entries in AHw, because it was copied as early as 1952. We are to be grateful to Prof. von Soden for finally making it available.

pārum itself, which describes the piece in the colophon, unfortunately remains enigmatic and unexplained.

The edition of the text has soared to new heights of Assyriological restraint by discussing the work without uttering a word about its content, let alone its literary style and structure, connections with other works, or individual message. This restraint is particularly admirable given the fact that even a superficial reading shows that in content and tone it contains what could be characterized as one of the earliest pieces of hard-core pornography known to us from Akkadian writings.

In order to call attention to a fascinating and titillating work and raise some of the difficulties facing a contemporary scholar when encountering such a text, I will be presumptuous and present here a normalized transliteration of the text (solely for the convenience of the reader) along with two English translations of this twenty-line ditty, followed by an explication. Alexander Heidel and his generation would certainly have rendered this text into Latin, indicating that it can be competently and safely read and understood only by one who is an initiate in a religious order.[2] Two translations are offered so as not to misinterpret or read into the text overtones and attitudes which the ancient writer, from a society culturally removed from my own, may not have had in mind.[3] The first rendition is quite literal. It uses sexual language which is clinical or archaic but avoids parlance which is particularly obscene on the one hand or euphemistic on the other. The second translation, on the other hand, is an attempt to render unabashedly what I perceive to be the lewd and jocular flavor of the text, so it uses more colloquial sexually suggestive language. It is only to be expected that people with different

2. See A. Heidel, *The Gilgamesh Epic and Old Testament Parallels* (Chicago, 1946) 21–22 (I iv 8–21), 27 (II ii 6–8).

3. To verify my feelings about the text and dispel suspicion that I was reading too much into the composition I showed it to several male and female colleagues at the Annenberg Research Institute, including the jubilarian, and at the Babylonian Section of the University Museum, as well as to some relatives and acquaintances with no familiarity with the ancient Near East. All asked found it both lewd and hilarious. Von Soden, in so pronouncedly avoiding the obscene aspects of the composition, has joined a backlash against what B. Landsberger perceived of as a pornographic bent among Assyriologists. For these opposing trends in scholarly circles, note the brief comments of J. S. Cooper ("Enki's Member: Eros and Irrigation in Sumerian Literature," in *DUMU$_2$-E$_2$-DUB-BA-A: Studies in Honor of Åke W. Sjöberg* [ed. H. Behrens et al.; Occasional Publications of the Samuel Noah Kramer Fund 11; Philadelphia, 1989] 87–89, esp. 88). For humor in Mesopotamian writings, see B. R. Foster, "Humor and Cuneiform Literature" (*JANESCU* 6 [1974] 69–85). Note especially his statement, "Humor is human and universal. People laugh at the same things; what varies from culture to culture is the restrictions, the relaxation of which gives rise to laughter and the modes of expression wit will employ. The humorous elements will always be the same."

sensitivities and from cultural backgrounds divergent from my own will certainly take issue with my choice of idioms.

Although lovers' dialogues are often used in erotic poetry from Mesopotamia, the present text is no lovers' dialogue and not erotic, as is indicated by the complete absence of figurative language or hint of any emotional attachment between the parties involved.[4] On the other hand, it is certainly not clinical. It is neither a medical text nor a love or potency incantation. Rather, it is crude and obscene and calls for the use of off-color terminology. There may be a humoristic, satirical bent to the composition that should influence the translation, but on this more will be said below.

Text

1.	*rīšātum*[*ma*]	*išdum ana ālim*
2.	^{d}*Telītum* [8–12 signs?]-*da-a-nim*	*rīšātumma išdum ana ālim*
3.	*i-ša*[-7–9 signs	*rīšātum*] *ma išdum ana ālim*
4.	*ku*[*lmašitum*?4–6 signs	*rīšātum*] *ma išdum ana ālim*
5.	*eṭ*[*lūtum* 5–7 signs	*rīšātum*] *ma išdum ana ālim*
6.	*ar*[*d*] *a*[*tum* 5–7	*rīšātum*] *ma išdum ana ālim*
7.	*i-ša*-x[7–9 signs	*rīšātum*] *ma išdum ana ālim*
8.	*ištēn il*[*likaššimma*	*rīšātum*] *ma išdum ana ālim*
9.	*alkī mugr*[*ī*] *nni* [3–4 signs	*rīšāt*] *umma išdum ana ālim*
10.	*u šanû illikaššimma*	*rīšātumma išdum ana ālim*
11.	*alkī lulappit ḫurdatki*	*rīšātumma išdum ana ālim*
12.	*ištuma amangurūkunuši*	*rīšātumma išdum ana ālim*
13.	*eṭlūt ālīkunu puḫḫirānimma*	*rīšātumma išdum ana ālim*
14.	*ana ṣilli dūrim ī nīlik*	*rīšātumma išdum ana ālim*
15.	*7 pantīša 7 qablīša*	*rīšātumma išdum ana ālim*
16.	*I šūši u I šūši iptanaššaḫū ana ūrīša*	*rīšātumma išdum ana ālim*
17.	*ītanḫū eṭlūtum ul innaḫ Ištar*	*rīšātumma išdum ana ālim*
18.	*šuknā eṭlūtum ana ḫurdati damiqtimma*	*rīšātumma išdum ana ālim*

4. For the language and motifs typical of love poetry see W. G. Lambert, "Devotion: The Languages of Religion and Love," in *Figurative Language in the Ancient Near East* (ed. Mindlen et al; London, 1987) 25–39. A motif found frequently in love poetry is going into a garden (see J. and Å. Westenholz, "Help for Rejected Suitors: The Old Akkadian Love Incantation MAD V 8," *Or* 46 [1977] 198–219 esp. 213ff.), but in our text Ištar invites the young men to the shadow of the wall, a place of prostitutes.

19. *ardatum ina qabêša* *rīšātumma išdum ana ālim*
20. *eṭlūtum išmû imgurū amassa* *rīšātumma išdum ana ālim*

---

21. *napḫar 20 pārum ša Ištar* MU.LUGAL *Hammurabim*
22. ^{md}ŠEG$_5$.ŠEG$_5$-*bēlu-rēṣūšu* LUGAL.E
23. *mār* ^{m}*Šumu-libši*
24. *išṭur*

First Translation

1. Jo[y] is a foundation for the city!
2. Telitum [x x x x x] x x x Joy ″. . . !
3. x [x x x x x x x Jo]y ″. . . !
4. Kul[mašitum x x x x x Jo]y ″. . . !
5. The young[men x x x x x x Jo]y ″. . . !
6. The young[girl x x x x x x Jo]y ″. . . !
7. x [x x x x x x x x x Jo]y ″. . . !
8. One comes [up to her (and says) Jo]y ″. . . !
9. Come, obey m[e x x x J]oy ″. . . !
10. and then another comes up to her (and says) Joy ″. . . !
11. "Come, let me caress your vulva." Joy ″. . . !
12. (She replies) "After I obey (the two of) you Joy ″. . . !
13. gather around me the young men of your city Joy ″. . . !
14. and let's go to the shadow of the wall." Joy ″. . . !
15. Seven (times) facing her chest
and seven (times) facing her haunches Joy ″ . . . !
16. sixty and another sixty (young men)
satisfy themselves again and again in her vagina. Joy ″. . . !
17. The young men are exhausted but Ištar is not exhausted Joy ″. . . !
18. (so she says) "Put it to the pretty vulva, young men!" Joy ″. . . !
19. When the young girl speaks Joy ″. . . !
20. the young men listened and obeyed her word. Joy ″. . . !

(Colophon)

21. A total of 20 lines). A *pārum* (composition) of Ištar.
The year when King Hammurapi became king
22. ^{md}ŠEG$_5$.ŠEG$_5$-bēlu-rēṣūšu
23. son of Šumu-libsi
24. wrote it.

Alternate Translation

1. Whoopee makes the town go around!
2. Telītum [x x x Who]opee ″. . . !
3. x [Who]opee ″. . . !
4. Kul[mašītum Who]opee ″. . . !
5. The jo[cks Whoo]pee ″. . . !
6. The ga[l Who]opee ″. . . !
7. x [Whoo]pee ″. . . !
8. One comes [on to her (and says) Who]opee ″. . . !
9. "Come, be my [(sex) slave," Wh]oopee ″. . . !
10. so another comes on to her (and says) Whoopee ″. . . !
11. "Come, let me pet your pudendum." Whoopee ″. . . !
12. (She replies) "After I slave to (both of) you Whoopee ″. . . !
13. gather the young men of your town to me Whoopee ″. . . !
14. and let's come over to the dark of the wall." Whoopee ″. . . !
15. Seven (times) to her gut
and seven (times) to her butt Whoopee ″. . . !
16. sixty and sixty more (jocks)
keep spending themselves between her thighs. Whoopee ″. . . !
17. The jocks all have groaned, (but) Ištar's not agroaning,
Whoopee ″. . . !
18. (so she says) "Sock it, O jocks, to the pretty pudendum!"
Whoopee ″. . . !
19. When the gal speaks Whoopee ″. . . !
20. the jocks listened and slaved to her command.
Whoopee ″. . . !

The Tone

No matter what its original genre and *Sitz im Leben*, the excerpt preserved on this tablet may be characterized as a "bawdy ballad," consisting of a narrative interspersed with dialogue. The situations described are also somewhat farcical (at least, from a masculine perspective). Contemporary scholars, inundated daily with sexual humor in their own societies, should not puritanically hesitate to identify such humor when it appears in an ancient culture; they would do well to let themselves snicker with the text as they read and interpret it. We will interpret it in this vein.

The Refrain

The main body of the text, made up of nineteen short verses (lines 2–20), is accented in every line by a refrain that repeats the first line of the composition, *rīšātumma išdum ana ālim.* Von Soden explains the refrain by speaking of a supposed "sumerischer Einfluss" or a background in "ein vor einem grösseren Kreis vorgetragenes Kultlied."[5] However, bearing in mind the text's theme and tone, it is reminiscent of colloquial obscene songs with lewd lyrics, such as "Barnacle Bill the Sailor" or "Roll Me Over in the Clover." It is to be intoned wildly by some young men out to find a good time with a local pickup, or on any other occasion when "boys will be boys."

The refrain expresses the theme of the piece: "Joy is the foundation of the city." The term *rīšātum,* which I have rendered 'joy' or 'whoopee', literally means 'mirth' or 'merrymaking'. In the context of this composition, it undoubtedly has the commonly attested secondary meaning associated with numerous terms for happiness, namely "(conjugal) bliss" or "joy (of sex)."[6] The message of the refrain is that sex is essential for the city or that sex is basic to urban life.[7]

The Vocabulary

The lewdness of the text is not in the lexicon, and this is one reason I chose not to use "dirty" words in translating it. The text uses no unusual lexemes that may be identified inherently as Akkadian "four-letter

5. For a refrain in a cultic love poem, see the "Love Lyrics of Nabû and Tašmetu," in A. Livingstone, *Court Poetry and Literary Miscellanea* (State Archives of Assyria 3; Helsinki, 1989) 35–37.

6. For joy as a metaphor for sexual relations in Biblical and Rabbinic Hebrew, in particular, and other Semitic languages, including Akkadian, in general, see G. A. Anderson, *A Time to Mourn, a Time to Dance: The Expression of Grief and Joy in Israelite Religion* (University Park, Penn., 1991) 27–37. For *rīšātum* see *rīšātu iššakkanūšu* 'he will enjoy himself (sexually)', CT 39, 44:18 (in sexual omens) and *rēšātim libbašu tušamla elṣiš* 'you happily filled his heart with joy' in W. Lambert, "Divine Love Lyrics from the Reign of Abi-Ešuh," *MIO* 12 (1966) 48:7, 8; *rēšāti mali,* ibid., 49:12, 13.

7. Von Soden takes the phrase to mean that joy is the basis of the city's cultic sphere. Unfortunately, there are no exact parallel usages of *išdum,* so that the exact nuance remains enigmatic. However, *išdum* of a particular, named city or country means, according to CAD I/J 237–38 s.v. *išdu* 2a and b, 'organization of a city or country', and when associated with *ummānum* 'army', it means 'discipline'. These usages, if transferred to our refrain, would give it a meaning something like 'sexual joy is how the city behaves', 'the city behaves licentiously', or 'sexual merriment is the way or law of the city'. We should also bear in mind that *išdu,* especially in parallelism with *zēru* ('seed') is a euphemism for penis. See CAD I/J 240 s.v. *išdu* 3e2′.

words," and it is doubtful whether the language possessed such a register. The lexeme *ūru*, which the narrator uses to describe the "goddess's" genitals in line 16, is a common anatomical term, usually rendered 'vagina', 'vulva', or 'pudendum'. It is derived from *erû* IV and is cognate with Hebrew *ʿerwâ* 'nakedness'. Its basic meaning is 'nakedness', and it is used to describe both male and female genitalia.[8] The word *ḫurdatum*, used by the young men as well as by the lady in conversation (11, 18), is, in contrast, rarer and more literary.[9] It occurs in two literary contexts: Gilgamesh VI 69 and in a newly published love song from Kish (Ki. 1063).[10] Interestingly, it appears in a medical text, BAM 248 II 30; but a commentary on that text[11] glosses it *ḫur-da-tú: ú-ru-u šá sin-niš-ti* and goes on to quote the passage from Gilgamesh VI 69. The necessity of explaining the word may indicate the rarity of the term and lack of familiarity with it at a later period. According to M. Gallery Kovacs, the word is used in Gilgamesh VI 69 because of its homonym, meaning 'date palm'.[12] Such a conditioned use would be another indication of the rarity of the word.[13]

The verbs used to designate sexual acts, *magāru* 'to comply with [sexually]' (lines 12, 20), *lupputu* 'to fondle, caress' (line 11), *šakānu* 'to place [insert the penis in the vagina]' (line 18), *pašāḫu* 'to be satisfied [from sexual intercourse]' (line 16), *anāḫu*- 'to get tired out (or to groan) [from

8. See R. D. Biggs, *ŠÀ.ZI.GA: Ancient Mesopotamian Potency Incantations* (TCS 2; Locust Valley, N.Y., 1967) 34.

9. The author may be indicating by this dichotomy in usage that *ḫurdatu* is a slang term used in speech, while *ūru* is a more refined term, suitable for the narrator. However, this distinction is hard to maintain because it would be ad hoc and cannot be applied to other texts. Enkidu, when propositioning Šamhāt, uses *ūru*, and the term also appears in the love incantation MAD V 8:16 (see Westenholz, "Help for Rejected Suitors"). Note also in the bilingual proverb collection (W. G. Lambert, *Babylonian Wisdom Literature* [Oxford, 1960; hereafter *BWL*] 242 14–16), where the Akkadian reads *ūrīmi damiq ina nišīja gummuranni* 'my vagina is fine, (yet) among my people (it is said of me) 'It is finished with you.' " According to Lambert, these are the words of an old prostitute, defending her ability to continue in her line of work. A poetic, euphemistic use of *ūru* is found in *BWL* 255:7–10, where the Akkadian reads *sarru murteddû ūrī // la kīnu šitta niggallašu* 'a liar chases women (lit. vaginas), the dishonest man has two sickles" (cf. CAD S 180b s.v. *sarru* A bilingual section).

10. See J. Westenholz, "A Forgotten Love Song," in *Language, Literature, and History: Philological and Historical Studies Presented to Erica Reiner* (ed. F. Rochberg-Halton; AOS 67; New Haven, Conn., 1987) 415–25, esp. 422 I 13′.

11. M. Civil, "Medical Commentaries from Nippur," *JNES* 33 (1974) 329–38, esp. 333, lines 40–41.

12. M. Gallery Kovacs, *The Epic of Gilgamesh* (Stanford, 1989) 53 n. 5.

13. For other Akkadian terms designating female genitalia, either anatomically or euphemistically (*biṣru, biṣṣūru, guruš-garaš, garištu, ḫallu, ḫanduttu, laqlaqqu, lib/pištu, ḫiṣbu, kuzbu, puridu, sūnu*, and *šasurru*) see CAD, AHw, and H. Holma, *Die Namen der Körperteile im Assyrisch-babylonischen* (Leipzig, 1911) 100–104.

sexual intercourse]' (line 17) are all common words, which are used sexually.[14]

The Cast

The characters in the text are some young men[15] and a female named Ištar. It is not completely certain whether she is the goddess, because her name is not written with the DINGIR sign, although there are attestations of the divine name without the determinative. If she is the goddess, she is playing a dual role. On the level of the narrative she is simply the girl whom the young men pick up. But since at the narrative's conclusion the girl turns out to be sexually invincible (see below), the author may have had the goddess in mind, lurking behind the heroine.

The Narrative

Regrettably, the beginning of the text is damaged. It mentions Ištar by her title Telītum 'the able one' and by terms often associated with this goddess, *kulmašītum*(?) and *ardatum* 'maiden', 'lass'. It also mentions 'the young men' *eṭlūtum*. Lines 3 and 7 both begin with the signs *i-ša-*, which may be the beginnings of verbs, and in line 2 the refrain is preceded with the remnants of a verbal form. If so, at least some of these

14. For more explicit terms, see CAD and AHw s.v. *nâku* and *naqābu*. Other terms used for intercourse include *alāku, garāšu, qerēbu,* and *ṭeḫû*. For *alāku* and *garāšu,* see Biggs, *ŠÀ.ZI.GA*, 8–10. It has been suggested to me by several people that *alkī* and *i nīlik* in lines 9, 11, and 14 and *illikaššimma* in lines 8 and 10 are to be explained sexually. However, the sexual connotations of *alāku* are present only in the combination *alāku ana FN*. Therefore, if they are found in our text they are present only in lines 8 and 10, and elsewhere only on a subsurface level. For this expression in Akkadian see Biggs; for the cognate term *hālak el hanna*ʿ*rah* in Amos 2:7, see S. Paul, "Two Cognate Semitic Terms for Mating and Copulation," *VT* 32 (1982) 492–94.

15. The term used, *eṭlūtu*, is a common designation for young men. It may have sexual overtones here, as it does in OB Gilgamesh P i 5, where Gilgamesh describes himself in a dream: *šamḫākuma attanallak ina birit eṭlūtim* 'I was walking about proudly (perhaps 'sexually aroused') among the (virile) young men'. The verb *šamḫāku* is certainly used here in anticipation of the subsequent appearance of the harlot Šamhat. For the sexual nuances of the entire passage in the Old-Babylonian version, see A. Draffkorn Kilmer, "A Note of an Overlooked Word-Play in the Akkadian Gilgamesh," in *ZIKIR ŠUMIM: Assyriological Studies Presented to F. R. Kraus on the Occasion of his Seventieth Birthday* (ed. G. van Driel et al.; Nederlands Instituut voor het nabije Oosten. Studia Francisci Scholten Memoriae Dicata 50; Leiden, 1982) 128–32. For the development of the later Ninevite version of this passage, see J. S. Cooper, "Gilgamesh Dreams of Enkidu: The Evolution and Dilution of Narrative," in *Essays on the Ancient Near East in Memory of Jacob Joel Finkelstein* (ed. M. de Jong Ellis; Memoirs of the Connecticut Academy of Arts and Sciences 19; Hamden, 1977) 39–44.

seven broken lines would not constitute a dramatis personae but would represent an integral part of the narrative.

Line 1 should be understood as an exposition of the theme and stand alone poetically. The six broken lines between the exposition and the dialogue (2–7) would represent either three couplets or two triplets. Since lines 2 and 6 begin with titles of Ištar (^{d}*Telītum, ardatum*) and line 4 may begin with a title of Ištar or a votary (*kulmašītum*), while lines 3 and 7 begin with the same verb, the three-couplet structure (2–3, 4–5, 6–7) seems more likely.

What remains of the narrative runs smoothly, coherently, and without interruption from line 8 to the end of the text. The young lady is approached in line 8 by one young man, who propositions her in general terms, *alkī mugrīnni* 'come, obey me'.[16] He is followed immediately by a second young man who is more explicit. Perhaps, having seen that his friend was not rebuffed for his advances, he musters up courage to outdo his fellow in forwardness. This young man invites the lady for foreplay,[17] obviously a synecdoche for sexual relations. Ištar is not one to decline such advances and, true to reputation, accepts, readily. As a matter of

16. The term *mugrānni* 'obey me', derived from *magāru*, is not particularly rare and has a wide range of meaning. Of particular interest to us are the cases where it is used in a master-servant relationship. We find the *-tan-* form in the comical satirical "Dialogue of Pessimism" in the master's address to the slave *arad mitanguranni* (see *BWL* 144–49: 1, 10, 17, 29, 39, 46, 53, 62, 70, 79). It is also used in KBo 1 12:7–16, edited by E. Ebeling, "Ein Hymnus auf die Suprematie des Sonnengottes in Exemplaren aus Assur und Bogazkoi," *Or* 23 (1954) 209–6, esp. 214:9. This text, which might be characterized as "wisdom" literature, presents instructions for the treatment of disobedient slaves. (See also CAD M/1 39b s.v. *magāru* 3a.) The use of the verb *magāru* in our text may indicate the dominance of the males and subservience of the female partner, roles that are reversed at the end of the text.

17. This act is to be compared with touching the '(place of) sexuality' (*kuzbam lapātum*) in an incantation published by S. Lackenbacher ("Note sur l'Ardat-Lili," *RA* 65 [1971] 119–54, esp. 136), and recently incorporated into a publication by M. J. Geller ("New Duplicates to SBTU II," *AfO* 35 (1988) 1–23, esp. 14). Although hidden by a very nonexplicit translation, this incantation, addressed to a demoness who is 'not like a girl' (*ardatu la šēmta*), describes in reverse order and in quite graphic language an act of lovemaking, something which the ardat-lili has never experienced. A 'penis has never ejaculated into her' (GIŠ *la-a ir-ḫ*[*u-u-si*]), a 'penis has never even penetrated/deflowered her' (GIŠ *la-a i-qí-pu-si*), 'in the lap of her husband no one has even fondled her sexual organs' (*ina su-un mu-ti-sá ku-uz-ba la il-pu-tu*), 'in her husband's lap no one has ever even removed her clothes' (*ina su-un mu-ti-šá ṣu-bat-sa la iš-ḫu-ṭu*), 'a nice (virile) young man has never even unclasped the clasps of her garment' (*eṭ-lu dam-qu ṣil-la-sá la ip-ṭu-ru*). This text demonstrates that, as we all know, fondling the naked genitalia follows undressing the girl and precedes penetration. *kuzbam lapātum* and *ḫurdatam lapātum* are, in light of this text and its clear orderly presentation of a sex act, not merely general descriptions (cf. Geller's "experienced sex") but specific designations of foreplay. On the absence of kissing in Mesopotamian foreplay, see J. S. Cooper, s.v. "Kuss" in *RLA* 6 (1980–83) 375–79.

fact, she immediately outdoes the two young men by offering herself not only to them but to the entire city. She invites all the young men in town down to the shadow of the city wall, assumedly to have a good time.[18] She uses the verb *i nīlik*, echoing the language of the two propositions, indicating her consent and any sexual connotations the seemingly innocuous verb *alāku* may have.

The shadow of the wall, where the rendezvous is to take place, seems to have been the area of the city frequented by prostitutes, the "red-light district." This is borne out by Enkidu's curse of Šamhat, in which he in fact determines the destiny of whores for all time. He says *ṣilli dūri lū manzazuki* 'the shadow of the wall will be the place where you stand', using the same expression as in our text. Male prostitutes also seem to have loitered in the shadow of the wall, as indicated by Ereškigal's curse of Aṣûšu-namir, which is identical to the one just mentioned ("Ištar's Descent to the Netherworld," line 103).[19] Note that the house of Rahab, the prostitute of Jericho known from the book of Joshua, was situated in the wall of the city (Josh 2:15).[20] Ištar refers to the city as 'your (pl.) city', perhaps indicating that she is a girl from out of town. She seems not to be a prostitute, however, since no price for her services is discussed (as it is in Gen 38:16–18).[21]

18. Our text reads *eṭlūt ālikunu puḫḫirānimma* 'gather around me all the young men of your city'. This may be compared with Gilgamesh's dream presaging the arrival of Enkidu, Gilgamesh OB P i 10–11, *Uruk mātum paḫir elīšu, eṭlūtum unaššaqū šēpēšu* 'The land of Uruk was assembled around it, the young men were kissing its feet'.

19. For a new edition of Enkidu's curse (UET VI 394) see now W. G. Lambert, "Prostitution," in *Außenseiter und Randgruppen* (ed. V. Haas; Xenia. Konstanzer Althistorische Vorträge und Forschungen 32; Konstanz, 1922) 127–61, esp. 129 line 25. Another denizen of the shadow of the wall was the dog, as shown by VS 17 8 edited by M. Sigrist, "On the Bite of a Dog," in *Love and Death in the Ancient Near East: Essays in Honor of Marvin H. Pope* (ed. J. H. Marks and R. M. Good; Guilford, 1987) 85–88, esp. 86, text 2, line 3: *ṣilli dūrim muzzazušu* 'the shadow of the wall is his station'. In the "Love Lyrics of Nabû and Tašmetu" the goddess is referred to as *ša* BÀD (*dūrim*) 'her of the wall' (SAA III 33 6). In the very next stanza Nabû's shelter is said to be the 'shade of a sprig of juniper' (*ṣīl kanni ša burāši puzar Nabium*...)'. These descriptions of the places where the two divine lovers are located may actually refer to a single place, the designation of which is broken up and distributed among the two stanzas. Both are in the shadow of the wall. If this passage does indeed refer to lovemaking in the shadow of the wall, it would indicate that this undesirable place, which was popular among prostitutes, was used for similar purposes by others as well.

20. Even if the second half of verse 15 is a gloss, as indicated by its absence in the LXX (see G. A. Cooke, *The Book of Joshua* [Cambridge, 1918] 14 ad loc.), this would not change the actual location of Rahab's establishment. See J. Bottéro, "'Free Love' and Its Disadvantages," in *Mesopotamia: Writing, Reasoning, and the Gods* (trans. Z. Bahrani and M. van de Mieroop; Chicago and London, 1992) 185–98, esp. 197.

21. See Ezek 16:33–34, where Jerusalem is described as looser than a whore, so loose that she even pays her partners for their services. For the fees of temple prostitutes in Mesopotamia, varying by the position, see Å. W. Sjöberg, *JCS* 29 (1977) 24 and B. Alster, "Marriage and

A total of 120 young men take their pleasures with the young lady. They have intercourse with her seven times from the back and seven from the front, although it is unclear in our text whether the sex acts "from the back" are anal intercourse[22] or vaginal intercourse with approach from the rear (as characteristic of Orpah, according to Rashi on *b. Soṭa* 42b). Although anal intercourse was popular in ancient Mesopotamia,[23] in this particular text the second possibility is more likely, because the description of the men's sexually satisfying themselves continuously (*iptanaššahū*) refers only to Ištar's vagina (*ana ūrīša*) and not her anus (*qinnatu*).

Also unclear is whether each of the men perform fourteen complete acts, reaching orgasm as many times, or whether each take seven thrusts in each position, ejaculating only twice! In the first case, Ištar would have experienced 14 × 120 = 1680 sexual encounters, while in the second eventuality, it would have occurred a mere 2 × 120 = 240. She must have thought that only the second possibility occurred, for when it is all over she still asks for more! The young men, on the other hand, surely think they have done the first, for they are all quite tired and undoubtedly quite proud of themselves for such a performance.

Such promiscuity is known from other places in ancient Near Eastern literature, although we must be aware of the likelihood that it was viewed differently in various cultures. In Mesopotamian literature Enkidu copulates[24] with Šamhat for six days and seven nights and she still

---

Love in the Sumerian Love Songs, with Some Notes on the Manchester Tammuz," in *The Tablet and the Scroll: Near Eastern Studies in Honor of William W. Hallo* (ed. M. E. Cohen et al.; Bethesda, Md., 1993) 15–27 (reference courtesy of S. Paul).

22. For anal intercourse in Mesopotamian texts, see CAD N/1 197–98 s.v. *nâku;* Q 250a s.v. *qiddatam,* 255b s.v. *qinnatu.* Anal intercourse was performed both homosexually and heterosexually. It could be preferred as a means of contraception, as indicated by the omen apodosis *entu aššum lā erîša qinnassa ušnâk* 'in order not to become pregnant the *entu*-priestess let her anus be penetrated' (according to Yohanan Muffs [personal communication], this text was presented to Moshe Held by Benno Landsberger to translate from English to Akkadian as an examination question at the University of Chicago). In our text, in which Ištar performs vaginal intercourse as well, there is certainly no contraceptive motive.

23. Note the relief reproduced by H. W. F. Saggs (*The Greatness That Was Babylon* (New York, 1962) fig. 60), described as a "cult scene of questionable nature." For terra-cotta reliefs depicting both anal and vaginal intercourse, see R. Opificius, *Das altbabylonische Terrakottarelief* (Untersuchungen zur Assyriologie und vorderasiatischen Archäologie 2; Berlin, 1961) 166–68; W. Andrae, *Die jungeren Ischtar-Tempel in Assur* (WVDOG 58; Leipzig, 1935) 90–93 and pls. 45–46; J. Spier, *Ancient Gems and Finger Rings: Catalogue of the Collections of the J. Paul Getty Museum* (Malibu, 1992) 61 no. 118 (last reference courtesy of Z. Zevit).

24. Gilgamesh I iv 21, *Enkidu tebīma Šamhat irhi,* should be translated 'Enkidu, erect, ejaculated (into) Šamhat' (cf. 'Enkidu was aroused and poured himself into Shamhat', in S. Dalley, *Myths from Mesopotamia: Creation, the Flood, Gilgamesh and Others* [Oxford, 1989] 25) rather than simply 'had intercourse with the harlot' (so M. Gallery Kovacs, *The Epic of Gilgamesh,* 9). For *tebû* as 'achieved erection' rather than simply 'be aroused sexually', see Biggs, *ŠÀ.ZI.GA,* 9.

gets the best of him, or, as the text puts it, he had his fill of her charms (Gilgamesh I iv 21–22).

At one point in the burlesque *aluzinnu*-text the actor/actress takes on the role of an oversexed but quite ugly woman and claims:[25]

18. *ina šinnisāti kī iāti ul ibašši . . .*
22. *kī maṣi ḫāmirī irammannimāku*
23. *kī ša alluttu aḫzu*
24. *ana panīšu û arkīšu issanaḫuramāku*

18. There is none like unto me among women . . .
22. so much does my husband (CAD A/2)/lover (Foster) love me
23. that like a trained (CAD A/2)/snared (Foster) crab
24. he keeps turning around forward and backward.

This text is admittedly enigmatic but it seems to contain an allusion to an oversexed wife and a worn-out, reluctant husband or lover.[26] Foster adds the words *from me* in parentheses at the end of the last line, implying that the "woman" is constantly in pursuit of her lover. CAD A/2 361a, s.v. *alluttu*, however, makes no interpretive additions to the text, leaving it to imply that the husband is constantly, incessantly making love with his wife.[27]

In the Ugaritic myths about Baal we find that this god made love with a cow, lying with her not only 77 times but mounting her 88 times (CTA 5 V 17–21) = *ANET*³ 139a).[28] This is a unique instance in which the massive sexual encounter results in conception, for the cow subsequently gives birth. There seems to be no lewd connotations in this text and there is certainly nothing humorous intended. Moreover, the text can hardly mean to imply that Baal was infertile and that it took him 88

25. For a new edition of the *aluzinnu*-text and discussion, see B. R. Foster, "Humor and Cuneiform Literature," *JANESCU* 6 (1974) 69–85, esp. 75–80.

26. This brings to my mind the Ropers—the landlords in the American TV comedy series "Three's Company."

27. In the Sumerian *balbale* to Inanna, published by S. N. Kramer (in *Proceedings of the American Philosophical Society* 107 [Philadelphia, 1963] 509–10), and later in *The Sacred Marriage Rite* ([Bloomington, 1969] 103–4), Kramer's rendition and interpretation have Dumuzi boasting that he made love to Inanna fifty times. However, T. Jacobsen ("The Sister's Message," *JANESCU* 5 [The Gaster Festschrift; 1973] 199–212) has offered a radically different reading of the entire passage, and Dumuzi's boast no longer exists. According to Jacobsen, Geshtinanna is speaking to Dumuzi, telling him about a conversation she had with Inanna while the two of them were lying in bed. I am grateful to Shalom Paul for bringing this text to my attention.

28. For a discussion of the passage, see P. J. van Zijl, *Baal: A Study of Texts in Connexion with Baal in the Ugaritic Epic* (AOAT 10; Neukirchen-Vluyn, 1972) 172–75.

times to impregnate his mate. Quite to the contrary, its main aim is to demonstrate Baal's fecundity, seen as directly proportional to his virility.

The motif of multiple sexual acts appears in Jewish writings from a considerably later period. Judg 5:27 is understood by Rabbi Johanan as alluding to Sisera's mating with Yael seven times before wearing himself out (*b. Yebam.* 103a). Rabbi Nahman reports in the name of Rav that Zimri son of Salu copulated with Cozbi[29] daughter of Zur 424 times, until his strength abated and he was killed by a zealous Phinehas (*b. Sanh.* 82b). According to a less imaginative opinion, Zimri copulated with Cozbi only 60 times, and as a result of this bout he was like a beaten egg and she was filled like a well-watered flower bed. Evaluating these texts, we should note that, apart from Yael, the men and women described are not positive figures and that their sexual prowess is probably not a laughing matter for the Rabbis who so describe them. Their sexual promiscuity is, rather, a measure of their moral depravity.[30]

Whatever the attitude towards the moral fiber of these oversexed personages is, in all these sexual marathons the women prove stronger than the men; and indeed, such is the case in our text. In our composition the men are exhausted, but Ištar is ready for more (line 17).

The young men, so it seems, may have gotten more than they bargained for. Von Soden remarks on the word *šuknā* in line 18: "Die genaue Bedeutungsnuance ist hier nicht ganz klar." In all due respect to the renowned lexikographer, the exact nuance of Ištar's asking for more ist *doch* ganz klar! She is simply saying "Do it to me again, boys." This time *she* is doing the propositioning, and the men have no choice but to try to satisfy her.

Ištar has proven herself more than equal to the whole town and may at this point be mocking her macho consorts. This possibility arises from a comparison of the initial proposition with Ištar's second proposition. The young man who propositioned her in the first place referred only to

29. This name is to be related to Akkadian *kuzbum*, as recognized already by P. Haupt in his glosses to C. J. Ball, *The Book of Genesis* (Leipzig, 1896) 96. It is semantically and functionally equivalent to Šamhat, the whore from the "Gilgamesh Epic" (see J. Greenfield, "Lexicographical Notes II," *HUCA* 30 [1959] 141–51, esp. 145 n. 23). According to the Rabbis (*b. Sanh.* 82b and *Tg. Yer.* Num 25:15), Cozbi had the nickname *Šewilnai*ʾ. Suggestions have been made to relate this term to various Persian or Arabic words meaning 'vagina' or 'whore', but these suggestions are now deemed incorrect. The term may be related to a supposed singular form, **šul*, of the Hebrew word *šulayim* 'margins, skirts', referring euphemistically to the vagina (cf. Jer 13:22, 26; Nah 3:5; Lam 1:9). Note Akkadian *sūnu*, which also indicates both the lap and the clothing covering the lap.

30. This is not to say that the Rabbis who made up these stories did not chuckle in the process or that the students who first heard their masters' explanations kept a straight face, but this can only be speculated on and is not indicated in the text.

her *ḫurdatum* 'pudendum'. She, however, when describing her vagina, uses the term *ḫurdatum damiqtum* 'pretty pudendum', thus adding the word *damiqtum* to what her second propositioner had designated. She may be imagined to be speaking in a mocking, pseudo-seductive sing-song, implying: the "pretty pudendum" you wanted so badly at first has proven a bit too much for you.

Additional light can be shed on Ištar's statement by comparing it with the bilingual proverb *BWL* 242:14–16, in which an old prostitute, commending her own wares, claims *ūrīmi damiq* 'my vagina is still pretty', that is to say, it still works well.[31] Ištar, using synonymous language after her sexual marathon with the 120 young men, is not only using words typical of prostitute's talk but is stating that she is still in working order and ready for more. This is in stark contrast to the men who have all tired themselves out.

The ownership of the female genitalia is further indication of the tone of the composition. When Ištar is first propositioned, the young man refers to her vagina as 'your' vagina. She, in contrast, uses no possessive pronoun now, thus disassociating herself from her own favors. In love lyrics such as Ki. 1063,[32] all parts of the female lover's body are referred to as 'ours', indicating love, sharing, and intimacy. In Ištar's famous marriage proposal to the gardener Išullanu,[33] the goddess likewise refers to 'our' vulva, indicating also more than a merely sexual encounter. The young men in our poem, however, refer to Ištar's vagina as 'yours', as Enkidu does in Gilgamesh I iv 9, 16 and III 43.[34] They have no intent of anything more than a sexual encounter with no strings attached. She, for her part, outdoes them in detachment and simply refers to her vagina neutrally, indicating perhaps her own even greater detachment and disinterest in the whole affair. The text may imply that one who has fooled around with Ištar has not gained any control over the goddess, for she detaches herself from her own sexual organs. One may enjoy Ištar's body and sexuality, for she is the ultimate sex object, but no one

31. Note as well UET VI 394:16 (Lambert, "Prostitution," 129), where Enkidu says *sūnuk*[*i*] *damqa qadūtum išeḫḫi* 'May beer dregs soil(?) your pretty (virile) lap'. *sūnu damqu* is another synonym of *ūru damqu* and *hurdatu damiqtu.* Also, see above, nn. 9 and 17.

32. Westenholz, "A Forgotten Love Song," esp. 417, with references to other texts and previous literature.

33. CAD Ḫ "emends" the text by translating 'put out your hand and touch my (text: our) vulva', but the reading *ḫur-da-at-na* in the medical commentary published by Civil (*JNES* 33 [1974] 332, 40), as well as the existence of the idiom in the newly published love poem, obviate this emendation.

34. But note also *ūrki ša šinātim* in MAD V 8:15–16 and *ina ūrīja ša šinātim* in C. Wilcke, "Liebesbeschwörungen aus Isin," *ZA* 75 (1985) 188–209, esp. 198:19.

may possess Ištar. This would be in keeping with the reputation of the goddess, as expressed in Gilgamesh's angry diatribe against her and her disastrous relationships with mortal men and beasts.[35]

The encounter ends a bit ironically, for the girl is now in control. The word *magārum,* used by the young man who initially propositioned Ištar (line 9) and by Ištar herself in accepting the proposition (line 12), is now used in describing the men's certainly forced response to her proposition (line 20). She has turned the tables on them. Figuratively speaking, they are now in a female superior, male inferior position. The guys are now Ištar's sexual slaves, and they must bend themselves to her.

If this twenty-line piece is indeed excerpted from a longer composition and if its background is a cultic setting or some temple festival, the festival would have been akin to Mardi Gras. If we insist on seeing this work as a small part of a larger cult drama, it can only be a vulgar scene aimed at titillating the rabble in the pit. The reason it would have been excerpted by ^{md}ŠEG$_5$.ŠEG$_5$-bēlu-rēṣūšu mār Šumu-libši is probably that the text piqued his prurient interests and he found it worthy of sharing with others. He may have been looking for "the good parts" of a longer work, in order to share them with his friends (just as I have done in publishing this discussion). If there is a religious message to the composition, as one might expect in a cult poem, it would be to extol the sexual prowess and conjugal invincibility of the second-millennium B.C.E. "Madonna"[36] goddess. She is untiring in providing endless sexual pleasure for everyone who so desires but, in the end, gets the best of him. We may certainly agree wholeheartedly with von Soden's concluding remark, "Die mütterliche Ištar vieler jünger Gebete wird in diesem Lied nirgends erkennbar."

It is just as likely, however, that the text was composed intentionally, perhaps by a puerile pupil used to writing "excerpts" and imitating classical literary patterns, as a bawdy song.[37] However, in mocking his heroes'

35. See T. Abusch, "Ishtar's Proposal and Gilgamesh's Refusal: An Interpretation of 'The Gilgamesh Epic' Tablet 6, Lines 1–79," *HR* 26 (1986) 143–87.

36. The similarities in personality and social role between the second-millennium B.C.E. Ištar and the second-millennium C.E. Madonna—both of them outrageous, antiestablishment, self-serving libertarians and sex symbols—are worthy of a separate study.

37. Two other obscene, although not specifically "pornographic" texts recently published are the "Warning to Bel-eṭir" and "Magic against Bel-eṭir," edited and translated without bowdlerizing by A. Livingstone, *Court Poetry and Literary Miscellanea,* 64–66 nos. 29 and 30 (see also p. xxviii). The first of these texts imitates the so-called *narû* literature, in general, and perhaps the Cuthean "Legend of Naram-Sin," in particular (especially the opening line, *ṭupšinna pitēma narâ šitassi*), while the second mimics an incantation. According to Livingstone, these two compositions are invectives against a historical figure and make references to other historical figures and events. Nonetheless, both are humorous satires of

machismo and showing his heroine to be the stronger of the sexes, our author should be hailed as one of the world's first known feminists!

---

the literary genres they are modeled after, using traditional literary patterns for obscene purposes. Could our text be religious satire, mocking either the goddess Ištar or one of her priestesses who takes her job a bit too seriously?

Some Reflections on Amarna Politics

WILLIAM L. MORAN

Mario Liverani has argued that the vassal correspondence in the Amarna letters was an exercise in mutual misunderstanding. In his opinion, the Egyptian administration wrote with a conception of suzerain-vassal relations that the vassals had only partially assimilated. Their letters often reflect a quite different conception and one totally alien to Egyptian thinking. Hence the ongoing misunderstanding, which was also fostered by the interference of linguistic substrates. This article offers a different interpretation of the evidence and denies any malentendu.

In 1967 Mario Liverani published an article entitled "Contrasti e confluenze di concezioni politiche nell'età di El-Amarna."[1] Though it appeared in a major Assyriological journal and argued for a radical revision of our thinking about Amarna politics, it was generally ignored by historians of the Amarna period. Perhaps in those "pre-Ebla" days *itala non leguntur* was still too true. Whatever the explanation, in 1983, when he returned to the subject, this time writing in English ("Political Lexicon and Political Ideologies in the Amarna Letters"),[2] Liverani could with good reason complain of the neglect that his work had received. And even now, writing a decade later, I am still unaware of any serious examination of Liverani's position. I wish, therefore, to fill this gap in Amarna studies, to make Liverani's position known and, in the spirit of friendly debate, to argue against it. I wish, too, of course, to salute Jonas Greenfield, no stranger to the Amarna world.

According to Liverani, in the correspondence between Egypt and its vassals in the Amarna period, there are discernible two political concepts or, more exactly, two lines of political behavior, deriving from different

1. M. Liverani, "Contrasti e confluenze de concezioni politiche nell' età di El-Amarna," *RA* 61 (1967) 1–18.

2. M. Liverani, "Political Lexicon and Political Ideologies in the Amarna Letters," *Berytus* 31 (1983) 41–56.

political, cultural, and social histories. One he calls Asiatic. Though he sees its diffusion from Anatolia across northern Mesopotamia and down through Syria and Palestine, he finds its classical expression in the Hittite vassal treaties. It is characterized by the presence of obligations that bind suzerain as well as vassal. The latter's oath of loyalty requires of him, inter alia, the acceptance of his master's friends and enemies as his own, and hence his renunciation of all aggression against a fellow vassal. To this the suzerain has a corresponding obligation, also solemnly ratified by oath, that as a reward for his loyalty the vassal be kept on his throne and hence defended from aggression.

Worlds apart is what Liverani calls the Egyptian conception of the vassal relationship. In this view, whereas the vassal has many obligations, the suzerain has none. As a god, the Pharaoh can be bound to no one. The theological absurdity of his being under oath, with its ensuing obligations, is reinforced by Egypt's profound ethnocentrism and consequent contempt for the barbarians abroad. A political arrangement of the Asiatic type is, therefore, unthinkable and completely alien to Egyptian thought and practice. Hence, the Egyptian vassal has no legal claims on his master and, however loyal, he may not, if attacked, demand to be defended. This he could expect only if purely Egyptian interests were at stake, and these—another important difference from Asiatic rule—do not necessarily involve the vassals' maintaining peaceful relations among themselves, provided they continue to serve Egypt.

The originality of Liverani's thesis is in his opinion that, whereas of course the directives and replies of the Pharaoh reflect a purely Egyptian viewpoint, this viewpoint is not completely shared by the vassals themselves, all of whom also betray in their letters the influence of the Asiatic institution. Liverani finds evidence of this anomaly in the numerous instances in which a vassal, in one way or another, insists on his loyalty and then, as if he were addressing an Asiatic overlord, demands help in defending himself against his enemies. The implied argument is naturally quite ineffective, especially since the enemy in question is almost always another Egyptian vassal. Indifferent to such quarrels insofar as the narrow interests of the conflicting parties are concerned, the Pharaoh usually refuses to intervene and tells the vassal to take care of himself. In short, the vassal correspondence is an exercise in mutual incomprehension to the extent that it is shot through with an intrusive element, a curious survival of a quite alien world of political discourse.

Can this possibly be right? This way of putting the question, even prior to a closer consideration of the evidence, seems legitimate, for to anyone recalling the historical context of the Amarna letters the improbability of such survival is immediately apparent. At the time the letters were written, Egyptian control of the area occupied by the vassals had been more or less firmly established since the reign of Thutmosis III. Experience of Egyptian rule was not something new; it had been a fact of political life for roughly a century. Whatever may have been the initial difficulties in grasping what an Egyptian regime meant and in adjusting to it, they should certainly have been surmounted by four or five generations of Syro-Palestinian princes.

Particularly difficult to understand is how a ruler in Byblos could have failed to see every implication of subjection to Egypt, for in the Amarna age Byblos had already been a center of profound Egyptian influence for over a millennium[3] and, with no exaggeration, its prince could boast that it had served Egypt from the most ancient days.[4] But even elsewhere, at least since the time of Thutmosis III, the sons of many local rulers had been held as hostages in Egypt, educated there and then returned to their native lands to succeed their fathers.[5] After years of such training and, presumably, indoctrination, could anyone have cherished the slightest illusion of enjoying any legal claims on his Egyptian master?

That, in fact, the Egyptian viewpoint was far from being unassimilated, Liverani himself has demonstrated, often with very perceptive observations.[6] Confining ourselves to a brief outline of his remarks, we find:

1. The vassals recognized the futility of arguing their case simply on the basis of their loyalty. Realizing that the Pharaoh was deaf to all but his own concerns, they tried to show that their enemies were really his enemies, and they warned that failure to defend them could only mean the loss of territory for the empire.
2. They adopted a purely Egyptian viewpoint of their duty to defend the city or territory where they were. The true Asiastic vassal saw himself as defending his own city for himself, and he expected to be helped in this by his lord. The vassals in the Amarna letters saw themselves quite differently: they were pure functionaries, defending city or territory, not for themselves, but for the king, and simply carrying out their duty to him.

3. Liverani ("Contrasti," 13 n. 6) acknowledges this dependence but in another context and for a different purpose.

4. *EA* 75:9, 88:45, 106:4, 116:56.

5. See, for example, D. B. Redford, *Akhenaten, the Heretic King* (Princeton, 1984), 25–26. The practice is well attested in the Amarna letters; cf. *EA* 59, 156, 180, 198, 296. W. F. Albright, "Cuneiform Material for Egyptian Prosopography 1500–1200 B.C.," *JNES* 5 (1946) 9–10, suggested that Amankhatpi of Tashul(a)tu in South Syria (*EA* 185–86) was a native Syrian who had acquired his Egyptian name while being raised in Egypt.

6. Liverani "Contrasti," 11–16.

3. The mentality of the functionary is also apparent in the resignations and requests for replacements that the vassals submit to the Pharaoh.[7] While such procedures make sense in a bureaucracy, for the holder of a throne with his own territory they are a form of political suicide, profiting no one.
4. The Amarna vassals also manifest a clear understanding and acceptance of their place in a hierarchy of authority. Such a hierarchy would be quite alien to an Asiatic vassal, who enjoyed a personal relationship with his lord and certain equality with other officials. His Egyptian counterpart was subordinated to Egyptian officials no less than to the Pharaoh, and to them, too, he owed a ready and unswerving obedience.

This description of the vassal mind only aggravates our initial doubts about the presence of any Asiatic elements in the thinking of the vassals. What seemed in the historical context of the Amarna letters to be quite unlikely now appears, from a psychological viewpoint, almost incomprehensible. If the vassals recognized the futility of assertions and proofs of loyalty, why did they cling to them? What is even harder to understand is, if they regarded themselves as pure functionaries, how could they return time and again to an argument that had no meaning at all? In fact, if Liverani is right, the self-image may change in the same breath, for a vassal may say not simply, "I am loyal, so protect me" (Asiatic vassal), but immediately add, "that I may guard the city for the king" (Egyptian functionary). This, I submit, is psychologically so implausible that, short of the most compelling evidence to the contrary, we must assume that protestations of loyalty and requests for help were made with an understanding consistent with the legal position of an Egyptian vassal and with the considerable evidence that the implications of such status were neither unfamiliar nor rejected.

One possibility that immediately suggests itself is that behind the assumption that protection is a reasonable reward for loyalty is the logic of enlightening the king with the fact that protecting his vassals is in his own best interests. Utter loyalty is something precious in any polity, and in a world of dubious allegiances its worth is only the greater. Rib-Hadda knows this and he claims that it has been recognized by his master: "He [the king] knows my loyalty! The king knows how often he has done some kindness to me because I am without duplicity. My only purpose is

7. I disagree with Liverani ("Contrasti," 13 n. 4) on the interpretation of *EA* 126:44–45. I maintain that in this passage the question is of Byblos's being abandoned, not by Rib-Hadda, but by the Pharaoh; for my arguments, see *The Amarna Letters* (Baltimore and London, 1992) *EA* 126 n. 7.

to serve the king, my lord."[8] Single-minded devotion is recognized and rewarded, and it becomes thereby the grounds of hope and expectations.

Its rarity must also be considered. "Moreover, give thought to me. Who will be loyal were I to die?"[9] "If the desire of the king is to guard his city and his servant, send a garrison to guard the city. [I] will guard it while I am [a]live. When [I] die, who is going to [gu]ard it?"[10] In neither passage may Rib-Hadda be said to be urging any personal claims; the Pharaoh's sovereign liberty to do what he will with Byblos and his servant could not be acknowledged more openly. What the vassal is doing is asking his master to consider the ways he has served him and the difficulty of replacing him with someone of comparable loyalty. This provides some understanding of what underlies the argument, "I am loyal, so protect me."

How far it is removed from the assertion of a legal right may be seen from the connotations of loyalty in some instances of its most formal expression, when a vassal identifies himself as an *arad kitti* 'loyal servant'. It belongs in the realm of expressions characteristic of the greeting formulas, in which the vassal professes his absolute servility and complete self-abasement. Thus Rib-Hadda of Byblos states: "I am a footstool for the feet of the king, my lord, and his loyal servant."[11] Compare this statement with the wording of the following: "Moreover, note that we have been loyal servants of the king from ancient times. Moreover, note that I am your loyal servant, but I have nothing but distress. Note this matter. Note that I am the dirt at your feet, O king."[12] Another example of self-abnegation is found in a letter from South Syria: "(PN), the loyal servant of the king, my lord, and the dirt at the feet of the king, my lord."[13] In the letters of Biridiya of Megiddo, the use of *arad kitti* is even more striking, for there it replaces all other expressions of abject humility and personal worthlessness—footstool, dirt at the feet, mire to be trodden on—and suffices as a declaration of complete submission.[14] The "loyal servant" is, therefore, the perfect slave, the pure instrument, one devoid of all personal autonomy in his relations with his master.

8. *EA* 119:39–44.

9. *EA* 114:68.

10. *EA* 130:44–52.

11. *EA* 106:6–7.

12. *EA* 116:55–60.

13. *EA* 192:4–5. In the correspondence of Ammunira of Beirut, "(your, the king's) servant" is frequently followed by "the dirt at (your, the king's feet)," both in the greeting formula (*EA* 141:4–5, 142:2–4, 143:3–5) and in the body of the letter (*EA* 141:11–12, 19–20; 143:11–12). In *EA* 141:39–40, "the servant of the king, (my) lord, and a footstool for his feet."

14. *EA* 242:5, 243:4, 246:4, 365:4.

He is also evident in the *arad kitti* who is involved in litigation with a rival ruler. The rival, he claims, is unjustly holding some of his property, and the writer asks the crown to intervene, going on to say: "May *any* property of mine in his possession be taken for the king, and let the loyal servant live for the king."[15] Though maintaining his rights against a fellow vassal, he readily yields whatever is his to his master and asks only that he live for him and his service.

Similar sentiments are expressed elsewhere: "If the king, my lord, loves his loyal servant, then send (back) the three men that I may live and guard the city for the king."[16] He dares not assert his master's devotion to him, but if it exists, then he appeals to it only that he may go on living and carrying out one of his fundamental responsibilities as a vassal. The cautionary clause is important, for it suggests the attitude that must underlie and qualify any apparently forthright "I am loyal, so protect me."

If the *arad kitti* speaks *de profundis*, conscious of his lowliness and uncertain of royal grace, he also speaks the truth, even the unpleasant truth: "Being a loyal servant of the king, the Sun, with my mouth I speak words to the king that are nothing but the truth."[17] This is the introduction to the body of the letter. Rib-Hadda then takes up three topics, each of which is introduced by either "may the king heed the words of his loyal servant" (11–13, first topic; 35–36, third topic) or "may my lord heed my words" (25, second topic). These repetitions, which structure the argument and are so resonant of the opening lines, serve to emphasize the truth and value of what Rib-Hadda asserts or advises. His loyalty, so insisted on, implies not a right to be heard, but the wisdom of doing so.

The same implications of veracity and reliability are stressed again by Rib-Hadda: "Treacherous words are now being spoken in the presence of the king, the Sun. I am your loyal servant, and whatever I know or have heard I write to the king, my lord."[18] Rib-Hadda goes on to discredit the idea that the followers of Aziru in Amurru could possibly resist Egyptian archers, and he recalls how right he proved to be in the past when at his urging the king's father sent archers and Aziru's father was captured. Rib-Hadda's loyalty means that he keeps the king fully in-

15. *EA* 105:81–83. Cf. "Everything belongs to the king" (*EA* 197:6).

16. *EA* 123:23–28.

17. *EA* 107:8–11. Note *arad kitti* and *kitta-ma* 'nothing but the truth'. The courage to report the unpalatable truth seems to be the point of *EA* 149:14–16. It is also claimed by ᶜAbdi-Kheba, who dares inform the court of the dire situation in South Palestine, and as a result he is slandered by his and the crown's enemies; see *EA* 286:22–24, 49, 63–64.

18. *EA* 108:20–25.

formed,[19] with the additional implication that no information is passed on to the king's enemies.[20] It also means that his advice can be trusted, a claim he can bolster with recent history.[21]

In other passages it is difficult to decide among the various connotations of and motivations associated with loyalty: personal value to the king, hope of reward, abasement and denial of personal interest, truthfulness and credibility.[22] When the king is urged to heed his loyal servant's words and is then asked for help, is the vassal reminding him that the crown's interests are involved? Is he asking to be rewarded for loyalty? Is he implying the purity of his motives? Is he guaranteeing the truth of the need or peril he describes? Often, one may suspect, he was vaguely aware of the whole register and would, if asked, exclude none of the possibilities. Like the poet, he would prefer not to join "that kingdom of

19. See also *EA* 145:23–26, 149:14–17, 151:49–51. Furnishing intelligence also appears as a vassal duty in Hittite and Assyrian treaties.

20. Supplying the enemy with information is treason; cf. *EA* 82:10–12, 147:66–69, 149:68–70.

21. *EA* 108:28–33 (the capture of ᶜAbdi-Ashirta), and see also 117:27–28, 132:16–18, 138: 33–34, and 362:20.

22. See *EA* 73:42; 80:17; 85:17, 63; 100:32; 101:38; 103:7, 24; 108:69; 109:42; 114:43; 116:55; 119:25; 139:30; 155:48; 180:19; 198:10; 241:19; 254:10–11. Occasionally, the stress is on how provocative loyalty is among the king's enemies, who make his servants pay for it. "For what reason is your loyal servant so treated? For service to you!" (*EA* 114:41–43; cf. 114:65–67, 100:15–18).

Cities also have *kittu*. They may be an *amat kitti* 'loyal maidservant' (*EA* 68:11, 74:7), or *āl/ālānī kitti* 'loyal city/cities' (*EA* 74:9, 56; 88:8, 44; 106:4; 127:25; 132:9; 138:37). According to Z. Kallai and H. Tadmor ("Bit Ninurta = Beth Horon: On the History of the Kingdom of Jerusalem in the Amarna Period," *ErIsr* 9 [1969] 138 n. 2 [Hebrew]), *ālānī kitti šarri* means 'cities under covenant with the king', not 'cities loyal to the king'. Against this view are several reasons: (1) In *EA* 74, *āl kittišu* (9) replaces *Gubla amat kitti ša šarri* (6–8), and the two expressions seem virtually synonymous. But *amat kitti* is obviously the feminine counterpart of *arad kitti*, and the latter does not mean simply 'one under covenant', i.e., 'vassal'. Not only is Yankhamu, the royal commissioner, an *arad kitti* (*EA* 118:56), but this quality is proposed as distinguishing him among the king's servants in general. Moreover, *arad kitti* is obviously a badge of distinction that a vassal parades before his master; it is not borne by his enemies, even though they are usually vassals like himself. For Rib-Hadda to call ᶜAbdi-Ashirta or Aziru an *arad kitti* is unthinkable, which it would not be if the expression simply meant a vassal under oath to the Pharaoh. (2) Again, in *EA* 74:9–10, the enormity of the scandal of the king's abandoning *āl kittīšu* is emphasized by Rib-Hadda's request, which he immediately urges, that the king should check in the royal archives to find out if there has ever been in Byblos a ruler who was not *arad kitti*. The presence of an *arad kitti* establishes Byblos as an *amat kitti*. (3) In *EA* 88:43–45, despite some question about the end of the passage, Byblos is certainly contrasted with other cities, and Rib-Hadda's argument would certainly be stronger if he could say, not that Byblos was Egypt's most ancient vassal, but that it had the longest record of loyalty.

single-eyed men to which language (as ordinarily used) aspires." For his purpose, better the richness of ambiguity.

The principal contribution of Liverani's later article in *Berytus*[23] is the discussion of four entries in the "Amarna political lexicon" as illustrative of the misunderstandings and cross-purposes that vitiated the political correspondence between Egypt and her Syro-Palestinian vassals.

The first entry is the verb *naṣāru* 'to protect'. According to Liverani, whereas an Asiatic vassal enjoys with his suzerain a personal relationship of mutual protection, his Egyptian counterpart is simply an impersonal cog in the bureaucratic machinery. When he is told, as he so often is, to protect himself and the place where he is, this is administrative jargon, meaning simply that he should be on the alert, do his job and stay where he has been put. The vassals do not understand this; when told to protect themselves, they think they are to do just that and so, like good Asiatics, under duress, they feel free to ask the Pharaoh for help or "salvific protection" (Liverani's term), in times of crisis.

Aiding and abetting this misapprehension is language interference: on the Egyptian side, because in Egyptian (*sꜣw*) 'to protect' also means 'to pay attention', Akkadian *naṣāru* is given this additional meaning, a plus alien to it in standard Akkadian. On the Canaanite side, on the basis of Canaanite *yšᶜ*, *naṣāru* is given another plus, the meaning not only of 'to protect', but 'to rescue, save'.

Comments: (1) The linguistic argument, which it must be noted, in its most controversial parts is never supported by the citation of a single text, is quite unconvincing. First of all, it is not true that in standard Akkadian *naṣāru* never means 'to pay attention'.[24] Second, in *EA*, *naṣāru* does not mean 'to rescue, save'.[25] Third, in Canaanite, *yšᶜ* does not mean 'to protect'.[26] (2) That the vassals should so universally and so persistently misunderstand the order to guard the place where they are,

23. Liverani, "Political Lexicon," 49–56.

24. See J.-M. Durand, *Archives épistolaires de Mari* 1/1 = (ARM 26; Paris, 1988) 391 n. 80 (end). Its appearance at Mari is especially relevant.

25. Of the meanings assigned to *naṣāru* in *EA*, Ebeling's glossary ([Vorderasiatische Bibliothek 2/2; Leipzig, 1915] 1483) is representative: *schützen, bewahren, auf der Hut sein, beobachten.* That Liverani in going against *opinio communis* and does not feel required to cite a single passage where the meaning is (*er*)*retten* is very hard to understand. Note that there are a few passages in which *naṣāru* is construed with *ištu*, but here the preposition is used in the sense of 'with', not 'from'; see the discussion in Moran, *The Amarna Letters*: *EA* 112 n. 1. It might also be remarked that, if *naṣāru* in *EA* means 'to rescue, save', not once, despite its great frequency, is it ever construed with *ištu qāt*, 'from the hand'. Contrast the two verbs that do mean 'rescue, save' in *EA*, *ekēmu* (*EA* 271:13, 274:10) and *šūzubu* (*EA* 62:30–31; 74:33, 44; 318:8), and cf. *hôšîaᶜ* / *hiṣṣîl miyyad* in Hebrew.

26. Again, a meaning asserted against the dictionaries, with no supporting evidence.

with not a word from Egypt to set them straight, seems extremely implausible. (3) If the vassals occasionally read more into the verb *naṣāru* than the Egyptians intend, this does not mean they do not understand their orders. Rather, they play the game of politics, ignore what is said and take the opportunity to state their case and their needs once more.

The second entry, and another source of tension, Liverani asserts, is the word *balāṭu*, both 'life' and 'to live'.[27] In *EA*, 'life' has two referents, one on the ideological level where all life, both now and in the hereafter, comes from the Pharaoh, and the other on the practical day-to-day level of 'victuals', the essentials of staying alive, with their ultimate source again the Pharaoh. Both uses, as Liverani admits, were familiar to the vassals, though naturally they were much more interested in the practical level, especially in times of food shortages. What is not clear is the basis of Liverani's claim that they could legitimately expect only life on the first level, in the form of ideology and propaganda. De facto, the Pharaoh provided for them in the past, and they appeal to this precedent.[28]

The third entry is the expression *šūšuru ana pānī* 'to prepare before the arrival'. Liverani has identified the underlying Egyptian expression, which, he maintains, though in general understood correctly by the vassals, was misunderstood in a small group of texts.[29] He may be right, but in the overall picture of political relations, such a misunderstanding seems trivial and of no real importance.

The last entry is the verb *qâlu*. According to Liverani, in good Akkadian *qâlu* means simply 'to keep quiet', but in *EA* it acquires a plus, the negative connotation of doing nothing, abstaining from action when the situation cries for it. Liverani traces this plus to Hebrew *dmm*, which means both 'to keep quiet' and 'to be still, inactive'. For the Egyptians, however, on the basis of *gr* in their own language, 'to keep quiet' suggests

27. Among the passages cited by Liverani is *EA* 369:18–23, with reference to my treatment of the text in "Amarna Glosses," *RA* 69 (1975) 151–53. It might be noted, however, that I argue there against any reading of *balāṭu* into the text.

28. See *EA* 112:50–51, 54–55; 121:11–17; 122:9–11, 24–31; 125:14–18; 130:21–30; cf., too, 68:27–28; 85:34–37; 86:32–35. Liverani himself ("Political Lexicon," 52) points to texts in which the Pharaoh boasts of having supplied foreigners with provisions.

29. They are *EA* 201–2, 203–6. The phrase *ana pānī*, according to Liverani, was taken in a spatial sense, and this prompted a reinterpretation of the verb to mean 'to make go straight'. Thus, the vassals saw their role to be that of guides. Since in *EA* 203–6 the expression is not 'to go before', but 'to be (at hand, available)', this suggests comparison with Hebrew *ḥāyâ lipnê* 'to be at the disposition of', and the vassals perhaps saw themselves as providing not so much guidance as assistance in general. It must also be noted that Liverani's denial of a temporal sense of *ana pānī* in good Akkadian is wrong. Such a sense is well attested in Old Babylonian (see Moran, *The Amarna Letters*, xxxi n. 100), and its presence in *EA* should be seen as one more provincial archaism (for a selective list, see ibid., xx nn. 40–41).

a different plus, the positive one of self-control. Hence, when Rib-Hadda asks why the Pharaoh keeps silent (and does nothing and neglects his own interests), the Pharaoh understands them to be asking why he exercises such admirable self-control—one more misunderstanding. The Pharaoh does nothing, just to make clear how absurd and useless Rib-Hadda's complaints really are.

Comments: (1) Liverani's description of the use of *qâlu* is very misleading. The negative implications of the verb reappear in Neo-Assyrian,[30] and they are already attested at Nuzi.[31] And given this early evidence, one can make a good case for an even earlier appearance in Old Babylonian.[32] (2) Hebrew *dmm* never connotes culpable or inexcusable negligence. (3) The Pharaoh's failure to act hardly requires recourse to language interference and the influence of an Egyptian verb.

As already noted, another important feature of Liverani's reconstruction of the Amarna age is his opinion that Egyptian policy was one of indifference to peace among vassals, provided they remained faithful to Egypt. To support this view he offers the evidence of two letters and the general consideration that, if intervassal wars were forbidden, we should have to admit Egyptian weakness or inertia and a certain inconsistency between actual practice and political thought.[33]

The first letter is *EA* 162, from Amenophis IV to Aziru in Amurru, and this is interpreted in the light of the latter's letters to the Egyptian court.[34] In these, as he harasses Egyptian vassals, foments sedition, sides with the rebels, and seizes new territory for himself, he goes on writing

30. See CAD Q 73b.

31. Ernest R. Lacheman, *Excavations at Nuzi V: The Palace and the Temple Archives* (HSS 14; Cambridge, Mass., 1950) no. 12:8–9; and see K. Deller, W. Mayer, and J. Oelsner, "Akkadische Lexikographie: *CAD Q*," *Or* n.s. 58 (1989) 266. This rules out Canaanite substrate influence.

32. See M. Stol, *Letters from Yale* (Altbabylonische Briefe 9; Leiden, 1981) no. 20:8, where F. Kraus (note a to translation) is quoted as favoring 'but you keep perfectly silent' (despite the waste just described), which fits the context admirably and was rejected by Stol only because the negative connotations of *qâlu* were otherwise unknown in Old Babylonian. The Nuzi evidence diminishes the force of this argument.

33. Liverani, "Contrasti," 10–11. Note especially 11 n. 2, where he writes that to hold that vassals were not free to attack one another would be to fall back into the opinion "che il comportamento abituale degli Egiziani nei rispetti di tali episodi fosse in disaccordo con le loro concezioni politiche, il che sembra difficile." The difficulty he does not explain; for a different view, see below.

34. The most recent translation of Aziru's letters is that of S. Izre'el, *Amurru Akkadian, with an Appendix of the History of Amurru by I. Singer* (HSS 41/1; Atlanta: 1991) 15–64. For a reexamination of the Aziru-Egypt correspondence and the historical context of *EA* 162, see I. Singer, HSS 41/2, 135–95, and in S. Izre'el and I. Singer, *The General's Letter from Ugarit: A Linguistic and Historical Reevaluation of RS 20.33* (*Ugaritica V, No. 20*) (Tel Aviv, 1990) 122–54.

to the court and pledging his fidelity. He has recognized (says Liverani) what Egypt requires of a vassal and he exploits the limitations of its goals. And when the king writes to him in *EA* 162, he is reproached only for his treatment of Rib-Hadda in exile and for consorting with an enemy of Egypt, and even this is done rather gently. All that is required of him is to conduct himself as a vassal. The Pharaoh's tacit acceptance of Amurru's expansion proves Aziru's assessment of Egyptian policy to be correct.

Now there is no denying the conciliatory tone of the letter, and Amenophis IV certainly seems to have acquiesced to Aziru's appropriations. It is questionable, however, whether from this any inference may be made about Egyptian policy in general. Amurru was a very special case. At the time *EA* 162 was written, the Hittite threat was obvious and Aziru was being lured to the Hittite side.[35] Egypt, it is clear, had decided that it needed his loyalty and needed it badly. Under the circumstances, it would have been folly not to connive at a fait accompli or to exercise the gentle art of persuasion towards a very critical ally, tempering threats with promises of reward.[36] But it must also be noted that, aggressive as Aziru undoubtedly was against his neighbors, he never admitted it.[37] Obviously, he did not feel he could make an open mockery of his loyalty by frankly admitting aggression, and his silence in this regard argues against Egyptian indifference to such hostilities.

The other text Liverani cites is a letter from Labᵓayu in Palestine.[38] Here, following Knudtzon's translation, he finds Labᵓayu openly admitting to the Pharaoh that he had occupied nearby Gezer; asking the king's acceptance of the situation, which he seems sure of, he goes on to pledge his loyalty. "Cosa si vuole di più? E in effetti non sembra che il faraone voglia di più."[39]

Since I have elsewhere argued at length against this interpretation, beginning with a radical revision of Knudtzon's translation,[40] I here state only my own opinion: Labᵓayu has been accused by Milkilu, the ruler of Gezer, of treason, and he replies to the accusations with a confession of what his crime really was—before a disloyal and hostile audience he had openly accepted his own vassal status and the obligations that it entails, while suggesting that his colleague Milkilu was himself a traitor. His entering Gezer argues courage and boldness rather than a

35. See especially lines 31–32.

36. Lines 33–38.

37. See Singer's remarks, *The General's Letter*, 135.

38. *EA* 253:11–35.

39. Liverani, "Contrasti," 10.

40. See my "Amarna Glosses," 147–51.

hostile occupation of the town, but if it looks as though he has occupied it, he has his defence ready: he was there to protect the interests of the crown.

On the other side of the ledger, unless one makes the vassals all hopelessly and blindly Asiatics, there is much evidence that, in principle, Egypt did not permit aggression against other vassals. Thus, Rib-Hadda frequently denounces ᶜAbdi-Ashirta and his successors for doing as they please;[41] and similar to this accusation is another, namely, that they seem to think that they are like the rulers of Khatti, Mittani, or Babylonia, that is, rulers independent of the authority of Egypt.[42] A display of aggressive independence seems to constitute a prima facie case of rebellion, a line of argument that is not easily reconciled with an alleged freedom to attack another vassal.

Such freedom is unknown in *EA* 139:11–17, where the killing of vassal kings and a royal commissioner, as well as breaching another's city walls, are declared, simply and without further qualification, as crimes (*arnu*) against the crown. And the murderers of the king of Tyre are eager to deny what they have done, insisting that their alleged victim is still alive.[43] Unless they are guilty of a crime and open to severe reprisals, why do they not simply admit the truth and reassure the king by promises of loyalty?

A ruler in South Palestine reports that the two sons of Labᵓayu have been constantly urging him to support their attack on the citizenry of Gina, who had slain their father. Though they threaten that he will pay for it if he refuses, he does just that, saying: "May the god of the king, my lord, preserve me from waging war against the people of Gina, servants of the king, my lord."[44] The only reason he gives for risking their fury is that the proposed victims are servants of the king. Is this an excess of piety, or is he only doing his duty? That it is the latter seems clear from what immediately follows. The writer requests that the king send an official to another ruler to tell him: "You will march against the two sons of Labᵓayu or you are a rebel against the king."[45] The close association between what he has done and what this ruler should do argues that, in his mind, the only alternative to refusing the sons of Labᵓayu is to become himself guilty of a crime against the crown.

41. *EA* 88:11, 108:12–13, 125:42–43, 126:11–12, 129:6, 139:11, 140:9–10. Note too, the condemnation of Aziru's having acted, if not disloyally, at least independently (*EA* 162:17ff.).

42. *EA* 76:12–13, 104:17–24, 116:67–71.

43. *EA* 89.

44. *EA* 250:20–22.

45. Lines 26–27.

One might cite other passages with the same general thrust,[46] but what is perhaps most striking and most relevant is the fact, that throughout *EA*, all wars are, in one way or another, wars of defence. A vassal admits only to defending himself and the crown or to carrying out rescue operations for innocent victims.[47] No one ever says, as Liverani thought Labʾayu did, that he has simply expanded his territory at the expense of another vassal. The argument from silence has a special validity here, because it is clear that many vassals were in fact aggressors. If, at least in theory, no special sanctions were attached to aggression, it is hard to see why absolutely no one ever admits the truth.

What, then, was Egyptian policy in this regard? It may be taken as axiomatic that one must distinguish between political ideas and political realities, recognizing that ideas may lag far behind realities. Not less axiomatic is the distinction between what a government says and what it does, between law and its enforcement, between a statement of policy and its implementation, between the power a government wills and the power it actually enjoys.[48]

That these axioms are pertinent to the present discussion was already implied in the consideration of Egypt-Amurru relations. The exigencies of the situation were such that Egypt was faced with a choice between either a much larger commitment of Egyptian forces or letting

46. For example, in *EA* 280:9–11: "The king, my lord, permitted me to wage war against Qeltu." The writer also promises, despite extreme provocation, to do nothing more until he hears from the king.

47. It seems a vassal was free to help his colleagues under attack (*EA* 256:21, 366:20–26) but was not obliged to, unless ordered by the king (cf. *EA* 92:30ff.). Noteworthy, too, is the fact that, critical as Rib-Hadda is of his fellow vassals, he never reproaches them for failure to send help. The apparent exception, the complaint against the kings of Beirut, Sidon, and Tyre (*EA* 92:29–40), is based on the fact of the Pharaoh's having ordered them to intervene on Rib-Hadda's behalf. On the other hand, Shuwardata seems to complain of having been abandoned by his brothers, who to judge from context were other vassals (*EA* 366:18–19). The whole question is complicated by the possibility that there were special alliances (cf. *EA* 136) or small leagues permitted by the Egyptians that could create special obligations.

48. These are commonplaces among observers of contemporary politics and sociologists of law; see, for example, T. W. Arnold, *The Symbols of Government* (New Haven and London, 1935; New York, 1962). Of the gaps between script and performance, two random illustrations: J. K. Hyde (*Society and Politics in Medieval Italy: The Evolution of Civil Life, 1000–1350* [New Studies in Medieval History; New York, 1973]) has shown that the social and political ideology of the Italian communes first found expression in the 15th century, approximately 300 years after it had taken form in the realities of social and political life and as it was in the course of disappearing; J. Hurstfield (*Freedom, Corruption and Government in Elizabethan England* [London, 1973]) has shown, inter alia, how far in Tudor England the working of a government could be from the way it would like to work, indeed from how it even thought it worked. Hence I do not agree with Liverani's "il che sembra difficile" (n. 33).

Amurru grow into a considerable power. In opting for the latter, it did not abolish its claims to absolute obedience, as ᶜAbdi-Ashirta and his successors acknowledged by paying them lip service. The political idea remained intact, though it no longer reflected the political reality.

In general, war and rebellion were chronic evils of the political order, and on the day-to-day level of administration Egyptian policy was probably about as tolerant as Liverani claims. But again we must question the legitimacy of inferences from what a government does or allows to what it says or claims. All that we may conclude is that the arrangement probably assured certain, perhaps short-sighted, Egyptian interests in the area, and that the limits of control, at least with the expenditure of resources Egypt was willing to make, had been reached. This does not mean that more far-reaching claims of control had been renounced in principle. Such a renunciation can be established only from statements of principle by either the governing or the governed. For the Amarna period, no such statements exist. On the contrary, from what the vassals say (and do not say) we can see what Egypt required them to say, that is, to acknowledge an absolute power that no longer existed, if indeed it ever did.

Pasūri-Dagan and Ini-Teššup's Mother

David I. Owen

The publication of the tablet Boston Museum of Fine Arts 1977.114 provides an insight into the role of the queen mother during the reign of Inni-Teššup, king of Karkemiš. Furthermore, the name of Inni-Teššup's mother, ^{fd}U-IR-*mi, is revealed for the first time. The text is a record of a legal decision that took place before the king in the city of Karkemiš, but the text must have come from the family archive of Pasūri-Dagan son of Akallina, presumably in or near the city of Emar or the town of Kulat(t)i.*

In 1977, the Museum of Fine Arts (MFA) in Boston acquired[1] a well-preserved cuneiform tablet,[2] impressed with a bilingual stamp seal of

Author's note: Next to a good joke, Jonas Greenfield appreciates most the discovery of a new text, regardless of its language, period or culture. His wide-ranging interests and curiosity have been the hallmarks of his long and distinguished career. It is thus a great pleasure to present him with the following text on the occasion of his jubilee.

1. My views on the sale and purchase of antiquities have been expressed in my paper, "The Illegal Antiquities Trade in Turkey: A Personal View," presented on December 29, 1971, at a symposium, "Looting the Past: An International Scandal," sponsored by the Society for American Archaeology at the annual meeting of the American Association for the Advancement of Science in Philadelphia. But this is not the place to expound on them. However, no matter how the eventual ownership of illegally exported antiquities is ultimately resolved, it is important that these documents and objects be fully published so that, at a minimum, their historical importance, albeit greatly diminished by their lack of context, be communicated. I wish to thank the authorities in the Egyptian Department at the Museum of Fine Arts, especially W. K. Simpson and T. Kendall, for entrusting the publication of this text to me and for their patience during the long and unexpected delay it took to bring it to press. I would also like to thank Dr. Kendall for providing me with the excellent photos.

2. The tablet is of the Syrian type, that is, narrower along the vertical axis, as opposed to the Syro-Hittite style, which is wider along the horizontal axis. See D. Arnaud's classification ("Catalogue des textes cunéiformes trouvés au cours des trois premières campagnes à Meskéné Qadime Ouest," *Annales archéologiques arabes syriennes* 25 [1975] 87–93) and the remarks of J. Huehnergard (*RA* 77 [1983] 12). On internal grounds, our tablet probably comes from Emar or a site in its vicinity, possibly from Pasūri-Dagan's archive itself.

Ini-Teššup, king of Karkemish.[3] It records a legal case heard before Ini-Teššup in which his previously unnamed mother, ^{d}U-IR-*mi*, and an otherwise unattested individual, Pasūri-Dagan, son of Akallina, were involved. For reasons unknown, Ini-Teššup's mother, the probable chief or favorite wife of Šaḫarunuwa, interceded in a dispute between Pasūri-Dagan, son of Akallina, and Ari-Teššup, a man from Aššur, concerning 45 shekels of silver that the latter owed him. If my understanding is correct, Ari-Teššup had gone to see Mašamuwa, the "director" (*muʾirru*), about the silver after Pasūri-Dagan had taken back the 45 shekels from him. In an unusual resolution, the king's mother (AMA.LUGAL) took the 45 shekels of silver away from Pasūri-Dagan and, instead of returning the silver as promised, provided a field, presumably of equal or greater value, in the town of Kulat(t)i, as compensation to Pasūri-Dagan.[4] Such a grant of land, even as compensation, appears to be in the tradition of the Hittite *Landschenkungsurkunden.*[5] It is not known why the dowager queen interceded on behalf of the "man from Aššur" or why a field was provided in lieu of the silver; nor is the role of the *muʾirru* clear. No related documents are known to me.[6] The text reads as follows.

3. For this royal seal, which exists in two examples, see C. F. A. Schaeffer, *Ugaritica* 3 (1939) 20–23, figs. 27–29. The impression on RS 17.230, fig. 29, appears to be from the same seal as MFA 1977.114.

4. I assume that the AMA.LUGAL is the equivalent of the AMA.GAL well known from other texts. The role of the AMA.GAL in the West Semitic, Syrian world may now be traced back to the Ebla documents of the mid-third millennium B.C.E., in which she plays a significant role in the royal household. M. Bonechi, commenting on the role of the AMA.GAL in Mari (*SEL* 7 [1990] 19–20), notes, "Il ruolo della regina-madre, che viene ormai riconosciuto come preminente nella Siria amorrea, e che andrà confrontato con quello dell'AMA.GAL.EN di Ebla." See also the remarks of C. H. Gordon, *Eblaitica* 2 (1990) 129–30; and M. G. Biga, "Femmes de la Famille royale d'Ebla," in *La Femme dans le Proche-Orient antique* (ed. J.-M. Durand; CRRAI 23; Paris: Editions Recherches sur les Civilisations, 1987) 41–47.

5. See K. K. Riemschneider, "Die hethitischen Landschenkungsurkunden," *MIO* 6 (1958) 328–81; K. Balkan, *Eine Schenkungsurkunde aus der althethitischen Zeit, gefunden in Inandık* (Anadolu Mediniyetlerini Araştırma vakfo yayınları 1; Ankara, 1973), and especially the chapter by G. Boyer, "La place des textes d'Ugarit dans l'histoire de l'ancien droit oriental," in J. Nougayrol et al., PRU 3, 283–308.

6. The Emar tablets that have been published so far are: D. Arnaud, *Emar* 6/3–4; idem, *Aula Orientalis* 2 (1984) 179–88; *Aula Orientalis* 5 (1987) 211–41; idem, *Textes syriens*; G. Beckman, *JCS* 40 (1988) 61–68; J. Huehnergard, "Five Tablets from the Vicinity of Emar," *RA* 77 (1983) 11–43; W. Meyer and G. Wilhelm, *Dammaziener Mitteilungen* 1 (1983) 249ff.; M. Sigrist, "Miscellanea," *JCS* 34 (1982) 242–52; A. Tsukimoto, "Sieben spätbronzezeitliche Urkunden aus Syrien," *ASJ* 10 (1988) 153–89; idem, "Akkadian Tablets in the Hirayama Collection I-III," *ASJ* 12 (1990) 177–259; *ASJ* 13 (1991) 275–333; *ASJ* 14 (1992) 289–310; and idem, "An Akkadian Field Sale Document Privately Held in Tokyo," *ASJ* 14 (1992) 311–16. Perhaps a related document will be found among the Emar tablets now in the hands of antiquities dealers, private collectors, and museums. So far, although I have had access to a number of these texts,

Text[7]

MFA 1977.114
7.6 × 5.6 cm
Copy and photos below

1. *a-na pa-ni* ^{I}*i-ni-*^{d}IM LUGAL KUR *kar-kà-miš*
2. DUMU ^{I}*ša-ḫa-ru-nu-wa* LUGAL KUR *kar-kà-miš*
3. DUMU.DUMU-*šu ša* ^{I}LUGAL-^{d}30 LUGAL KUR *kar-kà-miš-ma* UR.SAG
4. ^{I}*pa-sú-ri-*^{d}KUR DUMU ^{I}*a-kal-li-na*
5. *a-kán-na iq-bi ma-a* ^{I}*a-ri-*^{d}IM LÚ KUR *aš-šur*
6. 45 GÍN KÙ.BABBAR-*ia ú-ka-a-al-mi*
7. *i-na-an-na* ^{I}*a-ri-*^{d}IM
8. *iš-tu* KUR URU *aš-šur a-na* ^{lú}*mu-i*[*r-ri*]
9. *it-tal-kám*
10. *aš-šum* 45 GÌN KÙ.BABBAR-*ia*
11. *as-sa-bat-šu-mi*
12. *ù* ^{fd}U-IR-*mi* AMA.LUGAL
13. *iš-tu qa-ti-ia il-te-qè-mi*
14. *um-ma-a a-na-ku* KÙ.BABBAR-*ka*
15. *ú-šal-lam-ka-a-mi*
16. *i-na-an-na* ^{fd}U-IR-*mi* AMA.LUGAL

I have been unable to identify any related document or the participants directly involved in the court case.

To my knowledge, the major collections yet to be published are: (1) The Borowski collection in Jerusalem (ca. 30 texts), to be published by Joan Goodnick Westenholz et al. Thanks to her, I have been able to verify that none of the texts in that group relates to our document. (2) The R(osen) E(mar) collection in New York City (97 texts), now being prepared for publication by Professor Gary Beckman in his *Texts from the Vicinity of Emar in the Collection of Jonathan Rosen* (hereafter Beckman, *Rosen*). He too has provided me with references to the texts in his charge along with a preliminary manuscript of copies and accompanying transliterations. None of the Rosen tablets can be related to our text. (3) Isolated texts continue to appear in the hands of dealers and in private collections.

7. This text was read and discussed in a seminar on Emar tablets held at the École biblique in Jerusalem, Israel, in the spring of 1989, while I was a National Endowment for the Humanities Fellow at the Albright Institute of the American Schools of Oriental Research and a Fellow at the Sackler Institute of Advanced Studies, Tel Aviv University. I am indebted to the participants in that seminar, M. Sigrist, S. Izre'el, J. Westenholz, as well as M. Yamada, and J. Ikeda, doctoral students at Tel Aviv University, for their many helpful comments and observations, often based on unpublished texts at their disposal. Furthermore, I. Singer and R. Zadok of Tel Aviv University offered additional suggestions and references on readings of personal names, which proved to be quite helpful. D. Arnaud, long before his monumental publication of the Emar texts, was kind enough to comment on an early transliteration and copy of mine (letter of May 12, 1982) and to make a number of helpful suggestions.

17. *ki-i-mu-u* 45$^{!}$ GÍN KÙ.BABBAR *ša-a-šu*
18. A.ŠÀ *i-na* URU *ku-la-at-ti*
19. 2 *iku* GÍD.DA-*šu*
20. 1 *iku ru-pu-uš-šu*
21. ÚS.SA.DU AN.TA
22. ^{I}*ìl-lì-a-bi* DUMU ^{I}*tu-uq-na-ni*
23. *ù* ^{I}*mil-ki*-^{d}KUR DUMU ^{I}*tu-ri-ia*
24. ÚS.SA KI.TA
25. ^{I}*tu-ra*-^{d}KUR DUMU ^{I}*da-qa-ni*
26. SAG 1-KÁM LUGAL-*rum*
27. SAG [2-KÁM. . . .]
28. *a-na* [^{I}*pa-sú-ri*-^{d}KUR DUMU ^{I}] *a-kal-li-na*
29. *it-*[*ta-din ur-ra-am š*]*e-ra-am*
30. *aš-š*[*um* A.ŠÀ *ša-šu* ^{I}SUM-^{d}IM][8]
31. *a-n*[*a muḫ-ḫi* ^{I}*pa-sú-ri*-^{d}KUR]
32. [*la-a i-ra-ag-gu*$_{(5)}$*-um ù m*] *uḫ-ḫi* ^{I}SUM-^{d}IM
33. [^{I}*pa-sú-ri*-^{d}KUR *la-a i-ra-ag-gu*$_{(5)}$-] *um*
34. [*a-ḫu a-na a-ḫi la-a i-ra-ag-gu*$_{(5)}$*-um*]
35. *šu*[*m-ma i-ra-a*] *g*$^{?}$*-gu*$_{5}$*-um*
36. *ṭup-p*[*u an-nu-ú i-le-ʾe-e*] *-šu*

---

37. *ṭup-pa an-na-a a-na pa-ni* ^{I}*ú-ri*-^{d}I[M]
38. EN É *a-bu-us-sí*
39. *ša* ^{I}*i-ni*-^{d}IM LUGAL
40. ^{I}*ma-ša-mu-wa* GAL.UKKIN DUB.SAR
41. IN.SAR

TRANSLATION

1. Before Ini-Teššup, king of Karkamiš,
2. son of Šaḫarunuwa, king of Karkamiš,
3. grandson of Šarre-Kušuḫ, king of Karkamiš, the hero;
4. Pasūri-Dagan, son of Akallina,
5. spoke as follows: "Concerning Ari-Teššup, a man of Aššur,
6. 45 shekels of my silver he withholds.
7. And now, Ari-Teššup,
8. from the City of Aššur (has returned and) to the 'director'

8. The restorations suggested for the following lines are based on an estimate of line and sign spacing, traces of preserved signs, and comparisons with existing formulas in texts of similar genres. Other reconstructions are also possible here, but because these lines include the standard formulas for the ending of legal decisions, any variation in the reconstruction should not alter the understanding of the main points of the text.

9. has come.
10. As for the 45 shekels of my silver,
11. I had seized it.
12. But, ^{d}U-IR-*mi*, the king's mother,
13. took it (i.e., the silver) away from me
14. (saying) thus: 'I, your silver,
15. will pay back to you.'
16. But (now), ^{d}U-IR-*mi*, the king's mother,
17. instead of that 45$^{!}$ shekels of silver,
18. a field in the town of Kulat(t)i,
19. 2 *iku*s long
20. and 1 *iku* wide,
21. bordered along the upper side (by the properties of)
22. Ili-abi son of Tuqnani
23. and Milki-Dagan son of Turia
24. and along the lower side (by the property of)
25. Tura-Dagan son of Daqani,
26. along one side, by the king('s property),
27. along the other side by [PN's property],
28. to [Pasūri-Dagan son of] Akallina,
29. has g[iven." In the fu]ture,
30. conc[erning that field, Ari-Teššup]
31. [against Pasūri-Dagan]
32. [shall not raise a claim. And ag]ainst Ari-Teššup
33. [Pasūri-Dagan shall not raise a cla]im.
34. [One against the other shall not raise a claim].
35. I[f someone raises a] claim,
36. [this t]ablet [shall prevail over] him.

---

37. This tablet, before Uri-Teššup,
38. the master of the treasury
39. of Ini-Teššup, the king,
40. Mašamuwa, the "director," the scribe,
41. has written.

COMMENTS

Line 4. The reading of this name with *sú* is based on the spelling in Arnaud, *Emar* 6/3 215:27 where the name is written with *su* and where he is DUMU *ni-ra-ri*, obviously not the same individual. The name occurs again in A. Tsukimoto, *ASJ* 13 (1990) 303 (transliteration) and 329 (copy), no. 38:1 passim, where the patronymic is, unfortunately, broken.

More recently, the name occurs in two lists of witnesses (D. Arnaud, *Textes syriens de l'âge du bronze récent* [Aula Orientalis Supplementa 1; Barcelona, 1991; publ. 1992] texts 64:15 and 65:23) as the father of Mādī-Dagan, who may have been the chief scribe according to the seal on 64:20. If Pasūri-Dagan was a high-ranking official, as our text suggests, Mādī-Dagan the scribe may have been his son. Further documentation is necessary, however. The name Pasūri-Dagan was apparently not uncommon at Emar. Two additional references to a Pasūri-Dagan, each with different patronyms, appear in Beckman, *Rosen,* RE 63:28, 29 (seal), where ^{I}*pa-sú-ri-*^{d}KUR DUMU ^{f}*na-na* appears as a witness; and Beckman, *Rosen,* RE 67:13, where ^{I}*pa-sú-ri-*^{d}KUR DUMU *e-ri* appears as a witness.

On the reading ^{d}KUR = Dagan, see Arnaud, *RA* 68 (1974) 190. For the name Akallina, compare *A-kál-li* in Arnaud, *Emar* 6/3 8:31, passim and 9:27; and the variant orthographies in Beckman, *Rosen,* RE 21:11 *a-kal-li*; and idem, *Rosen,* RE 82:28, [IGI ^{I}z] *u-ḫal-ma* DUMU *a-ka-li,* without patronymics.

Line 5. It would be very interesting to know what connection Ari-Teššup, presumably a Hurrian, had with Aššur. He does not appear elsewhere.

Line 6. For *kullu,* 'to hold back (. . . as pledge, security, or for other reasons)', see CAD K 511 sub e.

Line 8. For *muʾirru* (= GAL.UKKIN) 'director', see CAD M/2 178 s.v.

Line 12. The name of the king's mother, presumably Ini-Teššup's, is probably to be read as Hurrian and not Hittite, but this cannot be determined with certainty. An exact parallel of the name, ^{fd}U-IR, is found in H. Klengel, KUB 40 80:11 and 16,[9] probably the same woman, given the rarity of the name. Similar name forms occur as ^{fd}SIN-IR (E. Laroche, *Les noms des Hittites* [Paris, 1966] 39, no. 132, which he reads as Hittite ^{f}Arma-IR-*i*) and DINGIR.MEŠ-IR (E. Edel, *Ägyptische Ärtze und ägyptische Medizin am hethitischen Königshof: Neue Funde von Keilschriftbriefen Ramses' II aus Boğazköy* [Opladen, 1976] 32ff.),[10] but I am not aware of any explicit writings for any of them. IR is apparently a phonetic spelling or variant orthography for ÌR, (*w*)*ardu,* according to Laroche (*Les noms des hittites,* sub no. 1745), following K. Balkan (*Letter of King Anum-Ḫirbi of Mama to King Warshama of Kanish* [Ankara, 1957] 23). See also the remarks of D. Hawkins on the reading of IR in *AnSt* 38 (1988) 105 n. 38. This convention is already attested in Ur III personal names, for which see D. I. Owen, *Selected Ur III Texts from the Harvard Semitic Museum* ([Materiali per

9. E. Laroche (*Catalogue des textes Hittites* [Paris, 1971] no. 297) describes H. Klengel, KBo 40 80, as a "document de procedure(?)." In this text lady ^{d}U-IR makes direct statements introduced by Akkadian *umma,* similar to standard letter form.

10. My thanks to Itamar Singer (Tel Aviv), who suggested this reading and who provided the references.

il vocabulario neosumerico 11; Rome, 1982] 12–13 sub no. 141, with previous literature). For personal names with the Luwian passive participial ending -(*m*)*mi* and other possible uses for this ending, see Laroche, *Les noms des hittites*, 330. Note also the recent observation by R. Beal that IR$^{TUM/TAM}$ 'Orakel(anfrage)' at Boğazköy is possibly an abbreviation *ER* for Akkadian *erištum*, the verb IR 'bitten, verlangen, durch Orakel ermitteln' being a back formation. G. Beckman, who pointed out this reference to me, further remarks that "perhaps this could be involved in these names in IR, and would allow participial interpretation: 'The one requested of Tarḫunta/the Gods'?? In any case, note that DINGIR.MEŠ.IR (Hattušili's sister) also shows i-complementation" (e-mail of January 30, 1992).

Line 18. Kulat(t)i, spelled here with double *t*, is known from the Emar texts, for which see below, comments to line 23. The town of Kullania, known from Alalaḫ sources, was equated by M. Astour with Kullata in the north Syrian list of Thutmoses III at Karnak (M. Astour, *JNES* 22 [1963] 225 no. 31), but it is unlikely that the Alalaḫ town is the same as the Kulat(t)i of the Emar sources. On the contrary, the Kullata of the Thutmoses III list is probably to be associated with the Kulat(t)i in the territory of Emar, a place not yet known when Astour wrote his article.

Line 19. The Emar texts dealing with fields regularly designate their lengths and widths, often adding the names of the adjoining fields. See Arnaud, *Emar* 6/3, passim, and the comments of A. Tsukimoto, *ASJ* 10 (1988) 165.

Line 22. A Tuqnani, father of Dagan-kabar, appears in Arnaud, *Emar* 6/3 336:23, and again in the same text, line 69, as father of Mašru and grandfather of I[. . .]-Dagan.[11]

Line 23. There is an Aḫi-Dagan, son of Dagan-kabar and grandson of Milki-Dagan, in Arnaud, *Emar* 6/3 115, who purchases a *bit-tuguru* with its wells in Kulat(t)i. Although the grandfather's name, Milki-Dagan, is not uncommmon in the Emar onomastica, the fact that this family resides in Kulat(t)i suggests that we are dealing here with the same person. If so, this would add another generation to their family tree, with Turia becoming the father of Milki-Dagan. For Turia, see Arnaud, *Emar* 6/3 64:12, where he appears as son of Zu-Aštari. The suggested connections between these individuals must be considered tentative.[12]

11. I am indebted to Carlo Zaccagnini and his doctoral student, Stefano Bassetti, at the University of Bologna, who provided me with an electronic corpus of the Emar texts, thereby allowing for thorough searches of the data.

12. The five generations would be:
Zu-Aštari → ? Turia → Milki-Dagan → Dagan-kabar → Aḫi-Dagan.

Line 25. Tura-Dagan son of Daqani occurs in a list of witnesses in Arnaud, *Textes syriens,* 56:17.

Line 32. On the use of *ragāmu* in Hittite land grants, see G. Boyer, PRU 3, 283ff. and the comments of A. Skaist, "A Unique Closing Formula in the Contracts from Ugarit," in *Society and Economy in the Eastern Mediterranean (c. 1500–1000* B.C.) (ed. M. Heltzer and E. Lipiński; Orientalia Louvaniensa Analecta 23; Louvain, 1988 [pub. 1989]) 151–59.

For the spelling of the name with SUM = *ari,* see J. Nougayrol, PRU 4, 171, text 17.42:1, passim.

Line 35. The broken sign before -gu_5-*um* does not appear to be an [*a*]*g,* although this is what is expected here. It looks more like a *mu.*

Line 37. For Uri-Teššup *bēl abussi,* see Arnaud, *Emar* 6/3 186:2, where Uri-Teššup is also involved in a division of property in Kulat(t)i. This is the second connection in this text with the town of Kulat(t)i.

Line 38. For *bēl abussi* 'master of the treasury', see CAD A/1 93 s.v. For *bēl bit abussi,* see also A. Goetze, *RHA* 54 (1952) 5–6. It is significant that this document was written before the 'master of the treasury'. No doubt the field was the property of the royal family and, as such, carried with it certain obligations for feudal dues. Note the important recent observations of Skaist on such obligations, as indicated in the texts from Ugarit and Karkemiš ("A Unique Closing Formula," 153).

Line 40. For Mašamuwa, see Laroche, *Les noms des hittites,* 115, no. 771; and A. Hagenbucher, *Texte der Hethiter* 15 (Heidelberg, 1989) 19 (reference courtesy of G. Beckman). He is known to have been an "ambassador" to Assyria under Muwatalli II and Urḫi-Teššup. If he is the same individual as the person in our text, this would have been late in his career. On the basis of my preliminary copy, Arnaud (letter of May 12, 1982) suggested we read here GAL.LÚ.MEŠ 'chief overseer'. However, if the suggested restoration in line 8 above is valid, the reading here of GAL.UKKIN is more likely. The sign does not appear to be LÚ (see photo) and is closer to the UKKIN known from contemporary texts. Collation on the photo confirms this. It is likely that Mašamuwa himself was the *muʾirru* to whom Ari-Teššup went to resolve the argument over the 45 shekels and perhaps the reason why such a prominent individual as the king's mother became involved.

Line 41. So translated in view of the accusatives in line 37.

Stamp seal. The stamp seal impression is from the bilingual royal seal of Ini-Teššup, well documented both at Ugarit and Emar. Another impression of this seal appears on Beckman, *Rosen,* RE 85, also written before Ini-Teššup. A photo is provided below for comparison. The use of the royal, dynastic seal on land grant legal documents appears to be related to feudal duties connected with the individual fields. See the comments of Skaist, "A Unique Closing Formula," 153ff.

obv.

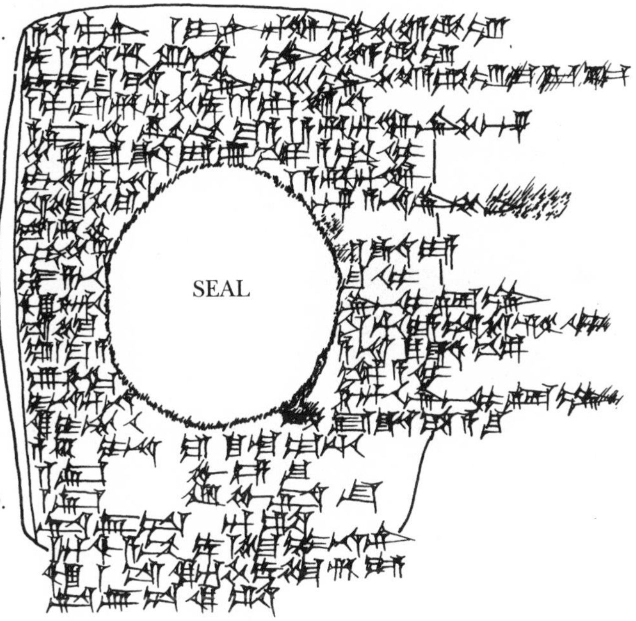

rev.

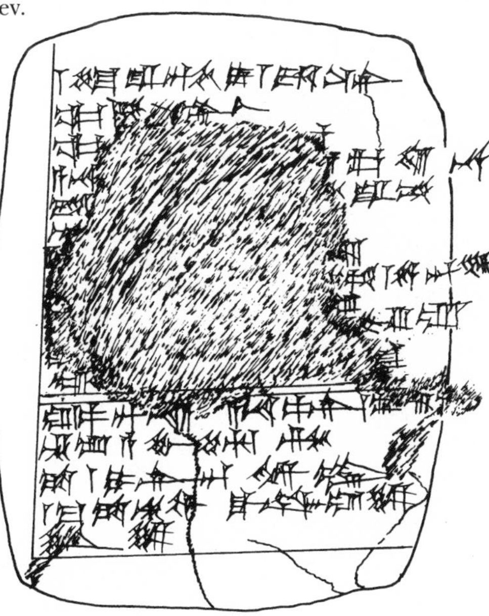

(MFA 1977.114)

obverse

right edge

lower edge

(MFA 1977.114)

upper edge

reverse

right edge

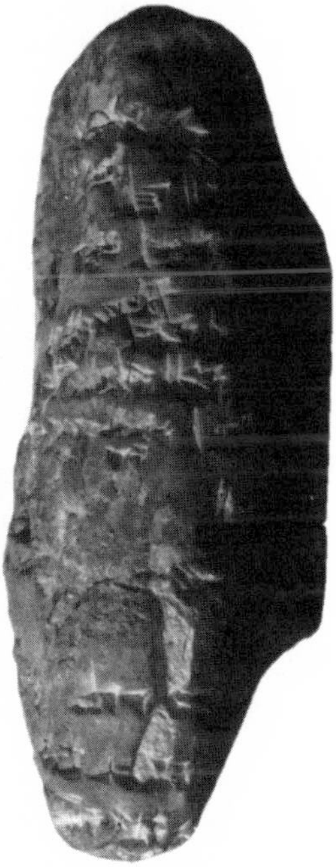

(MFA 1977.114)

Stamp Seal Impression

The "Plural of Ecstasy" in Mesopotamian and Biblical Love Poetry

Shalom M. Paul

Rapturous utterances of females in ecstatic amatory discourse in Sumerian, Akkadian, and biblical love lyrics are occasionally expressed by an unexpected shift from the first-person singular to the first-person plural. By this unique "plural of ecstasy," a woman gave ardent and passionate articulation to her highly charged sensuous state.

A very rare but misunderstood grammatical feature that occasionally appears in ancient Near Eastern and biblical love poetry is the employment of the first-person plural in ecstatic amatory discourse.[1] This psychological phenomenon, which I would like to designate the "plural of ecstasy,"

Author's note: This study is dedicated to my very dear friend, Jonas, whose "plurality" of interests and disciplines spans the entire realm of ancient Near Eastern and biblical literature.

I would like to express my deep sense of gratitude to Professor Jacob Klein for his thorough examination of the translation of the Sumerian love poems cited in this study and for his helpful annotations.

1. After independently reaching my conclusions, I discovered that this phenomenon was noted in passing by J. Goodnick Westenholz ("Love Lyrics from the Ancient Near East," in *Civilizations of the Ancient Near East* [ed. J. Sasson; New York, 1995]): "One noteworthy feature of the discourse is that female lovers commonly employed the first-person plural instead of the first-person singular especially when referring to bodily features, perhaps in the sense that they are sharing them with their lovers." Compare, too, her similar comments in "A Forgotten Love Song," in *Language, Literature and History: Philological and Historical Studies Presented to Erica Reiner* (ed. F. Rochberg-Halton; AOS 67; New Haven, 1987) 417. See also M. H. Pope, *Song of Songs* (AB 7C; Garden City, N.Y., 1977) 304 (citing S. N. Kramer, *The Sacred Marriage Rite* [hereafter, *SMR*] [Bloomington and London, 1969] 92), who states: ". . . there appears to be a common tradition of enallage in the sacred marriage songs, whatever the explanation, and it is the bride who refers to herself with plural pronouns in begging the love of the groom. Since the female in the sacred rite represented the great goddess, it may be that the shift to the plural was intended to suggest the excellence of divinity. Or, perhaps the priestess as surrogate both for the goddess and for mortal

replaces the otherwise expected first-person singular in rapturous utterances of the female lover.[2] Though its presence in Akkadian may be clearly demonstrated, its first attestations are apparently found in Sumerian love songs. The sudden and unexpected transition from singular to plural, which has baffled scholars, has usually been interpreted as reflecting the accompaniment of a female entourage which functioned as a lyric chorus. Though the presence of such an ensemble is attested occasionally in these love lyrics, it seems that it has been resorted to only in order to resolve these very few intriguing and puzzling passages. I would like to offer here an alternative solution to the problem, which may help shed new light on these passages (and perhaps on others as well). It seems that when a female lover gives ardent expression to her highly charged emotional state, she at times articulates her sensuous feelings in the *persona pluralis*. Possible examples of such a plural are found in the following excerpts from sacred and secular love poetry.[3]

Sumerian

SRT 5 [4]

This sacred marriage song relates how the goddess Inanna, while preparing herself by bathing and by donning her finery in fervent anticipation of her bridegroom's arrival in the bridal chamber, extols with intense excitement her recently attained youthful nubility:

---

females speaks for those who vicariously share her joy in the love of the king who represents the god." Since Pope did not take into account, however, that this plural also appears in secular poetry, the above explanations are not entirely tenable. For other ad hoc suggestions, see below, nn. 7, 8, 10, 17, and 27.

2. The female point of view is predominant in general in these love songs. See J. S. Cooper, "Enki's Member: Eros and Irrigation in Sumerian Literature," in *Dumu-e_2-dub-ba-a: Studies in Honor of Å. Sjöberg* (ed. H. Behrens; Philadelphia, 1989) 87–89.

3. Because of the intrinsic difficulties in understanding the genre of love poetry, the translations of these Sumerian poems often differ from one scholar to the next. This fact does not affect, however, the essential point of this paper, for the plural translation of the terms involved is not in question.

4. E. Chiera, *Sumerian Religious Texts* (Upland, Penn., 1924). For duplicate, see S. N. Kramer, "Cuneiform Studies and the History of Literature: The Sumerian Sacred Marriage Texts" (= *PAPS* 107, 1963) 521:N 4305 rev. ii. For translations (partial and complete), discussions, and comments, see S. N. Kramer, *SMR*, 97–98; B. Alster, "Sumerian Love Songs," *RA* 79 (1985) 146–52; A. Falkenstein, "Untersuchungen zur sumerischen Grammatik," *ZA* 45 (1939) 169–73; T. Jacobsen, "Religious Drama in Ancient Mesopotamia," in *Unity and Diversity* (ed. H. Goedicke and J. J. M. Roberts; Baltimore and London, 1975) 83; idem, *The Harps that Once*... (hereafter, *Harps*) (New Haven, 1987) 16–18; Y. Sefati, "Love Songs in Sumerian Literature: Critical Edition of the Dumuzi-Inanna Songs" (Ph.D. diss., Bar-Ilan University, 1985) 146–70 [Hebrew], who cites additional literature on p. 146.

39. Now *our* breasts (gaba-me) stand up![5]
40. Now hair has sprouted on *our* vulva (gal_4-la-me)![6]

Though Kramer, Jacobsen, and Sefati[7] refer this unexpected plural in her soliloquy to the supposed presence of female companions of the goddess,[8] the context clearly indicates that Inanna herself is speaking and, prior to the consummation of her union with her lover, is taking delightful exuberant pride in her own pudenda, which she refers to as 'our breasts' and 'our vulva'.[9]

PBS XII 52 obv. II–rev. I[10]

This royal love song begins with mí-ús-sá-m[e . . .] 'our son-in-law' (obv. lines 3′–4′), which Jacobsen explains as "a way of saying my

5. ba-gub-gub. Sum. gub = Akk. *zaqāpu*. Cf. KAR 472 ii 3: *šumma sinništu tulāša zaqpū* 'If a woman's breasts are erect'. For analogous Hebrew expressions, cf. שדי נכנו (Ezek 16:7); ושדי כמגדלות (Cant 8:10).

6. For sal-la = gal_4-la = *qallû* 'vulva', see Falkenstein, "Untersuchungen," 173. Note that in the passage from Ezekiel, which also describes the sexual maturation of a female (ותרבי ותגדלי), the mention of the 'well formed breasts' is followed by 'your (pubic) hair had sprouted' (ושערך צמח; Ezek 16:7). The connection with the Sumerian passage was also seen by M. Greenberg, *Ezekiel* (AB 22; Garden City, N.Y., 1973) 276.

7. Kramer, *SMR*, 98; Jacobsen, *Harps*, 18; Sefati, "Love Songs," 69. Sefati has noted this interchange on several occasions and refers to it on pp. 73–75, 112, 154 (n. 3), 167, 169, and 410. At times he suggests that -me may be an Emesal variant for -mu (p. 73). In other instances he relates the plural to a female chorus accompanying the bride to the groom. See, however, pp. 73–74, where he cites other, not strictly amatory, passages where the plural is seemingly inexplicable, since the reference is entirely to Inanna herself.

8. Note that 'singers' nar-e-ne appear in passing only once in the text, in line 28.

9. Alster ("Sumerian Love Songs," 146) notes and accepts the variant text, which renders both substantives as singular, ga-ba-mu 'my breasts' and gal_4-la-mà 'to my vulva'. This is a significant variant, since it proves that Inanna herself is the sole referent. (Could the scribe have deliberately emended the text to avoid the otherwise baffling plural and thereby harmonize these lines with the singular in line 43: [a] gal_4-la-mà-ke_4-eš / [b] gal_4-la-mu-šè? In such a case, our *lectio difficilior* definitely *praeferendum est.*) He also assumes (pp. 151–52) that the ensuing lines are all recited by the goddess alone:

> (41) Going to the lap of (my) bridegroom, let us rejoice! (42) Dance! Dance! (43) O Bau, let us rejoice over my vulva! (44) Dance! Dance! (45) (Until) the end, it will please him, it will please him!

Note that he omits from his translation ba-ba (line 41), which he explains "as an exclamatory expression," and ^{d}ba-u (line 43) is interpreted as a "scribal joke rendering this [i.e., ba-ba] expression." For interpretations of Baba, a pet name for Inanna and actually the wife of Ningirsu, see Jacobsen, *Harps*, 18; idem, *The Treasures of Darkness* (New Haven and London, 1976) 27–28, 81, 82, 156; Kramer, *SMR*, 152 n. 29; Falkenstein, "Untersuchungen," 169–71. As for Bau, the city goddess of Uruk, whose name is an onomatopoetic imitation of a dog's bark, "bow-wow," see T. Jacobsen, *Toward the Image of Tammuz and Other Essays on Mesopotamian History and Culture* (hereafter, *Tammuz*; ed. W. L. Moran; Cambridge, Mass., 1970) 33.

10. See S. Langdon, *Sumerian Grammatical Texts* (Philadelphia, 1917). For translations and discussion, see Alster, "Sumerian Love Songs," 128–35; Jacobsen, *Harps*, 91; Kramer,

'betrothed'."[11] Subsequently, the *amoreuse*, growing rapturous over her beloved's multilayered mane of hair, exclaims:

Obverse II

11. My (beloved) fit for the mane, my (beloved) fit for the mane,
12. My sweet one, my (beloved) fit for the mane,
13. Like a palm tree, my (beloved) fit for the mane,
14. My (beloved) exuberant like a tamarisk, my beloved fit for the mane.

Then, desirous of his close physical contact, she exclaims:

Reverse I

1. Man, who for your locks are acclaimed in the assembly,
2. My sweet, press (it) to *our* bosom (gaba-me-a).
3. Lad, who for your locks are honored in the assembly,
4. My brother of fairest face, press (it) to *our* bosom (gaba-me-a).

Though Kramer remarks, "It is not clear why the plural pronoun is used here,"[12] he does not resort to the assumption of a chorus, which is nowhere present. It is obvious that she is expressing her own rapturous state by means of the plural.

CBS 8530[13]

In a love song dedicated to the goddess Nanāja (= Inanna), a very erotic passage appears, replete with metaphors for sexual intercourse (obv. i 21–23):

Do not dig a canal, let me be your canal!
Do not plough a field, let me be your field!
Farmer, do not search for a wet place.
(My precious sweet one), let me be your wet place (i.e., vagina)!

SMR, 99–100; Sefati, "Love Songs," 301–16. See also Westenholz, "Forgotten Love Song," 417 n. 11. Kramer relates the plural to the parents of the girl; Alster, to a group of women.

11. Jacobsen (*Harps*, 87), states that this term 'stresses that he has been accepted by the family'. It is interesting to note that the plural occurs several times in lines 7–10:

(7) Wherever our parapet is, destroy our parapet!
(8) Our son-in-law, with whom we converse,
(9) When you touch (our) hair with your hand, what are you to us! (ta-me mu-un-gál) (or: then you are honey to us—reading the sign "ta" as "làl").
(10) When they have set you free, come to our house (é-me-eš-e)!

12. Kramer, *SMR*, 152 n. 31.

13. See B. Alster, "Marriage and Love in the Sumerian Love Songs," in *The Tablet and the Scroll: Near Eastern Studies in Honor of William W. Hallo* (ed. M. E. Cohen, D. C. Snell and D. B.

She then continues (lines 24–26):

> The [ditch(?)] is your furrow.
> *Our* little apples (i.e., breasts) (ḫasḫur tur-tur-me) are your desire!

Ni 2461[14]

This epithalamium is dedicated to Šusin (the fourth ruler of the Third Dynasty of Ur),[15] perhaps by his bride and reigning queen, Kubātum:[16]

9. Bridegroom, let me make all things sweet!
(Jacobsen: O! that you would do all the sweet things to me!)
10. My precious sweet, honey let me bring.
(Jacobsen: My sweet dear one, you bring that which will be honey sweet!)
11. In the bedchamber, honey filled,
(Jacobsen: In the bedroom's honey-sweet corner,)
12. Let *us* enjoy (ga-ba-ḫúl-ḫúl-le-en-dè-en) your sweet appeal (ḫi-li-ám-zè-ba-zu)!
(Jacobsen: Let *us* enjoy over and over your charms and sweetnesses!)
13. Bridegroom, let me make all things sweet!
(Jacobsen: O! that you would do all the sweet things to me!)

Within the literary inclusio of lines 9 and 13, "Bridegroom, let me make all things sweet!" (Jacobsen: "O! that you would do all the sweet things to me!"), which the bride addresses directly to her beloved spouse, she adds in the excitement of erotic ecstasy (line 12): "Let us (i.e., me) enjoy your sweet appeal!" (Jacobsen: "your charms and sweetnesses!"). The Sumerian word ḫi-li, as well as its Akkadian equivalent *kuzbu*, refer to attractive charm and sexual vigor. The mere thought of sharing his amatory delights explains this momentary passion-packed plural.

Weisberg; Bethesda, 1993) 15, 20. The text was first published by Å. W. Sjöberg ("Miscellaneous Sumerian Texts II," *JCS* 29 [1977] 21), but several of the restorations were made by Alster. For the similar metaphor of a "canal" in Egyptian love poetry, see below, n. 30.

14. See S. N. Kramer, M. Çiğ, and H. Kizilyay, "Five New Sumerian Literary Texts," *Belleten* 16 (1952) 360–63. Cf. Kramer, *SMR*, 92–93; idem, *The Sumerians* (Chicago, 1963) 254; Sefati, "Love Songs," 400–406. The first translation is based on Kramer's ("Five New Sumerian Literary Texts") and Alster's ("Sumerian Love Songs," 135–38), and is followed by Jacobsen's (*Harps*, 88). A different translation of Jacobsen's is found in *Tammuz*, 171.

15. Alster ("Sumerian Love Poetry," 135), assumes that the name Šusin does not refer to the king himself, but only serves as a metaphor employed by the woman for the man she loves.

16. For Kubātum, see Jacobsen, "The Reign of Ibbi-Suen," *JCS* 7 (1953) 46–47; P. Steinkeller, "More on the Ur III Royal Wives," *ASJ* 3 (1981) 80. For the identification of the bride who speaks here with Kubātum, see Jacobsen, *Tammuz*, 171.

N 3560 and duplicates[17]

The conclusion of another love song dedicated to Šusin may preserve an echo of this same use of the plural. His beloved pronounces an emotional blessing for his long life:

18. You are truly *our* lord! You are truly *our* lord (ù-mu-un-me)!
19. Silver wrought with lapis lazuli! You are truly *our* lord!
20. You are truly *our* farmer bringing in much grain!
21. He being the apple of *my* eye, being the lure of *my* heart,
22. May days of life dawn for him! May Shu-Suen [live long years]!

Though one cannot exclude the possibility of the presence of a chorus, the interchange between 'our' and 'my' is an indication of an individual speaker.

Yet another example of this interplay between the singular and plural may be found in the following Sacred Marriage song:

TMHNF 3, No. 24[18]

Here Inanna, who appears alone in this song, addresses Amaušum, the name of Dumuzi as god of the dates:[19]

Col. III

4. Come, rejoice to play, may you be *our* sun (^{d}utu-me)![20]
5. *My* Amaušum, let us embrace!
6. Come, rejoice to play, may you be *our* sun! (UD-me-en-dè-en)
7. Friend of An, lord of *my* choice (lit., my lord of heart),
8. (In) your pleasant mood, rejoice! May you be *our* sun (^{d}utu-me)!
9. Let *me* go to the lord; let *me* talk to him!

Akkadian

The examples from Akkadian love poetry for the "plural of ecstasy" are also few and far between, but they may be indisputably documented.

17. For translations and discussion, see Jacobsen (*Harps*, 93), whose translation is followed here; Kramer, *PAPS*, 508; idem, *SMR*, 95; idem, "Sumerian Sacred Marriage Texts," *ANET*, 644; Sefati, "Love Songs," 407–11 (on p. 410 he relates the plural, once again, to female companions).

18. For duplicate, see Kramer, *PAPS*, 107, 524:Ni 4552 rev. For translations and discussions, see S. N. Kramer and I. Bernhardt, *Sumerische literarische Texte aus Nippur*, vol. 1: *Mythen, Epen, Weisheitsliteratur und andere Literaturgattungen* (Berlin, 1961) 14; Kramer, *PAPS*, 524; Alster, "Sumerian Love Poetry," 152–55; Sefati, "Love Songs," 317–22.

19. For Amaušum, see Falkenstein, "Untersuchungen," 170 n. 2; Jacobsen, *Treasures of Darkness*, 26, 30–39; idem, *Tammuz*, 493, for multiple listings.

20. This is a term of endearment; cf. likewise Akk. *šamšu*, CAD Š/1 337, 3′.

Kich, B 472 i 9′–12′[21]

Jewelry is not only an indication of opulence and social status; it may also serve as a sexual allurement.[22] In this Old Babylonian poem the woman, in the course of extending an amorous invitation to her beloved for an erotic dalliance, portrays herself, in *waṣf*-like fashion, as being fully bedecked with the most precious of jewels. In this vivid and visual foreplay she tells her lover:

6′. Your love-making is sweet (*dādūka ṭābū*).[23]
7′. Waxing luxuriantly is your fruit (*muḫtanbū inbūka*),[24]
8′. (Of incense, my bed).

Then proceeding downwards, limb by limb, she excitedly exclaims:

9′. O by the diadem of *our* head (*rēšīni*),
the rings of *our* ears (*uznīni*),
10′. The mountains of *our* shoulders (*būdīni*),
the charms of *our* bosom (*irtīni*),
11′. the bracelet of date spadix charms of *our* wrists (*qātīni*),
12′. the belt of frog charms of *our* waist (*qablīni*)

All these personal adornments and allurements serve merely as a descriptive prelude to the "consummate" *pièce de resistance*:

13′. Reach forth with your left hand
and "honor" *our* vulva (*ḫurdatni*)![25]
14′. Play with *our* breasts (*tulīni*)!

21. H. de Genouillac, *Premières recherches archéologiques à Kich* (Paris, 1924), vol. 1. For a study of this poem, see Westenholz, "Forgotten Love Song," 415–25.

22. For the metaphor of jewelry, see J. G. Westenholz, "Metaphorical Language in the Poetry of Love in the Ancient Near East," in *La Circulation des biens, des personnes et des idées dans le Proche-Orient ancien: Actes de la XXXVIIIe Rencontre Assyriologique Internationale* (ed. D. Charpin and F. Joannès; Paris, 1992) 383–87.

23. Cf. Cant 1:2, טובים דדיך (מיין).

24. 'Fruit' has clear sexual overtones in Sumerian, Akkadian and Hebrew love lyrics. Cf., e.g., W. G. Lambert, "Devotion: The Languages of Religion and Love," in *Figurative Language in the Ancient Near East* (ed. M. Mendlin, M. J. Geller, and J. E. Wansbrough; London, 1987) 29ff.

25. For Akk. *ḫurdatu*, see Gilgamesh VI 69 (discussed below); M. Civil, "Medical Commentaries from Nippur," *JNES* 33 (1974) 332, lines 40–41: *ḫurdatu: ūru ša sinništi* 'vagina/vulva/pudendum of a woman' (note that the continuation of line 41 in this medical commentary contains the quotation from Gilgamesh VI 69); W. von Soden, "Ein spät-altbabylonisches *pārum*-Preislied für Ištar," *Or* 60 (1991) 340, line 11: *alkī lulappit ḫurdatki* 'Come, let me pet your vulva'!; line 18: *šuknā eṭlūtum ana ḫurdati damiqtimma* 'Put it (i.e., insert the penis) into the pretty vagina, young men!' For a further study and commentary on this blatantly pornographic piece, see V. Hurowitz's contribution to this volume, pp. 543–58.

Gilgamesh VI (7–9, 13–15), 68–69

Ishtar, totally stricken with the virile beauty of Gilgamesh, sensuously and brazenly offers herself to him, first as his lover and then as his wife:

6. Ishtar the princess looked covetously on the beauty of Gilgamesh.[26]
7. Come to me, Gilgamesh, be you (my) lover!
8. First give, O give me freely, your fruits of love!
9. You shall be my husband and I will be your wife.

Gilgamesh sarcastically rejects her seductive solicitations and her grandiose offer of sumptuous gifts by recalling, one by one, the dire fortunes of all his ill-fated predecessors, who succumbed to the goddess's enticement. In this catalog of forlorn and forsaken paramours, he also mentions Ishullanu, her father's orchardman, the only one prior to Gilgamesh who had the audacity to withstand her appeal—only to meet with a tragic end for which there was no appeal. Gilgamesh then quotes her shameless proposal:

68. My Ishullanu, let *us* have a taste (*i nīkul*)[27] of your strength (*kiššūtaki*)![28]
69. Stretch out[29] your hand (*qātka*)[30] and touch[31] *our* vulva (*ḫurdatni*)![32]

26. For the idiomatic expression, *ana . . . īnalīnā našû* here and in line 67 and its biblical interdialectal etymological and semantic cognate, נשא עינים אל 'to look at covetously', see my article, "Euphemistically 'Speaking' and a Covetous Eye," *HAR* 15 (Reuben Ahroni Volume; 1995).

27. B. Foster ("Gilgamesh: Sex, Love and the Ascent of Knowledge," in *Love and Death in the Ancient Near East: Essays in Honor of Marvin H. Pope* [hereafter, *Love and Death*] [ed. J. H. Marks and R. M. Good; Guilford, Conn., 1987] 35), attempts to explain this plural "as a term of endearment." According to him, "Ishtar begins with a first-person singular, but in an effort to preserve her dignity, turns to the first-person plural cohortative at the end."

For the corresponding sexual overtones of Heb. אכל, cf. Prov 30:20, Cant 5:1. Note, too, that the latter biblical citation, which abounds in sexual innuendos, begins: "I come into my garden (a well-established metaphor in love lyrics for feminine sexuality); I pluck (אריתי) my myrrh with my spice." For the figurative use of 'plucking' (Heb. ארה; see also M. Jastrow, *Dictionary of the Talmud Babli and Yerushalmi, Midrashic Literature and Targumim* [Philadelphia, 1903] 118, 'to pluck, esp. figs'), compare the employment of Akk. *qatāpu* 'to pluck' in the love song of Nabû and Tašmētu: *qatāpu ša inbīka ēnāja līmurāma* 'May my (Tašmētu's) eyes behold the plucking of your (Nabû's) fruit!' The Neo-Assyrian text is found in TIM 9 54 rev. 20 (cf. line 30). See A. Livingstone, *Court Poetry and Literary Miscellanea* (Helsinki, 1989) 35–37.

28. Note the unusual use of the feminine pronominal suffix, *-ki*. For words in Akkadian and Hebrew denoting 'strength', which, by extension, come to mean 'sexual vigor', see my forthcoming study.

29. For the reading *liš*(!) *tēṣâmma*, see W. von Soden, "Beiträge zum Verständnis des babylonischen Gilgameš-Epos," *ZA* 53 (1959) 26; cf. also CAD A/2 371, 5′ and L 84. Foster ("Gilgamesh," 35) also accepts this reading but remarks that the collation by P. Machinist and

C. B. F. Walker favors the reading *šú* (i.e., *šūṣâmma*). This reading is followed by Westenholz, "Forgotten Love Song," 417. For a duplicate, *šu-ṣa-am-ma*, see R. Frankena, "Nouveaux fragments de la sixième tablette de l'épopée de Gilgameš," in *Gilgameš et sa légende: Études recueilles par Paul Garelli à l'occasion de la VII*[e] *Rencontre Assyriologique Internationale (Paris, 1958)* (Paris, 1960) 120, ii 35.

30. Akk. *qātu*, as well as Heb. יד, Ugar. *yd*, and most likely Egyptian ḏr.t may also serve as euphemisms for the *membrum virile*. For Gilgamesh this was already noted by B. D. Eerdmans, "Der Ursprung der Ceremonien der Hosein-Feste," *ZA* 9 (1894) 297–98; P. Jensen, *OLZ* 29 (1926) 650. See, too, R. Campbell Thompson, *The Epic of Gilgamesh* (Oxford, 1930) 81 sub line 69; T. Jacobsen, "Two bal.bal.e Dialogues," in *Love and Death*, 61 n. 19. Cf. also CT 58, 13 (BM 88318), obv. 6–7; gal$_4$-la-mu . . . šu d[è-in-mar] cited by Alster, "Marriage and Love," 20. (This, of course, does not apply when the specific hand is designated in these erotic passages. For the 'left hand "honoring" the vulva', see the text from *Kich*, quoted in this study [above, p. 591]. For the "right hand," cf. SRT 31, lines 21–22: 'Your right hand should be placed on my vulva [šu-zi-da-zu gal$_4$-la-mà dè-em-mar]; your left hand [gùb-bu-zu] should be laid on my head', cited by Y. Sefati, "An Oath of Chastity in a Sumerian Love Song [SRT 31]?" in *Bar-Ilan Studies in Assyriology Dedicated to Pinḥas Artzi* [ed. J. Klein and A. Skaist; Ramat-Gan, 1990] 52–53; cf. 58–59).

For Biblical Hebrew, cf. Isa 57:8, 10 and Cant 5:4. See, e.g., Pope (*Song of Songs*, 517–19) and many other modern commentators; cf., too, M. Delcor, "Two Special Meanings of the Word יד in the Hebrew Bible," *JSS* 12 (1967) 230–40, esp. 234–40. For its appearance in Qumran Hebrew, see 1QS VII 13: ואשר יוציא ידו מתוחת בגדו והואה פוח ונראתה ערותו ונענש שלשים יום 'He who puts out his member (note that Heb. יוציא יד is the exact interdialectal cognate and semantic equivalent of the Akkadian expression found here, *qātam šūṣû*) from beneath his clothing, which is torn, and his nakedness is exposed, will be punished for thirty days'.

For Ugaritic, see "The Birth of the Gracious and Beautiful Gods," KTU 1.23, rev. 33–35, 37:

33. *tirkm.yd.il.kym* 'The organ of El is as long as the sea';
34. *wydil.kmdb.ark.yd.il.kym* 'And the organ of El is like the flood; the organ of El is like the sea';
35. *w.yd.il.kmdb* 'And the organ of El is like the flood'.

Nevertheless, the "long" and "short" of it is that El was not "up" to it, for the two females despondently remark:

37. *il.ḫṭh.nḫt.il.ymnn.mt.ydh* 'El, his rod is down, his love-staff droops' (see also lines 46–47).

For the ribald double-entendres here, see T. H. Gaster, *Thespis* (Garden City, N.Y., 1961) 428–30, notes. Such a meaning has also been suggested for the passage KTU 1.13, by J. C. de Moor ("An Incantation against Infertility (KTU 1.13)," *UF* 12 [1980] 306, 310), but his reconstructed text and interpretation are problematical.

For Egyptian, see A. Schott, *Altägyptische Liebeslieder* (Zürich, 1950) 56; M. V. Fox, *The Song of Songs and the Ancient Egyptian Love Songs* (Wiesbaden, 1985) 26, no. 18 (c): "Pleasant is the 'canal' within it, which your 'hand' scooped out." On p. 28, Fox remarks, "'Digging out' the blocked canal suggests defloration." Cf. also O. Keel, *Das Hohelied* (Zürich, 1986) 162; English trans. *The Song of Songs* (trans. F. J. Gaiser; Minneapolis, 1994) 192. See also above, n. 13.

31. Akk. *luput*. For another example of the sexual overtones of *lapātu*, see above, n. 25. See also J. Bottéro and S. N. Kramer, *Lorsque les dieux faisaient l'homme: Mythologie mésopotamienne* (Paris, 1989) 272: "Avance donc ta 'main' et me 'touche' la vulve!" Cf. p. 274: ". . . elle lui présent son sexe à 'toucher', en akkadien: *lapātu*—, euphemisme transparent . . . ."

32. For Akk. *ḫurdatu*, see above, n. 25.

In her enraptured and transported state, Ishtar's erotic desire is here expressed by the "plural of ecstasy."[33]

Late Babylonian Incipits

Two possible additional examples may be surmised from the incipits of the following Late Babylonian love poems;[34] but because they are incipits, it is impossible to arrive at a definitive conclusion:

KAR 158 Reverse ii 29 (p. 274)

atta māru[35] *rāʾimu dādīni*
'You (masculine) are the darling who is fond of *our* love-making'.

KAR 158 Reverse ii 20 (p. 273)

The incipit *šamša*[36] *ašni bēlani* is very enigmatic, except for the final word, *belāni*[37] '*our* darling lover'[38] (lit., '*our* lord').[39] *Bēlu* is a well-attested

33. Foster ("Gilgamesh," 35) remarks, "another royal plural"; but he also realizes, correctly, that there is an "intensification of Ishtar's desire."

For an interpretation of the Ishtar section in general, see T. Abusch, "Ishtar's Proposal and Gilgamesh's Refusal: An Interpretation of *The Gilgamesh Epic* Tablet 6, Lines 1–79" (*HR* 26 [1986] 143–87). For the personality of Ishtar here, see R. Harris, "Images of Women in the Gilgamesh Epic" in *Lingering over Words: Studies in Ancient Near Eastern Literature in Honor of William L. Moran* [ed. T. Abusch, J. Huehnergard, and P. Steinkeller; Atlanta, 1990] 219–30, esp. 226–28); and, in general, idem, "Inanna-Ishtar as Paradox and a Coincidence of Opposites" (*HR* 30 [1991] 261–78).

34. E. Ebeling, KAR I (= WVDOG 28). See idem, *Ein Hymnen-Katalog aus Assur* (Berlin, 1922). These incipits were employed by T. J. Meek in his studies on the Song of Songs: "Canticles and the Tammuz Cult," *AJSL* 39 (1922–23) 1–14; "Babylonian Parallels to the Song of Songs," *JBL* 43 (1924) 245–52; "The Song of Songs and the Fertility Cult," in *A Symposium on the Song of Songs* (ed. W. H. Schoff; Philadelphia, 1924) 48–79; *The Song of Songs: Introduction and Exegesis* (IB 5; New York and Nashville, 1956) 89–148. His entire theory, that the Song of Songs is a revised religious composition originally connected with the cult of Tammuz, has been completely rebutted.

For six other (partial) incipits, probably going back to the Old Babylonian Period, see I. L. Finkel, "A Fragmentary Catalogue of Love Songs," *ASJ* 10 (1988) 17–18.

35. For Akk. *māru* 'darling, lover', see CAD M/1 314. M. Held ("A Faithful Lover in an Old Babylonian Dialogue," *JCS* 15 [1961] 13) compares it to Heb. דוד, Cant 1:13, 14, 16; et al.

36. For *šamšu* as a term of endearment, see CAD Š/1 337.

37. For the pronominal suffix *-ni* (*-ani*) in Neo- and Late Babylonian, see W. von Soden, *Grundriss der akkadischen Grammatik* (Rome, 1952) 44 §42j, n. 12.

38. For Akk. *bēlu* as a term of endearment, see Held, "Faithful Lover," 13–14. For other examples in love poetry, see B. Foster, *Before the Muses* (2 vols.; Bethesda, Md., 1993) 1.98, line 11 ("Love Lyrics of Rim-Sin"); 2.902, line 15 ("Love Lyrics of Nabû and Tašmētu").

39. The incipit is cited in CAD Š/1 338, under *šamšu* 'sun', and on p. 400, under the verb *šanû*, but left untranslated both times.

term of endearment and is found in several other incipits:[40]

matima bēlu tēruba inanna
'When, O darling? Just now you have arrived!' (KAR 158 rev. ii 10).

sammūt erēni râmka bēlu
'Your love, O darling, is the fragrance of cedar' (KAR 158 rev. ii 21).

salīmka bēlī dāriam eleqqe nadnam
'I will win your favor, my darling, as a lasting gift'.[41]

bēlī ṣummâku râm[ka]
'My darling, I thirst for your love!'[42]

The plural 'our darling' in KAR 158 rev. ii 20 may similarly be a "plural of ecstasy."

Hebrew

This same phenomenon is also apparently present once or twice in the Song of Songs. However, since the reason for the enigmatic enallage[43] (i.e., shift in person) in these verses is not clear, biblical commentators, similar to their Sumerological colleagues, attempt to explain it by the sudden appearance of female companions, who supposedly function as a chorus in these otherwise personal ecstatic moments.

Song of Songs 1:4

This grammatically rapidly shifting verse commences with the young woman's rapturous plea: "Draw me after you, let us run!" Immediately following this direct second-person address to her lover, the next stich switches to the third-person: "The king brought me to his chambers." (Heb. מלך is to be understood as a term of endearment,[44] similar to Akk. *bēlu*, mentioned directly above [KAR 158 rev. ii 20]) and especially to Akk.

40. For examples, see Held, "Faithful Lover," 5, 13–14.

41. Ibid., 6, I 25–26; Foster (*Muses*, vol. 1, p. 93, line 25) translates: 'I shall have your eternal good will, darling, freely given'.

42. Held, "Faithful Lover," 8, III 12; for the similar metaphorical employment of Heb. צמא, see Ps 42:3, 63:2. Note, however, that von Soden (AHw 1536 sub *zummû(m)* II 2) reads *zummâku* 'I am deprived'.

43. For the phenomenon of enallage in Hebrew and Egyptian love poetry, see Fox, *Song of Songs*, 265–66. For Sumerian, see Sefati, "Love Songs," 73–75, 224; Kramer, *SMR*, 92. Compare also Pope, *Song of Songs*, 304.

44. Fox (*Song of Songs*, 98) compares it to the similar terms, 'my prince', 'prince of my heart', in Egyptian love poetry: "The lovers are called kings, princes, and queens because of the way love makes them feel about each other and about themselves."

šarru 'king', which is similarly employed in Babylonian love poetry incipits.[45] Cf. *ḫadiš akša šarru* 'Come here joyfully, O beloved [lit., O king]!' and *ārid kirî šarru ḫāṣibu erēni* 'The beloved [lit., the king] who goes down to the garden; he who trims the cedars'.)[46] The very thought or act of her lover's taking her to his private abode so arouses her passion that she joyously ejaculates: 'Let *us* delight and rejoice in you (נגילה ונשמחה בך)![47] *We* will praise (or, inhale)[48] your love-making more than wine (נזכירה דדיך מיין)!"[49] Obviously, this passionate damsel, in her fit of ecstasy, is referring solely to the sexual joys she alone will experience with her mate.

Song of Songs 2:15

The enigmatic but patently erotic overtones of this verse are palpable, אחזו־לנו שעלים שעלים קטנים מחבלים כרמים 'Catch *us* foxes, little foxes, spoilers of vineyards', especially when it is realized that כרם 'vineyard' is a well-attested poetic symbol for the female body, well-documented in Sumerian and Akkadian poetry, as well as in the Song of Songs itself (1:6, 8:12).[50] Thus it is possible that the 'us' (לנו) in the playful invitation 'Catch *us*' is the young lady's way of referring to herself in her enrap-

45. See J. A. Black, "Babylonian Ballads: A New Genre," *JAOS* 103 (1983) 25–34, esp. 29 n. 7, and 33 n. 19, for examples "of the use of *šarru* as an epithet of the male beloved in Babylonian amatory verse." See also Alster, "Marriage and Love," 16.

46. For Akk. *kirû* as a euphemism for the female pudenda, see Jacobsen, "bal.bal.e Dialogues," 62–63. For the idiom of 'going (down) to the garden' in Sumerian, Akkadian, Egyptian, and Hebrew love poetry, see Westenholz, "Metaphorical Language," 382; idem, "Love Lyrics."

47. Cf. the similar Sumerian expression in the love songs cited above (p. 589), ga-ba-ḫúl-ḫúl-le-en-dè-en. For the parallel pair, גיל and שמח, cf. Isa 25:9, 66:10; Joel 2:21, 23 et al. The two verbs also appear together in line 6 of the Ammonite Tell Siran inscription from ca. 600 B.C.E.: יגל וישמח. See K. P. Jackson, *The Ammonite Language of the Iron Age* (Chico, Cal., 1983) 35–44; W. E. Aufrecht, *A Corpus of Ammonite Inscriptions* (Lewiston, 1989) 203–11.

48. See R. Gordis (*The Song of Songs and Lamentations* [New York, 1974] 78), who translates Heb. נזכירה as 'inhale' and compares Lev 24:7, Isa 66:3, Hos 14:8, and Ps 20:4, citing medieval commentators.

49. R. E. Murphy (*The Song of Songs* [Hermeneia; Minneapolis, 1990] 127) notes the "ambiguity. It is not certain whether she is associating the 'maidens' with herself, or (more likely) speaking only of herself and the man she calls 'king'." On p. 128, he states, "The woman . . . involves the maidens." Murphy (*Song of Songs*, 139, 141) again resorts to a "plural group." Fox (*Song of Songs*, 114) conjectures that it "may be a 'plural of composition' referring to one girl's body" and cites *Gesenius' Hebrew Grammar* (Oxford, 1957) 397 §124b. See, however, Fox's note 23 (on p. 248, citing Westenholz in amatory contexts).

50. 'Vineyard' is also used in love poetry similarly to 'garden' to refer to the female pudenda. See above, n. 27. See my forthcoming study, "A Lover's Garden of Verses: Literal and Metaphorical Imagery in Ancient Near Eastern Love Poetry," *Moshe Greenberg Jubilee Volume* (forthcoming).

tured state. This becomes clear at the verse's amatory conclusion, in which she pointedly teases, '*Our* vineyard (כרמנו) is in blossom'.

In sum, in some very rare instances in Mesopotamian and biblical love poetry, there exists an unexpected shift from singular to plural that is occasioned by the passionate outburst of a female lover. Hopefully, others, in their examination of these love songs, will find additional examples to substantiate further this unique "plural of ecstasy."[51]

51. Could the following passage, taken from a Palestinian love song, reflect this same grammatical phenomenon?

> Examine me, O physician, as to what I suffer on behalf of the beloved one (*min il-ḥabîb*).
> By God, O Lord, this is a wondrous thing!
> Yet my heart melted for the beloved ones! (*ᶜala l-aḥbâb*).

The verses, cited by R. Gordis (*Song of Songs*, 34 and 88) in connection with Cant 5:1, are taken from St. H. Stephan, *Modern Palestinian Parallels to the Song of Songs* (Jerusalem, 1926) 80.

Water beneath Straw: Adventures of a Prophetic Phrase in the Mari Archives

Jack M. Sasson

The god Dagan of Terqa sends Zimri-Lim of Mari a message through a prophetess. Three different officials–the majordomo Sammetar, the priestess Inibshina, and the future Terqa governor Kibri-Dagan (via his son Kanisan)–convey this message to the king. Except for the statement "beneath straw runs water," however, each message reads differently from the other, and in this study I explain why. I also suggest a reason for the fact that Zimri-Lim did not follow Dagan's admonition.

In the study of the contexts, styles, and practitioners of ancient Near Eastern prophecy, whether as a goal in itself or as background to a better understanding of Hebrew prophecy, the archives recovered from Mari have deservedly received major attention. Among the documents recovered from the Old Babylonian palace, there were a number of letters that included divinely inspired messages intended for King Zimri-Lim, a contemporary of Hammurabi of Babylon.[1] In this essay, offered in tribute to a beloved colleague and an erstwhile teacher in my community

1. A useful recent overview that includes a bibliography is found in H. Huffmon, *ABD* 5.477–82. J.-M. Durand has collated, reedited, and enlarged the corpus of Mari letters with prophetic contents in a chapter of his 1988 book, *Archives épistolaires de Mari* 1/1 (ARM 26; Paris, 1988) 377–452. Other documents in the archives that have prophetic contents are nos. 346 and 371 in *Archives épistolaires de Mari* 1/2 (ed. D. Charpin et al.; ARM 26). Another example is now treated in J.-M. Durand, "Le Combat entre le Dieu de l'orage et la Mer," *MARI* 7 (1993) 43–47. Gripping as the evidence of Mari prophecy may be for students of the Bible, it should nevertheless be kept in mind that gods also channeled their wills through dreams and visions. At Mari, however, none of the preceding methods for learning the will of the gods was as highly regarded for its reliability as omens obtained by reading the livers of sacrificed animals; through inspection of fetuses (anomalous [*izbum*]; aborted [*iZ*$^?$*mum*]) and observation of astronomical oddities, natural phenomena (earthquakes, fire from heaven), and atypical meteorology (rain during summer, hail without rain, thunder without rain).

(Syrian Jews of Brooklyn), I want to focus on one prophecy, delivered by a single divine messenger but communicated to the king by at least three different Mari personalities, two high officials and a priestess. I want to suggest a reason for the fact that the language of one transmission differed from the other and that Zimri-Lim did not follow the will of Dagan, the source of the prophecy.

During the eighth month of Zimri-Lim's sixth or seventh year on the throne of Mari, Lupakhum, an *apīlum* ('mouthpiece') of Dagan, went on an errand for his king, who was then at Saggaratum.[2] We learn about it from a letter that Sammetar, then in charge at Mari, wrote the king (ARM 26 199):[3]

> Lupakhum, Dagan of Tuttul's *apīlum*, arrived here from Tuttul. He reported the information my lord entrusted to him, "Investigate for me (the oracles) before Dagan of Terqa." When he carried this message, he was given the following answer:
>
> > Wherever you go, happiness will constantly greet you. Battering ram and siege-tower are given to you; they will travel, as do companions, by your side.
>
> These are the words they told him when in Tuttul.
>
> No sooner did he arrive here from Tuttul than I had him escorted to Der so that he could carry my (door) bolt to the goddess Diritum. (Previously he had carried a *šernum* saying [to Diritum], "The *šernum* is not fastened and water will draw [it]. Reinforce the *šernum*.")[4] Now that he carried my (door) bolt, this is what was communicated (to the goddess Diritum):

2. See M.11436, cited by Durand, ARM 26/1 396: "1 shekel of silver, market weight, (given) to Lupakhum, the *apīlum* of Dagan, when he went to Tuttul. Month 8, day 7, year: Zimri-Lim consecrated a throne to Shamash." In the list of Zimri-Lim years with a known sequence, this is the fourth. To obtain a setting in his actual tenure, an objective that is still under debate, I have added, not completely arbitrarily, two years to that number.

3. On the chronology of posts held by Sammetar, see provisionally Durand, ARM 26/1 574–75.

4. We note that twice in the document Sammetar speaks of 'my bolt' *sikkurī*. The only hint given about the meaning of the symbolism is in information that is itself obscure. Sammetar reminds the king that "previously, he took a *šernum*, saying [to Diritum! note verbal form in line 21], 'the *šernum* is not fastened and water will draw (it). Reinforce the *šernum*.' " The form *i-SU-up-pu* in this quotation (*pānānum šernam saniqma mû i-Su-uP-Pu šernam dunnuni*) should be a middle weak verb, hence connected to *sâbum*, a verbing dealing with drawing water; but I do not know what *mû isubbū* means in the context. For *sanāqum*, said of bolts in line 20, see CAD S 140.

> You may count on a peace treaty with the lord of Eshnunna and therefore have become negligent; however, your watchmen should be strengthened more than previously.

Speaking to me,[5] this is what he said,

> The king may be planning to take a binding oath with the lord of Eshnunna without consulting God. This will be like the previous occasion, when the Benjaminites came down to settle in Saggaratum. Did I not tell the king, "Do not make covenants with the Benjaminites;[6] I shall send them among the . . .[7] their clans and God River will finish them off for you"? Now then, without consulting God, he ought not to take a binding oath.

Lupakhum spoke these words to me. Later, the next day in fact, a *qammātum*-woman of Dagan of Terqa came here to tell me:

> Beneath straw runs water. To make peace, they are constantly writing you and sending you their gods, but in their hearts they devise an entirely different "wind." The king must not take a binding oath without consulting God.

She requested and I gave her a *lakharum*-garment and a *ṣerretum*-broach. By the way, she gave Inibshina the high priestess her message at the temple of the goddess Belet-ekallim. Now I am sending to my lord all these messages that were reported to me. My lord should consider them and act according to his royal majesty. With regard to Yanṣib-Dagan, the soldier from Dashran whose head my lord ordered me to cut off, straightaway I sent Abi-epukh and when this man could not be found, Abi-epukh took his household and personnel into slavery. However, the next day a letter from Yasim-Dagan reached me saying that this

5. Durand has Lupakhum speak to Diritum. Charpin holds a position similar to mine; see his "Contexte historique et géographique des prophéties dans les textes de Mari," *Bulletin of the Canadian Society for Mesopotamian Studies* 23 (1992) 21–31.

6. Literally: "'to kill a donkey foal' of the Benjaminites." It is not at all clear whether the animal was slaughtered, as in Hebrew *šāḥaṭ*, or killed by breaking its neck, as in Hebrew *ᶜārap*, referring to a heifer killed for communal atonement for an unsolved murder. Charpin has published two versions of a letter that contain major testimony (and discrepancies) on this practice, one sent to the king and another to his private secretary, "Un Souverain éphémère en Ida-maraṣ: Išme-Addu of Ašnakkum," *MARI* 7 (1993) 185–87.

7. *Ina Bu ḫu Bu-ur-re-e qinnātišunu aṭarrassunūti* is a difficult phrase, because its second word is not attested elsewhere. Depending on which of its three initial signs is regarded as superfluous, it could be read {*BU*} *ḫuburrê* (Durand) or *buḫurrê*. *Qinnum* normally refers to 'clan, family' when in the feminine plural (as here) but refers to 'nests' when in the masculine plural. The verb *ṭarādum* is most commonly construed with animate objects as direct objects. Durand renders, "Je les (r)enverrai au milieu du dispersement de leurs nids. . . ."

man had just arrived there. My lord should now give me some indication of whether or not I should release his personnel.

This letter can be set within a fairly well understood context. No sooner had Zimri-Lim come to rule Mari than he was forced to battle the Benjaminites, a cluster of tribes that moved in and out of Mari territory. The struggle became even more dangerous to the stability of the new king's throne, especially because Eshnunna, a major power to the south of Mari, was supporting the tribal leaders. Zimri-Lim did succeed in defeating the tribes and was now contemplating accepting the peace overtures of Ibalpiel II, king of Eshnunna.[8] Let us inspect Sammetar's letter closely.

"Investigate for me (the oracles) before Dagan of Terqa," Zimri-Lim had asked Lupakhum. Lupakhum, however, stopped at Tuttul on the Balikh, where its own Dagan charged him to tell the king, "Wherever you go, happiness will constantly greet you. Battering ram and siege-tower are given to you; they will travel, as do companions, by your side." This report, then, was not of peace, but of war successfully negotiated.

Thus armed, Lupakhum traveled southward toward Mari. It is curious that we do not read that Lupakhum stopped at Terqa to petition Dagan, as bid by his king; but it remains possible that visiting Tuttul fulfilled this requirement. Lupakhum did not linger long at Mari. He took from Sammetar a bolt (whether real or decorative, we do not know)[9] and journeyed a day or so to a provincial town, Der, where the goddess Diritum resided. Whatever its symbolic value, the bolt seems to have had its effect on Lupakhum, for we find him admonishing the goddess: "You may count on a peace treaty with the lord of Eshnunna," he tells her, "and therefore have become negligent; however, your watchmen should be strengthened more than previously."

The wording of Lupakhum's admonition to Diritum is strikingly reminiscent of warnings that the gods repeatedly sent to Zimri-Lim; it may well be meant to hit its target by bouncing off the goddess. Sammetar twice refers to the bolt as being his property, and if his previous post at Terqa is at all relevant here, the bolt may have become instrumental in a cosmological test of wills that, as we know from other prophetic documents in Durand's volume (ARM 26 196), included a striking apocalyptic vision in which Dagan judges Tishpak and finds him wanting.

8. This complex story is well rehearsed in D. Charpin, "Un Traité entre Zimri-Lim de Mari et Ibâl-pî-El II d'Ešnunna," in *Marchands, Diplomates et Empereurs: Études sur la civilisation mésopotamienne offertes à Paul Garelli* (ed. D. Charpin and F. Joannès; Paris, 1991) 139–66.

9. See above, n. 4. ARM 21 230:4 lists a lapis-lazuli bolt for a piece of jewelry.

Be that as it may, Lupakhum next turns to Sammetar. Obviously speaking for Dagan and to Zimri-Lim, he reminds him how Dagan had orchestrated the defeat of the Benjaminites and warns, "Without consulting God, [Zimri-Lim] ought not take a binding oath [to the king of Eshnunna]." Sammetar himself deems this warning so crucial to his message that he uses two versions of it to frame the valuable lesson that Zimri-Lim should be drawing from recent history.

What is remarkable about Lupakhum's words as recorded by Sammetar is the absence of any clear indication that the *apīlum* was echoing words that reached him through a dream, vision, or trance. In fact, in a long and complex letter that recalls multiple oracles, we miss unequivocal references to formulas such as "thus speaks the god such and such." Moreover, not once is there any allusion to sending validating objects, such as fringes and hair from the clairvoyant, by which to enhance what is propitious or deflect what is sinister in a given prognostication. Dagan may well have had confidence in Lupakhum and may have trusted him to speak for him at many forums; yet on a decision with so much at stake, Zimri-Lim was being left to rely on Lupakhum's ex cathedra statements.

Sammetar may have recognized Zimri-Lim's dilemma over taking Lupakhum at his word, so he turns to a complementary prognostication. He writes, "Later, the next day in fact, a *qammātum*-woman of Dagan of Terqa came here to tell me: 'Beneath straw runs water.'[10] To make peace, they are constantly writing you and sending you their gods, but in their hearts they devise an entirely different 'wind'. The king must not take a binding oath without consulting God."

Notice how, as quoted, the god's words never identify the ruler who is so full of cunning. To connect the miscreant with Ibalpiel, Zimri-Lim had to move backwards in the text, locating the relevant information only in Lupakhum's twice-told warning. Had Zimri-Lim succumbed to such an obvious manipulation of mechanism, medium, and time, he might still have questioned the value of having to consult God, when God had just declared the potential ally to have had a conniving heart. Sammetar found it prudent, therefore, to shift the argument back to the *qammātum*. She has asked for handouts from the palace, he says of her, a sure sign that she feels her mission completed. If he had questions about

10. Whether to read the word *qammātum* or *qabbātum* is still at issue. See Durand, ARM 26/1 396 for diverse opinions, including his notion that *qammātum* is West Semitic for *kezertum*, a term referring to a type of female votaries distinguished for their piled-up hairdo. I have followed him here because of the spelling [*qa*-]*am-ma*-[*tim*] (genitive) in ARM 26 203:12′. It should be noted, however, that the "Mari" vocabulary for prophetic and divinatory personnel tends to divide among words related etymologically to 'seeing' or 'speaking', not 'standing', hence favoring *qabbātum* 'spokeswoman'.

her message or its delivery, Sammetar assures the king, a fuller explanation would come from Inibshina, the priestess and (half-)sister of the king, to whom the *qammātum* delivered the same message (*wûrtum*) at the temple of Belet-Ekallim in Mari.

Inibshina's own report on the matter was published long ago in Dossin's ARM 10 (80 = 26 197). The *qammātum*'s utterance is the core of her letter: "The friendship of Eshnunna's king is false: beneath straw runs water. I will gather him into the net that he knots (or: I knot). I will destroy his city and will ruin his wealth, untouched since of old."[11]

Inibshina enhances the urgency of this message by folding its words within two portions of an earlier oracle (*têrtum*)[12] that the goddess Annunitum communicated through Shelibum, a 'berdache' (*assinnu*, a gynepathic transvestite). For more details about the content of that particular oracle, Zimri-Lim had at hand a letter from Queen Shiptu (26 213),[13] who also conveyed specimens of Shelibum's hair and garment. But Inibshina was not content to use Annunitum's words just to envelope those of Dagan of Terqa; rather, she used selected sentiments from them to shape a terse censure of her king's behavior: *kiām ešme ummami ana ramānišu ištanarrar; ana ramānika la taštanarrar* 'I have heard it said that he *scintillates* on his own. Stop doing that!'

Inibshina's harangue includes difficult language, but whatever was its precise meaning (the difficulty is in the verb *šitarruru*[14]), the conviction and confidence with which she delivers the *qammātum*'s message is nevertheless evident. Indeed, as we return to it, we are struck by the sharpness of its tone compared with what is given in Sammetar's version. True, both want Zimri-Lim to avoid entanglement, but whereas Sammetar's *qammātum* warns of an unnamed opponent's craftiness and advises oracular consultation, Inibshina's *qammātum* is specific about Eshnunna's duplicity. However, she leaves Zimri-Lim no room to maneuver, for Dagan will already have destroyed Ibalpiel. Both Inibshina and Sammetar cite

11. Durand reads line 19: {*ŠU*} *šulputam ušalpat*. I am reminded of an OB passage cited in AHw 1269b: *mātu lā šulputtu uštalpat*. See also CAD L 92.

12. For usage of this term, see Durand, ARM 26/1 379–80.

13. Previously edited as ARM 10 7.

> Three days ago, in the temple of Annunitum, Shelibum went into a trance. Said Annunitum, "Zimri-lim, you will be tested through an uprising! Protect yourself by bidding loved and trustworthy servants to stand by you. Don't move about alone. As to those who test you, I will hand them over to you."

Durand(ARM 26/1 424) thinks that Inibshina is referring to 26 198. But the latter is hardly a prophecy.

14. CAD Š/2 58–59 (sub *šarāru* C) renders, "I have heard the following, 'He continually moves about (?) by himself,' you should not continually move about (?) by yourself."

the *qammātum*'s apothegmatic assertion, "Beneath straw runs water." But, whereas in Sammetar's version it requires a commentary to give it full sense, in Inibshina's account the aphorism reinforces Ibalpiel's character flaw. It has become, therefore, a moral indictment on which to justify the program of destruction Dagan is preparing for Eshnunna. Finally, while in Sammetar's version the *qammātum*'s warning is perfectly prosaic, or at best tries to play on *šārum* 'wind' and *šarrum* 'king', the *qammātum* of Inibshina turns out to be a fine punster, enveloping the series of reversals awaiting Ibalpiel in a parosonantic play on *šapal tibnim* (line 13) and on forms of *šulputum* (line 17).

If the letters of Sammetar and Inibshina left Zimri-Lim anxious about recovering Dagan's message, imagine how much more perplexed he must have been when not just one, but two more versions of essentially the same oracle reached him. Kibri-Dagan, who may have been Sammetar's son and who was probably writing from Terqa, very likely reported on the matter to the king, if not also to the king's private secretary Shunukhra-khalu. We know this because we have the letter the king received from Kibri-Dagan's "son" (real or otherwise), Kanisan, writing from Mari (ARM 26 202). Albeit without direct attribution, Kanisan cites his father's quotation of the *qammātum*'s iteration of Dagan's original words, and it too relies on the same adage, "beneath straw runs water":

> My father Kibri-Dagan wrote to me in Mari, "I have heard what was told [in Dagan's temple]. This is what was said, 'Beneath straw runs water.' He came, my lord's god; he has handed him his enemies. Now, as before, the ecstatic broke out into repeated declamation." This is what Kibri-Dagan wrote me.

Here, the imagination of Kibri-Dagan (or of Kanisan?) is strikingly circumscribed, setting the events in past time and using an obvious play on *alākum* by which to expound on our phrase, "Beneath straw runs water. He came, my lord's god; he has handed him his enemies."[15]

Whatever the original language of Dagan's sermon, we are left with only its avatars to inspect, obviously tailored by the personality of each dispatcher: Sammetar, Inibshina, Kibri-Dagan, if not also the *qammātum*.[16]

15. Kanisan continues by advising the king to consult the omens and to offer sacrifice. The reference to the male ecstatic (*muḫḫum*) is likely about another incident altogether, although it is not impossible that by the time Kibri-Dagan heard of the oracle, its source had become garbled. The pun in this version is connective: *mû illakū/illikma ilum.*

16. If three messages about the same affair are not enough, there is also ARM 26 203. This is a badly preserved text with a few lines about a *qammātum* who, upon delivering an

Table of Textual Comparisons

ARM 26 199 (Sammetar)	*ARM 26 197* (Inibshina)	*ARM 26 202* (Kanisan)
šapal in.nu.da (*tibnim*) *mû illakū ana salīmim ištanapparūnikkum ilīšunu iṭarradūnikkum u šāram šanêmma ina libbišunu ikappadū šarrum balum ilam išallu napištašu la ilappat*	*salīmātum ša awīl ešnunna daṣtumma šapal* in.nu.da (*tibnim*) *mû illakū u ana šêtim ša ukaṣṣaru akammissu alšu uhallaq u makkuršu ša ištu aqdami la šulput*[*tu*] *ušalpat*	*šapal* in.nu.da (*tibnim*) *mû illakū illikma ilum ša bēliya awilê ayyabīšu ana qātīšu umalli inanna* lú*muḫḫum kīma pananumma irṭub šitassam*
Beneath straw runs water. They keep on writing you about peacemaking; they send you their gods, but in their hearts they devise an entirely different "wind." The king must not take a binding oath without consulting God.	The friendship of Eshnunna's king is false: **beneath straw runs water**. I will gather him into the net that he knots (or: I knot); I will destroy his city and will ruin his wealth, untouched since of old.	**Beneath straw runs water**. He came, my lord's god; he has handed him enemies. (Now, as before, the ecstatic broke out into repeated declamation.)

The quotations we have examined differ in every way but in their recall of a deceptively opaque phrase.[17] Most scholars conjecture that the phrase "beneath straw runs water" is a warning against trickery; something like "still waters run deep" is one of its possible meanings.[18] But

oracle, is clipped of hair and garment fringes, after which she is rewarded with clothing. There is nothing in the document about water running beneath straw, but it may well have been a letter from Shiptu herself.

17. Diverse proposals are gathered in A. Marzal, *Gleanings from the Wisdom of Mari* (Studia Pohl 11; Rome, 1976) 27–29. A. Finet ("Citations littéraires dans la correspondance de Mari," *RA* 68 [1974] 31 and 42) has suggested that the imagery draws on brick-making technology. Straw is placed in pools of water before clay is added, and floating straw, he suggests, gives a false sense of security; but it is not clear to me how it does this. See also Finet's review of Marzal in *BiOr* 35 (1978) 222. Straw remains in place when loaded on a ship that itself floats on running water. This is the case reported in M. 13096, a Mari letter written by the same Sammetar (cited by Durand, "La Cité-état d'Imar à l'époque des rois de Mari," *MARI* 6 [1990] 46), but to concretize our phrase in this way would completely spoil the allusion.

18. In Akkadian the verb *alāku* construes with water readily (see CAD A/1 310 sub g) but hardly ever metaphorically. In Ugaritic it is said of 'wadis [*nḥl*] flowing like honey' (CTA 6 [UT 49] III 7, 13). In Hebrew *hālak* is commonly said of water, streams, rivers, and the sea, in some cases carrying more metaphoric sense than in others (see BDB, 232 sub 3; but Ezek 7:17, 21:12 [RSV 21:6] must be understood euphemistically). Other verbs are also used: *nāzal*, *yārad*,

such an interpretation depends too much on Inibshina's own setting for it. In actuality, *above running water there can only be moving straw,* and the moving straw would cause the rush of the water to be more obvious to the beholder.[19] The phrase could also be an allegory, but we elucidate the saying no better by assigning roles to straw or to running water.

I have pored over biblical, talmudic, and classical literature and have found straw and water, when directly linked in the same context, to deal almost exclusively with the care and feeding of beasts of burden. Our phrase could be a "riddle" which, by definition, needs an exact key to unlock it; or it could be an "enigma" which, by implication, can never have enough levels of meaning.[20] One recalls what is said in Num 12:6–8, that God spoke to the prophets in "riddles" (*bĕḥidôt),* except when addressing Moses.

I have two conclusions. First, whatever the *qammātum* said must have contained the phrase "beneath straw runs water," an expression that so baffled its hearers that, when they wrote to the king, they were uncharacteristically meticulous in reporting it. They quoted it accurately but also felt free to expound on it, offering their judgments to Zimri-Lim as if they were part of the *qammātum*'s discourse. This practice was common in the ancient Near East, where people who recorded *an orally delivered statement* did not feel obligated to register it in the precise form in which they heard it. As it reached different ears, the statement was shaped to suit the perspective of the hearer.[21] This is why I think it would be fruitless for us to search beyond this particular phrase for an "original" among the three formulations.[22]

šûb, nûs, ᵓāzal. In Hebrew gnomic literature 'deep waters' (*māyim ᶜamuqqîm*) is a metaphor for limitless resources or for profundity when said of conversation (*dibrê pî-ᵓîš,* Prov 18:4) and of 'stratagem/counsel/purpose' (*ᶜēṣâ,* Prov 20:5). Especially in the second case, whether 'deep waters' implies guidance or trickery is unclear.

19. It is important to recognize the fact that in all the references the texts are speaking of 'straw' (= in.nu.da *tibnum*), not of 'grass' or 'reed', two substances that theoretically could remain motionless when water runs beneath them.

20. I owe the suggestion for the term *enigma* to J.-M. Durand.

21. The topic deserves fuller treatment elsewhere. It would be interesting to contrast the precision with which *written* statements were transmitted. In most cases, since written statements were read aloud by scribes to illiterate officials, in transmission they tended to receive the same treatment as orally delivered declarations. This is in sharp contrast to occasions on which a scribe was given a whole document (or an extract thereof) to insert in a letter. Whenever we are able to compare an original with the document from which it was copied or excerpted, we find minor differences in "spelling" (number of cuneiform signs with which to write a word), "punctuation" (use of conjunctions), "orthography" (allocation of signs per line), or occasionally even the use of verbal tenses.

22. As does S. Parker, "Official Attitudes towards Prophecy at Mari and in Israel," *VT* 43 (1992) 59–60. He selects Inibshina's version as the most "authentic."

Why did Zimri-Lim fail to act on Dagan's warning? I need not debate the ardor of his piety and his understanding of philology to speculate that the versions of the divine message analyzed above would not have communicated to the king what Dagan really wanted of him. Had he nonetheless chosen to act on any of the versions of the prophecy, as received, he would have had no means of verifying or validating it.

Yet Zimri-Lim proved himself a shrewd reader of character, for despite his peace with Eshnunna, the cast of correspondents remained true to him: Lupakhum and Inibshina continued to serve him deep into his reign. Before he died a few months later, Sammetar did what the king bade him and once fussily inquired on how properly to welcome Eshnunna's delegation. The peace with Eshnunna gained Zimri-Lim a necessary respite without losing Yamkhad's support. Within four years Mari joined a coalition that brought Eshnunna to its knees.

I am just as keen to promote the second conclusion. Mari documents that recall movements of visionaries or cite the words of gods may turn out, on closer inspection, to deliver better insights on Mari personalities than on Mari prophecy.

Some di-til-la Tablets in the British Museum

Marcel Sigrist

The author presents six ditilla ('verdict') tablets, dealing with trials and verdicts in the city of Lagaš around 2000 B.C.E. The tablets provide a glimpse into the kind of social and family situations that could lead to contestation and trial.

Legal practice during the Ur III period (approximately 2100 to 2000 B.C.E.) is best known through the "di-til-la" tablets, which record the outcome of a legal dispute before the court. For this period most of the legal documents come from two cities, Lagaš and Umma, but the tell of Lagaš has yielded the largest quantity. So far, the other large cities of the time, such as Ur, Uruk, Drehem, and Nippur, have provided hardly any tablets of a legal nature.

The *ditilla* tablets were not the property of one of the parties in the legal battle; rather, they came from the central office of the provincial administration (the *ensi*), where they were kept in chronological sequence, in contrast to the following period, the Old Babylonian, when this type of document remained in the ownership of the winning party in the tribunal. These tablets were the archives of the central administration dealing with business and civil matters; among the civil archives are found the *ditilla* tablets, meaning 'the judgment is final', or *di nutilla* 'the judgment is not final'.

Dispensing justice was a royal privilege; it was therefore the king's representative in the provinces who would conduct the tribunal operations. Until the second regnal year of Amar-Sin, only the governor (*ensi*) is mentioned in the tablets. After that date, the judges also are mentioned; there may be two, three, or four judges, and in one case, seven. The city governor (*šagina*) is also mentioned. Besides royal justice, one should also note the existence of temple justice. In one instance the judges of the temple of Nanna are mentioned. It is difficult to define the role of the assembly (*puḫrum*), for lack of attestation. The commissioner (*maškim*) is always mentioned in the tablet. His role was to be present in the instruction of the case, from beginning to end, for the oath of the witnesses. Also mentioned is the person present during the trial (lú ki-ba gub-ba). Next to these is the group of the lú mar-za ki-ba gub-ba-me, men probably having a ritual function during the trial.

During the trial it was most important to be able to provide proof of the allegations made. Proof given by notables or important personalities was given a great deal of weight. The trial would end with a di-til-la when the party required to take an oath had done so. An oath was not necessary when a conditional verdict would clarify the matter. It was Falkenstein who inspired these studies, through his important publication, *Die neusumerischen Gerichtsurkunden.*[1]

While cataloging the Ur III tablets in the British Museum,[2] I came across some unpublished di-til-la tablets, which I am glad to be able to present here. All of the tablets deal with family matters: persons contesting their slavery status, the possibility of a widow's returning to her first husband's house, divorce for nonconsummation of a marriage, sharing the produce of an orchard among heirs and outsiders. In all of these cases, the factor of time is of the utmost importance. After a given span of time, situations or rights were challenged and it was up to the judges to deal with the new realities that had upset the social norms. Slavery was not meant to be permanent, the decisions of a father could not bind children for the future, and marriage had to have practical consequences for both parties.

Tablet 1 BM 19 356 (95 10-14 4)[3]

obv.	di-til-la	Verdict (concerning)
	| nin-kù-zu dumu ur-^{d}nanše	Nin-kuzu, the daughter of Ur-Nanše,
	ir$_{11}$ a-tu máš-šu-gíd-gíd-ke$_4$	slave of Atu the diviner,
	igi-ni in-gar-ra	who came (to the tribunal).
	mu-lugal	"In the name of the king!
	tukumbi u$_4$ 2-kam inim-lú-inim-ma	if in 2 days the word of the witnesses

1. A. Falkenstein, *Die neusumerischen Gerichtsurkunden* (3 vols.; BAW n.s. 39, 40, 44; Munich, 1956–57).

2. My thanks to the trustees of the British Museum for their kind permission to publish these tablets of the Western Asiatic Antiquities Collection.

3. I thank Dietz Otto Edzard for the readings proposed for this tablet.

na-ba-ša$_6$ dumu a-tu-ke4	(certifying) that Nabaša son of Atu
ama-gi$_4^{igi}$-mu in-gar-ra	gave me my liberty
mu-DU nu-mu-DU	I bring (everything is in order!); if I do not bring (the word of the witnesses)
géme ì-bí-la a-tu-ke$_4$-ne	the slave of the heirs of Atu
ḫa-a-me-èn	I will remain,"
bí-in-du$_{11}$-ga	did she declare.
mu u$_4$-gub-ba mu-lugal pàd-da-[ ]	because on the said day, according to the oath of the king,
nin-kù-zu lú-inim-ma	Nin-kuzu the witnesses (certifying)
ama-gi$_4^{igi}$-mu gar-ra	that "my liberty" has been granted
nu-mu-da-gub-ba-a-šè	could not bring
rev. géme ì-bí-la a-tu-ke$_4$-ne	as slave of the heirs of Atu
ba-ne-gin	she was given
lú-uru-sag maškim	Lu-urusag was the commissioner;
lú-dingir-ra	Lu-dingira
ur-^{d}ištaran	Ur-Ištaran (and)
lú-^{d}šára	Lu-Šara
di-ku$_5$-bi-me	were the judges.
mu ^{d}šu-^{d}EN.ZU	ŠS 6
lugal-e ^{d}na-rú-a	Construction of the great stele
maḫ ^{d}en-líl-lá mu-rú	to Enlil

Summary of the Case

Nin-kuzu, daughter of Ur-Nanše and slave of Atu, claims to have been freed by Nabaša, one of Atu's sons. She could not present actual witnesses to her manumission to the tribunal. Her claim was not accepted, and therefore she remained the slave of the heirs of Atu, the diviner.

Remarks on the Grammatical Construction of This Document

The text is divided into three sections from lines 2 to 4, lines 5 to 10 and lines 11 to 16. The first two sections end with two verbal forms in the genitive dependent on di-til-la: in-gar-ra et bí-in-du$_{11}$-ga. The decision starts and concludes with the expression mu . . . šè 'because . . . '; therefore, Nin-kuzu will remain forever the slave of Atu's heirs.

For the function of the *maškim*, the commissioner of the *ensi* attending the verdict, see the work of Falkenstein.[4] Judgments promulgated by two, three, or four judges are often attested. The two judges mentioned in this case are well known from other cases.

Tablet 2 BM 19 359 (95 10-14 7)

obv.	di-til-la	Verdict (concerning)
	| nin-barag-ge-si dumu ùr-re-ba-du$_7$	Ninbaragesi daughter of Urrebadu, whom,
	šám-til-la 3 gín kù-babbar-šè	for the full price of 3 shekels of silver,
	ùr-re-ba-du$_7$ ti-la-ra[5]	from Urrebadu, in his lifetime,
	šu ur-^{d}lama énsi-ka-ta	under the agreement of Ur-Lamma the governor,
	a-kal-la dumu ur-nìgin-gar-ke$_4$ in-ši-sa$_{10}$	Akalla son of Urnigingar bought;
	a-la dumu á-ra-da-na	Ala son of Aradana
rev.	lú-urub^{ki} dumu ur-nìgin-gar	Lu-urub son of Urnigingar
	lú inim-ma-bi-me	were the witnesses;
	nin-barag-ge-si ù ama-ni-e	Ninbaragesi and her mother
	lú inim-ma bí-gur	rejected these witnesses;
	a-kal-la	(but) Akalla
	nam-érim-àm	took the oath;
	géme a-kal-la ba-na-gi-in	(therefore) the maid-servant was attributed to Akalla.
	ti-é-maḫ-ta maškim	Tiemahta was the commissioner
	lú-^{d}šára	Lu-Šara (and)
	ur-^{d}ištaran	Ur-Ištaran
edge	di-ku$_5$-bi-me	were the judges.
	mu-ús-sa si-ma-núm^{ki} ba-ḫul	ŠS 4. Second year of the destruction of Simanum

COMMENTARY

While Urrebadu was still alive, his daughter Nin-baragesi was sold to Akalla (to be his servant or slave). There were two witnesses to the sale. Probably upon the death of her father, Nin-baragesi and her mother

4. Falkenstein, *Die neusumerischen Gerichtsurkunden*, 1.47–55.

5. The dative form is surprising. One would expect *-ta* to mark the sale of the young girl by her father.

contested the validity of the sale, its conditions, and its permanence, and therefore rejected the two men who were the witnesses. One should note that the sale was not due to depressed conditions. The text states precisely that the full price was paid and that the father agreed to it. In the last instance Akalla the buyer, now the owner of Nin-baragesi, could simply give in after the two witnesses had been rejected, losing his slave, or take the oath of the gods and so block the challenge to the validity of the sale. On the strength of the oath the judges agreed that the sale had really taken place and that Nin-baragesi was Akalla's servant.

The price of a female slave or servant varied between $\frac{1}{2}$ shekel and 10 shekels.[6] Nin-baragesi's price was very low, perhaps because she was still very young. But in no case may the sale be considered to have been due to generally depressed circumstances, in view of the explicit mention of 'for her full price'.

Tablet 3 BM 19 360 (95 10-14 8)

obv.	di-til-la	Verdict (concerning)
	| é ur-tur muhaldim	the house of Urtur the cook
	mu sila$_4$-tur dam ur-tur-ke$_4$	because Silatur the wife of Urtur,
	egir ur-tur ba-ug$_7$-ta	after the death of Urtur
	dam kúr-e ba-an-tuk-a-šè	another man married her,
	ur-^{d}lama dumu ur-tur-ra	(it is) to Ur-Lamma the son of Urtur
	ba-na-gi-in	(that the house) was given.
	sila$_4$-tur-e	Silatur
	túg in-ùr	deposited her garment.
	uru-ì-da-dù[7] maškim	Uru-idadu was the commissioner
rev.	lú-^{d}šára	Lu-Šara,
	lú-ib-gal	Lu-ibgal (and)
	ur-^{d}ištaran	Ur-Ištaran
	di-ku$_5$-bi-me	were the judges.
	mu-ús-sa si-ma-núm^{ki} ba-ḫul	ŠS 4. Second year after the destruction of Simanum

6. Falkenstein, *Die neusumerischen Gerichtsurkunden*, 1.89–90.

7. Falkenstein reads this name Uru-ì-da-zal. A closer examination of the tablet dictates the reading uru-ì-da-dù.

COMMENTARY

According to custom, Silatur came to live after her wedding in the house of her husband Urtur. After the death of her husband, to whom she had borne children, she remarried and most likely went to live in her second husband's house. Upon the death of her second husband, or after a divorce, Silatur wanted to return to her first husband's house, where her children lived. But Ur-Lamma, perhaps not her son but the son of Urtur, claimed that because she had left the house of her dead husband to enter her second husband's house, she had lost all rights to return to her first place or to bring any legal claim whatsoever against it. On this point the judges agreed with Ur-Lamma. Therefore Silatur was banned from returning to her first husband's house. The juridical expression to mark this loss of right is túg . . . ùr. This expression is already attested in many of the tablets published by Falkenstein. The custom continued for centuries throughout the Near East, as is noted in Meir Malul's study[8] and is found as far west as Ugarit and Emar. Several rituals mention the deposit of a garment on a chair or on a doorknob. This symbolic act signified the change in status of a person in respect to the house in which he or she had resided. The individual renounced all claim to rights and privileges as a member of the household. For Silatur this signified the definite loss of all rights to the house of Urtur, as well as complete dissolution of all familial bonds with the other members of her first husband's family.

The three judges active in this case are often mentioned in other cases from Tello.

Tablet 4 BM 22 867 (97 5-11 93)

obv.	di-til-la	Verdict (concerning)
	nin-inim-gi-na dumu lú-^{d}nanna-ka	Nin-inimgina daughter of Lu-Nanna (who)
	ur-^{d}ba-ba$_6$ dumu di-gi$_4$-di-gi$_4$-ke$_4$	(after) Ur-Baba the son of Digidigi
	in-tuk-àm	had married her
	nin-inim-gi-na-ke$_4$	(and after) Nin-inimgina
	é-lú-^{d}nanna ab-ba-na-ka	in the house of Lu-Nanna her father
	ur-^{d}ba-ba$_6$-ra	for Ur-Baba
	zag in-na-ús-sa-àm	had waited

8. M. Malul, *Studies in Mesopotamian Legal Symbolism* (AOAT 221; Neukirchen-Vluyn, 1988), in particular 160–208.

ur-^{d}ba-ba$_{6}$ gír-su^{ki}-a ti-la-a-ni	(while) Ur-Baba was living in Girsu
ama-ni-⟨⟨ni⟩⟩ iti 3-[àm]	(and) did not enter (during) 3 months
é-a nu-ši-ku$_{4}$-ra	the house of his spouse.
mu ur-^{d}ba-ba$_{6}$-ke$_{4}$	Because Ur-Baba
rev. du$_{11}$-ga-na ba-ni-gi-na-a-šè	agreed to her word
ur-^{d}ba-ba$_{6}$-ke$_{4}$	Ur-Baba
nin-inim-gi-na	Nin-inimgina
in-tag$_{4}$	divorced.
kal-la dumu ur-^{d}en-líl-lá maškim	Kalla the son of Ur-Enlil was the commissioner,
lú-ib-gal	Lu-ibgal
ur-^{d}ištaran	Ur-Ištaran
di-ku$_{5}$-bi-me	were the judges.
mu ^{d}Šu-^{d}EN.ZU lugal	ŠS 1

COMMENTARY

This verdict authorizes a divorce because of failure to consummate the marriage. The young husband, living in Girsu, did not come to live with his young bride in her father's house. May we conclude from this *ditilla* that the legal time limit for a young spouse to begin to cohabit with his wife was three months? We do not know who instituted the proceedings, the bride or her father. As the complaint was not rejected, the divorce could be pronounced without compensation. Why did the young spouse not enter his father-in-law's house? We can only guess. Very often, in cases when the son-in-law came to live with his bride, rather than the opposite, this indicated that he was rather poor and therefore remained more or less the servant, not son-in-law, of his wife's father. This could be the reason that Ur-Baba delayed cohabiting with his new bride for three months.

COMPOSITION OF THE TEXT

The form nu-ši-ku$_{4}$-ra of line 11 is a nominal form of the verb in the genitive dependent on ditilla. Two short sentences give the past events, lines 2–4 and 5–8. One should note that the writing of the sign ZAG at the beginning of line 8 is identical with the sign TAG$_{4}$ in line 15. I translate the expression zag . . . úš 'to wait'.[9]

9. M. L. Thomsen (*The Sumerian Language* [Copenhagen, 1984] 322) translates this compound verb 'to border on, to stand by, to set aside'.

Tablet 5 BM 25 077 (98 2-16 131)

obv.	di-til-la	Verdict (concerning)
	^{giš}kiri$_6$ ḫu-wa-wa šà ebiḫ^{ki}-ka	the orchard of Huwawa in Ebih
	lú-^{d}nin-gír-su ti-a	(which) Lu-Ningirsu, during his lifetime,
	ur-kù-nun-da in-da-an-be$_4$	divided with Urkununna;
	mu 10-àm in-da-an-kú-a	that during 10 years he ate with him from it
	lugal-nanga	Lugal-nanga
	^{d}Lamma[10]-ra	and Lammara
	nam-érim-àm	swore it.
	^{giš}kiri$_6$ ḫu-wa-wa ebiḫ^{ki}	Of the orchard of Huwawa in Ebih
rev.	ki-sá-a-bi	its possession (marked by the dividing wall)
	ki ur-kù-nun-ta	from Urkununna
	dumu lú-^{d}nin-gír-su-ke$_4$-ne	to the sons of Lu-Ningirsu
	ba-ne-gi-in	was granted to them.
	ab-ba-kal-la dumu ur-mes maškim	Abbakalla the son of Urmes was the commissioner
	šu-ì-lí	Šu-ili
	ur-^{d}ištaran	Ur-Ištaran
	ir$_{11}$-ḫùl-la	Ir-hulla
	di-ku$_5$-bi-me	were the judges
	lú-gír-su^{ki}	Lu-Girsu
	lú-nina^{ki} nu-bànda	Lu-Nina the inspector and
	lugal-síg-gíd dumu énsi	Lugal-siggid the son of the *ensi*,
	lú-mar-za ki-ba gub-ba-me	the *marza*-functionaries, attended.

During the ten years before his death, Lu-Ningirsu shared (divided) the produce of Huwawa's orchard in Ebih with Urkununna. Lugal-nanga and Lammara testified that this situation had lasted for ten years. Upon the death of Lu-Ningirsu, his sons requested that the orchard be put at their disposal again. We can only guess under what circumstances Lu-Ningirsu shared the produce of the orchard with Urkunnuna; perhaps it was in repayment of a debt. But because the orchard was never sold, the judges granted full possession of the orchard to Lu-Ningirsu's children.

10. Another reading suggested: DINGIR-dan.

To say this the judges use the word ki-sá, normally an expression for the outer wall of the orchard. This word was used, rather than simply 'the orchard', to express clearly that everything inside this wall was intended, that is, the orchard in its entirety and therefore also all of its produce.

In addition to the three presiding judges, three other functionaries, the lú marza, the inspector, and the son of the *ensi* of Lagaš, were present. The son of the *ensi* is mentioned in another tablet, dated to ŠS 6. Probably this tablet should be dated around the same time, although the date is broken off.

Tablet 6 BM 29 980 (99 1-16 17)

obv.	38 gur 70 sìla-ta	38 gur,[11] of 70 sìla each,
	lá-ni-àm	constitute the deficit
	A-kal-la ì-da-gál	of Akalla;
	iti ezem-^{d}bìl-ga-ka[12]	during the month "festival of Gilgames"
	šà umma^{ki}-ka	in Umma
	nì-ka$_9$-bi ba-ak	this account was done.
	igi nìgin-ki-du$_{10}$	(before) Niginkidu
	ba-lu$_5$ muḫaldim	Balu the cook
	ur-^{d}en.zu dumu ur-^{d}lugal-bàn-da	Ur-Sin son of Ur-Lugalbanda
	inim-ma dumu ur-[ ]	Inimma the son of [ ]
	lugal-ba-ta-è dumu ur-[ ]	Lugalbatae son of Ur-[ ]
rev.	ur-^{d}šul-[pa-è] dumu lú-^{d}[ ]	Ur-Šulpae son of Lu-[ ]
	hu-wa-wa dumu ku-li	Huwawa son of Kuli.
	igi lú-e-ne-šè	in front of these persons/ witnesses
	du$_{11}$-ga ba-an-gi	the matter was determined.
	mu en-nam-šita$_4$-^{d}šul-gi-ke$_4$-ba-	Year when the šita-priest who incessantly
	gub-⟨ba-šè⟩	prays for Šulgi was designated (Šulgi 28).
	kišib nìgin-ki-du$_{10}$	Instead of the seal of Niginkidu
	mu a-kal-la-šè íb-ra	the one of Akalla was rolled.

11. 8; 4.2. gur lugal.

12. The scribe omitted the sign mes.

COMMENTARY

This text does not mention *ditilla,* since it does not contain a legal decision. It is rather a written affirmation of the state of affairs in reference to the barley deficit of Akalla during the month of *ezem*-Gilgameš[13] in Umma. After this deposition was taken, an administrative sanction or judicial process could begin. This must have been a matter of some importance, because there are no less than seven witnesses who attested to the deficit of Akalla's account.

Tablet 7 BM 19102 (95 10-12 80)

obv.	nu-úr-ì-lí igi-ni ì-gá-ar	Nur-ili appeared (before the tribunal).
	ur-šu ù ku-li	Uršu and Kuli had
	ugula-ra maš-da in-na-ne-eš	complained to the overseer.
	a-šà ḫul-dím-ma-ta íb-ta-NE[14]	"He took him out from a bad field
	a-šà ša$_6$-ga bí-gin-ne bí-né-eš	in order to give him a good field," they had declared,
	nu-gi$_4$-né-eš	(but) they could not prove it.
	ur-é-gal-ke$_4$ 1 gín kù-babbar	"Ur-egal 1 shekel of silver
	lú-uru-da	to Lu-uru
	mu-šeš-tab-ba-na-še!	for his assistance
	in-na-sum bí-du$_{11}$	he gave," he stated.
	[ ]na/di-ku$_5$-e-ne	the judges?
	[ ]	
	[ ]	
rev.	[ ]	
	inim-má bí-du$_{11}$-nu-un.	a word they said

COMMENTARY

The few missing lines of this tablet make its interpretation very difficult. Apparently, Nur-ili was accused by Uršu and Kuli of having assigned somebody, in return for a bribe, to work in a better field than the one he was used to cultivating. Additionally, it was stated that what seemed to have been a bribe was in fact a payment by Lu-uruda to Ur-egal. Unfortunately, it is impossible to understand the connection between the two persons and the content of the trial.

13. The name of this month is unknown at Umma.

14. This form must be parsed: íb-ta-b-è.

Šīmu gamru: Its Function and History

Aaron Skaist

In the sale texts from Emar and Alalaḫ level VII of the second millennium the phrase ana šīmu gamer 'for the full price' is a complement of the verb 'to buy'. In the Old Babylonian sale deeds from Lower Mesopotamia, the analogous phrase šīmu gamru is part of the delivery-of-payment clause. The function of the phrase is the same in both areas: to protect the buyer against possible charges that he shortchanged the seller. The different position of the phrase in the sale texts from the various areas is a result of the history of the deeds in these areas. The article concludes with a brief look at the history of the phrase in texts of the late second and first millennia.

Function of šīmu gamru

The phrase šám-til-la-bi/ni-šè // *ana šīmu gamru* 'as its full price'[1] occurs in the great majority of sale deeds, from the Old Babylonian Period through the Neo-Babylonian Period. Why is the term for price in these deeds invariably written šám-til with the adjective til/*gamru*? So far, this phrase has not been the subject of a study defining its function or examining its history.

The operative section[2] of the Old Babylonian (ca. 1900–1600 B.C.E.) sale deed consists of two parts. One part describes the sale and concludes with the verb šám, while the other part records the payment of the price by the buyer and concludes with the verb lá. For example:

1. Object of sale
2. Seller
3. Buyer

1. The Akkadian equivalent of the Sumerian is to be found in B. Landsberger, MSL 1 27, tablet II, col. iii, line 44.

2. The term *operative section* to describe the section that records the transfer of rights was first used by R. Yaron, "The Schema of the Aramean Legal Document," *JSS* 2 (1957) 37.

4. Term for 'to buy'

---

5. Full price
6. Amount
7. Term for 'to pay'

In the sale texts from Lower Mesopotamia of the Old Babylonian Period, the phrase šám-til is part of the payment clause: for example, šám-til-la-bi/ni-šè x gín kù-babbar i-na-an-lá 'he (the buyer) weighed out x shekels of silver as its full price'. However, in contemporary sale texts found in Alalaḫ level VII in Syria,[3] the phrase is part of the sale clause: for example, Object of Sale, ki Seller, Buyer, *ana* x gín kù-babbar *ana šīm gamer išām* 'the buyer bought the object for x shekels of silver for the full price from the seller'. How is one to account for this difference? Is it functional, historical, or both?

In his recently published study of the Ur III Period sale documents, Steinkeller devoted one section to a study of the changes in the operative section of the sale deed, from the earliest sale deeds of the Fara Period (ca. 2600–2500 B.C.E.) through the Old Babylonian Period.[4] He first noted that the operative section of a sale document was either one-part or two-part, depending on whether the action of sale is described as one act or as two acts. From the Fara Period through the Ur III Period (ca. 2100–2000 B.C.E.), the one-part operative section predominated, though the two-part operative section was not unknown. In the Ur III Period, the standard form of sale text was a one-part operative type (Steinkeller called it Type A), which consisted of the following elements.

1. Object of Sale
2. Term for price
3. Amount
4. Seller (šè/-ra/-a)
   KI Seller (-ta)
5. Buyer(-e)
6. Term for 'to buy'

In the Old Babylonian Period in Lower Mesopotamia, however, the two-part operative document became the standard form of sale deed.

Steinkeller suggested that the reason that the older one-part operative sale text was abandoned was that it was not precise enough. Though the older texts recorded the purchase price, they did not record the

3. For the latest study of these texts, see B. Kienast, "Kauf," *RLA* 5.530–41.

4. P. Steinkeller, *Sale Documents of the Ur-III-Period* (Freiburger Altorientalische Studien 17; Wiesbaden, 1979) 22–29.

actual payment of the price, a fact of obvious importance to the buyer, who would want all possible protection against claims of nonpayment. Only the two-part operative type (already used in small numbers in the earlier periods) satisfied the needs of the buyer. Steinkeller noted that the only places in the Old Babylonian Period that consistently continued to use the older one-part operative type sale text were Early Eshnunna and Alalaḫ level VII.

There remains, however, the question why the people at Alalaḫ and early Eshnunna did not record the payment of the price. Why did they not feel the same need as the people of Lower Mesopotamia?

In fact, an examination of the Alalaḫ level VII sale texts shows that these sale deeds did indeed record the act of payment of the price. To be precise, they recorded not the payment of the price but rather its receipt.

At Alalaḫ the first part of the sale deed consisted of the following:

1. Object of Sale
2. ki Seller
3. Buyer
4. Term for price (*ana šīm gamer*)
5. Amount
6. Term for 'to buy'

This is then followed by the formula *apil libbašu ṭāb* 'it (the silver) was received, his (the seller's) heart is satisfied'. It seems clear, then, that the sale deeds from Alalaḫ level VII are to be seen as two-part operative section types. What may have misled Steinkeller is the fact that the first part of the Alalaḫ operative clause is clearly identical with the Ur III operative section (Type A), whereas in the Old Babylonian deeds from Lower Mesopotamia the notice of the price occurs only in the payment clause.

A comparison of the Alalaḫ receipt clause with the Old Babylonian delivery-of-payment clause should help to clarify the function of *šīmu gamru* in the latter deeds. At Alalaḫ the term *apil* records the fact that the seller received the price. That is to say, the buyer fulfilled his obligation toward the seller. The second term, *libbašu ṭāb,* records the acknowledgment that the seller received a specific sum, very likely the precise amount agreed upon in the first part of the operative section (see below, p. 622) and may not complain that he has been shortchanged.[5]

Now, in my view, this is the precise function of the term šám-til/*šīmu gamru* 'full price' in the delivery-of-payment clause. The verb lá/*išqul* 'to

5. See R. Westbrook, "The Phrase 'His Heart Is Satisfied' in Ancient Near Eastern Legal Sources," *JAOS* 111 (1991) 222.

weigh' records the weighing out or payment of the price by the buyer and is equivalent to the term *apil* at Alalaḫ. The description of the price as the 'full price' serves to protect the buyer against any possible future charges of shortchanging by the seller, which is the function of *libbašu ṭāb*.

What, then, is the function of *ana šīm gamer* in the first part of the operative section of the Alalaḫ sale texts? The fact that it is a complement of the verb 'to buy' and not of the verb of payment, would ostensibly be a clear indication that it cannot be the same as in the Old Babylonian texts from Lower Mesopotamia. Yet this is not necessarily so.

To describe an object as purchased at its 'full price' has no meaning if the price referred to in the sale document simply describes the price agreed upon by the parties. The price quoted in the text may or may not equal the actual value of the object sold. On the other hand, the price is best described as 'full price' when the price referred to is the price paid. Thus for example the buyer pays the full price, that is, the entire sum of silver agreed upon by the parties.

Now it is accepted that the function of the sale document in the Ur III Period was evidentiary.[6] The sale itself, that is, the transfer of ownership including the payment of the full price, was completed prior to the drawing up of the document. The price noted in the sale document thus refers not only to the price agreed upon but also to the price already paid. Hence, even if the notice concerning the price is placed before the verb šám 'to buy' and is not linked to the verb of payment, it refers to a price already paid and so may be described as a 'full price'.

Now the phrase šám-til does occur in a number of Ur III Period Type A sale deeds.[7] The description of the price šám as til 'complete' protects the buyer against any possible claims by the seller that he has not received the full price.[8] As was noted above, the first part of the operative section of the Alalaḫ level VII sale deed contains the same components as the Type A deed of the Ur III Period. Apart from the order of the elements,[9] the only significant change is the inclusion of the adjective *gamru* to describe the term for *šīmu* 'price'. In our view, the function of the phrase *ana šīm gamer* in the Alalaḫ texts has this same function.

6. See Steinkeller, *Sale Documents*, 139–49.

7. Ibid., nos. 65, 81, 94, 104, 117.

8. Another way of achieving this same aim was to include a completion-of-price clause in the sale deed as a *Schlussklausel* (ibid., pp. 30–33). Curiously, of all the Ur III sale deeds of the various types that contain the phrase šám-til, only two (ibid., nos. 61 and 94), both Type A, contain both šám-til and a completion-of-price clause.

9. At Alalaḫ the term for price and the amount are placed before the verb 'to buy', whereas in the Ur III texts they appear before the names of the seller and the buyer (ibid., 10).

The history of the sale deed in Syria prior to the Alalaḫ level VII texts is not known. Nevertheless, one may postulate that during the Ur III Period[10] and later, the Type A sale formulation was standard at Alalaḫ and that, at some time prior to the period of level VII, the phrase *ana šīm gamer* was introduced into the operative section. Its function would have been the same as in the Ur III sale texts.

Now in Lower Mesopotamia at the end of the Ur III Period (and somewhat later), a change occurred, and the two-part operative deed with a payment clause became standard. This brought about a change in the position of the term *šīmu gamru*, which was now no longer governed by the verb šám 'to buy' but by the verb 'to pay'.

At Alalaḫ the need to record the actual payment of the price was met differently. A receipt formula was added to the Type A formulation. However, the second half of the Alalaḫ operative section, in contrast to the Lower Mesopotamian deeds, did not contain the amount of the price. This very necessary bit of information was to be found in the first part of the operative section. The term *libbašu ṭāb* by itself only records the acknowledgment that the seller is satisfied with a sum of money. The presence of *ana šīm gamer* explicates that the seller is satisfied specifically with the precise amount agreed upon in the first part of the operative section and may no longer complain that he has been shortchanged.

In the early Eshnunna sale texts, the operative section is identical with Type A of the Ur III Period.[11] In certain sale texts, however, particularly those that record sales of palace property, we read kù-bi é-gal-la ba-an-ku_4 'the palace received the silver'. This clause is not to be taken as the second part of a two-part operative sale deed for two reasons: (1) the notice of the payment is preceded by a clause stating that the silver was weighed out, and (2) this clause occurs only in the sale deeds that record the sale of palace property.[12]

At this point it must be noted that the phrase *libbašu ṭāb* does occur in the Old Babylonian sale deeds from Lower Mesopotamia, but only in those from the Diyala River basin and from nearby Sippar in the extreme north of Lower Mesopotamia. It appears in these texts either as an independent clause, šà-ga-ni al-du_{10} 'his heart is satisfied', without reference to any other clause, or as part of the payment clause, *šīmam gamram libbašu ṭāb.* This latter formula, which clearly indicates that the seller is

10. See Kienast, "Kauf," *RLA* 5.531–32.

11. The formulas of the texts were published by R. M. Whiting, "Sealing Practices in House and Land Sale Documents at Eshnunna in the Isin-Larsa Period," in *Seals and Sealings in the Ancient Near East* (ed. M. Gibson and R. Biggs; Malibu, 1977) 70.

12. See Steinkeller (*Sale Documents*, 31), who compares this clause with the completion-of-payment clause.

satisfied with the price, is essentially a hybrid form, combining the *šīmam gamram* of the Old Babylonian delivery-of-payment clause with *libbašu ṭāb* of the receipt formula, which is a "periphery element."[13]

Later Reflections of šīmu gamru

The sale texts from Alalaḫ level VII that contain the phrase *ana šīm gamer* in the first part of the operative section and *libbašu ṭāb* in the second part of the operative section are neither isolated nor unique. Precisely the same formulation is to be found in the sale deeds discovered at Emar and its surrounding areas, which date from the 15th to 12th centuries B.C.E.[14] Curiously, though both formulas *šīmu gamru* and *ibbašu ṭāb* continued in use in the first millenium, their histories were different. Yet both may be traced to Syria and not to Lower Mesopotamia of the Old Babylonian Period.

In the fifth century B.C.E. Aramaic legal papyri discovered at Elephantine in Egypt, the term *ṭyb lbby* occurs as part of the receipt-of-payment clause. A number of years ago Muffs[15] treated the meaning of this term in a comprehensive monograph and concluded that it was a term of quittance. It expresses the recipient's satisfaction with the sum of money received and also the fact that the recipient has relinquished his claim to the object for which the money was paid.

Muffs went on to show that the Akkadian term *libbašu ṭāb*, which occurs in the Old Babylonian sale deed from Sippar and the Diyala region, has the same range of meaning and legal function as *ṭyb lbby* of the Aramaic papyri. Indeed he pointed out that the two terms are identical in their etymology, root metaphor, complements, and contextual range. He then concluded that the Aramaic term has definite historical connections with the Old Babylonian *libbašu ṭāb*. The precise definition of the term offered by Muffs has been justifiably challenged by Westbrook,[16] yet the fact remains that, as Muffs noted, the etymology, root metaphor, complements, and contextual range are identical.

What are the historical connections with the cuneiform legal tradition? Here Muffs strayed from the analysis of the term *ṭyb lbby* to a gen-

13. For a full discussion of the Old Babylonian Sippar and Diyala usage of *libbašu ṭāb*, see A. Skaist, "The Sale Contracts from Khafajah," in *Bar-Ilan Studies in Assyriology* (ed. J. Klein and A. Skaist; Ramat-Gan, 1990) 255–76.

14. The major publications of the sale deeds are: D. Arnaud, *Recherches au pays d'Aštata, Emar VI.1–3* (Paris, 1986); D. Arnaud, *Textes Syriens de l'age du bronze recent* (Barcelona, 1991); A. Tsukimoto, "Akkadian Tablets in the Hiryama Collection," *Acta Sumerologica* 12 (1990) 63–139.

15. Y. Muffs, *Studies in the Aramaic Legal Papyri from Elphantine* (Brill, 1969) 63–139.

16. Westbrook, "The Phrase 'His Heart Is Satisfied,'" 222.

eral analysis of the possible cuneiform connections of the Elephantine Aramaic papyri in general.[17] He argued that the phrase in question, or an analog, was used in what he calls fringe regions of cuneiform law, such as Susa, Kultepe, Nuzi, Alalaḫ, and Ras Shamra; and from there it was transmitted to the Aramaic texts from Elephantine. Muffs's difficulty is quite obvious, for there was no direct contact between the Aramaic papyrii and Old Babylonia.

When Muffs wrote his monograph, no first- or late second-millennium material that could have served as the direct antecedent of the fifth-century Aramaic papyri was available. The discovery of the sale deeds from Emar has greatly altered the picture. We now have texts from Syria from the late second millennium in which the term *libbašu ṭāb* is used precisely in the same fashion as in the Old Babylonian texts, the texts from Alalaḫ level VII,[18] and the papyri from Elephantine. The importance of the Emar texts is that they date from the time when the Arameans first appeared in Syria and Mesopotamia. Even though there is evidence that the people of Emar had contact with the Alamu,[19] one should not conclude that the Arameans borrowed the term directly from the people of Emar. Nevertheless, I do consider the texts from Emar, along with those from Alalaḫ level VII, to be representative of the usage current in that general area of Syria, a region that the Arameans penetrated, settled, and dominated.

The transfer of *libbašu ṭāb* may have taken place in the following fashion. An Aramean who purchased land from a native would have had the sale deed drawn up in the manner current in that area—very likely in Akkadian, as were all the available sale deeds. With the passage of time it was felt necessary to draw up the deeds in Aramaic. The simplest way of doing this would have been to translate the Akkadian directly into Aramaic. Thus it would have been possible for *libbašu ṭāb* to become *ṭyb lbby,* either as the accepted Aramaic equivalent or as a loan translation.

The formula *ana šīmišu gamru* continued in use in Lower Mesopotamia as part of the payment clause until approximately 1250 B.C.E. However, in the late Middle Babylonian deeds from the city of Ur,[20] the

17. Muffs, *Studies in the Aramaic Legal Papyri,* 173–94.

18. The major difference between the Alalaḫ level VII sale text operative section and the sale text operative section in the sale texts from Emar is that in the latter the receipt clause uses the phrase kù-babbar *maḫru* 'the silver was received' instead of the word *apil* found in the texts from Alalaḫ level VII.

19. The letter of Sîni-ṣūri (Arnaud, *Recherches au pays d'Aštata,* 263) contains a reference to two Aḫlamu men from the land of Suhi who arrived at Emar with a message from the *sakin* of the land of Suhi.

20. The texts were published by O. R. Gurney, UET VII, and transcribed and translated by him in *The Middle Babylonian Legal Texts from Ur* (Oxford, 1983).

statement šám-til-la-bi-šè or *ana šīmišu gamrūti* became part of the statement of sale.[21] It was now no longer linked to the verb lá/*šaqālum*, which in fact was no longer current in these deeds. The term in question was governed by the verb in-sa_{10}/*šīmu*, even though it was written in the text after the verb *šīmu*. Thus, for example, we read in one text,[22] which records the sale of a slave: $^{I.d}$utu-kar^{ir} *ki-i* $7\frac{1}{2}$ gín kù-gi in-$ša_{10}$ *a-na* šám-til-la-bi-šè 'Šamaš-ēṭir bought (a slave) for $7\frac{1}{2}$ shekels of silver as his full price'. This line is followed by a ruled line. Gurney[23] pointed out that the ruled line that regularly follows this phrase in the deeds from Ur and in one deed from Nippur links it closely with the statement of sale. He further noted that "the occasional ruling before the phrase suggests that the scribes may still have been aware of its original function, and it is noteworthy that in three texts it or a similar phrase is repeated as part of the receipt clause."

Coincidental with this change is another in the repayment clause of the late Middle Babylonian sale text. Instead of the Old Babylonian Period's description of the payment as an act on the part of the buyer, it is now described as an act on the part of the seller, who receives the price.

Yet another change that should be noted is the replacement of the oath clause, which is standard in the Old Babylonian sale texts, by a penalty clause providing for a financial penalty or even corporal punishment should the agreement be violated.

In my opinion, West Semitic influence was responsible for these changes. All three changes in the Middle Babylonian sale deed have their parallels in the sale texts from second-millenium Syria, at Alalaḫ and at Emar. It does not necessarily follow that the Middle Babylonians borrowed these elements directly from Emar, but the texts from Emar do attest to the fact that text formulations were used in Syria when the changes took place in Babylon, and this increases the probability that the changes resulted from contacts with the West.

21. Ibid., 5.
22. UET VII 21.
23. Gurney, *Middle Babylonian Legal Texts from Ur*, p. 5.

The God Athtar in the Ancient Near East and His Place in KTU 1.6 I

Mark S. Smith

The god Athtar is poorly understood in the Baal Cycle. Evidence from Ebla to South Arabia is surveyed in order to determine better the god's attributes and to ascertain his character in KTU 1.6 I. In many sources, Athtar is an astral deity and, contrary to what some scholars hold, he is also a god of natural irrigation, at least in Epigraphic South Arabic sources. He is not, however, an androgynous god, as some commentators propose. Different possibilities based on comparative evidence are entertained in order to explain his role in 1.6 I.

Introduction

The name of Jonas Greenfield is associated with the best work in West Semitic languages and literatures. I first met Jonas Greenfield at the Hebrew University in 1983–84. In his Ugaritic and West Semitic religion classes, he showed a mastery of texts from the broad range of Semitic languages. Professor Greenfield's sharp wit and relish for a good story punctuated class discussions, which usually concluded with his own incisive solution to difficult problems. My family's trips to Israel were also graced by the hospitality of Jonas and Bella Greenfield.

Jonas Greenfield's many insightful studies include studies of Ugaritic literature. In his contribution to a Festschrift honoring M. Delcor,[1] Greenfield observed that in 1.6 I, Athtar and *yd*^{c} *ylḥn* serve as foils to Baal.[2] Athtar and *yd*^{c} *ylḥn*, two candidates nominated in KTU 1.6 I to

1. J. C. Greenfield, "Ba^{c}al's Throne and Isa 6:1," in *Mélanges bibliques et orientaux en l'honneur de M. Mathias Delcor* (ed. A. Caquot, S. Légasse, and M. Tardieu; AOAT 215; Neukirchen-Vluyn, 1985) 193–98.

2. Most scholars hold these to be two different figures, but J. C. de Moor identifies the two as a single figure (*The Seasonal Pattern in the Ugaritic Myth of Ba*^{c}*lu, according to the Version of Ilimilku* [AOAT 16; Neukirchen-Vluyn, 1971] 202–3).

replace Baal as divine king, contribute to exalting Baal's kingship, for their inadequacies (manifest upon their attempts to assume the divine throne) underscore the strength and size of Baal. The arrangement of the material in this section of the Baal Cycle comports with Greenfield's point that Athtar and *yd*^{c} *ylḥn* function as foils to Baal. The large section, 1.5 VI–1.6 III, exhibits a concentric pentacolon (ABCB′A′):

- A Discovery of Baal's death (1.5 VI 3*–25)
  - B Anat searches for Baal and mourns him (1.5 VI 25–1.6 I 31)
    - C Nominations to replace Baal (1.6 I 32–67)
  - B′ Anat searches for Baal and destroys Mot (1.6 II)
- A′ Discovery of Baal's life (1.6 III).

This arrangement not only illustrates the balance and relationships between the columns; it also focuses attention on the events of the central section, indicating that Baal is irreplaceable. Once the central section illustrates this point through the negative portraits of the two nominees for kingship, the narrative moves inexorably towards Baal's return to life and kingship.[3] The word pair *yr*$^{\supset}$*a*$^{\supset}$*un*//*ṯt*^{c} in 1.5 II 7 is repeated as *yr*$^{\supset}$*u*// *ṯt*^{c} in 1.6 VI 30 and marks the episode of Baal's demise and its reversal.

The historical background to this presentation of Athtar is not transparent. Who is this figure who stands as a foil to Baal? A survey of other ancient Near Eastern sources may help to illuminate the character of Athtar in the Ugaritic texts.[4]

Syro-Mesopotamian Sources of Third and Second Millennia

A text from Farah (Farah III 110 i 3) dating to the 26th century contains the Sumerian proper name UR.^{d}*aš-tár* according to W. G. Lambert.[5]

3. See A. Waterston, "The Kingdom of ^{c}Aṯtar and His Role in the AB Cycle," *UF* 20 (1988) 363.

4. See A. Caquot, "Le Dieu ^{c}Athtar et les textes de Ras Shamra," *Syria* 35 (1958) 45–60; G. Garbini, "Sul nome ^{c}Athtar-^{c}Ashtar," *AION* 24 (1974) 409–10; J. Gray, "The Desert God ^{c}Aṯtr in the Literature and Religion of Canaan," *JNES* 8 (1949) 72–83; R. du Mesnil du Buisson, "^{c}Ashtart and ^{c}Ashtar à Ras-Shamra," *JEOL* 10 (1945–48) 406; A. Caquot, M. Sznycer, and A. Herdner, *Textes ougaritiques, tome 1: Mythes et légendes* (LAPO 7; Paris, 1974) 95. For general surveys of Athtar, see M. H. Pope, "^{c}Aṯtar," in *Götter und Mythen im Vorderen Orient* (ed. H. W. Haussig; Wörterbuch der Mythologie 1/1; Stuttgart, 1965) 249–50; U. Oldenburg, *The Conflict between El and Ba*^{c}*al in Canaanite Religion* (Leiden, 1969) 39–45; H. Gese, "Die Religionen Altsyriens," in *Die Religionen Altsyriens, Altarabiens und der Mandäer* (ed. H. Gese, M. Höfner, and K. Rudolph; Die Religionen der Menschheit 10/2; Stuttgart, 1970) 137–39; F. Stolz, *Strukturen und Figuren im Kult von Jerusalem: Studien zur altorientalischen vor- und frühisraelitischen Religion* (BZAW 118; Berlin, 1970) 182–94. For bibliography on Athtar up to 1988, see D. Pardee, "Ugaritic Proper Nouns," *AfO* 36–37 (1989–90) 466–70.

5. W. G. Lambert, "Pantheon of Mari," *MARI* 4 (1985) 537.

Ebla attests *aš-dár* and equates the name with Inanna.[6] On the basis of this identification, Xella takes *aš-dár* as Astarte,[7] but Archi and Heimpel prefer an equation with Athtar.[8] According to Heimpel, the basis of the equation of Athtar with Inanna is not anthropomorphic. He suggests rather that the two are equated because they both represent the Venus star, the male in the morning and the female at evening.[9] The name of the god appears also in proper names from Ebla, but it is less common in sacrificial lists.[10]

The Mari texts refer to ᵈMUŠ.US, which Lambert takes as Athtar, as opposed to ᵈMUŠ.ZA.ZA, which he suggests may be Athtart.[11] Mari also attests a "male Ishtar,"[12] who would seem to be Athtar. The inscription of Puzur-Astar mentions ᵈMUŠ.US, that is Astar, with Dagan and "Enki, lord of the assembly."[13] The title ᵈ*aš-tár-ṣa-ar-ba-at* seems to constitute the name of the god plus a geographical proper noun.[14]

The astral character of Athtar is evident at Emar. One text attests to ᵈ*Aš-tar* MUL 'Astar des étoiles'.[15] This occurrence is representative of the

6. W. Heimpel, "A Catalog of Near Eastern Venus Deities," *Syro-Mesopotamian Studies* 4/3 (1982) 14–15; M. Krebernik, "Zur Syllabar und Orthographie der lexikalischen Texte aus Ebla: Teil 2 (Glossar)," *ZA* 73 (1983) 31; P. Xella, "Aspekte religiöser Vorstellungen in Syrien nach den Ebla- und Ugarit-Texten," *UF* 15 (1983) 281–82, 290.

7. Cf. Emar ᶠ*Aštar-ummi* (see D. Arnaud, *Textes syriens de l'âge du bronze récent* [AOS 1; Barcelona, 1991] 85); Ugaritic *ᶜṯtrᵓum* (see F. Gröndahl, *Die Personnenamen der Texte aus Ugarit* [Studia Pohl 1; Rome, 1967] 46, 113). It is on the basis of this name, as well as the female-male interpretation of the Venus star, that some scholars consider Athtar to be androgynous. See Oldenburg, *Conflict between El and Baᶜal,* 39–45. There is no textual support for this interpretation. Furthermore, there is no evidence that Athtar symbolized both the male and female aspects that were associated with the Venus star. Rather, it stands to reason that Athtar and Athtart together symbolized these two aspects.

8. A. Archi, "Les Dieux d'Ebla au IIIᵉ millenaire avant J. C. et les dieux d'Ugarit," *Les Annales archéologiques arabes syriennes* 29–30 (1979–80) 169; Heimpel, "Catalog of Near Eastern Venus Deities," 14–15.

9. See Caquot, "Le Dieu ᶜAthtar," 51; T. Jacobsen, *The Treasures of Darkness: A History of Mesopotamian Religion* (New Haven, 1976) 140; J. J. M. Roberts, *The Earliest Semitic Pantheon: A Study of the Semitic Deities Attested in Mesopotamia before Ur III* (Baltimore, 1972) 39–40. For an example of the Mesopotamian astronomical observations of the Venus star, see Enuma Anu Enlil 50–51, VI 5 in E. Reiner, *Babylonian Planetary Omens, 2: Enuma Anu Enlil, Tablets 50–51* (in collaboration with D. Pingree; Bibliotheca Mesopotamica 2/2; Malibu, 1981) 48–49.

10. Archi, "Les Dieux d'Ebla," 171.

11. Lambert, "Pantheon of Mari," 53. See also Lambert, "Addenda to 'The Pantheon of Mari,'" *MARI* 6 (1990) 644. On the distinction between Athtar and Athtart at Mari, see also I. J. Gelb, "Mari and the Kish Civilization," in *Mari in Retrospect: Fifty Years of Mari and Mari Studies* (ed. G. D. Young; Winona Lake, Ind., 1992) 133.

12. Heimpel, "A Catalog of Near Eastern Venus Deities," 14.

13. Lambert ("Pantheon of Mari," 537) takes this reference to Enki as El.

14. Lambert, ibid., 529–30.

15. D. Arnaud, *Recherches au pays d'Aštata. Emar VI, tome 3: Texts sumériens et accadiens* (Paris, 1986) 373, text 378.39′.

understanding of the god, just as the same section presents other deities in ways characteristic of them: 'Ea of scribes, Nabu of schools, Ea of the forges'. Arnaud argues that ᵈNIN.URTA in the Emar texts is to be read as ᵈ*Aš-tar*, based on the double equation, Ninurta = Astabi and Astabi = Astar.[16] According to Arnaud, Athtar then was the city god of Emar. However, the equation is not secure since, as Fleming observes,[17] one text contains not only ᵈNIN.URTA (text 378, lines 7; 47′-48′ [partially reconstructed]), but also ᵈ*Aš-tar* MUL (line 39′).[18] The name of Athtar also appears as a theophoric element in several proper names.[19]

Ugaritic texts add further information about Athtar. In 1.6 I Athtar is presented as a warrior, albeit one who is inadequate for kingship. His epithet *ʿrẓ* is cognate with Biblical Hebrew *ʿārîṣ* 'powerful', which is applied to Yahweh in Jer 20:11.[20] The Ugaritic title need not be rendered 'terrible', but 'powerful' or the like.[21] This martial aspect is also reflected in the correspondence between the war-gods, Sumerian ᵈL[UGAR.MÁ]R?.DA,[22] Hurrian *aš-ta-bi-*[*n*]*i*?, and *aš-ta-ru*, in *Ugaritica* V, 137 iv b 16.[23] Athtar also appears in a hymn of the moon-goddess Nikkal (KTU 1.24.28). Athtar's place in this text may be due to his astral character.[24] Based on this evidence and other information pointing to Athtar's astral character in other sources, it is assumed that Athtar, like Ishtar, was associated with the planet Venus or "the Venus star," considered feminine in the evening and masculine in the morning.[25] At certain times of the year, the planet Venus appears in the western sky as a bright star just after sunset. At other times of the year, it appears in the eastern sky just before sunrise as a bright star.[26] Caquot deduces from 1.6 I 63 and 1.24.28 that Athtar once

16. Arnaud, *Textes syriens*, 15.

17. D. Fleming, *The Installation of Baal's Priestess at Emar: A Window on Ancient Syrian Religion* (HSS 42; Atlanta, 1992) 248–52, esp. 249 n. 186.

18. Arnaud, *Recherches au pays d'Aštata*, 372–73.

19. Arnaud, *Textes syriens*, 164; Fleming, *Installation of Baal's Priestess at Emar*, 221 n. 70.

20. Caquot, "Le Dieu ʿAthtar," 47.

21. See *UT* 19.1919: 'terrible, majestic'. De Moor (*Seasonal Pattern*, 202) translates *ʿrẓ* 'the tyrant' and notes the meaning 'mighty'. J. B. Burns ("*ʿArîṣ*: A 'Rich' Word," *The Bible Translator* 43 [1992] 124–30) argues that the basic meaning of the word in Biblical Hebrew is 'strong'. I wish to thank Professor Greenfield for drawing my attention to this point.

22. So restored by J. Huehnergard, *Ugaritic Vocabulary in Syllabic Transcription* (HSS 32; Atlanta, 1987) 164.

23. The name is read *aš-ta-bi-*[*n*]*i*? by Huehnergard (*Ugaritic Vocabulary*, 164); cf. P. D. Stern, *The Biblical* Ḥerem*: A Window on Israel's Religious Experience* (BJS 211; Atlanta, 1991) 35.

24. Caquot, "Le Dieu ʿAthtar," 47–49.

25. Gray, "Desert God ʿAṯtr"; Oldenburg, *Conflict between El and Baʿal*, 39–45.

26. See Gray, "Desert God ʿAṯtr"; idem, *Legacy of Canaan* (VTSup 5; 2d ed.; Leiden, 1965) 170; Pope, "ʿAṯtar," 249–50; Oldenburg, *Conflict between El and Baʿal*, 130; J. J. M. Roberts, *Earliest Semitic Pantheon*, 39; Caquot, Sznycer, and Herdner, *Textes ougaritiques*, 95.

held a high place in the pantheon, otherwise unattested in the Ugaritic myths. The Baal Cycle would reflect Baal's displacement of Athtar in importance,[27] a reconstruction that might explain why Athtart is connected with Baal.[28] Arnaud posits a reconstruction for Athtar at Emar,[29] which may also apply at Ugarit: perhaps at one time Athtart was Athtar's consort, and when Baal displaced Athtar, Athtart became his consort.

Athtar in the Ugaritic texts has been described in more general terms. Oberman viewed Athtar as Baal's "alter ego."[30] The opposite of Athtar, Baal is a warrior, endowed with all the tokens of kingship including a palace, wives, and a son.[31] Wyatt and Waterston[32] argue that Athtar,

27. W. F. Albright, *Yahweh and the Gods of Canaan: A Historical Analysis of Two Contrasting Faiths* (London, 1968; repr. Winona Lake, Ind., 1978) 231–32; Caquot, "Le Dieu ᶜAthtar," 58.

28. For the problem of whether or not Anat is the consort of Baal, see P. L. Day, "Why is Anat a Warrior and Hunter?" in *The Bible and the Politics of Exegesis: Essays in Honor of Norman K. Gottwald on His Sixty-Fifth Birthday* (ed. D. Jobling, P. L. Day, and G. T. Sheppard; Cleveland, 1991) 141–46, 329–32; idem, "Anat, Mistress of Animals," *JNES* (1992) 181–90; and N. Walls, *The Goddess Anat in Ugaritic Myth* (SBLDS 135; Atlanta, 1992). Day and Walls deny that Anat is the consort of Baal or that the two deities engage in sexual relations. The same argument might be used to suggest that Athtart is not the consort of Baal, but in Philo of Byblos's *Phoenician History* the two deities are said to rule together. In one New Kingdom text, Anat and Astarte are viewed as Seth's wives (see J. A. Wilson [trans.], "Egyptian Myths, Tales, and Mortuary Texts," *ANET,* 15; see also idem, "Egyptian Historical Texts," *ANET,* 250). This representation may reflect a West Semitic association of Astarte and Anat with Baal; if so, it would complicate the hypothesis that Anat is not Baal's consort. The relevance of this Egyptian evidence has been questioned by H. Te Velde (*Seth: God of Confusion* [2d ed.; Leiden, 1977] 29–30), seconded by Walls (*The Goddess Anat in Ugaritic Myth,* 145–46). Te Velde's chief argument is that, apart from this text, Anat is not called the consort of Seth. The uniqueness of this rendering of Astarte and Anat as the wives of Seth might be viewed as militating in favor of its authenticity as a witness to the West Semitic tradition. It also gives pause to Day's and Walls's dismissal of the Ugaritic evidence usually cited, because the pertinent texts are broken and less than explicit and because scholars may have held a bias toward the view that Baal and Anat engage in sexual relations. Even if they are not consorts, Baal and Athtart appear together in a number of contexts in the Ugaritic texts. Philo of Byblos likewise associates the two deities (*Praeparatio evangelica* 1.10.31; see H. W. Attridge and R. A. Oden, *Philo of Byblos, The Phoenician History: Introduction, Critical Text, Translation, Notes* [CBQMS 9; Washington, D.C., 1981] 54–55). A cylinder seal from second-millennium Bethel depicts a storm-god and a goddess with a hieroglyphic inscription with the name of Athtart (see H. Frankfort, *Cylinder Seals: A Documentary Essay on the Art and Religion of the Ancient Near East* [London, 1939] 289; reference courtesy of Elizabeth M. Bloch-Smith).

29. Arnaud, "La Religion à Emar," *Le Monde de la Bible* 20 (1981) 34. I wish to thank D. Pardee for providing me with a copy of this publication.

30. J. Obermann, *Ugaritic Mythology: A Study of Its Leading Motifs* (New Haven, 1948) 19.

31. The matter of wives and sons assumes that an heir is the point of 1.2 III 22. It would appear, however, that it is not Athtar but Yamm who is said not to have a wife.

32. N. Wyatt, "The AB Cycle and Kingship in Ugaritic Thought," *Cosmos* 2 (1986) 136–42; Waterston, "Kingdom of ᶜAṯtar."

like Baal, Yamm, and Mot, reigns as king over one part of the cosmos, namely the earth. Wyatt and Waterston assume that there were four major realms: Baal held heaven, Yamm the sea and rivers, Mot the underworld, and Athtar the earth. Yet this notion may not reflect Athtar's loss of status within the pantheon. The significance of Athtar's ascent and descent from the throne of Baal in 1.6 I is a matter of dispute that may be addressed following an examination of later sources.

Moabite, Aramaic, North Arabian, and Phoenician Sources

The name of Athtar appears in the ninth century Mesha stele (*KAI* no. 181:17) as the first element in the double name *ᶜštrkmš* 'Ashtar-Kemosh', a Moabite god. The name *ᶜštrkmš* has been thought to belong to a type of divine name characterized by Gordon as a "fusing of two different names."[33] It has also been argued that the name represents an equation of the two gods.[34] Stern treats **ᶜštr* as an epithet, "as a generalized form of the deity meaning, 'the warrior,' or the like,"[35] but the proposed meaning is otherwise unattested unless *ᶜštr* in the Deir ᶜAlla Inscription (combination I, line 14) were to be understood in this manner. Unfortunately, this line is poorly understood and consequently left untranslated in the edition of Hackett.[36] The Aramaic Sefire inscription contains another compound name, ᶜAttarsamak, who is said to be the king of Arpad (*KAI* nos. 222–24).[37] This name is also attested on an Aramaic seal dating to about 800.[38] Naveh notes the personal names *ᶜtrdrmy* from Hermapolis, *ᶜtrmlky* from Elephantine, and *ᶜtrswry* from Elephantine and Palmyra.[39] Another Aramaic seal of about the same date preserves the name *brᶜtr*, meaning either 'son of Athtar' or 'Athtar is

33. *UT* 8.61 n. 1; H. Barstad, *The Religious Polemics of Amos: Studies in the Preaching of Am 2, 7B–8, 4, 1–13, 5, 1–27, 6, 4–7, 8, 14* (VTSup 34; Leiden, 1984) 173; S. M. Olyan, *Asherah and the Cult of Yahweh in Israel* (SBLMS 34; Atlanta, 1988) 55. D. Holmès-Fredericq ("Possible Phoenician Influences in Jordan in the Iron Age," in *Studies in the History and Archaeology of Jordan III* [ed. A. Hadidi; Amman, 1987] 93) takes the double name as that of two deities but without explanation regards the first name as female "Ashtor."

34. S. Ackermann, *Under Every Green Tree: Popular Religion in Sixth-Century Judah* (HSM 46; Atlanta, 1992) 127.

35. Stern, *Biblical* Ḥerem, 37–38.

36. J. A. Hackett, *The Balaam Text from Deir ᶜAlla* (HSM 31; Chico, Cal., 1980) 29. P. K. McCarter ("The Balaam Texts from Deir ᶜAlla: The First Combination," *BASOR* 239 [1980] 49–60) translates *ᶜštr* as 'young'. If this word were related to the name of the god, then it would militate in favor of the non-Aramaic character of the dialect.

37. F. Rosenthal (trans.), "Canaanite and Aramaic Inscriptions," *ANET*, 659.

38. P. Bordreuil, *Catalogue des sceaux ouest-sémitiques inscrits de la Bibliothèque Nationale, du Musée du Louvre et du Musée biblique et Terre Sainte* (Paris, 1986) 76 no. 86.

39. J. Naveh, "A Nabatean Incantation Text," *IEJ* 29 (1979) 11–16.

pure'.[40] Caquot notes Athtar surviving as a theophoric element in the Palmyrene proper names *ᶜštwr* (*CIS* II 3933), *ᶜštwrgʾ* (4199) and *ᶜbdᶜštwr* (4418) and in the name of an ancestor of a family of converts called *barᶜaštōr* (*y. Bik.* 64a).[41]

The name *ᶜtršmn* 'Athtar of heaven' appears for the first time on an Aramaic seal that Bordreuil dates to the end of the ninth century.[42] The second element of Atarsamain's name has been taken as an indication of his astral status, in accordance with the astral character of the god, known from both earlier and later sources.[43] Cross regards the owner of the seal, Baraq, as an Aramaized Arab,[44] since "the god bears a favorite epithet of a North Arabian league." Neo-Assyrian sources provide further information about Athtar among the northern Arabs.[45] According to Esarhaddon, his father Sennacherib took the images of Arab gods as war booty, including that of Atarsamain, and Esarhaddon returned them.[46] Assurbanipal also mentions that he rounded up 'the people of Atarsamain' ([lu]*aʾlu ša* [d]*Ataršamain*).[47] This last phrase has a linguistic equivalent in Sabean *ʾhl ᶜṯtr* (*CIH* 434.1, 547.1),[48] which Biella translates

40. Bordreuil, *Catalogue des sceaux ouest-sémitiques,* 80 no. 93.

41. Caquot, "Le Dieu ᶜAthtar," 51. For further Aramaic proper names with **ᶜtr* as the theophoric element, see Bordreuil, *Catalogue des sceaux ouest-sémitiques,* 80.

42. Ibid., 75 no. 85. He regards this inscription as probably the oldest Aramaic cylinder seal inscription.

43. Albright, *Yahweh and the the Gods of Canaan,* 228. For criticisms of Albright's other identifications with Athtar, see F. M. Cross, *Canaanite Myth and Hebrew Epic* (Cambridge, Mass., 1973) 7 n. 13.

44. F. M. Cross, "The Seal of *Miqnêyaw,* Servant of Yahweh," in *Ancient Seals and the Bible* (ed. L. Gorelick and E. Williams-Forte; Malibu, 1983) 61.

45. See E. Ebeling, "Attar," *RLA* (Berlin, 1932) 1.312; M. Weippert, "Die Kämpfe des assyrischen Königs Assurbanipal gegen die Araber: Redactionskritische Untersuchung des Berichts in Prisma A," *WO* 7 (1973–74) 44–45; J. Teixidor, *The Pagan God: Popular Religion in the Greco-Roman Near East* (Princeton, 1977) 66–69.

46. A. L. Oppenheim (trans.), "Babylonian and Assyrian Historical Texts," *ANET,* 291.

47. See M. Weippert, "Die Kämpfe des assyrischen Königs Assurbanipal," 44–45; Oppenheim, *ANET,* 299; M. L. Barré, *The God-List in the Treaty between Hannibal and Philip V of Macedonia: A Study in Light of the Ancient Near Eastern Treaty Tradition* (JHNES; Baltimore, 1983) 161 n. 47. This translation might be supported by appeal to Arabic *ʾahl,* Epigraphic South Arabic *ʾhl* and Lihyanite *ʾl* 'people' (J. C. Biella, *Dictionary of Old South Arabic: Sabaean Dialect* [HSS 25; Chico, Cal., 1972] 7; Cross, "Epic Traditions," 36 n. 63). W. von Soden (AHw 39a) translates 'Beduinenstamm'. Cross argues that the context favors 'league, sacral confederation' (Cross, *Canaanite Myth and Hebrew Epic,* 7 n. 13, 105 n. 49; idem, "The Epic Traditions of Early Israel: Epic Narrative and the Reconstruction of Early Israelite Institutions," in *The Poet and the Historian: Essays in Literary and Historical Biblical Criticism* [ed. R. E. Friedman; Chico, Cal., 1983] 36 n. 63).

48. G. Ryckmans, *Les Noms propres sud-sémitiques, tome I: Répertoire analytique* (Bibliothèque du Muséon 2; Louvain, 1934) 27–28. Von Soden (AHw 39a) raises the possibility that Akkadian *aʾlu* may be a loanword from Arabic.

'clan of Athtar'.[49] Finally, Assurbanipal also addresses a prayer to Atarsamain.[50] Northern and central Arabian sources also attest to the names ᶜAttar and ᶜAttarsamain.[51]

The Phoenician evidence for the god Athtar is minimal at best. Garbini reads *lᶜštrḥn* in a fourth-century inscription from Byblos.[52]

Epigraphic South Arabic Sources

Epigraphic South Arabic inscriptions, hailing from the kingdoms of Hadramout, Maᶜin, Qataban and Sabaᵓ and dating from the eighth century B.C.E. to the 6th century C.E., attest to Athtar.[53] According to Jamme,[54] the name of Athtar is most frequently written *ᶜṯtr*, but sometimes it appears as (ᶜ)*str*, *ᶜtr*, and (ᶜ)*ṯt* in Sabaᵓ, and as *ᶜstrm* and (ᶜ)*ṯt* in Hadramout.[55] The god is well attested. J. Ryckmans regards him as the most important god of the South Arabian pantheon: "All the South Ara-

49. Biella, *Dictionary of Old South Arabic*, 7. Ryckmans (*Les Noms propres sud-sémitiques*, 27) translates 'la communauté de ᶜAṯtar' and explains that the expression refers to the "communauté de prêtres, ou confrèrie attachée à un temple de ᶜAṯtar." Similarly, Weippert ("Die Kämpfe des assyrischen königs Assurbanipal," 68–69) suggests 'Priester- oder Kultgenossenschaft' for *ᵓhl*. The *ᵓhl ᶜṯtr* is involved in the ritual hunt in *CIH* 547 (A. F. L. Beeston, "The Ritual Hunt: A Study in Old South Arabian Religious Practice," *Le Muséon* 61 [1948] 185, 196). In this context, Beeston translates *ᵓhl ᶜṯtr* as 'community of Athtar' and understands the phrase as a "religious collegium." For further discussion of Athtar and the sacred hunt, see G. Ryckmans, "Inscriptions sud-arabe: Quinzième série," *Le Muséon* 70 (1957) 109–10, 112; and M. Höfner, "Die vorislamischer Religionen Arabien," in *Die Religionen Altsyriens, Altarabiens und der Mandäer* (ed. H. Gese, M. Höfner, and K. Rudolph; Die Religionen der Menschheit 10/2; Stuttgart, 1970) 332–33.

50. M. Cogan, *Imperialism and Religion: Assyria, Judah and Israel in the Eighth and Seventh Centuries* B.C.E. (SBLMS 19; Missoula, Mont., 1974) 15–20; Barré, *The God-List*, 161 n. 47.

51. Höfner, "Die vorislamischer Religionen Arabien," 377. G. Ryckmans (*Les Noms propres sud-semitiques*, 27) notes also the Safaitic personal name *smᶜtr*. For early Islamic sources pertaining to Athtar, see T. Fahd, *Le Panthéon de l'arabie centrale à la veille de l'Hégire* (Institut français d'archéologie de Beyrouth bibliothèque archéologique et historique 88; Paris, 1968) 47, 54.

52. G. Garbini, "The God ᶜAštar in an Inscription from Byblos," *Or* 29 (1960) 322, who cites M. Dunand's earlier reading *lᶜštrt n* . . . .

53. The following description is based primarily on: Höfner, "Die vorislamischer Religionen Arabien," 268–71; A. Jamme, "Le Panthéon sud-arabe préislamique d'après les sources épigraphiques," *Le Muséon* 60 (1947) 85–97; idem, "La Religion sud-arabe préislamique," *Histoire des religions 4* (Paris, 1956) 264–65; G. Ryckmans, *Les Noms propres sud-sémitiques*, 27–28; idem, *Les religions arabes préislamiques* (2d ed.; Bibliothèque du Muséon 26; Louvain, 1951) 41–42; idem, "ᶜAṯtar-Ištar: Nom sumérien ou sémitique?" in *Herrmann von Wissmann-Festschrift* (ed. A. Leidlmair; Tübingen, 1962) 186–92. I wish to thank A. Jamme for commenting on an earlier draft of this section.

54. Jamme, "Le Panthéon sud-arabe préislamique," 85–86.

55. Ibid., 85–97; idem (trans.), "South Arabian Inscriptions," *ANET*, 663–69.

bian nations venerated him under the same name and he takes first place in enumerations of several gods."[56]

A number of inscriptions suggest that Athtar is an astral deity.[57] Some inscriptions bear witness to his title *šrqn*,[58] which commentators take, in Jamme's words, as an "epithet characterizing the star-god as 'the eastern.'"[59] In one Sabean inscription (*CIH* 149.2–3) Jamme reconstructs [*šr*]*qn* / *wǵrbn*, '[the ea]st and the west', which "marque les deux stades opposés de Vénus."[60]

Athtar is also called *yǵl* 'avenger' (*RES* 3978.1), *ʾb* 'father' (*RES* 2693.5) and *rfʾn* (*RES* 3978.1). G. Ryckmans takes the last as a sanctuary or an epithet, but Jamme and Höfner interpret it as an epithet meaning 'protector'.[61] Jamme also suggests that the term may be a place-name. Jamme[62] notes three further characteristics of Athtar: (1) he is the deity to whom people **rṯd* 'entrusted' things, because they believed that he was strong enough to protect their property; (2) the deity is mentioned commonly in the imprecations on tombs; and (3) he is qualified by the epithet *ʿzz* 'strong'.

The contextual evidence for Athtar as a waterer is less problematic. According to Jamme,[63] two other inscriptions, *RES* 4194.5 and *CIH* 47.2, suggest that Athtar was a god of irrigation. These inscriptions call Athtar *mnḍḥhmw*, which Jamme translates as 'leur divinité d'irrigation'. There is considerable disagreement over the value of this evidence. Höfner understands the epithet as "Bewässerungsgottheit" and translates the root **nḍḥ* 'mit Wasser bespregen, befeuchten'.[64] Van den Branden examines

56. J. Ryckmans, "South Arabia, Religion of," *ABD* 6.172.

57. Jamme, "Le Panthéon sud-arabe préislamique, 88–89; *ANET*, 663 n. 5; J. Ryckmans, "South Arabia," 172.

58. Jamme, "Le Panthéon sud-arabe préislamique," 88; *ANET*, 666–67.

59. Jamme, "Le Panthéon sud-arabe préislamique," 88; *ANET*, 666 n. 5. It has been supposed that Athtar has the epithet *ḏ-yhrq* 'he who sets', implying that Athtar was the evening star (G. Ryckmans, *Les Noms propres sud-sémitiques*, 28; Cross, *Canaanite Myth and Hebrew Epic*, 68). According to Jamme ("Le Panthéon sub-arabe préislamique," 92 n. 284), *RES* 4176.9 attests *byhrq* as a prepositional phrase. Jamme argues that this case shows that *yhrq* is to be interpreted not as an epithet but as a place-name. It is also claimed that in South Arabian inscriptions he is said also to be the firstborn of the moon-god. See Höfner, "Die vorislamischer Religionen Arabien," 249. Jamme disputes this view.

60. Jamme, "Le Panthéon sud-arabe préislamique," 88. See also Fahd, *Le Panthéon de l'arabie centrale*, 55.

61. See Jamme, "Le Panthéon sud-arabe préislamique," 89 and n. 257; Höfner, "Die vorislamischer Religionen Arabien," 498.

62. Jamme, "La Religion sud-arabe préislamique," 265.

63. Jamme, "Le Panthéon sud-arabe préislamique," 89; idem, "La Religion sud-arabe préislamiques," 264–65.

64. Höfner, "Die vorislamischer Religionen Arabien," 498, 515.

the context in which this title occurs and concludes that it may not refer to the role of irrigation as such, but to divine protection, another meaning known for the Arabic root **nḍḥ*.[65] The meaning of 'protection', however, stands outside the development of the basic fundamental meaning of the root. Hence, Athtar may have been attributed the role of waterer in this instance.

Jamme also notes another inscription, Fakhry 71.4–5.[66] In this text Athtar receives a gift 'in gratitude because he has vouchsa[fed] the spring storm [which was] an abundant irrigation' (*ḥmdm* / *bḏt* / [*wr*]*y* / *brq* / *ḏtᵓn* / *sqym* / *mhšfqm*).[67] G. Ryckmans questions the relative importance of this evidence for the character of Athtar, "c'est-à-dire remplaçent les divinités d'irrigation,"[68] which suggests that this feature of Athtar is a secondary development. Jamme similarly views the association of the role of irrigator of Athtar as "une reproduction fautive imputable au lapicide de l'énumération *habituelle* des noms divins."[69] It would appear then that Athtar was viewed occasionally as a provider of waters, but J. Ryckmans implies a more generous view of the evidence:

> ᶜAṯtar was the god of natural irrigation by rain, in contrast to the artificial irrigation of the arid zones, which depended on rainwater fallen elsewhere and conveyed and distributed by an irrigation network. This could explain a distinction between two kinds of Sabaean lands in the first centuries A.D.: the "domain (*mulk*) of ᶜAṯtar," in contrast to that "of Almaqah," the national god of Saba.[70]

The issue remains open.

In sum, the South Arabian evidence suggests that Athtar was an astral god who was considered a strong protector and occasionally a provider of water.

The Etymology of the Name of Athtar

Different cognates have been proposed for the name of Athtar. W. R. Smith, Gaster,[71] Gray, Ryckmans, and de Moor relate the name of Athtar

65. A. van den Branden, "Les Divinités sud-arabes *mnḍḥ* et *wrfw*," *BiOr* 16 (1959) 183–84

66. G. Ryckmans, *Les Religions arabes préislamiques*, 62.

67. Transcription and translation courtesy of A. Jamme.

68. G. Ryckmans, *Les Religions arabes préislamiques*, 41.

69. Jamme, "Le Panthéon sud-arabe préislamique," 89.

70. J. Ryckmans, "South Arabia," 172. The name of the god has been related to Arabic *ᶜaṯtarî* (see etymology section below), which refers to natural irrigation by water found on the surface running in channels or the like (E. W. Lane, *An Arabic-English Lexicon* [London, 1863–83; repr. Beirut, 1969] 1952).

71. Gaster (*Thespis*, 133 n. 35) suggests that **ᶜšr* in Ps 65:10 also shows this meaning, but this is disputed.

to Arabic *ᶜaṯtarî*, which is thought to refer to 'soil artificially irrigated', according to many ancient authorities.[72] Caquot and de Moor question the value of the Arabic cognate, but G. Ryckmans[73] relates the word to a Yemeni term *ᶜanṯarî* 'land thriving on water supply'.[74] The name of the god may have been the source of these nouns, however.

Ryckmans argues that the name of Athtar is also cognate with **ᶜtr* 'to be rich'.[75] Accordingly, Krebernik cites Biblical Hebrew **ᶜšr* and Aramaic **ᶜtr* as cognates.[76] The *-t-* is often explained as a *t-* infix plus metathesis.[77] Krebernik identifies the form with the Akkadian *PitRāS* form "mit begriffsintensivierender Bedeutung."[78] This infix is unusual, at best, for a divine name.

Leslau relates the god's name to Tigre *ᶜastär* 'heaven', Geᶜez *ᶜastar* 'sky', Amharic *astär* 'star' (from Geᶜez), and Bilin *astär* 'sky'.[79] These nouns appear to derive from the god's name and may provide further evidence that Athtar was considered an astral god.

Finally, based on his understanding of Athtar as *ᶜzz* 'strong', Jamme relates *ᶜṯtr* to Arabic *ᶜattâr* 'strong'.[80] Due to the unusual correspondence of consonants involved, this etymology has not met with general

72. G. Ryckmans, *Les Religions arabes préislamiques*, 41, 62; Oldenburg, *The Conflict between El and Baᶜal*, 39 n. 4. For a listing of some authorities, see W. R. Smith, *The Religion of the Semites: The Fundamental Institutions* (New York, 1972) 99–100 n. 2. See also de Moor, *Seasonal Pattern*, 205.

73. Caquot, "Le Dieu ᶜAthtar," 59; de Moor, *Seasonal Pattern*, 205 n. 4; G. Ryckmans, "ᶜAṯtar-Ištar," 190.

74. See M. Piamenta, *Dictionary of Post-Classical Yemeni Arabic* (Leiden, 1991) 2.316B, 324B. Reference courtesy of A. Jamme.

75. G. Ryckmans, "ᶜAṯtar-Ištar," 190.

76. Krebernik, "Zur Syllabar," 31. See also Akkadian *ešēru* 'to thrive, prosper' (of crops, animals, persons) (CAD E 354). It is possible that BH **ᶜšr* and Aramaic **ᶜtr*, as well as Akkadian *ešēru*, are related instead to Arabic **ǵṯr* 'to flourish' (used of land) and the noun *ǵaṯaran* 'abundance' (see Lane, *An Arabic-English Lexicon*, 2230). M. Delcor ("Astarté et la fécondité des troupeaux en Deut. 7,13 et parallèles," *UF* 6 [1974] 13) relates the name of the god instead to this root, but given the Ugaritic attestation of both *ᶜayin* and *ghayin*, this view is unwarranted. Krebernik also cites South Arabic **ᶜṯr* based on two citations by K. Conti Rossini (*Chrestomathia arabica meridionalis epigraphica* [Rome, 1931] 214). The first alleged attestation was based on a mistaken reading, as shown by Höfner ("Zur Interpretation altsüdarabischer Inschriften II," *WZKM* 43 [1936] 84; see also Biella, *Dictionary of Old South Arabic*, 389). The other attestation, *RES* 3306.405, is fragmentary and the text is poorly understood. The South Semitic evidence for **ᶜṯr* in this meaning is dubious. I wish to thank A. Jamme for pointing out these issues to me.

77. See F. Delitzsch, *Assyrische Grammatik* (Porta linguarum orientalium 10; Berlin, 1889) 178 (my thanks to A. Jamme for this reference); G. Ryckmans, *Les Noms propres sud-sémitiques*, 27; Delcor, "Astarté et la fécondité des troupeaux," 13; Krebernik, "Zur Syllabar," 31.

78. Von Soden, GAG §56n.

79. W. Leslau, *Comparative Dictionary of Geᶜez (Classical Ethiopic)* (Wiesbaden, 1987) 73.

80. Jamme, "La Religion sud-arabe préislamique," 265.

acceptance.[81] In sum, there is no clear Semitic etymology of the god's name.

Conclusion

Given the ancient Near Eastern evidence, approaches to the question of why Athtar represents an unsuitable candidate for kingship in KTU 1.2 III and 1.6 I have gravitated in two directions. On the basis of South Arabian sources and the putative Arabic cognate *ʿaṯṯari*, Jacobsen, Gaster, and Gray propose that Athtar is a god of irrigation and therefore serves as an apt foil to Baal's rains.[82] G. Ryckmans cites van Arendonk to the effect that in Arabic sources "*ʿiḏy baʿl* et *ʿaṯṯari* ont également été parfois employés indifféremment pour les terrains abreuvés par la pluie."[83] According to Smith,[84] *ʿaṯṯari* may have been originally distinguished as land watered by an artificial channel. The comparative evidence for this feature is late and relatively meager, and it is unclear whether it represents a development specific to Arabia. Moreover, no Ugaritic narrative explicitly mentions this putative function of Athtar. However, the notion may be older, and Ugarit may have inherited the tradition that Athtar was a producer of water. If so, Athtar's dominion over the earth in 1.6 I 65 might be intelligible from this point of view.[85] Indeed, this understanding would make sense out of 1.6 I 66–67. The reference to drawing water from containers (]*šʾabn brḫbt*//]*šʾabn bkknt*)[86] in these lines, if correct,[87] would be intelligible as references to water collected for irrigating land. Second, Caquot argues[88] that the Ugaritic texts may reflect the historical demise of Athtar's cult at the hands of the cult of Baal. Both were warrior-gods, but Baal was the divine patron of the Ugaritic dynasty.

81. G. Ryckmans, "ʿAṯtar-Ištar," 191.

82. Jacobsen, *Treasures of Darkness*, 140; Gaster, *Thespis* 127, 219; Gray, *Legacy of Canaan*, 170. For other scholars who hold this view, see de Moor, *Seasonal Pattern*, 205 n. 3.

83. G. Ryckmans, "ʿAṯtar-Ištar," 190 n. 31.

84. Smith, *Religion of the Semites*, 99 n. 2.

85. If so, Arabic *ʿaṯirat ʾarḍ* 'land (without herbage) that has *ʿiṯyar* dust' may reflect the god's association with the earth. See Lane, *Arabic-English Lexicon*, 1952.

86. J. C. L. Gibson, *Canaanite Myths and Legends* (2d. ed.; Edinburgh, 1978) 76; J. C. de Moor, *An Anthology of Religious Texts from Ugarit* (Leiden, 1987) 86. Like the other translators, Caquot, Sznycer, and Herdner (*Textes ougaritiques*, 258) render **šʾb* as 'puiser' but ask in note p if these lines do not allude to "un rituel d'hydrophorie." Perhaps most wisely, H. L. Ginsberg ("Ugaritic Myths, Epics, and Legends," *ANET*, 140) chose not to translates these lines.

87. The reading of the two instances of the verb is in doubt according to KTU, which instead reads]*hš*//]-*n* (see G. del Olmo Lete, *Mitos y leyendas de Canaan segun la tradición de Ugarit: Textos, versión y estudio* [Fuentes de la ciencia biblica 1; Madrid, 1981] 226).

88. Caquot, "Le Dieu ʿAthtar," 55. See also Gese, "Die Religionen Altsyriens," 138.

The geographical distribution of the cults of Baal and Athtar may clarify the status of Athtar at Ugarit.[89] The historical cult of Athtar may have been generally restricted to inland areas. Apart from the Ugaritic texts, there is no clear evidence for the cult of Athtar on the coast. There is no mention of Athtar in the Amarna letters, Egyptian sources mentioning West Semitic deities, the Bible, or Philo of Byblos. The single Phoenician attestation is debatable. In contrast, the cult of Baal is at home on the coast. It is tempting to view the conflict between Baal and Athtar in terms of the Arabic use of these gods' names for land fed by water. Smith remarks that *m. B. Bat.* 3:1 reflects the older use of *baᶜl* as land wholly dependent on rain and argues that the original contrast lay between land wholly dependent on rain as opposed to irrigated land.[90] The coastal regions received heavy rainfall, which precluded the need for either dry farming or irrigation. At Ugarit, for example, the rains occur over a period of seven or eight months and exceed 800 mm each year.[91] In contrast, many of the inland sites where Athtar is attested practiced either dry farming or natural irrigation. It might be argued, then, that in the environment of Ugarit, the god of the storm would naturally supplant the god of natural irrigation.

An additional consideration deserves notice. The Baal Cycle indicates that Athtar, unlike Baal, belongs to the family of El and Athirat, but the basis for this familial relationship is unclear. Given the wide attestation of Athtar as an astral deity, the basis for his relationship to El and Athirat may lie in the astral character of this family unit. Unfortunately, the evidence is extremely meager. In KTU 1.23.48–54, El is the father of Shahar and Shalim. Job 38:7 may preserve an old notion about the family of El in the parallel phrases *kôkĕbê bōqer* 'morning stars' // *kol-bĕnê ᵓĕlōhîm* 'all the divine sons' (or 'all the sons of God').[92] Epigraphic South Arabic sources may support this point. Athirat is the name of a Qatabanian solar goddess and spouse of the moon-god, according to Jamme.[93] El survives in South Arabian religion as well.[94] It must be emphasized that the Ugaritic evidence for the astral character of El and

89. Compare the comments of Gray (*Legacy of Canaan*, 170 n. 2): "The fertility function of the deity is not to be doubted, but in view of the preeminence of the cult of ᶜAṯtar in oases and lands bordering on the desert it seems more natural than the fertility-function of the deity in the settled lands."

90. Smith, *Religion of the Semites*, 102 n. 2. For subsequent modifications of this contrast, see ibid., 95–113, esp. 100, 102 n. 2.

91. M. Yon, "Ugarit: History and Archaeology," *ABD* 6.698.

92. Oldenburg, *Conflict between El and Baᶜal*, 18.

93. Jamme, "La Religion sud-arabe préislamique," 266. See also G. Ryckmans, *Les Religions arabes préislamiques*, 44.

94. U. Oldenburg, "Above the Stars of El: El in South Arabic Religion," *ZAW* 82 (1970) 187–208; J. Ryckmans, "South Arabia," 172.

Athirat's family is minimal. By the same token, this paucity of information may be due to the displacement of the family of El and Athirat by the Ugaritic cult of Baal, who does not belong to that family. Similarly, J. Ryckmans has suggested that the South Arabian cult of El was displaced by the cult of Athtar.[95]

In sum, the Ugaritic texts as well as the most proximate comparative evidence from Emar would suggest that Athtar is an astral deity who is considered a major warrior deity. The narratives of KTU 1.2 III and 1.6 I 63 stress that Athtar is not powerful enough to be king. Within the Ugaritic texts, Athtar is rendered as a weak god, perhaps a historical reflection of his cult's demise, as reflected in other sources from the Levantine coast. It would appear that at Ugarit Baal supplanted Athtar as the warrior-god who provides water.

95. So J. Ryckmans, "South Arabia," 172.

Index of Authors

Abegg, M. G. 208, 208 n. 7, 210 n. 10–11, 212–13, 213 n. 181, 216–17, 219, 221–22, 230, 236, 238, 240–41, 244–45, 250–51, 336, 336 n. 22, 338
Abou-Assaf, A. 394 n. 1
Abrahami, P. 46 n. 11
Abrahams, I. 205 n. 12
Abramsky, S. 367 n. 7
Abulafia, A. 509, 509 n. 5, 510
Abusch, T. 317 n. 1, 468 n. 2, 469 n. 3, 471 n. 9, 472 n. 11, 475 n. 19, 481 n. 31, 492 n. 65, 557 n. 35, 594 n. 33
Ackermann, S. 632 n. 34
Aharoni, Y. 286, 286 n. 12, 366 n. 4, 367 n. 11, 379 n. 1, 381
Aistleitner, J. 69 n. 2
Albrektson, B. 162, 162 n. 6
Albright, W. F. 48, 48 n. 22, 141, 141 n. 10, 151, 151 n. 22, 284 n. 3, 287 n. 18, 289, 347 n. 11, 398 n. 16, 561 n. 5, 631 n. 27, 633 n. 43
Allegro, J. M. 33 n. 9, 196 n. 8
Alster, B. 88 n. 44, 477 n. 22, 552 n. 21, 586 n. 4, 587 nn. 9–10, 588 n. 13, 589 n. 13, 589 n. 15, 590 n. 18, 596 n. 45
Alter, R. 15 n. 7
Amadasi Guzzo, M. G. 382 n. 12, 433, 433 n. 3, 434, 434 n. 6, 436 n. 14, 439, 439 n. 18, 439 n. 20, 496 n. 3, 499 n. 20, 501 n. 28, 503 n. 37
Amsler, S. 165 n. 19, 168 n. 24
Anawati, G. C. 22 n. 12
Andersen, F. I. 8 n. 2, 265 n. 8, 401 n. 19
Anderson, G. A. 548 n. 6
Andrae, W. 553 n. 23
Anklesaria, B. T. 412 n. 9, 413, 413 n. 14, 414 n. 26, 415
Archi, A. 177 n. 2, 629, 629 n. 8, 629 n. 10
Arnaud, D. 573 n. 2, 574 n. 6, 577–80, 624 n. 14, 625 n. 19, 629 n. 7, 629 n. 15, 630, 630 n. 16, 630 nn. 18–19, 631 n. 29
Arnold, T. W. 571 n. 48
Asmussen, J. P. 3 nn. 1–2
Assmann, J. 52 nn. 52–54
Astour, M. 283 n. 1, 579
Attridge, H. W. 631 n. 28
Aufrecht, W. E. 387 n. 5, 389, 389 n. 2, 394 n. 1, 395 n. 7, 596 n. 47
Avida, Y. 118, 118 n. 1, 119, 119 nn. 3–4, 119 n. 7, 121 nn. 9–10
Avigad, N. 368 n. 17, 368 n. 19, 387 n. 4, 394 n. 4, 439 n. 21
Avishur, Y. 77 n. 22

Bacher, W. 3 n. 3
Baillet, M. 40 n. 2, 182, 182 nn. 5–6, 185 nn. 18–19, 280 nn. 10–11
Bal^{c}amī 119 n. 6, 129 n. 27
Balkan, K. 574 n. 5, 578
Ball, C. J. 555 n. 29
Baltzer, K. 290 n. 24
Bardtke, H. 263, 263 n. 4
Bar-Maoz, Y. 89 n. 50
Barr, J. 8 n. 2, 70 n. 2, 165 n. 19, 451 n. 1
Barré, M. L. 633 n. 47, 634 n. 50
Barstad, H. 632 n. 33
Barthélemy, D. 208 n. 4
Bartoccini, R. 504 n. 40
Barton, G. A. 172 n. 35
Barucq, A. 51 n. 47
Basser, H. W. 198 n. 12
Baudissin, W. W. 163, 163 n. 9
Bauer, H. 7 n. 1, 9 nn. 5–6, 11 n. 14, 198 n. 15, 199 n. 22
Baumgarten, J. M. 33, 33 n. 9
Baumgartner, W. 70, 70 n. 3, 70 n. 6, 139 n. 4, 263, 365 n. 1, 439 n. 19
Beaulieu, P.-A. 535, 538, 538 n. 11, 538 n. 16
Beckman, G. 81 n. 8, 574 n. 6, 575 n. 6, 578–80
Beek, M. A. 152 n. 26
Beeston, A. F. L. 634 n. 49
Behrens, H. 544 n. 3
Bendor, S. 179 n. 14, 372 n. 38
Ben-Ḥayyim, Z. 70 n. 5
Ben Levi, J. 24 n. 22
Bentzen, A. 262 n. 3, 267 n. 12, 270–71, 271 nn. 14–15, 272, 272 n. 16, 274, 274 n. 19
Benz, F. L. 462 n. 3, 462 n. 5, 464 n. 6, 495 n. 1, 502 n. 33
Bergsträsser, G. 9 n. 6, 11 nn. 14–15
Bernhardt, I. 590 n. 18
Bertholet, A. 347 n. 8
Bresciani, E. 57 n.
Beyer, K. 62 n. 22, 343 n. 41, 391
Bialik, H. N. 14 n. 3

Bickerman, E. 175 n. 42, 322 n. 20
Biella, J. 48 n. 19, 633 n. 47, 634 n. 49, 637 n. 76
Biga, M. G. 574 n. 4
Biggs, R. D. 549 n. 8, 550 n. 14
Biran, A. 394 n. 3, 394 n. 6
Birot, M. 177 n. 1
Black, J. A. 596 n. 45
Blass, F. 454 n. 10
Blenkinsopp, J. 264 n. 6, 322 n. 18
Bloch, A. 14 nn. 1–2
Bloch, C. 14 nn. 1–2
Boehmer, R. M. 16 n. 11
Boer, P. A. H. de 51
Böhl, F. M. 86, 87 nn. 34–35
Bolle, K. W. 160, 160 n. 2
Bonechi, M. 574 n. 4
Bonnet, C. 499 n. 20, 500 n. 23
Bordreuil, P. 77 n. 22, 387 n. 9, 394 n. 1, 394 n. 5, 632 n. 38, 633, 633 nn. 40–42
Borger, R. 47 n. 17
Borowski, E. 385
Bossert, H. T. 385 n. 2
Böttcher, F. 99 n. 6
Bottéro, J. 46 n. 10, 552 n. 20, 593 n. 31
Bowman, R. A. 396, 396 n. 13
Boyer, G. 574 n. 5, 580
Brand, Y. 382 n. 14
Branden, A. van den 635, 636 n. 65
Braun, F. 58 nn. 2–3, 59 n. 8, 60 n. 12, 63 n. 28, 64 n. 29, 65 n. 35
Braun, R. 174 n. 39
Bresciani, E. 61 n. 15
Brinkman, J. A. 46 n. 7, 317 n. 1, 318 n. 6, 484 n. 43, 485 n. 44
Brinner, W. M. 22 n. 13, 24 n. 22
Brockelmann, C. 16 n. 8, 390
Bron, F. 395 n. 9
Brown, P. 64 n. 31
Brown, R. E. 208 n. 2
Brown, R. W. 64, 64 n. 30
Brownlee, W. H. 198 n. 12
Bruce, F. F. 454 n. 9
Brunner, H. 440 n. 28
Bruyère, B. 440 n. 28
Buber, M. 111 n. 24, 112 n. 30, 274, 274 n. 21
Buccellati, G. 151, 151 n. 23
Buchanan, B. 86 n. 31
Büchler, A. 33 n. 7
Buhl, F. 11 n. 14, 20 n. 6, 71, 71 n. 8
Buison, R. 628 n. 4
Burkert, W. 478 n. 26
Burnell, A. C. 412
Burns, J. B. 630 n. 21

Callaway, P. R. 37 n. 16
Campbell, R. M. 102 n. 2
Cantineau, J. 23 nn. 16–17, 25 n. 26, 25 n. 28, 26 n. 32
Caquot, A. 48 n. 20, 70 n. 2, 77 n. 22, 440 n. 28, 628 n. 4, 629 n. 9, 630, 630 n. 20, 630 n. 24, 630 n. 26, 631 n. 27, 633, 633 n. 41, 637–38, 637 n. 73, 638, n. 86, 638 n. 88
Cardona, G. R. 58 n. 2
Carmignac, J. 182 n. 4, 185 n. 16, 187 n. 26
Carruba, O. 426 n. 16
Cassin, E. 474 n. 15
Cassuto, U. 383, 383 n. 16
Castellino, G. 53 n. 57
Cazelles, H. 54 n. 60, 64 n. 31
Ceccaldi, G. C. 433 n. 1
Černý, J. 435 nn. 10–11
Charlesworth, J. H. 46 n. 4, 295 n. 8
Charpin, D. 82, 86 n. 29, 89, 89 nn. 49–51, 90 n. 57, 91 nn. 60–61, 93 n. 68, 599 n. 1, 601 nn. 5–6, 602 n. 8
Chiera, E. 586 n. 4
Chirichigno, G. C. 93 n. 69
Ch'u, T. 321 n. 17
Çiğ, M. 589 n. 14
Civil, M. 477 n. 22, 549 n. 11, 591 n. 25
Clements, R. E. 322 n. 19
Clifford, R. J. 487 n. 53, 488 n. 53
Cocquerillat, D. 536, 536 n. 1
Coelho, G. 412
Cogan, M. 322 n. 19, 323 n. 25, 634 n. 50
Cohen, J. 125 n. 19, 126 n. 23
Cohen, M. E. 553 n. 21
Comrie, B. 65 n. 36
Contenau, G. 535
Contini, R. 429 n. 40
Cooke, G. A. 552 n. 20
Cooper, J. S. 543 n. 3, 550 n. 15, 551 n. 17, 586 n. 2
Cornelius, F. 289 n. 22
Cotton, H. M. 453 nn. 4–7
Cowley, A. 57 n.
Cramer, W. 113 n. 38
Cross, F. M. 209, 334 n. 13, 389, 394 n. 5, 395 n. 11, 401 n. 20, 402 n. 21, 404 n. 23, 405 n. 24, 406 n. 26, 487 n. 53, 633, 633 nn. 43–44, 633 n. 47, 635 n. 59
Crüseman, J. 369 n. 21
Crüsemann, F. 320 n. 13
Cunchillos-Ilarri, J. L. 60 n. 13, 63 n. 27, 64 n. 31
Curtius, E. R. 66 n. 38

Dahood, M. 140, 140 n. 6, 141
Dalley, S. 317 n. 1, 318 n. 6, 553 n. 24
Danby, H. 380 nn. 3–4
Dandamayev, M. A. 523 n. 1
Dankwarth, G. 396, 396 n. 14
Dashian, J. 295 n. 9
Dauvillier, J. 412, 412 n. 5
Davies, D. 462 n. 4
Day, J. 476 n. 20

Day, P. L. 631 n. 28
Dayagi-Mendels, M. 385 n. 1, 387 n. 9
Debrunner, A. 454 n. 10
Delcor, M. 185 n. 16, 262 n. 3, 593 n. 30, 637 nn. 76–77
Delitzsch, F. 318 n. 7, 346 n. 5, 637 n. 77
Deller, K. 476 n. 20, 568 n. 31
Demsky, A. 367 n. 10
Díez Macho, A. 66, 66 n. 39
Di Lella, A. A. 262 n. 3
Dijk, J. van 46, 46 n. 5
Dillmann, A. 347 n. 8
Dion, P.-E. 49, 49 nn. 27–28, 49 n. 32, 59 n. 10, 61 n. 15, 62 n. 17
Diringer, D. 368 n. 15, 368 n. 18
Diyārbakrī 119, 119 n. 6, 129 n. 27
Dohaish, A. A. 64 n. 29
Dommershausen, W. 163 n. 10
Donner, H. 48 n. 26, 49, 49 n. 34, 52, 52 n. 51, 179 n. 14, 291, 291 n. 28
Dossin, G. 178 n. 10
Dothan, M. 394 n. 3
Dougherty, R. P. 535, 538, 538 n. 17
Douglas, M. 121 n. 11
Driver, G. R. 50, 50 n. 39, 89 n. 50, 323 n. 26
Driver, S. R. 88 n. 45
Dunand, M. 634 n. 52
Dunayevsky, I. 394 n. 3
Duncan-Jones, R. P. 444 n. 4
Dunsky, S. 130 n. 28
Dupont-Sommer, A. 49 n. 33, 50, 57 n. , 182 n. 3, 185 n. 17, 187 n. 25, 385 n. 3, 395 n. 10, 423, 423 n. 1, 424–30, 431 n. 46
Durand, J.-M. 46 n. 11, 178, 178 nn. 4–5, 425 n. 8, 566 n. 24, 599 n. 1, 600 nn. 2–3, 601 n. 5, 602, 603 n. 10, 604 nn. 11–13, 606 n. 17

ᶜEbād, A. 413 n. 22
Ebeling, E. 48, 48 n. 24, 535, 538 n. 13, 551 n. 16, 566 n. 25, 594 n. 34, 633 n. 45
Edel, E. 578
Edzard, D. O. 90, 90 n. 53, 475 n. 20, 476 n. 20
Eerdmans, B. D. 593 n. 30
Ehlich, K. 64 n. 31
Ehrlich, A. B. 350, 350 n. 19
Eichler, B. L. 85, 85 n. 25, 89, 89 n. 48
Eiland, M. 16 n. 10, 16 n. 13
Eilberg-Schwartz, H. 121 n. 11
Eisenman, R. H. 277 n. 1, 278 n. 4, 336, 336 nn. 23–25, 338, 340 n. 38
Eissfeldt, O. 261 n. 1, 369 n. 23, 370 n. 26, 372 n. 36
Elchouémi, M. 67 n. 48
Elgvin, T. 207 n. 1, 351, 355
Elkana, Y. 175 n. 41
Ellis, M. de J. 41 n. 7, 83 n. 16, 328 n. 3
Emeneau, M. B. 62 n. 19
Emerton, J. A. 289, 289 n. 20, 290 n. 24
Ephᶜal, I. 395 n. 9
Epstein, J. N. 32 n. 4
Erman, A. 435 n. 8
Even-Shoshan, A. 14 n. 3
Evetts, B. T. A. 523 n.
Ewald, H. G. A. 284

Fahd, T. 634 n. 51, 635 n. 60
Fales, F. M. 60 n. 13
Falkenstein, A. 477 n. 22, 586 n. 4, 587 n. 6, 587 n. 9, 590 n. 19, 610, 610 n. 1, 612, 612 n. 4, 613 nn. 6–7
Farber, W. 470 n. 8, 480 n. 29, 482 n. 33
Feinstein, M. 509 n. 5
Fensham, F. C. 141 n. 9
Février, J. G. 496 n. 2, 497 n. 6, 498, 498 n. 17, 504 n. 42
Field, F. 346 n. 5
Finet, A. 46 n. 10, 47 n. 17, 606 n. 17
Finkel, I. L. 478 n. 26, 483 n. 37, 487 n. 51, 594 n. 34
Finkelstein, J. J. 82 n. 10, 91 n. 59, 92, 92 n. 65
Finkelstein, L. 347 n. 10
Firestone, R. 20 n. 3, 20 n. 5
Fishelov, D. 14 n. 2
Fitzmyer, J. A. 14 n. 4, 15, 15 nn. 5–6, 50 n. 37, 59 nn. 9–10, 62 n. 21, 452 nn. 2–3
Fleisch, H. 23 n. 17
Fleischman, J. 88 n. 46
Fleming, D. 630 n. 17, 630 n. 19
Fohrer, G. 369 n. 24
Forbes, A. D. 8 n. 2, 265 n. 8
Foster, B. R. 481 n. 30, 544 n. 3, 554 n. 25, 592 n. 27, 592 n. 29, 594 n. 33, 594 n. 38, 595 n. 41
Foster, J. 412 n. 7
Fowler, J. D. 366 n. 3, 366 nn. 5–6, 367 n. 8, 368 n. 13, 368 n. 16
Fox, M. V. 171 n. 31, 173 n. 36, 593 n. 30, 595 nn. 43–44, 596 n. 49
Fraenkel, S. 183 n. 9
Frame, G. 538 n. 11
Frankel, S. 204 n. 8
Frankena, R. 87, 87 nn. 36–37, 593 n. 29
Frankfort, H. 631 n. 28
Freedman, D. N. 265 n. 8, 334 n. 11, 401 nn. 19–20
Frei, P. 425 n. 7, 429 n. 40
Frey, J. B. 31 n. 2
Frick, F. S. 367 n. 7
Friedman, M. 125 n. 20
Friedrich, J. 396, 396 n. 13, 397 n. 15, 495 n. 2, 496 n. 2, 497, 498, 498 nn. 12–13, 498 n. 15, 503, 503 n. 36
Frymer-Kensky, T. S. 164 n. 16, 477 n. 22, 477 n. 24

Galter, H. D. 324 n. 31
Garbini, G. 628 n. 4, 634, 634 n. 52
Garelli, P. 47 n. 14, 317 n. 1
Garfinkel, Y. 436 n. 12
Garnsey, P. 448, 448 n. 13
Garr, W. R. 502 n. 32
Gaster, T. H. 53, 593 n. 30, 636, 636 n. 71, 638, 638 n. 82
Geiger, A. 19 n. 2
Geiger, J. 453 nn. 4–6, 454 n. 7
Gelb, I. J. 47 n. 17, 177 n. 1, 629 n. 11
Geller, M. J. 475 n. 20, 551 n. 17
Genouillac, H. de 591 n. 21
George, A. R. 494 n. 75
Gera, D. L. 322 n. 21
Gerleman, G. 369 n. 22, 370 n. 25
German, F. H. 54 n. 61
Gerson, D. 109 nn. 8–9, 111 n. 25, 112 n. 27, 112 n. 31, 114 n. 50
Gese, H. 373 n. 42, 628 n. 4, 638 n. 88
Gesenius, W. 11 n. 14, 71, 97 n. 3, 139, 139 n. 3, 147 n. 18
Gibson, J. C. L. 61 n. 15, 69 n. 2, 140 n. 7, 150 n. 19, 394 n. 3, 638 n. 86
Gignoux, P. 281 n. 13, 415 nn. 29–30
Gilman, A. 64, 64 n. 30
Ginsberg, H. L. 70 n. 2, 77 n. 22, 138, 138 n. 2, 142 nn. 14–15, 638 n. 86
Ginsburger, M. 101 n. 1
Ginzberg, L. 36 nn. 12–15, 108 n. 4, 110 n. 11
Glueck, N. 285, 285 n. 9
Goetze, A. 82 n. 11, 580
Goitein, S. D. 20 n. 5, 109 n. 6
Goldingay, J. E. 262 n. 3
Goldschmidt, D. 203, 203 nn. 1–2, 204 nn. 8–9
Good, R. M. 552 n. 19
Goodchild, R. 503 n. 38, 504 n. 39
Gordis, D. M. 92 n. 64
Gordis, R. 172 n. 35, 198 n. 14, 596 n. 48, 597 n. 51
Gordon, C. H. 40 n. 5, 178 n. 8, 574 n. 4, 632
Goshen-Gottstein, M. 204 n., 205 n. 10
Grapow, H. 58 n. 5, 60 n. 14, 62 n. 17, 435 n. 8
Grave, C. 487 n. 52, 488 n. 53
Gray, J. 628 n. 4, 630 nn. 25–26, 636, 638, 638 n. 82, 639 n. 89
Grayson, A. K. 485 n. 44
Greenberg, M. 141, 141 n. 11, 587 n. 6
Greenfield, J. C. 41, 45 nn. 1–3, 49 n. 31, 57, 57 n. 1, 59 n. 10, 60 n. 11, 61 n. 16, 62, 62 n. 18, 62 n. 20, 62 n. 23, 63 nn. 24–25, 65 n. 33, 137 n. 1, 184 n. 13, 345 n., 348, 348 n. 14, 393 n., 395 n. 11, 428, 428 n. 33, 439 n. 21, 451 n. 1, 454 n. 8, 555 n. 29, 627 n. 1
Grelot, P. 45, 45 n. 4, 50, 50 nn. 40–41, 61 n. 15, 62 n. 18, 63 n. 25, 428 n. 31
Gressmann, H. 48 n. 24
Grintz, Y. M. 163 n. 11
Gröndahl, F. 629 n. 7
Groneberg, B. 86 n. 29, 484 n. 41
Gropp, G. 413, 413 n. 23, 414–15, 415 n. 31, 416
Grossfeld, B. 120 n. 8
Gruenwald, I. 478 n. 26
Guilbert, P. 182 n. 4
Guillard, R. 321 n. 17
Gunkel, H. 108 n. 3, 283, 283 nn. 1–2
Gunneweg, A. H. J. 367 n. 9
Gurney, O. R. 481 n. 30, 625 n. 20, 626 n. 21, 626 n. 23
Guyot, P. 321 n. 17
Gyekye, K. 66 n. 41

Haas, H. 475 n. 20
Hackett, J. A. 632, 632 n. 36
Hagenbucher, A. 580
Hahn, I. 427 n. 22
Halkin, F. 445 n. 5
Hall, I. H. 435, 435 n. 7, 436 n. 14
Hallo, W. W. 83 n. 20, 86 n. 31, 163 n. 10
Hamilton, G. J. 394 n. 1
Hammond, N. G. L. 174 n. 40
Haran, M. 367 n. 9, 371 n. 30
Harlez, B. de 413
Harris, R. 594 n. 33
Hartman, L. F. 262 n. 3
Hastings, J. 454 n. 9
Haug, M. 412, 412 n. 9
Haupt, P. 555 n. 29
Hawkins, D. 578
Hayes, J. P. 63 n. 24
Head, B. V. 440 n. 26
Heidel, A. 544, 544 n. 2
Heimpel, W. 629, 629 n. 6, 629 n. 8, 629 n. 12
Hekmat, A. 413 n. 22
Held, M. 53 n. 58, 594 n. 35, 594 n. 38, 595 nn. 40–41, 595 n. 42
Heltzer, M. 87 n. 38, 317 n. 1, 436 n. 12
Hengel, M. 170 n. 29, 174 n. 39, 174 n. 41, 454 n. 13, 455 n. 14, 458
Henning, W. B. 4 n. 15, 413, 413 n. 21, 414, 414 n. 27, 415
Herdner, A. 628 n. 4, 630 n. 26, 638 n. 86
Herodotus 322 n. 21
Herr, L. G. 387 n. 6, 387 nn. 8–9
Herzfeld, E. 413, 413 n. 15, 414
Hestrin, R. 385 n. 1, 387 n. 9
Hidal, S. 109 n. 8
Higger 212
Hill, G. F. 440 n. 26
Hillers, D. R. 52 n. 48, 63 n. 25
Hirsch, H. 53 n. 58

Höfner, M. 634 n. 49, 634 n. 51, 634 n. 53, 635, 635 n. 59, 635 n. 61, 635 n. 64, 637 n. 76
Hoftijzer, J. 36 n. 11, 63 n. 24, 96, 96 nn. 1–2, 99 n. 6, 186 n. 24, 390, 503 n. 36
Holladay, L. 365 n. 1
Hollander, H. W. 41 n. 7
Holma, H. 549 n. 13
Holmès-Fredericq, D. 632 n. 33
Honeyman, A. M. 381 n. 10
Horn, P. 4 n. 8, 4 nn. 10–14
Horovitz, H. S. 204 n. 7
Horovitz, J. 19, 19 n. 1, 20, 20 n. 4, 21, 21 nn. 7–11, 24, 27, 41 n. 11
Hrozný, B. 48
Huehnergard, J. 324 n. 28, 394 n. 1, 502 n. 34, 573 n. 2, 574 n. 6, 630 nn. 22–23
Huffmon, H. 599 n. 1
Humphreys, S. C. 175 n. 41
Hunger, H. 476 n. 21
Hunt, E. D. 314 n. 18
Hurowitz, V. 87, 87 n. 39, 88 n. 45, 478 n. 26, 591 n. 25
Hurstfield, J. 571 n. 48
Hurvitz, A. 76 n. 21, 195 n. 7, 334 n. 11
Hutter, M. 481 n. 30
Hyde, J. K. 571 n. 48

Ibn al-Athir 119
Ibn Janaḥ 74 n. 16, 345, 346 n. 3, 350, 350 n. 18
Ibh Shahin, Nissim ben Jacob 24 n. 22
Idel, M. 509 n. 5
Ingolt, H. 382 n. 11
Issaverdens, J. 295, 295 n. 5
Ivančik, A. 318 n. 6
Izre'el, S. 568 n. 34

Jackson, K. P. 596 n. 47
Jacobsen, T. 554 n. 27, 586 n. 4, 587, 587 n. 7, 587 nn. 9–10, 588 n. 11, 589, 589 n. 14, 589 n. 16, 590 n. 17, 590 n. 19, 593 n. 30, 596 n. 46, 629 n. 9, 638, 638 n. 82
Jagersma, H. 290 n. 25
Jakobson, R. 505, 505 n. 2
Jamme, A. 634, 634 nn. 53–55, 635, 635 nn. 57–63, 636, 636 n. 69, 637, 637 n. 80, 639 n. 93
Jastrow, M. 457 n. 21, 592 n. 27
Jastrow, O. 10 n. 9
Jean, C.-F. 186 n. 24, 390
Jean, H. 503 n. 36
Jenni, E. 172 n. 35
Jensen, P. 593 n. 30
Jepsen, A. 108 n. 3
Jeremias, J. 108 n. 5
Jespersen, O. 65 n. 36
Joannès, F. 526 n. 7, 536, 538 n. 11
Johnson, A. C. 444 n. 4
Jongeling, B. 280 n. 12
Jongeling, K. 495 n. 1, 496 n. 2, 497 n. 6, 498, 498 n. 14, 501 n. 28, 502 n. 31, 504 n. 41
Joseph, T. K. 412 n. 4, 412 n. 9, 413, 413 n. 15, 413 n. 17, 414, 414 n. 25, 415 n. 28
Josephus 33, 37, 42, 284, 338
Joüon, P. 183 n. 11

Kadish, G. E. 321 n. 16
Kaiser, O. 168 n. 23
Kallai, Z. 366 n. 4, 565 n. 22
Kamil, M. 57 n., 61 n. 15
Kara, J. 72 n. 13
Karageorghis, V. 382 n. 12, 433 n. 3, 434 n. 6, 436 n. 14, 439 n. 18, 439 n. 20, 440 n. 26
Kartun-Blum, R. 505 n. 1
Kasher, M. 204 n. 9
Kasovsky, Ch. Y. 71 n. 10, 76 n. 20
Kaufman, S. A. 59 n. 10, 323 nn. 22–23, 400, 400 n. 18, 402 n. 21, 427 n. 21, 476 n. 20
Kaufmann, Y. 161, 161 n. 3, 163, 163 n. 12, 164 n. 15
Kautsch, E. 97 n. 3
Kayatz, C. 52, 52 n. 51
Keel, O. 52, 52 n. 51, 593 n. 30
Keenan, J. G. 456 n. 17
Keil, C. F. 346 n. 5
Kelso, J. L. 381 n. 10
Kendall, D. 369 n. 21
Kienast, B. 620 n. 3, 623 n. 10
Kilian, R. 108 n. 3
Kilmer, A. D. 550 n. 15
Kinnier-Wilson, J. V. 317 n. 1
Kisāʾi 129 n. 27
Kister, M. 194 n. 6
Kittel, B. P. 185 n. 16
Kizilyay, H. 589 n. 14
Klein, M. L. 102 n. 2, 102 n. 4
Klengel, H. 578, 578 n. 9
Kloner, A. 462 n. 4
Knohl, I. 333 n. 11, 335 n. 18, 337 nn. 27–28, 339 n. 35
Knutsson, F. B. 60 n. 13, 64 nn. 31–32
Kobelski, P. J. 328 n. 3
Koch, K. 370 n. 26
Koehler, L. 70, 70 n. 3, 139 n. 4
Kohz, A. 58 n. 3
Komoróczy, G. 91 n. 59
König, E. 9 n. 6
Kooij, G. van der 36 n. 11
Kottsieper, I. 45, 46 n. 4, 47 n. 18
Kovacs, M. G. 549, 549 n. 12, 553 n. 24
Kraemer, C. J., Jr. 446 nn. 8–9
Kraemer, D. 92 n. 64

Krahmalkov, C. R. 368 n. 14, 502 n. 34
Kramer, S. N. 554 n. 27, 585 n. 1, 586 n. 4, 587, 587 n. 7, 587 nn. 9–10, 588 n. 12, 589 n. 14, 590 nn. 17–18, 593 n. 31, 595 n. 43
Kraus, F. R. 79, 79 n. 2, 82 n. 15, 83 n. 16, 83 n. 22, 84–86, 86 n. 32, 87–89, 90 n. 53, 90 n. 55, 93 n. 66, 568 n. 32
Krebernik, M. 177 n. 1, 629 n. 6, 637, 637 nn. 76–77
Krinski, J. L. 349, 350
Kristensen, A. L. 60 n. 13
Kronholm, T. 108 n. 1, 109 n. 8, 110 n. 11, 114 n. 49
Ktesias 322 n. 21
Kubíčková, V. 274 n. 22
Kugel, J. L. 325
Kuhn, H. W. 185 n. 17
Kuhn, K. G. 181 n. 1
Kümmel, H. 534–36, 538, 538 nn. 14–15
Kümmel, W. G. 458 n. 22
Kutscher, E. Y. 183 n. 11, 193 n. 1, 200, 200 n. 24, 361 n. 8
Kutscher, R. 201 nn. 31–32, 202
Kwasman, T. 476 n. 20
Kyrieleis, H. 395 n. 9

Labat, R. 47 n. 16
Lacheman, E. R. 568 n. 31
Lackenbacher, S. 551 n. 17
Lacoque, A. 262 n. 3
Laessøe, J. 86 n. 33, 473 n. 14
Lafont, B. 178, 178 n. 7
Lagarde, P. de 72 n. 11, 435 n. 11
Lagrange, M. J. 49 n. 29
Lambdin, T. O. 287 n. 17
Lambert, M. 99 n. 6, 201 n. 32
Lambert, W. G. 46, 46 nn. 8–9, 545 n. 4, 548 n. 6, 549 n. 9, 552 n. 19, 556 n. 31, 591 n. 24, 628, 628 n. 5, 629, 629 n. 11, 629 nn. 13–14
Landsberger, B. 90, 91 n. 58, 475 n. 20, 543 n. 3, 619 n. 1
Lane, E. W. 188 n. 33, 637 n. 76, 638 n. 85
Lanfranchi, G. B. 60 n. 13
Langdon, S. 587 n. 10
Laroche, E. 423, 426 n. 18, 578, 578 n. 9, 579–80
Larsen, M. T. 47 n. 14, 175 n. 41
Larson, E. 351 n.
Lassner, J. 129 n. 27, 130 n. 28, 131 n. 29, 131 n. 33
Lausberg, H. 66 n. 41
Layton, S. C. 179 n. 11, 394 n. 1, 394 n. 5
Leander, P. 7 n. 1, 9 nn. 5–6, 11 n. 14, 198 n. 15, 199 n. 22, 429 n. 35
Leclair, H. 446 n. 6
Leemans, W. F. 90, 90 n. 56
Lehmann, E. 475 n. 20
Lemaire, A. 367 n. 12, 381, 381 n. 9, 394 n. 5, 395 n. 9, 424 n. 3, 425 n. 8
Lemche, N. P. 108 n. 2
Le Roy, C. 432 n. 49
Leslau, W. 183 n. 8, 637, 637 n. 79
Levene, A. 109 n. 8
Levenson, J. D. 488 n. 53
Levi Della Vida, G. 496, 496 nn. 2–4, 497 nn. 8–11, 498 n. 18, 503, 503 n. 38, 504 n. 42
Levine, B. A. 32 nn. 3–4, 32 n. 6, 70, 70 nn. 4–5, 71 n. 9, 142 n. 15, 150 nn. 20–21, 168 n. 24
Levinson, S. C. 64 n. 31
Lewis, D. M. 322 n. 21
Lewis, N. 454 n. 8
Licht, J. 76 n. 19, 162 n. 5, 208, 208 n. 6
Liddell, H. G. 66 n. 40, 346 n. 1, 455 n. 15
Lidzbarski, M. 48 n. 26, 57 n.
Lieberman, S. J. 47 n. 17, 79 n. 2, 81 n. 5, 82 n. 13, 83, 83 n. 22, 84 n. 23, 88 nn. 46–47, 89 n. 52, 91 n. 59, 457 n. 19
Linant, P. 440 n. 27
Lindenberger, J. M. 45, 45 n. 4
Lipiński, E. P. 47 n. 17, 178 n. 10, 394 n. 5, 402 n. 21, 406 n. 25, 436 n. 12, 439 n. 23, 487 n. 52, 488 n. 53
Littmann, E. 58 n. 4, 497 n. 10, 498 n. 16
Littré, E. 184 n. 12
Liverani, M. 559, 559 nn. 1–2, 560, 561 n. 3, 561 n. 6, 562 n. 7, 566, 566 n. 23, 566 n. 25, 567, 567 nn. 27–29, 568, 568 n. 33, 569, 569 n. 39, 571, 571 n. 48, 572
Livingstone, A. 389 n., 548 n. 5, 557 n. 37, 592 n. 27
Lloyd, G. E. R. 175 n. 41
Lohse, E. 168 n. 23, 185 n. 17
Loukianoff, G. 440 n. 28
Lozachmeur, H. 424 n. 3
Luckenbill, D. 152 n. 25
Lundberg, M. 209 n. 9
Luzzatto 346 n. 5

Machinist, P. 324 n. 72, 592 n. 29
Macholz, G. C. 373 n. 42
MacKenzie, D. N. 415 n. 32
Maier, W. A. 163 n. 8
Maimonides 347 n. 7
Malkiel, Y. 16 n. 9
Malul, M. 614, 614 n. 8
Maori, Y. 204 n.
Marello, P. 178, 178 n. 3
Marks, J. H. 552 n. 19
Martínez, F. G. 208 n. 4, 280 n. 12
Marzal, A. 606 n. 17
Masica, C. P. 62 n. 19
Masᶜūdi 119
Mathews, H. J. 346 n. 2

Matter, E. A. 294 n. 2
Mayer, W. 473 n. 13, 568 n. 31
Mayerson, P. 448 nn. 11–12
Mazar, B. 151, 151 n. 24, 394 n. 3
McCarter, P. K., Jr. 169 n. 25, 320 n. 13, 632 n. 36
McCullough, W. S. 385 n. 2
McKane, W. 53, 53 n. 56, 54, 54 n. 59
Mércérian, J. 295 n. 6
Meek, T. J. 594 n. 34
Meier, C. 175 n. 41
Meier, G. 486 n. 46, 486 nn. 48–49, 490 n. 59, 491 n. 63, 492 n. 72
Meier, S. A. 66 n. 37, 66 n. 42
Melamed, E. Z. 363 n. 9
Mendelsohn, I. 320 n. 13
Menzel, B. 476 n. 20
Meshorer, Y. 453 n. 4
Mettinger, T. D. N. 323 n. 24
Metzger, H. 423
Metzger, M. 287 n. 19
Meyer, D. R. 179 n. 14
Meyer, W. 574 n. 6
Meyers, C. 126 n. 23
Michel, C. 47 n. 12
Michel, D. 174 n. 39
Mieroop, M. van de 93 n. 68
Miles, J. C. 89 n. 50
Milgrom, J. 69, 69 n. 1, 70, 71 n. 7, 71 n. 9, 348 n. 13
Milik, J. T. 61 n. 15, 207–8, 208 nn. 3–4, 212, 212 n. 13, 213, 213 n. 19, 215 n. 20, 217, 219, 221, 230, 236, 277, 277 n. 1, 278 nn. 2–3, 278 n. 5, 280 n. 10, 327 n. 1, 328 n. 3
Millard, A. R. 394 n. 1
Mingote, L. S. 426 n. 16
Mintz, A. 506 n. 4
Modi, J. J. 413, 413 nn. 12–13
Montgomery, J. A. 67 n. 46, 262 n. 3, 270
Moor, J. C. de 77 n. 22, 593 n. 30, 627 n. 2, 630 n. 21, 636–37, 637 nn. 72–73, 638 n. 82, 638 n. 86
Moore, C. A. 164 n. 13
Morag, S. 200 n. 23
Moran, W. L. 51 n. 43, 83 n. 22, 142, 566 n. 25, 567 n. 29
Moreshet, M. 193 n. 5
Moscati, S. 368 n. 20
Müller, C. 396, 396 n. 14
Muffs, Y. 284 n. 5, 624, 624 n. 15, 625, 625 n. 17
Murphy, R. E. 596 n. 49
Murray, R. 109 n. 8

Nashef, K. 484 n. 41
Naveh, J. 279 n. 9, 368 n. 19, 389, 389 n. 1, 394 n. 6, 395 n. 9, 399, 402 n. 21, 453 n. 4, 632 n. 39
Netter, S. Z. 349, 349 n. 16, 350
Neumann, G. 426, 426 nn. 15–16
Newsom, C. 279 n. 8
Nitzan, B. 76 n. 19, 197 n. 10, 198 n. 13
Noth, M. 108 n. 3, 286, 286 n. 10, 366 n. 3, 366 nn. 5–6, 367 n. 8, 368 n. 13
Nougayrol, J. 574 n. 5, 580
Nyberg, H. S. 290, 290 n. 27, 413, 413 nn. 18–20, 414, 416

Obermann, J. 631 n. 30
O'Callaghan, R. T. 285 n. 7
O'Connor, M. P. 96, 96 n. 2
Oded, B. 322 n. 19
Oden, R. A. 631 n. 28
Oelsner, J. 568 n. 31
Oesterley, W. O. E. 52
Ogden, G. 171 n. 31, 172 n. 34
Oldenburg, U. 628 n. 4, 629 n. 7, 630 nn. 25–26, 637 n. 72, 639 n. 92, 639 n. 94
O'Leary, D. 25 n. 28
Olivier, H. 91 n. 59
Olmo Lete, G. del 638 n. 87
Olyan, S. M. 632 n. 33
Opificius, R. 553 n. 23
Oppenheim, A. L. 53 n. 56, 88 n. 44, 164 n. 15, 317 n. 1, 318 n. 3, 318 n. 5, 319 n. 10, 348 n. 13, 478 n. 26, 527 n. 13, 528 n. 18, 633 nn. 46–47
Østrup, J. 58 n. 4
Otzen, B. 380, 380 n. 5
Owen, D. I. 86 n. 29, 573 n. 1, 578

Pagis, D. 505, 506, 506 n. 3, 512, 515–16, 519, 522
Palma, L. 436 n. 14, 438
Paper, H. H. 3 nn. 5–6, 4 n. 7
Pardee, D. 59 n. 7, 64 nn. 31–32, 65 n. 34, 66 nn. 43–44, 628 n. 4
Paret, R. 110 n. 19
Parker, S. 607 n. 22
Parkinson, D. B. 64 n. 29
Parpola, S. 45, 46 n. 6, 47, 47 nn. 14–15, 317 n. 1, 318 n. 6, 440 n. 25, 474 n. 15, 475 n. 17, 476 n. 20, 484 n. 41, 492 nn. 65–67, 492 n. 69, 492 n. 71
Paul, S. M. 77 n. 22, 162, 162 n. 7, 550 n. 14, 592 n. 26, 596 n. 50
Payne-Smith, R. 42 n. 12
Pedersen, J. 179 n. 14
Pelliot, P. 412 n. 6, 415 n. 28
Perkins, J. B. W. 500 n. 25
Perlmann, M. 22 n. 13, 23 n. 20
Pfeiffer, R. H. 87, 87 n. 41
Phelps, M. B. 209 n. 9
Piamenta, M. 637 n. 74
Pinches, T. G. 535
Pingree, D. 476 n. 21, 629 n. 9

Pintore, F. 366 n. 4
Pitard, W. T. 394 n. 5
Plöger, O. 52, 52 n. 50, 262 n. 3
Pope, M. H. 348 n. 12, 488 n. 53, 493 n. 73, 585 n. 1, 586 n. 1, 593 n. 30, 595 n. 43, 628 n. 4, 630 n. 26
Porten, B. 40 n. 6, 49, 49 nn. 33–34, 50, 50 n. 42, 57 n. 1, 59 n. 10, 60 n. 10, 61 n. 16, 62 n. 18, 62 n. 20, 62 n. 23, 63 nn. 24–25, 65 n. 33, 428 n. 31, 428 n. 33
Porteous, N. W. 262 n. 3
Postgate, J. N. 323 n. 23, 489 n. 57, 492 n. 68, 492 n. 70
Pritchard, J. B. 70 n. 2, 118 n. 2
Procksch, O. 283 n. 1, 290
Proietti, G. 499 n. 22
Pryke, E. J. 186 n. 23
Puech, É. 32 n. 5, 39, 39 n. 1, 40–43, 186 n. 22, 186 n. 24, 188 n. 34, 394 n. 6, 395 n. 9, 441 n. 29

Qimḥi, D. 147 n. 18, 350, 350 n. 18
Qimḥi, J. 345–46, 346 n. 3
Qimron, E. 29 n., 193 nn. 3–4, 196 n. 9, 212 n. 16, 351 n., 356, 358, 358 n. 6, 359, 359 n. 7, 454 n. 11

Rabin, I. A. 41 n. 11, 204 n. 7
Rabinowitz, I. 208, 208 n. 5, 212, 212 nn. 14–15
Rad, G. von 51, 286, 286 n. 10, 290 n. 26
Rainey, A. F. 48, 48 n. 25, 51 n. 43, 141, 141 n. 12, 324 n. 29
Ravnitzky, Y. H. 14 n. 3
Reade, J. 318 n. 4, 324 n. 31
Redford, D. B. 321 n. 16, 561 n. 5
Reed, S. 209 n. 9
Regelson, A. 505–6, 506 n. 3, 509, 509 n. 5, 510–12, 521
Reiner, E. 478 n. 25, 629 n. 9
Reinhold, G. G. G. 394 n. 5
Reinink, G. J. 59 n. 6
Rendsburg, G. A. 399 n. 17
Reynolds, J. M. 500 n. 25
Riemschneider, K. K. 574 n. 5
Rigaux, B. 208 n. 2
Ringgren, H. 165 n. 19, 167 n. 21
Robert, J. 457 n. 20
Robert, L. 457 n. 20
Roberts, J. J. M. 629 n. 9, 630 n. 26
Robertson, A. T. 454 n. 9
Rochberg-Halton, F. 164 n. 15
Röllig, W. 48 n. 26, 49, 49 n. 34, 395 n. 9, 496 n. 2, 498, 498 n. 14
Rofé, A. 319 n. 8
Rohrkopf, F. 454 n. 10
Rosenau, H. 109 n. 7
Rosenthal, F. 22 n. 13, 348 n. 13, 632 n. 37
Ross, J. F. 395 n. 11
Rossini, K. C. 637 n. 76
Rothkoff, A. 92 n. 64
Rowley, H. H. 370 n. 28
Rüger, H. P. 52, 52 n. 49
Ryckmans, G. 633 n. 48, 634 n. 49, 634 n. 51, 634 n. 53, 635, 635 n. 57, 635 n. 59, 636, 636 n. 66, 636 n. 68, 637, 637 nn. 72–73, 637 n. 77, 638, 638 n. 81, 638 n. 83, 639 n. 93
Ryckmans, J. 634, 635 n. 56, 636 n. 70, 637 n. 75, 639 n. 94, 640, 640 n. 95

Saadiah ben Joseph 118–24
Sack, R. H. 526 n. 5
Saggs, H. W. F. 553 n. 23
Salonen, E. 60 n. 13, 63 n. 27, 64 n. 31, 67 n. 45
Salzberger, G. 119 n. 6
Samely, A. 63 n. 26
Sanders, J. A. 344 n. 44
Sanjana, D. D. P. 413
Sarfatti, G. B. 379 n. 2
Sarghissian, B. 295 n. 4, 297 n. 14
Sarna, N. M. 284 n. 3
Satran, D. 313 n. 16
Sauneron, S. 53 n. 55, 64 n. 31
Schaeffer, C. F. A. 574 n. 3
Schapka, U. 4 nn. 16–20, 5 nn. 21–23
Schatz, W. 284 n. 4
Schechter, S. 120 n. 8
Schiffman, L. H. 219 n. 22, 224 n. 23, 226, 227 n. 24, 229 n. 25, 254
Schiffman, P. 92 n. 64
Schlatter, A. 454 n. 12
Scholem, G. 509 n. 5
Schott, A. 593 n. 30
Schröder, P. 434, 434 n. 5
Schubert, K. 58 n. 3
Schürer, E. 33 n. 8, 338 n. 29, 452 n. 2
Schuller, E. 201 n. 28
Schwenzner, W. 538 n. 11
Scott, R. 66 n. 40, 346 n. 1, 455 n. 15
Scullard, H. H. 174 n. 40
Sefati, Y. 586 n. 4, 587, 587 n. 7, 588 n. 10, 589 n. 14, 590 nn. 17–18, 593 n. 30, 595 n. 43
Segal, J. B. 448 n. 10
Segal, M. H. 203 n. 3
Segert, S. 29, 29 n. 1, 49 n. 35, 264 n. 5, 264 n. 7, 265 n. 9, 273 n. 18, 275 n. 25, 427 n. 27, 429 n. 35, 429 n. 37, 429 n. 41
Seifert, J. 274 n. 22
Seligmann, Y. A. 35 n. 10
Sellin, E. 48 n. 23
Selms, A. van 346 n. 6
Seux, J.-J. 50 n. 38
Shaffer, A. 179 n. 11, 393 n.
Shaked, S. 279 nn. 6–7, 279 n. 9
Sharp, R. 413

Shea, W. H. 368 n. 14
Shiff, L. 527 n. 11
Shiloh, Y. 462 n. 2
Shouriah, L. M. 412 n. 8, 413
Sidersky, D. 19 n. 2
Siegel, J. P. 354 n. 3
Sigrist, M. 552 n. 19, 574 n. 6
Simone, C. de 499 nn. 21–22
Singer, I. 569 n. 37, 578 n. 10
Sjöberg, Å. 477 n. 22, 552 n. 21, 589 n. 13
Skaist, A. 580, 624 n. 13
Skehan, P. 45 n. 1
Skinner, J. 284 n. 6, 285, 285 n. 8
Skjærvø, P. O. 281 n. 13
Slotty, F. 67 n. 47
Smith, D. L. 373 n. 41
Smith, G. A. 347
Smith, W. R. 636, 637 n. 72, 638, 638 n. 84, 639 n. 90
Soden, W. von 46, 47 n. 17, 317 n. 2, 318 n. 6, 319 n. 10, 383 n. 17, 543, 543 n. 1, 543 n. 3, 548, 548 n. 7, 555, 557, 591 n. 25, 592 n. 29, 594 n. 37, 595 n. 42, 633 nn. 47–48, 637 n. 78
Sokoloff, M. 206 n. 14, 347 n. 7
Soldt, W. H. van 48 n. 21
Sontheimer, W. 174 n. 40
Spar, I. 535
Speiser, E. A. 82 n. 11, 284, 284 n. 3, 289 n. 21, 487 n. 50
Sperber, A. 72 n. 11
Sperber, D. 446 n. 7
Spicehandler, E. 506 n. 4
Spier, J. 553 n. 23
Starcky, J. 39, 382 n. 11
Steiner, R. C. 275 n. 25
Steingass, F. 183 n. 8
Steinkeller, P. 85 n. 24, 589 n. 16, 620, 620 n. 4, 621, 622 nn. 6–9, 623 n. 12
Stemberger, G. 111 nn. 20–23, 113 n. 43
Stephan, H. 597 n. 51
Stern, P. D. 630 n. 23, 632 n. 35
Steuernagel, C. 347 n. 8
Stol, M. 85 n. 27, 568 n. 32
Stolper, M. W. 528 n. 15
Stolz, F. 628 n. 4
Stone, M. E. 41, 294 nn. 1–2, 295 n. 8, 296 nn. 10–11, 296 n. 13, 312–13, 313 nn. 15–16, 314 n. 17, 315, 315 n. 20
Strack, H. L. 111 nn. 20–23, 113 n. 43
Strassmaier, J. N. 523 n.
Strothmann, W. 71 n. 10
Strugnell, J. 197 n. 11
Suffrin, A. E. 159 n. 1, 164 n. 13
Sukenik, E. L. 182, 182 n. 2
Sweet, R. F. G. 81 nn. 5–6, 92 n. 63
Sznycer, M. 425 n. 9, 435 n. 6, 436 n. 13, 628 n. 4, 630 n. 26, 638 n. 86
Szubin, H. Z. 40 n. 6, 428 n. 31, 428 n. 33

al-Ṭabari, J. 22, 22 n. 13, 23, 23 n. 14, 23 nn. 19–20, 24, 24 nn. 23–25, 25, 25 nn. 28–30, 26, 26 n. 31, 26 n. 34, 119 n. 6
Tadmor, H. 317 n. 1, 320 n. 14, 322 n. 19, 323 n. 25, 324 n. 27, 324 n. 31, 565 n. 22
Tallqvist, K. 475 n. 20, 479 n. 27, 491 nn. 63–64
Talmon, S. 325, 328 nn. 2–4, 329 nn. 6–7, 333 n. 11, 335 n. 18, 337 nn. 27–28, 338 nn. 30–31, 339 nn. 35–36
Tammuz, O. 82, 82 n. 14
Tarragon, J.-M. de 150 nn. 20–21
Tawil, H. 348 n. 13
Te Velde, H. 631 n. 28
Teixidor, J. 394 n. 5, 424, 424 n. 6, 425 n. 7, 426, 426 n. 15, 426 n. 20, 427–28, 428 n. 29, 428 n. 32, 429, 429 n. 36, 429 n. 42, 430 n. 43, 433, 433 n. 4, 434, 436 n. 14, 438 nn. 16–17, 440 n. 29, 457 n. 18, 633 n. 45
Thackeray, H. St. J. 37
al-Thaᶜlabi, A. 23, 23 n. 15, 23 n. 19, 24–26, 26 n. 31, 26 n. 35, 119 n. 6, 129 n. 27
Thompson, H. O. 368 n. 14, 390
Thompson, R. C. 593 n. 30
Thompson, T. L. 108 n. 2
Thomsen, M. L. 615 n. 9
Toorn, K. van der 483 n. 39
Toy, C. J. 52
Tsukimoto, A. 574 n. 6, 577, 579, 624 n. 14

Ullendorff, E. 132 n. 36
Unger, E. 527 n. 13
Urbach, E. E. 36 n. 12, 40 n. 5
Utzschneider, H. 370 n. 26

Vajda, G. 20 n. 5
VanderKam, J. C. 339 n. 37
Van Seters, J. 283 n. 1, 289 n. 23
Vanstiphout, H. L. J. 59 n. 6
Vattioni, F. 50 n. 36
Vaux, R. de 108 n. 3, 208, 280 n. 10, 283 n. 1, 286, 286 n. 11, 323 n. 24, 370 n. 28, 371 nn. 30–31
Vellas, V. M. 262 n. 3
Vermes, G. 162 n. 5, 208 n. 4
Vogüé, M. de 387 n. 7
Vycichl, W. 435 nn. 10–11

Wacholder, B. Z. 208, 208 n. 7, 210 n. 10, 211 n. 11, 212–13, 213 n. 18, 216–17, 219, 221 n., 222, 230, 236, 238, 240–41, 244–45, 250–51, 336, 336 n. 22, 338, 340 n. 38
Walker, C. B. F. 477 n. 22, 593 n. 29
Wallach, Y. 505–6, 506 n. 3, 515–16, 519–21
Walls, N. 631 n. 28
Waltke, B. 96, 96 n. 2

Wasserfall, R. 126 nn. 21–22
Watanabe, K. 440 n. 25, 474 n. 15, 475 n. 17, 492 nn. 66–67, 492 n. 69, 492 n. 71
Waterston, A. 628 n. 3, 631, 631 n. 32, 632
Watt, W. M. 24 n. 21
Weber, R. 274 n. 20
Weidner, E. 319 n. 10, 484, 484 nn. 41–42, 494 n. 75
Weinberg, J. P. 365 n. 2, 367 n. 10, 370 n. 27, 370 n. 29, 372 n. 37, 373 nn. 39–40, 374 n. 44
Weinfeld, M. 91, 92 n. 62, 369 n. 21, 468 n. 1, 476 n. 20
Weippert, M. 633 n. 45, 633 n. 47, 634 n. 49
Weisberg, D. 536
Weiser, A. 108 n. 3
Weiss, M. 77 n. 22
Wenham, G. J. 290 n. 25
Wensinck, A. J. 24 n. 22
Wente, E. F. 62 n. 17
Werner, W. 162, 162 n. 6
West, E. W. 413, 413 n. 10, 416 n. 34
West, L. C. 444 n. 4
Westbrook, R. 85 n. 24, 86 n. 29, 90, 90 n. 54, 621 n. 5, 624 n. 16
Westendorf, W. 435 n. 10
Westenholz, Å. 545 n. 4, 556 n. 32
Westenholz, J. G. 545 n. 4, 549 n. 10, 556 n. 32, 575 n. 6, 585 n. 1, 588 n. 10, 591 nn. 21–22, 593 n. 29, 596 n. 46, 596 n. 49
Westermann, C. 108 n. 3, 284 n. 4, 373 n. 41
White, S. A. 338 n. 32
Whiting, R. M. 623 n. 11
Wilcke, C. 85 n. 24, 556 n. 34
Wilhelm, G. 574 n. 6
Williamson, H. G. M. 367 n. 10
Wilson, J. A. 631 n. 28
Wilson, R. R. 493 n. 73
Winckworth, C. P. T. 413, 413 n. 15, 414–15
Winston, D. 165 n. 17
Winter, I. 398 n. 16
Winter, M. M. 71 n. 10
Winter, W. 58 n. 3
Wise, M. 277 n. 1, 278 n. 4, 336, 336 nn. 23–25, 338
Wolff, H. W. 370 n. 29, 372 n. 35
Woude, A. S. van der 328 n. 3
Wright, A. G. 165, 165 n. 18
Wright, B. G. 313 n. 16
Wright, D. P. 69 n. 1, 334 n. 11
Wright, W. 446 n. 6, 448 n. 14
Wunsch, C. 537, 537 n. 8
Wyatt, N. 631, 631 n. 32, 632

Xella, P. 629, 629 n. 6
Xenophon 322 n. 21
Xlat'ec'i, G. 295 n. 6

Yaakov, Eliezer ben 347
Yadin, Y. 76 n. 19, 453 n. 4
Yahalom, Y. 8 n. 2, 200 n. 23
Yalon, H. 74 n. 14, 75 n. 17, 347 n. 7
Yardeni, A. 49, 49 n. 34, 50, 50 n. 42, 60 n. 10
Yaron, R. 619 n. 2
Yassif, E. 131 n. 30
Yon, M. 435 n. 6, 440 n. 27, 639 n. 91
Young, M. J. L. 64 n. 29
Younger, K. L. 49, 49 n. 30
Yovsēp'ianc', S. 295, 295 n. 3

Zadok, R. 484 n. 41, 488 n. 53
Zamakhsharī 119 n. 6, 129 n. 27
Závada, V. 274 n. 22
Zayadine, F. 368 n. 14, 391
Zeidel, M. 201 n. 29
Zevit, Z. 275 n. 24, 357 n. 5
Ziegler, K. 174 n. 40
Zijl, P. J. van 554 n. 28
Zilliacus, H. 59 n. 8
Zimmerli, W. 290 n. 26, 373 nn. 41–42, 374 n. 43
Zimmern, H. 318 n. 7
Zorn, J. 51 n. 43

Index of Scripture

Genesis
1–11 107–8
1:28 125
5:2 15
6:5 228
7:16 15
8:4 110, 110 n. 11
8:7 4
8:21 228
8:22 222
9:2 255
9:12 359
10:1 197 n. 10
10:24 287
11:1 285
11:10–26:35 108
11:16 287
11:31 109
12 14–15
12–25(26) 108
12:10–20 110
12:13 110 n. 14
12:15 110 nn. 16–17
12:17 110
12:17–20 111
13:10 289
14 283, 285–86, 288
14:1–11 284
14:3 286
14:5 287
14:6 287
14:10 287
14:11 284
14:12–13 284
14:13 287
14:14 284, 287, 290
14:15 145–46
14:17–24 111
14:18 111
14:18–20 284, 328 n. 3
14:19 287
15:4 112 n. 27
15:9–10 343 n. 42
16 112
16:12 112
17:12–13 87 n. 42
17:14 157
17:16 247
17:17 53

Genesis (cont.)
17:19–21 126 n. 23
17:23 87 n. 42
17:27 87 n. 42
18:1 113
18:11 346
18:12 349
18:12–15 53
18:15–33 113 n. 42
18:28 95
19 289
19:1–29 113 n. 45
19:30–38 113 n. 48
19:31–35 128
20 14
20:1–8 110
20:5 110 n. 14
20:9 219
21:9 53, 112
21:9–21 112
22 114
23:9 90 n. 54
24 114
24:1 347
24:12 169 n. 27
25:13–15 26
26:1–11 110
27:1 53 n. 57
27:20 169 n. 27
28:3–4 126 n. 23
30:11 163
30:13 163
31:40 72 n. 13, 73
31:46 63 n. 26
32:4–5 65
33:1 145
33:18 290
34:25–31 147
35:11–12 126 n. 23
37:36 321
38:1 201
38:6 15
38:6–30 125
38:16–18 552
39:1 321
39:15 55
40:20 213
41:3 55
41:43 380

Genesis (cont.)
45:5 162
46:33 171
47:3 171
47:27 126 n. 23
48:3–4 126 n. 23
49:7 147, 154

Exodus
1:15–22 357
1:22 357
3 358
3:3 358
3:15 357
4:23 358
4:30 358
5:1 358
6 358
6:23 367–68
7:3 358
7:9 358
7:13 358
7:16 358
7:20 359, 362
7:22 361
7:26 358
8:1 359, 362
8:2–3 362
8:3 359
8:13 359
8:16 358
8:17 359, 362
8:20 359
9:1 358
9:3 359
9:12 358, 361
9:13 358
9:14 359, 362
9:19 360
9:20 360
9:22 360
9:25 360
9:27 359
9:34 359
10:3 358
10:4–5 360
10:5 361, 363
10:15 360–61, 363
10:19 363

Exodus (cont.)
10:20 358, 361
10:22 360, 363
10:23 360, 363
10:27 358, 361
11:9 361
11:9–10 361
11:10 358, 361
12:15 157
12:16 337
12:19 157
12:26 204
14:8 358
15:3 219
15:14 95
19:5 247
21:2–4 91
21:5–6 91
21:6 87, 87 n. 39
24:1 367
24:6 381–82
24:7 87
24:9 367
24:18 316
25:2 371
28:1 367
28:11 51
33:1 316
33:20 315
34:29–35 346 n. 1
35:5 370
35:21 371
35:22 370
35:29 371
36:3 371

Leviticus
3:1 15
7:16 317
7:18 74
7:20 157
10:1 367
11:13 4
11:14 4
11:15 4
11:16 4
11:17 5
11:18 4–5
12:2 75
15:19 74–75
15:19–33 121 n. 11
15:20 75
15:24 75
15:25 75
15:26 75
15:33 75
16:30 42
16:34 252
17:10 157

Leviticus (cont.)
18:19 75, 121 n. 11, 122
18:29 134
19:7 74
19:18 227
19:19 41
20:3–6 157
20:4 250
20:18 75, 75 n. 18
20:21 74–75
22:11 87 n. 42
22:18 317, 371
22:21 317
22:23 317
23:8 337
23:9–21 339
23:11 339
23:15 339
23:16 339
23:30 157
23:39 337
24:7 596 n. 48
25:15–16 225
26 127
26:3–26 156 n. 27
26:9 126 n. 23, 127
26:21 168 n. 24
26:23 168 n. 24
26:24 168 n. 24
26:27 168 n. 24
26:28 168 n. 24
26:33 155
26:38 155–56
26:39–41 156
26:40 168 n. 24
26:41 154–55, 168 n. 24
26:44 73

Numbers
1:7 368
2:3 368
3:2 367
3:4 367
6:22–27 39
6:25 39
7:12 368–69
7:17 368
9:22 11
10:14 368
11:12 52
12:3 348 n. 13
12:6–8 607
12:8 316
13:2 173 n. 37
15:3 317
16:1 102, 104
16:1–18:27 102
16:3 104
16:7 173 n. 37

Numbers (cont.)
16:10 104
16:13 102, 104
16:16 104
16:28 104
16:29 104
16:31 104
17:3 102, 104
17:6 104
17:10 104–5
17:23 104–5
17:24 104–5
17:27 104–5
18:20 104–5
18:27 102, 104–5
21:18 369
22–24 35
24:7 197 n. 10
24:15–19 156
25:15 555 n. 29
26:54 194
26:60 367
26:61 367
27 54
27:12–26 54
27:21 197 n. 11
28:18 337
29:39 371
31:2 244
31:26 254
32:7 144
32:9 144
33:52 151
33:54 194

Deuteronomy
1:22 98
2:10–12 286
2:20 287
4:8 245
4:11 98, 98 n. 5
4:34 358
5:15 205 n. 10
5:23 98
6:20 204, 204 n. 9
6:21 204
6:22 358
7:3–4 134 n. 37
7:6 247
7:13 637 n. 76
7:19 358
7:26 74
8:3 96, 98
8:16 96, 98
8:20 157
9:1 157
9:3 157
11:28 252
12:2 151

Deuteronomy (cont.)
12:6 371
12:29 157
13:3 252
13:14 252
14:2 247
14:12 4
14:13 4
14:14 4
14:15 4
14:16 5
14:17 5
15:1–3 91
15:7–11 92
15:12–15 91
15:16–18 91
15:17 87 n. 40
15:18 92
16:8 337
17:18–20 197
18:1 40
18:12 157
19:1 157
22:9 41
23:1 320, 322
23:8 73
23:11 169–70
24:4 74
25:6 219
26:5 151–52
26:8 205 n. 10
28:29 244
28:68 216
29:2 358
29:10 342
29:19 219
31:2 345, 347, 349
32:3 178
32:7 195
32:22 188
34:7 345, 347–48, 350
34:11 358

Joshua
2:15 552
9 342 n. 40
9:11 255
9:21 342
9:27 342
14:8 144
18:6 163
18:8 163
18:10 163

Judges
1:23 173 n. 37
3:2 359
5:2 372
5:9 372

Judges (cont.)
5:27 555
7:20 245
8:1 98
9:4 152
11:18 98, 98 n. 5
13:12 171
18:29 290

1 Samuel
2:3 238
2:8 369
2:14 435 n. 9
5:2 55
6:9 163 n. 13, 169, 169 n. 28, 170
6:12 169 n. 28
7:1 366
8 320
8:14–15 320
8:15 320
9:3 153
9:20 153
16:8 366
17:13 366
17:32 144
20:26 169–70
22:2 152
25:31 66
30:7–8 197 n. 11
31:2 366

2 Samuel
4:4 52
6:3 366, 380
6:4 366
6:20 228
11–12 130
13 131 n. 32
13:1 15
13:3 367
13:5 367
13:32 367
13:35 367
14:27 15
15:16 145
17:25 31
18:14 143–44
19:36 348 n. 13

1 Kings
1:33 380
2:5 31
2:24 290
2:32 31
4:11 366
4:14 366
10:1–13 120
10:22 3

1 Kings (cont.)
11:1–2 134 n. 37
11:1–8 135
11:3 130
12–14 135
12:27 145
13:11–31 36
14:20 367
15:25 367
15:27 367
15:31 367
21:19 513
22:1–28 36
22:9 320

2 Kings
2:1–2 316
3:26 212
4:9 253
4:42 379, 383
8:6 320
9 319
9:8 151
9:31–33 319
10:1 52
10:5 52
10:15 367
10:16 380
10:19 151
11:4–9 337
18:17 323
19:18 151
20:18 322
21:3 151
23:1 320
23:13 74 n. 15
24:15 319
25:19 320

Isaiah
1:13 74
6:1 488, 627 n. 1
6:2–3 315
6:6–9 479 n. 28
6:12 157
10:31 73
11 191, 198
11:2 197
11:3 191, 195–97
11:8 55 n. 62
11:9 55
13:2 369
13:5 148
14 489
14:12 489
16:8 13
18:2 323
19:15 219
21:15 69, 73

Isaiah (cont.)
22:3 72
22:24–25 379, 382
25:9 596 n. 47
27:13 152
28 188
28:2 188
28:2–3 187
28:11 212
28:15 187, 187 n. 27, 188
28:17–18 188
28:18 187, 187 n. 27, 188
28–29 188
29:6 188
29:13–14 144
30:22 75, 75 n. 18
32:1 369
32:1–8 369
32:5 41, 369–70
32:7 369
32:8 369
33:3 72
33:15 195, 198
33:17 205
34:9 188
35:3–4 144
37:19 151
38:15 72
38:19 225
41:5 98 n. 4
41:7 139
41:22 221
42:9 221
43:9 221
43:18 221
45:7 203
46:8 144
46:9 221
48:3 221
49:17 132
50:6 346 n. 2
52:8 205–6
54:16 148
55:1 216
55:8–9 171 n. 31
55:11 212
56 322
56:3–4 321
56:5 325
57:8 593 n. 30
57:10 593 n. 30
58:2 256
59:20 252
59:23 52
61:8 212
65:11 163
66:3 596 n. 48
66:5 70–71, 77
66:10 596 n. 47

Isaiah (cont.)
66:12 55 n. 62
66:15 188

Jeremiah
1:10 151
2:5 72 n. 12
3:16 126 n. 23, 127
3:19 256
4:9 144
4:25 73
6:8 72
6:14 512
8:11 512
9:9 73
10:13 223
10:16 203 n. 3
12:2 145
12:3 219
13:7 216
13:8 148
13:22 555 n. 29
13:26 555 n. 29
15:13 216
16:3 236
17:8 13
18:7 151
18:11 171 n. 31, 229
18:18 54
20:11 630
21:8 256
22:3 244
22:13 227
22:23 148
23:1–4 153
23:3 126 n. 23, 127
23:5 127
26:19 161 n. 4
28:17 36
28–29 373
29:2 319
29:21–24 36
29:24–32 36
31:11 212
31:28 151
32:20 358
33:3 252
33:26 53 n. 57
34:14 92
34:19 320
35:6 367
35:8 367
37:12 146–47, 147 n. 18
38:7 320
41:16 319
43:8 319 n. 12
48:41 144
49:19 201 n. 29
49:22 144

Jeremiah (cont.)
49:24 148
49:38 157
50:6–7 153
50:54 201 n. 29
51:16 223
52:15 51

Ezekiel
3:5 212
3:6 212
4:11 223
4:16 223
6:3 151
7:17 606 n. 18
7:19 77
7:19–20 75
7:20 77
11:16 157
16:5 194
16:7 587 nn. 5–6
16:33–34 552 n. 21
18:6 75–76, 121 n. 11
18:24 227
20:6 256
20:15 256
21:12 606 n. 18
22:10 75, 121 n. 11
22:26 250
22:27 151
22:29 227
23:5 232
23:12 323
23:17 72
23:18 72
23:28 72
24:8 244
25 157
25:7 157
25:9 256
25:12 244
28:1–10 493
29:4 346 n. 2
31:3 13
32:9 252
34 153–54
34:2–5 153
34:15–16 153
36:9–11 126 n. 23, 127
36:17 75, 133
36:32 212
38–39 197 n. 10
40–48 373
44–45 54
44:8 98 n. 4
46:12 371

Hosea
4:15 143 n. 16

Hosea (cont.)
7:11 145
7:13 72
9:17 69
10:1–2 143, 145
10:1–8 142
10:2 142–43, 143 n. 16, 144
11:4 346 n. 2
13:15 233
14:1 143 n. 16
14:5 371
14:8 596 n. 48

Joel
1:11 151
2:21 596 n. 47
2:23 596 n. 47
3:1–3 148
3:1–9 148
3:2 148–49
3:3 149
3:4–9 149

Amos
1:5 152
1:6–8 152
1:9–10 152
2:7 550 n. 14
4:5 371
6:3 70–71, 77, 98 n. 4
7:9 53 n. 57
7:16 53 n. 57

Jonah
3:10 162 n. 4

Micah
1:4 315
2:10 148
3:3 435 n. 9
4:1 205 n. 12
6:8 244
7:9 247

Nahum
1:2 227
3:5 555 n. 29
3:7 72

Habakkuk
1:12–13 197

Zephaniah
2:5 156

Zechariah
1:16 206 n. 14
8:5 53

Zechariah (cont.)
11:7 148
11:24 148
13:2 35

Malachi
1:14 41 n. 8
2:5–6 163
3:16 222
3:24 145

Psalms
1:3 13
7:10 219
9:4 212
12:3 41, 143
16:5 163
17:2 205
17:3 219
17:4 193
17:14 139
19:7 222
20 48 n. 18
20:4 596 n. 48
30:5 254
31:12 72
34:12 193
35:10 212
39:5 168
42:3 595 n. 42
45:2 51
47:10 369
48:6 235
51 130
51:8 220
54:8 371
55:22 143
56:10 212
63:2 595 n. 42
68:3 315
68:10 371
74:20 185, 185 n. 19
77:6 170, 171 n. 31
78 352, 357, 362
78:43 358
78:44 359–60, 362
78:45 362
78:46 360, 363
78:47 360, 363
78:48 360, 362
78:50 359–60, 363
78:51 361
83:12 369
88:7 185
92:13 15
94:19 55 n. 62
97:5 315
97:12 254
99:3 253

Psalms (cont.)
99:5 253
102:13 172
105 352, 357, 362–63
105:26 357
105:27 358
105:28 360
105:29 359, 362
105:30 359, 362
105:31 359, 362
105:32–33 357
105:34–35 357
105:35 360, 363
105:36 357, 361
107:40–41 370
110 291
110:1–7 328 n. 3
110:3 371
113:7–8 370
115:5 194
115:7 194
119:7 256
119:24 55 n. 62
119:76 153
119:77 55 n. 62
119:106 256
119:108 371
119:164 256
135:7 223
135:9 358
137 263
140:6 148
143:3 185
145:2 228
145:16 236
149:7 196 n. 10

Job
5:26 347 n. 7
12:21 369
12:24 145
15:23 73
16:10 346 n. 2
18:18 69, 73
20:8 73
21:17 147–48
21:17–18 148
21:28 369–70
28:7 4
30:10 74 n. 15
30:15 369
30:30 188
33:6 182–83
34:18 370
38:7 639
38:24 146
38:41 4
39:3 148
39:8 173 n. 37

Job (cont.)
40:26 346
42:10 206 n. 14

Proverbs
1–8 54
1:2–6 54
2:13 222
2:16 143
3:18 55
3:19–20 55
5:10 143
6:23 256
7:5 143
8 54
8:12 53, 192
8:16 369
8:22 53
8:22–31 53
8:24–25 53–54
8:30 45–47 n. 17, 51
8:30–31 55 n. 62
9:1 53
12:16 225
13:23 227
16:8 227
16:10–15 54
16:33 163
17:3 219
17:7 369–70
17:20 45
17:26 369–70
18:4 607 n. 18
20:5 607 n. 18
21:27 74
24:7 254
25:2–7 54
26:5 123
26:28 143
28:27 250
30:20 592 n. 27
31:1 179
31:4 179

Ruth
2:3 168–69, 169 n. 26, 170
4:16 52
4:19 368
4:19–20 128
4:20 368

Canticles
1:2 591 n. 23
1:4 595
1:10 346 n. 2
1:13 594 n. 35
1:14 594 n. 35
1:16 594 n. 35
2:9 14 n. 1

Canticles (cont.)
4:15 14 n. 1
5:1 592 n. 27, 597 n. 51
5:4 593 n. 30
5:10–15 13
5:13 346 n. 2
7:2 47 n. 17, 51, 369
7:3 381–82
7:9 14, 14 n. 1, 16 n. 12
8:10 587 n. 5

Qohelet
1:2 165
1:4 171, 171 n. 33, 173 n. 38
1:10 171, 173 n. 38
1:12–2:23 172
1:12–2:26 168
1:13 168, 172–73, 173 n. 37
1:14 171
1:16–17 173 n. 38
1:17 173 n. 37
2:1 168, 173, 173 n. 37
2:3 168, 173 n. 37
2:4 171
2:4–6 390
2:10 167
2:11 171
2:12–13 173 n. 38
2:14 165–66, 170
2:15 165–66, 170, 173 n. 37
2:21 167, 172, 173 n. 38
3:5–6 154
3:11 166–67, 171–72, 172 n. 34–35, 173 n. 38
3:14 171, 173 n. 38
3:19–20 165–66
3:21–22 167
3:22 167
5:5 148
5:17 167
5:18 167
6:4 237
6:12 167
7:3 173 n. 37
7:4 173 n. 37
7:13 167, 171
7:14 167
7:17 166
7:23 167–68, 172–73, 173 nn. 37–38
7:23–28 168
7:25 168, 170, 170 n. 30, 171 n. 31, 173 nn. 37–38
7:27 170, 171 n. 31
7:27–28 170, 173 n. 38
7:29 171 n. 31, 173 n. 38
8:14 166, 171, 219

Qohelet (cont.)
8:17 166–67, 171, 172 n. 35
9:1 167, 173 n. 37, 219
9:2 165–66
9:3 165–66
9:4 167
9:5–6 167
9:6 167, 171, 173 n. 38
9:7 173 n. 37
9:9 167
9:10 166, 166 n. 20, 167, 170, 170 n. 30, 171, 171 nn. 31–32, 172, 173 n. 38
9:11 165–66
10:2 173 n. 37
10:10 173 n. 38
11:5 167, 172 n. 35
11:8 167
11:9 173 n. 36, 198
12:5 171, 173 n. 38
12:8 165
12:12 173 n. 36
12:13–14 173 n. 36

Lamentations
1:2 346
1:8 212
1:8–9 133
1:9 555 n. 29
1:17 73, 75, 133
2:13 201 n. 29
4 263
4:5 52 n. 48
4:16 139, 147
5 263

Esther
1:12 322
1:15 322
2:3 322
2:7 52
2:21 322
3:7 163, 163 n. 13
4:5 322
4:14 164 n. 13
6:1 73
6:9 380
6:14 322
7:9 322
9:24 163, 163 n. 13
9:24–26 164 n. 13

Daniel
1:1–2:4 262
1:3 322
1:7 322
1:10 322
1:18 322

Daniel (cont.)
2 66
2:13 428 n. 30
2:15 428 n. 30
2:16 430 n. 44
2:18 430 n. 44
2:20–23 273
2:30 66
2:36 67
2:49 430 n. 44
3 66
3:33 264, 273
4:6 219
4:7–9 273
4:11–14 273
4:31–32 264, 273
5:27 50 n. 37
6 316
6:27–28 273
7 54
7:9–10 273
7:13–14 273
7:16 430 n. 44
7:23–27 273
8 262, 268, 271–72
8–9 262
8–12 261–62
8:1–22 272
8:23 265–66
8:23–26 261–63, 265, 267, 272
8:24 266–67, 267 n. 12
8:24–25 266
8:25 266–67, 267 n. 12
8:26 220, 262, 266–67, 271
9 262, 268, 271–72
9:20–23 272
9:24 262, 267–69
9:24–27 261–63, 265–69, 272
9:25 267–69
9:25–26 263, 268
9:25–27 268
9:26 268–69
9:27 263, 268–69
10–11 271
10:1–11:2 272
10:5 271
10:5–6 262–63, 271
10:6 271
11 263, 271–72
11:2–45 261–63, 271–72, 274
11:10 272
11:16 256
11:24 272
11:35 272

Daniel (cont.)
11:40 272
11:41 256
12 262, 270–72
12:1 269–71
12:1–3 261–63, 265, 269, 271
12:1–4 272
12:2 270
12:3 262, 270–71
12:4 220, 262–63, 270–71
12:5 272
12:5–7 273
12:5–13 272
12:7 272–73
12:9 220, 273
12:9–13 272
12:10 272–73

Ezra
1:1–4 374
1:3 374
1:4 371
1:6 372
2:42 31
2:43–54 342, 342 n. 40
2:45 31
2:46 32
2:59–60 31
2:68 372
3:5 371–72
4:14–15 65
4:16 65
6 54
6:3–5 374
6:22 145
7:11–12 54
8:28 371
9:11 75, 133
10:25 334

Nehemiah
6:10 264
7:45 31
7:46–56 342, 342 n. 40
7:48 32
7:61–62 31
8:18 337
9:5–37 273
9:10 358
10:8 334
10:9 201, 337 n. 28
10:29 32
10:35 342
11:2 372
11:19 31

Nehemiah (cont.)
12:5 334
12:6 337

1 Chronicles
2:10 128, 368
2:13 366
2:17 31
2:28 367
2:30 367
2:55 367
3:18 367
3:20 462
5:29 367
6:7 368
6:27–41 290
8:30 367
8:33 366
9:17 31
9:36 367
9:39 366
10:2 366
13:7 366, 380
14:4 236
15:10 368
15:11 368
21:22 90 n. 54
21:24 90 n. 54
24 329
24:1 367
24:2 367
24:7 337
24:7–18 337
24:7–19 327–28
24:8 334, 340
24:9 334, 340
24:18 201
24:18 337 n. 28
28:21 370
29:5 372
29:6 372
29:9 372
29:14 372
29:17 372

2 Chronicles
9:21 3
17:16 372
18:1–27 36
26:15 171 n. 31
29:5 75
29:31 370
31:14 371
35:8 371
36:15 239

Deuterocanonical Books

2 Baruch
5:1 40

Ben Sira
1:28 41
8:13 188
37:19 225
40:8 72
41:11 195
42:9 72–73
44–49 264
44:1–9 264
51:24 203 n. 3

4 Esdras
4:25 40

4 Ezra
3:35 312
4:10–11 315
6:1 314
7:8 314
7:31–32 316
7:34–38 316
7:38 312
7:66 312
7:75 312–13
7:79 314
7:80–99 294
7:81–99 314
7:87 314
7:97 314
7:98 314–15
7:102–5 315
7:106–10 316

4 Ezra (cont.)
7:125 314
8:26–28 313
8:42 313
8:62 314
12:6 314
12:19–21 314
13:4 315
16 296

1 Maccabees
2:1 337
14:29 337

Wisdom
7:21 51
10:6 286

New Testament

Matthew
5:15 455
5:26 455
5:41 455
8:12 312
12:59 455
13:22 316
13:33 114 n. 56
17:25 455
22:13 312
22:17 455
22:19 452
25:30 312
27:26 455
27:27 455
27:65 455
27:66 455
28:11 455

Mark
4:21 455

Mark (cont.)
6:27 457
12:14 455
12:42 455
15:15 455
15:16 455

Luke
8:16 455
19:20 455
20:22 455
23:16 455
23:22 455
23:38 455

John
2:15 455
11:44 455
12:3 455
13:4 455
13:5 455

John (cont.)
19:19 452, 455
19:20 452
19:39 455
20:7 455

Acts
19:19 455

1 Corinthians
15:9 315

Galatians
3:16 114 n. 55
6:14 414

Hebrews
5:2 291
7:8 291

Index of Ancient Sources

Arabic Sources

al-Athīr, *Kāmil fi-Taʾrīkh* . 119, 119 n. 5
al-Ṭabarī, *Annales* ... 22–24, 22 n. 13, 119 n. 6
1.211 .... 24 n. 23
1.212 .... 24 n. 24
1.213 .... 24 n. 25
1.216 .... 23 n. 20
1.343 .... 23 n. 14
1.349 .... 23 n. 14
1.351 .... 26 n. 34
1.355 ..... 25 nn. 28–29, 26 n. 31
1.361–65 ...... 23 n. 19
1.371 .... 23 n. 14
al-Thaʿlabī, *ʿArāʾis* ...... 23, 23 n. 19, 26 n. 31, 26 n. 35, 119 n. 6
316 .... 129 n. 27
Balʿamī, *Taʾrīkh* .. 119 n. 6, 129 n. 27
CIH
47.2 635
149.2–3 635
434.1 633
547 .... 634 n. 49
547.1 633
Diyārbakrī, *K. al-Khamīs* 119, 119 nn. 5–6
1.278–79 ...... 129 n. 27
Kisāʾī, *Qiṣaṣ* ...... 119 n. 6, 129 n. 27
Masʿūdī, *Murūj al-dhahab* 119, 119 n. 5
Qiṣaṣ al-anbiyāʾ ... 19–20, 26
Qurʾān
2:175 .... 20 n. 6
2:179 .... 20 n. 6
4:46 .... 20 n. 6
6:74–84 ...... 110 n. 19
19:41–50 ..... 110 n. 19
21:51–73 ..... 110 n. 19
26:69–89 ..... 110 n. 19
29:16–27 ..... 110 n. 19
37:83–98 ..... 110 n. 19
43:26–28 ..... 110 n. 19
Yaʿqūbī, *Historiae* .. 119 n. 6
Zamakhsharī, *Kashshāf* .... 119 n. 6, 129 n. 27

Akkadian Sources

5 Rawl. 44, 111, 9′ ... 46 n. 6
A. 1146, lines 21, 24 178
A. 2090 178
Ammi-ditana, Edict 81
Ammi-ṣaduqa, Edict ..... 81, 81 n. 5, 82, 82 n. 10, 83, 83 n. 21, 84–86, 88–89, 89 n. 48, 90, 90 n. 55
Annals of Sennacherib col. V, lines 22–23 152 n. 25
ARM
1 42:42–43 .... 46 n. 11
1 43 .... 86 n. 33
1 85:17–19 .... 46 n. 11
10 (80 = 26 197) 604
21 230:4 .... 602 n. 9
26 .... 566 n. 24
26 196 602
26 197 606
26 199 .... 600, 606
26 202 605–6
26 377–452 .... 599 n. 1
26/1 379–80 .. 604 n. 12
ARM *(cont.)*
26/1 396 ...... 600 n. 2, 603 n. 10
26/1 424 ...... 604 n. 13
26/1 574–75 .... 600 n. 3
ARMT 15 .... 46 n. 10
BAM 248 II 30 549
BE X 54:4 .... 528 n. 15
BIN 1 97 .... 537 n. 4
BM
19 356 (95 10–14 4) 610–12
19 359 (95 10–14 7) 612–13
19 360 (95 10–14 8) 613–14
22 867 (97 5-11 93) 614–15
25 077 (98 2-16 131) 616–17
29 980 (99 1-16 17) 617–18
19102 (95 10-12 80) 618
78259 .... 81 n. 5
BWL 242:14–16 556
Camb. (Inscriptions of Cambyses, King of Babylon ... 527 n. 14
CBS 8530 588
Cleveland Public Library, White Collection 036422 531–42
CT
23, 10:14 ...... 317 n. 2
39, 44:18 ...... 548 n. 6
48, 35 .... 82 n. 10
55, 68 525
55, 96 .... 524, 527 n. 12, 528
55, 99 525
55, 173 ... 524, 527 n. 12, 529
55, 420 525
55, 483 526
55, 608 .... 525, 529
55, 692 525
55, 699 525
55, 763 .... 524, 530

CT *(cont.)*
55, 823 . . . . 526, 530
56, 551 526
57, 23 526
57, 118 525
57, 508 525
58, 13 . . . . 593 n. 30
Dar. (Inscriptions of Darius, King of Babylon) 523–28
EA
59 . . . . 561 n. 5
62:30–31 . . . . . 566 n. 25
68:11 . . . . 565 n. 22
68:27–28 . . . . . 567 n. 28
73:42 . . . . 565 n. 22
74:6–8 . . . . 565 n. 22
74:7 . . . . 565 n. 22
74:9 . . . . 565 n. 22
74:9–10 . . . . . . 565 n. 22
74:33 . . . . 566 n. 26
74:44 . . . . 566 n. 26
74:56 . . . . 565 n. 22
75:9 . . . . 561 n. 4
76:12–13 . . . . . 570 n. 42
80:17 . . . . 565 n. 22
82:10–12 . . . . . 565 n. 20
85:17 . . . . 565 n. 22
85:34–37 . . . . . 567 n. 28
85:63 . . . . 565 n. 22
86:32–35 . . . . . 567 n. 28
88:8 . . . . 565 n. 22
88:11 . . . . 570 n. 41
88:43–45 . . . . . 565 n. 22
88:44 . . . . 565 n. 22
88:45 . . . . 561 n. 4
89 . . . . 570 n. 43
92:29–40 . . . . . 571 n. 47
100:15–18 . . . . 565 n. 22
100:32 . . . . 565 n. 22
101:38 . . . . 565 n. 22
103:7 . . . . 565 n. 22
103:24 . . . . 565 n. 22
104:17–24 . . . . 570 n. 42
105:81–83 . . . . 564 n. 15
106:4 561 n. 4, 565 n. 22
106:6–7 . . . . . . 563 n. 11
107:8–11 . . . . . 564 n. 17
107:11–13 564
107:25 564
107:35–36 564
108:12–13 . . . . 570 n. 41
108:20–25 . . . . 564 n. 18
108:28–33 . . . . 565 n. 21
108:69 . . . . 565 n. 22
109:42 . . . . 565 n. 22
112 n. 1 . . . . . . 566 n. 25
112:50–51 . . . . 567 n. 28
112:54–55 . . . . 567 n. 28

EA (cont.)
114:41–43 . . . . 565 n. 22
114:43 . . . . 565 n. 22
114:65–67 . . . . . 565 n. 22
114:68 . . . . 563 n. 9
116:55 . . . . 565 n. 22
116:55–60 . . . . . 563 n. 12
116:56 . . . . 561 n. 4
116:67–71 . . . . . 570 n. 42
117:27–28 . . . . . 565 n. 21
118:56 . . . . 565 n. 22
119:25 . . . . 565 n. 22
119:39–44 . . . . . 563 n. 8
121:11–17 . . . . . 567 n. 28
122:9–11 . . . . . . 567 n. 28
122:24–31 . . . . . 567 n. 28
123:23–28 . . . . . 564 n. 16
125:14–18 . . . . . 567 n. 28
125:42–43 . . . . 570 n. 41
126 . . . . 562 n. 7
126:11–12 . . . . . 570 n. 41
126:44–45 . . . . . 562 n. 7
127:25 . . . . 565 n. 22
129:6 . . . . 570 n. 41
130:21–30 . . . . . 567 n. 28
130:44–52 . . . . . 563 n. 10
132:9 . . . . 565 n. 22
132:16–18 . . . . . 565 n. 21
136 . . . . 571 n. 47
138:33–34 . . . . . 565 n. 21
138:37 . . . . 565 n. 22
139:11 . . . . 570 n. 41
139:11–17 570
139:30 . . . . 565 n. 22
140:9–10 . . . . . . 570 n. 41
141:4–5 . . . . 563 n. 13
141:11–12 . . . . . 563 n. 13
141:19–20 . . . . . 563 n. 13
141:39–40 . . . . 563 n. 13
142:2–4 . . . . . . 563 n. 13
143:3–5 . . . . 563 n. 13
143:11–12 . . . . . 563 n. 13
145:23–26 . . . . . 565 n. 19
147:66–69 . . . . . 565 n. 20
149:14–16 . . . . . 564 n. 17
149:14–17 . . . . . 565 n. 19
149:68–70 . . . . . 565 n. 20
151:49–51 . . . . . 565 n. 19
155:48 . . . . 565 n. 22
156 . . . . 561 n. 5
162 . . 568, 568 n. 34, 569
162:17ff. . . . . . . 570 n. 41
162:31–32 . . . . . 569 n. 35
162:33–38 . . . . . 569 n. 36
180 . . . . 561 n. 5
180:19 . . . . 565 n. 22
185–86 . . . . 561 n. 5
192:4–5 . . . . 563 n. 13
197 142

EA (cont.)
197:6 . . . . 564 n. 15
197:33–34 142
198 . . . . 561 n. 5
198:10 . . . . 565 n. 22
201–2 . . . . 567 n. 29
203–6 . . . . 567 n. 29
241:19 . . . . 565 n. 22
242:5 . . . . 563 n. 14
243:4 . . . . 563 n. 14
246:4 . . . . 563 n. 14
250:20–22 . . . . 570 n. 44
250:26–27 . . . . 570 n. 45
253:11–35 . . . . 569 n. 38
254:10–11 . . . . 565 n. 22
256:21 . . . . 571 n. 47
271:13 . . . . 566 n. 25
274:10 . . . . 566 n. 25
274:14 141–42
280:9–11 . . . . . 571 n. 46
286:22–24 . . . . 564 n. 17
286:49 . . . . 564 n. 17
286:63–64 . . . . 564 n. 17
296 . . . . 561 n. 5
318:8 . . . . 566 n. 26
362:20 . . . . 565 n. 21
365:4 . . . . 563 n. 14
366:18–19 . . . . 571 n. 47
366:20–26 . . . . 571 n. 47
369:18–23 . . . . 567 n. 27
Emar
6/3 579
8:31 578
9:27 578
64:12 579
115 579
186:2 580
215:27 577
336:23 579
378:7 630
378:39′ 630
378:47′–48′ 630
6/3–4 . . . . 574 n. 6
Enuma Eliš
I 31 . . . . 53 n. 56
V 1–10 476
Esarhaddon, Succession Treaty . . . . . 475 n. 17
Esarhaddon, Treaty with Tyre IV 10–13 . . . 492
Farah III 110 i 3 628
GCCI II
26 527
98 . . . . 538 n. 17
407:2 . . . . 527 n. 8
Gilgamesh
I iv 8–21 . . . . . . 544 n. 2
I iv 9, 16 556
I iv 21 . . . . 553 n. 24

Gilgamesh *(cont.)*
I iv 21–22 554
II ii 6–8 . . . . 544 n. 2
III 43 556
VI 7–9 592
VI 13–15 592
VI 68–69 592
VI 69 549
IX ii 1–9 . . . . . 487 n. 50
Old Babylonian P
i 5 . . . . 550 n. 15
Old Babylonian P
i 10–11 . . . 552 n. 18
Hammurabi, Laws
(Codex) 79, 83, 86–88, 91–93
XI 11–13 . . . . . 115 n. 58
XXIV 22 . . . . . 110 n. 13
XXV 6 . . . . 110 n. 13
XLI 8 . . . . 112 n. 34
Hilprecht Collection in Jena
(HS 1879) . . . 543–58
K43+ . . . . 491 n. 64
K3394+, rev. 10 473
KAR
71 . . . . 491 n. 64
94:20 . . . . 486 n. 48
94:22 . . . . 486 n. 46
94:23 . . . . 486 n. 49
158 rev. ii 10 595
158 rev. ii 20 . . . 594, 595
158 rev. ii 21 595
158 rev. ii 29 594
472 ii 3 . . . . 587 n. 5
KBo 1 12:7–16 . . . 551 n. 16
Ki. 1063 (Love Song from
Kish) 549, 556
Kish B 572 i 9′–12′ 591
KUB 40 80:11, 16 578
Lab. 5 (Inscriptions of the
Reign of
Laborosoarchod) 525
LKA 155, rev, 25 . . 473 n. 14
M. 6060 178
MAD V 8:15–16 . . 556 n. 34
MAD V 8:16 . . . . . . 549 n. 9
Maqlû
I 1–36 . . . . 469, 472
I 1–72 468
I 18 . . . . 473 n. 13
I 31–33 . . . . . . 483 n. 36
I 37–41 469
I 37–60 468
I 37–72 . . . . 467, 467 n., 469, 490
I 38 485
I 42–45 . . . . 484–85, 488
I 42–49 469
I 43–45 485
Maqlû (cont.)
I 46–60 488
I 50–51 . . . . 482, 493
I 50–55 482
I 50–60 . . . 469, 479 n. 27
I 52–53 481–82
I 54–55 . . . . 477 n. 22
I 61–72 . . . . 469, 473
II 199–200 . . . . 473 n. 14
III 17 . . . . 183 n. 10
III 22′ff. 493
III 128–39 493
III 133–37 492
IV 50–60 479
VI 136–38 494
VI 145–47 494
VII 1–22 . . . . . . 483 n. 40
VII 8–9 481, 481 n. 32, 493
VII 8–11 . . . . . . 481, 482
VII 10–11 477 n. 22, 481
VII 11 . . . . 483 n. 40
VII 15 . . . . 483 n. 40
Incantation 2
(I 37–41) 469
Incantations 2–5 . . . 490
Incantation 3 (42–49) 470
Incantation 4 (50–60) 470
Incantation 5 (61–72) 470
MFA 1977.114 573–84
Middle Assyrian Law A
§47 475
MLC 1955 . . . . 81 n. 7
MUL.APIN I i 37 476
N 3560 590
NBC
6252 81
6311 . . . . 82, 93
8618 . . . . 81, 84
8702 82
8738 . . . . 82 n. 10
8819 . . . . 82 n. 10
8913 81
11507 . . . . 81 n. 7
Nbk. (Inscriptions of
Nabuchodonosor,
King of Babylon)
127 527
334 527
464 527
Nbn. (Inscriptions of
Nabonidus,
King of Babylon)
17 527
205 525
249 525
877 . . . . 525, 527 n. 9
Ni
2461 589
4552 . . . . 590 n. 18
OECT
10, 120:10–11 . 527 n. 10
11, 44 . . . . 492 n. 72
Or. Inst. A 3529 . . . 83 n. 17
PBS
2/I, 195:6 . . . . . 528 n. 16
12 52 obv. II–rev. I . . 587
RE (texts in the collection of
J. Rosen)
21:11 578
63:28 578
63:29 578
67:13 578
82:28 578
85 580
RS
17.230 . . . . 574 n. 3
22227 48
SAA III 33 6 . . . . . . 552 n. 19
Samsu-iluna
Edict . . . . 79, 81, 82, 83, 83 n. 21, 87
Letter to Ibbi-
Shahan 87–88
SRT
5 586
31 21–22 . . . . . 593 n. 30
STT 78 . . . . . . 491 nn. 62–64
TCL
12 115:11 535
17 76 82 n. 15, 83 n. 22
12 32 527
TMH
2/3 251 527
2/3 266 527
UET
IV 104 527
VI 394 . . . . 552 n. 19
VI 394:16 . . . . . 556 n. 31
VII . . . . 625 n. 20
VII 21 . . . . 626 n. 22
VS
3 18 527
6 63 527
6 252:15 . . . . . . 528 n. 17
6 287 525
17 8 . . . . 552 n. 19
YNER 10 535
YOR 5/2 535
YOS
3 2 . . . . 538 n. 16
3 22 . . . . 538 n. 13
3 46 . . . . 537 n. 9
6 6:4 . . . . 537 n. 6
6 5 . . . . 536 n. 2
6 12 . . . . 537 n. 4
6 35–36 . . . . 537 n. 4
6 43–45 . . . . 537 n. 4
6 45:3, 15 . . . . . 537 n. 7

YOS *(cont.)*
6 47 .... 537 n. 4
6 49 .... 537 n. 4
6 78 .... 537 nn. 4–5
6 84 .... 537 n. 4
6 85 .... 537 n. 3
6 129 .... 537 n. 10, 538
6 129:2 538
6 129:3 538
6 129:4 538
6 129:6 538
6 129:7 538
6 207 .... 538 n. 15
6 224:17–18 535
6 230:13 536
6 242 .... 537 n. 4
6 242:5 .... 538 n. 12
7 23:1 .... 538 n. 17
7 151 527
15 .... 82 n. 11
15 90 .... 82 n. 11

Classical Sources

Aesop, Life of 456
Herodotus
3.77 .... 322 n. 21
6.32 .... 322 n. 21
8.104–5 ...... 322 n. 21
Josephus
Ant.
1.171 284
13.10.7 §300 37
13.292 42
Josephus *(cont.)*
J.W.
1.2.8 §68–69 37
2.161–69 33
Life 1.2 338
Julian, *Misopogon*
369 II ...... 444 n. 1
Ktesias, *Persica* .... 322 n. 21
Marcellinus
XXX/VIII ... 444 n. 2
Philo of Byblos,
Praeparatio evangelica
1.10.31 .... 631 n. 28
Xenophon, *Cyr.* 7.5,
60–65 .... 322 n. 21

Papyri

Adon, Letter to
Pharaoh 57–67
Aḥiqar 50–51, 53–54
Aramaic
7 7 45
15 6 45
Amherst 63 261
Anastasi I 51
Aramaic Legal Papyri from Elephantine .... 624 n. 15
Arshama of Egypt,
Aramaic Dossier 50
Cave of Letters 457
no. 11: lines 6, 19 .. 454
no. 12: lines 1, 4 ... 454
no. 14: lines 12–13,
31 454
no. 16: lines 2, 4 ... 454
Hermopolis Papyri ... 57–67
5:7 390
Oxyrhynchus Papyrus
294.20 456
Padua Papyri 57–67
P. Ness. 65 446–47
P. Ness. 69 446–47
Saqqara Papyrus 50

Pseudepigraphical Literature

Apoc. Abr.
10:4 .... 40 n. 4
10:8 .... 40 n. 4
Apoc. of Sedrach 2:4 315
Apoc. Paul 11–16 314
2 Apoc. Bar. 51:1–6 314
Death of Adam 17 315
1 Enoch
10:9 41
18:12–16 ..... 477 n. 23
55:2 .... 40 n. 4
69:14–25 .... 40 n. 4
72–82 .... 343 n. 43
91:1 41
2 Enoch
8:1–8 315
22:1–2 315
Greek Ezra Apocalypse
1:21–23 313
1:24 312
4:38 312
5:26 312
6:21 313
Jubilees
7:1–6 .... 343 n. 42
16:20–31 42
21:5–20 42
21:12–14 42
23:21 .... 40 n. 3
32:9–15 42
34:18–29 42
36:7 .... 40 n. 3
Life of Adam and Eve 44 315
Questions of Ezra 293–316
A 1–10, B 4 297
A 11–15, B 6 297
A 16–30 297
A 31–40 297
B 10–14 297
T. Abraham
A 17:7 314
B 13:13 314
T. Levi 40, 187
4:3 40
9:6–14 42
9:12 42
18:3 40
35:9–21 343
36:19–21 343

Qumran Scrolls

CD
I 1 . . . . 195, 219
II 2 14 219
II 13 31
IV 5 31
VII 2–3 226
VII 6–9 33
VIII 16 194
VIII 26 243
IX 2–8 226
XII 19–21 224
XIII 18 244
XIV 22 226
1Q*27* . . . . . 192, 207–9, 211, 211 n. 12, 212, 214–15
1 i 8–12 211
1 ii 5–7 216
3 251
6 251
1QapGen . . 284–85, 287, 290
II 9 62
II 24 . . . . 65 n. 33
XIX 14–21 14
1QH
I 24–25 328
I 26 238
I 35 219
II 16–17 218
III 19–36 184
III 29–30, 36 189
III 30, 36 . . . . . . 186, 188
III 32 186
III 32–33 . 185 n. 19, 186
III 33 186
IV 14 41
IV 27–29 . . . . . . 43 n. 13
IV 36 229
V 12–VI 18 . . . . 182 n. 2, 185 n. 16
V 16 243
V 26 . . . . 185 n. 16
V 29–30 229
VI 188
VI 32 188
VI 35 . . . . 187, 188
VII 2–4 195
VII 4 224
VII 9 224
VII 20 195
X 28–29 194
XI 20–37 184
XI 30 187
XI 30–31, 37 189
XI 31 37 188
XI 31–32 187
XI 33 186
XI 33–34 186
1QH (*cont.*)
XI 34 186
XI 37 187
XII 4 222
XII 7 222
XII 8 213
XII 10 238
XII 32–33 184
XIII 12 . . . . 185 n. 16
XIII 19 212
XIV 188
XIV 21 200
XIV 33 188
XIV 38 . . . . 187, 188
XX 183
XX 35 182
XX 35–36 184
XXIII 183
XXIII 2, 7–8 184
XXIII 2, 16–17 184
XXIII 27–28 184
XXIII 28 182
XXIII 36–37 . . . 182, 184
1QH[a]
iii 30 . . . . 186 n. 22
iii 36 . . . . 186 n. 22
xi 31, 37 . . . . . . 186 n. 22
1QIsa[a] 198, 356, 361
15:6 361
23:6 201
35:8 201
43:17 183
XXVIII 356
XXX 356
XXXII 356
1QM
I 8–9 318
II 1 . . . . 254, 329
II 1–2 329
II 7 254
III 4 254
IV 6 31
IV 7 31
XI 2 40
XI 16 . . . . 197 n. 10
XIV 6 229
XVIII 2 . . . . 197 n. 10
1QpHab
V 1–8 197
VII 12–13 328
VIII 10–11 . . . . 199 n. 20
VIII 13 193
1QS
I 17 229
II 19–20 334
II 24 244
III 13–25 192
1QS (*cont.*)
III 15 . . . . 211 n. 11, 238
III 15–16 162
III 21 . . . . 222, 239
IV 11 222
IV 12 239
IV 15 193
IV 16 . . . . 194, 318
IV 24 194
IV 25 328
IX 2 . . . . 196 n. 9
IX 13–14 224
IX 17 . . . . 194, 200
V 4 244
V 25 . . . . 194, 244
VI 5 334
VI 8 334
VII 13 . . . . 593 n. 30
VII 19 334
VIII 2 244
VIII 16 195
X 329
X 10 222
X 27 244
XI 3–4 . . . . 211 n. 11
XI 7 . . . . 199 n. 17
XI 9 224
XI 21 . . 181–82, 182 n. 6
XI 21–22 184
1QSa
I 4 33
I 16 254
I 24 254
II 4–5 229
II 16 254
1QSb
IV 27 . . . . . . 40, 43 n. 13
V 20–29 . . . . . . 196 n. 10
2Q*26* 280
4Q*158*–4Q*186* . . . . . 196 n. 8
4Q*161* . . . . 191, 196–97, 197 n. 10
4Q*174* I 4 33
4Q*261* 341–42
4Q*285* . . . . 197 n. 10
4Q*299–301* 208
4Q*300* 207–10, 216–17
6–7 226
4Q*301* 207, 219
4Q*320* 339, 341
4Q*321* 333 n. 11, 335 n. 18, 337 n. 27, 339, 341
II 3 201
IV 8 201
V 2 201
IV 8 336
V 2 340

4Q*321* (*cont.*)
V 4 338
V 6 340
V 9 338
VI 7 . . . . 338, 340
4Q*322–324[a]* 337
4Q*323[a]*
2 2 . . . . 340 n. 38
3 3 . . . . 340 n. 38
4Q*323[c]* 1 4 . . . . . . 340 n. 38
4Q*325* miš D 327–44
4Q*326* . . . . 339 n. 35
I 4 338
4Q*327* . . . . . . 339 n. 35, 342
II 9 342
4Q*328* I 1 334
4Q*339* 33
1–2 35
1–9 35
3–9 36
4Q*340* 29
1–3 30
1–6 31
4–6 31
4Q*364* 201, 342
4Q*365[a]*
23 5 342
23 9 342
4Q*376* . . . . 197 n. 11
4Q*392* 2 2 358
4Q*400* 1 ii 19 191
4Q*403* 1 i 41 224
4Q*405* . . . . 334 n. 16
14–15 i 6 224
4Q*412* 3 1 245
4Q*413* 191
1 1 240
1 3 241
4Q*415* 2 ii 9 213
4Q*416*
1 4 250
1 6 250
1 15 . . . . 210 n. 10
2 iii 9–10 . . . . . 213 n. 18
4Q*416–419* 207
4Q*417* 2 i 8 . . 210 n. 10, 238
4Q*418* 41
2 7 . . . . 210 n. 10
9 8–9 . . . . 213 n. 18
43 5–6 . . . . 210 n. 10
43 6 238
55 5 238
69 ii 5 241
121 1 245
123 ii 2 222
123 3 . . . . 211 n. 11
169 3 244
170 3 244
214 2 245
4Q*419* 1 1–8 251
4Q*421*
1 ii 15 212
13 1–6 251
4Q*422* 358
1–9 351
5 10–11 359
10 . . . . 351, 356
10 1 354
10 1–12 356
10 2 . . . . 354, 357
10 3 . . . . 354, 357
10 4 . . . . 354, 357
10 5 355
10 5–7 358
10 6 . . . 352 n. 2, 355, 358
10 6–7 354
10 7 . . . . 354–56, 358, 361–63
10 7–8 359
10 7–10 354
10 8 . . . . . . 354, 355, 359, 362–63
10 8–9 362
10 9 . . . . 354–55, 360, 362–63
10 9–11 . . . . 360, 363
10 10 . . . . . . 354–55, 363
10 11 . . 354, 360–61, 363
10 12 . . . . 354, 361
10a–e 351–63
10b 354
10e 352, 354–55
III 352
4Q*427*
7 i + ii . . . . 201 n. 28
7 i 9 201
4Q*482*–4Q*520* . . . . . 182 n. 5
4Q*491* 201
11 i 17 201
4Q*501* 4 359
4Q*504* 181
1–2 iv 9–10 40
1–2 vii 7 185–86
4Q*508* 13 341–42
4Q*509* 131 ii 5 341
4Q*511* 181, 183
3–4 184
28–29 182–84
37 3–4 186
37 4 185–86
4Q*513* 3–4 338
4Q*520* 1 ii 4 212
4Q*522* i 11 201
4Q*542*
I 1 39
I 1–3 44
I 2 40
I 4–13 44
4Q*542* (*cont.*)
I 5–6 40
I 6–7 42
I 7–8 42
I 8–9 42
II 1–13 44
II 13 43
4QBéat. . . . . . . 182 n. 2, 185
4QFlor 33
4QMMT 41, 43, 197, 329
4QMysteries[a] . . . . . . 207–10, 214–16, 216 n. 21, 232
1 01–03 210
1 04–08 211
1 1–9 210
1 1–8 211
1 1–4 212
1 7 212
2 216
2a I 1–12 217
2a + 2c II 01–02 218
2a + 2c II 1–16 . . 217–18
2a + 2c II 3–15 219
2a + 2c II 4 218
2a + 2c II 7 218
2a + 2c II 8 219
2a + 2c II 10–12 219
2b 1–2 219
2b 1–5 220
2b 3–6 220
2b 01–03 220
3 214
3 1–4 215
3 01–04 215
3 (8)–(12) 215
3 1–3 216
4 1–5 220–21
4 4 221
5 1–5 221
5 1 222
5 2 222
5 4 222
6 I 1–17 222
6 I 1–19 223
6 I 4 223
6 I 5 223
6 I 9 223
6 I 18–19 223
6 II 1–20 224–25
7 1–6 226
8 1–11 227
9 1–5 228
10 1–11 229
11a–b 230
12–14 231
15 I–II 232
16–17 232
18–20 233
21–23 234

4QMysteries[a] (cont.)
24–26 235
27–28 236
28a–29 237
30–32 238
33–35 239
36–40 240
40 3 241
41–43 241
44 2 . . . . 241 n. 28
44–45 242
46 . . . . 241 n. 29
47 . . . . 241 n. 29
48–49 242
50 1–12 243
51–52 244
53–79 245–57
80 257
81–85 257–58
86–92 . . . . 259 n. 31
93–95 259
94 . . . . 259 n. 32

4QMysteries[a] (cont.)
96 . . . . 259 n. 33
97–98 259
99–101 . . . . 260 n. 34
102 260
4QS[a] . . . . 199 n. 19
4QS[d] 194, 200
VIII 6 200
4QS[j] 1, 8 181
4QTQahat . . . 39, 39 n. 1, 41
I 1 39
I 5 39
I 6–7 39
I 7–8 39
I 8–9 39
II 13 39
11QJér Nouv ar . . . 280 n. 12
11QMelch . . . . 328 n. 3
11QNJ 280
11QpaleoLev 25:32 199 n. 18
11QPs[a] XVI . . 329, 344 n. 44
11QShirShabb 2-1-9 9 . . 224

11QTemple
XI 10 338
XI 11 341
XVIII 9–12 338
XVIII 13–14 341
XIX 9 341
XXI 7–10 342
XXI 8 342
XXI 14 342
XXII 4 342
XXXVIII 4 341
XLIII 1 342
XLIII 1–4 342
XLIII 3 341
XLIII 6 338
XLIII 6–7 341
XLIII 9 342
XLIII 10 342
LVIII 15–21 196
LX 6 341

Rabbinic Sources

Mishna
Ber.
2:4 . . . . 205 n. 11
3:1 . . . . 205 n. 11
Ter. 4:7 380
Šabb.
1:2 . . . . 205 n. 11
18:1 . . . . 113 n. 41
Šeqal. 6:4 343
Sukk. 5:6–8 328
Ta^c an.
1:2 328
4:4 343
4:6 343
Yebam. 4:13 33
Qidd.
1:1 457
4:1 32
B. Bat. 3:1 639
Sanh. 1:5 35
Hor. 3:8 32
ᵓAbot
5:19 36
6:4 223
Zebaḥ.
14:2 . . . . 41 n. 10
8:1 . . . . 41 n. 10
9:3 . . . . 41 n. 10
Menaḥ. 7:2 380
Bek.
1:5 . . . . 41 n. 11
9:4 . . . . 41 n. 10

Tem.
2:3 . . . . 41 n. 10
6:1 . . . . 41 n. 10

Tosepta
Ber. 6.7 41
Yoma
2.2 40
4(3).14 381
Sukk. 4.24–25 338
B. Bat. 5.12 457
Zebaḥ.
8.2 . . . . 41 n. 10
9.5 . . . . 41 n. 10
15.20 . . . . 41 n. 10
Ḥul. 5.1 . . . . 41 n. 11

Midraš
ᵓAbot R. Nat. 8 122 nn. 12–13, 124 n. 16, 124 n. 18
Baraita Qinyan Torah . . . 223
Gen. Rab. 65, 346
40:6 . . . . 112 n. 30
41:2 110–11
43:6 . . . . 111 n. 26
44:9 . . . . 112 n. 29
44:14–16 . . . . . . 112 n. 29
45:9 112
48:10 . . . . 113 n. 41
48:16 346
61:2 . . . . 347 n. 7
79:1 . . . . 347 n. 7

Lev. Rab. 16:1 111
Midr. Hagadol . . . . . 346 n. 1
Midr. ha-Ḥêfeṣ . . . . 120, 120 n. 8, 124 n. 15, 129, 129 n. 26
Midr. Lekaḥ Ṭov . . . . 346 n. 1
Midr. Prov. . . . 120, 124 n. 15
4–7 . . . . 120 n. 8
40–41 . . . . 120 n. 8
Midr. 2 Sam. 7 33
Midr. Song of Songs 9 . . . . 134 n. 37
Midr. Song of Songs Rab. 9 . . . . . 130 n. 28
Midr. Tannaim 227 . 346 n. 1
Midr. Tanḥuma . . . 111 n. 24, 112 n. 30, 113 n. 44
Mek. Exod. 13:13 . . . 41 n. 11
Num. Rab. 20 36
Sepher Ha-galuj . . . . . 346 n. 2, 350 n. 18
Sipra Qedošim 11.1 . . 76 n. 21
Sipre 347
Sipre 91 457
Sipre Deut. . . . . . 36, 347 n. 10
Sop. 13:10 212
Yal. Gen. . . . . 111 n. 24
§8 . . . . 113 n. 41
§79 112

Jerusalem Talmud
Bik. 64 633

Pesaḥ. 10:4 . . . . 204 n. 6
Yoma
2.39 338
6.3 (43) 380
B. Qam. 9:5 446
Nid. 7.4 . . . . 124 n. 17

Babylonian Talmud
Ber.
3 . . . . 121 n. 10
8 . . . . 41 n. 9
11 203
12 337
Šab. 127 . . . . 113 n. 41
ᶜErub. 53 . . . . 124 n. 14
Pesaḥ. 54 41
Yoma
26 338
66 . . . . 381 n. 7
Sukk.
52 337
55–56 328
56 . . . . 337, 338
Taᶜan.
17 337
27 . . . . 328, 337, 340
28 343
29 338
Meg. 31 . . . . 112 n. 29
Moᶜed Qaṭ. 17 . . . . . 328, 338
Yebam.
64 . . . . 128 n. 24
101 337
103 555
Qidd. 70 32
Soṭa
6 . . . . 121 n. 10
33 37
14 113
42 553
B. Qam. 110 340
B. Meṣ. 87 . . . . 113 n. 41, 349
B. Bat. 120 349
Sanh.
21 . . 131 n. 32, 136 n. 38
49 346
73.1 36
82 . . . . 555 n. 29
93 . . . . 196 n. 10
Hor.
13 32
20 343
Ḥul. 11 43
ᶜArak.
11 338
12 328
13 . . . . 337, 340

Targums

Fragment Targum . . . 346 n. 1
Frag. Tg. Onq. 101–5
Palestinian Fragment-Targums
Paris 110 105
Vatican 440 105
Samaritan Targum . . 346 n. 3
Tg. Ezek. 18:6 . . . . . . 75 n. 18
Tg. Job . . . . 206 n. 14
Tg. Jonathan . . . . 346 n. 1
Tg. Lam. 1:17 76
Tg. Neof. . . . 40 n. 6, 346 n. 1
Tg. Onq. . . . . . . 213, 346 n. 1
Tg. Ps.-J. . . . . . 110 n. 11, 213
Tg. Pseudo–Ben Sira . . . . 131, 131 n. 29, 131 n. 31, 131 n. 35
Tg. Šênî . . . . 120, 120 n. 8, 130–31, 131 n. 3
Tg. Yer. Num 25:15 555 n. 29

West Semitic Inscriptions

ᵓAḥiram Inscription 404
Amman Citadel
Inscription 394–95, 399, 403, 405, 408
Arad
1 379
1:9–10 381
2 381
2:7 379
2:7–8 381
3:2–6 380
3:3–6 382
5:1–4 379
5:3 379
5:5–7 381
10 381
21:8 379
Assur Ostracon 57–67
Ben (Bir) Hadad,
Inscription 394, 400, 403, 405, 408
Bir Hadad, Stele . . . 394 n. 6
Bitia Inscription 496, 496 n. 5, 497, 497 n. 7, 504
CIS
I . . . . 433 n. 2
I 88 . . . . 434 n. 6
I 90 . . . . 434 n. 6
I 95 . . . . 436 n. 15
I 143 503
I 165 . . . . 439 n. 24
I 167 . . . . 439 n. 24
I 327:4–5 . . . . . 387 n. 10
I 3604 503
I 3709 503
I 3784 503
I 4503 503
I 4963 503
II 3933 633
II 4199 633
II 4418 633
CTA
5 V 17–21 554
6 III 7 . . . . 606 n. 18
6 III 13 . . . . 606 n. 18
Cyprus Museum,
Nicosia (inv.
Inscr. Ph. 13) . . . 438
Dan, Tel
Aramaic Stele . . . . . 394, 395 n. 6
Bowl Inscription 403
Jar Inscription 394
Deir ᶜAlla Inscription 36, 390
II 13 390
Dor, Tel, Phoenician
Ostraca 459–64
ᶜÊn Gev Inscription 400
Faḫariyeh, Tell, Bilingual
Inscription 393–409
Gezer Calendar 404
Gozan Pedestal
Inscription 394, 396–98, 400–401, 403, 405–6, 408
Hazaᵓel Inscriptions . . . 395, 398–400, 403, 405, 408
Ibn-Hani 77, 14 . . . . 51 n. 45
IPT (Iscrizioni puniche della Tripolitania)
10 (2) 503
17 (12) 496, 503

IPT (cont.)
21 (27) 497, 500–501
22 (28) 497, 501
23 (29) 496
24 (30) 500
25 503
26 (31) 496
27 (32) 501, 503
28 (33) 496
38 (44 f) 496
52 (44 t) 496
71 496
74 496
76 (6) 501
79 (38) 503
86 (51) 496
IRT (Inscriptions of Roman Tripolitania)
318 501
319 . . . . 501 n. 27
321 500
322 500
347 501
599 . . . . 503 n. 35
827 503
877 . . . . 504 n. 40
886 . . . . 504 n. 40
889 503–4
906 503
^{c}Izbet Ṣarṭah Ostracon 404, 407
KAI
10:5 . . . . 387 n. 10
11:1 . . . . 387 n. 10
19 . . . . 500 n. 23
24 . . . . 395 n. 8, 499
24:12 . . . . 387 n. 10
26 287
40 . . . . 500 n. 23
42 . . . . 500 n. 23
KAI (cont.)
43 . . . . 500 n. 23
60:3 . . . . 387 n. 10
66 503
69:12 . . . . 439 n. 24
74:9 . . . . 439 n. 24
178 . . . . 497, 503
179 503
181:17 632
202 . . . . 395 n. 11
214, 11 . . . . 48 n. 26
215, 2 49
222–24 632
277 499
Karatepe III 18 287
Kilamuwa Inscription . . 395, 397, 399, 405, 408
Kition Inscriptions . . 433–41
KTU
I, 4 v. 25 53
1.2 III 638, 640
1.5 II 7 628
1.5 VI 3–25 628
1.5 VI–1.6 III 628
1.5 VI 25–1.6 I 31 . . 628
1.6 I 627–40
1.6 I 32–67 628
1.6 I 63 630
1.6 I 65 638
1.6 I 66–67 638
1.6 II 628
1.6 III 628
1.6 VI 30 628
1.23 33–35 . . . . 593 n. 30
1.23 37 . . . . 593 n. 30
1.23.48–54 639
1.24.28 630
1.100 150
1.107 150
Lachish Letters 5–7 66
Luristan Bronze Jug Inscription 395, 405, 408
Mesha^{c} Inscription 399
Nora Fragment . . . 402 n. 21
Panammu
I, 14 . . . . 48 n. 26
II, 21 . . . . . . 48 n. 26, 49
Phoenician Stamp Seal *ḥrṣ* 385–87
PRU
3 11:4 . . . . 86 n. 33
3 283–308 . . . . . 574 n. 5
4 171 580
RES
1531 . . . . 436 n. 14
2693.5 635
3306.405 . . . . . 637 n. 76
3978.1 635
4176.9 . . . . 635 n. 59
4194.5 635
Sfiré
1 A 24 . . . 186, 186 n. 22
I A 4 . . . . 425 n. 8
I B 4–5 . . . . 425 n. 8
III 23.26 . . . . 425 n. 8
Siran Bottle Inscription 389–91
Ta^{c}anak, Tablet 1, line 20 48
Timnah Graffito 398
UT
8.61 . . . . 632 n. 33
19.1919 . . . . . . 630 n. 21
405 no. 1014 . . 387 n. 10
Xanthos Trilingual, lines 1–27 423–32
Zakkur Inscription 395, 398, 403, 405, 408

Miscellaneous Sources

Aḥiqar, Syriac, v. 10 45
British Library Or. 10794 . . . . . 102 n. 3
C.U.L. T-S B 12.20 . . . . . 102, 104–5
Enelow 874 (Saadiah ben Joseph) 120
Ephraem Syrus
Abr
IV [10–]11 113 n. 39
XV 14 . . . . . 113 n. 45
Azym II 7–8 . . . 111 n. 26
CNis (Carmena Nisibena)
XIII 11 . . . . 115 n. 59
Ephraem Syrus *CNis (cont.)*
XIX 1 . . . . . 112 n. 35
XXIV 1 . . . . 110 n. 18
XXXI 1 . . . . 114 n. 53
XXXI 10–12 . . . . 114 nn. 52–53
XXXI 15–16 114 n. 53
XXXII 2 . . . 114 n. 53
XXXIII 12–13 . . . . 114 n. 56
XXXIV 1 . . . 109 n. 10
XXXIV 7 . . 114 n. 57, 115 n. 58
XXXV 7 . . . 113 n. 45
Ephraem Syrus *CNis (cont.)*
XLI 16 . . . . 113 n. 45
XLIII 3 . . . . 110 n. 15
LVII 7–9 . . 113 n. 45, 113 n. 48
LXIII 1–4 . 114 n. 50
LXX 4–6 . . 114 n. 50
LXXII 3 . . . 114 n. 50
LXXII 5 . . . 113 n. 45
Crucif (de Crucifiixione)
II 7 . . . . 114 n. 50
III 7 . . . . . . 113 n. 38
V 9 . . . . 113 n. 46
VII 7 . . . . . . 110 n. 11

Ephraem Syrus *(cont.)*
Eccl (Hymnen de Ecclesia)
XI 3 . . . . . . 111 n. 25, 112 n. 27
XXIV 2–5[6] 112 n. 35
XLIII 2 . . . 112 n. 33
Epiph
V 3 . . . . 115 n. 59
VII 4 . . . . . . 114 n. 53
VIII 14 112 nn. 33–34
HdF (Hymnen de Fide)
V 17 . . 110 nn. 12–13
X 11 . . . . . . 112 n. 36, 113 n. 38
XXI 6 . . . . . 110 n. 13
LVI 3–6 . . . 114 n. 50
LVI 5–6 . . . 113 n. 42
LXXXI 13 . 113 n. 45
LXXXVII 3 110 n. 13
Jul (Contra Julianum)
IV 8 . . . . . . 110 n. 15
Nat (Hymnen de Nativitate)
I 25 . . . . . . 111 n. 25
I 84 . . . . . . 113 n. 40
II 18 . . . . . . 113 n. 42
VIII 13 . . . . 114 n. 50
IX 3 . . . . . . 111 n. 25

Ephraem Syrus *Nat (cont.)*
XIII 17 . . . . 112 n. 33
XIV 19 . . . . 115 n. 59
XVIII 30 . . . 114 n. 50
XX 1 . . . . . . 112 n. 32
XX 2 . 114 nn. 54–55
XX 4 . . . . . . 110 n. 16
XX 5 . . . . . . 112 n. 35
Parad
I 12 . . . . 113 n. 42
XII 5 . . . . . . 112 n. 28
Resurr (de Resurrectione)
III [1–]2 . . . 115 n. 59
Soq (Hymnen de Nativitate)
III 8 . . . . . . 112 n. 29, 114 n. 50
III 10 . . . . . 112 n. 37, 114 n. 50
Virg (Hymnen de Virginitate)
I 9 . . . . 110 n. 17
I 11 . . . . 113 n. 47
XXII 16–17 110 n. 14
XXXVIIIee 113 n. 46, 113 n. 48
XXXVIII 9 . . 113 n. 45
XXXVIII 13 113 n. 45
XLIV 1 . . . . 113 n. 42

Ephraem Syrus *Virg (cont.)*
XLIX 7–8 . 114 n. 56
XLIX 11 . . . . . 114 nn. 50–51
Fakhry 71.4–5 636
Judeo-Persian Job 3–5
Judeo-Persian Pentateuch (British Museum) . . . 3–5
Judeo-Persian Pentateuch (Vatican) 3–5
Keseçek Köyü, Cilician Inscriptions 430
Koṭṭayam Inscription . . . 416
Leipzig-Universität B.H. fol. 1 . . . . . 102 n. 3
Mount Thomas Cross, Pahlavi Inscription 411–22
Nürnberg-Stadtbibliothek Solger . . . . . . 102 n. 3
Paris Bibliothèque nationale Hébr. 110 . . . . . 102 n. 3
Peshiṭta
Genesis 16:12 112
Exodus 2:22 42
Exodus 12:48 42
Quilon Plate 412
SEG XXVIII 1302 . . 436 n. 12

Colophon

Production Staff at Eisenbrauns

Design	Jim Eisenbraun, Beverly Fields
Production management and quality control	Pam Nichols
Data entry	Barbara Manahan, Marlene Marsh
Electronic file conversion	Sam Heldenbrand, Barbara Manahan
Copy-editing	Beverly Fields
Typesetting	Jim Eisenbraun, Sam Heldenbrand
Illustration processing	Jennifer Ortega, Jim Eisenbraun
Proofreading	Pam Nichols, Marjory Hailstone, Marlene Marsh, Beverly Fields
Indexing	Waverly Conlan, Lee Belleman Barbara Manahan, Beverly Fields
Dustjacket design	Jennifer Ortega

Printed by Thomson-Shore, Dexter, Michigan, on 60 lb. Glatfelter natural neutral-pH recycled paper.